JURISPRUDENCE: READINGS AND CASES

JURISPRUDENCE: READINGS AND CASES

MARK R. MacGUIGAN
PH.D., J.S.D.

UNIVERSITY OF TORONTO PRESS

Second edition

Printed in Canada
Reprinted in 2018
ISBN 978-1-4875-7743-8 (paper)

To HARRY W. JONES

to whose inspiration and insight

I am deeply indebted

Preface

This book is composed of five chapters, each containing a series of cases which courts have disposed of according to a particular jurisprudential insight, followed by a series of readings which present the same insight from a more abstract and general point of view. My main purpose has been to present the ideas, whether of philosophers or jurists, with as much context as possible, in a form as near as possible to their natural habitat.

In order to attain comprehensive coverage of the field of jurisprudence I have had to compromise the ideal to some extent, though I hope not seriously. Articles and addresses could be included, by and large, without substantial omissions. Longer works presented more of a problem. It would, for example, have been impossible to include the whole of John Austin's *The Province of Jurisprudence Determined* without using up most of my allotted space. However, this particular problem was easily solved, for Austin's lectures 2, 3, and 4, which deal with his moral theory, are of no jurisprudential significance, since Austin expressly excluded morals from the province of jurisprudence; the solution was thus to include lecture 1, and the more important parts of lectures 5 and 6. Many other longer works were much harder to edit, but in every case my aim was to provide as much relevant material and as much continuity in reading as possible.

The question of the proper division of jurisprudence is not so much a matter of logic or science as of convenience. I have organized the book according to jurisprudential theories rather than according to problems or issues in the belief that this will allow a more integrated development of jurisprudential understanding. There are therefore chapters on positivism, natural law thought, and sociologism, and one on the judicial process which deals extensively with legal realism. Historical jurisprudence has been absorbed into sociological jurisprudence. I have thought it fitting, since this is the first Canadian book on jurisprudence, to add an appendix on the state of jurisprudence in Canada.

The chapter divisions are, of course, somewhat artificial, and may suit no teacher of jurisprudence but myself. Many teachers may not wish to make distinctions between positivism, naturalism, sociologism, and realism as clearcut as the chapter headings would suggest, though I hope the sequence of readings in each chapter and the editorial notes make it clear that these concepts are far from univocal and that many variations on themes shade over towards those developed by other schools. Even those teachers who do accept the divisions may very well wish to treat together readings which I have segregated in different chapters, such as Hart's *Positivism and the Separation of Law and Morals,* contained in Chapter II, and Fuller's reply, contained in Chapter III. But a book of materials such as this must have some structure; and this is the one I have found most useful. I should expect that other teachers might well use the same blocks to build different pyramids.

PREFACE

Though my own allegiance is for the most part to the school of natural law, I have striven for neutrality in the selection of cases and readings and in their editing. In the first (multilithed) edition of this book I attempted as well to write neutral notes with no critical comments, but my subsequent teaching experience has convinced me that students need a certain amount of evaluation in notes, even to enable them to disagree intelligently. However, I have kept the notes generally short, as I have the strong impression that most teachers of jurisprudence prefer to do their own editorializing.

I should like to express my gratitude to Miss Francess Halpenny and Mr. Hilary Marshall of the University of Toronto Press for their cooperation, to Mrs. Elizabeth Strand and Mrs. Honey Hecker of the Law School staff for their cheerful assistance in the labour of preparing the manuscript, and to Dean Wright and my colleagues for many helpful suggestions.

MARK R. MACGUIGAN

Faculty of Law
University of Toronto
January, 1966

Acknowledgements

Grateful acknowledgement is made for permission to reproduce extracts from the following works:

Aubert, Vilhelm, "The Concept of Law," (1964) 52 *Kentucky Law Journal* 363. (Reprinted by permission).

Brown, Brendan F., "Natural Law: Dynamic Basis of Law & Morals in the Twentieth Century" (1957) 31 *Tulane Law Review* 491. (Copyright 1956-1957 by the Tulane Law Review Association. Reprinted by permission).

Cardozo, Benjamin N., "Jurisprudence" [1932] *New York State Bar Association Report* 263. (Copyright 1932 by the New York State Bar Association. Reprinted by permission of the New York State Bar Association and of Columbia University, the residuary legatee of the literary estate of Benjamin Nathan Cardozo).
——— *The Nature of the Judicial Process.* (Copyright 1921 by Yale University Press. Reprinted by permission).

Cohen, Felix S., "Transcendental Nonsense and the Functional Approach," (1935) 35 *Columbia Law Review* 809. (Copyright 1935 by the Trustees of the Columbia Law Review. Reprinted by permission).

Cohen, Julius; Robson, Reginald A. H.; and Bates, Alan, *Parental Authority: The Community and the Law.* (Copyright © 1958 by Rutgers, The State University. Reprinted by permission of Rutgers University Press).

Coons, John E., *Legalism* (Reprinted by permission).

Dabin, Jean, *General Theory of Law.* (Reprinted by permission of the publishers from *The Legal Philosophies of Lask, Radbruch and Dabin,* trans. by Kurt Wilk, Cambridge, Mass.: Harvard University Press, Copyright, 1950, by The President and Fellows of Harvard College).

Dewey, John, "Logical Method and the Law" (1924) 10 *Cornell Law Quarterly* 17. (© Copyright 1924 by Cornell University. Reprinted by permission of Cornell Law Quarterly.)
——— "My Philosophy of Law," from *My Philosophy of Law.* (Copyright 1941 by the West Publishing Company. Reprinted by permission).

Ehrlich, Eugen, *Fundamental Principles of the Sociology of Law.* (Reprinted by permission of the publishers from Eugen Ehrlich, *Fundamental Principles of the Sociology of Law,* trans. by W. L. Moll, Cambridge, Mass.: Harvard University Press, Copyright, 1936, by The President and Fellows of Harvard College).

Frank, Jerome N., "Cardozo and the Upper-Court Myth," (1948) 13 *Law and Contemporary Problems* 369. (Reprinted from a book review, "Cardozo and the Upper-Court Myth," Vol. 13, No. 2 (Spring 1948) by permission from *Law and Contemporary Problems,* published by the Duke University School of Law, Durham, North Carolina. Copyright, 1948, by Duke University).

Freedman, Samuel, "Judges and the Law," (1962) 5 *Canadian Bar Association Journal* 208. (Reprinted by permission of the author).

FULLER, LON L., "The Case of the Speluncean Explorers" (1949) 62 *Harvard Law Review* 616 (Copyright re-assigned to author. Reprinted by permission).
——— *The Morality of Law*. (Copyright © 1964 by Yale University. Reprinted by permission of Yale University Press).
——— "Positivism and Fidelity to Law — A Reply to Professor Hart," (1958) 71 *Harvard Law Review* 630. (Copyright © 1958 by the Harvard Law Review Association. Reprinted by permission).

GOODHART, ARTHUR L., "Determining the Ratio Decidendi of a Case," (1930) 40 *Yale Law Journal* 161. (Copyright 1930-1931 by the Yale Law Journal Company. Reprinted by permission of the publisher and of the author.)

GRAY, J. C., *The Nature and Sources of Law*. (1909). (Reprinted by permission of Roland Gray, Jr., Boston, Mass.).

HAND, LEARNED, "The Speech of Justice," (1916) 29 *Harvard Law Review* 617. (Copyright 1916 by the Harvard Law Review Association. Reprinted by permission).

HART, H. L. A., *Definition and Theory in Jurisprudence* (1953). (Reprinted by permission of the Clarendon Press and of the author).
——— *The Concept of Law*. (© Oxford University Press 1961. Reprinted by permission of the Clarendon Press).
——— "Positivism and the Separation of Law and Morals," (1958) 71 *Harvard Law Review* 593. (Copyright © 1958 by the Harvard Law Review Association. Reprinted by permission).

HOBBES, THOMAS, *Leviathan*. Cambridge: the University Press. 1904. Text edited by A. R. Waller. (Reprinted by permission).

HUTCHESON, JOSEPH C. JR., "The Judgment Intuitive: The Function of the 'Hunch' in Judicial Decision," (1929) 14 *Cornell Law Quarterly* 274. (© Copyright 1929 by Cornell University. Reprinted by permission of Cornell Law Quarterly).

IHERING, RUDOLF VON, *Law as a Means to an End*. (Trans. by Isaac Husic, copyright 1913, Boston Book Co. Reprinted by permission of The Macmillan Company, New York.)

JOHN XXIII, POPE, *Pacem in Terris* (*Peace on Earth*) (1963). (Reprinted with permission from the America Press, 106 W. 56th Street, New York, New York 10019).

JONES, HARRY *W*., "Law and Morality in the Perspective of Legal Realism," (1961) 61 *Columbia Law Review* 799. (Copyright 1961 by the Directors of the Columbia Law Review Association, Inc. Reprinted by permission).
——— "The Rule of Law and the Welfare State," (1958) 58 Columbia Law Review 143. (Copyright 1958 by the Directors of the Columbia Law Review Association, Inc. Reprinted by permission).

KAYTON, IRVING, "Can Jurimetrics Be of Value to Jurisprudence?," (1964) 33 *George Washington Law Review* 287. (Copyright © 1964 by The George Washington Law Review. Reprinted by permission).

KELSON, HANS, *General Theory of Law and State*. (Copyright, New York: Russell & Russell, 1961. Reprinted by permission).
——— "The Pure Theory of Law and Analytical Jurisprudence" (1941) 55 *Harvard Law Review* 44. (Copyright 1941 by the Harvard Law Review Association. Reprinted by permission.)

LEVI, EDWARD H., *An Introduction to Legal Reasoning*. (Copyright 1948 by the University of Chicago. Reprinted from *An Introduction to Legal Reasoning* by Edward H. Levi by permission of the University of Chicago Press).

LLEWELLYN, KARL N., "On the Current Recapture of the Grand Tradition," in Llewellyn, *Jurisprudence: Realism in Theory and Practice*, 215-229, (© 1962 by The University of Chicago. Reprinted from *Jurisprudence: Realism in Theory and Practice* by Karl N. Llewellyn by permission of the University of Chicago Press).

——— "Some Realism about Realism — Responding to Dean Pound," (1931) 44 *Harvard Law Review 1222.* (Copyright 1931 by the Harvard Law Review Association. Reprinted by permission).

McWHINNEY, EDWARD, "Legal Theory and Philosophy of Law in Canada," from McWhinney (ed.), *Canadian Jurisprudence* (1959). (Reprinted by permission).

MEAD, MARGARET, "Some Anthropological Considerations Concerning Natural Law" (1961) 6 *Natural Law Forum 51.* (© 1961 by The University of Notre Dame. Reprinted by permission of the Natural Law Forum.)

OLIPHANT, HERMAN, "A Return to Stare Decisis," (1928) 14 *American Bar Association Journal* 71, 159. (Reprinted by permission).

O'MEARA, JOSEPH, "Natural Law and Everyday Law," (1960) 5 *Natural Law Forum* 83. (© 1960 by The University of Notre Dame. Reprinted by permission of the Natural Law Forum).

PASSERIN D'ENTREVES, A., "The Case for Natural Law Re-Examined," (1956) 1 *Natural Law Forum 5.* (© 1956 by The University of Notre Dame. Reprinted by permission of the Natural Law Forum).

POUND, ROSCOE, "My Philosophy of Law, "from *My Philosophy of Law.* (Copyright 1941 by the West Publishing Company. Reprinted by permission).

——— "A Survey of Social Interests," (1943) 57 Harvard Law Review 1. (Copyright 1943 by the *Harvard Law Review* Association. Reprinted by permission).

RAAB, CHARLES D., "Suggestions for a Cybernetic Approach to Sociological Jurisprudence," (1965) 17 *Journal of Legal Education* 377. (Reprinted from the *Journal of Legal Eduction,* Volume 17, No. 4, by permission from the Association of American Law Schools. Copyright 1965 by A.A.L.S.).

RAWLS, JOHN, "Justice as Fairness," (1957) 54 *Journal of Philosophy* 653. (Reprinted by permission of The Journal of Philosophy and of the author.)

ROBINSON, EDWARD S., *Law and the Lawyers* (1935). (Reprinted by permission of the Estate of Edward S. Robinson through William B. Gumbart, New Haven, Conn.).

ROSS, ALF, *On Law and Justice.* (Copyright 1959 by the University of California Press of Berkeley and Los Angeles, California. Reprinted by permission).

SALMOND, SIR JOHN, "The Names of the Law", Appendix 1, *Jurisprudence,* 9th ed. (1937), 669-679 (Reprinted by permission of Sweet & Maxwell, Ltd.).

SCHWARTZ, RICHARD D., "Field Experimentation in Sociolegal Research," (1961) 13 *Journal of Legal Education* 401. (Reprinted from the Journal of Legal Education, Volume 13, Number 4, by permission from the Association of American Law Schools. Copyright 1961 by A. A. L. S.).

SHAPIRO, MARTIN, "Political Jurisprudence," (1964) 52 *Kentucky Law Journal* 294. (Reprinted by permission).

SHKLAR, JUDITH N., *Legalism* (Reprinted by permission of the publishers from Judith Shklar, *Legalism,* Cambridge, Mass.: Harvard University Press, Copyright, 1965, by The President and Fellows of Harvard College).

STONE, JULIUS, *The Province and Function of Law* (1946), pp. 25-26. (Reprinted by permission).

THOMAS, AQUINAS, ST., Treatise on Law, *Summa Theologiae.* (Reprinted by permission of Basil Blackwell from Aquinas, *Selected Political Writings,* trans. J. G. Dawson, © Basil Blackwell and Mott, Ltd., 1959).

——— *Truth,* Vol. 3, trans. by Robert W. Schmidt, S. J. (Copyright 1954 Henry Regnery Company, Chicago, Illinois. Reprinted by permission).

WECHSLER, HERBERT, "The Nature of Judicial Reasoning," in Hook (ed.), *Law and Philosophy,* 293-296. (© 1964 by New York University. Reprinted by permission of New York University Press).

Editions used for other authors are as follows:

AUSTIN, JOHN, *The Province of Jurisprudence Determined,* vol. 1, *Lectures on Jurisprudence,* Robert Campbell (ed.), 4th ed. 1873, London: John Murray.

BENTHAM, JEREMY, *Principles of the Civil Code,* Part II, *The Works of Jeremy Bentham,* John Bowring (ed.), 1838, Edinburgh: William Tait.

——— *The Principles of Morals and Legislation,* Part I, *The Works of Jeremy Bentham,* John Bowring (ed.) 1838, Edinburgh: William Tait.

BLACKSTONE, WILLIAM, *Commentaries on the Laws of England,* William Draper Lewis (ed.) 1897, Philadelphia: Rees Welsh & Company.

JAMES, WILLIAM, "The Moral Philosopher and the Moral Life," pp. 184-215, *The Will To Believe and Other Essays in Popular Philosophy,* 1896, New York: Longmans Green and Co.

SAINT GERMAIN, CHRISTOPHER, *The Doctor and Student: Dialogues Between a Doctor of Divinity and a Student in the Laws of England.* William Muchall (ed.), 1874, Cincinnati: Robert Clarke & Co.

SAVIGNY, FRIEDRICH CARL VON, *Of the Vocation of Our Age for Legislation and Jurisprudence,* trans. by Abram Hayward, 1831, London: Littlewood & Co.

Grateful acknowledgement is also made to:

The Catholic Lawyer and the *Kentucky Law Journal* for permission to incorporate in editorial notes matter previously published in their pages; and to the West Publishing Company, Butterworth's, and the Incorporated Council of Law Reporting for England & Wales for permission to use extracts from cases.

Contents

Preface vii
Acknowledgements ix
Table of Cases xvii
Table of Authors xviii

Chapter I INTRODUCTION

Note on Jurisprudence 3
A. Cases
De Flaundres v. *Rycheman* 4
Note on the Word "Law" 5
The Case of the Speluncean Explorers 5
Hood & Sons v. *Du Mond* 23
Liversidge v. *Anderson* 28
B. Readings
Salmond, *Jurisprudence*: *The Names of the Law* 34
Shklar, *Legalism* 39
Coons, *Legalism* 45
Holmes, *The Path of the Law* 48
Jones, *The Rule of Law and the Welfare State* 62

Chapter II POSITIVISM

Note on Positivism 70
A. Cases
Jacobs v. *London Country Council* 71
Note on the *Jacobs Case* 76
Scruttons Ltd. v. *Midland Silicones* 76
Magor and St. Mellens R.D.C. v. *Newport Corporation* 88
British Movietonews Ld. v. *London and District Cinemas Ld.* 92
Note on Positivistic Cases 98
B. Readings
Note on Hume 99
Hobbes, *Leviathan* 99
Note on Hobbes 111
Bentham, *The Principles of Morals and Legislation* 113
Bentham, *Principles of the Civil Code* 121
Note on Bentham 130
Austin, *The Province of Jurisprudence Determined* 130
Note on Austinianism 157
Gray, *The Nature and Sources of Law* 158
Kelsen, *General Theory of Law and State* 166
Kelsen, *The Pure Theory of Law and Analytical Jurisprudence* 179
Hart, *Definition and Theory in Jurisprudence* 186
Hart, *Positivism and the Separation of Law and Morals* 193
Note on Hart 214
Hart, *The Concept of Law* 215

Rawls, *Justice as Fairness* 219
Note on Rawls 225
Ross, *On Law and Justice* 226
Note on Scandinavian Realism 236

CHAPTER III NATURAL LAW THOUGHT

Note on Natural Law Thought 239
A. CASES
Heydon's Case 242
Calvin's Case 243
Dr. Bonham's Case 244
Note on Coke and James I 244
Shaw v. *Director of Public Prosecutions* 245
Note on the *Shaw Case* 251
Barnette v. *West Virginia State Board of Education* 251
Lochner v. *New York* 255
Note on Laissez-Faire Economic Theory 258
Kintz v. *Harriger* 259
Sodero v. *Sodero* 261
Note on *Texada Mines* Case 263
R. v. *Hess* (No. 2) 263
Note on Civil Liberties 266
B. READINGS
St. Thomas Aquinas, *Truth* (*De Veritate*) 266
St. Thomas Aquinas, *Summa Theologiae* 268
Note on Law and Morals in Aquinas 282
Saint Germain, *The Doctor and Student* 284
Note on Hooker 290
Blackstone, *Commentaries on the Law of England* 291
Note on Blackstone 294
Dabin, *General Theory of Law* 295
Brown, *Natural Law: Dynamic Basis of Law and Morals* 310
A. P. d'Entrèves, *The Case for Natural Law Re-Examined* 317
Pope John XXIII, *Pacem in Terris* (*Peace on Earth*) 328
Note on the Changing Natural Law 332
Lon L. Fuller, *Positivism and Fidelity to Law* 333
Lon L. Fuller, *The Morality of Law* 356
Margaret Mead, *Some Anthropological Considerations Concerning Natural Law* 364

CHAPTER IV SOCIOLOGICAL JURISPRUDENCE

Note on Sociological Jurisprudence 368
A. CASES
Egerton v. *Brownlow* 370
M'Alister (*Donoghue*) v. *Stevenson* 375
Fender v. *Mildmay* 377
Petition of R.— 384
Repouille v. *U.S.* 386
Johnson v. *U.S.* 389
Fleming v. *Atkinson* 391
Note on Sociological Cases 393
B. READINGS
Savigny, *Of the Vocation of Our Age for Legislation and Jurisprudence* 393
von Ihering, *Law as a Means to an End* 401
Ehrlich, *Fundamental Principles of the Sociology of Law* 403
James, *The Moral Philosopher and the Moral Life* 427
Dewey, *My Philosophy of Law* 440
Note on Dewey 445

Pound, *A Survey of Social Interests* 445
Note on Pound 459
Pound, *My Philosophy of Law* 460
Cardozo, *The Nature of the Judicial Process* 465
Hand, *The Speech of Justice* 470
Cohen, Robson and Bates, *Parental Authority: The Community and the Law* 473
Raab, *Suggestions for a Cybernetic Approach to Sociological Jurisprudence* 486
Schwartz, *Field Experimentation in Sociological Research* 495
Note on Law and the Social Sciences 503

CHAPTER V THE JUDICIAL PROCESS

Note on American Legal Realism 506

A. CASES

London Street Tramways Company, Limited v. *L.C.C.* 508
Note on Precedent 509
Quinn v. *Leathem* 511
Young v. *Bristol Aeroplane Company, Limited* 513
Stuart v. *Bank of Montreal* 514
The Queen v. *Supertest Petroleum Corp. Ltd.* 516
Brown v. *Board of Education* 518
Hynes v. *New York Central R. Co.* 522
Rosenstiel v. *Rosenstiel* 524
Note on Judicial Legislation 531
Aero Spark Plug Co., Inc. v. *B. G. Corporation* 532
Ricketts v. *Pennsylvania R. Co.* 537

B. READINGS

Dewey, *Logical Method and the Law* 540
Oliphant, *A Return to Stare Decisis* 548
Goodhart, *Determining the Ratio Decidendi of a Case* 552
Note on Distinguishing 562
Levi, *An Introduction to Legal Reasoning* 563
Hutcheson, *The Judgment Intuitive* 566
Note on the Origins of Realism 571
Llewellyn, *Some Realism About Realism* 573
Robinson, *Law and the Lawyers* 579
Cardozo, *Jurisprudence* 588
Cohen, *Transcendental Nonsense and the Functional Approach* 597
Frank, *Cardozo and the Upper-Court Myth* 606
Llewellyn, *On the Current Recapture of the Grand Tradition* 614
Wechsler, *The Nature of Judicial Reasoning* 618
O'Meara, *Natural Law and Everyday Law* 620
Jones, *Law and Morality in the Perspective of Legal Realism* 627
Kayton, *Can Jurimetrics Be of Value to Jurisprudence?* 634

APPENDIX JURISPRUDENCE IN CANADA

Note on Canadian Jurisprudence 651
McWhinney, *Legal Theory and Philosophy of Law in Canada* 652
Freedman, *Judges and the Law* 658

Index 665

TABLE OF CASES

(Italicized page numbers indicate that the case is at least partly reproduced)

Abrams v. *U.S.* 642-3
Adamson v. *California* 259
Aero Spark Plug v. *B. G. Corp.* *532-7*
A.G.N.S.W. v. *Trethowan* 266
Barnette v. *W. Va. State Bd. of Ed.* *251-5*
Baxter v. *Baxter* 316
Best v. *Samuel Fox* 98
Betts v. *Brady* 648-9
Bonham's Case *244*, 315
Bourne v. *Keane* 509
Bowman v. *Secular Society* 240
British Movietonenews v. *London Cinemas* *92-8*
Brodwell v. *Ill.* 259
Brown v. *Board of Education* 496, *518-21*, 630-1
Buck v. *Bell* 316
Burnett v. *Coronado Oil* 510
Bushell's Case 663
Calvin's Case *243-4*, 315
De Flaundres v. *Rycheman* *4-5*
Dennis v. *U.S.* 644-6
Dickinson v. *Dodds* 556
Donoghue v. *Stevenson* 241, *375-7*, 659-60
Drew v. *The Queen* 518
Egerton v. *Brownlow* *370-5*, 447
Erie Railroad v. *Tompkins* 511, 657
Fender v. *Mildmay* *377-84*, 454
Fleming v. *Atkinson* *391-3*
Gideon v. *Wainright* 647-9
Hertz v. *Woodman* 510
Heydon's Case *242-3*
Hochster v. *Delatour* 553
Hood v. *Du Mond* *23-8*
Hynes v. *N.Y. Central Ry.* *522-4*
Ives v. *South Buffalo Ry. Co.* 259
Jacobs v. *L.C.C.* *71-6*
Johnson v. *U.S.* 389-91, 475
Kintz v. *Harriger* *259-61*
Liversidge v. *Anderson* *28-33*
Lochner v. *N.Y.* *255-8*
London Street Tramways v. *L.C.C.* *508-9*
Magor v. *Newport* *88-92*
Mahnich v. *Southern S.S.* 510
McBoyle v. *U.S.* 214
McCollum v. *Bd. of Education* 562
Omychund v. *Barker* 240
Oppenheim v. *Kridel* 393
Overseas Tankship v. *Morts Dock & Engineering* 393, 661
People v. *Vandewater* 558
Petition of R.—— *384-6*
Polemis, Re 661
Priestley v. *Fowler* 553
Printing and Numerical Registering Co. v. *Sampson* 258
Queen v. *Supertest Petroleum* *516-8*
Quinn v. *Leathem* *511-2*
R. v. *Dudley* 23
R. v. *Hess* (No. 2) *263-5*
Repouille v. *U.S.* *386-9*
Ricketts v. *Penn. Ry.* *537-40*
Rosenstiel v. *Rosenstiel* *524-31*
Russell v. *Russell* 454
Rylands v. *Fletcher* 159, 558-9
Saumur v. *City of Quebec* 266
Scruttons Ltd. v. *Midland Silicones* *76-87*
Shaw v. *D.P.P.* *245-51*
Smith v. *Allright* 510
Sodero v. *Sodero* *261-3*
Southern Pacific Co. v. *Jensen* 240, 532
Speluncean Explorers Case *5-23*
Stuart v. *Bank of Montreal* *514-6*
Swift v. *Tyson* 511
Switzman v. *Elbing* 266
Texada Mines Ltd. v. A.-G. B.C. 263
Trethowan's Case 266
Wagon Mound, The 393, 661
Washington v. *Dawson* 510
Whitney v. *Cal.* 643
Williams v. *Carwardine* 556
Woods Mfg. v. *The King* 518
Young v. *Bristol Aeroplane* *513-4*
Zorach v. *Clauson* 241, 562

TABLE OF AUTHORS AND JUDGES

(Italicized page numbers indicate a reading from an author or an opinion of a judge)

Abbott J. 266
Abinger, Lord 553
Adler 70, 239
Alderson B. 553, 660
Amos 196, *584-5*, 587
Angell 479
Antigone 302
Aristotle 316, 631
Atkin, Lord *32-3*, 241, *375-382*, 660
Aubert 237
Austin 53, 70-1, 112, *130-57*, 164, 179-86, 193-8, 203, 205, 209, 333-56, 444, 473, 651
Bacon 397, 399
Bain 428
Bates *473-86*
Bentham 53, 70, *113-30*, 148, 186, 190-1, 193-8, 203, 205, 346, 354, 418, 463, 589, 604
Bergbohm 345-6
Bergen J. *524-7*
Birkenhead, Lord 510
Black J. *26-7*, 259, 370, 562
Blackstone 70, 136, 145-6, 194-5, 202, *291-4*, 333, 486, 506, 600
Blaustein 510
Bohlen 590, 591
Boole 637, 648
Bracton 70, 240
Brandeis J. 25, 510, 583, 643-5
Brown, Brendan 239, 283, *310-7*
Brown, Jethro 157
Bryce, Lord 158
Buber 629
Buckland 158
Burlamaqui 239
Cahn 476-7
Campbell 236, 237
Cardozo J. 25, 368, 369, *465-9*, 474, 486, 488, 492, *522-4*, 568-9, *588-97*, 606-14, 622, 624, 626, 630, 635, 647, 658-9, 662
Chase J. *532-3*
Chroust 239
Cicero 37, 239
Cohen, Felix 294, *597-605*
Cohen, Julius *473-86*
Cohen, Morris R. 588, 595, 597
Coke 44, 244, 291, 508
Constable. 325
Cook 597
Coons *45-8*
Cowan 505
Crane J. 393
Dabin 282, *295-310*
Davies J. *514*
Davitt 507
Delos 324-5
Denning, Lord *82-7*, 89, 90-1, 95-6, 368
Descartes 61, 580
d'Entrèves, A.P. See Passerin
Desmond C. J. *527-9*
Deutsch 487, 490, 491, 495
Devlin, Lord 251
Dewey *440-5*, 480, *540-8*, 593, 655
Dicey 64-5
Dickinson 589, 590
Douglas J. 241, 563
Duguit 653
Durkheim 653
Eastwood 157
Ehrlich *403-27*, 479-80
Evershed, Lord 662
Field 510
Fortescue 240
Frank J. 201, 240, *388-9*, 474, 507, *533-40*, 571, 590, 597, *606-14*, 639, 655
Frankfurter J. 27-8, 370, 562, 661
Freedman J. A. *658-63*
Freud 503, 579
Friedmann 69
Fuller *5-23*, 212-3, 320-1, *333-64*, 573, 633
Geny 295, 595, 653
Gierke 405
Goodhart 76, 251, 511, *552-62*, 589, 597
Gray *158-65*, 196, 197, 333-4, 347, 474, 579-80, 597
Greene M. R. *513*
Greer L. J. 384
Grotius 146, 239, 443
Hägerström 200, 236-7
Hall 225
Halsbury, Earl of *508-9*, *511-2*
Hand J. 369, *386-8*, *389-91*, *470-2*, 607, 621, 622-6, 643-5
Hart *186-93*, *193-214*, 214, *215-9*, 333-56, 362-3, 507
Hayek 64-6
Hegel 61, 239, 447-8
Hoadly 162
Hobbes 53, 70-1, *99-111*, 111-3, 294
Hoebel 479
Hodson, Lord *251*
Hohfeld 622
Holland 157
Holmes J. 3, *48-62*, 193, 196, 236, 240, *257-8*, 315, 347, 368, 460, 474, 506, 532, 540, 543-4, 571-2, 588, 593, 597, 598-9, 604, 607, 624
Hooker 290-1, 323

Hughes C. J. 532
Hume 99, 480
Hutcheson J. *566-71*, 594, 661
Ihering 314, *401-2*, 418, 446, 474, 588, 601
Illum 236, 237-8
Jackson J. *23-6*
Jacobs 479
James I 244
James, William *427-40*, 465, 655
Jessel M. R. 258
John XXIII, Pope *328-32*, 332
Jones *62-9*, 214, 504, 507, *627-34*
Judson J. *391-3*
Justinian 70
Kant 61, 239, 318, 443, 460, 462
Kayton *634-50*
Keeton 157
Kellock J. 266
Kelsen 71, *166-86*, 199, 211, 235, 315, 337
King 241
Kohler 474
Kort 493, 648
Langdell 574, 654
Laskin 651
Lawlor 648
Levi *563-6*, 619
Llewellyn 479, 507, *573-9*, 588, 590-2, 597, 604, 613, *614-7*, 627, 633, 655
Locke J. 263
Locke, John 239
Lundstedt 236-7
MacMillan, Lord *31*, 660, 662
Macpherson 112
Maine 61, 164, 314, 410
Maitland 192, 607
Manning 158
Mansfield, Lord 148, 240, 246-7, 249, 352-3, 453, 455, 471, 663
Maritain 282, 325
Maugham, Viscount *29-31*
McCardie J. 557
McDougall 452
McKenna J 446-7
McWhinney *652-8*
Mead, Margaret *364-7*
Micklem 239, 323-4
Mill, James 428
Mill, J. S. 428
Montesquieu 202
Moore 479, 486, 575, 597
Morris, Lord *250-1*
Morton, Lord *89-92*
Nagel, Ernest 633
Nagel, Stuart S. 493
Neilsen 99, 219
Niebuhr 629
Northrop 479, 486
Odgen 130
O'Halloran J. A. *263-5*
Oliphant *548-52*, 597, 613
Olivecrona 236
O'Meara 325, 332, 333, 507, *620-7*
O'Sullivan 244
Parke B. *370-1*
Parker J. *251-5*
Passerin d'Entrèves 239, *317-28*, 332, 333
Patterson 71, 112, 157, 575
Peckham J. 203, *255-7*
Plato 70, 325, 326, 470
Pollock C. B. *371-5*
Pollock, Sir Frederick 158, 240, 244, 596, 607, 659
Porter, Lord 98-9
Pound 313-4, 368-9, *445-65*, 474, 486, 494, 495, 544, 571-2, 586, 588, 590, 597, 605, 613, 614, 624
Puchta 418
Pufendorf 146, 239
Raab *486-95*
Radbruch 205-8, 343-7
Radin 569, 597
Rand J. 266
Rawls *219-25*, 225-6
Read 651, 654, 655
Reid, Lord *79-82*, *247-50*
Roberts J. 510
Robinson *579-87*
Robson *473-86*
Rommen 322-3
Rooney 240
Roosevelt, Theodore 531
Rosenberg 503
Ross *226-36*, 236-7
Rousseau 318, 443
Russell, Bertrand 354
Russel, Lord *382-4*
Russell, Peter 651
Saint Germain *284-90*
Salmond J. A. *34-9*, 158, 199-200
Savigny *393-401*, 418, 588
Schwartz *495-503*
Scileppi J. *529-31*
Selznick 488, 490
Shapiro 369
Shklar *39-45*, 45-8, 71
Shuman 71
Simon, Viscount *93-8*
Simonds, Viscount 71, *76-9*, *88-9*, *98*, *245-7*
Slesser L. J. 332
Spencer 54, 258
Stone 3
Thomas Aquinas, St. 239, *266-82*, 282-4, 312-5, 322-5, 326, 332

Thomasius	239
Thorson P.	*516-8*
Tillich	628-9
Toqueville, de	42-3
Truro, Lord	375
Tucker, Lord	*92, 250*
Ulpian	3, 470
Vattel	239
Vico	326-7
Vinson C. J.	645-6
Walsh J.	*261-3*
Wanamaker J.	*259-61*
Warren C. J.	*518-21*
Weber	43
Wechsler	*618-9*, 619-20
Whitehead	354, 594, 624-6
Wiener	487, 492-3
Williams	5
Wild	322-3
Williston	538-9, 600
Winfield	369
Wittgenstein	212-3, 353-4, 363
Wrenbury, Lord	510
Wright, Cecil A.	651, 655
Wright, Lord	*32*, 76, *383-4*, 660
Wu	598
Wyzanski J.	*384-6*
Yntema	507, 597

JURISPRUDENCE: READINGS AND CASES

CHAPTER ONE

Introduction

The question of the proper definition and scope of jurisprudence is one on which it is impossible to get a consensus, for as long as there are differences in legal philosophy among jurisprudents so long will there be differences in their conceptions of jurisprudence. A jurisprudent's approach to the study of jurisprudence is a consequence of an already formulated jurisprudential position, and the continual determining and re-determining of the province of jurisprudence during the century or so of its recognized existence as a distinct discipline is a result of fundamental differences in jurisprudential theory.

To dispose first of a purely linguistic diffiiculty, we can find general agreement among all schools of thought that "jurisprudence", properly used, means something other than mere case law, the meaning which the word properly has in French and is sometimes loosely given in English. Holmes rightly draws this distinction in "The Path of the Law": "Jurisprudence, as I look at it, is simply law in its most generalized part. Every effort to reduce a case to a rule is an effort of jurisprudence, although the name as used in English is confined to the broadest rules and most fundamental conceptions."

But beyond this point there is little agreement. One attitude, based on the fundamental position that law is devoid of ethical and social values and that it should be sharply distinguished from other disciplines, is that jurisprudence should therefore avoid interdisciplinary questions and concentrate on the analysis of legal concepts. Holmes' view, at least in his more Austinian moments, is in fact not far from this. Another approach, founded on the basic insight that law rests on a bedrock of universally accepted moral principle, would dedicate jurisprudence exclusively to questions of justice in the law and the relationship of law to ethics. This is the tradition flowing from Ulpian's classic definition of jurisprudence as "the knowledge of divine and human things, the science of the just and the unjust" *(Juris prudentia est divinarum atque humanorum rerum notitia, justi atque injusti scientia).* In this approach jurisprudence tends to become a department of philosophy. A third view stems from the belief that the proper criterion of law is the way in which it operates and that one of the most important factors in determining its efficacy will be the extent of its correlation with the mores of the people. This approach tends to turn jurisprudence into a behavioral science. A fourth view is that, since law is nothing but process and that since the process is essentially a litigious one, jurisprudence should consist in a study of cases.

It would seem that the most fruitful approach to the teaching of jurisprudence is an "ecumenical" one, such as is found in the pluralistic, inter-disciplinary definition of Julius Stone:

> "Jurisprudence . . . is the lawyer's examination of the precepts, ideals and techniques of the law in the light derived from present knowledge in disciplines other than the law. . . . On the one hand, all the major branches which are generally admitted to the halls of jurisprudence are admissible by this test. Analytical jurisprudence is admissible as essentially a critique of law in terms of logic. . . . Historical jurisprudence is admissible insofar as it purports to interpret the development of law in terms of some theory of history. Also on this test

sociological jurisprudence is clearly not misnamed, for it reviews the law in the light of sociological knowledge, however that be defined. And insofar as economics, psychology, anthropology and the rest be regarded as disciplines distinct from sociology, they may each properly be credited with a respective approach to jurisprudence. The same is to be said of philosophy in its various branches, including notably the normative branches of ethics and politics. On the other hand, the various branches excluded from jurisprudence, by a consensus clearer than the reasons basing it, are justifiably excluded on this test. Thus the rebukes heaped upon 'medical jurisprudence', 'dental jurisprudence', and 'equity jurisprudence' are shown by this test to be justified by reasons other than the juristic *ipse dixit*."

(*The Province and Function of Law*, pp. 25-26)

It goes almost without saying, if jurisprudence is to be taken as the study of the interrelationship of law and other disciplines, that it must apply the insights and techniques of other disciplines in its own way for legal purposes, so that there is no necessary identity between the viewpoints of a jurisprudent and, say, a sociologist. In fact, the relationship between law and other disciplines is not entirely a one-sided one in which law is a parasite living on the fruits of others' labor, but is at least potentially one in which the other disciplines have something to gain from a study of law.

In addition to having a distinctive point of view, which will consist of a concern for the control of conduct through legal processes, jurispurudence must also be characterized by the generality of its interests. That is, it must be restricted to the general notions which transcend every particular field of law and must avoid the pitfall of succumbing to questions which more properly pertain to a particular field of law and which can be more adequately dealt with there. Of course, abstract questions concerning the nature of law have full significance only against a background of concrete controversies, but the teacher of jurisprudence has to assume, at least for practical reasons, that the materials of controversy in the various fields of contract, tort, property and crime have been presented by his colleagues in the courses devoted to those subjects. In keeping with this view, no explicit treatment of particular legal concepts like rights and liability is found in this book, though of course, many analytical problems are implicitly present. Nevertheless, since it is easier to proceed to the abstract from the concrete, there are in each section a number of cases which have been found to be fruitful in the stimulation of jurisprudential thought. Undoubtedly most of these cases also occupy important niches in their respective fields of law, but their jurisprudential treatment is probably more evaluative and less analytical than that of their particular field.

This first chapter contains a series of cases and readings without intrinsic connection to one another but which seem valuable as introductory material by virtue of their raising a wide range of jurisprudential questions. The chapter by no means attempts to define the province of jurisprudence; this is more properly the task of the whole book. All that it attempts to do is to sketch some of the main problems that have concerned jurisprudents over the years.

[N.B. As a general rule all footnotes have been omitted from the materials reproduced, and the footnotes retained have been renumbered].

A. CASES

DE FLAUNDRES v. RYCHEMAN

1346. Y.B. 19 Ed. III, Hil. pl. 3. Court of Common Pleas. (In translation)

SHARSULLE J.: No precedent is of such force as justice or that which is right.

R. THORPE (Counsel for the demandants): I think you will do as other judges have done in the same case, for otherwise we do not know what the law is.

HILLARY J.: Law is the will of the Justices.
STONORE C. J.: No. Law is justice, or that which is right.

Glanville L. Williams, "International Law and the Controversy Concerning the Word 'Law' " (1945) 22 *Brit. Y.B. Int. L.* 146, takes the extreme view that the jurisprudential controversy as to the word 'law' "is a verbal dispute, and nothing else" (p. 146) and that "Everyone is entitled for his own part to use words in any meaning he pleases; there is no such thing as an intrinsically 'proper' or 'improper' meaning of a word" (p. 148). In fine, "the only intelligent way to deal with a verbal question like that concerning the definition of the word 'law' is to give up thinking and arguing about it" (p. 163). However, it seems more reasonable to assume that the verbal dispute as to the proper use of the word conceals a genuine jurisprudential controversy as to the consequences for law of the adoption of a particular definition.

THE CASE OF THE SPELUNCEAN EXPLORERS

"In the Supreme Court of Newgarth," 4300, by Lon L. Fuller, (1949), 62 *Harvard Law Review* 616. Reprinted by permission of the author.

The defendants having been indicted for the crime of murder were convicted and sentenced to be hanged by the Court of General Instances of the County of Stowfield. They bring a petition of error before this Court. The facts sufficiently appear in the opinion of the Chief Justice.

TRUEPENNY, C. J.: The four defendants are members of the Speluncean Society, an organization of amateurs interested in the exploration of caves. Early in May of 4299 they, in the company of Roger Whetmore, then also a member of the Society, penetrated into the interior of a limestone cavern of the type found in the Central Plateau of this Commonwealth. While they were in a position remote from the entrance to the cave, a landslide occurred. Heavy boulders fell in such a manner as to block completely the only known opening to the cave. When the men discovered their predicament they settled themselves near the obstructed entrance to wait until a rescue party should remove the detritus that prevented them from leaving their underground prison. On the failure of Whetmore and the defendants to return to their homes, the Secretary of the Society was notified by their families. It appears that the explorers had left indications at the headquarters of the Society concerning the location of the cave they proposed to visit. A rescue party was promptly dispatched to the spot.

The task of rescue proved one of overwhelming difficulty. It was necessary to supplement the forces of the original party by repeated increments of men and machines, which had to be conveyed at great expense to the remote and isolated region in which the cave was located. A huge temporary camp of workmen, engineers, geologists and other experts was established. The work of removing the obstruction was several times frustrated by fresh landslides. In one of these, ten of the workmen engaged in clearing the entrance were killed. The treasury of the Speluncean Society was soon exhausted in the rescue effort, and the sum of eight hundred thousand frelars, raised partly by popular subscription and partly by legislative grant, was expended before the imprisoned men were rescued. Success was finally achieved on the thirty-second day after the men entered the cave.

Since it was known that the explorers had carried with them only scant provisions, and since it was also known that there was no animal or vegetable matter within the cave on which they might subsist, anxiety was early felt that they might meet death by starvation before access to them could be obtained. On the twentieth day of their imprisonment it was learned for the first time that they had taken with them into the cave a portable wireless machine capable of both sending and receiving messages. A similar machine was promptly installed in the rescue camp and oral communication established with the unfortunate men within the mountain. They asked to be informed how long a time would be required to release them. The engineers in charge of the project answered that at least ten days would be required even if no new landslides occurred. They then asked if any physicians were present, and were placed in communication with a committee of medical experts. The imprisoned men described their condition and the rations they had taken with them, and asked for a medical opinion whether they would be likely to live without food for ten days longer. The chairman of the committee of physicians told them that there was little possibility of this. The wireless machine within the cave then remained silent for eight hours. When communication was reestablished the men asked to speak again with the physicians. The chairman of the physicians' committee was placed before the apparatus and Whetmore, speaking on behalf of himself and the defendants, asked whether they would be able to survive for ten days longer if they consumed the flesh of one of their number. The physicians' chairman reluctantly answered this question in the affirmative. Whetmore asked whether it would be advisable for them to cast lots to determine which of them should be eaten. None of the physicians present was willing to answer the question. Whetmore then asked if there were among the party a judge or other official of the government who would answer this question. None of those attached to the rescue camp was willing to assume the role of adviser in this matter. He then asked if any minister or priest would answer their question, and none was found who would do so. Thereafter no further messages were received from within the cave, and it was assumed (erroneously, it later appeared) that the electric batteries of the explorers' wireless machine had become exhausted. When the imprisoned men were finally released it was learned that on the twenty-third day after their entrance into the cave Whetmore had been killed and eaten by his companions.

From the testimony of the defendants, which was accepted by the jury, it appears that it was Whetmore who first proposed that they might find the nutriment without which survival was impossible in the flesh of one of their own number. It was also Whetmore who first proposed the use of some method of drawing or casting lots, calling the attention of the defendants to a pair of dice he happened to have with him. The defendants were at first reluctant to adopt so desperate a procedure, but after the conversations by wireless related above, they finally agreed on the plan proposed by Whetmore. After much discussion of the mathematical problems involved, agreement was finally reached on a method of determining the issue by the use of the dice.

Before the dice were cast, however, Whetmore declared that he withdrew from the arrangement, as he had decided on reflection to wait for another week before embracing an expedient so frightful and odious. The others charged him with a breach of faith and proceeded to cast the dice. When it came Whetmore's turn, the dice were cast for him by one of the defendants, and he was asked to declare any objections he might have to the fairness of the throw. He stated that he had no such objections. The throw went against him and he was then put to death and eaten by his companions.

After the rescue of the defendants, and after they had completed a stay in a hospital where they underwent a course of treatment for malnutrition and shock, they were indicted for the murder of Roger Whetmore. At the trial, after the testimony had been concluded, the foreman of the jury (a lawyer by profession) inquired of the court whether the jury might not find a special verdict, leaving it to the court to say whether on the facts as found the defendants were guilty. After some discussion, both the Prosecutor and counsel for the defendants indicated their acceptance of this procedure, and it was adopted by the Court. In a lengthy special verdict the jury found the facts as I have related them above, and found further that if on these facts the defendants were guilty of the crime charged against them, then they found the defendants guilty. On the basis of this verdict, the trial judge ruled that the defendants were guilty of murdering Roger Whetmore. He then sentenced them to be hanged, the law of our Commonwealth permitting him no discretion with respect to the penalty to be imposed. After the release of the jury, its members joined in a communication to the Chief Executive asking that the sentence be commuted to an imprisonment of six months. The trial judge addressed a similar communication to the Chief Executive. As yet no action with respect to these pleas has been taken, as the Chief Executive is apparently awaiting our disposition of this petition of error.

It seems to me that in dealing with this extraordinary case the jury and the trial judge followed a course that was not only fair and wise, but the only course that was open to them under the law. The language of our statute is well known: "Whoever shall wilfully take the life of another shall be punished by death." N. C. S. A. (n. s.) 12-A. This statute permits of no exception applicable to this case, however our sympathies may incline us to make allowance for the tragic situation in which these men found themselves.

In a case like this the principle of executive clemency seems admirably suited to mitigate the rigors of the law, and I propose to my colleagues that we follow the example of the jury and the trial judge by joining in the communications they have addressed to the Chief Executive. There is every reason to believe that these requests for clemency will be heeded, coming as they do from those who have studied the case and had an opportunity to become thoroughly acquainted with all its circumstances. It is highly improbable that the Chief Executive would deny these requests unless he were himself to hold hearings at least as extensive as those involved in the trial below, which lasted for three months. The holding of such hearings (which would virtually amount to a retrial of the case) would scarcely be compatible with the function of the Executive as it is usually conceived. I think we may therefore assume that some form of clemency will be extended to these defendants. If this is done, then justice will be accomplished without impairing either the letter or spirit of our statutes or offering any encouragement for the disregard of law.

FOSTER, J.: I am shocked that the Chief Justice, in an effort to escape the embarrassments of this tragic case, should have adopted, and should have proposed to his colleagues, an expedient at once so sordid and so obvious. I believe that something more is on trial in this case than the fate of these unfortunate explorers, and that is the law of this Commonwealth. If this court declares that under our law these men have committed a crime, then our law is itself convicted in the tribunal of common sense, no matter what happens to the individuals involved in this petition of error. For us to assert that the law we uphold and expound compels us to a conclusion we are ashamed of, and from which we can only escape by appealing to a dispensation resting within the personal whim of the Executive, seems to me to amount to an admission that the law of this Commonwealth no longer pretends to incorporate justice.

For myself, I do not believe that our law compels the monstrous conclusion that these men are murderers. I believe, on the contrary, that it declares them to be innocent of any crime. I rest this conclusion on two independent grounds, either of which is of itself sufficient to justify the acquittal of these defendants.

The first of these grounds rests on a premise that may arouse opposition until it has been examined candidly. I take the view that the enacted or positive law of this Commonwealth, including all of its statutes and precedents, is inapplicable to this case, and that the case is governed instead by what ancient writers in Europe and America called "the law of nature."

This conclusion rests on the proposition that our positive law is predicated on the possibility of men's co-existence in society. When a situation arises in which the co-existence of men becomes impossible, then a condition that underlies all of our precedents and statutes has ceased to exist. When that condition disappears, then it is my opinion that the force of our positive law disappears with it. We are not accustomed to applying the maxim *cessante ratione legis, cessat ipsa lex* to the whole of our enacted law, but I believe that this is a case where it should be so applied.

The proposition that all positive law is based on the possibility of men's co-existence has a strange sound, not because the truth it contains is strange, but simply because it is a truth so obvious and pervasive that we seldom have occasion to give words to it. Like the air we breathe, it so pervades our environment that we forget that it exists until we are suddenly deprived of it. Whatever particular objects may be sought by the various branches of our law, it is apparent on reflection that all of them are directed toward facilitating and improving men's co-existence and regulating with fairness and equity the relations of their life in common. When the assumption that man may live together loses its truth, as it obviously did in this extraordinary situation where life only became possible by the taking of life, then the basic premises underlying our whole legal order have lost their meaning and force.

Had the tragic events of this case taken place a mile beyond the territorial limits of our Commonwealth no one would pretend that our law was applicable to them. We recognize that jurisdiction rests on a territorial basis. The grounds of this principle are by no means obvious and are seldom examined. I take it that this principle is supported by an assumption that it is only feasible to impose a single legal order upon a group of men living or residing together within the confines of a given area of the earth's surface. The premise that men shall co-exist in a group underlies, then, the territorial principle, as it does all of law. Now I contend that a case may be removed morally from the force of a legal order, as well as geographically. If we look to the purposes of law and government, and to the premises underlying our positive law, these men when they made their fateful decision were as remote from our legal order as if they had been a thousand miles beyond our boundaries. Even in a physical sense, their underground prison was separated from our courts and writ-servers by a solid curtain of rock that could be removed only after the most extraordinary expenditures of time and effort.

I conclude, therefore, that at the time Roger Whetmore's life was ended by these defendants, they were, to use the quaint language of nineteenth century writers, not in "a state of civil society" but in "a state of nature." This has the consequence that the law applicable to them is not the enacted and established law of this Commonwealth, but the law derived from those principles that were appropriate to their condition. I have no hesitancy in saying that under those principles they were guiltless of any crime.

What these men did was done in pursuance of an agreement accepted by all of them and first proposed by Whetmore himself. Since it was apparent that their extraordinary predicament made inapplicable the usual principles that regulate men's relations with one another, it was necessary for them to draw, as it were, a new charter of government appropriate to the situation in which they found themselves.

It has from antiquity been recognized that the most basic principle of law or government is to be found in the notion of contract or agreement. Ancient thinkers, expecially during the period from 1600 to 1900, used to base government itself on a supposed original Social Compact. Skeptics pointed out that this theory contradicted the known facts of history, and that there was no scientific evidence to support the notion that any government was ever founded in the manner supposed by the theory. Moralists replied that, if the Compact was a fiction from an historical point of view, the notion of compact or agreement furnished the only ethical justification on which the powers of government, which include that of taking life, could be rested. The powers of government can only be justified morally on the ground that these are powers that reasonable men would agree upon and accept if they were faced with the necessity of constructing anew some order to make their life in common possible.

Fortunately, our Commonwealth is not bothered by the perplexities that beset the ancients. We know as a matter of historical truth that our government was founded upon a contract or free accord of men. The archeological proof is conclusive that in the first period following the Great Spiral the survivors of that holocaust voluntarily came together and drew up a charter of government. Sophistical writers have raised questions as to the power of those remote contractors to bind future generations, but the fact remains that our government traces itself back in an unbroken line to that original charter.

If, therefore, our hangmen have the power to end men's lives, if our sheriffs have the power to put delinquent tenants in the street, if our police have the power to incarcerate the inebriated celebrant, these powers find their moral justification in that original compact of our forefathers. If we can find no higher source for our legal order, what higher source should we expect these starving unfortunates to find for the order they adopted for themselves?

I believe that the line of argument I have just expounded permits of no rational answer. I realize that it will probably be received with a certain discomfort by many who read this opinion, who will be inclined to suspect that some hidden sophistry must underlie a demonstration that leads to so many unfamiliar conclusions. The source of this discomfort is, however, easy to identify. The usual conditions of human existence incline us to think of human life as an absolute value, not to be sacrificed under any circumstances. There is much that is fictitious about this conception even when it is applied to the ordinary relations of society. We have an illustration of this truth in the very case before us. Ten workmen were killed in the process of removing the rocks from the opening to the cave. Did not the engineers and government officials who directed the rescue effort know that the operations they were undertaking were dangerous and involved a serious risk to the lives of the workmen executing them? If it was proper that these ten lives should be sacrificed to save the lives of five imprisoned explorers, why then are we told it was wrong for these explorers to carry out an arrangement which would save four lives at the cost of one?

Every highway, every tunnel, every building we project involves a risk to human life. Taking these projects in the aggregate we can calculate with some precision how many deaths the construction of them will require; statisticians can tell you the average cost in human lives of a thousand miles of a four-lane concrete highway. Yet we deliberately and knowingly incur and pay this cost on the assumption that the values obtained for those who survive outweigh the loss. If these things can be said of a society functioning above ground in a normal and ordinary manner, what shall we say of the supposed absolute value of a human life in the desperate situation in which these defendants and their companion Whetmore found themselves?

This concludes the exposition of the first ground of my decision. My second ground proceeds by rejecting hypothetically all the premises on which I have so far proceeded. I concede for purposes of argument that I am wrong in saying that the situation of these men removed them from the effect of our positive law, and I assume that the Consolidated Statutes have the power to penetrate five hundred feet of rock and to impose themselves upon these starving men huddled in their underground prison.

Now it is, of course, perfectly clear that these men did an act that violates the literal wording of the statute which declares that he who "shall wilfully take the life of another" is a murderer. But one of the most ancient bits of legal wisdom is the saying that a man may break the letter of the law without breaking the law itself. Every proposition of positive law, whether contained in a statute or a judicial precedent, is to be interpreted reasonably in the light of its evident purpose. This is a truth so elementary that it is hardly necessary to expatiate on it. Illustrations of its application are numberless and are to be found in every branch of the law. In *Commonwealth* v. *Staymore* the defendant was convicted under a statute making it a crime to leave one's car parked in certain areas for a period longer than two hours. The defendant had attempted to remove his car but was prevented from doing so because the streets were obstructed by a political demonstration in which he took no part and which he had no reason to anticipate. His conviction was set aside by this court, although his case fell squarely within the wording of the statute. Again, in *Fehler* v. *Neegas* a statute was before this court for construction in which the word "not" had plainly been transposed from its intended position in the final and most crucial section of the act. This transposition was contained in all the successive drafts of the act, where it was apparently overlooked by the draftsmen and sponsors of the legislation. No one was able to prove how the error came about, yet it was apparent that taking account of the contents of the statute as a whole, an error had been made, since a literal reading of the final clause rendered it inconsistent with everything that had gone before and with the object of the enactment as stated in its preamble. This Court refused to accept a literal interpretation of the statute, and in effect rectified its language by reading the word "not" into the place where it was evidently intended to go.

The statute before us for interpretation has never been applied literally. Centuries ago it was established that a killing in self-defense is excused. There is nothing in the wording of the statute that suggests this exception. Various attempts have been made to reconcile the legal treatment of self-defense with the words of the statute, but in my opinion these are all merely ingenious sophistries. The truth is that the exception in favor of self-defense cannot be reconciled with the *words* of the statute, but only with its *purpose*.

The true reconciliation of the excuse of self-defense with the statute making it a crime to kill another is to be found in the following line of reasoning. One of the principal objects underlying any criminal legislation is that of deterring men from crime. Now it is apparent that if it were declared to be the law that a killing in self-defense is murder such a rule could not operate in a deterrent manner. A man whose life is threatened will repel his aggressor, whatever the law may say. Looking therefore to the broad purposes of criminal legislation, we may safely declare that this statute was not intended to apply to cases of self-defense.

When the rationale of the excuse of self-defense is thus explained, it becomes apparent that precisely the same reasoning is applicable to the case at bar. If in the future any group of men ever find themselves in the tragic predicament of these defendants, we may be sure that their decision whether to live or die will not be controlled by the contents of our criminal code. Accordingly, if we read this statute intelligently it is apparent that it does not apply to this case. The withdrawal of this situation from the effect of the statute is justified by precisely the same considerations that were applied by our predecessors in office centuries ago to the case of self-defense.

There are those who raise the cry of judicial usurpation whenever a court, after analysing the purpose of a statute, gives to its words a meaning that is not at once apparent to the casual reader who has not studied the statute closely or examined the objectives it seeks to attain. Let me say emphatically that I accept without reservation the proposition that this court is bound by the statutes of our Commonwealth and that it exercises its powers in subservience to the duly expressed will of the Chamber of Representatives. The line of reasoning I have applied above raises no question of fidelity to enacted law, though it may possibly raise a question of the distinction between intelligent and unintelligent fidelity. No superior wants a servant who lacks the capacity to read between the lines. The stupidest housemaid knows that when she is told "to peel the soup and skim the potatoes" her mistress does not mean what she says. She also knows that when her master tells her to "drop everything and come running" he has overlooked the possibility that she is at the moment in the act of rescuing the baby from the drain barrel. Surely we have a right to expect the same modicum of intelligence from the judiciary. The correction of obvious legislative errors or oversights is not to supplant the legislative will, but to make that will effective.

I therefore conclude that on any aspect under which this case may be viewed these defendants are innocent of the crime of murdering Roger Whetmore, and that the conviction should be set aside.

TATTING, J.: In the discharge of my duties as a justice of this court I am usually able to dissociate the emotional and intellectual sides of my reactions, and to decide the case before me entirely on the basis of the latter. In passing on this tragic case I find that my usual resources fail me. On the emotional side I find myself torn between sympathy for these men and a feeling of abhorrence and disgust at the monstrous act they committed. I had hoped that I should be able to put these contradictory emotions to one side as irrelevant, and to decide the case on the basis of a convincing and logical demonstration of the result demanded by our law. Unfortunately, this deliverance has not been vouchsafed me.

As I analyse the opinion just rendered by my brother Foster I find that it is shot through with contradictions and fallacies. Let us begin with his first proposition: these men were not subject to our law because they were not in a "state of civil society" but in a "state of nature." I am not clear why this is so, whether it is because of the thickness of the rock that imprisoned them, or because they were hungry, or because they had set up a "new charter of government" by which the usual rules of law were to be supplanted by a throw of the dice. Other difficulties intrude themselves. If these men passed from the jurisdiction of our law to that of "the law of nature," at what moment did this occur? Was it when the entrance to the cave was blocked, or when the threat of starvation reached a certain undefined degree of intensity, or when the agreement for the throwing of the dice was made? These uncertainties in the doctrine proposed by my brother are capable of producing real difficulties. Suppose, for example, one of these men had had his twenty-first birthday while he was imprisoned within the mountain. On what date would we have to consider that he had attained his majority, – when he reached the age of twenty-one, at which time he was, by hypothesis, removed from the effects of our law, or only when he was released from the cave and became again subject to what my brother calls our "positive law"? These difficulties may seem fanciful, yet they only serve to reveal the fanciful nature of the doctrine that is capable of giving rise to them.

But it is not necessary to explore these niceties further to demonstrate the absurdity of my brother's position. Mr. Justice Foster and I are the appointed judges of a court of the Commonwealth of Newgarth, sworn and empowered to administer the laws of that Commonwealth. By what authority do we resolve ourselves into a Court of Nature? If these men were indeed under the law of nature, whence comes our authority to expound and apply that law? Certainly *we* are not in a state of nature.

Let us look at the contents of this code of nature that my brother proposes we adopt as our own and apply to this case. What a topsy-turvy and odious code it is! It is a code in which the law of contracts is more fundamental than the law of murder. It is a code under which a man may make a valid agreement empowering his fellows to eat his own body. Under the provisions of this code, furthermore, such an agreement once made is irrevocable, and if one of the parties attempts to withdraw the others may take the law into their own hands and enforce the contract by violence, – for though my brother passes over in convenient silence the effect of Whetmore's withdrawal, this is the necessary implication of his argument.

The principles my brother expounds contain other implications that cannot be tolerated. He argues that when the defendants set upon Whetmore and killed him (we know not how, perhaps by pounding him with stones) they were only exercising the rights conferred upon them by their bargain. Suppose, however, that Whetmore had had concealed upon his person a revolver, and that when he saw the defendants about to slaughter him he had shot them to death in order to save his own life. My brother's reasoning applied to these facts would make Whetmore out to be a murderer since the excuse of self-defense would have to be denied to him. If his assailants were acting rightfully in seeking to bring about his death, then of course he could no more plead the excuse that he was defending his own life than a condemned prisoner who struck down the executioner lawfully attempting to place the noose about his neck.

All of these considerations make it impossible for me to accept the first part of my brother's argument. I can neither accept his notion that these men were under a code of nature which this court was bound to apply to them, nor can I accept the odious and perverted rules that he would read into that code. I come now to the second part of my brother's opinion, in which he seeks to show that the defendants did not violate the provisions of N. C. S. A. (n. s.) § 12-A. Here the way, instead of being clear, becomes for me misty and ambiguous, though my brother seems unaware of the difficulties that inhere in his demonstrations.

The gist of my brother's argument may be stated in the following terms: No statute, whatever its language, should be applied in a way that contradicts its purpose. One of the purposes of any criminal statute is to deter. The application of the statute making it a crime to kill another to the peculiar facts of this case would contradict this purpose, for it is impossible to believe that the contents of the criminal code could operate in a deterrent manner on men faced with the alternative of life or death. The reasoning by which this exception is read into the statute is, my brother observes, the same as that which is applied in order to provide the excuse of self-defense.

On the face of things this demonstration seems very convincing indeed. My brother's interpretation of the rationale of the excuse of self-defense is in fact supported by a decision of this court, *Commonwealth* v. *Parry*, a precedent I happened to encounter in my research on this case. Though *Commonwealth* v. *Parry* seems generally to have been overlooked in the texts and subsequent decisions, it supports unambiguously the interpretation my brother has put upon the excuse of self-defense.

Now let me outline briefly, however, the perplexities that assail me when I examine my brother's demonstration more closely. It is true that a statute should be applied in the light of its purpose, and that *one* of the purposes of criminal legislation is recognized to be deterrence. The difficulty is that other purposes are also ascribed to the law of crimes. It has been said that one of its objects is to provide an orderly outlet for the instinctive human demand for retribution. *Commonwealth* v. *Scape*. It has also been said that its object is the rehabilitation of the wrong-doer. *Commonwealth* v. *Makeover*. Other theories have been propounded. Assuming that we must interpret a statute in the light of its purpose, what are we to do when it has many purposes or when its purposes are disputed?

A similar difficulty is presented by the fact that although there is authority for my brother's interpretation of the excuse of self-defense, there is other authority which assigns to that excuse a different rationale. Indeed, until I happened on *Commonwealth* v. *Parry* I had never heard of the explanation given by my brother. The taught doctrine of our law schools, memorized by generations of law students, runs in the following terms: The statute concerning murder requires a "wilful" act. The man who acts to repel an aggressive threat to his own life does not act "wilfully," but in response to an impulse deeply ingrained in human nature. I suspect that there is hardly a lawyer in this Commonwealth who is not familiar with this line of reasoning, especially since the point is a great favorite of the bar examiners.

Now the familiar explanation for the excuse of self-defense just expounded obviously cannot be applied by analogy to the facts of this case. These men acted not only "wilfully" but with great deliberation and after hours of discussing what they should do. Again we encounter a forked path, with one line of reasoning leading us in one direction and another in a direction that is exactly the opposite. This perplexity is in this case compounded, as it were, for we have to set off one explanation, incorporated in a virtually unknown precedent of this court, against another explanation, which forms a part of the taught legal tradition of our law schools, but which, so far as I know has never been adopted in any judicial decision.

I recognize the relevance of the precedents cited by my brother concerning the displaced "not" and the defendant who parked overtime. But what are we to do with one of the landmarks of our jurisprudence, which again my brother passes over in silence? This is *Commonwealth* v. *Valjean*. Though the case is somewhat obscurely reported, it appears that the defendant was indicted for the larceny of a loaf of bread and offered as a defense that he was in a condition approaching starvation. The court refused to accept this defense. If hunger cannot justify the theft of wholesome and natural food, how can it justify the killing and eating of a man? Again, if we look at the thing in terms of deterrence, is it likely that a man will starve to death to avoid a jail sentence for the theft of a loaf of bread? My brother's demonstrations would compel us to overrule *Commonwealth* v. *Valjean*, and many other precedents that have been built on that case.

Again, I have difficulty in saying that no deterrent effect whatever could be attributed to a decision that these men were guilty of murder. The stigma of the word "murderer" is such that it is quite likely, I believe, that if these men had known that their act was deemed by the law to be murder they would have waited for a few days at least before carrying out their plan. During that time some unexpected relief might have come. I realize that this observation only reduces the distinction to a matter of degree, and does not destroy it altogether. It is certainly true that the element of deterrence would be less in this case than is normally involved in the application of the criminal law.

There is still a further difficulty in my brother Foster's proposal to read an exception into the statute to favor this case, though again one not even intimated in his opinion. What shall be the scope of this exception? Here the men cast lots and the victim was himself originally a party to the agreement. What would we have to decide if Whetmore had refused from the beginning to participate in the plan? Would a majority be permitted to overrule him? Or, suppose that no plan were adopted at all and the others simply conspired to bring about Whetmore's death, justifying their act by saying that he was in the weakest condition. Or again, that a plan of selection was followed but one based on a different justification than the one adopted here, as if the others were atheists and insisted that Whetmore should die because he was the only one who believed in an after-life. These illustrations could be multiplied, but enough have been suggested to reveal what a quagmire of hidden difficulties my brother's reasoning contains.

Of course I realize on reflection that I may be concerning myself with a problem that will never arise, since it is unlikely that any group of men will ever again be brought to commit the dread act that was involved here. Yet, on still further reflection, even if we are certain that no similar case will arise again, do not the illustrations I have given show the lack of any coherent and rational principle in the rule my brother proposes? Should not the soundness of a principle be tested by the conclusions it entails without reference to the accidents of later litigational history? Still, if this is so, why is it that we of this court so often discuss the question whether we are likely to have later occasion to apply a principle urged for the solution of the case before us? Is this a situation where a line of reasoning not originally proper has become sanctioned by precedent, so that we are permitted to apply it and may even be under an obligation to do so?

The more I examine this case and think about it, the more deeply I become involved. My mind becomes entangled in the meshes of the very nets I throw out for my own rescue. I find that almost every consideration that bears on the decision of the case is counterbalanced by an opposing consideration leading in the opposite direction. My brother Foster has not furnished to me, nor can I discover for myself, any formula capable of resolving the equivocations that beset me on all sides.

I have given this case the best thought of which I am capable. I have scarcely slept since it was argued before us. When I feel myself inclined to accept the view of my brother Foster, I am repelled by a feeling that his arguments are intellectually unsound and approach mere rationalization. On the other hand, when I incline toward upholding the conviction I am struck by the absurdity of directing that these men be put to death when their lives have been saved at the cost of the lives of ten heroic workmen. It is to me a matter of regret that the Prosecutor saw fit to ask for an indictment for murder. If we had a provision in our statutes making it a crime to eat human flesh, that would have been a more appropriate charge. If no other charge suited to the facts of this case could be brought against the defendants, it would have been wiser, I think, not to have indicted them at all. Unfortunately, however, the men have been indicted and tried, and we have therefore been drawn into this unfortunate affair.

Since I have been wholly unable to resolve the doubts that beset me about the law of this case, I am with regret announcing a step that is, I believe, unprecedented in the history of this tribunal. I declare my withdrawal from the decision of this case.

KEEN, J.: I should like to begin by setting to one side two questions which are not before this court.

The first of these is whether executive clemency is affirmed. Under our system of government that is a question for the Chief Executive, not for us. I therefore disapprove of that passage in the opinion of the Chief Justice in which he in effect gives instructions to the Chief Executive as to what he should do in this case and suggests that some impropriety will attach if these instructions are not heeded. This is a confusion of governmental functions of which the judiciary should be the last to be guilty. I wish to state that if I were the Chief Executive I would go farther in the direction of clemency that the pleas addressed to him propose. I would pardon these men altogether, since I believe that they have already suffered enough to pay for any offense they may have committed. I want it to be understood that this remark is made in my capacity as a private citizen who by the accident of his office happens to have acquired an intimate acquaintance with the facts of this case. In the discharge of my duties as judge, it is neither my function to address directions to the Chief Executive, nor to take into account what he may or may not do in reaching my own decision, which must be controlled entirely by the law of this Commonwealth.

The second question that I wish to put to one side is that of deciding whether what these men did was "right" or "wrong," "wicked" or "good." That is also a question that is irrelevant to the discharge of my office as a judge sworn to apply, not my conceptions of morality, but the law of the land. In putting this question to one side I think I can also safely dismiss without comment the first and more poetic portion of my brother Foster's opinion. The element of fantasy contained in the arguments developed there has been sufficiently revealed in my brother Tatting's somewhat solemn attempt to take those arguments seriously.

The sole question before us for decision is whether these defendants did, within the meaning of N. C. S. A. (n. s.) § 12-A, wilfully take the life of Roger Whetmore. The exact language of the statute is as follows: "Whoever shall wilfully take the life of another shall be punished by death." Now I should suppose that any candid observer, content to extract from these words their natural meaning, would concede at once that these defendants wilfully took the life of Roger Whetmore.

Whence arise all the difficulties of the case, then, and the necessity for so many pages of discussion about what ought to be so obvious? The difficulties, in whatever tortured form that may present themselves, all trace back to a single source, and that is a failure to distinguish the legal and moral aspects of this case. To put it bluntly, my brothers do not like the fact that the written law requires the conviction of these defendants. Neither do I, but unlike my brothers I respect the obligations of an office that requires me to put my personal predilections out of my mind when I come to interpret and apply the law of this Commonwealth.

Now, of course, my brother Foster does not admit that he is actuated by a personal dislike of the written law. Instead he develops a familiar line of argument according to which the court may disregard the express language of a statute when something not contained in the statute itself, called its "purpose," can be employed to justify the result the court considers proper. Because this is an old issue between myself and my colleague, I should like, before discussing his particular application of the argument to the facts of this case, to say something about the historical background of this issue and its implications for law and government generally.

There was a time in this Commonwealth when judges did in fact legislate very freely, and all of us know that during this period some of our statutes were rather thoroughly made over by the judiciary. That was a time when the accepted principles of political science did not designate with any certainty the rank and function of the various arms of the state. We all know the tragic issue of that uncertainty in the brief civil war that arose out of the conflict between the judiciary, on the one hand, and the executive and the legislature, on the other. There is no need to recount here the factors that contributed to that unseemly struggle for power, though they included the unrepresentative character of the Chamber, resulting from a division of the country into election districts that no longer accorded with the actual distribution of the population, and the forceful personality and wide popular following of the then Chief Justice. It is enough to observe that those days are behind us, and that in place of the uncertainty that then reigned we now have a clear-cut principle, which is the supremacy of the legislative branch of our government. From that principle flows the obligation of the judiciary to enforce faithfully the written law, and to interpret that law in accordance with its plain meaning without reference to our personal desires or our individual conceptions of justice. I am not concerned with the question whether the principle that forbids judicial legislation is right or wrong, desirable or undesirable; I observe merely that it has become a tacit premise underlying the whole of the legal and governmental order I am sworn to administer.

Yet though the principle of the supremacy of the legislature has been accepted in theory for centuries, such is the tenacity of professional tradition and the force of fixed habits of thought that many of the judiciary have still not accommodated themselves to the restricted role which the new order imposes on them. My brother Foster is one of that group; his way of dealing with statutes is exactly that of a judge living in the thirty-nine hundreds.

We are all familiar with the process by which the judicial reform of disfavored legislative enactments is accomplished. Anyone who has followed the written opinions of Mr. Justice Foster will have had an opportunity to see it at work in every branch of the law. I am personally so familiar with it that in the event of my brother's incapacity I am sure I could write a satisfactory opinion for him without any prompting whatever, beyond being informed whether he liked the effect of the terms of the statute as applied to the case before him.

The process of judicial reform requires three steps. The first of these is to divine some single "purpose" which the statute serves. This is done although not one statute in a hundred has any such single purpose, and although the objectives of nearly every statute are differently interpreted by the different classes of its sponsors. The second step is to discover that a mythical being called "the legislator" in the pursuit of this imagined "purpose" overlooked something or left some gap or imperfection in his work. Then comes the final and most refreshing part of the task, which is, of course, to fill in the blank thus created. *Quod erat faciendum.*

My brother Foster's penchant for finding holes in statutes reminds one of the story told by an ancient author about the man who ate a pair of shoes. Asked how he liked them, he replied that the part he liked best was the holes. That is the way my brother feels about statutes; the more holes they have in them the better he likes them. In short, he doesn't like statutes.

One could not wish for a better case to illustrate the specious nature of this gap-filling process than the one before us. My brother thinks he knows exactly what was sought when men made murder a crime and that was something he calls "deterrence." My brother Tatting has already shown how much is passed over in that interpretation. But I think the trouble goes deeper. I doubt very much whether our statute making murder a crime really has a "purpose" in any ordinary sense of the term. Primarily such a statute reflects a deeply-felt human conviction that murder is wrong and that something should be done to the man who commits it. If we were forced to be more articulate about the matter, we would probably take refuge in the more sophisticated theories of the criminologists, which, of course, were certainly not in the minds of those who drafted our statute. We might also observe that men will do their own work more effectively and live happier lives if they are protected against the threat of violent assault. Bearing in mind that the victims of murders are often unpleasant people, we might add some suggestion that the matter of disposing of undesirables is not a function suited to private enterprise, but should be a state monopoly. All of which reminds me of the attorney who once argued before us that a statute licensing physicians was a good thing because it would lead to lower life insurance rates by lifting the level of general health. There is such a thing as over-explaining the obvious.

If we do not know the purpose of § 12-A, how can we possibly say there is a "gap" in it? How can we know what its draftsmen thought about the question of killing men in order to eat them? My brother Tatting has revealed an understandable, though perhaps slightly exaggerated revulsion to cannibalism. How do we know that his remote ancestors did not feel the same revulsion to an even higher degree? Anthropologists say that the dread felt for a forbidden act may be increased by the fact that the conditions of a tribe's life create special temptations toward it, as incest is most severely condemned among those whose village relations make it most likely to occur. Certainly the period following the Great Spiral was one that had implicit in it temptations to anthropophagy. Perhaps it was for that very reason that our ancestors expressed their prohibition in so broad and unqualified a form. All of this is conjecture, of course, but it remains abundantly clear that neither I nor my brother Foster knows what the "purpose" of § 12-A is.

Considerations similar to those I have just outlined are also applicable to the exception in favor of self-defense, which plays so large a role in the reasoning of my brothers Foster and Tatting. It is of course true that in *Commonwealth* v. *Parry* an *obiter dictum* justified this exception on the assumption that the purpose of criminal legislation is to deter. It may well also be true that generations of law students have been taught that the true explanation of the exception lies in the fact that a man who acts in self-defense does not act "wilfully," and that the same students have passed their bar examinations by repeating what their professors told them. These last observations I could dismiss, of course, as irrelevant for the simple reason that professors and bar examiners have not as yet any commission to make our laws for us. But again the real trouble lies deeper. As in dealing with the statute, so in dealing with the exception, the question is not the conjectural *purpose* of the rule, but its *scope*. Now the scope of the exception in favor of self-defense as it has been applied by this court is plain: it applies to cases of resisting an aggressive threat to the party's own life. It is therefore too clear for argument that this case does not fall within the scope of the exception, since it is plain that Whetmore made no threat against the lives of these defendants.

The essential shabbiness of my brother Foster's attempt to cloak his remaking of the written law with an air of legitimacy comes tragically to the surface in my brother Tatting's opinion. In that opinion Justice Tatting struggles manfully to combine his colleague's loose moralisms with his own sense of fidelity to the written law. The issue of this struggle could only be that which occurred, a complete default in the discharge of the judicial function. You simply cannot apply a statute as it is written and remake it to meet your own wishes at the same time.

Now I know that the line of reasoning I have developed in this opinion will not be acceptable with those who look only to the immediate effects of a decision and ignore the long-run implications of an assumption of a power of dispensation by the judiciary. A hard decision is never a popular decision. Judges have been celebrated in literature for their sly prowess in devising some quibble by which a litigant could be deprived of his rights where the public thought it was wrong for him to assert those rights. But I believe that judicial dispensation does more harm in the long run than hard decisions. Hard cases may even have a certain moral value by bringing home to the people their own responsibilities toward the law that is ultimately their creation, and by reminding them that there is no principle of personal grace that can relieve the mistakes of their representatives.

Indeed, I will go farther and say that the principles I have been expounding are not only those which are soundest for our present conditions, but that we would have inherited a better legal system from our forefathers if those principles had been observed from the beginning. For example, with respect to the excuse of self-defense, if our courts had stood steadfast on the language of the statute the result would undoubtedly have been a legislative revision of it. Such a revision would have drawn on the assistance of natural philosophers and psychologists and the resulting regulation of the matter would have had an understandable and rational basis, instead of the hodge-podge of verbalisms and metaphysical distinctions that have emerged from the judicial and professorial treatment of it.

These concluding remarks are, of course, beyond any duties that I have to discharge with relation to this case, but I include them here because I feel deeply that my colleagues are insufficiently aware of the dangers implicit in the conceptions of the judicial office advocated by my brother Foster.

I conclude that the conviction should be affirmed.

HANDY, J.: I have listened with amazement to the tortured ratiocinations to which this simple case has given rise. I never cease to wonder at my colleagues' ability to throw about every issue presented to them for decision an obscuring curtain of legalisms. We have heard this afternoon learned disquisitions on the distinction between positive law and the law of nature, the language of the statute and the purpose of the statute, judicial functions and executive functions, judicial legislation and legislative legislation. My only disappointment was that someone did not raise the question of the legal nature of the bargain struck in the cave, — whether it was unilateral or bilateral, and whether Whetmore could not be considered as having revoked an offer prior to action taken thereunder.

What have all these things to do with the case? The problem before us is what we, as officers of the government, ought to do with these defendants. That is a question of practical wisdom, to be exercised in a context, not of abstract theory, but of human realities. When the case is approached in this light, it becomes, I think, one of the easiest to decide that has ever been argued before this court.

Before stating my own conclusions about the merits of the case, I should like to discuss briefly some of the more fundamental issues involved, — issues on which my colleagues and I have been divided ever since I have been on the bench.

I have never been able to make my brothers see that government is a human affair, and that men are ruled, not by words on paper or by abstract theories, but by other men. They are ruled well when their rulers understand the feelings and conceptions of the masses subject to their government. They are ruled badly when the understanding is lacking.

Of all branches of the government, the judiciary is the most likely to lose its contact with the common man. The reasons for this are, of course, fairly obvious. Where the masses react to a situation in terms of a few salient features, we pick into little pieces every situation presented to us. Lawyers are hired by one another to see who can discover the greatest number of difficulties and distinctions in a single set of facts. Each side tries to find cases, real or imagined, that will embarrass the demonstrations of the other side. To escape this embarrassment, still further distinctions are invented and imported into the situation. When a set of facts has been subjected to this kind of treatment for a sufficient time, all the life and juice have gone out of it and we have left a handful of dust.

Now I realize that wherever you have rules and abstract principles lawyers are going to be able to make distinctions. To some extent the sort of thing I have been describing is a necessary evil attaching to any formal regulation of human affairs. But I think that the area which really stands in need of such regulation is greatly overestimated. There are, of course, a few fundamental rules of the game that must be accepted if the game is to go on at all. I would include among these the rules relating to the conduct of elections, the appointment of public officials, and the term during which an office is held. Here some restraint on discretion and dispensation, some adherence to form, some scruple for what does not fall within the rule, is, I concede, essential. Perhaps the area of basic principle should be expanded to include certain other rules, such as those designed to preserve the free civilmoign system.

But outside of these fields I believe that all government officials, including judges, will do their jobs best if they treat forms and abstract concepts as instruments. We should take as our model, I think, the good administrator, who accommodates procedures and principles to the case at hand, selecting from among the available forms those most suited to reach the proper result.

The most obvious advantage of this method of government is that it permits us to go about our daily tasks with efficiency and common sense. My adherence to this philosophy has, however, deeper roots. I believe that it is only with the insight this philosophy gives that we can preserve the flexibility essential if we are to keep our actions in reasonable accord with the sentiments of those subject to our rule. More governments have been wrecked, and more human misery caused, by the lack of this accord between ruler and ruled than by any other factor that can be discerned in history. Once drive a sufficient wedge between the mass of people and those who direct their legal, political and economic life, and our society is ruined. Then neither Foster's law of nature nor Keen's fidelity to written law will avail us anything.

Now when these conceptions are applied to the case before us, its decision becomes, as I have said, perfectly easy. In order to demonstrate this I shall have to introduce certain realities that my brothers in their coy decorum have seen fit to pass over in silence, although they are just as acutely aware of them as I am.

The first of these is that this case has aroused an enormous public interest, both here and abroad. Almost every newspaper and magazine has carried articles about it; columnists have shared with their readers confidential information as to the next governmental move; hundreds of letters-to-the-editor have been printed. One of the great newspaper chains made a poll of public opinion on the question,

"What do you think the Supreme Court should do with the Speluncean explorers?" About ninety percent expressed a belief that the defendants should be pardoned or let off with a kind of token punishment. It is perfectly clear, then, how the public feels about the case. We could have known this without the poll, of course, on the basis of common sense, or even by observing that on this court there are apparently four and a half men, or ninety percent, who share the common opinion.

This makes it obvious not only what we should do, but what we must do if we are to preserve between ourselves and public opinion a reasonable and decent accord. Declaring these men innocent need not involve us in any undignified quibble or trick. No principle of statutory construction is required that is not consistent with the past practices of this court. Certainly no layman would think that in letting these men off we had stretched the statute any more than our ancestors did when they created the excuse of self-defense. If a more detailed demonstration of the method of reconciling our decision with the statute is required, I should be content to rest on the arguments developed in the second and less visionary part of my brother Foster's opinion.

Now I know that my brothers will be horrified by my suggestion that this court should take account of public opinion. They will tell you that public opinion is emotional and capricious, that it is based on half-truths and listens to witnesses who are not subject to cross-examination. They will tell you that the law surrounds the trial of a case like this with elaborate safeguards, designed to insure that the truth will be known and that every rational consideration bearing on the issues of the case has been taken into account. They will warn you that all of these safeguards go for naught if a mass opinion formed outside this framework is allowed to have any influence on our decision.

But let us look candidly at some of the realities of the administration of our criminal law. When a man is accused of crime, there are, speaking generally, four ways in which he may escape punishment. One of these is a determination by a judge that under the applicable law he has committed no crime. This is, of course, a determination that takes place in a rather formal and abstract atmosphere. But look at the other three ways in which he may escape punishment. These are: 1) a decision by the Prosecutor not to ask for an indictment; 2) an acquittal by the jury; 3) a pardon or commutation of sentence by the executive. Can anyone pretend that these decisions are held within a rigid and formal framework of rules that prevents factual error, excludes emotional personal factors, and guarantees that all the forms of the law will be observed?

In the case of the jury we do, to be sure, attempt to cabin their deliberations within the area of the legally relevant, but there is no need to deceive ourselves into believing that this attempt is really successful. In the normal course of events the case now before us would have gone on all of its issues directly to the jury. Had this occurred we can be confident that there would have been an acquittal or at least a division that would have prevented a conviction. If the jury had been instructed that the men's hunger and their agreement were no defense to the charge of murder, their verdict would in all likelihood have ignored this instruction and would have involved a good deal more twisting of the letter of the law than any that is likely to tempt us. Of course the only reason that didn't occur in this case was the fortuitous circumstance that the foreman of the jury happened to be a lawyer. His learning enabled him to devise a form of words that would allow the jury to dodge its usual responsibilities.

My brother Tatting expresses annoyance that the Prosecutor did not, in effect, decide the case for him by not asking for an indictment. Strict as he is himself in complying with the demands of legal theory, he is quite content to have the fate of these men decided out of court by the Prosecutor on the basis of common sense. The Chief Justice, on the other hand, wants the application of common sense postponed to the very end, though like Tatting, he wants no personal part in it.

This brings me to the concluding portion of my remarks, which has to do with executive clemency. Before discussing that topic directly, I want to make a related observation about the poll of public opinion. As I have said, ninety percent of the people wanted the Supreme Court to let the men off entirely or with a more or less nominal punishment. The ten percent constituted a very oddly assorted group, with the most curious and divergent opinions. One of our university experts has made a study of this group and has found that its members fall into certain patterns. A substantial portion of them are subscribers to "crank" newspapers of limited circulation that gave their readers a distorted version of the facts of the case. Some thought that "Speluncean" means "cannibal" and that anthropophagy is a tenet of the Society. But the point I want to make, however, is this: although almost every conceivable variety and shade of opinion was represented in this group, there was, so far as I know, not one of them, nor a single member of the majority of ninety percent, who said, "I think it would be a fine thing to have the courts sentence these men to be hanged, and then to have another branch of the government come along and pardon them." Yet this is a solution that has more or less dominated our discussions and which our Chief Justice proposes as a way by which we can avoid doing an injustice and at the same time preserve respect for law. He can be assured that if he is preserving anybody's morale, it is his own, and not the public's, which knows nothing of his distinctions. I mention this matter because I wish to emphasize once more the danger that we may get lost in the patterns of our own thought and forget that these patterns often cast not the slightest shadow on the outside world.

I come now to the most crucial fact in this case, a fact known to all of us on this court, though one that my brothers have seen fit to keep under the cover of their judicial robes. This is the frightening likelihood that if the issue is left to him, the Chief Executive will refuse to pardon these men or commute their sentence. As we all know, our Chief Executive is a man now well advanced in years, of very stiff notions. Public clamor usually operates on him with the reverse of the effect intended. As I have told my brothers, it happens that my wife's niece is an intimate friend of his secretary. I have learned in this indirect, but, I think, wholly reliable way, that he is firmly determined not to commute the sentence if these men are found to have violated the law.

No one regrets more than I the necessity for relying in so important a matter on information that could be characterized as gossip. If I had my way this would not happen, for I would adopt the sensible course of sitting down with the Executive, going over the case with him, finding our (sic) what his views are, and perhaps working out with him a common program for handling the situation. But of course my brothers would never hear of such a thing.

Their scruple about acquiring accurate information directly does not prevent them from being very perturbed about what they have learned indirectly. Their acquaintance with the facts I have just related explains why the Chief Justice, ordinarily a model of decorum, saw fit in his opinion to flap his judicial robes in the face of the Executive and threaten him with excommunication if he failed to commute the sentence. It explains, I suspect, my brother Foster's feat of levitation by which a whole library of law books was lifted from the shoulders of these defendants. It explains also why even my legalistic brother Keen emulated Pooh-

Bah in the ancient comedy by stepping to the other side of the stage to address a few remarks to the Executive "in my capacity as a private citizen." (I may remark, incidentally, that the advice of Private Citizen Keen will appear in the reports of this court printed at taxpayers' expense.)

I must confess that as I grow older I become more and more perplexed at men's refusal to apply their common sense to problems of law and government, and this truly tragic case has deepened my sense of discouragement and dismay. I only wish that I could convince my brothers of the wisdom of the principles I I have applied to the judicial office since I first assumed it. As a matter of fact, by a kind of sad rounding of the circle, I encountered issues like those involved here in the very first case I tried as Judge of the Court of General Instances in Fanleigh County.

A religious sect had unfrocked a minister who, they said, had gone over to the views and practices of a rival sect. The minister circulated a handbill making charges against the authorities who had expelled him. Certain lay members of the church announced a public meeting at which they proposed to explain the position of the church. The minister attended this meeting. Some said he slipped in unobserved in a disguise; his own testimony was that he had walked in openly as a member of the public. At any rate when the speeches began he interrupted with certain questions about the affairs of the church and made some statements in defense of his own views. He was set upon by members of the audience and given a pretty thorough pommeling, receiving among other injuries a broken jaw. He brought a suit for damages against the association that sponsored the meeting and against ten named individuals who he alleged were his assailants.

When we came to the trial, the case at first seemed very complicated to me. The attorneys raised a host of legal issues. There were nice questions on the admissibility of evidence, and, in connection with the suit against the association, some difficult problems turning on the question whether the minister was a trespasser or a licensee. As a novice on the bench I was eager to apply my law-school learning and I began studying these questions closely, reading all the authorities and preparing well documented rulings. As I studied the case I became more and more involved in its legal intricacies and I began to get into a state approaching that of my brother Tatting in this case. Suddenly, however, it dawned on me that all these perplexing issues really had nothing to do with the case, and I began examining it in the light of common sense. The case at once gained a new perspective and I saw that the only thing for me to do was to direct a verdict for the defendants for lack of evidence.

I was led to this conclusion by the following considerations. The melee in which the plaintiff was injured had been a very confused affair, with some people trying to get to the center of the disturbance, while others were trying to get away from it; some striking at the plaintiff, while others were apparently trying to protect him. It would have taken weeks to find out the truth of the matter. I decided that nobody's broken jaw was worth that much to the Commonwealth. (The minister's injuries, incidentally, had meanwhile healed without disfigurement and without any impairment of normal faculties.) Furthermore, I felt very strongly that the plaintiff had to a large extent brought the thing on himself. He knew how inflamed passions were about the affair, and could easily have found another forum for the expression of his views. My decision was widely approved by the press and public opinion, neither of which could tolerate the views and practices that the expelled minister was attempting to defend.

Now, thirty years later, thanks to an ambitious Prosecutor and a legalistic jury foreman, I am faced with a case that raises issues which are at bottom much like those involved in that case. The world does not seem to change much, except that this time it is not a question of a judgment for five or six hundred frelars, but of the life or death of four men who have already suffered more torment and humiliation than most of us would endure in a thousand years. I conclude that the defendants are innocent of the crime charged, and that the conviction and sentence should be set aside.

TATTING, J.: I have been asked by the Chief Justice whether, after listening to the two opinions just rendered, I desire to reexamine the position previously taken by me. I wish to state that after hearing these opinions I am greatly strengthened in my conviction that I ought not to participate in the decision of this case.

The Supreme Court being evenly divided, the conviction and sentence of the Court of General Instances is AFFIRMED. It is ordered that the execution of the sentence shall occur at 6 A.M., Friday, April 2, 4300, at which time the Public Executioner is directed to proceed with all convenient dispatch to hang each of the defendants by the neck until he is dead.

Cf. *R.* v. *Dudley and Stephens* (1884), 14 *Q. B. D.* 273 where the master and mate of a yacht were indicted for the murder of a cabin-boy, whom they killed for food after 20 days without food in an open boat. The jury found a special verdict, which a five-judge court held had the legal effect of a conviction for murder. However, the automatic sentence of death passed by the Court was afterwards commuted by the Crown to six months' imprisonment.

HOOD & SONS v. DU MOND

Supreme Court of the United States, 1949.
336 U.S. 525, 93 L.Ed. 865, 69 S.Ct. 657.

MR. JUSTICE JACKSON delivered the opinion of the Court.: This case concerns the power of the State of New York to deny additional facilities to acquire and ship milk in interstate commerce where the grounds of denial are that such limitation upon interstate business will protect and advance local economic interests.

H. P. Hood & Sons, Inc., a Massachusetts corporation, has long distributed milk and its products to inhabitants of Boston. That city obtains about 90% of its fluid milk from states other than Massachusetts. Dairies located in New York State since about 1900 have been among the sources of Boston's supply, their contribution having varied but during the last ten years approximating 8%. The area in which Hood has been denied an additional license to make interstate purchases has been developed as a part of the Boston milk shed from which both the Hood Company and a competitor have shipped to Boston.

The state courts have held and it is conceded here that Hood's entire business in New York, present and proposed, is interstate commerce. This Hood has conducted for some time by means of three receiving depots, where it takes raw milk from farmers. Milk is not processed in New York but is weighed, tested and, if necessary, cooled and on the same day shipped fluid milk to Boston. Those existing plants have been operated under license from the State and are not in question here as the State has licensed Hood to continue them. The controversy concerns a proposed additional plant for the same kind of operation at Greenwich, New York.

Article 21 of the Agriculture and Markets Law of New York forbids a dealer to buy milk from producers unless licensed to do so by the Commissioner of Agriculture and Markets. For the license he must pay a substantial fee and furnish a bond to assure prompt payment to producers for milk. Under § 258, the Commissioner may not grant a license unless satisfied "that the applicant is qualified by character, experience, financial responsibility and equipment to properly conduct the proposed business." The Hood Company concededly has met all the foregoing tests and license for an additional plant was not denied for any failure to comply with these requirements.

The Commissioner's denial was based on further provisions of this section which require him to be satisfied "that the issuance of the license will not tend to a destructive competition in a market already adequately served, and that the issuance of the license will be in the public interest."

Upon the hearing pursuant to the statute, milk dealers competing with Hood as buyers in the area opposed licensing the proposed Greenwich plant. They complained that Hood, by reason of conditions under which it sold in Boston, had competitive advantages under applicable federal milk orders, Boston health regulations, and OPA ceiling prices. There was also evidence of a temporary shortage of supply in the Troy, New York market during the fall and winter of 1945-46. The Commissioner was urged not to allow Hood to compete for additional supplies of milk or to take on producers then delivering to other dealers.

The Commissioner found that Hood, if licensed at Greenwich, would permit its present suppliers, at their option, to deliver at the new plant rather than the old ones and for a substantial number this would mean shorter hauls and savings in delivery costs. The new plant also would attract twenty to thirty producers, some of whose milk Hood anticipates will or may be diverted from other buyers. Other large milk distributors have plants within the general area and dealers serving Troy obtain milk in the locality. He found that Troy was inadequately supplied during the preceding short season. . . .

Denial of the license was sustained by the Court of Appeals over constitutional objections duly urged under the Commerce Clause and, because of the importance of the questions involved, we brought the case here by certiorari.

Production and distribution of milk are so intimately related to public health and welfare that the need for regulation to protect those interests has long been recognized and is, from a constitutional standpoint, hardly controversial. Also, the economy of the industry is so eccentric that economic controls have been found at once necessary and difficult. These have evolved detailed, intricate and comprehensive regulations, including price-fixing. They have been much litigated but were generally sustained by this Court as within the powers of the State over its internal commerce as against the claim that they violated the Fourteenth Amendment. . . .

New York's regulations, designed to assure producers a fair price and a responsible purchaser, and consumers a sanitary and modernly equipped handler, are not challenged here but have been complied with. It is only additional restrictions, imposed for the avowed purpose and with the practical effect of curtailing the volume of interstate commerce to aid local economic interests, that are in question here, and no such measures were attempted or such ends sought to be served in the Act before the Court in the Eisenberg case.

Our decision in a milk litigation most relevant to the present controversy deals with the converse of the present situation. Baldwin v. Seelig, 294 U.S. 511. In that case, New York placed conditions and limitations on the local sale of milk imported from Vermont designed in practical effect to exclude it, while here its order proposes to limit the local facilities for purchase of additional milk so as to withhold milk from export. The State agreed then, as now, that the Commerce Clause prohibits it from directly curtailing movement of milk into or out of the

State. But in the earlier case, it contended that the same result could be accomplished by controlling delivery, bottling and sale after arrival, while here it says it can do so by curtailing facilities for its purchase and receipt before it is shipped out. In neither case is the measure supported by health or safety considerations but solely by protection of local economic interests, such as supply for local consumption and limitation of competition. This Court unanimously rejected the State's contention in the Seelig case and held that the Commerce Clause even in the absence of congressional action, prohibits such regulations for such ends. . . .

The Constitution, said Mr. Justice Cardozo for the unanimous Court, "was framed upon the theory that the peoples of the several states must sink or swim together, and that in the long run prosperity and salvation are in union and not division." He reiterated that the economic objective, as distinguished from any health, safety and fair-dealing purpose of the regulation, was the root of its invalidity. The action of the State would "neutralize the economic consequences of free trade among the states." "Such a power, if exerted, will set a barrier to traffic between one state and another as effective as if customs duties, equal to the price differential, has been laid upon the thing transported." "If New York, in order to promote the economic welfare of her farmers, may guard them against competition with the cheaper prices of Vermont, the door has been opened to rivalries and reprisals that were meant to be averted by subjecting commerce between the states to the power of the Nation." And again, "Neither the power to tax nor the police power may be used by the state of destination with the aim and effect of establishing an economic barrier against competition with the products of another state or the labor of its residents. Restrictions so contrived are an unreasonable clog upon the mobility of commerce. They set up what are equivalent to a rampart of customs duties designed to neutralize advantages belonging to the place of origin. They are thus hostile in conception as well as burdensome in result." . . .

This principle that our economic unit is the Nation, which alone has the gamut of powers necessary to control of the economy, including the vital power of erecting customs barriers against foreign competition, has as its corollary that the states are not separable economic units. As the Court said in Baldwin v. Seelig, 294 U.S. 511, 527, "what is ultimate is the principle that one state in its dealing with another may not place itself in a position of economic isolation." In so speaking it but followed the principle that the state may not use its admitted powers to protect the health and safety of its people as a basis for suppressing competition. In Buck v. Kuykendall, 267 U.S. 307, the Court struck down a state act because, in the language of Mr. Justice Brandeis, "Its primary purpose is not regulation with a view to safety or to conservation of the highways, but the prohibition of competition." The same argument here advanced, that limitation of competition would itself contribute to safety and conservation, and therefore indirectly serve an end permissible to the state, was there declared "not sound." 267 U.S. 307, 315. It is no better here. . . .

Our system, fostered by the Commerce Clause, is that every farmer and every craftsman shall be encouraged to produce by the certainty that he will have free access to every market in the Nation, that no home embargoes will withhold his export, and no foreign state will by customs duties or regulations exclude them. Likewise, every consumer may look to the free competition from every producing area in the Nation to protect him from exploitation by any. Such was the vision of the Founders; Such has been the doctrine of this Court which has given it reality. . . .

The State, however, contends that such restraint or obstruction as its order imposes on interstate commerce does not violate the Commerce Clause because the State regulation coincides with, supplements and is part of the federal regulatory scheme. This contention that Congress has taken possession of "the field" but shared it with the State, it is to be noted, reverses the contention usually made in comparable cases, which is that Congress has not fully occupied the field and hence the State may fill the void. The Court found "no federal approval or responsibility for the challenged features of this order."

Since the statute as applied violates the Commerce Clause and is not authorized by federal legislation pursuant to that Clause, it cannot stand. The judgment is reversed and the cause remanded for proceedings not inconsistent with this opinion.

It is so ordered.

MR. JUSTICE BLACK (dissenting): In this case the Court sets up a new constitutional formula for invalidation of state laws regulating local phases of interstate commerce. I believe the New York law is invulnerable to constitutional attack under constitutional rules which the majority of this Court have long accepted. The new formula subjects state regulations of local business activities to greater constitutional hazards than they have ever had to meet before. The consequences of the new formula, as I understand it, will not merely leave a large area of local business activities free from state regulation. All local activities that fall within the scope of this new formula will be free from any regulatory control whatever. For it is inconceivable that Congress could pass uniform national legislation capable of adjustment and application to all the local phases of interstate activities that take place in the 48 states. See Robertson v. California, 328 U.S. 440, 449, 459—460. It is equally inconceivable that Congress would attempt to control such diverse local activities through a "swarm of statutes only locally applicable and utterly inconsistent." Kidd v. Pearson, 128 U.S. 1, 21. . . .

Reconciliation of state and federal interests in regulation of commerce always has been a perplexing problem. The claims of neither can be ignored if due regard be accorded the welfare of state and nation. For in the long run the welfare of each is dependent upon the welfare of both. Injury to commercial activities in the states is bound to produce an injurious reaction on interstate commerce, and vice versa. The many local activities which are parts of interstate transactions have given rise to much confusion. The basic problem has always been whether the state or federal government has power to regulate such local activities, whether the power of either is exclusive or concurrent, whether the state has power to regulate until Congress exercises its supreme power, and the extent to which and the circumstances under which this Court should invalidate state regulations in the absence of an exercise of congressional power. This last question is the one here involved.

The Court strongly relies on Baldwin v. Seelig, 294 U.S. 511. But in that case the Court saw the New York law as a discriminatory "barrier to traffic between one state and another as effective as if customs duties, equal to the price differential, had been laid upon the thing transported." Baldwin v. Seelig, supra, at 521. The effect of the law, therefore, was precisely the same as though in order to protect its farmers from competition with Vermont milk, New York had imposed substantially higher taxes on sellers of Vermont produced articles than it imposed on sellers of New York produced articles. Under many previous decisions of this Court such discriminations against interstate commerce were not permitted. . . .

It was because New York attempted to project its law into Vermont that even its admitted health purpose was insufficient to outweigh Vermont's interest in controlling its own local affairs. Baldwin v. Seelig, supra, p. 524. Added to this was the Court's appraisal of the law as a plain discrimination against interstate commerce that would inescapably erect a barrier to suppress competitive sales of Vermont milk in New York, thus leading to retaliatory "rivalries and reprisals," at p. 522. Quite differently here New York has not attempted to regulate the price of milk in Massachusetts or the manner in which it will be distributed there; it has not attempted to put pressure on Massachusetts to reform its economic standards; its law is not hostile to interstate commerce in conception or operation; its purpose to conserve health and promote economic stability among New York producers is not stretched to the breaking point by an argument that New York cannot safely aid its own people's health unless permitted to trespass upon the power of Massachusetts to regulate local affairs in Massachusetts. Nor is this New York law, fairly administered as it has been, the kind that breeds "rivalries and reprisals." The circumstances and conditions that brought about invalidation of the law considered in the Baldwin case are too different from those here considered to rest today's holding on the Baldwin decision.

The sole immediate result of today's holding is that petitioner will be allowed to operate a new milk plant in New York. This consequence standing alone is of no great importance. But there are other consequences of importance. It is always a serious thing for this Court to strike down a statewide law. It is more serious when the state law falls under a new rule which will inescapably narrow the area in which states can regulate and control local business practices found inimical to the public welfare. The gravity of striking down state regulations is immeasurably increased when it results as here in leaving a no-man's land immune from any effective regulation whatever....

I would leave New York's law alone.

MR. JUSTICE MURPHY joins in this opinion.

MR. JUSTICE FRANKFURTER, with whom MR. JUSTICE RUTLEDGE joins (dissenting): If the Court's opinion has meaning beyond deciding this case in isolation, its effect is to hold that no matter how important to the internal economy of a State may be the prevention of destructive competition, and no matter how unimportant the interstate commerce affected, a State cannot as a means of preventing such competition deny an applicant access to a market within the State if that applicant happens to intend the out-of-state shipment of the product that he buys. I feel constrained to dissent because I cannot agree in treating what is essentially a problem of striking a balance between competing interests as an exercise in absolutes. Nor does it seem to me that such a problem should be disposed of on a record from which we cannot tell what weights to put in which side of the scales....

As I see the central issue, therefore, it is whether the difference in degree between denying access to a market for failure to comply with sanitary or bookkeeping regulations and denying it for the sake of preventing destructive competition from disrupting the market is great enough to justify a difference in result....

As matters now stand, however, it is impossible to say whether or not the restriction of competition among dealers in milk does in fact contribute to their economic well-being and, through them, to that of the entire industry. And if we assume that some contribution is made, we cannot guess how much. Why, when the State has fixed a minimum price for producers, does it take steps to keep competing dealers from increasing the price by bidding against each other for the existing supply? Is it concerned with protecting consumers from excessive prices? Or is it concerned with seeing that marginal dealers, forced by competition to pay more and charge less, are not driven either to cut corners in the maintenance of their plants or to close them down entirely? Might these consequences follow from operation at less than capacity? What proportion of capacity is necessary to enable the marginal dealer to stay in business? Could Hood's potential competitors in the Greenwich area maintain efficient and sanitary standards of operation on a lower margin of profit? How would their closing down affect producers? Would the competition of Hood affect dealers other than those in that area? How many of those dealers are also engaged in interstate commerce? How much of a strain would be put on the price structure maintained by the State by a holding that it cannot regulate the competition of dealers buying for an out-of-state market? Is this a situation in which State regulation, by supplementing federal regulation, is of benefit to interstate as well as to intrastate commerce?

We should, I submit, have answers at least to some of these questions before we can say either how seriously interstate commerce is burdened by New York's licensing power or how necessary to New York is that power. The testimony of the dealers with whom Hood seeks to compete is too inexplicit to supply the answers. Since the needed information is neither accessible to judicial notice nor within its proper scope, I believe we should seek further light by remanding the case to the courts of the State. It is a course we have frequently taken upon records no more unsatisfactory than this one. . . .

Broadly stated, the question is whether a State can withhold from interstate commerce a product derived from local raw materials upon a determination by an administrative agency that there is a local need for it. For me it has not been put to rest by Pennsylvania v. West Virginia. More narrowly, the question is whether the State can prefer the consumers of one community to consumers in other States as well as to consumers in other parts of its own territory. It is arguable, moreover, that the Commissioner was actuated not by preference for New York consumers, but by the aim of stablizing the supply of all the local markets, including Boston as well as Troy, served by the New York milkshed. It may also be that he had in mind the potentially harmful competitive effect of efforts by dealers supplying the Troy market to repair, by attracting new producers, the aggravation of Troy's shortage which would result from the diversion to Boston of part of Troy's supply. These too are matters as to which more light would be needed if it were now necessary to decide the question.

My conclusion, accordingly, is that the case should be remanded to the Supreme Court of Albany County for action consistent with the views I have stated.

LIVERSIDGE v. ANDERSON

House of Lords. [1942] A.C. 206; [1941] 3 All E.R. 338

Appeal from the Court of Appeal affirming an order of the King's Bench Division refusing the appellant's application for particulars of defence in an action by him against the Home Secretary for false imprisonment.

The appellant, who was detained by an order made by the respondent, Sir John Anderson, as Home Secretary, on May 26, 1940, under reg. 18B of the Defence (General) Regulations, 1939, claimed by his writ a declaration that his detention in Brixton prison was unlawful. The appellant applied for particulars (a) of the grounds on which the respondent had reasonable cause to believe the appellant to be a person of hostile associations and (b) of the grounds on which the respondent had reasonable cause to believe that by reason of such hostile associations it was necessary to exercise control over the appellant.

VISCOUNT MAUGHAM: My Lords, I think we should approach the construction of reg. 18B of the Defence (General) Regulations without any general presumption as to its meaning except the universal presumption, applicable to Orders in Council and other like instruments, that, if there is a reasonable doubt as to the meaning of the words used, we should prefer a construction which will carry into effect the plain intention of those responsible for the Order in Council rather than one which will defeat that intention. My Lords, I am not disposed to deny that, in the absence of a context, the prima facie meaning of such a phrase as "if A.B. has reasonable cause to believe" a certain circumstance or thing, it should be construed as meaning "if there is in fact reasonable cause for believing" that thing and if A.B. believes it. But I am quite unable to take the view that the words can only have that meaning. It seems to me reasonably clear that, if the thing to be believed is something which is essentially one within the knowledge of A.B. or one for the exercise of his exclusive discretion, the words might well mean if A.B. acting on what he thinks is reasonable cause (and, of course, acting in good faith) believes the thing in question.

In the present case there are a number of circumstances which tend to support the latter conclusion.

First, reg. 18B, paras. (I.) and (IA), alike require the Secretary of State to have reasonable cause to believe two different things. Taking the first paragraph, he must, in the first place, believe the person (*a*) to be of hostile origin or associations, or (*b*) to have been recently concerned in acts prejudicial to the public safety or the defence of the realm, or (*c*) in the preparation or instigation of such acts, or (*d*) to have been or to be a member of, or (*e*) to be active in the furtherance of the objects of organizations which are carefully defined by reference to the personal decision of the Home Secretary. Any one of these various circumstances is sufficient to satisfy the first fact which the Secretary of State must believe, and I do not doubt that a court could investigate the question whether there were grounds for a reasonable man to believe some at least of those facts if they could be put before the court. But then he must at the same time also believe something very different in its nature, namely, that by reason of the first fact, "it is necessary to exercise control over" the person in question. To my mind this is so clearly a matter for executive discretion and nothing else that I cannot myself believe that those responsible for the Order in Council could have contemplated for a moment the possibility of the action of the Secretary of State being subject to the discussion, criticism and control of a judge in a court of law. If, then, in the present case the second requisite, as to the grounds on which the Secretary of State can make his order for detention, is left to his sole discretion without appeal to a court, it necessarily follows that the same is true as to all the facts which he must have reasonable cause to believe.

Secondly, it is admitted that the Home Secretary can act on hearsay and is not required to obtain any legal evidence in such a case, and clearly is not required to summon the person whom he proposes to detain and to hear his objections to the proposed order. Since the Home Secretary is not acting judicially in such a case, it would be strange if his decision could be questioned in a court of law.

Thirdly, and this is of even greater importance, it is obvious that in many cases he will be acting on information of the most confidential character, which could not be communicated to the person detained or disclosed in court without the greatest risk of prejudicing the future efforts of the Secretary of State in this and like matters for the defence of the realm. A very little consideration will show that the power of the court (under s. 6 of the Act) to give directions for the hearing of proceeding in camera would not prevent confidential matters from leaking out, since such matters would become known to the person detained and to a number of other persons. It seems to me impossible for the court to come to a conclusion adverse to the opinion of the Secretary of State in such a matter. It is beyond dispute that he can decline to disclose the information on which he has acted on the ground that to do so would be contrary to the public interest, and that this privilege of the Crown cannot be disputed. It is not ad rem on the question of construction to say in reply to this argument that there are cases in which the Secretary of State could answer the attack on the validity of the order for detention without raising the point of privilege. It is sufficient to say that there must be a large number of cases in which the information on which the Secretary of State is likely to act will be of a very confidential nature. That must have been plain to those responsible in advising His Majesty in regard to the Order in Council, and it constitutes, in my opinion, a very cogent reason for thinking that the words under discussion cannot be read as meaning that the existence of "reasonable cause" is one which may be discussed in a court which has not the power of eliciting the facts which in the opinion of the Secretary of State amount to "reasonable cause."

Fourthly, it is to be noted that the person who is primarily entrusted with these most important duties is one of the principal Secretaries of State, and a member of the government answerable to Parliament for a proper discharge of his duties. I do not think he is at all in the same position, as, for example, a police constable. It is not wholly immaterial to note that the Secretary of State is provided with one or more advisory committees (para. (3.)), and that he has to report to Parliament at least once in every month as to the action taken by him and the orders he has made, and as to the number of cases in which he has declined to follow the advice of the advisory committee (para. (6.)). These provisions seem to point to the fact that the Secretary of State will be answerable to Parliament in carrying out duties of a very important and confidential nature. I have heard no explanation of the circumstance that no express provisions are made in the regulation as to an appeal from the Secretary of State's decision unless it is the fact that no such appeal was intended. It seems to me that, if any such appeal had been thought proper, it would have been to a special tribunal with power to inquire privately into all the reasons for the Secretary's action, but without any obligation to communicate them to the person detained. The objections to an appeal in a case of mere suspicion and in time of war are not far to seek, but, however that may be, an application to the High Court, with power to the judge to review the action of the Secretary of State, seems to be completely inadmissible, and I am unable to see that the words of the regulation in any way justify the conclusion that such a procedure was contemplated. . . .

Apart, however, from these considerations, I am of opinion that the arguments above enumerated in favour of the construction for which the Attorney-General contends must greatly outweigh any arguments which your Lordships have heard on the other side and that his construction must prevail. The result is that there is no preliminary question of fact which can be submitted to the courts and that in effect there is no appeal from the decision of the Secretary of State in these matters provided only that he acts in good faith. It follows, and it is not disputed by the appellant's counsel, that on this view the application for particulars must fail.

I can deal much more shortly with the question whether an onus is thrown on the first respondent, the Secretary of State who made the order for detention, to give evidence to show that he had reasonable cause to believe the appellant to be a person of hostile associations and that by reason thereof it was necessary to exercise control over him. The order on its face purports to be made under the regulation and it states that the Secretary of State had reasonable cause to believe the facts in question. In my opinion, the well known presumption omnia esse rite acta applies to this order, and, accordingly, assuming the order to be proved or admitted, it must be taken prima facie, that is until the contrary is proved, to have been properly made and that the requisite as to the belief of the Secretary of State was complied with. It will be noted that on the view I have expressed as to the construction of the regulation it is the personal belief of the Secretary of State that is in question, and that, if the appellant's contention on this point were correct, the same question would arise in the numerous cases where an executive order depends on the Secretary of State or some other public officer being "satisfied" of some fact or circumstance. It has never, I think, been suggested in such cases that the Secretary of State or public officer must prove that he was so "satisfied" when he made the order. Just as the fact that the act of the Secretary of State acting in a public office is prima facie evidence that he has been duly appointed to his office, so his compliance with the provision of the statute or the Order in Council under which he purported to act must be presumed unless the contrary is proved. There are scores of instances of such presumptions to be found in the books, none I think precisely in point, but many in which the principle was less necessary on the score of public convenience than the present. If an instance is required it may be found in the rule that where local authorities have made a rate under an Act, compliance with the formalities required by that Act will be presumed until the contrary is shown: *Reg.* v. *Reynolds.*

LORD MACMILLAN (concurring) . . . Courts may differ as to what is reasonable. A judge of first instance might hold the Secretary of State to have been justified in his belief, the Court of Appeal might take another view and this House might have its own view. In a matter at once so vital and so urgent in the interests of national safety, I am unable to accept a reading of the regulation which would prescribe that the Secretary of State may not act in accordance with what commends itself to him as a reasonable cause of belief without incurring the risk that a court of law would disagree with him, and also without the further liability that, should the court do so or if he cannot consistently with his duty disclose to the court the grounds of his belief, he will be mulcted in damages for false imprisonment as having acted outwith his powers.

My Lords, I make no apology for having discussed so fully the various aspects of the question before the House, for it is one of the highest importance. I yield to no one in my recognition of the value of the jealous scrutiny which our courts have always rightly exercised in considering any invasion of the liberty of the subject. But I remind myself, in Lord Atkinson's words, that "however precious the personal liberty of the subject may be there is something for which it may well be, to some extent, sacrificed by legal enactment, namely, national success in the war or escape from national plunder or enslavement": *Rex* v. *Halliday.* The liberty which we so justly extol is itself the gift of the law and as Magna Carta recognizes may by the law be forfeited or abridged. At a time when it is the undoubted law of the land that a citizen may by conscription or requisition be compelled to give up his life and all that he possesses for his country's cause it may well be no matter for surprise that there should be confided to the Secretary of State a discretionary power of enforcing the relatively mild precaution of detention.

LORD WRIGHT (concurring) . . . The appellant relies on the use of the word "reasonable" as qualifying the "cause to believe." It is said that "reasonable" necessarily implies an external standard to be applied by someone other than the Secretary, namely, by a judge. I cannot accept that contention, which seems to me to subordinate the whole substance of the enactment to a single word which itself is ambiguous and inconclusive. The word "reasonable" does indeed imply instructed and intelligent care and deliberation, the choice of the course which reason dictates. *But the choice is not necessarily that of an outsider.* If I am right in my view of the effect of the regulation, the choice can only be the choice of the minister. All the word "reasonable," then, means is that the minster must not lightly or arbitrarily invade the liberty of the subject. He must be reasonably satisfied before he acts, but it is still his decision and not the decision of anyone else. If in ordinary affairs I say that I reasonably believe in the truth of certain facts or in the propriety of certain conduct, I am prima facie adopting as my reason my own judgment. If I mean to refer to some external yardstick I should in general naturally say so expressly unless the contrary was clear from other circumstances. "Reasonable" connotes a quality or characteristic. Who is to decide on reasonableness is a different matter which depends on the circumstances.

LORD ATKIN (dissenting) I view with apprehension the attitude of judges who on a mere question of construction when face to face with claims involving the liberty of the subject show themselves more executive minded than the executive. Their function is to give words their *natural meaning*, not, perhaps, in war time leaning towards liberty, but following the dictum of Pollock C.B. in *Bowditch* v. *Balchin*, cited with approval by my noble and learned friend Lord Wright in *Barnard* v. *Gorman*: "In a case in which the liberty of the subject is concerned, we cannot go beyond the natural construction of the statute." In this country, amid the clash of arms, the laws are not silent. They may be changed, but they speak the same language in war as in peace. It has always been one of the pillars of freedom, one of the principles of liberty for which on recent authority we are now fighting, that the judges are no respecters of persons and stand between the subject and any attempted encroachments on his liberty by the executive, alert to see that any coercive action is justified in law. In this case I have listened to arguments which might have been addressed acceptably to the Court of King's Bench in the time of Charles I.

I protest, even if I do it alone, against a strained construction put on words with the effect of giving an uncontrolled power of imprisonment to the minister. To recapitulate: The words have only one meaning. They are used with that meaning in statements of the common law and in statutes. They have never been used in the sense now imputed to them. They are used in the Defence Regulations in the natural meaning, and, when it is intended to express the meaning now imputed to them, different and apt words are used in the regulations generally and in this regulation in particular. Even if it were relevant, which it is not, there is no absurdity or no such degree of public mischief as would lead to a non-natural construction.

I know of only one authority which might justify the suggested method of construction: " 'When I use a word,' Humpty Dumpty said in rather a scornful tone, 'it means just what I choose it to mean, neither more nor less.' 'The question is,' said Alice, 'whether you can make words mean so many different things.' 'The question is,' said Humpty Dumpty, 'which is to be master — that's all.' " ("Through the Looking Glass," c. vi.) After all this long discussion the question is whether the words "If a man has" can mean "If a man thinks he has." I am of opinion that they cannot, and that the case should be decided accordingly. . . .

It is surely incapable of dispute that the words "If A has X" constitute a condition the essence of which is the existence of X and the having of it by A. If it is a condition to a right (including a power) granted to A, whenever the right comes into dispute the tribunal whatever it may be that is charged with determining the dispute must ascertain whether the condition is fulfilled. In some cases the issue is one of fact, in others of both fact and law, but in all cases the words indicate an existing something the having of which can be ascertained. And the words do not mean and cannot mean "if A thinks that he has." "If A has a broken ankle" does not mean and cannot mean "if A thinks that he has a broken ankle." "If A has a right of way" does not mean and cannot mean "if A thinks that he has a right of way." "Reasonable cause" for an action or a belief is just as much a positive fact capable of determination by a third party as is a broken ankle or a legal right. If its meaning is the subject of dispute as to legal rights, then ordinarily the reasonableness of the cause, and even the existence of any cause is in our law to be determined by the judge and not by the tribunal of fact if the functions deciding law and fact are divided. Thus having established, as I hope, that the plain and natural meaning of the words "has reasonable cause" imports the existence of a fact or state of facts and not the mere belief by the person challenged that the fact or state of facts existed, I proceed to show that this meaning of the words has been accepted in innumerable legal decisions for many generations, that "reasonable cause" for a belief when the subject of legal dispute has been always treated as an objective fact to be proved by one or other party and to be determined by the appropriate tribunal. I will go further and show that until June or July of this year in connection with this reg. 18B, there never has been any other construction even submitted to the courts in whatever context the words are found. . . .

Of course, if the subjective theory is right and the Secretary of State has indeed unconditional power of imprisonment, it was enough for him to say that he exercised the power. But it seemed to be suggested in argument that, even if the power were conditional, yet it would be a good return by the Secretary of State to say that he had made the order in the terms of the regulation. This seems to me, with respect, to be fantastic. A minister given only a limited authority cannot make for himself a valid return by merely saying I acted as though I had authority. His ipse dixit avails nothing. A constable would make no valid return by saying: "I had reasonable cause for my arrest," or "I served the criminal at the time with a written notice that I was arresting him for reasonable suspicion of felony." However, on my view of this, the Secretary of State has made a return sufficient to indicate that the Divisional Court were right in refusing to order the writ to issue. I think that the appeal in this case should be dismissed.

B. READINGS

Sir John Salmond, 1862-1924
Justice of the Court of Appeal, New Zealand

JURISPRUDENCE
(1902; 9th ed., 1937)

The Names Of The Law

The first fact which an examination of juridical nomenclature reveals, is that all names for law are divisible into two classes, and that almost every language possesses one or more specimens of each. To the first class belong such terms as *jus*, *droit*, *recht*, *diritto*, *equity*. To the second belong *lex*, *loi*, *gesetz*, *legge*, *law*, and many others. It is a striking peculiarity of the English language that it does not possess any *generic* term falling within the first of these groups; for equity, in the technical juridical sense, means only a special department of civil law, not the whole of it, and therefore is not coextensive with *jus*, *droit*, and the other foreign terms with which it is classed. Since, therefore, we have in English no pair of contrasted terms adequate for the expression of the distinction between these two groups of names, we are constrained to have recourse to a foreign language, and we shall employ for this purpose the terms *jus* and *lex*, using each as typical of and representing all other terms which belong to the same group as itself.

What, then, are the points of difference between *jus* and *lex*; what is the importance and the significance of the distinction between the two classes of terms? In the first place *jus* has an ethical as well as a juridical application, while *lex* is purely juridical. *Jus* means not only law but also right. *Lex* means law and not also right. Thus our own *equity* has clearly the double meaning; it means either the rules of natural justice, or that special department of the civil law which was developed and administered in the Court of Chancery. The English *law*, on the other hand, has a purely juridical application; justice in itself, and as such, has no claim to the name of *law*. So also with *droit* as opposed to *loi*, with *recht* as opposed to *gesetz*, with *diritto* as opposed to *legge*.

If we inquire after the cause of this duplication of terms we find it in the double aspect of the complete juridical conception of law. Law arises from the union of justice and force, of right and might. It is justice recognised and established by authority. It is right realised through power. Since, therefore, it has two sides and aspects, it may be looked at from two different points of view, and we may expect to find, as we find in fact, that it acquires two different names. *Jus* is law looked at from the point of view of right and justice; *lex* is law looked at from the point of view of authority and force. *Jus* is the rule of right which becomes law by its authoritative establishment; *lex* is the authority by virtue of which the rule of right becomes law. Law is *jus* in respect of its *contents*, namely, the rule of right; it is *lex* in respect of its *source*, namely, its recognition and enforcement by the State. We see, then, how it is that so many words for law mean justice also; since justice is the content or subject-matter of law, and from this subject-matter law derives its title. We understand also how it is that so many words for law do not also mean justice; law has another side and aspect from which it appears, not as justice realised and established, but as the instrument through which its realisation and establishment are effected.

A *priori* we may presume that in the case of those terms which possess a double application, both ethical and legal, the ethical is historically prior, and the legal later and derivative. We may assume that justice comes to mean law, not that law comes to mean justice. This is the logical order, and is presumably the historical order also. As a matter of fact this presumption is, as we shall see, correct in the case of all modern terms possessing the double signification. In the case of *recht, droit, diritto, equity,* the ethical sense is undoubtedly primary, and the legal secondary. In respect of the corresponding Greek and Latin terms (*jus, dikaion*) the data would seem insufficent for any confident conclusion. The reverse order of development is perfectly possible; there is no reason why lawful should not come to mean in a secondary sense rightful, though a transition in the opposite direction is more common and more natural. The significant fact is the union of the two meanings in the same word, not the order of development.

A second distinction between *jus* and *lex* is that the former is usually *abstract*, the second *concrete*. The English term "law" indeed combines both these uses in itself. In its abstract application we speak of the law of England, criminal law, Courts of law. In its concrete sense, we say that Parliament has enacted or repealed a law. In foreign languages, on the other hand, this union of the two significations is unusual. *Jus, droit, recht* mean law in the abstract, not in the concrete. *Lex, loi, gesetz* signify, at least primarily and normally, a legal enactment, or a rule established by way of enactment, not law in the abstract. This, however, is not invariably the case. *Lex, loi,* and some other terms belonging to the same group have undoubtedly acquired a secondary and abstract signification in addition to their primary and concrete one. In medieval usage the law of the land is *lex terrae*, and the law of England is *lex et consuetudo Angliae*. So in modern French *loi* is often merely an equivalent for *droit*. We cannot therefore regard the second distinction between *jus* and *lex* as essential. It is closely connected with the first, but, though natural and normal, it is not invariable. The characteristic difference between English and foreign usage is not that our *law* combines the abstract and concrete significations (for so also do certain Continental terms), but that the English language contains no generic term which combines ethical and legal meanings as do *jus, droit,* and *recht*.

RECHT, DROIT, DIRITTO. – These three terms are all closely connected with each other and with the English *right*. The French and Italian words are derivatives of the Latin *directus* and *rectus*, these being cognate with *recht* and *right*. We may with some confidence assume the following order of development among the various ideas represented by this group of expressions:

1. The original meaning was in all probability *physical straightness*. This use is still retained in our *right* angle and *direct*. The root is RAG, to stretch or straighten. The group of connected terms ruler, *rex, rajah,* regulate, and others, would seem to be independently derived from the same root, but not to be in the same line of development as right and its synonyms. The ruler or regulator is he who keeps things straight or keeps order, not he who establishes the right. Nor is the right that which is established by a ruler.

2. In a second and derivative sense the terms used metaphorically to indicate moral approval – ethical rightness, not physical. Moral disapproval is similarly expressed by the metaphorical expressions wrong and tort, that is to say, crooked or twisted. These are metaphors that still commend themselves; for the honest man is still the straight and upright man, and the ways of wickedness are still crooked. In this sense, therefore, *recht, droit,* and *diritto* signify justice and right.

3. The first application being physical and the second ethical, the third is juridical. The transition from the second to the third is easy. Law is justice as recognised and protected by the State. The rules of law are the rules of right, as authoritatively established and enforced by tribunals appointed to that end.

What more natural, therefore, than for the ethical terms to acquire derivatively a juridical application? At this point, however, our modern English *right* has parted company with its Continental relatives. It has remained physical and ethical, being excluded from the juridical sphere by the superior convenience of the English *law*.

4. The fourth and last use of the terms we are considering may be regarded as derivative of both the second and third. It is that in which we speak of *rights*, namely, claims, powers, or other advantages conferred or recognised by the rule of right or the rule of law. That a debtor should pay his debt to his creditor is not merely right, it is *the* right of the creditor. Right is *his* right for whose benefit it exists. So, also, wrong is *the* wrong of him who is injured by it. The Germans distinguish this use of the term by the expression *subjectives Recht* (right as vested in a subject) as opposed to *objectives Recht,* namely, the rule of justice or of law as it exists objectively. The English *right* has been extended to cover legal as well as ethical *claims*, though it has, as we have seen, been confined to ethical *rules*.

A.-S. RIHT. – It is worthy of notice that the Anglo-Saxon *riht*, the progenitor of our modern *right*, possessed like its Continental relatives the legal in addition to the ethical meaning. The common law is *folc-riht*. The divine law is *godes riht*. A plaintiff claims property as "his by *folc-riht*", even as a Roman would have claimed it as being *dominus ex jure Quiritium*. The usage, however, did not prosper. It had to face the formidable and ultimately successful rivalry of the English (originally Danish) *law*, and even Norman-French, on its introduction into England, fell under the same influence. For a time, indeed, in the earlier books we find both *droit* and *ley* as competing synonyms, but the issue was never doubtful. The archaism of "common right" as a synonym for "common law" is the sole relic left in England of a usage universal in Continental languages.

EQUITY. – The English term "equity" has pursued the same course of development as the German *recht* and the French *droit*.

1. Its primitive meaning, if we trace the word back to its Latin source, *aequum*, is physical equality or evenness, just as physical straightness is the earliest meaning of right and its analogues.

2. Its secondary sense is ethical. Just as rightness is straightness, so equity is equality. In each case there is an easy and obvious metaphorical transition from the physical to the moral idea. Equity therefore is justice.

3. In a third and later stage of its development the word takes on a juridical significance. It comes to mean a particular portion of the civil law – that part, namely, which was developed by and administered in the Court of Chancery. Like *recht* and *droit* it passed from the sense of justice in itself to that of the rules in accordance with which justice is administered.

4. Fourthly and lastly we have to notice a legal and technical use of the term "equity", as meaning any claim or advantage recognised or conferred by a rule of equity, just as a right signifies any claim or advantage derived from a rule of right. An equity is an equitable, as opposed to a legal right. "When the equities are equal", so runs the maxim of Chancery, "the law prevails." So a debt is assignable "subject to equities".

JUS. – We have to distinguish in the case of *jus* the same three uses that have already been noticed in the case of *recht*, *droit*, and equity.

1. Right or Justice. . . .

2. Law. This is the most usual application of the term, the juridical sense having a much greater predominance over the ethical in the case of *jus*, than in that of its modern representatives *recht* and *droit*. *Jus*, in its ethical signification, is distinguished as *jus naturale*, and in its legal sense as *jus civile*. It is often con-

trasted with *fas*, the one being human and the other divine law. *Jus*, however, is also used in a wider sense to include both of these – *jus divinum et humanum.*

3. A right, moral or legal. . . .

The origin and primary signification of *jus* are uncertain. It is generally agreed, however, that the old derivation from *jussum* and *jubere* is not merely incorrect, but an actual reversal of the true order of terms and ideas. *Jussum* is a derivative of *jus*. *Jubere* is, in its proper and original sense, to declare, hold, or establish anything as *jus*. It was the recognised expression for the legitimate action of the Roman people. *Legem jubere* is to give to a statute (*lex*) the force of law (*jus*). Only in a secondary and derivative sense is *jubere* equivalent to *imperare*.

The most probable opinion is that *jus* is derived from the Aryan root YU, to join together (a root which appears also in *jugem*, *jungo*, and in the English *yoke*). It has been suggested accordingly that *jus* in its original sense means that which is fitting, applicable, or suitable. If this is so, there is a striking correspondence between the history of the Latin term and that of the modern words already considered by us, the primary sense in all cases being physical, the ethical sense being a metaphorical derivative of this, and the legal application coming last. The transition from the physical to the ethical sense in the case of the English *fit* and *fitting* is instructive in this connection. Another suggestion, however, is that *jus* means primarily that which is *binding* – the bond of moral and subsequently of legal obligation. But no definite conclusion on this matter is possible. . . .

LEX. – So far we have dealt solely with those words which belong to the class of *jus*, namely, those which possess a double signification, ethical and legal. We proceed now to the consideration of the second class, represented by *lex*. And first of *lex* itself. The following are its various uses given in what is probably the historical order of their establishment.

1. Proposals, terms, conditions, offers made by one party and accepted by another. . . .

2. A statute enacted by the *populus Romanus* in the *comitia centuriata* on the proposal of a magistrate. This would seem to be a specialised application of *lex* in the first-mentioned sense. . . .

3. Any statute howsoever made – whether by way of authoritative imposition, or by way of agreement with a self-governing people.

4. Any rule of action imposed or observed, eg., *lex loquendi*, *lex sermonis*. This is simply an analogical extension similar to that which is familiar in respect of the corresponding terms in modern languages, *law*, *loi*, *gesetz*.

5. Law in the abstract sense. *Lex*, so used, cannot be regarded as classical Latin, although in certain instances, as in Cicero's references to *lex naturae*, we find what seems a very close approximation to it. In medieval Latin, however, the abstract signification is quite common, as in the phrases *lex Romana*, *lex terrae*, *lex communis*, *lex et consuetudo*. *Lex* has become equivalent to *jus* in its legal applications. This use is still retained in certain technical expressions of private international law, such as *lex fori*, *lex domicilii*, and others.

It is possible that we have here an explanation of the very curious fact that so celebrated and important a word as *jus* failed to maintain itself in the Romance languages. Of the two terms *jus* and *lex*, bequeathed to later times by the Latin language, one was accepted (*loi* – *lex*) and the other rejected and supplanted by a modern substitute (*droit*, *diritto*). Why was this? May it not have been owing to that post-classical use of *lex* in the abstract sense, whereby it became synonymous and co-extensive with *jus*? If *lex Romana was jus civile*, why should the growing languages of modern Europe cumber themselves with both terms? The survivor of the two rivals was *lex*. At a later stage the natural evolution of thought and speech conferred juridical uses on the ethical terms *droit* and *diritto* and the ancient duality of legal nomenclature was restored.

6. Judgment. This, like the last and like the three following uses, is a medieval addition to the meanings of *lex*. . . .

7. The penalty, proof, or other matter imposed or required by a judgment; *lex ignea*, the ordeal of fire; *lex duelli*, trial by battle.

8. Legal rights, regarded collectively as constituting a man's legal standing or status. . . .

LAW. – Law is by no means the earliest legal term acquired by the English language. Curiously enough, indeed, it would seem not even to be indigenous, but to be one of those additions to Anglo-Saxon speech which are due to the Danish invasions and settlements. Of the earlier terms the commonest, and the most significant for our present purpose, is *dom*, the ancestor of our modern *doom*. A *dom* or *doom* is either (1) a law, ordinance, or statue or (2) a judgment. It does not seem possible to attribute with any confidence historical priority to either of these senses. In modern English the idea of judgment has completely prevailed over and excluded that of ordinance, but we find no such predominance of either meaning in Anglo-Saxon usage. The word has its source in the Aryan root DHA, to place, set, establish, appoint, and it is therefore equally applicable to the decree of the Judge and to that of the lawgiver. In the laws of King Alfred we find the term in both its senses. "These are the dooms which Almighty God himself spake unto Moses and commanded him to keep". "Judge then not one doom to the rich and another to the poor". In the following passage of the laws of Edgar the laws of the Danes are plainly equivalent to the dooms of the English: "I will that secular right stand among the Danes with as good laws as they best may choose. But with the English let that stand which I and my Witan have added to the dooms of my forefathers". . . .

Dom, together with all the other Anglo-Saxon legal terms, including, strangely enough, *right* itself, was rapidly superseded by *lagu*, which is the modern *law*. The new term makes its appearance in the tenth century, and the passage cited above from the laws of King Edgar is one of the earliest instances of its use. *Lagu* and law are derived from the root LAGH, to lay, settle, or place. Law is that which is laid down. There is a considerable conflict of opinion as to whether it is identical in origin with the Latin *lex* (*leg-*). Schmidt and others decide in the affirmative, and the probabilities of the case seem to favour this opinion. The resemblance between law and *lex* seems too close to be accidental. If this is so, the origin of *lex* is to be found in the Latin *lego*, not in its later sense of reading, but in its original sense of laying down or setting (as in the derivative *lectus*), which is also the primary signification of the Greek *lego*, the German *legen*, and the English *lay*. If this is so, then law and *lex* are alike that which is laid down, just as *Gesetz* is that which is set (*setzen*). This interpretation is quite consistent with the original possession by *lex* of a wider meaning than statute, as already explained. We still speak of laying down terms, conditions and propositions, no less than of laying down commands, rules and laws. *Lex*, however, is otherwise and variously derived from or connected with *ligare*, to bind, *legere*, to read, and *legein*, to say or speak.

It is true indeed that by several good authorities it is held that the original meaning of *lagu* and law is that which lies, not that which has been laid or settled – that which is customary, not that which is established by authority. The root LAGH, however, must contain both the transitive and intransitive senses, and I do not know what evidence there is for the exclusion of the former from the signification of the derivative *law*. Moreover, there seems no ground for attributing to *lagu* the meaning of custom. It seems from the first to have meant the product of authority, not that of use and wont. It is *statutum*, not *consuetudo*. As soon as we meet with it, it is equivalent to *dom*. The analogy also of *lex*, *gesetz*, *dom*, *thesmos*, and other similar terms is in favour of the interpretation here preferred.

Judith N. Shklar, 1928—
Associate Professor of Government, Harvard University

LEGALISM*
(1964)

What is legalism? It is the ethical attitude that holds moral conduct to be a matter of rule following, and moral relationships to consist of duties and rights determined by rules. Like all moral attitudes that are both strongly felt and widely shared it expresses itself not only in personal behavior but also in philosophical thought, in political ideologies, and in social institutions. As an historical phenomenon, it is, moreover, not something that can be understood simply by defining it. Such a morality must be seen in its various concrete manifestations, in its diverse applications, and in the many degrees of intensity with which men in different places and conditions have abided by it. It is, in short, a complex of human qualities, not a quantity to be measured and labeled.

Legalism, so understood, is thus often an inarticulate, but nonetheless consistently followed, individual code of conduct. It is also a very common social ethos, though by no means the only one, in Western countries. To a great extent it has provided the standards of organization and the operative ideals for a vast number of social groups, from governmental institutions to private clubs. Its most nearly complete expression is in the great legal systems of the European world. Lastly, it has also served as the political ideology of those who cherish these systems of law and, above all, those who are directly involved in their maintenance — the legal profession, both bench and bar. The court of law and the trial according to law are the social paradigms, the perfection, the very epitome, of legalistic morality. They are, however, far from being its only expressions. Indeed, they are inconceivable without the convictions, mores, and ideologies that must permeate any society which wishes to maintain them. Yet the spirit of legalism is not now, and never has been, the only morality among men even in generally legalistic societies. The full implications of this moral and political diversity, though its existence is commonly acknowledged and often regretted, has rarely been thoroughly investigated. This is by no means surprising, since almost all those who have devoted themselves to the study of legalistic morality and institutions have been their zealous partisans and promoters, anxious to secure their moral empire.

Even though it is no sign of disaffection for legalism to treat it as but one morality among others, such a view has not been congenial to any of the traditional theories of law. These have been devised almost exclusively by lawyers and philosophers who agree in nothing but in taking the prevalence of legalism and of law for granted, as something to be simply defined and analyzed. The consequences for legal theory have not been altogether fortunate. The urge to draw a clear line between law and non-law has led to the constructing of ever more refined and rigid systems of formal definitions. This procedure has served to iso-

*Reprinted by permission of the publishers from Judith Shklar, *Legalism*; Cambridge, Mass., Harvard University Press; Copyright 1965 by the President and Fellows of Harvard College.

late law completely from the social context within which it exists. Law is endowed with its own discrete, integral history, its own "science," and its own values, which are all treated as a single "block" sealed off from general social history, from general social theory, from politics, and from morality. The habits of mind appropriate, within narrow limits, to the procedures of law courts in the most stable legal systems have been expanded to provide legal theory and ideology with an entire system of thought and values. This procedure has served its own ends very well: it aims at preserving law from irrelevant considerations, but it has ended by fencing legal thinking off from all contact with the rest of historical thought and experience.

As an alternative to this unsatisfactory situation, it is suggested here that one ought not to think of law as a discrete entity that is "there," but rather to regard it as part of a social continuum. At one end of the scale of legalistic values and institutions stand its most highly articulate and refined expressions, the courts of law and the rules they follow; at the other end is the personal morality of all those men and women who think of goodness as obedience to the rules that properly define their duties and rights. Within this scale there is a vast area of social beliefs and institutions, both more and less rigid and explicit, which in varying degrees depend upon the legalistic ethos. This would provide an approach suitable to law as an historical phenomenon, and would replace the sterile game of defining law, morals, and politics in order to separate them as concepts both "pure" and empty, divorced from each other and from their common historical past and contemporary setting.

Lastly, there is legalism itself. To say that it is an ideology is to criticize only those of its traditional adherents who, in their determination to preserve law from politics, fail to recognize that they too have made a choice among political values. In itself this would hardly be a new accusation, nor a very important one. What does matter is again the intellectual consequences of this denial, and the attendant belief that law is not only separate from political life but that it is a mode of social action superior to mere politics. This is what will later be discussed as "the policy of justice," for legalism as an ideology does express itself in policies, in institutional structures, and in intellectual attitudes. As a social ethos which gives rise to the political climate in which judicial and other legal institutions flourish, legalism is beyond reproach. It is the rigidity of legalistic categories of thought, especially in appraising the relationships of law to the political environment within which it functions, that is so deleterious. This is the source of the artificiality of almost all legal theories and is what prevents its exponents from recognizing both the strengths and weaknesses of law and legal procedures in a complex social world.

Legalism as an ideology is the common element in all the various and conflicting modes of legal thinking that are to be discussed here. It is what gives legal thinking its distinctive flavor on a vast variety of social occasions, in all kinds of discourse, and among men who may differ in every other ideological respect. Legalism is, above all, the operative outlook of the legal profession, both bench and bar. Moreover, most legal theory, whether it be analytical positivism or natural law thinking, depends on categories of thought derived from this shared professional outlook. The tendency to think of law as "there" as a discrete entity, discernibly different from morals and politics, has its deepest roots in the legal profession's views of its own functions, and forms the very basis of most of our judicial institutions and procedures. That lawyers have particularly pronounced intellectual habits peculiar to them has often been noticed, especially by historians and other students of society whose views differ sharply from those of the legal profession. As one English lawyer has put it, "A lawyer is *bound* by certain habits of belief . . . by which lawyers, however dissimilar otherwise, are more closely linked than they are separated. . . A man who has had legal training is never quite the same again . . . is never able to look at institutions or administrative practices or even social or political policies, free from his legal habits or beliefs. It is not easy for a lawyer to become a political scientist. It is very difficult for him to become a sociologist or a historian. . . He is interested in relationships, in rights in something and against somebody, in relation to others. . . This is what is meant by the legalistic approach. . . A lawyer will fight to the death to defend legal rights against persuasive arguments based on expediency or the public interest or the social good. . . He distrusts them. . . He believes, as part of his mental habits, that they are dangerous and too easily used as cloaks for arbitrary action." . . .

The dislike of vague generalities, the preference for case-by-case treatment of all social issues, the structuring of all possible human relations into the form of claims and counterclaims under established rules, and the belief that the rules are "there" – these combine to make up legalism as a social outlook. When it becomes self-conscious, when it challenges other views, it is a full-blown ideology. Since lawyers are engaged in their daily lives with political or social conflicts of some kind, they are bound to run up against perspectives radically different from their own. As law serves ideally to promote the security of established expectations, so legalism with its concentration on specific cases and rules is, essentially, conservative. It is not, however, a matter of "masking" a specific class and economic interest. Not only do lawyerly interests often differ from those of other conservative social groups, businessmen's, for example, but legalism is no mask for anything. It is an openly, intrinsically, and quite specifically conservative view, because law is itself conservatizing ideal and institution. In its epitome, the judicial ethos, it becomes clear that this is the conservatism of consensus. It relies on what appears already to have been established and accepted. When constitutional and social changes have become inevitable and settled, the judiciary adapts itself to the new order. The "switch in time" from 1937 onward, after all, involved the whole federal bench eventually, not just one Supreme Court justice. For the judiciary to remain uncontroversial is the mark of neutral impartiality. Adjustment is therefore its natural policy, whenever possible. . . .

If many lawyers, in America especially, do recognize that the courts do legislate and make basic social choices, this is less true and even less accepted in other countries. Even in the United States, moreover, the public at large and important sections of the bar do not perceive their functions thus. The courts are expected to interpret the law, not to alter it. Professional ideology and public expectations, in fact, do mold the conduct of the judiciary and its perception of its role. To seek rules, or at least a public consensus that can serve in place of a rule, must be the judge's constant preoccupation, and it affects his choices in ways that are unknown to less constrained political agents. To avoid the appearance of arbitrariness is a deep inner necessity for him. The trouble is that the possibility of aloofness does not depend on the judge's behavior alone, but also on the public responses to it. In England, given the acceptance of Parliamentary sovereignty, the judiciary is not exposed to controversy as extensive as that in America. Here both the nature of the issues placed before the courts and the greater scope of choice available put the judiciary inevitably into the very midst of the great political battles of the nation. Elective state judiciaries, moreover, are bound to remain subject to public scrutiny, which the English judiciary is spared. . . .

Another instance of professional attitudes may be seen in the way in which such a citadel of conservative lawyerdom as the American Bar Association addresses itself to social issues. Matters are taken up one by one, in isolation from the social context and without discussion of the basic issue. Precisely because the A.B.A. regards itself as the official spokesman of the bar it must present its views in a formal manner that gives the appearance of being supra-political and almost without concrete content. It is the independence of the judiciary, the separation of powers, the preservation of fundamental rights, or just fairness, the policy of justice – never the specific social interests or purposes of policies – that is discussed. This formalism makes for adaptability in the long run, but it also represents a rooted conservatism. When it comes to changes that affect the judicial establishment directly, moreover, conservatism becomes immobility. An A.B.A.-sponsored survey of the American legal profession concluded that when it came to reforming procedure, for instance, lawyers were unreasonably obstinate. Observers of the English bar have reached the same conclusion. The English barrister tends to regard the common law as an inheritance to be preserved and technically perfected without being in any way altered. The changes that the bar wants, if any, are not those that the public is interested in. It is, moreover, doubtful that change of any kind is to its liking. "The lawyers could no doubt reform their education and training, reform the practice and processes of the law, even reform the law itself, if they felt like it. But probably they will not feel like it." On the contrary, the more the bar concentrates on formal perfection of established rules and procedures, the more removed it may become from the social ends that law serves. The judiciary, happily, is forced by the institutional demands of its office to keep moving.

The antiquity of legalism as an ideology is, in fact, one of the wonders of history. It is itself the expression of the continuity of the legal profession and its basic tasks. Whereas science has rendered the practice of modern medicine quite unlike the pre-nineteenth-century profession of the same name, the heirs of Coke resemble him closely in vocabulary, outlook, and concerns. De Tocqueville's description of the legalistic ethos is as accurate today as it was when it was written. Order and formality being the marks of the legal mind, he wrote, it is natural for lawyers to support the established social order. As long as they are not deprived of the authority which they regard as their due they will rally to the regime in power. The radical village lawyer of the French Revolution was an aberration that the aristocracy foolishly brought upon itself. In the normal course of events conservatism is inseparable from legalism. "If they prize freedom much, they generally value legality still more: they are less afraid of tyranny, than of arbitrary power." One might add that, if they fear tyranny, it is because it tends to be arbitrary, not because it is repressive. The fear of the arbitrary, however, is what gives legalism its political use. That is why it is not a conservatism without content. To the extent that change means uncertainty, the hatred of the arbitrary is inevitably conservative, but it is a conservatism that has a specific direction which distinguishes it from other conservatisms, especially on those occasions when the independence and professional standing of the bench and bar are directly involved; for they, and they alone, stand to protect "justice" against the arbitrariness and "expedience" of politics.

Almost a hundred years after de Tocqueville wrote, Max Weber could still present a picture of the ideology of the legal profession that was virtually unaltered. Lawyers remained as wedded to formal justice as ever and so to all the interests that relied on permanence and predictability in social procedures. Weber felt that this was even more true of the bureaucratized Continental lawyers than of those in common-law countries. And one can readily see how bureaucratic formalism would reinforce legalistic conservatism to a degree unknown in the Anglo-American legal systems where the free legal profession is less insulated from the shifts and turns of everyday politics. The liberalizing effect of involuntary politicization on the American higher bench, doomed to interpret and adapt its constitution, is evident enough. It is historical phenomena such as these, moreover, that make it so necessary to think of legalism as a matter of degree, rather than as either "there" or "not there," as lawyers think of law. Weber certainly thought of it dynamically, and he was far from complacent in his views of the intensification and rigidity of the legalism that he saw about him. If, as he argued, it was worse on the Continent than in England, his general remarks still are far from inapplicable to Anglo-American lawyerdom.

What he and de Tocqueville saw was that a legal caste, once it had established the "rule of law" securely against threats from absolutist arbitrariness, was bound to prefer order to liberty. What de Tocqueville called aristocratic habits of thought, Weber believed (rightly) to be more a matter of "internal professional ideology." The importance of the inner dynamic of legal reasoning and the professional preferences of lawyers tend to separate them from other social groups. Capitalist entrepreneurs have their own interest in stability and calculability, but the excessive formalities of lawyers' law are uncongenial to them. The conflct between jurists and psychiatrists is another example of tension engendered by incompatible professional views. As Weber was quick to note, these are not class struggles but acute differences between groups which belong to the same economic stratum in society. Looking at German lawyerdom mainly, he thought that its self-absorption, the extreme formalism of the legalistic spirit, would make it inevitably hostile not only to all radical social reform but to democracy in general. Since democracy was a radical ideal in Imperial Germany, he was quite right. However, as de Tocqueville noted, democracy is not necessarily incompatible with legalism. Law in America, then as now, is a profession open to talent, the poor boy's classical road to middle-class eminence. One might add that political democracy in America has been so conservative, in general, as to give the legalistic consciousness relatively little cause for complaint. Only occasionally, in the fear of radical state legislation and the Progressive movements for popular recall of the judiciary in the decades before the First World War, have legalism and democratic ideology clashed directly. Nevertheless, the main thrust of legalistic ideology is toward orderliness, and formalism can readily reinforce an inherent preference for authority. The ease with which German lawyers accepted "Adolf Légalité's" pretensions to legitimacy, the support they gave Nazism until its radical anti-legalistic tendencies revealed themselves (and even after), more than justify de Tocqueville's and Weber's suspicions. It cannot be repeated often enough that procedurally "correct" repression is perfectly compatible with legalism. That is the cost of conservative adaptability.

If traditionalism tends to favor liberal constitutionalism in America and England, as it did not in Germany, other aspects of legalism transcend the historic differences which Weber stressed so much and which certainly are very important. The differences in the respective attitudes of American lawyers, psychiatrists, and businessmen are still much as he described them. If the American corporation lawyer, the "house lawyer," comes to identify himself completely with the "organization" for which he works, there are lawyers who are wary of the informality of businessmen. There are, moreover, plenty of businessmen who find "lawyer's law," and expenses, unwelcome – and not only crude robber barons like Ryan and Whitney at that. The resort to arbitration under chamber of commerce auspices, from which lawyers were at first explicitly excluded, represented a significant preference for direct negotiations over formalism and, worse, litigation. On another level, businessmen do not want regulatory governmental agencies to become too courtlike, but prefer to maintain direct access to them in order to bargain with officials. The official program of the A.B.A., on the other hand, calls for judicialization. In this the lawyers, true to their ideology and habits, express their traditional distaste for the politics of negotiation, expediency, and arbitrariness. It is the popular acceptance of this legalism in America that surely contributes its share to the general cynicism toward politics as inevitably "dirty." The belief that negotiations aiming at peaceful settlements represent defeats for justice, for the politics of legalism, has led the official American bar to take at least one stand that separates it noticeably from most other conservative groups. From the first it has lent its support to international law, and especially to the International Court of Justice, on the ground that adjudication alone can prevent war and establish the reign of justice. Here, as in domestic politics, disputes between states are treated in isolation, apart from world politics in general. Here, too, the adjudicative process is held up as the model for government, the substitute for politics. So devoted a business lawyer as Joseph Choate headed the American delegation to the Second Hague Conference, and the "World Peace Through World Law" movement has today the ardent support of the A.B.A. This in itself would suffice to demonstrate the existence of a professional ideology among lawyers.

It also shows that lawyers are not indifferent to their public responsibilities, as has often been charged, but that they conceive of these in terms of their professional experiences and ideology. These give legalistic politics its identifying marks. It would be foolish to underestimate their prevalence or the depth of their roots in tradition, in the very structure of judicial institutions, and in the professional life of bench and bar. That is why one may well doubt the efficacy of the many schemes devised to reorient the thinking of lawyers by altering legal education in America. These proposals come mostly from academic lawyers who, like their medical-school counterparts, have a rather different view of their profession than do their client-oriented former students. Many academic lawyers would like to see a public-spirited political elite replace the private-law practicing lawyers whom they now teach. It is, to be sure, true that many lawyers do participate in politics. These men especially, but the profession as a whole, too, cannot, it is said, be prepared for their public duties by the case method or other traditional ways of teaching lawyers. Men as far apart in their political preferences as the late Justice Vanderbilt and Professor Hurst agree that special training for public service must replace the old curriculum.

That changes in the curriculum are the answer to all public deficiencies is, of course, in keeping with the great American tradition of painless reform. Everything from the study of Chaucer to the pursuit of "social science" has been proposed to this end. What has not been shown, however, is that changes in the content of courses alter the social behavior and attitudes of students once they enter upon their professional life. Given the very real demands for his services in our society, there is no reason why the young lawyer should not follow Lord Coke and make *meum* and *tuum* his favorite words, rather than the vocabulary of social science. Nor is there any reason to suppose that tinkering with the curriculum will, in the absence of significant social changes, alter traditional attitudes that are as firmly grounded as is legalism, not only among American lawyers but in popular opinion as well. The policy of justice, which despises arbitration, negotiations, bargaining, as mere "politics" arbitrary and expedient, will continue to appeal to lawyers. Adjudication of private *lites inter partes* will remain the model for public rectitude, the best way to solve all social conflicts, and "the law" will remain "there." Moreover, a great deal of analytical legal theory will continue to thrive on conceptions that have their roots in this nexus of beliefs. However formal the arguments and abstract the concepts, analytical jurisprudence reflects the same ideological climate as the legal profession as a whole, in spite of that minority of the legal profession in some American law schools which has long protested against formalism in jurisprudence, no less than against the ideological legalism of the bench and bar.

John E. Coons, 1929—
Professor of Law, Northwestern University

LEGALISM

(A paper delivered at the annual meeting of the Association of American Law Schools, 1965, as part of a panel discussion of the Shklar thesis)

Our subject – despite its name – is not simply a book on legalism . . . The book she has so beautifully written is a comment, rather, on the general problem of conceptualism in ethics, even though her examples have been largely limited to public law. She has adopted a meaning for legalism so broad that it could include questions ranging all the way from the destructibility of contingent remainders to the problem of the appropriate number of cocktails at the publishers' party. "What is legalism?" she asks. "It is the ethical attitude that holds moral conduct to be a matter of rule-following." This, then, is a book about an ethical attitude – an attitude holding that only specific verbal propositions have functional significance in moral and legal discourse; about an attitude that it can be a meaningful and sometimes necessary thing to construct and promulgate such formulas as "all dogs must be leashed" or "six martinis is too much." Dr. Shklar is a student of that insidious habit of human intelligence – generalization. Though her book is aimed at lawyers and speaks mostly of law, it is less a critique of lawyers and law than of all philosophies that strive to organize reality into verbal categories – in short, of practically all philosophies. Perhaps the book is not an outright rejection of conceptualism in ethics, but its author rather clearly wishes that it could be. She may suffer rules gladly for society's sake, but she does suffer. For her the center of ethical experience is not to be found in the hoary dicta of judges and moralists. It lies rather in a hope for something she describes as:

> . . . social diversity, inspired by that barebones liberalism which, having abandoned the theory of progress and every specific scheme of economics, is committed only to the belief that tolerance is a primary virtue and that a diversity of opinions and habits is not only to be endured but to be cherished and encouraged.

This – to me – sentimental attachment to diversity for its own sake informs the entire work. It may help to explain Dr. Shklar's ambivalent attitude of hostility coupled with occasional grudging admiration for what she supposes to be the mind of the American lawyer – he of the constipated psyche, hugging his comfort blanket of true rules, suspicious of diversity, yet oddly fastidious in supplying procedural equality for dissenters. So, at least, she seems to view him. This is not merely a book about an attitude. It is an attitude about an attitude.

Few of us would deny that conceptualism *can* be harmful in law as elsewhere. There is nothing like an overdose of hair splitting to render a legal or ethical system dysfunctional. . . . We can agree that the compartitioned mind is badly equipped for Law and Politics without concluding much at all about the bulk of the legal iceberg below the water line chosen by Dr. Shklar. I'd like to know what's going on in the murkier depths below the level of high policy. . . .

What most lawyers do believe in – but not much more – is the rare but real possibility of answering practical questions with civilized solutions. Where conceptualism promotes this end, it is available as our servant. Where it does not, then so much the worse for conceptualism. In fact, of course, many legal solutions are conceptualistic – or, if you prefer – legalistic. But to suppose that lawyers think of rules in ontological terms as "there" is to mistake the shorthand of professional discourse for the deposit of truth. We do not believe in the contingent remainder because it is there. It is there because we believe in it; or, perhaps more accurately, it works, therefore it is.

I believe the lawyer's attitude to be as skeptical as Dr. Shklar could possibly wish. We swim in a sea of indeterminacy, and, if we don't love it, we at least are aware of it. Our problem is not that of being fooled by concepts but of dominating them with practical reason. Where simplistic absurdities exist – and they do – we must slay them, and we do so with regularity. Yesterday we killed the fellow servant doctrine; today we have mortally wounded *Shelley's* case; tomorrow other ogres will fall. No doubt the failures, too, are numerous, but success is at least frequent enough to disallow legalism in the Shklaristic sense as the appropriate motif of the American bar. Even in, or perhaps especially in, the arena of high public policy so congenial to political scientist, legalism has been clearly the servant, not the master. In race relations, anti-trust policy, civil liberties, and criminal law, the courts have been anything but conceptualistic. Perhaps the geometry of one man-one vote should be viewed as an exception; but if attitudes are here the issue, I suspect that the legalistic apportionment decisions are applauded less by lawyers than by Doctor Shklar; American lawyers have always held a curious and abiding affection for sloppy pragmatism.

All that I have said amounts to this: there is no general problem of legalism but only problems of legalism. There are merely solutions that are dysfunctional – some because they are too conceptual, others perhaps because they are not sufficiently conceptual. It is our business and Dr. Shklar's to expose and correct them. She has ably identified several problems of excessive conceptualism at high levels. I would suggest another example that has previously occupied me – indeed, a pet of mine – one of a humbler character than war crimes but nonetheless important and pervasive. For lack of a better description, I would call it the cult of winner-take-all. It is imbedded in the unspoken premise that for any given dispute submitted to adjudication, only two solutions exist: for plaintiff or for defendant; it makes litigation what the game theorists describe as a zero sum game. A judge may strive for compromise in pre-trial, but his own decision from the bench must be polarized, however neatly the issues of fact and law may be balanced.

Now for most dispute situations, this all-or-nothing approach may have many advantages in terms of judicial administration and public policy, but as a universal principle of decision it is patent nonsense. It not only falsifies reality, but is frequently unjust to the losing party and the winner as well. In many stereotyped situations rules could be devised to effect compromise solutions more nearly reflecting the real equities. One thinks immediately of comparative negligence, but an even better case is that of the defrauded owner of a chattel versus the bona fide purchaser. In many such cases the equities suggest a split, and an intelligible rule could be framed to that end. Note, however, that I speak in terms of developing workable *rules* for compromise, not simply in terms of judicial discretion, though discretion would surely have its role to play. If this be legalism, make the most of it. It seems to me a functional legalism, and that, I submit, is the object of our quest.

This may appear a pedestrian concern juxtaposed to the great issues of war and peace that occupy Dr. Shklar. At bottom, however, is the identical question of the extent to which generalized solutions to ethical questions involve a sacrifice of human potential. Are rules of conduct inevitably prisons? Dr. Shklar is properly schizophrenic on this issue, but there is little doubt that rule-oriented systems cause her a good deal of uneasiness. I may be merely proving Dr. Shklar's fundamental point about lawyers' attitudes in what I'm about to say, but it is hard for me to think of rules as the enemy of freedom and diversity. It may be true, as Dr. Shklar suggests, that mystical moralists like Nietzsche or Sartre think of rules as confining and cold. But I expect that most men find mystical morality confining and cold – as confining and cold as the asylum that was eventually reserved for the original superman. Freedom is not the absence of form. Indeed, the history of human liberty is in large measure the history of form manifested in the organization and complication of matter and psyche. In the human species the development of structure is the beginning of choice; and the essence of structure is the development of rules. Under some circumstances even the most arbitrary of rules may serve to increase freedom – the rules of the road are the classic example.

But I would go even further in praise of rules: they are not merely a precondition of freedom. They are the guardians of the enthusiastic society, for they provide the limiting conditions under which romance is possible. Romance is not the offspring of formlessness; rather, it is the child of order. It depends in a fundamental way upon letting man know the risks he runs and then leaving him free to run them. Or – which is about the same thing – it depends upon perceiving the importance of the rules of any game in order to get any fun out of the playing. Bridge is really not much fun if trump keeps changing in the middle of the hand.

I'd like to illustrate this relation between rules and romance by returning for a moment to the nursery to examine what Chesterton called "the ethics of elfland." Let's take the case of Beauty and the Beast. Suppose we had reason to think that the witch who had hexed the handsome prince was really a pretty wishy-washy, discretion-oriented sort of witch who often relented when the chips were down. Even if Beauty lost her nerve and couldn't bring herself to kiss the poor ugly fellow, there still was a good chance the witch would give him his complexion back and he and Beauty would get married and live happily. I nearly said "ever after," but that would be up to the witch again, wouldn't it? If she changed her mind once, why not twice? And, for that matter, suppose Beauty and Prince didn't get along after all. Maybe the witch would let her off the hook and find another prince for her, and then another. . . . Romantic? Exciting?

Or suppose, on the other hand, the warmhearted heroine in her great charity summons her courage, kisses the beast, and he turns into . . . . a giraffe. Exciting? Romantic?

What was it about Beauty and the Beast, or even Cinderella, that made our childish hearts leap? Precisely this: we had confidence that the plan would be observed, the promise kept, the rule enforced. We were excited by the knowledge that what the girl did or failed to do really mattered. It was of no great importance that the rule itself be sensible but only that it be enforcible. We might hear the tale a hundred times, but there was always the chance that next time Beauty would not kiss the Beast, and we knew what the awful consequences would be – indeed, we insisted on them as the center and spice of the story.

On a larger scale, the same principle operates in Genesis. What a catastrophe for romance if God had said, "Well, Adam, you rascal, you've eaten the apple. I hope you won't do that again. Do try to be better." Adam's infidelity was in any event a disaster, but from the wreckage of Eden at least this was preserved by God's judgment: that what man does matters a very great deal. If God had merely shrugged, even this would have been lost, and our warm and comfortable Eden would be about as exciting as a cow pasture. If God could not be trusted to punish, He could not be trusted.

The application of this same line of thought to the institution of marriage is obvious, and brings the world of the fairy tale and of scripture across the borders of pure morality and into the world of the lawyer. The fascination and excitement of marriage has nothing to do with the physical. That aspect of the relation is quite imaginable even without the institution. The romance of marriage is in the commitment, in a man's willingness to cast his lot for life on a judgment that is both difficult and dangerous. Like accepting the challenge to a duel, it may be unwise, it may be regretted, it may be a disaster. But all this is simply to say that there is risk, and without risk there is no romance.

This line of thought can be carried too far, as perhaps I've unwittingly demonstrated. The content of the rules does make a difference. And, as Dr. Shklar demonstrates, a limited tyranny is conceivable, even under the rule of law. But at least insofar as legalism, like Mother Goose, preserves fidelity to human principle and institutions, it protects the essence of a zestful life. In preserving the rule of the game, the law keeps the game worth playing and continues to inspire the revolutionary notion that men can lead civilized lives, that society can provide freedom in order, and that the joy of responsible action is the primary spice of life.

An elaboration of Professor Coon's attack on "the cult of winner-take-all" is to be found in "Approaches to Court Imposed Compromise – The Uses of Doubt and Reason" (1964) 58 *Nw. U.L. Rev.* 50.

Oliver Wendell Holmes, Jr., 1841-1935
Harvard Law Professor, Judge and later Chief Justice of the Massachusetts Supreme Court, and Associate Justice of the United States Supreme Court 1902-1932.

THE PATH OF THE LAW
(1897)

When we study law we are not studying a mystery but a well-known profession. We are studying what we shall want in order to appear before judges, or to advise people in such a way as to keep them out of court. The reason why it is a profession, why people will pay lawyers to argue for them or to advise them, is that in societies like ours the command of the public force is intrusted to the judges in certain cases, and the whole power of the state will be put forth, if necessary, to carry out their judgments and decrees. People want to know under what circumstances and how far they will run the risk of coming against what is so much stronger than themselves, and hence it becomes a business to find out when this danger is to be feared. The object of our study, then, is prediction, the prediction of the incidence of the public force through the instrumentality of the courts.

The means of the study are a body of reports, of treatises, and of statutes, in this country and in England, extending back for six hundred years, and now increasing annually by hundreds. In these sibylline leaves are gathered the scattered prophecies of the past upon the cases in which the axe will fall. These are what properly have been called the oracles of the law. Far the most important and pretty nearly the whole meaning of every new effort of legal thought is to make these prophecies more precise, and to generalize them into a thoroughly connected system. The process is one, from a lawyer's statement of a case, eliminating as it does all the dramatic elements with which his client's story has clothed it, and retaining only the facts of legal import, up to the final analyses and abstract universals of theoretic jurisprudence. The reason why a lawyer does not mention that his client wore a white hat when he made a contract, while Mrs. Quickly would be sure to dwell upon it along with the parcel gilt goblet and the sea-coal fire, is that he foresees that the public force will act in the same way whatever his client had upon his head. It is to make the prophecies easier to be remembered and to be understood that the teachings of the decisions of the past are put into general propositions and gathered into text-books, or that statutes are passed in a general form. The primary rights and duties with which jurisprudence busies itself again are nothing but prophecies. One of the many evil effects of the confusion between legal and moral ideas, about which I shall have something to say in a moment, is that theory is apt to get the cart before the horse, and to consider the right or the duty as something existing apart from and independent of the consequences of its breach, to which certain sanctions are added afterward. But, as I shall try to show, a legal duty so called is nothing but a prediction that if a man does or omits certain things he will be made to suffer in this or that way by judgment of the court; and so of a legal right.

The number of our predictions when generalized and reduced to a system is not unmanageably large. They present themselves as a definite body of dogma which may be mastered within a reasonable time. It is a great mistake to be frightened by the ever-increasing number of reports. The reports of a given jurisdiction in the course of a generation take up pretty much the whole body of the law, and restate it from the present point of view. We could reconstruct the corpus from them if all that went before were burned. The use of the earlier reports is mainly historical, a use about which I shall have something to say before I have finished.

I wish, if I can, to lay down some first principles for the study of this body of dogma or systematized prediction which we call the law, for men who want to use it as the instrument of their business to enable them to prophesy in their turn, and, as bearing upon the study, I wish to point out an ideal which as yet our law has not attained.

The first thing for a business-like understanding of the matter is to understand its limits, and therefore I think it desirable at once to point out and dispel a confusion between morality and law, which sometimes rises to the height of conscious theory, and more often and indeed constantly is making trouble in detail without reaching the point of consciousness. You can see very plainly that a bad man has as much reason as a good one for wishing to avoid an encounter with the public force, and therefore you can see the practical importance of the distinction between morality and law. A man who cares nothing for an ethical rule which is believed and practised by his neighbors is likely nevertheless to care a good deal to avoid being made to pay money, and will want to keep out of jail if he can.

I take it for granted that no hearer of mine will misinterpret what I have to say as the language of cynicism. The law is the witness and external deposit of our moral life. Its history is the history of the moral development of the race. The practice of it, in spite of popular jests, tends to make good citizens and good men. When I emphasize the difference between law and morals I do so with reference to a single end, that of learning and understanding the law. For that purpose you must definitely master its specific marks, and it is for that I ask you for the moment to imagine yourselves indifferent to other and greater things.

I do not say that there is not a wider point of view from which the distinction between law and morals becomes of secondary or no importance, as all mathematical distinctions vanish in presence of the infinite. But I do say that that distinction is of the first importance for the object which we are here to consider – a right study and mastery of the law as a business with well understood limits, a body of dogma enclosed within definite lines. I have just shown the practical reason for saying so. If you want to know the law and nothing else, you must look at it as a bad man, who cares only for the material consequences which such knowledge enables him to predict, not as a good one, who finds his reasons for conduct, whether inside the law or outside of it, in the vaguer sanctions of conscience. The theoretical importance of the distinction is no less, if you would reason on your subject aright. The law is full of phraseology drawn from morals, and by the mere force of language continually invites us to pass from one domain to the other without perceiving it, as we are sure to do unless we have the boundary constantly before our minds. The law talks about rights, and duties, and malice, and intent, and negligence, and so forth, and nothing is easier, or, I may say, more common in legal reasoning, than to take these words in their moral sense, at some stage of the argument, and so to drop into fallacy. For instance, when we speak of the rights of man in a moral sense, we mean to mark the limits of interference with individual freedom which we think are prescribed by conscience, or by our ideal, however reached. Yet it is certain that many laws have been enforced in the past, and it is likely that some are enforced now, which are condemned by the most enlightened opinion of the time, or which at all events pass the limit of interference as many consciences would draw it. Manifestly, therefore, nothing but confusion of thought can result from assuming that the rights of man in a moral sense are equally rights in the sense of the Constitution and the law. No doubt simple and extreme cases can be put of imaginable laws which the statute-making power would not dare to enact, even in the absence of written constitutional prohibitions, because the community would rise in rebellion and fight; and this gives some plausibility to the proposition that the law, if not a part of morality, is limited by it. But this limit of power is not coextensive with any system of morals. For the most part it falls far within the lines of any such system, and in some cases may extend beyond them, for reasons drawn from the habits of a particular people at a particular time. I once heard the late Professor Agassiz say that a German population would rise if you added two cents to the price of a glass of beer. A statute in such a case would be empty words, not because it was wrong, but because it could not be enforced. No one will deny that wrong statutes can be and are enforced, and we should not all agree as to which were the wrong ones.

The confusion with which I am dealing besets confessedly legal conceptions. Take the fundamental question, What constitutes the law? You will find some text writers telling you that it is something different from what is decided by the courts of Massachusetts or England, that it is a system of reason, that it is a deduction from principles of ethics or admitted axioms or what not, which may or may not coincide with the decisions. But if we take the view of our friend the bad man we shall find that he does not care two straws for the axioms or deductions, but that he does want to know what the Massachusetts or English courts are likely to do in fact. I am much of his mind. The prophecies of what the courts will do in fact, and nothing more pretentious, are what I mean by the law.

Take again a notion which as popularly understood is the widest conception which the law contains – the notion of legal duty, to which already I have referred. We fill the word with all the content which we draw from morals. But what does it mean to a bad man? Mainly, and in the first place, a prophecy that if he does certain things he will be subjected to disagreeable consequences by way of imprisonment or compulsory payment of money. But from his point of view, what is the difference between being fined and being taxed a certain sum for doing a certain thing? That his point of view is the test of legal principles is shown by the many discussions which have arisen in the courts on the very question whether a given statutory liability is a penalty or a tax. On the answer to this question depends the decision whether conduct is legally wrong or right, and also whether a man is under compulsion or free. Leaving the criminal law on one side, what is the difference between the liability under the mill acts or statutes authorizing a taking by eminent domain and the liability for what we call a wrongful conversion of property where restoration is out of the question. In both cases the party taking another man's property has to pay its fair value as assessed by a jury, and no more. What significance is there in calling one taking right and another wrong from the point of view of the law? It does not matter, so far as the given consequence, the compulsory payment, is concerned, whether the act to which it is attached is described in terms of praise or in terms of blame, or whether the law purports to prohibit it or to allow it. If it matters at all, still speaking from the bad man's point of view, it must be because in one case and not in the other some further disadvantages, or at least some further consequences, are attached to the act by the law. The only other disadvantages thus attched to it which I ever have been able to think of are to be found in two somewhat insignificant legal doctrines, both of which might be abolished without disturbance. One is, that a contract to do a prohibited act is unlawful, and the other, that, if one of two or more joint wrongdoers has to pay all the damages, he cannot recover contribution from his fellows. And that I believe is all. You see how the vague circumference of the notion of duty shrinks and at the same time grows more precise when we wash it with cynical acid and expel everything except the object of our study, the operations of the law.

Nowhere is the confusion between legal and moral ideas more manifest than in the law of contract. Among other things, here again the so called primary rights and duties are invested with a mystic significance beyond what can be assigned and explained. The duty to keep a contract at common law means a prediction that you must pay damages if you do not keep it – and nothing else. If you commit a tort, you are liable to pay a compensatory sum. If you commit a contract, you are liable to pay a compensatory sum unless the promised event comes to pass, and that is all the difference. But such a mode of looking at the matter stinks in the nostrils of those who think it advantageous to get as much ethics into the law as they can. It was good enough for Lord Coke, however, and here, as in many other cases, I am content to abide with him. In *Bromage* v. *Genning*, a prohibition was sought in the King's Bench against a suit in the marches of Wales for the specific performance of a covenant to grant a lease, and Coke said that it would subvert the intention of the covenantor, since he intends it to be at his election either to lose the damages or to make the lease. Sergeant

Harris for the plaintiff confessed that he moved the matter against his conscience, and a prohibition was granted. This goes further than we should go now, but it shows what I venture to say has been the common law point of view from the beginning, although Mr. Harriman, in his very able little book upon contracts has been misled, as I humbly think, to a different conclusion.

I have spoken only of the common law, because there are some cases in which a logical justification can be found for speaking of civil liabilities as imposing duties in an intelligible sense. These are the relatively few in which equity will grant an injunction, and will enforce it by putting the defendant in prison or otherwise punishing him unless he complies with the order of the court. But I hardly think it advisable to shape general theory from the exception, and I think it would be better to cease troubling ourselves about primary rights and sanctions altogether, than to describe our prophecies concerning the liabilities commonly imposed by the law in those inappropriate terms.

I mentioned, as other examples of the use by the law of words drawn from morals, malice, intent, and negligence. It is enough to take malice as it is used in the law of civil liability for wrongs – what we lawyers call the law of torts – to show that it means something different in law from what it means in morals, and also to show how the difference has been obscured by giving to principles which have little or nothing to do with each other the same name. Three hundred years ago a parson preached a sermon and told a story out of Fox's *Book of Martyrs* of a man who had assisted at the torture of one of the saints, and afterward died, suffering compensatory inward torment. It happened that Fox was wrong. The man was alive and chanced to hear the sermon, and thereupon he sued the parson. Chief Justice Wray instructed the jury that the defendant was not liable, because the story was told innocently, without malice. He took malice in the moral sense, as importing a malevolent motive. But nowadays no one doubts that a man may be liable, without any malevolent motive at all, for false statements manifestly calculated to inflict temporal damage. In stating the case in pleading, we still should call the defendant's conduct malicious; but, in my opinion at least, the word means nothing about motives, or even about the defendant's attitude toward the future, but only signifies that the tendency of his conduct under the known circumstances was very plainly to cause the plaintiff temporal harm.

In the law of contract the use of moral phraseology has led to equal confusion, as I have shown in part already, but only in part. Morals deal with the actual internal state of the individual's mind, what he actually intends. From the time of the Romans down to now, this mode of dealing has affected the language of the law as to contract, and the language used has reacted upon the thought. We talk about a contract as a meeting of the minds of the parties, and thence it is inferred in various cases that there is no contract because their minds have not met; that is, because they have intended different things or because one party has not known of the assent of the other. Yet nothing is more certain than that parties may be bound by a contract to things which neither of them intended, and when one does not know of the other's assent. Suppose a contract is executed in due form and in writing to deliver a lecture, mentioning no time. One of the parties thinks that the promise will be construed to mean at once, within a week. The other thinks that it means when he is ready. The court says that it means within a reasonable time. The parties are bound by the contract as it is interpreted by the court, yet neither of them meant what the court declares that they have said. In my opinion no one will understand the true theory of contract or be able even to discuss some fundamental questions intelligently until he has understood that all contracts are formal, that the making of a contract depends not on the agreement of two minds in one intention, but on the agreement of two sets of of external signs – not on the parties' having *meant* the same thing but on their having *said* the same thing. Furthermore, as the signs may be addressed to one sense or another – to sight or to hearing – on the nature of the sign will depend the moment when the contract is made. If the sign is tangible, for instance, a letter, the contract is made when the letter of acceptance is delivered. If it is necessary that the minds of the parties meet, there will be no contract until the acceptance can be read – none, for example, if the acceptance be snatched from the hand of the offerer by a third person.

This is not the time to work out a theory in detail, or to answer many obvious doubts and questions which are suggested by these general views. I know of none which are not easy to answer, but what I am trying to do now is only by a series of hints to throw some light on the narrow path of legal doctrine, and upon two pitfalls which, as it seems to me, lie perilously near to it. Of the first of these I have said enough. I hope that my illustrations have shown the danger, both to speculation and to practice, of confounding morality with law, and the trap which legal language lays for us on that side of our way. For my part, I often doubt whether it would not be a gain if every word of moral significance could be banished from the law altogether, and other words adopted which should convey legal ideas uncolored by anything outside the law. We should lose the fossil records of a good deal of history and the majesty got from ethical associations, but by riding ourselves of an unnecessary confusion we should gain very much in the clearness of our thought.

So much for the limits of the law. The next thing which I wish to consider is what are the forces which determine its content and its growth. You may assume, with Hobbes and Bentham and Austin, that all law emanates from the sovereign, even when the first human beings to enunciate it are the judges, or you may think that law is the voice of the Zeitgeist, or what you like. It is all one to my present purpose. Even if every decision required the sanction of an emperor with despotic power and a whimsical turn of mind, we should be interested none the less, still with a view to prediction, in discovering some order, some rational explanation, and some principle of growth for the rules which he laid down. In every system there are such explanations and principles to be found. It is with regard to them that a second fallacy comes in, which I think it important to expose.

The fallacy to which I refer is the notion that the only force at work in the development of the law is logic. In the broadest sense, indeed, that notion would be true. The postulate on which we think about the universe is that there is a fixed quantitative relation between every phenomenon and its antecedents and consequents. If there is such a thing as a phenomenon without these fixed quantitative relations, it is a miracle. It is outside the law of cause and effect, and as such transcends our power of thought, or at least is something to or from which we cannot reason. The condition of our thinking about the universe is that it is capable of being thought about rationally, or, in other words, that every part of it is effect and cause in the same sense in which those parts are with which we are most familiar. So in the broadest sense it is true that the law is a logical development, like everything else. The danger of which I speak is not the admission that the principles governing other phenomena also govern the law, but the notion that a given system, ours, for instance, can be worked out like mathematics from some general axioms of conduct. This is the natural error of the schools, but it is not confined to them. I once heard a very eminent judge say that he never let a decision go until he was absolutely sure that it was right. So judicial dissent often is blamed, as if it meant simply that one side or the other were not doing their sums right, and, if they would take more trouble, agreement inevitably would come.

This mode of thinking is entirely natural. The training of lawyers is a training in logic. The processes of analogy, discrimination, and deduction are those in which they are most at home. The language of judicial decision is mainly the language of logic. And the logical method and form flatter that longing for certainty and for repose which is in every human mind. But certainty generally is illusion, and repose is not the destiny of man. Behind the logical form lies a judgment as to the relative worth and importance of competing legislative grounds, often an inarticulate and unconscious judgment, it is true, and yet the very root and nerve of the whole proceeding. You can give any conclusion a logical form. You always can imply a condition in a contract. But why do you imply it? It is because of some belief as to the practice of the community or of a class, or because of some opinion as to policy, or, in short, because of some attitude of yours upon a matter not capable of exact quantitative measurement, and therefore not capable of founding exact logical conclusions. Such matters really are battle grounds where the means do not exist for determinations that shall be good for all time, and where the decision can do no more than embody the preference of a given body in a given time and place. We do not realize how large a part of our law is open to reconsideration upon a slight change in the habit of the public mind. No concrete proposition is self evident, no matter how ready we may be to accept it, not even Mr. Herbert Spencer's "Every man has a right to do what he wills, provided he interferes not with a like right on the part of his neighbors."

Why is a false and injurious statement privileged, if it is made honestly in giving information about a servant. It is because it has been thought more important that information should be given freely, than that a man should be protected from what under other circumstances would be an actionable wrong. Why is a man at liberty to set up a business which he knows will ruin his neighbor? It is because the public good is supposed to be best subserved by free competition. Obviously such judgments of relative importance may vary in different times and places. Why does a judge instruct a jury that an employer is not liable to an employee for an injury received in the course of his employment unless he is negligent, and why do the jury generally find for the plaintiff if the case is allowed to go to them? It is because the traditional policy of our law is to confine liability to cases where a prudent man might have foreseen the injury, or at least the danger, while the inclination of a very large part of the community is to make certain classes of persons insure the safety of those with whom they deal. Since the last words were written, I have seen the requirement of such insurance put forth as part of the programme of one of the best known labor organizations. There is a concealed, half conscious battle on the question of legislative policy, and if any one thinks that it can be settled deductively, or once for all, I only can say that I think he is theoretically wrong, and that I am certain that his conclusion will not be accepted in practice *semper ubique et ab omnibus*.

Indeed, I think that even now our theory upon this matter is open to reconsideration, although I am not prepared to say how I should decide if a reconsideration were proposed. Our law of torts comes from the old days of isolated, ungeneralized wrongs, assaults, slanders, and the like, where the damages might be taken to lie where they fell by legal judgment. But the torts with which our courts are kept busy to-day are mainly the incidents of certain well known businesses. They are injuries to person or property by railroads, factories, and the like. The liability for them is estimated, and sooner or later goes into the price paid by the public. The public really pays the damages, and the question of liability, if pressed far enough, is really the question how far it is desirable that the public should insure the safety of those whose work it uses. It might be said that in such cases the chance of a jury finding for the defendant is merely a chance, once in a while rather arbitrarily interrupting the regular course of recovery, most likely in the case of an unusually conscientious plaintiff, and therefore better done away with. On the other hand, the economic value even of a life to the community can be estimated, and no recovery, it may be said, ought to go beyond that amount. It is conceivable that some day in certain cases we may find ourselves imitating, on a higher plane, the tariff for life and limb which we see in the *Leges Barbarorum*.

I think that the judges themselves have failed adequately to recognize their duty of weighing considerations of social advantage. The duty is inevitable, and the result of the often proclaimed judicial aversion to deal with such considerations is simply to leave the very ground and foundation of judgments inarticulate, often unconscious, as I have said. When socialism first began to be talked about, the comfortable classes of the community were a good deal frightened. I suspect that this fear has influenced judicial action both here and in England, yet it is certain that it is not a conscious factor in the decisions to which I refer. I think that something similar has led people who no longer hope to control the legislatures to look to the courts as expounders of the Constitutions, and that in some courts new principles have been discovered outside the bodies of those instruments, which may be generalized into acceptance of the economic doctrines which prevailed about fifty years ago, and a wholesale prohibition of what a tribunal of lawyers does not think about right. I cannot but believe that if the training of lawyers led them habitually to consider more definitely and explicitly the social advantage on which the rule they lay down must be justified, they sometimes would hesitate where now they are confident, and see that really they were taking sides upon debatable and often burning questions.

So much for the fallacy of logical form. Now let us consider the present condition of the law as a subject for study, and the ideal toward which it tends. We still are far from the point of view which I desire to see reached. No one has reached it or can reach it as yet. We are only at the beginning of a philosophical reaction, and of a reconsideration of the worth of doctrines which for the most part still are taken for granted without any deliberate, conscious, and systematic questioning of their grounds. The development of our law has gone on for nearly a thousand years, like the development of a plant, each generation taking the inevitable next step, mind, like matter, simply obeying a law of spontaneous growth. It is perfectly natural and right that it should have been so. Imitation is a necessity of human nature, as has been illustrated by a remarkable French writer, M. Tarde, in an admirable book, *Les Lois de l'Imitation*. Most of the things we do, we do for no better reason than that our fathers have done them or that our neighbors do them, and the same is true of a larger part than we suspect of what we think. The reason is a good one, because our short life gives us no time for a better, but it is not the best. It does not follow, because we all are compelled to take on faith at second hand most of the rules on which we base our action and our thought, that each of us may not try to set some corner of his world in the order of reason, or that all of us collectively should not aspire to carry reason as far as it will go throughout the whole domain. In regard to the law, it is true, no doubt, that an evolutionist will hesitate to affirm universal validity for his social ideals, or for the principles which he thinks should be embodied in legislation. He is content if he can prove them best for here and now. He may be ready to admit that he knows nothing about an absolute best in the cosmos, and even that he knows next to nothing about a permanent best for men. Still it is true that a body of law is more rational and more civilized when every rule it contains is referred articulately and definitely to an end which it subserves, and when the grounds for desiring that end are stated or are ready to be stated in words.

At present, in very many cases, if we want to know why a rule of law has taken its particular shape, and more or less if we want to know why it exists at all, we go to tradition. We follow it into the Year Books, and perhaps beyond them to the customs of the Salian Franks, and somewhere in the past, in the German forests, in the needs of Norman kings, in the assumptions of a dominant class, in the absence of generalized ideas, we find out the practical motive for what now best is justified by the mere fact of its acceptance and that men are accustomed to it. The rational study of law is still to a large extent the study of history. History must be a part of the study, because without it we cannot know the precise scope of rules which it is our business to know. It is a part of the rational study, because it is the first step toward an enlightened scepticism, that is, towards a deliberate reconsideration of the worth of those rules. When you get the dragon out of his cave on to the plain and in the daylight, you can count his teeth and claws, and see just what is his strength. But to get him out is only the first step. The next is either to kill him, or to tame him and make him a useful animal. For the rational study of the law the black-letter man may be the man of the present, but the man of the future is the man of statistics and master of economics. It is revolting to have no better reason for a rule of law than that so it was laid down in the time of Henry IV. It is still more revolting if the grounds upon which it was laid down have vanished long since, and the rule simply persists from blind imitation of the past. I am thinking of the technical rule as to trespass *ab initio*, as it is called, which I attempted to explain in a recent Massachusetts case.

Let me take an illustration, which can be stated in a few words, to show how the social end which is aimed at by a rule of law is obscured and only partially attained in consequence of the fact that the rule owes its form to a gradual historical development, instead of being reshaped as a whole, with conscious articulate reference to the end in view. We think it desirable to prevent one man's property being misappropriated by another, and so we make larceny a crime. The evil is the same whether the misappropriation is made by a man into whose hands the owner has put the property, or by one who wrongfully takes it away. But primitive law in its weakness did not get much beyond an effort to prevent violence, and very naturally made a wrongful taking, a trespass, part of its definition of the crime. In modern times the judges enlarged the definition a little by holding that, if the wrong-doer gets possession by a trick or device, the crime is committed. This really was giving up the requirement of a trespass, and it would have been more logical, as well as truer to the present object of the law, to abandon the requirement altogether. That, however, would have seemed too bold, and was left to statute. Statutes were passed making embezzlement a crime. But the force of tradition caused the crime of embezzlement to be regarded as so far distinct from larceny that to this day, in some jurisdictions at least, a slip corner is kept open for thieves to contend, if indicted for larceny, that they should have been indicted for embezzlement, and if indicted for embezzlement, that they should have been indicted for larceny, and to escape on that ground.

Far more fundamental questions still await a better answer than that we do as our fathers have done. What have we better than a blind guess to show that the criminal law in its present form does more good than harm? I do not stop to refer to the effect which it has had in degrading prisoners and in plunging them further into crime, or to the question whether fine and imprisonment do not fall more heavily on a criminal's wife and children than on himself. I have in mind more far-reaching questions. Does punishment deter? Do we deal with criminals on proper principles? A modern school of Continental criminalists plumes itself on the formula, first suggested, it is said, by Gall, that we must consider the criminal rather than the crime. The formula does not carry us very far, but the inquiries which have been started look toward an answer of my questions based on science for the first time. If the typical criminal is a degenerate, bound to swindle or to murder by as deep seated an organic necessity as that which makes the rattlesnake bite, it is idle to talk of deterring him by the classical method of imprisonment. He must be got rid of; he cannot be improved, or frightened out of his structural reaction. If, on the other hand, crime, like normal human conduct, is mainly a matter of imitation, punishment fairly may be expected to help to keep it out of fashion. The study of criminals has been thought by some well known men of science to sustain the former hypothesis. The statistics of the relative increase of crime in crowded places like large cities, where example has the greatest chance to work, and in less populated parts, where the contagion spreads more slowly, have been used with great force in favor of the latter view. But there is weighty authority for the belief that, however this may be, "not the nature of the crime, but the dangerousness of the criminal, constitutes the only reasonable legal criterion to guide the inevitable social reaction against the criminal."

The impediments to rational generalization, which I illustrated from the law of larceny, are shown in the other branches of the law, as well as in that of crime. Take the law of tort or civil liability for damages apart from contract and the like. Is there any general theory of such liability, or are the cases in which it exists simply to be enumerated, and to be explained each on its special ground, as is easy to believe from the fact that the right of action for certain well known classes of wrongs like trespass or slander has its special history for each class? I think that there is a general theory to be discovered, although resting in tendency rather than established and accepted. I think that the law regards the infliction of temporal damage by a responsible person as actionable, if under the circumstances known to him the danger of his act is manifest according to common experience, or according to his own experience if it is more than common, except in cases where upon special grounds of policy the law refuses to protect the plaintiff or grants a privilege to the defendant. I think that commonly malice, intent, and negligence mean only that the danger was manifest to a greater or less degree, under the circumstances known to the actor, although in some cases of privilege malice may mean an actual malevolent motive, and such a motive may take away a permission knowingly to inflict harm, which otherwise would be granted on this or that ground of dominant public good. But when I stated my view to a very eminent English judge the other day, he said: "You are discussing what the law ought to be; as the law is, you must show a right. A man is not liable for negligence unless he is subject to a duty." If our difference was more than a difference in words, or with regard to the proportion between the exceptions and the rule, then, in his opinion, liability for an act cannot be referred to the manifest tendency of the act to cause temporal damage in general as a sufficient explanation, but must be referred to the special nature of the damage, or must be derived from some special circumstances outside of the tendency of the act, for which no generalized explanation exists. I think that such a view is wrong, but it is familiar, and I dare say generally is accepted in England.

Everywhere the basis of principle is tradition, to such an extent that we even are in danger of making the role of history more important than it is. The other day Professor Ames wrote a learned article to show, among other things, that the common law did not recognize the defence of fraud in actions upon specialties, and the moral might seem to be that the personal character of the defence is due to its equitable origin. But if, as I have said, all contracts are formal, the difference is not merely historical, but theoretic, between defects of form which prevent a contract from being made, and mistaken motives which manifestly could not be considered in any system that we should call rational except against one who was privy to those motives. It is not confined to specialties, but is of universal application. I ought to add that I do not suppose that Mr. Ames would disagree with what I suggest.

However, if we consider the law of contract, we find it full of history. The distinctions between debt covenant, and assumpsit are merely historical. The classification of certain obligations to pay money, imposed by the law irrespective of any bargain as quasi contracts, is merely historical. The effect given to a seal is to be explained by history alone. Consideration is a mere form. Is it a useful form? If so, why should it not be required in all contracts? A seal is a mere form, and is vanishing in the scroll and in enactments that a consideration must be given, seal or no seal. Why should any merely historical distinction be allowed to affect the rights and obligations of business men?

Since I wrote this discourse I have come on a very good example of the way in which tradition not only overrides rational policy, but overrides it after first having been misunderstood and having been given a new and broader scope than it had when it had a meaning. It is the settled law of England that a material alteration of a written contract by a party avoids it as against him. The doctrine is contrary to the general tendency of the law. We do not tell a jury that if a man ever has lied in one particular he is to be presumed to lie in all. Even if a man has tried to defraud, it seems no sufficient reason for preventing him from proving the truth. Objections of like nature in general go to the weight, not to the admissibility, of evidence. Moreover, this rule is irrespective of fraud, and is not confined to evidence. It is not merely that you cannot use the writing, but that the contract is at an end. What does this mean? The existence of a written contract depends on the fact that the offerer and offeree have interchanged their written expressions, not on the continued existence of those expressions. But in the case of a bond, the primitive notion was different. The contract was inseparable from the parchment. If a stranger destroyed it, or tore off the seal, or altered it, the obligee could not recover, however free from fault, because the defendant's contract, that is, the actual tangible bond which he had sealed, could not be produced in the form in which it bound him. About a hundred years ago Lord Kenyon undertook to use his reason on this tradition, as he sometimes did to the detriment of the law, and, not understanding it, said he could see no reason why what was true of a bond should not be true of other contracts. His decision happened to be right, as it concerned a promissory note, where again the common law regarded the contract as inseparable from the paper on which it was written, but the reasoning was general, and soon was extended to other written contracts, and various absurd and unreal grounds of policy were invented to account for the enlarged rule.

I trust that no one will understand me to be speaking with disrespect of the law, because I criticise it so freely. I venerate the law, and especially our system of law, as one of the vastest products of the human mind. No one knows better than I do the countless number of great intellects that have spent themselves in making some addition or improvement, the greatest of which is trifling when compared with the mighty whole. It has the final title to respect that it exists, that it is not a Hegelian dream, but a part of the lives of men. But one may criticise even what one reveres. Law is the business to which my life is devoted, and I should show less than devotion if I did not do what in me lies to improve it, and, when I perceive what seems to me the ideal of its future, if I hesitated to point it out and to press toward it with all my heart.

Perhaps I have said enough to show the part which the study of history necessarily plays in the intelligent study of the law as it is to-day. In the teaching of this school and at Cambridge it is in no danger of being undervalued. Mr. Bigelow here and Mr. Ames and Mr. Thayer there have made important contributions which will not be forgotten, and in England the recent history of early English law by Sir Frederick Pollock and Mr. Maitland has lent the subject an almost deceptive charm. We must beware of the pitfall of antiquarianism, and must remember that for our purposes our only interest in the past is for the light it throws upon the present. I look forward to a time when the part played by history in the explanation of dogma shall be very small, and instead of ingenious research we shall spend our energy on a study of the ends sought to be attained and the reasons for desiring them. As a step toward that ideal it seems to me that every lawyer ought to seek an understanding of economics. The present divorce between the schools of political economy and law seems to me an evidence of how much progress in philosophical study still remains to be made. In the present state of political economy, indeed, we come again upon history on a larger scale, but there we are called on to consider and weigh the ends of legislation, the means of attaining them, and the cost. We learn that for everything we have we give up something else, and we are taught to set the advantage we gain against the other advantage we lose, and to know what we are doing when we elect.

There is another study which sometimes is undervalued by the practical minded, for which I wish to say a good word, although I think a good deal of pretty poor stuff goes under that name. I mean the study of what is called jurisprudence. Jurisprudence, as I look at it, is simply law in its most generalized part. Every effort to reduce a case to a rule is an effort of jurisprudence, although the name as used in English is confined to the broadest rules and most fundamental conceptions. One mark of a great lawyer is that he sees the application of the broadest rules. There is a story of a Vermont justice of the peace before whom a suit was brought by one farmer against another for breaking a churn. The justice took time to consider, and then said that he had looked through the statutes and could find nothing about churns, and gave judgment for the defendant. The same state of mind is shown in all our common digests and textbooks. Applications of rudimentary rules of contract or tort are tucked away under the head of Railroads or Telegraphs or go to swell treatises on historical subdivisions, such as Shipping or Equity, or are gathered under an arbitrary title which is thought likely to appeal to the practical mind, such as Mercantile Law. If a man goes into law it pays to be master of it, and to be a master of it means to look straight through all the dramatic incidents and to discern the true basis for prophecy. Therefore, it is well to have an accurate notion of what you mean by law, by a right, by a duty, by malice, intent, and negligence, by ownership, by possession, and so forth. I have in my mind cases in which the highest courts seem to me to have floundered because they had no clear ideas on some of these themes. I have illustrated their importance already. If a further illustration is wished, it may be found by reading the Appendix to Sir James Stephen's *Crimi-*

nal Law on the subject of possession, and then turning to Pollock and Wright's enlightened book. Sir James Stephen is not the only writer whose attempts to analyze legal ideas have been confused by striving for a useless quintessence of all systems, instead of an accurate anatomy of one. The trouble with Austin was that he did not know enough English law. But still it is a practical advantage to master Austin, and his worthy predecessors, Hobbes and Bentham, and his worthy successors, Holland and Pollock. Sir Frederick Pollock's recent little book is touched with the felicity which marks all his works, and is wholly free from the perverting influence of Roman models.

The advice of the elders to young men is very apt to be as unreal as a list of the hundred best books. At least in my day I had my share of such counsels, and high among the unrealities I place the recommendation to study the Roman law. I assume that such advice means more than collecting a few Latin maxims with which to ornament the discourse – the purpose for which Lord Coke recommended Bracton. If that is all that is wanted, the title *De Regulis Juris Antiqui* can be read in an hour. I assume that, if it is well to study the Roman Law, it is well to study it as a working system. That means mastering a set of technicalities more difficult and less understood than our own, and studying another course of history by which even more than our own the Roman law must be explained. If any one doubts me, let him read Keller's *Der Romische Civil Process und die Actionen*, a treatise on the praetor's edict, Muirhead's most interesting *Historical Introduction to the Private Law of Rome*, and, to give him the best chance, Sohm's admirable *Institutes*. No. The way to gain a liberal view of your subject is not to read something else, but to get to the bottom of the subject itself. The means of doing that are, in the first place, to follow the existing body of dogma into its highest generalizations by the help of jurisprudence; next, to discover from history how it has come to be what it is; and, finally, so far as you can, to consider the ends which the several rules seek to accomplish, the reasons why those ends are desired, what is given up to gain them, and whether they are worth the price.

We have too little theory in the law rather than too much, especially on this final branch of study. When I was speaking of history, I mentioned larceny as an example to show how the law suffered from not having embodied in a clear form a rule which will accomplish its manifest purpose. In that case the trouble was due to the survival of forms coming from a time when a more limited purpose was entertained. Let me now give an example to show the practical importance, for the decision of actual cases, of understanding the reasons of the law, by taking an example from rules which, so far as I know, never have been explained or theorized about in any adequate way. I refer to statutes of limitation and the law of prescription. The end of such rules is obvious, but what is the justification for depriving a man of his rights, a pure evil as far as it goes, in consequence of the lapse of time? Sometimes the loss of evidence is referred to, but that is a secondary matter. Sometimes the desirability of peace, but why is peace more desirable after twenty years than before? It is increasingly likely to come without the aid of legislation. Sometimes it is said that, if a man neglects to enforce his rights, he cannot complain if, after a while, the law follows his example. Now if this is all that can be said about it, you probably will decide a case I am going to put, for the plaintiff; if you take the view which I shall suggest, you possibly will decide it for the defendant. A man is sued for trespass upon land, and justifies under a right of way. He proves that he has used the way openly and adversely for twenty years, but it turns out that the plaintiff had granted a license to a person whom he reasonably supposed to be the defendant's agent, although not so in fact, and therefore had assumed that the use of the way was permissive, in which case no right would be gained. Has the defendant gained a right or not? If his gaining it stands on the fault and neglect of the landlord in the ordinary sense, as seems commonly to be supposed, there has been no such neglect, and the right of way has not been acquired. But if I were the defendant's counsel, I should suggest that the foundation of the acquisition of rights by lapse of time is to be looked for in the position of the person who gains them, not in that of the loser. Sir Henry Maine has made it fashionable to connect the archaic notion of property with prescription. But the connection is further back than the first recorded history. It is in the nature of man's mind. A thing which you have enjoyed and used as your own for a long time, whether property or an opinion, takes root in your being and cannot be torn away without your resenting the act and trying to defend yourself, however you came by it. The law can ask no better justification than the deepest instincts of man. It is only by way of reply to the suggestion that you are disappointing the former owner, that you refer to his neglect having allowed the gradual dissociation between himself and what he claims, and the gradual association of it with another. If he knows that another is doing acts which on their face show that he is on the way toward establishing such an association, I should argue that in justice to that other he was bound at his peril to find out whether the other was acting under his permission, to see that he was warned, and if necessary, stopped.

I have been speaking about the study of the law, and I have said next to nothing of what commonly is talked about in that connection – text-books and the case system, and all the machinery with which a student comes most immediately in contact. Nor shall I say anything about them. Theory is my subject, not practical details. The modes of teaching have been improved since my time, no doubt, but ability and industry will master the raw material with any mode. Theory is the most important part of the dogma of the law, as the architect is the most important man who takes part in the building of a house. The most important improvements of the last twenty-five years are improvements in theory. It is not to be feared as unpractical, for, to the competent, it simply means going to the bottom of the subject. For the incompetent, it sometimes is true, as has been said, that an interest in general ideas means an absence of particular knowledge. I remember in army days reading of a youth who, being examined for the lowest grade and being asked a question about squadron drill, answered that he never had considered the evolutions of less than ten thousand men. But the weak and foolish must be left to their folly. The danger is that the able and practical minded should look with indifference or distrust upon ideas the connection of which with their business is remote. I heard a story, the other day, of a man who had a valet to whom he paid high wages, subject to deduction for faults. One of his deductions was, "For lack of imagination, five dollars." The lack is not confined to valets. The object of ambition, power, generally presents itself nowadays in the form of money alone. Money is the most immediate form, and is a proper object of desire. "The fortune," said Rachel, "is the measure of the intelligence." That is a good text to waken people out of a fool's paradise. But, as Hegel says, "It is in the end not the appetite, but the opinion, which has to be satisfied." To an imagination of any scope the most far-reaching form of power is not money, it is the command of ideas. If you want great examples, read Mr. Leslie Stephen's *History of English Thought in the Eighteenth Century*, and see how a hundred years after his death the abstract speculations of Descartes had become a practical force controlling the conduct of men. Read the works of the great German jurists, and see how much more the world is governed to-day by Kant than by Bonaparte. We cannot all be Descartes or Kant, but we all want happiness. And happiness, I am sure from having known many successful men, cannot be won simply by being counsel for great corporations and having an income of fifty thousand dollars. An intellect great enough to win the prize needs other food besides success. The remoter and more general aspects of the law are those which give it universal interest. It is through them that you not only become a great master in your calling, but connect your subject with the universe and catch an echo of the infinite, a glimpse of its unfathomable process, a hint of the universal law.

The following are among the commentaries: Palmer, "Holmes, Hobbes and Hitler" (1945) 31 *A.B.A.J.* 569; Henry Hart, "Holmes' Positivism – An Addendum" (1951) 64 *Harv. L. Rev.* 929; Howe, "Holmes' Positivism – A Brief Rejoinder" (1951) 64 *Harv. L. Rev.* 937; MacGuigan, "The Problem of Law and Morals in Contemporary Jurisprudence" (1962) 8 *Catholic Law.* 293. On Holmes generally see also Wu, *Beyond East and West* 87-106 (1951), *Fountain of Justice*, passim (1955), and "Justice Holmes and the Common-Law Tradition" (1961) 14 *Vand. L. Rev.* 221.

Harry W. Jones, 1911–
Cardozo Professor of Jurisprudence
Columbia University

THE RULE OF LAW AND THE WELFARE STATE (1958)

How, if at all, can the values associated with the rule of law be achieved in today's welfare state? Though ponderous definitions would be out of place, it is unavoidable that some indication be given of the sense in which our crucial terms will be used. "Welfare state" is not used here as a derogatory epithet. In any decent political philosophy, the state is not an end in itself but an instrumentality to be appraised in terms of its contribution to the welfare of the individuals who compose the national community. The minimum-function state of the nineteenth century liberal tradition was not an anti-welfare conception. Rather, the English Whigs and their European and American counterparts held the deep conviction that the common good, the general welfare, is best promoted when state intervention in economic and social matters is kept to the lowest possible incidence.

The rise of the welfare state, as it is known today, proceeds from the triumph, in most of our western countries, of a new political philosophy. Changes in conditions and in majority political attitudes have made it the prevailing opinion today that the greater economic and social good of the greater number requires an abandonment of the "hands off" approach and the adoption of public measures directly and explicitly aimed at general economic betterment. The identifying characteristics of the welfare state are chiefly these: (1) a vast increase in the range and detail of government regulation of privately owned economic enterprise; (2) the direct furnishing of services by government to individual members of the national community – unemployment and retirement benefits, family allowances, low-cost housing, medical care, and the like; and (3) increasing government ownership and operation of industries and businesses which, at an earlier time, were or would have been operated for profit by individuals or private corporations.

How far must a particular country have gone, in one or more of the three directions just stated, before it can be characterized with certainty as a welfare state? Are Norway and Sweden already within the welfare state category? What of the United Kingdom, or France, or, for that matter, the United States? Clearly there is no hard and fast line but rather a continuum of increasing governmental intervention into affairs and concerns once thought of as inappropriate for state action. The most that can be said is that every western country has taken significant steps toward the welfare state destination but that some have gone considerably farther than the others in one or more of the welfare state directions. Traditional socialist theory, with its emphasis on governmental ownership and operation of the tools of production, offers the only approach to a sharper line of distinction. A "socialist" country, in which an appreciable portion of industrial enterprise is publicly owned and operated or definitely scheduled for future public management, is perhaps analytically different from a country in which movement towards the welfare state has gone as far as rigorous regulation and extensive provision of services but not as far as substantial government ownership and operation of industries and businesses.

Some explanation is imperative, also, as to the sense in which that elusive phrase, "the rule of law," is itself to be used in this discussion. It is difficult to define the term, even as understood in the United States. The term itself is not common coin in American legal theory; we are more likely to say "supremacy of law," "government under law" or (less accurately, I think) "government of laws and not of men." The one nugget of agreement discernible in the American writings is the idea, with which I devoutly agree, that state power is the great antagonist against which the rule of law must forever be addressed. The notion of an imposed or self-accepted constraint on governmental power may not exhaust the concept of the rule of law, but there is substantial agreement in American thought that the rule of law's great purpose is protection of the individual against state power-holders. Beyond this, it is difficult to find any common understanding among American lawyers, judges, and scholars as to the meaning, the essential attributes, of the rule of law. When an American writes or speaks on our general topic he usually begins with a confident assumption that everybody knows what the rule of law is and then devotes the rest of his time to a bold and eloquent statement in favor of it.

For want of a commonly understood American version of the rule of law, I will hazard my own understanding of the term's connotation in the American legal order. The rule of law is a tradition of decision, a tradition embodying at least three indispensable elements: *first*, that every person whose interests will be affected by a judicial or administrative decision has the right to a meaningful "day in court"; *second*, that deciding officers shall be independent in the full sense, free from external direction by political and administrative superiors in the disposition of individual cases and inwardly free from the influence of personal gain and partisan or popular bias; and *third*, that day-to-day decisions shall be reasoned, rationally justified, in terms that take due account both of the demands of general principle and the demands of the particular situation. This enumeration does not purport to exhaust the meaning of the "rule of law"; doubtless there are other essential attributes to be included in the term's full intension. But any American lawyer would say, I think, that the three features just given characterize the best of our legal institutions – for example, our criminal litigation when properly conducted – and make up the adjudicative ideal of our legal tradition.

Can this tradition, this adjudicative ideal, be carried over into the welfare state? Manifestly, the welfare state sets a harder and wider task for the rule of law. As government becomes regulator, dispenser of benefits, and mass employer, it draws to itself functions and responsibilities formerly dispersed among such other power centers as private companies, trade and labor associations, and charitable institutions. And there is danger that the man in the street will come to look at the state – source of so many of his most valued expectations – with a new affection that undermines the healthy suspicion with which the sturdy citizen of a free society should regard officialdom and all its works.

Does it follow, then, that the advent of the welfare state is attended, inevitably, by the decline and ultimate disappearance of the rule of law? This is the foreboding thesis of Friedrich A. Hayek's *The Road to Serfdom*, first published in England in 1944 and since very generally read in the United States and throughout Western Europe. Countless others have written to the same purpose and in the same vein, but it seems safe to say that Dr. Hayek's book is more widely known than any other single statement of the anti-welfare state position. Accordingly, I shall speak elsewhere in this paper of the "Hayek theorem" as a shorthand way of referring to the proposition that welfare state, by its inherent nature, is incompatible with the rule of law. This usage implies no singling out of Dr. Hayek's arguments but rather the use of the Hayek conclusions as fairly representative of the views of those who are convinced that the welfare state must have deadly impact on the traditional values of a legal order. To those of this conviction, there can be no useful discussion of ways and means to preserve the vitality of the rule of law in the administration of the welfare state. . . .

In Anglo-American legal philosophy at least, "the rule of law" is forever associated with Dicey, and it is appropriate to begin this section with some mention of that vigorous but not too precise writer. Jean Cocteau suggests that Baudelaire's prose is untranslatable because it "depends on inner rhythms indigenous to the French language." Dicey on the rule of law is similarly untranslatable, not because his words are English but because the very thought being communicated is inextricably bound up with English institutions. Consider these key passages from *The Law of the Constitution*:

> When we say that the . . . rule of law is a characteristic of the English constitution, we generally include under one expression at least three distinct though kindred conceptions.
>
> We mean, in the first place, that no man is punishable or can be lawfully made to suffer in body or goods except for a distinct breach of law established in the ordinary legal manner before the ordinary courts of the land. . . .
>
> We mean in the second place . . . not only that with us no man is above the law, but (what is a different thing) that here every man, whatever be his rank or condition, is subject to the ordinary law of the realm and amenable to the jurisdiction of the ordinary tribunals.
>
> There remains yet a third and different sense. . . . We may say that the constitution is pervaded by the rule of law on the ground that the general principles of the constitution (as for example the right to personal liberty, or the right of public meeting) are with us the result of judicial decisions determining the rights of private persons in particular cases brought before the courts; whereas under many foreign constitutions the security (such as it is) given to the rights of individuals results, or appears to result, from the general principles of the constitution.

There are, I believe, ideas of universal validity reflected in Dicey's "three meanings" of the rule of law. Aware as I am of the peril of taking Dicey out of his English constitutional context, I suggest these as Dicey's great ideas: (1) in a decent society it is unthinkable that government, or any officer of government, possesses arbitrary power over the person or the interests of the individual; (2) all members of society, private persons and government officials alike, must be equally responsible before the law; and (3) effective judicial remedies are more important than abstract constitutional declarations in securing the rights of the individual against encroachment by the state. These points all seem to me as valid in the welfare state as they were in nineteenth century England.

Whatever else may be read into the thought of Dicey, this sturdy foe of arbitrary power and faithful champion of the "ordinary courts" and the "ordinary law" did *not* say that the enactment of legislation designed to minimize existing economic inequalities violates the rule of law, and he did *not* say that the rule of law requires the determination of all particular controversies by essentially deductive reasoning from fixed principles. Dicey could not possibly have taken this second position, since that would have been to adopt a standard by which the common law of England itself would have to be found wanting. Any theory that tends to equate the rule of law with the formal generality of law must find other origin – as in the German constitutional theory that every law in the substantive sense must be, or have its basis in, an act of the legislature.

We pass now from Dicey to Hayek, from *The Law of the Constitution* to *The Road to Serfdom.* There are two main counts in Hayek's indictment of the welfare state as the deadly enemy of the rule of law. His first charge is that the national economic planning characteristic of the welfare state involves a deliberate discrimination by government between particular needs of different people and that this violates the rule of law principle of formal equality before the law. Consider this striking passage, which seems to condemn St. Thomas Aquinas equally with Harold Laski: "any policy aiming directly at a substantive ideal of distributive justice must lead to the destruction of the Rule of Law."

It is, of course, possible to reply to this argument on more or less formal, definitional grounds. One typical line of answer to Hayek is Kelsenian in terms: the rule of law has no reference to the relation between government and governed and is concerned only with the conformity of the law-applying function to the law-creating function. A second standard reply is that the rule of law has nothing whatever to do with substantive limitations on parliamentary action. Still another reply, which might certainly have been expected, is that Hayek is trying to add an ingredient of immutable *content* to a formal juristic concept and so, as the weary cliche would put it, "falling into the pit of natural law thinking."

Replies like these seem to me rather less than satisfactory, since their cumulative effect is a very drastic narrowing of the rule of law concept itself. Although I, too, think of the concept as a primarily procedural one, I am by no means sure that a meaningful rule of law has nothing whatever to say concerning the substantive content of legally enforced principles. A good case can be made that the concepts of the rule of law and of natural rights are at least fraternal twins; I would not foreclose the possibility that they may be identical twins. Be this as it may, I would prefer to reply to Hayek on more substantial grounds: that the mature law of any country is not and never has been as heedless of distributive justice – as blind to "the particular needs of different people" – as Hayek would have it. Countless examples spring to mind: the law of infants, bankruptcy legislation, homestead exemptions, water rights, individualization of punishment in criminal law, the common law's characteristic process of distinguishing cases on their facts. The perfection of formal equality is an abstraction that practical justice blows away, as it always has and must. The attainable ideal is that all laws should apply equally to all human beings unless, as Julius Stone puts it, "there is good reason to the contrary."

Interwoven with Hayek's attack on the egalitarian objectives of central economic planning is a second count of indictment, this one addressed to the crucial role of administrative discretion in the operations of the welfare state. The argument is a familiar one in the literature of administrative law: government regulatory and welfare programs can be carried into effect only by the delegation of discretionary power to "divers boards and authorities"; and the possession and exercise of such discretionary power contravenes the rule of law. Hayek's objections to discretionary power are in part theoretical and in part practical. Broad administrative discretion threatens the Kantian ideal that "man is free if he needs to obey no person but solely the laws" – an argument strikingly reminiscent of the contention often heard in the United States that discretionary administrative powers undermine a fundamental concept of "government of laws and not of men." In addition, and less philosophically, Hayek develops the charge that the possession of discretionary power destroys the predictability of decision which he sees as a major value of the rule of law. "The important question," says Hayek, "is whether the individual can foresee the action of the state and make use of this knowledge as a datum in forming his own plans. . . ." The paradox suggested is that discretion, without which government economic planning is unworkable, prevents reliable planning by the individual.

Without commenting at length on this aspect of Hayek's analysis, I will content myself with three points, each of them necessary, I think, to a full understanding of the Hayek theorem. (1) in Hayek's analysis, as in almost all of the writings condemnatory of administrative processes, discretion is equated with arbitrariness; there is no concession that discretionary power may be exercised in other than an arbitary way. (2) Hayek's counsel is one of despair and gives little attention to instruments of control that might be devised to prevent, or at least to minimize, the arbitrary exercise of discretionary power. (3) Hayek's entire chapter, and particularly his point that discretion destroys predictability, proceeds from the premise that discretion, leeway, and choice are far less significant in judicial administration of the "ordinary law" than twentieth century legal realism has shown them to be.

One can hardly quarrel too much with Hayek's opening principle, "that the discretion left to the executive organs wielding coercive power should be reduced as much as possible." That is rather like saying that force is bad per se and that Chicago and Naples should therefore not employ more policemen than they need. But how far is it possible to reduce the discretionary element without destroying a statute's effectiveness as an instrument of public policy? Experience is clear that it is not possible to draft effective legislation in many regulatory and welfare areas without leaving leeway for the exercise of administrative judgment in rule-making and adjudication. Is discretion such deadly poison to the rule of law that it is better to abandon deeply desired legislative objectives than to run the risk of possible arbitrary use of discretionary power?

There is reason and need in the welfare state to devise and perfect safeguards against the always present danger of abuse of administrative authority. Meaningful statutory standards, realistic procedural requirements, and discriminating techniques of judicial review are among the tools of control well along in course of development. Nor is it to be assumed that administrative officers are themselves alien to the tradition of honest judgment and fair decision embodied in the rule of law. It is not to be forgotten, as we admire the achievement of the French Conseil d'Etat, that its superb jurisdictional functioning is not wholly external, as in the case of American, English, or German judicial review. A strength of the Conseil d'Etat in the context of French political institutions is that the Conseil itself is *in* the administrative establishment even though it is not entirely *of* it.

Perhaps enough time has been given the mournful inquiry: Can the rule of law survive the rise in administrative power characteristic of the welfare state? The more rewarding question is the constructive one: Are there means by which the rule of law can be made to prevail throughout the entire range of welfare state administrative functioning?

The national state's minimum functions are the preservation of domestic order and the defense of national interests and integrity. If the state did no more, there would be relatively infrequent occasions for direct confrontation between the state's officials and its private citizens. Only a few in any national society have their plans actively interfered with by policemen, and fewer still come into direct touch with diplomatic officials or, in peace time, with officials of the military establishment.

In the welfare state, public power becomes an instrumentality for the achievement of purposes beyond the minimum objectives of domestic order and national defense. It is not enough that the national community be secure against internal disorder and external aggression; a society can be thus secure and well ordered and yet lack the attribute of distributive justice. But as social justice becomes a conscious end of state policy there is a vast and inevitable increase in the frequency with which ordinary citizens come into a relationship of direct encounter with state power-holders. The citizen's significant encounter now is not with the policeman or the criminal magistrate but with the official representing a regulatory authority, an administration of social insurances, or a state-operated economic enterprise. It is this dramatically increased incidence of encounter that sets the task of the rule of law in the welfare state.

At the first stage of the welfare state, old rights are subjected to new forms of limitation. Property and contract are the most obvious cases in point. It is not that the right of property or the right to contract were ever absolute; the maxim *sic utere* and the rule that courts will not enforce contracts against public policy are sufficient reminders that every legal system has put outside limits on the autonomy of property owners and contracting parties. But these outer bounds keep moving in as the area of individual decision in proprietary and contractual matters is narrowed in the welfare state. The state's commands must constantly be consulted when the individual is determining the use or disposition of his property, and many matters once left to private bargaining are now foreclosed by public statute or regulation. The doctrines and procedures of what Dicey called the "ordinary law" may give little specific help in working out the ultimate pattern by which old rights are to be adjusted to the social interests given preferred place in the welfare state. If the rule of law is to be fully meaningful in the contemporary setting of detailed regulation, there must be new acts of legal construction as momentous as those undertaken and performed by the great civil law codifiers and common law judges.

In any society, individuals will differ in natural gifts and economic position. Increased regulation of the stronger or more fortunate does not necessarily bring about a reduction in a society's net balance of individual self-assertion. In the welfare state – if and so long as it can be kept true to its avowed purposes – regulation is not an end in itself but a means of securing a greater measure of economic equality. A statute barring the forfeiture of premiums paid on a lapsed life-insurance policy diminishes freedom of contract only in the doctrinaire sense that insurers no longer can impose forfeiture clauses on a "take it or leave it" basis. Because of the inequality of bargaining power, such clauses were never the subject of genuine negotiation between insurer and insurance applicant. Similarly, it would be wildly unrealistic to see in a minimum wage law only an interference with the individual employee's right to contract for less than subsistence wages. What has happened in these and like instances is that areas of decision formerly subject to the rule of superior economic power have been brought, wisely or unwisely, within the reach of the rule of law. But whether looked at from the perspective of the persons regulated or from the perspective of those benefited by the regulation, there has been an increase in what I have called the incidence of encounter between the individual and the state power-holder and, with that increase, an expansion in the task of the rule of law.

Even more important than the regulatory aspect of the welfare state is its office as the source of new rights – for example, the expectations created by a comprehensive system of social insurance. I see no reason why the word "rights," with its unique emotive power, should be deemed inappropriate for these new expectations and preempted for use only in connection with such traditional interests as those in tangible property. For example, studies tell us that the typical middle income American reaches retirement age with a whole bundle of interests and expectations: as homeowner, as small investor, and as social security "beneficiary." Of these, his social security retirement benefits are probably his most important resource. Should this, the most significant of his rights, be entitled to a quality of protection inferior to that afforded his other interests? It becomes the task of the rule of law to surround this new "right" to retirement benefits with protections against arbitrary government action, with substantive and procedural safeguards that are as effective in context as the safeguards enjoyed by traditional rights of property in the best tradition of the older law.

To suggest, as I have, that the reasonable expectations of a social service beneficiary are as meaningful for the rule of law as the interests of an owner of investment securities or real property is in no way to urge a lowering of the standard of protection now extended by law to the more traditional interests. The goal, substantial parity of treatment, can be pursued by levelling up as well as by levelling down. The new expectations progressively brought into existence by the welfare state must be thought of not as privileges to be dispensed unequally or by arbitrary fiat of government officials but as substantial rights in the assertion of which the claimant is entitled to an effective remedy, a fair procedure, and a reasoned decision. Anything short of this leaves one man subject in his essential interests to the arbitrary will of another man who happens to partake of public power; and that kind of unequal and demeaning encounter is repugnant to every sense of the rule of law.

These comments, though impressionistic rather than exhaustive, should have given at least some idea of magnitude of the task ahead for the rule of law. For centuries our several western legal orders have pursued the ideal that individual rights be kept secure from infringement by other persons and, above all, from the arbitrary exercise of government power. Our concepts and procedures, in their best manifestations, furnish a surer protection than ever before to the essential rights that are first in any hierarchy of individual and social interests: freedom of religion, speech, suffrage, and press, and the related freedom from arbitrary detention. Beyond this, our legal orders have achieved a reasonably effective procedure for the vindication of such other traditional interests as property rights, contract rights, and rights to compensation for injury caused by another's fault. Now the welfare state brings its staggering volume of additional grist to the mills of justice: new rights in vast number and infinitely more widely dispersed among the citizenship than the old rights ever were. In the scale of legal valuation, these new and more widely asserted rights are outweighed only by the essential civil liberties; they are certainly as dear to their possessors as contract and property rights are to those who possess them.

Mass-produced goods rarely have the quality of goods made in far smaller quantity by traditional hand craftsmanship; an analogous problem challenges the welfare state. In an era when rights are mass produced, can the quality of their protection against arbitrary official action be as high as the quality of the protection afforded in the past to traditional legal rights less numerous and less widely dispersed among the members of society? Dicey accurately perceived it as a great strength of the rule of law in England that most questions of individual right came for decision to a small and homogeneous group of dedicated men, the judges of the "ordinary law." A thousand times as many deciding officers are needed to settle the issues presented by claimants of the new and more widely held rights of the welfare state. Is it beyond hope that this vast new company of officials can, in time, develop a tradition of decision worthy of being called, in Pound's fine phrase, an "ethos of adjudication"?

In the welfare state, the private citizen is forever encountering public officials of many kinds: regulators, dispensers of social services, managers of state-operated enterprises. It is the task of the rule of law to see to it that these multiplied and diverse encounters are as fair, as just, and as free from arbitrariness as are the familiar encounters of the right-asserting private citizen with the judicial officers of the traditional law.

There is a brilliant analysis of the same theme in the last chapter of Friedmann, *Law and Social Change in Contemporary Britain* 277-310 (1951). Professor Friedmann concludes that the planned state can be reconciled with the rule of law through the reduction of the sovereign privileges of the state to the absolute minimum, through the proper control of administrative discretion, through the subjection both of the Crown and its emanations to the common law in all commercial relations, and through more careful parliamentary control over planning activities.

CHAPTER TWO

Positivism

The history of Jurisprudence shows that there are two elements which have always been associated with the concept of law by philosophers. These are the reason element and the will or fiat element – the element of order discovered and that of order imposed, the given and the construed. Both elements have ancient supporting traditions in legal philosophy. We find Plato putting in the mouth of Thrasymachus in the *Republic* the words that "justice is the interest of the stronger." And the *Digest* of Justinian says "Whatever pleases the sovereign has the force of law." These are pure statements of the "will" position in law, that law is the will of the ruler.

Perhaps, therefore, the most fundamental problem of jurisprudence is embodied in the age-old (though etymologically incorrect) argument about the nature of law, whether *ius quia iustum* or *ius quia iussum*, whether law is essentially constituted by being just or by being commanded, whether it is essentially of reason or essentially of will. The mediæval tradition in English jurisprudence, which was based upon the Christian view of man as a rational being subject to eternal, natural, divine, and human law and upon the Christian view of human law as the complement and supplement of natural law, firmly adhered to a reason-theory of law. The viewpoint of this tradition is summed up in the famous words of Henry of Bracton, *rex non debet esse sub homine sed sub Deo et sub lege*, the king is under no man but is under God and the law: in other words, the king, though he has no earthly master, is subject both to the divine law of God and to the natural law of reason. This mediæval belief in the dependance of human law on higher law began to go out of favour in the sixteenth century and a new conception of law began to take hold. For a time the old and the new existed side by side, in uneasy combination; in Blackstone, for instance, we find, to adapt a phrase of Dr. Johnson's, these two most heterogeneous traditions yoked by violence together. But by the middle of the nineteenth century the struggle was clearly over, and the new tradition of legal positivism reigned supreme in English jurisprudence.

Positivism is essentially committed to a will-theory of law. In the words of Thomas Hobbes, its legitimate father, law "is not Counsell, but Command," and "Command is, where a man saith, *Doe this*, or *Doe not this*, without expecting other reason than the Will of him that sayes it." The essence of legal positivism is thus the belief that whatever the legislator posits as law, no more and no less, is law; one cannot go behind the command of the legislator to question its reasonableness, for the legislator's expressed will is, of itself, law. As Mortimer Adler has put it, "the real meaning of positivism involves . . . the notion of the arbitrary, an institution of the will as opposed to something natural, discovered by the intellect." [(1949) 1 Univ. N.D. Nat. Law Inst. Pregs. 65, 67].

In such a tradition legal obligation must be that necessity imposed upon one will by another will, a necessity of violence or coercion. Law is something not of reason but of will, and the consequence of this for almost all of the positivists is that it is therefore something wholly independent of morals. This is, for instance, a primary tenet of both Bentham and Austin. For them, law cannot ever create morals, nor morals ever judge law. Law and morals are not merely distinct, as in the mediæval tradition; rather they are wholly separate.

Though the separation of law and morals is in general a basic thesis of the legal positivists, it was not held at all by Hobbes, who adopted a much more extreme view of the relationship of law and morals, viz, the complete identification of the two. This view was not appealing to later positivists because it is necessarily tied up with state absolutism, but it is important because of the influence, both positive and negative, which it exerted on later positivism.

A theory usually associated with positivism is formalism, the view that judges are not entitled to legislate or to take into account extra-legal factors in reaching decisions. Austin and Hart both repudiate formalism, but it can be argued that they are inconsistent in so doing. Indeed, Professor Shklar would maintain that formalism is the very essence of positivism, for analytical theory "is more than anything an effort to enhance the formalism that is already a built-in feature of legal discourse" [*Legalism* 13 (1964)], and Professor Patterson notes "Kelsen's effort to squeeze the last drop of history, sociology and axiology out of the law and make it a 'pure' power system" [*Jurisprudence* 262 (1953)]. Dr. Shklar goes on to give one of the most vivid descriptions of formalism (33-4).

> "The idea of treating law as a self-contained system of norms that is 'there,' identifiable without any reference to the content, aim, and development of the rules that compose it, is the very essence of formalism, for formalism does not just involve treating law mechanically as a matter of logical deductions from given premises. It consists rather of treating law as an isolated block of concepts that have no relevant characteristics or functions apart from their possible validity or invalidity within a hypothetical system. But what aim is served by this 'homeless ghost'? Why do both the wide formalism that seeks a single universal pattern for all law and the narrow formalism that limits itself to analyzing the language used by lawyers in a municipal legal system insist on validation as the sole task worthy of legal theory? Is it really a self-evident procedure? To be sure, the question of what is valid *is* the one the practicing lawyer must ask in the course of his activities. There is, however, no reason to assume that it is the only intellectually worthwhile question to be asked about law. There is no particular reason why it is to be the only true form of legal thinking, or why formal definitions alone should prevail. On the contrary, the notion of the legal as something that begins at the outer door of the place of legislative activity and ends with a judicial decision is a highly artificial one. It is something that the legalistic ethos always demands, but it is not even partially realized under many historical circumstances. It corresponds to only one historical condition and to only one ideology. Yet these are the self-imposed boundaries of formalism. This narrowness is in itself unassailable as long as it does not pretend to exclusiveness or to the title of the one true method in legal theory.
>
> "This deliberate isolation of the legal system – the treatment of law as a neutral social entity – it itself a refined political ideology, the expression of a preference. As a description of law it does some considerable violence to political actualities."

Professor Samuel Shuman, *Legal Positivism: Its Scope and Limitations* (1963) argues that positivism has no necessary connection with analysis but that it is committed to some form of noncognitivism in ethics.

A. CASES

JACOBS v. LONDON COUNTY COUNCIL
House of Lords. [1950] 1 All E. R. 737

LORD SIMONDS: My Lords, on June 9, 1947, the appellant, Mrs. Jacobs, who lives at No. 255, Bennett's Castle Lane, Dagenham, in the county of Essex, left her house to visit a shop, No. 240, Bennett's Castle Lane, which is let by the respondents, the London County Council, to Smith Gard & Co., Ltd., pharmaceutical chemists. Bennett's Castle Lane is a highway vested in Ilford Borough Council and is within a large area laid out by the respondents as a housing estate known as the Becontree Estate. On that part of the estate which abuts on Bennett's Castle Lane the respondents built a number of shops (including No. 240) with flats above them. The frontages of these shops were set back from the pavement a distance of about ten feet six inches and the intervening space, which constituted a series of forecourts, was levelled and paved with paving-stones similar to those of the pavement of the highway. These forecourts were not fenced, but the paving-stones were so laid that there was a continuous line indicating which was forecourt and which was pavement. To the casual passer-by, however, the pavement of the highway and the forecourts were indistinguishable. Though there was at one time a dispute whether the forecourts were let with the adjoining shops, it is now clear that, at least so far as No. 240 is concerned, the forecourt was not included in the demise to Smith Gard & Co., Ltd., but was at all material times in both the ownership and the occupation of the respondents. In the forecourt in front of No. 240 at a distance of about two feet from the line marking the boundary between the pavement and the forecourt, there was a stop-cock which controlled the water supply to the flats above the shop. The paving-stones surrounding this stop-cock had sunk so that it projected to the extent of an inch and a quarter above them. The appellant, having on June 9, 1947, walked along the pavement until she was nearly opposite the shop, turned to her left and walked towards it. Perforce she crossed the forecourt and in doing so she caught her toe against the projecting stop-cock. She fell and sustained a somewhat serious injury in the fracture of her right patella.

In consequence she commenced action against the respondents in the Ilford County Court claiming damages. Her action was, in the first place, framed in negligence. She alleged that the respondents, as occupiers of the forecourt, had committed a breach of their duty to her as an invitee thereon. Alternatively, she laid her claim in nuisance, alleging that the condition of the stop-cock and surrounding paving-stones constituted a nuisance adjoining the highway whereby she had suffered injury. In the course of the proceedings the appellant's husband was joined as plaintiff, but nothing turns on this, or on the fact that, as I have already indicated, it was at one time in issue whether the respondents or Smith Gard & Co., Ltd., were occupiers of the forecourt. The learned county court judge found that the appellant had not herself been guilty of any negligence in not observing the condition of the paving-stones and stop-cock and that she was using reasonable care for her own safety. He further held that she was an invitee on the forecourt. Unfortunately, in an otherwise very clear judgment the learned judge did not state on what facts or for what reason he came to this conclusion. In regard to the respondents, he found that they did not take reasonable care to guard against such danger, or even to acquire knowledge of such danger arising, and that they ought to have known of it and failed to do so owing to their lack of reasonable care in the matter of inspection. On the alternative plea of nuisance also the learned judge found in favour of the appellant. In his opinion, the appellant, being lawfully on the land of the respondents and being injured by reason of a nuisance of their land, was entitled to succeed on this ground also. He thereupon awarded her general and special damages. The respondents appealed to the Court of Appeal (TUCKER ASQUITH and SINGLETON, L.J.J.), who unanimously reversed the judgment of the learned county court judge on both points.

On the first ground of claim, that of negligence, the question turns wholly on the category into which the appellant is to be placed. If she was an invitee on the forecourt of No. 240, then her claim is conceded by the respondents to be valid. If she was only a licensee, then she concedes that it is not. Invitee or licensee? That, then, is the question. For the respondents it is contended that the question is concluded in favour of licensee by the decision of this House in *Fairman* v. *Perpetual Investment Building Society*. For the appellant it is contended that the relevant observations of the noble and learned Lords who heard that case were *obiter dicta* and that it is not an authority binding on this House to the effect that a person in the position of the appellant, Mrs. Fairman, is in the category of licensee and not invitee, and, further, that in any event the circumstances of Mrs. Jacobs were different from those of Mrs. Fairman and Mrs. Jacobs, at any rate, was an invitee. My Lords, the appellant was, I think, encouraged to adopt the first branch of her contention by the observations of SCOTT, L.J., in *Haseldine* v. *Daw & Son, Ltd.* That learned lord justice (differing on this point from GODDARD, L.J.) expressed the opinion ([1941] 3 All E.R. 166) that the observations of the learned lords in *Fairman's* case on this question were all *obiter dicta* and he felt at liberty to state a different view of the law. So far as I have been able to discover, the opinion of SCOTT, L.J., has not received any support either in judicial decision or text-book of authority, and for a quarter of a century *Fairman's* case has been regarded as a definitive statement of the law. However, in the present case the learned lords justices who heard the appeal thought that the matter admitted of sufficient doubt to justify the admission of an appeal to this House. Hence it falls to your Lordships to determine what *Fairman's* case decided and for what proposition of law it is an authority, binding alike on this House and on every court of law in this country.

My Lords, I can entertain no doubt that *Fairman's* case decided that Mrs. Fairman was a licensee on the premises where she suffered damage and that that decision was the *ratio decidendi*, or a *ratio decidendi* (it matters not which), of the case. It is not, I think, always easy to determine how far, when several issues are raised in a case and a determination of any one of them is decisive in favour of one or other of the parties, the observations on other issues are to be regarded as *obiter*. That is the inevitable result of our system. For while it is the primary duty of a court of justice to dispense justice to litigants, it is its traditional role to do so by means of an exposition of the relevant law. Clearly, such a system must be somewhat flexible, with the result that in some cases judges may be criticised for diverging into expositions which could by no means be regarded as relevant to the dispute between the parties, and, in other cases, other critics may regret that an opportunity has been missed for making an oracular pronouncement on some legal problem which has long vexed the profession. However this may be, there is, in my opinion, no justification for regarding as *obiter dictum* a reason given by a judge for his decision, because he has given another reason also. If it were a proper test to ask whether the decision would have been the same apart from the proposition alleged to be *obiter*, then a case which *ex facie* decided two things would decide nothing. A good illustration will be found in *London Jewellers, Ltd.* v. *Attenborough*. In that case the determination of one of the issues depended on how far the Court of Appeal was bound by its previous decision in *Folkes* v. *King*, in which the court had given two grounds for its decision, the second of which as stated by GREER, L.J. ([1934] 2 K.B. 222), in *Attenborough's* case was that:

". . . where a man obtains possession with authority to sell, or to become the owner himself, and then sells, he cannot be treated as having obtained the goods by larceny by a trick."

In *Attenborough's* case it was contended that, since there was another reason given for the decision in *Folkes'* case, the second reason was *obiter*, but GREER, L.J, said ([1934] 2 K.B. 222) in reference to the argument of counsel:

"I cannot help feeling that if we were unhampered by authority there is much to be said for the proposition which commended itself to SWIFT, J., and which commended itself to me in *Folkes* v. *King*, but that view is not open to us in view of the decision of the Court of Appeal in *Folkes* v. *King*. In that case two reasons were given by all the members of the Court of Appeal for their decision and we are not entitled to pick out the first reason as the *ratio decidendi* and neglect the second, or to pick out the second reason as the *ratio decidendi* and neglect the first; we must take both as forming the ground of the judgment."

So, also, in *Cheater* v. *Cater* PICKFORD, L.J., after citing a passage from the judgment of MELLISH, L.J., in *Erskine* v. *Adeane*, said ([1918] 1 K.B. 252):

"That is a distinct statement of the law and not a *dictum*. It is the second ground given by the lord justice for his judgment. If a judge states two grounds for his judgment and bases his decision upon both, neither of those grounds is a *dictum*."

The principle, which can be thus simply stated, is not always easy of application, particularly where the judgments of an appellate court consisting of more than one judge have to be considered. An illuminating discussion of the difficulties that may then arise will be found in an article, "*Ratio Decidendi* and *Obiter Dictum* in Appellate Courts," by PROFESSOR PATON and G. SAWER in THE LAW QUARTERLY REVIEW, vol. 63, p. 461. It does not, however, appear to me that *Fairman's* case should cause any difficulty. In that case the defendants owned a block of flats which they let to various tenants, the defendants keeping possession and control of the common staircase giving access to the flats. The stairs were made of cement reinforced by iron bars embedded in the cement and running along the whole length of the tread. Owing to the wearing away of the cement, in some cases irregular depressions were scooped out behind the iron bars. The plaintiff, who lodged with her sister in a flat on the fourth floor, of which the sister's husband was tenant, while descending the stairs, caught her heel in a depression so formed, and fell and was injured. The trial judge found that the defendants were not guilty of negligence; that the state of the staircase was not dangerous at the time of the accident; and that the depression which caused the plaintiff to fall was not in the nature of a concealed danger or trap, but was obvious and could have been seen by the plaintiff if she had looked. He accordingly gave judgment for the defendants and his judgment was affirmed by the Court of Appeal. When the case came on appeal to this House, it was clear that it was important for the appellant to establish as high a degree of responsibility in the respondents as possible, and it was clear too that, if she was an invitee, that degree was higher than if she was a licensee. Accordingly, her counsel, after referring to *Miller* v. *Hancock* and stating the difference to which I have referred, urged that the appellant was "indirectly the invitee of the respondents." And so also counsel for the respondents opened his argument by saying: "*Qua* the respondents the appellant was not an invitee." Thus, while, no doubt, much argument ranged round other questions – what was the true inference to be drawn from the evidence, what was the measure of liability if the plaintiff was in fact an invitee, what was really decided in the much debated case of *Miller* v. *Hancock*, and so on – yet it was an issue clearly raised: What was the status of the appellant, invitee or licensee? And that issue was thus decided. LORD BUCKMASTER, finding himself unable to agree with the trial judge, held that the state of the staircase was a dangerous trap so that the appellant was entitled to succeed, whatever her status. It is possible that he would have decided in favour of invitee. That appears to be the purport of his final observation ([1923] A.C. 84). LORD ATKINSON decided (*ibid.*, 85) that she was *quoad* the landlord, when using the stairs, "at most merely his licensee." LORD SUMNER, after stating the relevant facts, said (*ibid.*, 92): "I think that the plaintiff was the defendants' licensee not their invitee," and went on to explain why. LORD WRENBURY, at an early stage of his opinion, said (*ibid.*, 95):

"It is well to define at the outset what, in my judgment, is the relation between the plaintiff and the landlord in respect of which she can sue."

He proceeded to define it thus (*ibid.*):

"She was, I think, the invitee of the tenant, and, in consequence, the licensee of the landlord."

Finally, LORD CARSON agreed in the conclusion reached by LORD BUCKMASTER. I do not find in his speech any reference to the immediate question. Thus, three of the five noble and learned Lords who heard the appeal decided that Mrs. Fairman was a licensee, not an invitee. To treat their deliberate conclusions as *obiter* would not be consonant with the principle which is, in my view, essential to our system of case law and precedent.

This House, then, is bound by *Fairman's* case. The question remains whether the facts of the case now under appeal distinguish it in principle. I have already set out the facts on which in *Fairman's* case the plaintiff was held to be a licensee. It would, in my opinion, be an unjustifiable refinement of the law for this House, which declared Mrs. Fairman to be a licensee, to declare Mrs. Jacobs to be other than a licensee. I can find no essential distinction between the two sets of facts. If there is one, it is, I think, to the disadvantage of Mrs. Jacobs, inasmuch as the forecourt on which she walked and fell was apparently, though not dedicated as a highway, open to the public at large, whether or not they were intending to enter the shop or even to gaze into its windows. I do not think that she had a higher right than any other member of the public, of whom it would be impossible to predicate that he had any common interest with the respondents in the forecourt. My Lords, I have deliberately used the expression "common interest," because in *Mersey Docks and Harbour Board* v. *Procter* (a case heard in this House just three months after judgment had been delivered in *Fairman's* case, LORD SUMNER said ([1923] A.C. 272):

"The leading distinction between an invitee and a licensee is that, in the case of the former, invitor and invitee have a common interest, while, in the latter, licensor and licensee have none."

It is possible that this House may on some future occasion have to examine further what for the purpose of this distinction constitutes a common interest, but it is clear that LORD SUMNER did not think that there was a common interest between Mrs. Fairman and the landlords of the block of flats in which she was the lodger of their tenant. A *fortiori*, as I think, there is no common interest here. Finally, my Lords, on this branch of the case I would say that I do not intend either to cast any doubt on, or to affirm, the authority of cases which have long been cited as examples of such a common interest, *e.g.*, the so-called dock cases and railway cases where the defendants were carrying on the business of a dock or railway undertaking and the plaintiffs, being lawfully on their premises, suffered injury thereon. It is not necessary to do so, and such a task should only be assumed where the facts of the case demand it, and then only after a more exhaustive examination of the authorities than the present appeal requires.

Since writing this part of my opinion, my attention has been called to a case recently tried in Eire. I refer to *Boylen* v. *Dublin Corpn.* in which the Irish Supreme Court distinguished *Fairman's* case. On that I make no comment, but I observe that BLACK J., in a reasoned judgment ([1949] I.R. 77), supported the view expressed by SCOTT, L.J., in *Haseldine's* case that the opinions given by the House in *Fairman's* case on the question of licensee or invitee were *obiter*.

The learned judge's observations led me to re-consider what I had written, but I am unable to come to a different conclusion. As I have already said, I recognise that the dividing line is difficult to draw, but it would, I think, be to deny the importance, I would say the paramount importance, of certainty in the law to give less than coercive effect to the unequivocal statement of the law made after argument by three members of this House in Fairman's case. Nor, perhaps I may add, are your Lordships entitled to disregard such a statement because you would have the law otherwise. To determine what the law is, not what it ought to be, is our present task.

It remains to examine the appellant's alternative claim, *viz.*, that the respondents were liable to her because the condition of the paving-stones round the stopcock constituted a nuisance adjoining the highway. . . . [The appeal was dismissed on this ground also].

LORDS NORMAND, MORTON of HENRYTON, MACDERMOTT, and RADCLIFFE concurred.

The *Jacobs* case has been subjected to strong criticism by Goodhart, "The 'I Think' Doctrine of Precedent: Invitors and Licensors" (1950) 66 L. Q. R. 374 and by Lord Wright (then retired), "The Law of 'Invitation' " (1950) 66 L. Q. R. 454.

Goodhart comments: "The *Jacobs Case* is of jurisprudential interest, not only because of the emphasis it places on the paramount importance of certainty in the law, but also because of the discussion it contains concerning the *ratio decidendi* of a case." Examining *Fairman's Case* he maintains that all three judges in the majority expressed a tentative 'I think' opinion on a point in the law of invitations which was not material in that case. He continues: "In the *Jacobs Case* their Lordships have held that these three 'I think' add up to an unequivocal declaration of the law which must be regarded as absolutely binding in all future cases. It is, of course, true that any judicial opinion concerning the law, even if expressed in tentative terms, is entitled to the greatest respect, but this seems to be the first instance in which such tentative opinions have been regarded as authoritative."

Lord Wright comments on the *Jacobs Case* in the course of a note on *Horton* v. *London Graving Dock:* "A very stringent and all pervading rule of precedents has been expressed by the House of Lords in *Jacobs' Case*, though sometimes in earlier judgments a different or at least more qualified rule had been stated. But an absolute assertion of the paramount importance of certainty in the law might well destroy the flexibility and sensitiveness to realism and facts and social values, which have been the pride of the common law. Great judges have said that the function of the common law was the perpetual quest for justice. I should be sorry if quest for certitude were substituted for quest for justice."

SCRUTTONS LTD. v. MIDLAND SILICONES

House of Lords. [1962] 1 All E.R. 1.

VISCOUNT SIMONDS: My Lords, the facts in this case are not in dispute. They are fully and accurately stated in the judgment of the learned trial judge, Diplock J., and I do not think it necessary to restate them. I come at once to the question of law which arises upon them.

The question is whether the appellants, a well-known firm of stevedores, who admittedly by their negligence caused damage to certain cargo consigned to the respondents under a bill of lading of March 26, 1957, can take advantage of a provision for limitation of liability contained in that document. In judgments, with which I entirely agree and to which, but for the importance of the case, I should think it necessary to add nothing, the learned judge and the Court of Appeal have unanimously answered the question in the negative.

The appellants' claim to immunity (for so I will call it for short) was put in a number of different ways, but I think that I do no injustice to the able argument of their counsel if I say that he rested in the main on the well-known case of *Elder, Dempster & Co. Ltd.* v. *Paterson, Zochonis & Co. Ltd.*, contending that that is an authority binding this House to decide in his favour.

Let me, then, get rid shortly of some of the other arguments advanced on behalf of the appellants.

In the first place, I see no reason for saying that the word "carrier" either in the bill of lading or in the United States Carriage of Goods by Sea Act, 1936 (which the bill of lading incorporated) means or includes a stevedore. This is a proposition which does not admit of any expansion. A stevedore is not a carrier according to the ordinary use of language and, so far from the context supplying an extended meaning to the latter word, the contrary is indicated, as Hodson L.J. points out, by clause 17 of the bill of lading which authorises the carrier or master to appoint stevedores.

Then to avert the consequences which would appear to follow from the fact that the stevedores were not a party to the contract conferring immunity on the carriers, it was argued that the carriers contracted as agents for the stevedores. They did not expressly do so: if then there was agency, it was a case of an agent acting for an undisclosed principal. I am met at once by the difficulty that there is no ground whatever for saying that the carriers were contracting as agent either for this firm of stevedores or any other stevedores they might employ. The relation of the stevedores in this case to the carriers was that of independent contractors. Why should it be assumed that the carriers entered into a contract of affreightment or into any part of it as agents for them?

Next it was urged that there was an implied contract between the cargo owners, the respondents, and the stevedores that the latter should have the benefit of the immunity clause in the bill of lading. This argument presents, if possible, greater difficulties. When A and B have entered into a contract, it is not uncommon to imply a term in order to give what is called "business efficacy" to it – a process, I may say, against the abuse of which the courts must keep constand guard. But it is a very different matter to infer a contractual relation between parties who have never entered into a contract at all. In the present case the cargo owners had a contract with the carrier which provided amongst other things for the unloading of their cargo. They knew nothing of the relations between the carrier and the stevedores. It was no business of theirs. They were concerned only to have the job done which the carriers had contracted to do. There is no conceivable reason why an implication should be made that they had entered into any contractual relation with the stevedores.

But, my Lords, all these contentions were but a prelude to one which, had your Lordships accepted it, would have been the foundation of a dramatic decision of this House. It was argued, if I understood the argument, that if A contracts with B to do something for the benefit of C, then C, though not a party to the contract, can sue A to enforce it. This is independent of whether C is A's undisclosed principal or a beneficiary under a trust of which A is trustee. It is sufficient that C is an "interested person." My Lords, if this is the law of England, then, subject always to the question of consideration, no doubt, if the carrier purports to contract for the benefit of the stevedore, the latter can enforce the contract. Whether that premiss is satisfied in this case is another matter, but, since the argument is advanced, it is right that I should deal with it.

Learned counsel for the respondents met it, as they had successfully done in the courts below, by asserting a principle which is, I suppose, as well established as any in our law, a "fundamental" principle, as Lord Haldane called it in *Dunlop Pneumatic Tyre Co. Ltd.* v. *Selfridge & Co. Ltd.*, an "elementary" principle, as it has been called times without number, that only a person who is a party to a contract can sue upon it. "Our law," said Lord Haldane, "knows nothing of a jus quaesitum tertio arising by way of contract." Learned counsel for the respondents claimed that this was the orthodox view and asked your Lordships to reject any proposition that impinged upon it. To that invitation I readily respond. For to me heterodoxy, or, as some might say, heresy, is not the more attractive because it is dignified by the name of reform. Nor will I easily be led by an undiscerning zeal for some abstract kind of justice to ignore our first duty, which is to administer justice according to law, the law which is established for us by Act of Parliament or the binding authority of precedent. The law is developed by the application of old principles to new circumstances. Therein lies its genius. Its reform by the abrogation of those principles is the task not of the courts of law but of Parliament. Therefore I reject the argument for the appellants under this head and invite your Lordships to say that certain statements which appear to support it in recent cases such as *Smith & Snipes Hall Farm* v. *River Douglas Catchment Board* and *White* v. *John Warwick & Co. Ltd.* must be rejected. If the principle of jus quaesitum tertio is to be introduced into our law, it must be done by Parliament after a due consideration of its merits and demerits. I should not be prepared to give it my support without a greater knowledge than I at present possess of its operation in other systems of law.

I come finally to the case which is said to require us to decide in favour of the appellants. The *Elder, Dempster* case has been the subject of so much analytical criticism, and so many different conclusions, that one may well despair of finding out what was decided by which of the five noble and learned Lords who took part in it. In the course of the discussion before your Lordships my mind turned to what was said by Lord Dunedin (who was himself a party to the *Elder, Dempster* decision some four years later in *Great Western Railway Co.* v. *Mostyn* (*Owners*)). He said: ". . . if from the opinions delivered it is clear – as is the

> case in most instances – what the ratio decidendi was which led to the judgment, then that ratio decidendi is also binding. But, if it is not clear, then I do not think it is part of the tribunal's duty to spell out with great difficulty a ratio decidendi in order to be bound by it. That is what the Court of Appeal has done here. With great hesitation they have added the opinion of Lord Haterley to that of Lord Cairns and then, with still greater difficulty, that of Lord Blackburn, and so have secured what they think was a majority in favour of Lord Cairns' very clear view. I do not think that the respect which they hold and have expressed for the judgments of your Lordships' House compelled them to go through this difficult and most unsatisfactory performance."

My Lords, Lord Dunedin's was a dissenting speech and at a latter date this House was able to ascertain the principle which was decided by that case and the case that he was discussing, *River Wear Commissioners* v. *Adamson* (see *Workington Harbour and Dock Board* v. *Towerfield* (*Owners*)). But that does not, I think, detract from the value and importance of his observations upon the ascertainment of the ratio decidendi of a decision which is said to bind this House. I would cast no doubt upon the doctrine of stare decisis, without which law is at hazard. But I do reserve the right at least to say of any decision of this House that it does not depart from a long-established principle, and particularly does not do so without even mentioning it, unless that is made abundantly clear by the majority of the noble Lords who take part in it. When, therefore, it is urged that the *Elder*, Dempster case decided that, even if there is no general exception to what I have called the fundamental rule that a person not a party to a contract cannot sue to enforce it, there is at least a special exception in the case of a contract for carriage of goods by sea, an exception which is to be available to every person, servant or agent of the contracting party or independent contractor, then I demand that that particular exception should be plainly deducible from the speeches that were delivered. Nor should I forget the warning given by Lord Halsbury in *Quinn* v. *Leathem* in a passage quoted by Diplock J. in this case, which I need not repeat. For it is undeniable that the facts in *Elder, Dempster* which enabled the House to hold that both shipowners and charterers could take advantage of a provision in a bill of lading, are remote from the facts of the present case. The question, then, is whether there is to be extracted from *Elder, Dempster* a decision that there is in a contract for carriage of goods by sea a particular exception to the fundamental rule in favour of all persons including stevedores and, presumably, other independent contractors. This question must clearly, in my opinion, be answered in the negative. . . .

I would dismiss this appeal with costs.

LORD REID: My Lords, the case for the respondents is simple. Goods which they had bought were damaged by the negligence of stevedores, who are the appellants. Before the damage occurred the property in the goods had passed to the respondents and they sue in tort for the amount of the loss to them caused by that damage. The appellants seek to take advantage of provisions in the bill of lading made between the sellers of the goods and the carrier. Those provisions in the circumstances of this case would limit liability to $500. They are expressed as being in favour of the carrier but the appellants maintain on a number of grounds that they can rely on these provisions with the result that, though the damage to the respondents' goods considerably exceeded $500, the respondents cannot recover more than the equivalent of that sum from them as damages. We were informed that questions of this kind frequently arise and that this action has been brought as a test case.

In considering the various arguments for the appellants, I think it is necessary to have in mind certain established principles of the English law of contract. Although I may regret it I find it impossible to deny the existence of the general rule that a stranger to a contract cannot in a question with either of the contracting parties take advantage of provisions of the contract, even where it is clear from the contract that some provision in it was intended to benefit him. That rule appears to have been crystallised a century ago in *Tweddle* v. *Atkinson* and finally established in this House in *Dunlop Pneumatic Co. Ltd.* v. *Selfridge & Co. Ltd.* There are, it is true, certain well-established exceptions to that rule – though I am not sure that they are really exceptions and do not arise from other principles. But none of these in any way touches the present case.

The actual words used by Lord Haldane in the *Dunlop* case were made the basis of an argument that, although a stranger to a contract may not be able to sue for any benefit under it, he can rely on the contract as a defence if one of the parties to it sues him in breach of his contractual obligation – that he can use the contract as a shield though not as a sword. I can find no justification for that. If the other contracting party can prevent the breach of contract well and good, but if he cannot I do not see how the stranger can. As was said in *Tweddle* v. *Atkinson*, the stranger cannot "take advantage" from the contract. . . .

Before dealing further with that case I think it necessary to make some general observations about the binding character of rationes decidendi of this House. Unlike most supreme tribunals this House holds itself bound by its own previous decisions. That was the decision of this House in *London Street Tramways Co. Ltd.* v. *London County Council.* It was founded on immemorial practice, and the justification given by Lord Halsbury L.C., with whom the other noble Lords concurred, was "the inconvenience – the disastrous inconvenience – of having each question subject to being reargued and the dealings of mankind rendered doubtful by reason of different decisions, so that in truth and in fact there would be no real final Court of Appeal." I have on more than one occasion stated my view that this rule is too rigid and that it does not in fact create certainty. In illustration of that I need go no further than the series of decisions in this House on workmen's compensation. But I am bound by the rule until it is altered.

But I can find no invariable practice with regard to rationes decidendi. In the first place it must be noted that only three years later Lord Halsbury said in *Quinn* v. *Leathem*:

> ". . . there are two observations of a general character which I wish to make, and one is to repeat what I have very often said before, that every judgment must be read as applicable to the particular facts proved, or assumed to be proved, since the generality of the expressions which may be found there are not intended to be expositions of the whole law, but governed and qualified by the particular facts of the case in which such expressions are to be found. The other is that a case is only an authority for what it actually decides. I entirely deny that it can be quoted for a proposition that may seem to follow logically from it."

And, if one has to assume that every case has a ratio decidendi to be extracted from the speeches in this House by the ordinary methods of construction of written documents, I think that quite a number of cases will be found of which the rationes decidendi have not in fact been followed. I give only a few examples which I happen to have noted from time to time. They may not be very modern, but, if there was no unbroken practice, modern pronouncements (in themselves at best only rationes decidendi) cannot have created a rule preventing your Lordships from exercising the full traditional jurisdiction of this House. A fairly recent example is *Goodman* v. *Saltash Corpn.*, and with that I couple a note by Mr. Macqueen to *Scott* v. *Maxwell* where, having dealt with the question of previous decisions being binding, he says: "Notwithstanding all this, it must be owned that one or two well known decisions of the House have been tabooed by the profession; not, however, by holding them to be wrong, but by making out invariably that they have no application to other cases. I think, however, it will be found that the House itself has never revoked what it has once deliberately laid down on an appeal or writ of error." And very soon after that was said Lord Chelmsford L.C. said in *Dundee Magistrates* v. *Morris*: ". . . your Lordships will probably think that *Ewan* v. *Provost of Montrose* can only be urged as an authority where the circumstances of the case to which it is sought to be applied are precisely similar to the circumstances of that case."

I would certainly not lightly disregard or depart from any ratio decidendi of this House. But there are at least three classes of case where I think we are entitled to question or limit it: first, where it is obscure, secondly, where the decision itself is out of line with other authorities or established principles, and thirdly, where it is much wider than was necessary for the decision so that it becomes a question of how far it is proper to distinguish the earlier decision. The first two of these grounds appear to me to apply to the present case.

It can hardly be denied that the ratio decidendi of the *Elder*, *Dempster* decision is very obscure. A number of eminent judges have tried to discover it, hardly any two have reached the same result, and none of the explanations hitherto given seems to me very convincing. It I had to try, the result might depend on whether or not I was striving to obtain a narrow ratio. So I turned to the decision itself. Two quite separate points were involved in the case. The first was whether the damage to the cargo was caused by bad stowage or by the ship being unseaworthy. This was very fully considered and the decision was bad stowage. On the conditions in the bill of lading this clearly freed the charterer of liability. The other question was whether those conditions were also available as a defence to the shipowner. From the report of the case it would seem that this was not very fully argued, and none of the three noble Lords who spoke devoted more than a page of print to it. They cannot have thought that any important question of law or any novel principle was involved. Lord Finlay said that a decision against the shipowner would be absurd and the other noble Lords probably thought the same. They must all have thought that they were merely applying an established principle to the facts of the particular case.

But when I look for such a principle I cannot find it, and the extensive and able arguments of counsel in this case have failed to discover it. The House sustained the dissenting judgment of Scrutton L.J. in the Court of Appeal (*Paterson, Zochonis & Co. Ltd.* v. *Elder, Dempster & Co. Ltd.*). The majority there did not have to consider this question, but Scrutton L.J. did and he also devoted less than a page to its consideration. His reasoning, though brief, is quite clear, but he gives no reason or authority for the proposition on which he bases his judgment and it is not derived from the argument as reported. He said: "The real answer to the claim is in my view that the shipowner is not in possession as a bailee, but as the agent of a person, the charterer, with whom the owner of the goods has made a contract defining his liability, and that the owner as servant or agent of the charterer can claim the same protection as the charterer. Were it otherwise there would be an easy way round the bill of lading in the case of every chartered ship; the owner of the goods would simply sue the owner of the ship and ignore the bill of lading exceptions, though he had contracted with the charterer for carriage on those terms and the owner had only received the goods as agent for the charterer." It is true that an unreasonable proposition is seldom good law, and, perhaps for that reason, it would seem that that great lawyer did not pause to consider how great an exception he was making to the rule that a stranger to a contract cannot take advantage from it. For he was saying in terms that servants and "agents" can take advantage of contracts made by their master or "principal." I would not dissent from a proposition that something of that kind ought to be the law if that was plainly the intention of the contract, and it may well be that this matter is worthy of consideration by those whose function it is to consider amending the law. But it seems to me much too late to do that judicially.

That this House made an exception to the general principle seems to me clear: the question we have now to consider is how wide an inroad did they make. It is very far from clear that any of those who spoke in this House intended to go all the way with Scrutton L.J.: if they had intended to do so it would have been easy to say so. And it is not clear just how far Scrutton L.J. himself intended to go. The use of the term "agent" is one difficulty: he cannot have been using that word accurately in its legal sense. The charterer or anyone else under obligation to do certain things employs servants or independent contractors and instructs them to do those things. But they do not act as agents; they have nothing to do with the party to whom their master or employer is under contractual obligation; their duty is to carry out the instructions of their master or employer under the contracts which they have made with him. But in the course of carrying out that duty they may by their own negligence do damage to the property of a third party, the person who has made a contract with their master or employer. On what ground are they to be better off than if they had damaged the property of some other person? On that analysis it becomes still more difficult to find a legal justification for what Scrutton L.J. said. And was there any implicit limitation to the rule which he enunciated? There seems to be no logical reason why it should be confined to carriage of goods by sea or indeed to carriage of any kind. If it is a good rule for bills of lading it would seem to be an equally good rule for all cases where the master or employer has some protection under a contract and employs someone else to do the things which have to be done under that contract. I must say I have considerable doubt whether Scrutton L.J. can really have intended this rule to be so far-reaching.

In such circumstances I do not think it is my duty to pursue the unrewarding task of seeking to extract a ratio decidendi from what was said in this House in *Elder, Dempster*. Nor is it my duty to seek to rationalise the decision by determining in any other way just how far the scope of the decision should extend. I must treat the decision as an anomalous and unexplained exception to the general principle that a stranger cannot rely for his protection on provisions in a contract to which he is not a party. The decision of this House is authoritative in cases of which the circumstances are not reasonably distinguishable from those which gave rise to the decision. The circumstances in the present case are clearly distinguishable in several respects. Therefore I must decide this case on the established principles of the law of England apart from that decision, and on that basis I have no doubt that this appeal must be dismissed.

LORD DENNING: My Lords, there are three contracts which fall for consideration in this case:

(1) *The Bill of Lading.* This evidenced a contract between the shipper and the carrier whereby the carrier agreed to carry a drum of silicone diffusion pump fluid by ship from New York to London and deliver it there to the consignee. In this contract the carrier stipulated that, in case of loss, damage or delay the value was to be deemed to be $500 and he was not to be liable for more than $500 per package "unless the nature and value thereof was declared by the shipper in writing before shipment and inserted in the bill of lading."

(2) *The Stevedoring Contract.* This was a contract between the carrier and the stevedores whereby the stevedores agreed to discharge the vessels of the carrier in the Port of London. The stevedores agreed to be responsible for any damage to or loss of cargo while being handled or stowed, unshipped or delivered. But the stevedores stipulated that they should have "such protection as is afforded by the terms, conditions and exceptions of the bills of lading." By this stipulation the stevedores clearly sought to be protected by the same conditions as the carrier was, so that they too would not be liable for more than $500 a package on undeclared cargo. It is noteworthy that so far as declared cargo was concerned, the stevedores agreed "to effect an insurance policy on Lloyds to cover any damage or loss on which a value in excess of $500 per package has been declared."

(3) *The Sale of the Goods.* This was a contract between the shipper and the consignee under which the property in the goods passed to the consignee whilst the goods were on board the ship. Thereupon there was transferred to the consignee all rights of suit and he was subject to the same liabilities in respect of the goods as if the contract contained in the bill of lading had been made with the consignee himself.

The shipper did not declare the value of the drum to the carrier, and its value was not inserted in the bill of lading. If a declaration of value had been made, the drum would have been included in a list of special cargo for the use of the carriers and the stevedores, and, in accordance with the usual practice, it would have been given special stowage: and it would, no doubt, have been covered by the insurance policy referred to in the stevedoring contract. But as there was no declaration of value in this case, the drum was dealt with as ordinary cargo, both by the carriers and the stevedores.

The drum was duly carried to London. The stevedores duly discharged the ship and put the drum into a shed. The consignees sent a lorry to take delivery of the drum. The stevedores were in the very act of lowering the drum on to the lorry when they negligently dropped it and some of the contents were lost. The drum was worth far more than $500 and the loss was far more than $500. If the consignee had sued the carrier for the loss, the consignee could not have recovered more than $500. If the carrier had sued the stevedores for the loss, the carrier could not have recovered more than $500. But it is said that the consignee can sue the stevedores in tort for negligence and recover the full value (£593 12s. 0d.) from them, despite the fact that the value was never declared as being in excess of $500 (£179 1s. 0d.).

Now, there are two principal questions in this case which need separate consideration: The first is whether the stevedores can rely on the limitation clause in the bill of lading to which they were *not* parties: The second is whether they can rely on the protection given by the stevedoring contract to which they *were* parties.

So far as the first question is concerned the stevedores rely on the reasoning of this House in the *Elder, Dempster* case, which was stated by Scrutton L.J. to be that "where there is a contract which contains an exemption clause, the servants or agents who act under that contract have the benefit of the exemption clause," see *Mersey Shipping & Transport Co. Ltd.* v. *Rea Ltd.* By "servants or agents" there the Lord Justice clearly means to comprehend all those who do the actual work in performance of the contract; "servants" being those under the direct control of the contracting party, and "agents" being those who are employed as sub-contractors for the purpose. The books are full of the use of the word "agent" in that sense: and I propose in this judgment to continue to use it so. And I think that the Lord Justice had in mind only exemption clauses in the carriage of goods. He knew as well as anyone that the law of England has always drawn a broad distinction between the carriage of goods and the carriage of passengers: see the classic judgment of the Court of Exchequer Chamber in *Readhead* v. *Midland Railway Co.*

My Lords, it is said that, in stating this proposition, for once Homer nodded and that this great master of our commercial law – and the members of this House too – overlooked the "fundamental principle" that no one who is not a party to a contract can sue or be sued upon it or take advantage of the stipulations or conditions that it contains. I protest they did nothing of the kind. You cannot understand the *Elder, Dempster case* without some knowledge of the previous law and I would draw the attention of your Lordships to it.

First of all let me remind your Lordships that this "fundamental principle" was a discovery of the nineteenth century. Lord Mansfield and Buller J. knew nothing of it. But in the nineteenth century it was carried to the most extravagant lengths. It was held that, where a duty to use reasonable care arose out of a contract, no one could sue or be sued for a breach of that contract except a party to it, see *Winterbottom* v. *Wright*, *Alton* v. *Midland Railway Co.* In the nineteenth century if a goods owner had sought to sue stevedores for negligence, as he has in this case, he would have failed utterly. The reason being that the duty of the stevedores to use reasonable care arose out of their contract with the carrier; and no one could sue them for a breach of that duty except the other party to the contract, namely, the carrier. If the goods were damaged, the only remedy of the owner of the goods was against the carrier with whom he contracted, and not against the stevedores with whom he had no contract. If proof were needed that the doctrine was carried so far, it is provided by the many cases in the middle of the nineteenth century where the owner of goods sent them by railway for "through transit" to a destination on another line. The first carrier carried them safely over his line but they were damaged by the negligence of the second carrier. It was repeatedly held that the goods owner had no remedy against the second carrier: for the simple reason that he had no contract with him. The owner's only remedy was against the first carrier with whom he contracted, see *Scothorn* v. *South Staffordshire Railway Co.* and not against the second carrier with whom he had no contract, see *Mytton* v. *Midland Railway Co.*, *Coxon* v. *Great Western Railway Co.* If the first carrier was exempted from liability by the conditions of the contract, the goods owner had no remedy at all: none against the first carrier because he was protected by the conditions: and none against the second carrier because he was "not liable at all." It was so held by this House in *Bristol & Exeter Railway Co.* v. *Collins*. See especially what Lord Chelmsford said with the entire agreement of Lord Brougham, and what Lord Cranworth said.

What an irony is here! This "fundamental principle" which was invoked 100 years ago for the purpose of holding that the agents of the carrier were "not liable at all" is now invoked for the purpose of holding that they are inescapably liable, without the benefit of any of the conditions of carriage. How has this come about?

The reason is because in the nineteenth century negligence was not an independent tort. . . .

This brings me to the *Elder, Dempster* case itself. . . . Two reasons were given for this decision.

The first reason, which I give in the words of Viscount Cave: The shipowners "were not directly parties to the contract; but they took possession of the goods (as Scrutton L.J. says) on behalf of and as the agents of the charterers, and so can claim the same protection as their principals." I feel no difficulty about the word "agents" in this context. It is clearly used to denote people employed as sub-contractors to do the work. Such people are entitled to the same protection as their principals. This was the proposition stated by Scrutton L.J. It was clearly approved not only by Viscount Cave but also by Viscount Finlay with the concurrence of Lord Carson. It was treated, too, as a correct proposition by Lord Sumner, with whom Lord Dunedin agreed, for he accepted that "the charterers *and their agents*" were not liable. Lord Sumner's only hesitation seems to have been whether in this case the shipowners took possession of the goods as "agents." They had a possessory lien for hire and might have been in possession on their own account. He put forward, therefore, another reason which he regarded as preferable.

The second reason. The shipowners were bailees and liable as such for negligence quasi ex contractu: but they were protected because the bailment to them was not a "bald bailment with unrestricted liability" but a "bailment upon terms, which include the exceptions and limitations stipulated in the known and contemplated form of bill of lading."

These two reasons were complementary and not alternative as is shown by the fact that Lord Carson agreed with both.

My Lords, I am not unduly attached to the strict doctrine of precedent but I should have thought there was good ground here to hold yourselves bound by the first reason in the *Elder, Dempster* case. Just as your Lordships held yourselves bound by a ratio decidendi of three out of five in *Fairman* v. *Perpetual Investment Building Society*, see *Jacobs* v. *London County Council*; and by ratio decidendi of four out of five in *Nicholls* v. *Austin (Leyton) Ltd.*, see *Close* v. *Steel Company of Wales Ltd.* So should you be bound by the reasoning in the *Elder, Dempster* case. I confess that I should do my best to distinguish it in some way if I was quite satisfied that it was wrong, but I am not in the least satisfied of this.

It is said that the decision is anomalous and contrary to principle but that is only because you are looking at it through the spectacles of 1961 and not those of 1924. Since the decision of *Donoghue* v. *Stevenson* in 1932 we have had negligence established as an independent tort in itself. Small wonder, then, that nowadays it is said that the tortfeasor cannot rely for his protection on provisions in a contract to which he was not a party. But the very point in the *Elder, Dempster* case was that the negligence there was not an independent tort in itself. It was negligence in the very course of performing the contract – done it is true by the sub-contractor and not by the principal – but if you permit the owner of the goods to sue the sub-contractor in tort for what is in truth a breach of the contract of carriage, then at least you should give him the protection of the contract. Were it otherwise there would be an easy way round the conditions of the contract of carriage. That is how the judges in the *Elder, Dempster* case looked at it and I am not prepared to say they were wrong. I am sure that the profession looked at it, too, at that time in the same way. If the draftsmen of the Hague Rules had thought in those days that the goods owner could get round the exceptions by suing the stevedores or the master in tort, they would surely have inserted provisions in those Rules to protect them. They did not do so because they did not envisage their being made liable at all.

But if you look at the *Elder, Dempster* case with the spectacles of 1961, then there is a way in which it can be supported. It is this: Even though negligence is an independent tort, nevertheless it is an accepted principle of the law of tort that no man can complain of an injury if he has voluntarily consented to take the risk of it on himself. This consent need not be embodied in a contract. Nor does it need consideration to support it. Suffice it that he consented to take the risk of injury on himself. So in the case of through transit, when the shipper of goods consigns them "at owner's risk" for the whole journey, his consent to take the risk avails the second carrier as well as the first, even though there is no contract between the goods owner and the second carrier. Likewise in the *Elder, Dempster* case the shipper, by exempting the charterers from bad stowage, may be taken to have consented to exempt the shipowners also. But I am afraid that this reasoning would not avail the stevedores in the present case: for the simple reason that the bill of lading is not expressed so as to protect the stevedores but only the "carrier." The shipper has therefore not consented to take on himself the risk of the negligence of the stevedores and is not to be defeated on that ground. But if the bill of lading were expressed in terms by which the owner of the goods consented to take on himself the risk of loss in excess of $500, whether due to the negligence of the carrier or the stevedores, I know of no good reason why his consent, if freely given, should not be binding on him. The case of *Cosgrove* v. *Horsfall* appears to suggest the contrary, but that was a contract for the carriage of passengers and not for the carriage of goods: and as I said in *Adler* v. *Dickson* it is not so easy to find an assent by a passenger to take the risk of personal injury on himself. The mere issue of a ticket or pass will not suffice.

I suppose, however, that I must be wrong about all this: because your Lordships, I believe, take a different view. But it means that I must go on to consider the second question, namely, whether the stevedores can avail themselves of the protection clause in their own "stevedoring contract." Here your Lordships are untrammelled by authority. The cases in the High Court of Australia and in the United States Supreme Court do not touch the point. The stevedores in those two cases, for aught that appears, had agreed to do their work on a "bald" stevedoring contract "with unrestricted liability": whereas here they stipulated that they should "have such protection as is afforded by the terms, conditions and exceptions of the bill of lading."

It is said here again that the owners of the goods cannot be affected by the "stevedoring contract" to which they were not parties: but it seems to me that we are now in a different branch of the law. When considering the contract between the carrier and the stevedores, it is important to remember that the carrier of goods, like a hirer, is a bailee: and the law of bailment is governed by somewhat different principles from those of contract or of tort: for "bailment," as Sir Percy Winfield said, "is more fittingly regarded as a distinct branch of the Law of Property, under the title Possession than as appropriate to either the law of contract or the law of tort," see The Province of the Law of Tort, p. 100. One special feature of the law of bailment is that the bailee can make a contract in regard to the goods which will bind the owner, although the owner is no party to the contract and cannot sue or be sued upon it. The contract must, no doubt, be of a category which the owner impliedly authorised the bailee to make, such as a contract for repair, storage, loading, unloading or removal; but, provided it is impliedly authorised, the true owner is bound by it. Thus if a bailee stores goods in a warehouse on his own account, and the warehouseman stipulates for a general lien on the terms usual in the trade, the owner of the goods is bound by it. He cannot claim the goods in defiance of the lien. Again, if the hirer of goods hands them to a furniture remover to be carried to his new home, and the remover stipulates, in the usual way of the trade, for exemption from liability for fire, the remover is entitled to the benefit of the exemption, not only as against the hirer, but also as against the owner. The reason for this may be seen by considering what would be the position if there were no exemption from liability. The bailee would then be able to recover the full value of the goods from the negligent wrongdoer, but he would have to account to the true owner for the proceeds, see *The Winkfield.* If the bailee is to be treated as the owner of the goods for the purpose thus of imposing full liability on the negligent wrongdoer, he is also to be treated as the owner for the purpose of exempting him from liability, at any rate where the true owner has impliedly authorised it. And, just as the original owner cannot sue in defiance of the exemption, nor can anyone who buys the goods from him: for the purchaser takes the goods subject to the subsisting bailment and the rights of anyone validly claiming under it, see *Jowitt & Sons* v. *Union Cold Storage Co.* . . .

Applying this principle, the question is: Did the owners of the goods impliedly authorise the carrier to employ the stevedores on the terms that their liability should be limited to $500? I think they did. Put in simple language, the shipper said to the carrier: "Please carry these goods to London and deliver them to the consignee. You may take it that they are not worth more than $500 so your liability is limited to $500. If they were worth more, we would declare it to you." The carrier carries them to London and says to the stevedores: "Please deliver these goods to the consignee. They have not been declared as being in excess of $500, so you need not insure them for more. You are to have the same protection as I have, namely, your liability is limited to $500." It is quite plain that the consignee cannot sue the carrier for more than $500, and the carrier cannot sue the stevedores for more than $500. But can the consignee turn round and say to the stevedores: "Although the goods were not declared as being worth more than $500, yet they were worth in fact $1,500 and I can make you liable for it"? I do not think our law permits him to do this. The carrier simply passed on the self-same limitation as he himself had, and this must have been within his implied authority. It seems to me that when the owner of goods allows the person in possession of them to make a contract in regard to them, then he cannot go back on the terms of the contract, if they are such as he expressly or impliedly authorised to be made, even though he was no party to the contract and could not sue or be sued upon it. It is just the same as if he stood by and watched it being made. And his successor in title is in no better position.

My Lords, I have dealt with this case at some length because it is the first case ever recorded in our English books where the owner of goods has sued a stevedore for negligence. If the owner can, by so doing, escape the exceptions in the contract of carriage and the limitations in the Hague Rules, it will expose a serious gap in our commercial law. It has great potentialities too. If you can sue the stevedore for his negligence in unloading, why should you not sue the master and officers of the ship for their negligence in the navigation or management of the ship? No longer need you worry about the limitation to £100 or £200 a package. You can recover the value of the most precious package without disclosing its nature or value beforehand. No longer need you worry about bringing an action within one year. You can bring it within six years. Nor are the potentialities limited to carriage by sea. They can be profitably extended to carriage by air and by road and rail. You have only to sue the servants of the carrier for negligence and you can get round all the exceptions and limitations that have hitherto been devised. No doubt the carrying company will stand behind its servants. It will foot the bill, as any good employer would, for the sake of good relations. But when you find that the carrying company has, in the long run, to pay for the damage, you see at once that you have turned the flank of the Hague Rules (for carriage by sea) and the Warsaw Convention (for carriage by air). The exemptions and limitations which are there so clearly given to the "carrier" do not avail his servants and agents when they are sued. By suing them, the goods owner will be able completely to upset the balance of risks as hitherto covered by insurance. No wonder that Parliament has already found it necessary to step in. It has done so in sections 2 and 3 of the Merchant Shipping (Liability of Shipowners and Others) Act, 1958: and sections 1, 5 and 10 and Schedule I, Article 25a of the Carriage by Air Act, 1961, which is not yet in force nor likely to be for some time. But these are only piecemeal efforts of very limited scope. Much more is needed if the law is such as your Lordships today declare it to be. For myself, however, I would not allow this gap to be driven in our commercial law. I would not give the "fundamental principle" of the nineteenth century a free rein. It should not have unbridled scope to defeat the intentions of business men. I would stand by the proposition stated by Scrutton L.J. and affirmed, as I believe, by this House 37 years ago.

I would allow this appeal.

[The concurring judgments of LORD KEITH OF AVONHOLM and LORD MORRIS OF BORTH-Y-GEST are omitted].

MAGOR AND ST. MELLONS RURAL DISTRICT COUNCIL v. NEWPORT CORPORATION

House of Lords. [1951] 2 All E. R. 839.

By the Newport Extension Act, 1934, s. 4, the boundary of the county borough of Newport was extended so as to include part of the area of the rural district of Magor and part of the area of the rural district of St. Mellons. The Act came into force on Apr. 1, 1935. By the Local Government Act, 1933, s. 151 and s. 152 (which are applied by s. 58 of the Act of 1934 where financial adjustments are necessary under the Act), provision is made for the adjustment of property, income, etc., between public bodies affected by any alteration in areas. Section 151 (1) enables public bodies so affected to settle any such adjustments by agreement. Section 152 (1) (b) provides that provision should (on an adjustment under s. 151) be made for payment to a local authority of such sum as may seem equitable in accordance with the rules contained in sched. V to the Act of 1933 in respect of any increase of burden which, as a consequence of any alteration of boundaries, would properly be thrown on the ratepayers of the area of that local authority in meeting the cost incurred by that local authority in the discharge of any of its functions. Rule 1 of sched. V provides that, in determining the sum to be paid, "regard shall be had to – (a) the difference between the burden on the ratepayers which will properly be incurred by the local authority in meeting the cost of executing any of their functions and the burden on the ratepayers which would properly have been incurred by the local authority in meeting such cost had no alteration of boundaries or other change taken place; (b) the length of time during which the increase of burden may be expected to continue." Before the Act of 1934 began to operate the Minister of Health made the County of Monmouth Review Order, 1935, which came into force on the same day as, but immediately after, the Act of 1934. The order abolished the rural district of Magor and the rural district of St. Mellons and formed a new rural district of Magor and St. Mellons, which included all the areas forming the two former rural districts except such parts thereof as were transferred to the borough of Newport by the Act of 1934 or to the areas of other authorities by the order. Under art. 53 of the order all property and liabilities of the dissolved district councils of Magor and St. Mellons were transferred to and vested in the new rural district council. "Property" in art. 53, it was provided, bore the same meaning as in the Local Government Act, 1888, which, in s. 100, defines it as including all property, real and personal, and all estates, interests, easements and rights, whether equitable or legal, in, to, and out of property, real and personal, including things in action. On a claim by the new rural district council of Magor and St. Mellons against the Newport Corporation for financial adjustment under the Act of 1934, it was accepted that, but for the order of 1935, the separate rural district councils for Magor and St. Mellons would each have been entitled to an adjustment under s. 151 of the Act of 1933.

LORD SIMONDS: My Lords, I have had the advantage of reading the opinion which my noble and learned friend, LORD MORTON OF HENRYTON, is about to deliver, and I fully concur in his reasons and conclusion, as I do in those of PARKER J., and the majority of the Court of Appeal. Nor should I have thought it necessary to add any observations of my own were it not that the dissenting opinion of DENNING, L.J., appears to invite some comment.

My Lords, the criticism which I venture to make of the judgment of the learned lord justice is not directed at the conclusion that he reached. It is after all a trite saying that on questions of construction different minds may come to different conclusions and I am content to say that I agree with my noble and learned friend. But it is on the approach of the lord justice to what is a question of construction and nothing else that I think it desirable to make some comment, for at a time when so large a proportion of the cases that are brought before the courts depend on the construction of modern statutes it would not be right for this House to pass unnoticed the propositions which the learned lord justice lays down for the guidance of himself and, presumably, of others. He said: ([1950] 2 All E. R. 1236):

> "We sit here to find out the intention of Parliament and of Ministers and carry it out, and we do this better by filling in the gaps and making sense of the enactment than by opening it up to destructive analysis."

The first part of this passage appears to be an echo of what was said in *Heydon's Case* three hundred years ago and, so regarded, is not objectionable. But the way in which the learned lord justice summarises the broad rules laid down by SIR EDWARD COKE in that case may well induce grave misconception of the function of the court. The part which is played in the judicial interpretation of a statute by reference to the circumstances of its passing is too well known to need restatement. It is sufficient to say that the general proposition that it is the duty of the court to find out the intention of Parliament – and not only of Parliament but of Ministers also – cannot by any means be supported. The duty of the court is to interpret the words that the legislature has used. Those words may be ambiguous, but, even if they are, the power and duty of the court to travel outside them on a voyage of discovery are strictly limited: see, for instance, *Assam Railway & Trading Co. Ltd.* v. *Inland Revenue Comrs.*, and, particularly, the observations of LORD WRIGHT ([1935] A.C. 458).

The second part of the passage that I have cited from the judgment of the learned lord justice is, no doubt, the logical sequel of the first. The court, having discovered the intention of Parliament and of Ministers too, must proceed to fill in the gaps. What the legislature has not written, the court must write. This proposition which restates in a new form the view expressed by the lord justice in the earlier case of *Seaford Court Estates, Ltd.* v. *Asher* (to which the lord justice himself refers), cannot be supported. It appears to me to be a naked usurpation of the legislative function under the thin disguise of interpretation, and it is the less justifiable when it is guesswork with what material the legislature would, if it had discovered the gap, have filled it in. If a gap is disclosed, the remedy lies in an amending Act. For the reasons to be given by my noble and learned friend I am of opinion that this appeal should be dismissed with costs.

LORD MORTON OF HENRYTON: My Lords, my noble and learned friend LORD GODDARD has asked me to say that he entirely agrees with the opinion which I am about to deliver. . . .

My Lords, my reasons for thinking that this appeal should be dismissed can be briefly stated, and I should have been content merely to express my agreement with the judgments of the majority of the Court of Appeal and of PARKER, J., but out of respect for the vigorous dissenting judgment of DENNING, L.J., I shall state my reasons in my own words and shall then go on to explain why I cannot agree with the reasoning or with the conclusion of DENNING, L.J.

It is clear from the opening words of s. 151 of the Act of 1933 that the only bodies which can claim a financial adjustment under that section are public bodies affected by an alteration of area as therein mentioned. The appellants are not such a body since they were not in existence when the areas of the old rural districts of Magor and St. Mellons were altered by the Act of 1934. They only came into existence immediately after that alteration. Consequently, they can make no claim in their own right to any financial adjustment under s. 151 and s. 152 of the Act of 1933. Their rights, if any, to claim such an adjustment depend entirely on art. 53 of the order of 1935, whereby the "property" so transferred included any rights to an adjustment which the rural district councils of Magor and St. Mellons respectively possessed immediately before they were dissolved. It is necessary, therefore, to consider what sum each of these two councils could have claimed under s. 152 of the Act of 1933 immediately before its abolition, and, as they would both be in the same position, I shall take, for the sake of simplicity, the case of the rural district council of St. Mellons. In order to receive any sum at all, that local authority would have had to prove that, in consequence of the alteration of boundaries brought about by the Act of 1934, an increase of burden would properly be thrown on the ratepayers of the rural district council of St. Mellons in meeting the cost incurred by that local authority in the discharge of any of its functions. The rural district council of St. Mellons could never prove any such thing. Immediately after the alteration of boundaries came the abolition of the rural district of St. Mellons and the dissolution of the council of that rural district. Therefore, no cost could be incurred by that local authority after the alteration of boundaries, and there could be no increase of burden to the ratepayers of that local authority in meeting such cost. Thus, the rural district council of St. Mellons could recover nothing under s. 152 (1) (b). The rules in sched. V to the Act of 1933 would afford them no assistance. These rules only come into operation if there is an "increase of burden to ratepayers" within s. 152 (1) (b) and they are directed to determining the sum to be paid in respect of that increase of burden. If there is no increase of burden which comes within s. 152 (1) (b) there is nothing on which the rules can operate. Any claim by the rural district council of Magor would be bound to fail for the same reasons. If I am right so far, any claim by the appellants must fail, since they can only claim as successors to the two rural district councils of Magor and St. Mellons and they can claim no higher rights than their predecessors in title. My Lords, I think it is manifest that in enacting s. 152 the legislature had in mind cases where the area of a local authority is altered and that local authority continues to exist after the alteration: see *Oxford City Council* v. *Oxfordshire County Council per* LORD RUSSELL OF KILLOWEN ([1938] 4 All E.R. 725). In such a case, if the wealthier portion of the area is lost, there is an increase of burden on the ratepayers in the area which remains, and s. 151 and s. 152 are directed to meeting such a case. The present case is one in which each of two local authorities loses a wealthy portion of its area and is abolished immediately after the loss occurs. It may well be that, if the legislature had contemplated such a state of affairs, some special provisions would have been inserted in the Act of 1933. What these provisions would have been can only be a matter of guesswork.

For the reasons which I have stated, I think that PARKER J., and the majority of the Court of Appeal arrived at the right conclusion. DENNING, L.J., however, took a different view, and I think I can only do justice to his reasoning if I set it out in full. After referring to the facts, and to the view expressed by PARKER, J., the learned lord justice continued ([1950] 2 All. E. R. 1235):

> "I cannot think that the judge is right about this. The Minister's order expressly provided that the property of the two rural district councils should be transferred to and vest in the combined council. The right of the two councils to compensation was clearly 'property' which vested in the combined council, and the judge so held, but he thought that the right was worth nothing because the two councils only lived for a moment of time after they had been shorn of

their rich grounds. Much as I respect his opinions, I cannot agree with him about this. The effect of the Minister's order was, if I may use a metaphor, not the death of the two councils, but their marriage. The burdens which each set of ratepayers had previously borne separately became a combined burden to be borne by them all together. So, also, the rights to which the two councils would have been entitled for each set of ratepayers separately became a combined right to which the combined council was entitled for them all together. This was so obviously the intention of the Minister's order that I have no patience with an ultra-legalistic interpretation which would deprive them of their rights altogether. I would repeat what I said in *Seaford Court Estates, Ltd.* v. *Asher*. We do not sit here to pull the language of Parliament and of Ministers to pieces and make nonsense of it. That is an easy thing to do, and it is a thing to which lawyers are too often prone. We sit here to find out the intention of Parliament and of Ministers and carry it out, and we do this better by filling in the gaps and making sense of the enactment than by opening it up to destructive analysis.

"It may be said that these heroics are out of place, and I agree they are, because I think that Parliament has really made its intention plain enough. The Act which conferred the title to compensation conferred it on each of the district councils, not in its own right, but in right of its ratepayers: (see s. 152 (1) (b) of the Act of 1933). The district council was the hand to receive the compensation, but it only received it so that it might give relief to the ratepayers for the increased burden which the change of boundaries cast on them. The amalgamation changed the legal identity of the two district councils, but it did not change the ratepayers at all, nor did it relieve them of their burdens: and there is no reason whatever why the amalgamated council should not claim the compensation due to the ratepayers.

"This enables me to show what I believe is the fallacy in the judgment of the learned judge. These are the steps in his argument. (i) Each district council only remained in existence for a moment of time after it was shorn of its rich grounds. (ii) Therefore, its increased burdens were to all intents and purposes nil. (iii) Therefore, it is entitled to nothing. (iv) The amalgamated council only takes over the property of the two district councils. (v) Therefore, as each of them was entitled to nothing, the amalgamated council is entitled to nothing. The fallacy in the whole of that argument is at the second step. It assumes that each district council was entitled in its own right in respect of its own increased burdens. On that basis it would, of course, be entitled to nothing, because it did not live long enough to bear any increased burden itself. The answer is, however, that it was never entitled in its own right at all. It was only entitled in right of its ratepayers in respect of their increased burdens, and their increased burdens did not last only for a moment of time. They lasted for years. Parliament expressly said that the arbitrator was to have regard to the length of time during which the increase of *burden on the ratepayers* might be expected to continue: see r. 1 (a) and (b) of sched. V of the Act of 1933; whereas the judge has limited the arbitrator to the length of time during which the rural district councils might be expected to continue, to wit, only a moment of time. The answer is that the right of each district council, even during that one moment, was a right to compensation for the whole length of time in the future during which the increased burden might be expected to fall on the ratepayers, and it was that right which devolved on the amalgamated council.

"In my judgment, therefore, amalgamation does not destroy the rights of those ratepayers whose councils are amalgamated. It only transfers them to the amalgamated body."

My Lords, I have already described this as a vigorous judgment, and it is certainly one which invites some comment. I feel sure that PARKER J., had no desire to defeat the Minister's intention by giving an ultra-legalistic interpretation to this order, nor did he wish to pull the language of the Act of 1933 and of the order of 1935 to pieces, or to make nonsense of them. He set out to interpret the Act and the order, and I agree with his interpretation. In so far as the intention of Parliament or of Ministers is revealed in Acts of Parliament or orders, either by the language used or by necessary implication, the courts should, of course, carry these intentions out, but it is not the function of any judge to fill in what he conceives to be the gaps in an Act of Parliament. If he does so, he is usurping the function of the legislature.

Passing from the observations which the learned lord justice himself describes as "heroics", I shall state why I cannot agree with his reasoning in the present case. I think the fundamental difference between us lies in the view which we take as to the effect of the order of 1935. The learned lord justice regards the order as bringing about, not the death of the two councils, but their marriage. I regard the order as effectively destroying each of the two councils by abolishing the rural districts of Magor and St. Mellons and dissolving their council. Immediately thereafter there came into existence a new corporate body, the appellant council. Members of the new council had to be elected, and the ratepayers, some of whom had formerly been ratepayers of Magor and some of St. Mellons, became ratepayers of the new rural district. The policy of the new council as regards expenditure might not be the same as that of either of the two dissolved councils. Neither the new council nor its ratepayers could make any claim to an adjustment under s. 151 and s. 152, since the corporate body was not affected by any alteration of areas, and these sections give no right to any ratepayers to make a claim in their own right. All that remains, in my view, is the right which the new council has as successor to the "property" of the two dissolved councils, and that right is worthless, for the reasons which I have already stated.

I have not thought it necessary to refer in detail to *Godstone Rural District Council* v. *Croydon Corpn.* or to the *Oxford City Council* case, but, in my view, the reasoning in each of these cases is entirely in harmony with the reasoning of PARKER, J., and the majority of the Court of Appeal in the present case. I would dismiss the appeal with costs.

LORD TUCKER: . . . I think it is clear that the situation which has arisen in the present case was never present to the minds of those responsible for the Local Government Act, 1933, and that the language is quite inappropriate to meet it. In these circumstances your Lordships would be acting in a legislative rather than a judicial capacity if the view put forward by DENNING, L.J., in his dissenting judgment were to prevail. I would dismiss the appeal.

[The dissenting judgment of LORD RADCLIFFE is omitted].

BRITISH MOVIETONEWS LD. v. LONDON AND DISTRICT CINEMAS LD.

House of Lords. [1951] 2 All E.R. 617; [1952] A.C. 166.

By an agreement dated July 25, 1941, a company carrying on business as film suppliers agreed to supply their newsreels to a company carrying on business as exhibitors for showing at a cinema at 10 guineas a week for a minimum period of 26 weeks, the agreement to be thereafter determinable by four weeks' notice; but there was a proviso that the exhibitors might terminate the agreement by one month's notice at any time after the first month. The newsreels were still being shown under the agreement when by the Cinematograph Film (Control) Order, 1943, made under Defence Regulation 55, which, in turn, had been made under the Emergency Powers (Defence) Act, 1939, no person in the film industry was to acquire or supply any film except under the authority of a licence granted by the Board of Trade. By section 1 (1) of the Act of 1939 Defence Regulations were authorized "for securing the public safety, the defence of the realm, the maintenance of public order and the efficient prosecution of any war in which His Majesty may be engaged, and for maintaining supplies and services essential to the life of the community." The effect of the Order was to restrict the consumption of raw film stock.

The parties to the original agreement made a supplemental agreement dated May 3, 1943, which recited the effect of the Order and provided (inter alia) that "during the continuance" of the Order (1) the original agreement was to remain in full force and effect "until such time as the said Order is cancelled" and thereafter for any unexpired period stipulated by the original agreement; (2) one copy of a newsreel might be used to serve two exhibitors during the same period and this was, if necessary, to be deemed to include newsreels supplied by other distributors; (3) the same rental was to be paid by the exhibitors, whoever supplied the newsreels; and (4) the conditions of the original agreement were to remain in force in so far as they were not excluded or modified by the supplemental agreement.

The Emergency Powers (Defence) Act, 1939, expired on February 24, 1946, and was replaced by the Supplies and Services (Transitional Powers) Act, 1945, section 1 (1) of which gave authority for directions by Order in Council that any Defence Regulation to which it applied should have effect "for the purpose of so maintaining, controlling and regulating supplies and services as (a) to secure a sufficiency of those essential to the well-being of the community or their equitable distribution or their availability at fair prices . . . " By subsection (3), where an Order in Council was made under that section all Orders made under the Regulation and in force when the date of the Order in Council came into operation should continue in force. It was directed that Defence Regulation 55 should continue in force (S.R. & O. 1945, No. 1618) and accordingly the Cinematograph Film (Control) Order, 1943, which was made under it, continued in force.

VISCOUNT SIMON: My Lords, the question involved in this appeal is not difficult to state, but in answering the question there has emerged a difference of opinion between Slade J., who tried the action and decided in favour of the appellant company, and the Court of Appeal (Bucknill and Denning L.J., and Roxburgh J.), which in a judgment prepared by Denning L.J. allowed the appeal of the respondent company. It now becomes necessary to decide which party in the litigation is right. Moreover, the judgment delivered in the Court of Appeal includes an expression of some general views as to the nature and extent of the judicial function in deciding the rights and obligations of parties under an executory contract which will require careful and candid consideration from the House. . . .

The respondent company next contend – and this raises the real difficulty – that "the Cinematograph Film (Control) Order, 1943," in the sense in which that expression is used in the supplemental agreement, was no longer "continuing" when they gave their notice to terminate, but that it had already been "cancelled" within the meaning of clause 1 (a) of that agreement on February 24, 1946. . . .

Defence Regulation 55 was one of the regulations originally made under the Act of 1939. The regulation authorized a competent authority (in the present case it was the Board of Trade) "so far as appears to that authority to be necessary in the interests of the defence of the realm or the efficient prosecution of the war, or for maintaining supplies and services essential to the life of the community" to provide (inter alia) "(a) for regulating . . . the . . . acquisition, use or consumption of articles of any description, and, in particular, for controlling the prices at which such articles may be sold." It was under this power that the Board of Trade made the Cinematograph Film (Control) Order, 1943. By paragraph 1 of that Order: "On and after April 8, 1943, no person carrying on a business in the course of which cinematograph film . . . is acquired or supplied, shall, except under the authority of a licence granted by the Board of Trade and subject to any limitation or condition attaching thereto, acquire or supply any such film."

The effect of this Order was, therefore, to control the supply of film to renters such as the appellant company and, as the recital of the supplemental agreement recognized, to restrict the consumption of raw film stock. One result of this scarcity would be to make it more difficult for renters to supply newsreels for the exclusive use of one exhibitor, and another result would be likely to be that the price charged to exhibitors in future contracts would rise. It was therefore in the interests of both parties to arrange for a more economical use of newsreels and, at the same time, to secure that existing prices charged to exhibitors should not be increased unreasonably. Both these purposes were secured by the supplemental agreement, the terms of which were settled by the organizations representing the two parties in a common form.

After the Supplemental Agreement was made, the Cinematograph Film (Control) Order, 1943, continued under the authority of Defence Regulation 55 without material change until it was revoked by the Cinematograph Film (Control) (Revocation) Order, 1950, made on September 4 of that year, which came into force on October 1, 1950. This, of course, is after the date of the writ in this action, or, indeed, of the judgment in the Court of Appeal which is now before the House. But, whereas Defence Regulation 55 derived its force originally from the Emergency Powers (Defence) Act, 1939, after February 24, 1946, its authority rested upon the Supplies and Services (Transitional Powers) Act, 1945. The question is whether, in these circumstances, the supplemental agreement, when referring to "the continuance" of the Order and to "such time as the said Order is cancelled," ought to be construed as referring to a period which ends when the statutory basis upon which Defence Regulation 55 rests is thus altered.

This is, primarily at any rate, a question of construction. The respondent company contend that the expression "during the continuance of the Cinematograph Film (Control) Order, 1943," means so long as the Order is and remains in force by virtue of the Emergency Powers (Defence) Act, 1939, or any statutory amendment of the enactment thereto, and the expression "until such time as the said Order is cancelled," means until the date when the Order ceases to be in force by virtue of the aforesaid authority, or until the date when the same is revoked, whichever shall be the earlier. This restricted construction is quite legitimate if that is, in the circumstances, the correct interpretation of the language used. But it is not the natural meaning of the words used and I can find no sufficient ground for construing them in this narrow sense. The economic considerations which must have influenced the parties in making the supplemental agreement did not change on February 24, 1946. The restriction in the consumption of raw film stock, which is referred to in the recital, continued after that date, and though a general licence was issued under the Order of July 15, 1946, for the acquisition of film used for other purposes, the restriction on film for newsreels continued until the cancellation of the Order late in 1950. The parties to the supplemental agreement chose to define the minimum period of its operation by reference to the continuance of the Order. What the length of that continuance might be was necessarily uncertain. It might have come to an end while the war was going on, if Defence Regulation 55 was revoked or if Parliament had not adopted addresses to continue in force the Emergency Powers (Defence) Act, 1939. In fact, the Order continued for five years after the fighting ceased, but all that time there was in operation a restriction on the consumption of raw film stock. And it was throughout the original order, not a new order in the same terms. I agree with Slade J. that the restricted meaning sought to be put on the language of the supplemental agreement by the respondent company is not the correct interpretation of the words used.

It is urged, in the alternative, that the supplemental agreement should be regarded as having terminated in February, 1946, owing to the operation of a doctrine "analogous to a frustration." But what is the change of circumstances in 1946 which would cause Mackinnon L.J.'s "officious bystander" (see *Shirlaw* v. *Southern Foundries* (1926) *Ld.*) to get instant acceptance from both sides if he suggested that of course the supplemental agreement would come to an end, although restriction on the consumption of raw film stock continued, if the Cinematograph Film (Control) Order, 1943, and Defence Regulation 55 are no longer authorized by the Emergency Powers (Defence) Act, 1939, but gain their validity from a later Act of Parliament? It is by no means clear to me that the parties would have assented. Hannen J., in *Bailey* v. *De Crespigny*, observed that "to hold a man liable by words, in a sense affixed to them by legislation subsequent to the contract, is to impose on him a contract he never made." But here, though the legislative authority behind the words of the Order altered, the words themselves mean the same thing throughout. This is not a case in which there has been "a vital change of the law . . . operating on the circumstances" (to use Lord Wright's phrase in *Joseph Constantine Steamship Line Ld.* v. *Imperial Smelting Corporation Ld.*); here the restriction on the consumption of raw film stock continued and the Order creating the restriction was not changed, vitally or at all.

I should have been glad to conclude at this point by expressing agreement with the careful judgment of Slade J., but my colleagues who heard this appeal concur with me in the view that it is desirable, in order to remove the possibility of misunderstanding hereafter, to refer to certain passages in the judgment delivered by Denning L.J. where phrases occur which give us some concern. I will quote from the revision of his written judgment. After a reference to the *Constantine* case and to *Denny, Mott & Dickson Ld.* v. *James B. Fraser & Co. Ld.* the judgment proceeds: "In these frustration cases, as Lord Wright said, the court really exercises a qualifying power – a power to qualify the absolute, literal or wide terms of the contract – in order to do what is just and reasonable in the new situation; and it can now by statute make ancillary orders to that end. Until recently the court only exercised this power when there was a frustrating event, that is a supervening event which struck away the foundations of the contract. But in the important decision of *Sir Lindsay Parkinson & Co. Ld.* v. *Commissioners of Works* this court exercised a like power when there was no frustrating event, but only an uncontemplated turn of events." The learned Lord Justice went on to give his account of the decision in *Parkinson's* case, which he stated was based on *Bush* v. *Whitehaven Trustees*, which in turn was based on the leading frustration case of *Jackson* v. *Union Marine Insurance Co. Ld.* He goes on: "The judgments show that, no matter that a contract is framed in words which, taken literally or absolutely, cover what has happened, nevertheless, if the ensuing turn of events was so completely outside the contemplation of the parties that the court is satisfied that the parties, as reasonable people, cannot have intended that the contract should apply to the new situation, then the court will read the words of the contract in a qualified sense; it will restrict them to the circumstances contemplated by the parties; it will not apply them to the uncontemplated turn of events, but will do therein what is just and reasonable. . . . This does not mean that the courts no longer insist on the binding force of contracts deliberately made. It only means that they will not allow the words, in which they happen to be phrased, to become tyrannical masters. The court qualifies the literal meaning of the words so as to bring them into accord with the true scope of the contract. Even if the contract is absolute in its terms, nevertheless if it is not absolute in intent, it will not be held absolute in effect. The day is done when we can excuse an unforeseen injustice by saying to the sufferer 'It is your own folly. You ought not to have passed that form of words. You ought to have put in a clause to protect yourself.' We no longer credit a party with the foresight of a prophet or his lawyer with the draftsmanship of a Chalmers. We realize that they have their limitations and make allowances accordingly. It is better thus. The old maxim reminds us that 'Qui haeret in litera, haeret in cortice,' which, being interpreted, means: He who clings to the letter, clings to the dry and barren shell, and misses the truth and substance of the matter. We have of late in this court paid heed to this warning, not only in *Parkinson's* case, but also in *John Lee & Son (Grantham) Ld.* v. *Railway Executive, Dennis Reed Ld.* v. *Goody,* and *Bennett, Walden & Co.* v. *Wood*, and we must pay like heed now."

With all respect to the learning and acumen of the learned Lord Justice, I do not agree that there has been a recent change as the result of which the courts now exercise a wider power in this regard than they previously used. Apart from the adjustment effected by the Law Reform (Frustrated Contracts) Act, 1943, which is quite irrelevant to the present point, there has been no recent change; the possibility that a fundamental alteration in circumstances may sometimes bring a contract to a premature end has long been recognized. The general principle upon which the court acts is well settled; so Lord Finlay L.C. stated in *Bank Line Ld.* v. *Arthur Capel & Co.* It can be found, for example, as Lord Porter observed in *Denny, Mott & Dickson Ld.* v. *James B. Fraser & Co. Ld.*, in Earl Loreburn's judgment in *F. A. Tamplin Steamship Co. Ld.* v. *Anglo-Mexican Petroleum Products Co. Ld.*, where it is thus expressed: "But a court can and ought to examine the contract and the circumstances in which it was made, not of course to vary, but only to explain it, in order to see whether or not from the nature of it the parties must have made their bargain on the footing that a particular thing or state of things would continue to exist. And if they must have done so, then a term to that effect will be implied, though it be not expressed in the contract. . . . No court has an absolving power, but it can infer from the nature of the contract and the surrounding circumstances that a condition which is not expressed was a foundation on which the parties contracted." While the principle remains the same, particular applications of it may greatly vary, and theoretical lawyers may debate whether the rule should be regarded as arising from an implied term, or because the basis of the contract no longer exists. In any view, it is a question of construction, as Lord Wright pointed out in *Constantine's* case, and as has been repeatedly asserted by other masters of the law.

When the authorities referred to by Denning L.J. as justifying the proposition that judges now exercise a wider power in these matters than they did some years ago are examined it will be found that they do not support any such notion. The decision of the Court of Appeal in Parkinson's case does not mark a new departure at all. No extracts from the judgments in that case were quoted by the Lord Justice on the ground that they were "so valuable that they should be read in full." When they are read in full, however, it seems to me indisputable that what was there decided was merely that, having regard to the terms of the variation deed and to the circumstances which led up to its execution, the deed could not, on its true construction, be interpreted as authorizing the Commissioners of Works at their pleasure to order an infinite quantity of extra work, to be executed over an unlimited time, on which the plaintiffs could never make any profit beyond the figure named. Asquith L.J.'s judgment makes it clear that the only question was this question of construction. He says: "Where the language of the contract is capable of a literal and wide, but also of a less literal and a more restricted, meaning, all relevant circumstances can be taken into account in deciding whether the literal or a more limited meaning should be ascribed to it." Cohen L.J. reached the same conclusion as a matter of construction, and incidentally expounded *Bush* v. *Whitehaven Trustees* – to which Denning L.J. also referred as though it embodied some new doctrine – in a way which shows that no novel principle was involved. Singleton L.J. was of the same opinion. In substance, the decision in *Parkinson's* case was that the work that had been executed by the contractors included more than was covered, on its true construction, by the variation deed, and that the cost of the uncovenanted addition had therefore to be paid for by a quantum meruit.

The three other cases referred to in the Court of Appeal's judgment as further illustrations of the expanded doctrine are equally mere applications of established rules of construction. In *John Lee & Son (Grantham) Ld.* v. *Railway Executive* Denning L.J. himself so explained the decision, preferring "a limited construction" of which the words were capable to the wider interpretation suggested. *Dennis Reed Ld.* v. *Goody* was again merely a case of interpreting the language of a contract; Denning L.J. was again a party to the decision and said so. *Bennett, Walden & Co.* v. *Wood* is also a pure case of construction; the Court of Appeal held that the words "in the event of our securing for you an offer" referred to a firm offer, which by acceptance would give rise to a contractual relationship. None of these three decisions illustrate the exercise of any recent extension of judicial practice or power.

It is of the utmost importance that the action of a court, when it decides that in view of a supervening situation the rights and obligations under a contract have automatically ceased, should not be misunderstood. The suggestion that an "uncontemplated turn of events" is enough to enable a court to substitute its notion of what is "just and reasonable" for the contract as it stands, even though there is no "frustrating event," appears to be likely to lead to some misunderstanding. The parties to an executory contract are often faced, in the course of carrying it out, with a turn of events which they did not at all anticipate – a wholly abnormal rise or fall in prices, a sudden depreciation of currency, an unexpected obstacle to execution, or the like. Yet this does not in itself affect the bargain they have made. If, on the other hand, a consideration of the terms of the contract, in the light of the circumstances existing when it was made, shows that they never agreed to be bound in a fundamentally different situation which has now unexpectedly emerged, the contract ceases to bind at that point – not because the court in its discretion thinks it just and reasonable to qualify the terms of the contract, but because on its true construction it does not apply in that situation. When it is said that in such circumstances the court reaches a conclusion which is "just and reasonable" (Lord Wright in Constantine's case) or one "which justice demands" (Lord Sumner in *Hirji Mulji* v. *Cheong Yue Steamship Co. Ld.*), this result is arrived at by putting a just construction upon the contract in accordance with an "implication . . . from the presumed common intention of the parties" (Lord Sumner in *Bank Line Ld.* v. *Arthur Capel & Co.*).

If the decisions in "frustration" cases are regarded as illustrations of the power and duty of a court to put the proper construction on the agreement made between the parties, having regard to the terms in which that agreement is expressed, and to the circumstances in which it was made, including any necessary implication, such decisions are seen to be examples of the general judicial function of interpreting a contract when there is disagreement as to its effect. What distinguishes "frustration" cases is that the interpretation involves the consequence that, in view of what has happened, further performance is automatically ended. This is because the frustrating event (such, for example, as war or prolonged delay) must be regarded as introducing a new situation to which no limit can be put. But there are, of course, many other examples where the court has to put an interpretation on the agreement made, not with the result that the contract is brought to an end by frustration, but with the result hat the contract goes on and continues to bind the parties according to its true construction. *Bennett, Walden & Co.* v. *Wood*, quoted by Denning L.J., is an obvious example. The advantage of approaching the topic in this way seems to me to be that it makes plain that in all cases alike the question is really at bottom a question of construction.

In my opinion the appeal succeeds, and I move that it be allowed with costs here and below.

LORD SIMONDS: It is no doubt essential to the life of the common law that its principles should be adapted to meet fresh circumstances and needs. But I respectfully demur to the suggestion that there has recently been, or need be, any change in the well known principles of construction or (except so far as the recent Act of 1943 provides) in the application of the law of frustration to commercial agreements, and, if indeed, as Denning L.J. appears to suggest, such cases as *John Lee & Son (Grantham) Ltd.* v. *Railway Executive, Dennis Reed Ld.* v. *Goody,* and *Bennett, Walden & Co.* v. *Wood*, illustrate such a change, they would have to be regarded as of doubtful authority. They can, however, be justified on more orthodox grounds.

I agree that the appeal should be allowed and the judgment of Slade J. restored.

LORD MORTON OF HENRYTON: My Lords, I agree with the opinions which have just been delivered and I do not desire to add any words of my own.

LORD TUCKER: My Lords, I agree that this appeal should be allowed for the reasons which have been stated by my noble and learned friend on the woolsack. I also desire to express my concurrence in the observations which he has made with regard to the judgment of the Court of Appeal delivered by Denning L.J.

Appeal allowed.

In *Best* v. *Samuel Fox & Co. Ltd.*, [1952] A.C. 716, 727 Lord Porter said: "I do not think it possible to say that a change in the outlook of the public, however great, must inevitably be followed by a change in the law of the country. The common law is a historical development rather than a logical whole, and the fact that a particular doctrine does not logically accord with another or others is no ground for its rejection." In that case the House of Lords held that a married woman whose husband has been injured by the negligence of the defendants had no right of action for the loss or impairment of consortium consequential on the injury, even though her husband would have had the right to bring such an action if she had been the one negligently injured.

Some other interesting cases of a positivistic tenor are: *Waghan* v. *Anon* (1346), Y. B. 20 Edw. 3, ii, R. S. 198-199; *Mirehouse* v. *Rennell* (1833), 8 Bing. 490, at 515-6; *Bright* v. *Hutton* (1852), 3 H. L. Cas. 341, at 388, 391-2; *Beamish* v. *Beamish* (1861), 9 H. L. Cas. 274; *R.* v. *Wheat R.* v. *Stocks*, [1921] 2 K. B. 119; *Commercial Credit Corporation* v. *Niagara Finance Corp Ltd.*, [1940] 3 D. L. R. 62; *Young* v. *Bristol Aeroplane Co. Ltd.*, [1944] 2 All E. R. 293; *Candler* v. *Crane, Christmas & Co.*, [1951] 2 K. B. 164; *A.-G. Can.* v. *Readers' Digest Association (Canada) Ltd.* (1961), 30 D. L. R. (2d) 296.

B. READINGS

In *A Treatise of Human Nature*, Vol. II, Bk. III, Part I, Sec. 1, David Hume wrote as follows: "In every system of morality which I have hitherto met with, I have always remarked, that the author proceeds for some time in the ordinary way of reasoning, and establishes the being of a God, or makes observations concerning human affairs; when of a sudden I am surprised to find, that instead of the usual copulations of propositions, *is*, and *is not*, I meet with no proposition that is not connected with an *ought*, or an *ought not*. This change is imperceptible; but is, however, of the last consequence. For as this ought, or ought not, expresses some new relation or affirmation, it is necessary that it should be observed and explained; and at the same time that a reason should be given, for what seems altogether inconceivable, how this new relation can be a deduction from others, which are entirely different from it. But as authors do not commonly use this precaution, I shall presume to recommend it to the readers; and am persuaded, that this small attention would subvert all the vulgar systems of morality, and let us see that the distinction of vice and virtue is not founded merely on the relations of objects, nor is perceived by reason." The position that no normative conclusion can be drawn from any factual premise has recently been dubbed "Hume's Hurdle" by Professor Kai Neilsen in *Law and Philosophy* 134 (Hook ed. 1964). There is a critical discussion of "Hume's Hurdle" by Professor Kenneth Stern in the same volume at pp. 247-259 and a sharp attack on it in Simonds, "The 'Natural Law' Controversy: Three Basic Logical Issues" (1960) 5 *Natural L.F.* 132, 133-137.

Thomas Hobbes, 1588-1679
Tutor in royal and noble households.

LEVIATHAN
(1651)

Chapter XII

OF THE NATURALL CONDITION OF MANKIND, AS CONCERNING THEIR FELICITY, AND MISERY

Nature hath made men so equall, in the faculties of body, and mind; as that though there bee found one man sometimes manifestly stronger in body, or of quicker mind then another; yet when all is reckoned together, the difference between man, and man, is not so considerable, as that one man can thereupon claim to himselfe any benefit, to which another may not pretend, as well as he. For as to the strength of body, the weakest has strength enough to kill the strongest, either by secret machination, or by confederacy with others, that are in the same danger with himselfe.

And as to the faculties of the mind . . . I find yet a greater equality amongst men . . . That which may perhaps make such equality incredible, is but a vain conceipt of ones owne wisdome, which almost all men think they have in a greater degree, than the Vulgar; that is, than all men but themselves, and a few others, whom by Fame, or for concurring with themselves, they approve . . . But this proveth rather than men are in that point equall, then unequall. For there is not ordinarily a greater signe of the equall distribution of any thing, than that every man is contented with his share.

From this equality of ability, ariseth equality of hope in the attaining of our Ends. And therefore if any two men desire the same thing, which neverthelesse they cannot both enjoy, they become enemies. . . .

And from this diffidence of one another there is no way for any man to secure himselfe, so reasonable, as Anticipation; that is, by force, or wiles, to master the persons of all men he can. . . . Also because there be some, that taking pleasure in contemplating their own power in the acts of conquest, which they pursue farther than their security requires; if others, that otherwise would be glad to be at ease within modest bounds, should not by invasion increase their power, they would not be able, long time, by standing only on their defence, to subsist. And by consequence, such augmentation of dominion over men, being necessary to a mans conservation, it ought to be allowed him.

Againe, men have no pleasure, (but on the contrary a great deal of griefe) in keeping company, where there is no power able to over-awe them all. For every man looketh that his companion should value him, at the same rate he sets upon himselfe. . . .

So that in the nature of man, we find three principall causes of quarrell. First Competition; Secondly, Diffidence; Thirdly, Glory.

The first, maketh men invade for Gain; the second, for Safety; and the third, for Reputation. . . .

Hereby it is manifest, that during the time men live without a common Power to keep them all in awe, they are in that condition which is called Warre; and such a warre, as is of every man, against every man. . . .

. . . In such condition, there is no place for Industry; because the fruit thereof is uncertain: and consequently no Culture of the Earth; no Navigation, nor use of the commodities that may be imported by Sea; no commodious Building; no Instruments of moving, and removing such things as require much force; no Knowledge of the face of the Earth; no account to Time; no Arts; no Letters; no Society; and which is worst of all, continuall feare, and danger of violent death; And the life of man, solitary, poore, nasty, brutish, and short. . . .

. . . The Desires, and other Passions of man, are in themselves no Sin. No more are the Actions, that proceed from those Passions, till they know a Law that forbids them: which till Lawes be made they cannot know: nor can any Law be made, till they have agreed upon the Person that shall make it.

It may peradventure be thought, there was never such a time, nor condition of warre as this: and I believe it was never generally so, over all the world: but there are many places, where they live so now. . . .

But though there had never been any time, wherein particular men were in a condition of warre one against another; yet in all times, Kings, and Persons of Soveraigne authority because of their Independency, are in continuall jealousies, and in the state and posture of Gladiators; having their weapons pointing, and their eyes fixed on one another; that is, their Forts, Garrisons, and Guns upon the

Frontiers of their King domes; and continuall Spyes upon their neighbours; which is a posture of War. But because they uphold thereby, the Industry of their Subjects; there does not follow from it, that misery, which accompanies the Liberty of particular men.

To this warre of every man against every man, this also is consequent; that nothing can be Unjust. The notions of Right and Wrong, Justice and Injustice have there no place. Where there is no common Power, there is no Law: where no Law, no Injustice. Force, and Fraud, are in warre, the two Cardinall vertues. Justice, and Injustice are none of the Faculties neither of the Body, nor Mind . . . It is consequent also to the same condition, that there be no Propriety, no Dominion, no *Mine* and *Thine* distinct; but onely that to be every mans, that he can get; and for so long, as he can keep it. . . .

Chapter XIV

Of the first and second NAURALL LAWES, and of CONTRACTS

. . . A LAW OF NATURE, (*Lex Naturalis,*) is a Precept, or generall Rule, found out by Reason, by which a man is forbidden to do, that, which is destructive of his life, or taketh away the means of preserving the same; and to omit, that, by which he thinketh it may be best preserved. For though they that speak of this subject, use to confound *Jus*, and *Lex*, *Right* and *Law*; yet they ought to be distinguished; because RIGHT, consisteth in liberty to do, or to forbeare; Whereas LAW, determineth, and bindeth to one of them: so that Law, and Right, differ as much, as Obligation, and Liberty; which in one and the same matter are inconsistent.

And because the condition of Man, (as hath been declared in the precedent Chapter) is a condition of Warre of every one against every one; in which case every one is governed by his own Reason; and there is nothing he can make use of, that may not be a help unto him, in preserving his life against his enemyes; It followeth, that in such a condition, every man has a Right to every thing; even to one anothers body. And therefore, as long as this naturall Right of every man to every thing endureth, there can be no security to any man, (how strong or wise soever he be,) of living out the time, which Nature ordinarily alloweth men to live. And consequently it is a precept, or generall rule of Reason, *That every man, ought to endeavour Peace, as farre as he has hope of obtaining it; and when he cannot obtain it, that he may seek, and use, all helps, and advantages of Warre.* The first branch of which Rule, containeth the first, and Fundamentall Law of Nature; which is, *to seek Peace, and follow it.* The Second, the summe of the Right of Nature; which is, *By all means we can, to defend our selves.*

From this Fundamentall Law of Nature, by which men are commanded to endeavour Peace, is derived this second Law; *That a man be willing, when others are so too, as farreforth, as for Peace, and defence of himselfe he shall think it necessary, to lay down this right to all things; and be contented with so much liberty against other men, as he would allow other men against himselfe.* For as long as every man holdeth this Right, of doing any thing he liketh; so long are all men in the condition of Warre. But if other men will not lay down their Right, as well as he; then there is no Reason for any one, to devest himselfe of his: For that were to expose himselfe to Prey, (which no man is bound to) rather than to dispose himselfe to Peace. This is that Law of the Gospell; *Whatsoever you require that others should do to you, that do ye to them.* And that Law of all men, *Quod tibi fieri non vis, alteri ne feceris.* . . .

The force of Words, being (as I have formerly noted) too weak to hold men to the performance of their Covenants; there are in mans nature, but two imaginable helps to strengthen it. And those are either a Feare of the consequence of breaking their word; or a Glory, or Pride in appearing not to need to breake it. This later is a Generosity too rarely found to be presumed on, especially in the pursuers of Wealth, Command, or sensuall Pleasure; which are the greatest part of Mankind. The Passion to be reckoned upon, is Fear. . . .

Chapter XV

OF OTHER LAWES OF NATURE.

From that law of Nature, by which we are obliged to transferre to another, such Rights, as being retained, hinder the peace of Mankind, there followeth a Third; which is this, *That men performe their Covenants made*: without which, Covenants are in vain, and but Empty words; and the Right of all men to all things remaining, wee are still in the condition of Warre.

And in this law of Nature, consisteth the Fountain and originall of JUSTICE. For where no Covenant hath preceded, there hath no Right been transferred, and every man has right to every thing; and consequently, no action can be Unjust. But when a Covenant is made, then to break it is *Unjust*: And the definition of INJUSTICE, is no other than *the not Performance of Covenant.* And whatsoever is not Unjust, is *Just.*

But because Covenants of mutuall trust, where there is a feare of not perfomance on either part, (as hath been said in the former Chapter,) are invalid; though the Originall of Justice be the making of Covenants; yet Injustice actually there can be none, till the cause of such feare be taken away; which while men are in the naturall condition of Warre, cannot be done. Therefore before the names of Just, and Unjust can have place, there must be some coercive Power, to compell men equally to the performance of their Covenants, by the terrour of some punishment, greater than the benefit they expect by the breach of their Covenant; and to make good that Propriety, which by mutuall Contract men acquire, in recompence of the universall Right they abandon: and such power there is none before the erection of a Common-wealth. And this is also to be gathered out of the ordinary definition of Justice in the Schooles: For they say, *that Justice is the constant Will of giving to every man his own.* And therefore where there is no *Own*, that is, no Propriety, there is no Injustice; and where there is no coerceive Power erected, that is, where there is no Commonwealth, there is no Propriety; all men having Right to all things: Therefore where there is no Common-wealth, there nothing is Unjust. So that the nature of Justice, consisteth in keeping of valid Covenants: but the Validity of Covenants begins not but with the Constitution of a Civill Power, sufficient to compell men to keep them: And then it is also that Propriety begins.

Chapter XVII

OF THE CAUSES, GENERATION, AND DEFINITION OF A COMMON-WEALTH.

The finall Cause, End, or Designe of men, (who naturally love Liberty, and Dominion over others,) in the introduction of that restraint upon themselves, (in which wee see them live in Common-wealths,) is the foresight of their own preservation, and of a more contented life thereby; that is to say, of getting themselves out from that miserable condition of Warre, which is necessarily consequent (as hath been shewn to the naturall Passions of men, when there is no visible Power to keep them in awe), and tye them by feare of punishment to the performance of their Covenants, and observation of those Lawes of Nature set down in the fourteenth and fifteenth Chapters.

For the Lawes of Nature (as *Justice*, *Equity*, *Modesty*, *Mercy*, and (in summe) *doing to others, as wee would be done to*,) of themselves, without the terrour of some Power, to cause them to be observed, are contrary to our naturall Passions, that carry us to Partiality, Pride, Revenge, and the like. And Covenants, without the Sword, are but Words, and of no strength to secure a man at all. Therefore notwithstanding the Lawes of Nature, (which every one hath then kept, when he has the will to keep them, when he can do it safely,) if there be no Power erected, or not great enough for our security; every man will, and may lawfully rely on his own strength and art, for caution against all other men. . . .

The only way to erect such a Common Power, as may be able to defend them from the invasion of Forraigners, and the injuries of one another, and thereby to secure them in such sort, as that by their owne industrie, and by the fruites of the Earth, they may nourish themselves and live contentedly; is, to conferre all their power and strength upon one Man, or upon one Assembly of men, that may reduce all their Wills, by plurality of voices, unto one Will: which is as much as to say, to appoint one Man, or Assembly of men, to beare their Person; and every one to owne, and acknowledge himselfe to be Author of whatsoever he that so beareth their Person, shall Act, or cause to be Acted, in those things which concerne the Common Peace and Safetie; and therein to submit their Wills, every one to his Will, and their Judgements, to his Judgment. This is more than Consent, or Concord; it is a reall Unitie of them all, in one and the same Person, made by Covenant of every man with every man, in such manner, as if every man should say to every man, *I Authorise and give up my Right of Governing my selfe, to this Man, or to this Assembly of men, on this condition, that thou give up thy Right to him, and Authorise all his Actions in like manner.* This done, the Multitude so united in one Person, is called a COMMON-WEALTH, in latine CIVITAS. This is the Generation of that great LEVIATHAN, or rather (to speake more reverently) of that *Mortall God*, to which wee owe under the *Immortall* God, our peace and defence. For by this Authoritie, given him by every particular man in the Common-Wealth, he hath the use of so much Power and Strength conferred on him, that by terror thereof, he is inabled to forme the wills of them all, to Peace at home, and mutuall ayd against their enemies abroad. And in him consisteth the Essence of the Common-wealth; which (to define it,) is *One Person, of whose Acts a great Multitude, by mutual Covenants one with another, have made themselves every one the Author*, to the end he *may use the strength and means of them all, as he shall think expedient, for their Peace and Common Defence.*

And he that carryeth this Person, is called SOVERAIGNE, and said to have *Soveraigne Power*; and every one besides, his SUBJECT.

The attaining to this Soveraigne Power, is by two wayes. One, by Naturall force; as when a man maketh his children, to submit themselves, and their children to his government, as being able to destroy them if they refuse; or by Warre subdueth his enemies to his will, giving them their lives on that condition. The other, is when men agree amongst themselves, to submit to some Man, or Assembly of men, voluntarily, on confidence to be protected by him against all others. This later, may be called a Politicall Common-wealth, or Commonwealth by *Institution*; and the former, a Common-wealth by *Acquisition*. And first, I shall speak of a Common-wealth by Institution.

Chapter XVIII

OF THE RIGHTS OF SOVERAIGNES BY INSTITUTION

A *Common-wealth* is said to be *Instituted*, when a *Multitude* of men do Agree, and *Covenant*, *every one*, *with every one*, that to whatsoever *Man*, or *Assembly of Men*, shall be given by the major part, the *Right* to *Present* the Person of them all, (that is to say, to be their *Representative*;) every one, as well he that *Voted for it*, as he that *Voted against it*, shall *Authorise* all the Actions and Judgements, of that Man, or Assembly of men, in the same manner, as if they were his own, to the end, to live peaceably amongst themselves, and be protected against other men.

From this Institution of a Common-wealth are derived all the *Rights*, and *Facultyes* of him, or them, on whom the Soveraigne Power is conferred by the consent of the People assembled.

First, because they Covenant, it is to be understood, they are not obliged by former Covenant to any thing repugnant hereunto. And Consequently they that have already Instituted a Common-wealth, being thereby bound by Covenant, to own the Actions, and Judgements of one, cannot lawfully make a new Covenant, amongst themselves, to be obedient to any other, in any thing whatsoever, without his permission. And therefore, they that are subjects to a Monarch, cannot without his leave cast off Monarchy, and return to the confusion of a disunited Multitude; nor transferre their Person from him that beareth it, to another Man, or other Assembly of men: for they are bound, every man to every man, to Own, and be reputed Author of all, that he that already is their Soveraigne, shall do, and judge fit to be done: so that any one man dissenting, all the rest should break their Covenant made to that man, which is injustice: and they have also every man given the Soveraignty to him that beareth their Person; and therefore if they depose him, they take from him that which is his own, and so again it is injustice. Besides, if he that attempteth to depose his Soveraign, be killed, or punished by him for such attempt, he is author of his own punishment, as being by the Institution, Author of all his Soveraign shall do: And because it is injustice for a man to do any thing, for which he may be punished by his own authority, he is also upon that title, unjust. And whereas some men have pretended for their disobedience to their Soveraign, a new Covenant, made, not with men, but with God; this also is unjust: for their is no Covenant with God, but by mediation of some body that representeth Gods Person; which none doth but Gods Lieutenant, who hath the Soveraignty under God. But this pretence of Covenant with God, is so evident a lye, even in the pretenders own consciences, that it is not onely an act of an unjust, but also of a vile, and unmanly disposition.

Secondly, Because the Right of bearing the Person of them all, is given to him they make Soveraigne, by Covenant onely of one to another, and not of him to any of them; there can happen no breach of Covenant on the part of the Soveraigne; and consequently none of his Subjects, by any pretence of forfeiture, can be freed from his Subjection. That he which is made Soveraigne maketh no Covenant with his Subjects beforehand, is manifest; because either he must make it with the whole multitude, as one party to the Covenant; or he must make a severall Covenant with every man. With the whole, as one party, it is impossible; because as yet they are not one Person: and if he make so many severall Covenants as there be men, those Covenants after he hath the Soveraignty are voyd, because what act soever can be pretended by any one of them for breach thereof, is the act both of himselfe, and of all the rest, because done in the Person, and by the Right of every one of them in particular. Besides, if any one, or more of them, pretend a breach of the Covenant made by the Soveraigne at his Institution; and others, or one other of his Subjects, or himselfe alone, pretend there was no such breach, there is in this case, no Judge to decide the controversie: it returns therefore to the Sword again; and every man recovereth the right of Protecting himselfe by his own strength, contrary to the designe they had in the Institution. It is therefore in vain to grant Soveraignty by way of precedent Covenant. The opinion that any Monarch receiveth his Power by Covenant, that is to say on Condition, proceedeth from want of understanding this easie truth, that Covenants being but words, and breath, have no force to oblige, contain, constrain, or protect any man, but what it has from the publique Sword; that is, from the untyed hands of that Man, or Assembly of men that hath the Soveraignty, and whose actions are avouched by them all, and performed by the strength of them all, in him united. But when an Assembly of men is made Soveraigne; then no man imagineth any such Covenant to have past in the Institution; for no man is so dull as to say, for example, the People of *Rome*, made a Covenant with the Romans, to hold the Soveraignty on such or such conditions; which not performed, the Romans might lawfully depose the Roman People. That men see not the reason to be alike in a Monarchy, and in a Popular Government, proceedeth from the ambition of some, that are kinder to the government of an Assembly, whereof they may hope to participate, than of Monarchy, which they despair to enjoy.

Thirdly, because the major part hath by consenting voices declared a Soveraigne; he that dissented must now consent with the rest; that is, be contented to avow all the actions he shall do, or else justly be destroyed by the rest. For if he voluntarily entered into the Congregation of them that were assembled, he sufficiently declared thereby his will (and therefore tacitely covenanted) to stand to what the major part should ordayne: and therefore if he refuse to stand thereto, or make Protestation against any of their Decrees, he does contrary to his Covenant, and therefore unjustly. And whether he be of the Congregation, or not; and whether his consent be asked, or not, he must either submit to their decrees, or be left in the condition of warre he was in before; wherein he might without injustice be destroyed by any man whatsoever.

Fourthly, because every Subject is by this Institution Author of all the Actions, and Judgments of the Soveraigne Instituted; it followes, that whatsoever he doth, it can be no injury to any of his Subjects; nor ought he to be by any of them accused of Injustice. For he that doth any thing by authority from another, doth therein no injury to him by whose authority he acteth: But by this Institution of a Common-wealth, every particular man is Author of all the Soveraigne doth; and consequently he that complaineth of injury from his Soveraigne, complaineth of that whereof he himselfe is Author; and therefore ought not to accuse any man but himselfe; no nor himselfe of injury; because to do injury to ones selfe, is impossible. It is true that they that have Soveraigne power, may commit Iniquity; but not Injustice, or Injury in the proper signification.

Fiftly, and consequently to that which was sayd last, no man that hath Soveraigne power can justly be put to death, or otherwise in any manner by his Subjects punished. For seeing every Subject is Author of the actions of his Soveraigne; he punisheth another, for the actions committed by himselfe. . . .

Chapter XXI

OF THE LIBERTY OF SUBJECTS.

. . . The Liberty of a Subject, lyeth therefore only in those things, which in regulating their actions, the Soveraign hath Praetermitted. . . .

To come now to the particulars of the true Liberty of a Subject; that is to say, what are the things, which though commanded by the Soveraign, he may neverthelesse, without Injustice, refuse to do; we are to consider, what Rights we passe away, when we make a Common-wealth; or (which is all one,) what Liberty we deny our selves, by owning all the Actions (without exception) of the Man, or Assembly we make our Soveraign. For in the act of our *Submission*, consisteth both our *Obligation*, and our *Liberty*; which must therefore be inferred by arguments taken from thence; there being no Obligation on any man, which ariseth not from some Act of his own; for all men equally, are by Nature Free. And because such arguments, must either be drawn from the expresse words, *I Authorise all his Actions*, or from the Intention of him that submitteth himself to his Power, (which Intention is to be understood by the End for which he so submitteth;) The Obligation, and Liberty of the Subject, is to be derived, either from those Words, (or others equivalent;) or else from the End of the Institution of Soveraignty; namely, the Peace of the Subjects within themselves, and their Defence against a common Enemy.

First therefore, seeing Soveraignty by Institution, is by Covenant of every one to every one; and Soveraignty by Acquisition, by Covenants of the Vanquished to the Victor, or Child to the Parent; It is manifest, that every Subject has Liberty in all those things, the right whereof cannot by Covenant be transferred. I have shewn before in the 14. Chapter, that Covenants, not to defend a mans own body, are voyd. Therefore,

If the Soveraign command a man (though justly condemned,) to kill, wound, or mayme himselfe; or not to resist those that assault him; or to abstain from the use of food, ayre, medicine, or any other thing, without which he cannot live; yet hath the man the Liberty to disobey.

If a man be interrogated by the Soveraign, or his Authority, concerning a crime done by himselfe, he is not bound (without assurance of Pardon) to confesse it; because no man (as I have shewn in the same Chapter) can be obliged by Covenant to accuse himselfe.

Again, the Consent of a Subject to Soveraign Power, is contained in these words, *I Authorise, or take upon me, all his actions*; in which there is no restriction at all, of his own former naturall Liberty: For by allowing him to *kill me*, I am not bound to kill my selfe when he commands me. 'Tis one thing to say, *Kill me, or my fellow, if you please*; another thing to say, *I will kill my selfe, or my fellow*. It followeth therefore, that

No man is bound by the words themselves, either to kill himselfe, or any other man; And consequently, that the Obligation a man may sometimes have, upon the Command of the Soveraign to execute any dangerous, or dishonourable Office, dependeth not on the Words of our Submission; but on the Intention; which is to be understood by the End thereof. When therefore our refusall to obey, frustrates the End for which the Soveraignty was ordained; then there is no Liberty to refuse: otherwise there is.

Upon this ground, a man that is commanded as a Souldier to fight against the enemy, though his Soveraign have Right enough to punish his refusall with death, may neverthelesse in many cases refuse, without Injustice; as when he substituteth a sufficient Souldier in his place: for in this case he deserteth not the service of the Common-wealth. And there is allowance to be made for naturall timorousnesse, not onely to women, (of whom no such dangerous duty is expected,) but also to men of feminine courage. When Armies fight, there is on one side, or both, a running away; yet when they do it not out of trechery, but fear, they are not esteemed to do it unjustly, but dishonourably. For the same reason, to avoyd battell, is not Injustice, but Cowardise. But he that inrowleth himselfe a Souldier, or taketh imprest mony, taketh away the excuse of a timorous nature; and is obliged, not onely to go to the battell, but also not to run from it, without his Captaines leave. And when the Defence of the Common-wealth, requireth at once the help of all that are able to bear Arms, every one is obliged; because otherwise the Institution of the Common-wealth, which they have not the purpose, or courage to preserve, was in vain.

To resist the Sword of the Common-wealth, in defence of another man, guilty, or innocent, no man hath Liberty; because such Liberty, takes away from the Soveraign, the means of Protecting us; and is therefore destructive of the very essence of Government. But in case a great many men together, have already resisted the Soveraign Power unjustly, or committed some Capitall crime, for which every one of them expecteth death, whether have they not the Liberty then to joyn together, and assist, and defend one another? Certainly they have: For they but defend their lives, which the Guilty man may as well do, as the Innocent. There was indeed injustice in the first breach of their duty; Their bearing of Arms subsequent to it, though it be to maintain what they have done, is no new unjust act. And if it be onely to defend their persons, it is not unjust at all. But the offer of pardon taketh from them, to whom it is offered, the plea of self-defence, and maketh their perseverance in assisting, or defending the rest, unlawfull.

As for other Lyberties, they depend on the Silence of the Law. In cases where the Soveraign has prescribed no rule, there the Subject hath the Liberty to do, or forbeare, according to his own discretion. And therefore such Liberty is in some places more, and in some lesse; and in some times more, in other times lesse, according as they that have the Soveraignty shall think most convenient. As for Example, there was a time, when in *England* a man might enter in to his own Land, (and dispossesse such as wrongfully possessed it,) by force. But in after-times, that Liberty of Forcible Entry, was taken away by a Statute made (by the King) in Parliament. And in some places of the world, men have the Liberty of many wives: in other places, such Liberty is not allowed.

If a Subject have a controversie with his Soveraigne, of debt, or of right of possession of lands or goods, or concerning any service required at his hands, or concerning any penalty, corporall, or pecuniary, grounded on a precedent Law; he hath the same Liberty to sue for his right, as if it were against a Subject; and before such Judges, as are appointed by the Soveraign. For seeing the Soveraign demandeth by force of a former Law, and not by vertue of his Power; he declareth thereby, that he requireth no more, then shall appear to be due by that Law. The sute therefore is not contrary to the will of the Soveraign; and consequently the Subject hath the Liberty to demand the hearing of his Cause; and sentence, according to that Law. But if he demand, or take any thing by pretence of his Power; there lyeth, in that case, no action of Law: for all that is done by him in Vertue of his Power, is done by the Authority of every Subject, and consequently, he that brings an action against the Soveraign, brings it against himselfe.

If a Monarch, or Soveraign Assembly, grant a Liberty to all, or any of his Subjects; which Grant standing, he is disabled to provide for their safety, the Grant is voyd; unlesse he directly renounce, or transferre the Soveraignty to another. For in that he might openly, (if it had been his will,) and in plain termes, have renounced, or transferred it, and did not; it is to be understood it was not his will; but that the Grant proceeded from ignorance of the repugnancy between such a Liberty and the Soveraign Power: and therefore the Soveraignty is still retayned; and consequently all those Powers, which are necessary to the exercising thereof; such as are the Power of Warre, and Peace, of Judicature, of appointing Officers, and Councellours, of levying Mony, and the rest named in the 18th Chapter.

The Obligation of Subjects to the Soveraign, is understood to last as long, and no longer, than the power lasteth, by which he is able to protect them. For the right men have by Nature to protect themselves, when none else can protect them, can by no Covenant be relinquished. The Soveraignty is the Soule of the Common-wealth; which once departed from the Body, the members doe no more receive their motion from it. The end of Obedience is Protection; which, wheresoever a man seeth it, either in his own, or in anothers sword, Nature applyeth his obedience to it, and his endeavour to maintaine it. And though Soveraignty, in the intention of them that make it, be immortall; yet is it in its own nature, not only subject to violent death, by forreign war; but also through the ignorance, and passions of men, it hath in it, from the very institution, many seeds of a naturall mortality, by Intestine Discord.

If a Subject be taken prisoner in war; or his person, or his means of life be within the Guards of the enemy, and hath his life and corporall Libertie given him, on condition to be Subject to the Victor, he hath Libertie to accept the condition; and having accepted it, is the subject of him that took him; because he had no other way to preserve himself. The case is the same, if he be deteined on the same termes, in a forreign country. But if a man be held in prison, or bonds, or is not trusted with the libertie of his bodie; he cannot be understood to be bound by Covenant to subjection; and therefore may, if he can, make his escape by any means whatsoever.

If a Monarch shall relinquish the Soveraignty, both for himself, and his heires; His Subjects returne to the absolute Libertie of Nature; because, though Nature may declare who are his Sons, and who are the nerest of his Kin; yet it dependeth on his own will, (as hath been said in the precedent chapter,) who shall be his Heyr. If therefore he will have no Heyre, there is no Soveraignty, nor Subjection. The case is the same, if he dye without known Kindred, and without declaration of his Heyre. For then there can no Heire be known, and consequently no Subjection be due.

If the Soveraign Banish his Subject; during the Banishment, he is not Subject. But he that is sent on a message, or hath leave to travell, is still Subject; but it is, by Contract between Soveraigns, not by vertue of the covenant of Subjection. For whosoever entreth into anothers dominion, is Subject to all the Laws thereof; unlesse he have a privilege by the amity of the Soveraigns, or by speciall licence.

If a Monarch subdued by war, render himself Subject to the Victor; his Subjects are delivered from their former obligation, and become obliged to the Victor. But if he be held prisoner, or have not the liberty of his own Body; he is not understood to have given away the Right of Soveraigntie; and therefore his Subjects are obliged to yield obedience to the Magistrates formerly placed, governing not in their own name, but in his. For, his Right remaining, the question is only of the Administration; that is to say, of the Magistrates and Officers; which, if he have not means to name, he is supposed to approve those, which he himself had formerly appointed.

Chapter XXV

OF COUNSELL

. . . COMMAND is, where a man saith, *Doe this*, or *Doe not this*, without expecting other reason than the Will of him that sayes it. From this it followeth manifestly, that he that Commandeth, pretendeth thereby his own Benefit: For the reason of his Command is his own Will onely, and the proper object of every mans Will, is some Good to himselfe.

COUNSELL, is where a man saith, *Doe*, or *Doe not this*, and deduceth his reasons from the benefit that arriveth by it to him to whom he saith it. And from this it is evident, that he that giveth Counsell, pretendeth onely (whatsoever he intendeth) the good of him, to whom he giveth it.

Therefore between Counsell and Command, one great difference is, that Command is directed to a mans own benefit; and Counsell to the benefit of another man. And from this ariseth another difference, that a man may be obliged to do what he is Commanded; as when he hath covenanted to obey: But he cannot be obliged to do as he is Counselled, because the hurt of not following it, is his own; or if he should covenant to follow it, then is the Counsell turned into the nature of a Command. A third difference between them is, that no man can pretend a right to be of another mans Counsell; because he is not to pretend benefit by it to himselfe: but to demand right to Counsell another, argues a will to know his designes, or to gain some other Good to himselfe; which (as I said before) is of every mans will the proper object. . . .

Chapter XXVI

OF CIVIL LAWES

4. The Law of Nature, and the Civill Law, contain each other, and are of equall extent. For the Lawes of Nature, which consist in Equity, Justice, Gratitude, and other morall Vertues on these depending, in the condition of meer Nature (as I have said before in the end of the 15th Cahpter,) are not properly Lawes, but qualities that dispose men to peace, and to obedience. When a Common-wealth is once settled, then are they actually Lawes, and not before; as being then the commands of the Common-wealth; and therefore also Civill Lawes: For it is the Soveraign Power that obliges men to obey them. For in the differences of private men, to declare, what is Equity, what is Justice, and what is morall Vertue, and to make them binding, there is need of the Ordinances of Soveraign Power, and Punishments to be ordained for such as shall break them; which Ordinances are therefore part of the Civill Law. The Law of Nature therefore is a part of the Civill Law in all Common-wealths of the world. Reciprocally also, the Civill Law is a part of the Dictates of Nature. For Justice, that is to say, Performance of Covenant, and giving to every man his own, is a Dictate of the Law of Nature. But every subject in a Common-wealth, hath covenanted to obey the Civill Law, (either one with another, as when they assemble to make a common Representative, or with the Representative it selfe one by one, when subdued by the Sword

they promise obedience, that they may receive life;) And therefore Obedience to the Civill Law is part also of the Law of Nature. Civill, and Naturall Law are not different kinds, but different parts of Law; whereof one part being written, is called Civill, the other unwritten, Naturall. But the Right of Nature, that is, the naturall Liberty of man, may by the Civill Law be abridged, and restrained: nay, the end of making Lawes, is no other, but such Restraint; without the which there cannot possibly be any Peace. And Law was brought into the world for nothing else, but to limit the naturall liberty of particular men, is such manner, as they might not hurt, but assist one another, and joyn together against a common Enemy. . . .

7. That Law can never be against Reason, Our Lawyers are agreed; and that not the Letter, (that is, every construction of it,) but that which is according to the Intention of the Legislator, is the Law. And it is true: but the doubt is, of whose Reason it is, that shall be received for Law. It is not meant of any private Reason; for then there would be as much contradiction in the Lawes, as there is in the Schooles; nor yet, (as Sr. *Ed. Coke* makes it,) an *Artificiall perfection of Reason, gotten by long study, observation, and experience,* (as his was.) For it is possible long study may encrease, and confirm erroneous Sentences: and where men build on false grounds, the more they build, the greater is the ruine: and of those that study, and observe with equall time, and diligence, the reasons and resolutions are, and must remain discordant: and therefore it is not that *Juris prudentia*, or wisedome of subordinate Judges; but the Reason of this our Artificiall Man the Common-wealth, and his Command, that maketh Law; And the Common-wealth being in their Representative but one Person, there cannot easily arise any contradiction in the Lawes; and when there doth, the same Reason is able, by interpretation, or alteration, to take it away. In all Courts of Justice, the Soveraign (which is the Person of the Commonwealth,) is he that Judgeth: The subordinate Judge, ought to have regard to the reason, which moved his Soveraign to make such Law, that his Sentence may be according thereunto; which then is his Soveraigns Sentence; otherwise it is his own, and an unjust one.

8. From this, that the Law is a Command, and a Command consisteth in declaration, or manifestation of the will of him that commandeth, by voyce, writing, or some other sufficient argument of the same, we may understand, that the Command of the Common-wealth, is Law onely to those, that have means to take notice of it. . . .

The Law of Nature excepted, it belongeth to the essence of all other Lawes, to be made known, to every man that shall be obliged to obey them, either by word, or writing, or some other act, known to proceed from the Soveraign Authority. For the will of another, cannot be understood, but by his own word, or act, or by conjecture taken from his scope and purpose; which in the person of the Common-wealth, is to be supposed alwaies consonant to Equity and Reason. . . .

All Laws, written, and unwritten, have need of Interpretation. . . .

The Interpretation of the Law of Nature, is the Sentence of the Judge constituted by the Soveraign Authority, to heare and determine such controversies, as depend thereon; and consisteth in the application of the Law to the present case. For in the act of Judicature, the Judge doth no more but consider, whither the demand of the party, be consonant to naturall reason, and Equity; and the Sentence he giveth is therefore the Interpretation of the Law of Nature which Interpretation is Authentique; not because it is his private Sentence; but because he giveth it by Authority of the Soveraign, whereby it becomes the Soveraigns Sentence; which is Law for that time, to the parties pleading.

But because there is no Judge Subordinate, nor Soveraign, but may erre in a Judgement of Equity; if afterward in another like case he find it more consonant to Equity to give a contrary Sentence, he is obliged to doe it. No mans error becomes his own Law; nor obliges him to persist in it. Neither (for the same reason) becomes it a Law to other Judges, though sworn to follow it. For though a wrong Sentence given by authority of the Soveraign, if he know and allow it, in such Lawes as are mutable, be a constitution of a new Law, in cases, in which every little circumstance is the same; yet in Lawes immutable, such as are the Lawes of Nature, they are no Lawes to the same, or other Judges, in the like cases for ever after. Princes succeed one another; and one Judge passeth, another commeth; nay, Heaven and Earth shall passe; but not one title of the Law of Nature shall passe; for it is the Eternall Law of God. Therefore all the Sentences of precedent Judges that have ever been, cannot all together make a Law contrary to naturall Equity: Nor any Examples of former Judges, can warrant an unreasonable Sentence, or discharge the present Judge of the trouble of studying what is Equity (in the case he is to Judge,) from the principles of his own naturall reason. For example sake, 'Tis against the Law of Nature, *To punish the Innocent*; and Innocent is he that acquitteth himselfe Judicially, and is acknowledged for Innocent by the Judge. Put the case now, that a man is accused of a capitall crime, and seeing the power and malice of some enemy, and the frequent corruption and partiality of Judges, runneth away for feare of the event, and afterwards is taken, and brought to a legall triall, and maketh it sufficiently appear, he was not guilty of the crime, and being thereof acquitted, is neverthelesse condemned to lose his goods; this is a manifest condemnation of the Innocent. I say therefore, that there is no place in the world, where this can be an interpretation of a Law of Nature, or be made a Law of Nature, or be made a Law by the Sentences of precedent Judges, that had done the same. . . .

What if the Leviathan, which Hobbes terms "the supreme Pastor" and endows with the power of regulating worship, forbids belief in Christ? Hobbes believes that such a command would of no effect, for belief and unbelief are not changed by commands. But he admits that the Leviathan would be entitled to command external profession of unbelief in Christ; since in external things men are subject to the power of the "Mortall God," they must obey it without compunction. Indeed, he is at pains to insist on the individual person's lack of guilt in such an act, affirming that "whatsoever a Subject . . . is compelled to in obedience to his Soveraign, and doth it not in order to his own mind, . . . that action is not his, but his Soveraigns; nor is it he that in this case denyeth Christ before men, but his Governour, and the law of his countrey."

Hobbes does admit that if a man receives contrary commands from God and the Leviathan, he ought to obey God's command if he can know with certainty what it is. But this proves to be a purely theoretical concession, for he maintains that in fact it is impossible to know whether a command is from God or not. What we do know with certainty is that the laws of nature are divine laws, and the chief of these is that men must obey the Leviathan whom they have created by mutual pact. Who can be so bold as to say that his judgment is superior to that of the Leviathan: "And in case a Subject be forbidden by the Civill Soveraign to profess some of those his opinions, upon what just ground can he disobey? Christian Kings may erre in deducting a Consequence, but who shall be Judge? Shall a private man Judge, when the question is of his own obedience? or shall any man Judg but he that is appointed thereto by the Church, that is by the Civill Soveraign that representeth it? . . . There can therefore be no contradiction between the Laws of God, and the Laws of a Christian Common-wealth."

There can be no contradiction between the laws of God and those of the Leviathan because the laws of the latter are presumptively good. The laws of man are not measured by those of God; rather those of God are measured by those of man. The Leviathan judges, but is not judged.

Patterson, *Jurisprudence* 83 (1953) states that Hobbes comes close to the imperative conception of law developed later by Austin; but he feels that Hobbes's command theory is a qualified one in that "the sovereign's right to command rests upon the social contract which is presupposed in the establishment of a sovereign." This much is undeniably true, but it does not seem to be the main reason why Hobbes is not to be considered squarely within the later imperative school. The principal reason why Hobbes does not fit into this school is not that he is not imperative enough but rather that he is too imperative. He carries the notion of law as the command of the sovereign much further than Austin because for him it includes morality too. The doctrine of the separation of law and morals which is characteristic of the imperative school proper has no place in Hobbes's theory. Law and morality are for him not separate; indeed they are not even distinct, but are one and the same. This identity does not result from the fact that the natural law, the source of morality, is a norm to which civil law conforms, but rather from the fact that the State determines both what is law and what is morality. The command of the Leviathan, backed by its coercive power, is law; it is also morality, because the State legislates for all human action. The Leviathan, in fine, is both Church and State.

For Hobbes, then, obligation rests ultimately upon the Leviathan's naked power, and he was indulging in no fanciful metaphor when he wrote in *A Dialogue of Common Laws* that phrase which is both memorable and terrifying: "in matter of government when nothing else is turned up, clubs are trumps." Stewart, "Hobbes among the Critics" (1958) 73 *Political Science Quarterly* 547, outlines the critical disagreement over the nature of legal obligation in Hobbes. Warrender, *The Political Philosophy of Hobbes* (1957), considers Hobbes as an exponent of a reason-theory of law, whereas Oakeshott, in his Introduction to *Leviathan* (1946), sees him as an upholder of a will-theory of law. Macpherson, *The Political Theory of Possessive Individualism* (1962) argues that an all-powerful sovereign is a necessary consequence of Hobbes' recognition that his society was a possessive market society.

The Austinian conception of sovereignty has its roots in Hobbes, but Austin introduces modifications which somewhat tame the absolutism of the Leviathan. The effect of the Austinian gloss on Hobbes is to turn Hobbes's philosophical principle that sovereign power is illimitable into a purely legal principle; for Austin it is only in the eyes of the law that the sovereign can be said to be unlimited in his power. Austin even takes this to be Hobbes's own meaning: "It is affirmed by Hobbes," he says, "that 'no law can be unjust'. . . . His meaning is obviously this: that 'no *positive* law is *legally* unjust.'" That this is Hobbes' view will not stand examination, but it is indubitably Austin's own view and it undeniably softens the impact of his theory of sovereignty. It goes no further than to say that every sovereign is legally despotic, a statement which Austin regards as a mere logical deduction from what is contained in his conception of positive law.

Further comment on the relationship between Austin and Hobbes may be given in Austin's own words:

"The capital errors in Hobbes's political treatises, are the following. – 1. He inculcates too absolutely the religious obligation of obedience to present or established government. He makes not the requisite allowance for the anomalous and excepted cases wherein disobedience is counselled by that very principle of utility which indicates the duty of submission. Writing in a season of civil discord, or writing in apprehension of its approach, he naturally fixed his attention to the glaring mischiefs of resistance, and scarcely adverted to the mischiefs which obedience occasionally engenders. And although his integrity was not less remarkable than the gigantic strength of his understanding, we may presume that his extreme timidity somewhat corrupted his judgment, and inclined him to insist unduly upon the evils of rebellion and strife. – 2. Instead of directly deriving the existence of political government, from a perception by the bulk of the governed of its great and obvious expediency, he ascribes the origin of sovereignty, and of independent political society, to a fictitious agreement or covenant."

Jeremy Bentham, 1748-1832
A man of independent means, able to devote his life to philosophy and law reform.

THE PRINCIPLES OF MORALS AND LEGISLATION (1789)

Chapter I

OF THE PRINCIPLE OF UTILITY

1. Nature has placed mankind under the governance of two sovereign masters, *pain* and *pleasure*. It is for them alone to point out what we ought to do, as well as to determine what we shall do. On the one hand the standard of right and wrong, on the other the chain of causes and effects, are fastened to their throne. They govern us in all we do, in all we say, in all we think: every effort we can make to throw off our subjection, will serve but to demonstrate and confirm it. In words a man may pretend to abjure their empire: but in reality he will remain subject to it all the while. The *principle of utility* recognises this subjection, and assumes it for the foundation of that system, the object of which is to rear the fabric of felicity by the hands of reason and of law. Systems which attempt to question it, deal in sounds instead of sense, in caprice instead of reason, in darkness instead of light. . . .

3. By utility is meant that property in any object, whereby it tends to produce benefit, advantage, pleasure, good, or happiness (all this in the present case comes to the same thing) or (what comes again to the same thing) to prevent the happening of mischief, pain, evil or unhappiness to the party whose interest is considered: if that party be the community in general, then the happiness of the community: if a particular individual, then the happiness of that individual.

Chapter III

OF THE FOUR SANCTIONS OR SOURCES OF PAIN AND PLEASURE

1. It has shown that the happiness of the individuals, of whom a community is composed, that is, their pleasures and their security, is the end and the sole end which the legislator ought to have in view: the sole standard, in conformity to which each individual ought, as far as depends upon the legislator, to be *made* to fashion his behaviour. But whether it be this or any thing else that is to be *done*, there is nothing by which a man can ultimately be *made* to do it, but either pain or pleasure. Having taken a general view of these two grand objects (*viz.* pleasure, and what comes to the same thing, immunity from pain) in the character of *final* causes; it will be necessary to take a view of pleasure and pain itself, in the character of efficient causes or means.

2. There are four distinguishable sources from which pleasure and pain are in use to flow: considered separately, they may be termed the *physical*, the *political*, the *moral*, and the *religious*: and inasmuch as the pleasures and pains belonging to each of them are capable of giving a binding force to any law or rule of conduct, they may all of them be termed *sanctions*. . . .

Chapter IV

VALUE OF A LOT OF PLEASURE OR PAIN, HOW TO BE MEASURED

1. Pleasures then, and the avoidance of pains are the *ends* which the legislator has in view: it behoves him therefore to understand their *value*. Pleasures and pains are the *instruments* he has to work with: it behoves him therefore to understand their force, which is again, in another point of view, their value.

2. To a person considered *by himself*, the value of a pleasure or pain considered *by itself*, will be greater or less, according to the four following circumstances:

(1) Its *intensity*.
(2) Its *duration*.
(3) Its *certainty* or *uncertainty*.
(4) Its *propinquity* or *remoteness*.

3. These are the circumstances which are to be considered in estimating a pleasure or a pain considered each of them by itself. But when the value of any pleasure or pain is considered for the purpose of estimating the tendency of any *act* by which it is produced, there are two other circumstances to be taken into the account; these are,

(5) Its *fecundity*, or the chance it has of being followed by sensations of the *same* kind: that is, pleasures, if it be pleasure: pains, if it be pain.

(6) Its *purity*, or the chance it has of *not* being followed by sensations of the *opposite* kind: that is, pains, if it be pleasure: pleasures, if it be pain.

These two last, however, are in strictness scarcely to be deemed properties of the pleasure or pain itself; they are not, therefore, in strictness to be taken into the account of the value of that pleasure or that pain. They are in strictness to be deemed properties only of the act, or other event, by which such pleasure or pain has been produced; and accordingly are only to be taken into the account of the tendency of such act or such event.

4. To a *number* of persons, with reference to each of whom the value of a pleasure or a pain is considered, it will be greater or less, according to seven circumstances: to wit, the six preceding ones; *viz.*

(1) Its *intensity*.
(2) Its *duration*.
(3) Its *certainty* or *uncertainty*.
(4) Its *propinquity* or *remoteness*.
(5) Its *fecundity*.
(6) Its *purity*.

And one other; to wit:

(7) Its *extent*; that is, the number of persons to whom it *extends*; or (in other words) who are affected by it.

5. To take an exact account, then, of the general tendency of any act, by which the interests of a community are affected, proceed as follows. Begin with any one person of those whose interests seem most immediately to be affected by it: and take an account,

(1) Of the value of each distinguishable *pleasure* which appears to be produced by it in the *first* instance.

(2) Of the value of each *pain* which appears to be produced by it in the *first* instance.

(3) Of the value of each pleasure which appears to be produced by it *after* the first. This constitutes the *fecundity* of the first *pleasure* and the impurity of the first *pain*.

(4) Of the value of each *pain* which appears to be produced by it after the first. This constitutes the *fecundity* of the first *pain*, and the *impurity* of the first pleasure.

(5) Sum up all the values of all the *pleasures* on the one side, and those of all the pains on the other. The balance, if it be on the side of pleasure, will give the *good* tendency of the act upon the whole, with respect to the interests of that *individual* person; if on the side of pain, the *bad* tendency of it upon the whole.

(6) Take an account of the *number* of persons whose interests appear to be concerned; and repeat the above process with respect to each. *Sum up* the numbers expressive of the degrees of *good* tendency, which the act has, with respect to each individual, in regard to whom the tendency of it is *good* upon the whole: do this again with respect to each individual, in regard to whom the tendency of it is *bad* upon the whole. Take the *balance*; which, if on the side of *pleasure*, will give the general *good tendency* of the act, with respect to the total number or community of individuals concerned; if on the side of pain, the general *evil tendency*, with respect to the same community.

6. It is not to be expected that this process should be strictly pursued previously to every moral judgment, or to every legislative or judicial operation. It may, however, be always kept in view: and as near as the process actually pursued on these occasions approaches to it, so near will such process approach to the character of an exact one. . . .

Chapter XVII

1. LIMITS BETWEEN PRIVATE ETHICS AND THE ART OF LEGISLATION.

6. As to ethics in general, a man's happiness will depend, in the first place, upon such parts of his behaviour as none but himself are interested in; in the next place, upon such parts of it as may affect the happiness of those about him. In as far as his happiness depends upon the first-mentioned part of his behaviour, it is said to depend upon his *duty to himself*. Ethics, then, in as far as it is the art of directing a man's actions in this respect, may be termed the art of discharging one's duty to one's self: and the quality which a man manifests by the discharge of this branch of duty (if duty it is to be called), is that of *prudence*. In as far as his happiness, and that of any other person or persons whose interests are considered, depends upon such parts of his behaviour as may affect the interests of those about him, it may be said to depend upon his *duty to others*; or, to use a phrase now somewhat antiquated, his *duty to his neighbour*. Ethics, then, in as far as it is the art of directing a man's actions in this respect, may be termed the art of discharging one's duty to one's neighbour. Now the happiness of one's neighbour may be consulted in two ways: 1. In a negative way, by forbearing to diminish it. 2. In a positive way, by studying to increase it. A man's duty to his neighbour is accordingly partly negative and partly positive: to discharge the negative branch of it, is *probity*: to discharge the positive branch, *beneficence*.

7. It may here be asked, how it is that upon the principle of private ethics, legislation and religion out of the question, a man's happiness depends upon such parts of his conduct as affect, immediately at least, the happiness of no one but himself: this is as much as to ask, What motives (independent of such as legislation and religion may chance to furnish) can one man have to consult the happiness of another? by what motives, or (which comes to the same thing) by what obligations, can he be bound to obey the dictates of *probity* and *bene-*

ficence? In answer to this, it cannot but be admitted, that the only interests which a man at all times and upon all occasions is sure to find adequate motives for consulting, are his own. Notwithstanding this, there are no occasions in which a man has not some motives for consulting the happiness of other men. In the first place, he has, on all occasions, the purely social motive of sympathy or benevolence: in the next place, he has, on most occasions, the semi-social motives of love of amity and love of reputation. The motive of sympathy will act upon him with more or less effect, according to the *bias* of his sensibility: the two other motives, according to a variety of circumstances, principally according to the strength of his intellectual powers, the firmness and steadiness of his mind, the quantum of his moral sensibility, and the characters of the people he has to deal with.

8. Now private ethics has happiness for its end: and legislation can have no other. Private ethics concerns every member; that is, the happiness and the actions of every member of any community that can be proposed: and legislation can concern no more. Thus far, then, private ethics and the art of legislation go hand in hand. The end they have, or ought to have, in view, is of the same nature. The persons whose happiness they ought to have in view, as also the persons whose conduct they ought to be occupied in directing, are precisely the same. The very acts they ought to be conversant about, are even in a *great measure* the same. Where, then, lies the difference? In that the acts which they ought to be conversant about, though in a great measure, are not *perfectly and throughout* the same. There is no case in which a private man ought not to direct his own conduct to the production of his own happiness, and of that of his fellow-creatures: but there are cases in which the legislator ought not (in a direct way at least, and by means of punishment applied immediately to particular individual acts) to attempt to direct the conduct of the several other members of the community. Every act which promises to be beneficial upon the whole to the community (himself included), each individual ought to perform of himself: but it is not every such act that the legislator ought to compel him to perform. Every act which promises to be pernicious upon the whole to the community (himself included), each individual ought to abstain from of himself; but it is not every such act that the legislator ought to compel him to abstain from.

9. Where, then, is the line to be drawn? – We shall not have far to seek for it. The business is to give an idea of the cases in which ethics ought, and in which legislation ought not (in a direct manner at least) to interfere. If legislation interferes in a direct manner, it must be by punishment. Now the cases in which punishment, meaning the punishment of the political sanction, ought not to be inflicted, have been already stated. If then, there be any of these cases in which, although legislation ought not, private ethics does or ought to interfere, these cases will serve to point out the limits between the two arts or branches of science. These cases, it may be remembered, are of four sorts: (1) Where punishment would be groundless. (2) Where it would be inefficacious. (3) Where it would be unprofitable. (4) Where it would be needless. Let us look over all these cases, and see whether in any of them there is room for the interference of private ethics, at the same time that there is none for the direct interference of legislation.

10. (1) First, then, as to the cases where punishment would be *groundless*. In these cases it is evident, that the restrictive interference of ethics would be groundless too. It is because, upon the whole, there is no evil in the act, that legislation ought not to endeavour to prevent it. No more, for the same reason, ought private ethics.

11. (2) As to the cases in which punishment would be *inefficacious*. These, we may observe, may be divided into two sets or classes. The first do not depend at all upon the nature of the act: they turn only upon a defect in the timing of the punishment. The punishment in question is no more than what, for any thing that appears, ought to have been applied to the act in question. It ought, however, to have been applied at a different time; viz. not till after it had been properly denounced. These are the cases of an *ex-post-facto* law; of a judicial sentence beyond the law; and of a law not sufficiently promulgated. The acts here in question then might, for any thing that appears, come properly under the department even of coercive legislation: of course do they under that of private ethics. As to the other set of cases, in which punishment would be inefficacious; neither do these depend upon the nature of the act, that is, of the *sort* of act: they turn only upon some extraneous *circumstances*, with which an act of *any* sort may chance to be accompanied. These, however, are of such a nature as not only to exclude the application of legal punishment, but in general to leave little room for the influence of private ethics. These are the cases where the will could not be deterred from any act, even by the extraordinary force of artificial punishment; as in the cases of extreme infancy, insanity, and perfect intoxication: of course, therefore, it could not by such slender and precarious force as could be applied by private ethics. The case is in this respect the same, under the circumstances of unintentionality with respect to the event of the action, unconsciousness with regard to the circumstances, and mis-supposal with regard to the existence of circumstances which have not existed; as also where the force, even of extraordinary punishment, is rendered inoperative by the superior force of a physical danger or threatened mischief. It is evident, that in these cases, if the thunders of the law prove impotent, the whispers of simple morality can have but little influence.

12. (3) As to the cases where punishment would be *unprofitable*. These are the cases which constitute the great field for the exclusive interference of private ethics. When a punishment is unprofitable, or in other words too expensive, it is because the evil of the punishment exceeds that of the offence. Now the evil of the punishment, we may remember, is distinguishable into four branches: (1) The evil or coercion, including constraint or restraint, according as the act commanded is of the positive kind or the negative. (2) The evil of apprehension. (3) The evil of sufferance. (4) The derivative evils resulting to persons in *connection* with those by whom the three above-mentioned original evils are sustained. Now with respect to those original evils, the persons who lie exposed to them may be two very different sets of persons. In the first place, persons who may have actually committed, or been prompted to commit, the acts really meant to be prohibited. In the next place, persons who may have performed, or been prompted to perform, such other acts as they fear may be in danger of being involved in the punishment designed only for the former. But of these two sets of acts, it is the former only that are pernicious: it is, therefore, the former only that it can be the business of private ethics to endeavour to prevent. The latter being by the supposition not mischievous, to prevent them is what it can no more be the business of ethics to endeavour at, than of legislation. It remains to show how it may happen, that there should be acts really pernicious, which, although they may very properly come under the censure of private ethics, may yet be no fit objects for the legislator to controul.

13. Punishment, then, as applied to delinquency, may be unprofitable in both or either of two ways: (1) By the expense it would amount to even supposing the application of it to be confined altogether to delinquency: (2) By

the danger there may be of its involving the innocent in the fate designed only for the guilty. First, then, with regard to the cases in which the expense of the punishment, as applied to the guilty, would outweigh the profit to be made by it. These cases, it is evident, depend upon a certain proportion between the evil of punishment and the evil of the offence. Now were the offence of such a nature, that a punishment which, in point of *magnitude*, should but just exceed the profit of it, would be sufficient to prevent it, it might be rather difficult perhaps to find an instance in which such punishment would clearly appear to be unprofitable. But the fact is, there are many cases in which a punishment, in order to have any chance of being efficacious, must, in point of magnitude, be raised a great deal above that level. Thus it is wherever the danger of detection is, or (what comes to the same thing,) is likely to appear to be, so small, as to make the punishment appear in a high degree uncertain. In this case it is necessary, as has been shown, if punishment be at all applied, to raise it in point of magnitude as much as it falls short in point of certainty. It is evident, however, that all this can be but guess-work: and that the effect of such a proportion will be rendered precarious, by a variety of circumstances: by the want of sufficient promulgation on the part of the law: by the particular circumstances of the temptation: and by the circumstances influencing the sensibility of the several individuals who are exposed to it. Let the *seducing* motives be strong, the offence then will at any rate be frequently committed. Now and then indeed, owing to a coincidence of circumstances more or less extraordinary, it will be detected and by that means punished. But for the purpose of example, which is the principal one, an act of punishment considered in itself, is of no use: what use it can be of, depends altogether upon the expectation it raises of similar punishment in future cases of similar delinquency. But this future punishment, it is evident, must always depend upon detection. If then the want of detection is such as must in general (especially to eyes fascinated by the force of the seducing motives) appear too improbable to be reckoned upon, the punishment, though it should be inflicted, may come to be of no use. Here, then, will be two opposite evils running on at the same time, yet neither of them reducing the quantum of the other: the evil of the disease and the evil of the painful and inefficacious remedy. It seems to be partly owing to some such considerations, that fornication for example, or the illicit commerce between the sexes, has commonly either gone altogether unpunished, or been punished in a degree inferior to that in which, on other accounts, legislators might have been disposed to punish it.

14. Second, with regard to the cases in which political punishment, as applied to delinquency, may be unprofitable, in virtue of the danger there may be of its involving the innocent in the fate designed only for the guilty. Whence should this danger, then, arise? From the difficulty there may be of fixing the idea of the guilty action; that is, of subjecting it to such a definition as shall be clear and precise enough to guard effectually against misapplication. This difficulty may arise from either of two sources: the one permanent, to wit, the nature of the *actions* themselves: the other occasional, I mean the qualities of the *men* who may have to deal with those actions in the way of government. In as far as it arises from the latter of these sources, it may depend partly upon the use which the *legislator* may be *able* to make of language; partly upon the use which, according to the apprehension of the legislator, the *judge* may be *disposed* to make of it. As far as legislation is concerned, it will depend upon the degree of perfection to which the arts of language may have been carried; in the first place, in the nation in general; in the next place, by the *legislator* in particular. It is to a sense of this difficulty, as it should seem, that we may attribute the caution with

which most legislators have abstained from subjecting to censure, on the part of the law, such actions as come under the notion of rudeness, for example, or treachery, or ingratitude. The attempt to bring acts of so vague and questionable a nature under the control of law, will argue either a very immature age, in which the difficulties which give birth to that danger are not descried; or a very enlightened age, in which they are overcome.

15. For the sake of obtaining the clearer idea of the limits between the art of legislation and private ethics, it may now be time to call to mind the distinctions above established with regard to ethics in general. The degree in which private ethics stands in need of the assistance of legislation, is different in the three branches of duty above distinguished. Of the rules of moral duty, those which seem to stand least in need of the assistance of legislation, are the rules of *prudence.* It can only be through some defect on the part of understanding, if a man be ever deficient in point of duty to himself. If he does wrong, there is nothing else that it can be owing to, but either some *inadvertence* or some *missupposal,* with regard to the circumstances on which his happiness depends. It is a standing topic of complaint, that a man knows too little of himself. Be it so: but is it so certain that the legislator must know more? It is plain, that of individuals the legislator can know nothing: concerning those points of conduct which depend upon the particular circumstances of each individual, it is plain, therefore, that he can determine nothing to advantage. It is only with respect to those broad lines of conduct in which all persons, or very large and permanent descriptions of persons, may be in a way to engage, that he can have any pretence for interfering; and even here the propriety of his interference will, in most instances, lie very open to dispute. At any rate, he must never expect to produce a perfect compliance by the mere force of the sanction of which he is himself the author. All he can hope to do, is to increase the efficacy of private ethics, by giving strength and direction to the influence of the moral sanction. With what chance of success, for example, would a legislator go about to extirpate drunkenness and fornication, by dint of legal punishment? Not all the tortures which ingenuity could invent would compass it: and, before he had made any progress worth regarding, such a mass of evil would be produced by the punishment, as would exceed, a thousand-fold, the utmost possible mischief of the offence. The great difficulty would be in the procuring evidence; an object which could not be attempted, with any probability of success, without spreading dismay through every family, tearing the bonds of sympathy asunder, and rooting out the influence of all the social motives. All that he can do, then, against offences of this nature, with any prospect of advantage, in the way of direct legislation, is to subject them, in cases of notoriety, to a slight censure, so as thereby to cover them with a slight shade of artificial disrepute.

16. It may be observed, that with regard to this branch of duty, legislators have, in general, been disposed to carry their interference full as far as is expedient. The great difficulty here is, to persuade them to confine themselves within bounds. A thousand little passions and prejudices have led them to narrow the liberty of the subject in this line, in cases in which the punishment is either attended with no profit at all, or with none that will make up for the expense.

17. The mischief of this sort of interference is more particularly conspicuous in the article of religion. The reasoning, in this case, is of the following stamp. There are certain errors, in matters of belief, to which all mankind are prone: and for these errors in judgment, it is the determination of a Being of infinite benevolence, to punish them with an infinity of torments. But from these errors the legislator himself is necessarily free: for the men who happen to be at hand

for him to consult with, being men perfectly enlightened, unfettered, and unbiassed, have such advantages over all the rest of the world, that when they sit down to inquire out the truth relative to points so plain and so familiar as those in question, they cannot fail to find it. This being the case, when the sovereign sees his people ready to plunge headlong into an abyss of fire, shall he not stretch out a hand to save them? Such, for example, seems to have been the train of reasoning, and such the motives, which led Lewis the XIVth into those coercive measures which he took for the conversion of heretics, and the confirmation of true believers. The ground-work, pure sympathy and loving-kindness: the superstructure, all the miseries which the most determined malevolence could have devised. But of this more fully in another place.

18. The rules of *probity* are those, which in point of expediency stand most in need of assistance on the part of the legislator, and in which, in point of fact, his interference has been most extensive. There are few cases in which it *would* be expedient to punish a man for hurting *himself*: but there are few cases, if any, in which it would *not* be expedient to punish a man for injuring his neighbour. With regard to that branch of probity which is opposed to offences against property, private ethics depends, in a manner, for its very existence upon legislation. Legislation must first determine what things are to be regarded as each man's property, before the general rules of ethics, on this head, can have any particular application. The case is the same with regard to offences against the state. Without legislation there would be no such thing as a *state*: no particular persons invested with powers to be exercised for the benefit of the rest. It is plain, therefore, that in this branch the interference of the legislator cannot any where be dispensed with. We must first know what are the dictates of legislation, before we can know what are the dictates of private ethics.

19. As to the rules of beneficence, these, as far as concerns matters of detail, must necessarily be abandoned in great measure to the jurisdiction of private ethics. In many cases the beneficial quality of the act depends essentially upon the disposition of the agent; that is, upon the motives by which he appears to have been prompted to perform it: upon their belonging to the head of sympathy, love of amity, or love of reputation; and not to any head of self-regarding motives, brought into play by the force of political constraint: in a word, upon their being such as denominate his conduct *free* and *voluntary*, according to one of the many senses given to those ambiguous expressions. The limits of the law on this head seem, however, to be capable of being extended a good deal farther than they seem ever to have been extended hitherto. In particular, in cases where the person is in danger, why should it not be made the duty of every man to save another from mischief, when it can be done without prejudicing himself, as well as to abstain from bringing it on him? This accordingly, is the idea pursued in the body of the work. [A woman's head-dress catches fire: water is at hand: a man, instead of assisting to quench the fire, looks on, and laughs at it. A drunken man, falling with his face downwards into a puddle, is in danger of suffocation: lifting his head a little on the one side would save him: another man sees this, and lets him lie. A quantity of gunpowder lies scattered about a room: a man is going into it with a lighted candle: another, knowing this, lets him go in without warning. Who is there that in any of these cases would think punishment misapplied?]

20. To conclude this section, let us recapitulate and bring to a point the difference between private ethics, considered as an art or science, on the one hand, and that branch of jurisprudence which contains the art or science of legislation, on the other. Private ethics teaches how each man may dispose

himself to pursue the course most conducive to his own happiness, by means of such motives as offer of themselves: the art of legislation (which may be considered as one branch of the science of jurisprudence) teaches how a multitude of men, composing a community, may be disposed to pursue that course which upon the whole is the most conducive to the happiness of the whole community, by means of motives to be applied by the legislator.

We come now to exhibit the limits between penal and civil jurisprudence. For this purpose it may be of use to give a distinct though summary view of the principal branches into which jurisprudence, considered in its utmost extent, is wont to be divided. . . .

Jeremy Bentham, 1748 - 1832

PRINCIPLES OF THE CIVIL CODE

Chapter II

DISTINCT OBJECTS OF THE CIVIL LAW

In this distribution of rights and obligations, the legislator, we have already said, should have for his object the happiness of the body politic. In inquiring more particularly in what this happiness consists, we find four subordinate objects – Subsistence, Abundance, Equality, Security.

The more perfect the enjoyment of all these particulars, the greater the sum of social happiness, and especially of that happiness which depends upon the laws.

It may be shown, that all the functions of the law may be referred to these four heads: to provide for subsistence; to secure abundance; to befriend equality; to maintain security.

This division does not possess all the clearness and precision which could be desired. The boundaries which separate these objects are not always easily determined; they approach at different points, and are confounded one with the other. But it is enough to justify this division, that it is the most complete, and that we shall be called in many circumstances to consider each of the objects it contains, separately and distinct from each of the others.

Subsistence, for example, is included in abundance; it is, however, properly mentioned separately, because the laws ought to do for subsistence many things which they ought not to permit to be done for abundance.

Security admits of as many distinctions as there are kinds of actions which may be opposed to it. It relates to the person, to the honour, to property, to condition.

Actions hurtful to security, when prohibited by the laws, receive the character of crimes.

Among these objects of the law, security is the only one which necessarily embraces the future: subsistence, abundance, equality, may be regarded for a moment only; but security implies extension in point of time, with respect to all the benefits to which it is applied. Security is therefore the principal object.

I have placed equality among the objects of the law. In an arrangement intended to give to every man the greatest possible amount of happiness, no reason can be assigned why the law should seek to give one man more than another. There are, however, good reasons why it should not do it. The advantage acquired by the one, can only exist in consequence of an equivalent disadvantage being borne by another. The advantage would only be enjoyed by the favoured party: the disadvantage would be felt by all those who were not thus favoured.

Equality may be fostered, both by protecting it where it exists, and by seeking to produce it where it does not exist. But here lies the danger: a single error may overturn the whole social order.

It may appear surprising, that liberty is not placed among the principal objects of the law. But in order that we may have clear notions, it is necessary to consider it as a branch of security: personal liberty is security against a certain species of injury which affects the person; whilst, as to political liberty, it is another branch of security – security against the injustice of the members of the Government. What relates to this object, belongs not to the civil, but to the constitutional code.

Chapter III

RELATION BETWEEN THESE OBJECTS

These four objects of the law appear very distinct to the mind, but they are much less so in practice. The same law may serve for several of them, because they are often united. What is done, for example, for the sake of subsistence and abundance.

But there are circumstances in which it is not possible to reconcile these objects: hence a measure suggested by one of them will be condemned by another. Equality, for example, would require a certain distribution of property, which is incompatible with security.

When this contradiction exists between these objects, it is necessary to find some means of deciding which ought to have the pre-eminence; otherwise, instead of guiding us in our researches, their consideration will serve only to augment our confusion.

At the first glance it is perceived, that subsistence and security rise together to the same height: abundance and equality are manifestly of an inferior order. Indeed, without security, equality itself could not endure a single day. Without subsistence, abundance cannot exist. The two first ends are like life itself: the two last are the ornaments of life.

In legislation, the most important object is security. If no direct laws are made respecting subsistence, this object will be neglected by no one. But if there are no laws respecting security, it will be useless to have made laws respecting subsistence: command production – command cultivation; you will have done nothing: but secure to the cultivator the fruits of his labour, and you most probably have done enough.

Security, we have observed, has many branches: it is necessary that one branch of security should give way to another. For example, liberty, which is one branch of security, ought to yield to general security, since it is not possible to make any laws but at the expense of liberty.

It is not possible, then, to obtain the greatest good, but by the sacrifice of some subordinate good. In distinguishing among these objects, which, on each occasion, deserves the pre-eminence, consists the difficulty of the legislative art. Each one claims pre-eminence in turn, and it sometimes requires a complex calculation to determine to which the preference is due.

Equality ought not to be favoured, except in cases in which it does not injure security; where it does not disturb the expectations to which the laws have given birth; where it does not derange the actually established distribution.

If all property were to be equally divided, the certain and immediate consequence would be, that there would soon be nothing more to divide. Every thing would be speedily destroyed. Those who had hoped to be favoured by the division, would not suffer less than those at whose expense it would be made. If the condition of the industrious were not better than the condition of the idle, there would be no reason for being industrious.

If the principle were established, that all men should possess *equal rights*, by a necessary train of consequences, all legislation would be rendered impossible. The laws never cease establishing inequalities, since they cannot bestow rights upon any, without imposing obligations upon others.

Declare that all men, that is, all the human race, have equal rights: there is an end of all subordination. The son has equal rights with his father; he has the same right to direct and to punish him; he has as much right in his father's house, as his father has himself. The maniac has the same right to shut up others, as they have to shut up him. The idiot has the same right to govern his family, as his family have to govern him. All this is included in the equality of rights: it means all this, or it means nothing at all. It is true, those who have maintained this doctrine of the equality of rights, have neither been fools nor idiots. They had no intention of establishing this absolute equality: they had in their minds some restrictions, some modifications, some explanations. But if they knew not how to speak in a sensible and intelligible manner, was it possible that the blind and ignorant multitude should better understand what they did not understand themselves? And if they proclaimed independence, was it not too certain that they would be listened to?

Chapter IV

OF LAWS RELATIVE TO SUBSISTENCE

What can the law do relative to subsistence? Nothing directly. All that the law can do is to create *motives*; that is to say, to establish rewards and punishments, by the influence of which, men shall be induced to furnish subsistence to themselves. But nature has created these motives, and given them sufficient energy. Before the idea of law was formed, *want* and *enjoyment* had done, in this respect, every thing which could have been done by the best concerted laws. Want, armed with every pain, and even death itself, had commanded labour, had sharpened courage, had inspired foresight, had developed all the faculties of man. Enjoyment, the companion of every satisfied want, had formed an inexhaustible fund of rewards for those who had overcome the obstacles and accomplished the designs of nature.

The force of the physical sanction being sufficient, the employment of the political sanction would be superfluous.

Besides, the motives furnished by the laws are always more or less precarious in their operation: this is a consequence of the imperfection of the laws themselves, or of the difficulty of establishing the necessary facts, before bestowing reward or punishment. The hope of impunity glides to the bottom of the heart, in all the intermediate degrees through which it is necessary to pass, before arriving at the accomplishment of the law. But those natural effects, which we may consider as the rewards and punishments of nature, do not admit of this uncertainty: there is no evasion, no delay, no favour: experience announces the event; experience confirms it – each succeeding day repeats the lesson of the past, and the uniformity of this course leaves no place for doubt. What can be added, by direct legislation, to the constant and irresistible power of these natural motives?

But the law may indirectly provide for subsistence, by protecting individuals whilst they labour, and by securing to them the fruits of their industry when they have laboured: *security* for the labourer – *security* for the fruits of labour. In these cases, the benefit of the law is inestimable.

Chapter V

OF LAWS RELATIVE TO ABUNDANCE

Shall laws be made, directing individuals not to be contented with subsistence alone, but to seek abundance? No: this would be a superfluous employment of artificial means, when the natural means are sufficient. The attractions of pleasure, the succession of wants, the active desire of adding to our happiness, will, under the safeguard of security, incessantly produce new efforts after new acquisitions. Wants and enjoyments, these universal agents in society, after having raised the first ears of corn, will by degrees erect the granaries of abundance, always increasing and always full. Desires extend themselves with the means of gratification; the horizon is enlarged in proportion as we advance; and each new want, equally accompanied by its pleasure and its pain, becomes a new principle of action. Opulence, which is only a comparative term, does not arrest this movement when once it is begun: on the contrary, the greater the means, the greater the field of operations, the greater the reward, and, consequently, the greater the force of the motive which actuates the mind. But in what does the wealth of society consist, if not in the total of the wealth of the individuals composing it? And what more is required than the force of these natural motives for carrying the increase of wealth to the highest possible degree?

We have seen that abundance is produced by degrees, by the continued operation of the same causes which had provided for subsistence: there is no opposition between these two objects. On the other hand, the greater the abundance, the more secure is subsistence. Those who have condemned abundance, under the name of luxury, have never understood this connexion.

Famines, wars, accidents of every kind, so often attack the resources of subsistence, that a society which has no superfluity would often be exposed to want necessaries. This is seen among savage nations: it is what has often been witnessed among all nations in the time of their ancient poverty; it is what has happened in our own days, in countries but little favoured by nature, such as Sweden, and in those countries in which the government has opposed the operations of commerce instead of protecting them; – whilst those countries in which luxury abounds, and where the governments are enlightened, are beyond the reach of famine. Such is the happy situation of England, where commerce is free. The gewgaw, useless in itself, obtains a value in exchange for necessaries: the manufactories of luxury are offices of insurance against want: the materials used in a brewery or a manufactory of starch, may be converted into a source of subsistence. How often has the keeping of dogs and horses been decried, as destroying the food of men! The profound politicians who would put down these expenses, do not rise one degree above those apostles of disinterestedness, who, for the purpose of producing abundance of corn, set fire to the granaries.

Chapter VI

PROPOSITIONS OF PATHOLOGY UPON WHICH THE ADVANTAGE OF EQUALITY IS FOUNDED

Pathology is a term used in medicine. It has not hitherto been employed in morals, but it is equally necessary there. When thus applied, moral *pathology* would consist in the knowledge of the feelings, affections, and passions, and their effects upon happiness. Legislation, which has hitherto been founded principally upon the quicksands of instinct and prejudice, ought at length to be placed upon the immoveable base of feelings and experience: a moral thermometer is required, which should exhibit every degree of happiness and suffering. The possession of such an instrument is a point of unattainable perfection; but it is right to contemplate it. A scrupulous examination of more or less, in point of pleasure or pain, may at first be esteemed a minute enterprise. It will be said that we must deal with generalities in human affairs, and be contented with a vague approximation. This is, however, the language of indifference or incapacity. The feelings of men are sufficiently regular to become the object of a science or an art; and till this is done, we can only grope our way by making irregular and ill-directed efforts. Medicine is founded upon the axioms of physical pathology: morals are the medicine of the soul: legislation is the practical branch; it ought, therefore, to be founded upon the axioms of mental pathology.

In order to judge of the effect of a portion of wealth upon happiness, it must be considered in three different states:

1*st*, When it has always been possessed.

2*d*, When it is about to be gained.

3*d*, When it is about to be lost.

General observation. – When the effect of a portion of wealth upon happiness is spoken of, it is always without reference to the sensibility of the particular individual, and the exterior circumstances in which he may be placed. Difference of character is inscrutable; and there are no two individuals whose circumstances are alike. If these two considerations were not laid on one side, it would be impossible to form a single general proposition: but though each of these propositions may be found false or inexact in each particular case, it will neither militate against their speculative correctness, nor their practical utility. It is sufficient, – 1*st*, If they approach more nearly to the truth than any others which can be substituted for them; and, 2*dly*, If they may be employed by the legislator, as the foundation of his labours, with less inconvenience than any others.

1. We proceed to the examination of the first case we have to examine – the effect of a portion of wealth when it has always been possessed.

1. *Each portion of wealth is connected with a corresponding portion of happiness.*

2. *Of two individuals, possessed of unequal fortunes, he who possesses the greatest wealth will possess the greatest happiness.*

3. *The excess of happiness on the part of the most wealthy will not be so great as the excess of his wealth.*

4. *For the same reason, the greater the disproportion between the two masses of wealth, the less the probability that there exists an equally great disproportion between the masses of happiness.*

5. *The more nearly the actual proportion approaches to equality, the greater will be the total mass of happiness.*

What is here said of wealth, ought not to be limited to pecuniary wealth: the term is used with a more extended signification, and includes every thing which serves for subsistence and abundance. It is for abbreviation's sake that *a portion of wealth* is spoken of, instead of *a portion of the matter of wealth*. . . .

Chapter VII

OF SECURITY

We have now arrived at the principal object of the Laws: the care of security.

This inestimable good is the distinctive mark of civilization: it is entirely the work of the laws. Without law there is no security; consequently no abundance, nor even certain subsistence. And the only equality which can exist in such a condition, is the equality of misery.

In order rightly to estimate this great benefit of the Laws, it is only necessary to consider the condition of savages. They struggle without ceasing against famine, which sometimes cuts off in a few days whole nations: rivalry with respect to the means of subsistence, produces among them the most cruel wars; and, like the most ferocious beasts, men pursue men, that they may feed on one another. The dread of this horrible calamity destroys amongst them the gentlest sentiments of nature: pity connects itself with insensibility in putting the old persons to death, because they can no longer follow their prey.

Examine also what passes at those periods, during which civilized societies almost return into the savage state: I refer to a time of war, when the laws which give security are in part suspended. Every instant of its duration is fruitful in calamity: at every step which it imprints upon the globe, at every movement which it makes, the existing mass of riches, the foundation of abundance and subsistence, is decreased and disappears: the lowly cottage, and the lofty palace are alike subject to its ravages; and often the anger or caprice of a moment consigns to destruction the slow productions of an age of labour.

Law alone has accomplished what all the natural feelings were not able to do: Law alone, has been able to create a fixed and durable possession which deserves the name of Property. The law alone could accustom men to submit to the yoke of foresight, at first painful to be borne, but afterwards agreeable and mild: it alone could encourage them in labour – superfluous at present, and which they are not to enjoy till the future. Economy has as many enemies as there are spendthrifts, or men who would enjoy, without taking the trouble to produce. Labour is too painful for idleness; it is too slow for impatience: Cunning and Injustice underhandedly conspire to appropriate its fruits; Insolence and Audacity plot to seize them by open force. Hence Security, always tottering, always threatened, never at rest, lives in the midst of snares. It requires in the legislator, vigilance continually sustained, and power always in action, to defend it against his constantly reviving crowd of adversaries.

The Law does not say to a man, "*Work and I will reward you*;" but it says to him, "*Work*, and by stopping the hand that would take them from you, *I will ensure to you the fruits* of your labour, its natural *and sufficient reward, which, without me, you could not preserve*." If industry creates, it is the law which preserves: if, at the first moment, we owe every thing to labour, at the second, and every succeeding moment, we owe every thing to the law.

In order to form a clear idea of the whole extent which ought to be given to the principle of security, it is necessary to consider, that man is not like the brutes, limited to the present time, either in enjoyment or suffering, but that he is susceptible of pleasure and pain by anticipation, and that it is not enough to guard him against an actual loss, but also to guarantee to him, as much as possible, his possessions against future losses. The idea of his security must be prolonged to him throughout the whole vista that his imagination can measure.

This disposition to look forward, which has so marked an influence upon the condition of man, may be called expectation – expectation of the future. It is by means of this we are enabled to form a general plan of conduct; it is by means of this, that the successive moments which compose the duration of life are not like insulated and independent points, but become parts of a continuous whole. Expectation is a chain which unites our present and our future existence, and passes beyond ourselves to the generations which follow us. The sensibility of the individual is prolonged through all the links of this chain.

The principle of security comprehends the maintenance of all these hopes; it directs that events, inasmuch as they are dependent upon the laws, should be conformed to the expectations to which the laws have given birth.

Every injury which happens to this sentiment produces a distinct, a peculiar evil, which may be called pain of disappointed expectation.

The views of jurists must have been extremely confused, since they have paid no particular attention to a sentiment so fundamental in human life: the word expectation is scarcely to be found in their vocabulary; an argument can scarcely be found in their works, founded upon this principle. They have followed it, without doubt, in many instances, but it has been from instinct, and not from reason.

If they had known its extreme importance, they would not have omitted to name it; to point it out, instead of leaving it in the crowd.

Chapter VIII

OF PROPERTY

That we may more completely estimate the advantage of the law, let us endeavour to form a clear idea of property. We shall see that there is no natural property – that property is entirely the creature of law.

Property is only a foundation of expectation – the expectation of deriving certain advantages from the thing said to be possessed, in consequence of the relations in which one already stands to it.

There is no form, or colour, or visible trace, by which it is possible to express the relation which constitutes property. It belongs not to physics, but to metaphysics: it is altogether a creature of the mind.

To have the object in one's hand – to keep it, to manufacture it, to sell it, to change its nature, to employ it – all these physical circumstances do not give the idea of property. A piece of cloth which is actually in the Indies may belong to me, whilst the dress which I have on may not be mine. The food which is incorporated with my own substance may belong to another, to whom I must account for its use.

The idea of property consists in an established expectation – in the persuasion of power to derive certain advantages from the object, according to the nature of the case.

But this expectation, this persuasion, can only be the work of the law. I can reckon upon the enjoyment of that which I regard as my own, only according to the promise of the law, which guarantees it to me. It is the law alone which allows me to forget my natural weakness: it is from the law alone that I can enclose a field and give myself to its cultivation, in the distant hope of the harvest.

But it may be said, What has served as a base to the law for the commencement of the operation, when it adopted the objects which it promised to protect under the name of property? In the primitive state, had not men a natural expectation of enjoying certain things – an expectation derived from sources anterior to the law?

Yes: they have had from the beginning, there have always been circumstances in which a man could secure by his own means the enjoyment of certain things: but the catalogue of these cases is very limited. The savage, who has hidden his prey, may hope to keep it for himself so long as his cave is not discovered; so long as he is awake to defend it; whilst he is stronger than his rivals: but this is all. How miserable and precarious is this method of possession! – Suppose, then, the slightest agreement among these savages reciprocally to respect each other's booty: this is the introduction of a principle, to which you can only give the name of law. A feeble and momentary expectation only results from time to time, from purely physical circumstances; a strong and permanent expectation results from law alone: that which was only a thread in a state of nature, becomes a cable, so to speak, in a state of society.

Property and law are born and must die together. Before the laws, there was no property: take away the laws, all property ceases.

With respect to property, security consists in no shock or derangement being given to the expectation which has been founded on the laws, of enjoying a certain portion of good. The legislator owes the greatest respect to these expectations to which he has given birth: when he does not interfere with them, he does all that is essential to the happiness of society; when he injures them, he always produces a proportionate sum of evil.

Chapter XII

SECURITY AND EQUALITY – MEANS OF RECONCILATION

Must there, therefore, be constant opposition, an eternal war between the two rivals, *Security* and *Equality*? Up to a certain point they are incompatible, but with a little patience and skill they may be brought by degrees to coincide.

Time is the only mediator between these contrary interests. Would you follow the counsels of equality without contravening those of security, wait for the natural period which puts an end to hopes and fears – the period of death.

When property is vacated by the death of the proprietors, the law may intervene in the distribution to be made, either by limiting in certain respects the power of disposing of it by will, with the design of preventing too great an accumulation of property in the hands of a single person, or by making the right of succession subservient to the purposes of equality, in case the deceased should not leave a husband, or wife, or relations, in the direct line, and should not have made use of his power of disposing of it by will. It passes then to new possessors, whose expectations are not formed, and equality may produce good to all, without deceiving the expectations of any. The principle only is indicated here: it will be more largely developed in the second Book.

When it regards the correction of a species of civil inequality such as slavery, the same attention ought to be paid to the rights of property; the operation should be gradual, and the subordinate object should be pursued without sacrificing the principal object. The men whom you would render free by these gradations, will be much more fitted for its enjoyment, than if you had led them to trample justice under foot, in order to introduce them to this new social condition.

We may observe, that in a nation which prospers by agriculture, manufactures, and commerce, there is a continual progress towards equality. If the laws do not oppose it – if they do not maintain monopolies – if they do not restrain trade and its exchanges – if they do not permit entails – large properties will be seen, without effort, without revolutions, without shock, to subdivide themselves by little and little, and a much greater number of individuals will participate in the advantage of moderate fortunes. This will be the natural result of the different habits formed by opulence and poverty. The first, prodigal and vain, seeks only to enjoy without creating: the second, accustomed to obscurity and to privations, finds its pleasures in its labours and its economy. From this arises the change which is going on in Europe, from the progress of arts and commerce, notwithstanding the obstacles of the laws. The ages of feudality are not long since passed by, in which the world was divided into two classes – a few great proprietors who were every thing, and a multitude of slaves who were nothing. These lofty pyramids have disappeared or have been lowered, and their debris has been spread abroad: industrious men have formed new establishments, of which the infinite number proves the comparative happiness of modern civilization. Hence we may conclude, that *security*, by preserving its rank as the supreme principle, indirectly conducts to the establishment of *equality*; whilst this latter, if taken as the basis of the social arrangement, would destroy security in establishing itself.

Chapter XIII

SACRIFICES OF SECURITY TO SECURITY

This title at first appears enigmatical, but the enigma is soon solved.

An important distinction is to be made between the ideal perfection of security, and that perfection which is practicable. The first requires that nothing should be taken from any one; the second is attained if no more is taken than is necessary for the preservation of the rest.

This sacrifice is not an attack upon security; it is only a defalcation from it. An attack is an unforeseen shock; an evil which could not be calculated upon; an irregularity which has no fixed principle: it seems to put all the rest in danger; it produces a general alarm. But this defalcation is a fixed deduction – regular, necessary, expected – which produces an evil of the first order, but no danger, no alarm, no discouragement to industry: the same sum of money, according to the manner in which it is levied upon the people, will possess the one or the other of these characters, and will produce, in consequence, either the deadening effects of insecurity, or the vivifying effects of security.

The necessity of these defalcations is evident. To work, and to guard the workmen, are two different, and, for a time, incompatible operations. It is therefore necessary, that those who create wealth by their labour should give up a portion of it to supply the wants of the guardians of the state: wealth can only be defended at its own expense.

Society, attacked by internal or external enemies, can only maintain itself at the expense of the security, not only of these enemies themselves, but even of those in whose protection it is engaged.

If there are any individuals who perceive not this necessary connexion, it is because, in this respect, as in so many others, the wants of to-day eclipse those of to-morrow. All government is only a tissue of sacrifices. The best government is that in which the value of these sacrifices is reduced to the smallest amount. The practical perfection of security is a quantity which unceasingly tends to approach to the ideal perfection, without ever being able to reach it.

I shall proceed to give a catalogue of those cases in which the sacrifice of some portion of security, in respect of property, is necessary for the preservation of the greater mass: –

1. General wants of the state for its defence against external enemies.
2. General wants of the state for defence against delinquents or internal enemies.
3. General wants of the state for the prevention of physical calamities.
4. Fines at the expense of offenders, on account of punishment, on account of indemnities in favour of the parties injured.
5. Incroachment upon the property of individuals, for the development of the

powers to be exercised against the above evils, by justice, by the police, by the army.

6. Limitations of the rights of property, or of the use which each proprietor may make of his own goods, in order to prevent his injuring himself or others. . . .

In *The Limits of Jurisprudence Defined*, c. 16 and c. 21, Bentham wrote:

"Interpretation may be distinguished into *strict* and *liberal.* It may be styled strict where you attribute to the legislator the will which at the time of making the law, as you suppose, he really entertained. It may be styled liberal where the will you attribute to him is not that which you suppose he really entertained, but a will which as you suppose he failed of entertaining only through inadvertency: insomuch that had the individual case which calls for interpretation been present to his view, he would have entertained that will, which by the interpretation put upon his law you act up to, as if it had been his in reality.

"I say through inadvertency: for to attribute to the legislator a will which you suppose him to have failed of entertaining through any other cause than inadvertency, that is from wrong judgment or perverse affections, and to act accordingly is not to interpret the law, but to act against it: which in a judge or other officer invested with powers of a public nature is as much as to over-rule it. . . . Let the judge be required wheresoever he determines in the way of liberal interpretation, to declare openly his having done so: at the same time drawing up *in terminis* a general provision expressive of the attention he thinks the case requires, which let him certify to the legislator: and let the alteration so made if not negatived by the legislator within such a time have the force of law. By this means the legislator would see what the Judge was doing: the Judge would be a counsel to him, not a control, the sceptre would remain unshaken in his hands. The experiments of the one would be corrected by the experience of the other: the simplicity of the legislative plan would be preserved from violation: the corrective applied would be applied, not in the obscure, voluminous and unsteady form of customary jurisprudence, but in the concise and perspicuous form of statute law. . . ."

On the question of civil disobedience there is a footnote in *The Theory of Legislation,* ed. C. K. Ogden (1931), p. 65: "Here we touch upon one of the most difficult of questions. If the law is not what it ought to be; if it openly combats the principle of utility; ought we to obey it? Ought we to violate it? Ought we to remain neuter between the law which commands an evil, and morality which forbids it? The solution of this question involves considerations both of prudence and benevolence. We ought to examine if it is more dangerous to violate the law than to obey it; we ought to consider whether the probable evils of obedience are less or greater than the probable evils of disobedience."

Ogden, in his edition of Bentham's *The Theory of Legislation* ix (1932), gives Bentham credit, directly or indirectly, for the following reforms in English law: the reform of the representative system in Parliament; the mitigation of the terrible criminal law: the improvement of prisons; the abolition of imprisonment for debt; reform of the law of evidence; reform of the Poor Law; the establishment of a national system of education; uniform and scientific methods of drafting Acts of Parliament; a general register of real property, of deeds and of all transactions; and the passing of public health legislation.

John Austin, 1790 - 1859
First Professor of Jurisprudence of the University of London.

THE PROVINCE OF JURISPRUDENCE DETERMINED (1832)

Lecture I

The matter of jurisprudence is positive law: law, simply and strictly so called: or law set by political superiors to political inferiors. But positive law (or law, simply and strictly so called) is often confounded with objects to which it is related by *resemblance*, and with objects to which it is related in the way of *analogy*: with objects which are *also* signified, *properly* and *improperly*, by the large and vague expression *law*. To obviate the difficulties springing from that confusion, I begin my projected Course with determining the province of jurisprudence, or with distinguishing the matter of jurisprudence from those various related objects: trying to define the subject of which I intend to treat, before I endeavour to analyze its numerous and complicated parts.

A law, in the most general and comprehensive acceptation in which the term, in its literal meaning, is employed, may be said to be a rule laid down for the guidance of an intelligent being by an intelligent being having power over him. Under this definition are included, and without impropriety, several species. It is necessary to define accurately the line of demarcation which separates these species from one another, as much mistiness and intricacy has been infused into the science of jurisprudence by their being confounded or not clearly distinguished. In the comprehensive sense above indicated, or in the largest meaning which it has, without extension by metaphor or analogy, the term *law* embraces the following objects: – Laws set by God to his human creatures, and laws set by men to men.

The whole or a portion of the laws set by God to men is frequently styled the law of nature, or natural law: being, in truth, the only natural law of which it is possible to speak without a metaphor, or without a blending of objects which ought to be distinguished broadly. But, rejecting the appellation Law of Nature as ambiguous and misleading, I name those laws or rules, as considered collectively or in a mass, the *Divine law*, or the *law of God*.

Laws set by men to men are of two leading or principal classes: classes which are often blended, although they differ extremely; and which, for that reason, should be severed precisely, and opposed distinctly and conspicuously.

Of the laws or rules set by men to men, some are established by *political* superiors, sovereign and subject: by persons exercising supreme and subordinate *government*, in independent nations, or independent political societies. (The aggregate of the rules thus established, or some aggregate forming a portion of that aggregate, is the appropriate matter of jurisprudence, general or particular.) To the aggregate of the rules thus established, or to some aggregate forming a portion of that aggregate, the term *law*, as used simply and strictly, is exclusively applied. But, as contradistinguished to *natural* law, or to the law of *nature* (meaning, by those expressions, the law of God), the aggregate of the rules, established by political superiors, is frequently styled *positive* law, or law existing *by position*. As contradistinguished to the rules which I style *positive morality*, and on which I shall touch immediately, the aggregate of the rules, established by political superiors, may also be marked commodiously with the name of *positive law*. For the sake, then, of getting a name brief and distinctive at once, and agreeably to frequent usage, I style that aggregate of rules, or any portion of that aggregate, *positive law*: though rules, which are *not* established by political superiors, are also *positive*, or exist *by position*, if they be rules or laws, in the proper signification of the term.

Though *some* of the laws or rules, which are set by men to men, are established by political superiors, *others* are *not* established by political superiors, or are *not* established by political superiors, in that capacity or character.

Closely analogous to human laws of this second class, are a set of objects frequently but *improperly* termed *laws*, being rules set and enforced by *mere opinion*, that is, by the opinions or sentiments held or felt by an indeterminate body of men in regard to human conduct. Instances of such a use of the term *law* are the expressions – 'The law of honour;' 'The law set by fashion;' and rules of this species constitute much of what is usually termed 'International law.'

The aggregate of human laws properly so called belonging to the second of the classes above mentioned, with the aggregate of objects *improperly* but by *close analogy* termed law, I place together in a common class, and denote them by the term *positive morality*. The name *morality* severs them from *positive law,* while the epithet *positive* disjoins them from the *law of God*. And to the end of obviating confusion, it is necessary or expedient that they *should* be disjoined from the latter by that distinguishing epithet. For the name *morality* (or *morals*), when standing unqualified or alone, denotes indifferently either of the following objects: namely, positive morality *as it is*, or without regard to its merits; and positive morality *as it would be*, if it conformed to the law of God, and were, therefore, deserving of *approbation*.

Besides the various sorts of rules which are included in the literal acceptation of the term law, and those which are by a close and striking analogy, though improperly, termed laws, there are numerous applications of the term law, which rest upon a slender analogy and are merely metaphorical or figurative. Such is the case when we talk of *laws* observed by the lower animals; of *laws* regulating the growth or decay of vegetables; of *laws* determining the movements of inanimate bodies or masses. For where *intelligence* is not, or where it is too bounded to take the name of *reason*, and, therefore, is too bounded to conceive the purpose of a law, there is not the *will* which law can work on, or which duty can incite of restrain. Yet through these misapplications of a *name*, flagrant as the metaphor is, has the field of jurisprudence and morals been deluged with muddy speculation.

Having suggested the *purpose* of my attempt to determine the province of jurisprudence: to distinguish positive law, the appropriate matter of jurisprudence, from the various objects to which it is related by resemblance, and to which it is related, nearly or remotely, by a strong or slender analogy: I shall now state the essentials of *a law* or *rule* (taken with the largest signification which can be given to the term *properly*).

Every *law* or *rule* (taken with the largest signification which can be given to the term *properly*) is a *command*. Or, rather, laws or rules, properly so called, are a *species* of commands.

Now, since the term *command* comprises the term *law*, the first is the simpler as well as the larger of the two. But, simple as it is, it admits of explanations. And, since it is the *key* to the sciences of jurisprudence and morals, its meaning should be analyzed with precision.

Accordingly, I shall endeavour, in the first instance, to analyze the meaning of '*command*:' an analysis which, I fear, will task the patience of my hearers, but which they will bear with cheerfulness, or, at least, with resignation, if they consider the difficulty of performing it. The elements of a science are precisely the parts of it which are explained least easily. Terms that are the largest, and, therefore, the simplest of a series, are without equivalent expressions into which we can resolve them concisely. And when we endeavour to *define* them, or to translate them into terms which we suppose are better understood, we are forced upon awkward and tedious circumlocutions.

If you express or intimate a wish that I shall do or forbear from some act, and if you will visit me with an evil in case I comply not with your wish, the *expression* or *intimation* of your wish is a *command*. A command is distinguished from other significations of desire, not by the style in which the desire is signified, but by the power and the purpose of the party commanding to inflict an evil or pain in case the desire be disregarded. If you cannot or will not harm me in case I comply not with your wish, the expression of your wish is not a command, although you utter your wish in imperative phrase. If you are able and willing to harm me in case I comply not with your wish, the expression of your wish amounts to a command, although you are prompted by a spirit of courtesy to utter it in the shape of a request. '*Preces* erant, sed *quibus contradici non posset*.' Such is the language of Tacitus, when speaking of a petition by the soldiery to a son and lieutenant of Vespasian.

A command, then, is a signification of desire. But a command is distinguished from other significations of desire by this peculiarity: that the party to whom it is directed is liable to evil from the other, in case he comply not with the desire.

Being liable to evil from you if I comply not with a wish which you signify, I am *bound* or *obliged* by your command, or I lie under a *duty* to obey it. If, in spite of that evil in prospect, I comply not with the wish which you signify, I am said to disobey your command, or to violate the duty which it imposes.

Command and duty are, therefore, correlative terms: the meaning denoted by each being implied or supposed by the other. Or (changing the expression) wherever a duty lies, a command has been signified; and whenever a command is signified, a duty is imposed.

Concisely expressed, the meaning of the correlative expressions is this. He who will inflict an evil in case his desire be disregarded, utters a command by expressing or intimating his desire: He who is liable to the evil in case he disregard the desire, is bound or obliged by the command.

The evil which will probably be incurred in case a command be disobeyed or (to use an equivalent expression) in case a duty be broken, is frequently called a *sanction*, or an *enforcement of obedience*. Or (varying the phrase) the command or the duty is said to be *sanctioned* or *enforced* by the chance of incurring the evil.

Considered as thus abstracted from the command and the duty which it enforces, the evil to be incurred by disobedience is frequently styled a *punishment*. But, as punishments, strictly so called, are only a *class* of sanctions, the term is too narrow to express the meaning adequately.

I observe that Dr. Paley, in his analysis of the term *obligation*, lays much stress upon the *violence* of the motive to compliance. In so far as I can gather a meaning from his loose and inconsistent statement, his meaning appears to be this: that, unless the motive to compliance be *violent* or *intense*, the expression or intimation of a wish is not a command, nor does the party to whom it is directed lie under a *duty* to regard it.

If he means, by a *violent* motive, a motive operating with certainty, his proposition is manifestly false. The greater the evil to be incurred in case the wish be disregarded, and the greater the chance of incurring it on that same event, the greater, no doubt, is the *chance* that the wish will *not* be disregarded. But no conceivable motive will *certainly* determine to compliance, or no conceivable motive will render obedience inevitable. If Paley's proposition be true, in the sense which I have now ascribed to it, commands and duties are simply impossible. Or, reducing his proposition to absurdity by a consequence as manifestly false, commands and duties are possible, but are never disobeyed or broken.

If he means by a *violent* motive, an evil which inspires fear, his meaning is simply this: that the party bound by a command is bound by the prospect of an evil. For that which is not feared is not apprehended as an evil; or (changing the shape of the expression) is not an evil in prospect.

The truth is, that the magnitude of the eventual evil, and the magnitude of the chance of incurring it, are foreign to the matter in question. The greater the eventual evil, and the greater the chance of incurring it, the greater is the efficacy of the command, and the greater is the strength of the obligation: Or, (substituting expressions exactly equivalent) the greater is the *chance* that the command will be obeyed, and that the duty will not be broken. But where there is the smallest chance of incurring the smallest evil, the expression of a wish amounts to a command, and, therefore, imposes a duty. The sanction, if you will, is feeble or insufficient; but still there *is* a sanction, and, therefore, a duty and a command.

By some celebrated writers (by Locke, Bentham, and, I think, Paley), the term *sanction*, or *enforcement of obedience*, is applied to conditional good as well as to conditional evil: to reward as well as to punishment. But, with all my habitual veneration for the names of Locke and Bentham, I think that this extension of the term is pregnant with confusion and perplexity.

Rewards are, indisputably, *motives* to comply with the wishes of others. But to talk of commands and duties as *sanctioned* or *enforced* by rewards, or to talk of rewards as *obliging* or *constraining* to obedience, is surely a wide departure from the established meaning of the terms.

If *you* expressed a desire that *I* should render a service, and if you proffered a reward as the motive or inducement to render it, *you* would scarcely be said to *command* the service, nor should *I*, in ordinary language, be *obliged* to render it. In ordinary language, *you* would *promise* me a reward, on condition of my rendering the service, whilst *I* might be *incited* or *persuaded* to render it by the hope of obtaining the reward.

Again: If a law hold out a *reward* as an inducement to do some act, an eventual *right* is conferred, and not an *obligation* imposed, upon those who shall act accordingly: The *imperative* part of the law being addressed or directed to the party whom it requires to *render* the reward.

In short, I am determined or inclined to comply with the wish of another, by the fear of disadvantage or evil. I am also determined or inclined to comply with the wish of another, by the hope of advantage or good. But it is only by the chance of incurring *evil*, that I am *bound* or *obliged* to compliance. It is only by conditional *evil*, that duties are *sanctioned* or *enforced*. It is the power and the purpose of inflicting eventual *evil*, and *not* the power and the purpose of imparting eventual *good*, which gives to the expression of a wish the name of a *command*.

If we put *reward* into the import of the term *sanction*, we must engage in a toilsome struggle with the current of ordinary speech; and shall often slide unconsciously, notwithstanding our efforts to the contrary, into the narrower and customary meaning.

It appears, then, from what has been premised, that the ideas or notions comprehended by the term *command* are the following. 1. A wish or desire conceived by a rational being, that another rational being shall do or forbear. 2. An evil to proceed from the former, and to be incurred by the latter, in case the latter comply not with the wish. 3. An expression or intimation of the wish by words or other signs.

It also appears from what has been premised, that command, duty, and sanction are inseparably connected terms: that each embraces the same ideas as the others, though each denotes those ideas in a peculiar order or series.

'A wish conceived by one, and expressed or intimated to another, with an evil to be inflicted and incurred in case the wish be disregarded,' are signified directly and indirectly by each of the three expressions. Each is the name of the same complex notion.

But when I am talking *directly* of the expression or intimation of the wish, I employ the term *command*: The expression or intimation of the wish being presented *prominently* to my hearer; whilst the evil to be incurred, with the chance of incurring it, are kept (if I may so express myself) in the background of my picture.

When I am talking *directly* of the chance of incurring the evil, or (changing the expression) of the liability or obnoxiousness to the evil, I employ the term *duty*, or the term *obligation*: The liability or obnoxiousness to the evil being put foremost, and the rest of the complex notion being signified implicitly.

When I am talking *immediately* of the evil itself, I employ the term *sanction*, or a term of the like import: The evil to be incurred being signified directly; whilst the obnoxiousness to that evil, with the expression or intimation of the wish, are indicated indirectly or obliquely.

To those who are familiar with the language of logicians (language unrivalled for brevity, distinctness, and precision), I can express my meaning accurately in a breath. – Each of the three terms *signifies* the same notion; but each *denotes* a different part of that notion, and *connotes* the residue.

Commands are of two species. Some are *laws* or *rules*. The others have not acquired an appropriate name, nor does language afford an expression which will mark them briefly and precisely. I must, therefore, note them as well as I can by the ambiguous and inexpressive name of '*occasional* or *particular* commands.'

The term *laws* or *rules* being not unfrequently applied to occasional or particular commands, it is hardly possible to describe a line of separation which shall consist in every respect with established forms of speech. But the distinction between laws and particular commands may. I think, be stated in the following manner.

By every command, the party to whom it is directed is obliged to do or to forbear.

Now where it obliges *generally* to acts or forbearances of a *class*, a command is a law or rule. But where it obliges to a *specific* act or forbearance, or to acts or forbearances which it determines *specifically* or *individually*, a command is occasional or particular. In other words, a class or description of acts is determined by a law or rule, and acts of that class or description are enjoined or forbidden generally. But where a command is occasional or particular, the act or acts, which the command enjoins or forbids, are assigned or determined by their specific or individual natures as well as by the class or description to which they belong.

The statement which I have given in abstract expressions I will now endeavour to illustrate by apt examples.

If you command your servant to go on a given errand, or *not* to leave your house on a given evening, to to rise at such an hour on such a morning, or to rise at that hour during the next week or month, the command is occasional or particular. For the act or acts enjoined or forbidden are specially determined or assigned.

But if you command him *simply* to rise at that hour, or to rise at that hour *always*, or to rise at that hour *till further orders*, it may be said, with propriety, that you lay down a *rule* for the guidance of your servant's conduct. For no specific act is assigned by the command, but the command obliges him generally to acts of a determined class.

If a regiment be ordered to attack or defend a post, or to quell a riot, or to march from their present quarters, the command is occasional or particular. But an order to exercise daily till further orders shall be given would be called a *general* order, and *might* be called a *rule*.

If Parliament prohibited simply the exportation of corn, either for a given period or indefinitely, it would establish a law or rule: a *kind* or *sort* of acts being determined by the command, and acts of that kind or sort being *generally* forbidden. But an order issued by Parliament to meet an impending scarcity, and stopping the exportation of corn *then shipped and in port*, would not be a law or rule, though issued by the sovereign legislature. The order regarding exclusively a specified quantity of corn, the negative acts or forbearances, enjoined by the command, would be determined specifically or individually by the determinate nature of their subject.

As issued by a sovereign legislature, and as wearing the form of a law, the order which I have now imagined would probably be *called* a law. And hence the difficulty of drawing a distinct boundary between laws and occasional commands.

Again: An act which is not an offence, according to the existing law, moves the sovereign to displeasure: and, though the authors of the act are legally innocent or unoffending, the sovereign commands that they shall be punished. As enjoining a specific punishment in that specific case, and as not enjoining generally acts or forbearances of a class, the order uttered by the sovereign is not a law or rule.

Whether such an order would be *called* a law, seems to depend upon circumstances which are purely immaterial: immaterial, that is, with reference to the present purpose, though material with reference to others. If made by a sovereign assembly, deliberately, and with the forms of legislation, it would probably be called a law. If uttered by an absolute monarch, without deliberation or ceremony, it would scarcely be confounded with acts of legislation, and would be styled an arbitrary command. Yet, on either of these suppositions, its nature would be the same. It would not be a law or rule, but an occasional or particular command of the sovereign One or Number.

To conclude with an example which best illustrates the distinction, and which shows the importance of the distinction most conspicuously, *judicial commands* are commonly occasional or particular, although the commands which they are calculated to enforce are commonly laws or rules.

For instance, the lawgiver commands that thieves shall be hanged. A specific theft and a specified thief being given the judge commands that the thief shall be hanged, agreeably to the command of the lawgiver.

Now the lawgiver determines a class or description of acts; prohibits acts of the class generally and indefinitely; and commands, with the like generality, that punishment shall follow transgression. The command of the lawgiver is, therefore, a law or rule. But the command of the judge is occasional or particular. For he orders a specific punishment, as the consequence of a specific offence.

According to the line of separation which I have now attempted to describe, a law and a particular command are distinguished thus. – Acts or forbearances of a class are enjoined *generally* by the former. Acts *determined specifically*, are enjoined or forbidden by the latter.

A different line of separation has been drawn by Blackstone and others. According to Blackstone and others, a law and a particular command are distinguished in the following manner. – A law obliges *generally* the members of the given community, or a law obliges *generally* persons of a given class. A particular command obliges a *single* person, or persons whom it determines *individually*.

That laws and particular commands are not to be distinguished thus, will appear on a moment's reflection.

For, *first*, commands which oblige generally the members of the given community, or commands which oblige generally persons of given classes, are not always laws or rules.

Thus, in the case already supposed; that in which the sovereign commands that all corn actually shipped for exportation be stopped and detained; the command is obligatory upon the whole community, but as it obliges them only to a set of acts individually assigned, it is not a law. Again, suppose the sovereign to issue an order enforced by penalties, for a general mourning, on occasion of a public calamity. Now, though it is addressed to the community at large, the order is scarcely a rule, in the usual acceptation of the term. For, though it obliges generally the members of the entire community, it obliges to acts which it assigns specifically, instead of obliging generally to acts or forbearances of a class. If the sovereign commanded that *black* should be the dress of his subjects, his command would amount to a law. But if he commanded them to wear it on a specified occasion, his command would be merely particular.

And, *secondly*, a command which obliges exclusively persons individually determined, may amount, notwithstanding, to a law or rule.

For example, A father may set a *rule* to his child or children: a guardian, to his ward: a master, to his slave or servant. And certain of God's *laws* were as binding on the first man, as they are binding at this hour on the millions who have sprung from his loins.

Most, indeed, of the laws which are established by political superiors, or most of the laws which are simply and strictly so called, oblige generally the members of the political community, or oblige generally persons of a class. To frame a system of duties for every individual of the community, were simply impossible: and if it were possible, it were utterly useless. Most of the laws established by political superiors are, therefore, *general* in a twofold manner: as enjoining or forbidding generally acts of kinds or sorts; and as binding the whole community, or, at least, whole classes of its members.

But if we suppose that Parliament creates and grants an office, and that Parliament binds the grantee to services of a given description, we suppose a law established by political superiors, and yet exclusively binding a specified or determinate person.

Laws established by political superiors, and exclusively binding specified or determinate persons, are styled, in the language of the Roman jurists, *privilegia*. Though that, indeed, is a name which will hardly denote them distinctly: for, like most of the leading terms in actual systems of law, it is not the name of a definite class of objects, but of a heap of heterogeneous objects.

It appears from what has been premised, that a law, properly so called, may be defined in the following manner.

A law is a command which obliges a person or persons.

But, as contradistinguished or opposed to an occasional or particular command, a law is a command which obliges a person or persons, and obliges generally to acts or forbearances of a class.

In language more popular but less distinct and precise, a law is a command which obliges a person or persons to a *course* of conduct.

Laws and other commands are said to proceed from *superiors*, and to bind or oblige *inferiors*. I will, therefore, analyze the meaning of those correlative expressions; and will try to strip them of a certain mystery, by which that simple meaning appears to be obscured.

Superiority is often synonymous with *precedence* or *excellence*. We talk of superiors in rank; of superiors in wealth; of superiors in virtue: comparing certain persons with certain other persons; and meaning that the former precede or excel the latter in rank, in wealth, or in virtue.

But, taken with the meaning wherein I here understand it, the term *superiority* signifies might: the power of affecting others with evil or pain, and of forcing them, through fear of that evil, to fashion their conduct to one's wishes.

For example, God is emphatically the superior of Man. For his power of affecting us with pain, and of forcing us to comply with his will, is unbounded and resistless.

To a limited extent, the sovereign One or Number is the superior of the subject or citizen: the master, of the slave or servant: the father, of the child.

In short, whoever can *oblige* another to comply with his wishes, is the *superior* of that other, so far as the ability reaches: The party who is obnoxious to the impending evil, being, to that same extent, the *inferior*.

The might or superiority of God, is simple or absolute. But in all or most cases of human superiority, the relation of superior and inferior, and the relation of inferior and superior, are reciprocal. Or (changing the expression) the party who is the superior as viewed from one aspect, is the inferior as viewed from another.

For example, To an indefinite, though limited extent the monarch is the superior of the governed: his power being commonly sufficient to enforce compliance with his will. But the governed, collectively or in mass, are also the superior of the monarch: who is checked in the abuse of his might by his fear of exciting their anger; and of rousing to active resistance the might which slumbers in the multitude.

A member of a sovereign assembly is the superior of the judge: the judge being bound by the law which proceeds from that sovereign body. But, in his character of citizen or subject, he is the inferior of the judge: the judge being the minister of the law, and armed with the power of enforcing it.

It appears, then, that the term *superiority* (like the terms *duty* and *sanction*) is implied by the term *command*. For superiority is the power of enforcing compliance with a wish: and the expression or intimation of a wish, with the power and the purpose of enforcing it, are the constituent elements of a command.

'That *laws* emanate from *superiors*' is, therefore, an identical proposition. For the meaning which it affects to impart is contained in its subject.

If I mark the peculiar source of a given law, or if I mark the peculiar source of laws of a given class, it is possible that I am saying something which may instruct the hearer. But to affirm of laws universally 'that they flow from *superiors*,' or to affirm of laws universally 'that *inferiors* are bound to obey them,' is the merest tautology and trifling.

Like most of the leading terms in the sciences of jurisprudence and morals, the term *laws* is extremely ambiguous. Taken with the largest signification which can be given to the term properly, *laws* are a species of *commands*. But the term is improperly applied to various objects which have nothing of the imperative character: to objects which are *not* commands; and which, therefore, are *not* laws, properly so called.

Accordingly, the proposition 'that laws are commands' must be taken with limitations. Or, rather, we must distinguish the various meanings of the term *laws*; and must restrict the proposition to that class of objects which is embraced by the largest signification that can be given to the term properly.

I have already indicated, and shall hereafter more fully describe, the objects improperly termed laws, which are *not* within the province of jurisprudence (being either rules enforced by opinion and closely analogous to laws properly so called, or being laws so called by a metaphorical application of the term merely). There are other objects improperly termed laws (not being commands) which yet may properly be included within the province of jurisprudence. These I shall endeavour to particularize: –

1. Acts on the part of legislatures to *explain* positive law, can scarcely be called laws, in the proper signification of the term. Working no change in the actual duties of the governed, but simply declaring what those duties *are*, they properly are acts of *interpretation* by legislative authority. Or, to borrow an expression from the writers on the Roman Law, they are acts of *authentic* interpretation.

But, this notwithstanding, they are frequently styled laws: *declaratory* laws, or declaratory statutes. They must, therefore, be noted as forming an exception to the proposition 'that laws are a species of commands.'

It often, indeed, happens (as I shall show in the proper place), that laws declaratory in name are imperative in effect: Legislative, like judicial interpretation, being frequently deceptive; and establishing new law, under guise of expounding the old.

2. Laws to repeal laws, and to release from existing duties, must also be excepted from the proposition 'that laws are a species of commands.' In so far as they release from duties imposed by existing laws, they are not commands, but revocations of commands. They authorize or permit the parties, to whom the repeal extends, to do or to forbear from acts which they were commanded to forbear from or to do. And, considered with regard to *this*, their immediate or direct purpose, they are often named *permissive laws*, or, more briefly and more properly, *permissions*.

Remotely and indirectly, indeed, permissive laws are often or always imperative. For the parties released from duties are restored to liberties or rights: and duties answering those rights are, therefore, created or revived.

But this is a matter which I shall examine with exactness, when I analyze the expressions 'legal right,' 'permission by the sovereign or state,' and 'civil or political liberty.'

3. Imperfect laws, or laws of imperfect obligation, must also be excepted from the proposition 'that laws are a species of commands.'

An imperfect law (with the sense wherein the term is used by the Roman jurist) is a law which wants a sanction, and which, therefore, is not binding. A law declaring that certain acts are crimes, but annexing no punishment to the commission of acts of the class, is the simplest and most obvious example.

Though the author of an imperfect law signifies a desire, he manifests no purpose of enforcing compliance with the desire. But where there is not a purpose of enforcing compliance with the desire, the expression of a desire is not a command. Consequently, an imperfect law is not so properly a law, as counsel, or exhortation, addressed by a superior to inferiors.

Examples of imperfect laws are cited by the Roman jurists. But with us in England, laws professedly imperative are always (I believe) perfect or obligatory. Where the English legislature affects to command, the English tribunals not unreasonably presume that the legislature exacts obedience. And, if no specific sanction be annexed to a given law, a sanction is supplied by the courts of justice, agreeably to a general maxim which obtains in cases of the kind.

The imperfect laws, of which I am now speaking, are laws which are imperfect, in the sense of *the Roman jurists*: that is to say, laws which speak the desires of political superiors, but which their authors (by oversight or design) have not provided with sanctions. Many of the writers on *morals*, and on the so called *law of nature*, have annexed a different meaning to the term *imperfect*. (Speaking of imperfect obligations, they commonly mean duties which are *not legal*:) duties imposed by commands of God, or duties imposed by positive morality, as contradistinguished to duties imposed by positive law. An imperfect obligation, in the sense of the Roman jurists, is exactly equivalent to no obligation at all. For the term *imperfect* denotes simply, that the law wants the sanction appropriate to laws of the kind. An imperfect obligation, in the other meaning of the expression, is a religious or a moral obligation. The term *imperfect* does not denote that the law imposing the duty wants the appropriate sanction. It denotes that the law imposing the duty is *not* a law established by a political superior: that it wants that *perfect*, or that surer or more cogent sanction, which is imparted by the sovereign or state.

I believe that I have now reviewed all the classes of objects, to which the term *laws* is improperly applied. The laws (improperly so called) which I have here lastly enumerated, are (I think) the only laws which are not commands, and which yet may be properly included within the province of jurisprudence. But though these, with the so called laws set by opinion and the objects metaphorically termed laws, are the only laws which *really* are not commands, there are certain laws (properly so called) which may *seem* not imperative. Accordingly, I will subjoin a few remarks upon laws of this dubious character.

1. There are laws, it may be said, which *merely* create *rights*: And, seeing that every command imposes a *duty*, laws of this nature are not imperative.

But, as I have intimated already, and shall show completely hereafter, there are not laws *merely* creating *rights*. There are laws, it is true, which *merely* create *duties*: duties not correlating with correlating rights, and which, therefore, may be styled *absolute*. But every law, really conferring a right, imposes expressly or tacitly a *relative* duty, or a duty correlating with the right. If it specify the remedy to be given, in case the right shall be infringed, it imposes the relative duty expressly. If the remedy to be given be not specified, it refers tacitly to preexisting law, and clothes the right which it purports to create with a remedy provided by that law. Every law, really conferring a right, is, therefore, imperative: as imperative, as if the relative duty, which it inevitably imposes, were merely absolute.

The meanings of the term *right*, are various and perplexed; taken with its proper meaning, it comprises ideas which are numerous and complicated; and the searching and extensive analysis, which the term, therefore, requires, would occupy more room than could be given to it in the present lecture. It is not, however, necessary, that the analysis should be performed here. I purpose, in my earlier lectures, to determine the province of jurisprudence; or to distinguish the laws established by political superiors, from the various laws, proper and improper, with which they are frequently confounded. And this I may accomplish exactly enough, without a nice inquiry into the import of the term *right*.

2. According to an opinion which I must notice *incidentally* here, though the subject to which it relates will be treated *directly* hereafter, *customary laws* must be excepted from the proposition 'that laws are a species of commands.'

By many of the admirers of customary laws (and, especially, of their German admirers), they are thought to oblige legally (independently of the sovereign or state), *because* the citizens or subjects have observed or kept them. Agreeably to this opinion, they are not the *creatures* of the sovereign or state, although the sovereign or state may abolish them at pleasure. Agreeably to this opinion, they are positive law (or law, strictly so called), inasmuch as they are enforced by the courts of justice: But, that notwithstanding, they exist *as positive law* by the spontaneous adoption of the governed, and not by position or establishment on the part of political superiors. Consequently, customary laws, considered as positive law, are not commands. And, consequently, customary laws, considered as positive law, are not laws or rules properly so called.

An opinion less mysterious, but somewhat allied to this, is not uncommonly held by the adverse party: by the party which is strongly opposed to customary law; and to all law made judicially, or in the way of judicial legislation. According to the latter opinion, all judge-made law, or all judge-made law established by *subject* judges, is purely the creature of the judges by whom it is established immediately. To impute it to the sovereign legislature, or to suppose that it speaks the will of the sovereign legislature, is one of the foolish or knavish *fictions* with which lawyers, in every age and nation, have perplexed and darkened the simplest and clearest truths.

I think it will appear, on a moment's reflection, that each of these opinions is groundless: that customary law is *imperative*, in the proper signification of the term; and that all judge-made law is the creature of the sovereign or state.

At its origin, a custom is a rule of conduct which the governed observe spontaneously, or not in pursuance of a law set by a political superior. The custom is transmuted into positive law, when it is adopted as such by the courts of justice, and when the judicial decisions fashioned upon it are enforced by the power of the state. But before it is adopted by the courts, and clothed with the legal sanction, it is merely a rule of positive morality: a rule generally observed by the citizens or subjects; but deriving the only force, which it can be said to possess, from the general disapprobation falling on those who transgress it.

Now when judges transmute a custom into a legal rule (or make a legal rule not suggested by a custom), the legal rule which they establish is established by the sovereign legislature. A subordinate or subject judge is merely a minister. The portion of the sovereign power which lies at his disposition is merely delegated. The rules which he makes derive their legal force from authority given by the state: an authority which the state may confer expressly, but which it commonly imparts in the way of acquiescence. For, since the state may reverse the rules which he makes, and yet permits him to enforce them by the power of the political community, its sovereign will 'that his rules shall obtain as law' is clearly evinced by its conduct, though not by its express declaration.

The admirers of customary law love to trick out their idol with mysterious and imposing attributes. But to those who can see the difference between positive law and morality, there is nothing of mystery about it. Considered as rules of positive morality, customary laws arise from the consent of the governed, and not from the position or establishment of political superiors. But, considered as moral rules turned into positive laws, customary laws are established by the state: established by the state directly, when the customs are promulged in its statutes; established by the state circuitously, when the customs are adopted by its tribunals.

The opinion of the party which abhors judge-made laws, springs from their inadequate conception of the nature of commands.

Like other significations of desire, a command is express or tacit. If the desire be signified by *words* (written or spoken), the command is express. If the desire be signified by conduct (or by any signs of desire which are *not* words), the command is tacit.

Now when customs are turned into legal rules by decisions of subject judges, the legal rules which emerge from the customs are *tacit* commands of the sovereign legislature. The state, which is able to abolish, permits its ministers to enforce them: and it, therefore, signifies its pleasure, by that its voluntary acquiescence, 'that they shall serve as a law to the governed.'

My present purpose is merely this: to prove that the positive law styled *customary* (and all positive law made judicially) is established by the state directly or circuitously, and, therefore, is *imperative*. I am far from disputing, that law made judicially (or in the way of improper legislation) and law made by statute (or in the properly legislative manner) are distinguished by weighty differences. I shall inquire, in future lectures, what those differences are; and why subject judges, who are properly ministers of the law, have commonly shared with the sovereign in the business of making it.

I assume, then, that the only laws which are not imperative, and which belong to the subject-matter of jurisprudence, are the following: – 1. Declaratory laws, or laws explaining the import of existing positive law. 2. Laws abrogating or repealing existing positive law. 3. Imperfect laws, or laws of imperfect obligation (with the sense wherein the expression is used by the Roman jurists).

But the space occupied in the science by these improper laws is comparatively narrow and insignificant. Accordingly, although I shall take them into account so often as I refer to them directly, I shall throw them out of account on other occasions. Or (changing the expression) I shall limit the term *law* to laws which are imperative, unless I extend it expressly to laws which are not.

Lecture V

. . . *The science of jurisprudence* (or, simply and briefly, *jurisprudence*) is concerned with positive laws, or with laws strictly so called, as considered without regard to their goodness or badness. . .

The body or aggregate of laws which may be styled the law of God, the body or aggregate of laws which may be styled positive law, and the body or aggregate of laws which may be styled positive morality, sometimes *coincide*, sometimes do *not* coincide, and sometimes *conflict*.

One of these bodies of laws *coincides* with another, when acts, which are enjoined or forbidden by the former, are also enjoined, or are also forbidden by the latter. – For example, The killing which is styled *murder* is forbidden by the positive law of every political society: it is also forbidden by a so called law which the general opinion of the society has set or imposed: it is also forbidden by the law of God as known through the principle of utility. The murderer commits a crime, or he violates a positive law: he commits a conventional immorality, or he violates a so called law which general opinion has established: he commits a sin, or he violates the law of God. He is obnoxious to punishment, or other evil, to be inflicted by sovereign authority: he is obnoxious to the hate and the spontaneous ill-offices of the generality or bulk of the society: he is obnoxious to evil or pain to be suffered here or hereafter by the immediate appointment of the Deity.

One of these bodies of laws does *not* coincide with another, when acts, which are enjoined or forbidden by the former, are not enjoined, or are not forbidden by the latter. – For example, Though smuggling is forbidden by positive law, and (speaking generally) is not less pernicious than theft, it is not forbidden by the opinions or sentiments of the ignorant or unreflecting. Where the impost or tax is itself of pernicious tendency, smuggling is hardly forbidden by the opinions or sentiments of any: And it is therefore practised by any without the slightest shame, or without the slightest fear of incurring general censure. Such, for instance, is the case where the impost or tax is laid upon the foreign commodity, not for the useful purpose of raising a public revenue, but for the absurd and mischievous purpose of protecting a domestic manufacture. – Offences against the game laws are also in point: for they are not offences against positive morality, although they are forbidden by positive law. A gentleman is not dishonoured, or generally shunned by gentlemen, though he shoots without a qualification. A peasant who wires hares escapes the censure of peasants, though the squires, as doing justiceship, send him to the prison and the tread-mill.

One of these bodies of the law *conflicts* with another, when acts, which are enjoined or forbidden by the former, are forbidden or enjoined by the latter. – For example, In most of the nations of modern Europe, the practice of duelling is forbidden by positive law. It is also at variance with the law which is received in most of those nations as having been set by the Deity in the way of express revelation. But in spite of positive law, and in spite of his religious convictions, a man of the class of gentlemen may be forced by the law of honour to give or to take a challenge. If he forbore from giving, or if he declined a challenge, he might incur the general contempt of gentlemen or men of honour, and might meet with slights and insults sufficient to embitter his existence. The negative *legal* duty which certainly is incumbent upon him, and the negative *religious* duty to which he believes himself subject, are therefore mastered and controlled by that positive *moral* duty which arises from the so called law set by the opinion of his class.

The simple and obvious considerations to which I have now adverted, are often overlooked by legislators. If they fancy a practice pernicious, or hate it they know not why, they proceed, without further thought, to forbid it by positive law. They forget that positive law may be superfluous or impotent, and therefore may lead to nothing but purely gratuitous vexation. They forget that the moral or the religious sentiments of the community may already suppress the practice as completely as it can be suppressed: or that, if the practice is favoured by those moral or religious sentiments, the strongest possible fear which legal pains can inspire may be mastered by a stronger fear of other and conflicting sanctions. [There are classes of useful acts which it were useless to enjoin, and classes of mischievous acts which it were useless to forbid: for we are sufficiently prone to the useful, and sufficiently averse from the mischievous acts, without the incentives and restraints applied by religious sanctions, or by sanctions legal or moral. And, assuming that general utility is the index to the Divine commands, we may fairly infer that acts of such classes are not enjoined or forbidden by the law of God: that he no more enjoins or forbids acts of the classes in question, than he enjoins or forbids such acts as are generally pernicious or useful.

[There are also classes of acts, generally useful or pernicious, which demand the incentives or restraints applied by religious sanctions, or by sanctions legal or moral. Without the incentives and restraints applied by religious sanctions, or applied by sanctions legal or moral, we are not sufficiently prone to those which are generally useful, and are not sufficiently averse from those which are generally pernicious. And, assuming that general utility is the index to the Divine commands, all these classes of useful, and all these classes of pernicious acts, are enjoined and forbidden respectively by the law of God.

Being enjoined or being forbidden by the Deity, all these classes of useful, and all these classes of pernicious acts, ought to be enjoined or forbidden by positive morality: that is to say, by the positive morality which consists of opinions or sentiments. But, this notwithstanding, some of these classes of acts ought not to be enjoined or forbidden by positive law. Some of these classes of acts ought not to be enjoined or forbidden even by the positive morality which consists of imperative rules.

Every act or forbearance that ought to be an object of positive law, ought to be an object of the positive morality which consists of opinions or sentiments. Every act or forbearance that ought to be an object of the latter, is an object of the law of God as construed by the principle of utility. But the circle embraced by the law of God, and which may be embraced to advantage by positive morality, is larger than the circle which can be embraced to advantage by positive law. Inasmuch as the two circles have one and the same centre, the whole of the region comprised by the latter is also comprised by the former. But the whole of the region comprised by the former is not comprised by the latter.

To distinguish the acts and forbearances that ought to be objects of law, from those that ought to be abandoned to the exclusive cognisance of morality, is, perhaps, the hardest of the problems which the science of ethics presents. The only existing approach to a solution of the problem, may be found in the writings of Mr. Bentham: who, in most of the departments of the two great branches of ethics, has accomplished more for the advancement of the science than all his predecessors put together. – See, in particular, *his Principles of Morals and Legislation*, ch. xvii.]

In consequence of the frequent coincidence of positive law and morality, and of positive law and the law of God, the true nature and fountain of positive law is often absurdly mistaken by writers upon jurisprudence. Where positive law has been fashioned on positive morality, or where positive law has been fashioned on the law of God, they forget that the copy is the creature of the sovereign, and impute it to the author of the model.

For example: Customary laws are positive laws fashioned by judicial legislation upon pre-existing customs. Now, till they become the grounds of judicial decisions upon cases, and are clothed with legal sanctions by the sovereign one or number, the customs are merely rules set by opinions of the governed, and sanctioned or enforced morally: Though, when they become the reasons of judicial decisions upon cases, and are clothed with legal sanctions by the sovereign one or number, the customs are rules of positive law as well as of positive morality. But, because the customs were observed by the governed before they were clothed with sanctions by the sovereign one or number, it is fancied that customary laws exist *as positive laws* by the institution of the private persons with whom the customs originated. – Admitting the conceit, and reasoning by analogy, we ought to consider the sovereign the author of the positive morality which is often a consequence of positive law. Where a positive law, not fashioned on a custom, is favourably received by the governed, and enforced by their opinions or sentiments, we must deem the so called law, set by those opinions or sentiments, a law imperative and proper of the supreme political superior.

Again: The portion of positive law which is parcel of the *law of nature* (or, in the language of the classical jurists, which is parcel of the *jus gentium*) is often supposed to emanate, even as positive law, from a Divine or Natural source. But (admitting the distinction of positive law into law natural and law positive) it is manifest that law natural, considered as a portion of positive, is the creature of human sovereigns, and not of the Divine monarch. To say that it emanates, as positive law from a Divine or Natural Source, is to confound positive law with law whereon it is fashioned, or with law whereunto it conforms.

[Austin's Note – on the prevailing tendency to confound what is with what ought to be law or morality, that is, 1st, to confound positive law with the science of legislation, and positive morality with deontology; and 2nly, to confound positive law with positive morality, and both with legislation and deontology.

The existence of law is one thing; its merit or demerit is another. Whether it be or be not conformable to an assumed standard, is a different enquiry. A law, which actually exists, is a law, though we happen to dislike it, or though it vary from the text, by which we regulate our approbation and disapprobation. This truth, when formally announced as an abstract proposition, is so simple and glaring that it seems idle to insist upon it. But simple and glaring as it is, when enunciated in abstract expressions the enumeration of the instances in which it has been forgotten would fill a volume.

Sir William Blackstone, for example, says, in his 'Commentaries,' that the laws of God are superior in obligation to all other laws; that no human laws should be suffered to contradict them; that human laws are of no validity if contrary to them; and that all valid laws derive their force from that divine original.

Now, he *may* mean that all human laws ought to conform to the divine laws. If this be his meaning, I assent to it without hesitation. The evils which we are exposed to suffer from the hands of God as a consequence of disobeying His commands are the greatest evils to which we are obnoxious; the obligations which they impose are consequently paramount to those imposed by any other laws, and if human commands conflict with the Divine law, we ought to disobey the command which is enforced by the less powerful sanction; this is implied in the term *ought*: the proposition is identical, and therefore perfectly indisputable – it is our interest to choose the smaller and more uncertain evil, in preference to the greater and surer. If this be Blackstone's meaning, I assent to his proposition, and have only to object to it, that it tells us just nothing.

Perhaps, again, he means that human lawgivers are themselves obliged by the Divine laws to fashion the laws which they impose by that ultimate standard, because if they do not, God will punish them. To this also I entirely assent: for if the index to the law of God be the principle of utility, that law embraces the whole of our voluntary actions in so far as motives applied from without are required to give them a direction conformable to the general happiness.

But the meaning of this passage of Blackstone, if it has a meaning, seems rather to be this: that no human law which conflicts with the Divine law is obligatory or binding; in other words, that no human law which conflicts with the Divine law *is a law*, for a law without an obligation is a contradiction in terms. I suppose this to be his meaning, because when we say of any transaction that it is invalid or void, we mean that it is not binding: as, for example, if it be a contract, we mean that the political law will not lend its sanction to enforce the contract.

Now, to say that human laws which conflict with the divine law are not binding, that is to say, are not laws, is to talk stark nonsense. The most pernicious laws, and therefore those which are most opposed to the will of God, have been and are continually enforced as laws by judicial tribunals. Suppose an act innocuous, or positively beneficial, be prohibited by the sovereign under the penalty of death; if I commit this act, I shall be tried and condemned, and if I object to the sentence, that it is contrary to the law of God, who has commanded that human lawgivers shall not prohibit acts which have no evil consequences, the Court of Justice will demonstrate the inconclusiveness of my reasoning by hanging me up, in pursuance of the law of which I have impugned the validity. An exception, demurrer, or plea, founded on the law of God was never heard in a Court of Justice, from the creation of the world down to the present moment.

But this abuse of language is not merely puerile, it is mischievous. When it is or what comes exactly to the same thing, the office or province of the juriconsult. said that a law ought to be disobeyed, what is meant is that we are urged to disobey it by motives more cogent and compulsory than those by which it is itself sanctioned. If the laws of God are certain, the motives which they hold out to disobey any human command which is at variance with them are paramount to all others. But the laws of God are not always certain. All divines, at least all reasonable divines, admit that no scheme of duties perfectly complete and unambiguous was ever imparted to us by revelation. As an index to the Divine will, utility is obviously insufficient. What appears pernicious to one person may appear beneficial to another. And as for the moral sense, innate practical principles, conscience, they are merely convenient cloaks for ignorance or sinister interest: they mean either that I hate the law to which I object and cannot tell why, or that I hate the law, and that the cause of my hatred is one which I find it incommodious to avow. If I say openly, I hate the law, *ergo*, it is not binding and ought to be disobeyed, no one will listen to me; but by calling my hate my conscience or my moral sense, I urge the same argument in another and a more plausible form: I seem to assign a reason for my dislike, when in truth I have only given it a sounding and specious name. In times of civil discord the mischief of this detestable abuse of language is apparent. In quiet times the dictates of utility are fortunately so obvious that the anarchical doctrine sleeps, and men habitually admit the validity of laws which they dislike. To prove by pertinent reasons that a law is pernicious is highly useful, for resistance, grounded on clear and definite prospects of good, is sometimes beneficial. But to proclaim generally that all laws which are pernicious or contrary to the will of God are void and not to be tolerated, is to preach anarchy, hostile and perilous as much to wise and benign rule as to stupid and galling tyranny.

In another passage of his 'Commentaries,' Blackstone enters into an argument to prove that a master cannot have a right to the labour of his slave. Had he contented himself with expressing his *disapprobation*, a very well-grounded one certainly, of the institution of slavery, no objection could have been made to his so expressing himself. But to dispute the existence or the possibility of the right is to talk absurdly. For in every age, and in almost every nation, the right has been given by positive law, whilst that pernicious disposition of positive law has been backed by the positive morality of the free or master classes.

Paley's admired definition of civil liberty appears to me to be obnoxious to the very same objection: it is a definition of civil liberty as it ought to be. 'Civil liberty,' he says, 'is the not being restrained by any law but which conduces in a greater degree to the public welfare;' and this is distinguished from *natural* liberty, which is the not being restrained at all. But when liberty is not exactly synonymous with right, it means, and can mean nothing else, but exemption from restraint or obligation, and is therefore altogether incompatible with law, the very idea of which implies restraint and obligation. But restraint is restraint although it be useful, and liberty is liberty though it may be pernicious. You may, if you please, call a useful restraint *liberty*, and refuse the name liberty to exemption from restraint when restraint is for the public advantage. But by this abuse of language you throw not a ray of light upon the nature of political liberty; you only add to the ambiguity and indistinctness in which it is already involved. I shall have to define and analyse the notion of liberty hereafter, on account of its intimate connexion with right, obligation, and sanction.

Grotius, Puffendorf, and the other writers on the so-called law of nations, have fallen into a similar confusion of ideas: they have confounded positive international morality, or the rules which actually obtain among civilised nations in their mutual intercourse, with their own vague conceptions of international morality as it *ought to be*, with that indeterminate something which they conceived it would be, if it conformed to that indeterminate something which they call the law of nature. Professor Von Martens, of Gottingen, who died only a few years ago, is actually the first of the writers on the law of nations who has seized this distinction with a firm grasp, the first who has distinguished the rules which ought to be received in the intercourse of nations, or which would be received if they conformed to an assumed standard of whatever kind, from those which *are* so received, endeavoured to collect from the practice of civilised communities what are the rules actually recognised and acted upon by them and gave to these rules the name of positive international law.

I have given several instances in which law and morality as they ought to be are confounded with the law and morality which actually exist. I shall next mention some examples in which positive law is confounded with positive morality, and both with the science of legislation and deontology.

Those who know the writings of the Roman lawyers only by hearsay are accustomed to admire their philosophy. Now this, in my estimation, is the only part of their writings which deserves contempt. Their extraordinary merit is evinced not in general speculation, but as expositors of the Roman law. They have seized its general principles with great clearness and penetration, have applied these principles with admirable logic to the explanation of details, and have thus reduced this positive system of law to a compact and coherent whole. But the philosophy which they borrowed from the Greeks, or which, after the examples of the Greeks they themselves fashioned, is naught. Their attempts to define jurisprudence and to determine the province of the jurisconsult are absolutely pitiable, and it is hardly conceivable how men of such admirable discernment should have displayed such contemptible imbecility.

At the commencement of the digest is a passage attempting to define jurisprudence. I shall first present you with this passage in a free translation, and afterwards in the original. 'Jurisprudence,' says this definition, 'is the knowledge of things divine and human; the science which teaches men to discern the just from the unjust.' 'Jusisprudentia est divinarum atque humanarum rerum notitia, justi atque injusti scientia.' In the excerpt from Ulpian, which is placed at the beginning of the Digest, it is attempted to define the office or province of the jurisconsult. 'Law,' says the passage, 'derives its name from justice, *justitia*, and is the science or skill in the good and the equitable. Law being the creature of justice, we the jurisconsults may be considered as her priests, for justice is the goddess whom we worship, and to whose service we are devoted. Justice and equity are our vocation; we teach men to know the difference between the just and the unjust, the lawful and the unlawful; we strive to reclaim them from vice, not only by the terrors of punishment, but also by the blandishment of rewards; herein, unless we flatter ourselves, aspiring to sound and real philosophy, and not like some whom we could mention, contenting ourselves with vain and empty pretension.' 'Juri operam daturum prius nosse oportet, unde nomen juris descendat. Est autem a justitia appellatum; nam, ut eleganter Celsus definit, jus est ars boni et aequi. Cujus merito quis nos sacerdotes appellet; justitiam namque colimus, et boni et aequi notitiam profitemur, aequum ab iniquo separantes, licitum ab illicito discernentes, bonos non solum metu poenarum verum etiam proemiorum quoque exhortatione efficere cupientes, veram, nisi fallor, philosophiam, non simulatam affectantes.'

Were I to present you with all the criticisms which these two passages suggest, I should detain you a full hour. I shall content myself with one observation on the scope and purpose of them both. This is, that they affect to define jurisprudence, Now jurisprudence, if it is anything, is the science of law, or at most the science of law combined with the art of applying it; but what is here given as a definition of it, embraces not only law, but positive morality, and even the test to which both these are to be referred. It therefore comprises the science of legislation and deontology. Further, it affirms that law is the creature of justice, which is as much as to say that it is the child of its own offspring. For when by *just* we mean anything but to express our own approbation we mean something which *accords with some given law*. True, we speak of law and justice, or of law and equity, as opposed to each other, but when we do so, we mean to express mere dislike of the law, or to intimate that it conflicts with another law, the law of God, which is its standard. According to this, every pernicious law is unjust. But, in truth, law is itself the standard of justice. What deviates from any law is unjust with reference to that law, though it may be just with reference to another law of superior authority. The terms just and unjust imply a standard, and conformity to that standard and a deviation from it; else they signify mere dislike, which it would be far better to signify by a grunt or a groan than by mischievous and detestable abuse of articulate language. But justice is commonly erected into an entity, and spoken of as a legislator, in which character it is supposed to prescribe the law, conformity to which it should denote. The veriest dolt who is placed in a jury box, the merest old woman who happens to be raised to the bench, will talk finely of equity or justice – the justice of the case, the equity of the case, the imperious demands of justice, the plain dictates of equity. He forgets that he is there to enforce *the law of the land*, else he does not administer that justice or that equity with which alone he is immediately concerned.

This is well known to have been a strong tendency of Lord Mansfield – a strange obliquity in so great a man. I will give an instance. By the English law, a promise to give something or to do something for the benefit of another is not binding without what is called a consideration, that is, a motive assigned for the promise, which motive must be of a particular kind. Lord Mansfield, however, overruled the distinct provisions of the law by ruling that moral obligation was a sufficient consideration. Now, moral obligation is an obligation imposed by opinion, or an obligation imposed by God: that is, moral obligation is anything which we choose to call so, for the precepts of positive morality are infinitely varying, and the will of God, whether indicated by utility or by a moral sense, is equally matter of dispute. This decision of Lord Mansfield, which assumes that the judge is to enforce morality, enables the judge to enforce just whatever he pleases.

I must here observe that I am not objecting to Lord Mansfield for assuming the office of a legislator. I by no means disapprove of what Mr. Bentham has chosen to call by the disrespectful, and therefore, as I conceive, injudicious, name of judge-made law. For I consider it injudicious to call by any name indicative of disrespect what appears to me highly beneficial and even absolutely necessary. I cannot understand how any person who has considered the subject can suppose that society could possibly have gone on if judges had not legislated, or that there is any danger whatever in allowing them that power which they have in fact exercised, to make up for the negligence or the incapacity of the avowed legislator. That part of the law of every country which was made by judges has been far better made than that part which consists of statutes enacted by the legislature. Notwithstanding my great admiration for Mr. Bentham, I cannot but think that, instead of blaming judges for having legislated, he should blame them for the timid, narrow, and piecemeal manner in which they have legislated, and for legislating under cover of vague and indeterminate phrases, such as Lord Mansfield employed in the above example, and which would be censurable in any legislator.]

Lecture VI

The superiority which is styled sovereignty, and the independent political society which sovereignty implies, is distinguished from other superiority, and from other society, by the following marks or characters. – 1. The *bulk* of the given society are in a *habit* of obedience or submission to a *determinate* and *common* superior: let that common superior be a certain individual person, or a certain body or aggregate of individual persons. 2. That certain individual, or that certain body of individuals, is *not* in a habit of obedience to a determinate human superior. Laws (improperly so called) which opinion sets or imposes, permanently affect the conduct of that certain individual or body. To express or tacit commands of other determinate parties, that certain individual body may yield occasional submission. But there is no determinate person, or determinate aggregate of persons, to whose commands, express or tacit, that certain individual or body renders habitual obedience.

Or the notions of sovereignty and independent political society may be expressed concisely this. – If a *determinate* human superior, *not* in a habit of obedience to a like superior, receive *habitual* obedience from the *bulk* of a given society, that determinate superior is sovereign in that society, and the society (including the superior) is a society political and independent.

To that determinate superior, the other members of the society are *subject*: or on that determinate superior, the other members of the society are *dependent*. The position of its other members towards that determinate superior, is *a state of subjection*, or *a state of dependence*. The mutual relation which subsists between that superior and them, may be styled *the relation of sovereign and subject*, or *the relation of sovereignty and subjection*.

Hence it follows, that it is only through an ellipsis, or an abridged form of expression, that the *society* is styled *independent*. The party truly independent (independent, that is to say, of a determinate human superior), is not the society, but the sovereign portion of the society: that certain member of the society, or that certain body of its members, to whose commands, expressed or intimated, the generality or bulk of its members render habitual obedience. Upon that certain person, or certain body of persons, the other members of the society are *dependent*: or to that certain person, or certain body of persons, the other members of the society are *subject*. By 'an independent political society,' or 'an independent and sovereign nation,' we mean a political society consisting of a sovereign and subjects, as opposed to a political society which is merely subordinate: that is to say, which is merely a limb or member of another political society, and which therefore consists entirely of persons in a state of subjection.

In order that a given society may form a society political and independent, the two distinguishing marks which I have mentioned above must unite. The *generality* of the given society must be in the *habit* of obedience to a *determinate* and *common* superior: whilst that determinate person, or determinate body of persons, must *not* be habitually obedient to a determinate person or body. It is the union of that positive, with this negative mark, which renders that certain superior sovereign or supreme, and which renders that given society (including that certain superior) a society political and independent.

From the various shapes which sovereignty may assume or from the various possible forms of supreme government, I proceed to the limits, real and imaginary, of sovereign or supreme power.

Subject to the slight correctives which I shall state at the close of my discourse, the essential difference of a positive law (or the difference that severs it from a law which is not a positive law) may be put in the following manner. – Every positive law, or every law simply and strictly so called, is set, directly or circuitously, by a sovereign person or body, to a member or members of the independent political society wherein that person or body is sovereign or supreme. Or (changing the expression) it is set, directly or circuitously, by a monarch or sovereign number, to a person or persons in a state of subjection to its author.

Now it follows from the essential difference of a positive law, and from the nature of sovereignty and independent political society, that the power of a monarch properly so called, or the power of a sovereign number in its collegiate and sovereign capacity, is incapable of *legal* limitation. A monarch or sovereign number bound by a legal duty, were subject to a higher or superior sovereign: that is to say, a monarch or sovereign number bound by a legal duty, were sovereign and not sovereign. (Supreme power limited by positive law, is a flat contradiction in terms.)

Nor would a political society escape from legal despotism, although the power of the sovereign were bounded by legal restraints. The power of the superior sovereign immediately imposing the restraints, or the power of some other sovereign superior to that superior, would still be absolutely free from the fetters of positive law. For unless the imagined restraints were ultimately imposed by a sovereign not in a state of subjection to a higher or superior sovereign, a series of sovereigns ascending to infinity would govern the imagined community. Which is impossible and absurd.

Monarchs and sovereign bodies have attempted to oblige themselves, or to oblige the successors to their sovereign powers. But in spite of the laws which sovereigns have imposed on themselves, or which they have imposed on the successors to their sovereign powers, the position that 'sovereign power is incapable of legal limitation' will hold universally or without exception.

The immediate author of a law of the kind, or any of the sovereign successors to that immediate author, may abrogate the law at pleasure. And though the law be not abrogated, the sovereign for the time being is not constrained to observe it by a legal or political sanction. For if the sovereign for the time being were legally bound to observe it, that present sovereign would be in a state of subjection to a higher or superior sovereign.

As it regards the successors to the sovereign or supreme powers, a law of the kind amounts, at the most, to a rule of positive morality. As it regards its immediate author, it is merely a law by a metaphor. For if we would speak with propriety, we cannot speak of a law set by a man to himself: though a man may adopt a principle as a guide to his own conduct, and may observe it as he would observe it if he were bound to observe it by a sanction.

The laws which sovereigns affect to impose upon themselves, or the laws which sovereigns affect to impose upon their followers, are merely principles or maxims which they adopt as guides, or which they commend as guides to their successors in sovereign power. A departure by a sovereign or state from a law of the kind in question, is not illegal. If a law which it sets to its subjects conflict with a law of the kind, the former is legally valid, or legally binding. . . .

. . . I am led to consider the meanings of the epithet *unconstitutional*, as it is contradistinguished in the epithet *illegal*, and as it is applied to conduct of a monarch, or to conduct of a sovereign number in its collegiate and sovereign capacity. The epithet *unconstitutional*, as thus opposed and applied, is sometimes used with a meaning which is more general and vague, and is sometimes used with a meaning which is more special and definite. I will begin with the former.

1. In every, or almost every, independent political society, there are principles or maxims which the sovereign habitually observes, and which the bulk of the society, or the bulk of its influential members, regard with feelings of approbation. Not unfrequently, such maxims are expressly adopted, as well as habitually observed, by the sovereign or state. More commonly, they are not expressly adopted by the sovereign or state, but are simply imposed upon it by opinions prevalent in the community. Whether they are expressly adopted by the sovereign or state, or are simply imposed upon it by opinions prevalent in the community, it is bound or constrained to observe them by merely moral sanctions. Or (changing the phrase) in case it ventured to deviate from a maxim of the kind in question, it would not and could not incur a legal pain or penalty, but it probably would incur censure, and might chance to meet with resistance, from the generality or bulk of the governed.

Now, if a law or other act of a monarch or sovereign number conflict with a maxim of the kind to which I have adverted above, the law or other act may be called *unconstitutional* (in that more general meaning which is sometimes given to the epithet). For example: The *ex post facto* statutes which are styled acts of attainder, may be called *unconstitutional*, though they cannot be called *illegal*. For they conflict with a principle of legislation which parliament has habitually observed, and which is regarded with approbation by the bulk of the British community.

In short, when we style an act of a sovereign an *unconstitutional* act (with that more general import which is sometimes given to the epithet), we mean, I believe, this: That the act is inconsistent with some given principle or maxim: that the given supreme government has expressly adopted the principle, or, at least, has habitually observed it: that the bulk of the given society, or the bulk of its influential members, regard the principle with approbation: and that, since the supreme government has habitually observed the principle, and since the bulk of the society regard it with approbation, the act in question must thwart the expectations of the latter, and must shock their opinions and sentiments. Unless we mean this, we merely mean that we deem the act in question generally pernicious: or that, without a definite reason for the disapprobation which we feel, we regard the act with dislike.

2. The epithet *unconstitutional* as applied to conduct of a sovereign, and as used with the meaning which is more special and definite, imports that the conduct in question conflicts with *constitutional law*.

And here I would briefly remark, that I mean by the expression *constitutional law*, the positive morality, or the compound of positive morality and positive law, which fixes the constitution or structure of the given supreme government. I mean the positive morality, or the compound of positive morality and positive law, which determines the character of the person, or the respective characters of the persons, in whom, for the time being, the sovereignty shall reside: and, supposing the government in question an aristocracy or government of a number, which determines moreover the mode wherein the sovereign powers shall be shared by the constituent members of the sovereign number or body. . . .

Again: An act of the British parliament vesting the sovereignty in the king, or vesting the sovereignty in the king and the upper or lower house, would essentially alter the structure of our present supreme government, and might therefore be styled with propriety an *unconstitutional* law. In case the imagined statute were also generally pernicious, and in case it offended moreover the generally or bulk of the nation, it might be styled *irreligious* and *immoral* as well as *unconstitutional*. But to call it *illegal* were absurd: for if the parliament for the time being be sovereign in the united kingdom, it is the author, directly or circuitously, of all our positive law, and exclusively sets us the measure of legal justice and injustice.

[It is affirmed by Hobbes, in his masterly treatises on government, that 'no law can be unjust:' which proposition has been deemed by many, an immoral or pernicious paradox. If we look at the scope of the treatises in which it occurs, or even at the passages by which it is immediately followed, we shall find that the proposition is neither pernicious nor paradoxical, but is merely a truism put in unguarded terms. His meaning is obviously this: that 'no *positive* law is *legally* unjust.' And the decried proposition, as thus understood, is indisputably true. For positive law is the measure or test of legal justice and injustice: and, consequently, if positive law might be legally unjust, positive law might be unjust as measured or tried by itself. In the passages immediately following, he tells us that positive law may be generally pernicious; that is to say, may conflict with the Divine law which general utility indicates, and, as measured or tried by that law, may be unjust. He might have added, that it also may be unjust as measured by positive morality, although it must needs be just as measured by itself, and although it happen to be just as measured by the law of God.

For *just* or *unjust*, *justice* or *injustice*, is a term of relative and varying import. Whenever it is uttered with a determinate meaning, it is uttered with relation to a determinate law which the speaker assumes as a standard of comparison. This is hinted by Locke at the end of the division of laws which I have inserted in my fifth lecture; and it is, indeed, so manifest, on a little sustained reflection, that it hardly needs the authority of that great and venerable name.]

But when I affirm that the power of a sovereign is incapable of legal limitation, I always mean by a 'sovereign,' a monarch properly so called, or a sovereign number in its collegiate and sovereign capacity. Considered collectively, or considered in its corporate character, a sovereign number is sovereign and independent: but, considered severally, the individuals and smaller aggregates composing that sovereign number are subject to the supreme body of which they are component parts. Consequently, though the body is inevitably independent of legal or political duty, any of the individuals or aggregates whereof the body is composed may be legally bound by laws of which the body is the author. For example: A member of the house of lords, or a member of the house of commons, may be legally bound by an act of parliament, which, as one of the sovereign legislature, he has concurred with others in making. Nay, he may be legally bound by statutes, or by rules made judicially, which have immediately proceeded from subject or subordinate legislatures: for a law which proceeds immediately from a subject or subordinate legislature is set by the authority of the supreme. . . .

But if sovereign or supreme power be incapable of legal limitation, or if every supreme government be legally absolute, wherein (it may be asked) doth political liberty consist, and how do the supreme governments which are commonly deemed free, differ from the supreme governments which are commonly deemed despotic?

I answer, that political or civil liberty is the liberty from legal obligation, which is left or granted by a sovereign government to any of its own subjects: and that, since the power of the government is incapable of legal limitation, the government is legally free to abridge their political liberty, at its own pleasure or discretion. I say it is *legally* free to abridge their political liberty, at its own pleasure or discretion. For a government may be hindered by *positive morality* from abridging the political liberty which it leaves or grants to its subjects: and it is bound by the *law of God*, as known through the principle of utility, not to load them with legal duties which general utility condemns. – There are kinds of liberty from legal obligation, which will not quadrate with the foregoing description: for persons in a state of nature are independent of political duty, and independence of political duty is one of the essentials of sovereignty. But *political* or *civil* liberty supposes political society, or supposes a *polis* or *civitas*: and it is the liberty from legal obligation which is left by a state to its subjects, rather than the liberty from legal obligation which is inherent in sovereign power.

Political or civil liberty has been erected into an idol, and extolled with extravagant praises by doting and fanatical worshippers. But political or civil liberty is not more worthy of eulogy than political or legal restraint. Political or civil liberty, like political or legal restraint, may be generally useful, or generally pernicious; and it is not as being liberty, but as conducing to the general good, that political or civil liberty is an object deserving applause.

To the ignorant and bawling fanatics who stun you with their pother about liberty, political or civil liberty seems to be the principal end for which government ought to exist. But the final cause or purpose for which government ought to exist, is the furtherance of the common weal to the greatest possible extent. And it must mainly attain the purpose for which it ought to exist, by two sets of means: *first*, by conferring such rights on its subjects as general utility commends, and by imposing such relative duties (or duties corresponding to the rights) as are necessary to the enjoyment of the former: *secondly*, by imposing such absolute duties (or by imposing such duties without corresponding rights) as tend to promote the good of the political community at large, although they promote not specially the interests of determinate parties. Now he who is clothed with a legal right, is also clothed with a political liberty: that is to say, he has the liberty from legal obligation, which is necessary to the enjoyment of the right. Consequently, in so far as it attains its appropriate purpose by conferring rights upon its subjects, government attains that purpose through the medium of political liberty. But since it must impose a duty wherever it confers a right, and should also impose duties which have no corresponding rights, it is less through the medium of political liberty, than through that of legal restraint, that government must attain the purpose for which it ought to exist. To say that political liberty ought to be its principal end, or to say that its principal end ought to be legal restraint, is to talk absurdly: for each is merely a mean to that furtherance of the common weal, which is the only ultimate object of good or beneficent sovereignty. But though both propositions are absurd, the latter of the two absurdities is the least remote from the truth. – As I shall show hereafter, political or civil liberties rarely exist apart from corresponding legal restraints. Where persons in a state of subjection are free from legal duties, their liberties (generally speaking) would be nearly useless to themselves, unless they were protected in the enjoyment of their liberties, by legal duties on their fellows: that is to say, unless they had legal rights (importing such duties on their fellows) to those political liberties which are left them by the sovereign government. I am legally free, for example, to move from place to place, in so far as I can move from place to place consistently with my legal obligations: but this my political liberty would be but a sorry liberty, unless my fellow-subjects were restrained by a political duty from assaulting and imprisoning my body. Through the ignorance or negligence of a sovereign government, some of the civil liberties which it leaves or grants to its subjects, may not be protected against their fellows by answering legal duties: and some of those civil liberties may perhaps be protected sufficiently by religious and moral obligations. But, speaking generally, a political or civil liberty is coupled with a legal right to it: and, consequently, political liberty is fostered by that very political restraint from which the devotees of the idol liberty are so fearfully and blindly averse. . . .

I now have defined or determined the general notion of sovereignty, including the general notion of independent political society: And, in order that I might further elucidate the nature or essence of sovereignty, and of the independent political society which sovereignty implies, I have considered the possible forms of supreme political government with the limits, real or imaginary, of supreme political power. To complete my intended disquisition on the nature or essence of sovereignty, and of the independent political society that sovereignty implies, I proceed to the *origin* or *causes* of the habitual or permanent obedience, which, in every society political and independent, is rendered by the bulk of the community to the monarch or sovereign number. In other words, I proceed to the origin or causes of political government and society.

The proper purpose or end of a sovereign political government, or the purpose or end for which it ought to exist, is the greatest possible advancement of human happiness: Though, if it would duly accomplish its proper purpose or end, or advance as far as is possible the weal or good of mankind, it commonly must labour directly and particularly to advance as far as is possible the weal of its own community. The good of the universal society formed by mankind, is the aggregate good of the particular societies into which mankind is divided: just as the happiness of any of those societies is the aggregate happiness of its single or individual members. Though, then, the weal of mankind is the proper object of a government, or though the test of its conduct is the principle of general utility, it commonly ought to consult directly and particularly the weal of the particular community which the Deity has committed to its rule. If it truly adjust its conduct to the principle of general utility, it commonly will aim immediately at the particular and more precise, rather than the general and less determinate end.

It were easy to show, that the general and particular ends never or rarely conflict. Universally, or nearly universally, the ends are perfectly consistent, or rather are inseparably connected. An enlightened regard for the common happiness of nations, implies an enlightened patriotism; whilst the stupid and atrocious patriotism which looks exclusively to country, and would further the interests of country at the cost of all other communities, grossly misapprehends and frequently crosses the interests that are the object of its narrow concern. – But the topic which I now have suggested, belongs to the province of ethics, rather than the province of jurisprudence. It belongs especially to the peculiar department of ethics, which is concerned with international morality: which affects to determine the morality that ought to obtain between nations, or to determine the international morality commended by general utility.

From the proper purpose or end of a sovereign political government, or from the purpose or end for which it ought to exist, we may readily infer the causes of that habitual obedience which would be paid to the sovereign by the bulk of an enlightened society. Supposing that a given society were adequately instructed or enlightened, the habitual obedience to its government which was rendered by the bulk of the community, would exclusively arise from reasons bottomed in the principle of utility. If they thought the government accomplished perfectly its proper purpose or end, this their conviction or opinion would be their motive to obey. If they deemed the government faulty, a fear that the evil of resistance might surpass the evil of obedience, would be their inducement to submit: for they would not persist in their obedience to a government which they deemed imperfect, if they thought that a better government might probably be got by resistance, and that the probable good of the change outweighed its probable mischief.

Since every actual society is inadequately instructed or enlightened, the habitual obedience to its government which is rendered by the bulk of the community, is partly the consequence of custom: They partly pay that obedience to that present or established government, because they, and perhaps their ancestors, have been in a habit of obeying it. Or the habitual obedience to the government which is rendered by the bulk of the community, is partly the consequence of prejudices: meaning by 'prejudices,' opinions and sentiments which have no foundation whatever in the principle of general utility. If, for example, the government is monarchical, they partly pay that obedience to that present or established government because they are fond of monarchy inasmuch as it is monarchy, or because they are fond of the race from which the monarch has descended. Or if, for example, the government is popular, they partly pay that obedience to that present or established government, because they are fond of democracy inasmuch as it is democracy, or because the word 'republic' captivates their fancies and affections.

But though that habitual obedience is partly the consequence of custom, or though that habitual obedience is partly the consequence of prejudices, it partly arises from a reason bottomed in the principle of utility. It partly arises from a perception, by the generality or bulk of the community, of the expediency of political government: or (changing the phrase) it partly arises from a preference, by the generality or bulk of the community, of any government to anarchy. If, for specific reasons, they are attached to the established government, their general perception of the utility of government concurs with their special attachment. If they dislike the established government, their general perception of the utility of government controls and masters their dislike. They detest the established government: but if they would change it for another by resorting to resistance, they must travel to their object through an intervening anarchy which they detest more.

The habitual obedience to the government which is rendered by the bulk of the community, partly arises, therefore, in almost every society, from the cause which I now have described: namely, a perception, by the bulk of the community, of the utility of political government, or a preference by the bulk of the community, of any government to anarchy. And this is the only cause of the habitual obedience in question, which is common to all societies, or nearly all societies. It therefore is the only cause of the habitual obedience in question, which the present general disquisition can properly embrace. The causes of the obedience in question which are peculiar to particular societies, belong to the province of statistics, or the province of particular history.

The only general cause of the *permanence* of political governments, and the only general cause of the *origin* of political governments, are exactly or nearly alike. Though every government has arisen in part from specific or particular causes, almost every government must have arisen in part from the following general cause: namely, that the bulk of the natural society from which the political was formed, were desirous of escaping to a state of government, from a state of nature or anarchy. If they liked specially the government to which they submitted, their general perception of the utility of government concurred with their special inclination. If they disliked the government to which they submitted, their general perception of the utility of government controlled and mastered their repugnance. . . .

Every government has arisen through the *consent* of the people, or the bulk of the natural society from which the political was formed. For the bulk of the natural society from which a political is formed, submit *freely* or *voluntarily* to the inchoate political government. Or (changing the phrase) their submission is a consequence of *motives*, or they *will* the submission which they render.

But a special approbation of the government to which they freely submit, or a preference of that government to every other government, may not be their motive to submission. Although they submit to it freely, the government perhaps is forced upon them: that is to say, they could not withhold their submission from that particular government, unless they struggled through evils which they are loath to endure, or unless they resisted to the death. Determined by a fear of the evils which would follow a refusal to submit, (and, probably, by a general perception of the utility of political government,) they freely submit to a government from which they are specially averse.

The expression 'that every government arises through the people's *consent*,' is often uttered with the following meaning: That the bulk of a natural society about to become a political, or the inchoate subjects of an inchoate political government, *promise*, expressly or tacitly, to obey the future sovereign. The expression, however, as uttered with the meaning in question, confounds *consent* and *promise*, and therefore is grossly incorrect. That the inchoate subjects of every inchoate government *will* or *consent* to obey it, is one proposition: that they promise, expressly or tacitly, to render it obedience, is another proposition. Inasmuch as they actually obey, they will or consent to obey: or their will or consent to obey, is evinced by their actual obedience. But a will to render obedience, as evinced by actual obedience, is not of necessity a tacit promise to render it: although by a promise to render obedience, a will or consent to render it is commonly expressed or intimated.

That the inchoate subjects of every inchoate government *promise* to render it obedience, is a position involved by an hypothesis which I shall examine in the the next section.

In every community ruled by a monarch, the subject members of the community lie under duties to the monarch; and in every community ruled by a sovereign body, the subject members of the community (including the several members of the body itself), lie under duties to the body in its collective and sovereign capacity. In every community ruled by a monarch, the monarch lies under duties towards his subjects: and in every community ruled by a sovereign body, the collective and sovereign body lies under duties to its subjects (including its own members considered severally).

The duties of the subjects towards the sovereign government, are partly religious, partly legal, and partly moral.

The religious duties of the subjects towards the sovereign government, are creatures of the Divine law as known through the principle of utility. If it thoroughly accomplish the purpose for which it ought to exist, or further the general weal to the greatest possible extent, the subjects are bound religiously to pay it habitual obedience. And, if the general good which probably would follow submission outweigh the general good which probably would follow resistance, the subjects are bound religiously to pay it habitual obedience, although it accomplish imperfectly its proper purpose or end. – The legal duties of the subjects towards the sovereign government, are creatures of positive laws which itself has imposed upon them, or which are incumbent upon them by its own authority and might. – The moral duties of the subjects towards the sovereign government, are creatures of positive morality. They mainly are creatures of law (in the improper acceptation of the term) which the general opinion of the community itself sets to its several members.

The duties of the sovereign government towards the subjects are partly religious and partly moral. If it lay under legal duties towards the subjects, it were not a supreme, but were merely a subordinate government.

Its religious duties towards the subjects, are creatures of the Divine law as known through the principle of utility. It is bound by the Divine law as known through the principle of utility, to advance as far as is possible the weal or good of mankind: and, to advance as far as is possible the weal or good of mankind, it commonly must labour directly and particularly to advance as far as is possible the happiness of its own community. – Its moral duties towards the subjects, are creatures of positive morality. They mainly are creatures of laws (in the improper acceptation of the term) which the general opinion of its own community lays or imposes upon it.

It follows from the foregoing analysis, that the duties of the subjects towards the sovereign government, with the duties of the sovereign government towards the subjects, originate respectively in three several sources: namely, the Divine law (as indicated by the principle of utility), positive law, and positive morality. And, to my understanding, it seems that we account sufficiently for the origin of those obligations, when we simply refer them to those their obvious fountains. It seems to my understanding, that an ampler solution of their origin is not in the least requisite, and, indeed, is impossible. But there are many writers on political government and society, who are not content to account for their origin, by simply referring them to those their manifest sources. It seems to the writers in question, that we want an ampler solution of the origin of those obligations, or, at least, of the origin of such of them as are imposed by the law of God. And, to find that ampler solution which they believe requisite, those writers resort to the hypothesis of the *original covenant* or *contract*, or the *fundamental civil pact*. . . .

Since the 1870's English jurisprudence has been strongly Austinian. Austin's most faithful disciples have been the following: Sir William Markby, *Elements of Law* (1871); Sheldon Amos, *A Systematic View of the Science of Jurisprudence* (1872), *The Science of Law* (1875); Sir Thomas Erskine Holland, *The Elements of Jurisprudence* (1880); William Edward Hearn, *The Theory of Legal Duties and Rights* (1883); W. Jethro Brown, *The Austinian Theory of Law* (1906); R. A. Eastwood and G. W. Keeton, *The Austinian Theories of Law and Sovereignty* (1929).

However, in the course of the century his views have also been subjected to considerable criticism. Much of the criticism has centred not so much on the volitional as on the technical aspects of the imperative theory, and the use of the term "command" itself, Patterson points out, "has been more widely criticized than any other part of Austin's conception" (*Jurisprudence* 90). Criticism of this kind has come even from those most sympathetic to Austin. Holland, for example, objects to the characterization of law as command because it is unable to explain satisfactorily such things as declaratory laws and laws repealing laws. He suggests instead a definition of law as a "proposition announcing the will of the State" (12th ed. 1916, 88-89), which will be able to explain indicative-mood laws as well as imperative-mood ones. Eastwood and Keeton, the most authentic Austinians of the twentieth century, though they maintain that law is most properly defined in terms of command, admit that there is more to law than command. Kelsen attacks the notion of command for introducing into law a psychological element which has no place there, viz, the sanction-induced state of fear which leads to obedience; for him behavioural motives have no place in "pure" law than moral and religious elements. Yet all of these jurisprudents would probably agree with Jethro Brown that the most serious criticism that could be urged against Austin's positivism was, not its positive errors, but its inadequacy, and certainly all would maintain the necessity of the complete separation of law and morals.

But other thinkers object to the very separation of law and morals posited by Austin and to the will-theory of law on which it is based. Sir Frederick Pollock takes

Austin to task for maintaining that law is essentially sanction. "Law is enforced by the State because it is law," he insists; "it is not law merely because the State enforces it." (*A First Book of Jurisprudence* 29 [1918]). For Lord Bryce, too, force is not an essential constituent but a consequent of legal order; "it is by the natural or providential order of things, and in virtue of the constitution of man as a social being, that men are grouped into communities under leaders who judge among them," he says, and adds that "the same influences which have drawn men together keep them together, and make them willingly yield to the State the physical strength . . . needful for its purposes." (*Studies in History and Jurisprudence*, II, 501-502 [1901]) Sir John Salmond's view is that the imperative theory grossly oversimplifies the concept of law by excluding from it all notes except that of force. The note of justice is equally essential, he argues, for "law is not right alone, or might alone, but the perfect union of the two." (*Jurisprudence* 52 [7th ed. 1924]). Even Professor Hart, who is obviously quite well disposed towards Austin, hits at the roots of the command theory.

Manning's gloss on Austin plays down the place of sanction in positivism. He compares the sovereign to a sheep-dog and maintains that the sovereign's duty is merely to round up marginal cases. Not all the sheep are or want to be marginal cases. Indeed, he points out, "the flock owes its continued existence as such not merely to the sheep-dog, but to the fact that the average sheep is content to trot along in the middle, and rarely if ever becomes a marginal case." ["Austin Today: or 'the Province of Jurisprudence' Re-examined" in *Modern Theories of Law* 180, 194 (1933)]. He maintains, moreover, that the obedience even of the marginal cases is not necssarily due to fear of the dog.

The change in attitude towards Austin even during this century is described by Buckland, *Some Reflections on Jurisprudence* 2: "The analysis of legal concepts is what jurisprudence meant for the student in the days of my youth. In fact it meant Austin. He was a religion; today he seems to be regarded rather as a disease."

For recent criticisms of Austin and positivism generally see MacGuigan, "Law, Morals, and Positivism" (1961) 4, *U. of Toronto L. J.* 1, and Stumpf, "Austin's Theory of the Separation of Law and Morals" (1961) 14, *Vand. L. Rev.* 117.

John Chipman Gray, 1839 - 1915
Professor of Law, Harvard University

THE NATURE AND SOURCES OF LAW (1909)

Chapter IV

THE LAW

SEC. 191. The Law of the State or of any organized body of men is composed of the rules which the courts, that is, the judicial organs of that body, lay down for the determination of legal rights and duties. The difference in this matter between contending schools of Jurisprudence arises largely from not distinguishing between the Law and the Sources of the Law. On the hand, to affirm the existence of *nicht positivisches Recht*, that is, of Law which the courts do not follow, is declared to be an absurdity; and on the other hand, it is declared to be an absurdity to say that the Law of a great nation means the opinions of half-a-dozen old gentlemen, some of them, conceivably, of very limited intelligence. The truth is, each party is looking at but one side of the shield. If those half-a-dozen old gentlemen form the highest judicial tribunal of a country, then no rule or principle which they refuse to follow is Law in that country. However desirable, for instance, it may be that a man should be obliged to make gifts which he has promised to make, yet if the courts of a country will not compel him to keep his promise, it is not the Law of that country that promises to make a gift are binding. On the other hand, those six men seek the rules which they follow not in their own whims, but they derive them from sources often of the most general and permanent character, to which they are directed, by the organized body to which they belong, to apply themselves. . . .

SEC. 215. To come, then, to the question whether the judges discover preexisting Law, or whether the body of rules that they lay down is not the expression of preexisting Law, but the Law itself. Let us take a concrete instance: On many matters which have come in question in various jurisdictions, there is no doctrine received *semper, ubique, et ab omnibus*. For instance, Henry Pitt has built a reservoir on his land, and has filled it with water; and, without any negligence on his part, either in the care or construction of his reservoir, it bursts, and the water, pouring forth, floods and damages the land of Pitt's neighbor, Thomas Underhill. Has Underhill a right to recover compensation from Pitt? In England, in the leading case of *Rylands* v. *Fletcher*, it was held that he could recover, and this decision has been followed in some of the United States – for instance, in Massachusetts; but in others, as, I believe, in New Jersey, the contrary is held.

SEC. 216. Now, suppose that Pitt's reservoir is in one of the newer States, say Utah, and suppose, further, that the question has never arisen there before; that there is no statute, no decision, no custom on the subject; the court has to decide the case somehow; suppose it should follow *Rylands* v. *Fletcher* and should rule that in such cases the party injured can recover. The State, then, through its judicial organ, backed by the executive power of the State, would be recognizing the rights of persons injured by such accidents, and, therefore, the doctrine of *Rylands* v. *Fletcher* would be undoubtedly the present Law in Utah.

SEC. 217. Suppose, again, that a similar state of facts arises in the adjoining State of Nevada, and that there also the question is presented for the first time, and that there is no statute, decision, or custom on the point; the Nevada court has to decide the case somehow; suppose it should decline to follow *Rylands* v. *Fletcher*, and should rule that in such cases the party injured is without remedy. Here the State of Nevada would refuse to recognize any right in the injured party and, therefore, it would unquestionably be the present Law in Nevada that a person injured by such an accident would have no right to compensation.

SEC. 218. Let us now assume that the conditions and habits of life are the same in these two adjoining States; that being so, these contradictory doctrines cannot both conform to an ideal rule of Law, and let us, therefore, assume that an all-wise and all-good intelligence, considering the question, would think that one of these doctrines was right and the other wrong, according to the true standard of morality, whatever that may be. It matters not, for the purposes of the discussion, which of the two doctrines it is, but let us suppose that the intelligence aforesaid would approve *Rylands* v. *Fletcher*; that is, it would think the Law as established in Nevada by the decision of its court did not conform to the eternal principles of right.

SEC. 219. The fact that the ideal theory of Law disapproved the Law as established in Nevada would not affect the present existence of that Law. However wrong intellectually or morally it might be, it would be the Law of the State today. But what was the Law in Nevada a week before a rule for decision of such questions was adopted by the courts of that State? Three views seem possible: *first*, that the Law was then ideally right, and contrary to the rule now declared and practised on; *second*, that the Law was then the same as is now declared and practised; *third*, that there was then no Law on the matter.

SEC. 220. The first theory seems untenable on any notion of discovery. A discoverer is a discoverer of that which is, – not of that which is not. The result of such a theory would be that when Underhill received the injury and brought his suit, he had an interest which would be protected by the State, and that it now turns out that he did not have it, – a contradiction in terms.

SEC. 221. We have thus to choose between the theory that the Law was at that time what it now is, and the theory that there was than no law at all on the subject. The latter is certainly the view of reason and of common sense alike. There was, at the time in question, *ex hypothesi,* no statute, no precedent, no custom on the subject; of the inhabitants of the State not one out of a hundred had an opinion on the matter or had ever thought of it; of the few, if any, to whom the question had ever occurred, the opinions were, as likely as not, conflicting. To say that on this subject there was really Law existing in Nevada, seems only to show how strong a root legal fictions can strike into our mental processes.

SEC. 222. When the element of long time is introduced, the absurdity of the view of Law preexistent to its declaration is obvious. What was the Law in the time of Richard Coeur de Lion on the liability of a telegraph company to the persons to whom a message was sent? It may be said that though the Law can preexist its declaration, it is conceded that the Law with regard to a natural force cannot exist before the discovery of the force. Let us take, then, a transaction which might have occurred in the eleventh century: A sale of chattels, a sending to the vendee, his insolvency, and an order by the vendor to the carrier not to deliver. What was the Law on stoppage *in transitu* in the time of William the Conqueror?

SEC. 223. The difficulty of believing in preexisting Law is still greater when there is a change in the decision of the courts. In Massachusetts it was held in 1849, by the Supreme Judicial Court, that if a man hired a horse in Boston on a Sunday to drive to Nahant, and drove instead to Nantasket, the keeper of the livery stable had no right to sue him in trover for the conversion of the horse. But in 1871 this decision was overruled, and the right was given to the stablekeeper. Now, did stable-keepers have such rights, say, in 1845? If they did, then the court in 1849 did not discover the Law. If they did not, then the court in 1871 did not discover the Law.

SEC. 224. And this brings us to the reason why courts and jurists have so struggled to maintain the preexistence of the Law, why the common run of writers speak of the judges as merely stating the Law, and why Mr. Carter, in an advance towards the truth, says of the judges that they are discoverers of the Law. That reason is the unwillingness to recognize the fact that the courts, with the consent of the State, have been constantly in the practice of applying in the decision of controversies, rules which were not in existence and were, therefore, not knowable by the parties when the causes of controversy occurred. It is the unwillingness to face the certain fact that courts are constantly making *ex post facto* Law.

SEC. 225. The unwillingness is natural, particularly on the part of the courts, who do not desire to call attention to the fact that they are exercising a power which bears so unpopular a name, but it is not reasonable. Practically in its application to actual affairs, for most of the laity, the Law, except for a few crude notions of the equity involved in some of its general principles, is all *ex post facto.* When a man marries, or enters into a partnership, or buys a piece of land, or engages in any other transaction, he has the vaguest possible idea of the Law governing the situation, and with our complicated system of Jurisprudence, it is impossible it should be otherwise. If he delayed to make a contract or do an act until he understood exactly all the legal consequences it involved, the contract would never be made or the act done. Now the Law of which a man has no knowledge is the same to him as if it did not exist.

Chapter V

THE COURTS

SEC. 266. *The Limits of Judicial Power.* Thus far we have seen that the Law is made up of the rules for decision which the courts lay down; that all such rules are Law; that rules for conduct which the courts do not apply are not Law; that the fact that the courts apply rules is what makes them Law; that there is no mysterious entity "The Law" apart from these rules; and that the judges are rather the creators than the discoverers of the Law.

SEC. 267. Is the power of the judges, then, absolute? Can the comparatively few individuals who fill judicial position in the State, for instance, lay down rules for the government of human intercourse at their bare pleasure or whim? Not so; the judges are but organs of the State; they have only such power as the organization of the State gives them; and what that organization is, is determined by the wills of the real rulers of the State.

SEC. 268. Who are the rulers of a State, is a question of fact and not of form. In a nominal autocracy, the real rulers may be a number of court favorites or the priests of a religion; and in a democracy, the real ruler may be a demagogue or political boss.

SEC. 269. It is conceivable that a body of judges may be the ruling wills of a community, and then they hold their powers by virtue of dominating other wills, but this, except in a very primitive community, can hardly ever be the case. The half-a-dozen elderly men sitting on a platform behind a green or red cloth, with very probably not commanding wills or powerful physique, can exercise their functions only within those limits which the real rulers of the State allow for the exercise; for the State and the court as an organ thereof are the product of the wills of those rulers.

SEC. 273. The power of the rulers of the State or other community in reference to its judicial organs or courts is exercised in a twofold way, – first, by creating them, and secondly, in laying down limits for their action, or, in other words, indicating the sources from which they are to derive the rules which make up the Law. From what *sources* does the State or other community direct its judges to obtain the Law? These sources are defined for the most part in a very vague and general way, but one rule is clear and precise. The State requires that the acts of its legislative organ shall bind the courts, and so far as they go, shall be paramount to all other sources. This may be said to be a necessary consequence from the very conception of an organized community of men.

SEC. 274. The other sources from which courts may draw their general rules are fourfold, – judicial precedents, opinions of experts, customs, and principles of morality (using morality as including public policy). Whether there is any precedent, expert opinion, custom, or principle from which a rule can be drawn, and whether a rule shall be drawn accordingly, are questions which, in most communities, are left to the courts themselves, and yet there are probably in every community limits within or beyond which courts may, or, on the other hand, cannot, seek for rules from the sources mentioned, although the limits are not precisely defined. Take, for instance, a country where the English Common Law has prevailed. If a court in such a country should, in matters not governed by statute, absolutely refuse to follow any judicial precedents, it is not likely that the rulers of the country would recognize the doctrine of that court as Law; or, if a court should frame a rule based upon the principle that infanticide was not immoral, that rule would not be the Law.

SEC. 275. Though the commands by the rulers of a community as to the limits within which these last four classes of sources are to be sought by the courts are indefinite, while the command that legislative acts must be followed by the courts is precise and peremptory, the fact is that this latter rule, in its working, is almost as indefinite as those which are imposed on the courts with reference to the other sources; for, after all, it is only words that the legislature utters; it is for the courts to say what those words mean; that is, it is for them to interpret legislative acts; undoubtedly there are limits upon their power of interpretation, but these limits are almost as undefined as those which govern them in their dealing with the other sources.

SEC. 276. And this is the reason why legislative acts, statutes, are to be dealt with as sources of Law, and not as part of the Law itself, why they are to be coordinated with the other sources which I have mentioned. It has been sometimes said that the Law is composed of two parts, – legislative law and judge-made law, but, in truth, all the Law is judge-made law. The shape in which a statute is imposed on the community as a guide for conduct is that statute as interpreted by the courts. The courts put life into the dead words of the statute. To quote again from Bishop Hoadly, a sentence which I have before given: "Nay, whoever hath an *absolute authority* to *interpret* any written or spoken laws, it is *He* who is truly the Law Giver to all intents and purposes, and not the Person who first wrote and spoke them." I will return to this later. . . .

Chapter VIII

STATUTES

SEC. 366. *Interpretation of Statutes.* It may be urged that if the Law of a society be the body of rules applied by its courts, then statutes should be considered as being part of the Law itself, and not merely as being a source of the Law; that they are rules to be applied by the courts directly, and should not be regarded merely as fountains from which the courts derive their own rules. Such a view is very common in the books. And if statutes interpreted themselves, this would be true; but statutes do not interpret themselves; their meaning is declared by the courts, and *it is with the meaning declared by the courts, and with no other meaning, that they are imposed upon the community as Law.* True though it be, that, of all the sources from which the courts draw the Law, statutes are the most stringent and precise, yet the power of the judges over the statutes is very great; and this not only in countries of the Common Law, but also on the Continent of Europe, where the office of judge is less highly esteemed. . . .

SEC. 368. A judge puts before himself the printed page of the statute book; it is mirrored on the retina of his eye, and from this impression he has to reproduce the thought of the law-giving body. The process is far from being merely mechanical; it is obvious how the character of the judge and the cast of his mind must affect the operation, and what a different shape the thought when reproduced in the mind of the judge may have from that which it bore in the mind of the lawgiver. This is true even if the function of the judge be deemed only that of attempting to reproduce in his own mind the thought of the lawgiver; but as we shall see in a moment, a judge, starting from the words of a statute, is often led to results which he applies as if they had been the thought of the legislature, while yet he does not believe, and has no reason to believe, that his present thought is the same as any thought which the legislature really had. . . .

SEC. 370. But the matter does not rest here. A fundamental misconception prevails, and pervades all the books as to the dealing of the courts with statutes. Interpretation is generally spoken of as if its chief function was to discover what the meaning of the Legislature really was. But when a Legislature has had a real intention, one way or another, on a point, it is not once in a hundred times that any doubt arises as to what its intention was. If that were all that a judge had to do with a statute, interpretation of statutes, instead of being one of the most difficult of a judge's duties, would be extremely easy. The fact is that the difficulties of so-called interpretation arise when the Legislature has had no meaning at all; when the question which is raised on the statute never occurred to it; when what the judges have to do is, not to determine what the Legislature did mean on a point which was present to its mind, but to guess what it would have intended on a point not present to its mind, if the point had been present. If there are any lawyers among those who honor me with their attendance, let them consider any dozen cases of the interpretation of statutes, as they have occurred consecutively in their reading or practice, and they will, I venture to say, find that in almost all of them it is probable, and that in most of them it is perfectly evident, that the makers of the statutes had no real intention, one way or another, on the point in question; that if they had, they would have made their meaning clear; and that when the judges are professing to declare what the Legislature meant, they are, in truth, themselves legislating to fill up *casus omissi*. . . .

SEC. 379. But, on the other hand, it has been said over and over again, both in the Civil and in the Common Law, that the courts must not undertake to make the legislature say what it has not said. Is not the true rule that the judge should give to the words of a statute the meaning which they would have had, *if he had used them himself*, unless there be something in the circumstances which makes him believe that such was *not* the *actual* meaning of the legislature?. . . .

Chapter XIII

MORALITY AND EQUITY

SEC. 642. When a case comes before a court for decision, it may be that nothing can be drawn from the sources heretofore mentioned; there may be no statute, no judicial precedent, no professional opinion, no custom, bearing on the case somehow; the decision of cases is what courts are for. The French Code Civil says: "*Le juge qui refusera de juger sous pretexte du silence, de l'obscurite, ou de l'insufficiance de la loi, pourra etre poursuivi comme coupable de deni de justice.*" And I do not know of any system of Law where a judge is held to be justified in refusing to pass upon a controversy because there is no person or book or custom to tell him how to decide it. He must find out for himself; he must determine what the Law ought to be; he must have recourse to the principles of morality.

SEC. 643. In organized communities, political or other, the courts, in laying down rules for the decision of cases, are hemmed in and limited in many ways; the duty and responsibility of considering what rules they ought to apply is largely taken away from them, and there is imposed upon them, or they impose upon themselves, by reason of statutes, precedents, professional opinion or custom, lines of conduct to be followed without regard to their moral character; but where these limitations have not been imposed, then it is safe to say that in all civilized societies the courts are impliedly directed to decide in accordance with the precepts of morality.

SEC. 644. Of course, I take morality in its largest sense, and mean by moral conduct, right conduct. In many, perhaps in most, of the questions, which are raised in the Law, morality presents itself in the guise of public policy. But even when the motive of the judge is simply to bring one doctrine into harmony with another doctrine, or to extend a doctrine by analogy, he is acting in an ethical way, for it is a good thing in itself that the rules of the Law should be harmonious, and should be extended harmoniously.

SEC. 645. It is from this source that a great amount of our Law is drawn. In fact it is the way in which most new Law is now brought in, except what is due to the statutebook; and it should be observed that this source not only works alone when the others fail, but that when the others are in operation, this mingles with them and largely influences their direction and effect. Whether a statute shall be interpreted one way or another is often determined by the moral character which the one or the other interpretation will give to it; and there are few judicial precedents or professional opinions or customs whose position as sources of Law is not strengthened or weakened by the fact of their agreeing or disagreeing with sound ethical principles. In fact, in a large number of cases, the sources of the Law are indistinguishably joined.

SEC. 646. Austin, in his Province of Jurisprudence Determined, having devoted the first lecture to a consideration of the Nature of Law, takes up in the second the question of the index to the unrevealed Divine Law, and discusses it at great length through three lectures; as is well known, he arrives at the conclusion that utility is the index of the Divine Law and the test or morality.

SEC. 647. It is hard to defend Austin's consistency in thus giving up so large a part of the volume to a discusion on the test of morality. The main thesis of the book is to show that positive Law is the command of the Sovereign; that its existence and force are in no way dependent upon the ethics of its contents; and that positive Law is the subject-matter of Jurisprudence as compared with the Science of Legislation. And this has often been remarked upon. Thus Sir Henry Maine: – "The truth is that Austin's system is consistent with *any* ethical theory; and if Austin seems to assert the contrary, I think the cause is to be sought in his firm conviction of the truth of his own ethical creed, which, I need not say, was Utilitarianism in its earlier shape. Devotion to this philosophy, coupled with what I hold to be a faulty arrangement, has produced the most serious blemish in the 'Province of Jurisprudence Determined.' The second, third, and fourth lectures are occupied with an attempt to identify the law of God and the law of Nature (so far as these last words can be allowed to have any meaning) with the rules required by the theory of utility. . . . Taken at its best, it is a discussion belonging not to the philosophy of Law, but to the philosophy of Legislation. The jurist, properly so called, has nothing to do with any ideal standard of Law or morals."

SEC. 648. From Austin's point of view, his discussion of the test of morality may not be justifiable, but when we believe the doctrines of morality to be a source, and one of the main sources, from which the Law is drawn, they are as appropriate for the consideration of Jurisprudence as are the statutes, precedents, professional opinions, or customs to which the courts have recourse for their rules.

SEC. 649. Indeed, if Jurisprudence is to be a progressive science, it must take cognizance of the changes which knowledge or ignorance has produced in human beliefs and ideals. Take three communities, let them have the same statutes and the other sources of Law the same, but let the courts of one of them adopt the Koran as its index of morality, another the Bible as interpreted in England one hundred and fifty years ago, and another the scheme of morals, whatever it may be, which prevails, say in France, at the present day, the Laws of those three communities will show before long a varying development.

SEC. 650. What is the true test of morality is not a question which can be answered here. It is obvious that it is very important for the theory of the Law. To take an instance: In many of the States, the question of the liability of the Pullman Car Company for the loss by theft from a sleeping car of a commercial traveller's bag containing samples of hat pins, is a novel one, and the judges are or will be called on to make Law upon it. What question should a judge ask? Should it be, "What protection of a sample bag is desirable to secure the greatest happiness of the greatest number?" or should it be, "What is my intuitive moral sense on the subject of Pullman cars?" or again, should it be, "What it God's revealed or unrevealed will touching bagmen?" or again, "What dealing with drummers is most in accordance with the Freedom of the Will?" or, "What protection to hat pins is most according to Nature?" or is it a mixed affair to which two or more of these tests should be applied? It is conceivable that application of these different tests might lead to different results.

SEC. 651. But although the test selected for determining the morality of a course of conduct and, therefore, the propriety of a decision, is theoretically of the first importance, yet it must be admitted that the conscious adoption of one test rather than another by a judge is not of so much practical consequence as might at first be supposed, for, by a familiar principle of human nature, when a man thinks that a thing ought to be done, he will not find it difficult to make it stand all the tests of morality that may be applied to it, and he will come to the conclusion that the greatest happiness of the greatest number, the dictates of conscience, the will of God, the Freedom of Will, and Nature unite in demanding it.

SEC. 652. Whatever may be the test to establish the ultimate principles of morality, the doctrine of utility must be all-important in working out details. But whose good should a court seek, the good of the community whose organ it is, or the good of the world at large? Should it, for instance, give preference to the domestic over the foreign creditors of a bankrupt? The true doctrine, though I advance this with some diffidence, would seem to be that the position of the courts should be much the same as that of a private individual. With an individual, regard for himself, for his family, and for others, all go to make up a complete morality; so, with a judge, as an organ of the State, regard for the members of the State and for persons not members of the State should be joined. The science of ethics, whatever it may do in the future, has as yet made trifling progress in settling any practical rules for the decision of such questions. . . .

Hans Kelsen, 1881–

Professor of Law, University of Vienna; Professor of Political Science, University of California at Berkeley.

GENERAL THEORY OF LAW AND STATE
(1945)
X. The Legal Order

A. THE UNITY OF A NORMATIVE ORDER

a. The Reason of Validity: the Basic Norm

The legal order is a systems of norms. The question then arises: What is it that makes a system out of a multitude of norms? When does a norm belong to a certain system of norms, an order? This question is in close connection with the question as to the reason of validity of a norm.

In order to answer this question, we must first clarify the grounds on which we assign validity to a norm. When we assume the truth of a statement about reality, it is because the statement corresponds to reality, because our experience confirms it. The statement "A physical body expands when heated" is true, because we have repeatedly and without exception observed that physical bodies expand when they are heated. A norm is not a statement about reality and is therefore incapable of being "true" or "false," in the sense determined above. A norm is either valid or non-valid. Of the two statements: "You shall assist a fellowman in need," and "You shall lie whenever you find it useful," only the first, not the second, is considered to express a valid norm. What is the reason?

The reason for the validity of a norm is not, like the test of the truth of an "is" statement, its conformity to reality. As we have already stated, a norm is not valid because it is efficacious. The question why something ought to occur can never be answered by an assertion to the effect that something occurs, but only by an assertion that something ought to occur. In the language of daily life, it is true, we frequently justify a norm by referring to a fact. We say, for instance: "You shall not kill because God has forbidden it in one of the Ten Commandments"; or a mother says to her child: "You ought to go to school because your father has ordered it." However, in these statements the fact that God has issued a command or the fact that the father has ordered the child to do something is only apparently the reason for the validity of the norms in question. The true reason is norms tacitly presupposed because taken for granted. The reason for the validity of the norm, You shall not kill, is the general norm, You shall obey the commands of God. The reason for the validity of the norm, You ought to go to school, is the general norm, Children ought to obey their father. If these norms are not presupposed, the references to the facts concerned are not answers to the questions why we shall not kill, why the child ought to go to school. The fact that somebody commands something is, in itself, no reason for the statement that one ought to behave in conformity with the command, no reason for considering the command as a valid norm, no reason for the validity of the norm the contents of which corresponds to the command. The reason for the validity of a norm is always a norm, not a fact. The quest for the reason of validity of a norm leads back, not to reality, but to another norm from which the first norm is derivable in a sense that will be investigated later. Let us, for the present, discuss a concrete example. We accept the statement "You shall assist a fellowman in need," as a valid norm because it follows from the statement "You shall love your neighbor." This statement we accept as a valid norm, either because it appears to us as an ultimate norm whose validity is self-evident, or – for instance – Christ has bidden that you shall love your neighbor, and we postulate as an ultimate valid norm the statement "You shall obey the commandments of Christ." The statement "You shall lie whenever you find it useful," we do not accept as a valid norm, because it is neither derivable from another valid norm nor is it in itself an ultimate, self-evidently valid norm.

A norm the validity of which cannot be derived from a superior norm we call a "basic" norm. All norms whose validity may be traced back to one and the same basic norm form a system of norms, or an order. This basic norm constitutes, as a common source, the bond between all the different norms of which an order consists. That a norm belongs to a certain system of norms, to a certain normative order, can be tested only by ascertaining that it derives its validity from the basic norm constituting the order. Whereas as "is" statement is true because it agrees with the reality of sensuous experience, an "ought" statement is a valid norm only if it belongs to such a valid system of norms, if it can be derived from a basic norm presupposed as valid. The ground of truth of an "is" statement is its conformity to the reality of our experience; the reason for the validity of a norm is a presupposition, a norm presupposed to be an ultimately valid, that is, basic norm. The quest for the reason of validity of a norm is not – like the quest for the cause of an effect – a *regressus ad infinitum*; it is terminated by a highest norm which is the last reason of validity within the normative system, whereas a last or first cause has no place within a system of natural reality.

b. The Static System of Norms

According to the nature of the basic norm, we may distinguish between two different types of orders or normative systems: static and dynamic systems. Within an order of the first kind the norms are "valid" and that means, we assume that the individuals whose behavior is regulated by the norms "ought" to behave as the norms prescribe, by virtue of their contents: Their contents has an immediately evident quality that guarantees their validity, or, in other terms: the norms are valid because of their inherent appeal. This quality the norms have because they are derivable from a specific basic norm as the particular is derivable from the general. The binding force of the basic norm is itself self-evident, or at least presumed to be so. Such norms as "You must not lie," "You must not deceive," "You shall keep your promise," follow from a general norm prescribing truthfulness. From the norm "You shall love your neighbor" one may deduce such norms as "You must not hurt your neighbor," "You shall help him in need," and so on. If one asks why one has to love one's neighbor, perhaps the answer will be found in some still more general norm, let us say the postulate that one has to live "in harmony with the universe." If that is the most general norm of whose validity we are convinced, we will consider it as the ultimate norm. Its obligatory nature may appear so obvious that one does not feel any need to ask for the reason of its validity. Perhaps one may also succeed in deducing the principle of truthfulness and its consequences from this "harmony" postulate. One would then have reached a norm on which a whole system of morality could be based. However, we are not interested here in the question of what specific norm lies at the basis of such and such a system of morality. It is essential only that the various norms of any such system are implicated by the basic norm as the particular is implied by the general, and that, therefore, all the particular norms of such a system are obtainable by means of an intellectual operation, viz., by the inference from the general to the particular. Such a system is of a static nature.

c. The Dynamic System of Norms

The derivation of a particular norm may, however, be carried out also in another way. A child, asking why it must not lie, might be given the answer that its father has forbidden it to lie. If the child should further ask why it has to obey its father, the reply would perhaps be that God has commanded that it obey its parents. Should the child put the question why one has to obey the commands of God, the only answer would be that this is a norm beyond which one cannot look for a more ultimate norm. That norm is the basic norm providing the foundation for a system of dynamic character. Its various norms cannot be obtained from the basic norm by any intellectual operation. The basic norm merely establishes a certain authority, which may well in turn vest norm-creating power in some other authorities. The norms of a dynamic system have to be created through acts of will by those individuals who have been authorized to create norms by some higher norm. This authorization is a delegation. Norm creating power is delegated from one authority to another authority; the former is the higher, the latter the lower authority. The basic norm of a dynamic system is the fundamental rule according to which the norms of the system are to be created. A norm forms part of a dynamic system if it has been created in a way that is – in the last analysis – determined by the basic norm. A norm thus belongs to the religious system just given by way of example if it is created by God or originates in an authority having its power from God, "delegated" by God.

B. THE LAW AS A DYNAMIC SYSTEM OF NORMS

a. The Positivity of Law

The system of norms we call a legal order is a system of the dynamic kind. Legal norms are not valid because they themselves or the basic norm have a content the binding force of which is self-evident. They are not valid because of their inherent appeal. Legal norms may have any kind of content. There is no kind of human behavior that, because of its nature, could not be made into a legal duty corresponding to a legal right. The validity of a legal norm cannot be questioned on the ground that its contents are incompatible with some moral or political value. A norm is a valid legal norm by virtue of the fact that it has been created according to a definite rule and by virtue thereof only. The basic norm of a legal order is the postulated ultimate rule according to which the norms of this order are established and annulled, receive and lose their validity. The statement "Any man who manufactures or sells alcoholic liquors as beverages shall be punished" is a valid legal norm if it belongs to a certain legal order. This it does if this norm has been created in a definite way ultimately determined by the basic norm of that legal order, and if it has not again been nullified in a definite way, ultimately determined by the same basic norm. The basic norm may, for instance, be such that a norm belongs to the system provided that it has been decreed by the parliament or created by custom or established by the courts, and has not been abolished by a decision of the parliament or through custom or a contrary court practice. The statement mentioned above is no valid legal norm if it does not belong to a valid legal order – it may be that no such norm has been created in the way ultimately determined by the basic norm, or it may be that, although a norm has been created in that way, it has been repealed in a way ultimately determined by the basic norm.

Law is always positive law, and its positivity lies in the fact that it is created and annulled by acts of human beings, thus being independent of morality and similar norm systems. This constitutes the difference between positive law and natural law, which, like morality, is deduced from a presumably self-evident basic norm which is considered to be the expression of the "will of nature" or of "pure reason." The basic norm of a positive legal order is nothing but the fundamental rule according to which the various norms of the order are to be created. It qualifies a certain event at the initial event in the creation of the various legal norms. It is the starting point of a norm-creating process and, thus, has an entirely dynamic character. The particular norms of the legal order cannot be logically deduced from this basic norm, as can the norm "Help your neighbor when he needs your help" from the norm "Love your neighbor." They are to be created by a special act of will, not concluded from a premise by an intellectual operation.

b. Customary and Statutory Law

Legal norms are created in many different ways: general norms through custom or legislation, individual norms through judicial and administrative acts or legal transactions. Law is always created by an act that deliberately aims at creating law, except in the case when law has its origin in custom, that is to say, in a generally observed course of conduct, during which the acting individuals do not consciously aim at creating law; but they must regard their acts as in conformity with a binding norm and not as a matter of arbitrary choice. This is the requirement of so-called *opinio juris sive necessitatis*. The usual interpretation of this requirement is that the individuals constituting by their conduct the law-creating custom must regard their acts as determined by a legal rule; they must believe that they perform a legal duty or exercise a legal right. This doctrine is not correct. It implies that the individuals concerned must act in error: since the legal rule which is created by their conduct cannot yet determine this conduct, at least not as a legal rule. They may erroneously believe themselves to be bound by a rule of law, but this error is not necessary to constitute a law-creating custom. It is sufficient that the acting individuals consider themselves bound by any norm whatever.

We shall distinguish between statutory and customary law as the two fundamental types of law. By statutory law we shall understand law created in a way other than by custom, namely, by legislative, judicial, or administrative acts or by legal transactions, especially by contracts and (international) treaties.

C. THE BASIC NORM OF A LEGAL ORDER

a. The Basic Norm and the Constitution

The derivation of the norms of a legal order from the basic norm of that order is performed by showing that the particular norms have been created in accordance with the basic norm. To the question why a certain act of coercion – e.g., the fact that one individual deprives another individual of his freedom by putting him in jail – is a legal act, the answer is: because it has been created in conformity with a criminal statute. This statute, finally, receives its validity from the constitution, since it has been established by the competent organ in the way the constitution prescribes.

If we ask why the constitution is valid, perhaps we come upon an older constitution. Ultimately we reach some constitution that is the first historically and that was laid down by an individual usurper or by some kind of assembly. The validity of this first constitution is the last presupposition, the final postulate, upon which the validity of all the norms of our legal order depends. It is postulated that one ought to behave as the individual, or the individuals, who laid down the first constitution have ordained. This is the basic norm of the legal order under consideration. The document which embodies the first constitution is a real constitution, a binding norm, only on the condition that the basic norm is presupposed to be valid. Only upon this presupposition are the declarations of those to whom the constitution confers norm-creating power binding norms. It is this presupposition that enables us to distinguish between individuals who are legal authorities and other individuals whom we do not regard as such, between acts of human beings which create legal norms and acts which have no such effect. All these legal norms belong to one and the same legal order because their validity can be traced back – directly or indirectly – to the first constitution. That the first constitution is a binding legal norm is presupposed, and the formulation of the presupposition is the basic norm of this legal order. The basic norm of a religious norm system says that one ought to behave as God and the authorities instituted by Him command. Similarly, the basic norm of a legal order prescribes that one ought to behave as the "fathers" of the constitution and the individuals – directly or indirectly – authorized (delegated) by the constitution command. Expressed in the form of a legal norm: coercive acts ought to be carried out only under the conditions and in the way determined by the "fathers" of the constitution or the organs delegated by them. This is, schematically formulated, the basic norm of the legal order of a single State, the basic norm of a national legal order. It is to the national legal order that we have here limited our attention. Later, we shall consider what bearing the assumption of an international law has upon the question of the basic norm of national law.

b. The Specific Function of the Basic Norm

That a norm of the kind just mentioned is the basic norm of the national legal order does not imply that it is impossible to go beyond that norm. Certainly one may ask why one has to respect the first constitution as a binding norm. The answer might be that the fathers of the first constitution were empowered by God. The characteristic of so-called legal positivism is, however, that it dispenses with any such religious justification of the legal order. The ultimate hypothesis of positivism is the norm authorizing the historically first legislator. The whole function of this basic norm is to confer law-creating power on the act of the first legislator and on all the other acts based on the first act. To interpret these acts of human beings as legal acts and their products as binding norms, and that means to interpret the empirical material which presents itself as law as such, is possible only on the condition that the basic norm is presupposed as a valid norm. The basic norm is only the necessary presupposition of any positivistic interpretation of the legal material.

The basic norm is not created in a legal procedure by a law-creating organ. It is not – as a positive legal norm is – valid because it is created in a certain way by a legal act, but it is valid because it is presupposed to be valid; and it is presupposed to be valid because without this presupposition no human act could be interpreted as a legal, especially as a norm-creating, act.

By formulating the basic norm, we do not introduce into the science of law any method. We merely make explicit what all jurists, mostly unconsciously, assume when they consider positive law as a system of valid norms and not only as a complex of facts, and at the same time repudiate any natural law from which positive law would receive its validity. That the basic norm really exists in the juristic consciousness is the result of a simple analysis of actual juristic statements. The basic norm is the answer to the question: how – and that means under what condition – are all these juristic statements concerning legal norms, legal duties, legal rights, and so on possible?

c. The Principle of Legitimacy

The validity of legal norms may be limited in time, and it is important to notice that the end as well as the beginning of this validity is determined only by the order to which they belong. They remain valid as long as they have not been invalidated in the way which the legal order itself determines. This is the principle of legitimacy.

This principle, however, holds only under certain conditions. It fails to hold in the case of a revolution, this word understood in the most general sense, so that it also covers the so-called *coup d'Etat*. A revolution, in this wide sense, occurs whenever the legal order of a community is nullified and replaced by a new order in an illegitimate way, that is in a way not prescribed by the first order itself. It is in this context irrelevant whether or not this replacement is affected through a violent uprising against those individuals who so far have been the "legitimate" organs competent to create and amend the legal order. It is equally irrelevant whether the replacement is effected through a movement emanating from the mass of the people, or through action from those in government positions. From a juristic point of view, the decisive criterion of a revolution is that the order in force is overthrown and replaced by a new order in a way which the former had not itself anticipated. Usually, the new men whom a revolution brings to power annul only the constitution and certain laws of paramount political significance, putting other norms in their place. A great part of the old legal order "remains" valid also within the frame of the new order. But the phrase "they remain valid," does not give an adequate description of the phenomenon. It is only the contents of these norms that remain the same, not the reason of their validity. They are no longer valid by virtue of having been created in the way the old constitution prescribed. That constitution is no longer in force; it is replaced by a new constitution which is not the result of a constitutional alteration of the former. If laws which were introduced under the old constitution "continue to be valid" under the new constitution, this is possible only because validity has expressly or tacitly been vested in them by the new constitution. The phenomenon is a case of reception (similar to the reception of Roman law). The new order "receives," i.e., adopts, norms from the old order; this means that the new order gives validity to (puts into force) norms which have the same content as norms of the old order. "Reception" is an abbreviated procedure of law-creation. The laws which, in the ordinary inaccurate parlance, continue to be valid are, from a juristic viewpoint, new laws whose import coincides with that of the old laws. They are not identical with the old laws, because the reason for their validity is different. The reason for their validity is the new, not the old, constitution, and between the two continuity holds neither from the point of view of the one nor from that of the other. Thus, it is never the constitution merely but always the entire legal order that is changed by a revolution.

This shows that all norms of the old order have been deprived of their validity by revolution and not according to the principle of legitimacy. And they have been so deprived not only *de facto* but also *de jure*. No jurist would maintain that even after a successful revolution the old constitution and the laws based thereupon remain in force, on the ground that they have not been nullified in a manner anticipated by the old order itself. Every jurist will presume that the old order – to which no political reality any longer corresponds – has ceased to be valid, and that all norms, which are valid within the new order, receive their validity exclusively from the new constitution. It follows that, from this juristic point of view, the norms of the old order can no longer be recognized as valid norms.

d. Change of the Basic Norm

It is just the phenomenon of revolution which clearly shows the significance of the basic norm. Suppose that a group of individuals attempt to seize power by force, in order to remove the legitimate government in a hitherto monarchic State, and to introduce a republican form of government. If they succeed, if the old order ceases, and the new order begins to be efficacious, because the individuals whose behavior the new order regulates actually behave, by and large, in conformity with the new order, then this order is considered as a valid order. It is now according to this new order that the actual behavior of individuals is interpreted as legal or illegal. But this means that a new basic norm is presupposed. It is no longer the norm according to which the old monarchical constitution is valid, but a norm according to which the new republican constitution is valid, a norm endowing the revolutionary government with legal authority. If the revolutionaries fail, if the order they have tried to establish remains inefficacious, then, on the other hand, their undertaking is interpreted, not as a legal, a law-creating act, as the establishment of a constitution, but as an illegal act, as the crime of treason, and this according to the old monarchic constitution and its specific basic norm.

e. The Principle of Effectiveness

If we attempt to make explicit the presupposition on which these juristic considerations rest, we find that the norms of the old order are regarded as devoid of validity because the old constitution and, therefore, the legal norms based on this constitution, the old legal order as a whole, has lost its efficacy; because the actual behavior of men does no longer conform to this old legal order. Every single norm loses its validity when the total legal order to which it belongs loses its efficacy as a whole. The efficacy of the entire legal order is a necessary condition for the validity of every single norm of the order. A *conditio sine qua non*, but not a *conditio per quam*. The efficacy of the total legal order is a condition, not the reason for the validity of its constituent norms. These norms are valid not because the total order is efficacious, but because they are created in a constitutional way. They are valid, however, only on the condition that the total order is efficacious; they cease to be valid, not only when they are annulled in a constitutional way, but also when the total order ceases to be efficacious. It cannot be maintained that, legally, men have to behave in conformity with a certain norm, if the total legal order, of which that norm is an integral part, has lost its efficacy. The principle of legitimacy is restricted by the principle of effectiveness.

f. Desuetudo

This must not be understood to mean that a single legal norm loses its validity, if that norm itself and only that norm is rendered ineffective. Within a legal order which as a whole is efficacious there may occur isolated norms which are valid and which yet are not efficacious, that is, are not obeyed and not applied even when the conditions which they themselves lay down for their application are fulfilled. But even in this case efficacy has some relevance to validity. If the norm remains permanently inefficacious, the norm is deprived of its validity by "desuetudo." "Desuetudo" is the negative legal effect of custom. A norm may be annulled by custom, viz., by a custom contrary to the norm, as well as it may be created by custom. Desuetudo annuls a norm by creating another norm, identical in character with a statute whose only function is to repeal a previously valid statute. The much-discussed question whether a statute may also be invalidated by desuetudo is ultimately the question whether custom as a source of law may be excluded by statute within a legal order. For reasons which will be given later, the question must be answered in the negative. It must be assumed that any legal norm, even a statutory norm, may lose validity by desuetudo.

However, even in this case it would be a mistake to identify the validity and the efficacy of the norm; they are still two different phenomena. The norm annulled by desuetudo was valid for a considerable time without being efficacious. It is only an enduring lack of efficacy that ends the validity.

The relation between validity and efficacy thus appears to be the following: A norm is a valid legal norm if (a) it has been created in a way provided for by the legal order to which it belongs, and (b) if it has not been annulled either in a way provided for by that legal order or by way of desuetudo or by the fact that the legal order as a whole has lost its efficacy.

g. The "Ought" and the "Is"

The basic norm of a national legal order is not the arbitrary product of juristic imagination. Its content is determined by facts. The function of the basic norm is to make possible the normative interpretation of certain facts, and that means, the interpretation of facts as the creation and application of valid norms. Legal norms, as we pointed out, are considered to be valid only if they belong to an order which is by and large efficacious. Therefore, the content of a basic norm is determined by the facts through which an order is created and applied, to which the behavior of the individuals regulated by this order, by and large, conforms. The basic norm of any positive legal order confers legal authority only upon facts by which an order is created and applied which is on the whole effective. It is not required that the actual behavior of individuals be in absolute conformity with the order. On the contrary, a certain antagonism between the normative order and the actual human behavior to which the norms of the order refer must be possible. Without such a possibility, a normative order would be completely meaningless. What necessarily happens under the laws of nature does not have to be prescribed by norms: the basic norm of a social order to which the actual behavior of the individuals always and without any exception conforms would run as follows: Men ought to behave as they actually behave, or: You ought to do what you actually do. Such an order would be as meaningless as an order with which human behavior would in no way conform, but always and in every respect contradict. Therefore, a normative order loses its validity when reality no longer corresponds to it, at least to a certain degree. The validity of a legal order is thus dependent upon its agreement with reality, upon its "efficacy." The relationship which exists between the validity and efficacy of a legal order – it is, so to speak, the tension between the "ought" and the "is" – can be determined only by an upper and a lower borderline. The agreement must neither exceed a certain maximum nor fall below a certain minimum.

h. Law and Power (Right and Might)

Seeing that the validity of a legal order is thus dependent upon its efficacy, one may be misled into identifying the two phenomena, by defining the validity of law as its efficacy, by describing the law by "is" and not by "ought" statements. Attempts of this kind have very often been made and they have always failed. For, if the validity of law is identified with any natural fact, it is impossible to comprehend the specific sense in which law is directed towards reality and thus stands over against reality. Only if law and natural reality, the system of legal norms and the actual behavior of men, the "ought" and the "is," are two different realms, may reality conform with or contradict law, can human behavior be characterized as legal or illegal.

The efficacy of law belongs to the realm of reality and is often called the power of law. If for efficacy we substitute power, then the problem of validity and efficacy is transformed into the more common problem of "right and might." And then the solution here presented is merely the precise statement of the old truth that though law cannot exist without power, still law and power, right and might, are not the same. Law is, according to the theory here presented, a specific order or organization of power.

i. The Principle of Effectiveness as Positive Legal Norm (International and National Law)

The principle that a legal order must be efficacious in order to be valid is, in itself, a positive norm. It is the principle of effectiveness belonging to international law. According to this principle of international law, an actually established authority is the legitimate government, the coercive order enacted by this government is the legal order, and the community constituted by this order is a State in the sense of international law, insofar as this order is, on the whole, efficacious. From the standpoint of international law, the constitution of a State is valid only if the legal order established on the basis of this constitution is, on the whole, efficacious. It is this general principle of effectiveness, a positive norm of international law, which, applied to the concrete circumstances of an individual national legal order, provides the individual basic norm of this national legal order. Thus, the basic norms of the different national legal orders are themselves based on a general norm of the international order. If we conceive international law as a legal order to which all the States (and that means all the national legal orders) are subordinated, then the basic norm of a national legal order is not a mere presupposition of juristic thinking, but a positive legal norm, a norm of international law applied to the legal order of a concrete State. Assuming the primacy of international law over national law, the problem of the basic norm shifts from the national to the international legal order. Then the only true basic norm, a norm which is not created by a legal procedure but presupposed by juristic thinking, is the basic norm of international law.

j. Validity and Efficacy

That the validity of a legal order depends upon its efficacy does not imply, as pointed out, that the validity of a single norm depends upon its efficacy. The single legal norm remains valid as long as it is part of a valid order. The question whether an individual norm is valid is answered by recourse to the first constitution. If this is valid, then all norms which have been created in a constitutional way are valid, too. The principle of effectiveness embodied in international law refers immediately only to the first constitution of a national legal order, and therefore to this order only as a whole.

The principle of effectiveness may, however, be adopted to a certain extent also by national law, and thus within a national legal order the validity of a single norm may be made dependent upon its efficacy. Such is the case when a legal norm may lose its validity by desuetudo.

D. THE STATIC AND THE DYNAMIC CONCEPT OF LAW

If one looks upon the legal order from the dynamic point of view, as it has been expounded here, it seems possible to define the concept of law in a way quite different from that in which we have tried to define it in this theory. It seems especially possible to ignore the element of coercion in defining the concept of law.

It is a fact that the legislator can enact commandments without considering it necessary to attach a criminal or civil sanction to their violation. If such norms are also called legal norms, it is because they were created by an authority which, according to the constitution, is competent to create law. They are law because they issue from a law-creating authority. According to this concept, law is everything that has come about in the way the constitution prescribes for the creation of law. This dynamic concept differs from the concept of law defined as a coercive norm. According to the dynamic concept, law is something created by a certain process, and everything created in this way is law. This dynamic concept, however, is only apparently a concept of law. It contains no answer to the question of what is the essence of law, what is the criterion by which law can be distinguished from other social norms. This dynamic concept furnishes an answer only to the question whether or not and why a certain norm belongs to a system of valid legal norms, forms a part of a certain legal order. And the answer is, a norm belongs to a certain legal order if it is created in accordance with a procedure prescribed by the constitution fundamental to this legal order.

It must, however, be noted that not only a norm, i.e., a command regulating human behavior, can be created in the way prescribed by the constitution for the creation of law. An important stage in the law-creating process is the procedure by which general norms are created, that is, the procedure of legislation. The constitution may organize this procedure of legislation in the following way: two corresponding resolutions of both houses of parliament, the consent of the chief of State, and publication in an official journal. This means that a specific form of law-creation is established. It is then possible to clothe in this form any subject, for instance, a recognition of the merits of a statesman. The form of a law – a declaration voted by parliament, consented to by the chief of State, published in the official journal – is chosen in order to give to a certain subject, here to the expression of the nation's gratitude, the character of a solemn act. The solemn recognition of the merits of a statesman is by no means a norm, even if it appears as the content of a legislative act, even if it has the form of a law. The law as the product of the legislative procedure, a statute in the formal sense of the term, is a document containing words, sentences; and that which is expressed by these sentences need not necessarily be a norm. As a matter of fact, many a law – in this formal sense of the term – contains not only legal norms, but also certain elements which are of no specific legal, i.e. normative, character, such as, purely theoretical views concerning certain matters, the motives of the legislator, political ideologies contained in references such as "justice" or "the will of God," etc., etc. All these are legally irrelevant contents of the statute, or, more generally, legally irrelevant products of the law-creating process. The law-creating process includes not only the process of legislation, but also the procedure of the judicial and administrative authorities. Even judgments of the courts very often contain legally irrelevant elements. If by the term "law" is meant something pertaining to a certain legal order, then law is anything which has been created according to the procedure prescribed by the constitution fundamental to this order. This does not mean, however, that everything which has been created according to this procedure is law in the sense of a legal norm. It is a legal norm only if it purports to regulate human behavior, and if it regulates human behavior by providing an act of coercion as sanction.

XI. The Hierarchy of the Norms

B. THE DIFFERENT STAGES OF THE LEGAL ORDER

g. Creation of Law and Application of Law

1. Merely Relative Difference between Law-creating and Law-applying Function

The legal order is a system of general and individual norms connected with each other according to the principle that law regulates its own creation. Each norm of this order is created according to the provisions of another norm, and ultimately according to the provisions of the basic norm constituting the unity of this system of norms, the legal order. A norm belongs to this legal order only because it has been created in conformity with the stipulations of another norm of the order. This regressus finally leads to the first constitution, the creation of which is determined by the presupposed basic norm. One may also say that a norm belongs to a certain legal order if it has been created by an organ of the community constituted by the order. The individual who creates the legal norm is an organ of the legal community because and insofar as his function is determined by a legal norm of the order constituting the legal community. The imputation of this function to the community is based on the norm determining the function. This explanation, however, does not add anything to the previous one. The statement "A norm belongs to a certain legal order because it is created by an organ of the legal community constituted by this order" and the statement "A norm belongs to a legal order because it is created according to the basic norm of this legal order" assert one and the same thing.

A norm regulating the creation of another norm is "applied" in the creation of the other norm. Creation of law is always application of law. These two concepts are by no means as the traditional theory presumes, absolute opposites. It is not quite correct to classify legal acts as law-creating and law-applying acts; for, setting aside two borderline cases of which we shall speak later, every act is, normally, at the same time a law-creating and law-applying act. The creation of a legal norm is – normally – an application of the higher norm, regulating its creation, and the application of a higher norm is – normally – the creation of a lower norm determined by the higher norm. A judicial decision, e.g., is an act by which a general norm, a statute, is applied but at the same time an individual norm is created obligating one or both parties to the conflict. Legislation is creation of law, but taking into account the constitution, we find that it is also application of law. In any act of legislation, where the provisions of the constitution are observed, the constitution is applied. The making of the first constitution can likewise be considered as an application of the basic norm.

2. Determination of the Law-creating Function

As pointed out, the creation of a legal norm can be determined in two different directions: the higher norm may determine: (1) the organ and the procedure by which a lower norm is to be created, and (2) the contents of the lower norm. Even if the higher norm determines only the organ, and that means the individual by which the lower norm has to be created, and that again means authorizes this organ to determine at his own discretion the procedure of creating the lower norm and the contents of this norm, the higher norm is "applied" in the creation of the lower norm. The higher norm must at least determine the organ by which the lower norm has to be created. For a norm the creation of which is not determined at all by another norm cannot belong to any legal order. The individual creating a norm cannot be considered the organ of a legal community, his norm-creating function cannot be imputed to the community, unless in performing the function he applies a norm of the legal order constituting the community. Every law-creating act must be a law-applying act, i.e., it must apply a norm preceding the act in order to be an act of the legal order or the community constituted by it. Therefore, the norm-creating function has to be conceived of as a norm-applying function even if only its personal element, the individual who has to create the lower norm, is determined by the higher norm. It is this higher norm determining the organ which is applied by every act of this organ.

That creation of law is at the same time application of law, is an immediate consequence of the fact that every law-creating act must be determined by the legal order. This determination may be of different degrees. It can never be so weak that the act ceases to be an application of law. Nor can it be so strong that the act ceases to be a creation of law. As long as a norm is established through the act, it is a law-creating act, even if the function of the law-creating organ is in a high degree determined by the higher norm. This is the case when not only the organ and the law-creating procedure but also the contents of the norm to be created are determined by a higher norm. However, in this case, too, an act of law-creating exists. The question whether an act is creation or application of law is in fact quite independent of the question as to the degree to which the acting organ is bound by the legal order. Only acts by which no norm is established may be merely application of law. Of such a nature is the execution of a sanction in a concrete case. This is one of the two borderline cases mentioned above. The other is the basic norm. It determines the creation of the first constitution; but being presupposed by juristic thinking, its presupposition is not itself determined by any higher norm and is therefore no application of law.

h. Individual Norms Created on the Basis of General Norms

1. The Judicial Act as Creation of an Individual Norm

As an application of law, traditional doctrine considers above all the judicial decision, the function of courts. When settling a dispute between two parties or when sentencing an accused person to a punishment, a court applies, it is true, a general norm of statutory or customary law. But simultaneously the court creates an individual norm providing that a definite sanction shall be executed against a definite individual. This individual norm is related to the general norms as a statute is related to the constitution. The judicial function is thus, like legislation, both creation and application of law. The judicial function is ordinarily determined by the general norms both as to procedure and as to the contents of the norm to be created, whereas legislation is usually determined by the constitution only in the former respect. But that is a difference in degree only.

2. The Judicial Act as a Stage of the Law-creating Process

From a dynamic standpoint, the individual norm created by the judicial decision is a stage in a process beginning with the establishment of the first constitution, continued by legislation and custom, and leading to the judicial decisions. The process is completed by the execution of the individual sanction. Statutes and customary laws are, so to speak, only semi-manufactured products which are finished only through the judicial decision and its execution. The process through which law constantly creates itself anew goes from the general and abstract to the individual and concrete. It is a process of steadily increasing individualization and concretization.

The general norm which, to certain abstractly determined conditions, attaches certain abstractly determined consequences, has to be individualized and concretized in order to come in contact with social life, to be applied to reality. To this purpose, in a given case it has to be ascertained whether the conditions, determined *in abstracto* in the general norm, are present *in concreto*, in order that the sanction, determined *in abstracto* in the general norm, may be ordered and executed *in concreto*. These are the two essential elements of the judicial function. This function has, by no means, as is sometimes assumed, a purely declaratory character. Contrary to what is sometimes asserted, the court does not merely formulate already existing law. It does not only "seek" and "find" the law existing previous to its decision, it does not merely pronounce the law which exists ready and finished prior to its pronouncement. Both in establishing the presence of the conditions and in stipulating the sanction, the judicial decision has a constitutive character. The decision applies, it is true, a preexisting general norm in which a certain consequence is attached to certain conditions. But the existence of the concrete conditions in connection with the concrete consequence is, in the concrete case, first established by the court's decision. Conditions and consequences are connected by judicial decisions in the realm of the concrete, as they are connected by statutes and rules of customary law in the realm of the abstract. The individual norm of the judicial decision is the necessary individualization and concretization of the general and abstract norm. Only the prejudice, characteristic of the jurisprudence of continental Europe, that law is, by definition, only general norms, only the erroneous identification of law with the general rules of statutory and customary law, could obscure the fact that the judicial decision continues the law-creating process from the sphere of the general and abstract into that of the individual and concrete.

3. The Ascertainment of the Conditioning Facts

The judicial decision is clearly constitutive as far as it orders a concrete sanction to be executed against an individual delinquent. But it has a constitutive character also, as far as it ascertains the facts conditioning the sanction. In the world of law, there is no fact "in itself," no "absolute" fact, there are only facts ascertained by a competent organ in a procedure prescribed by law. When attaching to certain facts certain consequences, the legal order must also designate an organ that has to ascertain the facts in the concrete case and prescribe the procedure which the organ, in so doing, has to observe. The legal order may authorize this organ to regulate its procedure at its own discretion; but organ and procedure by which the conditioning facts are to be ascertained must be – directly or indirectly – determined by the legal order, to make the latter applicable to social life. It is a typical layman's opinion that there are absolute, immediately evident facts. Only by being first ascertained through a legal procedure are facts brought into the sphere of law or do they, so to speak, come into existence within this sphere. Formulating this in a somewhat paradoxically pointed way, we could say that the competent organ ascertaining the conditioning facts legally "creates" these facts. Therefore, the function of ascertaining facts through a legal procedure has always a specifically constitutive character. If, according to a legal norm, a sanction has to be executed against a murderer, this does not mean that the fact of murder is "in itself" the condition of the sanction. There is no fact "in itself" that A has killed B, there is only my or somebody else's belief of knowledge that A has killed B. A himself may either acquiesce or deny. From the point of view of law, however, all these are no more than private opinions without relevance. Only the establishment by the competent organ has legal relevance. If the judicial decision has already obtained the force of law, if it has become impossible to replace this decision by another because there exists the status of *res judicata* – which means that the case has been definitely decided by a court of last resort – then the opinion that the condemned was innocent is without any legal significance. As already pointed out, the correct formulation of the rule of law is not "If a subject has committed a delict, an organ shall direct a sanction against the delinquent," but "If the competent organ has established in due order that a subject has committed a delict, then an organ shall direct a sanction against this subject."

Hans Kelsen, 1881–

THE PURE THEORY OF LAW AND ANALYTICAL JURISPRUDENCE

III. The Concept of the Norm

Since the pure theory of law limits itself to cognition of positive law, and excludes from this cognition the philosophy of justice as well as the sociology of law, its orientation is much the same as that of so-called analytical jurisprudence, which found its classical Anglo-American presentation in the work of John Austin. Each seeks to attain its results exclusively by analysis of positive law. While the pure theory of law arose independently of Austin's famous *Lectures on General Jurisprudence*, it corresponds in important points with Austin's doctrine. It is submitted that where they differ the pure theory of law has carried out the method of analytical jurisprudence more consistently than Austin and his followers have succeeded in doing.

This is true especially as to the central concept of jurisprudence, the norm. Austin does not employ this concept, and pays no attention to the distinction between "is" and "ought" that is the basis of the concept of the norm. He defines law as "rule," and "rule" as 'command." He says, Every *law* or *rule* . . . is a *command*. Or, rather, laws or rules, properly so called, are a *species* of commands."

A command is the expression of the will of an individual directed to the conduct of another individual. If it is my will that someone behave in a certain manner, and if I exprcss my will as regards this other individual in a certain way, my expression is a command. Thus a command consists of two elements: a wish directed toward someone else's behavior, and its expression in one way or another. There is a command only so long as both the will and its expression are present. If someone issues a command to me, and before its execution I have adequate reason to assume that it is no longer his will, then neither is it any longer a command, even though the expression of his will should remain. But a so-called 'binding" command is said to persist even if the will, the psychic phenomenon, has lapsed. More accurately, however, that which persists is not really the command, but rather my obligation. A command, on the other hand, is essentially a willing and its expression.

Hence legal rules, which according to Austin constitute the law, are not actually commands. They exist, that is to say, they are valid and obligate individuals, even if the will by which they were created has long ceased to be. It may even be said to be doubtful whether some instances in which legal obligations exist as to certain behavior ever represented the real will of anyone. An example will illustrate this.

If one calls a statute constitutionally enacted by a legislature a command, or, what amounts to the same thing, the "will" of the legislators, this expression has almost nothing to do with the true concept of "command." The statute is valid, that is, binding, even after all the members of the legislature that enacted it have died; then, therefore, the content of the statute is no longer the "will" of anyone, at least not of anyone competent to will it. Thus binding law cannot be the psychological will of the law-makers even though a real act of will is necessary to make the law. And an analysis of the constitutional process by which a statute comes into being shows that even the act creating a binding law need by no means represent any will to the behavior required by the statute. The statute is enacted when a majority of the legislators have voted for a bill submitted to them. The content of the statute is not the "will" of the legislators who vote against the bill; their will is expressly contrary. Yet their expressions of will are just as essential to the existence of the statute as are the expressions of will of the members who voted for it. The statute is an enactment of the whole legislature, including the minority, but this obviously does not mean that its content is the will – in the psychological sense – of all the members of the legislature. Even if one takes into consideration only the majority that voted for the bill, the assertion that the statute was the will of the majority is patent fiction. Voting for a bill by no means implies actually "willing" the content of the statute. Psychologically one can "will" only something of which one has an idea; one cannot "will" something of which one knows nothing. And it is indubitable that in very many if not all cases, a large proportion of the members of a legislature who vote for a bill either do not know its content or know it very superficially. That a legislator raises his hand or says "Aye" when the vote is being taken does not mean that he has made the content of the bill the content of his own will, in the way in which a man who "commands" another to act in a certain way "wills" this conduct.

Clearly, therefore, if a particular law is called a command, or, what amounts to the same thing, the "will" of the law-maker, or if law in general is called the "command" or "will" of the "state," this can be taken as only a figurative expression. As is usually the case, an analogy lies at its root. When definite human behavior is "enacted," "provided," "prescribed," in a rule of law, the enactment is quite similar to a true command. But there is an important difference. The statement that a command exists means that a psychic phenomenon – a will – is directed toward certain human behavior. Human behavior is enacted, provided, or prescribed by a rule of law without any psychic act of will. Law might be termed a "depsychologized" command. This appears in the statement that man "ought" to conduct himself according to the law. Herein lies the importance of the concept of "ought," here is revealed the necessity for the concept of the norm. A norm is a rule stating that an individual ought to behave in a certain way, but not asserting that such behavior is the actual will of anyone.

A comparison of the "ought" of the norm with a command is apt only to a very slight extent. The law enacted by the legislator is a "command" only if it is assumed that a "command" has binding force. A command which has binding force is, indeed, a norm. But without the concept of the norm, the law can be described only with the help of a fiction, and Austin's assertion that legal rules are "commands" is a superfluous and dangerous fiction of the "will" of the legislator or the state.

IV. The Element of Coercion

In accordance with the assertions of analytical jurisprudence, the pure theory of law regards the element of coercion as an essential characteristic of the law. Austin and his followers characterize law as "enforcible" or as a rule "enforced" by a given authority. By this they mean that the legal order "commands" the individual to act in a certain fashion, and "forces" men in a specific way to obey the commands of the legal order. The specific means by which the law "enforces" the obedience of individuals consists in inflicting an evil called a sanction in case of disobedience. The "coercion" which according to this view is characteristic of the law is a psychic one; obedience to the commands of the law is achieved through fear of the sanction.

From the standpoint of a strictly analytical method, this formulation is not correct. It has reference to the behavior of the citizen and the organs applying the law, but it may well be doubted whether the lawful behavior of individuals is brought about by fear of the threatened sanction. So far as we know anything about the motives for the behavior of individuals, we may surmise that moral or religious motives, for instance, are important, and even perhaps more effective than fear, of the sanction of the law. And psychic coercion is not a specific element of the law. Moral and religious norms as well are coercive in this psychological sense. For the rest, this question as to the motives for lawful behavior is beside the purpose of cognition directed only to the content of the legal order.

We are here in the presence of a problem of sociological, not analytical or mormative jurisprudence. The latter can only affirm that the law sets up coercive measures as sanctions that are to be directed under definite conditions against definite individuals. From this standpoint, it is not the psychic coercion that proceeds from the idea men have of the law, but the outward sanctions which it provides that are of the law's essence.

Among the conditions to which the law attaches the sanction as a consequence, the delict is decisively important. The delict – with a limitation to be mentioned later – is conduct of the individual against whom this sanction is directed which is the opposite of the conduct that the law prescribes. Hence the sanction is provided for the very case where the law fails in a concrete instance to achieve its purpose, for the case in which obedience to the law does not receive the enforcement that Austin maintains is essential to law. Hence the law is not, as Austin formulates it, a rule "enforced" by a specified authority, but rather a norm which provides a specific measure of coercion as sanction. The nature of the law will not be grasped if one characterizes it as does Austin, as a command to conduct oneself lawfully. The law is a decree of a measure of coercion, a sanction, for that conduct called "illegal," a delict; and this conduct has the character of "delict" because and only because it is a condition of the sanction.

The legal norm refers to the conduct of two entities: the citizen, against whose delict the coercive measure of the sanction is directed; and the organ that is to apply the coercive measure to the delict. The function of the legal norm consists in attaching the sanction as a consequence to certain conditions among which the delict plays a leading part. Looked at from a sociological point of view, the essential characteristic of law, by which it is distinguished from all other social mechanisms, is the fact that it seeks to bring about socially desired conduct by acting against contrary socially undesired conduct – the delict – with a sanction which the individual involved will deem an evil. Analytical jurisprudence takes into consideration only the content of the legal order, and hence only the connection between delict and sanction.

Although Austin recognizes the essential significance of the sanction for the concept of law, he fails to define the legal norm in a manner corresponding to this understanding. The pure theory of law is only drawing an obvious conclusion when it formulates the legal norm (using the term in a descriptive sense) as a hypothetical judgment, in which the delict appears as an essential condition, the sanction as the consequence. The sense in which condition and consequence are connected in the legal norm is that of "ought." If one steals, he ought to be punished; if one does not make good tortious damage, civil execution ought to issue against him. This concept of the legal norm is the fundamental concept of normative jurisprudence. All other concepts, especially those of legal duty and right, are derived from it.

VIII. The Law and the State

It is one of the characteristics of Austin's doctrine that it has no legal concept of the state. The concept of an "independent political society" plays a certain role in his teachings, but it is not a legal concept, and Austin himself does not call this "independent political society" a state. By it he means a society consisting of a sovereign and subjects. The sovereign may be an individual or a group, but never all the persons comprising the political society. Austin says occasionally "law is the creature of the sovereign or state," but "state" here obviously means not a political society, but rather the bearer of the sovereignty within the society. For the rest, Austin seldom uses the word "state," and reveals a disinclination for the concept. When he says that all law is created by the "state," he means: "Every positive law . . . is set by a sovereign person, or a sovereign body of persons," that is to say, by that portion of the political society in which the sovereignty resides.

As all law emanates from the sovereign, the sovereign himself is not subject to the law. One of the main principles of Austin's theory is that sovereign power "is incapable of *legal* limitation." The essence of sovereignty consists, according to Austin, in the fact that the individual or group designated as sovereign will "not be habitually obedient to a determinate human superior." This concept of the sovereign is sociological or political, but not juristic – yet it is an essential element of Austin's jurisprudence, which teaches that law is to be understood only as the command of the sovereign. This is difficult to reconcile with the theoretic method of analytical jurisprudence, which derives its concepts only from an analysis of positive law. In the norms of positive law no such thing as a "sovereign," a person or group "incapable of legal limitation," can be found. The central difficulty is that the jurisprudence of Austin, while it deals with the concept of a sovereign which is not the state but only an organ of the state, does not concern itself at all with the problem of the state itself.

On this point there is a great difference between Austin's analytical jurisprudence and the pure theory of law. The latter does not deny the traditional view that the state is a political society; but it shows that a number of individuals can form a social unit, a "society" or better, "community," only on the basis of an order, or, in other words, that the element constituting the political community is an order. The state is not its individuals; it is the specific union of individuals, and this union is the function of the order which regulates their mutual behavior. Only in this order does the social community exist at all. It is a political community, because and to the extent that the specific means by which this regulatory order seeks to attain its end is the decreeing of measures of coercion. The legal order is such a coercive order, as we have seen. One of the distinctive results of the pure theory of law is its recognition that the coercive order which constitutes the political community we call a state, is a legal order. What is usually called the legal order of the state, or the legal order set up by the state, is the state itself.

Law and state are usually held to be two distinct entities. But if it be recognized that the state is by its very nature an ordering of human behavior, that the essential characteristic of this order, coercion, is at the same time the essential element of the law, this traditional dualism can no longer be maintained. By subsuming the concept of the state under the concept of a coercive order which can only be the legal order, by giving up a concept of the state distinct in principle from the concept of law, the pure theory of law realizes a tendency inherent in the doctrine of Austin. Austin rightly felt that a *political* concept of the state had no place in a juristic theory. Hence he seeks to dispense with it. But he substitutes for it another political concept, that of the "sovereign," instead of establishing a *legal* concept of the state.

The state which "possesses" a legal order is imagined as a person. This "person" is only a personification of the unity of the legal order. The dualism of state and law arises from hypostatizing the personification, asserting this figurative expression to be a real being, and so opposing it to the law. If, however, juristic thinking is freed from this fiction, then all the problems concerning the relation of state and law are revealed as illusory. Thus the much-mooted question whether the state creates the law is answered by saying that men create the law, on the basis of its own definite norms. The individuals who create the law are organs of the legal order, or, what amounts to the same thing, organs of the state. They are organs because and to the extent that they fulfill their functions according to the provisions of the legal order which constitutes the legal community. For an individual to be an organ of the state means only that certain acts performed by him are attributed to the state, that is, are referred to the unity of the legal order. If it be asked why a certain act of an individual is imputed to the state, there is no other answer than that this conduct is determined by the legal order. The criterion of this imputation of a human act to the state is purely juristic in character. If a norm of the legal order is created in accordance with the stipulations of another norm of this legal order, then the individual who creates the law is an organ of the legal order, an organ of the state. In this sense it can be said that the state creates the law, but this means only that the law regulates its own creation.

If one resolves the dualism of law and the state, if one recognizes the state as a legal order, then the so-called elements of the state – territory and population – appear as the territorial and personal spheres of validity of the national legal order. What Austin calls the "sovereign" appears as the order's highest organ, and sovereignty is then not a characteristic of the individual or group of individuals comprising this organ, but a characteristic of the state itself. For sovereignty to be a characteristic of the *national* legal order, however, can mean only that above this order no higher order is assumed.

IX. International and National Law

If there is a legal order superior to the national legal orders, it must be international law. Whether it is really law in the same sense as national law, and whether as a legal order, it stands above the national legal orders, are the two decisive questions. Austin answers both negatively, admitting the validity of international law only as "positive international morality." Therefore the theory of international law, like the theory of the state, is eliminated from the province of Austin's jurisprudence. The pure theory of law, on the other hand, shows that it is quite possible to consider international law as real law, since it contains all the essential elements of a legal order. It is a coercive order in the same sense as national law: it obligates states to definite behavior, in that it provides sanctions against contrary conduct. The sanctions provided by international law are reprisals and war. The pure theory of law attempts to prove that according to international law not only reprisals but war, as well, is permissible only as a reaction against a wrong that has been suffered. The pure theory of law shows that the principle of *bellum justum* is a principle of positive international law. International law is real law, but it is primitive law. This is so especially because the reaction against the delict, the execution of the sanction, is left to the state itself, the very subject whose rights are infringed, instead of being delegated to a central organ as is the case in the national legal order. Thus the international legal order is radically decentralized, and for this very reason the international community constituted by international law is not a state, but only a union of states. A certain degree of centralization is essential to the state. Similarly the completely decentralized community of a primitive tribe is not a state, although there is no doubt that the order constituting it is a legal order.

There are today two opposing views in regard to the relation between national and international law, the one dualistic and the other monistic. The former maintains that national law and international law are two completely distinct and mutually independent systems of norms, like positive law and morality, for instance. The pure theory of law shows that such a dualistic concept of the relation between national and international law is logically impossible, and that none of the followers of the dualistic theory is able to maintain his point of view consistently. If one assumes that two systems of norms are considered as valid simultaneously from the same point of view, one must also assume a normative relation between them; one must assume the existence of a norm or order that regulates their mutual relations. Otherwise insoluble contradictions between the norms of each system are unavoidable, and the logical principle that excludes contradictions holds for the cognition of norms as much as for the cognition of natural reality. When positive law and morality are asserted to be two distinct mutually independent systems of norms, this means only that the jurist, in determining what is legal, does not take into consideration morality, and the moralist, in determining what is moral, pays no heed to the prescriptions of positive law. Positive law and morality can be regarded as two distinct and mutually independent systems of norms, because and to the extent that they are not conceived to be simultaneously valid from the same point of view. But once it is conceded that national and international law are both positive law, it is obvious that both must be considered as valid simultaneously from the same juristic point of view. For this reason, they must belong to the same system of norms, they must in some way supplement each other.

The monistic theory meets this logical requirement. It regards national and international law as one system of norms, as a unity. Opinions differ, however, as to how this whole is constructed. Some assert international law to be a part of national law, those norms of national law that regulate the relation of the state to other states. The rules admitted to be international law can bind the individual state only when the latter recognizes them and thereby takes them over into its own legal order. This is the theory of the primacy of national law, obviously proceeding from the idea that the state is sovereign, that is, that the national legal order is an order of the highest rank, above which no other order can be deemed valid. As this is true for each of the many national legal orders, there is, according to this theory, not one international law, but as many as there are national legal orders. In truth, there is no international law at all as such, but only national law. The relationship between the different national legal orders can be established only from the point of view of one given order, whose norms alone determine its relations to the other orders. From such a point of view, that is, from the standpoint of a definite national legal order, all other orders appear not as sovereign, but rather as delegated orders. They are systems of valid norms only to the extent that they are recognized as such by the state whose legal order constitutes the point of departure.

The pure theory of law shows that this monistic theory is indeed logically possible, but that it is not consonant with the idea that all states or national legal orders are of the same rank. The primacy of national law means the primacy of one national legal order not only in regard to international law, but in regard to all the other national legal orders as well. The idea quite generally held, that all states form a community in which they stand side by side on a footing of equality, is possible only on the assumption that above the states, or above the national legal orders, there is a legal order that makes them equal by defining their mutual spheres of validity. This order can be only international law. The pure theory of law shows by an analysis of positive international law that it actually does perform the function just mentioned, and hence can be regarded, if one foregoes the assumption of the sovereignty of the individual states, as a system of norms standing above the national legal orders, according them equal rank, and binding them together into a universal legal order. This is the theory of the primacy of international law, the theoretic basis for which was revealed for the first time by the pure theory of law.

There is nothing to prevent this interpretation of the legal material except the idea of the sovereignty of the state. One of the most important results of the pure theory of law is that sovereignty, in the specific sense which this idea has in a theory of law, is not a real characteristic of a real thing. Sovereignty is a judgment of value and as such it is an assumption. The individualistic philosophy of the 18th and 19th centuries proceeded from the idea that the human individual was sovereign, i.e., of the highest value. From this it was concluded that a social order can be binding on the individual only when it is recognized by the individual as binding. From this came the doctrine of the social contract, which still has its exponents; but today the inclination is rather to a universalistic philosophy of values according to which the community is superior to the individual.

In the sphere of international relations the view that the state is essentially sovereign is an individualistic philosophy, based on the individuality of the state. The dogma of sovereignty is not the result of scientific analysis of the phenomenon of the state, but the assumption of a philosophy of values. Consequently it cannot be contradicted scientifically. One can only show that an interpretation which proceeds from another assumption – namely, from that of the sovereignty of the international legal community – is just as possible, and that positive international law itself, so far as its validity is admitted, requires this interpretation.

The analysis of positive international law made by the pure theory of law shows that its norms are incomplete norms, which need supplementing by the norms of the national legal orders. The generally accepted proposition that international law obligates only states means not that international law does not obligate individuals, but rather that while, like every law, it obligates individuals, it does so indirectly, through the medium of national legal orders. To say that international law obligates a state to certain conduct means that international law obligates an individual as an organ of this state to such conduct, but that international law determines directly only the conduct, leaving the national legal order to determine the individual whose conduct forms the content of the international obligation. Thus international law presupposes the simultaneous validity of national legal orders within one and the same system of legal norms that embraces international law as well.

A generally recognized principle of international law, formulated in the usual manner, reads as follows: if a power is established anywhere, in any manner, which is able to ensure permanent obedience to its coercive order among the individuals whose behavior this order regulates, then the community constituted by this coercive order is a state in the sense of international law. The sphere in which this coercive order is permanently effective is the territory of the state; the the individuals who live in the territory are the people of the state in the sense of positive international law. This is the principle of effectiveness, so important throughout international law. By this legal principle, international law defines the territorial and personal spheres of validity of the national legal orders, spheres which each state is bound to respect. By it also is determined the validity of the national orders. These are valid, in the sense of international law, because and to the extent that they satisfy the requirement of effectiveness. If jurisprudence, as we have shown, considers a legal norm as valid only when it belongs to a legal order which is in the main effective, it is using a principle of positive law itself, a principle of international law.

Since the national legal orders find the reason for their validity in the international legal order, which at the same time defines their spheres of validity, the international legal order must be superior to each national order. Thus it forms, together with them, one uniform universal legal system.

As it is the task of natural science to describe its object – reality – in one system of natural laws, so it is the task of jurisprudence to comprehend all human law in one system of norms. This task Austin's jurisprudence did not see; the pure theory of law, imperfect and inaccurate though it may be in detail, has gone a measurable distance toward its accomplishment.

H. L. A. Hart, 1907–
Professor of Jurisprudence, University of Oxford

DEFINITION AND THEORY IN JURISPRUDENCE (1953)

II

Long ago Bentham issued a warning that legal words demanded a special method of elucidation and he enunciated a principle that is the beginning of wisdom in this matter though it is not the end. He said we must never take these words alone, but consider whole sentences in which they play their characteristic role. We must take not the *word* "right" but the sentence "You have a right" not the *word* "State" but the sentence "He is a member or an official of the State". His warning has largely been disregarded and jurists have continued to hammer away at single words. This may be because he hid the product of his logical insight behind technical terms of his own invention "Archetypation", "Phraseoplerosis", and the rest; it may also be because his further suggestions were not well adapted to the peculiarities of legal language which as part of the works of "Judge & Co." was perhaps distasteful to him. But in fact the language involved in the enunciation and application of rules constitutes a special segment of human discourse with special features which lead to confusion if neglected. Of this type of discourse the law is one very complex example and sometimes to see its features we need to look away from the law to simpler cases which in spite of many differences share these features. The economist or the scientist often uses a simple model with which to understand the complex; and this can be done for the law. So in what follows I shall use as a simple analogy the rules of a game which at many vital points have the same puzzling logical structure as rules of law. And I shall describe four distinctive features which show, I think, the method of elucidation we should apply to the law and why the common mode of definition fails.

1. First, let us take words like "right" or "duty" or the names of corporations not alone but in examples of typical contexts where these words are at work. Consider them when used in statements made on a particular occasion by a judge or an ordinary lawyer. They will be statements such as "A has a right to be paid £10 by B". "A is under a duty to fence off this machinery." "A & Company, Ltd. have a contract with B." It is obvious that the use of these sentences silently assumes a special and very complicated setting, namely the existence of a legal system with all that this implies by way of general obedience, the operation of the sanctions of the system, and the general likelihood that this will continue. But though this complex situation is assumed in the use of these statements of rights or duties they do not *state* that it exists. There is a parallel situation in a game. "He is out" said in the course of a game of cricket has as its proper context the playing of the game with all that *this* implies by way of general compliance by both the players and the officials of the game in the past, present, and future. Yet one who says "He is out" does not state that a game is being played or that the players and officials will comply with the rules. "He is out" is an expression used to appeal to rules, to make claims, or give decisions under them; it is not a statement *about* the rules to the effect that they will be enforced or acted on in a given case nor any other kind of statement *about* them. The analysis of statements of rights and duties as predictions ignores this distinction, yet it is just as erroneous to say that "A has a right" is a prediction that a Court or official will treat A in a certain way as to say that "He is out" is a prediction that the umpire is likely to order the batsman off the field or the scorer to mark him out. No doubt, when someone has a legal right a corresponding prediction will normally be justified but this should not lead us to identify two quite different forms of statement.

2. If we take "A has a right to be paid £10 by B" as an example, we can see what the distinctive function of this form of statement is. For it is clear that as well as presupposing the existence of a legal system, the use of this statement has also a special connexion with a particular rule of the system. This would be made explicit if we asked "Why has A this right"? For the appropriate answer could only consist of two things: first, the statement of some rule or rules of law (say those of Contract), under which given certain facts certain legal consequences follow; and secondly, a statement that these facts were here the case. But again it is important to see that one who says that "A has a right" does not *state* the relevant rule of law; and that though, given certain facts, it is correct to say "A has a right" one who says this does not state or describe those facts. He has done something different from either of these two things: he has drawn a conclusion from the relevant but unstated rule, and from the relevant but unstated facts of the case. "A has a right" like "He is out" is therefore the tail-end of a simple legal calculation: it records a result and may be well called a conclusion of law. It is not therefore used to predict the future as the American Realists say; it refers to the present as their opponents claim but unlike ordinary

statements does not do this by describing present or continuing facts. This it is – this matter of principle – and not the existence of stray exceptions for lunatics or infants that frustrates the definition of a right in factual terms such as expectations or powers. A paralysed man watching the thief's hand close over his gold watch is properly said to have a right to retain it as against the thief, though he has neither expectation or power in any ordinary sense of these words. This is possible just because the expression "a right" in this case does not describe or stand for any expectation, or power, or indeed anything else, but has meaning only as part of a sentence the function of which as a whole is to draw a conclusion of law from a specific kind of legal rule.

3. A third peculiarity is this: the assertion "Smith has a right to be paid £10" said by a judge in deciding the case has a different status from the utterance of it out of court, where it may be used to make a claim, or an admission and in many other ways. The Judge's utterance is official, authoritative and, let us assume, final; the other is none of these things, yet in spite of these differences the sentences are of the same sort: they are both conclusions of law. We can compare this difference in spite of similarity with 'He is out' said by the umpire in giving his decision and said by a player to make a claim. Now of course the unofficial utterance may have to be withdrawn in the light of a later official utterance but this is not a sufficient reason for treating the first as a prophecy of the last for plainly not all mistakes are mistaken predictions. Nor surely need the finality of a judge's decision either be confused with infallibility or tempt us to *define* laws in terms of what Courts do, even though there are many laws which the Courts must first interpret before they can apply. We can acknowledge that what the scorer says is final; yet we can still abstain from defining the notion of a score as what the scorer says. And we can admit that the umpire may be wrong in his decision though the rules give us no remedy if he is, and though there may be doubtful cases which he has to decide with but little help from the rules.

4. In any system legal or not, rules may for excellent practical reasons attach identical consequences to any one of a set of very different facts. The rule of cricket attaches the same consequence to the batsman's being bowled, stumped, or caught. And the word "out" is used in giving decisions or making claims under the rule and in other verbal applications of it. It is easy to see here that no one of these different ways of being out is more essentially what the word means than the others, and that there need be nothing common to all these ways of being out other than their falling under the same rule though there *may* be some similarity or analogy between them. But it is less easy to see this in those important cases where rules treat a *sequence* of different actions or states of affairs in a way which unifies them. In a game a rule may simply attach a single consequence to the successive actions of a set of different men – as when a team is said to have won a game. A more complex rule may prescribe that what is to be done at one point in a sequence shall depend on what was done or occurred earlier: and it may be indifferent to the identity of the persons concerned in the sequence so long as they fall under certain defining conditions. An example of this is when a team permitted by the rules of a tournament to have a varying memberships is penalized only in the third round – when the membership has changed – for what was done in the first round. In all such cases a sequence of action or states of affairs is unified simply by falling under certain rules; they *may* be otherwise as different as you please. Here can be seen the essential elements of the language of legal corporations. For in law, the lives of ten men that overlap but do not coincide may fall under separate rules under which they have separate rights and duties and then they are a collection of individuals for the law; but their actions

may fall under rules of a different kind which make what is to be done by any one or more of them depend in complex ways on what was done or occurred earlier. And then we may speak in appropriately unified ways of the sequence so unified, using a terminology like that of corporation law which will show that it is *this* sort of rule we are applying to the facts. But here the unity of the rule may mislead us when we come to define this terminology. It may cast a shadow: we may look for an identical continuing thing or person or quality *in* the sequence. We may find it – in "corporate spirit". This is real enough; but it is a secret of success not a criterion of identity.

III

These four general characteristics of legal language explain both why definition of words like "right", "duty", and "corporation" is baffled by the absence of some counterpart to "correspond" to these words, and also why the unobvious counterparts which have been so ingeniously contrived – the future facts, the complex facts or the psychological facts – turn out not to be something in terms of which we can define these words although to be connected with them in complex or indirect ways. And the fundamental point that the primary function of these words is not to stand for or describe anything but a distinct function, makes it vital to attend to Bentham's warning that we should not, as does the traditional method of definition, abstract words like "right" and "duty," "state", or "corporation" from the sentences in which alone their full function can be seen, and then demand of them so abstracted their genus and differentia.

Let us see what the use of this traditional method of definition presupposes and what the limits of its efficacy are, and why it may be misleading. It is of course the simplest form of definition, and also a peculiarly satisfying form because it gives us a set of words which can always be substituted for the word defined whenever it is used; it gives us a comprehensible synonym or translation for the word which puzzles us. It is peculiarly appropriate where the words have the straightforward function of standing for some kind, of thing, or quality, person, process, or event, for here we are not mystified or puzzled about the general characteristics of our subject-matter, but we ask for a definition simply to locate within this familiar general kind or class some special subordinate kind or class. Thus since we are not puzzled about the general notions of furniture or animal we can take a word like "chair" or "cat" and give the principle of its use by first specifying the general class to which what it is used to describe belongs, and then going on to define the specific differences that mark it off from other species of the same general kind. And of course if we are *not* puzzled about the general notion of a corporate body but only wish to know how one species (say a College) differs from another (say a limited Company) we can use this form of definition of single words perfectly well. But just because the method is appropriate at this level of inquiry, it cannot help us when our perplexities are deeper. For if our question arises, as it does with fundamental legal notions because we are puzzled about the general category to which something belongs and how some general type of expression relates to fact, and not merely about the place within that category, then until the puzzle is cleared up this form of definition is at the best unilluminating and at the worst profoundly misleading. It is unilluminating because a mode of definition designed to locate some subordinate species within some familiar category cannot elucidate the characteristics of some anomalous category; and it is misleading, because it will suggest that what is in fact an anomalous category is after all some species of the familiar. Hence if applied to legal words like "right", "duty", "state", or "corporation" the common mode of definition suggests that these words like ordinary words stand for or describe some thing, person, quality, process, or event; when the difficulty of finding these becomes apparent, different contrivances varying with tastes are used to explain or explain away the anomaly. Some say the difference is that the things for which these legal words stand are real but not sensory, others that they are fictious entities, others that these words stand for plain fact but of a complex, future, or psychological variety. So this standard mode of definition forces our familiar triad of theories into existence as a confused way of accounting for the anomalous character of legal words.

How then shall we define such words? If definition is the provision of a synonym which will not equally puzzle us these words cannot be defined. But I think there is a method of elucidation of quite general application and which we can call definition, if we wish. Bentham and others practised it, though they did not preach it. But before applying it to the highly complex legal cases, I shall illustrate it from the simple case of a game. Take the notion of a trick in a game of cards. Somebody says "What is a trick?" and you reply "I will explain: when you have a game and among its rules is one providing that when each of four players has played a card then the player who has put down the highest card scores a point, in these circumstances that player is said to have 'taken a trick' ". This natural explanation has not taken the form of a definition of the single word "trick": no synonym has been offered for it. Instead we have taken a sentence in which the word "trick" plays its characteristic role and explained it first by specifying the conditions under which the whole sentence is true, and secondly by showing how it is used in drawing a conclusion from the rules in a particular case. Suppose now that after such an explanation your questioner presses on: "That is all very well, that explains 'taking a trick'; but I still want to know what the word 'trick' means just by itself. I want a definition of 'trick'; I want something which can be substituted for it whenever it is used." If we yield to this demand for a single word definition we might reply: "The trick is just a collective name for the four cards." But someone may object: "The trick is not just a name for the four cards because these four cards will not always constitute a trick. It must therefore be some entity to which the four cards belong." A third might say: "No, the trick is a fictitious entity which the players pretend exists and to which by fiction which is part of the game they ascribe the cards." But in so simple a case we would not tolerate these theories, fraught as they are with mystery and empty of any guidance as to the use made of the word within the game: we would stand by the original twofold explanation; for this surely gave us all we needed when it explained the conditions under which the statement "He has taken a trick" is true and showed us how it was used in drawing a conclusion from the rules in a particular case.

If we turn back to Bentham we shall find that when his explanation of legal notions is illuminating as it very often is, it conforms to this method though only loosely. Yet curiously what he tells us to do is something different: it is to take a word like "right" or "duty" or "state": to embody it in a sentence such as "you have a right" where it plays a characteristic role and then to find a *translation* of it into what we should call factual terms. This he called the method of paraphrase – giving phrase for phrase not word for word. Now this method is applicable to many cases and has shed much light; but it distorts many legal words like 'right' or 'duty' whose characteristic role is not played in statements of fact but in conclusions of law. A paraphrase of these in factual terms is not possible and when Bentham proffers such a paraphrase it turns out not to be one at all.

But more often and much to our profit he does not claim to paraphrase: but he makes a different kind of remark, in order to elucidate these words – remarks such as these: "What you have a right to have me made do, is that which I am liable according to law upon a requisition made on your behalf to be punished for not doing" or "To know how to expound a right carry your eye to the act which in the circumstances in question would be a violation of that right; the law creates the right by forbidding that act." These, though defective, are on the right lines. They are not paraphrases but they specify some of the conditions necessary for the truth of a sentence of the form "You have a right". Bentham shows us how these conditions include the existence of a law imposing a duty on some other person; and moreover, that it must be a law which provides that the breach of the duty shall be visited with a sanction if you or someone on your behalf so choose. This has many virtues. By refusing to identify the meaning of the word "right" with any psychological or physical fact it correctly leaves open the question whether on any given occasion a person who has a right has in fact any expectation or power; and so it leaves us free to treat men's expectations or powers as what in general men will have if there is a system of rights, and as part of what a system of rights is generally intended to secure. Some of the improvements which should be made on Bentham's efforts are obvious. Instead of characterizing a right in terms of punishment many would do so in terms of the remedy. But I would prefer to show the special position of one who has a right by mentioning not the remedy but the choice which is open to one who has a right as to whether the corresponding duty shall be performed or not. For it is, I think, characteristic of those laws that confer rights (as distinguished from those that only impose obligations) that the obligation to perform the corresponding duty is made by law to depend on the choice of the individual who is said to have the right or the choice of some person authorized to act on his behalf.

I would therefore tender the following as an elucidation of the expression "a legal right": (1) A statement of the form "X has a right" is true if the following conditions are satisfied:

(a) There is in existence a legal system.

(b) Under a rule or rules of the system some other person Y is, in the events which have happened, obliged to do or abstain from some action.

(c) This obligation is made by law dependent on the choice either of X or some person authorized to act on his behalf so that either Y is bound to do or abstain from some action only if X (or some authorized person) so chooses or alternatively only until X (or such person) chooses otherwise. (2) A statement of the form "X has a right" is used to draw a conclusion of law in a particular case which falls under such rules.[1]

[1] This deals only with a right in the first sense (correlative to duty) distinguished by Hohfeld. But the same form of elucidation can be used for the cases of 'liberty', 'power', and 'immunity' and will I think show what is usually left unexplained viz: why these four varieties in spite of differences are referred to as 'rights'. The unifying element seems to be this: in all four cases the law specifically recognizes the choice of an individual either negatively by not impeding or obstructing it (liberty and immunity) or affirmatively by giving legal effect to it (claim and power). In the negative cases there is no law to interfere if the individual chooses to do or abstain from some action (liberty) or to retain his legal position unchanged (immunity); in the affirmative cases the law gives legal effect to the choice of an individual that some other person shall do or shall abstain from some action or that the legal position of some other person shall be altered. Of course when we say in any of these four senses that a person has a right we are not referring to any *actual* choice that he has made but either the relevant rules of law are such that *if* he chooses certain consequences follow, or there are no rules to impede his choice *if* he makes it. If there are legal rights which cannot be waived these would need special treatment.

IV

. . . Such was Maitland's question: When Nusquamia owes you money who owes you this? How should it be answered? Surely only by ceasing to batter our heads against the single word: Nusquamia. Pressing the question "Who or what when Nusquamia owes you £1,000 is it which owes you this?" is like demanding desperately: "When you lost that game what was it that you lost?" To the question so pressed the only answer is to repeat "a game", as to the other the only answer is to repeat "Nusquamia". This, of course, tells us precisely nothing but is at least neither mystifying nor false. To elucidate it we must obey Bentham's first injunction: we must take the whole statement "Nusquamia owes you £1,000" and describe its use perhaps as follows:

1. Here in the territory of Nusquamia there is a legal system in force; under the laws of this system certain persons on complying with certain conditions are authorized for certain purposes to do actions analogous to those required to make a contract of loan between private individuals.

2. When such persons do such acts certain consequences, analogous to those attached to the similar actions of private individuals, follow, including the liability of persons designated by law to repay the sums of money out of funds defined by law.

3. The expression "Nusquamia owes you £1,000" does not state the existence of these rules nor of these circumstances, but is true in a particular case when they exist, and is used in drawing a conclusion of law from these rules in a particular case.

How much detail should be given depends on the degree to which the questioner is puzzled. If all that he is puzzled by his inability to say who or what Nusquamia is and the inadequacies of theories to explain this, he may be content with what has been done. But of course he may be puzzled by the notion of one and the same legal system existing throughout the lives of different men in terms of which this elucidation of "Nusquamia" has been offered.[1] If so this in its turn must be elucidated as it can be in the same manner.

There is of course nothing in this method to prevent its application to the ephemeral technical one-man Company which Realists regarded as a difficulty for their theory. To explain what a limited Company is we must refer to the relevant legal rules, which determine the conditions under which a characteristic sentence like "Smith & Co. owe White £10" is true. Then we must show how the name of a limited Company functions as part of a conclusion of law which is used to apply both special Company rules and also rules such as those of contract which were originally worked out for individuals. It will, of course, be necessary to stress that under the special conditions defined by the special rules, other rules are applied to the conduct of individuals in a manner radically different from though still analogous to that in which such rules apply to individuals apart from such special conditions. This we could express by restating the familiar principle of our Company law "A Company is a distinct entity from its members" as: "The name of a limited Company is used in conclusions of law which apply legal rules in special circumstances in a manner distinct from though analogous to those in which such rules are applied to individuals apart from such circumstances." This restatement would show that we have to do not with

[1] That is, we must elucidate the expression 'the same legal system' by showing what are the conditions sufficient for the truth of statements of the form 'The same legal system is in force in England now as in 1900'. The fundamental question here is the elucidation of the expression 'the same rule'.

anomalous or fictitious entities, but with a new and extended though analogous use of legal rules and of the expressions involved in them.

H. L. A. Hart, 1907–

POSITIVISM AND THE SEPARATION OF LAW AND MORALS

In this article I shall discuss and attempt to defend a view which Mr. Justice Holmes, among others, held and for which he and they have been much criticized. But I wish first to say why I think that Holmes, whatever the vicissitudes of his American reputation may be, will always remain for Englishmen a heroic figure in jurisprudence. This will be so because he magically combined two qualties: one of them is imaginative power, which English legal thinking has often lacked; the other is clarity, which English legal thinking usually possesses. The English lawyer who turns to read Holmes is made to see that what he had taken to be settled and stable is really always on the move. To make this discovery with Holmes is to be with a guide whose words may leave you unconvinced, sometimes even repelled, but never mystified. Like our own Austin, with whom Holmes shared many ideals and thoughts, Holmes was sometimes clearly wrong; but again like Austin, when this was so he was always wrong clearly. This surely is a sovereign virtue in jurisprudence. Clarity I know is said not to be enough; this may be true, but there are still questions in jurisprudence where the issues are confused because they are discussed in a style which Holmes would have spurned for its obscurity. Perhaps this is inevitable: jurisprudence trembles so uncertainly on the margin of many subjects that there will always be need for someone, in Bentham's phrase, "to pluck the mask of Mystery" from its face. This is true, to a pre-eminent degree, of the subject of this article. Contemporary voices tell us we must recognize something obscured by the legal "positivists" whose day is now over: that there is a "point of intersection between law and morals," or that what is and what *ought* to be are somehow indissolubly fused or inseparable, though the positivists denied it. What do these phrases mean? Or rather which of the many things that they *could* mean, *do* they mean? Which of them do "positivists" deny and why is it wrong to do so?

I

I shall present the subject as part of the history of an idea. At the close of the eighteenth century and the beginning of the nineteenth the most earnest thinkers in England about legal and social problems and the architects of great reforms were the great Utilitarians. Two of them, Bentham and Austin, constantly insisted on the need to distinguish, firmly and with the maximum of clarity, law as it is from law as it ought to be. This theme haunts their work, and they condemned the natural-law thinkers precisely because they had blurred this apparently simple but vital distinction. By contrast, at the present time in this country and to a lesser extent in England, this separation between law and morals is held to be superficial and wrong. Some critics have thought that it blinds men to the true nature of law and its roots in social life. Others have thought it not only intellectually misleading but corrupting in practice, at its worst apt to weaken resistance to state tyranny or absolutism, and at its best apt to bring law into disrespect. The nonpejorative name "Legal Positivism," like most terms which are used as missiles in intellectual battles, has come to stand for a baffling multitude of different sins. One of them is the sin, real or alleged, of insisting, as

Austin and Bentham did, on the separation of law as it is and law as it ought to be.

How then has this reversal of the wheel come about? What are the theoretical errors in this distinction? Have the practical consequences of stressing the distinction as Bentham and Austin did been bad? Should we now reject it or keep it? In considering these questions we should recall the social philosophy which went along with the Utilitarians' insistence on this distinction. They stood firmly but on their own utilitarian ground for all the principles of liberalism in law and government. No one has ever combined, with such even-minded sanity as the Utilitarians, the passion for reform with respect for law together with a due recognition of the need to control the abuse of power even when power is in the hands of reformers. One by one in Bentham's works you can identify the elements of the *Rechtstaat* and all the principles for the defense of which the terminology of natural law has in our day been revived. Here are liberty of speech, and of press, the right of association, the need that laws should be published and made widely known before they are enforced, the need to control administrative agencies, the insistence that there should be no criminal liability without fault, and the importance of the principle of legality, *nulla poena sine lege*. Some, I know, find the political and moral insight of the Utilitarians a very simple one, but we should not mistake this simplicity for superficiality nor forget how favorably their simplicities compare with the profundities of other thinkers. Take only one example: Bentham on slavery. He says the question at issue is not whether those who are held as slaves can reason, but simply whether they suffer. Does this not compare well with the discussion of the question in terms of whether or not there are some men whom Nature has fitted only to be the living instruments of others? We owe it to Bentham more than anyone else that we have stopped discussing this and similar questions of social policy in that form.

So Bentham and Austin were not dry analysts fiddling with verbal distinctions while cities burned, but were the vanguard of a movement which laboured with passionate intensity and much success to bring about a better society and better laws. Why then did they insist on the separation of law as it is and law as it ought to be? What did they mean? Let us first see what they said. Austin formulated the doctrine:

"The existence of law is one thing; its merit or demerit is another. Whether it be or be not is one enquiry; whether it be or be not conformable to an assumed standard, is a different enquiry. A law, which actually exists, is a law, though we happen to dislike it, or though it vary from the text, by which we regulate our approbation and disapprobation. This truth, when formally announced as an abstract proposition, is so simple and glaring that it seems idle to insist upon it. But simple and glaring as it is, when enunciated in abstract expressions the enumeration of the instances in which it has been forgotten would fill a volume.

"Sir William Blackstone, for example, says in his "Commentaries" that the laws of God are superior in obligation to all other laws; that no human laws should be suffered to contradict them; that human laws are of no validity if contrary to them; and that all valid laws derive their force from that Divine original.

"Now, he *may* mean that all human laws ought to conform to the Divine laws. If this be his meaning, I assent to it without hesitation. . . . Perhaps, again, he means that human lawgivers are themselves obliged by the Divine laws to fashion the laws which they impose by that ultimate standard, because if they do not, God will punish them. To this also I entirely assent. . . .

"But the meaning of this passage of Blackstone, if it has a meaning, seems rather to be this: that no human law which conflicts with the Divine law is obligatory or binding; in other words, that no human law which conflicts with the Divine law *is a law*. . . ."

Austin's protest against blurring the distinction between what law is and what it ought to be is quite general: it is a mistake, whatever our standard of what ought to be, whatever "the text by which we regulate our approbation or disapprobation." His examples, however, are always a confusion between law as it is and law as morality would require it to be. For him, it must be remembered, the fundamental principles of morality were God's commands, to which utility was an "index": besides this there was the actual accepted morality of a social group or "positive" morality.

Bentham insisted on this distinction without characterizing morality by reference to God but only, of course, by reference to the principles of utility. Both thinkers' prime reason for this insistence was to enable men to see steadily the precise issues posed by the existence of morally bad laws, and to understand the specific character of the authority of a legal order. Bentham's general recipe for life under the government of laws was simple: it was "*to obey punctually*; *to censure freely*." But Bentham was especially aware, as an anxious spectator of the French revolution, that this was not enough: the time might come in any society when the law's commands were so evil that the question of resistance had to be faced, and it was then essential that the issues at stake at this point should neither be oversimplified nor obscured. Yet, this was precisely what the confusion between law and morals had done and Bentham found that the confusion had spread symmetrically in two different directions. On the one hand Bentham had in mind the anarchist who argues thus: "This ought not to be the law, therefore it is not and I am free not merely to censure but to disregard it." On the other hand he thought of the reactionary who argues: "This is the law, therefore it is what it ought to be" and thus stifles criticism at its birth. Both errors, Bentham thought, were to be found in Blackstone: there was his incautious statement that human laws were invalid if contrary to the law of God, and "that spirit of obsequious *quietism* that seems constitutional in our Author" which "will scarce ever let him recognise a difference" between what is and what ought to be. This indeed was for Bentham the occupational disease of lawyers: "[I]n the eyes of lawyers – not to speak of their dupes – that is to say, as yet, the generality of non-lawyers – the *is* and *ought to be* . . . were one and indivisible." There are therefore two dangers between which insistence on this distinction will help us to steer: the danger that law and its authority may be dissolved in man's conceptions of what law ought to be and the danger that the existing law may supplant morality as a final test of conduct and so escape criticism.

In view of later criticisms it is also important to distinguish several things that the Utilitarians did not mean by insisting on their separation of law and morals. They certainly accepted many of the things that might be called "the intersection of law and morals." First, they never denied that, as a matter of historical fact, the development of legal systems had been powerfully influenced by moral opinion, and, conversely, that moral standards had been profoundly influenced by law, so that the content of many legal rules mirrored moral rules or principles. It is not in fact always easy to trace this historical causal connection, but Bentham was certainly ready to admit its existence; so too Austin spoke of the "frequent coincidence" of positive law and morality and attributed the confusion of what law is with what law ought to be to this very fact.

Secondly, neither Bentham nor his followers denied that by explicit legal provisions moral principles might at different points be brought into a legal system and form part of its rules, or that courts might be legally bound to decide in accordance with what they thought just or best. Bentham indeed recognized, as Austin did not, that even the supreme legislative power might be subjected to legal restraints by a constitution and would not have denied that moral principles, like those of the fifth amendment, might form the content of such legal constitutional restraints. Austin differed in thinking that restraints on the supreme legislative power could not have the force of law, but would remain merely political or moral checks; but of course he would have recognized that a statute, for example, might confer a delegated legislative power and restrict the area of its exercise by reference to moral principles.

What both Bentham and Austin were anxious to assert were the following two simple things: first, in the absence of an expressed constitutional or legal provision, it could not follow from the mere fact that a rule violated standards of morality that it was not a rule of law; and, conversely, it could not follow from the mere fact that a rule was morally desirable that it was a rule of law.

The history of this simple doctrine in the nineteenth century is too long and too intricate to trace here. Let me summarize it by saying that after it was propounded to the world by Austin it dominated English jurisprudence and constitutes part of the framework of most of those curiously English and perhaps unsatisfactory productions – the omnibus surveys of the whole field of jurisprudence. A succession of these were published after a full text of Austin's lectures finally appeared in 1863. In each of them the utilitarian separation of law and morals is treated as something that enables lawyers to attain a new clarity. Austin was said by one of his English successors, Amos, "to have delivered the law from the dead body of morality that still clung to it"; and even Maine, who was critical of Austin at many points, did not question this part of his doctrine. In the United States men like N. St. John Green, Gray, and Holmes considered that insistence on this distinction had enabled the understanding of law as a means of social control to get off to a fruitful new start; they welcomed it both as self-evident and as illuminating – as a revealing tautology. This distinction is, of course, one of the main themes of Holmes' most famous essay "The Path of the Law," but the place it had in the estimation of these American writers is best seen in what Gray wrote at the turn of the century in *The Nature and Sources of the Law*. He said:

"The great gain in its fundamental conceptions which Jurisprudence made during the last century was the recognition of the truth that the Law of a State . . . is not an ideal, but something which actually exists. . . . [i]t is not that, which ought to be, but that which is. To fix this definitely in the Jurisprudence of the Common Law, is the feat that Austin accomplished."

II

So much for the doctrine in the heyday of its success. Let us turn now to some of the criticisms. Undoubtedly, when Bentham and Austin insisted on the distinction between law as it is and as it ought to be, they had in mind *particular* laws the meanings of which were clear and so not in dispute, and they were concerned to argue that such laws, even if morally outrageous, were still laws. It is, however, necessary, in considering the criticisms which later developed, to consider more than those criticisms which were directed to this particular point if we are to get at the root of the dissatisfaction felt; we must also take account of the objection that, even if what the Utilitarians said on this particular point were true, their insistence on it, in a terminology suggesting a general cleavage between what is and ought to be law, obscured the fact that at other points there is an essential point of contact between the two. So in what follows I shall consider not only criticisms of the particular point which the Utilitarians had in mind, but also the claim that an essential connection between law and morals emerges if we examine how laws, the meanings of which are in dispute, are interpreted and applied in concrete cases; and that this connection emerges again if we widen our point of view and ask, not whether every particular rule of law must satisfy a moral minimum in order to be a law, but whether a system of rules which altogether failed to do this could be a legal system.

There is, however, one major initial complexity by which criticism has been much confused. We must remember that the Utilitarians combined with their insistence on the separation of law and morals two other equally famous but distinct doctrines. One was the important truth that a purely analytical study of legal concepts, a study of the meaning of the distinctive vocabulary of the law, was as vital to our understanding of the nature of law as historical or sociological studies, though of course it could not supplant them. The other doctrine was the famous imperative theory of law – that law is essentially a command.

These three doctrines constitute the utilitarian tradition in jurisprudence; yet they are distinct doctrines. It is possible to endorse the separation between law and morals and to value analytical inquiries into the meaning of legal concepts and yet think it wrong to conceive of law as essentially a command. One source of great confusion in the criticism of the separation of law and morals was the belief that the falsity of any one of these three doctrines in the utilitarian tradition showed the other two to be false; what was worse was the failure to see that there were three quite separate doctrines in this tradition. The indiscriminate use of the label "positivism" to designate ambiguously each one of these three separate doctrines (together with some others which the Utilitarians never professed) has perhaps confused the issue more than any other single factor. [It may help to identify five (there may be more) meanings of "positivism" bandied about in contemporary jurisprudence:

(1) the contention that laws are commands of human beings.

(2) the contention that there is no necessary connection between law and morals or law as it is and ought to be.

(3) the contention that the analysis (or study of the meaning) of legal concepts is (a) worth pursuing and (b) to be distinguished from historical inquiries into the causes or origins of laws, from sociological inquiries into the relation of law and other social phenomena, and from the criticism or appraisal of law whether in terms of morals, social aims, "functions," or otherwise.

(4) the contention that a legal system is a "closed logical system" in which correct legal decisions can be deduced by logical means from predetermined legal rules without reference to social aims, policies, moral standards, and

(5) the contention that moral judgments cannot be established or defended, as statements of facts can, by rational argument, evidence, or proof ("noncognitivism" in ethics).

Bentham and Austin held the views described in (1), (2), and (3) but not those in (4) and (5). Opinion (4) is often ascribed to analytical jurists, but I know of no "analyst" who held this view.] Some of the early American critics of the Austinian doctrine were, however, admirably clear on just this matter. Gray, for example, added at the end of the tribute to Austin, which I have already quoted, the words, "He may have been wrong in treating the Law of the State as being the command of the sovereign" and he touched shrewdly on many points where the command theory is defective. But other critics have been less clear-headed and have thought that the inadequacies of the command theory which gradually came to light were sufficient to demonstrate the falsity of the separation of law and morals.

This was a mistake, but a natural one. To see how natural it was we must look a little more closely at the command idea. The famous theory that law is a command was a part of a wider and more ambitious claim. Austin said that the notion of a command was "the *key* to the sciences of jurisprudence and morals," and contemporary attempts to elucidate moral judgments in terms of "imperative" or "prescriptive" utterances echo this ambitious claim. But the command theory, viewed as an effort to identify even the quintessence of law, let alone the quintessence of morals, seems breathtaking in its simplicity and quite inadequate. There is much, even in the simplest legal system, that is distorted if presented as a command. Yet the Utilitarians thought that the essence of a legal system could be conveyed if the notion of a command were supplemented by that of a habit of obedience. The simple scheme was this: What is a command? It is simply an expression by one person of the desire that another person should do or abstain from some action, accompanied by a threat of punishment which is likely to follow disobedience. Commands are laws if two conditions are satisfied: first, they must be general; second, they must be commanded by what (as both Bentham and Austin claimed) exists in every political society whatever its constitutional form, namely, a person or a group of persons who are in receipt of habitual obedience from most of the society but pay no such obedience to others. These persons are its sovereign. Thus law is the command of the uncommanded commanders of society – the creation of the legally untrammelled will of the sovereign who is by definition outside the law.

It is easy to see that this account of a legal system is threadbare. One can also see why it might seem that its inadequacy is due to the omission of some essential connection with morality. The situation which the simple trilogy of command, sanction, and sovereign avails to describe, if you take these notions at all precisely, is like that of a gunman saying to his victim, "Give me your money or your life." The only difference is that in the case of a legal system the gunman says it to a large number of people who are accustomed to the racket and habitually surrender to it. Law surely is not the gunman situation writ large, and legal order is surely not to be thus simply identified with compulsion.

This scheme, despite the points of obvious analogy between a statute and a command, omits some of the most characteristic elements of law. Let me cite a few. It is wrong to think of a legislature (and a fortiori an electorate) with a changing membership, as a group of persons habitually obeyed: this simple idea is suited only to a monarch sufficiently long-lived for a "habit" to grow up. Even if we waive this point, nothing which legislators do makes law unless they comply with fundamental accepted rules specifying the essential lawmaking procedures. This is true even in a system having a simple unitary constitution like the British. These fundamental accepted rules specifying what the legislature must do to legislate are not commands habitually obeyed, nor can they be expressed as habits of obedience to persons. They lie at the root of a legal system, and what is most missing in the utilitarian scheme is an analysis of what it is for a social group and its officials to accept such rules. This notion, not that of a command as Austin claimed, is the "key to the science of jurisprudence," or at least one of the keys.

Again, Austin, in the case of a democracy, looked past the legislators to the electorate as "the sovereign" (or in England as part of it). He thought that in the United States the mass of the electors to the state and federal legislatures were the sovereign whose commands, given by their "agents" in the legislatures, were law. But on this footing the whole notion of the sovereign outside the law being "habitually obeyed" by the "bulk" of the population must go: for in this case the "bulk" obeys the bulk, that is, it obeys itself. Plainly the general acceptance of the authority of a law-making procedure, irrespective of the changing individuals who operate it from time to time, can be only distorted by an analysis in terms of mass habitual obedience to certain persons who are by definition outside the law, just as the cognate but much simpler phenomenon of the general social acceptance of a rule, say of taking off the hat when entering a church, would be distorted if represented as habitual obedience by the mass to specific persons.

Other critics dimly sensed a further and more important defect in the command theory, yet blurred the edge of an important criticism by assuming that the defect was due to the failure to insist upon some important connection between law and morals. This more radical defect is as follows. The picture that the command theory draws of life under law is essentially a simple relationship of the commander to the commanded, of superior to inferior, of top to bottom; the relationship is vertical between the commanders or authors of the law conceived of as essentially outside the law and those who are commanded and subject to the law. In this picture no place, or only an accidental or subordinate place, is afforded for a distinction between types of legal rules which are in fact radically different. Some laws require men to act in certain ways or to abstain from acting whether they wish to or not. The criminal law consists largely of rules of this sort: like commands they are simply "obeyed" or "disobeyed." But other legal rules are presented to society in quite different ways and have quite different functions. They provide facilities more or less elaborate for individuals to create structures of rights and duties for the conduct of life within the coercive framework of the law. Such are the rules enabling individuals to make contracts, wills, and trusts, and generally to mould their legal relations with others. Such rules, unlike the criminal law, are not factors designed to obstruct wishes and choices of an antisocial sort. On the contrary, these rules provide facilities for the realization of wishes and choices. They do not say (like commands) "do this whether you wish it or not," but rather "if you wish to do this, here is the way to do it." Under these rules we exercise powers, make claims, and assert rights. These phrases mark off characteristic features of laws that confer rights and powers; they are laws which are, so to speak, put at the disposition of individuals in a way in which the criminal law is not. Much ingenuity has gone into the task of "reducing" laws of this second sort to some complex variant of laws of the first sort. The effort to show that laws conferring rights are "really" only conditional stipulations of sanctions to be exacted from the person ultimately under a legal duty characterizes much of Kelsen's work. Yet to urge this is really just to exhibit dogmatic determination to suppress one aspect of the legal system in order to maintain the theory that the stipulation of a sanction, like Austin's command, represents the quintessence of law. One might as well urge that the rules of baseball were "really" only complex conditional directions to the scorer and that this showed their real or "essential" nature.

One of the first jurists in England to break with the Austinian tradition, Salmond, complained that the analysis in terms of commands left the notion of a right unprovided with a place. But he confused the point. He argued first, and correctly, that if laws are merely commands it is inexplicable that we should have come to speak of legal rights and powers as conferred or arising under them, but then wrongly concluded that the rules of a legal system must necessarily be connected with moral rules or principles of justice and that only on this footing could the phenomenon of legal rights be explained. Otherwise, Salmond thought, we would have to say that a mere "verbal coincidence" connects the concepts of legal and moral right. Similarly, continental critics of the Utilitarians, always alive to the complexity of the notion of a subjective right, insisted that the command theory gave it no place. Hagerstrom insisted that if laws were merely commands the notion of an individual's right was really inexplicable, for commands are, as he said, something which we either obey or we do not obey; they do not confer rights. But he, too, concluded that moral, or, as he put it, commonsense, notions of justice must therefore be necessarily involved in the analysis of any legal structure elaborate enough to confer rights.

Yet, surely these arguments are confused. Rules that confer rights, though distinct from commands, need not be moral rules or coincide with them. Rights, after all, exist under the rules of ceremonies, games, and in many other spheres regulated by rules which are irrelevant to the question of justice or what the law ought to be. Nor need rules which confer rights be just or morally good rules. The rights of a master over his slaves show us that. "Their merit or demerit," as Austin termed it, depends on how rights are distributed in society and over whom or what they are exercised. These critics indeed revealed the inadequacy of the simple notions of command and habit for the analysis of law; at many points it is apparent that the social acceptance of a rule or standard of authority (even if it is motivated only by fear or superstition or rests on inertia) must be brought into the analysis and cannot itself be reduced to the two simple terms. Yet nothing in this showed the utilitarian insistence on the distinction between the existence of law and its "merits" to be wrong.

III

I now turn to a distinctively American criticism of the separation of the law that is from the law that ought to be. It emerged from the critical study of the judicial process with which American jurisprudence has been on the whole so benefically occupied. The most skeptical of these critics – the loosely named "Realists" of the 1930's – perhaps too naively accepted the conceptual framework of the natural sciences as adequate for the characterization of law and for the analysis of rule-guided action of which a living system of law at least partly consists. But they opened men's eyes to what actually goes on when courts decide cases, and the contrast they drew between the actual facts of judicial decision and the traditional terminology for describing it as if it were a wholly logical operation was usually illuminating; for in spite of some exaggeration the "Realists" made us acutely conscious of one cardinal feature of human language and human thought, emphasis on which is vital not only for the understanding of law but in areas of philosophy far beyond the confines of jurisprudence. The insight of this school may be presented in the following example. A legal rule forbids you to take a vehicle into the public park. Plainly this forbids an automobile, but what about bicycles, roller skates, toy automobiles? What about airplanes? Are these, as we say, to be called "vehicles" for the purpose of the rule or not? If we are to communicate with each other at all, and if, as in the most elementary form of law, we are to express our intentions that a certain type of behavior be regulated by rules, then the general words we use – like "vehicle" in the case I consider – must have some standard instance in which no doubts are felt about its application. There must be a core of settled meaning, but there will be, as well, a penumbra of debatable cases in which words are neither obviously applicable nor obviously ruled out. These cases will each have some features in common with the standard case; they will lack others or be accompanied by features not present in the standard case. Human invention and natural processes continually throw up such variants on the familiar, and if we are to say that these ranges of facts do or do not fall under existing rules, then the classifier must make a decision which is not dictated to him, for the facts and phenomena to which we fit our words and apply our rules are as it were *dumb*. The toy automobile cannot speak up and say, "I am a vehicle for the purpose of this legal rule," nor can the roller skates chorus, "We are not a vehicle." Fact situations do not await us neatly labeled, creased, and folded, nor is their legal classification written on them to be simply read off by the judge. Instead in applying legal rules, someone must take the responsibility of deciding that words do or do not cover some case in hand with all the practical consequences involved in this decision.

We may call the problems which arise outside the hard core of standard instances or settled meaning "problems of the penumbra"; they are always with us whether in relation to such trivial things as the regulation of the use of the public park or in relation to the multidimensional generalities of a constitution. If a penumbra of uncertainty must surround all legal rules, then their application to specific cases in the penumbral area cannot be a matter of logical deduction, and so deductive reasoning, which for generations has been cherished as the very perfection of human reasoning, cannot serve as a model for what judges, or indeed anyone, should do in bringing particular cases under general rules. In this area men cannot live by deduction alone. And it follows that if legal arguments and legal decisions of penumbral questions are to be rational, their rationality must lie in something other than a logical relation to premises. So if it is rational or "sound" to argue and to decide that for the purposes of this rule an airplane is not a vehicle, this argument must be sound or rational without being logically conclusive. What is it then that makes such decisions correct or at least better than alternative decisions? Again, it seems true to say that the criterion which makes a decision sound in such cases is some concept of what the law ought to be; it is easy to slide from that into saying that it must be a moral judgment about what law ought to be. So here we touch upon a point of necessary "intersection between law and morals" which demonstrates the falsity or, at any rate, the misleading character of the Utilitarians' emphatic insistence on the separation of law as it is and ought to be. Surely, Bentham and Austin could only have written as they did because they misunderstood or neglected this aspect of the judicial process, because they ignored the problems of the penumbra.

The misconception of the judicial process which ignores the problems of the penumbra and which views the process as consisting pre-eminently in deductive reasoning is often stigmatized as the error of "formalism" or "literalism." My question now is, how and to what extent does the demonstration of this error show the utilitarian distinction to be wrong or misleading? Here there are many issues which have been confused, but I can only disentangle some. The charge of formalism has been leveled both at the "positivist" legal theorist and at the courts, but of course it must be a very different charge in each case. Leveled at the legal theorist, the charge means that he has made a theoretical mistake about the character of legal decision; he has thought of the reasoning involved as consisting in deduction from premises in which the judges' practical choices or decisions play no part. It would be easy to show that Austin was guiltless of this error; only an entire misconception of what analytical jurisprudence is and why he thought it important has led to the view that he, or any other analyst, believed that the law was a closed logical system in which judges deduced their decisions from premises. On the contrary, he was very much alive to the character of language, to its vagueness or open character; he thought that in the penumbral situation judges must necessarily legislate, and, in accents that sometimes recall those of the late Judge Jerome Frank, he berated the common-law judges for legislating feebly and timidly and for blindly relying on real or fancied analogies with past cases instead of adapting their decisions to the growing needs of society as revealed by the moral standard of utility. The villains of this piece, responsible for the conception of the judge as an automaton, are not the Utilitarian thinkers. The responsibility, if it is to be laid at the door of any theorist, is with thinkers like Blackstone and, at an earlier stage, Montesquieu. The root of this evil is preoccupation with the separation of powers and Blackstone's "childish fiction" (as Austin termed it) that judges only "find," never "make," law.

But we are concerned with "formalism" as a vice not of jurists but of judges. What precisely is it for a judge to commit this error, to be a "formalist," "automatic," a "slot machine"? Curiously enough the literature which is full of the denunciation of these vices never makes this clear in concrete terms; instead we have only descriptions which cannot mean what they appear to say: it is said that in the formalist error courts make an excessive use of logic, take a thing to "a dryly logical extreme," or make an excessive use of analytical methods. But just how in being a formalist does a judge make an excessive use of logic? It is clear that the essence of his error is to give some general term an interpretation which is blind to social values and consequences (or which is in some other way stupid or perhaps merely disliked by critics). But logic does not prescribe interpretation of terms; it dictates neither the stupid nor intelligent interpretation of any expression. Logic only tells you hypothetically that *if* you give a certain term a certain interpretation then a certain conclusion follows. Logic is silent on how to classify particulars – and this is the heart of a judicial decision. So this reference to logic and to logical extremes is a misnomer for something else, which must be this. A judge has to apply a rule to a concrete case – perhaps the rule that one may not take a stolen "vehicle" across state lines, and in this case an airplane has been taken. He either does not see or pretends not to see that the general terms of this rule are susceptible of different interpretations and that he has a choice left open uncontrolled by linguistic conventions. He ignores, or is blind to, the fact that he is in the area of the penumbra and is not dealing with a standard case. Instead of choosing in the light of social aims, the judge fixes the meaning in a different way. He either takes the meaning that the word most obviously suggests in its ordinary nonlegal context to ordinary men, or one which the word has been given in some other legal context, or, still worse, he thinks of a standard case and then arbitrarily identifies certain features in it – for example, in the case of a vehicle, (1) normally used on land, (2) capable of carrying a human person, (3) capable of being self-propelled – and treats these three as always necessary and always sufficient conditions for the use in all contexts of the word "vehicle," irrespective of the social consequences of giving it this interpretation. This choice, not "logic," would force the judge to include a toy motor car (if electrically propelled) and to exclude bicycles and the airplane. In all this there is possibly great stupidity but no more "logic," and no less, than in cases in which the interpretation given to a general term and the consequent application of some general rule to a particular case is consciously controlled by some identified social aim.

Decisions made in a fashion as blind as this would scarcely deserve the name of decisions; we might as well toss a penny in applying a rule of law. But it is at least doubtful whether any judicial decisions (even in England) have been quite as automatic as this. Rather, either the interpretations stigmatized as automatic have resulted from the conviction that it is fairer in a criminal statute to take a meaning which would jump to the mind of the ordinary man at the cost even of defeating other values, and this itself is a social policy (though possibly a bad one); or much more frequently, what is stigmatized as "mechanical" and "automatic" is a determined choice made indeed in the light of a social aim but of a conservative social aim. Certainly many of the Supreme Court decisions at the turn of the century which have been so stigmatized represent clear choices in the penumbral area to give effect to a policy of a conservative type. This is peculiarly true of Mr. Justice Peckham's opinions defining the spheres of policy power and due process.

But how does the wrongness of deciding cases in an automatic and mechanical way and the rightness of deciding cases by reference to social purposes show that the utilitarian insistence on the distinction between what the law is and what it ought to be is wrong? I take it that no one who wished to use these vices of formalism as proof that the distinction between what is and what ought to be is mistaken would deny that the decisions stigmatized as automatic are law; nor would he deny that the system in which such automatic decisions are made is a legal system. Surely he would say that they are law, but they are bad law, they ought not to be law. But this would be to use the distinction, not to refute it; and of course both Bentham and Austin used it to attack judges for failing to decide penumbral cases in accordance with the growing needs of society.

Clearly, if the demonstration of the errors of formalism is to show the utilitarian distinction to be wrong, the point must be drastically restated. The point must be not merely that a judicial decision to be rational must be made in the light of some conception of what ought to be, but that the aims, the social policies and purposes to which judges should appeal if their decisions are to be rational, are themselves to be considered as part of the law in some suitably wide sense of "law" which is held to be more illuminating than that used by the Utilitarians. This restatement of the point would have the following consequence: instead of saying that the recurrence of penumbral questions shows us that legal rules are essentially incomplete, and that, when they fail to determine decisions, judges must legislate and so exercise a creative choice between alternatives, we shall say that the social policies which guide the judges' choice are in a sense there for them to discover; the judges are only "drawing out" of the rule what, if it is properly understood, is "latent" within it. To call this judicial legislation is to obscure some essential continuity between the clear cases of the rule's application and the penumbral decisions. I shall question later whether this way of talking is salutory, but I wish at this time to point out something obvious, but likely, if not stated, to tangle the issues. It does not follow that, because the opposite of a decision reached blindly in the formalist or literalist manner is a decision intelligently reached by reference to some conception of what ought to be, we have a junction of law and morals. We must, I think, beware of thinking in a too simple-minded fashion about the word "ought." This is not because there is no distinction to be made between law as it is and ought to be. Far from it. It is because the distinction should be between what is and what from many different points of view ought to be. The word "ought" merely reflects the presence of some standard of criticism; one of these standards is a moral standard but not all standards are moral. We say to our neighbour, "You ought not to lie," and that may certainly be a moral judgment, but we should remember that the baffled poisoner may say, "I ought to have given her a second dose." The point here is that intelligent decisions which we oppose to mechanical or formal decisions are not necessarily identical with decisions defensible on moral grounds. We may say of many a decision: "Yes, that is right; that is as it ought to be," and we may mean only that some accepted purpose or policy has been thereby advanced; we may not mean to endorse the moral propriety of the policy or the decision. So the contrast between the mechanical decision and the intelligent one can be reproduced inside a system dedicated to the pursuit of the most evil aims. It does not exist as a contrast to be found only in legal systems which, like our own, widely recognize principles of justice and moral claims of individuals.

An example may make this point plainer. With us the task of sentencing in criminal cases is the one that seems most obviously to demand from the judge the exercise of moral judgment. Here the factors to be weighed seem clearly to be moral factors: society must not be exposed to wanton attack; too much misery must not be inflicted on either the victim or his dependents; efforts must be made to enable him to lead a better life and regain a position in the society whose laws he has violated. To a judge striking the balance among these claims, with all the discretion and perplexities involved, his task seems as plain an example of the exercise of moral judgment as could be; and it seems to be the polar opposite of some mechanical application of a tariff of penalties fixing a sentence careless of the moral claims which in our system have to be weighed. So here intelligent and rational decision is guided however uncertainly by moral aims. But we have only to vary the example to see that this need not necessarily be so and surely, if it need not necessarily be so, the Utilitarian point remains unshaken. Under the Nazi regime men were sentenced by courts for criticism of the regime. Here the choice of sentence might be guided exclusively by consideration of what was needed to maintain the state's tyranny effectively. What sentence would both terrorize the public at large and keep the friends and family of the prisoner in suspense so that both hope and fear would cooperate as factors making for subservience? The prisoner of such a system would be regarded simply as an object to be used in pursuit of these aims. Yet, in contrast with a mechanical decision, decision on these grounds would be intelligent and purposive, and from one point of view the decision would be as it ought to be. Of course, I am not unaware that a whole philosophical tradition has sought to demonstrate the fact that we cannot correctly call decisions or behavior truly rational unless they are in conformity with moral aims and principles. But the example I have used seems to me to serve at least as a warning that we cannot use the errors of formalism as something which per se demonstrates the falsity of the utilitarian insistence on the distinction between law as it is and law as *morally* it ought to be.

We can now return to the main point. If it is true that the intelligent decision of penumbral questions is one made not mechanically but in the light of aims, purposes, and policies, though not necessarily in the light of anything we would call moral principles, is it wise to express this important fact by saying that the firm utilitarian distinction between what the law is and what it ought to be should be dropped? Perhaps the claim that it is wise cannot be theoretically refuted for it is, in effect, an *invitation* to revise our conception of what a legal rule is. We are invited to include in the "rule" the various aims and policies in the light of which its penumbral cases are decided on the ground that these aims have, because of their importance, as much right to be called law as the core of legal rules whose meaning is settled. But though an invitation cannot be refuted, it may be refused and I would proffer two reasons for refusing this invitation. First, everything we have learned about the judicial process can be expressed in other less mysterious ways. We can say laws are incurably incomplete and we must decide the penumbral cases rationally by reference to social aims. I think Holmes, who had such a vivid appreciation of the fact that "general propositions do not decide concrete cases," would have put it that way. Second, to insist on the utilitarian distinction is to emphasize that the hard core of settled meaning is law in some centrally important sense and that even if there are borderlines, there must first be lines. If this were not so the notion of rules controlling courts' decisions would be senseless as some of the "Realists" – in their most extreme moods, and, I think, on bad grounds – claimed.

By contrast, to soften the distinction, to assert mysteriously that there is some fused identity between law as it is and as it ought to be, is to suggest that all legal questions are fundamentally like those of the penumbra. It is to assert that there is no central element of actual law to be seen in the core of central meaning which rules have, that there is nothing in the nature of a legal rule inconsistent with *all* questions being open to reconsideration of the light of social policy. Of course, it is good to be occupied with the penumbra. Its problems are rightly the daily diet of the law schools. But to be occupied with the penumbra is one thing, to be preoccupied with it another. And preoccupation with the penumbra is, if I may say so, as rich a source of confusion in the American legal tradition as formalism in the English. Of course we might abandon the notion that rules have authority; we might cease to attach force or even meaning to an argument that a case falls clearly within a rule and the scope of a precedent. We might call all such reasoning "automatic" or "mechanical," which is already the routine invective of the courts. But until we decide that this *is* what we want, we should not encourage it by obliterating the Utilitarian distinction.

IV

The third criticism of the separation of law and morals is of a very different character; it certainly is less an intellectual argument against the Utilitarian distinction than a passionate appeal supported not by detailed reasoning but by reminders of a terrible experience. For it consists of the testimony of those who have descended into Hell, and, like Ulysses or Dante, brought back a message for human beings. Only in this case the Hell was not beneath or beyond earth, but on it; it was a Hell created on earth by men for other men.

This appeal comes from those German thinkers who lived through the Nazi regime and reflected upon its evil manifestations in the legal system. One of these thinkers, Gustav Radbruch, had himself shared the "positivist" doctrine until the Nazi tyranny, but he was converted by this experience and so his appeal to other men to discard the doctrine of the separation of law and morals has the special poignancy of a recantation. What is important about this criticism is that it really does confront the particular point which Bentham and Austin had in mind in urging the separation of law as it is and as it ought to be. These German thinkers put their insistence on the need to join together what the Utilitarians separated just where this separation was of most importance in the eyes of the Utilitarians; for they were concerned with the problem posed by the existence of morally evil laws.

Before his conversion Radbruch held that resistance to law was a matter for the personal conscience, to be thought out by the individual as a moral problem, and the validity of a law could not be disproved by showing that its requirements were morally evil or even by showing that the effect of compliance with the law would be more evil than the effect of disobedience. Austin, it may be recalled, was emphatic in condemning those who said that if human laws conflicted with the fundamental principles of morality then they cease to be laws, as talking "stark nonsense."

> "The most pernicious laws, and therefore those which are most opposed to the will of God, have been and are continually enforced as laws by judicial tribunals. Suppose an act innocuous, or positively beneficial, be prohibited by the sovereign under the penalty of death; if I commit this act, I shall be tried and condemned, and if I object to the sentence, that it is contrary to the law of God . . . the court of justice will demonstrate the inconclusiveness of my reasoning by hanging me up, in pursuance of the law of which I have impugned the validity. An exception, demurrer, or plea, founded on the law

of God was never heard in a Court of Justice, from the creation of the world down to the present moment."

These are strong, indeed brutal words, but we must remember that they went along – in the case of Austin and, of course, Bentham – with the conviction that if laws reached a certain degree of iniquity then there would be a plain moral obligation to resist them and to withhold obedience. We shall see, when we consider the alternatives, that this simple presentation of the human dilemma which may arise has much to be said for it.

Radbruch, however, had concluded from the ease with which the Nazi regime had exploited subservience to mere law – or expressed, as he thought, in the "positivist" slogan "law as law" (*Gesetz als Gesetz*) – and from the failure of the German legal profession to protest against the enormities which they were required to perpetrate in the name of law, that "positivism" (meaning here the insistence on the separation of law as it is from law as it ought to be) had powerfully contributed to the horrors. His considered reflections led him to the doctrine that the fundamental principles of humanitarian morality were part of the very concept of *Recht* or Legality and that no positive enactment or statute, however clearly it was expressed and however clearly it conformed with the formal criteria of validity of a given legal system, could be valid if it contravened basic principles of morality. This doctrine can be appreciated fully only if the nuances imported by the German word *Recht* are grasped. But it is clear that the doctrine meant that every lawyer and judge should denounce statutes that transgressed the fundamental principles not as merely immoral or wrong but as having no legal character, and enactments which on this ground lack the quality of law should not be taken into account in working out the legal position of any given individual in particular circumstances. The striking recantation of his previous doctrine is unfortunately omitted from the translation of his works, but it should be read by all who wish to think afresh on the question of the interconnection of law and morals.

It is impossible to read without sympathy Radbruch's passionate demand that the German legal conscience should be open to the demands of morality and his complaint that this has been too little the case in the German tradition. On the other hand there is an extraordinary naivete in the view that insensitiveness to the demands of morality and subservience to state power in a people like the Germans should have arisen from the belief that law might be law though it failed to conform with the minimum requirements of morality. Rather this terrible history prompts inquiry into why emphasis on the slogan "law is law," and the distinction between law and morals, acquired a sinister character in Germany, but elsewhere, as with the Utilitarians themselves, went along with the most enlightened liberal attitudes. But something more disturbing than naivete is latent in Radbruch's whole presentation of the issues to which the existence of morally iniquitous laws give rise. It is not, I think, uncharitable to say that we can see in his argument that he has only half digested the spiritual message of liberalism which he is seeking to convey to the legal profession. For everything that he says is really dependent upon an enormous overvaluation of the importance of the bare fact that a rule may be said to be a valid rule of law, as if this, once declared was conclusive of the final moral question: "Ought this rule of law to be obeyed?" Surely the truly liberal answer to any sinister use of the slogan "law is law" or of the distinction between law and morals is, "very well, but that does not conclude the question. Law is not morality; do not let it supplant morality."

However, we are not left to a mere academic discussion in order to evaluate the plea which Radbruch made for the revision of the distinction between law and morals. After the war Radbruch's conception of law as containing in itself the essential moral principle of humanitarianism was applied in practice by German courts in certain cases in which local war criminals, spies, and informers under the Nazi regime were punished. The special importance of these cases is that the persons accused of these crimes claimed that what they had done was not illegal under the laws of the regime in force at the time these actions were performed. This plea was met with the reply that the laws upon which they relied were invalid as contravening the fundamental principles of morality. Let me cite briefly one of these cases.

In 1944 a woman, wishing to be rid of her husband, denounced him to the authorities for insulting remarks he had made about Hitler while home on leave from the German army. The wife was under no legal duty to report his acts, though what he had said was apparently in violation of statutes making it illegal to make statements detrimental to the government of the Third Reich or to impair by any means the military defense of the German people. The husband was arrested and sentenced to death, apparently pursuant to these statutes, though he was not executed but was sent to the front. In 1949 the wife was prosecuted in a West German court for an offense which we would describe as illegally depriving a person of his freedom (*rechtswidrige Freiheitsberaubung*). This was punishable as a crime under the German Criminal Code of 1871 which had remained in force continuously since its enactment. The wife pleaded that her husband's imprisonment was pursuant to the Nazi statutes and hence that she had committed no crime. The court of appeal to which the case ultimately came held that the wife was guilty of procuring the deprivation of her husband's liberty by denouncing him to the German courts, even though he had been sentenced by a court for having violated a statute, since, to quote the words of the court, the statute "was contrary to the sound conscience and sense of justice of all decent human beings." This reasoning was followed in many cases which have been hailed as a triumph of the doctrines of natural law and as signaling the overthrow of positivism. The unqualified satisfaction with this result seems to me to be hysteria. Many of us might applaud the objective – that of punishing a woman for an outrageously immoral act – but this was secured only by declaring a statute established since 1934 not to have the force of law, and at least the wisdom of this course must be doubted. There were, of course, two other choices. One was to let the woman go unpunished; one can sympathize with and endorse the view that this might have been a bad thing to do. The other was to face the fact that if the woman were to be punished it must be pursuant to the introduction of a frankly retrospective law and with a full consciousness of what was sacrificed in securing her punishment in this way. Odious as retrospective criminal legislation and punishment may be, to have pursued it openly in this case would at least have had the merits of candour. It would have made plain that in punishing the woman a choice had to be made between two evils, that of leaving her unpunished and that of sacrificing a very precious principle of morality endorsed by most legal systems. Surely if we have learned anything from the history of morals it is that the thing to do with a moral quandary is not to hide it. Like nettles, the occasions when life forces us to choose between the lesser of two evils must be grasped with the consciousness that they are what they are. The vice of this use of the principle that, at certain limiting points, what is utterly immoral cannot be law or lawful is that it will serve to cloak the true nature of the problems with which we are faced and will encourage the romantic optimism that all the values we cherish ultimately will fit into a single system, that no one of them has to be sacrificed or compromised to accommodate another.

"All Discord Harmony not understood
All Partial Evil Universal Good"

This is surely untrue and there is an insincerity in any formulation of our problem which allows us to describe the treatment of the dilemma as if it were the disposition of the ordinary case.

It may seem perhaps to make too much of forms, even perhaps of words, to emphasize one way of disposing of this difficult case as compared with another which might have led, so far as the woman was concerned, to exactly the same result. Why should we dramatize the difference between them? We might punish the woman under a new retrospective law and declare overtly that we were doing something inconsistent with our principles as the lesser of two evils; or we might allow the case to pass as one in which we do not point out precisely where we sacrifice such a principle. But candour is not just one among many minor virtues of the administration of law, just as it is not merely a minor virtue of morality. For if we adopt Radbruch's view, and with him and the German courts make our protest against evil law in the form of an assertion that certain rules cannot be law because of their moral iniquity, we confuse one of the most powerful, because it is the simplest, forms of moral criticism. If with the Utilitarians we speak plainly, we say that laws may be law but too evil to be obeyed. This is a moral condemnation which everyone can understand and it makes an immediate and obvious claim to moral attention. If, on the other hand, we formulate our objection as an assertion that these evil things are not law, here is an assertion which many people do not believe, and if they are disposed to consider it at all, it would seem to raise a whole host of philosophical issues before it can be accepted. So perhaps the most important single lesson to be learned from this form of the denial of the Utilitarian distinction is the one that the Utilitarians were most concerned to teach: when we have the ample resources of plain speech we must not present the moral criticism of institutions as propositions of a disputable philosophy.

V

I have endeavored to show that, in spite of all that has been learned and experienced since the Utilitarians wrote, and in spite of the defects of other parts of their doctrine, their protest against the confusion of what is and what ought to be law has a moral as well as an intellectual value. Yet it may well be said that, though this distinction is valid and important if applied to any particular law of a system, it is at least misleading if we attempt to apply it to "law," that is, to the notion of a legal system, and that if we insist, as I have, on the narrower truth (or truism), we obscure a wider (or deeper) truth. After all, it may be urged, we have learned that there are many things which are untrue of laws taken separately, but which are true and important in a legal system considered as a whole. For example, the connection between law and sanctions and between the existence of law and its "efficacy" must be understood in this more general way. It is surely not arguable (without some desperate extension of the word "sanction" or artificial narrowing of the word "law") that every law in a municipal legal system must have a sanction, yet it is at least plausible to argue that a legal system must, to be a legal system, provide sanctions for certain of its rules. So too, a rule of law may be said to exist though enforced or obeyed in only a minority of cases, but this could not be said of a legal system as a whole.

Perhaps the differences with respect to laws taken separately and a legal system as a whole are also true of the connection between moral (or some other) conceptions of what law ought to be and law in this wider sense.

This line of argument, found (at least in embryo form) in Austin, where he draws attention to the fact that every developed legal system contains certain fundamental notions which are "necessary" and "bottomed in the common nature of man," is worth pursuing – up to a point – and I shall say briefly why and how far this is so.

We must avoid, if we can, the arid wastes of inappropriate definition, for, in relation to a concept as many-sided and vague as that of a legal system, disputes about the "essential" character, or necessity to the whole, of any single element soon begin to look like disputes about whether chess could be "chess" if played without pawns. There is a wish, which may be understandable, to cut straight through the question whether a legal system, to be a legal system, must measure up to some moral or other standard with simple statements of fact: for example, that no system which utterly failed in this respect has ever existed or could endure; that the normally fulfilled assumption that a legal system aims at some form of justice colours the whole way in which we interpret specific rules in particular cases, and if this normally fulfilled assumption were not fulfilled no one would have any reason to obey except fear (and probably not that) and still less, of course, any moral obligation to obey. The connection between law and moral standards and principles of justice is therefore as little arbitrary and as "necessary" as the connection between law and sanctions, and the pursuit of the question whether this necessity is logical (part of the "meaning" of law) or merely factual or causal can safely be left as an innocent pastime for philosophers.

Yet in two respects I should wish to go further (even though this involves the use of a philosophical fantasy) and show what could intelligibly be meant by the claim that certain provisions in a legal system are "necessary." The world in which we live, and we who live in it, may one day change in many different ways; and if this change were radical enough not only would certain statements of fact now true be false and vice versa, but whole ways of thinking and talking which constitute our present conceptual apparatus, through which we see the the world and each other, would lapse. We have only to consider how the whole of our social, moral, and legal life, as we understand it now, depends on the contingent fact that though our bodies do change in shape, size, and other physical properties they do not do this so drastically nor with such quicksilver rapidity and irregularity that we cannot identify each other as the same persistent individual over considerable spans of time. Though this is but a contingent fact which may one day be different, on it at present rest huge structures of our thought and principles of action and social life. Similarly, consider the following possibility (not because it is more than a possibility but because it reveals why we think certain things necessary in a legal system and what we mean by this): suppose that men were to become invulnerable to attack by each other, were clad perhaps like giant land crabs with an impenetrable carapace, and could extract the food they needed from the air by some internal chemical process. In such circumstances (the details of which can be left to science fiction) rules forbidding the free use of violence and rules constituting the minimum form of property – with its rights and duties sufficient to enable food to grow and be retained until eaten – would not have the necessary non-arbitrary status which they have for us, constituted as we are in a world like ours. At present, and until such radical changes supervene, such rules are so fundamental that if a legal system did not have them there would be no point in having any other rules at all. Such rules overlap with basic moral principles vetoing murder, violence, and theft; and so we can add to the factual statement that all legal systems in fact coincide with morality at such vital points, the statement that this is, in this sense, necessarily so. And why not call it a "natural" necessity?

Of course even this much depends on the fact that in asking what content a legal system must have we take this question to be worth asking only if we who consider it cherish the humble aim of survival in close proximity to our fellows. Natural-law theory, however, in all its protean guises, attempts to push the argument much further and to assert that human beings are equally devoted to and united in their conception of aims (the pursuit of knowledge, justice to their fellow men) other than that of survival, and these dictate a further necessary content to a legal system (over and above my humble minimum) without which it would be pointless. Of course we must be careful not to exaggerate the differences among human beings, but it seems to me that above this minimum the purposes men have for living in society are too conflicting and varying to make possible much extension of the argument that some fuller overlap of legal rules and moral standards is "necessary" in this sense.

Another aspect of the matter deserves attention. If we attach to a legal system the minimum meaning that it must consist of general rules – general both in the sense that they refer to courses of action, not single actions, and to multiplicities of men, not single individuals – this meaning connotes the principle of treating like cases alike, though the criteria of when cases are alike will be, so far, only the general elements specified in the rules. It is, however, true that *one* essential element of the concept of justice is the principle of treating like cases alike. This is justice in the administration of the law, not justice of the law. So there is, in the very notion of law consisting of general rules, something which prevents us from treating it as if morally it is utterly neutral, without any necessary contact with moral principles. Natural procedural justice consists therefore of those principles of objectivity and impartiality in the administration of the law which implement just this aspect of law and which are designed to ensure that rules are applied only to what are genuinely cases of the rule or at least to minimize the risks of inequalities in this sense.

These two reasons (or excuses) for talking of a certain overlap between legal and moral standards as necessary and natural, of course, should not satisfy anyone who is really disturbed by the Utilitarian or "positivist" insistence that law and morality are distinct. This is so because a legal system that satisfied these minimum requirements might apply, with the most pedantic impartiality as between the persons affected, laws which were hideously oppressive, and might deny to a vast rightless slave population the minimum benefits of protection from violence and theft. The stink of such societies is, after all, still in our nostrils and to argue that they have (or had) no legal system would only involve the repetition of the argument. Only if the rules failed to provide these essential benefits and protection for anyone – even for a slave-owning group – would the minimum be unsatisfied and the system sink to the status of a set of meaningless taboos. Of course no one denied those benefits would have any reason to obey except fear and would have every moral reason to revolt.

VI

I should be less than candid if I did not, in conclusion, consider something which, I suspect, most troubles those who react strongly against "legal positivism." Emphasis on the distinction between law as it is and law as it ought to be may be taken to depend upon and to entail what are called "subjectivist" and "relativist" or "noncognitive" theories concerning the very nature of moral judgments, moral distinctions, or "values." Of course the Utilitarians themselves (as distinct from later positivists like Kelsen) did not countenance any such theories, however unsatisfactory their moral philosophy may appear to us now. Austin thought ultimate moral principles were the commands of God, known to us by revelation or through the "index" of utility, and Bentham thought they were verifiable propositions about utility. Nonetheless I think (though I cannot prove) that insistence upon the distinction between law as it is and ought to be has been, under the general head of "positivism," confused with a moral theory according to which statements of what is the case ("statements of fact") belong to a category or type radically different from statements of what ought to be ("value statements"). It may therefore be well to dispel this source of confusion.

There are many contemporary variants of this type of moral theory: according to some, judgments of what ought to be, or ought to be done, either are or include as essential elements expressions of "feeling," "emotion," or "attitudes" or "subjective preferences"; in others such judgments both express feelings or emotions or attitudes and enjoin others to share them. In other variants such judgments indicate that a particular case falls under a general principle or policy of action which the speaker has "chosen" or to which he is "committed" and which is itself not a recognition of what is the case but analogous to a general "imperative" or command addressed to all including the speaker himself. Common to all these variants is the insistence that judgments of what ought to be done, because they contain such "noncognitive" elements, cannot be argued for or established by rational methods as statements of fact can be, and cannot be shown to follow from any statement of fact but only from other judgments of what ought to be done in conjunction with some statement of fact. We cannot, on such a theory, demonstrate, *e.g.*, that an action was wrong, ought not to have been done, merely by showing that it consisted of the deliberate infliction of pain solely for the gratification of the agent. We only show it to be wrong if we add to those verifiable "cognitive" statements of fact a general principle not itself verifiable or "cognitive" that the infliction of pain in such circumstances is wrong, ought not to be done. Together with this general distinction between statements of what is and what ought to be go sharp parallel distinctions between statements about means and statements of moral ends. We can rationally discover and debate what are appropriate means to given ends, but ends are not rationally discoverable or debatable; they are "fiats of the will," expressions of "emotions," "preferences," or "attitudes."

Against all such views (which are of course far subtler than this crude survey can convey) others urge that all these sharp distinctions between is and ought, fact and value, means and ends, cognitive and noncognitive, are wrong. In acknowledging ultimate ends or moral values we are recognizing something as much imposed upon us by the character of the world in which we live, as little a matter of choice, attitude, feeling, emotion as the truth of factual judgments about what is the case. The characteristic moral argument is not one in which the parties are reduced to expressing or kindling feelings or emotions or issuing exhortations or commands to each other but one by which parties come to acknowledge after closer examination and reflection that an initially disputed case falls within the ambit of a vaguely apprehended principle (itself no more "subjective," no more a "fiat of our will" than any other principle of classification) and this has as much title to be called "cognitive" or "rational" as any other initially disputed classification of particulars.

Let us now suppose that we accept this rejection of "non-cognitive" theories of morality and this denial of the drastic distinction in type between statements of what is and what ought to be, and that moral judgments are as rationally defensible as any other kind of judgments. What would follow from this as to the nature of the connection between law as it is and law as it ought to be? Surely, from this alone, nothing. Laws, however morally iniquitous, would still (so far as this point is concerned) be laws. The only difference which the acceptance of this view of the nature of moral judgments would make would be that the moral iniquity of such laws would be something that could be demonstrated; it would surely follow merely from a statement of what the rule required to be done that the rule was morally wrong and so ought not to be law or conversely that it was morally desirable and ought to be law. But the demonstration of this would not show the rule not to be (or to be) law. Proof that the principles by which we evaluate or condemn laws are rationally discoverable, and not mere "fiats of the will," leaves untouched the fact that there are laws which may have any degree of iniquity or stupidity and still be laws. And conversely there are rules that have every moral qualification to be laws and yet are not laws.

Surely something further or more specific must be said in disproof of "non-cognitivism" or kindred theories if ethics is to be relevant to the distinction between law as it is and law as it ought to be, and to lead to the abandonment at some point or some softening of this distinction. No one has done more than Professor Lon Fuller of the Harvard Law School in his various writings to make clear such a line of argument and I will end by criticising what I take to be its central point. It is a point which again emerges when we consider not those legal rules or parts of legal rules the meanings of which are clear and excite no debate but the interpretation of rules in concrete cases where doubts are initially felt and argument develops about their meaning. In no legal system is the scope of legal rules restricted to the range of concrete instances which were present or are believed to have been present in the minds of legislators; this indeed is one of the important differences between a legal rule and a command. Yet, when rules are recognized as applying to instances beyond any that legislators did or could have considered, their extension to such new cases often presents itself not as a deliberate choice or fiat on the part of those who so interpret the rule. It appears neither as a decision to give the rule a new or extended meaning nor as a guess as to what legislators, dead perhaps in the eighteenth century, would have said had they been alive in the twentieth century. Rather, the inclusion of the new case under the rule takes its place as a natural elaboration of the rule, as something implementing a "purpose" which it seems natural to attribute (in some sense) to the rule itself rather than to any particular person dead or alive. The Utilitarian description of such interpretative extension of old rules to new cases as judicial legislation fails to do justice to this phenomenon; it gives no hint of the differences between a deliberate fiat or decision to treat the new case in the same way as past cases and a recognition (in which there is little that is deliberate or even voluntary) that inclusion of the new case under the rule will implement or articulate a continuing and identical purpose, hitherto less specifically apprehended.

Perhaps many lawyers and judges will see in this language something that precisely fits their experience; others may think it a romantic gloss on facts better stated in the Utilitarian language of judicial "legislation" or in the modern American terminology of "creative choice."

To make the point clear Professor Fuller uses a nonlegal example from the philosopher Wittgenstein which is, I think, illuminating.

> "Someone says to me: "Show the children a game." I teach them gaming with dice and the other says "I did not mean that sort of game." Must the exclusion of the game with dice have come before his mind when he gave me the order?"

Something important does seem to me to be touched on in this example. Perhaps there are the following (distinguishable) points. First, we normally do interpret not only what people are trying to do but what they say in the light of assumed common human objectives so that unless the contrary were expressly indicated we would not interpret an instruction to show a young child a game as a mandate to introduce him to gambling even though in other contexts the word "game" would be naturally so interpreted. Second, very often, the speaker whose words are thus interpreted might say: "Yes, that's what I mean [or "that's what I meant all along"] though I never thought of it until you put this particular case to me." Third, when we thus recognize, perhaps after argument or consultation with others, a particular case not specifically envisaged beforehand as falling within the ambit of some vaguely expressed instruction, we may find this experience falsified by description of it as a mere decision on our part so to treat the particular case, and that we can only describe this faithfully as coming to realize and to articulate what we "really" want or our "true purpose" – phrases which Professor Fuller uses later in the same article.

I am sure that many philosophical discussions of the character of moral argument would benefit from attention to cases of the sort instanced by Professor Fuller. Such attention would help to provide a corrective to the view that there is a sharp separation between "ends" and "means." But I think the relevance of his point to the issue whether it is correct or wise to insist on the distinction between law as it is and law as it ought to be is very small indeed. Its net effect is that in interpreting legal rules there are some cases which we find after reflection to be so natural an elaboration or articulation of the rule that to think of and refer to this as "legislation," "making law," or a "fiat" on our part would be misleading. So, the argument must be, it would be misleading to distinguish in such cases between what the rule is and what it ought to be – at least in some sense of ought. We think it ought to include the new case and come to see after reflection that it really does. But even if this way of presenting a recognizable experience as an example of a fusion between is and ought to be is admitted, two caveats must be borne in mind. The first is that "ought" in this case need have nothing to do with morals for the reasons explained already in section III: there may be just the same sense that a new case will implement and articulate the purpose of a rule in interpreting the rules of a game or some hideously immoral code of oppression whose immorality is appreciated by those called in to interpret it. They too can see what the "spirit" of the game they are playing requires in previously unenvisaged cases. More important is this: after all is said and done we must remember how rare in the law is the phenomenon held to justify this way of talking, how exceptional is this feeling that one way of deciding a case is imposed upon us as the only natural or rational elaboration of some rule. Surely it cannot be doubted that, for most cases of interpretation, the language of choice between alternatives, "judicial legislation" or even "fiat" (though not arbitrary fiat), better conveys the realities of the situation.

Within the framework of relatively well-settled law there jostle too many alternatives too nearly equal in attraction between which judge and lawyer must uncertainly pick their way to make appropriate here language which may well describe those experiences which we have in interpreting our own or others' principles of conduct, intention, or wishes, when we are not conscious of exercising a deliberate choice, but rather of recognising something awaiting recognition. To use in the description of the interpretation of laws the suggested terminology of a fusion or inability to separate what is law and ought to be will serve (like earlier stories that judges only find, never make, law) only to conceal the facts, that here if anywhere we live among uncertainties between which we have to choose, and that the existing law imposes only limits on our choice and not the choice itself.

For a recent commentary see Breckenridge, "Legal Positivism and Natural Law: The Controversy Between Professor Hart and Professor Fuller" (1965) 18 *Vand. L. Rev.* 945.

Professor Hart based his discussion of the German Wife's Case on the account of it appearing in (1951) 64 *Harv. I. Rev.* 1005. It has since been shown by Dr. H. O. Pappe of the Australian National University "On the Validity of Judicial Decisions in the Nazi Era" (1960) 23 *M. L. R.* 260 that this account is misleading in that the German Court actually decided the case on the ground that she had no duty to inform against her husband and did so for purely personal reasons; the Court accepted the theoretical possibility that statutes in conflict with natural law might be invalid, but held that the statute here did not violate the natural law. Hart therefore advises, *The Concept of Law* 254 n. 204 (1961), that the case as discussed in the article above must be regarded as hypothetical.

In place of the deposed doctrine of command Hart in effect substitutes a system of accepted rules as the basis of law. He describes these rules in *The Concept of Law* 78-79 (1961): "We have already seen the need, if we are to do justice to the complexity of a legal system, to discriminate between two different though related types. Under rules of the one type, which may well be considered the basic or primary type, human beings are required to do or abstain from certain actions, whether they wish to or not. Rules of the other type are in a sense parasitic upon or secondary to the first; for they provide that human beings may by doing or saying certain things introduce new rules of the primary type, extinguish or modify old ones, or in various ways determine their incidence or control their operations. Rules of the first type impose duties; rules of the second type confer powers, public or private. Rules of the first type concern actions involving physical movement or changes; rules of the second type provide for operations which lead not merely to physical movement or change, but to the creation or variation of duties or obligations. . . . We shall make the general claim that in the combination of these two types of rule there lies what Austin wrongly claimed to have found in the notion of coercive orders, namely, 'the key to the science of jurisprudence'. We shall not indeed claim that wherever the word 'law' is 'properly' used this combination of primary and secondary rules is to be found; for it is clear that the diverse range of cases of which the word 'law' is used are not linked by any such simple uniformity, but by less direct relations – often of analogy of either form or content to a central case. What we shall attempt to show is that most of the features of law which have proved most perplexing and have both provoked and eluded the search for definition can best be rendered clear, if these two types of rule and the interplay between them are understood. We accord this union of elements a central place because of thir explanatory power in elucidating the concepts that constitute the framework of legal thought. . . ."

The vehicle problem in Hart's article is based on *McBoyle* v. *U.S.* (1930) 283 U.S. 25 where the Supreme Court of the United States held that an aircraft is not a motor vehicle for purposes of the National Motor Vehicle Theft Act, which forbids the transport of stolen motor vehicles in interstate or foreign commerce. Unquestionably one of the realists Hart has in mind is Professor Harry Jones, who used the *McBoyle* problem as his principal example in "Statutory Doubts and Legislative Intention" (1940) 40 *Col. L. Rev.* 957.

H. L. A. Hart, 1907–

THE CONCEPT OF LAW
(1961)

. . . Reflection on some very obvious generalizations – indeed truisms – concerning human nature and the world in which men live, show that as long as these hold good, there are certain rules of conduct which any social organization must contain if it is to be viable. Such rules do in fact constitute a common element in the law and conventional morality of all societies which have progressed to the point where these are distinguished as different forms of social control. With them are found, both in law and morals, much that is peculiar to a particular society and much that may seem arbitrary or a mere matter of choice. Such universally recognized principles of conduct which have a basis in elementary truths concerning human beings, their natural environment, and aims, may be considered the *minimum content* of Natural Law, in contrast with the more grandiose and more challengeable constructions which have often been proffered under that name. In the next section we shall consider, in the form of five truisms, the salient characteristics of human nature upon which this modest but important minimum rests.

2. THE MINIMUM CONTENT OF NATURAL LAW

In considering the simple truisms which we set forth here, and their connexion with law and morals, it is important to observe that in each case the facts mentioned afford a *reason* why, given survival as an aim, law and morals should include a specific content. The general form of the argument is simply that without such a content laws and morals could not forward the minimum purpose of survival which men have in associating with each other. In the absence of this content men, as they are, would have no reason for obeying voluntarily any rules; and without a minimum of co-operation given voluntarily by those who find that it is in their interest to submit to and maintain the rules, coercion of others who would not voluntarily conform would be impossible. It is important to stress the distinctively rational connexion between natural facts and the content of legal and moral rules in this approach, because it is both possible and important to inquire into quite different forms of connexion between natural facts and legal or moral rules. Thus, the still young sciences of psychology and sociology may discover or may even have discovered that, unless certain physical, psychological, or economic conditions are satisfied, e.g. unless young children are fed and nurtured in certain ways within the family, no system of laws or code of morals can be established, or that only those laws can function successfully which conform to a certain type. Connexions of this sort between natural conditions and systems of rules are not mediated by *reasons*; for they do not relate the existence of certain rules to the conscious aims or purpose of those whose rules they are. Being fed in infancy in a certain way may well be shown to be a necessary condition or even a *cause* of a population developing or maintaining a moral or legal code, but it is not a *reason* for their doing so. Such causal connexions do not of course conflict with the connexions which rest on purposes or conscious aims; they may indeed be considered more important or fundamental than the latter, since they may actually explain why human beings have those conscious aims or purposes which Natural Law takes as its starting-points. Causal explanations of this type do not rest on truisms nor are they mediated by conscious aims or purposes: they are for sociology or psychology like other sciences to establish by the methods of generalization and theory, resting on observation and, where possible, on experiment. Such connexions therefore are of a different kind from those which relate the content of certain legal and moral rules to the facts stated in the following truisms.

(i) *Human vulnerability.* The common requirements of law and morality consist for the most part not of active services to be rendered but of forbearances, which are usually formulated in negative form as prohibitions. Of these the most important for social life are those that restrict the use of violence in killing or inflicting bodily harm. The basic character of such rules may be brought out in a question: If there were not these rules what point could there be for beings such as ourselves in having rules of *any* other kind? The force of this rhetorical question rests on the fact that men are both occasionally prone to, and normally vulnerable to, bodily attack. Yet though this is a truism it is not a necessary truth; for things might have been, and might one day be, otherwise. There are species of animals whose physical structure (including exoskeletons or a carapace) renders them virtually immune from attack by other members of their species and animals who have no organs enabling them to attack. If men were to lose their vulnerability to each other there would vanish one obvious reason for the most characteristic provision of law and morals: *Thou shalt not kill.*

(ii) *Approximate equality.* Men differ from each other in physical strength, agility, and even more in intellectual capacity. Nonetheless it is a fact of quite major importance for the understanding of different forms of law and morality, that no individual is so much more powerful than others, that he is able, without co-operation, to dominate or subdue them for more than a short period. Even the strongest must sleep at times and when asleep, loses temporarily his superiority. This fact of approximate equality, more than any other, makes obvious the necessity for a system of mutual forbearance and compromise which is the base of both legal and moral obligation. Social life with its rules requiring such forbearances is irksome at times; but it is at any rate less nasty, less brutish, and less short than unrestrained aggression for beings thus approximately equal. It is, of course, entirely consistent with this and an equal truism that when such a system of forbearance is established there will always be some who will wish to exploit it, by simultaneously living within its shelter and breaking its restrictions. This, indeed is, as we later show, one of the natural facts which makes the step from merely moral to organized, legal forms of control a necessary one. Again, things might have been otherwise. Instead of being approximately equal there might have been some men immensely stronger than others and better able to dispense with rest, either because some were in these ways far above the present average, or because most were far below it. Such exceptional men might have much to gain by aggression and little to gain from mutual forbearance or compromise with others. But we need not have recourse to the fantasy of giants among pygmies to see the cardinal importance of the fact of approximate equality: for it is illustrated better by the facts of international life, where there are (or were) vast disparities in strength and vulnerability between the states. This inequality, as we shall later see, between the units of international law is one of the things that has imparted to it a character so different from municipal law and limited the extent to which it is capable of operating as an organized coercive system.

(*iii*) *Limited altruism.* Men are not devils dominated by a wish to exterminate each other, and the demonstration that, given only the modest aim of survival, the basic rules of law and morals are necessities, must not be identified with the false view that men are predominantly selfish and have no disinterested interest in the survival and welfare of their fellows. But if men are not devils, neither are they angels; and the fact that they are a mean between these two extremes is something which makes a system of mutual forbearances both necessary and possible. With angels, never tempted to harm others, rules requiring forbearances would not be necessary. With devils prepared to destroy, reckless of the cost to themselves, they would be impossible. As things are, human altruism is limited in range and intermittent, and the tendencies to aggression are frequent enough to be fatal to social life if not controlled.

(*iv*) *Limited resources.* It is a merely contingent fact that human beings need food, clothes, and shelter; that these do not exist at hand in limitless abundance; but are scarce, have to be grown or won from nature, or have to be constructed by human toil. These facts alone make indispensable some minimal form of the institution of property (though not necessarily individual property), and the distinctive kind of rule which requires respect for it. The simplest forms of property are to be seen in rules excluding persons generally other than the "owner" from entry on, or the use of land, or from taking or using material things. If crops are to grow, land must be secure from indiscriminate entry, and food must, in the intervals between its growth or capture and consumption, be secure from being taken by others. At all times and places life itself depends on these minimal forbearances. Again, in this respect, things might have been otherwise than they are. The human organism might have been constructed like plants, capable of extracting food from air, or what it needs might have grown without cultivation in limitless abundance.

The rules which we have so far discussed are *static* rules, in the sense that the obligations are not variable by individuals. But the division of labour, which all but the smallest groups must develop to obtain adequate supplies, brings with it the need for rules which are *dynamic* in the sense that they enable individuals to create obligations and to vary their incidence. Among these are rules enabling men to transfer, exchange, or sell their products; for these transactions involve the capacity to alter the incidence of those initial rights and obligations which define the simplest form of property. The same inescapable division of labour, and perennial need for co-operation, are also factors which make other forms of dynamic or obligation-creating rule necessary in social life. These secure the recognition of promises as a source of obligation. By this device individuals are enabled by words, spoken or written, to make themselves liable to blame or punishment for failure to act in certain stipulated ways. Where altruism is not unlimited, a standing procedure providing for such self-binding operations is required in order to create a minimum form of confidence in the future behaviour of others, and to ensure the predictability necessary for co-operation. This is most obviously needed where what is to be exchanged or jointly planned are mutual services, or wherever goods which are to be exchanged or sold are not simultaneously or immediately available.

(*v*) *Limited understanding and strength of will.* The facts that make rules respecting persons, property, and promises necessary in social life are simple and their mutual benefits are obvious. Most men are capable of seeing them and of sacrificing the immediate short-term interests which conformity to such rules demands. They may indeed obey, from a variety of motives: some from prudential calculation that the sacrifices are worth the gains, some from a disinterested interest in the welfare of others, and some because they look upon the rules as worthy of respect in themselves and find their ideals in devotion to them. On the other hand, neither understanding of long-term interest, nor the strength or goodness of will, upon which the efficacy of these different motives towards obedience depends, are shared by all men alike. All are tempted at times to prefer their own immediate interests and, in the absence of a special organization for their detection and punishment, many would succumb to the temptation. No doubt the advantages of mutual forbearance are so palpable that the number and strength of those who would co-operate voluntarily in a coercive system will normally be greater than any likely combination of malefactors. Yet, except in very small closely-knit societies, submission to the system of restraints would be folly if there were no organization for the coercion of those who would then try to obtain the advantages of the system without submitting to its obligations. "Sanctions" are therefore required not as the normal motive for obedience, but as a *guarantee* that those who would voluntarily obey shall not be sacrificed to those who would not. To obey, without this, would be to risk going to the wall. Given this standing danger, what reason demands is *voluntary* co-operation in a *coercive* systtm.

It is to be observed that the same natural fact of approximate equality between men is of crucial importance in the efficacy of organized sanctions. If some men were vastly more powerful than others, and so not dependent on their forbearance, the strength of the malefactors might exceed that of the supporters of law and order. Given such inequalities, the use of sanctions could not be successful and would involve dangers at least as great as those which they were designed to suppress. In these circumstances instead of social life being based on a system of mutual forbearances, with force used only intermittently against a minority of malefactors, the only viable system would be one in which the weak submitted to the strong on the best terms they could make and lived under their "protection". This, because of the scarcity of resources, would lead to a number of conflicting power centres, each grouped round its "strong man": these might intermittently war with each other, though the natural sanction, never negligible, of the risk of defeat might ensure an uneasy peace. Rules of a sort might then be accepted for the regulation of issues over which the "powers" were unwilling to fight. Again we need not think in fanciful terms of pygmies and giants in order to understand the simple logistics of approximate equality and its importance for law. The international scene, where the units concerned have differed vastly in strength, affords illustration enough. For centuries the disparities between states have resulted in a system where organized sanctions have been impossible, and law has been confined to matters which did not affect "vital" issues. How far atomic weapons, when available to all, will redress the balance of unequal power, and bring forms of control more closely resembling municipal criminal law, remains to be seen.

The simple truisms we have discussed not only disclose the core of good sense in the doctrine of Natural Law. They are of vital importance for the understanding of law and morals, and they explain why the definition of the basic forms of these in purely formal terms, without reference to any specific content or social needs, has proved so inadequate. Perhaps the major benefit to jurisprudence from this outlook is the escape it affords from certain misleading dichotomies which often obscure the discussion of the characteristics of law. Thus, for example, the traditional question whether every legal system *must* provide for sanctions can be presented in a fresh and clearer light, when we command the view of things presented by this simple version of Natural Law. We shall no longer have to choose between two unsuitable alternatives which are often taken as exhaustive: on the one hand that of saying that this is required by "the" meaning of the words "law" or "legal system", and on the other that of saying that it is "just a fact" that most legal systems do provide for sanctions. Neither of these alternatives is satisfactory. There are no settled principles forbidding the use of the word "law" of systems where there are no centrally organized sanctions, and there is good reason (though no compulsion) for using the expression of "international law" of a system, which has none. On the other hand we do need to distinguish the place that sanctions must have within a municipal system, if it is to serve the minimum purposes of beings constituted as men are. We can say, given the setting of natural facts and aims, which make sanctions both possible and necessary in a municipal system, that this is a *natural necessity*; and some such phrase is needed also to convey the status of the minimum forms of protection for persons, property, and promises which are similarly indispensable features of municipal law. It is in this form that we should reply to the positivist thesis that "law may have any content". For it is a truth of some importance that for the adequate description not only of law but of many other social institutions, a place must be reserved, besides definitions and ordinary statements of fact, for a third category of statements: those the truth of which is contingent on human beings and the world they live in retaining the salient characteristics which they have.

In one of the most trenchant attacks of recent years on the natural law theory Professor Kai Neilsen refers with approval to what he terms Hart's "aseptic, demythologized" conception of natural law: *Law and Philosophy* 124 (Hook ed. 1964).

John Rawls, 1921-
Professor of Philosophy, Harvard University

JUSTICE AS FAIRNESS (1957)

The fundamental idea in the concept of justice is that of fairness. It is this aspect of justice for which utilitarianism, in its classical form, is unable to account, but which is represented, even if misleadingly so, in the idea of the social contract. To establish these propositions I shall develop, but of necessity only very briefly, a particular conception of justice by stating two principles which specify it and by considering how they may be thought to arise. The parts of this conception are familiar; but perhaps it is possible by using the notion of fairness as a framework to assemble and to look at them in a new way.

1. Throughout I discuss justice as a virtue of institutions constituting restrictions as to how they may define offices and powers, and assign rights and duties; and not as a virtue of particular actions, or persons. Justice is but one of many virtues of institutions, for these may be inefficient, or degrading, or any of a number of things, without being unjust. Essentially justice is the elimination of arbitrary distinctions and the establishment, within the structure of a practice, of a proper balance between competing claims. I do not argue that the principles given below are *the* principles of justice. It is sufficient for my purposes that they be typical of the family of principles which might reasonably be called principles of justice as shown by the background against which they may be thought to arise.

The first principle is that each person participating in a practice, or affected by it, has an equal right to the most extensive liberty compatible with a like liberty for all; and the second is that inequalities are arbitrary unless it is reasonable to expect that they will work out for everyone's advantage and unless the offices to which they attach, or from which they may be gained, are open to all. These principles express justice as a complex of three ideas: liberty, equality, and reward for contributions to the common advantage.

The first principle holds, of course, only *ceteris paribus*: while there must always be a justification for departing from the initial position of equal liberty (which is defined by the pattern of rights and duties), and the burden of proof is placed upon him who would depart from it, nevertheless, there can be, and often there is, a justification for doing so. One can view this principle as containing the principle that similar cases be judged similarly, or if distinctions are made in the handling of cases, there must be some relevant difference between them (a principle which follows from the concept of a judgment of any kind). It could be argued that justice requires only an equal liberty; but if a greater liberty were possible for all without loss or conflict, then it would be irrational to settle on a lesser liberty. There is no reason for circumscribing rights until they mutually interfere with one another. Therefore no serious distortion of the concept of justice is likely to follow from including within it the concept of the greatest equal liberty instead of simply equal liberty.

The second principle specifies what sorts of inequalities are permissible, where by inequalities it seems best to understand not any difference between Offices and positions, since structural differences are not usually an issue (people do not object to there being different offices as such, and so to there being the offices of president, senator, governor, judge, and so on), but differences in the benefits and burdens attached to them either directly or indirectly, such as prestige and wealth, or liability to taxation and compulsory service. An inequality is allowed only if there is reason to believe that the practice with the inequality will work to the advantage of *every* party. This is interpreted to require, first, that there must normally be evidence acceptable to common sense and based on a common fund of knowledge and belief which shows that this is in fact likely to be the case. The principle does not rule out, however, arguments of a theological or metaphysical kind to justify inequalities (e.g., a religious basis for a caste system) provided they belong to common belief and are freely acknowledged by people who may be presumed to know what they are doing.

Second, an inequality must work for the common advantage; and since the principle applies to practices, this implies that the representative man in *every* office or position of the practice, when he views it as a going institution, must find it reasonable to prefer his condition and prospects with the inequality to what they would be without it. And finally, the various offices to which special benefits and burdens attach arė required to be open to all; and so if, for example, it is to the common advantage to attach benefits to offices (because by doing so not only is the requisite talent attracted to them, but encouraged to give its best efforts once there), they must be won in a fair compeittion in which contestants are judged on their merits. If some offices were not open, those excluded would normally be justified in feeling wronged, even if they benefited from the greater efforts of those who were allowed to compete for them. Assuming that offices are open, it is necessary only to consider the design of the practices themselves and how they jointly, as a system, work together. It is a mistake to fix attention on the varying relative positions of particular persons and to think that each such change, as a once-for-all transaction, must be in itself just. The system must be judged from a general point of view: unless one is prepared to criticize it from the standpoint of a representative man holding some particular office, one has no complaint against it.

2. Given these principles, one might try to derive them from *a priori* principles of reason, or offer them as known by intuition. These are familiar steps, and, at

least in the case of the first principle, might be made with some success. I wish, however, to look at the principles in a different way.

Consider a society where certain practices are already established, and whose members are mutually self-interested: their allegiance to the established practices is founded on the prospect of self-advantage. It need not be supposed that they are incapable of acting from any other motive: if one thinks of the members of this society as families, the individuals thereof may be bound by ties of sentiment and affection. Nor must they be mutually self-interested under all circumstances, but only under those circumstances in which they ordinarily participate in their common practices. Imagine also that the persons in this society are rational: they know their own interests more or less accurately; they are capable of tracing out the likely consequences of adopting one practice rather than another and of adhering to a decision once made; they can resist present temptations and attractions of immediate gain; and the knowledge, or the perception, of the difference between their condition and that of others is not, in itself, a source of great dissatisfaction. Finally, they have roughly similar needs and interests and are sufficiently equal in power and ability to assure that in normal circumstances none is able to dominate the others.

Now suppose that on some particular occasion several members of this society come together to discuss whether any of them has a legitimate complaint against their established institutions. They try first to arrive at the principles by which complaints, and so practices themselves, are to be judged. Their procedure for this is the following: each is to propose the principles upon which he wishes his complaints to be tried with the understanding that, if acknowledged, the complaints of others will be similarly tried, and that no complaints will be heard at all until everyone is roughly of one mind as to how complaints are to be judged. They understand further that the principles proposed and acknowledged on this occasion are to be binding on future occasions. Thus each will be wary of proposing principles which give him a peculiar advantage, supposing them to be accepted, in his present circumstances, since he will be bound by it in future cases the circumstances of which are known and in which the principle might well be to his detriment. Everyone is, then, forced to make in advance a firm commitment, which others also may reasonably be expected to make, and no one is able to tailor the canons of a legitimate complaint to fit his own special condition. Therefore each person will propose principles of a general kind which will, to a large degree, gain their sense from the various applications to be made of them. These principles will express the conditions in accordance with which each is least unwilling to have his interests limited in the design of practices on the supposition that the interests of others will be limited likewise. The restrictions which would so arise might be thought of as those a person would keep in mind if he were designing a practice in which his enemy were to assign him his place.

In this account of a hypothetical society the character and respective situations of the parties reflect the circumstances in which questions of justice may be said to arise, and the procedure whereby principles are proposed and acknowledged represents constraints, analogous to those of having a morality, whereby rational and mutually self-interested parties are brought to act reasonably. Given all conditions as described, it would be natural to accept the two principles of justice. Since there is no way for anyone to win special advantage for himself, each might consider it reasonable to acknowledge equality as an initial principle. There is, however, no reason why they should regard this position as final; for if there are inequalities which satisfy the second principle, the immediate gain which equality would allow can be considered as intelligently invested in view of its future return. If as is quite likely, these inequalities work as incentives to draw out better efforts, the members of this society may look upon them as concessions to human nature: they, like us, may think that people ideally should want to serve one another. But as they are mutually self-interested, their acceptance of these inequalities is merely the acceptance of the relations in which they actually stand. They have no title to complain of one another. And so, provided the conditions of the principle are met, there is no reason why they should reject such inequalities in the design of their social practices. Indeed, it would be short-sighted of them to do so, and could result, it seems, only from their being dejected by the bare knowledge, or perception, that others are better situated. Each person will, however, insist on a common advantage, for none is willing to sacrifice anything for the others.

These remarks are not, of course, offered as a proof that persons so circumstanced would settle upon the two principles, but only to show that the principles of justice could have such a background; and so can be viewed as those principles which mutually self-interested and rational persons, when similarly situated and required to make in advance a firm commitment, could acknowledge as restrictions governing the assignment of rights and duties in their common practices, and thereby accept as limiting their rights against one another.

3. That the principles of justice can be regarded in this way is an important fact about them. It brings out the idea that fundamental to justice is the concept of fairness which relates to right dealing between persons who are cooperating with or competing against one another, as when one speaks of fair games, fair competition, and fair bargains. The question of fairness arises when free persons, who have no authority over one another, are engaging in a joint activity and amongst themselves settling or acknowledging the rules which define it and which determine the respective shares in its benefits and burdens. A practice will strike the parties as fair if none feels that, by participating in it, he, or any of the others, is taken advantage of, or forced to give in to claims which he does not regard as legitimate. This implies that each has a conception of legitimate claims which he thinks it reasonable that others as well as himself should acknowledge. If one thinks of the principles of justice as arising in the way described, then they do define this sort of conception. A practice is just, then, when it satisfies the principles which those who participate in it could propose to one another for mutual acceptance under the aforementioned circumstances. Persons engaged in a just, or fair, practice can face one another honestly, and support their respective positions, should they appear questionable, by reference to principles which it is reasonable to expect each to accept. It is this notion of the possibility of mutual acknowledgment which makes the concept of fairness fundamental to justice. Only if such acknowledgment is possible, can there be true community between persons in their common practices; otherwise their relations will appear to them as founded to some extent on force and violence. If, in ordinary speech, fairness applies more particularly to practices in which there is a choice whether to engage or not, and justice to practices in which there is no choice and one must play, the element of necessity does not alter the basic conception of the possibility of mutual acceptance, although it may make it much more urgent to change unjust than unfair institutions.

Now if the participants in a practice accept its rules as fair, and so have no complaint to lodge against it, there arises a prima facie duty (and a corresponding prima facie right) of the parties to each other to act in accordance with the practice when it falls upon them to comply. When any number of persons engage in a practice, or conduct a joint undertaking, according to rules, and thus restrict their liberty, those who have submitted to these restrictions when required have a right to a similar acquiescence on the part of those who have benefited by their submission. These conditions will, of course, obtain if a practice is correctly acknowledged to be fair, for in this case, all who participate in it will benefit from it. The rights and duties so arising are special rights and duties in that they depend on previous voluntary actions–in this case, on the parties' having engaged in a common practice and accepted its benefits. It is not, however, an obligation which presupposes a deliberate performative act in the sense of a promise, or contract, and the like. It is sufficient that one has knowingly participated in a practice acknowledged to be fair and accepted the resulting benefits. This prima facie obligation may, of course, be overridden: it may happen, when it comes one's turn to follow a rule, that other considerations will justify not doing so. But one cannot, in general, be released from this obligation by denying the justice of the practice only when it falls on one to obey. If a person rejects a practice, he should, as far as possible, declare his intention in advance, and avoid participating in it or accepting its benefits.

This duty may be called that of fair play, which is, perhaps, to extend the ordinary notion; for acting unfairly is usually not so much the breaking of any particular rule, even if the infraction is difficult to detect (cheating), but taking advantage of loopholes or ambiguities in rules, availing oneself of unexpected or special circumstances which make it impossible to enforce them, insisting that rules be enforced when they should be suspended, and, more generally, acting contrary to the intention of a practice. (Thus one speaks of the sense of fair play: acting fairly is not simply following rules; what is fair must be felt or perceived.) Nevertheless, it is not an unnatural extension of the duty of fair play to have it include the obligation which participants in a common practice owe to each other to act in accordance with it when their performance falls due. Consider the tax dodger, or the free rider.

The duty of fair play stands beside those of fidelity and gratitude as a fundamental moral notion; and like them it implies a constraint on self-interest in particular cases. I make this point to avoid a misunderstanding: the conception of the mutual acknowledgment of principles under special circumstances is used to analyze the concept of justice. I do not wish to imply that the acceptance of justice in actual conduct depends solely on an existing equality of conditions. My own view, which is perhaps but one of several compatible with the preceding analysis, and which I can only suggest here, is that the acknowledgment of the duty of fair play, as shown in acting on it, and wishing to make amends and the like when one has been at fault, is one of the forms of conduct in which participants in a common practice show their recognition of one another as persons. In the same way that, failing a special explanation, the criterion for the recognition of suffering is helping him who suffers, acknowledging the duty of fair play is the criterion for recognizing another as a person with similar capacities, interests, and feelings as oneself. The acceptance by participants in a common practice of this duty is a reflection in each of the recognition of the aspirations of the others to be realized by their joint activity. Without this acceptance they would recognize one another as but complicated objects in a complicated routine. To recognize another as a person one must respond to him and act towards him as one; and these forms of action and response include, among other things, acknowledging the duty of fair play. These remarks are unhappily obscure; their purpose here is to forestall the misunderstanding mentioned above.

The conception at which we have arrived, then, is that the principles of justice may be thought of as arising once the constraints of having a morality are imposed upon rational and mutually self-interested parties who are related and situated in a special way. A practice is just if it is in accordance with the principles which all who participate in it might reasonably be expected to propose or to acknowledge before one another when they are similarly circumstanced and required to make a firm commitment in advance; and thus when it meets standards which the parties could accept as fair should occasion arise for them to debate its merits. Once persons knowingly engage in a practice which they acknowledge to be fair and accept the benefits of doing so, they are bound by the duty of fair play which implies a limitation on self-interest in particular cases.

Now if a claim fails to meet this conception of justice there is no moral value in granting it, since it violates the conditions of reciprocity and community amongst persons: he who presses it, not being willing to acknowledge it when pressed by another, has no grounds for complaint when it is denied; whereas him against whom it is pressed can complain. As it cannot be mutually acknowledged, it is a resort to coercion: granting the claim is only possible if one party can compel what the other will not admit. Thus in deciding on the justice of a practice it is not enough to ascertain that it answers to wants and interest in the fullest and most effective manner. For if any of these be such that they confllict with justice, they should not be counted; their satisfaction is no reason for having a practice. It makes no sense to concede claims the denial of which gives rise to no complaint in preference to claims the denial of which can be objected to. It would be irrelevant to say, even if true, that it resulted in the greatest satisfaction of desire.

4. This conception of justice differs from that of the stricter form of utilitarianism (Bentham and Sidgwick), and its counterpart in welfare economics, which assimilates justice to benevolence and the latter in turn to the most efficient design of institutions to promote the general welfare. Now it is said occasionally that this form of utilitarianism puts no restrictions on what might be a just assignment of rights and duties. But this is not so. Beginning with the notion that the general happiness can be represented by a social utility function consisting of the sum of individual utility functions with identical weights (this being the meaning of the maxim that each counts for one and no more than one), it is commonly assumed that the utility functions of individuals are similar in all essential respects. Differences are laid to accidents of education and upbringing, and should not be taken into account; and this assumption, coupled with that of diminishing marginal utility, results in a prima facie case for equality. But even if such restrictions are built into the utility function, and have, in practice, much the same result as the application of the principles of justice (and appear, perhaps, to be ways of expressing these principles in the language of mathematics and psychology), the fundamental idea is very different from the conception of justice as reciprocity. Justice is interpreted as the contingent result of a higher order administrative decision whose form is similar to that of an entrepreneur deciding how much to produce of this or that commodity in view of its marginal revenue, or to that of someone distributing goods to needy persons according to the relative urgency of their wants. The choice between practices is thought of as being made on the basis of the allocation of benefits and burdens to individuals (measured by the present capitalized value of the utility of these benefits over the full period of the practice's existence) which results from the distribution of rights and duties established by a practice. The individuals receiving the benefits are not thought of as related in any way: they represent so many different directions in which limited resources may be allocated. Preferences and interest are taken as given; and their satisfaction has value irrespective of the relations between persons which they represent and the claims which the parties are prepared to make on one another.

This value is properly taken into account by the (ideal) legislator who is conceived as adjusting the rules of the system from the center so as to maximize the present capitalized value of the social utility function. The principles of justice will not be violated by a legal system so conceived provided these executive decisions are correctly made; and in this fact the principles of justice are said to find their derivation and explanation.

Some social decisions are, of course, of an administrative sort; namely, when the decision turns on social utility in the ordinary sense: on the efficient use of common means for common ends whose benefits are impartially distributed, or in connection with which the question of distribution is misplaced, as in the case of maintaining public order, or national defense. But as an interpretation of the basis of the principles of justice the utilitarian conception is mistaken. It can lead one to argue against slavery on the grounds that the advantages to the slaveholder do not counter-balance the disadvantages to the slave and to society at large burdened by a comparatively inefficient system of labor. The conception of justice as fairness, when applied to the offices of slaveholder and slave, would forbid counting the advantages of the slaveholder at all. These offices could not be founded on principles which could be mutually acknowledged, so the question whether the slaveholder's gains are great enough to counter-balance the losses to the slave and society cannot arise in the first place.

The difference between the two conceptions is whether justice is a fundamental moral concept arising directly from the reciprocal relations of persons engaging in common practices, and its principles those which persons similarly circumstanced could mutually acknowledge; or whether justice is derivative from a kind of higher order executive decision as to the most efficient design of institutions conceived as general devices for distributing benefits to individuals the worth of whose interests is defined independently of their relations to each other. Now even if the social utility function is constructed so that the practices chosen by it would be just, at least under normal circumstances, there is still the further argument against the utilitarian conception that the various restrictions on the utility function needed to get this result are borrowed from the conception of justice as fairness. The notion that individuals have similar utility functions, for example, is really the first principle of justice under the guise of a psychological law. It is assumed not in the manner of an empirical hypothesis concerning actual desires and interests, but from sensing what must be laid down if justice is not to be violated. There is, indeed, irony in this conclusion; for utilitarians attacked the notion of the original contract not only as a historical fiction but as a superfluous hypothesis: they thought that utility alone provides sufficient grounds for all social obligation, and is in any case the real basis of contractual obligations. But this is not so unless one's conception of social utility embodies within it restrictions whose basis can be understood only if one makes reference to one of the ideas of contractarian thought: that persons must be regarded as possessing an original and equal liberty, and their common practices are unjust unless they accord with principles which persons so circumstanced and related could freely accept.

This paper is an abbreviated version of the paper of the same title published in (1958) 67 *Phil. Rev.* 164.

In a companion paper, "Justice as Fairness: A Modernized Version of the Social Contract" (1957) 54 *J. of Phil.* 662, Professor Everett Hall comments on Professor Rawls' new form of the old social contract theory and points critically to "the lack of any inherent connection between justice as fairness (equality in natural rights) and its authentication as consent. The one need not actually have been arrived at by the other; the one is not deductively derivable from the other. . . . Is there some other kind of divination our author is trusting? I do find a possibility. . . . It operates through an association in his mind between violence and unfairness, and by obversion, consent and justice. . . . Both fairness and peaceful agreement are goods; unfairness and violence are equally evils. This normative association, however, does not show how either member in each of these pairs demands the other" (666-667).

See also Rawls' papers, "Two Concepts of Rules" (1955) 64 *Phil. Rev.* 3, "Constitutional Liberty and the Concept of Justice" in *Nomos VI: Justice* 98 (Friedrich and Chapman ed. 1963), and "Legal Obligation and the Duty of Fair Play" in *Law and Philosophy* 3 (Hook ed. 1964). The latter two papers are contributions to symposiums, and in *Law and Philosophy* the ten companion papers in "The Law and Ethics" section of the book are in large part commentaries on Rawls' paper.

Alf Ross, 1899-
Professor of Law, University of Copenhagen

ON LAW AND JUSTICE
(Danish ed. 1953; English ed. 1958)

§3 PRELIMINARY ANALYSIS OF THE CONCEPT "VALID LAW"

Let us imagine that two persons are playing chess, while a third person looks on.

If the onlooker knows nothing about chess he will not understand what is going on. From his knowledge of other games he will probably conclude that it is some sort of game. But he will not be able to understand the individual moves or to see any connection between them. Still less will he have any notion of the problems involved in any particular disposition of the pieces on the board.

If the onlooker knows the rules of chess, but beyond that not much about the theory of the game, his experience of the others' play changes character. He will understand that the horse's "irregular" movement is the prescribed knight's move. He is in a position to recognise the movements of the pieces in turn as moves prescribed by the rules. Within limits he is even able to predict what will take place. For he knows that the players take turns to make a move, and that each move has to fall within the total of possibilities allowed by the rules in any given disposition of the pieces. But beyond that, especially if the players are more than mere beginners, a great deal will appear puzzling. He does not understand the players' strategy, and has no eye for the tactical problems of the situation. Why, for example, does White not take the bishop? For a complete understanding of the game a knowledge not only of the rules of chess but also of a certain amount of the theory of the game is essential. The likelihood of being able to predict the next move increases if account is take not only of the rules of play but also of the theory of the game and the understanding each player has of it. Finally there must also be taken into account the purpose governing the play of the individual players. It is normally assumed that a player plays to win. But there are also other possibilities (for example, to let his opponent win, or to experiment and try out the value of a certain move).

These considerations of the game of chess contain a peculiar and interesting lesson. Here before us we have a series of human actions (the movements of the hands to change the position of certain objects in space) and we may well suppose that these together with other bodily processes (breathing, psychophysical processes, etc.) constitute a course of events which follow certain biological and physiological laws. Nevertheless, it is obvious that it is beyond the limit of all reasonable possibility to give an account of this course of events in such a way that the individual moves of chess can be explained and predicted on a biological and physiological basis.

The problem presents a quite diffferent aspect if we go to another level of observation and interpret the course of events in the light of the rules and theory of chess. Certain items of the whole series of events, namely, the moving of the pieces, stand out then as being actions relevant to chess or significant for chess. The movement of the pieces is not looked on as merely changing the position of objects in space, but as moves in the game, and the game becomes a significant coherent whole, because the moves reciprocally motivate each other and are construed as attack and defence in accordance with the theoretical principles of the game. If we watch the players we understand each move made by each player from the point of view of their consciousness of the rules of chess together with the knowledge we assume them to have to the theory of the game, and the goal they have set themselves in the game. Further it is also possible to ignore the persons of the players and understand the game on its own in its abstract significance (a game in a book of chess).

It must be noted that the "understanding" we are thinking of here is of a kind other than causal. We are not operating here with laws of causation. The moves do not stand in any mutually causal relation. The connection between them is established by way of the rules and theory of chess. The connection is one of meaning.

It can further be stated that fellowship is an essential factor in a game of chess. By this I mean that the aims and interests pursued and the actions conditioned by these can only be conceived of as a link in a greater whole which includes the actions of another person. When two men dig a ditch together, they are doing nothing that each one of them could not equally well do on his own. It is quite otherwise in chess. It is not possible for one person on his own to set himself the goal of winning at chess. The actions which make up playing chess can only be performed when playing in turns with a second person. Each player has his part to play, but each part only achieves significance when the second player fulfils his role.

Fellowship is also revealed in the intersubjective character of the rules of chess. It is essential that they should be given the same interpretation, at least by the two players in a given game. Otherwise there would be no game, and the separate moves would remain in isolation with no coherent meaning.

Now all this shows that the game of chess can be taken as a simple model of that which we call a social phenomenon. Human social life in a community is not a chaos of mutually isolated individual actions. It acquires the character of community life from the very fact that a large number (not all) of individual actions are relevant and have significance in relation to a set of common conceptions of rules. They constitute a significant whole, bearing the same relation to one another as move and countermove. Here, too, there is mutual interplay, motivated by and acquiring its significance from the common rules of the social "game." And it is the consciousness of these rules which makes it possible to understand and in some measure to predict the course of events.

I will now examine more closely what a rule of chess actually is, and in what way it is possible to establish what the rules are which govern the game of chess.

I have in mind here the primary rules of chess, those which determine the arrangement of the pieces, the moves, "taking," and the like, and not rules of chess theory.

As to the latter a few remarks will suffice. Like other technological rules they obviously are of the nature of hypothetical theoretical pronouncements. They assume the existence of the primary rules of chess and indicate the consequences which different openings and gambits will lead to in the game, judged in relation to the chance of winning. Like other technological rules their directive force is conditioned by an interest – in this example the interest in the winning of the game. If a player does not have this interest, then the theory of the game is without importance to him.

The primary rules of chess, on the other hand, are directives. Although they are formulated as assertions about the "ability" or "power" of the pieces to move and "take," it is clear that they are intended to indicate how the game is to be played. They aim directly, that is, unqualified by any underlying objective, to motivate the player; they tell him, as it were: This is how it is played.

These directives are felt by each player to be socially binding; that is to say, a player not only feels himself spontaneously motivated ("bound") to a certain method of action but is at the same time certain that a breach of the rules will call forth a reaction (protest) on the part of his opponent. And in this way they are clearly distinguished from the rules of skill contained in the theory. A stupid move can arouse astonishment, but not a protest.

On the other hand, the rules of chess are not tinged with morality; this is the result of the fact that normally no one really wants to break them. The wish to cheat at a game must be due to the fact that a player has an aim other than merely to win according to the rules of the game; for example, he may want to be admired or to win a sum of money which is at stake. This latter aim is often present at a game of cards, and it is well known that the demand for honourable play here takes on a moral value.

How is it possible then to establish which rules (directives) govern the game of chess?

One could perhaps think of approaching the problem from the behaviourist angle – limiting oneself to what can be established by external observation of the actions and then finding certain regularities. But in this way an insight into the rules of the game would never be achieved. It would never be possible to distinguish actual custom, or even regularities conditioned by the theory of the game, from the rules of chess proper. Even after watching a thousand games it would still be possible to believe that it is against the rules to open with a rook's pawn.

The simplest thing, perhaps, would be to go by certain authoritative rulings, for example, rulings given at chess congresses, or information contained in recognised textbooks on chess. But even this might not be sufficient, since it is not certain that such declarations are adhered to in practice. Sometimes games are played in fact in many varying ways. Even in a classic game like chess variations of this kind can occur (for example, the rule about "taking" *en passant* is not always adhered to). This problem of what rules govern "chess" must therefore, strictly speaking, be understood to refer to the rules which govern an actual game between two specific persons. It is their actions, and theirs alone, which are bound up in a significant whole, and governed for both of them by the rules.

Thus we cannot but adopt an introspective method. The problem is to discover which rules are actually felt by the players to be socially binding, in the sense indicated above. The first criterion is that they are in fact effective in the game and are outwardly visible as such. But in order to decide whether rules that are observed are more than just customary usage or motivated by technical reasons, it is necessary to ask the players by what rules they feel themselves bound.

Accordingly we can say: a rule of chess "is valid" means that within a given fellowship (which fundamentally comprises the two players of an actual game) this rule is effectively adhered to, because the players feel themselves to be socially bound by the directive contained in the rule. The concept of validity (in chess) involves two elements. The one refers to the actual effectiveness of the rule which can be established by outside observation. The other refers to the way in which the rule is felt to be motivating, that is, socially binding.

There is a certain ambiguity in the concept "rule of chess." The rules of chess have no reality and do not exist apart from the experience of the players, that is, their ideas of certain patterns of behaviour and, associated therewith, the emotional experience of the compulsion to obey. It is possible to abstract the meaning of an assertion purely as a thought content (" 2 and 2 make 4") from the apprehension of the same by a given person at a given time; and in just the same way it is also possible to abstract the meaning of a directive ("the king has the power of moving one square in any direction") from the concrete experience of the directive. The concept "rule of chess" must therefore in any accurate analysis be divided into two: the experienced ideas of certain patterns of behaviour (with the accompanying emotion) and the abstract content of those ideas, the norms of chess.

Thus the norms of chess are the abstract idea content (of a directive nature) which make it possible, as a scheme of interpretation, to understand the pheomena of chess (the actions of the moves and the experienced patterns of action) as a coherent whole of meaning and motivation, a game of chess; and along with other factors, within certain limits to predict the course of the game.

The phenomena of chess and the norms of chess are not mutually independent, each of them having their own reality; they are different sides of the same thing. No biological-physical action is as such regarded as a move of chess. It acquires this quality only by being interpreted in relation to the norms of chess. And conversely, no directive idea content has as such the character of a valid norm of chess. It acquires this quality only by the fact that it can, along with others, be effectively applied as a scheme of interpretation for the phenomena of chess. The phenomena of chess become phenomena of chess only when placed in relation to the norms of chess and vice versa.

The purpose of this discussion of chess has undoubtedly become clear by now. It is a pointer toward the statement that the concept "valid norm of chess" may function as the model for the concept "valid law" which is the real object of our preliminary considerations.

The law too may be regarded as consisting partly of legal phenomena and partly of legal norms in mutual correlation.

Observing the law as it functions in society we find that a large number of human actions are interpreted as a coherent whole of meaning and motivation by means of legal norms as the scheme of interpretation. A purchases a house from B. It turns out that the house is full of termites. A asks B for a reduction in the purchase price, but B will not agree. A brings an action against B, and the judge in accordance with the law of contract orders B to pay to A a certain sum of money within a given time. B does not do this. A has the sheriff levy upon the personal property of B which is then sold in auction. This sequence of events comprises a whole series of human actions, from the establishment of the law of contract to the auction. A biological-physical consideration of these actions cannot reveal any causal connection between them. Such connections lie within each single individual. But we interpret them with the aid of the reference scheme "valid law" as legal phenomena constituting a coherent whole of meaning and motivation. Each one of these actions acquires its legal character only when this is done. A's purchase of the house happens by word of mouth or with the aid of written characters. But these become a "purchase" only when seen in relation to the legal norms. The various actions are mutually motivating just like the moves in chess. The judge, for example, is motivated by A's and B's parts in the deal (and the further circumstances in connection with it, the condition of the house), and by the precedents establishing the law of contract. The whole proceeding has the character of a "game," only according to norms which are far more complicated than the norms of the game of chess.

On the basis of what has been said, the following hypothesis is advanced: The concept "valid (Illinois, California, common) law" can be explained and defined in principle in the same manner as the concept "valid (for any two players) norm of chess." That is to say, "valid law" means the abstract set of normative ideas which serve as a scheme of interpretation for the phenomena of law in action, which again means that these norms are effectively followed, and followed because they are experienced and felt to be socially binding.[1]

This conclusion may perhaps be thought commonplace, and it may seem that a vast apparatus of reasoning has been employed to this end. This might be true if the problems were approached by a person with no preconceived notions. But it would not be true for an historical approach. By far the greater part of all writers on jurisprudence up to the present have maintained that the concept "valid law" cannot be explained without recourse to the metaphysical. The law according to this view is not merely an empirical phenomenon. When we say that a rule of law is "valid" we refer not only to something factual, that can be observed, but also to a "validity" of a metaphysical character. This validity is alleged to be a pure concept of reason of divine origin or existing *a priori* (independent of experience) in the rational nature of man. And eminent writers on jurisprudence who deny such spiritual metaphysics have nevertheless been of the opinion that the "validity" of the law can only be explained by means of specific postulates.

Seen in this light our preliminary conclusion will, I trust, not be called commonplace. This analysis of a simple model is calculated to raise doubts as to the necessity of metaphysical explanations of the concept of law. Who would ever think of tracing the valid norm of chess back to an *a priori* validity, a pure idea of chess, bestowed upon man by God or deduced by man's eternal reason? The thought is ridiculous, because we do not take chess as seriously as law – because stronger emotions are bound up with the concepts of law. But this is no reason for believing that logical analysis should adopt a fundamentally different attitude in each of the two cases.

Of course many problems still remain before the concept "valid law" is satisfactorily analysed. But there is no need to go further into the matter at this point. This preliminary study is sufficient to serve as a basis for a survey of the various branches of the study of law, and for determining the proper place of "jurisprudence."

§8 THE VALIDITY OF THE LEGAL SYSTEM

The point from which we set out is the hypothesis that a system of norms is "valid" if it is able to serve as a scheme of interpretation for a corresponding set of social actions in such a way that it becomes possible for us to comprehend this set of actions as a coherent whole of meaning and motivation, and within certain limits to predict them. This capacity within the system is based on the fact that

1 By the judge and other legal authorities applying the law (§ 8).

the norms are effectively complied with, because they are felt to be socially binding.

What, now, are those social facts which as legal phenomena constitute the counterpart of the legal norms? They must be the human actions regulated by the legal norms. These, as we have seen, are in the last analysis norms determining the conditions under which force shall be exercised through the machinery of the State; or – briefly – norms for the ordering by the courts of the exercise of force. It follows that the legal phenomena as the counterpart of the norms must be the decisions of the courts. It is here that we must seek for the effectiveness that is the validity of law.

A national law system, considered as a valid system of norms, can accordingly be defined as the norms which actually are operative in the mind of the judge, because they are felt by him to be socially binding and therefore obeyed. The test of the validity is that on this hypothesis – that is, accepting the system of norms as a scheme of interpretation – we can comprehend the actions of the judge (the decisions of the courts) as meaningful responses to given conditions and within certain limits predict them – in the same way as the norms of chess enable us to understand the moves of the players as meaningful responses and predict them.

The action of the judge is a response to a number of conditions determined by the legal norms – that a contract of sale has been performed, that the seller has not delivered, that the buyer has given notice in due time, and so on. Also these conditioning facts acquire their specific meaning as legal acts through an interpretation in the light of the ideology of the norms. For this reason they might be included under the term legal phenomena in the wider sense or law in action.

Only the legal phenomena in the narrower sense, however – the application of the law by the courts – are decisive in determining the validity of the legal norms. In contrast to generally accepted ideas it must be emphasised that the law provides the norms for the behaviour of the courts, and not of private individuals. The effectiveness which conditions the validity of the norms can therefore be sought solely in the judicial application of the law, and not in the law in action among private individuals. If, for example, criminal abortion is prohibited, the true content of the law consists in a directive to the judge that he shall under certain conditions impose a penalty for criminal abortion. The decisive factor determining that the prohibition is valid law is solely the fact that it is effectively upheld by the courts where breaches of the law are brought to light and prosecuted.[1] It makes no difference whether the people comply with or frequently ignore the prohibition. This indifference results in the apparent paradox that the more effectively a rule is complied with in extrajudicial legal life, the more difficult it is to ascertain whether the rule possesses validity, because the courts have that much less opportunity to manifest their reaction.

In the foregoing, the terms "the judge" and "the courts" have been used indiscriminately. When we are speaking of a national law system, it is assumed that we are dealing with a set of norms which are supraindividual in the sense that they are particular to the nation, varying from nation to nation, not from one individual judge to another. For this reason it makes no difference whether one refers to "the judge" or to "the courts." So far as the individual judge is motivated

1 The term "courts" is here understood as a comprehensive term for the authorities which combine to administer the criminal prosecutions: police, prosecuting authority and court. If the police regularly omit to investigate certain breaches of the law, or if the prosecuting authority regularly omits to bring a prosecution, the penal law loses its character of valid law, notwithstanding its application at rare intervals in the courts.

by particular, personal ideas, these cannot be assigned to the law of the nation, although they are a factor which must be considered by anyone interested in forecasting a concrete legal decision.

When the basis for the validity of the law is sought in the decisions of the courts, the chain of reasoning may appear to be working in a circle. For it may be adduced that the qualification of judge is not merely a factual quality but can only be assigned by reference to valid law, in particular to the rules of public law governing the organisation of the courts and the appointment of judges. Before I can ascertain whether a certain rule of private law is valid law, therefore, I have to establish what is valid law in these other respects. And what is the criterion for this?

The answer to this problem is that the legal system forms a whole integrating the rules of private law with the rules of public law. Fundamentally, validity is a quality ascribed to the system as a whole. The test of the validity is that the system in its entirety, used as a scheme of interpretation, makes us to comprehend, not only the manner in which the judges act, but also that they are acting in the capacity as "judges." There is no Archimedes point for the verification, no part of the law which is verified before any other part.

The fact that fundamentally the entire legal system undergoes verification need not exclude the possibility of investigating whether a definite individual rule is valid law. It merely implies that the problem cannot be solved without reference to "valid law" as a whole. These more particular problems of verification are discussed in §§9 and 10.

The concept of the validity of the law rests, according to the explanation offered in this section, on hypotheses concerning the spiritual life of the judge. What is valid law cannot be ascertained by purely behaviouristic means, that is, by external observation of regularity in the reactions (customs) of the judges. Throughout a lengthy period the judge may have exhibited a certain typical reaction; for example, he may have imposed penalties for criminal abortion. Suddenly this reaction changes, because a new law has been promulgated. Validity cannot be ascertained by recourse to a more general, externally observable custom, namely, that of "obeying the legislator." For it is not possible from external observation to identify the "legislator" who is being obeyed. Purely external observation might lead one to the conclusion that obedience was paid to the persons, mentioned by their names, who at the time of observation were members of the legislature. But one day this too is changed. One can continue in this way right up to the constitution, but there is nothing to prevent the constitution from being changed too one day.

A behaviouristic interpretation, then, achieves nothing. The changing behaviour of the judge can only be comprehended and predicted through ideological interpretation, that is, by means of the hypothesis of a certain ideology which animates the judge and motivates his actions.

Another way of expressing the same thing is to say that law presupposes, not only regularity in the judge's mode of action, but also his experience of being bound by the rules. In the concept of validity two points are involved: partially the outward observable and regular compliance with a pattern of action, and partly the experience of this pattern of action as being a socially binding norm. Not every outward observable custom in the game of chess is an expression of a valid norm of chess, as, for example, not to open with a rook's pawn; in the same way not every outward and observable regularity in the reactions of the judge is the expression of a valid norm of law. It may be, for example, that a custom has developed of imposing only fines as the penalties for certain breaches of the law even though imprisonment is also authorised. Now it must, to be sure, be added that the customs of judges show a strong inclination to develop into binding norms, and that a custom will, in that case, be construed as the expression of valid law. But this is not the case so long as it is nothing more than a factual custom.

This twofold point in the concept of validity explains the dualism which has always marked this concept in current metaphysical theory of law. According to this theory valid law means both an order which is in fact effective and an order which possesses "binding force" derived from *a priori* principles; law is at the same time something factual in the world of reality and something valid in the world of ideas. It is not difficult to see that this dualism of viewpoint may lead to both logical and epistemological complications which find expression in a number of antinomies in the theory of law. It leads consistently to a metaphysical assertion that existence itself in its innermost being is valid (Hegel). Like most metaphysical constructions, the construction of the immanent validity of positive law rests on a misinterpretation of certain experiences, in this case the experience that the law is not merely a factual, customary order, but an order which is experienced as being socially binding. The traditional conception, therefore, with the metaphysics removed, can be appropriated in support of my own view so far as it is opposed to a purely behaviouristic interpretation of the validity of the law.

§ 13 DISCUSSION: IDEALISM AND REALISM IN JURISPRUDENCE

The interpretation of the concept "valid law" offered in the foregoing chapters differs sharply from the traditional view prevailing particularly in Continental jurisprudence. It may be characterised as jurisprudential realism and placed in contrast to jurisprudential idealism.

The latter rests on the assumption that there exist two different "worlds" corresponding with two different methods of cognition. First, "the world of reality," comprising all the physical and psychical phenomena in time and space which we apprehend through the experience of the senses. And then "the world of ideas or validity" comprising various sets of absolutely valid normative ideas (the true, the good and the beautiful) which we apprehend immediately by our reason. This latter cognition is thus independent of the experience of the senses and is therefore called *a priori*.

Jurisprudential idealism further assumes that the law belongs to both these worlds. Cognition of law, therefore, is simultaneously based on external experience as well as on *a priori* reasoning. The law is a phenomenon of reality so far as its content is a historical fact varying according to time and place, having been created by men and dependent on external factors of power. But that this content has "validity" as law, is something that cannot be observed in experience. What "validity" is does not permit of further description. It is an *a priori* concept, given in an irreducible direct intuition of reason. But validity is not merely a quality perceived by intuition; it is also a claim, absolutely binding on human action and human volition. Only he who obeys the valid claim acts "rightly." This "rightness" no more admits of explanation or proof than does validity itself. It is merely another aspect of the concept of validity.

The difference between law and morality can, according to idealistic views, be expressed as follows: While the moral norm, also according to its content, originates in pure reason, validity of the law is attached to an earthly and temporal content – the "positive" law with its historically determined content. Morality is pure validity; the law is simultaneously phenomenon and validity, a cross between reality and idea, or a revelation of a validity of reason in the world of reality.

Idealism occurs in two main varieties which could be called the material and the formal. . . .

The underlying thought in jurisprudential realism is the desire to understand the cognition of law in conformity with the ideas of the nature, problems and method of science as worked out by modern, empiristic philosophy. Several philosophical trends – logical empirism, the Uppsala philosophy, the Cambridge school, and others – find common ground in the rejection of metaphysics, speculative cognition based on *a priori* apprehension by reason. There is only one world and one cognition. All science is ultimately concerned with the same body of facts, and all scientific statements about reality – that is, those which are not purely logical-mathematical – are subject to experimental test.

From the standpoint of such presuppositions a specific "validity" cannot be admitted, neither in terms of a material *a priori* idea of justice nor as a formal category. Ideas of validity are metaphysical constructions built on a false interpretation of the "binding force" experienced in the moral consciousness. Like all other social sciences the study of law must in the final analysis be a study of social phenomena, the life of a human community; and jurisprudence must have as its task the interpretation of the "validity" of the law in terms of social effectivity, that is, a certain correspondence between a normative idea content and social phenomena. In this chapter I have attempted to show how this task can be fulfilled.

> In American jurisprudence the term "realism" is used primarily in a sense other than that indicated here, namely, as designating scepticism against legal concepts and rules and the part they play in the administration of justice (§9, note 4). At the same time, however, the American school of thought is also "realistic" in the sense in which we have used the term, to the extent that it looks on the law as a social phenomenon determined by the application of the law by the courts. . . .
>
> The trend in jurisprudence describing itself as sociological consists in the main of idealism in disguise (§1, notes 24 and 25).

This is the relative position of the two main tendencies in jurisprudence, metaphysical idealism and scientific realism. The ultimate struggle between them cannot be carried out within the province of jurisprudence itself, but must be fought out on the battlefield of general philosophy. The debate between idealism and realism in jurisprudence necessarily loses itself in fundamental problems of epistemology. Concerning these, the legal philosopher cannot be asked more than to outline the main features of the philosophical basis on which he builds. Further, I am convinced that legal metaphysics will gradually disappear in the same way as metaphysics in the natural sciences has all but disappeared: not so much because of the logical arguments against its tenability as because the interest in metaphysical constructions gradually fades away with the development of a regular science which proves its worth. Who nowadays would think of "refuting" the belief in the Philosopher's Stone? Let the dead bury their dead.

On the other hand, it is within the province of jurisprudence to offer a criticism of idealism in its application to the problems of legal theory. One of the great difficulties of idealistic jurisprudence has been to explain how it is possible that the act of legislation as a social phenomenon can produce anything more than social effects, namely, valid obligations of an *a priori* nature. If idealism is taken seriously – if certain actually maintained rules or systems are denied the character of law because they do not harmonise with a presupposed ideal of justice – then this leads to an inexpedient limitation of the concept of law. It is an elementary, scientific principle that an object must be defined according to objective qualities and not according to any evaluation. It is irrelevant, for example, whether Hitler's Jewish laws or certain foreign laws permitting polygamy are considered to conflict with the idea of law; it remains still an inescapable, practical task to expose these actually effective rules in connection with the system in which they occur. To me it seems preposterous to express moral disapproval by excluding these subjects from the province of legal science. The idea of law, if it can be admitted at all, can therefore at the most be a regulative legal-political idea, but not a constitutive moment in the concept of law. If one tries to lessen the claim of idealism by saying that positive law at any rate must be an attempt at realising justice, this introduces among the objective facts of the law a subjective factor of intention which is difficult to explain. Attempts can succeed or fail. Is the unsuccessful attempt also law? The construction would appear to be as arbitrary as if one were to maintain that a dog is an unsuccessful attempt at creating a cat.

Finally, if one radically rejects every ethical censure, as Kelsen does, and simply accepts as valid law the order which is actually upheld, specific validity as a categorical form becomes a superfluous drape. The impossibility of Kelsen's attempt, in determining the nature of positive law, to ignore psychological and social reality becomes apparent when we reach the initial hypothesis (basic norm or *Grundnorm*). As long as we remain on the lower steps of the legal system, it is possible to postpone the problem of the validity of the norm by referring back to a superior norm. But this procedure cannot be employed when we come to the initial hypothesis. At this point the question of the relation of the norm to reality becomes inescapably urgent. If the system is to make sense, it is clear that the initial hypothesis cannot be chosen arbitrarily. Kelsen himself says that it must be chosen in such a way that it covers the system which is actually in effect. But it is then clear that, in reality, effectivity is the criterion for positive law; and that the initial hypothesis, once we know what is positive law, in reality only has the function of investing it with the "validity" which is demanded by the metaphysical interpretation of legal consciousness, though no one knows what it is. The initial hypothesis is the ultimate source from which validity wells forth and branches out through the whole system. It might be possible to pass this over as a superfluous but harmless construction were it not that it results in shutting the eyes to a closer analysis of the criterion of effectivity. By making validity an internormative relation (deriving the validity of one norm from the validity of another) Kelsen has at the outset precluded himself from dealing with the heart of the problem of the validity of the law – the relation between the normative idea content and the social reality.

§14 DISCUSSION: PSYCHOLOGICAL AND BEHAVIOURISTIC REALISM AND THEIR SYNTHESIS

All theories of realism agree in interpreting the validity of law in terms of the social effectiveness of the legal norms. A valid norm differs from a mere draft statute or a demand for reform because the normative idea content of the valid norm is active in the legal life of the community – there is a law in action corresponding to the law in norms. The task is to define more precisely this "being active." On this point the theories differ. There are two approaches which could be called the psychological and the behaviouristic branch of legal realism.

Psychological realism finds the reality of law in psychological facts. A norm is valid if it is accepted by popular legal consciousness. The fact that such a rule is also upheld by the courts is in this view derivative and secondary, a normal consequence of the popular legal consciousness which is determinative also for the reactions of the judge. The actual criterion is not the upholding as such, but the determining factor behind it.

In order to test whether a given rule is valid law, we must therefore, according to this view, make certain social-psychological inquiries. We shall have to inquire whether the rule is accepted by the popular legal consciousness. We are told that this investigation may be easy, if the rule is found in a statute adopted in a constitutional manner; for the popular legal consciousness has, above all, as its indirect and formalised content the belief that law is law, and that the law must be obeyed. The public generally accepts that anything established according to the constitution has a claim to be respected as law. . . .

Such a definition cannot be accepted. It must be assumed that, at least within certain limits, it is possible to define a national law system as an externally given, inter-subjective phenomenon, and not merely as a subjective opinion which can be measured by means of a Gallup poll among professors of law. If there are fairly certain grounds for the assumption that a given rule will be taken as a basis for the decisions of the courts of the country, then that rule is valid national law as understood generally by lawyers, and it is irrelevant what views may exist in the legal consciousness of Professor Illum or of anyone else.

Behaviouristic realism finds the reality of law in the actions of the courts. A norm is valid if there are sufficient grounds to assume that it will be accepted by the courts as a basis for their decisions. The fact that such norms are consistent with the prevailing legal consciousness is, according to this view, derivative and secondary, a normal but not essential presupposition for the acceptance by the courts. The contrast of this view with the psychological theory can be expressed as follows: While the latter defines the validity of the law in such a way that we have to say *the law is applied because it is valid*, the behaviourist theory defines the concept in such a way that we have to say *the law is valid because it is applied.*

Views along similar lines have played an important part in American realism which dates back to Oliver Wendell Holmes, who as early as 1897 formulated the later frequently quoted opinion: "The prophecies of what the courts will do in fact, and nothing more pretentious, are what I mean by the law."

A purely behaviouristic interpretation of the concept of validity is, however, not feasible, because it is impossible to predict the behaviour of the judge by a purely external observation of custom. The law is more than a familiar, habitual order.

To arrive at a tenable interpretation of the validity of the law is possible only by a synthesis of psychological and behaviouristic views, as I have attempted to explain in the present chapter. The view is behaviouristic so far as it is directed toward finding consistency and predictability in the externally observed verbal behaviour of the judge. It is psychological so far as the consistency referred to is a coherent whole of meaning and motivation, only possible on the hypothesis that in his spiritual life the judge is governed and motivated by a normative ideology of a known content.

Ross' book was reviewed by Campbell (1959) 22 M. L. R. 703 and by Hart under the title "Scandinavian Realism" in [1959] *Camb. L. J.* 233.

It is possible to speak of a Scandinavian Realist *movement* because of the common approach taken to jurisprudential problems by jurisprudents in the Scandinavian countries. The leading figures in the movement are the Swedish philosopher Axel Hägerström (1868-1939), the Swedish law professors Vilhelm Lundstedt (1882-1955) and Karl Olivecrona (1897-), and the Danish law professor Alf Ross. The Scandinavians share a common empiricism and a common aversion to "higher law" theories, transcendentalism, and metaphysics; in their view law consists of observable facts which like any other facts can be known through empirical science.

The most radically empirical and anti-ideological of the group is Lundstedt. He believes that legal rules are in no sense normative, not even in the Kelsenian sense, but are as purely instrumental as the "rules" of engineering; in fact, even to call them rules distorts the reality. Thus not only are natural law and the common sense of justice unreal, but so are such concepts as legal rights, legal duties, and legal relationships. One should speak of legal activities rather than of legal rules, rights, etc., for law is nothing other than the activities carried on in its name. In fact, it is nothing other than life itself: "Law is nothing but the very life of mankind in organized groups and the conditions which make possible the peaceful co-existence of masses of individuals in social groups and their co-operation for other ends than mere existence and propagation" [*Legal Thinking Revised* 8 (1956)]. The only possible justification for legal activities is that they are indispensable for the existence of society, though he somewhat inconsistently often refers to social welfare as the end of law. As Professor A. H. Campbell put it in a review of his book in (1958) 21 M. L. R. 566, 568: "Although we have some doubt whether metaphysic does not slip in some-somewhere at the apex of Lundstedt's system, we can admire the ruthless gusto with which he expels it at all lower levels."

For good analyses of the Scandinavian Realists generally see Lloyd, *Introduction to Jurisprudence* 237-248 (1959) and Aubert, "The Concept of 'Law' " (1964) 52 *Ky L. J.* 363. Aubert writes, at 369-372:

> "Let us start with a brief consideration of one definition which ties the concept of law to a certain type of empirical data: the legal beliefs of the citizens. In his book *Codes and Law* the Danish jurist Illum states: 'A rule is not a legal rule simply because it has come about as a product of a social mechanism which has found its expression in the founding of a state. Those rules which are produced in this manner become law only by becoming an integral part of the people's common legal beliefs.' Now, Illum holds the opinions of lawyers to be the most important source of information concerning the content of these legal beliefs. But he makes it clear that conformity to the convictions also of lay-people affected by the rules in question, is a necessary condition for the validity of said rules. Illum is fully aware of the consequence of this definition, that there exists no uniform legal conviction with respect to any rule. 'One searches for the law, but finds only the specific beliefs of specific people concerning the contents of the legal system. There are as many varieties of law as there exist legal convictions'. . . .
>
> "The point of view adopted by Illum in such an extreme form, has also been maintained by Alf Ross in his earlier work [*Towards a Realistic Jurisprudence* (1954)]. In his earlier phase it seems as if the conformity of the citizens' behaviour to rules was a necessary condition for the validity of these rules as law. If the behaviour of the people deviated massively from the rules they could not make claim to legal validity. At the same time Ross demanded that the obedience of the citizens be based upon motives of a certain disinterested kind, if it were to be interpreted as evidence for the validity of rules.
>
> "Illum, and Ross in his earlier works, developed concepts of 'valid law' which have a democratic orientation. . . . Today, however, other types of 'realistic' definitions of law loom larger in the legal philosophical debates. They can perhaps be said to have a more authoritarian orientation in so far as they attempt to anchor the concept of law in the legal enforcement machinery, or more specifically, in judicial opinion and behaviour.
>
> "Within Scandinavian philosophy of law, the Uppsala philosophers especially have sought a definition of 'law' along these lines. The leading representatives of this school of thought, Hägerström and Lundstedt, arrived at first at the conclusion that terms like 'valid law', 'right', 'obligation' have no empirical referents. To use such terms was characterized as metaphysics, and as such unworthy of endeavors making scientific claims. At the same time as they maintained this point of view they suggested that legal terms could be given a meaning so as to

have them refer to empirical invariances, namely invariances in the behavior of the law-enforcing agencies. . . . This definition is clearly at variance with Illum's point of view, that the concept of "valid law" presupposes the existence of regularly occurring opinions and actions on part of the citizens. . . ."

CHAPTER THREE

Natural Law Thought

There is a strong tendency today to identify natural law theory with the Catholic Church. This tendency has a certain foundation in the accidents of history and contemporary reality, for it is a fact that most Catholic jurisprudents are natural lawyers while most non-Catholic ones are not. Although the reformers Luther, Calvin and Zwingli continued to accept the conception of natural law after the break with Rome in the sixteenth century, their theologies were not wholly compatible with it, and contemporary Protestant theologians are generally unsympathetic to natural law theory. But even apart from the facts that historically natural law was a development of Greek philosophy rather than of Catholic theology and that some of the most distinguished exponents of natural law theory today, men such as Nathaniel Micklem and Mortimer Adler, are not members of the Catholic Church, it can be clearly established that there is no essential dependence of natural law thought on Catholic theology. (Whether there is an essential dependence of Catholic theology on "rationalist" philosophy and therefore on natural law thought is fortunately not a problem for jurisprudents). As Dr. Brendan Brown has put it, "The tenet that the Catholic Church, through its divine mission, has the right and duty to decide the content of the natural law when reasonable men disagree is not a part of the natural law but of the supernatural law" [(1959) 48 *Geo. L. J.* 192, 196].

Indeed, as one of the wisest of contemporary natural lawyers has remarked, "there is really not one tradition of natural law, but many" [d'Entrèves, *Natural Law* 11 (1951)], and only a few of these traditions could be considered in any sense Catholic. One of the earliest statements is the Stoic version in Cicero's *Republic*: "[T]hose creatures who have received the gift of reason from Nature have also received right reason, and therefore they have also received the gift of law, which is right reason applied to command and prohibition. And if they have received law, they have received justice also. Now all men have received reason; therefore all men have received justice. . . . True law is right reason in agreement with Nature; it is of universal application, unchanging and everlasting. . . . We cannot be freed from its obligations by Senate or People, and we need not look outside ourselves for an expounder or interpreter of it. . . . [O]ne eternal and unchangeable law will be valid for all nations and for all times, and there will be one master and one ruler, that is, God, over us all, for He is the author of this law, its promulgator, and its enforcing judge." The most important mediæval theory of natural law was that of Thomas Aquinas, and then follow the "natural rights" theories of Grotius (1583-1645), Pufendorf (1632-1694), Locke (1632-1704), Thomasius (1655-1728), Burlamaqui (1694-1748), Vattel (1714-1767), Kant (1724-1804) and the theorists of the American Revolution of 1776 and the French Revolution of 1789. In d'Entrèves' opinion [*Natural Law* 72 (1951)] "it is with Hegel that the final break with natural law occurs in legal as well as in political theory", for his theory of the rational will and ethical state is incompatible with a higher law viewpoint.

With such a variety of natural law philosophers and philosophies it may well seem difficult to find a common thread. In the view of Dr. Anton-Hermann Chroust there are four universal characteristics of natural law thought which vary in the emphasis placed upon them at a different times: "(a) Natural Law usually consists of one or several generalized, but nevertheless essentially concrete, moral or legal 'values' or 'value judgments'; (b) these 'value judgments' are, in accordance with their 'absolute source' – 'Nature' Revelation (God), or Reason – universally valid and immutable; (c) they are within the reach of human reason properly employed and, therefore, the objects of ratiocination; (d) once perceived in their absoluteness and 'pure rationality' they overrule every form of Positive Law". . . . [I]t never ceases to search for a unifying higher point of view which would endow the notion of law with something above its naive 'givenness'. . . . [*Interpretations of Modern Legal Philosophies* 72. (1947)] Obviously the *content* of the natural law will vary with the particular natural lawyer – as is well illustrated by the collection of cases in the first section of this chapter.

The effect of natural law theories, and particularly that of St. Thomas Aquinas, upon the common law was considerable in its formative years: see O'Sullivan, *The Inheritance of the Common Law* (1950). The influence of Aquinas on Sir John Fortescue is well known, since it is directly acknowledged by that English jurist [*De Natura Legis Naturae*, c. 16, 26; *De Laudibus Legum Angliae*, c. 9; *The Governance of England*, ch. 1], but the similarity between the thought of Bracton and that of St. Thomas is not so well known. Dean Rooney, *Lawlessness, Law and Sanction* 76 (1937) states that "Bracton's concept of sanction and the concomitant definition of law will be found to involve practically the same essential factors as that of St. Thomas." Solicitor-General Murray, later Lord Mansfield, was speaking as a natural lawyer when he argued: "All occasions do not arise at once; . . . a statute very seldom can take in all cases, therefore the common law, that works itself pure by rules drawn from the fountain of justice, is for this reason superior to an act of parliament" [*Omychund* v. *Barker* (1744) 1 Atk. 21, 33; 26 E.R. 15, 22-23]. As for the conception of the "reasonable man", Sir Frederick Pollock observed: "St. German pointed out as early as the sixteenth century that the words 'reason' and 'reasonable' denote for the common lawyer the ideas which the civilian or canonist puts under the head of 'Law of Nature.' Thus natural law may fairly claim, in principle though not by name, the reasonable man of English and American law and all his works, which are many" [*Essays in the Law* 69 (1922); this remark of Pollock's is quoted with approval by Circuit Judge Frank in *Beidler & Bookmyer, Inc.* v. *Universal Insurance Co.* (1943) 134 F. 2d 828, 830 n. 7]. But that natural law is not always welcomed as a source today is indicated by the words of Mr. Justice Holmes in *Southern Pacific Co.* v. *Jensen* (1917), 244 U.S. 205, 222: "The common law is not a brooding omnipresence in the sky but the articulate voice of some sovereign or quasi-sovereign that can be identified. . . ." Certainly the common law is no longer receptive to the infusion of natural law as such, and *a fortiori* is no longer distinctively Christian.

The relationship of Christianity and the law was considered in the famous case of *Bowman* v. *Secular Society*. The issue in the case was whether the Secular Society could claim a legacy under a will in the light of its professedly un-Christian aims. If English law were intrinsically Christian, it would be against the policy of the law to allow a non-Christian missionary society to obtain the assistance of legal institutions, and so the Court had to decide the true relationship of Christianity and the law. In the course of his decision, Lord Sumner said:

> "My Lords, with all respect for the great names of the lawyers who have used it, the phrase 'Christianity is part of the law of England' is not really law; it is rhetoric. . . . One asks what part of our law may Christianity be, and what part of Christianity may it be that is part of our law? Best C.J. once said in *Bird* v. *Holbrook* (a case of injury by setting a spring-gun): 'There is no act which Christianity forbids, that the law will not reach: if it were otherwise, Christianity would not be, as it has always been held to be, part of the law of England'; but this was rhetoric too. Spring-guns, indeed, were got rid of, not by Christianity, but by Act of Parliament. 'Thou shalt not steal' is part of our law. 'Thou shalt not commit adultery' is part of our law, but another part. 'Thou shalt love thy neighbor as thyself' is not part of our law at all. Christianity has tolerated chattel slavery; not so the present law of England. Ours is, and always has been, a Christian State. The English family is built on Christian ideas, and if the national

religion is not Christian there is none. English law may well be called Christian law, but we apply many of its rules and most of its principles, with equal justice and equally good government, in heathen communities, and its sanctions, even in Courts of conscience, are material and not spiritual." [[1917] A.C. 406, 464].

Christian morals are thus not a theoretical part of the law; what they are is a sociological fact of which the law must take cognizance. This is also the burden of the statement by Mr. Justice Douglas in the United States Supreme Court in the 1952 case of *Zorach* v. *Clauson*: "We are a religious people whose institutions presuppose a Supreme Being" [(1952) 343 U.S. 306, 313]. Christian morality is a fact in Anglo-American-Canadian society. But even if the morality were non-Christian, this would also be a social fact for the State to accept and utilize.

What form do morals assume when incorporated in law? The best answer to this question is found in *Donoghue* v. *Stevenson* where Lord Atkin said:

"Acts or omissions which any moral code would censure cannot in a practical world be treated so as to give a right to every person injured by them to demand relief. In this way rules of law arise which limit the range of complainants and the extent of their remedy. The rule that you are to love your neighbour becomes in law, you must not injure your neighbour; and the lawyer's question, Who is my neighbour? receives a restricted reply. You must take reasonable care to avoid acts or omissions which you can reasonably foresee would be likely to injure your neighbour. Who, then, in law, is my neighbour? The answer seems to be – persons who are so closely and directly affected by my act that I ought reasonably to have them in contemplation as being so affected when I am directing my mind to the acts or omissions which are called in question."

Thus even where it is clear that the core of a legal rule is moral, the expression of the legal rule will be distinctively juridical.

One of the most topical jurisprudence issues today is that of disobedience to unjust laws. This issue was raised on this continent by the 1962 Saskatchewan medicare dispute between the government and the medical profession and, most dramatically, by racial events of the last few years in the United States. One view is that expressed by the late President Kennedy in an address to the people of the United States on September 30, 1962: "Americans are free . . . to disagree with the law – but not to disobey it." Another view is expressed by Rev. Martin Luther King in his moving "Letter from Birmingham City Jail" of April 16, 1963:

"There are *just* laws and there are *unjust* laws. I would be the first to advocate obeying just laws. One has not only a legal but moral responsibility to obey just laws. Conversely, one has a moral responsibility to disobey unjust laws. I would agree with Saint Augustine that 'An unjust law is no law at all.'

"Now what is the difference between the two? How does one determine when a law is just or unjust? A just law is a man-made code that squares with the moral law or the law of God. An unjust law is a code that is out of harmony with the moral law. To put it in the terms of Saint Thomas Aquinas, an unjust law is a human law that is not rooted in eternal and natural law. Any law that uplifts human personality is just. Any law that degrades human personality is unjust. All segregation statutes are unjust because segregation distorts the soul and damages the personality. . . .

"Let us turn to a more concrete example of just and unjust laws. An unjust law is a code that a majority inflicts on a minority that is not binding on itself. This is difference made legal. On the other hand a just law is a code that a majority compels a minority to follow that it is willing to follow itself. This is *sameness* made legal.

"Let me give another explanation. An unjust law is a code inflicted upon a minority which that minority had no part in enacting or creating because they did not have the unhampered right to vote."

There is a sense in which the question of obedience to law is a problem solely for the natural lawyer. The positivist is concerned by hypothesis with the validity and legality of law, not with its efficacy or justice. Validity and legality are purely formal concepts: law is valid, it is "legal," if it is enacted or adjudicated into being in the proper form. Efficacy and justice on the other hand, are concerned with the content of the legal rule: a law is efficacious when it is actually being obeyed by the people whose conduct it aims to govern, and it is just when it should be obeyed by them. The natural lawyer is interested in efficacy and justice as well as in validity and legality, and so it would appear that only for him is conformity to law a problem *qua* jurisprudent or even *qua* jurist. Of course he is more interested in justice than in efficacy, but in order to know whether a law, even a morally good one, can be borne by a particular people at a particular time, he must also know whether it is or will be efficacious. For example, moralists appear to be reaching the conclusion that a law outlawing professional boxing would be good, but it is highly doubtful whether it would yet be supported by popular feeling. For the natural lawyer, then, the ultimate theoretical question in jurisprudence "what is law?" has as a counterpart at the other end of the scale an ultimate practical question (and one by no means unrelated to the first theoretical question) "should this particular law be obeyed?"

Yet it would seem that to the more sophisticated positivist today, fidelity to law has also become a jurisprudential issue.

On the theory of resistance see Drinan "Changing Role of the Lawyer in an Era of Non-Violent Action" (1964) 1 *Law in Transition Q.* 123, and MacGuigan, "Civil Disobedience and Natural Law" (1964) 52 *Ky. L. J.* 346, reprinted in (1965) 11 *Catholic Law.* 118.

On natural law generally see Rommen, *The Natural Law* (1947), Wu, *Fountain of Justice* (1955), and the recent symposium on natural law in *Law and Philosophy* (Hook ed. 1964).

A. CASES

HEYDON'S CASE
1584. 3 Co. Rep. 7a.

[The statute 31 H. 8 c. 13 avoided estates for life made by religious within the previous year. Held, that a copyhold was an estate for life within the statute and that a lease of it by a religious house was therefore void].

And after all the Barons openly argued in Court in the same term, *scil.* Pasch. 26 Eliz. and it was unanimously resolved by Sir Roger Manwood, Chief Baron, and the other Barons of the Exchequer, that the said lease made to Heydon of the said parcels, whereof Ware and Ware were seised for life by copy of court-roll, was void; for it was agreed by them, that the said copyhold estate was an estate for life, within the words and meaning of the said Act. And it was resolved by them, that for the sure and true interpretation of all statutes in general (be they penal or beneficial, restrictive or enlarging of the common law,) four things are to be discerned and considered:

1st. What was the common law before the making of the Act.

2nd. What was the mischief and defect for which the common law did not provide.

3rd. What remedy the Parliament hath resolved and appointed to cure the disease of the commonwealth.

And, 4th. The true reason of the remedy; and then the office of all the Judges is always to make such construction as shall suppress the mischief, and advance the remedy, and to suppress subtle inventions and evasions for continuance of the mischief, and *pro privato commodo*, and to add force and life to the cure and remedy, according to the true intent of the makers of the Act, *pro bono publico*. And it was said, that in this case the common law was, that religious and ecclesiastical persons might have made leases for as many years as they pleased, the mischief was that when they perceived their houses would be dissolved, they made long and unreasonable leases: and ecclesiastical houses which should be dissolved after the Act (as the said college in our case was) that all leases of any land, whereof any estate or interest for life or years was then in being, should be void; and their reason was, that it was not necessary for them to make a new lease so long as a former had continuance; and therefore the intent of the Act was to avoid doubling of estates, and to have but one single estate in being at a time: for doubling of estates implies in itself deceit, and private respect, to prevent the intention of the Parliament. And if the copyhold estate for two lives, and the lease for eighty shall stand together, there will be doubling of estates *simul & semel*, which will be against the true meaning of Parliament.

And in this case it was debated at large, in what cases the general words of Acts of Parliament shall extend to copyhold or customary estates, and in what not; and therefore this rule was taken and agreed by the whole Court, that when an Act of Parliament doth alter the service, tenure, interests of the land, or other thing, in prejudice of the lord, or of the custom of the manor, or in prejudice of the tenant, there the general words of such Act of Parliament shall not extend to copyholds: but when an Act of Parliament is generally made for the good of the weal public, and no prejudice can accrue by reason of alteration of any interest, service, tenure, or custom of the manor, there many times copyhold and customary estates are within the general purview of such acts. . . .

CALVIN'S CASE
1609. 7 Co. Rep. 1a.

[The question for determination was whether the plaintiff Robert Calvin, who was born in Scotland after the accession of James I to the throne of England was an alien and so disqualified from bringing an action for lands within England. It was held by an assembly of judges that he was not an alien and might hold lands in England].

Now followeth the Second Part, De Legibus, wherein these parts were considered: first that the ligeance or faith of the subject is due unto the King by the law of nature: secondly, that the law of nature is part of the law of England: thirdly, that the law of nature was before any judicial or municipal law: fourthly, that the law of nature is immutable.

The law of nature is that which God at the time of creation of the nature of man infused into his heart, for his preservation and direction; and this is *lex aeterna*, the moral law, called also the law of nature. And by this law, written with the finger of God in the heart of man, were the people of God a long time governed, before the law was written by Moses, who was the first reporter or writer of law in the world. The apostle in the second chapter to the Romans saith, *Cum enim gentes quae legem non habent naturaliter ea quae legissunt faciunt.* And this is within the command of that moral law, *honora patrem*, which doubtless doth extend to him that is *pater patriae*. And that Apostle saith *Omnis anima potestatibus sublimioribus subdita sit.* And these be the words of the Great Divine, *Hoc Deus in Sacris Scripturis jubet, hoc lex naturae dictari, ut quilibet subditus obediate superio*, and Aristotle, nature's secretary, lib. 5. AEthic. saith, that *jus naturale est, quod apud omnes homines eandem habet potentiam.* And herewith doth agree Bracton, lib. 1. cap. 5. and Fortescue, cap. 8. 12. 13. and 16. Doctor and Student, cap. 2. and 4. And the reason hereof is, for that God and nature is one to all, and therefore the law of God and nature is one to all. By this law of nature is the faith, ligeance, and obedience of the subject due to his Sovereign or superior. . . .

Wherefore to conclude this point (and to exclude all that hath been or could be objected against it) it the obedience and ligeance of the subject to his sovereign be due by the law of nature, if that law be parcel of the laws, as well of England, as of all other nations, and is immutable, and that *postnati* and we of England are united by birth-right, in obedience and ligeance (which is the true cause of natural subjection) by the law of nature; it followeth that Calvin the plaintiff being born under one ligeance to one King, cannot be an alien born. . . .

DR. BONHAM'S CASE

1611. 8 Co. Rep. 113b.

[This was an action for false imprisonment brought by Thomas Bonham, doctor in philosophy and physic. He had taken the degree of Doctor of Physic in the University of Cambridge but was imprisoned by the College of Physicians and Others for practising physic without leave of the College. Judgment was given for the plaintiff].

The censors cannot be judges, ministers, and parties; judges to give sentence or judgment; ministers to make summons; and parties to have the moiety of the forfeiture, *quia aliquis non debet esse Judex in propria causa, imo iniquum est aliquem suae rei esse judicem*; and one cannot be Judge and attorney for any of the parties, Dyer 3 E. 6. 65. 38 E. 3. 15. 8 H. 6. 19 b. 20 a. 21 E. 4. 47 a. & c. And it appears in our books, that in many cases, the common law will controul Acts of Parliament, and sometimes adjudge them to be utterly void: for when an Act of Parliament is against common right and reason, or repugnant, or impossible to be performed, the common law will controul it, and adjudge such Act to be void; and, therefore, in 8 E. 3. 30 a. b. *Thomas Tregor's case* on the statute of W. 2. c. 38. *et* Artic' Super Chartras, c. 9. Herle saith, some statutes are made against law and right, which those who made them perceiving, would not put them in execution. . . .

In 1616 there followed the dispute between Coke and James I in the Star Chamber, reported in O'Sullivan, *The Inheritance of the Common law* 83-84 (1950):

JAMES: It is atheism and blasphemy to dispute what God can do. Good Christians content themselves with His Will revealed in His Word. So it is presumption and high contempt in a subject to dispute what a King can do or say, that a King cannot do this or that; but rest in that which is the King's Will revealed in his Law.

COKE: Your Majesty, the law is the golden measure to try the causes of his subjects, and which protects His Majesty in safety and peace. The King cannot take any case out of his Courts and give judgment upon it himself. The judgments are always given *per curiam* and the judges are sworn to execute justice according to the Law and Customs of England.

JAMES: This means that I shall be under the law which it is treason to affirm.

COKE: Sir, Bracton saith: *Quod rex non debet esse sub homine sed sub Deo et sub lege*: That the King ought to be under no man but under God and the Law.

'His Majesty fell into that high indignation as the like was never known in him, looking and speaking fiercely, with bended fist offering to strike him, which the Lord Coke, perceiving, fell flat on all fower.'

Cf. Pollock, "Judicial Caution and Valour" (1929) 45 L.Q.R. 293, 295: "Caution and valour are both needed for the fruitful constructive interpretation of legal principles. The Court should be ever valiant to override the merely technical difficulties of professional thinking, and also current opinions having some show of authority, in the search for a solution which will be acceptable and in a general way intelligible to reasonable citizens. . . ."

SHAW v. DIRECTOR OF PUBLIC PROSECUTIONS
House of Lords [1961] 2 All E.R. 446.

VISCOUNT SIMONDS: My Lords, the appellant, Frederick Charles Shaw, was, on September 21, 1960, convicted at the Central Criminal Court on an indictment containing three counts which alleged the following offences: (1) Conspiracy to corrupt public morals; (2) living on the earnings of prostitution contrary to section 30 of the Sexual Offences Act, 1956, and (3) publishing an obscene publication contrary to section 2 of the Obscene Publications Act, 1959. He appealed against conviction to the Court of Criminal Appeal on all three counts. His appeal was dismissed but that court certified that points of law of general public importance were involved in the decisions on the first and second counts and gave him leave to appeal on them to his House. They refused so to certify in respect of the third count. I propose, my Lords, to deal in this opinion in the first place with the second count, for I have had the privilege of reading the speech which my noble and learned friend Lord Tucker is about to deliver on the first count, and so fully agree with him, that I find it convenient to add some general observations which can be regarded as supplementary to what he says.

My Lords, the particulars of the offence charged in the second count were that on divers days unknown between October 1, 1959, and July 23, 1960, the appellant lived wholly or in part on the earnings of prostitutes. Before I refer to the statute on which the charge is based I must refer briefly to the relevant facts.

When the Street Offences Act, 1959, came into operation it was no longer possible for prostitutes to ply their trade by soliciting in the streets, and it became necessary for them to find some other means of advertising the services that they were prepared to render. It occurred to the appellant that he could with advantage to himself assist them to this end. The device that he adopted was to pubish on divers days between the dates mentioned in the particulars of offences a magazine or booklet which was called "Ladies' Directory." It contained the names, addresses and telephone numbers of prostitutes with photographs of nude female figures, and in some cases details which conveyed to initiates willingness to indulge not only in ordinary sexual intercourse but also in various perverse practices. Learned counsel for the appellant made some point of the fact that the magazine contained also advertisements of models and clubs. I therefore mention it, but I do not think that is of any importance. The profit derived by the appellant from their enterprise was two-fold. From the prostitutes whom he canvassed and advertised he received fees ranging from two guineas for quarter-page advertisements without photographs to ten guineas for full-page advertisements with photographs. There was evidence that one issue produced from this source a sum of £250 19s. Secondly, the appellant sold copies of the magazine to a Mr. Blass, the proprietor of a sweet and cigarette kiosk, and perhaps, though this is not very clear, to other persons at a price of five shillings per copy. The weekly sales of Mr. Blass were said by him to have started at 30 to 40 and eventually reached about 80. It is manifest that the appellant received substantial sums from his undertaking. It is also clear from the evidence that the prostitutes paid for advertisement out of the earnings of their profession and that they or some of them obtained custom by means of it.

It is in these circumstances that the question must be asked whether the appellant lived wholly or in part on the earnings of prostitution. . . .

My Lords, as I have already said, the first count in the indictment is "Conspiracy to corrupt public morals," and the particulars of offence will have sufficiently appeared. I am concerned only to assert what was vigorously denied by counsel for the appellant, that such an offence is known to the common law, and that it was open to the jury to find on the facts of this case that the appellant was guilty of such an offence. I must say categorically that, it it were not so, Her Majesty's courts would strangely have failed in their duty as servants and guardians of the common law. Need I say, my Lords, that I am no advocate to the right of the judges to create new criminal offences? I will repeat well-known words: "Amongst many other points of happiness and freedom which your Majesty's subjects have enjoyed there is none which they have accounted more dear and precious than this, to be guided and governed by certain rules of law which giveth both to the head and members that which of right belongeth to them and not by any arbitrary or uncertain form of government." These words are as true today as they were in the seventeenth century and command the allegiance of us all. But I am at a loss to understand how it can be said either that the law does not recognise a conspiracy to corrupt public morals or that, though there may not be an exact precedent for such a conspiracy as this case reveals, it does not fall fairly within the general words by which it is described. I do not propose to examine all the relevant authorities. That will be done by my noble and learned friend. The fallacy in the argument that was addressed to us lay in the attempt to exclude from the scope of general words acts well calculated to corrupt public morals just because they had not been committed or had not been brought to the notice of the court before. It is not thus that the common law has developed. We are perhaps more accustomed to hear this matter discussed upon the question whether such and such a transaction is contrary to public policy. At once the controversy arises. On the one hand it is said that it is not possible in the twentieth century for the court to create a new head of public policy, on the other it is said that this is but a new example of a well-established head. In the sphere of criminal law I entertain no doubt that there remains in the courts of law a residual power to enforce the supreme and fundamental purpose of the law, to conserve not only the safety and order but also the moral welfare of the State, and that it is their duty to guard it against attacks which may be the more insidious because they are novel and unprepared for. That is the broad head (call it public policy if you wish) within which the present indictment falls. It matters little what label is given to the offending act. To one of your Lordships it may appear an affront to public decency, to another considering that it may succeed in its obvious intention of provoking libidinous desires, it will seem a corruption of public morals. Yet others may deem it aptly described as the creation of a public mischief or the undermining of moral conduct. The same act will not in all ages be regarded in the same way. The law must be related to the changing standards of life, not yielding to every shifting impulse of the popular will but having regard to fundamental assessments of human values and the purposes of society. Today a denial of the fundamental Christian doctrine, which in past centuries would have been regarded by the ecclesiastical courts as heresy and by the common law as blasphemy, will no longer be an offence if the decencies of controversy are observed. When Lord Mansfield, speaking long after the Star Chamber had been abolished, said [*Rex.* v. *Delaval* (1763) 2 Burr. 1434, 1439], that the Court of King's Bench was the custos morum of the people and had the superintendency of offences contra bonos mores, he was asserting, as I now assert, that there is in that court a residual power, where no statute has yet intervened to supersede the common law, to superintend those offences which are prejudicial to the public welfare. Such occasions will be rare, for Parliament has not been slow to legislate when attention has been sufficiently aroused. But gaps remain and will always remain since no one can foresee every way in which the wickedness of man may disrupt the order of society. Let me take a single instance to which my noble and learned friend Lord Tucker refers. Let it be supposed that at some future perhaps, early, date homosexual practices between adult consenting males are no longer a crime. Would it not be an offence if even without obscenity, such practices were publicly advocated and encouraged by pamphlet and advertisement? Or must we wait until Parliament finds time to deal with such conduct? I say, my Lords, that if the common law is powerless in such an event, then we should no longer do her reverence. But I say that her hand is still powerful and that it is for Her Majesty's judges to play the part which Lord Mansfield pointed out to them.

I have so far paid little regard to the fact that the charge here is of conspiracy. But, if I have correctly described the conduct of the appellant, it is an irresistible inference that a conspiracy between him and others to do such acts is indictable. It is irrelevant to this charge that section 2(4) of the Obscene Publications Act, 1959, might bar proceedings against him if no conspiracy were alleged. It may be thought superfluous, where that Act can be invoked, to bring a charge also of conspiracy to corrupt public morals, but I can well understand the desirability of doing so where a doubt exists whether obscenity within the meaning of the Act can be proved.

I will say a final word upon an aspect of the case which was urged by counsel. No one doubts – and I have put it in the forefront of this opinion – that certainty is a most desirable attribute of the criminal and civil law alike. Nevertheless there are matters which must ultimately depend on the opinion of a jury. In the civil law I will take an example which comes perhaps nearest to the criminal law – the tort of negligence. It is for a jury to decide not only whether the defendant has committed the act complained of, but whether in doing it he has fallen short of the standard of care which the circumstances require. Till their verdict is given it is uncertain what the law requires. The same branch of the civil law supplies another interesting analogy. For, though in the Factory Acts and the regulations made under them, the measure of care required of an employer is defined in the greatest detail, no one supposes that he may not be guilty of negligence in a manner unforeseen and unprovided for. That will be a matter for the jury to decide. There are still, as has recently been said, "unravished remnants of the common law."

So in the case of a charge of conspiracy to corrupt public morals the uncertainty that necessarily arises from the vagueness of general words can only be resolved by the opinion of twelve chosen men and women. I am content to leave it to them.

The appeal on both counts should, in my opinion, be dismissed.

LORD REID: In my opinion there is no such general offence known to the law as conspiracy to corrupt public morals. Undoubtedly there is an offence of criminal conspiracy and undoubtedly it is of fairly wide scope. In my view its scope cannot be determined without having regard first to the history of the matter and then to the broad general principles which have generally been thought to underlie our system of law and government and in particular our system of criminal law.

It appears to be generally accepted that the offence of criminal conspiracy was the creature of the Star Chamber. So far as I am able to judge the summary in Kenny's Outlines of Criminal Law, section 59, 17th ed., p. 88, is a fair one. There it is said that the criminal side of conspiracy was "emphasised by the Star Chamber which recognised its possibilities as an engine of government and moulded it into a substantive offence of wide scope whose attractions were such that its principles were gradually adopted by the common law courts." The Star Chamber perhaps had more merits than its detractors will admit but its methods and principles were superseded and what it did is of no authority today. The question is how far the common law courts in fact went in borrowing from it. . . .

There are two competing views. One is that conspiring to corrupt public morals is only one facet of a still more general offence, conspiracy to effect public mischief; and that, like the categories of negligence, the categories of public mischief are never closed. The other is that, whatever may have been done two or three centuries ago, we ought not now to extend the doctrine further than it has already been carried by the common law courts. Of course I do not mean that it should only be applied in circumstances precisely similar to those in some decided case. Decisions are always authority for other cases which are reasonably analogous and are not properly distinguishable. But we ought not to extend the doctrine to new fields. . . .

Even if there is still a vestigial power of this kind it ought not, in my view, to be used unless there appears to be general agreement that the offence to which it is applied ought to be criminal if committed by an individual. Notoriously, there are wide differences of opinion today as to how far the law ought to punish immoral acts which are not done in the face of the public. Some think that the law already goes too far, some that it does not go far enough. Parliament is the proper place, and I am firmly of opinion the only proper place, to settle that. When there is sufficient support from public opinion, Parliament does not hesitate to intervene. Where Parliament fears to tread it is not for the courts to rush in.

Before turning to the question whether the authorities on a fair construction warrant indictment on this charge, I must notice the offence of conspiring to effect public mischief. . . .

In my judgment this House is in no way bound and ought not to sanction the extension of "public mischief" to any new field, and certainly not if such extension would be in any way controversial. Public mischief is the criminal counterpart of public policy, and the criminal law ought to be even more hesitant than the civil law in founding on it in some new aspect. I think that the following comments are as valid today as they were in 1824: "I am not much disposed to yield to arguments of public policy. I think the courts of Westminster Hall . . . have gone much further than they were warranted in going in question of policy: they have taken on themselves, sometimes, to decide doubtful questions of policy; and they are always in danger of so doing because courts of law look only at the particular case, and have not the means of bringing before them all those considerations which ought to enter into the judgment of those who decide on questions of policy" (*per* Best J. C. in *Richardson* v. *Mellish*). "I . . . protest . . . against arguing too strongly upon public policy – it is a very unruly horse and when once you get astride it you never know where it will carry you. It may lead you from the sound law. It is never argued at all but when other points fail" (*per* Burrough J.).

It may, perhaps, be said that there is no question here of creating a new offence because there is only one offence of conspiracy – agreeing or acting in concert to do an unlawful act. In a technical sense that is true. But in order to extend this offence to a new field the court would have to create a new unlawful act: it would have to hold that conduct of a kind which has not hitherto been unlawful in this sense must now be held to be unlawful. It appears to me that the objections to that are just as powerful as the objections to creating a new offence. The difference is a matter of words; the essence of the matter is that a type of conduct for the punishment of which there is no previous authority now for the first time becomes punishable solely by a decision of a court.

I therefore proceed to consider the authorities on the footing that the courts cannot now create a new offence, or a new kind of criminal conspiracy, or at least that, if any such power still exists, this is not a proper sphere in which to exercise it. . . .

But in argument more stress was put on words which are reported to have been used by the judges than on the actual decisions, and in particular on the statement by Lord Mansfield and others that the Court of King's Bench was custos or censor morum. It was said that they thereby decided or recognised that any conspiracy to corrupt morals or, as the learned trial judge put it in the present case, "to lead morally astray" was an indictable offence. I do not think so. As the reports of those days are not full reports of the judgments, we do not have the precise context, but I think it much more probable that those judges were intending to say that they then had power to create new offences, that this power extended to the moral field, and that the acts in these particular cases should be held to be punishable. It must be observed that these references to the court being censor or custos morum occur equally in decisions in cases of conspiracy and in cases against individuals. In the eighteenth century courts created new offences in the field of morals both against individuals (see, for example, *Curl's* case) and against combinations. So if, contrary to my view, the references established a general offence of conspiring to corrupt public morals, then surely they must also have established that it is a general offence for an individual to act so as to corrupt public morals or to attempt to do so. If it was established in the eighteenth century that there was a general offence of conspiring to corrupt public morals (or to lead members of the public morally astray) then, as the essence of criminal conspiracy is doing or agreeing to do an unlawful act, it must follow that for two centuries every act which has tended to lead members of the public astray morally has been an unlawful act, and the respondent's argument would apply equally to make unlawful every act which tends to lead a single individual morally astray. In the unending controversy about the proper relationship between law and morals no one seems to have suspected that. Hitherto, I think, there has been a wide measure of agreement with Professor Kenny's view that only *certain* acts which are *outrageously* immoral are unlawful in this sense.

I claim little knowledge of the history of English criminal law – any such knowledge that I may have is of a different system. But it seems that most crimes must have been the creation of judges of a remoter time, because Parliament played a comparatively small part, and there was no reception of any foreign system. And it seems that they proceeded piecemeal, taking care no doubt to move in advance of contemporary opinion, and that they did not first invent a general theory or a general offence and then apply it at once to a wide variety of particular cases. A somewhat similar situation arose in connection with equally general statements by equally eminent judges that Christianity is part of the law of England. That was dealt with in this House in *Bowman* v. *Secular Society Ltd.* [[1917] A.C. 406], where it seems to me that more attention was paid to what the courts had in fact done than to the language that judges had used in doing it. . . .

Finally I must avert to the consequences of holding that this very general offence exists. It has always been thought to be of primary importance that our law, and particularly our criminal law, should be certain: that a man should be able to know what conduct is and what is not criminal, particularly when heavy penalties are involved. Some suggestion was made that it does not matter if this offence is very wide: no one would ever prosecute and if they did no jury would ever convict if the breach was venial. Indeed, the suggestion goes even further: that the meaning and application of the words "deprave" and "corrupt" (the traditional words in obscene libel now enacted in the 1959 Act) or the words "debauch" and "corrupt" in this indictment ought to be entirely for the jury, so that any conduct of this kind is criminal if in the end a jury think it so. In other words, you cannot tell what is criminal except by guessing what view a jury will take, and juries' views may vary and may change with the passing of time. Normally the meaning of words is a question of law for the court. For example, it is not left to a jury to determine the meaning of negligence: they have to consider on evidence and on their own knowledge a much more specific question – Would a reasonable man have done what this man did? I know that in obscene libel the jury has great latitude but I think that it is an understatement to say that this has not been found wholly satisfactory. If the trial judges charge in the present case was right, if a jury is entitled to water down the strong words "deprave," "corrupt" or "debauch" so as merely to mean lead astray morally, then it seems to me that the court has transferred to the jury the whole of its functions as censor morum, the law will be whatever any jury may happen to think it ought to be, and this branch of the law will have lost all the certainty which we rightly prize in other branches of our law.

LORD TUCKER: My Lords, I have referred to this case as, in my opinion, the decision of the present and other similar cases does not depend upon the label which is to be attached to a particular conspiracy. Can it be doubted that a conspiracy to corrupt public morals is a conspiracy to effect a public mishief? Is it to be said that a conspiracy to sell decorated domestic pottery in the home market by means of devices contrived to evade the object of Board of Trade orders is a criminal conspiracy but an agreement to do acts calculated to corrupt public morals is not? Suppose Parliament tomorrow enacts that homosexual practices between adult consenting males is no longer to be criminal, is it to be said that a conspiracy to further and encourage such practices amongst adult males could not be the subject of a criminal charge fit to be left to a jury? Similarly, with regard to a conspiracy to encourage and promote Lesbianism today, or incestuous sexual intercourse in the year 1907? My Lords, if these questions are to be answered in the negative I would expect to find some clear authority during the past centuries which would justify such an answer. I know of none. . . .

LORD MORRIS OF BORTH-Y-GEST: . . . I join, however, with those of your Lordships who affirm that the law is not impotent to convict those who conspire to corrupt public morals. The declaration of Lord Mansfield (see *Jones* v. *Randall*, that "whatsoever is contrary, bonos mores est [sic] decorum, the principles of our law prohibit, and the King's court, as the general censor and guardian of the public manners, is bound to restrain and punish," is echoed and finds modern expression in Kenny's Outlines of Criminal Law (17th ed., section 451, p. 393) in the statement that agreements by two or more persons may be criminal if they are agreements to do acts which are outrageously immoral or else are in some way extremely injurious to the public. There are certain manifestations of conduct which are an affront to and an attack upon recognised public standards of morals and decency, and which all well-disposed persons would stigmatise and condemn as deserving of punishment. The cases afford examples of the conduct of individuals which has been punished because it outraged public decency or because its tendency was to corrupt the public morals.

It is said that there is a measure of vagueness in a charge of conspiracy to corrupt public morals, and also that there might be peril of the launching of prosecutions in order to suppress unpopular or unorthodox views. My Lords, I entertain no anxiety on these lines. Even if accepted public standards may to some extent vary from generation to generation, current standards are in the keeping of juries, who can be trusted to maintain the corporate good sense of the community and to discern attacks upon values that must be preserved. If there were prosecutions which were not genuinely and fairly warranted juries would be quick to perceive this. There could be no conviction unless 12 jurors were unanimous in thinking that the accused person or persons had combined to do acts which were calculated to corrupt public morals. My Lords, as time proceeds our criminal law is more and more being codified. Though it may be that the occasions for presenting a charge such as that in count 1 will be infrequent, I concur in the view that such a charge is contained within the armour of the law, and that the jury were in the present case fully entitled to decide the case as they did.

I would dismiss the appeal.

LORD HODSON: My Lords, I am in full agreement with the speeches by my noble and learned friend on the Woolsack, and by my noble and learned friend Lord Tucker, and wish only to add a few sentences on the first count.

I am wholly satisfied that there is a common law misdemeanour of conspiracy to corrupt public morals. The judicial precedents which have been cited show conclusively to my mind that the courts have never abandoned their function as custodes morum by surrendering to the legislature the right and duty to apply established principles to new combinations of circumstances. . . .

Since a criminal indictment is followed by the verdict of a jury it is true that the function of custos morum is in criminal cases ultimately performed by the jury, by whom, on a proper direction, each case will be decided. This I think is consonant with the course of the development of our law. One may take, as an example, the case of negligence where the standard of care of the reasonable man is regarded as fit to be determined by the jury. In the field of public morals it will thus be the morality of the man in the jury box that will determine the fate of the accused, but this should hardly disturb the equanimity of anyone brought up in the traditions of our common law.

I would dismiss the appeal. *Appeal dismissed.*

In a note on this case, entitled "The Shaw Case: The Law and Public Morals" (1961) 77 *L. Q. R.* 560 Dr. Goodhart defends the result against an attack by Glanville Williams.

The *Shaw* case has been the prime exhibit in the continuing debate over Lord Devlin's thesis that "it is not possible to set theoretical limits to the power of the State to legislate against immorality" and that the only criterion for such legislation is the existence of "a real feeling of reprobation" of the conduct in question [*The Enforcement of Morals* 14, 17 (1959)]. The Devlin thesis has produced spirited controversy: Hart, "Immorality and Treason", *The Listener*, July 30, 1959, p. 162: Wolheim, "Crime, Sin and Mr. Justice Devlin", *Encounter*, Nov. 1959, p. 39; Rostow, "The Enforcement of Morals" [1960] *Camb. L. J.* 174; Hart, "The Use and Abuse of the Criminal Law" (1961) 4 *Oxford Law.* 7; Devlin, "Law, Democracy, and Morality" (1962) 110 *U. Pa. L. Rev.* 635; Hughes, "Morals and the Criminal Law" (1962) 71 *Yale L. J.* 662; Hart, *Law, Liberty, and Morality* (1963); Williams, "Authoritarian Morals and the Criminal Law" [1966] *Crim. L.R.* 132.

BARNETTE v. WEST VIRGINIA STATE BOARD OF EDUCATION
Federal District Court for Southern District of West Virginia.
1942. 47 F. Supp. 251

PARKER, Circuit Judge delivered the judgment of the Court. This is a suit by three persons belonging to a sect known as "Jehovah's Witnesses", who have children attending the public schools of West Virginia, against the Board of Education of that state. It is brought by plaintiffs in behalf of themselves and their children and all other persons in the State of West Virginia in like situation, and its purpose is to secure an injunction restraining the State Board of Education from enforcing against them a regulation of the Board requiring children in the public schools to salute the American flag. They allege that they and their children and other persons belonging to the sect of "Jehovah's Witnesses" believe that a flag salute of the kind required by the Board is a violation of the second commandment of the Decalogue, as contained in the 20th chapter of the Book of Exodus; that because of this belief they cannot comply with the regulation of the Board; that, if they fail to comply, the children will be expelled from school, and thus be deprived of the benefits of the state's public school system; and that plaintiffs, in such event, will have to provide them education in private schools at great expense or be subjected to prosecution for crime for failing to send them to school, as required by the compulsory school attendance law of the state. They contend, therefore, that the regulation amounts to a denial of religious liberty and is violative of rights which the first amendment to the federal Constitution protects against impairment by the federal government and which the 14th Amendment protects against impairment by the states.

A motion has been made to dismiss the bill on the ground that the regulation of the Board is a proper exercise of power vested in it by the State of West Virginia, and that, under the doctrine of *Minersville School District* v. *Gobitis*, 310 U. S. 586, 60 S. Ct. 1010, 84 L. Ed. 1375, 127 A. L .R. 1493, the flag salute which it requires cannot be held a violation of the religious rights of plaintiffs. The case was heard on application for interlocutory injunction; but the parties have agreed that it be submitted for final decree on the bill and motion to dismiss. No question is raised as to jurisdiction; and it appears from the face of the bill that the case is one arising under the Constitution of the United States involving, as to each plaintiff, a sum in excess of $3,000., since it is alleged that each of plaintiffs would be required to incur expense in excess of that amount if their children should be excluded from the public schools. And it seems clear that there is jurisdiction, irrespective of the amount involved, since the suit is for the protection of rights and privileges guaranteed by the due process clause of the 14th Amendment, and jurisdiction is given by Judicial Code . . . There is, therefore, but one question for our decision, viz.: Whether children who for religious reasons have conscientious scruples against saluting the flag of the country can lawfully be required to salute it. We think that this question must be answered in the negative.

Ordinarily we would feel constrained to follow an unreversed decision of the Supreme Court of the United States, whether we agreed with it or not. It is true that decisions are but evidences of the law and not the law itself; but the decisions of the Supreme Court must be accepted by the lower courts as binding upon them if any orderly administration of justice is to be attained. The developments with respect to the Gobitis case, however, are such that we do not feel that it is incumbent upon us to accept it as binding authority. Of the seven justices now members of the Supreme Court who participated in that decision, four have given public expression to the view that it is unsound, the present Chief Justice in his dissenting opinion rendered therein and three other justices in a special dissenting opinion in *Jones* v. *City of Opelika*, 316 U. S. 584, 62 S Ct. 1231, 1251, 86 L. Ed. 1691. The majority of the court in *Jones* v. *City of Opelika*, moreover, thought it worth while to distinguish the decision in the Gobitis case, instead of relying upon it as supporting authority. Under such circumstances and believing, as we do, that the flag salute here required is violative of religious liberty when required of persons holding the religious views of plaintiffs, we feel that we would be recreant to our duty as judges, if through a blind following of a decision which the Supreme Court itself has thus impaired as an authority, we should deny protection to rights which we regard as among the most sacred of those protected by constitutional guarantees.

There is, of course, nothing improper in requiring a flag salute in the schools. On the contrary, we regard it as a highly desirable ceremony calculated to inspire in the pupils a proper love of country and reverence for its institutions. And, from our point of view, we see nothing in the salute which could reasonably be held a violation of any of the commandments in the Bible or of any of the duties owing by man to his Maker. But this is not the question before us. Admittedly plaintiffs and their children do have conscientious scruples, whether reasonable or not, against saluting the flag, and these scruples are based on religious grounds. If they are required to salute the flag, or are denied rights or privileges which belong to them as citizens because they fail to salute it, they are unquestionably denied that religious freedom which the Constitution guarantees. The right of religious freedom embraces not only the right to worship God according to the dictates of one's conscience, but also the right "to do, or forbear to do, any act, for conscience sake, the doing or forbearing of which, is not prejudicial to the public weal". Chief Justice Gibson in Commonwealth v. Lesher, 17 Serg. & R., Pa., 155.

Courts may decide whether the public welfare is jeopardized by acts done or omitted because of religious belief; but they have nothing to do with determining the reasonableness of the belief. That is necessarily a matter of individual conscience. There is hardly a group of religious people to be found in the world who do not hold to beliefs and regard practices as important which seem utterly foolish and lacking in reason to others equally wise and religious; and for the courts to attempt to distinguish between religious beliefs or practices on the ground that they are reasonable or unreasonable would be for them to embark upon a hopeless undertaking and one which would inevitably result in the end of religious liberty. There is not a religious persecution in history that was not justified in the eyes of those engaging in it on the ground that it was reasonable and right and that the persons whose practices were suppressed were guilty of stubborn folly hurtful to the general welfare. The fathers of this country were familiar with persecution of this character; and one of their chief purposes in leaving friends and kindred and settling here was to establish a nation in which every man might worship God in accordance with the dictates of his own conscience and without interference from those who might not agree with him. The religious freedom guaranteed by the 1st and 14th Amendments means that he shall have the right to do this, whether his belief is reasonable or not, without interference from anyone, so long as his action or refusal to act is not directly harmful to the society of which he forms a part.

This does not mean, of course, that what a man may do or refrain from doing in the name of religious liberty is without limitations. He must render to Caesar the things that are Caesar's as well as to God the things that are God's. He may not refuse to bear arms or pay taxes because of religious scruples, nor may he engage in polygamy or any other practice directly hurtful to the safety, morals, health or general welfare of the community. See cases cited in *Minersville School District* v. *Gobitis*, 3 Cir. 10 F2d. 63, 68. To justify the overriding of religious scruples, however, there must be a clear justification therefor in the necessities of national or community life. Like the right of free speech, it is not to be overborne by the police power, unless its exercise presents a clear and present danger to the community. Cf. *Herndon* v. *Lowry*, 301 U. S. 242, 57 S. Ct. 732, 739, 81,

L. Ed. 1066, where it was said: "The power of a state to abridge freedom of speech and of assembly is the exception rather than the rule and the penalizing even of utterances of a defined character must find its justification in a reasonable apprehension of danger to organized government. The judgment of the Legislature is not unfettered. The limitation upon individual liberty must have appropriate relation to the safety of the state." Religious freedom is no less sacred or important to the future of the Republic than freedom of speech; and if speech tending to the overthrow of the government but not constituting a clear and present danger may not be forbidden because of the guaranty of free speech, it is difficult to see how it can be held that conscientious scruples against giving a flag salute must give way to an educational policy having only indirect relation, at most, to the public safety. Surely, it cannot be that the nation is endangered more by the refusal of school children, for religious reasons, to salute the flag than by the advocacy on the part of grown men of doctrines which tend towards the overthrow of the government.

The suggestion that the courts are precluded by the action of state legislative authorities in deciding when rights of religious freedom must yield to the exercise of the police power would, of course, nullify the constitutional guaranty. It would not be worth the paper it is written on, if no legislature or school board were bound to respect it except in so far as it might accord with the policy they might choose to follow. For the courts to so hold would be for them to abdicate the most important duty which rests on them under the Constitution. The tyranny of majorities over the rights of individuals or helpless minorities has always been recognized as one of the great dangers of popular government. The fathers sought to guard against this danger by writing into the Constitution a bill of rights guaranteeing to every individual certain fundamental liberties, of which he might not be deprived by any exercise whatever of governmental power. This bill of rights is not a mere guide for the exercise of legislative discretion. It is a part of the fundamental law of the land, and is to be enforced as such by the courts. If legislation or regulations of boards conflict with it, they must give way; for the fundamental law is of superior obligation. It is true of freedom of religion, as was said of freedom of speech in Schneider v. State, 308 U. S. 147, 161, 60 S. Ct. 146, 151, 84 L. Ed. 155: "In every case, therefore, where legislative abridgment of the rights is asserted, the courts should be astute to examine the effect of the challenged legislation. Mere legislative preferences or beliefs respecting matters of public convenience may well support regulation directed at other personal activities, but be insufficient to justify such as diminishes the exercise of rights so vital to the maintenance of democratic institutions. And so, as cases arise, the delicate and difficult task falls upon the courts to weigh the circumstances and to appraise the substantiality of the reasons advanced in support of the regulation of the free enjoyment of the rights."

Can it be said by the Court, then, in the exercise of the duty to examine the regulation here in question, that the requirement that school children salute the flag has such direct relation to the safety of the state, that the conscientious objections of plaintiffs must give way to it? Or to phrase the matter differently, must the religious freedom of plaintiffs give way because there is a clear and present danger to the state if these school children do not salute the flag, as they are required to do? It seems to us that to ask these questions is to answer them, and to answer them in the negative. As fine a ceremony as the flag salute is, it can have at most only an indirect influence on the national safety: and no clear and present danger will result to anyone if the children of this sect are allowed to refrain from saluting because of their conscientious scruples, however groundless we may personally think these scruples to be. It certainly cannot strengthen the

Republic, or help the state in any way, to require persons to give a salute which they have conscientious scruples against giving, or to deprive them of an education because they refuse to give it. As was well said by Justice Lehman of New York in his concurring opinion in *People* v. *Sandstrom*, 279 N. Y. 523, 18 N. E. 2d 840, 847: "The salute of the flag is a gesture of love and respect – fine when there is real love and respect back of the gesture. The flag is dishonored by a salute by a child in reluctant and terrified obedience to a command of secular authority which clashes with the dictates of conscience".

The salute to the flag is an expression of the homage of the soul. To force it upon one who has conscientious scruples against giving it, is petty tyranny unworthy of the spirit of this Republic and forbidden, we think, by the fundamental law. This court will not countenance such tyranny but will use the power at its command to see that rights guaranteed by the fundamental law are respected. We are not impressed by the argument that the powers of the School Board are limited by reason of the passage of the joint resolution of June 22, 1942, pertaining to the use and display of the flag; but we are clearly of opinion that the regulation of the Board requiring that school children salute the flag is void in so far as it applies to children having conscientious scruples against giving such salute and that, as to them, its enforcement should be enjoined. Injunctive order will issue accordingly.

Injunction granted.

[On appeal to the U. S. Supreme Court, 319 U. S. 624, the judgment of the three-judge District Court was upheld and *Minersville School District* v. *Gobitis* overruled].

LOCHNER v. NEW YORK

United States Supreme Court. 1904. 198 U. S. 45.

MR. JUSTICE PECKHAM delivered the opinion of the court: The indictment, it will be seen, charges that the plaintiff in error violated the one hundred and tenth section of article 8, chapter 415, of the Laws of 1897, known as the labor law of the State of New York, in that he wrongfully and unlawfully required and permitted an employee working for him to work more than sixty hours in one week. There is nothing in any of the opinions delivered in this case, either in the Supreme Court or the Court of Appeals of the State, which construes the section, in using the word "required," as referring to any physical force being used to obtain the labor of an employee. It is assumed that the word means nothing more than the requirement arising from voluntary contract for such labor in excess of the number of hours specified in the statute. There is no pretense in any of the opinions that the statute was intended to meet a case of involuntary labor in any form. All the opinions assume that there is no real distinction, so far as this question is concerned, between the words "required" and "permitted." The mandate of the statute that "no employee shall be required or permitted to work," is the substantial equivalent of an enactment that "no employee shall contract or agree to work," more than ten hours per day, and as there is no provision for special emergencies the statute is mandatory in all cases. It is not an act merely fixing the number of hours which shall constitute a legal day's work, but an absolute prohibition upon the employer, permitting, under any circumstances, more than ten hours work to be done in his establishment. The employee may desire to earn the extra money, which would arise from his working more than the prescribed time, but this statute forbids the employer from permitting the employee to earn it.

The statute necessarily interferes with the right of contract between the employer and employees, concerning the number of hours in which the latter may labor in the bakery of the employer. The general right to make a contract in relation to his business is part of the liberty of the individual protected by the Fourteenth Amendment of the Federal Constitution. *Allgeyer* v. *Louisiana*, 165 U. S. 578. Under that provision no State can deprive any person of life, liberty or property without due process of law. The right to purchase or to sell labor is part of the liberty protected by this amendment, unless there are circumstances which exclude the right. There are, however, certain powers, existing in the sovereignty of each State in the Union, somewhat vaguely termed police powers, the exact description and limitation of which have not been attempted by the courts. Those powers, broadly stated and without, at present, any attempt at a more specific limitation, relate to the safety, health, morals and general welfare of the public. Both property and liberty are held on such reasonable conditions as may be imposed by the governing power of the State in the exercise of those powers, and with such conditions the Fourteenth Amendment was not designed to interfere. *Mugler* v. *Kansas*, 123 U. S. 623; *In re Kemmler*, 136 U. S. 436; *Crowley v. Christensen*, 137 U. S. 86; *In re Converse*, 137 U. S. 624.

The State, therefore, has power to prevent the individual from making certain kinds of contracts, and in regard to them the Federal Constitution offers no protection. If the contract be one which the State, in the legitimate exercise of its police power, has the right to prohibit, it is not prevented from prohibiting it by the Fourteenth Amendment. Contracts in violation of a statute, either of the Federal or state government, or a contract to let one's property for immoral purposes, or to do any other unlawful act, could obtain no protection from the Federal Constitution, as coming under the liberty of person or of free contract. Therefore, when the State, by its legislature, in the assumed exercise of its police powers, has passed an act which seriously limits the right to labor or the right of contract in regard to their means of livelihood between persons who are *sui juris* (both employer and employee), it becomes of great importance to determine which shall prevail – the right of the individual to labor for such time as he may choose, or the right of the State to prevent the individual from laboring or from entering into any contract to labor, beyond a certain time prescribed by the State. . . .

The question whether this act is valid as a labor law, pure and simple, may be dismissed in a few words. There is no reasonable ground for interfering with the liberty of person or the right of free contract, by determining the hours of labor, in the occupation of a baker. There is no contention that bakers as a class are not equal in intelligence and capacity to men in other trades or manual occupations, or that they are not able to assert their rights and care for themselves without the protecting arm of the State, interfering with their independence of judgment and of action. They are in no sense wards of the State. Viewed in the light of a purely labor law, with no reference whatever to the question of health, we think that a law like the one before us involves neither the safety, the morals nor the welfare of the public, and that the interest of the public is not in the slightest degree affected by such an act. The law must be upheld, if at all, as a law pertaining to the health of the individual engaged in the occupation of a baker. It does not affect any other portion of the public than those who are engaged in that occupation. Clean and wholesome bread does not depend upon whether the baker works but ten hours per day or only sixty hours a week. The limitation of the hours of labor does not come within the police power on that ground.

It is a question of which of two powers or rights shall prevail – the power of the State to legislate or the right of the individual to liberty of person and freedom of contract. The mere assertion that the subject relates though but in a remote degree to the public health does not necessarily render the enactment valid. The act must have a more direct relation, as a means to an end, and the end itself must be appropriate and legitimate, before an act can be held to be valid which interferes with the general right of an individual to be free in his person and in his power to contract in relation to his own labor. . . .

. . . We do not believe in the soundness of the views, which uphold this law. On the contrary, we think that such a law as this, although passed in the assumed exercise of the police power, and as relating to the public health, or the health of the employees named, is not within that power, and is invalid. The act is not, within any fair meaning of the term, a health law, but is an illegal interference with the rights of individuals, both employers and employees, to make contracts regarding labor upon such terms as they may think best, or which they may agree upon with the other parties to such contracts. Statutes of the nature of that under review, limiting the hours in which grown and intelligent men may labor to earn their living, are mere meddlesome interferences with the rights of the individual, and they are not saved from condemnation by the claim that they are passed in the exercise of the police power and upon the subject of the health of the indidual whose rights are interfered with, unless there be some fair ground, reasonable in and of itself, to say that there is material danger to the public health or to the health of the employees, if the hours of labor are not curtailed. If this be not clearly the case the individuals, whose rights are thus made the subject of legislative interference, are under the protection of the Federal Constitution regarding their liberty of contract as well as of person; and the legislature of the State has no power to limit their right as proposed in this statute. All that it could properly do has been done by it with regard to the conduct of bakeries, as provided for in the other sections of the act, above set forth. These several sections provide for the inspection of the premises where the bakery is carried on, with regard to furnishing proper wash-rooms and water-closets, apart from the bake-room, also with regard to providing proper drainage, plumbing and painting; the sections, in addition, provide for the height of the ceiling, the cementing or tiling of floors, where necessary in the opinion of the factory inspector, and for other things of that nature; alterations are also provided for and are to be made where necessary in the opinion of the inspector, in order to comply with the provisions of the statute. These various sections may be wise and valid regulations, and they certainly go to the full extent of providing for the cleanliness and the healthiness, so far as possible, of the quarters in which bakeries are to be conducted. Adding to all these requirements, a prohibition to enter into any contract of labor in a bakery for more than a certain number of hours a week, is, in our judgment, so wholly beside the matter of a proper, reasonable and fair provision, as to run counter to that liberty of person and of free contract provided for for in the Federal Constitution. . . .

It is manifest to us that the limitation of the hours of labor as provided for in this section of the statute under which the indictment was found, and the plaintiff in error convicted, has no such direct relation to and no such substantial effect upon the health of the employee, as to justify us in regarding the section as really a health law. It seems to us that the real object and purpose were simply to regulate the hours of labor between the master and his employees (all being men, *sui juris*), in a private business, not dangerous in any degree to morals or in any real and substantial degree, to the health of the employees. Under such circumstances the freedom of master and employee to contract with each other in relation to their employment, and in defining the same, cannot be prohibited or interfered with, without violating the Federal Constitution. . . .

MR. JUSTICE HOLMES (dissenting): I regret sincerely that I am unable to agree with the judgment in this case, and that I think it my duty to express my dissent.

This case is decided upon an economic theory which a large part of the country does not entertain. If it were a question whether I agreed with that theory, I should desire to study it further and long before making up my mind. But I do not conceive that to be my duty, because I strongly believe that my agreement or disagreement has nothing to do with the right of a majority to embody their opinions in law. It is settled by various decisions of this court that state constitutions and state laws may regulate life in many ways which we as legislators might think as injudicious or if you like as tyrannical as this, and which equally with this interfere with the liberty to contract. Sunday laws and usury laws are ancient examples. A more modern one is the prohibition of lotteries. The liberty of the citizen to do as he likes so long as he does not interfere with the liberty of others to do the same, which has been a shibboleth for some well-known writers, is interfered with by school laws, by the Post Office, by every state or municipal institution which takes his money for purposes thought desirable, whether he likes it or not. The Fourteenth Amendment does not enact Mr. Herbert Spencer's Social Statics. The other day we sustained the Massachusetts vaccination law. *Jacobson* v. *Massachussetts*, 197 U. S. 11. United States and state statutes and decisions cutting down the liberty to contract by way of combination are familiar to this court. *Northern Securities Co.* v. *United States*, 193 U.S. 197. Two years ago we upheld the prohibition of sales of stock on margins or for future delivery in the constitution of California. *Otis* v. *Parker*, 17 US. 606. The decision sustaining an eight hour law for miners is still recent. *Holden* v. *Hardy*, 169 U.S. 366. Some of these laws embody convictions or prejudices which judges are likely to share. Some may not. But a constitution is not intended to embody a particular economic theory, whether of paternalism and the organic relation of the citizen to the State or of *laissez faire*. It is made for people of fundamentally differing views, and the accident of our finding certain opinions natural and familiar or novel and even shocking ought not to conclude our judgment upon the question whether statutes embodying them conflict with the Constitution of the United States.

General propositions do not decide concrete cases. The decision will depend on a judgment or intuition more subtle than any articulate major premise. But I think that the proposition just stated, if it is accepted, will carry us far toward the end. Every opinion tends to become a law. I think that the word liberty in the Fourteenth Amendment is perverted when it is held to prevent the natural outcome of a dominant opinion, unless it can be said that a rational and fair man necessarily would admit that the statute proposed would infringe funamental principles as they have been understood by the traditions of our people and our law. It does not need research to show that no such sweeping condemnation can be passed upon the statute before us. A reasonable man might think it a proper measure on the score of health. Men whom I certainly could not pronounce unreasonable would uphold it as a first instalment of a general regulation of the hours of work. Whether in the latter aspect it would be open to the charge of inequality I think it unnecessary to discuss.

HARLAN, WHITE and DAY J.J. also dissented.

Cf. with the majority opinion the view of Sir George Jessel M. R. in *Printing and Numerical Registering Co.* v. *Sampson* (1875) L. R. 19 Eq. 462, 465: "If there is one thing more than any other which public policy requires, it is that men of full age and competent understanding shall have the utmost liberty of contracting, and that contracts, when entered into freely and voluntarily, shall be enforced by courts of justice."

In *Ives* v. *South Buffalo Ry. Co.* (1911), 201 N. Y. 271, 64 N. E. 431, a New

York court held unconstitutional as depriving the employer of his property without due process of law a section of the Workmen's Compensation Act which imposed absolute liability on certain employers for injuries to workmen independent of negligence or default on the part of the employer.

However, not all decisions reflecting adherence to laissez-faire economic theory are based, even implicitly, on a natural-law theory. Further, even when a majority opinion is scornfully described as a natural-law one by a dissenting judge in the same case, as was the majority opinion in *Adamson* v. *California* (1947) 332 U. S. 46, 69-70 by Black J., the accusation is not always justified, and it might well be contended that Black's dissenting view, that the privilege against self-incrimination is protected against interference by the States by the Fourteenth Amendment, is more truly based on a natural-law theory than the majority view.

A list of State regulatory statutes that have been struck down by the U.S. Supreme Court is given by Black J. in a footnote in the *Adamson* Case (fn. 12, p. 83).

In *Bradwell* v. *Illinois* (1872) 16 Wall. 130, 140 the natural law was invoked to exclude women from the practice of law.

KINTZ v. HARRIGER

Supreme Court of Ohio. 1919. 99 Ohio State 240; 124 N. E. 168

WANAMAKER J. The sole question in this case is whether or not perjured testimony given under oath before a grand jury is privileged, that is, protected by public policy, or whether it may be the basis of a civil action in malicious prosecution. The court of common pleas held it was not privileged. The Court of Appeals held that it was privileged. The case is here as one of public or great general interest. The authorities cited by the Court of Appeals and by counsel for defendant in error in his brief in this case may fairly be said to sustain the judgment of the Court of Appeals. The weight of precedent for a century and more, in both American and English ruling cases, is undoubtedly to this effect.

This question has not heretofore been squarely or directly decided by the Supreme Court of Ohio, and we therefore approach it in the light of fundamental facts and primary principles, rather than upon mere precedent.

Before we ever had an English Magna Charta, or an American Bill of Rights in the form of a Constitution, federal or state, one of the most sacred rights of the citizen was the right to a good name and reputation and to be protected in the enjoyment of that good name and reputation. Our constitutional fathers must have so regarded it or they would not have specially designated it in the organic law of our state.

This primary and precious right solemnly proclaimed in Holy Writ, in the lives and literature of our own people, in our Constitutions and Bills of Rights, is too sacred a thing to be denied or destroyed by a mere "Thus saith the court."

Precedents are valuable for information, admonition, and as milestones in the nation's progress. But they do not necessarily imply the last word of wisdom. They are not always to be adopted. They are quite frequently to be avoided. They are worth exactly what they weigh in right and reason when applied to the particular circumstances of each particular case. They must always have due regard to the natural equities of each special case.

It was an easy step from the dogma, the king can do no wrong, to the corollary, the king's councilor, the king's chancellor, the court can do no wrong. The courts are fallible, though some of us seem fearful of admitting it. The judicial records show that we have reversed not only other courts, but we have reversed even ourselves, and wisely, too; and so it will ever be. The old doctrine that the regular orderly processes of the court cannot be inquired into, though tainted with fraud and perjury, where personal rights are lost or damages sustained, finds little favor in these modern times, when justice is the goal of all good government, judicial no less than legislative or administrative.

It is, to say the least, a singular sort of logic that holds that any ordinary citizen, in any ordinary conversation, by the use of false and malicious slander, wrongs another citizen, for which the latter has a right of action in damages, but that when the wrong-doer, in order to give additional credibility and sanction to his wrong, uses a court of justice as the vehicle for his perjury in the assassination of character, a public policy should intervene to protect him in his wrong-doing and save him from redressing the grievous injury he has committed against his fellow citizen. What do courts mean when they say that a public policy demands the absolute privilege of such testimony?

A correct definition, at once concise and comprehensive, of the words "public policy" has not yet been formulated by our courts. Indeed, the term is as difficult to define with accuracy as the words "fraud," "equity," "welfare." In substance, it may be generally said to be the community common sense and common conscience extended and applied throughout the state to matters of public morals, public health, public safety, public welfare, and the like. It is that general and well-settled public opinion relating to man's plain, palpable duty to his fellow man, that has due regard to all circumstances of each particular situation.

Our written public policies are put into our Constitutions, our statutes, and ordinances, but our unwritten public policies rest largely in judicial judgment and public opinion. Manifestly, when the Constitution of the state declares and defines certain public policies, such public policies must be paramount, though a score of statutes conflict and a multitude of judicial decisions be to the contrary. No General Assembly is above the plain potential provisions of the Constitution, and no court, however sacred or powerful, has the right to declare any public policy that clearly contravenes or nullifies the rights declared in the Constitution. . . . What is the particular policy under whose mask it is sought to invoke the absolute privilege of protection to the perjured witness in this case? It is undoubtedly regard for the ancient doctrine of giving absolute immunity and protection to judicial proceedings in due course of law. . . .

The doctrine as announced from leading cases appears at 25 Cyc. 376, in these words:

"The doctrine of absolute privilege is founded on the principle that in certain cases it is advantageous for the public interest that persons should not be in any way fettered in their statements and is confined to cases where the public service or the due administration of justice requires that a person shall speak his mind freely."

No quarrel can be had with this doctrine when fairly interpreted and applied. If it be manifestly "advantageous for the public interests that persons should not be in any way fettered in their statements," and if "the due administration of justice requires that a person shall speak his mind freely," then it must be conceded that the public right should be paramount to any private right. But surely the word "fettered" here is not to be used in the broad sense that perjured testimony may be offered. Surely the oath that the witness takes before the grand jury, in and of itself, fetters him to the truth. It is only when he violates the obligation of that oath that he commits the wrong. Moreover, "that a person shall speak his mind freely" accords with the doctrine of freedom of speech and freedom of press; but that same constitutional right is qualified by the fact that he shall be responsible for its abuse.

The whole duty of courts is to ascertain the facts, the truth, in any given controversy, and then apply the fundamental principles of justice to that truth, and when by any species of jugglery it is claimed that the courts should announce a public policy that works out the greatest injustice, bottomed upon the grossest untruth, well, it is just such hairsplitting distinctions as these that have to frequently undermined, and justly undermined, public confidence in our courts.

If this prosecution had been started before a magistrate, upon an affidavit falsely, willfully, and maliciously made, including the identical matters testified to before the grand jury, the rule is well settled in Ohio, though it is with regret that I say many states hold to the contrary, that such perjured affidavit can be made the basis of an action in malicious prosecution.

Why then should there be any different rule applied when, instead of doing it publicly before the magistrate, by affidavit, the wrongdoer does it in the secret chambers of the grand jury room, and thereby obtains the sanction of an official action by having the charge found and presented by the grand jury as an official arm of the court?

It surely is a distinction without any difference, except that before the justice of the peace the charge was that of the prosecuting witness alone, whereas by indictment the prosecuting witness wrongfully caused it to be made the official charge of a grand jury in the court of common pleas. True, one qualification has been placed by those courts holding for complete immunity, to wit, as long as such evidence is relevant to the matter concerning which it is given. If irrelevant, therefore, these same courts have held that it may be used as the basis of a suit in damages for malicious prosecution, though given under the cover of a grand jury.

How are these two positions distinguished? Obviously upon the basis that in one the evidence is relevant, and in the other irrelevant. But both do damage, that which is relevant more frequently than that which is irrelevant. Yet how can such a distinction apply to an obvious and admitted falsehood? A falsehood is relevant to nothing. It fits no truth. It does not even fit another falsehood. After all, it is but the "tangled web."

Oaths are too lightly regarded nowadays, not only before the grand jury, but in trial courts; aye, in every place where they are required for some qualification. It is high time indeed for the public to know what the oath implies, the obligation which it carries, and that one may not maliciously assassinate the good name of another under the mask of an oath before a grand jury and then have a court of justice intervene to protect him from such a rank wrong. . . .

Courts have gone a long way in protecting the bona fides of the individual. But where the facts are not only not convincing, but concededly to the contrary, it is inexcusable, especially upon the part of a court, to extend its powers for the protection of such infamy.

The judgment of the Court of Appeals is therefore reversed, and the judgment of the court of common pleas affirmed.

Judgment reversed.

NICHOLS, C. J., and JONES, MATTHAIS, JOHNSON, and DONAHUE, J. J., concur.
ROBINSON, J., not participating.

SODERO v. SODERO

Supreme Court of New York. 1945. 56 N. Y. S. 2d. 823.

WALSH, Justice: Plaintiff seeks a declaratory judgment that plaintiff is the lawful wife of defendant Cesare Sodero, that defendants are not husband and wife, and that an Arkansas decree granting a divorce to defendant Cesare Sodero from plaintiff is invalid. There is practically no dispute about the facts. Plaintiff and defendant Sodero were married in Egypt in 1906. They came to this country in 1907 and have been domiciled in New York State since then. They had five children. In 1921 plaintiff obtained a decree of separation against defendant Sodero on the ground of cruel and inhuman treatment.

At the close of Sodero's professional engagements in and near New York, in June, 1944, he went to Arkansas, and arrived at Hope in that State on June 9, 1944. He testified that he was suffering from a form of arthritis and went there to take mineral baths at Hot Springs, a distance of 40 to 50 miles from Hope. Between June and September he took the full course of 21 baths. While there he learned of the favorable divorce laws and decided to divorce the plaintiff. This knowledge was evidently gained very quickly and the plans made immediately, because after a residence in the State of 61 or 62 days, the minimum being two months, his complaint was prepared and the "warning order" to plaintiff was issued. The final decree of divorce was granted on September 12, 1944, about 95 days after his arrival in Hope, the minimum required residence before decree, under Arkansas statute, being three months. The ground for the absolute divorce was that the parties had not lived together as husband and wife since 1919 (Arkansas statute required three years), and the separation was without any reasonable cause on the part of the plaintiff. . . .

The marriage in question is contrary to the natural law and to the express provisions of New York statute. The court realizes that a discussion of the natural law or a finding under it is not necessary for the determination of this case. However, the point should not be unanswered.

The court assumes that defendants use the term "natural law" in its proper sense. The imperatives of natural law are not the same for the lower animals as they are for man. The moral law as promulgated to man by the light of reason is rightly called the natural law. It was defined by Sophocles and Cicero, Kant, Blackstone and Kent and mentioned in the Declaration of Independence as "the laws of nature and of Nature's God". Cicero, who lived before Christianity was born and did not have the benefit of the Old Testament, gives this excellent summary:

"Right reason is indeed a true law, in accord with nature, diffused among all men, unchangeable, eternal. By its commands it calls men to their duty, by its prohibitions it deters them from vice. * * *
There shall no longer be one law at Rome and another at Athens, nor shall it prescribe one thing to-day and another one tomorrow, but one and the same law, eternal and immutable, shall be prescribed for all nations and all times, and the God who shall prescribe, introduce and promulgate this law shall be the one common Lord and Supreme ruler of all, and whosoever will refuse obedience to Him shall be filled with confusion, as this very act will be a virtual denial of his human nature; and should he escape a present punishment, he shall endure heavy chastisement hereafter." De Republica, Bk. III, Ch. 23.

The natural law was codified in the Ten Commandments. By the natural law, the unity of the matrimonial bond and its indissolubility and permanency are essential properties of conjugal society. Polygamy is opposed to the unity of the bond. When defendant Sodero with one wife in New York married another woman, even in Arkansas, he was then united to more than one person, in violation of the natural law. The natural law is not restricted by State boundaries.

The Arkansas marriage is contrary to the express provisions of New York statute. Domestic Relations Law § 6, provides: "A marriage is absolutely void if contracted by a person whose husband or wife by a former marriage is living." Defendant Sodero did not come within the exceptions of that section. Since his attempted divorce was invalid, he was in no better position to remarry than if he did not have the Arkansas decree. This does not mean that New York State is legislating for Arkansas, but it has the power to legislate and adjudicate for its own citizens and has the obligation to do so for their protection and the general welfare of the family and the home, the preservation of which is vital to the nation.

Judgment for the plaintiff is granted to declare plaintiff is the lawful wife of defendant Cesare Sodero, that the Arkansas decree of divorce is invalid, and that the defendants are not husband and wife. Submit judgment on notice.

In *Texada Mines Ltd.* v. *A.-G. B.C.* (1960) 24 D.L.R. (2d) 81, 86, Locke J., delivering the judgment of the Court, said:

"The true nature of this legislation is not to be determined alone from the language of the statute and, as was done in this Court in the reference *Re Alberta Legislation* . . . and by the Judicial Committee on the appeal . . . where other statutes of the Legislature passed prior to and contemporaneously with the Act dealing with the taxation of banks were considered, statutes such as the *Iron Bounty Act*, the *Taxation Act* and history of each of these statutes and evidence as to the effect of the legislation upon iron mining in the Province may properly be considered in determining what is its true nature."

Held that, when considered in the light of the Iron Bounty Act passed contemporaneously with it and in the light of the history of the matter, the Mineral Property Taxation Act was *ultra vires* as imposing an export tax.

R. v. HESS. (No. 2)

British Columbia Court of Appeal (single judge in Chambers). [1949] 4 D. L. R. 199.

O'HALLORAN J. A.: Irving Hess was convicted in the Vancouver Police Court on October 27, 1949 of possession of narcotic drugs under s. 4(1) (d) of the *Opium and Narcotic Drug Act*, 1929 (Can.), c. 49, and sentenced to 3 years' imprisonment and a fine. His appeal to this Court was allowed on December 22, 1948 (Sidney Smith J. A. Dissenting), his conviction quashed, and a verdict of aquittal directed to be entered [94 Can. C. C. 48]. The formal order for judgment of this Court was entered on Janurary 10, 1949.

Despite the judgement of this Court that entitled Hess to his freedom, the officers of the Crown detained him in custody under s. 1025A [enacted 1938, c. 44, s. 49] of the *Cr. Code*, pending the determination of an appeal by the Attorney-General of the Province to the Supreme Court of Canada, notice whereof I am informed was served on Hess on January 15, 1949. Counsel for Hess made application for bail to the Chief Justice of the Court of Appeal who referred it to me. The application was argued before me on January 19th. On January 20th I granted bail upon the applicant's own recognizance without sureties in the sum of $10 cash, stating that since vital questions in our system of law were involved, I would shortly hand down extended reasons.

Section 1025A reads: "*Except as provided by subsection four of section one thousand and thirteen*, in any case where the Attorney General has a right of appeal from a judgment of aquittal or setting aside of a conviction under this Part *the person* so acquitted or whose conviction is set aside shall, unless the Attorney General shall within the time limited for appeal notify, in writing, the proper officer having custody of such person that he does not intend to appeal, *remain in custody until the expiration of the time limited for such appeal . . . and if an appeal is taken such person shall remain in custody until the determination of such appeal*: *Provided that a judge of the court to which the appeal is taken may*, if it seems fit, on application of such person admit him to bail pending the determination of such appeal *and the time during which such person is so admitted to bail shall not count as part of any term of imprisonment under his sentence.*" . . .

The section tends to flout the authority and jurisdiction of the Courts. The last line of s. 1025A provides that the time a person is out on bail after acquittal shall not count as part of any term of imprisonment "under his sentence". When a conviction is quashed on appeal, the sentence naturally falls with it. How s. 1025A can treat as an existing thing, a sentence which disappeared with the quashing of the conviction, is beyond me. The section is built upon the theory that a conviction or acquittal remains in a state of suspension until an appeal has been determined by a Court of Appeal or the Supreme Court of Canada. That of course is a fundamental fallacy as was pointed out in the bail decision of *R.* v. *Goverluk* . . .

The acquitted man may well ask why he is required to give bail to realize the liberty the Court of Appeal has already given him. If he is detained after acquittal it must be on some charge against him. But there is no charge against the man before me on this application. The highest Court in this Province has said he is not guilty of the very charge upon which he is detained. He may well complain that this is an invasion of his constitutional rights presently mentioned. No argument for his detention upon "state necessity" has been advanced, nor can it be, for it was exploded long ago by Lord Camden L. C. J. in *Entick* v. *Carrington* (1765), 19 St. Tr. 1030 at p. 1073. The whole conception of bail in s. 1025A is unreal. The man is being treated as if he were still guilty of the crime with which he was charged, notwithstanding the Court of Appeal has found him not guilty.

Nor can any comfort be found in the circumstance that some words in s. 1025A may seem to sanction this weird result, and thus make it "technically legal". But the Courts are concerned with the substance and not the form. In *R.* v. *Brixton Prison* (*Governor*) (1916), 86 L.J.K.B. 62 at p. 66 Low J. said: "I do not agree that it is for the Executive to come here and simply say, 'The man is in custody, and therefore the right of the High Court to interfere does not apply, because the custody is at the moment technically legal'."

The learned Judge gave this answer: "I say that that answer of the Crown will not do if this Court is satisfied that what is really in contemplation is the exercise of an abuse of power. The arm of the law would have grown very short, and the power of the Court very feeble, if that were the case."

It is part of the common law of England, that Parliament shall respect the decisions of the Courts. If Parliament may assume the power to set aside a decision of the Court, or interfere with the enforcement of its judgments because it does not like a decision or a judgment then there is really no use for Courts at all in our constitutional sense, for then the people would be saddled with a judiciary whose first law would be to decide a case in accordance with the wishes of the dominant party then in control of the machinery of the State. It would break down the independence of the judiciary and destroy the judicial system Canada and its common law Provinces have inherited.

If Parliament has the constitutional power to direct a Government functionary to detain an acquitted man until the determination of the appeal which a Crown officer may take against such acquittal, it must also have the constitutional power to direct its functionary to detain the acquitted man for a much longer period, in fact to speak in what I hope are significant terms, to detain him at will in a concentration camp. There may be people who think Parliament has that power. I do not; I could not reach that viewpoint without blurring or rubbing out the dividing line between our constitutional democratic system and the totalitarian system in its various forms past and present. My reading of constitutional history convinces me that the dividing line is found in the common law in England which runs in the common law Provinces of Canada.

It may be said there is provision for bail in s. 1025A. But it is discretionary in the Judge. But why should a man have to give bail when he is detained for no offence known to our law. Nor is the bail allowed as of right. And the man might not be able to provide the stipulated bail; it has cost him money to contest his case through two Courts and make final provision for the third Court contest. Furthermore a Parliament which could give the powers of detention contained in s. 1025A, and by consequence the power to confine him at will in a concentration camp, could enact legislation denying bail. It may be said Parliament would not do such a thing, or even if the power existed in a Government functionary, that he would not exercise it. There are many answers, but the one which history prompts is that a Parliament which will flout the decision of the Courts will not stop there, if it finds it expedient to go further to achieve its ends. That is one reason why throughout the centuries the common law Courts have been the guardians of the liberties of the people.

The applicant in this case having been acquitted by the Court of Appeal and entitled to his liberty is arbitrarily detained. He has committed no crime, he is guilty of no offence against the State; but he is detained only at the whim of the Attorney-General. It has been pointed out previously (a) this man was denied bail for 24 days; (b) that tactics of a delaying expensive and obstructive character surrounded his application for bail even after the lapse of 24 days and (c) that he is an acquitted person with no charge laid against him. It is curious how these kind of things repeat themselves periodically in one form or another in constitutional history. Lord Chief Justice Coke and his brother Judges determined to resist the efforts of King James I (1603-1625) to subject persons to arrest and imprisonment by a Court of High Commission without proper trial. . . .

I conclude that the purported powers in s. 1025A to deny an acquitted person bail, to obstruct and delay his application therefor, and to detain him in custody for an offence of which the Court has acquitted him and when there is no offence charged against him are all contrary to the *written* constitution of the United Kingdom, as reflected in *Magna Carta* (1215), the *Petition of Right* (1628), the *Bill of Rights* (1689) and the *Act of Settlement* (1700-1). I conclude further that the opening paragraph of the preamble to the *B.N.A. Act*, 1867, which provided for a "Constitution similar in principle to that of the United Kingdom", thereby adopted the same constitutional principles, and hence s. 1025A is contrary to the Canadian Constitution, and beyond the competence of Parliament or any provincial Legislature to enact so long as our Constitution remains in its present form of a constitutional democracy. (And see O'Halloran J.A., "Inherent Rights" in the Fall, Winter and Spring issues of Osgoode Hall Obiter Dicta, 1947-48.)

I am not primarily concerned with any jurisdiction I may or may not possess to grant bail under s. 1025A. For reasons stated I cannot construe that section to harmonize with the jurisdiction and independence of the Court of which I am a member, and to fit into the pattern of the constitutional framework of Canada. I am concerned with the enforcement of a judgment of this Court which s. 1025A has been invoked to flout. My inherent jurisdiction to make the bail order I did applies equally whether the applicant's detention is purely a civil matter in the sense of s. 92(13) of the *B.N.A. Act*, and outside the operation of the criminal law as (I think it is), or alternatively whether his detention comes within the scope of criminal procedure or the criminal law in the sense of s. 91(27) of the *B.N.A. Act*.

S. 1025A of the Criminal Code was dropped in the 1954 revision.

In *Saumur* v. *City of Quebec & A.-G. Que.*, [1953] 4 D. L. R. 641, where a by-law of the City of Quebec providing that no one might distribute any pamphlet or tract in the city streets without the written permission of the chief of police was held invalid, Kellock J. raised (at 694 and 696), without answering it, the question whether such legislation violating the freedom of religion is *intra vires* even of the Parliament of Canada, and Rand J. said (at 670): "Strictly speaking, civil rights arise from positive law; but freedom of speech, religion and the inviolability of the person, are original freedoms which are at once the necessary attributes and modes of self-expression of human beings and the primary conditions of their community life within a legal order."

In *Switzman* v. *Elbling & A.G. Que.* (1957), 7 D. L. R. 2d 337, 371 Abbott J. said: "Although it is not necessary, of course, to determine this question for the purposes of the present appeal, the Canadian Constitution being declared to be similar in principle to that of the United Kingdom, I am also of opinion that as our Constitutional Act now stands, Parliament itself could not abrogate this right of discussion and debate."

These dicta apart, there is no Canadian authority which puts civil liberties beyond the reach of legislation, as the Bill of Rights does in the United States.

In *A.G. N.S.W.* v. *Trethowan,* [1932] A.C. 526, the Judicial Committee of the Privy Council held that, because of s. 7A of the Constitution Act, which provided that no Bill for abolishing the Legislative Council should be presented to the Governor for His Majesty's assent until it had been approved by a majority of the electors voting in a referendum, two Bills passed in 1930 by both houses of the legislature, one to repeal s. 7A and the other to abolish the Legislative Council, were invalid. See McWhinney, "Trethowan's Case Reconsidered" (1955) 2 *McGill L. J.* 32.

B. READINGS

St. Thomas Aquinas, 1225-1274
Dominican friar and Professor of Theology

TRUTH (DE VERITATE)
(1256-1259)

Question 22, Articles 1 and 5

All things, not only those which have knowledge but also those which are without it, tend to good. To understand this it will help to bear in mind that some of the ancient philosophers taught that well-suited effects in nature come about from the necessity of their prior causes, though the natural causes themselves have not been disposed in that particular way with a view to the suitability of the effects. With this opinion the Philosopher finds fault, because according to it, unless such suitabilities and aptnesses were in some sense intended, they would come about by chance and so would not happen most of the time but only rarely, like other things which we say happen by chance. Hence we must say that all natural things are ordained and disposed to their well-adapted effects.

There are two ways in which a thing may be ordained or directed to something else as its end: (1) by itself, as a man directs himself to the place where he is going; and (2) by something else, as an arrow is aimed at a definite spot by the archer. Nothing can direct itself to an end unless it knows the end, for the one directing must have knowledge of that to which he directs. But even things which do not know the end can be directed to a definite end, as is evident from the arrow.

This can come about in two ways. (1) Sometimes what is directed to an end is merely driven or moved by the one directing it without acquiring from the director any form by which such a direction or inclination belongs to it. Such an inclination, like that by which the arrow is aimed by the archer at a definite target, is violent. (2) Sometimes what is directed or inclined to an end acquires from the director or mover some form by which such an inclination belongs to it. In that case the inclination will be natural, having a natural principle. Thus He who gave heaviness to the stone inclined it to be borne downward naturally. In this way the one who begets them is the mover in regard to heavy and light things, according to the Philosopher.

It is after this fashion that all natural things are inclined to what is suitable for them, having within themselves some principle of their inclination in virtue of which that inclination is natural, so that in a way they go themselves and are not merely led to their due ends. Things moved by violence are only led, because they contribute nothing to the mover. But natural things go to their ends inasmuch as they cooperate with the one inclining and directing them through a principle implanted in them.

What is directed or inclined to something by another is inclined to that which is intended by the one inclining or directing it. The arrow for example, is directed to the same target at which the archer aims. Consequently, since all natural things have been inclined by a certain natural inclination toward their ends by the prime mover, God, that to which everything is naturally inclined must be what is willed or intended by God. But since God can have no end for His will other than Himself and He is the very essence of goodness, all other things must be naturally inclined to good. To desire or have appetency (*appetere*) is nothing else but to strive for something (*ad aliquid petere*), stretching, as it were, toward something which is destined for oneself.

Accordingly, since all things are destined and directed by God to good, and this is done in such a way that in each one is a principle by which it tends of itself to good as if seeking good itself, it is necessary to say that all things naturally tend to good. If all things were inclined to good without having within themselves any principle of inclination, they could be said to be led to good, but not to be tending toward it. But in virtue of an innate principle all things are said to tend to good as if reaching for it of their own accord. For this reason it is said in Wisdom (8:1) that divine wisdom "ordereth all things sweetly" because each one by its own motion tends to that for which it has been divinely destined. . . .

4. When we say that all things tend to good, good is not to be restricted to this or that but to be taken in its generality, because each being naturally tends to a good suitable to itself. If, notwithstanding, the term *good* is limited to some single good, that will be the act of being. Nor is this prevented by the fact that all things have the act of being, because whatever has being desires its continuance and what actually has being in one way has it only potentially in another. Thus air is actually air and potentially fire. And so what actually has being desires to be actually.

[In Article 2 St. Thomas makes the point that "all things naturally tend to God implicitly, but not explicitly." In Article 3 he says that "to tend, though in one way common to all things, is in another way restricted to animals, inasmuch as in them there is found appetite and what moves the appetite," i.e., a power of desiring and a power of knowing. In Article 4 he proves that the rational appetite or will is a power distinct from the sense appetite].

As can be gathered from the words of Augustine, necessity is of two kinds: (1) the necessity of force; and this can by no means apply to the will; and (2) the necessity of natural inclination, as we say that God necessarily lives; and with such necessity the will necessarily wills something.

For an understanding of this it should be noted that among things arranged in an order the first must be included in the second, and in the second must be found not only what belongs to it by its own nature but also what belongs to it according to the nature of the first. Thus it is the lot of man not only to make use of reason, as belongs to him in accordance with his specific difference, *rational*; but also to make use of senses and food, as belong to him in accordance with his genus, *animal* or *living being*. In like manner we see among the senses that the sense of touch is a sort of foundation for the other senses and that in the organ of each sense there is found not only the distinctive characteristic of the sense whose proper organ it is, but also the characteristics of touch. Thus the eye not only senses white and black as the organ of sight, but also as the organ of touch senses heat and cold and is destroyed by an excess in them.

Now nature and the will stand in such an order that the will itself is a nature, because whatever is found in reality is called a nature. There must accordingly be found in the will not only what is proper to the will but also what is proper to nature. It belongs to any created nature, however, to be ordained by God for good, naturally tending to it. Hence even in the will there is a certain natural appetite for the good corresponding to it. And it has, moreover, the tendency to something according to its own determination and not from necessity. This belongs to it inasmuch as it is the will.

Just as there is an ordination of nature to the will, there is, moreover, a parallel ordination of the things which the will naturally wills to those in regard to which it is determined of itself and not by nature. Thus, just as nature is the foundation of will, similarly the object of natural appetite is the principle and foundation of the other objects of appetite. Now among the objects of appetite the end is the foundation and principle of the means to the end, because the latter, being for the sake of the end, are not desired except by reason of the end. Accordingly what the will necessarily wills, determined to it by a natural inclination, is the last end, happiness, and whatever is included in it: to be, knowledge of truth, and the like. But it is determined to other things, not by a natural inclination, but by so disposing itself without any necessity.

Although the will wills the last end by a certain necessary inclination it is nevertheless in no way to be granted that it is forced to will it. For force is nothing else but the infliction of some violence. According to the Philosopher that is violent "whose principle is outside it with the being which suffers the violence contributing nothing." The throwing of a stone upward would be an example, because the stone of itself is not at all inclined to that motion. But seeing that the will is an inclination by the fact of its being an appetite, it cannot happen that the will should will anything without having an inclination to it. Thus it is impossible for the will to will anything by force or violently even though it does will something by a natural inclination. It is therefore evident that the will does not will anything necessarily with the necessity of force, yet it does will something necessarily with the necessity of natural inclination.

SUMMA THEOLOGIAE
(1269-1270)

LAW IN GENERAL (Qu. 90)

(1)[1] Law is a rule or measure of action in virtue of which one is led to perform certain actions and restrained from the performance of others. The term 'law'

[1] These paragraph numbers refer to the article within a question from which the excerpt is taken.

derives [etymologically] from 'binding,' because by it one is bound to a certain course of action. But the rule and measure of human action is reason, which is the first principle of human action: this is clear from what we have said elsewhere. It is reason which directs action to its appropriate end; and this, according to the philosopher, is the first principle of all activity. . . .

Reason has power to move to action from the will, as we have shown already: for reason enjoins all that is necessary to some end, in virtue of the fact that the end is desired. But will, if it is to have the authority of law, must be regulated by reason when it commands. It is in this sense that we should understand the saying that the will of the prince has the power of law.[2] In any other sense the will of the prince becomes an evil rather than law.

(2) Since every part bears the same relation to its whole as the imperfect to the perfect, and since one man is a part of that perfect whole which is the community, it follows that the law must have as its proper object the well-being of the whole community. So the Philosopher, in his definition of what pertains to law, makes mention both of happiness and of political union. He says (*Ethics* V, chap. 1): 'We call that legal and just which makes for and preserves the well-being of the community through common political action': and the perfect community is the city, as is shown in the first book of the *Politics* (chap. 1).

(3) Law, strictly understood, has as its first and principal object the ordering of the common good. But to order affairs to the common good is the task either of the whole community or of some one person who represents it. Thus the promulgation of law is the business either of the whole community or of that political person whose duty is the care of the common good. Here as in every other case it is the one who decrees the end who also decrees the means thereto. . . .

A private person has no authority to compel right living. He may only advise; but if his advice is not accepted he has no power of compulsion. But law, to be effective in promoting right living must have such compelling force; as the Philosopher says (*X Ethics*, chap. 9). But the power of compulsion belongs either to the community as a whole, or to its official representative whose duty it is to inflict penalties, as we shall see later. He alone, therefore, has the right to make laws. . . .

Just as one man is a member of a family, so a household forms part of a city: but a city is a perfect community, as is shown in the first book of the *Politics*. Similarly, as the well-being of one man is not a final end, but is subordinate to the common good, so also the well-being of any household must be subordinate to the interests of the city, which is a perfect community. So the head of a family may make certain rules and regulations, but not such as have, properly speaking, the force of law.

(4) From the foregoing we may gather the correct definition of law. It is nothing else than a rational ordering of things which concern the common good; promulgated by whoever is charged with the care of the community.

THE VARIOUS TYPES OF LAW (Qu. 91.)

(1) *The Eternal Law*

As we have said above, law is nothing else but a certain dictate of the practical reason 'in the prince' who rules a perfect community. It is clear, however, supposing the world to be governed by divine providence as we demonstrated in the First Part, that the whole community of the Universe is governed by the divine

[2] The reference is to the text in the Roman law: *'Quod principi placuit legis habet vigorem.' (Dig.*, I, iv, 1, Ulpianus.)

reason. Thus the rational guidance of created things on the part of God, as the Prince of the universe, has the quality of law. . . . This we can call the eternal law.

(2) *The Natural Law*

Since all things which are subject to divine providence are measured and regulated by the eternal law – as we have already shown – it is clear that all things participate to some degree in the eternal law; in so far as they derive from it certain inclinations to those actions and aims which are proper to them. But of all others, rational creatures are subject to divine providence in a very special way; being themselves made participators in providence itself, in that they control their own actions and the actions of others. So they have a certain share in the divine reason itself, deriving therefrom a natural inclination to such actions and ends as are fitting. This participation in the eternal law by rational creatures is called the natural law. Thus when the Psalmist said (*Psalm* IV, 6): 'Offer up the sacrifice of justice,' he added, as though being asked the question, what is the sacrifice of justice, 'Many say, who sheweth us good things?', and then replied saying: 'The light of Thy countenance, O Lord, is signed upon us.' As though the light of natural reason, by which we discern good from evil, and which is the natural law, were nothing else than the impression of the divine light in us. So it is clear that the natural law is nothing else than the participation of the eternal law in rational creatures.

(3) *Human Law*

Just as in speculative reason we proceed from indemonstrable principles, naturally known, to the conclusions of the various sciences, such conclusions not being innate but arrived at by the use of reason; so also the human reason has to proceed from the precepts of the natural law, as though from certain common and indemonstrable principles, to other more particular dispositions. And such particular dispositions, arrived at by an effort of reason, are called human laws: provided that the other conditions necessary to all law, which we have already noted, are observed. So Cicero says (*De Invent. Rhetor.* II, 53): 'Law springs in its first beginnings from nature: then such standards as are judged to be useful become established by custom: finally reverence and holiness add their sanction to what springs from nature and is established by custom.'

(4) *The Necessity for a Divine Law*

In addition to natural law and to human law there had of necessity to be also a divine law to direct human life: and this for four reasons. In the first place because it is by law that man is directed in his actions with respect to his final end. If, therefore, man were destined to an end which was no more than proportionate to his natural faculties, there would be no need for him to have any directive on the side of reason above the natural law and humanly enacted law which is derived from it. But because man is destined to an end of eternal blessedness, and this exceeds what is proportionate to natural human faculties as we have already shown, it was necessary that he should be directed to this end not merely by natural and human law, but also by a divinely given law. – Secondly: because of the uncertainty of human judgement, particularly in matters that are contingent and specific, it is often the case that very differing judgements are passed by various people on human activities; and from these there proceed different, and even contrary, laws. In order, therefore, that man should know without any doubt what he is to do and what to avoid, it was necessary that his actions should be directed by a divinely given law, which is known to be incapable of error. – Thirdly: because laws are enacted in respect of what is capable of being judged. But the judgement of man cannot reach to the hidden interior actions of the soul, it can only be about external activities which are apparent. Nevertheless, the perfection of virtue requires that a man should be upright in both classes of actions. Human law being thus insufficient to order and regulate interior actions, it was necessary that for this purpose there should also be a divine law. – Fourthly: because, as Augustine says (I *De Lib. Arb.*), human law can neither punish nor even prohibit all that is evilly done. For in trying to prevent all that is evil it would render impossible also much that is good; and thus would impede much that is useful to the common welfare and therefore necessary to human intercourse. In order, therefore, that no evil should go unforbidden and unpunished it was necessary that there should be a divine law which would prohibit all manner of sin.

THE EFFECTS OF LAW (Qu. 92.)

(1) *The Moral Object of Law*

It is clear that the true object of law is to induce those subject to it to seek their own virtue. And since virtue is 'that which makes its possessor good,' it follows that the proper effect of law is the welfare of those for whom it is promulgated: either absolutely or in some certain respect. If the intention of the law-giver is directed to that which is truly good, that is to the common good regulated by divine justice, it will follow that man will, by such a law, be made unconditionally good. If on the other hand the intention of the law-giver is directed, not to that which is absolutely good, but merely to what is useful – in that it is pleasurable to himself or contrary to divine justice – then such a law does not make men good unconditionally, but only in a certain respect; namely, in so far as it has reference to some particular political regime. In this sense good is to be found even in those things which are intrinsically evil: as when a man is termed a good thief, because he is expert in attaining the object he sets before himself. . . .

The goodness of any part is to be considered with reference to the whole of which it forms a part: so Augustine says (III *Confess.*, 8): 'All parts are base which are not fittingly adapted to their whole.' So, all men being a part of the city, they cannot be truly good unless they adapt themselves to the common good. Nor can the whole be well constituted if its parts be not properly adapted to it. So it is impossible for the welfare of the community to be in a healthy state unless the citizens are virtuous: or at least such of them as are called to take up the direction of affairs. It would be sufficient for the common well-being if the rest were virtuous to the extent of obeying the commands of the ruler. So the Philosopher says (III *Polit.*, 2): 'A ruler must have the virtue of a truly upright man: but not every citizen is bound to reach a similar degree of uprightness.'. . .

Tyrannical law, not being according to reason, is not law at all in the true and strict sense, but is rather a perversion of law. It does, however, assume the nature of law to the extent that it provides for the well-being of the citizens. Thus it bears relationship to law in so far as it is the dictate to his subjects of some one in authority; and to the extent that its object is the full obedience of those subjects to the law. For them such obedience is good, not unconditionally, but with respect to the particular regime under which they live.

In the second article of question 92 on the effects of law St. Thomas establishes that the acts of law are command, prohibition, permission and punishment:

"The precepts of law concern human acts, for law directs human acts, as was established above. Now there are three kinds of human acts. For, as stated above, some acts are generically good (viz. acts of virtue), and with respect to them the law orders or commands, for the law orders all acts of virtue (*Ethics*, V, 1). Some acts are generically evil (viz. acts of vice), and with respect to them the law prohibits. Some acts are generically indifferent, and with respect to them the law permits; and all acts that are not wholly good or wholly evil may be said to be indifferent.

"But the means by which law induces obedience is the fear of punishment, and in this respect punishment may be said to be the effect of law."

THE ETERNAL LAW (Qu. 93.)

(1) *Its Derivation from the Divine Wisdom*

Just as in the mind of every artist there already exists the idea of what he will create by his art, so in the mind of every ruler there must already exist an ideal of order with respect to what shall be done by those subject to this rule. And just as the ideal of those things that have yet to be produced by any art is known as the exemplar, or actual art of the things so to be produced, the ideal in the mind of the ruler who governs the actions of those subject to him has the quality of law – provided that the conditions we have already mentioned above are also present. Now God, in His wisdom, is the creator of all things, and may be compared to them as the artist is compared to the product of his art; we have shown in Part I. Moreover he governs all actions and movements of each individual creature, as we also pointed out. So, as the ideal of divine wisdom, in so far as all things are created by it, has the quality of an exemplar or art or idea, so also the ideal of divine wisdom considered as moving all things to their appropriate end has the quality of law. Accordingly, the eternal law is nothing other than the ideal of divine wisdom considered as directing all actions and movements.

(3) *All Law derives ultimately from the Eternal Law*

In every case of ruling we see that the design of government is passed from the head of the government to his subordinate governors; just as the scheme of what shall be done in a city derives from the king to his subordinate ministers by statute; or again, in artistic construction, the plan of what is to be made is passed from the architect to the subordinate operators. Since, then, the eternal law is the plan of government in the supreme governor, all schemes of government in those who direct as subordinates must derive from the eternal law. Consequently, all laws, so far as they accord with right reason, derive from the eternal law. For this reason Augustine says (*I De Lib. Arb.*): "In human law nothing is just or legitimate if it has not been derived by men from the eternal law." . . .

Human law has the quality of law only in so far as it proceeds according to right reason: and in this respect it is clear that it derives from the eternal law. In so far as it deviates from reason it is called an unjust law, and has the quality not of law but of violence. Nevertheless, even an unjust law, to the extent it retains the appearance of law through its relationship to the authority of the lawgiver, derives in this respect from the eternal law. "For all power is from the Lord God" (*Rom.* XII, 1).

THE NATURAL LAW (Qu. 94.)

(2) *Precepts of the Natural Law*

The first part of article 2 is as follows:

"The precepts of natural law are to practical reason as the first principles of demonstrations are to speculative reason: both are self-evident [*per se* known] principles. Now something can be self-evident in two ways – either in itself or in relation to us. A proposition is said to be self-evident in itself when its predicate is contained in the notion of its subject, even though to a person who does not know the definition of the subject it does not appear to be self-evident. For example, the proposition *Man is a rational being* is self-evident in its very nature because to say *man* is to say a *rational being;* and yet to a person who does not know the definition of man, the proposition is not self-evident. And therefore, as Boethius says, certain axioms or propositions are universally self-evident, viz. those propositions whose terms are universally known, as *Every whole is greater than its part*, and *Things equal to one and the same thing are equal to one another.*

"But some propositions are self-evident only to the wise, since they alone know the meaning of the terms. And so to a person who knows that an angel is not a body, it is self-evident that an angel does not have dimensions, but it is not obvious to the unlearned, for they do not understand it."

[Obviously, although he does not state the conclusion here, at least the most general principles of natural law are in the class of universally self-evident propositions. Aquinas admits in article 6 that the *deduced* principles of natural law may by accident be unknown to some men, as a result of faulty reasoning or of mistaken social customs or of personal depravity].

"Now an order is to be found in those things that fall under man's apprehension. For the first thing that he knows is being, since the discernment of being is included in all other knowledge. Therefore the first indemonstrable principle is that one cannot simultaneously affirm and deny, which is based on the notion of being and non-being; and all other principles are founded on this one (Metaph. IV, 9).

"Just as being is the first thing apprehended by speculative reason, so good is the first thing apprehended by practical reason, since practical reason is oriented to action and every agent acts for an end because it appears good to him. Therefore the first principle of practical reason is one founded on the notion of good, viz. that good is what all things seek after. And so the first precept of law is that good is to be done and pursued and evil to be avoided. All other precepts of natural law are based on this one, so that the precepts of natural law are constituted by what is naturally apprehended by practical reason as good or bad for man.

"But since good has the character of an end and evil does not, all those things to which man has a natural inclination are naturally apprehended by reason as good, and consequently to be pursued, and their contraries as evil and to be avoided."

The order of the precepts of the natural law corresponds to the order of our natural inclinations. For there is in man a natural and initial inclination to good which he has in common with all substances; in so far as every substance seeks its own preservation according to its own nature. Corresponding to this inclination, the natural law contains all that makes for the preservaiton of human life, and all that it opposed to its dissolution. Secondly, there is to be found in man a further inclination to certain more specific ends, according to the nature which man shares with other animals. In virtue of this inclination there pertains to the natural law all those instincts 'which nature has taught all animals,' such as sexual relationship, the rearing of off-spring, and the like. Thirdly, there is in man a certain inclination to good, corresponding to his rational nature: and this inclination is proper to man alone. So man has a natural inclination to know the truth about God and to live in society. In this respect there come under the natural law, all actions connected with such inclinations: namely, that a man should avoid ignorance, that he must not give offence to others with whom he must associate and all actions of like nature.

(4) *The Universality of the Natural Law*

As we have just said, all those actions pertain to the natural law to which man has a natural inclination: and among such it is proper to man to seek to act according to reason. Reason, however, proceeds from general principles to matters of detail, as is proved in the *Physics* (Book I, 1). The practical and the speculative reason, however, go about this process in different ways. For the

[1] This is the definition of Ulpian in the *Digest*, I, i, 1.

speculative reason is principally employed about necessary truths, which cannot be otherwise than they are; so that truth is to be found as surely in its particular conclusions as in general principles themselves. But practical reason is employed about contingent matters, into which human actions enter: thus, though there is a certain necessity in its general principles, the further one departs from generality the more is the conclusion open to exception.

So it is clear that as far as the general principles of reason are concerned, whether speculative or practical, there is one standard of truth or rightness for everybody, and that this is equally known by every one. With regard to the particular conclusions of speculative reason, again there is one standard of truth for all; but in this case it is not equally known to all: it is universally true, for instance, that the three interior angles of a triangle equal two right angles; but this conclusion is not known by everybody. When we come to the particular conclusions of the practical reason, however, there is neither the same standard of truth or rightness for every one, nor are these conclusions equally known to all. All people, indeed, realize that it is right and true to act according to reason. And from this principle we may deduce as an immediate conclusion that debts must be repaid. This conclusion holds in the majority of cases. But it could happen in some particular case that it would be injurious, and therefore irrational, to repay a debt; if for instance, the money repaid were used to make war against one's own country. Such exceptions are all the more likely to occur the more we get down to particular cases: take, for instance, the question of repaying a debt together with a certain security, or in some specific way. The more specialized the conditions applied, the greater is the possibility of an exception arising which will make it right to make restitution or not.

So we must conclude that the law of nature, as far as general first principles are concerned, is the same for all as a norm of right conduct and is equally well known to all. But as to more particular cases which are conclusions from such general principles it remains the same for all only in the majority of cases, both as a norm and as to the extent to which it is known. Thus in particular instances it can admit of exceptions: both with regard to rightness, because of certain impediments, (just as in nature the generation and change of bodies is subject to accidents caused by some impediment), and with regard to its knowability. This can happen because reason is, in some persons, depraved by passion or by some evil habit of nature; as Caesar relates in *De Bello Gallico* (VI, 23), of the Germans, that at one time they did not consider robbery to be wrong; though it is obviously against natural law.

(5) *The Immutability of Natural Law*

There are two ways in which natural law may be understood to change. One, in that certain additions are made to it. And in this sense there is no reason why it should not change. Both the divine law and human laws do, in fact, add much to the natural law which is useful to human activity.

Or again the natural law would be understood to change by having something subtracted from it. If, for instance, something ceased to pertain to the natural law which was formerly part of it. In this respect, and as far as first principles are concerned, it is wholly unchangeable. As to secondary precepts, which, as we have said, follow as immediate conclusions from first principles, the natural law again does not change; in the sense that it remains a general rule for the majority of cases that what the natural law prescribes is correct. It may, however, be said to change in some particular case, or in a limited number of examples; because of some special causes which make its observation impossible; as we have already pointed out. . . .

Things may be said to pertain to the natural law for two reasons. First, if there is a natural inclination to them: as, for example, that it is wrong to do injury to one's neighbour. Secondly, if nature does not lead us to do what is contrary. So we might say that man has a natural right to go naked because, nature not having provided him with clothing he has had to fashion it for himself. In this sense the "common possession of all things and the equal liberty of all"[1] can be said to pertain to the natural law. For neither private possession nor servitude were imposed by nature: they are the adoptions of human reason in the interests of human life. And in these cases the natural law is not altered but is added to.

HUMAN LAW. (QU. 95)

(1) *The Necessity for Human Laws.*

From the foregoing it is clear that there is in man a natural aptitude to virtuous action. But men can achieve the perfection of such virtue only by the practice of a 'certain discipline.' – And men who are capable of such discipline without the aid of others are rare indeed. – So we must help one another to achieve that discipline which leads to a virtuous life. There are, indeed, some young men, readily inclined to a life of virtue through a good natural disposition or upbringing, or particularly because of divine help; and for such, paternal guidance and advice are sufficient. But there are others, of evil disposition and prone to vice, who are not easily moved by words. These it is necessary to restrain from wrongdoing by force and by fear. When they are thus prevented from doing evil, a quiet life is assured to the rest of the community; and they are themselves drawn eventually, by force of habit, to do voluntarily what once they did only out of fear, and so to practice virtue. Such discipline which compels under fear of penalty is the discipline of law. Thus the enactment of laws was necessary to the peaceful and virtuous life of men. And the Philosopher says (I *Politics*, 2): 'Man, when he reaches the perfection of virtue is the best of all animals: but if he goes his way without law and justice he becomes the worst of all brutes.' For man, unlike other animals, has the weapon of reason with which to exploit his base desires and cruelty.

The answers to the arguments in this article are of interest:

"Men who are well disposed are led to virtue more properly by admonition than by compulsion, but those who are evilly disposed can be brought to virtue only by compulsion. . . .

"As the Philosopher says (*Rhet.*, I, 1), it is better that all matters be settled by legislation than left to the discretion of judges. There are three reasons for this. First, it is easier to find a few wise men to frame right laws than the many who would be needed to judge rightly in each case. Second, those who make the laws have a long time for consideration, whereas judgment in a case has to be given at once; and it is easier to see what is right by considering many instances than by considering a single one. Third, legislators judge in universal terms and for the future, whereas those who sit on lawsuits judge existing controversies, and their judgment may be affected by love, hate or avarice.

"Since the living justice necessary for the judge is not found in many men, and since it can be perverted, it was necessary, whenever possible, for the law to be settled by legislation and for very few matters to be left to the discretion of men. . . .

"Some particular instances which cannot be covered by the law must necessarily be left to judges, as the Philosopher says in the same place – (*Rhet.*, I, 1) for example, concerning something that has happened or not happened, and the like."

[1] The definition is from St. Isidore of Seville, *Etymologiae*, V, 4.

(2) *The Subordination of Human Laws to the Natural Law.*

Saint Augustine says (I *De Lib. Arbitrio*, 5): "There is no law unless it be just." So the validity of law depends upon its justice. But in human affairs a thing is said to be just when it accords aright with the rule of reason: and, as we have already seen, the first rule of reason is the natural law. Thus all humanly enacted laws are in accord with reason to the extent that they derive from the natural law. And if a human law is at variance in any particular with the natural law, it is no longer legal, but rather a corruption of law.

But it should be noted that there are two ways in which anything may derive from natural law. First, as a conclusion from more general principles. Secondly, as a determination of certain general features. The former is similar to the method of the sciences in which demonstrative conclusions are drawn from first principles. The second way is like to that of the arts in which some common form is determined to a particular instance: as, for example, when an architect, starting from the general idea of a house, then goes on to design the particular plan of this or that house. So, therefore, some derivations are made from the natural law by way of formal conclusion: as the conclusion, "Do no murder," derives from the precept, "Do harm to no man." Other conclusions are arrived at as determinations of particular cases. So the natural law establishes that whoever transgresses shall be punished. But that a man should be punished by a specific penalty is a particular determination of the natural law.

Both types of derivation are to be found in human law. But those which are arrived at in the first way are sanctioned not only by human law, but by the natural law also; while those arrived at by the second method have the validity of human law alone.

(4) *The Divisions of Human Law*

Many elements enter into the notion of human law which may be taken as grounds for its classification. In the first place it is clear from what we have said above that the essential characteristic of human law is that it derived from natural law. From this point of view positive law may be divided into the law of nations (*ius gentium*) and civil law (*ius civile*): and this corresponds to the twofold derivation from natural law which we have already examined. To the law of nations pertain all those conclusions which are directly derived from natural law as immediate conclusions. Such are the norms governing buying and selling and other similar activities which are necessary to social intercourse: these derive from natural law because man is naturally a social animal as the Philosopher proves in the First Book of *Politics* (chapter 1). Those norms which derive from the natural law as particular applications, on the other hand, make up the civil law which any city determines according to its particular requirements.

The second essential characteristic of human law is that it is directed to the common welfare of the city. From this point of view human laws may be divided according to the different offices of those who are specially charged with the common welfare: there are the priests who pray to God for the people; the rulers who govern the community; and the soldiers who fight for its safety. To each of these categories there corresponds a particular code.

The third essential characteristic of human law is that it should be promulgated by the ruler of the civil community, as we have already said. From this point of view human laws may be distinguished according to the different political regimes. One of these, as the Philosopher says in the *Politics* (III, 5), is monarchy, which occurs when the city is governed by one man: to this correspond the "constitutions of princes". Another form of government is aristocracy, that is government by the best and the nobility: to this corresponds the "opinions of the wise" and the "counsels of the senate". Another is oligarchy, or government by the rich and powerful: and to this corresponds the "praetorian law" which is also known as the 'ius honorarium'. Then there is government by the entire people or democracy: and to this corresponds the "plebiscite". Lastly there is the tyrannical regime which is entirely corrupt, and which in consequence has no corresponding law. There is, in addition, another form of mixed government, constituted from all the elements just mentioned, and this is the best form of government. In this, law is enacted according to the definition of Isidore (*Etym.* V, 10): "by the common sanction of nobles and people."

A fourth essential characteristic of law is that it is directive of human actions. From this point of view laws may be distinguished according to their different objects, and are sometimes named according to their authors: so we speak of the "Julian law concerning adultery" and the "Cornelian Law concerning assassination," etc. The reference being not to the author but the matter with which they deal.

THE POWERS OF HUMAN LAW (QU. 96.)

(1) *Its Generality*

Whatever exists in virtue of some end must be proportionate to that end. But the end of law is the common welfare: for, as Isidore says (*Etym.* II, 10): "Laws must be formulated, not in view of some particular interest, but for the general benefit of the citizens." So human laws must be related to the common welfare. But the common well being is made up of many different elements. It is, therefore, necessary that the law should take account of these diverse elements, both with respect to persons and to affairs, and with reference to different times. For the political community is composed of many persons; its welfare entails much varied provision; and such provision is not confined to any one period of time, but should continue through successive generations of citizens: as St. Augustine says in *De Civitate Dei* (XXII, 6).

(2) *Its Limits*

Laws when they are passed should take account of the condition of the men who will be subject to them; for, as Isidore says (*Etym.* II, 10): the law should be "possible both with regard to nature and with regard to the custom of the country." But capacity to act derives from habit, or interior disposition: not everything that is possible to a virtuous man is equally possible to one who lacks the habit of virtue; just as a child is incapable of doing all that a grown man can do. For this reason there is not the same law for children and for adults: there are many things permitted to children which are punished by the law, and even abhorred, in adults. Equally, it is possible to permit many things to those not far advanced in virtue which would not be tolerated in a virtuous man.

Now human law is enacted on behalf of the mass of men, the majority of whom are far from perfect in virtue. For this reason human law does not prohibit every vice from which virtuous men abstain; but only the graver vices from which the majority can abstain; and particularly those vices which are damaging of others, and which, if they were not prohibited, would make it impossible for human society to endure: as murder, theft, and suchlike, which are prohibited by human law.

(3) The object of the different virtues may be considered either with respect to the private benefit of the individual person, or with respect to the general welfare of the community. So, for example, the virtue of fortitude may be exercised by a person either for the protection of the city or in defence of the rights of his

friends: and similarly with respect to the other virtues. Law, however, as we have said, regards the common welfare. So there is no virtue whose practice may not be prescribed by law. At the same time not every act of all virtues is ordered by the law, but only those which may be directed towards the common welfare; either directly, when something is done explicitly for the common benefit; or indirectly, as when, for example, the legislator enacts certain provisions relative to good discipline, which accustom the citizens to respect the common need for justice and peace.

(4) *The Obligation of Human Law*

Laws enacted by men are either just or unjust. If just, they draw from the eternal law, from which they derive, the power to oblige in conscience; as is said in the book of *Proverbs* (VIII, 15): 'By me kings reign, and lawgivers decree just things.' Now laws can be considered just, either with respect to their object, that is when they are directed to the common welfare; or with respect to their author, that is when the law which is enacted does not exceed the powers of him who enacts it; or again with reference to their form, when the burdens they impose upon the citizens are distributed in such proportion as to promote the common welfare. For since every man is part of the community, all that any man is or has, has reference to the community: just as any part belongs, in that which it is, to the whole. For this reason nature is seen to sacrifice a part for the preservation of the whole. In the light of this principle, laws which observe due proportion in the distribution of burdens are just, and oblige in conscience; they are legitimate laws.

Contrariwise, laws may be unjust for two reasons. Firstly, when they are detrimental to human welfare, being contrary to the norms we have just established. Either with respect to their object, as when a ruler enacts laws which are burdensome to his subjects and which do not make for common prosperity, but are designed better to serve his own cupidity and vainglory. Or with respect to their author, if a legislator should enact laws which exceed the powers vested in him. Or, finally with respect to their form, if the burdens, even though they are concerned with the common welfare, are distributed in an inequitable manner throughout the community. Laws of this sort have more in common with violence than with legality: for, as St. Augustine says, in the *De Libro Arbitrio* (I, 5): 'A law which is not just cannot be called a law.' Such laws do not, in consequence, oblige in conscience, except, on occasion, to avoid scandal or disorder. For in this case a man may be bound even to give up his rights, as St. Matthew teaches (V, 40 – 41): 'Whosoever will force thee one mile, go with him other two: and if a man take away thy coat, let go thy cloak also unto him.'

Secondly, laws may be unjust through being contrary to divine goodness: such tyrannical laws enforcing idolatry, or any other action against the divine law. Such laws may under no circumstances be obeyed: for, as it is said (*Acts* V, 29): 'We must obey God rather than man.'

(5) *Its Powers of Compulsion*

Law, as we see from what has been said, has two essential characteristics: the first, that of a rule directive of human action: the second, that of power to compel. So there are two ways in which a man may be subject to the law. Either as that which is ruled is subject to the rule. And, in this respect, all who are subject to a certain power are subject also to the laws which emanate from that power. First, when a person is wholly absolved from such subjection. So the citizens of one city or realm are not bound by the laws of the ruler of another city or realm, just as they do not come under his dominion. Secondly, when persons are subject to a higher law. So for instance, one who is subject to a proconsul must obey his command, but not in those matters in which he is dispensed by the emperor: for in these matters, being subject to higher commands, he is not bound by the orders of a subordinate. In such a case it happens that one who is subject to a certain law in principle, is in certain matters exempt from it, being subject in such matters to a higher law.

The second way in which a man may be said to be subject to the law is as one who is constrained to what constrains him. In this sense virtuous and just men are not subject to the law, but only the wicked. For whatever pertains to constraint and to violence is against the will. But the will of the good is at one with the law, whereas in the bad the will is opposed to the law. So, in this sense, the good are not under the law, but only the bad. . . .

A ruler is said to be above the law[1] with respect to its constraining force: for nobody can be constrained by himself; and law derives its power of constraint only from the power of the ruler. So it is said that the prince is above the law, because if he should act against the law nobody can bring a condemnatory judgment against him. So commenting on the text of *Psalm* L (verse 6) 'To thee only have I sinned' etc., the Gloss explains that 'there is no man who can judge the actions of a king.' – But with respect to the directive power of law, a ruler is voluntarily subject to it, in conformity with what is laid down in the [*Decretals*, I, II, 6]: 'Whoever enacts a law for another should apply the same law to himself. And we have it on the authority of the wise man that you should subject yourself to the same law which you promulgate.' And in the *Codex*, the Emperors, Theodosius and Valentinian, write to the Prefect Volusianus: "It is a saying worthy of the majesty of a ruler, if the prince professes himself bound by the laws: for even our authority depends upon that of the law. And, in fact, the most important thing in government is that power should be subject to laws." The Lord also reproves those who 'say and do not do'; and who 'bind heavy and insupportable burdens for others, but with a finger of their own they will not move them' (*Matthew*, XXIII, 3, 4). So, in the judgment of God a ruler is not free from the directive power of the law; but should voluntarily and without constraint fulful it. – A ruler is above the law also in the sense that he may, if it be expedient, change the law, or dispense from it according to time and to place.

(6) *The Interpretation of Human Laws. Exceptional Cases*

As we have said above, all law is directed to the common well-being of men, and for this reason alone does it obtain the power and validity of law: so to the extent that it falls short of this object it has no power of obligation. So the Jurisconsult[2] says that 'neither justice nor equity permit that what has been usefully established in the interests of men should be made harsh and damaging to the community through too rigid an interpretation.' Now it frequently happens that the observance of a certain rule, though generally useful to the community, is, in certain other cases, extremely damaging. For the legislator, not being able to foresee all particular cases, frames the law to meet what is commonly the case, and with a view to its general usefulness. Consequently, if it should happen that the observance of such a law would be damaging to the general well-being it should not be observed. So, for example, in a city during a state of siege there might be a law ordering that all gates should be kept closed, and such a regulation would, in general, be useful to the common welfare. But if it should happen that the enemy were pursuing some of the citizens on whom the safety of the city depended, it would be a disaster for the city if the gates were not opened to them.

[1] This principle also derives from Roman law: '*Princeps legibus solutus est*' (*Dig.*, I, iii, 31, Ulpianus).

[2] *Dig.*, I, iii, 25 (Modestinus).

In such a case the gates should obviously be opened, against the letter of the law, but for the sake of the common welfare which the legislator intended.

It must, however, be borne in mind, that if the decision on the letter of the law is not a matter of immediate danger which requires prompt action, it is not open to anybody to act as interpreter of what is and what is not in the public interest: such decision belongs rightly to rulers, and it is to meet such cases that they have authority to dispense from the law. When, however, danger is so imminent that there is no time to refer the matter to the authorities, necessity itself carries its own dispensation: for necessity knows no law.

THE MUTABILITY OF HUMAN LAW (Qu. 97.)

(1) *Reasons for Such Mutability*

As we have said above, human law is a certain dictate of reason by which human actions are regulated. From this point of view there can be two causes which justify a changing of human law. The first is on the part of reason: the second on the part of men whose actions are regulated by the law. On the part of reason because it would seem natural for human reason to proceed by stages from the imperfect to the more perfect. So we see in speculative science that those who first began to philosophize arrived at an incomplete system which their successors later elaborated into something more perfect. It is the same also in practical affairs. For those who first set themselves to consider what was useful to the common well-being of man, not being able to solve the entire problem themselves, established certain regulations which were imperfect and deficient in many respects; and these regulations were later modified by their successors to retain those which were the least defective from the point of view of the public interest.

On the part of men, whose actions are regulated by law, changes in law may be justified on account of altered circumstances: for according to the different circumstances in which men are found, different standards obtain. St. Augustine gives an example of this in (I *De Lib. Arbitrio*, 6) "If a people is orderly, serious-minded and jealously observes the public interest, there is justification for a law which confers upon them the faculty of electing their own magistrates for the administration of public affairs. But if that people should gradually become dishonest, and the elections become corrupt, so that the government falls into the hands of dishonourable and vicious men, then it is right that the power of electing to office should be taken from them and that a return should be made to limited suffrage for the few and honest."

(2) *The Limits of Such Mutability*

As has been said, change in human law is justified only to the extent that it benefits the general welfare. Now the very fact of change in the law is, in a certain sense, detrimental to the public welfare. This is because, in the observance of law, custom is of great importance: so much so, that any action which is opposed to general custom, even if itself of little importance, always seems more serious. So when law is changed its coercive power is diminished, to the extent that custom is set aside. Thus human law should never be changed unless the benefits which result to the public interest are such as to compensate for the harm done. This may be the case if the new statutes contain great and manifest advantages; or if there is urgent necessity due to the fact that the old law contains evidence injustice, or its observance is excessively harmful. So the Jurisconsult[1] says that 'in passing new constitutions their utility must be very evident before renouncing those laws which have been regarded as equitable.'

[1] *Dig.*, I, iv, 2 (Ulpianus).

(3) *The Value of Custom*

All law proceeds from the reason and will of a legislator: divine and natural law from the rational will of God; human law from man's will, regulated by reason. Now reason and will in man are manifested in action both by word and by deed: for the test of what one considers good is to be found in the way one acts. Now it is clear that by words, which are the expression of the interior motions and concepts of the human reason, law can be changed and also explained. In the same way law can be changed and explained by means of actions, many times repeated, such a result in custom: and it can thus happen that new customs arise, which have the validity of law; in the sense that such exterior actions, frequently verified, clearly manifest the interior movement of the will and the concept of reason. For whatever is done frequently would seem to result from a deliberate judgement of reason. In this sense custom has the power of law, it may annul law and it may act as the interpreter of law. . . .

The community within which a custom becomes established may be of two conditions. If it is a case of a free community possessing the right to enact its own laws, the consent of the whole community in the observance of a certain custom has more value than the authority of the ruler, whose power to enact laws derives from the fact that he represents the community. In this case it is open to the entire community, though not to single individuals, to establish a law. – If, on the other hand, it is a community which does not enjoy the right to establish its own laws or to abrogate a law emanating from some superior authority, a custom which becomes established in such a community may, nevertheless, attain the status of law if it continues to be tolerated by those whose duty it is to legislate for the community. For, from the fact that it is so tolerated, it follows that the legislator approved what is established by the custom.

THE DIFFERENCE BETWEEN LEGAL AND MORAL OBLIGATION

Law and the Practice of Virtue (Qu. 100, Art. 9.)

As we have shown above, a precept of law has power to compel: thus whatever is obliged by law may be said to fall directly under the precept of law. But the compulsion of law obtains through fear of penalty, as is shown in the tenth book of the *Ethics*; for those matters may be said to come strictly under the precept of law for which a legal penalty is inflicted. Hence divine law differs from human law in the imposition of its penalties. For a legal penalty is inflicted only for those matters about which the law-giver is competent to judge, since the law punishes in view of a judgement passed. Now man, the maker of human law, can pass judgement only upon external actions, because 'man seeth those things that appear,' as we are told in the first book of *Kings*. God alone, the divine Law-giver, is able to judge the inner movements of the will, as the Psalmist says, "The searcher of hearts and reins is God."

In view of this we must conclude that the practice of virtue is in one respect subject both to human and to divine law, while in another respect it is subject to divine but not to human law. Again there is a third sense in which it is affected neither by divine nor by human law. Now the mode of the practice of virtue consists, according to Aristotle (II *Ethics*, 4), in three things. The first of these is that a person should act knowingly. And this is subject to judgement both by divine and by human law. For whatever a man does in ignorance he does accidentally, and in consequence both human and divine law must consider the question of ignorance in judging whether certain matters are punishable or pardonable.

The second point is that a man should act voluntarily, deliberately choosing a particular action for its own sake. This involves a twofold interior action of the will and of intention, and of these we have already spoken above. Divine law alone is competent to judge of these, but not human law. For human law does not punish the man who meditates murder but does not commit it, though divine law does punish him, as we are told by *St. Matthew* (V, 22): "Whosoever is angry with his brother shall be in danger of the judgement."

The third point is that a man should act upon a firm and unchanging principle; and such firmness proceeds strictly from habit, and obtains when a man acts from a rooted habit. In this sense the practice of virtue does not fall under the precept either of divine or of human law for no man is punished for breaking the law, either by God or by man, if he duly honours his parents, though lacking the habit of filial piety.

With regard to the content of natural law, there have been among disciples of St. Thomas two views as to its inclusiveness, views to which Dabin has given the names of "maximalist" and minimalist." The maximalists are those who give the natural law the greatest possible extension. They hold that it includes the whole content of the natural moral order, that is, all propositions that can be rationally deduced from the primal propositions. In order to make such a vast body of propositions logically manageable, they are forced to distinguish "primary," "secondary," "tertiary," and perhaps further kinds of precepts to indicate the extent of the deduction necessary for their derivation. The minimalists, on the other hand, are those who give the natural law the least possible extension. They hold that the natural law includes not all moral precepts which are according to nature but merely those few which are self-evident, and to which the characteristics of universality, immutability, and necessity can be attributed. There are, of course, variations on both of these views. For instance, Maritain, *Man and the State* 85-93 (1951) holds a maximalist view with regard to the ontological element he discerns in natural law and a minimalist view regard to the gnoseological element.

St. Thomas' own usage of the terms "primary" and "secondary" in relation to the precepts of natural law gives some shadow of authenticity to the maximalist position, but despite his occasionally inconsistent use of terms, his own words and the logical implications of his doctrine of natural law make it clear that for him natural law has a minimal extension, and includes only those principles that are self-evident, universal, immutable, and necessary.

With regard to St. Thomas' conception of morality, the important point is that his is not a legalistic morality. The essence of legalism in ethics is the belief that a human act, that is, an act proceeding from reason and will, is not by itself a moral act, but that it becomes a moral act only by conforming to some extrinsic rule or law. The consequences of this view are that the norm of morality is conformity to law; that there can be morality only where there is law; and that since law is conceived of as being imposed on the individual extrinsically, morality is an extrinsicism. Moral rules are rules set by an authority and man must submit himself to them because, if he does not, he will be leading a life wholly lacking in moral worth. This, then, is the legalistic conception of moral life: action in submission to extrinsic rules.

This view of morality is incompatible with that of St. Thomas Aquinas. St. Thomas does not distinguish between a moral act and a human act. A human act is any act proceeding from reason and will. It is reason, therefore, the distinguishing characteristic of the voluntary act, which is the norm of morality. Reason is not for Aquinas, as for the legalists, morally neutral, but is on the contrary the very standard of the moral life. Reason does not need to be dignified by any extrinsic rule in order to become moral. It is rather itself that which dignifies. A reasonable act, by the very fact that it is reasonable, is moral.

In a moral universe such as that posited by Aquinas God is present not as legislator but as creator. Man does not take his moral rules from any extrinsic legislator, not even God. Morality comes from within the person, not from another person, not even if that other person is a divine person. Of course God has created man and his nature and so is in this indirect sense the author of morals. Hence God in a sense imposes morality upon man, but not by legislating it. He imposes it only by, as it were, imposing upon man his nature. God makes man and man makes morality – or rather man finds morality, in his own nature and in other natures.

The effect of morals upon law varies according to the derivation of the legal rules involved. As we have seen, legal rules are derived from natural law through the moral "law" in two ways, by conclusion and by determination. We might cast this difference in derivation into the traditional common law distinction between *mala per se* and *mala prohibita,* but we can also adopt the terminology suggested by Dr. Brendan Brown and refer to these rules as "static" and "dynamic" norms respectively. Static norms are those which are ascertained deductively, whereas dynamic norms are those which are instituted with the aid of induction. The more basic judge-made rules and many constitutional and equitable norms are static or deduced, but by far the greater number of explicit legal rules are dynamic and not logically necessary. However, underlying the dynamic rules in almost every part of law there are unspoken static rules which are implicitly part of law. For example, underlying the law that one who fraudulently and without colour of right takes anything with the intention of depriving the owner of it is guilty of theft and is subject to certain penalties there is the implicit moral judgment that theft is wrong. The fact, therefore, that static rules are in an explicit way such a small part of law is no gauge of their importance, for implicitly they are the basis of all law.

Morals has a substantive effect upon the static norms of positive law and a merely adjectival effect upon the dynamic norms. The static norms, since they can be deduced from the principles of the natural law, fall within natural morality. They are concerned with things good or bad in themselves and are thus necessary conclusions from the principles. Hence the content of the rule as formulated by the science of morals is taken over into law; for the legislator, though he does have the choice – except in the case of moral precepts absolutely necessary for the preservation of society, such as the prohibition of murder – whether to adopt a moral precept or not and make it a static norm, does not have the option of changing the content of the rule, since it is the product of right reason and just as binding on the legislator as on the moralist. Morals, therefore, dictates the very substance of the static norms.

The effect of morals upon dynamic norms is different because these norms govern morally indifferent acts. They operate in a sphere in which institution rather than rationality predominates, though reason is not, of course, excluded. Here the legislator has no obligation regarding the contents of the laws he makes. His sole obligation is to proceed reasonably. This obligation, though single, is not inconsiderable. St. Thomas says that laws must be just in a threefold way: in their end, that is, they must be ordained to the common good; in their author, that is, their making must be within the legislator's power; and in their form, that is, their incidence must be according to a proportional equality established by the common good. To be wholly just, a law must be just in all of these ways. The first requirement is clearly substantive but the second is adjectival and the third has at least a strong adjectival aspect. Thus, though morals affects the substance of the static rules, it affects the dynamic rules only by imposing procedural requirements.

But the relationship of law and morals comprises more than the penetration of morals into law. There is a mutual interpenetration of law and morals. Again the effect depends upon whether static or dynamic legal norms are involved. Static norms cannot affect the natural moral order because they are repetitions of what is already in it, adding merely the authoritative command of the state to the internal commands of reason. Dynamic norms, however, contribute to the contents of morality. They cannot, of course, add to the natural moral order, except accidentally, because the acts which they command or forbid are in themselves morally indifferent. But the totality of morality, morality in the concrete, is more than intrinsic morality. Indeed in the concrete every act is either good or bad: for an act has goodness or badness not only from its object, which determines its species, but also from the circumstances accidental to it, and every act has some circumstance which makes it good or bad, even if it is only the end it intends. Thus, though dynamic legal rules are incapable of adding to the natural moral order, since they are not in themselves either good or bad, they are able to add to the sum total of morality. This is possible because the necessity of a political authority to guide the many to the attainment of the common good of the community is an inescapable conclusion from the natural law principle of seeking the common good, and because this authority, once established, proceeds by instituting rules of conduct which are the most feasible and convenient means to the attainment of the end, the common good; and, once the means have been determined by the superior wisdom of the legislator, the citizens must accept them as *the* ways of achieving the common good, or else the very purpose of the legislator's authority will be frustrated. Thus obedience to the commands of the legislator becomes a moral obligation in the concrete, even though it is not a moral obligation in the abstract because of the absence of a necessary relationship to the natural law. The determination of the ruler, even though merely prudential and contingent, binds the subject in conscience.

Thus there is for St. Thomas a mutual interpenetration of law and morals. Some moral obligations are also legal obligations (static norms), and all legal obligations are moral obligations, either primarily and necessarily (static norms) or secondarily and prudentially (dynamic norms). In fact, St. Thomas even goes so far as to say that legislative determinations which are unjust (and therefore, by his definition, not law at all) may sometimes be binding in conscience for prudential reasons, that is, in order to avoid the greater evils of scandal and disturbance.

On St. Thomas generally see MacGuigan, "St. Thomas and Legal Obligation" (1961) 35 New Scholasticism 281 (and see also the criticism of the article by Stevens, "Moral Obligation in St. Thomas" (1962) 40 *Mod. Schlmn.*; "Positive Law and the Moral Law" (1961) 2 *Current Law and Social Problems* 89; "The Liberalism of St. Thomas" (1962) 4 *Crosslight* 36; and "Civil Disobedience and Natural Law" (1964) 52 *Ky. L.J.* 346; Davitt, "Law as Means to End – Thomas Aquinas" (1961) 14 *Vand. L. Rev* 65; and "St. Thomas Aquinas and the Natural Law" in *Origins of the Natural Law* 26 (Harding ed. 1954).

Christopher Saint Germain, 1460 (?)-1540
Lawyer

THE DOCTOR AND STUDENT: DIALOGUES BETWEEN A DOCTOR OF DIVINITY AND A STUDENT IN THE LAWS OF ENGLAND. (1518)

A Doctor of divinity, that was of great acquaintance and familiarity with a student in the laws of England, said thus unto him: I have had a great desire of long time to know whereupon the law of England is grounded; but because the most part of the law of England is written in the French tongue, therefore I cannot, through mine own study, attain to the knowledge thereof; for in that tongue I am nothing expert. And because I have found thee a faithful friend to me in all my business, therefore I am bold to come to thee before any other, to know thy mind, what be the very grounds of the law of England, as thou thinkest.

Stud. That would ask a great leisure, and it is also above my cunning to do it: nevertheless, that thou shalt not think that I would wilfully refuse to fulfil thy desire, I shall with good will do that in me is to satisfy thy mind. But I pray thee that thou wilt first shew me somewhat of other laws that pertain most to this matter, and that doctors treat of, how laws have been begun; and then I will gladly shew thee, as methinketh, what be the grounds of the law of England.

Doct. I will with good will do as thou sayest. Wherefore thou shalt understand that doctors treat of four laws, the which (as me seemeth) pertain most to this matter. The first is the *law eternal.* The second is the *law of nature* of reasonable creatures, the which, as I have heard say, is called by them that be learned in the law of England, the *law of reason.* The third is the *law of God.* The fourth is the *law of man.* And therefore I will first treat of the *law eternal.*

Dialogue 1

CHAPTER 1: Of the law eternal

Like as there is in every artificer a reason of such like things as are to be made by his craft: so likewise it behoveth that in every governor there be reason and a foresight in the governing of such things as shall be orderd and done by him to them that he hath the governance of. And forasmuch as Almighty God is the creator and maker of all creatures, to which he is compared as a workman to his works, and is also the governor of all deeds and movings that be found in any creature: therefore as the reason of the wisdom of God (inasmuch as creatures be created by him) is the reason and foresight of all crafts and works that have been or shall be; so the reason of the wisdom of God, moving all things by wisdom made to a good end, obtaineth the name and reason of a law, and that is called the law eternal.

And this law eternal is called the first law: and it is well called the first, for it was before all other laws, and all other laws be derived of it. Whereupon St. Augustine saith, in his first book of *free arbitrement*, that in *temporal laws nothing is righteous ne lawful, but that the people have derived to them out of the law eternal.* Wherefore every man hath right and title to have that he hath righteously, and of right wise judgment of the first reason, which is the law eternal.

Stud. But how may this law eternal be known? For, as the apostle writeth in the second chapter of his first epistle to the Corinthians, *quae sunt Dei nemo scit, nisi Spiritus Dei*; that is to say, no man knoweth what is in God but the Spririt of God; wherefore it seemeth that he openeth his mouth against heaven, that attempteth to know it.

Doct. This law eternal no man may know, as it is in itself, but only blessed souls that see God face to face. But Almighty God of his goodness sheweth of it as much to his creatures as is necessary for them, for else God should bind his creatures to a thing impossible; which may in no wise be thought in him. Therefore it is to be understood that three manner of ways Almighty God maketh this law eternal know to his creatures reasonable. *First*, by the light of natural reason; *secondly*, by heavenly revelation; *thirdly*, by the order of a prince, or any other secondary governor that hath power to bind his subjects to a law.

And when the law eternal or the will of God is known to his creatures reasonable by the light of natural understanding, or by the light of natural reason, that is called the *law of reason*: and when it is shewed by heavenly revelation in such manner as hereafter shall appear, then it is called the *law of God*: and when it is shewed unto him by the order of a prince, or of any other secondary governor that hath a power to set a law upon his subjects, then it is called the *law of man*, though originally it be made of God. For laws made by man that hath received thereto power of God, be made by God. Therefore the said three laws, that is to say the law of reason, the law of God, and the law of man, the which hath several names after the manner as they be shewed to a man, be called in God one law eternal. . . .

Chapter II:
Of the law of reason, the which by doctors is called the law of nature of reasonable creatures

First it is to be understood, that the *law of nature* may be considered in two manners, that is to say, generally and specially. When it is considered generally, then it is referred to all creatures, as well reasonable as unreasonable: for all unreasonable creatures live under a certain rule to them given by nature, necessary to them for the conservation of their being. But of this law it is not our intent to treat at this time. The law of nature specially considered, which is also called the *law of reason*, pertaineth only to creatures reasonable, that is, man, which is created to the image of God.

And this law ought to be kept as well among Jews and Gentiles, as among christian men: and this law is always good and righteous, stirring and inclining a man to good, and abhorring evil. And as to the ordering of the deeds of man, it is preferred before the law of God, and it is written in the heart of every man, teaching him what is to be done, and what is to be fled; and because it is written in the heart, therefore it may not be put away, ne it is never changeable by no diversity of place, ne time: and therefore against this law, prescription, statute nor custom may not prevail: and if any be brought in against it, they be not prescriptions, statutes or customs, but things void and against justice. And all other laws, as well the laws of God as to the acts of men, as other, be grounded thereupon.

Stud. Sith the law of reason is written in the heart of every man, as thou hast said before, teaching him what is to be done, and what is to be fled, and the which thou sayest may never be put out of the heart, what needeth it then to have any other law brought in to order the acts and deeds of the people?

Doct. Though the law of reason may not be changed, nor wholly put away; nevertheless, before the law written, it was greatly lett and blinded by evil customs, and by many sins of the people, beside our original sin; insomuch that it might hardly be discerned what was righteous, and what was unrighteous, and what was good, and what evil. Wherefore it was necessary, for the good order of the people, to have many things added to the law of reason, as well by the church as by secular princes, according to the manners of the country and of the people where such additions should be exercised. And this law of reason differeth from the law of God in two manners. For the law of God is given by the revelation of God; and this law is given by a natural light of understanding. And also the law of God ordereth a man of itself, by a nigh way, to the felicity that ever shall endure; and the law of reason ordereth a man to the felicity of this life.

Stud. But what be the things that the law of reason teaches to be done, and what to be fled? I pray thee shew me.

Doct. The law of reason teacheth, that good is to be loved, and evil is to be fled: also that thou shalt do to another, that thou wouldest another should do unto thee; and that we may do nothing against truth; and that a man must live peacefully with others; that justice is to be done to every man; and also that wrong is not to be done to any man; and that also a trespasser is worthy to be punished; and such other. Of the which follow divers other secondary commandments, the which be as necessary conclusions derived of the first. As of that commandment, that good is to be beloved; it followeth, that a man should love his benefactor: for a benefactor, in that he is a benefactor, includeth in him a reason of goodness, for else he ought not to be called a benefactor; that is to say, a good doer, but an evil doer: and so in that he is a benefactor, he is to be beloved in all times and in all places. And this law also suffereth many things to be done: as that it is lawful to put away force with force; and that it is lawful for every man to defend himself and his goods against an unlawful power. And this law runneth with every man's law, and also with the law of God, as to the deeds of man, and must be always kept and observed, and shall always declare what ought to follow upon the general rules of the law of man, and shall restrain them if they be anything contrary unto it.

And here it is to be understood, that after some men, the law whereby all things were in common, was never of the law of reason, but only in the time of extreme necessity. For they say, that the law of reason may not be changed; but they say, it is evident, that the law whereby all things should be in common, is changed: wherefore they conclude, that was never the law of reason.

Chapter IV: Of the law of man.

The *law of man* (the which sometime is called the *law positive*) is derived by reason, as a thing which is necessary, and probably following of the law of reason and of the law of God. And that is called *probable*, in that it appeareth to many, and especially to wise men to be true. And therefore in every law positive well made, is somewhat of the law of reason, and of the law of God; and to discern the law of God and the law of reason from the law positive is very hard. And though it be hard, yet it is much necessary in every moral doctrine, and in all laws made for the commonwealth. And that the law of man be just and rightwise, two things be necessary, and that is to say, wisdom and authority. Wisdom that he may judge after reason what is to be done for the commonalty, and what is expedient for a peaceable conservation and necessary sustentation of them; authority, that he have authority to make laws. For the law is derived of *ligare*, that is to say, to bind. But the sentence of a wise man doth not bind the commonalty, if he have no rule over them. Also to every good law be required these properties: that is to say, that it be honest, rightwise, possible in itself, and after the custom of the country, convenient for the place and time, necessary, profitable, and also manifest, that it be not captious by any dark sentences, ne mixt with any private wealth, but all made for the commonwealth. And after St. Bridget, in the fourth book, in the hundred and twenty-ninth chapter, every good law is ordained to the health of the Soul, and to the fulfilling of the laws of God, and to induce the people to fly evil desires, and to do good works. Also the cardinal of Camerer writeth, Whatsoever is righteous in the law of man, is righteous in the law of God. For every man's law must be consonant to the law of God. And therefore the laws of princes, the commandments of prelates, the statutes of commonalties, ne yet the ordinance of the church, is not righteous nor obligatory, but it be consonant to the law of God.

And of such a law of man that is consonant to the law of God, it appeareth who hath right to lands and goods and who not: for whatsoever a man hath by such laws of man, he hath righteously; and whatsoever he hath against such laws, is unrighteously had.

For laws of man not contrary to the law of God, nor to the law of reason, must be observed in the law of the soul: and he that despiseth them, despiseth God, and resisteth God. And furthermore, as Gratian saith, because evil men fear to offend, for fear of pain; therefore it was necessary that divers pains should be ordained for divers offences, as physicians ordained divers remedies for several diseases. And such pains be ordained by the makers of laws, after the necessity of the time, and after the disposition of the people. And though that law that ordained such pains hath thereby a conformity to the law of God, (for the law of God commandeth that the people shall take away evil from among themselves;) yet they belong not so much to the law of God, but that other pains (standing the first principles) might be ordained and appointed therefore. That is the law that is called most properly the *law positive*, and the *law of man.*

And the philosopher said in the third book of his *ethics*, that *the intent of a maker of a law is to make the people good, and to bring them to virtue.* And although I have somewhat in general shewed thee whereupon the law of England is grounded (for necessity it must be grounded of the said laws, that is to say, of the law eternal, of the law of reason, and of the law of God:) nevertheless I pray thee shew me more specially whereupon it is grounded, as thou thinkest, as thou before has promised to do.

Stud. I will with good-will do therein that lieth in me, for thou hast shewed me a right, plain, and straight way thereto. Therefore thou shalt understand that the law of England is grounded upon six principal grounds. *First*, It is grounded on the *law of reason. Secondly*, On the *law of God. Thirdly,* On divers general *customs of the realm. Fourthly*, On divers *principles* that be called *maxims. Fifthly*, On divers *particular customs. Sixthly*, On divers *statutes* made in parliaments by the king, and by the common council of the realm. On which grounds I shall speak in order as they be rehearsed before. And first of the *law of reason.*

Chapter V: Of the first ground of the law of England

The first ground of the law of England is the *law of reason*, whereof thou hast treated before in the second chapter, the which is kept in this realm, as it is in all other realms, and as of necessity it must needs be, (as thou hast said before.)

Doct. But I would know what is called the *law of nature* after the laws of England.

Stud. It is not used among them that be learned in the laws of England to reason what thing is commanded or prohibited by the law of nature, and what not, but all the reasoning in that behalf is under this manner. As when any thing is grounded upon the law of nature, they say, that reason will that such a thing be done; and if it be prohibited by the law of nature, they say it is against reason, or that reason will not suffer that to be done.

Doct. Then I pray thee shew me what they that be learned in the laws of the realm hold to be commanded or prohibited by the law of nature, under such terms, and after such manner, as is used among them that be learned in the said laws.

Stud. There be put by them that be learned in the laws of England two degrees of the law of reason, that is to say, the law of reason *primary*, and the law of reason *secondary.* By the law of reason *primary* be prohibited in the laws of England murder (that is, the death of him that is innocent), perjury, deceit, breaking of the peace, and many other like. And by the same law also it is lawful for a man to defend himself against an unjust power, so he keep due circumstance. And also if any promise be made by menace to the body, it is by the law of reason void in the laws of England. The other is called the law of *secondary* reason, the which is divided into two branches, that is to say, into a law of secondary reason *general*, and into a law of secondary reason *particular.* The law of a secondary reason *general* is grounded and derived of the general law, or general custom of property, whereby goods moveable and immoveable be brought into a certain property, so that every man may know his own thing. And by this branch be prohibited in the laws of England disseisins, trespass in lands and goods, rescuss, theft, unlawful with-holdings of another man's goods, and such other. And by the same law it is a ground in the law of England that satisfaction must be made for a trespass, and that restitution must be made of such goods as one man hath that belong to another man; the debts must be paid, covenants fulfilled, and such other. And because disseisins, trespass in lands and goods, theft, and other had not been known, if the law of property had not been ordained; therefore all things that be derived by reason out of the said law of property, be called *the law of reason secondary general*, for the law of property is generally kept in all countries.

The law of reason *secondary particular* is the law that is derived of divers customs general and particular, and of divers maxims and statutes ordained in this realm. And it is called *the law of reason secondary particular*, because the reason in that case is derived of such a law that is only holden for the law in this realm, and in none other realm.

Doct. I pray thee shew me some special case of such a law of reason secondary particular, for an example.

Stud. There is a law in England, which is a law of custom, that if a man take a distress lawfully, that he shall put it in pound overt, there to remain till he be satisfied of that he distrained for. And then thereupon may be asked this question, that if the beasts die in pound for lack of meat, at whose peril die they? whether die they at the peril of him that distrained, or of him that oweth the beasts?

Doct. If the law be as thou sayest, and that a man for a just cause taketh a distress, and putteth it in the pound overt, and no law compelleth him that distrained to give them meat, then it seemeth of reason that if the distress die in pound for lack of meat, that it died at the peril of him that oweth the beasts, and not of him that distrained; for in him that distrained there can be assigned no default, but in the other may be assigned a default, because the rent was unpaid.

Stud. Thou hast given a true judgment, and who hath taught thee to do so but reason derived of the said general custom? And the law is so full of such secondary reasons derived out of the general customs and maxims of the realm, that some men have affirmed that all the law of the realm is the law of reason. But that cannot be proved, as me seemeth, as I have partly shewed before, and more fully will shew after. And it is not much used in the laws of England, to reason what law is grounded upon the law of the first reason primary, or on the law of reason secondary, for they be most commonly openly known of themselves; but for the knowledge of the law of reason secondary is greater difficulty, and therefore therein dependeth much the manner and form of arguments in the laws of England.

And it is to be noted, that all the deriving of reason in the law of England proceedeth of the first principles of the law, or of something that is derived of them: and therefore no man may right wisely judge, no groundly reason in the laws of England, if he be ignorant in the first principles. Also all birds, fowls, wild beasts of forest and warren, and such other, be excepted by the laws of England out of the said general law and custom of property: for by the laws of the realm no property may be of them in any person, unless they be tame. Nevertheless the eggs of hawk, herons, or such other as build in the ground of any person, be adjudged by the said laws to belong to him that oweth the ground.

Chapter XVI: *What is equity?*

Doct. Equity is a right wiseness that considereth all the particular circumstances of the deed, the which also is tempered with the sweetness of mercy. And such an equity must always be observed in every law of man, and in every general rule thereof: and that knew he well that said thus, *Laws covet to be ruled by equity.* And the wise man saith, *Be not overmuch right wise*; *for extreme right wiseness is extreme wrong*: as who saith, If thou take all that the words of the law giveth thee thou shalt sometime do against the law. And for the plainer declaration what equity is, thou shalt understand, that sith the deeds and acts of men, for which laws have been ordained, happen in divers manners infinitely, it is not possible to make any general rule of the law, but that it shall fail in some case: and therefore makers of law take heed to such things as may often come and not to every particular case, for they could not though they would. And therefore, to follow the words of the law were in some case both against justice and the commonwealth. Wherefore in some cases it is necessary to love the words of the law, and to follow that reason and justice requireth, and to that intent equity is ordained; that is to say, to temper and mitigate the rigour of the law. And it is called also by some men *epieikeia*: the which is no other thing but an exception of the law of God, or the law of reason, from the general rules of the law of men, when they by reason of their generality, would in any particular case judge against the law of God or the law of reason: the which exception is secretly understood in every general rule of every positive law. And so it appeareth, that equity taketh not away the very right, but only that that seemeth to be right by the general words of the law. Nor it is not ordained against the cruelness of the law, for the law in such case generally taken is good in himself; but equity followeth the law in all particular cases where right and justice requireth, notwithstanding the general rule of the law be to the contrary. Wherefore it appeareth, that if law were made by man without any such exception expressed or implied, it were manifestly unreasonable, and were not to be suffered: for such causes might come, that he that would observe the law should break both the law of God and the law of reason. As if a man make a vow that he will never eat white-meat, and after it happeneth him to come there where he can get no other meat: in this case it behoveth him to break his avow, by his equity or *epieikeia*, as it is said before. Also if a law were made in a city, that no man under the pain of death should open the gates of the city before the sun-rising; yet if the citizens before that hour flying from their enemies, come to the gates of the city, and one for saving of the citizens openeth the gates before the hour appointed by the law, he offendeth not the law, for that case is excepted from the said general law by equity, as is said before. And so it appeareth that equity rather followeth the intent of the law, than the words of the law. And I suppose that there be in like wise some like equities grounded on the general rules of the law of the realm. . . .

The legal theory of the Anglican churchman Richard Hooker is very close to that of Aquinas and St. Germain. In his *Of the Laws of Ecclesiastical Polity* his general description of law is that it is "any kind of rule or canon, whereby actions are framed" (I, c. 3), and further on (I, c. 10) he writes: "Now as the learned in the laws of this land observe, that our statutes sometimes are only the affirmation or ratification of that which common law was held before; so here it is not to be omitted that generally all laws human, which are made for the ordering of political societies, be either such as establish some duty whereunto all men by the law of reason did before stand bound; or else such as make that a duty now which before was none. The one sort we may for distinction's sake call 'mixedly,' and the other 'merely' human. . . . Which law in this case we termed *mixed,* because the matter whereunto it bindeth is the same which reason necessarily doth require at our hands, and from the Law of Reason it differeth in the manner of binding only. For whereas men before stood bound in conscience to do as the Law of Reason teacheth, they are now by virtue of human law become constrainable, and if they outwardly transgress, punishable. As for laws which are *merely* human, the matter of them is any thing which reason doth but probably teach to be fit and convenient; so that till such time as law hath passed amongst men about it, of itself it bindeth no man."

Coke, too, indicated some adherence to the same theory when he wrote (*Institutes, Commentary on Littleton, First Institute,* s. 138) that "Reason is the life of the law; nay the Common Law itself is nothing else but reason."

Sir William Blackstone, 1723-1780
First Vinerian Professor of Law, Oxford University

COMMENTARIES ON THE LAWS OF ENGLAND (1765)

Law, in its most general and comprehensive sense, signifies a rule of action; and is applied indiscriminately to all kinds of action, whether animate or inanimate, rational or irrational. Thus we say, the laws of motion, of gravitation, of optics, or mechanics, as well as the laws of nature and of nations. And it is that rule of action which is prescribed by some superior, and which the inferior is bound to obey.

Thus, when the supreme Being formed the universe, and created matter out of nothing, he impressed certain principles upon that matter, from which it can never depart, and without which it would cease to be. When he put that matter into motion, he established certain laws of motion, to which all movable bodies must conform. And, to descend from the greatest operations to the smallest, when a workman forms a clock, or other piece of mechanism, he establishes, at his own pleasure, certain arbitrary laws for its direction, – as that the hand shall describe a given space in a given time, to which law as long as the work conforms, so long it continues in perfection, and answers the end of its formation.

If we farther advance, from mere inactive matter to vegetable and animal life, we shall find them still governed by laws, more numerous indeed, but equally fixed and invariable. The whole progress of plants, from the seed to the root, and from thence to the seed again; the method of animal nutrition, digestion, secretion, and all other branches of vital economy; are not left to chance, or the will of the creature itself, but are performed in a wondrous involuntary manner, and guided by unerring rules laid down by the great Creator.

This, then, is the general signification of law, a rule of action dictated by some superior being; and, in those creatures that have neither the power to think, nor to will, such laws must be invariably obeyed, so long as the creature itself subsists, for its existence depends on that obedience. But laws, in their more confined sense, and in which it is our present business to consider them, denote the rules, not of action in general, but of *human* action or conduct; that is, the precepts by which man, the noblest of all sublunary beings, a creature endowed with both reason and free-will, is commanded to make use of those facilities in the general regulation of his behaviour.

Man considered as a creature, must necessarily be subject to the laws of his Creator, for he is entirely a dependent being. A being, independent of any other, has no rule to pursue, but such as he prescribes to himself; but a state of dependence will inevitably oblige the inferior to take the will of him on whom he depends as the rule of his conduct; not, indeed, in every particular, but in all those points wherein his dependence consists. This principle, therefore, has more or less extent and effect, in proportion as the superiority of the one and the dependence of the other is greater or less, absolute or limited. And consequently, as man depends absolutely upon his Maker for everything, it is necessary that he should, in all points, conform to his Maker's will.

This will of his Maker's is called the law of nature. For as God, when He created matter, and endued it with a principle of mobility, established certain rules for the perpetual direction of that motion, so, when he created man, and endued him with free-will to conduct himself in all parts of life, he laid down certain immutable laws of human nature, whereby that free-will is in some degree regulated and restrained, and gave him also the faculty of reason to discover the purport of those laws.

Considering the Creator only as a being of infinite *power*, he was able unquestionably to have prescribed whatever laws he pleased to His creature, man, however unjust or severe. But, as he is also a being of infinite *wisdom*, he has laid down only such laws as were founded in those relations of justice that existed in the nature of things antecedent to any positive precept. These are the eternal immutable laws of good and evil, to which the Creator himself, in all his dispensations, conforms; and which he has enabled human reason to discover, so far as they are necessary for the conduct of human actions. Such, among others, are these principles: that we should live honestly, should hurt nobody, and should render to every one his due; to which three general precepts Justinian has reduced the whole doctrine of law.

But if the discovery of these first principles of the law of nature depended only upon the due exertion of right reason, and could not otherwise be obtained than by a chain of metaphysical disquisitions, mankind would have wanted some inducement to have quickened their inquiries, and the greater part of the world would have rested content in mental indolence, and ignorance of its inseparable companion. As, therefore, the Creator is a being not only of infinite *power*, and *wisdom*, but also of infinite *goodness*, he has been pleased so to contrive the constitution and frame of humanity, that we should want no other prompter to inquire after and pursue the rule of right, but only our own self-love, that universal principle of action. For he has so intimately connected, so inseparably interwoven the laws of eternal justice with the happiness of each individucal, that the latter cannot be attained but by observing the former; and, if the former be punctually obeyed, it cannot but induce the latter. In consequence of which mutual connection of justice and human felicity, he has not perplexed the law of nature with a multitude of abstracted rules and precepts, referring merely to the fitness or unfitness of things, as some have vainly surmised, but has graciously reduced the rule of obedience to this one paternal precept, "that man should pursue his own true and substantial happiness." This is the foundation of what we call ethics, or natural law; for the several articles into which it is branched in our systems, amount to no more than demonstrating that this or that action tends to man's real happiness, and therefore very justly concluding that the performance of it is part of the law of nature; or, on the other hand, that this or that action is destructive of man's real happiness, and therefore that the law of nature forbids it.

This law of nature, being coeval with mankind, and dictated by God himself, is of course superior in obligation to any other. It is binding over all the globe in all countries, and at all times: no human laws are of any validity, if contrary to this; and such of them as are valid derive all their force and all their authority, mediately or immediately, from this original.

But, in order to apply this to the particular exigencies of each individual, it is still necessary to have recourse to reason, whose office it is to discover, as was before observed, what the law of nature directs in every circumstance of life, by considering what method will tend the most effectually to our own substantial happiness. And if our reason were always, as in our first ancestor before his transgression, clear and perfect, unruffled by passions, unclouded by prejudice, unimpaired by disease or intemperance, the task would be pleasant and easy; we should need no other guide but this. But every man now finds the contrary in his own experience; that his reason is corrupt, and his understanding full of ignorance and error.

This has given manifold occasion for the benign interposition of divine Providence, which, in compassion to the frailty, the imperfection, and the blindness of human reason, hath been pleased, at sundry times and in divers manners, to discover and enforce its laws by an immediate and direct revelation. The doctrines thus delivered we call the revealed or divine law, and they are to be found only in the holy scriptures. These precepts, when revealed, are found upon comparison to be really a part of the original law of nature, as they tend in all their consequences to man's felicity. But we are not from thence to conclude that the knowledge of these truths was attainable by reason, in its present corrupted state; since we find that, until they were revealed, they were hid from the wisdom of ages. As then the moral precepts of this law are indeed of the same original with those of the law of nature, so their intrinsic obligation is of equal strength and perpetuity. Yet undoubtedly the revealed law is of infinitely more authenticity than that moral system which is framed by ethical writers, and denominated the natural law; because one is the law of nature, expressly declared so to be by God himself; the other is only what, by the assistance of human reason, we imagine to be that law. If we could be as certain of the latter as we are of the former, both would have an equal authority; but, till then, they can never be put in any competition together.

Upon these two foundations, the law of nature and the law of revelation, depend all human laws; that is to say, no human laws should be suffered to contradict these. There are, it is true, a great number of indifferent points in which both the divine law and the natural leave a man at his liberty, but which are found necessary, for the benefit of society, to be restrained within certain limits. And herein it is that human laws have their greatest force and efficacy; for, with regard to such points as are not indifferent, human laws are only declaratory of, and act in subordination to, the former. To instance in the case of murder: this is expressly forbidden by the divine, and demonstrably by the natural law; and, from these prohibitons, arises the true unlawfulness of this crime. Those human laws that annex a punishment to it do not at all increase its moral guilt, or superadd any fresh obligation, *in foro conscientiae*, to abstain from its perpetration. Nay, if any human law should allow or enjoin us to commit it, we are bound to transgress that human law, or else we must offend both the natural and the divine. But, with regard to matters that are in themselves indifferent, and are not commanded or forbidden by those superior laws, – such, for instance, as exporting of wool into foreign countries, – here the inferior legislature has scope and opportunity to interpose, and to make that action unlawful which before was not so.

If man were to live in a state of nature, unconnected with other individuals, there would be no occasion for any other laws than the law of nature, and the law of God. Neither could any other law possibly exist: for a law always supposes some superior who is to make it; and, in a state of nature, we are all equal, without any other superior but Him who is the author of our being. But man was formed for society; and, as is demonstrated by the writers on this subject, is neither capable of living alone, nor indeed has the courage to do it. However, as it is impossible for the whole race of mankind to be united in one great society, they must necessarily divide into many, and form separate states, commonwealths, and nations, entirely independent of each other, and yet liable to a mutual intercourse. Hence arises a third kind of law to regulate this mutual intercourse, called "the law of nations," which, as none of these states will acknowledge a superiority in the other, cannot be dictated by any, but depends entirely upon the rules of natural law, or upon mutual compacts, treaties, leagues, and agreements between these several communities: in the construction also of which compacts we have no other rule to resort to, but the law of nature; being the only one to which all the communities are equally subject; and therefore the civil law very justly observes, that *quod naturalis ratio inter omnes homines constituit, vocatur jus gentium.*

Thus much I thought it necessary to premise concerning the law of nature, the revealed law, and the law of nations, before I proceeded to treat more fully of the principal subject of this section, municipal or civil law; that is, the rule by which particular districts, communities, or nations, are governed; being thus defined by Justinian, "*jus civile est quod quisque sibi populus constituit.*" I call it *municipal* law, in compliance with common speech; for, though strictly that expression denotes the particular customs of one single *municipium* or free town, yet it may with sufficient propriety be applied to any one state or nation which is governed by the same laws and customs.

Municipal law, thus understood, is properly defined to be "a rule of civil conduct prescribed by the supreme power in a state, commanding what is right and prohibiting what is wrong." . . .

Felix Cohen, "Transcendental Knowledge and the Functional Approach" (1935), 35 *Columbia Law Review* 809, 838 writes: "The confusion and ambiguity which infest the classical conception of law, as formulated by Blackstone and implicitly accepted by most modern legal writers, arise from the attempts in effect to superimpose the picture of law drawn by the tender-minded hypocrite, Coke, upon the picture executed by the tough-minded cynic, Hobbes, and to give us a composite photograph. Law, says Blackstone, is 'a rule of civil conduct prescribed by the supreme power in a State (Hobbes speaking) commanding what is right and prohibiting what is wrong (Coke speaking)'. Putting these two ideas together, we have a fertile source of confusion, which many important legal scholars since Blackstone have found about as useful in legal polemics as the ink with which a cuttlefish befuddles his enemies.

"Those theorists who adhere to the Blackstonian definition of law are able to spin legal theories to the heart's content without fear of refutation. If legislatures or courts disagree with a given theory, it is a simple matter to show that this disagreement is unjust, unreasonable, monstrous and, therefore, not 'sound law.' On the other hand, the intruding moralist who objects to a legal doctrine on the ground that it is unjust or undesirable can be told to go back to the realm of morality he came from, since the law is the command of the sovereign and not a matter of moral theory. Perhaps the chief usefulness of the Blackstonian theory is the gag it places upon legal criticism. Obviously, if the law is something that commands what is right and prohibits what is wrong, it is impossible to argue about the goodness or badness of any law, and any definition that deters people from criticism of the law is very useful to legal apologists for the existing order of society. As a modern authority on legal reasoning declares, 'Thus all things made legal are at the same time legally ethical because it is law, and the law must be deemed ethical or the system itself must perish'."

See also Boorstin, *The Mysterious Science of Law* (1941); Hart, "Blackstone's

Use of the Law of Nature" (1956) *Butterworth's South African L. Rev.* 169; McKnight, "Blackstone, Quasi-Jurisprudent" (1959) 13 *Sw. L. J.* 399.

Jean Dabin, 1889-
Professor of Law, Catholic University of Louvain

GENERAL THEORY OF LAW

(French ed. 1944; reprinted by permission of the publishers from *The Legal Philosophies of Lask, Radbruch, and Dabin*, trans. by Kurt Wilk, Cambridge, Mass.: Harvard University Press, Copyright 1950 by the President and Fellows of Harvard College.

98. *Explanation of the Terms "Given" and "Construed."* These are the terms in which Geny has posed the problem, terms no doubt a little simple. But since the formulation has become classic among legal theorists, it seems useful to preserve it while rendering more precise its meaning, which certainly needs explanation.

A thing is given when it exists as an object outside of any productive intervention of man: Such as God, nature, human beings and their relations, the contingent facts of history. A thing is construed when, taken by itself, it has its cause in the efficient activity of man: Such as a house, a poem, a syllogism, the state. It is clear, further, that the "construed," once it has been given reality, becomes something "given" for everybody, including its author: A given relative datum, if one likes the term, whereas the thing that owes nothing to human causality is a given absolute. Now, with regard to the "given," to whatever category it may belong – physical, metaphysical, or historical – the attitude of man is that of knowledge, of science; with regard to the "construed," man, who by definition is the constructor, is operative and, in this sense, makes a work of art or of technology. On the one hand, the attitude of investigation or reception; on the other, creative operation.

This is not to say that the work of knowledge would exclude all construction: In its raw state, the "given" is difficult to seize for the human mind; at least there is needed for its comprehension an operation of the intelligence which cannot proceed without a certain more or less deforming conceptual elaboration. In relation to the "raw fact," the "scientific fact" is "construed." Yet the whole effort of science tends to as exact as possible a restitution of the real, naturally in accordance with the means at the disposal of science. On the contrary, the work of the man of art or of technology arrives at something new, which may well have retained from the real its materials (by contrast with pure creation) or the reason for its being (by contrast with aimless work), but which nevertheless in its actual form did not before exist in reality. Thus understood, the distinction appears hardly contestable. At bottom, it fits in with the classical distinction between the speculative or theoretical sciences, which confine themselves to considering things from the standpoint of their truth alone, and the practical sciences which, aiming at action, tend to evolve rules of action, which is here called "Construing."

100. *Statement of the Question.* After these differentiations, with which category is the law to be ranked? Is the law, as regards its content, "given," apart from all human elaboration, or is it rather "construed" by men, by the professional jurist or the people? And, since the terms are interrelated, is the law, as something "given," an object of science, that is, something to be found and registered, or is it, as something "construed," a work of art or of a technique?

Let us first of all remark that the law may be contemplated from two points of view: In its historical existence, and in its essence.

101. *In Its Historical Existence, the Law Is "Given."* In its historical existence the law is obviously "given," an object of science, whether we deal with contemporary law or ancient law, with national law, foreign law, or international law. This given law, if it is in force, will no doubt require application to special cases, which belongs to a certain art rather than to science. But with a reservation for application to special cases, the historically given law, in force or not, does present itself as a reality, susceptive of a properly scientific, speculative knowledge. Again, the law of a country or of a group of countries or, if that is possible, of the entire world may be studied not as static, at an arrested moment of time, but in its evolution in the course of the ages. This is the viewpoint proper to the historian. Finally the law may be studied from a strictly sociological viewpoint, in its relations with the social life either of a country or an epoch or in general. Anyway, the activity is one of science: The science of the national or foreign law, the science of legal history, the science of the sociology of law. The attempt is made to analyze and to understand certain phenomena as such or by comparison, namely, phenomena of legal rules. This is the science of the established law, which is eventually to complete and crown some general theory: A "philosophy" of such a legal system, a "philosophy" of legal history, "principles" of the sociology of law.

102. *But What about Law in Its Essence*? But outside of the "existential" law – present, past, future, or merely possible – there is law pure and simple, denuded of any form of concrete existence. It is in relation to the law as thus understood, in the state of essence, that our question is raised. In it one at once discerns the interest in an exact appraisal of the lawyer's mission. If the law is "given," at least for the jurist, it will be enough to gather the "given" thing in the reality that supplies it. According to the more or less "positive" nature of the given, the method of knowledge will vary: Properly scientific or philosophical, even theological (in the eventuality that something given that is juridical has been revealed). But the search always sets itself only one aim: To find out the law where it is, as something given. An appeasing doctrine! The jurist is a man of science: His conclusions have the objectivity and certainty of science. The authentic rule, issuing from the given, has the validity of the propositions of science: Imagination is excluded. Contrariwise, if the law is construed, the door is open to the arbitrary subjectivism of the author of the rule. Even if the construction should be subjected to principles, the solutions evolved in applying them could only be vacillating, disputable and disputed.

But whatever may be the security – real or fancied – which one expects from a "scientific" conception of the law, it is impossible to found security upon error. The law will be even more arbitrary, or in any case more tyrannical, if it presents itself in the name of something given that would lack objective reality. It is truth, then, that it matters to seek even when it should appear less agreeable, less comfortable than error.

111. *Return to the Problem: Is There a Legal 'Given'?* Such, rapidly sketched, according to some of their typical interpreters, are the present theories concerning the nature of the "given" in the law. But prior to any discussion of the nature of law, the initial question remains: Is it correct to say that the law – the law as here defined, in the sense of a societal rule of the state or between states – is *given*, if only in part? Is the truth not rather that the law is not at all given, that following the logical definition of the "construed" as a work produced by man, the law is wholly "construed," down to its most substantial foundation?

Contrary to prevailing opinion, we would here take the part of the theory of *total* "construction" and try to prove it, first negatively, through a critique of the two kinds of conceptions of the "given," and then in a direct manner, through an analysis of the process of elaboration of the law.

125. *To Say "Prudent" Is Not to Say "Arbitrary."* From saying that the law is "construed" wholly and down to its foundations it does not follow that construction can take place in an arbitrary fashion or even with the freedom of artistic creation, precisely because it is a work of prudential reason. To say reason is to say submission to truth in all its forms, theoretical and practical. To say prudence is to say, a path to follow and hence a method. No doubt there remains room in the concrete work of elaboration for a certain proportion of arbitrary will. But the margin is enclosed within relatively narrow limits: Those which trace the unbreakable "given" of external realities, on the one hand, and the more supple "given" of the method of elaboration, on the other. We may also note that on reflection the idea of a "given" law no more excludes the arbitrary than that of a "construed" law includes it. All depends on the origin assigned to the "given": If the "given" is in the consciousness of the mass, or *a fortiori* in the will of the strongest, the law thus given will indeed exclude the arbitrariness of the jurist who is bound by that "given," but not that of the consciousness or will of those who created the "given."

But let us look more closely at the limits imposed upon construction.

126. *The Factual Presuppositions of the Jurist's Legal Rule.* The jurist does not draw his rule *ex nihilo* and he does not build it up in a vacuum. Like any rule whatsoever the law is based upon facts. By "facts," in the widest sense, we understand all realities whatsoever, no matter of what nature they may be or to what discipline they may belong, that are capable of interesting the jurist in elaborating his own system, whether as underlying, substructural facts or as surrounding, environmental facts.

This definition includes, first, the facts properly so called, that is, facts of the Is (*Sein*). These are the facts concerning man, for whom, and also by whom, the rule exists: Physiological, psychological, economic, sociological, political, historical ones; facts concerning God, the author and sovereign Lord of man and creatures. All the sciences – sciences properly so called, metaphysics, theology – thus become "auxiliary sciences" of law. The truths they propose are for the jurist so many precedent "given" things which in a certain manner always bind him, whether they have the character of necessity or belong to the domain of pure accident.

At the outset, the jurist will accept them as they are, being unable to change anything in them. He will even take them as points of departure of his law, by way of conditions or presuppositions, except for translating the scientific realties into concepts manageable by the use of categories, legal presumptions, and other processes of formal legal technique. In this sense it is exact to say unqualifiedly: *Ex facto oritur jus*; the facts are sources of law, generative elements of legal rules and solutions. For instance, that paternity is not susceptible of being established directly, at least in the present state of science; that material things are divided into movables and immovables; that man is endowed with personality; that he has an instinct of sociability; that in the ranks of society there are individuals of feeble mind, and of various kinds – these are inescapable facts, for the jurist as for everybody, which entail consequences in the field of the legal discipline.

But even where facts depend upon the free will of men, facts of conduct that the jurist with his law could lay his hands on, these facts continue to be present and consequently to bind the jurist by reason of their existence alone. Whether he adapts himself to them or approves them, or again claims to rectify, to correct or repress them, they are, and by that token they count. In this sense again the statement is true, this time in a relative manner: *Ex facto oritur jus*. Not because the law would always have to bow before the facts of conduct, since its mission is on the contrary to appraise and govern them; but because these facts can exercise an influence upon the decision to be adopted by the legislator. This is so especially for the facts constituting the social environment, which represent the surrounding air of forces, ideas, interests and wants, always moving, sometimes antagonistic, in the midst of which the law is to evolve. Now, to the extent that the facts constituting the environment are dependent upon human freedom, it is clear that the jurist, before assuming an attitude with regard to them, must endeavor to comprehend them, which presupposes knowledge and experience of that social environment.

127. *Moral or Technical Precepts and Existing Law as Presupposed Facts.* Nor is this all. The facts composing the "given" that precedes the law embrace not merely the facts pure and simple which are objects of speculative science. They also embrace all the rules of action, without distinction between human activity (*agere, agibilia*) and technical or artistic activity (*facere, factibilia*). There exists a mass of techniques, belonging to the most varied fields: The techniques of business, of banking, of insurance; the techniques of building machines, tools and apparatus; the techniques of ocean navigation and of air navigation; medical and surgical technique; techniques of aesthetic, scientific, literary work, and of legislative work, too, etc. For the jurist, the rules, procedures, and prescriptions of the different arts or techniques are obviously given as facts. In so far as the law is concerned with technical fields the jurist is consequently bound by the "given" of the technique which will provide him with the basic elements of his construction.

The same remark applies to rules of nontechnical human activity: The rule of morals or the rule of already established law (facts of the Ought (*Sollen*)). For the jurist, the moral rule is given not only as to its first principles of natural law and justice but also to the ultimate conclusions and determinations therefrom, the product of the work of specialists in ethics. Although those conclusions and above all the determinations are themselves in part "construed," what is thus "construed" by the moralist becomes "given" for the jurist. The same holds for existing law in relation to the work of elaboration of a new rule: for the construing jurist, the existing law, which is itself in its entirety "construed," becomes a legal "given" inasmuch as it is a historical reality. And it is quite certain that the jurist, in making his rule, could not detach himself from this historical legal "given," whether he wishes to complete or perfect, or even to reform or reverse, the existing law.

But take care to note: These latter "given" factors remain prelegal, subject to auxiliary sciences, the science of natural law and morals, the science of the existing law or of legal history. Though they may very closely touch the elaboration of the law – which precludes their being called "metajuridical" – yet they do not constitute the legal "given" of the rule to be construed. This is obvious for the preexisting law, since by hypothesis one seeks to modify it; it is also true of the "given" of the moral rule, of natural law, and of justice. The jurist receives morals and moral solutions as "given" at their specific place and level, inasmuch as they are a moral "given." He does not have to receive them as a legal "given," that is, as a completely prepared "given" of his own rule. On this new level, he will make such use of them as is prescribed by the rule of prudence related to his special work, the work of the law to be elaborated. Sometimes, then, prudence will dictate that one sanction the moral "given," sometimes it will command a different attitude: A refusal to intervene or a new arrangement of the moral "given."

204. *First Principles and Secondary Precepts.* As to the extent of the "given" of nature and of what must therefore be referred to natural law, views are divided. The traditional school reserves the name natural, with the characteristics of universality, immutability, and certainty inherent in that quality, to altogether general and ncessary "first principles," distinguishing them even from "secondary precepts" or "particular conclusions quite close to the first principles." Other interpretations, of later date, include within natural law not only the first principles, but the more or less close conclusions evolved from the first principles by way of rational argumentation. So there exists, historically at least, a "minimalist" conception of natural law, limited to the strict and direct "given" of the inclinations of nature, and another, "maximalist" one, extending to the solutions that are the proper work of reason in starting from the natural "given," without, however, any clearly traced boundary lines between the successive zones of first principles, secondary precepts, and their more or less close conclusions.

The disadvantage of the strict conception evidently is to reduce the concrete content of natural law to rather vague generalities, which gives rise to the objection (an unjust one, incidentally) of useless verbalism; the dangers of the broad conception lie in lending the validity of natural law, that is, absolute authority, to solutions endowed with truth merely relative to the cases. The present tendency is toward the minimum conception. On the one hand, one fears being unable to account for the "legitimate variation" of positive rules. On the other hand, one mistrusts logical apriorism in the domain of the moral and social sciences.

205. *Subject Matter of Natural Law: The Totality of the Duties of Man.* As regards the subject matter of natural law, or equality of the natural legal rule with which it is synonymous, it embraces all orders of duties imposed by nature, and consequently not only the duty of justice (*suum cuique tribuere*) or, more broadly, the duties *ad alterum*, but also the duties toward God, the duties toward oneself, the duties deduced from the idea of the family (giving rise to the concept of natural family law), the duties of the political order, incumbent upon subjects as well as upon rulers, at home and abroad (natural political law). Adopting another principle of division, St. Thomas Aquinas classifies "the natural inclinations from which the order of the precepts of natural law flows" as follows: An inclination, common to all substances, toward the conservation of their being according to its proper nature; an inclination, common to men and animals, toward the union of the male and female, the education of the youth, and similar things; an inclination, proper to man, toward the goods conforming to his nature as a rational being, such as the desire to know God and to live in society, which impels him to avoid ignorance, not to do wrong to his neighbor with whom he must maintain relations, and other things of that kind. It is not hard to recognize in that classification the principles corresponding to the totality of the duties of man: Toward himself, toward his family, toward God, toward his neighbor, toward society.

207. *The Ambiguity of the Concept of Natural Law.* For here at last is the ambiguity which has not ceased to befog the concept of natural law from the day the state began to legislate: To what sort of regulation is the natural law related? To the regulation which, aiming at the moral perfection of men, obligates them before their conscience and before God to practice the good and avoid the bad, in short, the moral rule? Or to the regulation of societal origin, laid down by

(domestic or international) public authority with a view to the temporal public good (of individuals or states), in short, the legal rule? Or again to both sorts of rules cumulatively, whether they are considered as distinct at least in form or taken for inseparable at least up to a certain point? In a word, is natural law the directing principle of morals or of law?

The question no doubt was less important practically in periods of not very complex civilization when the civil law was most often content with the role of servant and executor of morals. But in our times, with the three fold phenomenon of the increase of wants, above all material wants, the development of technology, and the emergence of the masses, the civil law is led to formulate many requirements which bear no more than an indirect relationship to morality. Hence the present interest of the problem as to the order of regulation to which the rule of conduct called natural law belongs.

215. *Moral and Political But No Juridical Natural Law.* To sum up. First, there exists a moral natural law which is fundamental to the moral conduct of individuals as well as to the positive moral rule, and in every domain including the social domain (social morals) and without distinction between outward and inner acts. This rule of itself obliges only in the internal forum and not before the state, its police and its courts. Second, there also exists a political natural law which, based upon the political instinct of man, establishes political society and all that is essential to it, especially the public authority and the civil law, the latter being considered not in its concrete dispositions but in its principle and its method of elaboration. This political natural law is undoubtedly dependent upon moral natural law because morals governs everything human. But it is in turn the starting point of a new system of properly social (indeed, societal) institutions and rules, inspired by the idea of the public good (at once moral, utilitarian and technical) and governing only the outward acts of man as a member of the group. Third, there exists no juridical natural law in the sense of solutions or even mere directives given in advance to the authority charged with the establishment of the civil law according to the public good. No doubt there are principles commonly accepted in the laws of the countries of the same level of civilization: *Jus gentium* or "general principles of law." But one could not without ambiguity and danger credit natural law with principles which, on the one hand, are very heterogeneous, since one finds there commingled rules of morals, of common sense, and of social utility – and which, on the other hand, lack the characteristics of necessity and universality inherent in the idea of nature. The practice of civilized countries, even supported by wisdom and experience, is not synonymous with natural inclination.

216. *The Dualism of "Natural Law –Positive Law" Replaced by "Morals – Law."* If these views are correct, they yield an important result concerning the statement of the problem here under discussion. One must no longer speak of relationships between natural law and positive law (at least when by positive law one understands, as is customary, the law of the jurists, the civil law, and not the positive moral law or rule). One must speak of relationships between morals, not only natural but also positive, and the civil law, that is to say, the law. This statement does correspond to reality. On the one hand, what makes its appearance throughout natural law is indeed morals. On the other hand, the law has relationships with kinds of values other than the ethical values. By comparison, the traditional statement errs both by lack of precision and by confusion. It does not bring out with precision that natural law above all signifies morals. At the same time, that statement leads us to believe that natural law covers all values whatever of interest to the jurist.

244. *Restatement of the Problem.* We are now in a position, after this long preamble, to define the exact role of the two factors of natural law and justice in the elaboration of the law.

To sum up. Natural law represents the category of the moral rule; and although the concept is technically limited to the first principles of morality, that limitation is without interest to the jurist, who is bound to accept all of morals as given, not only in its first principles but in the subordinate conclusions and determinations evolved by moral science and eventually by the positive rule of the moral law. That is why hereafter natural law will be spoken of in the sense of the moral norm, and vice versa. As to justice, it represents one of the principal rules of morals, that which regards the right of another to be respected and satisfied, either that of particular private persons (particular justice: Commutative and distributive) or that of the public community (legal justice), the latter form of justice outranking the particular justices which are subordinate to it as the parts are to the whole.

Now the elaboration of the law proceeds by considering, first, the public good of the community under contemplation, and secondly, the resources and "possibilities" of the implementation of the law. The question proposed, then, reduces itself to the study of the relationships between natural law (i.e., morals) and justice, on the one hand, and the social-political element of the public good and the technical element of regulation, on the other. Furthermore, nothing new is to be expected of this comparison, for the principles have been set forth in the chapter on the method of elaboration of the law, and we are concerned with nothing more than putting certain aspects thereof into fuller relief.

245. *There Could Be No Public Good Against Morals.* A first point could arouse no controversy: A legal rule positively contrary to morals must be condemned as contrary to the public good. For notwithstanding the difference of the concepts, there is no conceivable divorce of the demands of morals from the requirements of the public good. There is no public good against morals because morals governs man and the public is composed of men. By what route or detour could that which would be bad for man be transformed into a good for the public? It is irrelevant in this regard that the public good is but an intermediary good, consisting simply in an environment favorable to the action of individuals and groups. How could that environment be useful to man, not only from the moral but also from the material point of view, if it is the result of measures reproved by morals? The advantage will be but illusory or fugitive, and ultimately it is man who will pay the price of immoral policies. It also matters little that the public good has purely temporal or even material and technical aspects. Morals does not reign solely over virtue, or rather, everything is a matter of virtue, including the activities of the purely temporal, material, and technical order. More, the first condition of the public good in all domains is respect for the moral rule, both of precept and of counsel, in the choice of means as of ends. And there is no room for distinctions according to the orders of relations. Whether the relationships involved are of the private or of the political order, on the domestic or on the international plane, any legal rule that violates morals at the same time violates the public good. No solution is politically good that would be morally bad: An immoral or amoral conception of politics is a politically false conception, always for the reason that politics is human and all that is human is, if not moral, at least subject to morals.

As concerns justice especially, a conflict with the public good is even less conceivable inasmuch as justice, in the form of legal justice at any rate, is defined by the public good, always reserving the rights of morality in general. Therefore, all that is laid down by the law in conformity with the public good is at once in conformity with justice. This conformity, moreover, is presumed to exist, for it is the prerogative of authority to benefit from "previous obedience": Until proof to the contrary the authority is deemed to be right.

246. *Examples and Cases of Application.* In applying these principles it can be said, in the first place, that the law cannot command what morals forbids, nor can it forbid what morals commands. The classical example, although it concerns a precept for a particular case and not a statutory rule, is that of Antigone. Creon's edict forbidding the burial of the corpse of Antigone's brother was immoral and unjust as contrary to *pietas* (*eusebeia*) toward the dead of the family and the infernal gods (Sophocles, *Antigone*, verses 745, 749, 924). But there are other historical or imaginable examples: Laws enforcing sacrifices to false gods or prohibiting worship of the true God; laws requiring apostasy, dueling, abortion, euthanasia; laws prohibiting acts of liberality *inter vivos* or by will. The contradiction does not have to be immediate. It suffices that the law by its disposition tends to discourage the virtuous act in setting up impediments (formalities, delays, taxes) or to encourage the vicious act in setting up advantages (prizes, remissions). It also suffices that the law turns away from action which morals merely counsels, or that it impels toward the commission of what morals calls imperfection: In each of these ways the moral ideal is being checked. Other laws are immoral by contradicting the principles of "institutional morals," being that part of morals which governs the natural social structures; such are the laws admitting a free union instead of or besides marriage, or those ignoring the authority of parents over their children. Finally, there are the laws that are immoral by attacking the principles of political morals: Oppressive laws which under the pretext of the good of the community or the state deprive individuals, nationals or aliens, of their essential liberties, such as the right to marry; or partial laws which violate distributive justice to the detriment or in favor of a fraction of the public (party, class, race, or any social category whatever).

Most of the time, no doubt, the legislator enacting an immoral rule believes it to be moral. But it also happens that he thinks he will be able to attain a certain goal of the public good, for instance, an addition of power for the state, without having to concern himself with the moral value of the means, or by persuading himself that every useful means is necessarily moral. This, precisely, is the amoral or immoral conception of politics in its repercussion upon the law.

247. *Confusions to Be Avoided in Appraising the Immoral Character of Laws.* But one must understand the assumption correctly, and not qualify as "contrary to morals" a policy or a law that would not merit that reproach. Everything permitted by morals, whether as being indifferent by its object or on the ground of a capacity for choice left to the individual, need not necessarily receive the consecration of the law. It is the right and the duty of the legislator to declare illicit the morally indifferent act which under the circumstances would be prejudicial to the public good. By virtue of that very prohibition, the morally indifferent act becomes morally bad, for the act contrary to the public good, denounced as such by a law charged with watching over the public good, is from the outset an immoral act. In the same way, a capacity to act which morals sanctions but which under the circumstances would be prejudicial to the public good could be legitimately suppressed by a law, and that suppression would be binding even in conscience.

On stronger grounds, one must not call legislation immoral that would regulate the rights of everyone toward other private persons, or toward the state as functioning for the good of the total community rather than of the right of everyone taken in isolation. There will perhaps result from such regulation some diminution of the right of the one correlative to an augmentation of the right of the other. But there is nothing immoral in that modification, because morals itself prescribes the subjection of the particular good to the general good (moral virtue of legal justice); provided, however, that the law leave the particular person favored by its disposition free to renounce the advantage or in other ways to reestablish the equilibrium. For the solutions of the public good are not incompatible with practicing the virtues of moderation and equity; the contrary is true.

248. *The Law Is Not Bound to Consecrate Every Rule of Morals.* Is this to say that, everywhere and always, where morals commands or forbids, the law is under an obligation to follow and sanction the prescription of morals? Not at all. The prohibition of contradicting does not involve the obligation of sanctioning; and the public good, which is not compatible with any kind of immoral law, does not necessarily require the intervention of a law in order to compel respect for morals. No doubt every virtuous act is useful, every vicious act is harmful, not only to its author but to the entire community, inasmuch as it contributes to the formation of a public environment either virtuous or vicious. Such an environment could indeed result only from the acts of particular individuals, who always originate what is public. But the question is not whether the practicing of every virtue and every vice influences the public. The question is whether it is good for the public that every virtue give rise to a legal imperative, every vice to a censure or repression. Now, in the first place, morals imposed under threat of compulsion no longer is morals. Objectively, materially, the precept will perhaps be obeyed and morals, in this sense, satisfied. But by reason of the compulsion and inasmuch as the obedience is due only to the compulsion, the observance of the rule has lost all moral value. Hence one may ask if a law serves the public good when its intervention has the effect of sacrificing the subjective to the objective element in morals, in short, of suppressing morality under color of saving morals.

249. *The "Discipline of the Laws" and Virtue.* To be sure, one may invoke the necessity of a "discipline" for the perfection of virtue, and the educational action of laws which would engender a habit favorable to the spontaneous fulfillment of duty. But that is a matter of experience, depending upon the mentality of peoples. In fact it often happens, especially in our modern times, that the result of the intervention is rather negative. When virtue claims to impose itself by force, if only by the force of a law, it runs the risk of arousing a state of mind hostile to the law and to virtue, which is a pity both for morality and for legality: In such a case, a moralizing law becomes in all respects demoralizing. No doubt, again, the effect of every law, including every civil law, is to render men good not only inasmuch as they obey that law (for it is virtuous to obey a just law) but also inasmuch as it imposes upon them what the public good prescribes. But it does not follow that a law, or at least a civil law, is qualified to repress all vices and to command actions fulfilling all virtues. It is incumbent upon moral laws to render man good as regards all virtues because their competence, in matters of virtue, is direct and general. As to civil laws, "bearing upon the governance of commonwealths," their moralizing effect is limited to the virtue which concerns the public good, to wit, legal justice. Civil laws render men good as regards the virtue of legal justice, the requirements of which they show them and make more precise, at least to the extent of what they are in a position to obtain from the subjects and therefore to impose upon them. Thus civil laws do not even render men good as regards the totality of legal justice; they render them good as regards that justice only according to the possible, taking account of the moral level of the people, the state of public opinion, and the principle of efficiency proper to the civil law. Again,

what matters from our point of view is less the effect of a law than its end; or, if one prefers, the effect can be legitimately pursued only within the framework of the end. Now the end of civil laws is not immediately to moralize man; it is to procure the public good, that is to say, an environment, an intermediary good, and moreover an effective public good, therefore, one calculated by the standard of realities.

250. *The Law and the Ideal Type of the Family.* The same maxim must guide the laws in the elaboration of the legal regime of the natural groups, particularly the family. For instance, institutional morals is not content with just any marriage implying a certain stability, as a rule for the union of sexes; its ideal is that of the one and indissoluble marriage, which alone perfectly realizes the individual and familial ends of marriage. But how can one expect the laws to escape from realities where the mores are not, or not yet, at the height of this ideal – to proscribe polygamy among polygamous peoples, to restore the indissolubility of marriage among peoples accustomed to divorce? Has the Church not taken centuries to make the barbarian peoples accept its matrimonial legislation, to abolish slavery (encouragement of emancipations), to extirpate the scourge of private wars (institution of the Truce of God)? Before commanding in a imperative manner by its legislation, the Church recommended, preached, educated, often compromised with the "hardness of hearts."

251. *The Capacity of Morals for "Ordination to the Public Good."* The problem of the relations between law and morals finds its definitive answer in the following formulation: The jurist will retain only those of the rules of morals whose consecration or confirmation by the law will in fact under the circumstances be found useful to the public good and practicable with regard to the technical equipment of the jurist. On the one hand, none of the divisions or parts of morals, none of its rules or its virtues, is excluded from the possibility of consecration; on the other, the latter will take place only as far as the public good in the particular case will derive an advantage from it and the technique will oppose no obstacle to it. The capacity for "ordination" to the public good in its different forms – political public good where the state is concerned, social public good where the community embraced within the framework of the state is concerned – this is the first essential condition of the "subsumption" of morals into law. This first condition, indeed, implies the second, relating to technique, for a rule technically inapplicable and hence useless will very rarely be advantageous to the public good. It will have been noted that the criterion is not only conformity to the public good of the *attitudes* to be required of the subjects, but also and above all conformity to the public good of the *intervention* of a law prescribing for the subjects such attitudes, even if these conform to the public good. Besides the content of a law, the very principle of its intervention must therefore be considered.

252. *The Moral Precepts Susceptible of Consecration by the Law.* What, then, are the moral precepts that may be ordained for the public good by the intermediary of the laws? Here political prudence comes in, and especially legislative prudence, whose role is precisely that of discerning solutions most adequate to the circumstances of times, places, and cases. Although these solutions are variable in concrete cases, it is not impossible to assign to the work of prudence if not an inflexible method, at least a marching order of general though provisional value.

Among the rules of morals, the jurist constructing civil laws will at the outset introduce a distinction between the rules governing relationships with others and the rules regarding duties toward God and toward one's self. On the one hand, the duties towards God and the duties toward oneself exist independently of any form of social life; on the other hand, the legal rule is a social rule, and therefore one presupposing other persons. It is clear that the public good, the end of the legal rule, is more directly concerned with the relationships between men than with the relationships of man with God or his conduct toward himself. These latter spheres of duties can affect the public only indirectly, incidentally. Now logic commands one to apply one's self in the first place to what makes up the direct subject matter of the law, unhampered by any ulterior view of the "incidental" matter.

In the second place, the jurist will distinguish among the moral rules governing the relationships among men those implying something due which is capable of exaction: The debt of justice in its three forms, commutative, distributive, and legal, and also the debts that may be called familial, between spouses, between parents and children, and between relatives, in which the necessary institution of the family consists. As for moral prescriptions other than those of justice, the measure of interest the jurist accords them will depend on the degree of their proximity to justice: A closer interest for the annexed virtues of justice, by reason of their analogy to the principal virtue; a more remote interest where the ground of the debt decreases of disappears, as in the case of beneficence and liberality.

253. *Justice as the Precept Most Obviously Fit for Consecration.* On several grounds, justice is somehow the natural subject matter of the legal system. First, because fulfillment of the moral duty of justice is most indispensable to the public good. As for injustice among private persons, it is in reaction to this "common evil" that the concept of a public good was born in which the first element is order and peace guaranteed by the force of the community organized in the state. At all times justice has been placed in the first rank of that *ratio qua societas hominum inter ipsos et vitae quasi communitas continetur*. The state would fail in its mission, the public good would not be realized, if justice between individuals was not respected. What about legal justice and distributive justice? Here the question does not even arise. Legal justice is the virtue most necessary to the public good precisely because its object is the public good (of the state or of the public). It is in legal justice that law and morals meet so closely as almost to merge. Is not the object of the moral precept of legal justice that which is fixed by a law? The same goes for distributive justice. The state may well produce the most abundant public good and yet its effort will turn into civil war, that is, public evil, if it distributes it contrary to equity. Neither is it conceivable that a civil law could depart from distributive justice, because the latter is the moral norm to which the rulers, the authors of the civil law, are subject in their professional capacity.

It is true that the two justices, commutative and distributive, which refer to the particular good, are like every particular virtue subordinate to legal justice, which is qualified to regulate the content thereof, that is to say, the particular right of everyone, according to the requirements of the public good. But that subordination is not the work of civil laws. It results, as has been said, from morals itself, which demands the subordination in the temporal order of the particular [private] good to the public good so that on this point the harmony between the two rules is complete.

254. *Exceptional Rectification of the Two Particular Justices on the Ground of Legal Justice.* Yet it would be a mistake to believe that the solutions given by commutative and distributive justice on the basis of the individual right alone would always or even frequently call for rectification on the ground of legal justice. Not only is there no necessary opposition between the public good and

the particular justices, but such opposition is also relatively rare. The public good in application will on the contrary demand respect for the particular justices. It must not be forgotten that individuals are the beginning and the end of the state and the public good – that one must therefore start from them as one must finally revert to them. That is why on the methodical level the jurist constructing the law will at once proceed to the solutions of particular justice: Commutative for the relationships among private persons, distributive for what is due to the citizens from the state, thus consecrating the particular right *a priori* according to the title of each one considered individually. Nor will any rectification whatever be operative on the ground of the public good except where proof has been made beyond any doubt that the consecration of the right of the individual according to the standard of particular justice either involves positive damage to the public good in the special case or does not permit the attainment of an advantage remotely compensating the evil inherent in a rectification of justice.

Therefore, when it is recommended that the jurist take justice in its three forms for the basic matter of his rules, it is appropriate to make this more precise by the following complementary distinction. In the relationships between private persons, the justice primarily to be considered is commutative justice; in what concerns the rights of citizens against the state, it will be distributive justice – the domain of legal justice being provisionally limited to the obligations of the citizen toward the state (societal justice). Legal justice as general justice which governs the other virtues, including the two particular justices, will be called upon only secondarily, after demonstration of the insufficiency of the solutions of the particular justices with respect to the public good. Ordinarily, the public good is best served when every one of the members of the public sees what constitutes his own right consecrated in the most exact manner.

255. *Special Structural Adaptability of Justice for the Legal Rule.* Justice is the preferred matter of the legal order for a second reason, which has to do with its particular structure. Indeed, justice is distinguished by the characteristics of objectivity, externality, and clarity, which render it eminently adaptable for the legal imperative. On the one hand, unlike the virtues which relate to the passions, justice governs the action of the subject relative to the right of another. Now to decree respect for the right of another, and at the same time to assure the execution of that precept, is undoubtedly less difficult than to foresee and prescribe the environment conducive to virtue in the matter of passions. No civil law could reach them except in acts that translate them outwardly, whereas operative action – of commission or omission – alone suffices to satisfy justice, at least materially. Moreover, the object of justice, to wit, the right of another, is a thing given in external reality, while the virtues regulating the passions have their seat in the subject himself. By reason of this objectivity, the solution of justice has general validity, like the legal rule, obligating everybody uniformly, without distinction according to the subject who is under obligation, while the just measure in respect to passions is a matter of the special case, depending upon individual situations and circumstances.

On the other hand, unlike the other virtues *ad alterum*, justice shows the peculiarity of clear determination as to persons and things. Its beneficiary is the determinate person, individual or collectivity, in whom the right exists; the debtor is either everybody or such and such an individual or collectivity. Similarly, the object of the right is determined or determinable: Such and such a thing, service, or attitude; that alone is someone's due because it alone is "his own." Now again this clarity lends itself to the logical and precise mechanism of the legal rule. True, the determination is far from being as perfect in the two justices of the political order, legal and distributive justice, as in commutative justice. There is some leeway in the appraisal of what is due to the state and the public (legal justice) or what is coming to each one in the distribution of the public good (distributive justice). Nevertheless, the principles according to which prudence must make the concrete determination are outlined in an objective manner. It is indeed the reason of being of the state and of the laws to lay down terms for the original indeterminacy of all that falls within the political.

256. *Like the Legal Duty, the Duty of Justice Is Capable of Exaction.* Justice is the obvious matter of the legal order for a third reason, to wit, that the debt of justice is capable of being exacted. Because its object is the right of another and that right of another is its holder's own, he has the right to exact respect for it if need be by force. Morally, by its nature, justice implies the right to repel unjust aggression: This is the case of vindication which may be permissible and sometimes is a virtue, according to the circumstances. Now, similarly, by its nature the legal rule is capable of exaction and proceeds by way of compulsion: What is required by the public good or decided upon in conformity with it calls for being carried out, voluntarily or by force. Thus when the law takes over on its account the moral precept of justice, the compulsion with which it accompanies it does not constitute an innovation. Especially as regards commutative justice, the consecration of a law does nothing but replace the very insufficient (and for the public good deadly) mode of private compulsion with the regulated mode of public compulsion. The change touches only the form of compulsion and not its principle. Contrariwise, the moral duties incapable of exaction are as such repugnant to compulsion, which is foreign to them and even denatures them. Beneficence and liberality imposed by compulsion remain benefits materially; they have lost their character of virtuous acts. It requires precisely a basis in legal justice to render legitimate a command which makes them – on this new ground – capable of exaction.

257. *The Law and the Annexed Virtues of Justice, Especially Faith in Promises.* By the very reason of their participation in justice, the annexed virtues of justice, at least those among them which embody more fully the objective structure of justice, participate in the aptness of their principal virtue for legal consecration. What we have here especially in mind is faith in promises. Not only does the party who violates his promise offend the other contracting party to whom he owes his pledged faith, but also all social life is impossible if promises made are not kept at all. Confidence and credit have their sole basis in faith; and faithlessness in promises is undoubtedly as damaging to the public good as are attacks against the right of another. From that side, the situation is clear: The intervention of the laws to sanction faith in promises is not only justified but required. From the side of formal realization of the intervention, the situation is no less clear. The object of faith in promises can be "grasped" quite as much as the object of the debt of commutative justice – even more so, for the promise has formally determined it. The only difference is in respect to exaction. Contrary to what is due in justice, what is promised to another is not coming to him as something that belongs to him, directly or by equivalent; hence the strict exaction of justice cannot enter the arena. Yet faith in promises is so much required by the public good that one should not be astonished to see the laws confer upon it the capability of exaction which it does not of itself possess. In that manner, the moral debt of honesty, which engenders faith in promises, is transformed into a legal debt, which may henceforth be exacted on the ground of legal justice.

258. *The Law and the Constituent Principles of the Family.* Lastly, among the

moral principles whose place is marked in the law, there are to be counted the constituent rules of the family, the rules which define the family as an institution. Family relationships – between spouses, between parents and children, even between relatives – bear a double aspect according to whether they are viewed from within or from without. Seen from their inner or intimate side, family relationships belong above all to that part of morals which governs sentiments and acts resulting from sentiments. In the first rank of these sentiments we find love, a special love of familial character, which is further differentiated according to the diverse psychological and moral categories of conjugal love, paternal and maternal love, filial love, fraternal love, etc. But the law is powerless with respect to the duty of love and even, to a degree, the duty of familial piety inasmuch as it involves love. Contrariwise, with regard to the traits by which the family is set apart as an institution and which belong to the institutional part of morals, the powerlessness of the law disappears. It is not impossible for a law to decree that only the legitimate union, that is, marriage, shall be endowed with legal effects; that this union shall be one and indissoluble, at least in principle; that it shall entail reciprocal duties of cohabitation, faithfulness, aid, and support; that parents ought to give their children during their formative period nourishment and education; that children in turn are under the obligation of docility; that the family group shall have a head, the husband and father, charged with authority – and responsibility – toward his wife and children, – all this according to the moral conceptions prevalent in the people under contemplation.

To what extent do the constituent principles of the law of domestic relations approach the type of justice? In the absence of justice toward the family as a body (because the family, while forming a group and a community, is not a moral person), it is not forbidden to speak of a sort of justice between spouses, which gives them rights that may be exacted from one another, or a sort of justice between parents and children, which makes them creditors (or debtors) of education, nourishment, docility, etc. But this matters little from our point of view. It is enough that the constituent principles of the family evidently concern the "public." Now it may be affirmed beyond doubt: The family concerns the public good at least as much as it concerns justice, as clearly and as closely. Is the family not one of the bases of the social and political order of a country? It it not the root of life, and thus of peoples and states? Does one not find it omnipresent, actively and passively, with regard to the particular individuals who are subjects of justice? That is why the law will at once come to the aid of the familial institution, as it comes to the aid of individuals in commutative and distributive justice, and of the state and the public in legal justice.

259. *Yet the Normal Order of Consecration Is Subject to Derogation.* It is granted, again, that these interventions of the law take place not directly in favor of justice, or in favor of the family, but inasmuch as these values – and their legal protection itself – effectively realize the public good in the circumstances, and on the condition also that the intervention should not be technically incapable of realization. Such being the point of view of the jurist, it is possible that the marching order outlined above in a theoretical manner, starting *de eo quod plerumque fit*, must undergo certain derogations in practice. Thus some moral rules that would normally require the consecration of the law might have to go without it, while others which normally would not require it would have to obtain it.

There could be no question here of drawing up a systematic list of these exceptional cases, their general theory having been presented. Let us confine ourselves to some suggestions, limited to the law of private relations, since in the relationships of the political order the rule of the law itself undertakes, by order of morals, to determine the requirements of legal and distributive justice.

260. *Cases Where the Law Abstains from Consecrating Justice.* It has already been observed, with supporting examples, how commutative justice (and equally so its annex, faith in promises) often enough had to withdraw before more or less urgent considerations of the social order: Economic, political, psychological (such as the concern for security). Even in morals, general justice normally prevails over particular justice. But there is another set where the law foregoes sanctioning commutative justice. Either it refers for the determination of their respective rights to the regulation agreed upon between the interested parties although this may not always conform to natural justice. Or again it leaves the field free to individual activities, where these usually work spontaneously in the direction of justice, or where political prudence or the insufficiency of legal equipment makes it advisable to tolerate them wholly or in part even though they are unjust.

261. *Cases Where the Law Goes Beyond the Framework of Justice.* Also, contrariwise, the law pushes beyond commutative justice, sanctioning moral rules other than the rule of justice. It draws first of all upon those virtues *ad alterum*, annexed to justice, where the debt is but moral: Not only fidelity to the pledged word, which is as indispensable to social life as is strict justice, but also, for instance, gratitude and sometimes beneficence and liberality. So-called "social legislation" is full of precepts imposing obligations upon employers to which on the part of the workers no strict right corresponds and which often fall within gratuitous assistance. But these virtues are eminently "social," more social in certain respects than justice. For if justice is the necessary condition of life in society in rendering to each his own, the social virtues, by their disinterested altruistic character, positively tighten the social bond. Hence it will be seen that the law, concerned with concord and fraternity among the members of the group, is led to promulgate statutes "of social solidarity," where the required attitudes become a matter of legal justice by reason of their "ordination" for the public good. Furthermore, social relations do not exist solely between equals: At their basis is authority. That is why the law prescribes obedience to authorities not only in the state but also in the private groups, in the first place the family. Although obedience is but an annexed virtue of justice, it will be seen that laws come to the aid of the hierarchies which make up the organic unity of social life.

But the law does not entrench itself in the field of the virtues *ad alterum*. Stepping beyond the circle of justice and the social virtues, it represses some shortcomings in duties toward one's self (e.g., the attempt at suicide, drunkenness, certain alienations of essential rights or liberties), some shortcomings in duties toward God (e.g., blasphemy, sacrilege, perjury), or again acts of cruelty to animals. Why? Not because commutative justice would be involved, but because these offenses affect the public, causing trouble or damage in the social environment.

Lastly, beyond justice and even morals, one will have to indicate the innumerable measures of prudence laid down by the law to the end of preventing the violation of the moral precepts it has taken up and sanctioned. Such are the regulations designed to police traffic, industry and labor, and commerce, but also to protect the rights of the persons engaged in those activities against encroachments. Now these preventive measures, though in part ordained for justice, are in themselves means indifferent to justice.

262. *"Just Laws" and Laws Consecrating Justice Are Not Synonymous.* Finally, one will have to guard against confounding just laws and laws which consecrate justice. A law is just when it prescribes what is within its role to prescribe. In this sense, a just law is a law adjusted to its end, the public good, and to its

proper means of realization, in short, a law conforming to the legal method. This, the rule of natural law being unaffected, is the *regula rationis* in matters of positive law. Now while ordinarily a just law is a law which consecrates justice, this is not always so. That is all the difference between the lawyer's justice, which is a matter of prudence, and the moralist's justice, which is a matter of truth or science.

Brendan F. Brown, 1898–
Professor of Law, Loyola University of New Orleans.

NATURAL LAW: DYNAMIC BASIS OF LAW AND MORALS IN THE TWENTIETH CENTURY (1957)

I

NATURAL LAW IS THE COMMON BASIS OF LAW AND MORALS

All law originates in the eternal law, that timeless divine plan of government which directs all actions to their appointed ends. This plan is a rule and measure of the whole community of the universe. All other types of law are only limited participations in this plan.

Natural law is a sharing in the eternal law by man. It is that aspect of the eternal law which directs the behavior of human beings, as distinguished from other forms of creation. The eternal law is the cause of the natural law and exists in man as an imprint on his reason.

The natural law proceeds ultimately from the intellect and will of a Divine Lawgiver, but is made known immediately through reason. It is a source of obligation because it conforms to the essence of rational human nature, and because it has been ordained by the Creator of nature. It is truly law for it is an ordinance for the common good of man and has been promulgated in his intellect by Him Who has the care of all things.

The natural law creates the norm of an objective morality. The *mores* of various peoples in different periods of history do not constitute this norm. But customs will have the force of law if they are an expression of the natural law.

Certain obligations to God, to others, and to sub-human creation result from the natural law. The principal mutual obligations of human beings toward each other are justice and charity. Both moralists and jurists are concerned with the achievement of justice. But the formal object of each is different. The moralist is concerned with the *virtue* of justice, one of the cardinal moral virtues, while the jurist is interested in justice not so much as a virtue or interior disposition, but as a factor of the social order. The jurist focuses his attention upon order and exterior peace, which result from the proper social attitude of the citizen. The jurist looks at the object of the virtue of justice insofar as it commands the attitudes of individuals and even imposes itself upon them by social force and constraint if necessary. But in final analysis, both law and morals are founded on the natural law.

Human law and morals are connected, but distinct, sciences. Their formal objects are different. Morals is the higher of the two norms. Both have the common power to direct and the same subject matter of human conduct. Both seek the same mutual establishment of friendship and orderly relationships among men in society. Both preserve the moral order. They share the same ends.

But law and morals have different sanctions. The sanction of law is primarily exterior; that of ethics, interior. The authority to compel pertains only to law. Law and morals differ, therefore, in the means which they use for the realization of their common ends, and in the respective functions which they perform.

The boundary line between law and morals continually shifts. This is so because enforcement is the distinctive quality of positive law in relation to morals. The lawmaker transforms morals into law whenever public opinion deems this necessary for the well being of the community.

Law seeks to enforce only those minimum standards of moral conduct which are indispensable for the common good. It does not compel all ethical obligations. It is not able to do so. But it should enforce those moral duties which are immediately necessary for the good of society.

Law must be possible in regard to the nature of things as well as the customs of the country. Hence, it does not prohibit all evil activities from which good men refrain. It forbids only the more serious acts of injustice from which the greater part of the community can abstain.

Law is formulated for the majority of men, most of whom are imperfect in virtue. But law does not endorse the moral wrongs which it does not endeavor to prevent. It does not disapprove the virtues which it does not promote.

Finally, law is educative, as well as coercive. It should lead men to virtue gradually, but not abruptly. It should do this affirmatively by regulating human conduct so that men may habitually seek the ends in which their perfection will be found. It must do it negatively by restraining them from doing evil; some must "be dragged by an exterior force to the fulfillment of the justice of the law." Some will obey the law only because of the fear of penalties, not out of the love of justice. Good men will regard just law as a preparation for virtue regardless of the penalties attached. It is not necessary, therefore, to choose between law and morals as if they were completely unrelated.

II

In the first place, the natural law is immutable in some respects. Its starting point, namely, do good and avoid evil, is an indemonstrable moral fact, falling within the apprehension of the practical aspect of reason, which is principally concerned with ends and means. This starting point corresponds to the proposition that the same thing may not be affirmed and denied at the same time, which comes within the apprehension of the speculative phase of reason. This phase has mainly to do with cause and effect.

The obvious deductions which flow from the self evident, intuitively perceived, starting point are absolute and immutable. Examples of such conclusions are the moral precepts of the Decalogue, social relationships, self preservation, care of off-spring, and the like. These conclusions follow directly from the essential attributes of human nature. Like the properties of a triangle, these conclusions do not change since the essence of human nature does not vary.

The natural law is discoverable by reason alone. It is knowable proximately through the conscience, at least with regard to its more fundamental norms. Its most basic precept, namely, that man must live in accordance with his rational nature so as to do good and avoid evil, is manifest to all. Indeed, it is impossible for its primary principles to remain unknown. But varying gradations and methods of reasoning are required to reach the sub-norms of the natural law. Obvious conclusions can easily be deduced by reason. But the remote conclusions are reached only after considerable study and reasoning.

Man's knowledge of the primary immutable principles may not change, but the natural law may vary both subjectively and objectively with regard to its inferior norms, namely, those detailed proximate conclusions which are drawn from the first category of moral values by deduction, and manifestly from all succeeding categories. In a subjective sense, human knowledge of the remote conclusions of the natural law may increase from time to time. Knowledge within the field of morals grows analogous to that which takes place in regard to other sciences. This knowledge evolves by deductive reasoning. This proceeds from major premises which change as a result of induction based on observation and experience.

New moral judgments with regard to right and wrong may emerge. Thus experience has demonstrated that excessive inbreeding interferes with the primary end of marriage, i.e., the healthy propagation of the human race. This led to a recognition of the evil of marriage within particular degrees of kinship, and resulted in the establishment of the forbidden degrees.

In an objective sense, the remote conclusions of the natural law may be enlarged and contracted. Thus a change in historical and sociological facts may enlarge the natural law by introducing new secondary or inferior conclusions. These would be for the benefit of human life. Again, changing facts may contract the remote principles of the natural law by subtraction, so that a norm which the natural law prescribes in one period may not be commanded at another.

Thus at one time in the Middle Ages, the lending of money at interest was contrary to a remote conclusion of the natural law. This was deduced from the primary precept, "Thou shalt not steal." But with the rise of capitalism and the initiation of the industrial revolution, a conclusion was added which approved the lending of money at a reasonable rate.

Not all the deductions drawn from the primary precepts of the natural law are universally true. They are binding in a majority of cases, but not in all. Exceptional facts may interfere with the observance of these precepts in cases of unusual occurrence. The reason is that these precepts depend not only on deductive conclusions but also upon specific ultimate facts. The particular rationally deduced conclusion from the primary principles of the natural law is only tentative. It will change with the addition, subtraction, or alteration of ultimate facts.

St. Thomas Aquinas has illustrated this point by the example of property entrusted by A to B. It is a mandate of a remote conclusion of the natural law that such property ought to be returned to its owner. This mandate holds true in a majority of cases under ordinary circumstances. But it would not be binding "if it would be injurious, and therefore unreasonable, to restore the goods held in trust." This would be the situation if the property in question were demanded in order to wage an unjust war against one's country. The precept "Property held in trust must be returned to its owner" becomes still more mutable the more multiple the factual details become. An example would be if the parties had agreed upon a deed of trust specifying the duration of the relationship and the precise conditions upon which the property was to be returned.

Thus the natural law provides a dynamic, as well as a static, basis for the moral order by sanctioning evolution within the fixed orbit of the natural tendencies and inclinations of rational human nature. It preserves a delicate and essential balance between the eternal and the temporal good. It distinguishes in kind between the enduring and permanent facts which are beyond the scope of sense, and those which exist in the world of changeable things. It allows for differences of fact-content which exist in various principles. It promotes moral growth toward the morally unchangeable.

In the second place, human law bears an immutable and absolute relationship to the natural law. The juridicity of human law arises from this relationship. Human law has the character of law to the extent that it is derived from the natural law, which is the first rule of reason. The force of a law depends on its justice, which in turn is determined by its reasonableness.

An enactment or a case-decision which is contrary to the natural law may have the appearance of law, but it is not law. Unjust human law does not bind in conscience. But prudence may dictate obedience to certain types of unjust law to avoid public disturbance, as where an unjust law takes away a person's right to a thing forbidden, but does not oblige him to do something intrinsically wrong.

The absolute relationship between natural law and human law requires that human lawmakers reinforce the primary and necessary conclusions of the natural law by means of state-law. If this were not done, some members of the community might not be aware of these conclusions, or else might not be inclined to obey. Besides human reason must devise certain discretionary rules left undetermined by the natural law.

The norms of state-law fall within two spheres, one static and the other dynamic. The fundamental static norms of such law are deduced from an analysis of the nature of man and all his essential relationships. These norms are recognized by all civilized societies to some extent, depending upon their particular level of intelligence. But the dynamic or inferior norms of human positive law express values which are in the nature of temporary generalizations of morals pertaining to the culture of the particular time or place. These dynamic norms are ascertained inductively by way of determinations of the superior principles of the natural law. They are syntheses produced by induction from a variety of facts.

Analysis, synthesis, deduction and induction are rooted in reason. It is reason which deduces the moral norm which forbids theft and confers the right of property from the total expression of the moral law, do good and avoid evil. It is also reason which determines by induction the particular type of property-law which should guarantee the right of property in a particular legal system. This induction will proceed consciously or subconsciously from the consideration of many factors, such as the customs and psychology of the people, their political, economic, and industrial environment, the nature and quantity of the land, and the like.

According to the natural law, human law must be changed whenever it becomes obsolete. Human skill may find more effective methods for implementing the primary principles of the natural law. Lawmakers may discover more successful ways of effectuating the mandate of those principles of positive law which stem from the necessary premises of the natural law. Again, they may make better determinations, or choices, in the discretionary area of human law. The natural law performs the vital function of providing a critical norm for every positive legal order.

Hence, facts and conclusions therefrom may and do change law and morals except insofar as these latter are founded on the first principles of the natural law. But the inferior norms underlying law and morals do not result entirely from facts which are known by the senses. Moral norms, as such, may not be extracted entirely from sense-facts which belong to a different order than value-judgments.

III

Roscoe Pound has written that "next to the nature of law, nineteenth century jurists were troubled about the relation of law and morals." They were disturbed because the Analytical School of Austin which had detached law from morals was proving socially inadequate to solve the contemporary problems of justice. It was becoming increasingly clear that morals, in some sense, must be restored to positive law, if the legal order was to function effectively.

The moral norm of abstract natural rights, based on a state of nature or a social compact, had proven sociologically unsatisfactory. Indeed the Analytical School had gained wide acceptance because it had offset the extreme subjectivism and the excessive tendency toward deduction of the Law of Nature School, which ignored or slighted experience. The Historical School of Maine had reintroduced the factor of experience by its investigations into cultural anthropology and ancient legal systems. But it could not offer the legislator any principle except that of history which would constitute an assured basis of creative law making for the future. In the nineteenth century, legal philosophers had so forgotten the Thomistic doctrine of the natural law as to cause Jhering, one of the founders of the Sociological School of Jurisprudence, to exclaim that he probably would not have written his entire book, if he had been aware of the doctrines of Thomas Aquinas.

The chief problem of Jurisprudence in the twentieth century has been that of how best to restore morals to law in a social context. Various solutions have been proposed by way of juristic doctrine, but none equals that of the Thomistic natural law. No other doctrine offers a greater promise of a legal order which will have the stability of human nature, yet will have sufficient flexibility to meet the ever changing needs of society. No other doctrine can guarantee so well that the legal order will be truly rational with regard to the content of its legal precepts, and its jural postulates. All other doctrines have a blind spot in their failure to locate the source of the authority which communicates stability to law and morals. Stability as well as flexibility is required for a legal order. But the concept of stability has no final significance, if all ideals admit of change, however slow that change may be.

The Sociological School of Jurisprudence attempted a solution with considerable functional success. Jhering had done much in Europe, beginning in the latter part of the nineteenth century, to build law on a morality of interests. These were antecedent to legal rights. Roscoe Pound protested against the abuse of liberty of contract, in the first decade of the twentieth century, and initiated the School of Sociological Jurisprudence in this country. The dominant thought of this School is that the individual, public and social interests behind the law are to be classified and appraised in terms of the moral ideals of the particular epoch. Legal stability and change are to be reconciled by an analysis from case to case of these interests. Legal rights are merely recognitions of certain interests. Social interests are the most important. They should prevail over the interests of the individual in case of an irreconcilable conflict. Society is regarded as an entity, a faceless mass.

The Sociological School thus far in the twentieth century has made many valuable legislative and judicial contributions to law. Scholastic Jurists, following the Thomistic concept of natural law, have approved these contributions. This is so because the present postulates of American civilization happen to conform, generally speaking, to the morals of the objective natural law.

But the doctrinal weakness of the theory of interests is the absence of any truly permanent norm for determining which interest ought to be legally recognized in the name of social utility. The chief cleavage of thought between the Sociological School and the Scholastic is that the former admits no absolute limit in regard to the satisfaction of social interests. The latter relies on the authority of the restraining first principles of the natural law to guarantee human rights forever.

Secondly, Kelsen has argued that his system of jurisprudence is dynamic and that of natural law is static. Kelsen maintains that the idea of justice is irrational. He excluded it from the field of jurisprudence. His pure theory of law and his hierarchy of juridical norms proceeding from a neo-Kantian logicism is disguised positivism. By conforming law to the ultimate, arbitrary norm of the majority, Kelsen enables law to grow, but not in any particular direction. His pure theory of law can contain any legal content which force chooses to put into it.

According to natural law, social progress does not consist in mere change. Kelsen's fear "that natural law derives the legal order from certain meaningful notions of justice," which "hold the legal order within a frame and freeze it into rigidity," sprang from a misunderstanding of the Thomistic concept. Lon Fuller has correctly refuted Kelsen with regard to this attack upon natural law by stating that it is a "plain fact that ideas are capable of growth."

Both Kelsen and Thomas Aquinas divided law into its static and its dynamic parts. Both agreed that a norm which is directly deduced from a basic norm, without any induction, belongs to a static order. But they fundamentally disagreed in that Kelsen made both types of law mere postulates, while St. Thomas rooted them in reason. Kelsen maintained that the practical reason, which perceives means and ends, as distinguished from the pure reason, which recognizes causes and effects, was actually not reason, but only sentiment. St. Thomas held, however, that each is an essential function of the single faculty of human reason. This is so even though the practical reason deals at times with contingent matters of detail wherein there cannot be absolute rectitude in moral matters.

Thirdly, Holmes, though a man of deep seated moral beliefs, professed a legal philosophy which was static rather than dynamic. It did not provide an ideal toward which the actual might move. General acceptance was his immediate measure of morality, and force the final criterion. His concept of law and morals lacked a vital principle of purposeful growth. Paradoxically, many of his decisions were not consistent with his formal philosophy.

Holmes attacked natural law jurisprudence without distinguishing between the numerous legal philosophies which have adopted that name. Apparently he was not aware of the tremendous dynamism of the Thomistic notion of the natural law. Doctrinally, he would not face up to the compelling fact of the permanence and intrinsic dignity of human personality. In one sense, he unknowingly proved the existence of natural law by absolutely denying that it had universal validity in regard to time and place.

IV

The philosophy of an objective natural law has been accepted for the most part in American constitutional theory. This acceptance is manifested, for example, by the doctrine of judicial supremacy. Historical evidence shows that the Constitution of the United States with its Bill of Rights, like Magna Carta, was an implementation of the natural law. According to the doctrine of judicial supremacy, an act of a legislature which is contrary to the Constitution does not have the force of law, although it may have the appearance of such. Since the Constitution is natural law which has been clothed with positive law, the doctrine of judicial supremacy upholds the legal philosophy of *Bonham's Case* and *Calvin's Case*, decided in the first part of the seventeenth century by Sir Edward Coke. These cases held in effect that legislation which violates the natural law is not law, and hence is not entitled to obedience.

The Anglo-American judiciary has adhered, generally speaking, to the body of ethical values which underlie Western civilization. These values were approved centuries ago, beginning at least as far back as Aristotle, by natural law, whether it be the *jus naturale* of the pagan world, or the *lex naturalis* of the Christian. But in adhering to these values, judges have not been sufficiently concerned with their source, or degree of permanence. At times the relation between natural law and positive law will be affirmed, as in the case of *Seidenberg* v. *Seidenberg* [126 F. Supp. 19] decided in 1954 by Judge Alexander Holtzoff of the United States District Court for the District of Columbia. He there stated: "The family is the foundation of society. The duty of a married man to support and protect his wife and children is inherent in human nature. It is a part of Natural Law, as well as a requirement of the law of every civilized country."

But the natural law jurist fears that if all these values are regarded merely as tentative generalizations, the day may come when their rejection may be hailed with moral approval. Indeed, specific cases may be considered to show that judges in courts of last resort at times will decide a case in contravention of the norms of the natural law. They do so because they do not trace their moral starting point far enough back so as to relate it to a primary precept of the natural law. Two classical examples may be cited, one in England, and the other in the United States.

The first case is *Baxter* v. *Baxter* [[1948] A.C. 274] decided in the House of Lords in 1948. The facts were that A sued B for an annulment on the grounds that there never was a marriage, because it had never been consummated from the time of the ceremony in 1934 until they separated in 1944. B refused intercourse, unless A took contraceptive precautions which prevented insemination. A complied, but consistently objected. He contended that "one of the principal ends, if not the principal end of marriage," was the procreation of children. The House of Lords denied the decree of nullity on the grounds that consummation had no essential relation to the procreation of children. The opinion stated in effect that such procreation was not the principal end of marriage.

In reaching this decision, the House of Lords apparently believed in all honesty that it was not violating the essence of Christian marriage, to which it specifically referred. But a scholastic critique of the case would conclude that it was in direct conflict with a primary principle of the natural law. It is an obvious deduction from the self evident truth that good must be done and evil avoided, that the human race must survive, and that this can only be achieved by means of some kind of an institution of marriage for the procreation and rearing of offspring. No induction is required to know that persons who have excluded procreation by a positive act of the will have not contracted marriage. This is an absolute and immutable principle which no change of facts will ever vitiate. This does not mean, however, that all persons must marry, but that the institution of marriage has for its primary purpose the survival-interest of humanity.

The second case is *Buck* v. *Bell* [(1927) 274 U.S. 200], decided by the Supreme Court of the United States in 1927. The facts were that the plaintiff in error was a feeble minded woman who had been committed to a state institution for epileptics and the mentally deranged. Her mother was in the same institution. She in turn was the mother of an illegitimate feeble minded child. The plaintiff in error had committed no crime which would warrant capital punishment. The State of Virginia passed a statute which vested discretion in the superintendents of certain mental institutions to sterilize mental defectives under careful medical and legal safeguards. The majority of the United States Supreme Court held that this statute was valid under the Fourteenth Amendment, for it did not deny due process and equal protection. Mandatory sterilization was compared with compulsory vaccination.

The major premise upon which this case was decided violated the natural law. The scholastic jurist would rather compare sterilization with killing than with vaccination. Sterilization is the mutilation not only of a member of the body, but also of an important faculty. Hence it may not be inflicted upon the morally innocent any more than capital punishment. Sterilization is in derogation of a fundamental precept of the natural law because of the necessary deductive relation which exists between the avoidance of moral evil and the killing of part of a person who has not withdrawn himself from the order of reason by the commission of grave crime.

In conclusion, it is the duty of the legal profession to understand that the separation of morals from the natural law is the first step toward detachment of the Common Law from its ancient moorings. Recognition of this duty is perhaps one of the reasons for the increasing interest in natural law by the American Bar Association as expressed by numerous recent articles on that subject in its Journal. The revival of natural law jurisprudence will succeed to the extent of the knowledge of that particular type of natural law doctrine which this article details.

A.P. d'Entrèves, 1902–
Professor of Political Science, University of Turin; Formerly Serena Professor of Italian Studies, Oxford University.

THE CASE FOR NATURAL LAW RE-EXAMINED (1956)

Any analysis of the relationship between law and morals must lead to the recognition that there is a difference between legal and moral obligation, a difference that does not necessarily entail separation. There must be a name for the relationship between the two, for the principle that spans the chasm that divides them, thus bringing law and morals into harmony. I have suggested elsewhere that this is one of the meanings, one of the essential meanings, in which the term "natural law" has been used through the ages. It is a convenient name for indicating the ground of obligation of law, which alone can ensure that the law itself is obeyed not only *propter iram* but *propter conscientiam.* And it is a no less convenient name for indicating the limits of the obligatoriness of the law, the crucial point: on it depends whether the injunction of the law is more than mere coercion.

Let me then turn back for a moment and survey our progress so far. If we have not yet found a definition of natural law, we have at any rate come across a number of things which seem to be implied in natural law thinking. We have found that law is no mere command, no arbitrary choice, for it involves a problem of obligation; we have found that it is impossible to understand this problem of obligation without examining the relationship between law and morals; and I have just suggested that, to express the "point of intersection" between law and morals, our benighted forbears had a name, natural law. And yet I doubt that natural law thinkers, old and new, would rest content with a definition of natural law as nothing but a name for the moral foundation of law, as nothing but the attempt to explain law in terms not of force or convention, but of obligation. They would, I surmise, consider such a definition as inadequate, and I think they would be right. For the most important feature of natural law is to stress not only the existence of a problem, but actually to provide an answer to it. Natural law theorists would point out that not all solutions of the problem of law and morals are equally valid, and that, it if were matter merely of explaining the obligatoriness of the law, Rousseau's general will can do that very well. They would emphatically assert that the only valid ground of legal obligation is given by a Law – an unwritten law, an ideal law – to which we can and must refer as the model or standard on which all laws depend and from which they derive their obligation.

We are thus brought to the third, and perhaps the most important, of the three characteristics of natural law thinking, the one to which I propose to devote my last two lectures. Needless to say, I shall endeavor to approach this last and most awkward side of my subject with the same caution I have practiced so far. I hope you will bear me no grudge for doing so. There are, after all, many mansions in the House of the Father; and if all natural law theorists agree on the existence of the ideal law, they have differed, and are bound to differ, in the manner of conceiving and defining it. We must therefore examine these differences with an open mind: this, at any rate, is my own personal conviction, and it is based not only on my own misgivings, but on the belief, which I have stressed from the start, that our purpose here is to find a common ground of understanding, and not to hoist a banner or to put forward a "blueprint" of ready-made solutions.

In brief, then, what I propose to do is to examine how, in different times and in different ways, the ideal law has been conceived and defined. In my mind, these conceptions and definitions seem to fall, roughly, under three main types or headings. These are and must be purely provisional headings. I think in fact that the moment we start classifying "types" or "patterns of thought" we run the risk of killing the very thing we are studying. But in very rough outline it seems that the notion of natural law has been, and can be, worked out in three different directions. The first is that of the ideal or natural law as a kind of "technology"; the second I would call the notion of natural law as an "ontology"; and the third might perhaps best be described as a "deontology". . . .

III. THE KNOWLEDGE OF AN IDEAL LAW: THE CHALLENGE OF NATURAL LAW THEORIES

MY TASK in the last two lectures is the examination of the various types or headings under which the attempts to define natural law – as the ideal or standard by which all laws can be valued and on which their obligation depends – may be classified. Before beginning this examination, and before even trying to explain if not to justify my headings, one point, which is a common mark of all and each of such attempts, calls for attention.

There is no denying that the very assertion of the existence and possibility of knowledge of an ideal law is the most serious challenge which natural law theory offers modern thought. Natural law is a stumbling block, indeed perhaps a scandal to the modern: and the reason, so we are told, is that the distinction between "fact" and "value," the opposition, in other words, between what *is* and what *ought to be*, has become, after Kant, the cornerstone of modern ethics. Kant's doctrine of the "autonomy of the will" is usually taken to mark the end of the natural law tradition.

I do not propose to discuss this view at this stage, a view which – to my mind at any rate – is subject to many reservations. But I would like to point out that if we want to go back to the real source of the distinction between "fact" and "value," if we want to have before our eyes – as we have on some other occasions – a clear and downright statement of the case, we can do no better than turn to a passage from Hume: "I cannot forbear adding to these reasonings an observation, which may, perhaps, be found of some importance. In every system of morality which I have hitherto met with, I have always remarked, that the author proceeds for some time in the ordinary way of reasoning, and establishes the being of a God, or makes observations concerning human affairs: when of a sudden I am surprised to find, that instead of the usual copulations of propositions, *is*, and *is not*, I meet with no proposition that is not connected with an *ought*, or an *ought not*. This change is imperceptible; but it is, however, of the last consequence. For as this *ought*, or *ought not*, expresses some new relation or affirmation, it is necessary that it should be observed and explained; and at the same time that a reason should be given, for what seems altogether unconceivable, how this new relation can be a deduction from others, which are entirely different from it."

I doubt that the main objection to natural law thinking could be put forward with more clarity and cogency than in this classic statement. It is the objection to what in the language of the modern semanticists is called the passage from the indicative to the imperative mood, an objection, one must admit, based on a perfectly accurate description of what natural law theorists are ultimately after. Rather than countering the objection forthwith, I am inclined to accept the description, and indeed enlarge it so far as to venture a new definition of natural law as the attempt to bridge the chasm between *is* and *ought*, between "fact" and "value." The classification I have proposed is in fact nothing other than the story of these different attempts: it remains to see to what extent they have been and can hope to be successful.

One first attempt is that of conceiving natural law as a "technology." This is an ugly word, which has gained undue popularity. This is what makes me specially reluctant to use it. But I have my reasons for doing so. Technology, according to the *Oxford Dictionary*, means "science of the industrial arts." But I do not think that I am forcing that meaning unduly by suggesting that it is a convenient name for indicating the knowledge of the rules of a particular art or craft – the "know-how," as the phrase now goes. And I believe that to many jurists, old and new, natural law was just this: the knowledge of the right rule, of the correct solution to a given problem in law, the answer that lies "in the nature of things," and which it is only a matter of finding and applying in order to have good laws.

Such at any rate – unless I am grossly mistaken – seems to have been in its broadest sense the Roman conception of natural law, on the importance of which I need hardly linger. Right at the beginning of the *Digest* we find the jurist Celsus defining law – *jus* – as *ars boni et aequi*. Surely, an "art" has its rules. Surely, therefore, there must be some means, some instrument for finding out the *bonum et aequum*. *Jus naturale* was that instrument. I am well aware of the ambiguities of the texts that have been handed down to us by Justinian. They are, and always will be, a matter of controversy. Of, late, the most authoritative interpreters have warned us against the mistake of conceiving the Roman notion of *jus naturale* as a philosophical construction. They draw a sharp line between the sweeping generalizations of such writers as Cicero and Seneca, and the "professional constructions" of the lawyers who are included in Justinian's book. *Jus naturale* was to these lawyers not a complete and ready-made system of rules, but essentially a means of interpretation, almost, as it were, the "trick of the trade" which they resorted to and used in a masterly fashion. In shaping a body of laws which would apply to the whole civilized world they had no abstract theories in mind, but aimed at the workable and practical.

If we consider and compare the several definitions of natural law which are contained in the first section of the *Digest* we undoubtedly find many contradictions. But these contradictions, however puzzling, are comparatively much less important than the fundamental agreement on one point, viz., on the view that there is no problem in law that cannot be solved, provided the *constans et perpetua voluntas* is there, *jus suum cuique tribuere.* "What natural reason dictates to all men," "what nature has taught all animals" – this is what the jurist and the lawgiver must keep in mind if they are to do their job well and construct a system that may prove *semper bonum et aequum.*

Clearly, this is not a philosophical proposition. It looks much rather like the "science of an art" according to the definition in the *Oxford Dictionary.* I cannot help being reminded, in connection with this Roman notion of natural law, of what seems to me a modern version of the same conception. I am thinking of Professor Fuller's assertion of the existence of a "natural order" underlying group life, which it is the task of the judge – and the lawgiver – to discover. I would almost be tempted to apply to the Roman notion of natural law his remark, that there is "nothing mystical" about it, that our attitude in approaching this kind of natural law is not "that of one doing obeisance before an altar, but more like that of a cook trying to find the secret of a flaky pie crust, or of an engineer trying to devise a means of bridging a ravine." I rather like to think of the Roman lawyers as cooks and engineers. The pie they cooked and the bridge they built were certainly remarkably good if they proved so successful all through the ages. Their "technology" was excellent. They did find the best working law for long centuries.

I would hardly dare to press my parallel much further. Yet, in another place, Professor Fuller provides me with some additional proof of what I have called the "technological" approach to our problem. "Because of the confusions invited by the term 'natural law' " he has recently recommended a new name for the field of study which natural law used to cover; and he suggests the term "eunomics" for "the science, theory or study of good order and workable arrangements." "Eunomics," Professor Fuller assures us, "involves no commitment to "ultimate ends." Its primary concern "is with the means aspect of the means-end relation." I surmise that one of the tasks of "eunomics" would be to discover the "natural laws of social order" as the best working laws in view of the particular ends of a given society.

Now Professor Fuller's theory provides me with the best definition of what I have called the technological notion of natural law. But it also provides me with the main objection which I would move against that notion. In plain, everyday language, the objection is that the "best working" law is not necessarily the "best" law. But that objection can also be put in more philosophical idiom by recalling the capital distinction between "technical" and "categorical" imperatives, a distinction which, to my mind, could hardly be more pertinent than in this case. The distinction is the one which Kant makes in the *Foundations of the Metaphysics of Morals*, sect. 2: "All imperatives command either hypothetically or categorically. The former present the practical necessity of a possible action as a means to achieving something else which one desires (or which one may possibly desire). The categorical imperative would be one which presented an action as of itself objectively necessary, without regard to any other end." Subsequently, Kant distinguishes hypothetical imperatives as "technical" (belonging to art), and "pragmatic" (belonging to welfare).

If anything, both the *jus naturale* of the Roman lawyers and Professor Fuller's "natural law of the social order" are hypothetical or technical imperatives in the Kantian sense. They are hypothetical inasmuch as they are means to an end, and technical insofar as they pertain to an "art" – though if one chose to call them "pragmatic" according to Kant's definition this would not alter their "hypothetical" character. If there were any doubts about it, here is an illustration given by Professor Fuller which clearly indicates the "technical" character of the law which, to him as to the Romans, lies in the *natura rei*. Suppose a man wants to assemble an engine: he can obviously do so only if he knows the proper rules of his job. There is no doubt that one such rule (and probably one only) exists. My comment would be that the finding out of this rule has nothing to do with the decision to do the job: our man could very well give up his attempts to assemble the engine and turn to some more congenial occupation. To determine the means for an end is quite different matter from ascertaining the "objective necessity" of the end itself: in other words, there is no warrant for turning a technical (hypothetical) imperative into a categorical one.

To conceive natural law as a "technology" is not to help us solve our problem of obligation. There is no intention to belittle its value and use; indeed these may be great within proper limits. By the help of *jus naturale* the Roman jurists worked out a system of laws which fitted men's needs for many centuries. And the modern lawgiver must keep the "nature of things" in mind, if he wants his laws to be fitting and efficient. I guess this is what is meant by saying – in the current jargon – that laws must conform to the existing "sociological requirements." The penalty for disregarding such requirements may be a heavy one. "Lawgivers are normally fairly sensible and therefore avoid imposing laws . . . which can be obeyed only by a wide departure from normal or probable behaviour. . . . Sometimes they go wrong on this (as the legislators of the United States did with the 18th Amendment) – and then there is trouble. Rationing and restrictions always breed black markets. But . . . lawgivers do not have to act sensibly nor do they have to consider exclusively the interests of their own social group. There is a statistical probability that they will do so, but to suppose that there is any necessity in all this is simply to become confused about the logical grammar of 'law'."

Once again I have quoted from Mr. Weldon's little book [*The Vocabulary of Politics*]. I think his rather caustic remarks bring out very neatly the point I have been trying to make. There is no proper link between "statistical probability" and moral obligation. The penalty for disregarding the "nature of things" or the "sociological requirements" does not provide any ground for asserting the absolute validity of the rules or laws deduced from them. Actually such laws are nothing more than statements of facts, even though cloaked in an "ought" proposition – as when we say: "if you want to accelerate you ought to press the pedal." It is a delusion to think that they can provide that bridge between the *is* and the *ought*, between "facts" and "values" which we are seeking.

With all its great credentials – which it would be blindness to deny –natural law as a technology does not provide the answer to our problem. Or, if it does so, it is only by assuming an end as the only right end to pursue, by surreptitiously introducing a "value" behind the "fact," and discarding the "hypothetical" for a "categorical" imperative. Personally, I am not sure that the Roman lawyers did not after all do something of the sort, and I am quite willing to admit that, if this were proved to be so, my strictures on the *jus naturale* would no longer be valid. But in that case we would probably have to subsume the Roman theory of natural law into that second category of natural law thinking to which I am now turning.

I shall devote the remainder of this lecture to examining this second type – if I may call it so – of natural law theory. I must say at once that this second type seems by far the most solidly grounded. The reservations which I shall have to make about it are not so much reservations on its philosophical basis, which is a very strong one; they are inspired by the very difficulty it presents for the common man, as well as by some serious misgivings about its supposed implications.

The second type has a name, a name which it deliberately gives itself. So this time I need not spend many words to justify my terminology. It is the ontological conception of natural law – the doctrine of natural law as an "ontology". With regard to the problem of bridging the chasm between *is* and *ought*, between "fact" and "values," this doctrine would appear to seize the bull by its horns, and to reply to Hume's challenge: there is no such chasm; your distinction is a wrong one. The ontological approach welds together being and oughtness, and maintains that the very notion of natural law stands and falls on that identification. This point is so important that I would like to clarify and emphasize it with the help of two quotations.

My first quotation comes from Professor Rommen. "The natural law . . . depends on the science of being, on metaphysics. Hence every attempt to establish the natural law must start from the fundamental relation of being and oughtness, of the real and the good." From Professor Wild I am selecting the following sentence: "All genuine natural law philosophy . . . must be unreservedly ontological in character. It must be concerned with the nature of existence in general, for it is only in the light of such basic analysis that the moral structure of human life can be more clearly understood." The fact that two thinkers approaching the problem from different angles agree so completely on this point seems to me particularly eloquent. Professor Rommen has a further and important remark: "The idea of natural law obtains general acceptance only in the periods when metaphysics, queen of the sciences, is dominant. It recedes or suffers an eclipse, on the other hand, when being . . . and oughtness, morality and law, are separated, when the essence of things and their ontological order are viewed as unknowable."

This last contention seems indeed to have very wide implications. It might be taken to mean that the very notion of natural law is an indication of "metaphysical" thinking. Thus it would open up some very interesting lines of research on the "metaphysics" underlying some "modern" conceptions of natural law – such as the conceptions of natural law which were so prominent and indeed so effective in the seventeenth and the eighteenth century. But this is clearly not what Professor Rommen has in mind, for to him there is one system, and one system only, which bases natural law on the "ontological order of things" – and this is the system of Thomist philosophy. There is no denying that St. Thomas Aquinas' doctrine of natural law still represents the most carefully thought out presentation of the ontological view, the most complete and thoroughgoing development both of its assumptions and of its implications.

I do not think that I need spend many words on the merits of St. Thomas doctrine of natural law. Personally, I would like to stress that in the eyes of the historian that doctrine is the embodiment of a great tradition, the tradition that proceeds from Greek and Roman thought and is welded to Christianity. In my view a further merit of the Thomist conception of natural law is that it does not reject that technical notion of natural law which the Roman lawyers had emphasized. On the contrary, it makes the largest possible use of it; it is just because St. Thomas was well trained in the law that his natural law has an eminently practical and realistic cast.

It is, beyond that, an almost unique example of closely knit philosophical argumentation. Its basis – in Professor Rommen's words – is a "conception of an order of reality" established in its essence by God's wisdom, and proceeding in its existence from God's will. It therefore provides an answer to each and every problem touched upon in this discussion: the relationship between reason and will in law, as well as the relationship between moral and legal obligation. In fact, if natural law is to be defined as the bridge between *is* and *ought*, between facts and values, St. Thomas' definition of it stands out for its cogency and conciseness: *lex naturalis nihil aliud est quam participatio legis aeternae in rationali creatura.* In the general "order of reality" man participates because he is a rational being, and hence has the possibility of attaining a knowledge of it. That knowledge thus becomes the condition and the source of all laws pertaining to men: "being themselves made participators in Providence itself, in that they control their own actions and the actions of others."

So brief a summary can hardly do justice to St. Thomas' theory of natural law. For my part I have tried to do it justice on another occasion, and my purpose here is merely to recall it as a perfect illustration of the "ontological" approach to our problem. Henceforward I shall willfully assume the role of the *advocatus diaboli,* trying to lay bare the reasons which make for its unpopularity outside a restricted circle of orthodox Thomists. I am still arguing on the assumption that we are here to find a common ground for our case. I still have Professor Goodhart's remark in mind, that "the real difficulty lies in finding a common basic premise."

Now it seems to me that in our divided world the first and most serious stumbling block to the Thomist conception of natural law lies precisely in its premise, in that metaphysical premise which both Professor Rommen and Professor Wild tell us is essential to the proper construction of natural law. It is the premise of a divine order of the world, which St. Thomas recalls at the very beginning of his theory of law, and from which he infers, with unimpeachable logic, the most detailed and specified consequences: *supposito quod mundus divina providentia regatur, ut in Primo habitum est.* Once that premise is granted, the whole majestic edifice of laws can be established on it: eternal law, the natural law, human and divine laws, all are ultimately based on and justified through the existence of a supreme, benevolent Being. In the words of a great English writer, who was also a good Thomist: "Of Law there can be no less acknowledged, than that her seat is the bosom of God, her voice the harmony of the world."

I have described this premise of the belief in God and in God's action in the world as a stumbling block. I need hardly add that I would not like to see my words misinterpreted. To be sure, such a belief, far from being a stumbling block to the Christian, is in fact the very essence of his faith. Yet even on this point, as we all well know, Christians have been, and perhaps still are divided. I had my good reasons for taking my last quotation from a Protestant writer, Richard Hooker. Protestant theology has not always been friendly towards the idea of natural law. Thomist natural law is only too often considered to be the exclusive preserve of Roman Catholics. There are, however, encouraging signs that such prejudices are gradually being overcome and the way paved for better understanding among Christians.

In a recent book on the *Law and the Laws* Dr. Nathaniel Micklem, Principal of Mansfield College, the Congregational Hall of Oxford, frankly recognizes that there was a break in the natural law tradition at the time of the Reformation. He points out that natural law plays very little part in Protestant theology, a least in the theology of the early reformers. But he remarks, "if the reformers were more pessimistic than the medieval Church they doubted neither that there is a law of nature nor that we may have cognizance of it, *nec tamen extincta est penitus notitia naturalis de Deo* (Melanchton)." Actually, Dr. Micklem concludes, the view that natural law commands – that there is an intimate connection between nature, reason and law – "is no fanciful or esoteric theological speculation but a reminder of the *philosophia perennis* significant alike to jurisprudence and theology."

The last remark undoubtedly shows how very far a modern Protestant theologian can go towards paying homage to the Thomist conception of the law of nature. But the world is not peopled only by Catholics and Protestants. The modern student of law need not necessarily be a Christian. In fact, lawyers have never had a very good reputation on that score: *Juristen böse Christen*! For the agnostic jurist of the present day, and perhaps indeed for the modern man who lives in a "de-christianized world," it will be very difficult to accept the notion of natural law, if that acceptance is made conditional on the acceptance of the metaphysical premise: *supposito quod mundus divina providentia regatur*. This, to my mind, is the first difficulty for the "ontological" theory of natural law – a difficulty which may not be a difficulty at all if we simply take the line: "Well, this is natural law. Take it or leave it." But we are here to find, if possible, a way of making the argument for natural law acceptable also to people who do not share our own premises.

The second objection is a more practical one. I have spoken of *Juristen* as *böse Christen*. Since I can well expect that such a description might not only cause offense but sound grossly exaggerated, let me try to define their attitude in more general terms as the attitude of men who, having to do with the everyday life and practice of the law, have little time for metaphysical cogitations. It might therefore happen that they accept the "ontological" notion of natural law because of their religious beliefs, as an essential part of Christian ethics, yet without probing into the problem more deeply; or else that they may have some slight feeling of impatience or embarrassment at being constantly reminded of the necessity of a philosophical and metaphysical training. I am not inventing this objection just for the sake of the argument. A discussion has lately taken place in Italy among Catholic lawyers on the subject of natural law. In reading the reports of that frank and very interesting discussion I think that the feelings I have described can be clearly detected. I would like to quote from the important contribution of Father Joseph Delos, O.P., to the discussion.

Father Delos takes his start from the general idea that inspired the discussion, the idea that there must be "a principle which provides the condition *sine qua non* of positive law." "Certainly," he says, "this is our common thought. I am taking this agreement into account in order to ask one further question. How are we lawyers to find and to clarify that principle?

"Let me explain my question: the theologian studies and works out that principle, he knows its origin and assesses its value; but we are not theologians. The philosopher does the same: but we are not philosophers. We are lawyers, and this means that we are addicted to a particular science which has an object of its own: the rule of positive law. Is there no way, no method which we can call our own? I believe there is; and thus that 'principle which provides the condition *sine qua non* of positive law' may in turn be explored by the theologian, by the philosopher – be a moralist or a metaphysician – and by the jurist as well, each of them doing his job with the method that is proper to his own discipline; and this third manner – that of the jurist – of presenting a truth that is essentially one, will not fail to be an enrichment of human knowledge. Let me add that for many lawyers this will be the main way – for some indeed the only way – of satisfying their intellectual needs."

I have cited this passage at length because it seems to me in many ways of great significance. If a theologian and a philosopher of Father Delos' calibre declares *nous ne sommes pas des theologiens, nous ne sommes pas des philosophes*, this can surely not be taken merely as a profession of modesty. It rather means that, *qua* jurist, he feels that he must as it were divest himself of his quality, of his capacity as a theologian or a philosopher, and that he must do so in order to make his position equal to that of the jurist, and understandable to him. There is, there must be *un chemin, une méthode* proper to the jurist – and different from that of the metaphysician and the theologian. For my part, I cannot help reading Father Delos' words as a healthy reminder that is better not to drive too many metaphysical nails into the jurist's head in our presentation of the case for natural law. Surely that case can be made without running the risk that, in refusing the "metaphysical premise," he may refuse natural law as well, thus throwing away the baby with the bath water.

The points I have raised so far are less objections than subjects of meditation. Now I must limit myself to a very brief mention of one or two further points which I think can be raised – and are often raised with regard to the ontological approach to natural law. One of them is the mistake of stressing its deductive possibilities too much, and thus turning it into the "blueprint of detailed solutions" against which Dean O'Meara so rightly warns us. This is precisely the mistake Mr. Constable makes – and I hope he will not take my comment ill – in his recent essay, *What does Natural Law Jurisprudence Offer*? Mr. Constable believes that, from a Thomist notion of natural law, based on the idea of "order," there can be inferred the idea of an "organic community," based on the idea of "service," "guided" – I am quoting his words – by "some persons or groups of persons" having "a clear insight into the nature of goodness."

I can only register quite frankly and openly my dissent from such views, and declare that if these were the implications of natural law, personally I would find it impossible to accept them. If not indeed of Plato's Republic, Mr. Constable's "organic community" seems to me to smack of that "corporativist" idea against which no lesser authority than Professor Maritain has warned us in his admirable essay, *The Rights of Man and Natural Law*, where he denounced it as one of the "temptations" deriving "from old concepts formerly in favor in certain Christian circles."

Let us be quite chary in drawing conclusions from "natural law" which might turn into a highly controversial political program. Let us not forget that the "organic theory of society" has in recent days been a welcome excuse for the suppression of individual freedom. Let us, above all, practice a healthy distrust of any "persons or groups" who claim to have "a clear insight into the nature of goodness."

With these last two points, we have come to the crux of the problem. The ontological theory of natural law is a great and impressive construction. But it does not seem to take into sufficient account those aspects of natural law that have become the lasting inheritance of modern man. With its insistence on the objective notion of "order" and law, it tends to disregard or to belittle the importance of the subjective notion of a claim and a right. In one word, it does not adquately stress that idea of "natural rights" which has become part and parcel of modern civilization. "We hold . . . that all men . . . are endowed by their Creator with certain unalienable Rights." Americans, after all, have proclaimed this doctrine to the world, and have inserted it in the *Declaration of Independence*.

No doubt the "ontologist" may point out that there is no "right" without "law," and that the very notion of subjective claim presupposes that of an objective order. And he will be perfectly justified in doing so, and this is where the ontological argument is indeed unassailable. But I seriously doubt that he can find any clear assertion of the claim – of "natural rights" – in his sources, whether in Plato or in St. Thomas Aquinas. This claim is in fact a modern development of "natural law," and for a recognition of "natural rights" the time was not ripe either in classical days or in the Middle Ages.

The same reservation should be made, I believe, with regard to the "clear insight into the nature of goodness," that is, to the authoritative interpretation of natural law which seems implied in the ontological position. Quite apart from the fact that an undue stress on the possibility of such authoritative interpretation runs the risk of converting natural law into a new kind of positivism, it is quite clear that such a notion can only be a further stumbling block to the modern. I sincerely hope that I will not be accused of conceding too much to some recent attacks on the revival of natural law as a cloak for the introduction of "authoritarian systems. If those shafts are aimed at the Church, I would like to say that they miss the mark insofar as the *magisterium* of the Church, which Catholics accept in the interpretation of moral truths, is after all based itself on a free acceptance. But the fact remains that, if the recognition of a "natural order of things" is linked to the idea of an authoritative interpretation through the Church or any given society, the revival of natural law will automatically rule out all those *qui foris sunt*, who do not belong to that society. Surely this is not what the conveners of this meeting had in mind. I propose to examine in my concluding lecture the possibilities of hope left for us in that revival.

IV. VALUE JUDGMENTS AND THE NATURAL LAW

IF BOTH natural law as a technology and natural law as an ontology are open to objections and encounter difficulties, is there a way of presenting the case for natural law in a manner which might – even if it did not ensure general acceptance – at least make that notion less obnoxious to the modern world at large? To avoid misgivings, I might as well begin by saying that, if I borrow the name for third kind of approach to natural law from the founder of utilitarianism, this should not be taken to mean that I am a follower of Bentham and pleading a merely utilitarian approach to our problem. It just happens that the word "deontology" seems to provide one of those convenient labels which must, however, always be used with necessary caution.

Can we agree, at least, on certain things that are binding? The problem is all here, in this very plain, simple question.

In order to develop my arguement, I am going back first of all to the image of the "bridge" – the bridge between fact and value, between what *is* and what *ought to be*. This time I am taking my text from an author who, though not very widely known in Anglo-Saxon countries, has of late been the subject of some very admirable work here in America. He is a fellow-countryman of mine, and his name is dear to all Italians.

At the beginning of his *Scienza Nuova* Giambattista Vico has a remark which seems important for the problem we are discussing. This remark is put forward in the form of two "axioms" or *Degnità* – the fundamental exposition of principles by which Vico prefaces his study of history and philosphy. I shall quote them here in the English translation which has recently been made of his work by two American scholars.

Degnità CXI: "The certitude of laws is an obscurity of judgment, backed only by authority, so that we find them harsh in application, yet are obliged to apply them by their certitude. In good Latin *certum* means *'particularized,'* or, *as the schools* say, 'individuated'; so that, in over-elegant Latin, *certum* and *commune* are opposed to each other."

Degnità CXIII: "The truth of the laws is a certain light and splendor with which natural reason illuminates them; so that jurisconsults are often in the habit of saying *verum est* for *aequum est.*"

I am quite ready to grant that the two passages I have quoted are far from being easy to interpret. But, to put it briefly, Vico's idea seems to be that in every law one can find an element which he calls the *certum* (the element of authority), and an element which he calls the *verum* (the element of "truth," which is discovered by "reason"). *Certum and Verum*, authority and reason, are the two facets of the law, two aspects of the same thing, two different angles from which all law can be considered. Sometimes the *certum* may obscure the *verum*, authority takes the place of judgement, and laws are obeyed only because of their "certitude." But there is no law which, illuminated by the light of reason, does not reveal an element of *verum*, the "truth" which it contains, like a soft kernel within the hard shell of authority that enfolds it: though it may happen that this very authority is the value of the law, that "certitude" is itself a valuable guarantee against the disrupting forces of anarchy, so as to justify the old Roman adage *dura lex sed lex* – which Vico would like to read: *lex dura est sed certa est.*

I believe that these ideas can shed some light on the problem which we are discussing, that they do constitute a new approach to the question of the bridge between *is* and *ought*, between facts and values. For indeed, insofar as every law is a compound of *certum* and *verum*, every law is in itself a bridge over the chasm – or at any rate an attempt at bridging it. For every law is no doubt a factual proposition, inasmuch as it is a particular authoritative statement. But it is also and at the same time – insofar as it aims at a particular end, and is not a senseless imposition – a statement about "values". . . .

What I want considered is this idea: it is possible in each and every legal proposition to ascertain the "value" it contains – even down to traffic regulations if you please, since there can be no doubt about the "value" they protect, that of our own personal safety. I know full well the ambiguity of the word "value" which I am using in this context; I would be quite willing to use a different word if I could think of a better one. My point is of far greater relevance, and far more controversial: for it amounts to nothing less than admitting that we have gone all this long way to find the ground of obligation of law without realizing that this ground does not lie outside, but within the law itself, that it must be sought in the interplay of the *verum* and the *certum*, in the ideal principle which is at work in every law despite the material circumstances that engross it. For each and every law is indeed nothing other than a "normative translation" of a particular value: we must try and break the shell in order to get to the kernel. And if a particular rule will not yield an answer to our quest, it is to the general system of which that rule is a part that we must turn, and we will no doubt find it. . . . .

So much for the *verum* and the *certum* of the law and for the presence of a value judgment in every legal proposition. I have been very agreeably surprised to come across some interesting work lately done in this country on lines singularly akin to the one I have been indicating. I refer to Professor McDougal's program of "value clarification." I believe as he does that there is a new and fascinating line of enquiry open to jurisprudence. My only difference with Professor McDougal is, that while he seems to think of the "values" underlying a given legal proposition or a given legal order as "preferences," as "goals," as "objects of decision," I would plead that they should also and foremost be considered and studied as "grounds of obligation." In fact, I believe that it is here the notion of natural law as a "deontology" can, if at all, find its justification: for the problem of natural law is to me essentially that of the intersection between the legal proposition and the value that underlies it, the ascertainment of the element of obligation that makes us feel we are obeying the law not merely because of its "certitude," – to use Vico's expression again – but because of the element of "truth" it contains, a truth carrying conviction. The difficulty of course is to persuade ourselves that such "values" are "objective qualities" in the law itself and not mere subjective or emotional reactions on our part, devoid of any universality. . . . For my part, I believe that in every human society, in fact in "Human nature" itself, there are certain ultimate standards or values which determine approval or disapproval, assent or dissent; and I believe that it is these same values that determine our judgment as to whether a law is "just" or "unjust": in other words – to use a very ancient language that seems perfectly appropriate at this point – whether we are bound in conscience to obey it or not. To ascertain such values may be thought a modest – or an immodest – undertaking. Yet I think that, failing all other ways, such an undertaking is well worth attempting, and may even in the end lead us to a much greater amount of agreement than we might expect. Personally, I am quite willing to accept Mr. McDougal's "tabulation" of the values which correspond to "our present-day democratic preferences for a peaceful world" as a very near approximation of the values I have in mind. Surely it is only his modesty as a field worker, his concern with a purely "scientific" presentation of the case, that prevents Professor McDougal from seeing such values not only as resulting from our "democratic preferences," but as corresponding for a very large part to what *semper et ubique* has been thought *bonum et aequum*. In fact, they are in many points reminiscent of what our benighted forebears would have called "natural law."

Pope John XXIII, 1881-1963.

PACEM IN TERRIS (PEACE ON EARTH) (1963)

Order Among Men

(8) First of all, it is necessary to speak of the order which should exist among men.

(9) Any human society, if it is to be well-ordered and productive, must lay down as a foundation this principle, namely, that every human being is a person, that is, his nature is endowed with intelligence and free will. By virtue of this, he has rights and duties of his own, flowing directly and simultaneously from his very nature. These rights are therefore universal, inviolable and inalienable. . . .

RIGHTS

(11) Beginning our discussion of the rights of man, we see that every man has the right to life, to bodily integrity, and to the means which are necessary and suitable for the proper development of life. These means are primarily food, clothing, shelter, rest, medical care, and finally the necessary social services. Therefore, a human being also has the right to security in cases of sickness, inability to work, widowhood, old age, unemployment, or in any other case in which he is deprived of the means of subsistence through no fault of his own.

Rights Pertaining to Moral and Cultural Values

(12) By the natural law, every human being has the right to respect for his person, to his good reputation, to freedom in searching for truth and – within the limits laid down by the moral order and the common good – in expressing and communicating his opinions, and in pursuit of art. He has the right, finally, to be informed truthfully about public events.

(13) The natural law also gives man the right to share in the benefits of culture, and therefore the right to a basic education or to technical or professional training in keeping with the stage of educational development in the country to which he belongs. Every effort should be made to insure that persons be enabled, on the basis of merit, to go to higher studies, so that, as far as possible, they may occupy posts and take on responsibilities in human society in accordance with their natural gifts and the skills they have acquired.

Right to Worship God According to Conscience

(14) Every human being has the right to honor God according to the dictates of an upright conscience, and the right to profess his religion privately and publicly. For, as Lactantius so clearly taught: *We were created for the purpose of showing to the God who bore us the due submission we owe Him, of recognizing Him alone, and of serving Him. We are obliged and bound by this duty to God; from this, religion itself receives its name.*

And on this point Our predecessor of immortal memory, Leo XIII, declared: *This genuine, this honorable freedom of the sons of God, which most nobly protects the dignity of the human person, is greater than any violence or injustice; it has always been sought by the Church, and always most dear to her. This was the freedom which the Apostles claimed with intrepid constancy, which the apologists defended with their writings, and which the martyrs in such numbers consecrated with their blood.*

Right to Choose Freely One's State of Life

(15) Human beings have, in addition, the right to choose freely the state of life which they prefer. They therefore have the right to set up a family, with equal rights and duties for man and woman, and also the right to follow a vocation to the priesthood or the religious life.

(16) The family, grounded on marriage freely contracted, monogamous and indissoluble, must be considered the first and essential cell of human society. To it must be given, therefore, every consideration of an economic, social, cultural and moral nature which will strength its stability and facilitate the fulfillment of its specific mission.

(17) Parents, however, have a prior right in the support and education of their children.

Economic Rights

(18) When we turn to the economic sphere, it is clear that human beings have the natural right to free initiative in the economic field and the right to work.

(19) Indissolubly linked with those rights is the right to working conditions in which physical health is not endangered, morals are safeguarded and young people's normal development is not impaired. Women have the right to working conditions in accordance with their requirements and their duties as wives and mothers.

(20) From the dignity of the human person there also arises the right to carry on economic activities according to the degree of responsibility of which one is capable. Furthermore – and this must be specially emphasized – there is the worker's right to a wage determined according to criteria of justice. This means,

therefore, one sufficient, in proportion to the available resources, to give the worker and his family a standard of living in keeping with human dignity. In this regard, Our predecessor Pius XII said:

To the personal duty to work imposed by nature, there corresponds and follows the natural right of each individual to make of his work the means to provide for his own life and the lives of his children; so profoundly is the empire of nature ordained for the preservation of man.

(21) The right to private property, even of productive goods, also derives from the nature of man. This right, as We have elsewhere declared, *is a suitable means for safeguarding the dignity of the human person and for the exercise of responsibility in all fields; it strengthens and gives serenity to family life, thereby increasing the peace and prosperity of the state.*

(22) However, it is opportune to point out that there is a social duty inherent in the right of private property.

Right of Assembly and Association

(23) From the fact that human beings are by nature social, there arises the right of assembly and association. They have also the right to give the societies of which they are members the form they consider most suitable for the aim they have in view, and to act within such societies on their own initiative and responsibility in order to achieve their desired objectives.

(24) We Ourselves strongly cautioned in the encyclical *Mater et Magistra* that, for the achievement of ends which individual human beings cannot attain except by association, it is necessary and indispensable to set up a great variety of intermediate groups and bodies in order to guarantee the dignity of the human person and safeguard a sufficient sphere of freedom and responsibiiity.

Right to Emigrate And Immigrate

(25) Every human being must also have the right to freedom of movement and of residence within the confines of his own country, and, when there are just reasons for it, the right to emigrate to other countries and take up residence there. The fact that one is a citizen of a particular state does not detract in any way from his membership in the human family, nor from his citizenship in the world community and his common tie with all men.

Political Rights

(26) The dignity of the human person involves, moreover, the right to take an active part in public affairs and to contribute one's part to the common good of the citizens. For, as Our predecessor of happy memory, Pius XII, pointed out: *The human individual, far from being an object and, as it were, a merely passive element in the social order, is in fact, must be and must continue to be, its subject, its foundation and its end.*

(27) The human person is also entitled to a juridical protection of his rights, a protection that should be efficacious, impartial and in conformity with true norms of justice.

As Our predecessor Pius XII warns: *That perpetual privilege proper to man, by which every individual has a claim to the protection of his rights, and by which there is assigned to each a definite and particular sphere of rights, immune from all arbitrary attacks, is the logical consequence of the order of justice willed by God.*

DUTIES

Rights And Duties Linked In The One Person

(28) The natural rights with which We have been dealing are, however, inseparably connected, in the very person who is their subject, with just as many respective duties. And rights as well as duties find their source, their sustenance and their inviolability in the natural law which grants or enjoins them.

(29) For example, the right of every man to life is correlative with the duty to preserve it; his right to a decent standard of living, with the duty of living it becomingly; and his right to investigate the truth freely, with the duty of pursuing it ever more completely and profoundly.

Reciprocity Of Rights And Duties Between Persons

(30) Once this is admitted, it is also clear that in human society to one man's natural right there corresponds a duty in other persons: the duty, namely, of acknowledging and respecting the right in question. For every fundamental human right draws its indestructible moral force from the natural law, which, in granting it, imposes a corresponding obligation. Those, therefore, who claim their own rights, yet altogether forget or neglect to carry out their respective duties, are people who build with one hand and destroy with the other.

(31) Since men are social by nature, they are meant to live with others and to work for one another's welfare. Hence, a well-ordered human society requires that men recognize and observe their mutual rights and duties. It also demands that each contribute generously to the establishment of a civic order in which rights and duties are progressively more sincerely and effectively acknowledged and fulfilled.

(32) It is not enough, for example, to acknowledge and respect every man's right to the means of subsistence. One must also strive to insure that he actually has enough in the way of food and nourishment.

(33) The society of men must not only be organized but must also provide them with abundant resources. This certainly, requires that they recognize and fulfill their mutual rights and duties. It also requires that they all collaborate in the many enterprises that modern civilization either allows or encourages or even demands.

An Attitude Of Responsibility

(34) The dignity of the human person also requires that every man enjoy the right to act freely and responsibly. For this reason, in social relations especially man should exercise his rights, fulfill his obligations and, in the countless forms of collaboration with others, act chiefly on his own responsibility and initiative. This is to be done in such a way that each one acts on his own decision, of set purpose and from a consciousness of his obligation, without being moved by force or pressure brought to bear on him externally.

For any human society that is established on the sole basis of force must be regarded as simply inhuman, inasmuch as the freedom of its members is repressed, when in fact they should be provided with appropriate incentives and means for developing and perfecting themselves.

Social Life In Truth, Justice, Charity, Freedom

(35) A political society is to be considered well-ordered, beneficial and in keeping with human dignity if it is grounded on truth. As the Apostle Paul exhorts us: *Wherefore, put away lying and speak truth each one with his neighbor, because we are members of another.* This indeed will be the outcome when reciprocal

rights and duties are sincerely recognized.

Furthermore, human society will be such as We have just described it, if the citizens, guided by justice, apply themselves seriously to respecting the rights of others and discharging their own duties; if they are moved by such fervor of charity as to make their own the needs of others, and share with others their own goods; if, finally, they everywhere work for a progressively closer fellowship in the world of spiritual values. Moreover, human society is realized in freedom, that is to say, by ways and means in keeping with the dignity of its citizens, who accept the responsibility of their actions precisely because they are by nature rational beings.

(36) Human society, venerable brothers and beloved children, ought to be regarded above all as a spiritual reality; one in which men communicate knowledge to each other in the light of truth; in which they can enjoy their rights and fulfill their duties, and are inspired to strive for goods of the spirit. Society should enable men to share in and enjoy every legitimate expression of beauty. It should encourage them constantly to pass on to others all that is best in themselves, while they strive to make their own the spiritual achievements of others. These are the values which continually give life and basic orientation to cultural expressions, economic and social institutions, political movements and forms, laws and all other structures by which society is outwardly established and constantly developed.

(37) The order which prevails in society is by nature moral. Grounded as it is in truth, it must function according to the norms of justice, it should be inspired and perfected by mutual love, and finally it should be brought to an ever more refined and human balance in full freedom. . . .

It is evident from the views of John XXIII and d'Entrèves presented in this chapter and those of Dean O'Meara presented in Chapter V that the abstract and objective character of the traditional Catholic natural law theories is undergoing a searching re-examination, and many traditionally held positions are being challenged.

First, an edict not in accord with reason was traditionally said to be lawlessness or violence rather than law – neither was it law nor should it be called law. Today Catholic thinkers are beginning to be willing to grant the use of the name 'law' to all enactments of the State, if only to avoid continuous and fruitless semantic bickering. Moreover, many Catholic jurisprudents would grant the effective reality as well as the name. Dean O'Meara of Notre Dame Law School says: "Law is law, whether it be good or bad." Sir Henry Slesser, formerly a Lord Justice of Appeal in England, writes:

> "In general . . . I would prefer the views of Cardozo . . . that my duty as a Judge must be 'to objectify the law, not my own aspirations, convictions and philosophies, but those of men and women of my time'. This seems to me to introduce that objective reference which is so essential in valid judgment. I, personally, may believe in the indissolubility of the married state, I may regard it as sacramental, but that should not influence me as a Judge. Assuming that the people as a whole, both through Parliament and in their minds, have accepted divorce as a legal and social institution, I ought not to hesitate to apply an approval of a morality based upon that assumption." [*The Art of Judgment* 38 (1962)].

Both O'Meara and Slesser conceive it to be a Catholic judge's duty to resign, rather than to attempt to subvert the law from the Bench, but both also feel that such an extreme step is not likely to be necessary.

Second, although St. Thomas himself gave the legislative element of law its due place, there has always been a tendency among Christian philosophers to stress the static, derived element. Today it is clearly recognized that by far the greater part of law is invented, not discovered. There is a new stress on the dynamic, inductive aspect of law.

Third, there was for centuries an alliance between natural law theory and the old Blackstonian theory of pre-existing rules of law which judges found but did not make, whereas it now appears to many natural lawyers that this alliance exaggerates the rational, derived element of human positive law at the expense of the volitional, legislative element, and that such an exaggeration is a gross distortion of natural law theory, which should rather ally itself with legal realism in an acceptance of judicial creativity.

Not all of the innovations will prove of lasting value. Many progressive natural lawyers will undoubtedly draw the line at Dean O'Meara's too ready concession that natural law must be content to be a non-reason theory and particularly at his statement: "I do not envisage natural law as the arbiter of legal validity." Whatever conclusion is reached as to the use of the word "law" and as to the consequences for the judge, it is not likely that there will be a complete abandonment of the moral critique of law.

But d'Entrèves and O'Meara make a powerful case for the view that natural law theory must do a better job than it has of respecting the integrity and autonomy of the legal order. In a word, it must become less abstract. In this regard the existentialist emphasis of John XXIII in making the person (rather than an abstract principle) the foundation of natural law is likely to be of profound significance.

For a natural law statement sympathetic to legal realism see MacGuigan, "The Problem of Law and Morals in Contemporary Jurisprudence" (1962) 8 *Catholic Law.* 293.

Lon L. Fuller, 1902–
Carter Professor of General Jurisprudence, Harvard University.

POSITIVISM AND FIDELITY TO LAW – A REPLY TO PROFESSOR HART

II. THE DEFINITION OF MORALITY

It is characteristic of those sharing the point of view of Professor Hart that their primary concern is to preserve the integrity of the concept of law. Accordingly, they have generally sought a precise definition of law, but have not been at pains to state just what it is they mean to exclude by their definitions. They are like men building a wall for the defense of a village, who must know what it is they wish to protect, but who need not, and indeed cannot, know what invading forces those walls may have to turn back.

When Austin and Gray distinguish law from morality, the word "morality" stands indiscriminately for almost every conceivable standard by which human conduct may be judged that is not itself law. The inner voice of conscience, notions of right and wrong based on religious belief, common conceptions of decency and fair play, culturally conditioned prejudices – all of these are grouped together under the heading of "morality" and are excluded from the domain of law. For the most part Professor Hart follows in the tradition of his predecessors. When he speaks of morality he seems generally to have in mind all sorts of extra-legal notions about "what ought to be," regardless of their sources, pretensions, or intrinsic worth. This is particularly apparent in his treatment of the problem of interpretation, where uncodified notions of what ought to be are viewed as affecting only the penumbra of law, leaving its hard core untouched.

Toward the end of the essay, however, Professor Hart's argument takes a turn that seems to depart from the prevailing tenor of his thought. This consists in reminding us that there is such a thing as an immoral morality and that there are many standards of "what ought to be" that can hardly be called moral. Let us grant, he says, that the judge may properly and inevitably legislate in the penumbra of a legal enactment, and that this legislation (in default of any other standard) must be guided by the judge's notions of what ought to be. Still, this would be true even in a society devoted to the most evil ends, where the judge would supply the insufficiencies of the statute with the iniquity that seemed to him most apt for the occasion. Let us also grant, says Professor Hart toward the end of his essay, that there is at times even something that looks like discovery in the judicial process, when a judge by restating a principle seems to bring more clearly to light what was really sought from the beginning. Again, he reminds us, this could happen in a society devoted to the highest refinements of sin, where the implicit demands of an evil rule might be a matter for discovery when the rule was applied to a situation not consciously considered when it was formulated.

I take it that this is to be a warning addressed to those who wish "to infuse more morality into the law." Professor Hart is reminding them that if their program is adopted the morality that actually gets infused may not be to their liking. If this is his point it is certainly a valid one, though one wishes it had been made more explicitly, for it raises much the most fundamental issue of his whole argument. Since the point is made obliquely, and I may have misinterpreted it, in commenting I shall have to content myself with a few summary observations and questions.

First, Professor Hart seems to assume that evil aims may have as much coherence and inner logic as good ones. I, for one, refuse to accept that assumption. I realize that I am here raising, or perhaps dodging, questions that lead into the most difficult problems of the epistemology of ethics. Even if I were competent to undertake an excursus in that direction, this is not the place for it. I shall have to rest on the assertion of a belief that may seem naive, namely, that coherence and goodness have more affinity than coherence and evil. Accepting this belief, I also believe that when men are compelled to explain and justify their decisions, the effect will generally be to pull those decisions toward goodness, by whatever standards of ultimate goodness there are. Accepting these beliefs, I find a considerable incongruity in any conception that envisages a possible future in which the common law would "work itself pure from case to case" toward a more perfect realization of iniquity.

Second, if there is a serious danger in our society that a weakening of the partition between law and morality would permit an infusion of "immoral morality," the question remains, what is the most effective protection against this danger? I cannot myself believe it is to be found in the positivist position espoused by Austin, Gray, Holmes, and Hart. For those writers seem to me to falsify the problem into a specious simplicity which leaves untouched the difficult issues where real dangers lie.

Third, let us suppose a judge bent on realizing through his decisions an objective that most ordinary citizens would regard as mistaken or evil. Would such a judge be likely to suspend the letter of the statute by openly invoking a "higher law"? Or would he be more likely to take refuge behind the maxim that "law is law" and explain his decision in such a way that it would appear to be demanded by the law itself?

Fourth, neither Professor Hart nor I belong to anything that could be said in a significant sense to be a "minority group" in our respective countries. This has its advantages and disadvantages to one aspiring to a philosophic view of law and government. But suppose we were both transported to a country where our beliefs were anathemas, and where we, in turn, regarded the prevailing morality as thoroughly evil. No doubt in this situation we would have reason to fear that the law might be covertly manipulated to our disadvantage; I doubt if either of us would be apprehensive that its injunctions would be set aside by an appeal to a morality higher than law. If we felt that the law itself was our safest refuge, would it not be because even in the most perverted regimes there is a certain hesitancy about writing cruelties, intolerances, and inhumanities into law? And is it not clear that this hesitancy itself derives, not from a separation of law and morals, but precisely from an identification of law with those demands of morality that are the most urgent and the most obviously justifiable, which no man need be ashamed to profess?

Fifth, over great areas where the judicial process functions, the danger of an infusion of immoral, or at least unwelcome, morality does not, I suggest, present a real issue. Here the danger is precisely the opposite. For example, in the field of commercial law the British courts in recent years have, if I may say so, fallen into a "law-is-law" formalism that constitutes a kind of belated counterrevolution against all that was accomplished by Mansfield. The matter has reached a stage approaching crisis as commercial cases are increasingly being taken to arbitration. The chief reason for this development is that arbitrators are willing to take into account the needs of commerce and ordinary standards of commercial fairness. I realize that Professor Hart repudiates "formalism," but I shall try to show later why I think his theory necessarily leads in that direction.

Sixth, in the thinking of many there is one question that predominates in any discussion of the relation of law and morals, to the point of coloring everything that is said or heard on the subject. I refer to the kind of question raised by the Pope's pronouncement concerning the duty of Catholic judges in divorce actions. This pronouncement does indeed raise grave issues. But it does not present a problem of the relation between law, on the one hand, and, on the other, generally shared views of right conduct that have grown spontaneously through experience and discussion. The issue is rather that of a conflict between two pronouncements, both of which claim to be authoritative; if you will, it is one kind of law against another. When this kind of issue is taken as the key to the whole problem of law and morality, the discussion is so denatured and distorted that profitable exchange becomes impossible. In mentioning this last aspect of the dispute about "positivism," I do not mean to intimate that Professor Hart's own discussion is dominated by any *arrière-pensée*; I know it is not. At the same time I am quite sure that I have indicated accurately the issue that will be uppermost in the minds of many as they read his essay.

In resting content with these scant remarks, I do not want to seem to simplify the problem in a direction opposite to that taken by Professor Hart. The questions raised by "immoral morality" deserve a more careful exploration than either Professor Hart or I have offered in these pages.

III. THE MORAL FOUNDATION OF A LEGAL ORDER

Professor Hart emphatically rejects "the command theory of law," according to which law is simply a command backed by a force sufficient to make it effective. He observes that such a command can be given by a man with a loaded gun, and "law surely is not the gunman situation writ large." There is no need to dwell here on the inadequacies of the command theory, since Professor Hart has already revealed its defects more clearly and succinctly than I could. His conclusion is that the foundation of a legal system is not coercive power, but certain "fundamental accepted rules specifying the essential lawmaking procedures."

When I reached this point in his essay, I felt certain that Professor Hart was about to acknowledge an important qualification on his thesis. I confidently expected that he would go on to say something like this: I have insisted throughout on the importance of keeping sharp the distinction between law and morality. The question may now be raised, therefore, as to the nature of these fundamental rules that furnish the framework within which the making of law takes place. On the one hand, they seem to be rules, not of law, but of morality. They derive their efficacy from a general acceptance, which in turn rests ultimately on a perception that they are right and necessary. They can hardly be said to be law in the sense of an authoritative pronouncement, since their function is to state when a pronouncement is authoritative. On the other hand, in the daily functioning of the legal system they are often treated and applied much as ordinary rules of law are. Here, then, we must confess there is something that can be called a "merger" of law and morality, and to which the term "intersection" is scarcely appropriate.

Instead of pursuing some such course of thought, to my surprise I found Professor Hart leaving completely untouched the nature of the fundamental rules that make law itself possible, and turning his attention instead to what he considers a confusion of thought on the part of the critics of positivism. Leaving out of account his discussion of analytical jurisprudence, his argument runs something as follows: Two views are associated with the names of Bentham and Austin. One is the command theory of law, the other is an insistence on the separation of law and morality. Critics of these writers came in time to perceive – "dimly" Professor Hart says – that the command theory is untenable. By a loose association of ideas they wrongly supposed that in advancing reasons for rejecting the command theory they had also refuted the view that law and morality must be sharply separated. This was a "natural mistake," but plainly a mistake just the same.

I do not think any mistake is committed in believing that Bentham and Austin's error in formulating improperly and too simply the problem of the relation of law and morals was part of a larger error that led to the command theory of law. I think the connection between these two errors can be made clear if we ask ourselves what would have happened to Austin's system of thought if he had abandoned the command theory.

One who reads Austin's Lectures V and VI cannot help being impressed by the way he hangs doggedly to the command theory, in spite of the fact that every pull of his own keen mind was toward abandoning it. In the case of a sovereign monarch, law is what the monarch commands. But what shall we say of the "laws" of succession which tell who the "lawful" monarch is? It is of the essence of a command that it be addressed by a superior to an inferior, yet in the case of a "sovereign many," say, a parliament, the sovereign seems to command itself since a member of parliament may be convicted under a law he himself drafted and voted for. The sovereign must be unlimited in legal power, for who could adjudicate the legal bounds of a supreme lawmaking power? Yet a "sovereign many" must accept the limitation of rules before it can make law at all. Such a body can gain the power to issue commands only by acting in a "corporate capacity"; this it can do only by proceeding "agreeably to the modes and forms" established and accepted for the making of law. Judges exercise a power delegated to them by the supreme lawmaking power, and are commissioned to carry out its "direct or circuitous commands." Yet in a federal system it is the courts which must resolve conflicts of competence between the federation and its components.

All of these problems Austin sees with varying degrees of explicitness, and he struggles mightily with them. Over and over again he teeters on the edge of an abandonment of the command theory in favor of what Professor Hart has described as a view that discerns the foundations of a legal order in "certain fundamental accepted rules specifying the essential lawmaking procedures." Yet he never takes the plunge. He does not take it because he had a sure insight that it would forfeit the black-and-white distinction between law and morality that was the whole object of his Lectures – indeed, one may say, the enduring object of a dedicated life. For if law is made possible by "fundamental accepted rules" – which for Austin must be rules, not of law, but of positive morality – what are we to say of the rules that the lawmaking power enacts to regulate its own lawmaking? We have election laws, laws allocating legislative representation to specific geographic areas, rules of parliamentary procedure, rules for the qualification of voters, and many other laws and rules of similar nature. These do not remain fixed, and all of them shape in varying degrees the lawmaking process. Yet how are we to distinguish between those basic rules that owe their validity to acceptance, and those which are properly rules of law, valid even when men generally consider them to be evil or ill-advised? In other words, how are we to define the words "fundamental" and "essential" in Professor Hart's own formulation: "certain fundamental accepted rules specifying the essential lawmaking procedure"?

The solution for this problem in Kelsen's theory is instructive. Kelsen does in fact take the plunge over which Austin hesitated too long. Kelsen realizes that before we can distinguish between what is law and what is not, there must be an acceptance of some basic procedure by which law is made. In any legal system there must be some fundamental rule that points unambiguously to the source from which laws must come in order to be laws. This rule Kelsen called "the basic norm." In his own words,

> "The basic norm is not valid because it has been created in a certain way, but its validity is assumed by virtue of its content. It is valid, then, like a norm of natural law. . . . The idea of a pure positive law, like that of natural law, has its limitations."

It will be noted that Kelsen speaks, not as Professor Hart does, of "fundamental rules" that regulate the making of law, but of a single rule or norm. Of course, there is no such single rule in any modern society. The notion of the basic norm is admittedly a symbol, not a fact. It is a symbol that embodies the positivist quest for some clear and unambiguous test of law, for some clean, sharp line that will divide the rules which owe their validity to their source and those which owe their validity to acceptance and intrinsic appeal. The difficulties Austin avoided by sticking with the command theory, Kelsen avoids by a fiction which simplifies reality into a form that can be absorbed by positivism.

A full exploration of all the problems that result when we recognize that law becomes possible only by virtue of rules that are not law, would require drawing into consideration the effect of the presence or absence of a written constitution. Such a constitution in some ways simplifies the problems I have been discussing, and in some ways complicates them. In so far as a written constitution defines basic lawmaking procedure, it may remove the perplexities that arise when a parliament in effect defines itself. At the same time, a legislature operating under a written constitution may enact statutes that profoundly affect the lawmaking procedure and its predictable outcome. If these statutes are drafted with sufficient cunning, they may remain within the frame of the constitution and yet undermine the institutions it was intended to establish. If the "court-packing" proposal of the 'thirties does not illustrate this danger unequivocally, it at least suggests that the fear of it is not fanciful. No written constitution can be self-executing. To be effective it requires not merely the respectful deference we show for ordinary legal enactments, but that willing convergence of effort we give to moral principles in which we have an active belief. One may properly work to amend a constitution, but so long as it remains unamended one must work with it, not against it or around it. All this amounts to saying that to be effective a written constitution must be accepted, at least provisionally, not just as law, but as good law.

What have these considerations to do with the ideal of fidelity to law? I think they have a great deal to do with it, and that they reveal the essential incapacity of the positivistic view to serve that ideal effectively. For I believe that a realization of this ideal is something for which we must plan, and that is precisely what positivism refuses to do.

Let me illustrate what I mean by planning for a realization of the ideal of fidelity to law. Suppose we are drafting a written constitution for a country just emerging from a period of violence and disorder in which any thread of legal continuity with previous governments has been broken. Obviously such a constitution cannot lift itself unaided into legality; it cannot be law simply because it says it is. We should keep in mind that the efficacy of our work will depend upon general acceptance and that to make this acceptance secure there must be a general belief that the constitution itself is necessary, right, and good. The provisions of the constitution should, therefore, be kept simple and understandable, not only in language, but also in purpose. Preambles and other explanations of what is being sought, which would be objectionable in an ordinary statute, may find an appropriate place in our constitution. We should think of our constitution as establishing a basic procedural framework for future governmental action in the enactment and administration of laws. Substantive limitations on the power of government should be kept to a minimum and should generally be confined to those for which a need can be generally appreciated. In so far as possible, substantive aims should be achieved procedurally, on the principle that if men are compelled to act in the right way, they will generally do the right things.

These considerations seem to have been widely ignored in the constitutions that have come into existence since World War II. Not uncommonly these constitutions incorporate a host of economic and political measures of the type one would ordinarily associate with statutory law. It is hardly likely that these measures have been written into the constitution because they represent aims that are generally shared. One suspects that the reason for their inclusion is precisely the opposite, namely, a fear that they would not be able to survive the vicissitudes of an ordinary exercise of parliamentary power. Thus, the divisions of opinion that are a normal accompaniment of lawmaking are written into the document that makes law itself possible. This is obviously a procedure that contains serious dangers for a future realization of the ideal of fidelity to law.

I have ventured these remarks on the making of constitutions not because I think they can claim any special profundity, but because I wished to illustrate what I mean by planning the conditions that will make it possible to realize the ideal of fidelity to law. Even within the limits of my modest purpose, what I have said may be clearly wrong. If so, it would not be for me to say whether

I am also wrong clearly. I will, however, venture to assert that if I am wrong, I am wrong significantly. What disturbs me about the school of legal positivism is that it not only refuses to deal with problems of the sort I have just discussed, but bans them on principle from the province of legal philosophy. In its concern to assign the right labels to the things men do, this school seems to lose all interest in asking whether men are doing the right things.

IV. THE MORALITY OF LAW ITSELF

Most of the issues raised by Professor Hart's essay can be restated in terms of the distinction between order and good order. Law may be said to represent order *simpliciter*. Good order is law that corresponds to the demands of justice, or morality, or men's notions of what ought to be. This rephrasing of the issue is useful in bringing to light the ambitious nature of Professor Hart's undertaking, for surely we would all agree that it is no easy thing to distinguish order from good order. When it is said, for example, the law simply represents that public order which obtains under all governments – democratic, Fascist, or Communist – the order intended is certainly not that of a morgue or cemetery. We must mean a functioning order, and such an order has to be at least good enough to be considered as functioning by some standard or other. A reminder that workable order usually requires some play in the joints, and therefore cannot be too orderly, is enough to suggest some of the complexities that would be involved in any attempt to draw a sharp distinction between order and good order.

For the time being, however, let us suppose we can in fact clearly separate the concept of order from that of good order. Even in this unreal and abstract form the notion of order itself contains what may be called a moral element. Let me illustrate this "morality of order" in its crudest and most elementary form. Let us suppose an absolute monarch, whose word is the only law known to his subjects. We may further suppose him to be utterly selfish and to seek in his relations with his subjects solely his own advantage. This monarch from time to time issues commands, promising rewards for compliance and threatening punishment for disobedience. He is, however, a dissolute and forgetful fellow, who never makes the slightest attempt to ascertain who have in fact followed his directions and who have not. As a result he habitually punishes loyalty and rewards disobedience. It is apparent that this monarch will never achieve even his own selfish aims until he is ready to accept that minimum self restraint that will create a meaningful connection between his words and his actions.

Let us now suppose that our monarch undergoes a change of heart and begins to pay some attention to what he said yesterday when, today, he has occasion to distribute bounty or to order the chopping off of heads. Under the strain of this new responsibility, however, our monarch relaxes his attention in other directions and becomes hopelessly slothful in the phrasing of his commands. His orders become so ambiguous and are uttered in so inaudible a tone that his subjects never have any clear idea what he wants them to do. Here, again, it is apparent that if our monarch for his own selfish advantage wants to create in his realm anything like a system of law he will have to pull himself together and assume still another responsibility.

Law, considered merely as order, contains, then, its own implicit morality. This morality of order must be respected if we are to create anything that can be called law, even bad law. Law by itself is powerless to bring this morality into existence. Until our monarch is really ready to face the responsibilities of his position, it will do no good for him to issue still another futile command, this time self-addressed and threatening himself with punishment if he does not mend his ways.

There is a twofold sense in which it is true that law cannot be built on law. First of all, the authority to make law must be supported by moral attitudes that accord to it the competency it claims. Here we are dealing with a morality external to law, which makes law possible. But this alone is not enough. We may stipulate that in our monarchy the accepted "basic norm" designates the monarch himself as the only possible source of law. We still cannot have law until our monarch is ready to accept the internal morality of law itself.

In the life of a nation these external and internal moralities of law reciprocally influence one another; a deterioration of the one will almost inevitably produce a deterioration in the other. So closely related are they that when the anthropologist Lowie speaks of "the generally accepted ethical postulates underlying our . . . legal institutions as their ultimate sanction and guaranteeing their smooth functioning," he may be presumed to have both of them in mind.

What I have called "the internal morality of law" seems to be almost completely neglected by Professor Hart. He does make brief mention of "justice in the administration of the law," which consists in the like treatment of like cases, by whatever elevated or perverted standards the word "like" may be defined. But he quickly dismisses this aspect of law as having no special relevance to his main enterprise.

In this I believe he is profoundly mistaken. It is his neglect to analyze the demands of a morality of order that leads him throughout his essay to treat law as a datum projecting itself into human experience and not as an object of human striving. When we realize that order itself is something that must be worked for, it becomes apparent that the existence of a legal system, even a bad or evil legal system, is always a matter of degree. When we recognize this simple fact of everyday legal experience, it becomes impossible to dismiss the problems presented by the Nazi regime with a simple assertion: "Under the Nazis there was law, even if it was bad law." We have instead to inquire how much of a legal system survived the general debasement and perversion of all forms of social order that occurred under the Nazi rule, and what moral implications this mutilated system had for the conscientious citizen forced to live under it.

It is not necessary, however, to dwell on such moral upheavals as the Nazi regime to see how completely incapable the positivistic philosophy is of serving the one high moral ideal it professes, that of fidelity to law. Its default in serving this ideal actually becomes most apparent, I believe, in the everyday problems that confront those who are earnestly desirous of meeting the moral demands of a legal order, but who have responsible functions to discharge in the very order toward which loyalty is due.

Let us suppose the case of a trial judge who has had an extensive experience in commercial matters and before whom a great many commercial disputes are tried. As a subordinate in a judicial hierarchy, our judge has of course the duty to follow the law laid down by his supreme court. Our imaginary Scrutton has the misfortune, however, to live under a supreme court which he considers woefully ignorant of the ways and needs of commerce. To his mind, many of this court's decisions in the field of commercial law simply do not make sense. If a conscientious judge caught in this dilemma were to turn to the positivistic philosophy what succor could he expect? It will certainly do no good to remind him that he has an obligation of fidelity to law. He is aware of this already and painfully so, since it is the source of his predicament. Nor will it help to say that if he legislates, it must be "interstitially," or that his contributions must be "confined from molar to molecular motions." This mode of statement may be congenial to those who like to think of law, not as a purposive thing, but as an expression of the dimensions and directions of state power. But I cannot believe that the essentially trite idea behind this advice can be lifted by literary eloquence to the point where it will offer any real help to our judge; for one thing, it may be impossible for him to know whether his supreme court would regard any particular contribution of his as being wide or narrow.

Nor is it likely that a distinction between core and penumbra would be helpful. The predicament of our judge may well derive, not from particular precedents, but from a mistaken conception of the nature of commerce which extends over many decisions and penetrates them in varying degrees. So far as his problem arises from the use of particular words, he may well find that the supreme court often uses the ordinary terms of commerce in senses foreign to actual business dealings. If he interprets those words as a business executive or accountant would, he may well reduce the precedents he is bound to apply to a logical shambles. On the other hand, he may find great difficulty in discerning the exact sense in which the supreme court used those words, since in his mind that sense is itself the product of a confusion.

Is it not clear that it is precisely positivism's insistence on a rigid separation of law as it is from law as it ought to be that renders the positivistic philosophy incapable of aiding our judge? Is it not also clear that our judge can never achieve a satisfactory resolution of his dilemma unless he views his duty of fidelity to law in a context which also embraces his responsibility for making law what it ought to be?

The case I have supposed may seem extreme, but the problem it suggests pervades our whole legal system. If the divergence of views between our judge and his supreme court were less drastic, it would be more difficult to present his predicament graphically, but the perplexity of his position might actually increase. Perplexities of this sort are a normal accompaniment of the discharge of any adjudicative function; they perhaps reach their most poignant intensity in the field of administrative law.

One can imagine a case – surely not likely in Professor Hart's country or mine – where a judge might hold profound moral convictions that were exactly the opposite of those held, with equal attachment, by his supreme court. He might also be convinced that the precedents he was bound to apply were the direct product of a morality he considered abhorrent. If such a judge did not find the solution for his dilemma in surrendering his office, he might well be driven to a wooden and literal application of precedents which he could not otherwise apply because he was incapable of understanding the philosophy that animated them. But I doubt that a judge in this situation would need the help of legal positivism to find these melancholy escapes from his predicament. Nor do I think that such a predicament is likely to arise within a nation where both law and good law are regarded as collaborative human achievements in need of constant renewal, and where lawyers are still at least as interested in asking "What is good law?" as they are in asking "What is law?"

V. THE PROBLEM OF RESTORING RESPECT FOR LAW AND JUSTICE AFTER THE COLLAPSE OF A REGIME THAT RESPECTED NEITHER

After the collapse of the Nazi regime the German courts were faced with a truly frightful predicament. It was impossible for them to declare the whole dictatorship illegal or to treat as void every decision and legal enactment that had emanated from Hitler's government. Intolerable dislocations would have resulted from any such wholesale outlawing of all that occurred over a span of twelve years. On the other hand, it was equally impossible to carry forward into the new government the effects of every Nazi perversity that had been committed in the name of law; any such course would have tainted an indefinite future with the poisons of Nazism.

This predicament – which was, indeed, a pervasive one, affecting all branches of law – came to a dramatic head in a series of cases involving informers who had taken advantage of the Nazi terror to get rid of personal enemies or unwanted spouses. If all Nazi statutes and judicial decisions were indiscriminately "law," then these despicable creatures were guiltless, since they had turned their victims over to processes which the Nazis themselves knew by the name of law. Yet it was intolerable, especially for the surviving relatives and friends of the victims, that these people should go about unpunished, while the objects of their spite were dead, or were just being released after years of imprisonment, or, more painful still, simply remained unaccounted for.

The urgency of this situation does not by any means escape Professor Hart. Indeed, he is moved to recommend an expedient that is surely not lacking itself in a certain air of desperation. He suggests that a retroactive criminal statute would have been the least objectionable solution to the problem. This statute would have punished the informer, and branded him as a criminal, for an act which Professor Hart regards as having been perfectly legal when he committed it.

On the other hand, Professor Hart condemns without qualification those judicial decisions in which the courts themselves undertook to declare void certain Nazi statutes under which the informer's victims had been convicted. One cannot help raising at this point the question whether the issue as presented by Professor Hart himself is truly that of fidelity to law. Surely it would be a necessary implication of a retroactive criminal statute against informers that, for purposes of that statute at least, the Nazi laws as applied to the informers or their victims were to be regarded as void. With this turn the question seems no longer to be whether what was once law can now be declared not to have been law, but rather who should do the dirty work, the courts or the legislature.

But, as Professor Hart himself suggests, the issues at stake are much too serious to risk losing them in a sematic tangle. Even if the whole question were one of words, we should remind ourselves that we are in an area where words have a powerful effect on human attitudes. I should like, therefore, to undertake a defense of the German courts, and to advance reasons why, in my opinion, their decisions do not represent the abandonment of legal principle that Professor Hart sees in them. In order to understand the background of those decisions we shall have to move a little closer within smelling distance of the witches' caldron than we have been brought so far by Professor Hart. We shall have also to consider an aspect of the problem ignored in his essay, namely, the degree to which the Nazis observed what I have called the inner morality of law itself.

Throughout his discussion Professor Hart seems to assume that the only difference between Nazi law and, say, English law is that the Nazis used their laws to achieve ends that are odious to an Englishman. This assumption is, I think, seriously mistaken, and Professor Hart's acceptance of it seems to me to render his discussion unresponsive to the problem it purports to address.

Throughout their period of control the Nazis took generous advantage of a device not wholly unknown to American legislatures, the retroactive statute curing past legal irregularities. The most dramatic use of the curative powers of such a statute occurred on July 3, 1934, after the "Roehm purge." When this intra-party shooting affair was over and more than seventy Nazis had been – one can hardly avoid saying – "rubbed out," Hitler returned to Berlin and procured from his cabinet a law ratifying and confirming the measures taken between June 30, and July 1, 1934, without mentioning the names of those who were now considered to have been lawfully executed. Some time later Hitler declared that during the Roehm purge "the supreme court of the German people . . . consisted of myself," surely not an overstatement of the capacity in which he acted if one takes seriously the enactment confering retroactive legality on "the measures taken."

Now in England and America it would never occur to anyone to say that "it is in the nature of law that it cannot be retroactive," although, of course, constitutional inhibitions may prohibit certain kinds of retroactivity. We would say it is normal for a law to operate prospectively, and that it may be arguable that it ought never operate otherwise, but there would be a certain occult unpersuasiveness in any assertion that retroactivity violates the very nature of law itself. Yet we have only to imagine a country in which *all* laws are retroactive in order to see that retroactivity presents a real problem for the internal morality of law. If we suppose an absolute monarch who allows his realm to exist in a constant state of anarchy, we would hardly say that he could create a regime of law simply by enacting a curative statute conferring legality on everything that had happened up to its date and by announcing an intention to enact similar statutes every six months in the future.

A general increase in the resort to statutes curative of past legal irregularities represents a deterioration in that form of legal morality without which law itself cannot exist. The threat of such statutes hangs over the whole legal system, and robs every law on the books of some of its significance. And surely a general threat of this sort is implied when a government is willing to use such a statute to transform into lawful execution what was simple murder when it happened.

During the Nazi regime there were repeated rumors of "secret laws." In the article criticized by Professor Hart, Radbruch mentions a report that the wholesale killings in concentration camps were made "lawful" by a secret enactment. Now surely there can be no greater legal monstrosity than a secret statute. Would anyone seriously recommend that following the war the German courts should have searched for unpublished laws among the files left by Hitler's government so that citizens' rights could be determined by a reference to these laws?

The extent of the legislator's obligation to make his laws known to his subjects is, of course, a problem of legal morality that has been under active discussion at least since the Secession of the Plebs. There is probably no modern state that has not been plagued by this problem in one form or another. It is most likely to arise in modern societies with respect to unpublished administrative directions. Often these are regarded in quite good faith by those who issue them as effecting only matters of internal organization. But since the procedures followed by an administrative agency, even in its "internal" actions, may seriously affect the rights and interests of the citizen, these unpublished, or "secret," regulations are often a subject for complaint.

But as with retroactivity, what in most societies is kept under control by the tacit restraints of legal decency broke out in monstrous form under Hitler. Indeed, so loose was the whole Nazi morality of law that it is not easy to know just what should be regarded as an unpublished or secret law. Since unpublished instructions to those administering the law could destroy the letter of any published law by imposing on it an outrageous interpretation, there was a sense in which the meaning of every law was "secret." Even a verbal order from Hitler that a thousand prisoners in concentration camps be put to death was at once an administrative direction and a validation of everything done under it as being "lawful."

But the most important affronts to the morality of law by Hitler's government took no such subtle forms as those exemplified in the bizarre outcroppings I have just discussed. In the first place, when legal forms became inconvenient, it was always possible for the Nazis to bypass them entirely and "to act through the party in the streets." There was no one who dared bring them to account for whatever outrages might thus be committed. In the second place, the Nazi-dominated courts were always ready to disregard any statute, even those enacted by the Nazis themselves, if this suited their convenience or if they feared that a lawyer-like interpretation might incur displeasure "above."

This complete willingness of the Nazis to disregard even their own enactments was an important factor leading Radbruch to take the position he did in the articles so severely criticized by Professor Hart. I do not believe that any fair appraisal of the action of the postwar German courts is possible unless we take this factor into account, as Professor Hart fails completely to do.

These remarks may seem inconclusive in their generality and to rest more on assertion than evidentiary fact. Let us turn at once, then, to the actual case discussed by Professor Hart.

In 1944 a German soldier paid a short visit to his wife while under travel orders on a reassignment. During the single day he was home, he conveyed privately to his wife something of his opinion of the Hitler government. He expressed disapproval of (sich abfällig geäussert über) Hitler and the other leading personalities of the Nazi party. He also said it was too bad Hitler had not met his end in the assassination attempt that had occurred on July 20th of that year. Shortly after his departure, his wife, who during his long absence on military duty "had turned to other men" and who wished to get rid of him, reported his remarks to the local leader of the Nazi party, observing that "a man who would say a thing like that does not deserve to live." The result was a trial of the husband by a military tribunal and a sentence of death. After a short period of imprisonment, instead of being executed, he was sent to the front again. After the collapse of the Nazi regime, the wife was brought to trial for having procured the imprisonment of her husband. Her defense rested on the ground that her husband's statements to her about Hitler and the Nazis constituted a crime under the laws then in force. Accordingly, when she informed on her husband she was simply bringing a criminal to justice.

This defense rested on two statutes, one passed in 1934, the other in 1938. Let us first consider the second of these enactments, which was part of a more comprehensive legislation creating a whole series of special wartime criminal offenses. I reproduce below a translation of the only pertinent section:

> The following persons are guilty of destroying the national power of resistance and shall be punished by death: Whoever publicly solicits or incites a refusal to fulfill the obligations of service in the armed forces of Germany, or in armed forces allied with Germany, or who otherwise publicly seeks to injure or destroy the will of the German people or an allied people to assert themselves stalwartly against their enemies.

It is almost inconceivable that a court of present-day Germany would hold the husband's remarks to his wife, who was barred from military duty by her sex, to be a violation of the final catchall provision of this statute, particularly when it is recalled that the text reproduced above was part of a more comprehensive enactment dealing with such things as harboring deserters, escaping military duty by self-inflicted injuries, and the like. The question arises, then, as to the extent to which the interpretive principles applied by the courts of Hitler's government should be accepted in determining whether the husband's remarks were indeed unlawful.

This question becomes acute when we note that the act applies only to *public* acts or utterances, whereas the husband's remarks were in the privacy of his own home. Now it appears that the Nazi courts (and it would be noted we are dealing with a special military court) quite generally disregarded this limitation and extended the act to all utterances, private or public. Is Professor Hart prepared to say that the legal meaning of this statute is to be determined in the light of this apparently uniform principle of judicial interpretation?

Let us turn now to the other statute upon which Professor Hart relies in assuming that the husband's utterance was unlawful. This is the act of 1934, the relevant portions of which are translated below:

> (1) Whoever publicly makes spiteful or provocative statements directed against, or statements which disclose a base disposition toward, the leading personalities of the nation or of the National Socialist German Workers' Party, or toward measures taken or institutions established by them, and of such a nature as to undermine the people's confidence in their political leadership, shall be punished by imprisonment.
> (2) Malicious utterances not made in public shall be treated in the same manner as public utterances when the person making them realized or should have realized they would reach the public.
> (3) Prosecution for such utterances shall be only on the order of the National Minister of Justice; in case the utterance was directed against a leading personality of the National Socialist German Workers' Party, the Minister of Justice shall order prosecution only with the advice and consent of the Representative of the Leader.
> (4) The National Minister of Justice shall, with the advice and consent of the Representative of the Leader, determine who shall belong to the class of leading personalities for purposes of Section 1 above.

Extended comment on this legislative monstrosity is scarcely called for, overlarded and undermined as it is by uncontrolled administrative discretion. We may note only: first, that it offers no justification whatever for the death penalty actually imposed on the husband, though never carried out; second, that if the wife's act in informing on her husband made his remarks "public," there is no such thing as a private utterance under this statute. I should like to ask the reader whether he can actually share Professor Hart's indignation that, in the perplexities of the postwar reconstruction, the German courts saw fit to declare this thing not a law. Can it be argued seriously that it would have been more beseeming to the judicial process if the post-war courts had undertaken a study of "the interpretative principles" in force during Hitler's rule and had then solemnly applied those "principles" to ascertain the meaning of this statute? On the other hand, would the courts really have been showing respect for Nazi law if they had construed the Nazi statutes by their own, quite different, standards of interpretation?

Professor Hart castigates the German courts and Radbruch, not so much for what they believed had to be done, but because they failed to see that they were confronted by a moral dilemma of a sort that would have been immediately apparent to Bentham and Austin. By the simple dodge of saying, "When a statute is sufficiently evil it ceases to be law," they ran away from the problem they should have faced.

This criticism is, I believe, without justification. So far as the courts are concerned, matters certainly would not have been helped if, instead of saying, "This is not law," they had said, "This is law but it is so evil we will refuse it." Surely moral confusion reaches its height when a court refuses to apply something it admits to be law, and Professor Hart does not recommend any such "facing of the true issue" by the courts themselves. He would have preferred a retroactive statute. Curiously, this was also the preference of Radbruch. But unlike Professor Hart, the German courts and Gustav Radbruch were living participants in a situation of drastic emergency. The informer problem was a pressing one, and if legal institutions were to be rehabilitated in Germany it would not do to allow the people to begin taking the law into their own hands, as might have occurred while the courts were waiting for a statute.

As for Gustav Radbruch, it is, I believe, wholly unjust to say that he did not know he was faced with a moral dilemma. His postwar writings repeatedly stress the antinomies confronted in the effort to rebuild decent and orderly government in Germany. As for the ideal of fidelity to law, I shall let Radbruch's own words state his position:

> We must not conceal from ourselves – especially not in the light of our experiences during the twelve-year dictatorship – what frightful dangers for the rule of law can be contained in the notion of "statutory lawlessness" and in refusing the quality of law to duly enacted statutes.

The situation is not that legal positivism enables a man to know when he faces a difficult problem of choice, while Radbruch's beliefs deceive him into thinking there is no problem to face. The real issue dividing Professors Hart and Radbruch is: How shall we state the problem? What is the nature of the dilemma in which we are caught?

I hope I am not being unjust to Professor Hart when I say that I can find no way of describing the dilemma as he sees it but to use some such words as the following: On the one hand, we have an amoral datum called law, which has the peculiar quality of creating a moral duty to obey it. On the other hand, we have a moral duty to do what we think is right and decent. When we are confronted by a statute we believe to be thoroughly evil, we have to choose between those two duties.

If this is the positivist position, then I have no hesitancy in rejecting it. The "dilemma" it states has the verbal formulation of a problem, but the problem it states makes no sense. It is like saying I have to choose between giving food to a starving man and being mimsy with the borogoves. I do not think it is unfair to the positivistic philosophy to say that it never gives any coherent meaning to the moral obligation of fidelity to law. This obligation seems to be conceived as sui generis, wholly unrelated to any of the ordinary, extralegal ends of human life. The fundamental postulate of positivism – that law must be strictly severed from morality – seems to deny the possibility of any bridge between the obligation to obey law and other moral obligations. No mediating principle can measure their respective demands on conscience, for they exist in wholly separate worlds.

While I would not subscribe to all of Radbruch's post-war views – especially those relating to "higher law" – I think he saw, much more clearly than does Professor Hart, the true nature of the dilemma confronted by Germany in seeking to rebuild her shattered legal institutions. Germany had to restore both respect for law and respect for justice. Though neither of these could be restored without the other, painful antinomies were encountered in attempting to restore both at once, as Radbruch saw all too clearly. Essentially Radbruch saw the dilemma as that of meeting the demands of order, on the one hand, and those of good order, on the other. Of course no pat formula can be derived from this phrasing of the problem. But, unlike legal positivism, it does not present us with opposing demands that have no living contact with one another, that simply shout their contradictions across a vacuum. As we seek order, we can meaningfully remind ourselves that order itself will do us no good unless it is good for something. As we seek to make our order good, we can remind ourselves that justice itself is impossible without order, and that we must not lose order itself in the attempt to make it good.

VI. THE MORAL IMPLICATIONS OF LEGAL POSITIVISM

We now reach the question whether there is any ground for Gustav Radbruch's belief that a general acceptance of the positivistic philosophy in pre-Nazi Germany made smoother the route to dictatorship. Understandably, Professor Hart regards this as the most outrageous of all charges against positivism.

Here indeed we enter upon a hazardous area of controversy, where ugly words and ugly charges have become commonplace. During the last half century in this country no issue of legal philosophy has caused more spilling of ink and adrenalin than the assertion that there are "totalitarian" implications in the views of Oliver Wendell Holmes, Jr. Even the most cautiously phrased criticisms of that grand old figure from the age of Darwin, Huxley, and Haeckel seem to stir the reader's mind with the memory of past acerbities. It does no good to suggest that perhaps Holmes did not perceive all the implications of his own philosophy, for this is merely to substitute one insult for another. Nor does it help much to recall the dictum of one of the closest companions of Holmes' youth – surely no imperceptive observer – that Holmes was "composed of at least two and a half different people rolled into one, and the way he keeps them together in one tight skin, without quarreling any more than they do, is remarkable."

In venturing upon these roughest of all jurisprudential waters, one is not reassured to see even so moderate a man as Professor Hart indulging in some pretty broad strokes of the oar. Radbruch disclosed "an extraordinary naïvete" in assessing the temper of his own profession in Germany and in supposing that its adherence to positivism helped the Nazis to power. His judgment on this and other matters shows that he had "only half digested the spiritual message of liberalism" he mistakenly thought he was conveying to his countrymen. A state of "hysteria" is revealed by those who see a wholesome reorientation of German legal thinking in such judicial decisions as were rendered in the informer cases.

Let us put aside at least the blunter tools of invective and address ourselves as calmly as we can to the question whether legal positivism, as practiced and preached in Germany, had, or could have had, any causal connection with Hitler's ascent to power. It should be recalled that in the seventy-five years before the Nazi regime the positivistic philosophy had achieved in Germany a standing such as it enjoyed in no other country. Austin praised a German scholar for bringing international law within the clarity-producing restraints of positivism. Gray reported with pleasure that the "abler" German jurists of his time were "abjuring all '*nicht positivisches Recht*,' " and cited Bergbohm as an example. This is an illuminating example, for Bergbohm was a scholar whose ambition was to make German positivism live up to its own pretensions. He was distressed to encounter vestigial traces of natural-law thinking in writings claiming to be positivistic. In particular, he was disturbed by the frequent recurrence of such notions as that law owes its efficacy to a perceived moral need for order, or that it is in the nature of man that he requires a legal order, etc. Bergbohm announced a program, never realized, to drive from positivistic thinking these last miasmas from the swamp of natural law. German jurists generally tended to regard the Anglo-American common law as a messy and unprincipled conglomerate of law and morals. Positivism was the only theory of law that could claim to be "scientific" in an Age of Science. Dissenters from this view were characterized by positivists with that epithet modern man fears above all others: "naïve." The result was that it could be reported by 1927 that "to be found guilty of adherence to natural law theories is a kind of social disgrace."

To this background we must add the observation that the Germans seem never to have achieved that curious ability possessed by the British, and to some extent by the Americans, of holding their logic on short leash. If a German writer had hit upon the slogan of American legal realism, "Law is simply the behavior patterns of judges and other state officials," he would not have regarded this as an interesting little conversation-starter. He would have believed it and acted on it.

German legal positivism not only banned from legal science any consideration of the moral ends of law, but it was also indifferent to what I have called the inner morality of law itself. The German lawyer was therefore peculiarly prepared to accept as "law" anything that called itself by that name, was printed at government expense, and seemed to come "*von oben herab*."

In the light of these considerations I cannot see either absurdity or perversity in the suggestion that the attitudes prevailing in the German legal profession were helpful to the Nazis. Hitler did not come to power by a violent revolution. He was Chancellor before he became the Leader. The exploitation of legal forms started cautiously and became bolder as power was consolidated. The first attacks on the established order were on ramparts which, if they were manned by anyone, were manned by lawyers and judges. These ramparts fell almost without a struggle.

Professor Hart and others have been understandably distressed by references to a "higher law" in some of the decisions concerning informers and in Radbruch's postwar writings. I suggest that if German jurisprudence had concerned itself more with the inner morality of law, it would not have been necessary to invoke any notion of this sort in declaring void the more outrageous Nazi statutes.

To me there is nothing shocking in saying that a dictatorship which clothes itself with a tinsel of legal form can so far depart from the morality of order, from the inner morality of law itself, that it ceases to be a legal system. When a system calling itself law is predicated upon a general disregard by judges of the terms of the laws they purport to enforce, when this system habitually cures its legal irregularities, even the grossest, by retroactive statutes, when it has only to resort to forays of terror in the streets, which no one dares challenge, in order to escape even those scant restraints imposed by the pretence of legality – when all these things have become true of a dictatorship, it is not hard for me, at least, to deny to it the name of law.

I believe that the invalidity of the statutes involved in the informer cases could have been grounded on considerations such as I have just outlined. But if you were raised with a generation that said "law is law" and meant it, you may feel the only way you can escape one law is to set another off against it, and this perforce must be a "higher law." Hence these notions of "higher law," which are a justifiable cause for alarm, may themselves be a belated fruit of German legal positivism.

It should be remarked at this point that it is chiefly in Roman Catholic writings that the theory of natural law is considered, not simply as a search for those principles that will enable men to live together successfully, but as a quest for something that can be called "a higher law." This identification of natural law with a law that is above human laws seems in fact to be demanded by any doctrine that asserts the possibility of an authoritative pronouncement of the demands of natural law. In those areas affected by such pronouncements as have so far been issued, the conflict between Roman Catholic doctrine and opposing views seems to me to be a conflict between two forms of positivism. Fortunately, over most of the area with which lawyers are concerned, no such pronouncements exist. In these areas I think those of us who are not adherents of its faith can be grateful to the Catholic Church for having kept alive the rationalistic tradition in ethics.

I do not assert that the solution I have suggested for the informer cases would not have entailed its own difficulties, particularly the familiar one of knowing where to stop. But I think it demonstrable that the most serious deterioration in legal morality under Hitler took place in branches of the law like those involved in the informer cases; no comparable deterioration was to be observed in the ordinary branches of private law. It was in those areas where the ends of law were most odious by ordinary standards of decency that the morality of law itself was most flagrantly disregarded. In other words, where one would have been most tempted to say, "This is so evil it cannot be a law," one could usually have said instead, "This thing is the product of a system so oblivious to the morality of law that it is not entitled to be called a law." I think there is something more than accident here, for the overlapping suggests that legal morality cannot live when it is severed from a striving toward justice and decency.

But as an actual solution for the informer cases, I, like Professors Hart and Radbruch, would have preferred a retroactive statute. My reason for this preference is not that this is the most nearly lawful way of making unlawful what was once law. Rather I would see such a statute as a way of symbolizing a sharp break with the past, as a means of isolating a kind of cleanup operation from the normal functioning of the judicial process. By this isolation it would become possible for the judiciary to return more rapidly to a condition in which the demands of legal morality could be given proper respect. In other words, it would make it possible to plan more effectively to regain for the ideal of fidelity to law its normal meaning.

VII. THE PROBLEM OF INTERPRETATION: THE CORE AND THE PENUMBRA

It is essential that we be just as clear as we can be about the meaning of Professor Hart's doctrine of "the core and the penumbra," because I believe the casual reader is likely to misinterpret what he has to say. Such a reader is apt to suppose that Professor Hart is merely describing something that is a matter of everyday experience for the lawyer, namely, that in the interpretation of legal rules it is typically the case (though not universally so) that there are some situations which will seem to fall rather clearly within the rule, while others will be more doubtful. Professor Hart's thesis takes no such jejune form. His extended discussion of the core and the penumbra is not just a complicated way of recognizing that some cases are hard, while others are easy. Instead, on the basis of a theory about language meaning generally, he is proposing a theory of judicial interpretation which is, I believe, wholly novel. Certainly it has never been put forward in so uncompromising a form before.

As I understand Professor Hart's thesis (if we add some tacit assumptions implied by it, as well as some qualifications he would no doubt wish his readers to supply) a full statement would run something as follows: The task of interpretation is commonly that of determining the meaning of the individual words of a legal rule, like "vehicle" in a rule excluding vehicles from a park. More particularly, the task of interpretation is to determine the range of reference of such a word, or the aggregate of things to which it points. Communication is possible only because words have a "standard instance," or a "core of meaning" that remains relatively constant, whatever the context in which the word may appear. Except in unusual circumstances, it will always be proper to regard a word like "vehicle" as embracing its "standard instance," that is, that aggregate of things it would include in all ordinary contexts, within or without the law. This meaning the word will have in any legal rule, whatever its purpose. In applying the word to its "standard instance," no creative role is assumed by the judge. He is simply applying the law "as it is."

In addition to a constant core, however, words also have a penumbra of meaning which, unlike the core, will vary from context to context. When the object in question (say, a tricycle) falls within this penumbral area, the judge is forced to assume a more creative role. He must now undertake, for the first time, an interpretation of the rule in the light of its purpose or aim. Having in mind what was sought by the regulation concerning parks, ought it to be considered as barring tricycles? When questions of this sort are decided there is at least an "intersection" of "is" and "ought," since the judge, in deciding what the rule "is," does so in the light of his notions of what "it ought to be" in order to carry out its purpose.

If I have properly interpreted Professor Hart's theory as it affects the "hard core," then I think it is quite untenable. The most obvious defect of his theory lies in its assumption that problems of interpretation typically turn on the meaning of individual words. Surely no judge applying a rule of the common law ever followed any such procedure as that described (and, I take it, prescribed) by Professor Hart; indeed, we do not normally even think of his problem as being one of "interpretation." Even in the case of statutes, we commonly have to assign meaning, not to a single word, but to a sentence, a paragraph, or a whole page or more of text. Surely a paragraph does not have a "standard instance" that remains constant whatever the context in which it appears. If a statute seems to have a kind of "core meaning" that we can apply without a too precise inquiry into its exact purpose, this is because we can see that, however one might formulate the precise objective of the statute, *this* case would still come within it.

Even in situations where our interpretive difficulties seem to head up in a single word, Professor Hart's analysis seems to me to give no real account of what does or should happen. In his illustration of the "vehicle," although he tells us this word has a core of meaning that in all contexts defines unequivocally a range of objects embraced by it, he never tells us what these objects might be. If the rule excluding vehicles from parks seems easy to apply in some cases, I submit this is because we can see clearly enough what the rule "is aiming at in general" so that we know there is no need to worry about the difference between Fords and Cadillacs. If in some cases we seem to be able to apply the rule without asking what its purpose is, this is not because we can treat a directive arrangement as if it had no purpose. It is rather because, for example, whether the rule be intended to preserve quiet in the park, or to save carefree strollers from injury, we know, "without thinking," that a noisy automobile must be excluded.

What would Professor Hart say if some local patriots wanted to mount on a pedestal in the park a truck used in World War II, while other citizens, regarding the proposed memorial as an eyesore, support their stand by the "no vehicle" rule? Does this truck, in perfect working order, fall within the core or the penumbra.

Professor Hart seems to assert that unless words have "standard instances" that remain constant regardless of context, effective communication would break down and it would become impossible to construct a system of "rules which have authority." If in every context words took on a unique meaning, peculiar to that context, the whole process of interpretation would become so uncertain and subjective that the ideal of a rule of law would lose its meaning. In other words, Professor Hart seems to be saying that unless we are prepared to accept his analysis of interpretation, we must surrender all hope of giving an effective meaning to the ideal of fidelity to law. This presents a very dark prospect indeed, if one believes, as I do, that we cannot accept his theory of interpretation. I do not take so gloomy a view of the future of the ideal of fidelity to law.

An illustration will help to test, not only Professor Hart's theory of the core and the penumbra, but its relevance to the ideal of fidelity to law as well. Let us suppose that in leafing through the statutes, we come upon the following enactment: "It shall be a misdemeanor, punishable by a fine of five dollars, to sleep in any railway station." We have no trouble in perceiving the general nature of the target toward which this statute is aimed. Indeed, we are likely at once to call to mind the picture of a disheveled tramp, spread out in an ungainly fashion on one of the benches of the station, keeping weary passengers on their feet and filling their ears with raucous and alcoholic snores. This vision may fairly be said to represent the "obvious instance" contemplated by the statute, though certainly it is far from being the "standard instance" of the physiological state called "sleep."

Now let us see how this example bears on the ideal of fidelity to law. Suppose I am a judge, and that two men are brought before me for violating this statute. The first is a passenger who was waiting at 3 A.M. for a delayed train. When he was arrested he was sitting upright in an orderly fashion, but was heard by the arresting officer to be gently snoring. The second is a man who had brought a blanket and pillow to the station and had obviously settled himself down for the night. He was arrested, however, before he had a chance to go to sleep. Which of these cases presents the "standard instance" of the word "sleep"? If I disregard that question, and decide to fine the second man and set free the first, have I violated a duty of fidelity to law? Have I violated that duty if I interpret the word "sleep" as used in this statute to mean something like "to spread oneself out on a bench or floor to spend the night, or as if to spend the night"?

Testing another aspect of Professor Hart's theory, is it really ever possible to interpret a word in a statute without knowing the aim of the statute? Suppose we encounter the following incomplete sentence: "All improvements must be promptly reported to . . . ." Professor Hart's theory seems to assert that even if we have only this fragment before us we can safely construe the word "improvement" to apply to its "standard instance," though we would have to know the rest of the sentence before we could deal intelligently with "problems of the penumbra." Yet surely in the truncated sentence I have quoted, the word "improvement" is almost as devoid of meaning as the symbol "X."

The word "improvement" will immediately take on meaning if we fill out the sentence with the words, "the head nurse," or, "the Town Planning Authority," though the two meanings that come to mind are radically dissimilar. It can hardly be said that these two meanings represent some kind of penumbral accretion to the word's "standard instance." And one wonders, parenthetically, how helpful the theory of the core and the penumbra would be in deciding whether, when the report is to be made to the planning authorities, the word "improvement" includes an unmortgageable monstrosity of a house that lowers the market value of the land on which it is built.

It will be instructive, I think, to consider the effect of other ways of filling out the sentence. Suppose we add to, "All improvements must be promptly reported to . . . ." the words, "the Dean of the Graduate Division." Here we no longer seem, as we once did, to be groping in the dark; rather, we seem now to be reaching into an empty box. We achieve a little better orientation if the final clause reads, "to the Principal of the School," and we feel completely at ease if it becomes, "to the Chairman of the Committee on Relations with the Parents of Children in the Primary Division."

It should be noted that in deciding what the word "improvement" means in all these cases, we do not proceed simply by placing the word in some general context, such as hospital practice, town planning, or education. If this were so, the "improvement" in the last instance might just as well be that of the teacher as that of the pupil. Rather, we ask ourselves, What can this rule be for? What evil does it seek to avert? What good is it intended to promote? When it is "the head nurse" who receives the report, we are apt to find ourselves asking, "Is there, perhaps, a shortage of hospital space, so that patients who improve sufficiently are sent home or are assigned to a ward where they will receive less attention? If "Principal" offers more orientation than "Dean of the Graduate Division," this must be because we know something about the differences between primary education and education on the postgraduate university level. We must have some minimum acquaintance with the ways in which these two educational enterprises are conducted, and with the problems encountered in both of them, before any distinction between "Principal" and "Dean of the Graduate Division" would affect our interpretation of "improvement." We must, in other words, be sufficiently capable of putting ourselves in the position of those who drafted the rule to know what they thought "ought to be." It is in the light of this "ought" that we must decide what the rule "is."

Turning now to the phenomenon Professor Hart calls "preoccupation with the penumbra," we have to ask ourselves what is actually contributed to the process of interpretation by the common practice of supposing various "borderline" situations. Professor Hart seems to say, "Why, nothing at all, unless we are working with problems of the penumbra." If this is what he means, I find his view a puzzling one, for it still leaves unexplained why, under his theory, if one is dealing with a penumbral problem, it could be useful to think about other penumbral problems.

Throughout his whole discussion of interpretation, Professor Hart seems to assume that it is a kind of cataloguing procedure. A judge faced with a novel situation is like a library clerk who has to decide where to shelve a new book. There are easy cases: the *Bible* belongs under Religion, *The Wealth of Nations* under Economics, etc. Then there are hard cases, when the librarian has to exercise a kind of creative choice, as in deciding whether *Das Kapital* belongs under Politics or Economics, *Gulliver's Travels* under Fantasy or Philosophy. But whether the decision where to shelve is easy or hard, once it is made all the librarian has to do is to put the book away. And so it is with judges, Professor Hart seems to say, in all essential particulars. Surely the judicial process is something more than a cataloguing procedure. The judge does not discharge his responsibility when he pins an apt diagnostic label on the case. He has to do something about it, to treat it, if you will. It is this larger responsibility which explains why interpretive problems almost never turn on a single word, and also why lawyers for generations have found the putting of imaginary borderline cases useful, not only "on the penumbra," but in order to know where the penumbra begins.

These points can be made clear, I believe, by drawing again on our example of the statutory fragment, which reads, "All improvements must be promptly reported to . . . ." Whatever the concluding phrase may be, the judge has not solved his problems simply by deciding what kind of improvement is meant. Almost all of the words in the sentence may require interpretation, but most obviously this is so of "promptly" and "reported." What kind of "report" is contemplated: a written note, a call at the office, entry in a hospital record? How specific must it be? Will it be enough to say "a lot better," or "a big house with a bay window"?

Now it should be apparent to any lawyer that in interpreting words like "improvement," "prompt," and "report," no real help is obtained by asking how some extralegal "standard instance" would define these words. But, much more important, when these words are all parts of a single structure of thought, they are in interaction with one another during the process of interpretation. "What is an 'improvement'? Well, it must be something that can be made the subject of a report. So, for purposes of this statute 'improvement' really means 'reportable improvement.' What kind of 'report' must be made? Well, that depends upon the sort of 'improvement' about which information is desired and the reasons for desiring the information."

When we look beyond individual words to the statute as a whole, it becomes apparent how the putting of hypothetical cases assists the interpretative process generally. By pulling our minds first in one direction, then in another, these cases help us to understand the fabric of thought before us. This fabric is something we seek to discern, so that we may know truly what it is, but it is also something that we inevitably help to create as we strive (in accordance with our obligation of fidelity to law) to make the statute a coherent, workable whole.

I should have considered all these remarks much too trite to put down here if they did not seem to be demanded in an answer to the theory of interpretation proposed by Professor Hart, a theory by which he puts such store that he implies we cannot have fidelity to law in any meaningful sense unless we are prepared to accept it. Can it be possible that the positivistic philosophy demands that we abandon a view of interpretation which sees as its central concern, not words, but purpose and structure? If so, then the stakes in this battle of schools are indeed high.

I am puzzled by the novelty Professor Hart attributes to the lessons I once tried to draw from Wittgenstein's example about teaching a game to children. I was simply trying to show the role reflection plays in deciding what ought to be done. I was trying to make such simple points as that decisions about what ought to be done are improved by reflection, by an exchange of views with others sharing the same problems, and by imagining various situations that might be presented. I was assuming that all of these innocent and familiar measures might serve to sharpen our perception of what we were trying to do, and that the product of the whole process might be, not merely a more apt choice of means for the end sought, but a clarification of the end itself. I had thought that a famous judge of the English bench had something like this in mind when he spoke of the common law as working "itself pure." If this view of the judicial process is no longer entertained in the country of its origin, I can only say that, whatever the vicissitudes of Lord Mansfield's British reputation may be, he will always remain for us in this country a heroic figure of jurisprudence.

I have stressed here the deficiencies of Professor Hart's theory as that theory affects judicial interpretation. I believe, however, that its defects go deeper and result ultimately from a mistaken theory about the meaning of language generally. Professor Hart seems to subscribe to what may be called "the pointer theory of meaning," a theory which ignores or minimizes the effect on the meaning of words of the speaker's purpose and structure of language. Characteristically, this school of thought embraces the notion of "common usage." The reason is, of course, that it is only with the aid of this notion that it can seem to attain the inert datum of meaning it seeks, a meaning isolated from the effects of purpose and structure.

It would not do to attempt here an extended excursus into linguistic theory. I shall have to content myself with remarking that the theory of meaning implied in Professor Hart's essay seems to me to have been rejected by three men who stand at the very head of modern developments in logical analysis: Wittgenstein, Russell, and Whitehead. Wittgenstein's posthumous *Philosophical Investigations* constitutes a sort of running commentary on the way words shift and transform their meanings as they move from context to context. Russell repudiates the cult of "common usage," and asks what "instance" of the word "word" itself can be given that does not imply some specific intention in the use of it. Whitehead explains the appeal that "the deceptive identity of the repeated word" has for modern philosophers; only by assuming some linguistic constant (such as the "core of meaning") can validity be claimed for procedures of logic which of necessity move the word from one context to another.

VIII. THE MORAL AND EMOTIONAL FOUNDATIONS OF POSITIVISM

If we ignore the specific theories of law associated with the positivistic philosophy, I believe we can say that the dominant tone of positivism is set by a fear of a purposive interpretation of law and legal institutions, or at least by a fear that such an interpretation may be pushed too far. I think one can find confirmatory traces of this fear in all of those classified as "positivists" by Professor Hart, with the outstanding exception of Bentham, who is in all things a case apart and who was worlds removed from anything that could be called *ethical* positivism.

Now the belief that many of us hold, that this fear of purpose takes a morbid turn in positivism, should not mislead us into thinking that the fear is wholly without justification, or that it reflects no significant problem in the organization of society.

Fidelity to law *can* become impossible if we do not accept the broader responsibilities (themselves purposive, as all responsibilities are and must be) that go with a purposive interpretation of law. One can imagine a course of reasoning that might run as follows: This statute says absinthe shall not be sold. What is its purpose? To promote health. Now, as everyone knows, absinthe is a sound, wholesome, and beneficial beverage. Therefore, interpreting the statute in the light of its purpose, I construe it to direct a general sale and consumption of that most healthful of beverages, absinthe.

If the risk of this sort of thing is implicit in a purposive interpretation, what measures can we take to eliminate it, or to reduce it to bearable proportions? One is tempted to say, "Why, just use ordinary common sense." But this would be an evasion, and would amount to saying that although we know the answer, we cannot say what it is. To give a better answer, I fear I shall have to depart from these high standards of clarity Professor Hart so rightly prizes and so generally exemplifies. I shall have to say that the answer lies in the concept of *structure*. A statute or a rule of common law has, either explicitly, or by virtue of its relation with other rules, something that may be called a structural integrity. This is what we have in mind when we speak of "the intent of the statute," though we know it is men who have intentions and not words on paper. Within the limits of that structure, fidelity to law not only permits but demands a creative role from the judge, but beyond that structure it does not permit him to go. Of course, the structure of which I speak presents its own "problems of the penumbra." But the penumbra in this case surrounds something real, something that has a meaning and integrity of its own. It is not a purposeless collocation of words that gets its meaning on loan from lay usage.

It is one of the great virtues of Professor Hart's essay that it makes explicit positivism's concern for the ideal of fidelity to law. Yet I believe, though I cannot prove, that the basic reason why positivism fears a purposive interpretation is not that it may lead to anarchy, but that it may push us too far in the opposite direction. It sees in a purposive interpretation, carried too far, a threat to human freedom and human dignity.

Let me illustrate what I mean by supposing that I am a man without religious beliefs living in a community of ardent Protestant Christian faith. A statute in this community makes it unlawful for me to play golf on Sunday. I find this statute an annoyance and accept its restraints reluctantly. But the annoyance I feel is not greatly different from that I might experience if, though it were lawful to play on Sunday, a power failure prevented me from taking the streetcar I would normally use in reaching the course. In the vernacular, "it is just one of those things."

What a different complexion the whole matter assumes if a statute compels me to attend church, or, worse still, to kneel and recite prayers! Here I may feel a direct affront to my integrity as a human being. Yet the purpose of both statutes may well be to increase church attendance. The difference may even seem to be that the first statute seeks its end slyly and by indirection, the second, honestly and openly. Yet surely this is a case in which indirection has its virtues and honesty its heavy price in human dignity.

Now I believe that positivism fears that a too explicit and uninhibited interpretation in terms of purpose may well push the first kind of statute in the direction of the second. If this is a basic concern underlying the positivistic philosophy, that philosophy is dealing with a real problem, however inept its response to the problem may seem to be. For this problem of the impressed purpose is a crucial one in our society. One thinks of the obligation to bargain "in good faith" imposed by the National Labor Relations Act. One recalls the remark that to punish a criminal is less of an affront to his dignity than to reform and improve him. The statutory preamble comes to mind: the increasing use made of it, its legislative wisdom, the significance that should be accorded to it in judicial interpretation. The flag salute cases will, of course, occur to everyone. I myself recall the splendid analysis by Professor von Hippel of the things that were fundamentally wrong about Nazism, and his conclusion that the grossest of all Nazi perversities was that of coercing acts, like the putting out of flags and saying, "Heil Hitler!" that have meaning only when done voluntarily, or, more accurately, have a meaning when coerced that is wholly parasitic on an association of them with past voluntary expressions.

Questions of this sort are undoubtedly becoming more acute as the state assumes a more active role with respect to economic activity. No significant economic activity can be organized exclusively by "don'ts." By its nature economic production requires a co-operative effort. In the economic field there is special reason, therefore, to fear that "This you may not do" will be transformed into "This you must do – but willingly." As we all know, the most tempting opportunity for effecting this transformation is presented by what is called in administrative practice "the prehearing conference," in which the negative threat of a statute's sanctions may be used by its administrators to induce what they regard, in all good conscience, as "the proper attitude."

I look forward to the day when legal philosophy can address itself earnestly to issues of this sort, and not simply exploit them to score points in favor of a position already taken. Professor Hart's essay seems to me to open the way for such a discussion, for it eliminates from the positivistic philosophy a pretense that has hitherto obscured every issue touched by it. I mean, of course, the pretense of the ethical neutrality of positivism. That is why I can say in all sincerity that, despite my almost paragraph-by-paragraph disagreement with the views expressed in his essay, I believe Professor Hart has made an enduring contribution to legal philosophy.

Lon L. Fuller, 1902-

THE MORALITY OF LAW

The Neutrality of the Law's Internal Morality toward Substantive Aims

In presenting my analysis of the law's internal morality I have insisted that it is, over a wide range of issues, indifferent toward the substantive aims of law and is ready to serve a variety of such aims with equal efficacy. One moral issue in lively debate today is that of contraception. Now it is quite clear that the principles of legality are themselves incapable of resolving this issue. It is also clear that a legal system might maintain its internal integrity whether its rules were designed to prohibit or to encourage contraception.

But a recognition that the internal morality of law may support and give efficacy to a wide variety of substantive aims should not mislead us into believing that *any* substantive aim may be adopted without compromise of legality. Even the adoption of an objective like the legal suppression of contraception may, under some circumstances, impair legal morality. If, as sometimes seems to be the case, laws prohibiting the sale of contraceptives are kept on the books as a kind of symbolic act, with the knowledge that they will not and cannot be enforced, legal morality is seriously affected. There is no way to quarantine this contagion against a spread to other parts of the legal system. It is unfortunately a familiar political technique to placate one interest by passing a statute, and to appease an opposing interest by leaving the statute largely unenforced.

One of the tasks of the present chapter is to analyze in general terms the manner in which the internal and external moralities of law interact. . . .

Legality as a Condition of Efficacy

I think I need not repeat here the argument implicit in my whole second chapter that the internal morality of the law is not something added to, or imposed on, the power of law, but is an essential condition of that power itself. If this conclusion is accepted, then the first observation that needs to be made is that law is a precondition of good law. A conscientious carpenter, who has learned his trade well and keeps his tools sharp, might, we may suppose, as well devote himself to building a hangout for thieves as to building an orphans' asylum. But it still remains true that it takes a carpenter, or the help of a carpenter, to build an orphans' asylum, and that it will be a better asylum if he is a skillful craftsman equipped with tools that have been used with care and kept in proper condition.

If we had no carpenters at all it would be plain that our first need would be, not to draft blueprints for hospitals and asylums or to argue about the principles of good design, but to recruit and train carpenters. It is in this sense that much of the world today needs law more than it does good law. . . .

Legality and Justice

One deep affinity between legality and justice has often been remarked and is in fact explicitly recognized by Hart himself (p. 202). This lies in a quality shared by both, namely, that they act by known rule. The internal morality of the law demands that there be rules, that they be made known, and that they be observed in practice by those charged with their administration. These demands may seem ethically neutral so far as the external aims of law are concerned. Yet, just as law is a precondition for good law, so acting by known rule is a precondition for any meaningful appraisal of the justice of law. "A lawless unlimited power" expressing itself solely in unpredictable and patternless interventions in human affairs could be said to be unjust only in the sense that it does not act by known rule. It would be hard to call it unjust in any more specific sense until one discovered what hidden principle, if any, guided its interventions. It is the virtue of a legal order conscientiously constructed and administered that it exposes to public scrutiny the rules by which it acts.

It is now generally forgotten by what dodges the Nazis avoided that public disclosure. During their regime there appeared in many German shop windows a sign reading "Jüdisches Geschäft." No law was ever passed requiring the display of such signs. They were installed at the "request" of Party members who went about distributing them to the stores where their display was thought appropriate. The explanation of this procedure current among the German citizenry was that the Nazis knew that a formal and published legal enactment would invite foreign criticism. This ruse was in fact partly successful. At times when an influx of foreigners was expected, say, during a commercial fair, the signs were, again at the request of the Party, temporarily removed. In Berlin, where a great many foreign visitors were coming and going at all times, signs were not used at all. Instead stores of Jewish ownership were "requested" by the Party to use a distinctive paint around the frames of their display windows. The casual foreign visitor would be likely to observe the frequency with which this color was used, but generally remained ignorant of its significance and that it had been used in compliance with a rule that was never enacted publicly.

In our own country it is quite common for the practices of governmental agencies to be controlled by unwritten and unpublished rules. Sometimes these rules are quite innocent in substance, though a lack of knowledge of them may handicap the citizen in dealing with the agency. At other times these undeclared rules are far from innocent. A particularly brutal instance of such a rule was revealed recently in Boston. It appears that when an arrested person is detained in jail overnight, it is the practice to require him to sign a paper releasing the police from all civil liability for acts connected with his arrest and detention. Signing such a paper is a condition of his discharge from custody. No doubt many a police officer, quite unreflective about this practice, has applied it with a sense of conscientiously observing standard operating procedure. It is hard to imagine any lawmaker who would be willing to authorize such a procedure by a published rule.

So far I have spoken as if the affinity between legality and justice consisted simply in the fact that a rule articulated and made known permits the public to judge of its fairness. The affinity has, however, deeper roots. Even if a man is answerable only to his own conscience, he will answer more responsibly if he is compelled to articulate the principles on which he acts. Many persons occupying positions of power betray in their relations with subordinates uniformities of behavior that may be said to constitute unwritten rules. It is not always clear that those who express these rules in their actions are themselves aware of them. It has been said that most of the world's injustices are inflicted, not with the fists, but with the elbows. When we use our fists we use them for a definite purpose, and we are answerable to others and to ourselves for that purpose. Our elbows, we may comfortably suppose, trace a random pattern for which we are not responsible, even though our neighbor may be painfully aware that he is being systematically pushed from his seat. A strong commitment to the principles of legality compels a ruler to answer to himself, not only for his fists, but for his elbows as well.

Legal Morality and Laws Aiming at Alleged Evils That Cannot Be Defined

The simple demand that rules of law be expressed in intelligible terms seems on its face ethically neutral toward the substantive aims law may serve. If any principle of legal morality is, in Hart's words, "compatible with very great iniquity," this would seem to be it. Yet if a legislator is attempting to remove some evil and cannot plainly identify the target at which his statute is directed, it is obvious he will have difficulty in making his laws clear. I have already tried to illustrate this point by a reference to statutes designed to prevent "a return of the old saloon." In that case, however, we have to do with legislative foolishness, rather than with anything touching on iniquity.

It is quite otherwise with laws attempting to make legal rights depend on race. It is common today to think of the government of South Africa as combining a strict observance of legality with the enactment of a body of law that is brutal and inhuman. This view could only arise because of the now inveterate confusion between deference for constituted authority and fidelity to law. An examination of the legislation by which racial discrimination is maintained in South Africa reveals a gross departure from the demands of the internal morality of law.

The following extracts are taken from a careful and objective study of the racial laws enacted by the Union of South Africa:

> The Legislation abounds with anomalies and the same person may, in the result, fall into different racial categories under different statutes . . . the Minister of the Interior on the 22nd March 1957, stated that approximately 100,000 race classification cases were then pending before the Director of Census and Statistics which were regarded as "borderline cases" . . . As the present sudy has revealed, the absence of uniformity of definition flows primarily from the absence of any uniform or scientific basis of race classification . . . In the final analysis the legislature is attempting to define the indefinable.

Even the South African judge who in his private life shares the prejudices that have shaped the law he is bound to interpret and apply, must, if he respects the ethos of his calling, feel a deep distaste for the arbitrary manipulations this legislation demands of him.

It should not be supposed it is only in South Africa that statutes attaching legal consequences to differences in race have given rise to serious difficulties of interpretation. In 1948 in *Perez* v. *Sharp* the Supreme Court of California held unconstitutional a statute providing that "no license may be issued authorizing the marriage of a white person with a Negro, mulatto, mongolian or member of the Malay race." The holding that the statute was invalid was rested in part on the ground that it did not meet the constitutional requirement "that a law be definite and its meaning ascertainable by those whose rights and duties are governed thereby."

Our naturalization laws now expressly provide that the "right of a person to become a naturalized citizen . . . shall not be denied . . . because of race." The Supreme Court is thus now safe from the danger of getting itself entangled in its own interpretations as it did in 1922 and 1923. In *Ozawa* v. *United States* the Court had to give some meaning to a provision restricting naturalization to "white persons." The court observed, "Manifestly, the test afforded by the mere color of the skin of each individual is impracticable as that differs greatly among persons of the same race." In an attempt to achieve something like scientific exactitude the Court declared that "white person" should be interpreted to mean a person of the Caucasian race. In a case argued a few months after this decision, the applicant for citizenship was a high-caste Hindu. His counsel introduced rather convincing proof that among anthropologists employing the term "Caucasian," he would be assigned to that race. The Court observed that the term Caucasian was unknown to those who drafted the statute in 1790, and that "as used in the science of ethnology, the connotation of the word is by no means clear and the use of it in its scientific sense as an equivalent for the words of the statute . . . would simply mean the substitution of one perplexity for another . . . The words of familiar speech, which were used by the original framers of the law, were intended to include only the type of man whom they knew as white."

Finally, by a bitter irony the Israeli High Court of Justice has encountered well-nigh insoluble problems in trying to give some simple and understandable interpretation to the Law of Return granting citizenship automatically to immigrants who are "Jews." On December 6, 1962, a divided Court held that a Roman Catholic monk was not a Jew for purposes of this law. His counsel argued that, being of Jewish parentage, he was by rabbinical law still a Jew. The Court conceded that this was true, but said that the question was not one of religious law but of the secular law of Israel. By that law he was no longer a Jew because he had embraced the Christian religion.

The View of Man Implicit in Legal Morality

I come now to the most important respect in which an observance of the demands of legal morality can serve the broader aims of human life generally. This lies in the view of man implicit in the internal morality of law. I have repeatedly observed that legal morality can be said to be neutral over a wide range of ethical issues. It cannot be neutral in its view of man himself. To embark on the enterprise of subjecting human conduct to the governance of rules involves of necessity a commitment to the view that man is, or can become, a responsible agent, capable of understanding and following rules, and answerable for his defaults.

Every departure from the principles of the law's inner morality is an affront to man's dignity as a responsible agent. To judge his actions by unpublished or retrospective laws, or to order him to do an act that is impossible, is to convey to him your indifference to his powers of self-determination. Conversely, when the view is accepted that man is incapable of responsible action, legal morality loses its reason for being. To judge his actions by unpublished or retrospective laws is no longer an affront, for there is nothing left to affront – indeed, even the verb "to judge" becomes itself incongruous in this context; we no longer judge a man, we act upon him.

Today a whole complex of attitudes, practices, and theories seems to drive us toward a view which denies that man is, or can meaningfully strive to become, a responsible, self-determining center of action. The causes of this development are of the most varied sort; in their motivation they seem to run the gamut from the basest to the most noble. . . .

The Problem of the Limits of Effective Legal Action

So far in this chapter I have attempted to show that the internal morality of law does indeed deserve to be called a "morality." I hope I have demonstrated that an acceptance of this morality is a necessary, though not a sufficient condition for the realization of justice, that this morality is itself violated when an attempt is made to express blind hatreds through legal rules, and that, finally, the specific morality of law articulates and holds before us a view of man's nature that is indispensable to law and morality alike.

It is now time to turn to the limits of legal morality and to an analysis of the situations in which an application of this morality may be inappropriate and damaging.

But first note must be taken of a confusion that threatens our subject. Let me give an historical instance of this confusion. In his essay *On Liberty* Mill had written:

> The object of this Essay is to assert one simple principle, as entitled to govern absolutely the dealings of society with the individual by way of compulsion and control, whether the means used be physical force in the form of legal penalties, or the moral coercion of public opinion. That principle is, that . . . the only purpose for which power can be rightfully exercised over any member of a civilized community, against his will, is to prevent harm to others. His own good, either physical or moral, is not sufficient warrant.

In his famous reply to Mill, James Fitzjames Stephens sought to refute Mill's "one simple principle" by pointing out that the British citizen has power exercised over him to extract taxes which go in support of the British Museum, an institution obviously designed, not to protect the citizen from harm, but to improve him.

What is illustrated here is a confusion between law in the usual sense of rules of conduct directed toward the citizen, and governmental action generally. Mill was arguing that "physical force in the form of *legal penalties*" should not itself be used as a direct instrument for improving the citizen. Certainly he did not intend to assert that the government should never use funds raised through taxes – enforced, if necessary, by coercive measures – to provide facilities that will enable the citizen to improve himself.

The confusion Stephen introduced in his controversy with Mill represents a fairly subtle representative of its class. A more thorough piece of obfuscation is found in the following passage from a famous anthropologist:

> Law has been often used as an instrument of legislative omnipotence. There was an attempt to make a whole nation sober by law. It failed. [At this point we may say, so far, so good.] In Nazi Germany a whole nation is being transformed into a gang of bloodthirsty world-bandits through the instrumentality of law, among others. This, we hope, will fail again. The Italian dictator is trying to make his intelligent, cynical, and peace-loving people into courageous heroes. The fundamentalists have tried in some states of this Union to make people God-fearing and bibliolatric by law. A

great communistic Union has tried to abolish God, marriage, and the family, again by law.

This identification of law with every conceivable kind of official act has become so common that when one finds an author about to discuss, in Pound's famous phrase, "the limits of effective legal action," one is not sure whether the subject will be the attempted legal suppression of homosexuality or the failure of the government to convert the power of the tides into electricity at Passamaquoddy. . . .

The Problem of Defining the Moral Community

So far in these pages a basic question has been passed over in silence. This is the question, Who are embraced in the moral community, the community within which men owe duties to one another and can meaningfully share their aspirations? In plain straightforward modern jargon the question is, Who shall count as a member of the in-group?

This is a problem that has bothered all moral philosophers. Within a functioning community, held together by bonds of mutual interest, the task of drafting a moral code is not difficult. It is comparatively easy to discern in this situation certain rules of restraint and cooperation that are essential for satisfactory life within the community and for the success of the community as a whole. But this confidence in moral judgment is bought at a cost, for if there are no rational principles for determining who shall be included in the community, the internal code itself rests on what appears to be an essentially arbitrary premise.

Is there any resolution for this dilemma? If so, it cannot be obtained from the morality of duty for that morality is essentially a morality of the in-group. It presupposes men in living contact with one another, either through an explicit reciprocity or through relations of tacit reciprocity embodied in the forms of an organized society.

A measure of resolution can, however, be obtained from the morality of aspiration. The most eloquent expression of this possibility is found in the Bible. The morality of duty expounded in the Old Testament includes the command: Thou shalt love thy neighbor as thyself. The New Testament tells of an encounter between a lawyer and Jesus that turned on this command. The lawyer, perceiving that the passage contained a point of difficulty, wishes to test Jesus' powers of exegesis. He asked, "And who is my neighbor?"

On this occasion Jesus does not answer, "Your neighbor is everyone; you are bound to love all men everywhere, even your enemies." Instead he relates the parable of the Good Samaritan. A certain man had been struck down by thieves and left half dead. Two of his community brothers passed him by without offering aid. Then one of the despised Samaritans – definitely a member of the out-group – bound up his wounds and took him into care. Jesus ends with the question: "Which now of these three, thinkest thou, was neighbor unto him that fell among the thieves?"

The meaning of this parable is, I believe, not that we should include everyone in the moral community, but that we should aspire to enlarge that community at every opportunity and to include within it ultimately, if we can, all men of good will.

But this still leaves a certain difficulty. The morality of aspiration speaks, not imperatively, but in terms of praise, good counsel, and encouragement. Is there no firmer basis for deciding the question of the membership of the moral community?

I believe that in one situation there is. I shall put this situation abstractly, though it is far from being hypothetical. Within a given political society there are men commonly described as being of different races. These men have lived together for many years. Each group has enriched the idiom, the thought, the music, the humor, and the artistic life of the other. They have together produced a common culture. Is there no moral principle that can imperatively condemn drawing a line between them, and denying to one group access to the essentials on which a satisfactory and dignified life can be built?

I believe there is. In this case the morality of aspiration speaks in terms fully as imperative as those characteristic of the morality of duty, so that the distinction between the two at this point breaks down. The morality of aspiration is after all a morality of *human* aspiration. It cannot refuse the human quality to human beings without repudiating itself.

In the Talmud there is a passage that reads, "If I am not for myself, who shall be for me? If I am for myself alone, what am I?" If we put this in the plural, we have, "If we are not for ourselves, who shall be for us? If we are for ourselves alone, what are we?" Whatever answer we may give to this last question, it must be predicated on the assumption that we are above all else human beings. If we have to qualify our answer by adding some biological tag line to our own title, then we deny the human quality to ourselves in an effort to justify denying it to others.

The Minimum Content of a Substantive Natural Law

In seeking to know whether it is possible to derive from the morality of aspiration anything more imperative than mere counsel and encouragement, I have then so far concluded that, since the morality of aspiration is necessarily a morality of human aspiration, it cannot deny the human quality to those who possess it without forfeiting its integrity. Can we derive more than this?

The problem may be stated in another form. In my third chapter I treated what I have called the internal morality of law as itself presenting a variety of natural law. It is, however, a procedural or institutional kind of natural law, though, as I have been at pains in this chapter to show, it affects and limits the substantive aims that can be achieved through law. But can we derive from the morality of aspiration itself any proposition of natural law that is substantive, rather than procedural, in quality?

In his *Concept of Law* H. L. A. Hart presents what he calls "the minimum content of natural law" (pp. 189-95). Starting with the single objective of human survival, conceived as operating within certain externally imposed conditions, Hart derives, by a process I would describe as purposive implication, a fairly comprehensive set of rules that may be called those of natural law. What is expounded in his interesting discussion is a kind of minimum morality of duty.

Like every morality of duty this minimum natural law says nothing about the question, Who shall be included in the community which accepts and seeks to realize cooperatively the shared objective of survival? In short, who shall survive? No attempt is made to answer this question. Hart simply observes that "our concern is with social arrangements for continued existence, not with those of a suicide club."

In justifying his starting point of survival Hart advances two kinds of reasons. One amounts to saying that survival is a necessary condition for every other human achievement and satisfaction. With this proposition there can be no quarrel.

But in addition to treating survival as a precondition for every other human good, Hart advances a second set of reasons for his starting point – reasons of a very different order. He asserts that men have properly seen that in "the modest aim of survival" lies "the central indisputable element which gives empirical good sense to the terminology of Natural Law." He asserts further that in the teleological elements that run through all moral and legal thinking there is "the tacit assumption that the proper end of human activity is survival." He observes that "an overwhelming majority of men do wish to live, even at the cost of hideous misery."

In making these assertions Hart is, I submit, treading more dubious ground. For he is no longer claiming for survival that it is a necessary condition for the achievement of other ends, but seems to be saying that it furnishes the core and central element of all human striving. This, I think, cannot be accepted. As Thomas Aquinas remarked long ago, if the highest aim of a captain were to preserve his ship, he would keep it in port forever. As for the proposition that the overwhelming majority of men wish to survive even at the cost of hideous misery, this seems to me of doubtful truth. If it were true, I question whether it would have any particular relevance to moral theory.

Hart's search for a "central indisputable element" in human striving raises the question whether in fact this search can be successful. I believe that if we were forced to select the principle that supports and infuses all human aspiration we would find it in the objective of maintaining communication with our fellows.

In the first place – staying within the limits of Hart's own argument – man has been able to survive up to now because of his capacity for communication. In competition with other creatures, often more powerful than he and sometimes gifted with keener senses, man has so far been the victor. His victory has come about because he can acquire and transmit knowledge and because he can consciously and deliberately effect a coordination of effort with other human beings. If in the future man succeeds in surviving his own powers of self-destruction, it will be because he can communicate and reach understanding with his fellows. Finally, I doubt if most of us would regard as desirable survival into a kind of vegetable existence in which we could make no meaningful contact with other human beings.

Communication is something more than a means of staying alive. It is a way of being alive. It is through communication that we inherit the achievements of past human effort. The possibility of communication can reconcile us to the thought of death by assuring us that what we achieve will enrich the lives of those to come. How and when we accomplish communication with one another can expand or contract the boundaries of life itself. In the words of Wittgenstein, "The limits of my language are the limits of my world."

If I were asked, then, to discern one central indisputable principle of what may be called substantive natural law – Natural Law with capital letters – I would find it in the injunction: Open up, maintain, and preserve the integrity of the channels of communication by which men convey to one another what they perceive, feel, and desire. In this matter the morality of aspiration offers more than good counsel and the challenge of excellence. It here speaks with the imperious voice we are accustomed to hear from the morality of duty. And if men will listen, that voice, unlike that of the morality of duty, can be heard across the boundaries and through the barriers that now separate men from one another.

See Summers, "Professor Fuller on Morality and Law" (1965) 18 *J. Legal Ed.* 1 and the symposium on Fuller in (1965) 11 *Vill. L. Rev.* 624; also Palms. "The Natural Law Philosophy of Lon L. Fuller" (1965) 11 *Catholic Law* 94.

In The Law In Quest of Itself 5 (1940) Fuller described natural law as follows:

"Natural law . . . is the view which denies the possibility of a rigid separation of the *is* and the *ought,* and which tolerates a confusion of them in practice."

Margaret Mead, 1901-
Professor of Anthropology, Columbia University, and Professor of Psychiatry, University of Cincinnati

SOME ANTHROPOLOGICAL CONSIDERATIONS CONCERNING NATURAL LAW (1961)

AMONG THE VARIETY of contributions which anthropology, as the comparative study of cultures with particular emphasis upon the study of living societies without a written tradition, may make to the study of natural law, I propose to deal here with three: (1) what anthropology can say about the universality, as evidenced by all known cultures, of the recognitions peculiar to natural law; (2) what case studies of primitive or exotic societies, which have come newly in contact with our elaborated system of Western law, can contribute; and (3) what the attempt to distill the essence of something as culturally embedded as our own legal system can contribute to the process of diffusion of historical systems of law.

I

In asking what conceptions of human rights are universal to all known cultures, it is, of course, necessary to recognize that we can only ask this question about the assemblage of societies that have been observed and recorded. Inevitably, our universe excludes all cultures that have vanished without leaving any record, and the steadily shrinking number of existing cultures that exist in the present but have not yet been studied. The culturally regulated relationship among persons within a given environment is characterized both by certain persistent regularities, due to the species-specific characteristics of human beings, and a wide variety of forms having historical uniqueness. It is only those areas of human life which are most closely based in our common biological heritage in which we may not expect still to find, among existing cultures, instances which alter existing generalizations.

Nevertheless, the systematic observations of constancies among all known cultures make it highly probable that the kinds of cultural behavior found in all of them have been an integral part of their survival system up to the present time. Among such constancies we may note the distinction between the sacredness of human life within and without the group, or the existence of a category of murder – a type of killing that is different from all other killings, falling in specified ways within the circle of protected persons. The distinctions vary from one group to another; a newborn infant may be excluded, or an adulterer caught *in flagrante delicto*; expected revenge may even take the form of a man's obligation to kill the foster father, who once killed his father, married his mother, and reared him from childhood. But the categories of justified versus unjustified killing remain for all known societies. As human beings, to survive, must live in aggregations of more than one biological family, this distinction can be regarded as a vital one for the development of a viable society. The extension of the category of those whose killing constitutes murder, in contradistinction to legitimate vengeance, or conventional head hunting or warfare, has been a conspicuous marker of the evolution of civilizations in spite of its carrying with it the inescapable corollary of increasing the number of those who become at one stroke – as with a declaration of war – legitimate victims.

With the same universality we find incest rules governing the three primary incest relationships – mother-son, father-daughter, and brother-sister – occurring in all known societies. Although in special cases they may be occasionally waived, as in royal marriages between brother and sister, or in cases of small in-marrying groups in which there are no possible mates, such exceptions are treated as exceptions, marking royalty off from commoners or signaling a desperate population emergency. The circumstance that the taboo is frequently broken – especially in the father-daughter form – under conditions of cultural breakdown, only serves to demonstrate that its maintenance is socio-cultural rather than instinctive. Clinical and anthropological evidence suggests that the attraction and repulsion of members of a biological family are such that social regulation has been necessary. The function of the incest taboo may be seen as preventing competition among members of the same sex within the family group during the long period when human young are not mature enough to fend for themselves, and as providing forms in which the search for mates outside the immediate family strengthens ties within families.

It is in those instances where incest rules have been elaborated to include large numbers of persons, all members of one clan, all members of one village or district, etc., that the compensatory need for religio-legal devices for breaking a rule that has become too onerous is found, and the complementary right to find a mate is brought into relief. Again those instances in which marriage is denied require strong cultural elaborations or religious and ethical sanctions, in which individuals become completely dedicated to a religious life.

Finally, in spite of the widespread notions of primitive communism, there is no known culture without some institution of private property. The forms in which this is expressed may appear bizarre – the right to a name, or the right to certain forms of privacy such as the right to sleep without being awakened, or to eat without being spoken to – but the association of social identity with rights against the invasion of others is universal. Practices such as the destruction or interment of an individual's personal possessions, weapons, tools, dress and adornment, etc., combined with ownership of camping sites and hunting territories by larger corporate groups, have misled some observers into thinking that no property was held by individuals. Experience with attempts to impose modern ideas of state capitalism or collective ideologies upon "communistic" primitive people very rapidly exposes the error of this assumption.

Effective use of case studies from primitive cultures requires a recognition that no matter how primitive the people under discussion are, rules concerning the sacredness of life (under some circumstances), rules concerning the prohibition of incest in the primary familial relationships in most circumstances, and rules governing an individual's rights over some differentiated physical or cultural items will be found. That such recognitions have been universal in the past does not, however, argue conclusively for their necessary continuance in the future. But they appear to have provided a minimal culturally transmitted ethical code without which human societies were not viable. The English geneticist C. H. Waddington has argued persuasively, on purely naturalistic grounds, that the capacity to accept a division of behavior into that which is right and that which is wrong, is a distinctively human species-specific type of behavior which has played an essential part in the evolution of culture.

"Natural law" might thus be defined as those rules of behavior which had developed from a species-specific capacity to ethicalize as a feature of those examples of such ethicalizing that appear in all known societies.

III

Meanwhile as contact between different parts of the world becomes more rationalized and self-conscious, new approaches to the problems of culture contact have emerged. Instead of the earlier haphazard reliance on accidents of personnel and period, any segment of Western culture involved in the process of diffusion can be scrutinized for suitability. The science of nutrition provides a useful model for such scrutiny, as methods of assaying both the nutritional status of human beings and the nutritional content of foodstuffs are available. In the old haphazard style of culture contact, whether nutritional information was diffused by bringing students from the less developed countries to the more developed, or by exporting experts from the scientifically specialized centers, the result was substantially the same. The scientific core of information about calories, types of balance among proteins, carbohydrates, and fats, and the need for essential vitamins and minerals, was diffused surrounded by a large amount of cultural baggage peculiar to the country where the science of nutrition had been elaborated. Such cultural baggage included such items as an insistence on animal milk as a substitute for mother's milk, and styles of food preparation, meal arrangement, etc., which were alien to the importing countries, irrelevant to basic nutritional needs, incompatible with the local food resources. Today we know that there are two possibilities: for the importing country with an old literate tradition, i.e., Java, Burma, Thailand, Lebanon, students can be trained in the science of nutrition in such a way that they can take the basic scientific knowledge back to their own countries, and embody the principles they have learned in the dietary practices of their own culture; or where the underdeveloped country lacks in literate tradition, an expert can be sent to that country to work out ways of applying the nutritional principles there within the limits of the local conditions. The basic principles of nutritional science may be regarded as universals, derived from man's biology and from the biochemical composition of specific foods grown on specific types soil. They are as applicable in one culture as in another, and we may expect to add to our understanding of the nutritional process as intensive scientific investigation proceeds in the laboratories of modern industrialized societies. Stripped of the cultural traditions of the country within which the science of nutrition had developed, it can be applied anywhere.

Although a system of jurisprudence provides us with a very different set of problems, it would be worthwhile, I believe, to experiment with the model of stripped universals when we are faced with attempts to diffuse our legal system beyond the boundaries of the civilization within which it grew. We have seen that recognition of natural rights, to life, property, and reproduction, is found in all societies, although with profound variations in interpretation. However, when Western law and traditional law or primitive custom have confronted each other, it is rather the question of sanctions, authority, order which have constituted the aspects of the law which have become salient. It would be worthwhile to undertake a series of intensive explorations of societies on the verge of intensive modernization who are at the moment attempting to formulate their legal systems, relying variously upon British, American, Swiss, French, Soviet models and others. In each such case two sets of cultural envelopes are involved, the culturally embedded system of the donor or model country, and the culture of the receiver or model-seeking country. If such situations were analyzed with a view to finding a minimal set of legal principles which might be regarded as stripped universals, the creation of new legal systems might be effectively streamlined in contrast to the present attempt to tinker with models which are hoary with specific traditional accretions, many of which are inappropriate in the new situation. Is it possible to regard law as having such a set of universals, which can in any way be compared with scientific study of the law by way of the study of comparative legal systems, each seen as part of a particular culture and one link in a long historical chain of legal inventions?

CHAPTER FOUR

Sociological Jurisprudence

Sociological jurisprudence, both in its origins and in its development, is inextricably intertwined with the name of Roscoe Pound, the Dean of Harvard Law School from 1916 to 1936. Although he was not the first jurisprudent to perceive that law is not an end in itself but a means to the achievement of social goals (Holmes, for example, spoke in 1897 of the judicial duty of "weighing considerations of social advantage") and although his characteristic theme of law as social engineering was in fact borrowed from von Ihering's work of 1877, *Law as a Means to an End,* it was he who first clearly enunciated the sociological theory in the United States, the country that was to become the principal home of the sociological school, and who developed and popularized it in the greater number of his hundreds of articles and score of books. His famous paper of 1907, "The Need of a Sociological Jurisprudence" [19 Green Bag 607], the year following his equally famous address before the American Bar Association, "The Causes of Popular Dissatisfaction With the Administration of Justice" [29 Rep. A. B. A., Pt. I, 395], may justly be taken as the starting point of sociological jurisprudence as a coherent movement.

Pound has drawn a distinction between the sociology of law and sociological jurisprudence ["Sociology of Law and Sociological Jurisprudence" (1943 5 *U. Toronto L. J.* 1]. The former is sociology proper; the latter is jurisprudence. The sociology of law will be interested in law as one of the means of social control, whereas sociological jurisprudence will stress the peculiar characteristics of the legal order; "jurists look primarily at their special subject and set it off for that purpose", Pound remarks, "while sociologists may be looking at social control as a whole, and so even what seems to the jurists a deep cleavage seems to the sociologist no more than a scratch" [3-4]. The sociology of law is the more general approach and presumably may be as consistent with other jurisprudential theories as with sociological jurisprudence, at least if sociological jurisprudence goes beyond methodology to imply a value theory.

Despite its differentiation from the sociology of law, sociological jurisprudence has remained to some extent dependent upon sociology and has developed with the continuing development of sociology (which is itself largely a twentieth-century phenomenon), although it is largely the product of jurists rather than of sociologists. In fact, its development might be said to be primarily the result of the considerable effect of sociological theories in the early part of the century upon Pound and Holmes. [A good historical study is to be found in Geis, "Sociology and Sociological Jurisprudence: Admixture of Lore and Law" (1964) 52 *Ky. L. J.* 267].

One of Pound's most important contributions to sociological jurisprudence is the notion of an inventory of interests, a listing of all the interests which are pressing for recognition in society at a particular time. As presented by Pound, such as inventory is axiologically neutral, with no spelling out of the relative importance of the conflicting interests. Actually what sociological jurisprudents have in mind is that jurists should accept the order of values of the society in which they live. As Cardozo put it, the judge is "under a duty to conform to the accepted standards of the community, the mores of the times."

The question of how a judge is to know what the moral standards of the community are has proved a troublesome one for the sociologists. The Denning approach, that the judge should rely on his own moral sense as indicative of the moral views of his age, has not been generally acceptable. [For a discussion of Lord Denning's views, see Dowrick, *Justice According to the English Common Lawyers* 92 (1961)]. Logically it might seem that there should be a poll of popular opinion every time a new issue is to be decided, for only in this way could there be a scientific basis for decision. But most sociologists acknowledge the impracticability of a "Gallup-Poll" approach to judicial decision, and so in practice they are more likely to follow Judge Hand's view that a judge should make the best guess he can as to how a poll would turn out and make this the determining factor in his judicial work. Cardozo's view was rather that only the views of the élite should be taken into account: "It is the customary morality of right-minded men and women which [the judge] is to enforce by his decree". Another possibility is that sociological surveys should be made in certain crucial areas of the law without reference to particular litigation, and that these surveys should be used by courts to decide issues not only in those areas (which would be far too limited to cover a significant number of cases) but also in other areas by use of analogy. But it is probably true to say that in general the sociologists have reconciled themselves to the impossibility of a strictly scientific solution and have settled for a rule-of-thumb approximation of what they think a scientific social survey would discover. What the sociological school does insist on is that to the extent that he can ascertain what the mores of the people are, the judge is bound to follow them. In practice this would admittedly often result in the judge's equation of the community's moral sense with his own, but if the judge did recognize that his own view was not in accord with that of fellow countrymen he would be obliged to forego his own view in the interests of the community.

A legal conception which often conceals the presence of values in decision-making is that of public policy. Professor Winfield has defined public policy as "a principle of judicial legislation or interpretation founded on the current needs of the community" ["Public Policy in the English Common Law" (1928) 42 Harv. L. Rev. 76, 92], but as the cases in the first section show, not all judges have recognized either the character or the importance of questions of public policy.

In addition to sociological jurisprudence proper the so-called "new jurisprudence", which refuses to recognize any barriers between law and politics, has a strong sociological bent and may be said to be merely a radical sociologism. Professor Martin Shapiro has given this new jurisprudence the name of "political jurisprudence", and because of its current importance it is worth considering at some length his analysis of it:

> "I believe that . . . a new movement is afoot in legal theory, and I propose to call it political jurisprudence.
>
> "This new movement is essentially an extension of certain elements of sociological jurisprudence and judicial realism, combined with the substantive knowledge and methodology of political science. Its foundation is the sociological jurist's premise that law must be understood not as an independent organism but an integral part of the social system. Political jurisprudence is in one sense an attempt to advance sociological jurisprudence by greater specialization. It seeks to overcome the rather nebulous and over general propositions of the earlier movement by concentrating on the specifically political aspects of law's interaction with society and describing the concrete impact of legal arrangements on the distribution of power and rewards among the various elements in a given society.
>
> "From judicial realism, political jurisprudence derives a peculiar concern for the attitudes and behavior of judges and the environment of judicial decision. Indeed, many of the political jurists have devoted most of their efforts to devising a methodology that will allow them to refine and systematize the impressionistic insights of the realists by isolating and measuring the strength and direction of judicial attitudes and relating them to the actual patterns of decision.
>
> "Moreover, the new jurisprudence shares with all modern American thinking about law, the premise that judges make rather than simply discover law. Without this premise there could be no political jurisprudence, for one of the central concerns of politics is power and power implies choice. If the judge had no

choice between alternatives, if he simply applied the rule supplied him by the tablets and reached the conclusion commanded by an inexorable legal logic, he would be of no more interest politically than the IBM machine that we could soon design to replace him. . . .

"The core of political jurisprudence is a vision of courts as political agencies and judges as political actors. Any given court is thus seen as a part of the institutional structure of American government basically similar to such other agencies as the ICC, the House Rules Committee, the Bureau of the Budget, the city council of Omaha, the Forestry Service and the Strategic Air Command. Judges take their places with the commissioners, congressmen, bureaucrats, city councilmen, and technicians who make the political decisions of government. In short, the attempt is to intellectually integrate the judicial system into the matrix of government and politics in which it actually operates and to examine courts and judges as participants in the political process, rather than presenting law, with a capital L, as an independent area of substantive knowledge. Quite fundamentally, political jurisprudence subordinates the study of law, in the sense of a concrete and independent system of prescriptive statements, to the study of men, in this instance those men who fulfill their political functions by the creation, application and interpretation of law." ["Political Jurisprudence" (1964) 52 *Ky. L. J.* 294, 294-297].

Discussion of political jurisprudence has principally taken the form of a continuing debate on the role of the United States Supreme Court between judicial activists and judicial self-deniers, with Mr. Justice Black and Mr. Justice Frankfurter serving as the prototypes of the respective views. The entrants in the lists are too numerous to be catalogued here.

Political jurisprudence has emerged concomitantly with another novelty, quantification of statistical analysis – the quantitative measurement, principally through the use of electronic computers, of large samples of data – and political jurisprudence appears to be largely dependent upon this new technique. It is well to keep in mind that data analysis is only a tool and is not itself essentially committed to any theory of jurisprudence. A statistical study of precedents might, for example, be used either for the positivist purpose of establishing how the courts must decide a new case in the same area or for the realist purpose of prediction. As used for purposes of political jurisprudence in the last decade, quantification has been devoted to behavioral studies of the judiciary. Thus there have been studies of judicial attitudes on such matters as civil liberties, analyses of particular courts as small groups in terms of leadership and bloc formation, and accounts of the social background of judges and its effect on their decision-making. The best account of these developments is in *Judicial Decision-Making* (Schubert ed. 1963).

A. CASES

EGERTON v. BROWNLOW
House of Lords. 1853. 4 H.L.C. 1; 10 E.R. 359

[The will of the Earl of Bridgewater provided for certain contingent gifts subject to the proviso that if the beneficiary died without having acquired the title of Duke or Marquis of Bridgewater, the estate should cease and become absolutely void. The House of Lords held 4-1 that the condition was void as against public policy, thereby reversing the judgment of the majority of the judges. The judgments reproduced are from the lower court hearing.]

PARKE B.: . . . The Principal question argued at your Lordships' bar was that the provisoes were illegal. I am of opinion that none of them was illegal. The main ground in which it is argued that the provisoes are illegal, is that they are against "public policy." This is a vague and unsatisfactory term, and calculated to lead to uncertainty and error, when applied to the decision of legal rights; it is capable of being understood in different senses; it may, and does, in its ordinary sense, mean "political expedience," or that which is best for the common good of the community; and in that sense there may be every variety of opinion, according to education, habits, talents, and dispositions of each person, who is to decide whether an act is against public policy or not. To allow this to be a ground of judicial decision, would lead to the greatest uncertainty and confusion. It is the province of the statesman, and not the lawyer, to discuss, and of the legislature to determine, what is the best for the public good, and to provide for it by proper enactments. It is the province of the judge to expound the law only; the written from the statutes: the unwritten or common law from the decisions of our predecessors and of our existing courts, from textwriters of acknowledged authority, and upon the principles to be clearly deduced from them by sound reason and just inference; not to speculate upon what is the best, in his opinion, for the advantage of the community. Some of these decisions may have no doubt been founded upon the prevailing and just opinions of the public good; for instance, the illegality of covenants in restraint of marriage or trade. They have become a part of the recognized law, and we are therefore bound by them, but we are not thereby authorized to establish as law everything which we may think for the public good, and prohibit everything which we think otherwise. The term "public policy" may indeed be used only in the sense of the policy of the law, and in that sense it forms a just ground of judicial decision. It amounts to no more than that a contract or condition is illegal which is against the principle of the established law. If it can be shown that any provision is contrary to well-decided cases, or the principle of decided cases, and void by analogy to them, and within the same principle, the objection ought to prevail. But we are clearly of opinion that this cannot be shown here. . . .

POLLOCK C.B.: . . . This doctrine of the public good or the public safety, or what is sometimes called "public policy," being the foundation of law, is supported by decisions in every branch of the law; and an unlimited number of cases may be cited as directly and distinctly deciding upon contracts and covenants as the avowed broad ground of the public good and on that alone; and the name and authority of nearly all the great lawyers (whose decisions and opinions have been extensively reported) will be found associated with this doctrine in some shape or other. It is distinctly laid down by Coke (66 a), "*nihil quod est inconveniens est licitum.*"

It is above a hundred years ago that Lord Hardwicke, in *The Earl of Chesterfield* v. *Janseen* (1 Atk. 352), thus expressed himself in giving judgment, alluding to marriage-brokage bonds: "The Court relieves for the sake of the public as a general mischief." May I venture to ask your Lordships whether peerage-brokage bonds would be entitled to greater favour? Lord Hardwicke continues: "So in bargains to procure offices, neither of the parties is defrauded, but it serves to introduce unworthy objects into public offices, and therefore for the sake of the public the bargain is rescinded." And again: "Political arguments, in the fullest sense of the word, as they concern the government of a nation, must be, and have always been of great weight in the consideration of this Court; and though there may be no *dolus malus* in contracts as to other persons, yet, if the rest of mankind are concerned as well as the parties, it may properly be said that it regards the public utility."

So in *Lawton* v. *Lawton* (*id.* 16), the same eminent Judge said, "These reasons of public benefit and convenience weigh greatly with me, and are a principal ingredient in my present opinion."

In *May* v. *Brown* (3 Bar. and Cres. 131), Mr. Justice Holroyd (a lawyer of no mean authority) said, "The argument *'ab inconvenienti'* is of importance in considering what the law is, and there cannot be any doubt that the reception of this evidence would tend to great inconvenience and injustice."

I have seen indeed a reference to the case of *Mellish* and *Richardson* (2 Bing. 229), where Chief Justice Best and Mr. Justice Burrough expressed opinions on the subject of deciding matters of law on the ground of public policy; but in that case those learned individuals did not disaffirm the doctrine, but merely laid down that (as a ground of decision) it ought to be used with great care and caution; Chief Justice Best said he would not decide on a doubtful question of policy, and Mr. Justice Burrough merely said, You must not argue too strongly on public policy; and so far from Lord Chief Justice Best being of opinion that public policy was not a ground of legal decision, it appears that in the case of *Gifford* v. *Lord Yarborough* (5 Bin. 169) Lord Chief Justice Best in delivering the unanimous opinion of the Judges to your Lordships' House four years after *Mellish* and *Richards* was decided, said, "The Judges are therefore warranted by justice, by public policy, by the opinions of learned writers, and the authority of decided cases, in giving the answer they have directed me to give;" and the same learned Chief Justice, in *Fletcher* v. *Lord Sondes* (3 Bing. 590), in stating his opinion to your Lordships' House, said, "I am aware these are rather considerations of policy than law; but, my Lords, if there be any doubt what is the law, Judges solve such doubts by considering what will be the good or bad effects of their decision;" (and he adds) "That doctrine cannot be law which injures the rights of individuals, and will be productive of evil to the Church and to the community." These are the deliberate and well considered expressions of Lord Chief Justice Best, probably written down with care before they were delivered to your Lordships. I may add that in the same case of *Fletcher* v. *Lord Sondes*, another of the learned Judges, Mr. Baron Hullock (3 Bing. 538), in stating his opinion to this House, said, "The bond in this case operates equally against public policy (alluding to the case of *The Bishop of London* v. *Fytche*), and is, therefore, on that ground equally void and illegal."

Now, the principle that certain contracts are illegal, and therefore void, because they are against public policy or the public good, is familiar to every lawyer. Why are seamen not allowed to insure their wages (which is their part of the adventure), as well as the owner of his ship, or the merchant his goods? Because it is for the public good that they should have no motive to relax in their exertions to preserve the ship and cargo. Why are trustees not allowed to enter into contracts with their cestuique trust? Why was it held by Lord Ellenborough unlawful for the putative father of an illegitimate child to compound with the parish and to pay or secure a gross sum to the parish, they taking the chance of the expense being more or less? Because it was against public policy. And this doctrine has been confirmed in several cases in every court in Westminster Hall. So in the case of wagers, it is now fully established that no contract in the nature of a wager is valid which is against public policy. It is true in *Walcot* v. *Tappin* (1 Keble, 56 and 65), and in *Andrews* v. *Herne* (1 Lev. 33), which, though so differently named, turn out to be the same case, the plaintiff was allowed to recover twenty pounds from the defendant who had betted that sum against twenty shillings paid to him on the event of Charles Stuart becoming King of England in six months. No objection was taken to the unlawfulness of the bet, and the royalist who had backed his sovereign recovered against the republican who had betted twenty to one against him; but in *Good* v. *Elliott* (3 T.R. 693), Buller, J. pronounces the contract illegal; and in *Gilbert* v. *Sykes* (16 East, 150), Mr. Le Blanc expressly says no such action could now be maintained.

In that last case of *Gilbert* and *Sykes*, Lord Ellenborough lays down, "Wherever the tolerating of any species of contract has a tendency to produce a public mischief or inconvenience, such a contract has been held to be void:" and he cites the authority of Lord Mansfield in *Jones* v. *Randall* (Cowp. Rep. 37). The result of the cases seems to establish this distinction: that, where a contract is directly opposed to public welfare, it is void, though the parties may have a real interest in the matter, and an apparent right to deal with it; but where the contract is altogether gratuituous, and the parties have no interest but what they themselves create by the contract, it is sufficient that there be any tendency whatever to public mischief to render the contract void. An attention to this distinction will reconcile all the cases, and will furnish an answer to much that has been said in favour of this condition. This condition is purely gratuitous. If, therefore, it has any tendency to public mischief, it is void.

There is one other case I am desirous of mentioning, *Norman* v. *Cole* (3 Esp. 253), a decision of Lord Eldon's when Chief Justice of the Common Pleas. A sum of money had been lodged to assist in procuring a pardon, and the action was brought to recover it back. I cite the case not for the particular decision (it was held that the action would not lie), but for the principle laid down by Lord Eldon: he says, "Where a person interposes his interest and good offices to procure a pardon, it ought to be done gratuituously, and not for money." The doing an act of that description should proceed from pure motives, not from pecuniary ones; and it is the pecuniary motive that exists in this case, and that was created expressly that it might operate as a pecuniary motive, that constitutes, in my opinion, the vice of the condition. The allusion in the last case to a pardon induces me to put this case to your Lordships: suppose some member of the Derwentwater family were to become immensely wealthy, and were to leave large possessions to a relative, with a condition that, unless he procured the reversal of the attainder and the restoration of the peerage, he should forfeit the estates, and they should go over to another devisee: would such a condition be good? would it be good in respect of the reversal of the attainder? I cannot entertain a doubt that it would be clearly bad. Would it be good for a restoration or revival of the peerage? It seems to me impossible to distinguish this last case from that now before your Lordships; it is the very case under discussion. My Lords, after all these authorities, am I not justified in saying that, were I to discard the public welfare from my consideration, I should abdicate the functions of my office – I should shrink from the discharge of my duty? I think I am not permitted merely to follow the particular decisions of those who have had the courage to decide before me, but in a new and unprecedented case to be afraid of imitating their example. I think I am bound to look for the principles of former decisions, and not to shrink from applying them with firmness and caution to any new and extraordinary case that may arise.

The conclusions to which I have arrived, from the decided cases and the principles they involve, are, that all matters relating to the public welfare – all acts of the legislature or the executive – must be decided and determined upon their own merits only; and that it is against the public interest (and therefore not lawful) for any one officiously, wantonly, and capriciously, without any motive but his own will, to create any pecuniary interest or other bias of any sort in the decision of a matter of a public nature, and which involves the public welfare, the party creating that interest having no special and particular individual interest in the subject-matter with which he intermeddles. My Lords, in the case of wagers and contracts this has been repeatedly and solemnly decided by all the Courts (and the case of conditions is an *a fortiori* case). It is no doubt some restraint upon the freedom of human action, and some limit to the contracts a man may make and to the mode in which he may use or dispose of his property, but (as far as wagers are concerned) it was (before the late Act of Parliament) the clear, settled, established law of the land, vouched by the decisions of every Court in Westminster Hall, spread over a period of upwards of a century; and the Judges who have concurred in these decisions include every illustrious name that has adorned the profession of the law during that time. In principle I cannot find any distinction between a wager during life and a condition annexed to a legacy or devise to take effect after death: the mischief of both is precisely the same. If there be any distinction in respect of the right to dispose of property, it ought rather (as it seems to me) to be in favour of the right of the owner to dispose of it as he pleases while alive; but I think there is no distinction, and I am of opinion that, according to the law of England, the owner of property cannot make any matter the subject of a condition to operate after his death which he could not have made the subject of a contract or a wager during his life; I think no man can leave his property clogged and conditioned by his own personal views of public affairs, or by his posthumous ambition (if I may so call it); he cannot make his political opinions run (like a covenant) with his land; he may leave it to whom he pleases, but it must be unfettered by any condition bearing upon matters connected with the public welfare, as to which he must leave those who come after him to decide, and to act upon their own view of the merits of any public question, unfettered by any condition which may create a motive or exercise an influence that would disturb a judgment that ought to be founded on the public good alone.

My Lords, it may be that Judges are no better able to discern what is for the public good than other experienced and enlightened members of the community; but that is no reason for their refusing to entertain the question, and declining to decide upon it. Is it, or is it not, a part of our common law, that in a new and unprecedented case, where the mere caprice of a testator is to be weighed against the public good, the public good should prevail? In my judgment, it is. Whether the public good is really concerned in this condition, and the principle which it involves, is the question for the consideration of your Lordships; and your Lordships will have to decide whether or not it be mischievous to the community at large that every branch of the public service, civil and military, every department of the state, should be besieged by persons who, at the peril of losing their estates, are making every effort to obtain offices for which they may be unfit, and to procure titles and distinctions of which they may be unworthy; that no man should be able to accept or decline public service without searching the wills at Doctors Commons to see whether he may not thereby call into action some condition precedent or subsequent which may ruin himself or some very near relation; that an able statesman or a victorious general should (in some period of great emergency) have to choose whether he will save his country and lose his estate, or save his estate by declining the public service; and finally (in addition to the present complicated system of conveyancing) that the real and ultimate ownership of a large portion of the landed property of the kingdom should remain in abeyance till it appeared whether one member of a family would become a bishop, another member of another family a common law or equity judge, who should (thirty years hence) have the custody of the great or privy seal; or, whether the members of the learned professions in London should one day have the privilege of returning members to parliament, and whether the young gentleman now at school should become one of such members, and afterwards a peer of the realm. My Lords, I am not sure that some limit may not be discovered to the fanciful vagaries and capricious conditions with which property may be bequeathed, though it touch not the public interest; but the moment conditions (in this case a series of conditions) are introduced, which in principle have a strong tendency opposed to the public welfare, the common law, which favours not conditions, but deems them odious, is strong enough to stay the evil and repress the mischief; and in a perfectly new case (a case altogether *primae impressionis*) I think the Judges are bound to hold fast to the principles of the common law, to remember the maxim *salus reipublicae suprema lex*, and if the condition be really in principle against the public good, to pronounce it in their judgment void.

It only remains for me (on this point) to inquire whether this particular condition, the obtaining a peerage by Lord Alford within a limited period, is a condition which falls within the principle I have endeavoured to establish; and I am of opinion that is is. . . .

In the House of Lords (H.L. Cas. 196; E.R. 437) Lord Truro defined public policy as follows: "Public Policy, in relation to this question, is that principal of law which holds that no subject can lawfully do that which has a tendency to be injurious to the public or against the public good – which may be termed the policy of the law, or public policy in relation to the law."

M'ALISTER (or DONOGHUE) v. STEVENSON
House of Lords. [1932] All E.R. Rep. 1; [1932] A.C. 562

The appellant, a shop assistant, sought to recover from the respondent, an aerated water manufacturer, on the ground of his alleged negligence, £500 as damages for the injurious effects alleged to have been produced on her by the presence of a snail in a bottle of ginger beer manufactured by the respondent and ordered for the appellant in a shop in Paisley by a friend of the appellant. In consequence of her having drank part of the contaminated contents of the bottle the appellant alleged that she contracted a serious illness. The bottle was stated to have been dark opaque glass, so that the condition of its contents could not be ascertained by inspection, and to have been closed with a metal cap, while on the side was a label bearing the name of the respondent.

LORD ATKIN. The sole question for determination in this case is legal: Do the averments made by the pursuer in her pleading, if true, disclose a cause of action? I need not restate the particular facts. The question is whether the manufacturer of an article of drink sold by him to a distributor in circumstances which prevent the distributor or the ultimate purchaser or consumer from discovering by inspection any defect is under any legal duty to the ultimate purchaser or consumer to take reasonable care that the article is free from defect likely to cause injury to health. I do not think a more important problem has occupied your Lordships in your judicial capacity, important both because of its bearing on public health and because of the practical test which it applies to the system of law under which it arises. The case has to be determined in accordance with Scots law, but it has been a matter of agreement between the experienced counsel who argued this case, and it appears to be the basis of the judgments of the learned judges of the Court of Session, that for the purposes of determining this problem the law of Scotland and the law of England are the same. . . . The law of both countries appears to be that in order to support an action for damages for negligence the complainant has to show that he has been injured by the breach of a duty owed to him in the circumstances by the defendant to take reasonable care to avoid such injury. In the present case we are not concerned with the breach of the duty; if a duty exists, that would be a question of fact which is sufficiently averred and for the present purposes must be assumed. We are solely concerned with the question whether as a matter of law in the circumstances alleged the defender owed any duty to the pursuer to take care. . . .

At present I content myself with pointing out that in English law there must be, and is, some general conception of relations giving rise to a duty of care, of which the particular cases found in the books are but instances. The liability for negligence, whether you style it such or treat it as in other systems as a species of "culpa", is no doubt based upon a general public sentiment of moral wrongdoing for which the offender must pay. But acts or omissions which any moral code would censure cannot in a practical world be treated so as to give a right to every person injured by them to demand relief. In this way rules of law arise which limit the range of complainants and the extent of their remedy. The rule that you are to love your neighbour becomes in law, you must not injure your neighbour; and the lawyer's question, Who is my neighbour? receives a restricted reply. You must take reasonable care to avoid acts or omissions which you can reasonably foresee would be likely to injure your neighbour. Who, then, in law, is my neighbour? The answer seems to be – persons who are so closely and directly affected by my act that I ought reasonably to have them in contemplation as being so affected when I am directing my mind to the acts or omissions which are called in question. . . .

There will, no doubt, arise cases where it will be difficult to determine whether the contemplated relationship is so close that the duty arises. But in the class of case now before the Court I cannot conceive any difficulty to arise. A manufacturer puts up an article of food in a container which he knows will be opened by the actual consumer. There can be no inspection by any purchaser and no reasonable preliminary inspection by the consumer. Negligently in the course of preparation he allows the contents to be mixed with poison. It is said that the law of England and Scotland is that the poisoned consumer has no remedy against the manufacturer. My Lords, if this were the result of the authorities, I should consider the result a grave defect in the law and so contrary to principle that I should hesitate long before following any decision to that effect which had not the authority of this House. I would point out that in the assumed state of the authorities not only would the consumer have no remedy against the manufacturer, he would have none against anyone else, for in the circumstances alleged there would be no evidence of negligence against anyone other than the manufacturer, and except in the case of a consumer who was also a purchaser no contract and no warranty of fitness, and in the case of the purchase of a specific article under its patent or trade name, which might well be the case in the purchase of some articles of food and drink, no warranty protecting the purchaser-consumer. There are other instances of articles of food and drink where goods are sold intended to be used immediately by the consumer, such as many forms of goods sold for cleaning purposes, when the same liability must exist. The doctrine supported by the decision below would not only deny a remedy to the consumer who was injured by consuming bottled beer or chocolates poisoned by the negligence of the manufacturer, but also the user of what should be a harmless proprietary medicine, an ointment, a soap, a cleaning fluid or cleaning powder. I confine myself to articles of common household use, where everyone, including the manufacturer, knows that the articles will be used by persons other than the actual ultimate purchaser – namely, by members of his family and his servants, and, in some cases, his guests. My Lords, I do not think so ill of our jurisprudence as to suppose that its principles are so remote from the ordinary needs of civilized society and the ordinary claims which it makes upon its members as to deny a legal remedy where there is so obviously a social wrong. . . .

My Lords, if your Lordships accept the view that the appellant's pleading discloses a relevant cause of action, you will be affirming the proposition that by Scots and English law alike a manufacturer of products which he sells in such a form as to show that he intends them to reach the ultimate consumer in the form in which they left him, with no reasonable possibility of intermediate examination, and with the knowledge that the absence of reasonable care in the preparation or putting up of the products is likely to result in injury to the consumer's life or property, owes a duty to the consumer to take that reasonable care. It is a proposition that I venture to say no one in Scotland or England who was not a lawyer would for one moment doubt. It will be an advantage to make it clear that the law in this matter, as in most others, is in accordance with sound common sense. I think that this appeal should be allowed.

[The concurring judgments of LORD MACMILLAN and LORD THANKERTON and the dissenting judgments of LORD BUCKMASTER and LORD TOMLIN are omitted. For a parallel U.S. case see *MacPherson* v. *Buick* (1916), 217 N.Y. 382].

FENDER v. MILDMAY

House of Lords. [1937] 3 All E.R. 402; [1938] A.C. 1

LORD ATKIN: My Lords, this is an appeal by the plaintiff from an order of the Court of Appeal, who by a majority affirmed a judgment of HAWKE, J., on the trial of the action before himself and a special jury. The action was for breach of promise of marriage. The jury found for the plaintiff for £2,000 damages. HAWKE, J., entered judgment for the defendant, holding that the promise of marriage was unenforceable, as being contrary to public policy. The defendant, who was married at the time, met the plaintiff at a nursing-home, where she was a nurse. He told her that he was unhappy with his wife, and later asked her whether if his wife divorced him, she would marry him after the divorce. She consented, and thereupon sexual relations took place between them. The wife petitioned for a divorce on the ground of his adultery with the plaintiff, and a decree *nisi* was pronounced on Jan. 16, 1933. In Feb. and Apr., 1933, the defendant promised to marry the plaintiff immediately after the decree had been made absolute. These are promises for breach of which the present action was brought. The parties continued their relations until June, 1933, when, by the agency of his solicitor's clerk, the defendant intimated to the plaintiff that he did not intend to marry her. The decree was made absolute on July 31, 1933. In August, the defendant again repudiated his promise, and, in May, 1934, he married another lady. The question is whether a promise made by one spouse, after a decree *nisi* has been pronounced, to marry a third party, after the decree has been made absolute, is void on the grounds of public policy. I state it in these simple terms because it was not suggested in argument, and indeed could not be, that it made any difference whether the promise was made by petitioner or by respondent, and, if by the latter, to the man or woman with whom the adultery charged in the petition had been committed. Is it, then, contrary to public policy that a promise, made between decree *nisi* and decree absolute, to marry after decree absolute should be enforceable? It is not without significance that there is no judicial authority on this matter. The nearest authority in the English courts that has been found consists of two cases in 1908 which were not concerned with divorce proceedings, but decided that promises, made by a married man to a woman who knew he was married, that he would marry her after the death of his wife were contrary to public policy and void. It will be necessary to refer to these cases later, but I propose, in the first instance, to say something upon the doctrine of public policy generally. My Lords, from time to time judges of the highest reputation have uttered warning notes as to the danger of permitting judicial tribunals to roam unchecked in this field. The "unruly horse" of HOBART, C. J., is commonplace. I will content myself with two passages, both of which have the authority of the approval of the EARL OF HALSBURY, L.C., in *Janson* v. *Driefontein Mines, Ltd.* [(1902) A.C. 484]:

"To avow or insinuate that it might, in any case, be proper for a judge to prevent a party from availing himself of an indisputable principle of law, in a court of justice, upon the ground of some notion of fancied policy or expedience, is a new doctrine in Westminster Hall, and has a direct tendency to render all law vague and uncertain [MARSHALL ON INSURANCE, 3rd Edn., p. 32]."

[The second quotation, from Baron Parke's judgment in *Egerton*, is omitted]. I will add three other well known propositions.

"It must not be forgotten that you are not to extend arbitrarily those rules which say that a given contract is void as being against public policy, because if there is one thing which more than another public policy requires it is that men of full age and competent understanding shall have the utmost liberty of contracting, and that their contracts when entered into freely and voluntarily shall be held sacred and shall be enforced by courts of justice" [*per* JESSEL, M. R., in *Printing and Numerical Registering Co.* v. *Sampson,* at p. 465].

"Certain kinds of contracts have been held void at common law on this ground – a branch of the law, however, which certainly should not be extended, as judges are more to be trusted as interpreters of the law than as expounders of what is called public policy" [*per* CAVE, J., in *Re Mirams,* at p. 595].

"Public policy is always an unsafe and treacherous ground for legal decision, and in the present case it would not be easy to say on which side the balance of convenience would incline" [*per* LORD DAVEY, in *Janson* v. *Driefontein Consolidated Mines, Ltd.* (1), at p. 500].

In *Janson* v. *Driefontein Consolidated Mines, Ltd.*, the EARL OF HALSBURY, L.C., indeed appeared to decide that the categories of public policy are closed, and that the principle could not be involved anew unless the case could be brought within some principle of public policy already recognised by the law. I do not find, however, that this view received the express assent of the other members of the House, and it seems to me, with respect, too rigid. On the other hand, it fortifies the serious warning, illustrated by the passages cited above, that the doctrine should be invoked only in clear cases, in which the harm to the public is substantially incontestable, and does not depend upon the idiosyncratic inferences of a few judicial minds. I think that this should be regarded as the true guide. In popular language, following the wise aphorism of SIR GEORGE JESSEL, M.R., cited above, the contract should be given the benefit of the doubt.

But there is no doubt that the rule exists. In cases where the promise is to do something contrary to public policy, which, for short, I will call a harmful thing, or where the consideration for the promise is the doing, or the promise to do, a harmful thing, a judge, though he is on slippery ground, at any rate has a chance of finding a footing. The contract is unreasonably to restrict a man's economic activities, to procure a marriage between two persons, to oust the jurisdiction of the court. These things are decided to be harmful in themselves. To do them is injurious to public interests. But the doctrine does not extend only to harmful acts, it has to be applied to harmful tendencies. Here the ground is still less safe, and more treacherous. One cannot resist the tendency test. It was applied in this House in that remarkable case *Egerton* v. *Brownlow* (*Earl*), not, indeed, to a contract, but to a condition. In that case, the seventh Earl of Bridgewater had attached a condition to limitations under his will that, if the person taking did not in his lifetime acquire the title and dignity of Duke or Marquess of Bridgewater, the estates were to pass over from his heirs male to other reversionaries subject to a like condition. The fulfilment of the condition of the grant of an honour by the Crown was of necessity lawful, but the majority of the learned Lords, LYNDHURST, BROUGHAM, TRURO and ST. LEONARDS, differing from LORD CRANWORTH, L.C., and from the advice of the majority of the judges, held that the condition was bad, inasmuch as it had the tendency to cause the holder of the estates to use unlawful and corrupt means to secure the rank of a peer, which involved public duties as legislator and the like. I do not stay to comment. I doubt whether at the present day such a tendency would be held to exist, or to invalidate such a condition. It has been negatived in recent times in the case of a similar condition of obtaining a baronetcy: *Re Wallace*, *Champion* v. *Wallace*. The uncertainty of "tendencies" as a criterion of rights is illustrated by the rule, much in vogue in earlier days, and in countries other than our own, that seamen could not validly insure their future wages, which then depended upon the ship earning freight. Such insurance would have a tendency, so it was supposed, to induce seamen to relax their efforts to bring the ship to port, being more interested, one must suppose, in those days, in their wages than in their safety. This rule is expressly abrogated in our country by the Marine Insurance Act. But, assuming, as we must, that the harmful tendency of a contract must be examined, what is meant by tendency? It can only mean, I venture to think, that, taking that class of contract as a whole, the contracting parties will generally, in a majority of cases, at any rate, in a considerable number of cases, be exposed to a real temptation, by reason of the promises to do something harmful, i.e., contrary to public policy, and that it is likely that they will yield to it. All kinds of contracts provide motives for improper actions, e.g., benefits deferred until the death of a third party, and contracts of insurance. To avoid a contract, it is not enough that it affords a motive to do wrong: it must surely be shown that such a contract generally affords a motive, and that it is likely to be effective. Tendency I find defined in the Oxford Dictionary as a constant disposition to move or act toward some present end or purpose. I think that, even in *Egerton* v. *Brownlow* (*Earl*), this element of what I may call "effective motive" was assumed by the majority. . . .

I think the substance of these judgments is that you must have a general rule, a general tendency to wrong, to which there may be exceptions, but, if the contract has to be applied to an act of social or other relations, in which there will be generally no tendency to do wrong, though there may be exceptions, the contract will not be avoided. A rule is not proved by exceptions, unless the exceptions themselves lead one to infer a rule.

The evil tendency, in such a contract as the present, has been expressed in various ways by the judges. HAWKE, J., said that the promise was inconsistent with the obligations of the subsisting marriage, and the mutual loyalty required in marriage. He also thought that the wife might have changed her mind, and induced the husband to return to her. He seems to suggest an approval of the suggestion that such contracts have a tendency to create immoral relations. SLESSER, L.J., appears to apply the principles which had been expressed by PHILLIMORE, J., in *Spiers* v. *Hunt*, and the Court of Appeal in *Wilson* v. *Carnley*, in respect of promises to marry another after the death of the promisor's spouse. He cites PHILLIMORE, J.:

"The tendency of such a contract is to make the husband in thought, if not in deed, unfaithful to his wife. In certain cases it might even lead to crime. Its very probable result is sexual immorality."

He cites VAUGHAN WILLIAMS, L.J. who said that such a contract, i.e., to marry after the death of the wife, had a tendency to make the husband do something which was in contravention of the obligations which are recognised in this country as owing from a husband to a wife, FARWELL, L.J., who thought it was not only inconsistent with that affection which ought to subsist between married persons but was also calculated to act as a direct inducement to immorality, and KENNEDY, L. J., who said that it was against public policy, as tending to immorality. He himself also thought that the contract was void, because it must necessarily tend to prevent reconciliation. GREENE, L.J., thought that the contract in this case was void, because it tended to induce the promisor to act contrary to the rules of morality, it tended to encourage or facilitate immorality. It also tended to prevent reconciliation. Inasmuch as the judgments below were largely based on the cases of *Spiers* v. *Hunt* and *Wilson* v. *Carnley*, it is necessary to say something about those decisions. They were both cases in which a husband during the lifetime of his wife had promised to marry another woman on the death of his wife. In the first case, the promise to marry after the death was express; in the second, it was implied from the fact that both parties knew the wife to be alive. In the first case, immoral relations followed the promise; in the second case, there is no statement that they did. Husband and wife in both cases were living together in normal conditions, though, in the former case, the wife was already an invalid, though she survived the promise seven or eight years. Here the judges appear to have thought that a promise made in such circumstances tended to cause immoral relations. They may be right. Speaking for myself, I really do not know whether that result would follow as a rule. I can only say that, if the lady yields to a promise with such an indefinite date, she is probably of a yielding disposition, and it would appear difficult to predicate that immorality is either facilitated or accelerated by the promise. As to the suggestion that such a promise is bad, because it tends to induce the husband to murder his wife, I reject this ground altogether. ALDERSON, B., in *Egerton* v. *Brownlow* (*Earl*) incontinently classes such objections as ridiculous. They appear to afford another instance of the horrid suspicions to which high-minded men are sometimes prone. But I think that there is real substance in the objection that such a promise tends to produce conduct which violates the solemn obligations of married life. The obligations are not all included in the legal phrase rendering conjugal rights, but it can hardly be doubted that a betrothal to another would almost necessarily interfere with, hamper, and embarrass the married *consortium* which, on the hypothesis, is existing, and will continue to exist. If the moral ideal and the legal obligation are expressed in the promise to love and to cherish, it may well be doubted whether they can exist unimpaired in the presence of a betrothal to another.

But what application has this reasoning to circumstances as they exist after decree *nisi*? Not only are the parties not living together but they are not entitled to require that conjugal rights should be restored. The *consortium* is broken. The petitioning spouse has in effect said, "You have in such a degree violated your marriage obligations that I am proposing to treat myself as free, and I obtain an order from the court which, after 6 months, unless it is shown that I have done something to justify the court in interfering, will put our marriage to an end." It is said that the status of marriage exists until decree absolute. Of course it does. It is said that, if either of the spouses has immoral intercourse with a third party, he or she commits adultery. Certainly. That follows from the continued existence of the status of marriage. But let us consider how far the normal obligations and conditions of marriage continue in ordinary circumstances, after decree *nisi*. They have disappeared. There is no *consortium*, and the parties are living apart. They owe no duties each to the other to perform any kind of matrimonial obligation. The custody of the children is provided for by the court. The maintenance of the wife, if petitioner, is similarly provided for: the petitioning spouse has said: "I have done with you." In these circumstances, what possible effect can a promise to marry a third person have by way of interference with matrimonial obligations? There is no single duty which is being observed by either to the other, and it appears to me merely fanciful to suggest that the public interests are in any respect being impaired. If a respectable man, whose wife has fled with the lodger, leaving the children in his charge, engages himself to another respectable person, to marry her as soon as he is free, no public interests suffer. In my opinion, they benefit. Similarly in the converse case of a wife whose husband is living with another woman, of whose child he is the father. Does either of these persons still owe any kind of duty to love or cherish the other spouse, to whom no doubt he or she is still married, or owe him or her any duty which, in the interests of themselves or of the public, will be impaired by a promise to marry a third person when free? From the point of view of law, it ought to be remembered, as an essential factor in this discussion, that, by legislation, it has been established that it is not contrary to public policy that married persons should obtain a divorce, and not contrary to public policy that, immediately after final divorce, either of them should marry. To me, I must confess it appears lamentable that the law should set its ban upon promises made to do a lawful act by persons who, in the interval between the promise and its fulfilment, do nothing, and are not induced by the promise to do anything, contrary to the public interests. I dismiss with some indignation the idea that public policy is to be involved, on the ground that such promises tend to immorality. No doubt a promise to marry is one of the weapons of the seducer, but no one has yet sought to invalidate on this ground a promise to marry made by unmarried persons, and I am quite unable to see why any different view should be taken of promises to marry which differ only in respect of the short period, six months or less, which must elapse between promise and performance.

It remains to consider the ground for avoiding such promises, that they tend to prevent reconciliation. On this part of the case, I would wish to refer to what I have already written on "tendency." If the public policy of enforcing contracts to do lawful acts is to be maintained, it must be defeated only where there is a practical danger of injury to the public by enforcing particular classes of contracts. There must be a general tendency to harm. This topic is sometimes discussed as though a petition for divorce, and the proceedings taken to obtain a decree, were casual steps in matrimonial life, capable of being, and indeed likely to be, retraced at any time before decree absolute. In fact, they constitute the most serious and deliberate decision which a man or woman now takes. I should say that it is very seldom that parties hurry into divorce. There is much consideration and much advice tendered before a matrimonial offence or offences are regarded as decisive. The fact, at any rate, is that, in an enormous proportion of cases, when once a petitioner has got as far as decree *nisi*, no reconciliation does, or, in most cases, can, take place. The parties have shown themselves not to be of a reconciling mind. No doubt figures could be obtained, but, from the information available to the public, it is obvious that the number of decrees *nisi* that are not made absolute, in relation to those granted, expressed as a percentage, would be a minute fraction of 1 per cent. In other words there are no facts upon which the alleged general tendency can act. The so-called exceptions are the rule, and the working of the alleged rule is acutely exceptional. I come, therefore, to the conclusion that to enforce a contract such as that under discussion would harm no public interest, would leave all the obligations of marriage unimpaired, while the performance of the contract is innocent, in accordance with the policy of the law, and, in some circumstances, very much to be encouraged.

I attach importance to repelling the attack upon such contracts, for I seem to detect a resurgence of ecclesiastical principles as expressed in ecclesiastical law, which at one time found favour with common law judges, and certainly with equity judges, where they had to deal with separation agreements, and which were finally repressed more than 100 years ago. . . .

LORD RUSSELL OF KILLOWEN: My Lords, when England was a Catholic country, matrimony was a sacrament, conferred upon themselves by the spouses. This sacramental nature of marriage, the holy state of matrimony, was the basis of the civil law of Europe with regard to it. When, in the reign of Elizabeth, England abandoned the old faith, and became a Protestant country, matrimony ceased, according to the new dispensation, to be ranked among the sacraments of the Gospel. The 25th of the 39 Articles so provided. The status of marriage became the product or result of a contract between the parties. But the obligations resulting from the status, the solemnity of the status, the importance to a civilised community of its maintenance, remained almost unimpaired. Until the first Divorce Act, in 1857, the marriage tie was indissoluble except by legislation. The question now arises whether, as a result of that Act, and subsequent divorce legislation, there has come about such an alteration in the public view of the status of marriage, its obligations, and the importance of its maintenance, that, without any offence to public policy or public opinion, a spouse may validly contract to marry another, provided only that the jurisdiction of the divorce court has been invoked in relation to his or her existing marriage.

My Lords, I use those words advisedly, because, as it seems to me, every argument for the appellant which depends upon the existence of a decree *nisi* is applicable to a case where the suit has not yet proceeded beyond the presentation of the petition. The decree *nisi*, as I understand it, effects nothing. It does not dissolve the marriage. The parties are just as much man and wife as they were before. It is true that the right to *consortium* could not be enforced; that duty and obligation between spouses is no doubt in suspense. So it is once a petition for divorce has been presented. Other duties and obligations, however, remain. The duty and obligation to refrain from sexual intercourse with others, surely continues. To break it would be to commit bigamy. I confess that I do not understand how the existence of a decree *nisi* is really relevant or essential to this case. The parties at the time of the contract are either married or not. If they are married, can either of them, while still married, enter into an enforceable contract to marry someone else? . . .

Counsel for the appellant contended that the solemnity of the institution of marriage was in no way involved in the appeal, and that the tendency of his argument was to uphold the marriage tie. With all respect to him and those who share his view, I cannot agree. The institution of marriage has long been on a slippery slope. What was once a holy estate, enduring for the joint lives of the spouses, is steadily assuming the characteristics of a contract for a tenancy at will. For myself, I am glad that the opinion which I have formed of the law which is applicable to this case is consistent with the view that the obligations of married people do not cease, in the eye of the law, until, in the eye of the same law, they cease to be married, and that the married state, so long as it lasts, is still a status of sufficient solemnity to justify the words of FARWELL, L.J., when he said, in *Wilson* v. *Carnley* at p. 740:

"Speaking for myself, I find it impossible to realise the position of a man who in the lifetime of his wife, deliberately affiances himself to another woman."

In conclusion, I would point out that the decision which I would wish this House to reach in this case will in no way hinder any persons who desire to marry after divorce from taking that step. It will only compel a person already married to await with decency until he or she is no longer a married man or woman before becoming the subject of a fresh betrothal.

LORD WRIGHT: I must first attempt to explain what I think to be the modern law in regard to the duty of the court concerning rules based on public policy in this connection. In one sense, every rule of law, either common law or equity, which has been laid down by the courts, in that course of judicial legislation which has evolved the law of this country, has been based on considerations of public interest or policy. In that sense, SIR GEORGE JESSEL, M.R., referred to the paramount public policy that people should fulfil their contracts. But public policy in the narrower sense means that there are considerations of public interest which require the courts to depart from their primary function of enforcing contracts, and exceptionally to refuse to enforce them. Public policy in this sense is disabling. It is important to determine, first of all, on what principles a judge should exercise this peculiar and exceptional jurisdiction when a question of public policy is raised. What is, I think, now clear is that public policy is not a branch of law to be extended, as LORD BLANESBURGH, then YOUNGER, L.J., said in *Re Wallace, Champion* v. *Wallace*, at p. 303; to the same effect the EARL of HALSBURY, L.C., in *Janson* v. *Driefontein Consolidated Mines, Ltd., at* p. 491, said: "I deny that any court can invent a new head of public policy." The EARL OF HALSBURY, L.C., further denied the right of a judge or a court to declare that such and such things are, in his or their view, contrary to public policy. The view of the law which has prevailed is that stated by PARKE, B., in *Egerton* v. *Brownlow* (*Earl*) at p. 123. His statement has several times been quoted with approval in this house. . . .

I have found it necessary to state my opinion on this matter because it has been at least suggested, if not overtly argued, that a judge has peculiar powers in a question of public policy in acting upon his individual views or predilection, and can on these grounds refuse to enforce a contract or disposition of property *ex facie* valid. That was the view expressed, in sharp contrast to the views of PARKE, B., and ALDERSON, B., which I have quoted, by POLLOCK, C.B., in the same case of *Egerton* v. *Brownlow* (*Earl*). He said, at p. 151:

"It may be that judges are not better able to discern what is for the public good than other experienced and enlightened members of the community; but that is no reason for their refusing to entertain the question, and declining to decide upon it."

While it is true that a judge is entitled to have, and even state, on proper occasions, his personal opinions, on questions of public interest, it is a different matter if he claims to base his judicial decisions on his personal opinions. Hence the modern acceptance of the contrasted view of PARKE, B., which I have explained. It is true that the majority of the House in *Egerton* v. *Brownlow* (*Earl*) came to the conclusion advised by POLLOCK, C.B., and not that advised by PARKE, B., and the eight judges who agreed with him, but there was no need for such extreme reasoning to support their judgement, which, indeed, was a legitimate extension of *Kingston (Earl)* v. *Pierepont (Lady Elizabeth)*, and depended on the view that the condition in question was aimed at, and tended to exercise, a corrupt influence on the Government in regard to the appointment to high dignity in the state, that is, a dukedom or marquisate. Later the Court of Appeal, in *Re Wallace, Champion* v. *Wallace*, refused to extend this doctrine to a baronetcy. The only place in which I have found the *dictum* of POLLOCK, C.B., quoted in *Speyer's* case, at p. 79, by LORD HALDANE, but only with very qualified approval. It was not necessary for the decision, and finds no reflection in the opinions of his colleagues, either the two who agreed with him or the two who dissented. In view of the passages I have quoted from later judges, it is, I think, clear that this *dictum* of POLLOCK, C.B., and certain observations in *Egerton* v. *Brownlow (Earl)* to a similar effect, cannot be regarded as fixing the modern law, which, in my opinion, is as stated by PARKE, B.

[The concurring judgment of LORD THANKERTON and the dissenting judgment of LORD ROCHE are omitted].

[In the Court of Appeal Greer L.J. said, [1936] 1 K.B. 111, 117-18, 154 L.T. 94, 96:

"I cannot myself see that after a decree nisi a promise by the respondent to marry if and when the decree is made absolute is contrary to public policy. If that promise be made to a third person, not a party to the divorce proceedings, who is perfectly innocent, it seems to me impossible to hold that such a promise has any tendency to cause immoral relations. In such a case I think it has quite the opposite tendency, because the contracting parties have every reason to expect that they will be free in a short time to make a regular union; and they are unlikely to be tempted by the promise of marriage to indulge in sexual intercourse before the period arrives when they are free to marry and may lawfully have such intercourse. In a case like the present where the promise was made by the respondent to his partner in the act of adultery on which the decree nisi was founded, I also think it is not contrary to public policy that they should bind themselves if and when the decree is made absolute to marry one another and make lawful the relations between them. I should think public policy would be rather to encourage them in the event of their being free to become married people. Consider the circumstances in which persons in the position in which the plaintiff and the defendant found themselves after the decree nisi are placed. If the woman says to the respondent: 'Now in all probability you will be freed from the marriage bond in about six months when the decree is made absolute: will you marry me then?" what is he to answer? Is it in the interests of morality, decency or public policy that he should say "No"? By "No" he might mean: "No, I prefer to maintain the status quo and continue to have you as my mistress"; or he might mean: "No, I prefer to retain my freedom to throw you over and marry some one else, or remain unmarried." In my judgment morality, decency, and public policy are in favour of his answering in the affirmative and promising, as the defendant did, that as soon as it should become lawful for him to do so he would by marriage regularize the irregular union he had formed, and that this contract should be held binding in law. The chance of a reconciliation with the petitioning wife is so remote that I think it may be disregarded."]

PETITION OF R —

United States District Court, D. Massachusetts, 1944.
56 F. Supp. 969

WYZANSKI, District Judge: The issue before me is whether Florence R— "has been and still is a person of good moral character" within the meaning of ss. 307 (a) (3) of the Nationality Act of 1940, 54 Stat. 1137, 1142, 8 U.S.C.A. ss. 707(a) (3), so that she may be naturalized as a citizen of the United States.

Florence R— was born under the name of S— F— S in Esthonia. In 1928 she immigrated to the United States; and on June 15, 1941, she went through a marriage ceremony in Connecticut with Harry R—, a naturalized citizen domiciled in Massachusetts. Together they then established and have since maintained a matrimonial domicil in this Commonwealth.

Many years ago Harry R— had married another woman. These two persons, at some time prior to June 15, 1941, while domiciled in Massachusetts, and without going to Mexico, had been awarded a decree by a Mexican tribunal. This divorce was invalid because Massachusetts does not recognize the right of a foreign country to exercise through its courts jurisdiction to dissolve a marriage when both spouses are domiciled in Massachusetts. *Bergeron* v. *Bergeron*, 287 Mass. 524, 527-529, 192 N.E. 86; American Law Institute, Restatement, Conflict of Laws ss. 111.

There is no evidence that either Harry R— or Florence R— knew that the divorce proceedings were invalid until in the spring of this year the officials of the Immigration and Naturalization Service informed Florence R—. After receiving this information Florence R— continued to live in the same home with Harry R—, and I suppose that, in the absence of direct evidence and as an inference from the circumstances under which they lived and from their ages, I must presume that they engaged in acts of sexual intercourse.

Under the law of Massachusetts those acts of Florence R— were criminal. This Commonwealth regards it as fornication if a woman has sexual intercourse with a man to whom she is not married. Mass. G. L. (Ter. Ed.) c. 272 § 18; c. 277 § 39. This is so even though she has gone through a marriage ceremony with that man in good faith, sincerely but erroneously believing that the man was validly divorced. See *Jekshewitz* v. *Groswald*, 265 Mass. 413, 418, 164 N. E. 609, 62 A.L.R. 525. Compare *Commonwealth* v. *Thompson*, 11 Allen, Mass., 23, 87 Am. Dec. 685; *Commonwealth* v. *Hayden*, 163 Mass. 453, 457, 40 N. E. 846, 28 L.R.A. 318, 47 Am. St. Rep. 468; *Commonwealth* v. *Mixer*, 107 Mass. 141, 142, 93 N.E. 249, 31 L.R.A., N.S. 467, 20 Ann. Ca 1152; *McGrath* v. *Sullivan*, 303 Mass. 327, 331, 21 N.E. 2d 533. By reiteration, the local courts have emphasized their doctrine that purity of motive, and ignorance of the facts or the law are of no consequence.

I, therefore, am squarely faced with the necessity of deciding whether under the Nationality Act a woman lacks "good moral character" if she has committed the crime of fornication by having sexual intercourse with a man with whom she went through a marriage ceremony in good faith, sincerely but erroneously believing the man was divorced.

A somewhat similar issue has been before the courts previously. The earlier authorities tended to take a mechanical view of the question. Their approach was that if the petitioner had engaged in sexual acts which were unlawful under the criminal code, then the petitioner was not of good moral character. Later cases, notably Petition of Schlau, D.C.S.D.N.Y. 1941, 41 F. Supp. 161; In re Schlau, 2 Cir., 1943, 136 F. 2d 480, while they are distinguishable, show a tendency to investigate the particular conduct and to measure it less by statutory and judge-made rules than by the usages of the society in which the petitioner moves.

Ordinarily, if Congress leaves a case to a judge to decide, it expects him to appraise the facts by technical criteria. He has not the freedom which a jury so often exercises to disregard the letter of the law and apply the sentiment of the community. But there are exceptional cases in which the judge enjoys a broader scope. By using in the Nationality Act a phrase so popular as "good moral character" Congress seems to have invited the judges to concern themselves not only with the technicalities of the criminal law, but also with the norms of society and the way average men of good will act, in short, with what Eugen Ehrlich in Fundamental Principles of the Sociology of Law (translated by W. L. Moll, Harvard University Press, 1936), p. 501, calls "the ascertainment of the living law." Cf. Note, 43 Harvard Law Review 117.

In the light of the living law I cannot say that Florence R— has done anything which the community regards as reprehensible. She herself has been married only once and has never procured any divorce. She and Harry R— live together in the same way as any lawfully married couple. Undoubtedly they are received among their friends and acquaintances as though their marriage were valid.

Moreover, the husband's prior divorce would seem normal to many laymen. They would see no moral difference between a person in moderate circumstances who had secured a divorce from Mexico by mail and a more affluent person who had secured a divorce in person in Nevada after establishing a domicil there. To laymen any distinction would rest on "purely abstract legal reason." It would represent a rule which, while in theory maintaining equality, in practice established a different standard for the poor and the rich. Compare the caustic remarks of Mr. Justice Maule quoted by Roscoe Pound, The Spirit of the Common Law (Boston 1921) pp. 210-212. It would disregard the fact that in our society Mexican and Nevada divorces both pass as being more or less respectable and represent the mores of the day. Compare Ehrlich, Fundamental Principles of the Sociology of the Law, supra, p. 491.

I therefore conclude that proof that a petitioner has committed fornication at least in the circumstances of this case is not an adequate ground for saying that the petitioner is not "of good moral character." I do not find it necessary to decide whether it would be a ground for denying citizenship if a petitioner had committed fornication for commercial motives, or with a minor, or under circumstances different from those here involved.

Petition for citizenship granted.

REPOUILLE v. UNITED STATES

Circuit Court of Appeals, Second Circuit, 1947. 165 F. 2d 152

Appeal from the District Court of the United States for the Eastern District of New York.

Naturalization proceeding by Louis Loftus Repouille against the United States. From an order of the District Court for the Eastern District of New York granting the alien's petition for naturalization, the United States appeals.

Order reversed and petition dismissed.

Before L. Hand, Augustus N. Hand and Frank, Circuit Judges.

L. Hand, Circuit Judge: The District Attorney, on behalf of the Immigration and Naturalization Service, has appealed from an order, naturalizing the appellee, Repouille. The ground of the objection in the district court and here is that he did not show himself to have been a person of "good moral character" for the five years which preceded the filing of his petition. The facts were as follows. The petition was filed on September 22, 1944, and on October 12, 1939, he had deliberately put to death his son, a boy of thirteen, by means of chloroform. His reason for this tragic deed was that the child had "suffered from birth from a brain injury which destined him to be an idiot and a physical monstrosity, malformed in all four limbs. The child was blind, mute, and deformed. He had to be fed; the movements of his bladder and bowels were involuntary, and his entire life was spent in a small crib." Repouille had four other children at the time towards whom he has always been a dutiful and responsible parent; it may be assumed that his act was to help him in their nurture, which was being compromised by the burden imposed upon him in the care of the fifth. The family was altogether dependent upon his industry for its support. He was indicted for manslaughter in the first degree; but the jury brought in a verdict of manslaughter in the second degree with a recommendation of the "utmost clemency"; and the judge sentenced him to not less than five years nor more than ten, execution to be stayed, and the defendant to be placed on probation, from which he was discharged in December, 1945. Concededly, except for this act he conducted himself as a person of "good moral character" during the five years before he filed his petition. Indeed, if he had waited before filing his petition from September 22, to October 14, 1944, he would have had a clear record for the necessary period, and would have been admitted without question.

Very recently we had to pass upon the phrase "good moral character"in the Nationality Act; and we said that it set as a test, not those standards which we might ourselves approve, but whether "the moral feelings, now prevalent generally in this country" would "be outraged" by the conduct in question: that is, whether it conformed to "the generally accepted moral conventions current at the time." In the absence of some national inquisition, like a Gallup poll, that is indeed a difficult test to apply; often questions will arise to which the answer is not ascertainable, and where the petitioner must fail only because he has the affirmative. Indeed, in the case at bar itself the answer is not wholly certain; for we all know that there are great numbers of people of the most unimpeachable virtue, who think it morally justifiable to put an end to a life so inexorably destined to be a burden to others, and – so far as any possible interest of its own is concerned – condemned to a brutish existence, lower indeed than all but the lowest forms of sentient life. Nor is it inevitably an answer to say that it must be immoral to do this, until the law provides security against the abuses which would inevitably follow, unless the practice were regulated. Many people – probably most people – do not make it a final ethical test of conduct that it shall not violate law; few of us exact of ourselves or of others the unflinching obedience of a Socrates. There being no lawful means of accomplishing an end, which they believe to be righteous in itself, there have always been conscientious persons who feel no scruple in acting in defiance of a law which is repugnant to their personal convictions, and who even regard as martyrs those who suffer by doing so. In our own history it is only necessary to recall the Abolitionists. It is reasonably clear that the jury which tried Repouille did not feel any moral repulsion at his crime. Although it was inescapably murder in the first degree, not only did they bring in a verdict that was flatly in the face of the facts and utterly absurd – for manslaughter in the second degree presupposes that the killing had not been deliberate – but they coupled even that with a recommendation which showed that in substance they wished to exculpate the offender. Moreover, it is also plain, from the sentence which he imposed, that the judge could not have seriously disagreed with their recommendation.

One might be tempted to seize upon all this as a reliable measure of current morals; and no doubt it should have its place in the scale; but we should hesitate to accept it as decisive, when, for example, we compare it with the fate of a similar offender in Massachusetts who, although he was not executed, was imprisoned for life. Left at large as we are, without means of verifying our conclusion, and without authority to substitute our individual beliefs, the outcome must needs be tentative; and not much is gained by discussion. We can say no more than that, quite independently of what may be the current moral feeling as to legally administered euthanasia, we feel reasonably secure in holding that only a minority of virtuous persons would deem the practise morally justifiable, while it remains in private hands, even when the provocation is as overwhelming as it was in this instance.

However, we wish to make it plain that a new petition would not be open to this objection; and that the pitiable event, now long passed, will not prevent Repouille from taking his place among us as a citizen. The assertion in his brief that he did not "intend" the petition to be filed until 1945, unhappily is irrelevant; the statute makes crucial the actual date of filing.

Order reversed; petition dismissed without prejudice to the filing of a second petition.

FRANK, Circuit Judge (dissenting): This decision may be of small practical import to this petitioner for citizenship, since perhaps, on filing a new petition, he will promptly become a citizen. But the method used by my colleagues in disposing of this case may, as a precedent, have a very serious significance for many another future petitioner whose "good moral character" may be questioned (for any one of a variety of reasons which may be unrelated to a "mercy killing") in circumstances where the necessity of filing a new petition may cause a long and injurious delay. Accordingly, I think it desirable to dissent.

The district judge found that Repouille was a person of "good moral character." Presumably, in so finding, the judge attempted to employ that statutory standard in accordance with our decisions, i.e., as measured by conduct in conformity with "the generally accepted moral conventions at the time." My colleagues, although their sources of information concerning the pertinent mores are not shown to be superior to those of the district judge, reject his finding. And they do so, too, while conceding that their own conclusion is uncertain, and (as they put it) "tentative." I incline to think that the correct statutory test (the test Congress intended) is the attitude of our ethical leaders. That attitude would not be too difficult to learn; indeed, my colleagues indicate that they think such leaders would agree with the district judge. But the precedents in this circuit constrain us to be guided by contemporary public opinion about which, cloistered as judges are, we have but vague notions. (One recalls Gibbon's remark that usually a person who talks of "the opinion of the world at large" is really referring to "the few people with whom I happened to converse.")

Seeking to apply a standard of this type, courts usually do not rely on evidence but utilize what is often called the doctrine of "judicial notice," which, in matters of this sort, properly permits informal inquiries by the judges. [In this very case, my colleagues have relied on informally procured information with reference to "the fate of a similar offender in Massachusetts."] However, for such a purpose (as in the discharge of many other judicial duties), the courts are inadequately staffed, so that sometimes "judicial notice" actually means judicial ignorance. [Think how any competent administrative agency would act if faced with a problem like that before us here.]

But the courts are not utterly helpless; such judicial impotence has its limits. Especially when an issue importantly affecting a man's life is involved, it seems to me that we need not, and ought not, resort to our mere unchecked surmises, remaining wholly (to quote my colleagues' words) "without means of verifying our conclusions." Because court judgments are the most solemn kind of governmental act – backed up as they are, if necessary, by the armed force of the government – they should, I think, have a more solid foundation. I see no good reason why a man's rights should be jeopardized by judges' needless lack of knowledge.

I think, therefore, that, in any case such as this, where we lack the means of determining present-day public reactions, we should remand to the district judge with these directions: The judge should give the petitioner and the government the opportunity to bring to the judge's attention reliable information on the subject, which he may supplement in appropriate way. All the data so obtained should be put of record. On the basis thereof, the judge should reconsider his decision and arrive at a conclusion. Then, if there is another appeal, we can avoid sheer guessing, which alone is now available to us, and can reach something like an informed judgment. [Of course, we cannot thus expect to attain certainty, for certainty on such a subject as public opinion is unattainable.]

JOHNSON v. UNITED STATES

United States Court of Appeals, Second Circuit, 1951. 186 F. 2d 588.

L. HAND, Chief Judge: The United States appeals from an order admitting Johnson, an alien, to citizenship on the ground that the evidence did not show that he had been a person of "good moral character" for the five years preceding the filing of his petition on June 27, 1944. The petitioner was born in Russia on April 28, 1897, and was admitted to this country on June 3, 1913; he has always lived here, was married on November 14, 1923, and has a son born on April 19, 1926. The most intelligible way to present the other evidence in the record is in the sequence in which the "Naturalization Service" apparently discovered it. On July 11, 1944, about two weeks after the petition was filed, the Probation Officer of the Domestic Relations Court in the City of New York answered an inquiry of the "Naturalization Petitions Section" that Johnson and his wife had been "known to this Court since 1931"; that on April 15, 1940, he "was placed under order of $15 a week," and that a warrant had been issued for him on July 1, 1940, which had never been executed. The "Naturalization Petitions Section" next procured an affidavit from Johnson's wife on December 30, 1944, in which she said that he left her in 1932 and that the Domestic Relations Court had ordered him to pay her $20 a week which he never completely performed. The affidavit continued that in November, 1944, she had haled him once more into court and he "promised" to pay her six dollars a week, which also he failed to do, and that, for the preceding ten years he had been living with a married woman, who at the time he began to live with her was only twenty years old. Finally, it alleged that he had once paid his wife $12 for four weeks and "recently" $6 for two weeks; that their son, who was in the Army, had allowed her an "allotment"; "but I think my husband should support me." On May 25, 1945, the Probation Officer wrote again that the order of the Domestic Relations Court had been "modified" on July 21 to $10 but that Johnson had paid nothing after April 3, 1945, so far as the records showed. On February 24, 1945, Johnson answered his wife's affidavit with one of his own in which he swore that he had lived with her till 1932 when they had been "dispossessed," and had separated until 1935, when they again lived together for three months. They separated finally, he swore, "because she was always demanding money" which he did not have, because he was out of a steady job till 1936; though they had been "many times" in court, and in November, 1944, her allowance had been reduced to six dollars a week which he had paid except for the last two weeks. He denied that he had "been living with any other woman since I left my wife," although he had taken one to dances and had visited another at the farm where she lived with her husband.

Apparently no further inquiries were made for two years, but on December 11, 1946, Johnson swore to another affidavit in the first part of which he declared that he had refused (apparently at an examination before some official) to answer as to his relations with a woman named Urich, because it might incriminate him. However, he did admit that they had occupied an apartment together from December 1944 to January 1945, though innocently; but he still refused to answer whether their relations had also been equally innocent during the whole of the five years before June 27, 1944, when he filed his petition. Finally, when the hearing came on before the judge he admitted that he had lived in illicit relations with Urich between 1939 and 1942, when she broke down nervously and had to go to a hospital till 1944; yet, when she came out in 1944 and resumed living with him for a month or so their relations were innocent, as he had said before. The evidence taken as a whole leaves it uncertain why Johnson left his wife in 1935. On the one hand she swore that his liaison with Urich began ten years before December 30, 1944; on the other, he swore that he did not begin with Urich until two years later, which does not accord with hers. All that was clearly proved was that for five years – from 1937 to 1942 – he was living with a paramour.

We held in *Estrin* v. *United States*, 2 Cir., 80 F. 2d 105, that even a single lapse from marital fidelity, if there were no "extenuating circumstances," was not consistent with the requirement of five years of unbroken "good moral character." That decision we regarded as still law when we decided Petitions of Rudder, 2 Cir., 159 F. 2d 695, eleven years later; and still holds good. Moreover, it rests upon the applicant to prove the "extenuating circumstances." We thought that the applicants in Petitions of Rudder, supra, had done so. In all four cases the relation had continued for many years with all the circumstances of lawful marriage except legal sanction. In one case the applicant's paramour had been divorced from her husband, but had neglected to get leave from the proper court to marry again, as the law required. In two others she was a woman separated from her husband, and was married to the applicant as soon as she was freed by the death of, or divorce from, her husband. In the fourth the applicant's wife, from whom he had been separated for fifteen years, had refused to give him a divorce; and the liaison did not begin until six or seven years after he had left her. We must own that the statute imposes upon courts a task impossible of assured execution; people differ as much about moral conduct as they do about beauty. There is not the slightest doubt that to many thousands of our citizens nothing will excuse any sexual irregularity, for some indeed this extends even to the subsequent marriage of an innocent divorced spouse. On the other hand there are many thousands who look with a complaisant eye upon putting an easy end to one union and taking on another. Our duty in such cases, as we understand it, is to divine what the "common conscience" prevalent at the time demands; and it is impossible in practice to ascertain what in a given instance it does demand. We should have no warrant for assuming that it meant the judgment of some ethical elite, even if any criterion were available to select them. Nor is it possible to make use of general principles, for almost every moral situation is unique; and no one could be sure how far the distinguishing features of each case would be morally relevant to one person and not to another. Theoretically, perhaps we might take as the test whether those who would approve the specific conduct would outnumber those who would disapprove; but it would be fantastically absurd to try to apply it. So it seems to us that we are confined to the best guess we can make of how such a poll would result.

In the case at bar the difficulties are not, however, very formidable. As we have said, we start with the premise that Johnson left his wife in 1935, and that his meretricious union with Urich began at least in 1937 and continued for five years. Such a situation does not seem to us to fall within our decision in the case of Jannibelli, that one of the four applicants in Petitions of Rudder, supra, whose case is the nearest. True, it did not appear why Jannibelli had originally left his wife, but that was fifteen years before he filed his petition instead of nine as here; and the new union had lasted for eight or nine years and was continuing at the time of the hearing. Perhaps we should have insisted that Jannibelli prove why he had continued to live separate from his wife during the five years before he filed his petition; perhaps it was not a good answer that the separation went back so far. Be that as it may, even though we may have been too lenient then, the situation here calls for more explanations than Johnson could, or would, give. On this record it is left in doubt whether he did not without any just excuse desert his wife and child, and – at most only two years later – begin a liaison with a younger woman. Moreover, it is also doubtful whether he has not continually neglected to pay even those progressively reduced allowances which the court made to his wife. This combination of factors satisfies us that by the standard of the prevailing "common conscience" he did not prove himself a person of "good moral character," as the statute uses those words.

Order reversed; petition denied.

FLEMING v. ATKINSON

Supreme Court of Canada. 1959. 18 D.L.R. (2d) 81.

JUDSON J.: The accident which gives rise to this litigation happened on a country road in the Province of Ontario on a summer afternoon between the plaintiff, the driver of a motor vehicle, and 3 cows, part of a larger herd belonging to the defendant, which was grazing on the side of the road. Both the learned trial Judge [1955] 4 D.L.R. 408, O.R. 565] and the Court of Appeal [5 D.L.R. (2d) 309, [1956] O.R. 801] have found that there were was nothing unusual in the presence of these animals on the highway and that their owner made no effort to keep them within the boundaries of his property, the fences of which were in a state of very poor repair. The defendant's appeal to this Court raises squarely the question whether an adjoining owner owes a duty of reasonable care to users of the highway to prevent domestic animals, not known to be dangerous, from straying on to the highway. *Searle* v. *Wallbank* [1947] A.C. 341, followed in Ontario in *Noble* v. *Calder*, [1952], 3 D.L.R. 651, O.R. 577, both deny the existence of any such duty. The judgment under appeal has found the defendant, the owner of the animals, partly responsible for this accident, a distinction having been drawn on the facts between the present case and *Noble* v. *Calder*. I think it desirable now when the matter is in this Court for the first time to examine further into the nature of the obligation, if any.

There were two reasons implicit in the judgment in *Searle* v. *Wallbank* for the rejection of the duty. The first is based upon the history of the highways of England, which came into being largely as a result of dedication by adjoining owners, who gave to the public no more than a right of passage which had to be exercised subject to the risk of straying animals. The second is based upon the facts as they existed until the advent of fast-moving traffic. It is put in this way by Maugham L.C. at p. 353: "No facts in my opinion have been established which would tend to show that farmers and others at some uncertain date in our lifetime became subject for the first time to an onerous and undefined duty to cyclists and motorists which never previously existed." It is beyond dispute that for centuries straying animals on the highway did not present any risk to slow-moving traffic. The only risk in the situation arose when an animal *mansuetae naturae* showed a vicious propensity, and for this the owner was only liable on proof of *scienter*.

I an in complete agreement with the reasons of Roach J.A. in the judgment under appeal when he says that the historical basis for the rule in *Searle* v. *Wallbank*, dependent as it is upon the peculiarities of highway dedication in England, has never existed in Ontario. This seems to me to be of the greatest significance when considering the rights of the public on these highways. The public right of passage on the highways of Ontario was never subject to the risk of straying animals for the historical reasons given in *Searle* v. *Wallbank*. For the most part the highways of Ontario did not come into being as a result of dedication by adjoining owners. They were created when the Province was surveyed. The fee remained in the Crown and it is now vested either in the Crown in right of the Province or in the municipalities. This distinction between the legal position in England, where the ownership of the fee in the highways still remains in the adjoining owners, and that in Ontario, where the fee is in the highway authority, was traced in detail by Boyd C. in *Ricketts* v. *Markdale* (1900), 31 O.R. 610. How, in these circumstances, can an adjoining owner acquire any right to permit his animals to stray on the highway? Against the highway authority, his animals are trespassers. His right is the same as that of any other member of the public and no higher, namely, the right of passage for himself and his animals, the right of access to his property and special rights which are of no significance in this inquiry, such as the right of purchase when highways are closed and the right to occupy unopened road allowances. There is therefore no reason for giving adjoining owners any special rights to permit the straying of animals. This alone is sufficient to distinguish the law of Ontario from the law of England and to render the principle stated in *Searle* v. *Wallbank* inapplicable here.

The other foundation for the principle of immunity in favour of the adjoining owner was that until the advent of fast-moving traffic no cause of action could possibly have existed. There was in fact no real risk worthy of judicial consideration from the mere presence of straying animals on the highway. There was nothing that called for the interference of the law in this situation. But does it follow as a consequence of this that there can be no cause of action today when the facts are entirely different and when there has been a developing law of negligence for the last 150 years? As was pointed out by the learned editor in 66 L.Q. Rev. 456, the real objection to the decision in *Searle* v. *Wallbank* is that a conclusion of fact has hardened into a rule of law when the facts upon which the original conclusion was based no longer exist: "As long as the conclusion of fact and the rule of law were not in conflict this shift from the one to the other passed unnoticed, but now that 'the experience of centuries' is no longer valid under the changed conditions of modern motor traffic it is not surprising that the law on this point is subject to criticism."

A rule of law has, therefore, been stated in *Searle* v. *Wallbank* and followed in *Noble* v. *Calder* which has little or no relation to the facts or needs of the situation and which ignores any theory of responsibility to the public for conduct which involves forseeable consequences of harm. I can think of no logical basis for this immunity and it can only be based upon a rigid determination to adhere to the rules of the past in spite of changed conditions which call for the application of rules of responsibility which have been worked out to meet modern needs. It has always been assumed that one of the virtues of the common law system is its flexibility, that it is capable of changing with the times and adapting its principles to new conditions. There has been conspicuous failure to do this in this branch of the law and the failure has not passed unnoticed. It has been criticized in judicial decisions (including the one under appeal), in the texts and by the commentators.

The anomalous nature of the rule is emphasized by comparison with the rights and obligations existing between adjoining owners. In this situation the owner of the animals must keep them upon his land under control and is liable for trespass if they escape and do such damage as it is in their nature to commit. The right of action for trespass exists also in the owner of the soil of a highway if cattle depasture his herbage. An owner may only drive his animals onto the highway for the purpose of passage and if he does so he must exercise reasonable care while they are using the highway for this purpose. By contrast, the rule is said to be one of non-liability if the animals are permitted to stray. Further, what difference is there between driving the animals onto the highway and turning them loose on the property when it must be apparent, as in the present case, that sooner or later they will be on the highway?

My conclusion is that it is open to this Court to apply the ordinary rules of negligence to the case of straying animals and that the principles enunciated in *Searle* v. *Wallbank*, dependent as they are upon historical reasons, which have no relevancy here, and upon a refusal to recognize a duty now because there had been previously no need of one, offer no obstacle. . . .

[FAUTEUX and ABBOTT JJ. concurred with JUDSON, J. The concurring judgment of RAND J., joined in by TASCHEREAU J., and the dissenting judgments of LOCKE and CARTWRIGHT JJ. are omitted].

In *Oppenheim* v. *Kridel* (1923), 140 N.E. 227, 230 (N.Y.C.A.), Crane J., speaking for 5 of 6 judges, said: "The common law is not rigid and inflexible, a thing dead to all surrounding and changing conditions, it does expand with reason. The common law is not a compendium of mechanical rules, written in fixed and indelible characters, but a living organism which grows and moves in response to the larger and fuller development of the nation." Held, that a wife as well as a husband has a cause of action for criminal conversation.

In *Overseas Tankship (U.K.) Ltd.* v. *Morts Dock & Engineering Co. Ltd.* (The Wagon Mound) [1961] A.C. 388, 422, Viscount Simonds said, in refusing to follow In re Polemis, [1921] 3 K.B. 560: "it does not seem consonant with current ideas of justice or morality that for an act of negligence, however slight or venial, which results in some trivial foreseeable damage the actor should be liable for all consequences however unforeseeable and however grave, so long as they can be said to be 'direct'."

B. READINGS

Friedrich Carl von Savigny, 1779-1861
Professor of Roman Law, University of Berlin

OF THE VOCATION OF OUR AGE FOR LEGISLATION AND JURISPRUDENCE (1814)

II Origin of Positive Law

We first inquire of history, how law actually developed itself amongst nations of the nobler races; the question – What may be good, or necessary, or, on the contrary, censurable herein, – will be not at all prejudiced by this method of proceeding.

In the earliest times to which authentic history extends, the law will be found to have already attained a fixed character, peculiar to the people, like their language, manners and constitution. Nay, these phenomena have no separate existence, they are but the particular faculties and tendencies of an individual people, inseparably united in nature, and only wearing the semblance of distinct attributes to our view. That which binds them into one whole is the common conviction of the people, the kindred consciousness of an inward necessity, excluding all notion of an accidental and arbitrary origin.

How these peculiar attributes of nations, by which they are first individualized, originated – this is a question which cannot be answered historically. Of late, the prevalent opinion has been that all lived at first a sort of animal life, advancing gradually to a more passable state, until at length the height on which they now stand, was attained. We may leave this theory alone, and confine ourselves to the mere matter of fact of that first authentic condition of the law. We shall endeavour to exhibit certain general traits of this period, in which the law, as well as the language, exists in the consciousness of the people.

This youth of nations is poor in ideas, but enjoys a clear perception of its relations and circumstances, and feels and brings the whole of them into play; whilst we, in our artificial complicated existence, are overwhelmed by our own riches, instead of enjoying and controlling them. This plain natural state is particularly observable in the law; and as, in the case of an individual, his family relations and patrimonial property may possess an additional value in his eyes from the effect of association, – so on the same principle, it is possible for the rules of the law itself to be amongst the objects of popular faith. But these moral faculties require some bodily existence to fix them. Such, for language, is its constant uninterrupted use; such, for the constitution, are palpable and public powers, – but what supplies its place with regard to the law? In our times it is supplied by rules, communicated by writing and word of mouth. This mode of fixation, however, presupposes a high degree of abstraction, and is, therefore, not practicable in the early time alluded to. On the contrary, we then find symbolical acts universally employed where rights and duties were to be created or extinguished: it is their palpableness which externally retains law in a fixed form; and their solemnity and weight correspond with the importance of the legal relations themselves, which have been already mentioned as peculiar to this period. In the general use of such formal acts, the Germanic races agree with the ancient Italic, except that, amongst these last, the forms themselves appear more fixed and regular, which perhaps arose from their city constitutions. These formal acts may be considered as the true grammar of law in this period; and it is important to observe that the principal business of the early Roman jurists consisted in the preservation and accurate application of them. We, in latter times, have often made light of them as the creation of barbarism and superstition, and have prided ourselves on not having them, without considering that we, too, are at every step beset with legal forms, to which, in fact, only the principal advantages of the old forms are wanting, – namely, their palpableness, and the popular prejudice in their favour, whilst ours are felt by all as something arbitrary, and therefore burthensome. In such partial views of early times we resemble the travellers, who remark, with great astonishment, that in France the little children, nay, even the common people, speak French with perfect fluency.

But this organic connection of law with the being and character of the people, is also manifested in the progress of the times; and here, again, it may be compared with language. For law, as for language, there is no moment of absolute cessation; it is subject to the same movement and development as every other popular tendency; and this very development remains under the same law of inward necessity, as in its earliest stages. Law grows with the growth, and strengthens with the strength of the people, and finally dies away as the nation loses its nationality. But this inward progressive tendency, even in highly cultivated times, throws a great difficulty in the way of discussion. It has been maintained above, that the common consciousness of the people is the peculiar seat of law. This, for example, in the Roman law, is easily conceivable of its essential parts, such as the general definition of marriage, of property, &c. &c., but with regard to the endless detail, of which we have only a remnant in the Pandects, every one must regard it as impossible.

This difficulty leads us to a new view of the development of law. With the progress of civilization, national tendencies become more and more distinct, and what otherwise would have remained common, becomes appropriated to particular classes; the jurists now become more and more a distinct class of the kind; law perfects its language, takes a scientific direction, and, as formerly it existed in the consciousness of the community, it now devolves upon the jurists, who thus, in this department, represent the community. Law is henceforth more artificial and complex, since it has a twofold life; first, as part of the aggregate existence of the community, which it does not cease to be; and, secondly, as a distinct branch of knowledge in the hands of the jurists. All the latter phenomena are explicable by the co-operation of those two principles of existence; and it may now be understood, how even the whole of that immense detail might arise from organic causes, without any exertion of arbitrary will or intention. For the sake of brevity, we call, technically speaking, the connection of law with the general existence of the people – the political element; and the distinct scientific existence of law – the technical element.

At different times, therefore, amongst the same people, law will be natural law (in a different sense from our law of nature), or learned law, as the one or the other principle prevails, between which a precise line of demarcation is obviously impossible. Under a republican constitution, the political principle will be able to preserve an immediate influence longer than in monarchical states; and under the Roman republic in particular, many causes co-operated to keep this influence alive, even during the progress of civilization. But in all times, and under all constitutions, this influence continues to shew itself in particular applications, as where the same constantly-recurring necessity makes a general consciousness of the people at large possible. Thus, in most cities, a separate law for menial servants and house-renting will grow up and continue to exist, equally independent of positive rules and scientific jurisprudence: such laws are the individual remains of the primitive legal formations. Before the great overthrow of almost all institutions, which we have witnessed, cases of this sort were of much more frequent occurrence in the small German states than now, parts of the old Germanic institutions having frequently survived all revolutions whatever. The sum, therefore, of this theory is, that all law is originally formed in the manner, in which, in ordinary but not quite correct language, customary law is said to have been formed: i.e. that it is first developed by custom and popular faith, next by jurisprudence, – everywhere, therefore, by internal silently-operating powers, not by the arbitrary will of a law-giver.

This state of things has hitherto been only historically set forth; whether it be praiseworthy and desirable, the following enquiry will show. But even in an historical point of view, this state of law requires to be more accurately defined. In the first place, in treating of it, a complete undisturbed national development is assumed; the influence of an early connection with foreign jurisprudence will, farther on, be illustrated by the example of Germany. It will likewise appear, that a partial influence of legislation on jurisprudence may sometimes produce a beneficial, and sometimes an injurious, effect. Lastly, there are great variations within the limits of the validity and application of the law. For, as the same nation branches off into many stocks, and states are united or disunited, the same law may sometimes be common to several independent states; and sometimes, in different parts of the same state, together with the same fundamental principles, a great diversity of particular provisions may prevail. . . .

III. *Legislative Provisions and Law Books.*

LEGISLATION, properly so called, not unfrequently exercises an influence upon particular portions of the law; but the causes of this influence vary greatly. In the first place, the legislator, in altering the existing law, may be influenced by high reasons of state. When, in our time, unprofessional men speak of the necessity of new legislation, they commonly mean that only of which the settlement of the rights of land-owners is one of the most striking examples. The history of the Roman law, also, supplies examples of this kind, – a few in the free times of the republic, – the important *Lex Julia et Papia Poppaea*, in the time of Augustus, – and a great number since the Christian emperors. That enactments of this kind easily become a baneful corruption of the law, and that they should be most sparingly employed, must strike any one who consults history. In these, the technical part of law is only looked at for the sake of the form and the connection with the whole remaining law, which connection makes this branch of legislation more difficult than it is commonly supposed to be. Of a much less doubtful character is a second influence of legislation upon the law. Particular rules, indeed, may be doubtful, or from their very nature may have varying and ill-defined limits, as, for example, all prescription; whilst the administration of the law requires limits defined with the greatest possible precision. Here a kind of legislation may be introduced, which comes to the aid of custom, removes these doubts and uncertainties, and thus brings to the light, and keeps pure, the real law, the proper will of the people. The Roman government had, for this purpose, an excellent institution in in the Praetorian Edicts, an institution which, under certain conditions, might even exist in monarchical states.

But these kinds of partial influence are not intended when, as in our times, the necessity of a code is spoken of. Rather, in this case, the following is meant: – The nation is to examine its whole stock of law, and put it into writing, so that the book, thus formed, shall henceforth be not one amongst other legal authorities, but that all others which have been hitherto in force, shall be in force no longer. The first question, therefore, is, where are the materials for this code to come from? According to a theory already mentioned, it has been maintained by many, that these are to be supplied by the universal law of nature, without reference to any thing existing. But those who had to do with the execution of such plans, or were otherwise acquainted with practical law, have laid no stress upon this extravagant and wholly groundless theory; and it is unanimously agreed that the existing law is to be laid down with merely such alterations and improvements as might be thought necessary on grounds of expediency. That this was the prevalent opinion when the new codes were framed, will appear hereafter. The substance of a code would, accordingly, be two-fold; it would be composed partly of the existing law, and partly of new provisions. So far as the last are concerned, their occurrence on the occasion of a code, is obviously a matter of accident; they might have been proposed singly at any other time, and, what is more, there might be no want of them, at any time the code is formed. In Germany, in particular, these new provisions would often be but apparently new, since that which was new in one state might have been already in force in another; so that the question would relate, not to new laws, but to already existing laws of kindred nations, with a mere change of jurisdiction. Not, therefore, to confuse our inquiry, we will lay new laws entirely aside, and look only to the essentials of the code. In this case we must consider the code as the exposition of the aggregate existing law, with exclusive validity conferred by the state itself.

That we should consider this last as essential in an understanding of the kind, is natural in times so fruitful in writing as ours; when, with such a number of authors and such a rapid succession of books and authorities, no particular book can preserve a predominant and lasting influence otherwise than through the authority of the state. In fact, however, it may well be thought that a work of the kind might be accomplished by private jurists, without requisition or confirmation on the part of the state. This was often the case with the old German law, and we should have a good deal of trouble to make our forefathers understand that difference between a law book, as a private production, and a real code, which we consider so natural and necessary. For the present, however, we have only to do with the notion peculiar to our times. Nevertheless it is clear, that this difference consists merely in the originating cause and the confirmation on the part of the state, not in the nature of the work itself, for this in every case is wholly technical, and as such belongs to the jurists; since, as regards the substance of the code we are supposing, the political element of the law has long worked itself out, and there is nothing to do but to discriminate and expound the result, which is the peculiar function of technical jurisprudence.

The requisites of such a code, and the expectations from it, are of two kinds. With regard to the condition of the law itself, the highest degree of precision is to be looked for, and, at the same time, the highest degree of uniformity in the application. The limits of its jurisdiction are to be more clearly defined and regulated, since a general national law is to replace a varying customary law. We here confine ourselves to the first benefit, as the second will be best discussed further on, in particular application to Germany.

That this first benefit depends upon the excellence of the execution, must be obvious to all, and, therefore, in this respect, it is just as possible to lose as to gain. Well deserving of consideration is what Bacon, from the magnitude of his intellect and his experience, said of a work of the kind. He is of opinion, that it should never be engaged in without a pressing necessity, and even then with particular care of the legal authorities in force; by, in the first place, the scrupulous adoption of every thing that is applicable in them, and, secondly, by their being preserved and constantly consulted. Above all, he says, the work should only be undertaken in times which in civilization and knowledge surpass the preceding, for it would be truly lamentable were the productions of former times to be mutilated by the ignorance of the present. It is not difficult to say what is here required: the existing law, which is not to be changed, but retained, must be thoroughly understood and properly expressed. *That* (the understanding of it) concerns the substance, *this* (the expression) the form.

As regards the substance, the most important and difficult part is the completeness of the code, and upon this point we have only fully to comprehend the following proposition, in which all agree.

The code, then, as it is intended to be the only law authority, is actually to contain, by anticipation, a decision for every case that may arise. This has been often conceived, as if it were possible and advantageous to obtain, by experience, a perfect knowledge of the particular cases, and then to decide each by a corresponding provision of the code. But whoever has considered law-cases attentively, will see at a glance that this undertaking must fail, because there are positively no limits to the varities of actual combinations of circumstances. In all the new codes, indeed, all appearance of an attempt to obtain this material perfection has been given up, without, however, establishing any thing in its stead. But there is certainly a perfection of a different kind, which may be illustrated by a technical expression of geometry. In every triangle, namely, there are certain data, from the relations of which all the rest are necessarily deducible: thus, given two sides and the included angle, the whole triangle is given. In like manner, every part of our law has points by which the rest may be given: these may be termed the leading axioms. To distinguish these, and deduce from them the internal connection, and the precise degree of affinity which subsist between all juridical notions and rules, is amongst the most difficult of the problems of jurisprudence. Indeed, it is peculiarly this which gives our labours the scientific character. If then the code be formed in a time which is unequal to this art, the following evils are inevitable: The administration of justice is ostensibly regulated by the code, but really by something else, external to the code, acting as the true dominant authority. This false appearance, however, is productive of the most disastrous effects. For the code, by its novelty, its connection with the prevailing notions of the age, and its external influence, will infallibly attract all attention to itself, away from the real law-authority; so that the latter, left in darkness and obscurty, will derive no assistance from the moral energies of the nation, by which alone it can attain to a satisfactory state. That this is no groundless apprehension, will appear further on when we come to treat of the new codes: and it will be seen that not only the substance itself, but the very notion and general nature of this true governing source of law is misunderstood, as it then appears under the most opposite names, sometimes as natural law (*Naturrecht*), sometimes as *jurisprudence*, sometimes as analogical law. If to this imperfect knowledge of the leading principles, be added the abovementioned aim at material completeness, particular decisions unnoticed by the framers, will be constantly crossing and contradicting each other, which will gradually come to light by practice only, and, in the case of a bad administration of justice, not even by that. This result would be clearly inevitable, so far as contemporaries are concerned, were an age, without being fully qualified, to fix its legal notions by legislative authority in this manner; but the effect of it would be no less injurious to succeeding times. For if, in these, circumstances should be favourable for a revision of the law, nothing would be more conducive to the end in view than the being extensively connected with preceding intelligent times; but the code now stands between, impeding and throwing difficulties in the way of this connection on all sides. Besides, in the partial dealing with an established positive law, there is the risk of being overwhelmed by mere texts, and every sort of relief must, on the other hand, be very welcome: an imperfect code, however, more than any thing else, must confirm the supremacy of this dead spiritless mode of treating the law.

But, besides the substance, the form of the code must be taken into consideration, for the framer may have fully studied the law on which he is at work, and his production may, notwithstanding, fail of its end, if he have not withal the art of exposition. What this exposition ought to be, is better shown by instances of successful or unsuccessful application, than by general rules. It is commonly required that the language of the law should be particularly distinguished by brevity. Certainly brevity may be extremely effective, as is clear from the examples of the Roman Decrees and Edicts. But there is also a dry, inexpressive brevity, adopted by him who does not understand the use of language as an instrument, and which remains wholly ineffective; numerous examples of it are to be found in the laws and records of the middle ages. On the other hand, diffuseness in law authorities may be very exceptionable, nay, wholly intolerable, as in many of the constitutions of Justinian, and in most of the novels of the Theodosian Code; but there is also an intelligent and very effective diffuseness, and this is discernible in many parts of the Pandects.

Putting together what has been said above concerning the requisites of a really good code, it is clear that very few ages will be found qualified for it. Young nations, it is true, have the clearest perception of their law, but their codes are defective in language and logical skill, and they are generally incapable of expressing what is best, so that they frequently produce no individual image, whilst their matter is in the highest degree individual. The laws of the middle ages, already quoted, are examples of this; and had we the twelve tables complete before us, we should probably find something of the sort, only in a less degree. In declining ages, on the other hand, almost every thing is wanting – knowledge of the matter, as well as language. There thus remains only a middle period; that which, (as regards the law, although not necessarily in any other respect,) may be accounted the summit of civilization. But such an age has no need of a code for itself: it would merely compose one for a succeeding and less fortunate age, as we lay up provisions for winter. But an age is seldom disposed to be so provident for posterity.

VI. *Our Vocation for Legislation*

The grounds upon which the necessity of a code for Germany is usually rested, have been spoken of in the preceding chapter; we have now to consider the capacity for the undertaking. Should there be any deficiency in this respect, our condition, which we are anxious to improve, would necessarily be deteriorated by a code.

Bacon required that the age in which a code should be formed, should excel preceding ages in intelligence, from which it follows, as a necessary conclusion, that this capacity must have been denied to many an age, which, in other respects, may be regarded as in a high state of cultivation. Very recently, the opponents of the Roman law have not unfrequently laid particular stress upon such arguments as the following: – Reason is common to all nations and ages alike, and as we have, moreover, the experience of former times to resort to, all that we do must infallibly be better than all that has been done before. – But even this opinion, that every age has a vocation for every thing, is a prejudice of the most dangerous kind. In the fine arts we are obliged to acknowledge the contrary; why are we unwilling to make the same admission, with respect to the government and the law?

If we examine the expectations of unprofessional men from a code, these will be found to vary with the objects of law; and here, also, the twofold element of all law, which I have termed the political and the technical, is manifest. In some of these objects they take an immediate lively interest; others they give up, as indifferent matters of juridical technicality. The former is more the case in family law; the latter in property law, mostly in its general fundamental principles. We will take, as representatives of these different kinds of objects, *marriage* and *property*; what is about to be said of them is to be taken to apply to the whole class to which they belong. . . .

Unluckily, during the whole of the eighteenth century Germany was very poor in great jurists. There were numbers of laborious men, it is true, by whom very valuable preparatory labours were executed, but more than this was seldom done. A two-fold spirit is indispensable to the jurist; the historical, to seize with readiness the peculiarities of every age and every form of law; and the systematic, to view every notion and every rule in lively connection and co-operation with the whole, that is, in the only true and natural relation. This twofold scientific spirit is very rarely found amongst the jurists of the eighteenth century; and, in particular, some superficial speculations in philosophy had an extremely unfavourable effect. A just appreciation of the time in which one lives is very difficult: still, unless all signs deceive, a spirit has come upon our science, capable of elevating it for the future to the rank of a national system. Little, indeed, of this improvement is yet produced, and upon this ground I deny our capacity for the production of a good code. Many may look upon this judgment as overstrained, but I challenge them to shew me one out of the no small number of systems of Roman-Germanic law, which is not merely capable of being made useful in promoting this or that particular end – for of such we have many – but which is really good as a book. This praise, however, can only be bestowed, when the exposition has a distinctive self-dependent form, and, at the same time, renders the matter more vividly perceptible. Thus, for example, in the Roman law, the point would be to catch the method of the old jurists, the spirit which animates the Pandects; and I should rejoice to become acquainted with any one of our systems with which it were possible for this to be the case. As no work of the kind, though talents and assiduity have not been wanting, has ever yet succeeded, I maintain that, in our age, a good code is not practicable; for with regard to this, the undertaking is the same, only more difficult. There is yet another test of our capacity: if we compare our juridical literature with the progress of German literature in general, and consider whether the first has kept pace with the latter, the result will be unfavourable, and we shall find them bearing a very different relation to each other than that borne by the Roman jurists to the literature of Rome. There is nothing degrading in this conclusion, for the task imposed upon us is really very great, – beyond comparison, more difficult than that of the Roman jurists. But we are not to mistake the magnitude of the task from indolence or self-conceit; we are not to believe ourselves at the goal, when we are still far from it.

If then, we have really nothing which is necessary to the formation of a good code, we are not to believe that the actual undertaking would be nothing more than a disappointment, which, at the worst, would merely not have advanced us. The great danger inevitably impending when a very defective and shallow state of knowledge is fixed by positive authority, has been already spoken of; and this danger would be great in proportion to the vastness of the undertaking and its connection with the wakening spirit of nationality. Examples, near at hand, often afford, in matters of this kind, a less significant illustration; to make clear, therefore, what may be the result of such a proceeding, I will refer to the time immediately following the decline of the Roman empire in the West, where an imperfect state of legal knowledge was fixed exactly in this manner. The only case which here offers a comparison, is the Edict of Theodoric, because in this alone the existing law was to be stated in new form. I am far from believing that, what we might produce, would be exactly like this edict; for the times are really very different. The Romans, in the year 500, found some difficulty in saying what they thought – we possess some skill in composition: moreover, there were, at that time, no juridical writers – we have no want of these. But the similarity is not to be mistaken in this: that there was then a mass of historical matter to be expressed, which was not comprehended, nor could be mastered, and which in its new form we find some difficulty in recognising. In one respect, too, the disadvantage is on our side: in the year 500, there was nothing to spoil. In our time, on the contrary, vigorous exertions are undeniably making, and it is impossible to say how much good we subtract from the future by confirming present deficiencies. For "*ut corpora lente augescunt, cito extinguuntur; sic ingenia studiaque oppresseris facilius quam revocaveris.*"

An important point still remains to be considered, – the language. I ask of any one who knows what good appropriate expression is, and who does not regard language as a common tool, but as a scientific instrument, whether we possess a language in which a code could be composed? I am far from questioning the strength of the old German language; but that even this is not now fit for the purpose, is to me a proof the more, that we are behindhand in this circle of thought. The moment our science improves, it will be seen of how much avail our language, by its freshness and primitive vigour, will prove. What is more, I believe that, of late, we have even retrograded in this respect. I know no German law of the eighteenth century, which, in weight and vigour of expression, could be compared with the Criminal Ordinances of Charles the Fifth.

I know what answer might be given to these reasons; even admitting all of them, it may be said, the powers of the human mind are boundless, and by reasonable exertion a work, even in these times, might be soon produced, in which none of these defects would be traceable. Well, any one may make the attempt, our age is not an inattentive one, and there is no danger that actual success will be overlooked.

I have hitherto investigated the fitness of our times for a general system of legislation, as if nothing of the kind had ever been undertaken. I now turn to the codes which recent times have actually produced.

On the Field-Carter argument over codifications, which was of some importance in the United States in the latter part of the nineteenth century, see Hall, *Readings in Jurisprudence* 119-121 (1938) and Patterson, *Jurisprudence* 421-425 (1953).

Rudolf von Ihering, 1818-1892
Professor of Law at several German Universities

LAW AS A MEANS TO AN END

(German ed. 1877-1882; Husik trans. copyright by The Macmillan Company 1914; reprinted by permission.)

Chapter VII

SOCIAL MECHANICS, OR THE LEVERS OF SOCIAL MOVEMENT

Social Mechanics. This is the picture of society as life presents it daily to our eyes. Thousands of rollers, wheels, knives, as in a mighty machine, move restlessly, some in one direction, some in another, apparently quite independent of one another as if they existed only for themselves, nay in apparent conflict, as if they wanted mutually to annihilate each other – and yet all work ultimately together harmoniously for *one purpose*, and one *single* plan rules the whole. What compels the elementary forces of society to order and co-operation; who indicates to these their paths and their motions? The machine *must* obey the master; the laws of mechanics enable him to *compel* it. But the force which moves the wheelwork of human society is the human *will*; that force which, in contrast to the forces of nature, boasts of its freedom; but the will in that function is the will of thousands and millions of individuals, the struggle of interests, of the opposition of efforts, egoism, self-will, insubordination, inertia, weakness, wickedness, crime. There is no greater miracle in the world than the disciplining and training of the human will, whose actual realization in its widest scope we embrace in the word society.

The sum of impulses and powers which accomplish this work I call *social mechanics*. If these were wanting, who would assure society that the moving forces upon which she counts might not one day refuse their service, or take a direction hostile to her purposes; that the will might not one day at this or that point rise in revolt against the role assigned to it and bring the whole wheelwork to a standstill? Temporarily such standing still actually takes place at individual points; yea, even shocks which seem to threaten the entire existence of society, just as in the human body. But the vital force of society is so strong and indestructible that she always quickly overcomes these disturbances; in place of anarchy, order as a rule at once steps in again – every social disturbance is only a search for a new and better order – anarchy is only a means, never an end, something temporary, never anything permanent; the struggle of anarchy with society always ends with the victory of the latter.

But this means nothing else than that the society possesses a compelling power over the human will; that there is a *social* mechanics to compel the human will just as there is a *physical* mechanics to force the machine. This social mechanics is identical with the principle of leverage, by means of which society sets the will in motion for her purposes, or in short, *the principle of the levers of social motion*.

There are *four* such levers. Two of them have egoism as their motive and presupposition; I call them the *lower* or *egoistic* social levers; they are *reward* and *coercion*. Without them social life cannot be thought, no *commerce* without reward, and no *law* or *State* without coercion; they represent therefore the elementary assumptions of society; the necessary impulses which can nowhere be wanting and are not wanting, though their condition be ever so rudimentary or degenerate. Opposed to these are two other impulses which have not egoism as their motive and presupposition, but on the contrary the denial thereof; and as they come into play not in the lower region of purely individual purposes, but in the higher region of universal purposes, I call them the *higher*; or, since, as I shall show later (Chapter IX), society is the source of morality, the *moral* or *ethical* levers of social motion. They are the *Feeling of Duty* and of *Love*; the former the prose, the latter the poetry of the moral spirit.

Of the two egoistical levers, coercion holds psychologically the lowest position. Reward stands psychologically a degree higher, for reward appeals to the freedom of the subject; it expects its success exclusively from the free resolve of the latter. In an indolent person reward fails of its purpose, whereas coercion proves its power over him also, for it either excludes freedom entirely, where it operates mechanically, or limits it, where it operates psychologically (p. 17). Coercion addresses itself to man at his lowest; it denotes the lowest point of social mechanics; which should therefore in reality begin with coercion. But the point of view from which we have to consider those two levers is not the manner of their psychological influence upon the individual, but their practical significance for society; and if we apply the point of view of social formation to the two motives as a standard of measurement, there can be no doubt that the social organization of reward – commerce, is to be designated as lower in comparison with that of coercion – the *law* and the *State*. Hence an exposition which has made if its task to rise from the lower to the higher in its consideration of society, must begin with reward, as we are going to do. . . .

Eugen Ehrlich, 1862-1922
Professor of Law Czernowitz University, now in the Ukraine

FUNDAMENTAL PRINCIPLES OF THE SOCIOLOGY OF LAW

Reprinted by permission of the publishers from *Fundamental Principles of the Sociology of Law* by Eugen Ehrlich, 1936, translated by W. L. Moll, Cambridge, Mass.; Harvard University Press, Copyright 1936 by The President and Fellows of Harvard College.)

FOREWORD

It is often said that a book must be written in a manner that permits of summing up its content in a single sentence. If the present volume were to be subjected to this test, the sentence might be the following: At the present as well as at any other time, the center of gravity of legal development lies not in legislation, nor in juristic science, nor in judicial decision, but in society itself. This sentence, perhaps, contains the substance of every attempt to state the fundamental principles of the sociology of law.

Paris, on Christmas Day, 1912. THE AUTHOR

II

THE INNER ORDER OF THE SOCIAL ASSOCIATIONS

It is axiomatic that all study in the field of social science is based on the concept of human society. Society is the sum total of the human associations that have mutual relations with one another. And these associations that constitute human society are very heterogeneous. The state, the nation, the community of states which are bound together by the ties of international law, i.e. the political, economic, intellectual, and social association of the civilized nations of the earth extending far beyond the bounds of the individual state and nation, the religious communions and the individual churches, the various sects and religious groups, the corporations, the classes, the professions, the political parties within the state, the families in the narrowest and in the widest sense, the social groups and cliques – constitute a society to the extent that acting and reacting upon one another is at all perceptible among them. . . .

The inner order of the associations of human beings is not only the original, but also, down to the present time, the basic form of law. The legal proposition not only comes into being at a much later time, but is largely derived from the inner order of the associations. In order to explain the beginnings, the development, and the nature of law, one must first of all inquire into the order of the associations. All attempts that have been made until now to comprehend the nature of law have failed because the investigation was not based on the order of the associations but on the legal propositions.

The inner order of the associations is determined by legal norms. Legal norms must not be confused with legal propositions. The legal proposition is the precise, universally binding formulation of the legal precept in a book of statutes or in a law book. The legal norm is the legal command, reduced to practice, as it obtains in a definite association, perhaps of very small size, even without any formulation in words. As soon as there are legal propositions within an association that have actually become effective, they give rise to legal norms. But in every society there is a much greater number of legal norms than of legal propositions; for there always is much more law that is applicable to individual cases than is applicable to all relations of a similar kind; much more law than the contemporary jurists who have attempted to formulate it in words have realized. Every modern legal historian knows how small a portion of the law that was valid at the time is contained in the Twelve Tables or in the *Lex Salica.* Modern codes are in the same case. In the past centuries, all legal norms that were determinative of the inner order of the associations were based upon custom, upon contracts, and upon articles of association of corporations. In the main, this is the situation today.

III

THE SOCIAL ASSOCIATIONS AND THE SOCIAL NORMS

A social association is a plurality of human beings who, in their relations with one another, recognize certain rules of conduct as binding, and, generally at least, actually regulate their conduct according to them. These rules are of various kinds: rules of law, of morals, of religion, of ethical custom, of honor, of decorum, of tact, of etiquette, of fashion. To these may be added some of lesser importance, e.g. rules of games, the rule that one must wait one's turn, for instance at the ticket window or in the waiting room of a busy physician. These rules are social facts, the resultants of the forces that are operative in society, and can no more be considered separate and apart from society, in which they are operative, than the motion of the waves can be computed without considering the element in which they move. As to form and content, they are norms, abstract commands and prohibitions, concerning the social life within the association and directed to the members of the association. In addition to rules of conduct of this kind, there are rules that are not norms because they do not refer to the social life of human beings: e.g. the rules of language, of taste, or of hygiene.

The legal norm, therefore, is merely one of the rules of conduct, of the same nature as all other rules of conduct. For reasons readily understood, the prevailing school of juristic science does not stress this fact, but, for practical reasons, emphasizes the antithesis between law and the other norms, expecially the ethical norms, in order to urge upon the judge at every turn as impressively as possible that he must render his decisions solely according to law and never according to other rules. . . .

Not all human associations are being regulated by legal norms, but manifestly only those associations are parts of the legal order whose order is based upon legal norms. The sociology of law deals exclusively with these; the others are the subject matter of other branches of sociology. Among the legal associations there are some that are readily recognizable by external criteria, i.e. those that jurists style juristic persons, corporations, institutions, foundations, and, first and foremost, the state. But even in public law, there are numerous legal associations that have no legal personality; such as administrative boards, public institutions, the people, the army, the various classes, ranks, and professions. Much more of this is to be found in private law.

In all legal associations the legal norm constitutes the backbone of the inner order; it is the strongest support of their organization. By organization we mean that rule in the association which assigns to each member his relative position in the association (whether of domination or of subjection) and his function. This rule may deal not only with the relation of man to man, but also with the relation of man to things. Indirectly it deals with the relation of man to man even in the latter case. For the owner of articles of consumption determines what performance is to be rendered in return by those at whose disposal he places the goods; the owner of the factory determines the order in the factory and its management; the creditor determines the fate of the subject matter of the obligation, and often of the debtor; just as often, however, it is the debtor that determines the fate of the subject matter of the obligation and of the creditor, for, being the possessor of the thing, he has a great deal of legal power over it. But only those rules of law have a share in the creation of the legal order of the association that have actually become rules of conduct in the association, i.e. that are being recognized and followed by men, in a general way at least. Rules of law that have remained mere norms for decision, that become effective only in the very rare cases of legal controversy, do not take part in the ordering of the associations. This may be said, *a fortiori*, of those legal propositions, in reality quite numerous, that do not affect life at all. The same holds true for the norms of morality, ethical custom, and religion. It is always necessary therefore to ask not only how much of what has been promulgated by the lawgiver, proclaimed by the founder of a religion, or taught by the philosopher has been applied by the courts, preached from the pulpits, or taught in books or schools, but how much has actually been practiced and lived. Only that which becomes part and parcel of life becomes a living norm; everything else is mere doctrine, norm for decision, dogma, or theory. Norms of ethical custom, of honor, of decorum, of tact, of etiquette, of fashion are only rules of human conduct; and though a new code of honor (rules for the duel) should appear at every moment, it would remain absolutely without any significance whatever if it did not actually become part and parcel of life.

The first and most important function of the sociological science of law, therefore, is to separate those portions of the law that regulate, order, and determine society from the mere norms for decision, and to demonstrate their organizing power. This was recognized first of all in *Staatsrecht* (public law in the narrow sense) and in administrative law. Indeed hardly anyone doubts today that *Staatsrecht* is an ordering of the state, whose purpose is not to decide legal disputes, but to determine the positions and the functions of the organs of the state, as well as the duties and functions of the authorities of the state. But the state is above all a social association; the forces that are operative in the state are social forces; everything that proceeds from the state, the activity of the authorities of the state and particularly legislation by the state, is something that is done by society through the association created for that purpose, i.e. the state. The same classes, orders, and interests that control society prevail in the state; and if the state makes war on any one of these, we know that the state has passed under the control of one of the others. *Staatsrecht* (public law in the narrow sense) therefore comprises both a state and a social ordering. . . .

Gierke contrasts the law of the state and of the corporations of public and private law, which he styles social law, with the entire remaining private law, which he styles individual law. But this antithesis is unwarranted. There is no individual law. All law is social law. Life knows not man as an utterly detached, individual, and isolated being, nor does the law know such a being. The law always sees in man solely a member of one of the countless associations in which life has placed him. These associations, inasmuch as they bear a legal stamp, are being ordered and regulated by law and the other social norms; it is the norms that assign to each individual his position of domination or of subjection and his function. It is true, membership in the association occasionally, but by no means always, gives rise to individual rights and duties of the individual, but this is not its purpose, is not its essential content. . . .

The contract, then, is the juristic form for the distribution and utilization of the goods and personal abilities (services) that are in existence in society. Not only the making of the contract, but also its content, is a result of social interrelations. In connection with any one of the ordinary contracts of daily life, it may suffice to raise the question which part of it is peculiar to this specific contract and which part is determined by the social order and by the organization of economic life and of commercial intercourse, in order to satisfy ourselves of the extent to which the latter elements preponderate. The fact that we are in a position today to satisfy our needs as to food, clothing, and housing by means of the everyday contracts of sale and lease and the contracts for work and labor, we owe to the other fact that in the community in which we live commerce and production of goods have been regulated sufficiently to make this manner of satisfying one's needs possible. Assuredly five hundred years ago this was not possible anywhere, and there is many a part of the world in which it is not possible today. One cannot rent a dwelling in a mountain village where there are none to let; one cannot provide oneself daily with food and clothing unless they are offered for sale in the vicinity; and one cannot hire a man to perform services which are not being rendered in exchange for wages in the form of money. This applies, self-evidently, not only to the subject matter of the contract but to every individual provision of the contract. If one examines a contract point by point, one can easily find the social reason why it is worded exactly as it is. It may be the fact that one of the parties occupies a position of social or economic advantage over the other, or the condition of the market, or the custom of the particular line of business. A person who has changed his residence will notice at once that he is making contracts of an entirely different nature from those that he made before. And though he be ever so firmly resolved not to change his mode of living in any way, the world round about him has changed, and he must conform to it even in his contractual intent. In England, as a rule, one does not rent an apartment but a whole house; one does not purchase one's daily supply of meat at the butcher's, but has it delivered weekly at one's residence. Accordingly rental contracts and contracts for the purchase of meat in England have a quite different content from those on the Continent. The writer has intentionally chosen contracts of the retail trade as illustrations, for in these the peculiar features of each individual case appear most clearly. It has often been shown to what extent the contracts of the wholesale trade and of industry are merely expressions of the general conditions of the market or of the special needs of the particular economic sphere. Most written contracts are drawn up according to printed forms, the content of which often is not made known to the parties, for it is determined by society quite independently of their individual wills. Nevertheless, it is true that the individualizing data that are written into the form are also a result of social interrelations. . . .

The entire private law therefore, inasmuch as it has an organizing content, is social law in precisely the same sense as the law of the state and the law of corporations. It is always concerned with the human associations: it determines the position of the individual in the group of working human beings and the relation of the group to its tools. Like *Staatsrecht* (public law in the narrow sense) and the law of corporations, private law primarily creates associations, not individual rights and duties; and though individual spheres arise for the individual in the organized community, this is a reflex effect of organization, in public law no less than in private law. The fact that in this case the association is not based on a constitution or on articles of association, but on the law of things and of contract and on the order of the family, must not hide this great truth from us, for in this case the law of things and of contract and the order of the family serve the same purpose that is accomplished elsewhere by a constitution or by articles of association. A hermit may have a truly "individual sphere" not only in the juristic but also in the sociological and economic sense, but a man living among men cannot. One may have individual rights in economically insignificant articles of use and consumption, e.g. in clothing, in jewelry, in a portfolio, or in stationery, but even in the matter of the furnishings of a dwelling, except in the case of single men or women, there is the common use by the family. And even the true individual rights are social rights, to the same extent at least as is the legal claim of the member of the commune to participation in the use of the pasture belonging to the commune or of the member of a reading club to participation in the use of the books and periodicals. In conceding to the individual the possession of these things and permitting him to dispose of them according to his pleasure, society regulates their use and consumption; ownership of the goods which it concedes to the individual is merely a result of this social order. The individual enjoys this ownership as a member of an ordered community which respects private ownership and protects it without, in the case of certain things, concerning itself about the way in which they are being utilized. Society could regulate individual use and consumption in a manner quite different from, and much more detailed than, the manner in which it does this today, and we shall be convinced of this at a much earlier date perhaps than we should like as soon as the exhaustion of the resources of nature, which is even now threatening, shall have drawn much nearer. Whenever society actually accords to the individual an individual sphere, it refrains, on principle, from any and all interference. The inner life of the adult man, for instance, is his individual sphere; it lies within the domain of art, of religion, of philosophy, but not of law or of the extra-legal social norms.

The jural associations of human society therefore are, in the main, the following: the state with its courts and magistracies; the family, and the other bodies, associations, and communities with or without juristic personality; associations created by means of contract and inheritance, and, in particular, national and world-wide economic systems. Possession and ownership, which for the purposes of sociological discussions might be treated as, to a certain extent, convertible terms, real rights and claims based on obligation, create the inner order of these associations. This is the part that law plays in the ordering of the political, intellectual, economic, and social life of present-day society. This by no means exhausts the entire material of the law, but it is the part of the law which has power to regulate and order. Apart from this, there is another part of the law, which does not directly regulate and order the associations, but only protects them against attacks. It is connected with the social associations as a sort of seconday order; it maintains and strengthens them, but does not give them shape or form. This applies to the law of procedure before the courts and other tribunals; for it is merely a part of the order of the tribunals which have been created for the protection of social institutions; it is without direct influence upon society. It applies also to penal law, for the latter creates no social institutions; it merely protects goods that are already in existence in society and institutions that have already been established. And, lastly, it applies also to all those provisions of the material private law that concern only the protection afforded by law; like penal law, they create neither goods nor social institutions; they but regulate the already existing protection afforded by the courts and other tribunals. These norms did not come into being within the social associations themselves as the inner order of the latter, but arose in juristic law or in the law created by the state. All rights of monopoly, especially patent rights and copyrights, are created by the state. They consist in a command, addressed to all who are subjected to the will of the state, except the person who holds the right, to refrain from engaging in any activity in a certain sphere. Norms of similar nature have occasionally arisen in juristic law also.

And now we must point out the significance, but slightly considered hitherto, of the extra-legal norms for the inner ordering of the associations. The statement that legal institutions are based exclusively on legal norms is not true. Morality, religion, ethical custom, decorum, tact, even etiquette and fashion, do not order the extra-legal relations only; they also affect the legal sphere at every turn. Not a single one of the jural associations could maintain its existence solely by means of legal norms; all of them, at all times, require the aid of extra-legal norms which increase or eke out their force. Nothing short of the cooperation of the social norms of every description can offer a complete picture of the social mechanism. . . .

IV

SOCIAL AND STATE SANCTION OF THE NORMS

Sanction is not a peculiarity of the legal norms. The norms of ethical custom, morality, religion, tact, decorum, etiquette, and fashion would be quite meaningless if they did not exercise a certain amount of coercion. They too constitute the order of the human associations, and it is their specific function to coerce the individual members of the association to submit to the order. All compulsion exercised by the norms is based upon the fact that the individual is never actually an isolated individual; he is enrolled, placed, embedded, wedged, into so many associations that existence outside of these would be unendurable, often even impossible, to him. We are speaking now of basic facts of the inner, the emotional, life of man. The psychic needs of ordinary commonplace creatures, who everywhere constitute the compact majority, must indeed be appraised none too highly; nevertheless there is no one to whom country, native land, religious communion, family, friends, social relations, political party, are mere words. Most people perhaps will set little store by one or the other of these, but doubtless there would be very few who do not cling with all their hearts and minds to one group at least. It is within his circle that each man seeks aid in distress, comfort in misfortune, moral support, social life, recognition, respect, honor. In the last analysis it is his group that supplies him with everything that he sets store by in life. But the importance of these associations is not limited to these moral, intangible considerations, for on them depends success in one's profession and business. On the other hand, one's profession and business draw one into a number of professional and business associations. . . .

A man therefore conducts himself according to law, chiefly because this is made imperative by his social relations. In this respect the legal norm does not differ from the other norms. The state is not the only association that exercises coercion; there is an untold number of associations in society that exercise it much more forcibly than the state. One of the most vigorous of these associations is the family. Modern legislation more and more does away with the possibility of execution of a decree for the restitution of conjugal relations. But even if the family law were abolished in its entirety, families would not bear in aspect much different from that which they bear today; for fortunately the family law requires state sanction only in rare instances. If the workman, the employee, the officeholder, the military officer, do not perform their contractual and official duties from a sense of duty, they do so because they wish to rise to better ones. The physician, the attorney, the mechanic, the merchant, are interested in exact performance of their contracts because they wish to satisfy their patients, clients, and customers and to increase the number of the latter; at any rate, because they wish to establish or strengthen their credit. Penalty and levy of execution is the last thing that enters their minds. There are large mercantile houses which, as a matter of principle, do not bring suit on a matter arising in their commercial relations, and as a rule do not permit themselves to be sued, but satisfy even an unfounded claim in full. They meet refusal of payment and frivolous demands by severing commercial relations. To this extent their own power is sufficient unto them; to this extent they can dispense with the aid of the courts and with legal protection. Likewise persons of superior social position avoid litigation of controversies, e.g. with servants, employees, workmen, mechanics. Their social and economic influence affords sufficient protection from imposition. For decades the English trade unions have declined all recognition by the state, thereby consciously and intentionally foregoing legal protection. Manifestly they did not fare badly by doing so. Modern trusts and cartels have at their disposal a complete system of means of coercion, by which they are enabled, without ever calling upon the power of the state or upon the courts, to enforce their just, as well as their often altogether unjustifiable, demands against everyone who happens to come within their sphere of power. . . .

To consider the right of compulsory execution, as jurists often do, as the basis of the legal order involves a tremendous overestimation of its scope. Limited in its effectiveness to a small fraction of legal life, i.e. the obligation to pay money, it is secondary even within this sphere to the force of the social interrelations which urge us to perform our obligations. There can be no doubt that the creditor usually makes a correct calculation as to whether credit may safely be granted to the debtor, i.e. that the considerations which prompt him to extend credit coincide with those that prompt the debtor to meet his obligations. In fact, a person to whom his personal reputation, his social standing, his business relations, in short his credit, mean anything surely will never even think of hazarding a compulsory execution. All these things mean too much to him to endanger them for the sake of a momentary advantage. The gambler pays his unenforceable gambling debts under a merely social compulsion, and the average man is at least as sensitive to social sanction as the average gambler. Even unenforceable debts arising from stock-exchange differences are usually being paid, although in these cases the social and economic consequences of failure to do so are much less than in case of true business debts. The generally known ineffectiveness of the usury laws demonstrates that the persons from whom usury is being exacted can be compelled to pay even without compulsory execution. The reports of mercantile credit associations show that the well known purely economic means of coercion, to wit boycott and black list, are effective even where compulsory execution has remained altogether fruitless. Nothnagel, in the book referred to above, mentions older mateial, which however is still valuable. Compulsory execution, like penalty, we may therefore say, exists only for those that have come down in the world and for those whom society has cast out. It is effective against the reckless borrower, the cheat, the bankrupt, and against him who has become insolvent through misfortune. However much of a burden these classes of borrowers may be on business life, they are too insignificant to warrant the statement that the value of the legal order depends upon the protection it affords against such elements.

On the whole the effect of the coercive order of the state is limited to protection of one's person, of one's possession, and of claims against those who are outside of the pale of society. Whatsoever else the state may do in order to maintain the law is of much less significance, and one might reasonably maintain that society would not go to pieces even if the state should exercise no coercion whatever. . . .

In view of the coercion by means of which the social associations enforce observance of the norms, it may be said that the individual manifestly is at all times both active and passive; every member of the association takes part in bringing pressure to bear, and every individual, in turn, must submit to pressure. The coercive power of the norms – a fact of mass psychology – posits at the same time the observance of the latter – a fact of individual psychology. It would be a mistake, nevertheless, to lay too much stress upon this particular fact. With the great mass of men who throughout their whole lives permit themselves, without objection, to be fitted into the vast social mechanism, it is not a matter of conscious thinking, but of unconsciously habituating themselves to the emotions and thoughts of their surroundings, which are with them from the cradle to the grave. The most important norms function only through suggestion. They come to man in the form of commands or of prohibitions; they are addressed to him without a statement of the reason on which they are based; and he obeys them without a moment's reflection. They have not subdued man but have educated him. They are being impressed upon his mind in his childhood; an "It is not done," "It is not proper," "Thus hath God commanded" follows him through his whole life. And he submits with a willingness which is the greater the more emphatically experience brings home to him the advantages of obedience and the disadvantages of disobedience. The advantages and disadvantages are not only social but also individual; for he who obeys a command is spared the arduous labor of doing his own thinking, and the still more arduous labor of making his own decision. Liberty and independence are ideals of the poet, the artist, and the thinker only. The average man is a Philistine, without much appreciation of these things. He loves that to which he has become habituated, the instinctive, and hates nothing more than intellectual exertion. That is the reason why women become enthusiastic over men of strong will. The latter make their decisions for them, and do not even give the thought of resistance opportunity to arise. For all the trouble and pains that they are thereby freed from they are sincerely grateful to their husbands.

In this way, obedience to norms ultimately impresses its stamp upon the whole man. It makes not only the individual act, but the man himself, just, moral, faithful, tenacious of ethical custom, dignified, tactful, honorable, well-mannered, modern. He submits to the norms from conviction, and this imparts stability to his conduct. After the social pressure which is brought to bear upon the individual in each case by the habit of obedience to the norms has fashioned the character of the individual, it can no longer be effectively counteracted by the other influences. The social norms give shape and form to the individuality of man. . . .

VI

THE NORMS FOR DECISION

Courts do not come into being as organs of the state, but of society. . . .

The courts decide on the basis of their norms for decision whether a social norm has been transgressed or not. The prevailing juristic science takes for granted that it must be a legal norm that has been transgressed, that the object for which courts have been erected is not the protection of non-legal norms. But it is evident that this can apply only to the organs of the state for the administration of justice. And even as to these it is true only if we call every norm according to which a court renders a decision a legal norm. But if we do that, the question becomes a mere question of terminology. If we consider the inner content of the norms according to which the courts must render their decisions – and that is the only fair way to proceed – we shall be convinced that the non-legal norms play an important role even in the courts of the state. . . .

All of this, of course, does not mean that the courts should, without more ado, render their decisions according to non-legal norms. All legal propositions are not suitable for norms for decisions; *a fortiori* all non-legal norms, taken indiscriminately, are still less so. To make a proper selection is a task of enormous difficulty – a task which makes much higher demands upon the powers of the judge than the mere application of law. The strong tendency on the Continent to make the judge merely a ministerial servant of the statute who has no right to exercise any discretion whatever arises, I am convinced, from a suspicion that he is not equal to so difficult a task. . . .

VII

THE STATE AND THE LAW

The sociological science of law, therefore, will not be able to state the difference between law and morals in a brief simple formula in the manner of the juristic science that has hitherto been current. Only a thorough examination of the psychic and social facts, which at the present time have not even been gathered, can shed light upon this difficult question. Though we are well aware of the great degree of caution made imperative by the present state of juristic science, we may perhaps be permitted to assume, at this time, the following essential characteristics of law. The legal norm regulates a matter which, at least in the opinion of the group within which it has its origin, is of great importance, of basic significance. The individual act which is commanded by the legal proposition may not be of great weight, as for instance in the case of statutes regulating foods, or concerning prevention of fires or infectious diseases of cattle, but we must always consider the consequences if violations of these statutes should assume the dimension of a mass phenomenon. Only matters of lesser significance are left to other social norms. Therefore the proposition, "Thou shalt honor thy father and thy mother" is considered a legal proposition only where the organization of the state and of society is based chiefly on the order of the family. A community which conceives of God as being in an immediate relation to its affairs will be inclined to elevate religious norms to the rank of legal norms. On the other hand, the legal norm, as contrasted with the other norms, can always be stated in clear definite terms. It thereby gives a certain stability to the associations that are based on legal norms, whereas associations not based on legal norms, e.g. political parties, religious communions, groups of relatives, social relations, are characterized by a looseness, a lack of stability, until they assume a legal form. Norms of morality, too, of ethical custom, of decorum, often become legal norms as soon as they lose their universal character, and, couched in clear precise terms, assume basic significance for the legal order of society. In this way, the Roman *prudentes* and the praetor often succeeded in introducing them into the legal system; in this way, equity arose in England, which is today a system of law as fully developed as the common law. It may well be possible therefore that the normal precept of good faith in contractual relations may, in the course of time, be compressed into a series of definite and clear legal propositions.

Correct observation therefore underlies the habit of speaking of the heteronomy of law and of the autonomy of morals. This is not a matter of essential characteristics but of differences of degree. In the case of legal norms, society devotes much more thought to the matter of formulating than in the case of norms of morals and of the other non-legal norms; in view of the importance it attaches to law it is anxious to have not merely a general direction, but a detailed precept. Everyone ought to be able to know from the mere wording of the legal norm how he is to regulate his conduct in a given case; whereas the non-legal norms, couched as they are, in general terms, are little more than general guides; and on this basis, everyone must make his own rules of conduct in the individual case. It is true therefore that, in the case of norms of morality, it is to a much greater extent a matter of the inner attitude of mind than in the case of law. A man without any inner sense of law knows how to perform his contracts, respect the property right of others; but in order to be able to conduct himself correctly from the point of view of morals, religion, ethical custom, decorum, etiquette, and fashion, he requires a sense of morality, religion, ethical custom, decorum, tact, etiquette, and fashion. Without this sense, he cannot hit upon the correct thing. For this reason, when non-legal norms are involved, the center of gravity is inwardly within a man's self to a much greater extent than when legal norms are involved.

If we bear these characteristics in mind, it may be possible to give a more exact definition of the legal norm. Legal norms are those norms that flow from the facts of the law, to wit from usages, which assign to each member of the social association his position and function, from the relations of domination and subjection, from the relations arising from possession, from articles of association, from contracts, from testamentary and other dispositions; furthermore, those norms are legal norms that arise from the legal propositions of state and of juristic law. . . . But this proposition is not convertible. Not all norms that arise in this way are legal norms. These characteristics therefore do not furnish a positive delimitation of legal norms from other norms. Such delimitation would require first of all a thorough study of the nature of the non-legal norms.

Whether we can consider a norm which is socially valid but which violates a prohibition issued by the state a legal norm in the sociological sense, is a question of social power. The decisive question in this connection is whether or not it releases the overtones of feeling which are peculiar to the legal norm, the *opinio necessitatis* of the common law jurists. It is precisely in this matter that the juristic science of the Continental common law, in a manner deserving our deepest gratitude, has prepared the ground for the work of the sociology of law through its doctrine of the so-called abrogative power of customary law; it has assumed and demonstrated that legal propositions that are in conflict with the legal consciousness may languish and die. . . .

IX

THE STRUCTURE OF THE LEGAL PROPOSITION

The immediate basis of the legal order of human society is the facts of the law: usage, relations of domination, relations of possession, declarations of will, particularly in their most important forms, to wit: articles of association, contract, and testamentary disposition. From these facts the rules of conduct which determine the conduct of man in society derive. These facts alone, therefore, and not the legal propositions, according to which the courts render decisions, and according to which the administrative tribunals of the state proceed, are of authoritative significance for the legal order in human society. Nevertheless the legal propositions gain significance for the latter inasmuch as the decisions of the courts and the measures taken by the administrative agencies affect the facts of the law and thus bring about changes in the existing usages, relations of domination, relations of possession, articles of association, contracts, and testamentary disposition, i.e. on this presupposition the decisions of the courts and the measures taken by the administrative agencies, which are based on the legal propositions, in turn produce norms which regulate the social conduct of human beings. New facts of the law therefore can be established not only, as in past centuries, by the application of force, or, as is usual in our days, by the silent, unobserved sway of social forces, i.e. particularly by new kinds of associations, new kinds of agreements, and testamentary dispositions, but also, at least indirectly, by means of legal propositions. For this purpose however it is not sufficient that the legal proposition should have formal validity, or that it should be applied in isolated cases; for an isolated fact is not a social fact. It is necessary for this purpose that men regulate their conduct according to the legal proposition. A legal proposition which dictates to the courts and administrative tribunals the course of action which they are to follow contains what amounts to a legal norm for the courts and administrative tribunals as soon as these bodies actually carry it out; it becomes a rule of conduct only when the social relations are actually being ordered thereby.

The legal norms which are deriving from the legal propositions, therefore, always have reference to social relations, but the nature of this reference varies. The sum total of the legal norms which have validity for courts and other tribunals has never been identical with the sum total of social law; there have always been a number of social legal relations which have been free from all intrusion from this quarter. . . . Every legal proposition that contains a norm attaches a command or a prohibition to a given state of facts as the legal consequence of the latter. The state of facts which conditions the norm, the command, or the prohibition, is a fact of the law, i.e. a usage, a relation of domination or of possession, or a declaration of the will. In the case of a legal proposition which functions as a norm, we are always concerned, therefore, with the relation of the command or the prohibition which as been converted into a norm to one of the above named facts of the law. We must accordingly distinguish three classes of legal propositions.

In the first place there are legal propositions that accord the protection of the courts and other tribunals to the facts of the law as they exist in society. They do this either unconditionally or under certain conditions by recognizing the usages of the associations as being legally effective, protecting relations of domination and of possession, enforcing contracts and testamentary directions. In all these instances the norms of the legal proposition conform as a matter of logical necessity to the norms which derive directly from the facts of the law, i.e. from usage, domination, possession, declaration of the will. These are the norms that result "from the concept," "from the nature of the thing." This is the proper place in law for the logical element, and logical necessity is raised to a sort of mathematical precision in so far as the concept of value enters in; for value, in fact, partakes of the nature of the mathematical: it is an equation. This juristic mathematics, "an arithmetic of concepts," therefore is found in the law of claims for damages and unjust enrichment; in the law of claims arising from contracts in which value is given for value, from contracts of barter, and from contracts for furnishing things for use. Distinguished from legal propositions of this kind are those that negate existing facts of the law or that self-actively create facts of the law. On the basis of legal propositions courts and other state tribunals artificially create or dissolve associations, establish or abolish relations of domination, give, take away, or transfer possession, rescind articles of association, contracts, testamentary declarations of the will, or occasionally create them by compulsion. Under this head are found chiefly the legal propositions that decree expropriation or forfeiture of things; that declare certain relations invalid, null, voidable, or punishable. . . .

A third species of legal propositions attaches legal consequences to facts of the law, quite independently of the norms that result from the usages, the relations of domination and of possession, and the dispositions created by these facts. Let us bear in mind certain rights and duties connected with ownership . . . and trade rights, the obligation to pay taxes, the duty to insure in connection with certain contracts, the duty of the owner of poisons and explosives to give notice.

The norms prescribed by the legal proposition therefore can either secure absolute enforcement for the norms that flow from the facts of the law or they can hinder them or invalidate them; and, lastly, they can attach legal consequences to them that bear no relation whatsoever to the legal consequences that flow from the facts. Accordingly the legal order which society self-actively creates for itself in the facts of the law, in the existing usages, relations of domination, and of possession, articles of association, contracts, testamentary dispositions, is brought face to face with a legal order which is created by means of legal propositions, and enforced solely by means of the activity of the courts and the other tribunals of the state. And norms, rules of conduct, flow from this second legal order no less than from the former, to the extent that it protects, gives form and shape to, modifies, or perhaps abolishes the facts of the law. And only those norms that are contained in these two legal orders constitute the whole law of society. The important thing for the norms of the second legal order is not the distribution of interests in the individual social associations, but the distribution in society as a whole, which comprises all the associations within a certain territory. The second legal order then is an order which has been imposed by society upon the associations.

The juristic writer, the teacher of law, and the legislator, who formulate the legal proposition, always act as persons commissioned by society, whether it be in virtue of the confidence which society placed in them, as in the case of the Roman and of the common law jurists up to the time of the recent codifications, or in virtue of social or official position, or, as in the case of the legislator, upon the authority of the constitution of the state. The form and the content of a legal proposition are the result of the joint labors of society and of the individual jurist, and the sociology of law will have to distinguish the contribution of the former clearly from that of the latter. . . .

The decision as to the interests involved in a dispute is entrusted by the state to the jurist when it is clearly indicated neither by the general interest nor by the distribution of power in society as a whole. This situation may be brought about by various causes. In the first place very often the parties to the dispute are quite unaware of the great social interests involved in the decision; very often the latter are distributed among the various classes and ranks in such a manner as to place them above the struggles of class and rank; in many cases these social interests are too inconsiderable and insignificant to become involved in the dispute. Very often, too, the possessors of power, who are called upon to render the decision, are not at all involved in the conflict of interests. The most important cause however is the fact that the powers that are engaged in the struggle in behalf of the different interests counterbalance one another or that the influences that proceed from the groups that are most powerful politically, economically, or socially, are checked or thwarted by other social tendencies, which are based on religious, ethical, scientific, or other ideological convictions.

When the jurist is asked to draw the line between the conflicting interests independently, he is asked, by implication, to do it according to justice. This implies, in the first place, something negative. He is asked to arrive at a decision without any consideration of expediency and uninfluenced by the distribution of power. In recent times, it is true, it has often been said that justice, too, is a matter involving questions of power. If the writer means to say that the idea of justice, on which the decision is based, must have attained a certain power in the body social at the time when it influences the judicial finding of norms or the activity of the state, he is indeed stating a truth, but it is a self-evident truth; and a self-evident truth does not require statement. But if he means to say that, under the cloak of justice, effect is always being given to the influence of political, social, or economic position, the statement is manifestly incorrect. A legal norm whose origin can be traced to such influences is usually stigmatized by the very fact as something unjust. Justice has always weighted the scales solely in favor of the weak and the persecuted. A just decision is a decision based on grounds which appeal to a disinterested person; it is a decision which is rendered by a person who is not involved in the conflict of interests, or which, even though it be rendered by a person involved in this conflict, nevertheless is such as a disinterested person would render or approve of. It is never based on taking advantage of a position of power. When a person who is in a position of power acts justly, he acts against his own interest, at any rate against his immediate interest, prompted by religious, ethical, scientific, or other ideological considerations; perhaps merely by considerations of prudent policy. The parties of political and social justice, e.g. the doctrinaire liberals, the English Fabians, the German Social-political or National-Socialist parties, the French Solidarists, find their adherents chiefly among ideologists who are not personally interested in the political and social conflicts of interests. In this fact lies their strength and also their weakness.

But all of these are negative characteristics. Which are the positive characteristics of justice? The catch phrase about balancing of interests which is so successful at the present time is not an answer to this question; for the very question is: What is it that gives weight to the interests that are to be balanced? Manifestly it is not the balancing jurist, writer or teacher, judge or legislator, but society itself. The function of the jurist is merely to balance them. There are trends caused by the interests that flourish in society which ultimately influence even persons that are not involved in these conflicting interests. The judge who decides according to justice follows the tendency that he himself is dominated by. Justice therefore does not proceed from the individual, but arises in society.

The role of the person rendering the decision is of importance only inasmuch as, within certain limitations, he can select the solution which corresponds most nearly to his personal feelings. But in doing this, he cannot disregard the social basis of the decision. If a Spartacus, favored by fortune, had abolished slavery in antiquity, or if the socialists should abolish private property, let us say in a beleaguered city, as was done in Paris during the days of the Commune, these facts would have nothing to do with justice. And a judge who, in a decision which he renders, recognizes private property in means of production in spite of the fact that he is a socialist, or who admits the defense that the debt sued upon in a stock-exchange transaction is a gaming debt although in his opinion the setting-up of this plea is a breach of good faith, does not thereby contradict himself. In doing these things he is merely being guided by social tendencies against his own individual feeling in the matter. A rebellious slave, the government of a beleaguered city, like that of Paris during the Commune, can indeed proceed according to their individual feelings, but they can do so only because they have been removed from social influences by the force of circumstances. Justice is a power wielded over the minds of men by society.

It is the function of juristic science, in the first place, to record the trends of justice that are found in society, and to ascertain what they are, whence they come, and whither they lead; but it cannot possibly determine which of these is the only just one. In the forum of science, they are all equally valid. What men consider just depends upon the ideas they have concerning the end of human endeavor in this world of ours, but it is not the function of science to dictate the final ends of human endeavor on earth. That is the function of the founder of a religion, of the preacher, of the prophet, of the preacher of ethics, of the practical jurist, of the judge, of the politician. Science can be concerned only with those things that are susceptible of scientific demonstration. That a certain thing is just is no more scientifically demonstrable than is the beauty of a Gothic cathedral or of a Beethoven symphony to a person who is insensible to it. All of these are questions of the emotional life. Science can ascertain the effects of a legal proposition, but it cannot make these effects appear either desirable or loathsome to man. Justice is a social force, and it is always a question whether it is potent enough to influence the disinterested persons whose function it is to create juristic and statute law.

But although science can teach us nothing concerning the ends, once the end is determined, it can enlighten us as to the means to that end. The practical technical rules that perform this function are based on the results of pure science. There is no science that teaches men that they ought to be healthy, but practical medical science teaches men who desire to be healthy what they can do, according to the present state of the natural sciences, to bring about that result. Practical juristic science is concerned with the manner in which the ends may be attained that men are endeavoring to attain through law, but it must utilize the results of the sociology of law for this purpose. The legal proposition is not only the result, it is also a lever, of social development; it is an instrumentality in the hands of society whereby society shapes things within its sphere of influence according to its will. Through the legal proposition man acquires a power, limited though it be, over the facts of the law; in the legal proposition a willed legal order is brought face to face with the legal order which has arisen self-actively in society. . . .

What can the sociology of law offer to juristic science in this sphere? The ultimate ends of our pilgrimage on this earth doubtless shall ever remain hidden from our eyes, but we can, at any rate, overlook a small part of the way. The highest aim of all science is to vouchsafe to us a glimpse of the future; the investigator gradually becomes a seer. As the physicist endeavors to determine the course of a cannon-ball in advance, so the disciples of the social sciences endeavor to calculate in advance the unifying regularities in the course of the future development of social happenings. They can point to many great successes, particularly in the general sphere of economics, and every advance in sociological study will bring new successes.

Sociology teaches us the laws governing the development of human society and the effects of the legal propositions. It teaches juristic science how the legal propositions may be adapted to the laws of social development in accordance with their effects. Sociology indeed is just as far from teaching us that we must regulate our lives according to these scientific laws in the matter of our legal propositions and our conduct generally as the natural sciences are from telling us that we must be healthy. But men usually wish to do that which is expedient, just as, with very rare exceptions, they desire to be well. Accordingly on the basis of the results of the steady progress of the science of sociology, juristic science will be in a correspondingly better position to tell the judge and the legislator when they are resisting the laws of development and failing to understand the effects of the legal propositions, they are bootlessly frittering social forces away. . . .

There is no formula in which the idea of justice is summed up and fully expressed; it is a term that expresses a way and a goal – a goal which lies in the sunlit distance, which the human mind can divine, but not know, and a way which man must tread with faltering and uncertain steps. He who shall be able to speak the last word on the subject of justice will thereby have found the law of the development of the human race, perhaps of the universe. Meanwhile science must rest content to contemplate the line of development which has been graven into the past and to divine that which the near future will trace out for it.

It is a long way that leads from the inner order of the associations to the legal propositions of our codes and juristic handbooks. In primitive times only the legal propositions governing procedure and the regulations concerning penalties are being created; and they are being created solely according to considerations of expediency. The norms that are contained in these propositions belong to those that constitute the second order of society, for they do not order and regulate the associations directly but are designed merely to ward off dangers. The norms of the first order, which are required by the exigencies of litigation, do not as yet exist in the form of legal propositions; they derive from the inner order of the associations through universalization and reduction to unity, or they are being obtained by a process of free finding, and are not being developed into universally valid legal propositions until a later time. At the same time the legal propositions of the second order grow in number and power, an ever richer procedural law develops, the regulations as to penalties are being converted, in part, into a law of damages, and, in part, into a law of crimes. Finally state law arises as the norm for the decisions of the courts, and as the basis for action by the state.

At each of these stages, society is as active as the jurist. Every legal proposition is shaped out of materials furnished by society, but the shaping is done by the jurist. It is indeed the norms that are already prevailing in society that, universalized and reduced to unity, become legal propositions; but in the last analysis, the jurist decides what is to be universalized and reduced to unity, which of the various orders of the family that come within his sphere he is to treat as the model order according to which he decides the controversies that arise in the others, which of the various contents of contracts that occur furnishes the standard for the decision of controversies arising from all like contracts. The purpose of the free finding of norms is merely to eke out and to take the place of the inner order of the associations where the latter fails in the adjudication of litigation; and the whole "second order" is destined, from the very beginning, to surround the inner order of the associations, as it is being created anew every moment by usage, relations of domination and of possession, with a wall of defense against attack and danger. The law governing interference by society and the state with the inner order of the associations also proceeds at all times from a larger social or state association, which is endeavoring to exert influence over the smaller associations of which it is composed. However great the extent to which these norms arise from the relations already existing in society, the jurist who transforms them into legal propositions must supply not only the wording but also a great deal of the content. But the jurist who in this manner places the stamp of his personality upon the legal proposition in turn is subjected to the influence of society. Its distribution of power, its ideas of the general interest, its trends of justice dictate to him what he is to universalize and reduce to unity, what norms he is to find for the relation that is in dispute, what is to be protected against attack and danger, what is to be surrendered to the latter, where the self-created order of the associations is to be modified or abolished. Only a small part of the legal proposition therefore is the expression of the personality of its author to such an extent that one might assume that it would not have been worded as it is had it been created by a different person. And even at this point we must not fail to observe to what extent every man, even the most individual genius, is a resultant of the influences of his environment, that every man can be born and work only in a given society, that everywhere else he would be impossible and would make shipwreck.

The prevailing school of jurisprudence, which sees in every legal proposition only the expression of the "will of the lawgiver," altogether fails to recognize the important part of society in its creation. The teachers of the Natural Law School, in their day, had a much deeper insight into the matter inasmuch as they endeavored to base the law upon the sense of justice, i.e. upon the social trends of justice; Savigny and Puchta with their doctrine of the popular consciousness of right and law as the basis of legal development merely restated thoughts of the natural law in terms of a social point of view. Bentham, by his principle of utility, with which Jhering's *Zweck im Rechte* coincides in the main, for the first time, in a comprehensive manner, directed attention to the general interest, which, it is true, he often enough confused with the interest of a single class, the bourgeois middle class. The materialistic interpretation of history went much further than the natural law doctrine, than the Historical School, than Bentham and Jhering. It pointed out to what extent the law, and therefore also the legal propositions, are a superstructure erected on the foundation of the economic order, and also to what extent the legal propositions are being fashioned and created under the pressure of the distribution of power in society. But in doing this it became biassed, for it intentionally excluded from its consideration the element of human personality, the trends of justice as well non-economic influences which it always, and occasionally in an extremely arbitrary manner, traced back to economic ones, and usually, though quite unintentionally, all consideration of the general interest. The sociology of law must not overlook any of these things; it must consider everything that takes part in the creation of the legal proposition.

XXI

THE METHODS OF THE SOCIOLOGY OF LAW

II. The Study of the Living Law

The reason why the dominant school of legal science so greatly prefers the legal proposition to all other legal phenomena as an object of investigation is that it tacitly assumes that the whole law is to be found in the legal propositions. It is assumed furthermore that since, at the present time, all legal propositions are to be found in the statutes, where they are readily accessible to anyone, all that is necessary in order to get a knowledge of the law of the present time is to gather the material from the statutes, to ascertain the content of this material by one's own individual interpretation, and to utilize this interpretation for the purpose of juristic literature and judicial decision. Occasionally one meets with the further idea that legal propositions may arise independently of statute. In Germany the usual belief is that they can be found in juristic literature; in France, in judicial decisions. "Customary law," on the other hand, in the prevailing view, is so unimportant that no effort is being put forth to ascertain its content by scientific methods, much less to create methods for its investigation. Only the teachers of, and writers on, commercial law still concern themselves with usage, in this case, with business custom. This explains why the efforts of those who are carrying on research in law at the present time are bent upon ascertaining the legal propositions of the past, which are not so readily accessible to us as those that are contained in modern statutes. It is believed that the scientific result of the labor expended upon the study of the law of the past consists not only in a knowledge of the development of law, which of course means only the development of legal propositions, but also in an historical understanding of the law of the present; for the law, i.e. according to the tacit assumption the legal propositions of the present time, is rooted in the past. These, I take it, are the lines of thought on which the method of research in the field of law has hitherto been based.

But the statement that the whole law is not contained in the legal propositions applies to a much greater degree to the law that is in force today than to the law of the past. For the men who composed the Twelve Tables, the *Lex Salica*, and the *Sachsenspiegel* actually had a direct personal knowledge of the law of their own time, and their endeavor was to gather up this law with which they dealt, and to formulate it in legal propositions. This however does not apply, even approximately, to the most important part of the legal material with which the jurists of the present day are concerned, i.e. the codes. For in contrast to what once upon a time the jurists had in mind under all circumstances, vaguely at least, the compilers of the modern codes very often did not have the slightest intention whatever of stating the law of their own time and of their own community. They draw their legal material, first, from the compilation of Justinian, from which, self-evidently, they are likely to obtain reliable information on almost any other subject than the law of their own time, i.e. of the eighteenth or of the nineteenth century; secondly, from older statements of law, which, even if they met the requirements of their own time, do not meet those of the time of the legislator; thirdly, from juristic literature, which was chiefly concerned with the interpretation of older laws and of older codes, and, in any case, did not belong to the time of the code in question. The truth of this statement appears most clearly in the case of the German Civil Code, the sources of which have been almost exclusively text-books of pandect law, earlier German statutes and compilations of law, and foreign codifications. Accordingly our codes are uniformly adapted to a time much earlier than their own, and all the juristic technique in the world would be unable to extract the actual law of the present from it, for the simple reason that it is not contained therein. But the territory within which our codes are valid is so vast, the legal relations with which they deal are so incomparably richer, more varied, more subject to changes than they have ever been, that the mere idea of making complete presentation in a code would be monstrous. To attempt to imprison the law of time or of a people within the sections of a code is about as reasonable as to attempt to confine a stream within a pond. The water that is put in the pond is no longer a living stream but a stagnant pool, and but little water can be put in the pond. Moreover, if one considers that the living law had already overtaken and grown away from each one of these codes at the very moment the latter were enacted, and is growing away from them more and more every day, one cannot but realize the enormous extent of this as yet unplowed and unfurrowed field of activity which is being pointed out to the modern legal investigator.

It could not be otherwise. The legal propositions are not intended to present a complete picture of the state of the law. The jurist draws them up with a view to existing practical needs, and with a view to what he is interested in for practical reasons. He will not put forth the effort to formulate legal propositions with reference to matters that lie outside of his sphere of interest, perhaps for the sole reason that they are not within the jurisdiction of the courts before which he practices, or because they do not concern his clients. Since commercial law lay outside of the usual sphere of interest of the Roman jurist, we find that the commercial law of the Roman sources is utterly inadequate; and for the very same reason the Romans and, until quite recently, the modern jurists have very little to say about labor law. Even Eyke von Repgow did not deal with the law of cities and with the customs of manors because it lay outside of his immediate sphere of interest.

On the other hand, the attempt to arrive at an understanding of the present through the study of history or of prehistoric times, i.e. of ethnology, is an error in principle. To explain something, according to a saying of Mach's, is to replace a mystery that one is not accustomed to. Now the present contains fewer mysteries that we are not accustomed to than does the past. The paleontologist will understand the nature and the functions of the organs of a fossil animal only if he understands the nature and the functions of the organs of living animals. But the zoölogist cannot learn the physiology of the animals which he is studying from the paleontologist; he will have recourse to paleontology only for the purpose of getting a picture of the development of the present-day animal kingdom. We arrive at an understanding of the past through the present, and not vice versa. Accordingly the history of law and ethnological legal science will not be of value for the understanding of the existing law but only for the study of the development of law.

As a result of the methods employed by modern legal science, the present state of our law is, in a great measure, actually unkown to us. We often know nothing, not only of things that are remote but also of things that happen before our very eyes. Almost every day brings some juristic surprise which we owe to a lucky accident, to a peculiar lawsuit, or to an article in the daily papers. This surprise may concern the peasant tenants in Schwarzenberg, or puzzling heritable building rights in the heart of the city of Vienna, in the Brigittenau, or peculiar relations involving heritable leases in Berhomet, in Bukowina. But he who observes life with careful attentiveness knows that these are not isolated occurrences. We are groping in the dark everywhere. And we cannot plead the excuse that the legal historian can avail himself of, i.e. that a bit of the past has been irrecoverably lost. We need but open our eyes and ears in order to learn everything that is of significance for the law of our time. . . .

Note also the law of the family. The first thing that attracts the attention of the observer is the contrast between the actual order of the family and that which the codes decree. I doubt whether there is a country in Europe in which the relation between husband and wife, parents and children, between the family and the outside world, as it actually takes form in life, corresponds to the norms of the positive law; or in which the members of the family, in which there is a semblance of proper family life, would as much as think of attempting to enforce the rights against one another that the letter of the law grants to them. It is evident therefore that in this case, too, the positive law is far from giving a picture of that which actually takes place in life. So much the less must legal science and doctrine confine itself to giving an exposition of the content of the statutes; it must seek to ascertain the actual forms that the family relations assume, which are essentially uniform and typical although they differ in the various classes of society and in the various parts of the country. We shall not discuss in this connection whether the statute has lost its mastery over life or whether it never had it; whether life, in the process of growth, has developed beyond the statute and grown away from it or whether it never corresponded to it. In this connection, too, science fulfills its function as the theory of law and right very poorly if it merely presents that which is prescribed by the statute and fails to tell what actually takes place. . . .

The only branch of law the juristic science of which is based not merely incidentally, but throughout, on actual usage is commercial law. . . .

This then is the *living* law in contradistinction to that which is being enforced in the courts and other tribunals. The living law is the law which dominates life itself even though it has not been posited in legal propositions. The source of our knowledge of this law is, first, the modern legal document; secondly, direct observation of life, of commerce, of customs and usages, and of all associations, not only of those that the law has recognized but also of those that it has overlooked and passed by, indeed even of those that it has disapproved.

In our day, doubtless, the most important source of knowledge of the living law is the modern legal document. Even today one of these documents is being studied very extensively, to wit the judicial decision, but not in the sense we have in mind here. It is not being treated as evidence of the living law, but as a work of juristic literature which is to be examined not as to the truth of the legal relations described therein and as to the living law that is to be extracted therefrom, but as to the correctness of the statutory interpretations and of the juristic constructions contained therein. . . .

I myself entertained this idea when about a quarter of a century ago I began to work at my book on the declaration of the will by silence. My intention was to study more than six hundred volumes of decisions of German, Austrian, and French courts, and on the basis of these decisions to present a picture of what judicial decisions had made of the declaration of the will of silence. Before long however my attention was arrested by, and occupied with, what actually took place rather than by the judicial decision. As a result my book contains, to a great extent at least, a statement of the facts on which the judicial decisions had been rendered, as they actually happened in life, and a statement of the significance of the silent declaration of the will in legal life. In this book, I actually, though unconsciously, applied the sociological method of legal science, for which I subsequently sought to establish a theoretical basis.

At a later time, however, I realized that this method is not quite sufficient. Even the judicial decisions do not give a perfect picture of legal life. Only a tiny bit of real life is brought before the courts and other tribunals; and much is excluded from litigation either on principle or as a matter of fact. Moreover the legal relation which is being litigated shows distorted features which are quite different from, and foreign to, the same relation when it is in repose. Who would judge our family life or the life of our societies by the law-suits that arise in the families or in the societies? The sociological method therefore demands absolutely that the results which are obtained from the judicial decisions be supplemented by direct observation of life.

And for this very purpose the modern business document offers a basis which can become at least as fruitful as the method of past millennia and centuries. A glance at modern legal life shows that it is predominantly controlled not by statute law but by the business document. Non-compulsory law is set aside by the content of the business document. The living law must be sought in marriage contracts, in contracts of purchase, of usufructuary lease, in contracts for building loans, for loans secured by hypothecs, in testaments, and in contracts of inheritance, in articles of association of societies and of business partnerships, and not in the sections of the codes. In all of these contracts, there is, in addition to the individual content which applies only to the particular transaction, a typical, ever recurring content. This typical content is basically the most important thing in the document. If our literary jurists were well advised, they would concern themselves primarily with it, as did the Romans, who, in their commentaries on the edict and in their *libri iuris civilis*, wrote long disquisitions on the ever recurring *duplae stipulatio* and the *institutio ex re certa*. In that case we probably should have more monographs on the beer-seller of the breweries, or on the contracts for the processing of sugar beets by the sugar factories, or on the sale of a physician's practice, than on the concept of the juristic person or the construction of a pledge right in one's own *res* (*Sache*). Of course it is a new task for the jurist to make use of a modern document for the purposes of theoretical and of practical legal science. But the historian, particularly the legal historian, is quite familiar with the study of documents, and the latter might, at the beginning at least, render valuable services both to the theoretical and to the practical jurist. The science of historical documents has developed a technique that is one of the most delicate and difficult things in scientific work, and the industry and labor of a lifetime will scarcely suffice for the mastery of all its refinements. But in the case of the modern document tasks must be fulfilled which in part are quite different from those involved in the case of the historical document and which are by no means lighter.

Above all, we must endeavor to treat the document as a part of the living law, and to derive the living law from it as the Romans did in their law of contracts and of testaments. The titles of the Digest *de contrahenda emptione, de actionibus emti venditi, de evictionibus et duplae stipulatione, pro socio, de stipulatione servorum,* and those that deal with the law of testaments and legacies, can still serve as models everywhere. It is a matter of the utmost importance that present-day theoretical and practical science should at last concern itself not with Roman, but with present-day contracts and documents. It would be the first task of modern legal science to examine the documents as to the part of their content that is of general importance, typical, and ever recurring, to treat juristically and to evaluate them from every angle according to their importance from the point of view of society, economics, and legislative policy.

In this way we could at last get a picture of what is taking place among us in the sphere of the document. Although in general the documents are alike, they differ very much in details according to localities, classes, ranks, races, and creeds. It seems likely that we must perform the function of legal statistics by means of the devices of the science of documents. It will not be possible to do this without new methods. But what splendid results are beckoning to the jurist in this connection, especially if he succeeds in laying bare the historical, economic, or social presuppositions of these diversities.

Still the value of the document would be greatly overestimated if one should think that one could, without more ado, read the living law from it. It is not at all conclusively established that the document as a whole contains and bears witness to the living law. The living law is not the part of the content of the document that the courts recognize as binding when they decide a legal controversy, but only that part which the parties actually observe in life. The effects of the transactions that are evidenced by documents cannot be learned without more ado from their enforceable legal consequences. Could anyone infer from the articles of association of a society or of a share company that the seemingly plenipotent meetings of the shareholders usually turn out to be utterly insignificant gatherings of yes-men? But the legally operative content of the document gives no reliable information as to the effects not intended by the parties nor yet as to those intended. There is much in the document that is simply traditional; this part is copied from a form book by the person who drafts the document, but it never reaches the consciousness of the parties. They will therefore neither demand nor grant the things provided for therein, and will be very much surprised to hear of them when, in the event of litigation, the document gets into the hands of a lawyer who insists upon them in court. There are other provisions which the parties will permit to be embodied in the document only in order to be prepared for the worst. It is self-evident that they are not to be mentioned as long as there is no controversy. The other party understands this very well. He accepts the most extreme rigors of a contract of this sort calmly, but haggles most obstinately over all provisions that are intended to be taken seriously. If one reads a contract of usufructuary lease prepared by the administrator of the Prussian crown-lands or of the Greek-Oriental religious foundation of Bukowina, one marvels how it is possible for the lessee to move at all within this barbed-wire fence of paragraphs. Nevertheless the lessee gets on very well. No use is ever being made of all of these contractual penalties, of the clauses appointing stated times, of the short-term notices to quit, of the forfeitures of security, of the right to compensation for damage done, as long as it is possible to get on with the lessee at all. One who is engaged in the practical affairs of life is anxious to deal peaceably with people. He is not interested in carrying on litigation even if he is bound to win.

The standard therefore according to which the Sociological School of jurisprudence must test, not only the legal propositions, but also the legal document, is actual life. Here too it must observe the distinction between the law that is enforced by the courts and the living law. The entire valid content of the document is law that is enforced by the courts (i.e. norm for decision), for, in case the parties resort to litigation, the decision will hinge upon it; but it is living law only in so far as the parties habitually insist upon it even if they do not wish to risk litigation. Failure to observe this heterogeneousness of the component parts of the document embodying the contract results in an erroneous and distorted picture of life itself. But the contrast is of the utmost importance for the administration of justice and for legislation as well. It is questionable whether the latter should lend themselves to permitting those things to be taken seriously which were never intended to be taken seriously.

Of course we can learn only so much of the living law from the document as has been embodied therein. How shall we quarry that part of the living law that has not been embodied in a legal document but which nevertheless is a large and important part thereof? There is no other means but this, to open one's eyes, to inform oneself by observing life attentively, to ask people, and note down their replies. To be sure, to ask a jurist to learn from actual observation and not from sections of a code or from bundles of legal papers is to make an exacting demand upon him; but it is unavoidable, and marvelous results can be achieved in this manner.

From the great number of things that deserve being studied in this manner, I would select only a few. First of all the old law that still survives. The old law, which is popular law and not merely juristic law, lives on under a thin surface of modern statute law, and dominates the conduct and the legal consciousness of the people. The legal historian can not only find many things here as to which his sources are silent, but he can actually observe many things which are generally believed to belong to a time that is long since past. In doing this he can disregard the legal document; for it is well known how often it is but a poor compromise between that which is traditional and the demands of modern law, e.g. in the law of inheritance among the peasants, and in the matrimonial regime. But it is necessary to focus attention to a much greater extent than has been done hitherto upon those parts of the old law that still exist among the people though they are not embodied in legal documents, especially since it is doubtful whether it can hold its own much longer against the impact of modern commercial life. . . .

The germs of new law that are viable are probably of greater importance to the jurist than such dying survivals. And here we are confronted by a peculiar fact. It is generally believed that the knowledge that law is in never-ending process of development is an enduring achievement of the historical school, and one would think that this is accepted as true not only as to times long since past but also as to the last century. But science and theory are making a peculiar use of this bit of academic wisdom. So far as the ancient Romans or the Germans down to the fourteenth and fifteenth centuries are concerned, jurists are wide awake to the development of legal institutions, e.g. of the family, of the relations of personal subjection, of ownership of land, of contracts. Statutes, which are of no significance in those days, are scarcely being mentioned. But for the later period, this kind of legal history breaks down altogether, and for the last century, the science of the Historical School resolves itself altogether into a history of legislation. Jurists seem to assume that in this period legal institutions develop only through changes in the paragraphs of the codes. What is the meaning of this? Has the non-statutory development of legal institutions ceased altogether in the nineteenth century? But today, just as in antiquity and in the Middle Ages, legal history is based not so much upon the emergence and the disappearance of legal propositions that have been formulated in words as upon the emergence of new legal institutions and the gradual assumption of a new content by those that are already in existence. No legal historian will admit that the basic legal relations in Germany, let us say, of the sixteenth century, coincide with those of the fifteenth, or that the changes, some of which were very sweeping ones, took place solely as a result of legislation, which was enacted very rarely and was not very sweeping. Does this not hold true for the nineteenth century as well, a period which was so highly agitated socially, economically, and politically that one may say that until that time mankind had never experienced its like? It is a question of what one means by development. The family law has undergone development. This means exactly what it meant in the Middle Ages, i.e. that the relations of husband and wife, of parents and children, now bear a different stamp. Ownership of land has undergone development even apart from the fact that the soil was freed by statute and by administrative action from the burdens and charges resting upon it; this means that there is a different system of landholding in vogue because different kinds of real and obligatory rights have been established with reference to the soil, and also because the economy of the peasant and of the great landowner has undergone a change. The law of contract has undergone development; this development is based on the fact that new kinds of contracts have come into use and that the contracts of the traditional kind now have a different content. The law of inheritance has undergone development; this means, chiefly, that division of inheritance, testaments, and other dispositions *mortis causa* now have a content quite different from that which they had a century ago. Compared with these revolutionary changes, the changes brought about by legislation are negligible.

The sociology of law then must begin with the ascertainment of the living law. Its attention will be directed primarily to the concrete, not the abstract. It is only the concrete that can be observed. What the anatomist places under the microscope is not human tissue in the abstract but a specific tissue of a specific human being; the physiologist likewise does not study the functions of the liver of mammals in the abstract, but those of a specific liver of a specific mammal. Only when he has completed the observation of the concrete does he ask whether it is universally valid, and this fact, too, he endeavors to establish by means of a series of concrete observations, for which he has to find specific methods. The same may be said of the investigator of law. He must first concern himself with concrete usages, relations of domination, legal relations, contracts, articles of association, dispositions by last will and testament. It is not true, therefore, that the investigation of the living law is concerned only with "customary law" or with "business usage." If one does any thinking at all when one uses these words – which is not always the case – one will realize that they do not refer to the concrete, but to that which has been universalized. But only the concrete usages, the relations of domination, the legal relations, the contracts, the articles of association, the dispositions by last will and testament, yield the rules according to which men regulate their conduct. And it is only on the basis of these rules that the norms for decision that the courts apply and the statutory provisions that alone have hitherto occupied the attention of jurists arise. The great majority of judicial decisions are based on the concrete usages, relations of possession, contracts, articles of association, and dispositions by last will and testament, that the courts have found to exist. If we would comprehend the universalizations, the reductions to unity, and the other methods of finding norms that the judge and the lawgiver employ, we must first of all know the basis upon which they were carried out. The more we know of the Roman banking system, the better shall we understand *receptum* and *litteris contrahere*. Does this not hold true for the law of our day? To this extent Savigny was right when he said that the law – and by law he means above all the legal proposition – can be understood only from its historical connection; but the historical connection does not lie in the hoary past, but in the present, out of which the legal proposition grows.

But the scientific significance of the living law is not confined to its influence upon the norms for decision which the courts apply or upon the content of statutes. The knowledge of the living law has an independent value, and this consists in the fact that it constitutes the foundation of the legal order of human society. In order to acquire a knowledge of this order we must know the usages, relations of domination, legal relations, contracts, articles of association, declaration by last will and testament, quite independently of the question whether they have already found expression in a judicial decision or in a statute or whether they will ever find it. The provisions contained in the new German Commercial Code regulating stock exchanges, banks, publishing houses, and other supplementary provisions were full of gaps when they were enacted and, for the most part, have become antiquated today. Modern commerce, especially the export trade, has meanwhile created an enormous number of new forms, which ought to be the subject matter of scientific study as well as those that have been enumerated in the statute. Very much that is of genuine value can be found on this point in the literature on the science of commerce that is blossoming forth so abundantly. A part of the order in the sphere of mining and navigation has been made accessible to legal science through mining law, maritime law, and the law of inland navigation, but for the most part this has long since become antiquated. The factory, the bank, the railroad, the great landed estate, the labor union, the association of employers, and a thousand other forms of life – each of these likewise has an order, and this order has a legal side as well as that of the mercantile establishment, which is being regulated in detail only by the Commercial Code. In addition there are countless forms in which the activity of these associations manifests itself outwardly, above all the contracts. In studying the manufacturing establishment, the legal investigator must pursue the countless, highly intricate paths that lead from the the acceptance of the order to the delivery of the finished products to the customer, to wit the position of the representative and of the commercial traveler, the three departments that are to be found in every manufacturing establishment (the sales department, the technical department, and the manufacturing department), the arrival of the orders, the preparation and the preservation of drawings, the computation of the cost of the undertaking, the sale price, the calculation for the purpose of checking up, the execution of the order on the basis of the drawings, the functions of the manufacturing department, of the master workman, the management of the warehouse, the computation of wages by the piece and by time, the distribution of wages among the individual workmen, the importance of the certificate showing that material has been handed over, the price list, the supervision at the gates by porters. Of equal importance for the legal side of the order of the undertaking is the keeping of books, the taking of inventories, the supervision over the warehouse, the preservation of drawings and models, the employment of workmen and of apprentices, the working regulations, and the committees of the workmen.

Economists, it is true, have often been engaged in investigations of the kind demanded here. But this has by no means rendered the work of the jurist superfluous. The jurist and the economist are dealing everywhere with the same social phenomena. Property, money, bills of exchange, share companies, credit, law and right of inheritance – it would be difficult to find a single object that the science of law is not concerned with as much as economics. But the jurist and the economist are dealing with different aspects of the same social phenomena. One concerns himself with their economic significance and scope; the other, with their legal regulation and their legal consequences. Though the jurist can be taught much by the economist, and the economist by the jurist, the questions which the identical objects of investigation pose to their respective sciences are absolutely distinct; and for this very reason no part of the labor which is necessary for both may be thrust upon one of them alone.

The investigation of the living law will of course render neither the historical nor the ethnological method superfluous; for we can learn the laws governing the development of society only by studying the historic and the prehistoric (ethnological) facts. But the historical and the ethnological methods are indispensable, too, for the understanding of the state of the law of the present time. It is true we shall never understand the past but through the present; but the path to the understanding of the innermost nature of the present lies through the understanding of the past. Within every part of the present lies its entire past, which can be clearly discerned by the eye that is able to look into these depths. . . .

In order to understand the actual state of the law we must institute an investigation as to the contribution that is being made by society itself as well as by state law, and also as to the actual influence of the state upon social law. We must know what kinds of marriages and families exist in a country, what kinds of contracts are being entered into, what their content is as a general rule, what kinds of declarations by last will and testament are being drawn up, how all of these things ought to be adjudged according to the law that is in force in the courts and other tribunals, how they are actually being adjudged, and to what extent these judgments and other decisions are actually effective. An investigation of this sort will reveal that although the legislation of two different countries may be identical, e.g. of France and Roumania, the law of one country may differ from that of the other; that in spite of the fact that the courts and other tribunals of Bohemia, Dalmatia, and Galicia apply the same code, the law of these countries is by no means the same; and that because of the differences in the actual state of the law, there is no uniform law even in the various parts of Germany in spite of the Civil Code, quite apart from the particular divergencies of legislation.

Of course our knowledge in this sphere will always remain full of gaps, and unsatisfactory, and doubtless it is much easier and much more pleasant to study a few codes together with illustrative material and explanatory notes than to ascertain the actual state of the law. But it certainly is not the function of science to seek easy and pleasant tasks but great and productive ones. We know in part, and the science of law is no exception to this; the more truly scientific it will become, the more perfect it will be.

This exposition would altogether fail of its purpose if it were understood to convey the idea that I mean to say that the methods which I have indicated in any way exhaust the methodology of the sociology of law. New scientific aims will always make new scientific methods necessary. For this reason, in order to prove that the possibilities are unlimited, I wish to point out a few things. Political geography as created by Ratzel and as it is understood today by Brunhes in France is in fact sociology with a geographic method. As early as the fifties of the last century Le Play, a Frenchman, in his *science social* based his investigations at all points on the local conditions of social life, and the school which he founded is zealously continuing the work he began. In his book on irrigation in Spain, Egypt, and Algiers, which is at least as interesting, even to the jurist, as any work on the history of law or on ethnology, Brunhes points out that there is a great number of legal formations which are associated everywhere with the kind and nature of the irrigation plants and the amount of their output. The reason why the Arabs of the desert do not recognize property rights in the sandy plain of the desert but only in the trees of the oases cannot be given by ethnology and legal history but only by the peculiar economic institutions of the desert.

Many decades ago Ofner of Vienna pointed out the possibility of instituting a direct investigation of the sense of law and right by means of juristic experiment. A year ago Kobler discussed the idea in detail in the Vienna *Juristische Blätter*, and actually instituted experiments in the *Freie juristische Vereinigung*, which he himself had founded. Actual or fictitious law cases, even entire court proceedings, are being submitted to the persons who are being used for the experiment, who must not be jurists, and who are requested to express an opinion on them. They can do this only by relying on their sense of law and right. Is not everyone reminded of the psychometry of the school of Fechner and Wundt? These tests are open to the same objections that have been urged against psychometry. The person who permits himself to be used for the experiment is not in his usual frame of mind, and he knows, too, that his judgment does not decide the case; the fictitious case arouses no passions, does not agitate the emotions, but addresses itself to the intellect alone. These are sources of error which a correct method must compute and take into account. In spite of this however the attempt will produce valuable results, provided one does not forget about the sources of error.

Method is as infinite as science itself.

William James, 1842-1910
Professor of Philosophy, Harvard University

THE MORAL PHILOSOPHER AND THE MORAL LIFE (1891)

The main purpose of this paper is to show that there is no such thing possible as ethical philosophy dogmatically made up in advance. We all help to determine the content of ethical philosophy so far as we contribute to the race's moral life. In other words, there can be no final truth in ethics any more than in physics, until the last man has had his experience and said his say. In the one case as in the other, however, the hypotheses which we now make while waiting, and the acts to which they prompt us, are among the indispensable conditions which determine what that 'say' shall be.

First of all, what is the position of him who seeks an ethical philosophy? To begin with, he must be distinguished from all those who are satisfied to be ethical sceptics. He *will* not be a sceptic; therefore so far from ethical scepticism being one possible fruit of ethical philosophizing, it can only be regarded as that residual alternative to all philosophy which from the outset menaces every would-be philosopher who may give up the quest discouraged, and renounce his original aim. That aim is to find an account of the moral relations that obtain among things, which will weave them into the unity of a stable system, and make of the world what one may call a genuine universe from the ethical point of view. So far as the world resists reduction to the form of unity, so far as ethical propositions seem unstable, so far does the philosopher fail of his ideal. The subject-matter of his study is the ideals he finds existing in the world; the purpose which guides him is this ideal of his own, of getting them into a certain form. This ideal is thus a factor in ethical philosophy whose legitimate presence must never be overlooked; it is a positive contribution which the philosopher himself necessarily makes to the problem. But it is his only positive contribution. At the outset of his inquiry he ought to have no other ideals. Were he interested peculiarly in the triumph of any one kind of good, he would *pro tanto* cease to be a judicial investigator, and become an advocate for some limited element of the case.

There are three questions in ethics which must be kept apart. Let them be called respectively the *psychological* question, the *metaphysical* question, and the *casuistic* question. The psychological question asks after the historical *origin* of our moral ideas and judgements; the metaphysical question asks what the very *meaning* of the words "good," "ill," and "obligation" are; the casuistic question asks what is the *measure* of the various goods and ills which men recognize, so that the philosopher may settle the true order of human obligations.

I

The psychological question is for most disputants the only question. When your ordinary doctor of divinity has proved to his own satisfaction that an altogether unique faculty called "conscience" must be postulated to tell us what is right and what is wrong; or when your popular-science enthusiast has proclaimed that "apriorism" is an exploded superstition, and that our moral judgments have gradually resulted from the teaching of the environment, each of these persons thinks that ethics is settled and nothing more is to be said. The familiar pair of names, Intuitionist and Evolutionist, so commonly used now to connote all possible differences in ethical opinion, really refer to the psychological question alone. The discussion of this question hinges so much upon particular details that it is impossible to enter upon it at all within the limits of this paper. I will therefore only express dogmatically my own belief, which is this, – that the Benthams, the Mills, and the Bains have done a lasting service in taking so many of our human ideals and showing how they must have arisen from the association with acts of simple bodily pleasures and reliefs from pain. Association with many remote pleasures will unquestionably make a thing significant of goodness in our minds; and the more vaguely the goodness is conceived of, the more mysterious will its source appear to be. But it is surely impossible to explain all our sentiments and preferences in this simple way. The more minutely psychology studies human nature, the more clearly it finds there traces of secondary affections, relating the impressions of the environment with one another and with our impulses in quite different ways from those mere associations of coexistence and succession which are practically all that pure empiricism can admit. Take the love of drunkenness; take bashfulness, the terror of high places, the tendency to seasickness, to faint at the sight of blood, the susceptibility to musical sounds; take the emotion of the comical, the passion for poetry, for mathematics, or for metaphysics, – no one of these things can be wholly explained by either association or utility. They *go with* other things that can be so explained, no doubt; and some of them are prophetic of future utilities, since there is nothing in us for which some use may not be found. But their origin is in incidental complications to our cerebral structure, a structure whose original features arose with no reference to the perception of such discords and harmonies as these.

Well, a vast number of our moral perceptions also are certainly of this secondary and brain-born kind. They deal with directly felt fitnesses between things, and often fly in the teeth of all the prepossessions of habit and presumptions of utility. The moment you get beyond the coarser and more commonplace moral maxims, the Decalogues and Poor Richard's Almanacs, you fall into schemes and positions which to the eye of common sense are fantastic and over-strained. The sense for abstract justice which some persons have is as eccentric a variation, from the natural-history point of view, as is the passion for music or for the higher philosophical consistencies which consumes the soul of others. The feeling of the inward dignity of certain spiritual attitudes, as peace, serenity, simplicity, veracity, and of the essential vulgarity of others, as querulousness, anxiety, egoistic fussiness, etc., – are quite inexplicable except by an innate preference of the more ideal attitude for its own pure sake. The nobler thing tastes better, and that is all that we can say. "Experience" of consequences may truly teach us what things are *wicked*, but what have consequences to do with what is *mean* and *vulgar*? If a man has shot his wife's paramour, by reason of what subtile repugnancy in things is it that we are so disgusted when we hear that the wife and the husband have made it up and are living comfortably together again? . . . All these subtilities of the moral sensibility go as much beyond what can be ciphered out from the "laws of association" as the delicacies of sentiment possible between a pair of young lovers go beyond such precepts of the "etiquette to be observed during engagement" as are printed in manuals of social form.

No! Purely inward forces are certainly at work here. All the higher, more penetrating ideals are revolutionary. They present themselves far less in the guise of effects of past experience than in that of probable causes of future experience, factors to which the environment and the lessons it has so far taught us must learn to bend.

This is all I can say of the psychological question now. In the last chapter of a recent work I have sought to prove in a general way the existence, in our thought, of relations which do not merely repeat the couplings of experience. Our ideals have certainly many sources They are not all explicable as signifying corporeal pleasures to be gained, and pains to be escaped. And for having so constantly perceived this psychological fact, we must applaud the intuitionist school. Whether or not such applause must be extended to that school's other characteristics will appear as we take up the following questions.

The next one in order is the metaphysical question, of what we mean by the words, "obligation," "good," and "ill."

II

First of all, it appears that such words can have no application or relevancy in a world in which no sentient life exists. Imagine an absolutely material world, containing only physical and chemical facts, and existing from eternity without a God, without even an interested spectator: would there be any sense in saying of that world that one of its states is better than another? Or if there were two such worlds possible, would there be any rhyme or reason in calling one good and the other bad, – good or bad positively, I mean, and apart from the fact that one might relate itself better than the other to the philosopher's private interests? But we must leave these private interests out of the account, for the philosopher is a mental fact, and we are asking whether goods and evils and obligations exist in physical facts *per se*. Surely there is no *status* for good and evil to exist in, in a purely insentient world. How can one physical fact, considered simply as a physical fact, be "better" than another? Betterness is not a physical relation. In its mere Material capacity, a thing can no more be good or bad than it can be pleasant or painful. Good for what? Good for the production of another physical fact, do you say? But what in a purely physical universe demands the production of that other fact? Physical facts simply *are* or are *not*; and neither when present or absent, can they be supposed to make demands. If they do, they can only do so by having desires; and then they have ceased to be purely physical facts, and have become facts of conscious sensibility. Goodness, badness, and obligation must be *realized* somewhere in order really to exist; and the first step in ethical philosophy is to see that no merely inorganic "nature of things" can realize them. Neither moral relations nor the moral law can swing *in vacuo*. Their only habitat can be a mind which feels them; and no world composed of merely physical facts can possibly be a world to which ethical propositions apply.

The moment one sentient being, however, is made a part of the universe, there is a chance for goods and evils really to exist. Moral relations now have their *status*, in that being's consciousness. So far as he feels anything to be good, he *makes* it good. It *is* good, for him; and being good for him, is absolutely good, for he is the sole creator of values in that universe, and outside of his opinion things have no moral character at all.

In such a universe as that it would of course be absurd to raise the question of whether the solitary thinker's judgments of good and ill are true or not. Truth supposes a standard outside of the thinker to which he must conform; but here the thinker is a sort of divinity, subject to no higher judge. Let us call the supposed universe which he inhabits a *moral solitude*. In such a moral solitude it is clear that there can be no outward obligation, and that the only trouble the god-like thinker is liable to have will be over the consistency of his own several ideals with one another. Some of these will no doubt be more pungent and appealing than the rest, their goodness will have a profounder, more penetrating taste; they will return to haunt him with more obstinate regrets if violated. So the thinker will have to order his life with them as its chief determinants, or else remain inwardly discordant and unhappy. Into whatever equilibrium he may settle, though, and however he may straighten out his system, it will be a right system; for beyond the facts of his own subjectivity there is nothing moral in the world.

If now we introduce a second thinker with his likes and dislikes into the universe, the ethical situation becomes much more complex, and several possibilities are immediately seen to obtain.

One of these is that the thinkers may ignore each other's attitude about good and evil altogether, and each continue to indulge his own preferences, indifferent to what the other may feel or do. In such a case we have a world with twice as much of the ethical quality in it as our moral solitude, only it is without ethical unity. The same object is good or bad there, according as you measure it by the view which this one or that one of the thinkers takes. Nor can you find any possible ground in such a world for saying that one thinker's opinion is more correct than the other's, or that either has the truer moral sense. Such a world, in short, is not a moral universe but a moral dualism. Not only is there no single point of view within it from which the values of things can be unequivocally judged, but there is not even a demand for such a point of view, since the two thinkers are supposed to be indifferent to each other's thoughts and acts. Multiply the thinkers into a pluralism, and we find realized for us in the ethical sphere something like that world which the antique sceptics conceived of, – in which individual minds are the measures of all things, and in which no one "objective" truth, but only a multitude of "subjective" opinions, can be found.

But this is the kind of world with which the philosopher, so long as he holds to the hope of a philosophy, will not put up. Among the various ideals represented, there must be, he thinks, some which have the more truth or authority; and to these the others *ought* to yield, so that system and subordination may reign. Here in the word "ought" the notion of *obligation* comes emphatically into view, and the next thing in order must be to make its meaning clear.

Since the outcome of the discussion so far has been to show us that nothing can be good or right except so far as some consciousness feels it to be good or thinks it to be right, we perceive on the very threshold that the real superiority and authority which are postulated by the philosopher to reside in some of the opinions, and the really inferior character which he supposes must belong to others, cannot be explained by any abstract moral "nature of things" existing antecedently to the concrete thinkers themselves with their ideals. Like the positive attributes good and bad, the comparative ones better and worse must be *realized* in order to be real. If one ideal judgment be objectively better than another, that betterness must be made flesh by being lodged concretely in some one's actual perception. It cannot float in the atmosphere, for it is not a sort of meteorological phenomenon, like the aurora borealis or the zodiacal light. Its *esse* is *percipi*, like the *esse* of the ideals themselves between which it obtains. The philosopher, therefore, who seeks to know which ideal ought to have supreme weight and which one ought to be subordinated, must trace the ought itself to the *de facto* constitution of some existing consciousness, behind which, as one of the data of the universe, he as a purely ethical philosopher is unable to go. This consciousness must make the one ideal right by feeling it to be right, the other wrong by feeling it to be wrong. But now what particular consciousness in the universe *can* enjoy this prerogative of obliging others to conform to a rule which it lays down?

If one of the thinkers were obviously divine, while all the rest were human, there would probably be no practical dispute about the matter. The divine thought would be the model, to which the others should conform. But still the theoretic question would remain, What is the ground of the obligation, even here?

In our first essays at answering this question, there is an inevitable tendency to slip into an assumption which ordinary men follow when they are disputing with one another about questions of good and bad. They imagine an abstract moral order in which the objective truth resides; and each tries to prove that this pre-existing order is more accurately reflected in his own ideas than in those of his adversary. It is because one disputant is backed by this overarching abstract order that we think the other should submit. Even so, when it is a question no longer of two finite thinkers, but of God and ourselves, – we follow our usual habit, and imagine a sort of *de jure* relation, which antedates and overarches the mere facts, and would make it right that we should conform our thoughts to God's thoughts, even though he made no claim to that effect, and though we preferred *de facto* to go on thinking for ourselves.

But the moment we take a steady look at the question, *we see not only that without a claim actually made by some concrete person there can be no obligation, but that there is some obligation wherever there is a claim.* Claim and obligation are, in fact, coextensive terms; they cover each other exactly. Our ordinary attitude of regarding ourselves as subject to an overarching system of moral relations, true "in themselves," is therefore either an out-and-out superstition, or else it must be treated as a merely provisional abstraction from that real Thinker in whose actual demand upon us to think as he does our obligation must be ultimately based. In a theistic-ethical philosophy that thinker in question is, of course, the Deity to whom the existence of the universe is due.

I know well how hard it is for those who are accustomed to what I have called the superstitious view, to realize that every *de facto* claim creates in so far forth an obligation. We inveterately think that something which we call the "validity" of the claim is what gives to it its obligatory character, and that this validity is something outside of the claim's mere existence as a matter of fact. It rains down upon the claim, we think, from some sublime dimension of being, which the moral law inhabits, much as upon the steel of the compass-needle the influence of the Pole rains down from out of the starry heavens. But again, how can such an inorganic abstract character of imperativeness, additional to the imperativeness which is in the concrete claim itself, *exist*? Take any demand, however slight, which any creature, however weak, may make. Ought it not, for its own sole sake, to be satisfied? If not, prove why not. The only possible kind of proof you could adduce would be the exhibition of another creature who should make a demand that ran the other way. The only possible reason there can be why any phenomenon ought to exist is that such a phenomenon actually is desired. Any desire is imperative to the extent of its amount; it *makes* itself valid by the fact that it exists at all. Some desires, truly enough, are small desires; they are put forward by insignificant persons, and we customarily make light of the obligations which they bring. But the fact that such personal demands as these impose small obligations does not keep the largest obligations from being personal demands.

If we must talk impersonally, to be sure we can say that "the universe" requires, exacts, or makes obligatory such or such an action, whenever it expresses itself through the desires of such or such a creature. But it is better not to talk about the universe in this personified way, unless we believe in a universal or divine consciousness which actually exists. If there be such a consciousness, then its demands carry the most of obligation simply because they are the greatest in amount. But it is even then not *abstractly* right that we should respect them. It is only *concretely* right, – or right after the fact, and by virtue of the fact, that they are actually made. Suppose we do not respect them, as seems largely to be the case in this queer world. That ought not to be, we say; that is wrong. But in what way is this fact of wrongness made more acceptable or intelligible when we imagine it to consist rather in the laceration of an *a priori* ideal order than in the disappointment of a living personal God? Do we, perhaps, think that we cover God and protect him and make his impotence over us less ultimate, when we back him up with this *a priori* blanket from which he may draw some warmth of further appeal? But the only force of appeal to *us*, which either a living God or an abstract ideal order can wield, is found in the 'everlasting ruby vaults' of our own human hearts, as they happen to beat responsive and not irresponsive to the claim. So far as they do feel it when made by a living consciousness, it is life answering to life. A claim thus livingly acknowledged is acknowledged with a solidity and fullness which no thought of an 'ideal' backing can render more complete; while if, on the other hand, the heart's response is withheld, the stubborn phenomenon is there of an impotence in the claims which the universe embodies, which no talk about an eternal nature of things can glaze over or dispel. An ineffective *a priori* order is as impotent a thing as an ineffective God;

and in the eye of philosophy, it is as hard a thing to explain.

We may now consider that what we distinguished as the metaphysical question in ethical philosophy is sufficiently answered, and that we have learned what the words "good," "bad," and "obligation" severally mean. They mean no absolute natures, independent of personal support. They are objects of feeling and desire, which have no foothold or anchorage in Being, apart from the existence of actually living minds.

Wherever such minds exist, with judgments of good and ill, and demands upon one another, there is an ethical world in its essential features. Were all other things, gods and men and starry heavens, blotted out from this universe, and were there left but one rock with two loving souls upon it, that rock would have as thoroughly moral a constitution as any possible world which the eternities and immensities could harbor. It would be a tragic constitution, because the rock's inhabitants would die. But while they lived, there would be real good things and real bad things in the universe; there would be obligations, claims, and expectations; obediences, refusals, and disappointments; compunctions and longings for harmony to come again, and inward peace of conscience when it was restored; there would, in short, be a moral life, whose active energy would have no limit but the intensity of interest in each other with which the hero and heroine might be endowed.

We, on this terrestrial globe, so far as the visible facts go, are just like the inhabitants of such a rock. Whether a God exist, or whether no God exist, in yon blue heaven above us bent, we form at any rate an ethical republic here below. And the first reflection which this leads to is that ethics have as genuine and real a foothold in a universe where the highest consciousness is human, as in a universe where there is a God as well. 'The religion of humanity' affords a basis for ethics as well as theism does. Whether the purely human system can gratify the philosopher's demand as well as the other is a different question, which we ourselves must answer ere we close.

III

The last fundamental question in Ethics was, it will be remembered, the casuistic question. Here we are, in a world where the existence of a divine thinker has been and perhaps always will be doubted by some of the lookers-on, and where, in spite of the presence of a large number of ideals in which human beings agree, there are a mass of others about which no general consensus obtains. It is hardly necessary to present a literary picture of this, for the facts are too well known. The wars of the flesh and the spirit in each man, the concupiscences of different individuals pursuing the same unshareable material or social prizes, the ideals which contrast so according to races, circumstances, temperaments, philosophical beliefs, etc., – all form a maze of apparently inextricable confusion with no obvious Ariadne's thread to lead one out. Yet the philosopher, just because he is a philosopher, adds his own peculiar ideal to the confusion (with which if he were willing to be a sceptic he would be passably content), and insists that over all these individual opinions there is a *system of truth* which he can discover if he only takes sufficient pains.

We stand ourselves at present in the place of that philosopher, and must not fail to realize all the features that the situation comports. In the first place we will not be sceptics; we hold to it that there is a truth to be ascertained. But in the second place we have just gained the insight that that truth cannot be a self-proclaiming set of laws, or an abstract 'moral reason,' but can only exist in act, or in the shape of an opinion held by some thinker really to be found. There is, however, no visible thinker invested with authority. Shall we then simply proclaim our own ideals as the lawgiving ones? No; for if we are true philosophers we must throw our own spontaneous ideals, even the dearest, impartially in with that total mass of ideals which are fairly to be judged. But how then can we as philosophers ever find a test; how avoid complete moral scepticism on the one hand, and on the other escape bringing a wayward personal standard of our own along with us, on which we simply pin our faith?

The dilemma is a hard one, nor does it grow a bit more easy as we resolve it in our minds. The entire undertaking of the philosopher obliges him to seek an impartial test. That test, however, must be incarnated in the demand of some actually existent person; and how can he pick out the person save by an act in which his own sympathies and prepossessions are implied?

One method indeed presents itself, and has as a matter of history been taken by the more serious ethical schools. If the heap of things demanded proved on inspection less chaotic than at first they seemed, if they furnished their own relative test and measure, then the casuistic problem would be solved. If it were found that all goods *qua* goods contained a common essence, then the amount of this essence involved in any one good would show its rank in the scale of goodness, and order could be quickly made; for this essence would be *the* good upon which all thinkers were agreed, the relatively objective and universal good that the philosopher seeks. Even his own private ideals would be measured by their share of it, and find their rightful place among the rest.

Various essences of good have thus been found and proposed as bases of the ethical system. Thus, to be a mean between two extremes; to be recognized by a special intuitive faculty; to make the agent happy for the moment; to make others as well as him happy in the long run; to add to his perfection or dignity; to harm no one; to follow from reason or flow from universal law; to be in accordance with the will of God; to promote the survival of the human species on this planet, – are so many tests, each of which has been maintained by somebody to constitute the essence of all good things or actions so far as they are good.

No one of the measures that have been actually proposed has, however, given general satisfaction. Some are obviously not universally present in all cases, – *e.g.*, the character of harming no one, or that of following a universal law; for the best course is often cruel; and many acts are reckoned good on the sole condition that they be exceptions, and serve not as examples of a universal law. Other characters, such as following the will of God, are unascertainable and vague. Others again, like survival, are quite indeterminate in their consequences, and leave us in the lurch where we most need their help: a philosopher of the Sioux Nation, for example, will be certain to use the survival-criterion in a very different way from ourselves. The best, on the whole, of these marks and measures of goodness seems to be the capacity to bring happiness. But in order not to break down fatally, this test must be taken to cover innumerable acts and impulses that never *aim* at happiness; so that, after all, in seeking for a universal principle we inevitably are carried onward to the most universal principle, – *that the essence of good is simply to satisfy demand*. The demand may be for anything under the sun. There is really no more ground for supposing that all our demands can be accounted for by one universal underlying kind of motive than there is ground for supposing that all physical phenomena are cases of a single law. The elementary forces in ethics are probably as plural as those of physics are. The various ideals have no common character apart from the fact that they are ideals. No single abstract principle can be so used as to yield to the philosopher anything like a scientifically accurate and genuinely useful casuistic scale.

A look at another peculiarity of the ethical universe, as we find it, will still further show us the philosopher's perplexities. As a purely theoretic problem, namely, the casuistic question would hardly ever come up at all. If the ethical philosopher were only asking after the best *imaginable* system of goods he would indeed have an easy task; for all demands as such are *prima facie* respectable, and the best simply imaginary world would be one in which *every* demand was gratified as soon as made. Such a world would, however, have to have a physical constitution entirely different from that of the one which we inhabit. It would need not only a space, but a time, 'of *n*-dimensions,' to include all the acts and experiences incompatible with one another here below, which would then go on in conjunction, – such as spending our money, yet growing rich; taking our holiday, yet getting ahead with our work; shooting and fishing, yet doing no hurt to the beasts; gaining no end of experience, yet keeping our youthful freshness of heart; and the like. There can be no question that such a system of things, however brought about, would be the absolutely ideal system; and that if a philosopher could create universes *a priori*, and provide all the mechanical conditions, that is the sort of universe which he should unhesitatingly create.

But this world of ours is made on an entirely different pattern, and the casuistic question here is most tragically practical. The actually possible in this world is vastly narrower than all that is demanded; and there is always a *pinch* between the ideal and the actual which can only be got through by leaving part of the ideal behind. There is hardly a good which we can imagine except as competing for the possession of the same bit of space and time with some other imagined good. Every end of desire that presents itself appears exclusive of some other end of desire. Shall a man drink and smoke, *or* keep his nerves in condition? – he cannot do both. Shall he follow his fancy for Amelia, *or* Henrietta? – both cannot be the choice of his heart. Shall he have the dear old republican party, *or* a spirit of unsophistication in public affairs? he cannot have both, etc. So that the ethical philosopher's demand for the right scale of subordination in ideals is the fruit of an altogether practical need. Some part of the ideal must be butchered, and he needs to know which part. It is a tragic situation, and no mere speculative conundrum, with which he has to deal.

Now *we* are blinded to the real difficulty of the philosopher's task by the fact that we are born into a society whose ideals are largely ordered already. If we follow the ideal which is conventionally highest, the others which we butcher either die and do not return to haunt us; or if they come back and accuse us of murder, every one applauds us for turning to them a deaf ear. In other words, our environment encourages us not to be philosophers but partisans. The philosopher, however, cannot, so long as he clings to his own ideal of objectivity, rule our any ideal from being heard. He is confident, and rightly confident, that the simple taking counsel of his own intuitive preferences would be certain to end in a mutilation of the fulness of the truth. The poet Heine is said to have written 'Bunsen' in the place of 'Gott' in his copy of that author's work entitled "God in History," so as to make it read "Bunsen in der Geschichte." Now, with no disrespect to the good and learned Baron, it is not safe to say that any single philosopher, however wide his sympathies, must be just such a Bunsen in der Geschichte of the moral world, so soon as he attempts to put his own ideas of order into that howling mob of desires, each struggling to get breathing-room for the ideal to which it clings? The very best of men must not only be insensible, but be ludicrously and peculiarly insensible, to many goods. As a militant, fighting freehanded that the goods to which he *is* sensible may not be submerged and lost from out of life, the philosopher, like every other human being, is in a natural position. But think of Zeno and of Epicurus, think of Calvin and of Paley. think of Kant and Schopenhauer, of Herbert Spencer and John Henry Newman, no longer as one-sided champions of special ideals, but as school-masters deciding what all must think, – and what more grotesque topic could a satirist wish for on which to exercise his pen? The fabled attempt of Mrs. Partington to arrest the rising tide of the North Atlantic with her broom was a reasonable spectacle compared with their effort to substitute the content of their clean-shaven systems for that exuberant mass of goods with which all human nature is in travail, and groaning to bring to the light of day. Think, furthermore, of such individual moralists, no longer as mere school-masters, but as pontiffs armed with the temporal power, and having authority in every concrete case of conflict to order which good shall be butchered and which shall be suffered to survive, – and the notion really turns one pale. All one's slumbering revolutionary instincts waken at the thought of any single moralist wielding such powers of life and death. Better chaos forever than an order based on any closet-philosopher's rule, even though he were the most enlightened possible member of his tribe. No! if the philosopher is to keep his judicial position, he must never become one of the parties to the fray.

What can he do, then, it will now be asked, except to fall back on scepticism and give up the notion of being a philosopher at all?

But do we not already see a perfectly definite path of escape which is open to him just because he is a philosopher, and not the champion of one particular ideal? Since everything which is demanded is by that fact a good, must not the guiding principle for ethical philosophy (since all demands conjointly cannot be satisfied in this poor world) be simply to satisfy at all times *as many demands as we can*? That act must be the best act, accordingly, which makes for the *best whole*, in the sense of awakening the least sum of dissatisfactions. In the casuistic scale, therefore, those ideals must be written highest which *prevail at the least cost*, or by whose realization the least possible number of other ideals are destroyed. Since victory and defeat there must be, the victory to be philosophically prayed for is that of the more inclusive side, – of the side which even in the hour of triumph will to some degree do justice to the ideals in which the vanquished party's interests lay. The course of history is nothing but the story of men's struggles from generation to generation to find the more and more inclusive order. *Invent some manner* of realizing your own ideals which will also satisfy the alien demands, – that and that only is the path of peace! Following this path society has shaken itself into one sort of relative equilibrium after another by a series of social discoveries quite analogous to those of science. Polyandry and polygamy and slavery, private warfare and liberty to kill, judicial torture and arbitrary royal power have slowly succumbed to actually aroused complaints; and though some one's ideals are unquestionably the worse off for each improvement, yet a vastly greater total number of them find shelter in our civilized society than in the older savage ways. So far then, and up to date, the casuistic scale is made for the philosopher already far better than he can ever make it for himself. An experiment of the most searching kind has proved that the laws and usages of the land are what yield the maximum of satisfaction to the thinkers taken all together. The presumption in cases of conflict must always be in favor of the conventionally recognized good. The philosopher must be a conservative, and in the construction of his casuistic scale must put the things most in accordance with the customs of the community on top.

And yet if he be a true philosopher he must see that there is nothing final in any actually given equilibrium of human ideals, but that, as our present laws and customs have fought and conquered other past ones, so they will in their turn be overthrown by any newly discovered order which will hush up the complaints that they still give rise to, without producing others louder still. "Rules are made for man, not man for rules," – that one sentence is enough to immortalize Green's Prolegomena to Ethics. And although a man always risks much when he breaks away from established rules and strives to realize a larger ideal whole than they permit, yet the philosopher must allow that it is at all times open to any one to make the experiment, provided he fear not to stake his life and character upon the throw. The pinch is always here. Pent in under every system of moral rules are innumerable persons whom it weighs upon, and goods which it represses; and these are always rumbling and grumbling in the background, and ready for any issue by which they may get free. See the abuses which the institution of private property covers, so that even to-day it is shamelessly asserted among us that one of the prime functions of the national government is to help the adroiter citizens to grow rich. See the unnamed and unnamable sorrows which the tyranny, on the whole so beneficent, of the marriage-institution brings to so many, both of the married and the unwed. See the wholesale loss of opportunity under our *regime* of so-called equality and industrialism, with the drummer and the counter-jumper in the saddle, for so many faculties and graces which could flourish in the feudal world. See our kindliness for the humble and the outcast, how it wars with that stern weeding-out which until now has been the condition of every perfection in the breed. See everywhere the struggle and the squeeze; and everlastingly the problem how to make them less. The anarchists, nihilists, and free-lovers; the free-silverites, socialists, and single-tax men; the free-traders and civil-service reformers; the prohibitionists and anti-vivisectionists; the radical darwinians with their idea of the suppression of the weak, – these and all the conservative sentiments of society arrayed against them, are simply deciding through actual experiment by what sort of conduct the maximum amount of good can be gained and kept in this world. These experiments are to be judged, not *a priori*, but by actually finding, after the fact of their making, how much more outcry or how much appeasement comes about. What closet-solutions can possibly anticipate the result of trials made on such a scale? Or what can any superficial theorist's judgment be worth, in a world where every one of hundreds of ideals has its special champion already provided in the shape of some genius expressly born to feel it, and to fight to death in its behalf? The pure philosopher can only follow the windings of the spectacle, confident that the line of least resistance will always be towards the richer and the more inclusive arrangement, and that by one tack after another some approach to the kingdom of heaven is incessantly made.

IV

All this amounts to saying that, so far as the casuistic question goes, ethical science is just like physical science, and instead of being deducible all at once from abstract principles, must simply bide its time, and be ready to revise its conclusions from day to day. The presumption of course, in both sciences, always is that the vulgarly accepted opinions are true, and the right casuistic order that which public opinion believes in; and surely it would be folly quite as great, in most of us, to strike out independently and to aim at originality in ethics as in physics. Every now and then, however, some one is born with the right to be original, and his revolutionary thought or action may bear prosperous fruit. He may replace old "laws of nature" by better ones; he may, by breaking old moral rules in a certain place, bring in a total condition of things more ideal than would have followed had the rules been kept.

On the whole, then, we must conclude that no philosophy of ethics is possible in the old-fashioned absolute sense of the term. Everywhere the ethical philosopher must wait on facts. The thinkers who create the ideals come he knows not whence, their sensibilities are evolved he knows not how; and the question as to which of two conflicting ideals will give the best universe then and there, can be answered by him only through the aid of the experience of other men. I said some time ago, in treating of the 'first' question, that the intuitional moralists deserve credit for keeping most clearly to the psychological facts. They do much to spoil this merit on the whole, however, by mixing with it that dogmatic temper which, by absolute distinctions and unconditional 'thou shalt nots,' changes a growing, elastic, and continuous life into a superstitious system of relics and dead bones. In point of fact, there are no absolute evils, and there are no non-moral goods; and the *highest* ethical life – however few may be called to bear its burdens – consists at all times in the breaking of rules which have grown too narrow for the actual case. There is but one unconditional commandment, which is that we should seek incessantly, with fear and trembling, so to vote and to act as to bring about the very largest total universe of good which we can see. Abstract rules indeed can help; but they help the less in proportion as our intuitions are more piercing, and our vocation is the stronger for the moral life. For every real dilemma is in literal strictness a unique situation; and the exact combination of ideals realized and ideals disappointed which each decision creates is always a universe without a precedent, and for which no adequate previous rule exists. The philosopher, then, *qua* philosopher, is not better able to determine the best universe in the concrete emergency than other men. He sees, indeed, somewhat better than most men what the question always is, – not a question of this good or that good simply taken, but of the two total universes with which these goods respectively belong. He knows that he must vote always for the richer universe, for the good which seems most organizable, most fit to enter into complex combinations, most apt to be a member of a more inclusive whole. But which particular universe this is he cannot know for certain in advance; he only knows that if he makes a bad mistake the cries of the wounded will soon inform him of the fact. In all this the philosopher is just like the rest of us non-philosophers, so far as we are just and sympathetic instinctively, and so far as we are open to the voice of complaint. His function is in fact indistinguishable from that of the best kind of statesman at the present day. His books upon ethics, therefore, so far as they truly touch the moral life, must more and more ally themselves with a literature which is confessedly tentative and suggestive rather than dogmatic, – I mean with novels and dramas of the deeper sort, with sermons, with books on statecraft and philanthropy and social economical reform. Treated in this way ethical treatises may be voluminous and luminous as well; but they never can be *final*, except in their abstractest and vaguest features; and they must more and more abandon the old-fashioned, clear-cut, and would-be 'scientific' form.

V

The chief of all the reasons why concrete ethics cannot be final is that they have to wait on metaphysical and theological beliefs. I said some time back that real ethical relations existed in a purely human world. They would exist even in what we called a moral solitude if the thinker had various ideals which took hold of him in turn. His self of one day would make demands on his self of another; and some of the demands might be urgent and tyrannical, while others were gentle and easily put aside. We call the tyrannical demands *imperatives*. If we ignore these we do not hear the last of it. The good which we have wounded returns to plague us with interminable crops of consequential damages, compunctions, and regrets. Obligation can thus exist inside a single thinker's consciousness; and perfect peace can abide with him only so far as he lives according to some sort of a casuistic scale which keeps his more imperative goods on top. It is the nature of these goods to be cruel to their rivals. Nothing shall avail when weighed in the balance against them. They call out all the mercilessness in our disposition, and do not easily forgive us if we are so soft-hearted as to shrink from sacrifice in their behalf.

The deepest difference, practically, in the moral life of man is the difference between the easy-going and the strenuous mood. When in the easy-going mood the shrinking from present ill is our ruling consideration. The strenuous mood, on the contrary, makes us quite indifferent to present ill, if only the greater ideal be attained. The capacity for the strenuous mood probably lies slumbering in every man, but it has more difficulty in some than in others in waking up. It needs the wilder passions to arouse it, the big fears, loves, and indignations; or else the deeply penetrating appeal of some one of the higher fidelities, like justice, truth, or freedom. Strong relief is a necessity of its vision; and a world where all the mountains are brought down and all the valleys are exalted is no congenial place for its habitation. This is why in a solitary thinker this mood might slumber on forever without waking. His various ideals, known to him to be mere preferences of his own, are too nearly of the same denominational value: he can play fast or loose with them at will. This too is why, in a merely human world without God, the appeal to our moral energy falls short of its maximal stimulating power. Life, to be sure, is even in such a world a genuinely ethical symphony; but it is played in the compass of a couple of poor octaves, and the infinite scale of values fails to open up. Many of us, indeed, – like Sir James Stephen in those eloquent "Essays by a Barrister," – would openly laugh at the very idea of the strenuous mood being awakened in us by those claims of remote posterity which constitute the last appeal of the religion of humanity. We do not love these men of the future keenly enough; and we love them perhaps the less the more we hear of their evolutionized perfection, their high average longevity and education, their freedom from war and crime, their relative immunity from pain and zymotic disease, and all their other negative superiorities. This is all too finite, we say; we see too well the vacuum beyond. It lacks the note of infinitude and mystery, and may all be dealt with in the don't-care mood. No need of agonizing ourselves or making others agonize for these good creatures just at present.

When, however, we believe that a God is there, and that he is one of the claimants, the infinite perspective opens out. The scale of the symphony is incalculably prolonged. The more imperative ideals now begin to speak with an altogether new objectivity and significance, and to utter the penetrating, shattering, tragically challenging note of appeal. They ring out like the call of Victor Hugo's alpine eagle, "qui parle au precipice et que le gouffre entend," and the strenuous mood awakens at the sound. It saith among the trumpets, ha, ha! it smelleth the battle afar off, the thunder of the captains and the shouting. Its blood is up; and cruelty to the lesser claims, so far from being a deterrent element, does but add to the stern joy with which it leaps to answer to the greater. All through history, in the periodical conflicts of puritanism with the don't-care temper, we see the antagonism of the strenuous and genial moods, and the contrast between the ethics of infinite and mysterious obligation from on high, and those of prudence and the satisfaction of merely finite need.

The capacity of the strenuous mood lies so deep down among our natural human possibilities that even if there were no metaphysical or traditional grounds for believing in a God, men would postulate one simply as a pretext for living hard, and getting out of the game of existence its keenest possibilities of zest. Our attitude towards concrete evils is entirely different in a world where we believe there are none but finite demanders, from what it is in one where we joyously face tragedy for an infinite demander's sake. Every sort of energy and endurance, of courage and capacity for handling life's evils, is set free in those who have religious faith. For this reason the strenuous type of character will on the battle-field of human history always outwear the easy-going type, and religion will drive irreligion to the wall.

It would seem, too, – and this is my final conclusion, – that the stable and systematic moral universe for which the ethical philosopher asks is fully possible only in a world where there is a divine thinker with all-enveloping demands. If such a thinker existed, his way of subordinating the demands to one another would be the finally valid casuistic scale; his claims would be the most appealing; his ideal universe would be the most inclusive realizable whole. If he now exist, then actualized in his thought already must be that ethical philosophy which we seek as the pattern which our own must evermore approach. In the interests of our own ideal of systematically unified moral truth, therefore, we, as would-be philosophers, must postulate a divine thinker, and pray for the victory of the religious cause. Meanwhile, exactly what the thought of the infinite thinker may be is hidden from us even were we sure of his existence; so that our postulation of him after all serves only to let loose in us the strenuous mood. But this is what it does in all men, even those who have no interest in philosophy. The ethical philosopher, therefore, whenever he ventures to say which course of action is the best, is on no essentially different level from the common man. "See, I have set before thee this day life and good, and death and evil; therefore, choose life that thou and thy seed may live," – when this challenge comes to us, it is simply our total character and personal genius that are on trial; and if we invoke any so-called philosophy, our choice and use of that also are but revelations of our personal aptitude or incapacity for moral life. From this unsparing practical ordeal no professor's lectures and no array of books can save us. The solving word, for the learned and the unlearned man alike, lies in the last resort in the dumb willingnesses and unwillingnesses of their interior characters, and nowhere else. It is not in heaven, neither is it beyond the sea; but the word is very nigh unto thee, in thy mouth and in thy heart, that thou mayest do it.

John Dewey, 1859-1952
Professor of Philosophy, Columbia University

MY PHILOSOPHY OF LAW

When the question of the nature of law is examined in the light of the doctrines of various schools and the controversies between them, it is found to break up into at least three distinct yet related questions. The three issues concern the *source* of law, its *end*, and its *application*, including under this last head questions of the methods by which law is and can be made effective.

The problems involved in the discussion about law that can be called philosophical seem to arise from the need for having some principles which can be employed to justify and/or criticize existing legal rules and practices. This need and motive are perhaps most clearly manifested in those philosophies which made an explicit distinction between what they called positive law on one side and the law of nature on the other hand, the latter being employed as the end positive laws ought to realize and the standard to which they should conform. This particular formulation is at present in vogue only in the school of thought that remains faithful to the general line of ideas formulated in the Middle Ages and that continued to influence continental writers on law through the seventeenth century. But the distinction between what happens to exist at a given time and what might and should be, and the need for such a conception of the latter as will provide "principles" for organizing, justifying, and or disapproving and reforming some aspects of what exists seem to be back of all movements that fall in the field of legal philosophy.

From this point of view, discussion of the source and the end of law can be brought under a single head, that of the *standard* or criterion by which to evaluate existing legal regulations and practices. The question of what law *is* then reduces itself to a question of what it is believed regulations and practices *should be*. According to traditions that are highly influential, determination of the end and standard is intimately bound up with determination of an *ultimate* source – as is obvious when the Will or Reason of God, or the ultimate and intrinsic Law of Nature, is held to be the source of law. What lies back of this identification of source with end and standard is the belief that unless a source higher and more fixed than that of experience can be found, there is no sure ground for any genuinely philosophic valuation of law as it actually exists. This appeal to a source is not, then, the same as appeal to origin in time, since that last procedure links the matter up with experience, and with all the defects that the classic tradition attaches to whatever is experiential.

These preliminary remarks have a double purpose. On one hand, they are designed to express the belief that there is a genuine and important matter involved in the discussions called "legal philosophy"; the question, namely of the ground upon which existing legal affairs, including rules of law, the work of legislation, judicial decisions, and administrative practices, can be legitimately and profitably evaluated. The other point is that as matter of fact legal philosophies have reflected and are sure to continue to reflect movements of the period in which they are produced, and hence cannot be separated from what these movements stand for.

This last remark is a sweeping one. To many persons, it will seem to beg all the important questions with which legal philosophy is concerned. However, upon the side of past systems, it signifies that they have to be viewed in connection with actual cultural and social movements of the periods in which they appeared. The view also holds that the real significance of those philosophies is increased when they are viewed as manifestations of efforts put forth practically. For upon an exclusively intellectual basis, the various legal philosophies are in such conflict with one another as to indicate that all alike are attempting the impossible. On the view here suggested, they have all the importance that is possessed by the movements they reflect; their conflicts are proofs of a certain vital genuineness. On the same score, if different contributions to this volume represent incompatible positions, it is because they express different attitudes toward practical questions of what should be done and how best to do it. At all events, what I myself have to say is put forth in this spirit. Fundamentally, a program for action to be tested in action is set forth, not something that can be judged (beyond assertions of fact and matters of logical consistency) on a purely intellectual basis.

The standpoint taken is that law is through and through a social phenomenon;

social in origin, in purpose or end, and in application. Now one cannot utter or write the word "social" without being aware of all the ambiguities and controversies that attend the meaning of the words *society* and *social*. Here what was just said may be objected to on the ground that it tries to explain what is obscure, namely the nature of law, by reference to something still more obscure, namely, society. For the purpose of the present topic, however, it is needful to make only two statements regarding what is denoted by "social." It is postulated that whatever else social means it applies, first, to human *activities*, and secondly to these activities, as forms of behavior, as *inter*-activities. By saying that social facts, or phenomena, are activities, it is meant, negatively, that they are *not* facts of the kind indicated when "fact" is taken to mean something done, finished, and over with; and positively that they are processes, things going *on*. Even in the case of past events, when social facts are under consideration, it is important to recognize that they represent slices of time having a dimension long enough to cover initial conditions and a later stage of issue or outcome, the latter being in its turn an *on*going. With reference to law, this position signifies that law must be viewed both as intervening in the complex of other activities, and as itself a social process, not something that can be said to be done or to happen at a certain date. The first part of the foregoing statement means that "law" cannot be set up as if it were a separate entity, but can be discussed only in terms of the social conditions in which it arises and of what it concretely does there. It is this fact which renders the use of the word "law" as a single general term rather dangerous, making it needful to state explicitly that the word is used as a summary term to save repeating legal rules, legislative and administrative activities (as far as the latter influence the course of human activities), judicial decisions, etc.

The second part of the statement involves the conclusion that what is called *application* is not something that happens *after* a rule or law or statute is laid down but is a necessary part of them; such a necessary part indeed that in given cases we can judge what the law *is* as matter of fact only by telling how it operates, and what are its effects in and upon the human activities that are going on. For special purposes, the signification of "applicability" may be restricted much more technically. But from the standpoint that can be called philosophical, application must be taken broadly. A given legal arrangement *is* what it *does*, and what it does lies in the field of modifying and/or maintaining human activities as going concerns. Without application there are scraps of paper or voices in the air but nothing that can be called law.

It might seem as if what is conveyed by saying that social activities are *inter*-activities were already included in the word "*social*," since social means association. By calling especial attention to this trait, however, we indicate that there is a *de facto*, though not necessarily *de jure* or moral, reciprocity in every fact of social behavior. A *trans*-action does not just go across in a one-way direction, but is a two-way process. There is reaction as well as action. While it is convenient to view some human beings as agents and others as patients (recipients), the distinction is purely relative; there is no receptivity that is not also a re-*action* or response, and there is no agency that does not also involve an element of receptivity. The emphasis upon agreement, contract, consensus, in various political and legal philosophies is in effect a recognition of this aspect of social phenomena, although a rather overidealized expression of it.

Social processes have conditions which are stable and enduring as compared with the multitudes of special actions composing the process. Human beings form habits as surely as they perform special deeds, and habits, when embodied in interactivities, are customs. These customs are, upon the view here taken, the *source* of law. We may use the analogy, or if one prefers, the metaphor, of a river valley, a stream, and banks. The valley in its relation to surrounding country, or as the "lie of the land," is the primary fact. The stream may be compared to the social process, and its various waves, wavelets, eddies, etc., to the special acts which make up a social process. The banks are stable, enduring conditions, which limit and also direct the course taken by the stream, comparable to customs. But the permanence and fixity of the banks, as compared with the elements of the passing stream, is relative, not absolute. Given the lie of the land, the stream is an energy which carves its way from higher to lower levels and thereby, when viewed as a long run (in time as well as in space) process, it forms and reforms its own banks. Social customs, including traditions, institutions, etc., are stable and enduring as compared with special deeds and with the serial arrangement of these acts which forms a process. But they, and therefore the legal regulations which are their precipitated formulations, are only relatively fixed. They undergo, sooner or later, more slowly or more rapidly, the attrition of ongoing processes. For while they constitute the *structure* of the processes that go *on*, they are the structure *of* the processes in the sense that they arise and take shape within the processes, and are not forced upon the processes from without.

Habit and custom introduce factors into the constitution of human activities which were not taken account of by earlier philosophers who called themselves empirical; factors which, when they are taken account of, profoundly modify the demand for an origin and source of law outside of time, and for a standard or norm that is outside of and independent of experience. As for the first point, earlier empirical philosophers in their revolt against universals and principles that were alleged to be immutable and eternal, beyond criticism and beyond alteration, often pulverized experience, and reduced all general and enduring factors in it to the general names they bore. Every habit and every custom is, however, general within certain limits. It arises out of interaction of environing conditions, which change slowly, with needs and interests of human beings which also endure with but slight change throughout considerable periods of time. Limitation of space does not permit an adequate statement of the nature of the connections that exist between habits and rules of law. But it is clear without extended argument that explicit enactment of a custom into law, however the enactment takes place, reinforces and often extends the relatively enduring and stable character of custom, thus modifying its general character.

It is possible that the bearing of the generality of custom and law, as structural conditions of social activities, upon mooted problems of legal philosophical doctrine is not readily apparent. The point is that recognition of this aspect of social phenomena makes it unnecessary to appeal, on *practical* grounds, to an outside source. As a matter of pure metaphysical theory, a person may continue to have a very low opinion of time and of things affected by temporal conditions. But from any practical standpoint, recognition of the relatively slow rate of change on the part of certain constituents of social action is capable of accomplishing every useful, every *practically* needed, office that has led in the past and in other cultural climes to setting up external sources such as the Will or Reason of God, the Law of Nature in medieval theory and in philosophers like Grotius and his successors, the General Will of Rousseau, and the Practical Reason of Kant.

What has been said does not apply to the doctrine that *sovereignty* is the source of law. Sovereignty is used to denote something which is at least of the nature of a social fact, something existing *within* social activities and relations and not outside of them. Unless I am mistaken, the fact that this view which once highly commended itself to students of politics and of jurisprudence no longer exercises any great appeal indicates why a brief statement about it will suffice. For (unless again I am much mistaken) the view already wears a certain antiquarian air, so that it is hard even in imagination to see why once it had such a vogue. Seen in perspective, this doctrine owed its force to two things. It got away from making law depend upon outside metaphysical sources; it instituted in their place reliance upon conditions and agencies to which some verifiable empirical meaning could be given. In the second place, sovereignty is a *political* term, and the vogue of the doctrine coincided with that immense outburst of legislative activity which took place in the field conventionally labeled "political." The Austinian theory of the source of law may be said to constitute a rationalized approbation of a movement to bring legal rules and arrangements within the scope of deliberate purposive action, at the expense of the comparatively unplanned results of customs interpreted in judicial decisions. The doctrine has lost much of its original appeal because development of the social sciences, viz., of history, anthropology, sociology, and psychology, has tended to make sovereignty at best an expression of the working of a vast multitude of social forces, and at worst a pure abstraction. The sovereignty doctrine of the source of law thus represents a transition from acceptance of "sources" outside of social actions into one within them, but a transition which fastened on only one social factor and froze that one in isolation. When it was discovered that social customs, and to some extent social interests, lord it over any specific set of persons who can be picked out and called "sovereign," the doctrine declined. The growing tendency to interpret political activities in connection with economic factors acted, of course, in the same direction.

So far the topic of end and standard has not received attention. It may be urged that if the account that has been given of the experiential source of law is accepted, it only strengthens the case for an end and standard that lie outside of actual social activities. For, it is argued, the fact that such and such customs and laws have grown up is no sign that they *should* exist; it furnishes no test for their value. In short, we come here upon the large problem of "value in relation to fact," and upon the conclusion, held by many that they are so separate that standards for judging the value of what exists must have *their* source as standards outside of any possible empirical field.

With reference to this issue, recognition of the on-going character of social facts as continuing activities is of fundamental importance. If what are taken to be social facts are chopped off by being regarded as closed and completely ended, then there is much to be said on theoretical grounds for the view that the standard for evaluating them must lie outside the field of actual existences. But if they are on-going, they have consequences; and consideration of consequences may provide ground upon which it is decided whether they be maintained intact or be changed.

When it stated that there is much to be said *theoretically* for the view that an outside end and standard are needed if social facts are not taken as going concerns, it is not meant that much can be said in favor of the applicability of such standard to actual social conditions, with which, by definition, they have nothing to do. It is undeniable that different standards, so different as to conflict with one another, have been held and used a different places and times in the past. Their conflict is sufficient evidence that they were not derived from any *a priori* absolute standard. Denial of the possibility of extracting a standard from actual social activities is thus in effect a denial that an absolute standard, even if it exists, ever had any influence or effect. *For what reason is there for thinking that the standards now put forth by those who appeal to a non-empirical absolute end, will have a different fortune from those put forward in the past?*

The usual way of meeting difficulties of this type is to admit that a distinction must be made between *form*, which is absolute, and its contents or filling, which are historical and relative. The admission is fatal to everything which the doctrine of absolute ends was framed to meet. For according to the admission, all concrete valuations must be based upon what is admitted to be experiential and temporal.

On the view here presented, the standard is found in consequences, in the *function* of what goes on socially. If this view were generally held, there would be assurance of introduction on a large scale of the rational factor into concrete evaluations of legal arrangements. For it demands that intelligence, employing the best scientific methods and materials available, be used, to investigate, in terms of the context of actual situations, the consequences of legal rules and of proposed legal decisions and acts of legislation. The present tendency, hardly more as yet than in a state of inception, to discuss legal matters in their concrete social setting, and not in the comparative vacuum of their relations to one another, would get the reinforcement of a consistent legal theory. Moreover, when it is systematically acknowledged in practice that social facts are going concerns and that all legal matters have their place *within* these ongoing concerns, there will be a much stronger likelihood than at present that new knowledge will be acquired of a kind which can be brought to bear upon the never-ending process of improving standards of judgment.

In *Human Nature and Conduct* 239-241 (1922) he wrote: "Many men are now aware of the harm done in legal matters by assuming the antecedent existence of fixed principles under which every new case may be brought. They recognize that this assumption merely puts an artificial premium on ideas developed under bygone conditions, and that their perpetuation in the present works inequity. Yet the choice is not between throwing rules previously developed and sticking obstinately by them. The intelligent alternative is to revise, adapt, expand and alter them. The problem is one of continuous, vital readaptation. . . . [A]ll principles are empirical generalizations from the ways in which previous judgments of conduct have practically worked out. When this fact is apparent, these generalizations will be seen to be not fixed rules for deciding doubtful cases, but instrumentalities for their investigation, methods by which the net value of past experience is rendered available for present scrutiny of new perplexities. Then it will also follow that they are hypotheses to be tested and revised by their further working."

Roscoe Pound, 1870-1964
Dean of Law and Carter Professor of Jurisprudence, Harvard University

A SURVEY OF SOCIAL INTERESTS

There has been a notable shift throughout the world from thinking of the task of the legal order as one of adjusting the exercise of free wills to one of satisfying wants, of which free exercise of the will is but one. Accordingly, we must start today from a theory of interests, that is, of the claims or demands or desires which human beings, either individually or in groups or associations or relations, seek to satisfy, of which, therefore, the adjustment of relations and ordering of conduct through the force of politically organized society must take account. I have discussed the general theory of interests, the classification of interests, and the details of individual interests in other places. It is enough to say here that the classification into individual interests, public interests, and social interests was suggested by Jhering. As I should put it, individual interests are claims or demands or desires involved immediately in the individual life and asserted in title of that life. Public interests are claims or demands or desires involved in life in a politically organized society and asserted in title of that organization. They are commonly treated as the claims of a politically organized society thought of as a legal entity. Social interests are claims or demands or desires involved in social life in civilized society and asserted in title of that life. It is not uncommon to treat them as the claims of the whole social group as such.

But this does not mean that every claim or demand or desire which human beings assert must be put once for all for every purpose into one of these three categories. For some purposes and in some connections it is convenient to look at a given claim or demand or desire from one standpoint. For other purposes or in other connections it is convenient to look at the same claim or demand or the same type of claims or demands from one of the other standpoints. When it comes to weighing or valuing claims or demands with respect to other claims or demands, we must be careful to compare them on the same plane. If we put one as an individidual interest and the other as a social interest we may decide the question in advance in our very way of putting it. For example, in the "truck act" cases one may think of the claim of the employer to make contracts freely as an individual interest of substance. In that event, we must weigh it with the claim of the employee not to be coerced by economic pressure into making contracts to take his pay in orders on a company store, thought of as an individual interest of personality. If we think of either in terms of a policy we must think of the other in the same terms. If we think of the employee's claim in terms of a policy of assuring a minimum or a standard human life, we must think of the employer's claim in terms of a policy of upholding and enforcing contracts. If the one is thought of as an individual interest and the other as a social interest, our way of stating the question may leave nothing to decide.

In general, but not always, it is expedient to put claims or demands in their most generalized form, i.e., as social interests, in order to compare them. But where the problems are relatively simple, it is sometimes possible to take account of all the factors sufficiently by comparing individual interests put directly as such. It must be borne in mind that often we have here different ways of looking at the same claims or same type of claims as they are asserted in different titles. Thus, individual interests of personality may be asserted in title of or subsumed under the social interest in the general security, or the social interest in the individual life, or sometimes from different standpoints or in different aspects, both of them. Again, individual interests in the domestic relations may be subsumed under the social interest in the security of social institutions of which domestic institutions are the oldest and by no means the least important. Again, the public interest in the integrity of the state personality may be thought of as the social interest in the security of social institutions of which political institutions are one form. When we have recognized and legally delimited and secured an interest, it is important to identify the generalized individual interest behind and giving significance and definition to the legal right. When we are considering what claims or demands to recognize and within what limits, and when we are seeking to adjust conflicting and overlapping claims and demands in some new aspect or new situation, it is important to subsume the individual interests under social interests and to weigh them as such.

Some years ago one of the justices of our highest Court, [McKenna, J.], dissenting from the judgment of that Court in the *Arizona Employers' Liability Cases*, told us that there was a "menace in the . . . . judgment to all rights, subjecting them unreservedly to conceptions of public policy." Undoubtedly, if certain legal rights were definitely established by the Constitution there would be a menace to the general security if the Court which must ultimately interpret and apply the provisions of that instrument were to suffer a state legislature to infringe those legal rights on mere considerations of political expediency. But it was only the ambiguity of the term "right," a word of many meanings, and want of clear understanding of what our law has been seeking to achieve through the obscure conception of "public policy" that made it possible to think of the decision in question in such a way. The "rights" of which Mr. Justice McKenna spoke were not legal rights in the same sense as my legal right to the integrity of my physical person or my legal right of ownership in my watch. They are individual wants, individual claims, individual interests, which it was felt ought to be secured through legal rights or through some other legal machinery. In other words, there was a policy of securing them. The Fourteenth Amendment did not set up these or any other individual interests as absolute legal rights. It imposed a standard upon the legislator. It said to him that if he trenched upon these individual interests he must not do so arbitrarily. His action must have some basis in reason. It is submitted that that basis must be the one upon which the common law has always sought to proceed, the one implied in the very term "due process of law," namely, a weighing or balancing of the various interests which overlap or come in conflict and a rational reconciling or adjustment. Thus the public policy of which Mr. Justice McKenna spoke is seen to be something at least on no lower plane than the so-called rights. As the latter term refers to individual interests which we feel ought to be secured by law, the former refers to social interests which we feel the law ought to or which in fact the law does secure in delimiting individual interests and establishing legal rights. There is a policy in the one case as much as in the other. The body of the common law is made up of adjustments or compromises of conflicting individual interests in which we turn to some social interest, frequently under the name of public policy, to determine the limits of a reasonable adjustment.

In the common law we have been wont to speak of social interests under the name of "public policy." Thus when a great judge was called on to weigh certain claims with reference to the social interest in the security of political institutions, he said that a "great and overshadowing public policy" forbade applying to the case one of the most fundamental principles of the law. Again, when it seemed to a majority of the Supreme court of the United States that the validity of an acquisition from the Federal Government ought to be put at rest as against a claim of fraud, although limitation did not run against the Government, the Court spoke of the "policy" behind the statute of limitations and invoked the doctrine of election of remedies as expressing the same policy. So, too, when a great teacher of law wished to say that another fundamental legal doctrine was sometimes limited in its application because of the social interest in the general security, he stated that "except in certain cases based on public policy" the law of today makes liability dependent upon fault. But this limitation of the application of principles, or setting off of exceptions, on grounds of public policy, was felt to be something abnormal. The classical expression of this feeling is in the opinions of the judges in *Egerton* v. *Lord Brownlow*. Although the case was decided ultimately on the ground of public policy, the remarks of the judges have colored all subsequent judicial thinking on the subject. From the seventeenth century to the end of the nineteenth, juristic theory sought to state all interests in terms of individual natural rights. Moreover, the nineteenth century, under the influence of Hegel, wrote legal history as the unfolding in human experience of an idea of liberty, as an outcome of the clash of individual free wills, leading to the discovery of the invisible bounds within which each might realize a maximum of self-assertion. Thus for a time social interests were pushed into the background. It was said that public policy was "a very unruly horse, and when once you get astride it you never know where it will carry you." It was conceived that a court should be slow and cautious in taking public policy into account, and that if rules of law were to be limited in their application, or if exercise of individual powers of action was to be held down upon such grounds, the matter ought to be left to the legislature.

Questions of public policy came up in three forms: (1) in connection with the validity of testamentary dispositions. Thus different social interests were weighed of conditions in conveyances and testamentary gifts; (3) in connection with the validity of testamentary dispositions. Thus different social interests were weighed against a policy in favor of free contract ("right" of free contract) and a policy in favor of free disposition of property which was taken to be involved in the security of acquisitions and to be a corollary of individual interests of substance (rights of property). Accordingly, distrust of public policy grew out of a feeling that security of acquisitions and security of transactions were paramount policies. " . . . if there is one thing," said Sir George Jessel, "which more than another public policy requires it is that men of full age and competent understanding shall have the utmost liberty of contracting, and that their contracts . . . shall be enforced by Courts of justice."

In truth, the nineteenth-century attitude toward public policy was itself only the expression of a public policy. It resulted from a weighing of the social interest in the general security against other social interests which men had sought to secure through an overwide magisterial discretion in the stage of equity and natural law.

Thus the conception of public policy was never clearly worked out, nor were the several policies recognized by the common law defined as were the individual interests to which the juristic thought of the last century gave substantially its whole attention. The books are full of schemes of natural rights. There are no adequate schemes of public policies. Often the weighing of social interests is disguised by reasoning about "causation," or by the drawing of what seem on their face arbitrary distinctions. But three general types of policies are clearly recognized as such in the law books of the last century. First and most numerous are policies with reference to the security of social institutions. As to political institutions, there is a recognized policy against acts promotive of crime or violation of law – in other words, a policy of upholding legal institutions and a policy against acts prejudicially affecting the public service performed by public officers. As to domestic institutions, there is the well-known policy against acts affecting the security of the domestic relations, or in restraint of marriage. As to economic institutions, there are the policy against acts destructive of competition, the policy against acts affecting commercial freedom, and the policy against permanent or general restrictions on the free use and transfer of property. Secondly, there are policies with reference to maintaining the general morals. Thus there is a recognized policy against acts promotive of dishonesty. Also there is a recognized policy against acts offending the general morals. Thirdly, there are policies with reference to the individual social life: a policy against things tending to oppression, and a policy against general or extensive restrictions upon individual freedom of action. Some of the policies with respect to economic institutions suggest this same interest in the individual life.

In one way or another most of the social interests of which the law must take account today are at least suggested in the list of those recognized as policies in the common law. Yet one social interest which has governed the ideas of lawyers at all times and has played a controlling part in the thought of the immediate past is relatively little stressed as a policy. The social interest in the general security seems to have been thought of as something apart, as something involved in the very idea of law and entering into every legal relation as a necessary element. This appears clearly in nineteenth-century theories as to the end of law and in nineteenth-century juristic method.

Jurists of the last century thought of law as involving restraints on liberty which might only be justified so far as it was necessary in order to maintain liberty. Hence, they conceived that the legal order was to be held down to the minimum which was required to protect the individual against aggression and to secure the harmonious co-existence of the free will of each and the free will of all. But this is only a way of stating a paramount social interest in the general security in terms of individual liberty. Again, men strove zealously in the last century to insure complete security through absolute certainty and uniformity in judicial administration. When the eighteenth-century idea that these things might be attained through a complete and perfect code broke down, they sought to achieve them through a method of mechanical logical deduction from fixed legal conceptions. As this also broke down at many points, lawyers sought the same ends through universal definitions of absolute rights. But behind the quest of certainty and uniformity is their real end – the social interest in the general security. Attempts to administer justice with an eye solely to that one social interest have broken down because of the pressure of other social interests which it has proved impossible to ignore. Exclusive attention to security led jurists to seek abstract, universal, eternal adjustments or harmonizings of conflicting or overlapping interests which were too abstract to prove workable. We have learned slowly that it is the problem – namely, to satisfy human claims and demands and desires – that is constant, not the exact machinery of satisfying them. To go back to the illustrations of the "truck acts," in rural, pioneer, agricultural America there was no call to limit the contracts a laborer might make as to taking his pay in goods. To have imposed a limitation would have interfered with individual freedom of industry and contract without any corresponding gain in securing some other interest. On the other hand, in industrial America of the end of the nineteenth century, a regime of unlimited free contract between employer and employee in certain enterprises led not to conservation but to destruction of values. It led to sacrifice of the social interest in the human life of the individual worker. Hence we began to put limits to liberty of contract between employer and employee and to require wages to be paid in money. It was inevitable that the statutes imposing these limits should be bitterly opposed by a generation which could only think of contracts of employment in terms of individual rights and security of transactions.

Not only did our thinking in the last century deceive itself in supposing that it was proceeding solely on the basis of individual liberty and individual rights deduced therefrom, it deceived itself quite as much in its interpretation of legal development. The conception that pressure of individual interests brought about state and law and fashioned legal institutions has no historical warrant. On the contrary, from the first, the controlling factor is the need of the social group to be secure against those forms of action and courses of conduct which threaten its existence. This paramount social interest is the first interest of any sort to be given legal recognition. It is not too much to say that law in the lawyer's sense of that term arose and primitive law existed simply to maintain one narrow phase of this interest, namely, the social interest in peace and order.

It must be borne in mind that juristic thinking became fixed to no small extent in the mold of the strict law. That mold was largely shaped by the circumstance that in its beginnings law was no more than a means toward the peaceable ordering of society, a regulative agency by which men were restrained and the general security was maintained. Law retains this character of a regulative agency and means toward peaceable ordering, although other functions and other ends become manifest as it develops. Thus the interests which were paramount while law was formative left their mark upon it and fixed the lines of legal thought. In the beginning, in order to establish a peaceable ordering of society, the legal order had to undertake two tasks. It had to regulate self-redress and ultimately to supersede it. It had also to prevent aggression. The simple program of primitive law deals only with assault, homicide, and larceny, which are causes of private war, and with impiety, which it was believed might cause interposition of the gods in the form of natural calamities. In the last century it was easy to say that the former (*i. e.*, giving a remedy for aggression) is private law, the securing of individual interests, while the latter (i.e., putting down impiety) is criminal law – the securing of social interests as such. It is true that putting down private war grew into private law, and in the eighteenth and nineteenth centuries we came to think of it in terms of individual interests only. When self-redress and private war had been put down for centuries, men saw only that the legal order prevented or repaired infringements of individual interests. In primitive society, however, the chief significance of aggression on individuals was that it was certain to lead to private war. Where only the interests of the individual were involved we have another story. As such primitive law ignores him. It was only the free man, head of a household and able to disturb the peace of society, who had standing in the old Roman law to call upon the law for redress. In a society in which groups of kindred are the significant element, a wrong involves much more than the mere injury to John Doe or Richard Roe. In this stage of the strict law men have discovered how to secure the social interest in peace and order by means of legal remedies given to injured individuals.

In a later stage of legal development, the individual human being, the moral unit, becomes the legal unit, and the law seeks to transmute his moral duties into legal duties. In the maturity of law, legal rights are put behind the duties and remedies and orderings and appear to be the ultimate ends for which the legal order exists. It was natural, in that period of legal development, to write legal history from an abstract individualist standpoint and to interpret it as a working out of restrictions upon individual agression in order to secure individual freedom of action. On the contrary, individual freedom of action as an end is something which came into juristic thinking in modern times, as we began to be conscious of a social interest in the individual human life. Individual legal rights were worked out in the endeavor to maintain the social interest in the general security.

Thus the formal remedies of the strict law, the abstract individualist legal philosophy of the nineteenth century, the individualist interpretation of legal history by the historical jurists, in short, the whole training of the lawyer, led him to think of the legal order exclusively in terms of individual rights. When the social interest in the general security is to be weighed in the scale, the courts have had little difficulty. But when other social interests are involved, it has been usual to employ a vague conception of "policy," of which courts and lawyers are rightly mistrustful, since the policies are largely ill-defined and in their application have been felt to leave too much scope for the personal equation of the particular tribunal. Hence pressure of new social interests has given the courts pause and sometimes has led them to cast doubt upon the method of dealing with individual interests which consciously or unconsciously the law has always employed. Today, jurists are having to consider all manner of problems arising from consciousness of new social interests, or at least from new phases of old ones. In contrast to nineteenth-century attempts to state the end of the legal order in terms of security of acquisitions and security of transactions, attempts have been made to state it in terms of the social interest in the individual life, or to value that interest along with the interest in the general security on which the last century insisted almost exclusively. Nor is this change confined to legal thought. Concrete individualization rather than abstract treatment is insisted upon today in every department of human activity. In law this means increased regard for the circumstances of the actual case and results in a continually increasing resort to administrative tribunals or to administrative methods. When we try to generalize the process for legal and judicial purposes, it appears as a conscious recognition of the social interest in the individual life. In criminal law we speak of a "socialized" punitive justice.

An important phase of the social interest in the individual life calls for security to free and spontaneous self-assertion and is connected easily with the juristic thought of the immediate past. But there are many conditions in the life of today in which other phases of this interest must come into account and may call for restrictions upon abstract self-assertion. Thus American legislation restricted the power of Indian allottees to dispose of the tracts allotted to them. British legislation limited the *jus disponendi* of Irish tenants, suddenly turned into proprietors and without experience of economic freedom. Courts of equity avoided sailors' contracts, contracts with heirs and sales of reversions and expectancies, and agreements with debtors clogging their equity of redeeming mortgaged property where there was an economic pressure and only an abstract, theoretical freedom of contract. Back of these doctrines of equity was a dim recognition of a social interest of which we have come to be fully conscious. Today our statute books are full of such restrictions. We do not ask: What will promote the maximum abstract freedom of contract as an item of the general abstract freedom taken to be the end of law? We ask instead: Is it wise social engineering, under the actual social and economic conditions of the time and place, to limit free self-assertion, or what in appearance is free self-assertion, for a time in certain situations? Does it secure a maximum of our scheme of interests as a whole, with the least sacrifice, to leave persons in certain relations free to contract as they choose or as their necessities may seem to dictate, or should we rather limit what is not under actual conditions a free choice? Such a mode of thinking does not fit easily into the method of hard and fast conceptions on which the last generation relied to maintain the general security. A generation ago modern social legislation presented itself to the judicial mind as involving, on the one hand, a natural right of free contract, guaranteed by the Constitution as a part of liberty, and, on the other hand, a hard and fast conception of the police power of the state, defined in terms of public health, safety, and morals. Thus courts were not unlikely to reach an *impasse* and there were sure to be judicial dissents. The net result was to break down the method of conceptions, when used as a method of applying a standard, and to take account of an increasing number of social interests as such. In reality, the courts were using an ideal of the end of law as a measure of reasonableness or of "public purpose," since the "police power" was the power of the government to achieve its ends in ways not forbidden by the fundamental law established in the Constitution.

Perhaps enough has been said to show the practical importance of recognizing social interests as such, instead of thinking of policies, and of a more complete statement of them and a more adequate classification. Yet a satisfactory starting point for such a classification requires some consideration. A generation ago, as a matter of course, we should have relied upon logical deduction. We should have deduced the several social interests as presuppositions of generalized social existence. But schemes of necessary presuppositions of law or of legal institutions seem to me to be at bottom schemes of observed elements in actual legal systems, systematically arranged, reduced to their lowest terms, and deduced, as one might say, to order. I doubt the ability of the jurist to work out deductively, the necessary jural presuppositions of society in the abstract.

At one time it seemed that a more attractive starting point might be found in social psychology. One need only turn to the list of so-called instincts in any of the older social psychologies in order to see an obvious relation between interests, as the jurist now uses that term, or what we had been wont to call natural rights or public policies, on the one hand, and these "instincts" or whatever they are now called, on the other hand. Thus in McDougall's *Social Psychology* we used to find an instinct of repugnance and "predisposition to aesthetic discrimination." In jurisprudence we must consider a social interest in aesthetic surroundings which the law is beginning grudgingly to recognize. In McDougall we used to find an instinct of self-abasement, and in jurisprudence we must consider the so-called right of privacy. Again, to take so-called instincts with which the law has always had much to do, there is evident relation between the "instinct of pugnacity" and the law as to self-defense; between the "instinct of self-assertion" and the anxiety of the law that the will of the individual shall not be trodden upon; between the "instinct of acquisition" and the individual interests of substance and the social interest in the security of acquisitions; between the "instinct of gregariousness" and loyalty and veracity as tendencies or habits connected therewith, and the social interest in the security of transactions. But in the last two decades, after a bitter controversy among sociologists and social psychologists, and redefinitions and substitute categories, most of what was accepted a generation ago in this connection has been pretty much given up. Certainly we can no longer build on McDougall's scheme and such definitions and classifications as are suggested today are remote from what we need in jurisprudence.

If we may not rely upon logical deduction nor upon a theory and classification of what were formerly called instincts, there remains a less pretentious method which may none the less be upon surer ground. If legal phenomena are social phenomena, observation and study of them as such may well bear fruit for social science in general as well as for jurisprudence. Why should not the lawyer make a survey of legal systems in order to ascertain just what claims or demands or desires have pressed or are now pressing for recognition and satisfaction and how far they have been or are now recognized and secured? This is precisely what has been done in the case of individual interests, in the schemes of natural rights, although the process has usually been covered up by a pretentious fabric of logical deduction. The same method may well be applied to social interests, and this should be done consciously and avowedly, as befits the science of today. It is true that objection has been made to this because the same social interest appears behind many legal institutions and doctrines and precepts, and legal institutions and doctrines and precepts almost always have behind them, not one social interest or a simple adjustment or compromise of two, but a complex harmonizing of many. Yet it is of the first importance to perceive this, to note what those interests are, to see how they are adjusted or harmonized or compromised, and to inquire why it is done in this way rather than in another. The first step in such an investigation is a mere survey of the legal order and an inventory of the social interests which have pressed upon lawmakers and judges and jurists for recognition.

In such a survey and inventory, first place must be given to the social interest in the general security – the claim or want or demand, asserted in title of social life in civilized society and through the social group, to be secure against those forms of action and courses of conduct which threaten its existence. Even if we accept Durkheim's view that it is what shocks the general conscience, not what threatens the general security, that is repressed, I suspect that the general conscience reflects experience or superstition as to the general safety. A common-law judge observed that there would be no safety for human life if it were to be considered as law that drunkenness could be shown to negative the intent element of crime where a drunk man kills while intoxicated though he would never do such a thing when sober. It should be noted how the exigencies of the general security outweighed the traditional theory of the criminal law.

This paramount social interest takes many forms. In its simplest form it is an interest in the general safety, long recognized in the legal order in the maxim that the safety of the people is the highest law. It was recognized in American constitutional law in the nineteenth century by putting the general safety along with the general health and general morals in the "police power" as a ground of reasonable restraint to which natural rights must give way. In another form, quite as obvious today but not so apparent in the past, before the nature and causes of disease were understood, it is an interest in the general health. In another form, recognized from the very beginnings of law, it is an interest in peace and public order. In an economically developed society it takes on two other closely related forms, namely, a social interest in the security of acquisitions and a social interest in the security of transactions. The two last came to be well understood in the nineteenth century, in which they were more or less identified with individual interests of substance and individual interests in freedom of contract. Yet a characteristic difference between the law of the eighteenth century and the law of the nineteenth century brings out their true nature. Eighteenth-century courts, taking a purely individualist view, regarded the statute of limitations as something to be held down as much as possible and to be evaded in every way. Lord Mansfield in particular, under the influence of natural-law ideas and thinking of the statute only as an individual plea which enabled the individual interest of a plaintiff to be deprived of legal security, sought out numerous astute contrivances to get around its most obvious provisions. If one said, "I am ready to account, but nothing is due you," if he made provision in his will for the payment of his "just debts," owing them to present their claims, in these and like cases it was held there was an acknowledgement sufficing to take a barred debt out of the statute. Modern courts came to see that there was something more here than the individual interests of plaintiff and defendant. They came to see that the basis of the statute was a social interest in the security of acquisitions, which demands that titles shall not be insecure by being open to attack indefinitely, and a social interest in the security of transactions which demands that the transactions of the past shall not be subject to inquiry indefinitely, so as to unsettle credit and disturb business and trade. If we compare the French rule, *en tout cas de meuble possession vaut titre*, with the Roman doctrine that no one can transfer a greater title than he has, if we note the growth of the idea of negotiability in the law everywhere, and in our law both by legislation and by judicial decision, we may see something of how how far recognition of the social interest in the security of transactions went in the maturity of law.

Other examples of recognition of the security of transactions may be seen in the presumption as to transactions of a corporation through its acting officers, the stress which the courts put upon *stare decisis* in cases involving commercial law, and the doctrine allowing only the sovereign to challenge *ultra vires* conveyances of corporations. As to recognition of the social interest in the security of acquisitions, note the insistence of the courts upon *stare decisis* where rules of property are involved. In such cases it is an established proposition that it is better that the law be settled than that it be settled right.

Second, we may put the social interest in the security of social institutions – the claim or want or demand involved in life in civilized society that its fundamental institutions be secure from those forms of action and courses of conduct which threaten their existence or impair their efficient functioning. Looking at them in chronological order, this interest appears in three forms.

The first is an interest in the security of domestic institutions, long recognized in the form of a policy against acts affecting the security of domestic relations or in restraint of marriage. Legislation intended to promote the family as a social institution has been common. There is a policy against actions by members of the family against each other. Today, although the law is becoming much relaxed, this social interest is still weighed heavily against the individual claims of married persons in most divorce legislation. It still weighs heavily against individual claims in the law as to illegitimate children. At times this has been carried so far that great and numerous disabilities have attached to such children lest recognition of their individual interests should weaken a fundamental social institution. The movement to give independence to married women has had collateral effects of impairing the security of this interest, and the balance is not easy to make nor to maintain. The tendency to relax the rules which formerly obtained is brought out in *Russell* v. *Russell*, in which two of the five law lords dissented as to application of the policy of "preservation of the sanctity of married life," and *Fender* v. *St. John Mildmay*, in which again two of five law lords dissented as to the rule concerning the validity of a promise of marriage before a divorce proceeding has been finally determined. There are, however, recent cases which tend to uphold the policy formerly well established.

It is no doubt too soon to be sure of even the path which juristic thought of the immediate future will follow. But increased weight given to the social interest in the individual life in the concrete, instead of upon abstract liberty, seems to be indicated. There is emphasis upon the concrete claims of concrete human beings . . . Family law, in which there must be a balance between the security of social institutions and the individual life, is necessarily much affected by such a change. In another part of the law, the social interest in the security of domestic institutions still weighs heavily, in comparison, however, with the general security. A wife is not to be held as accessory after the fact for harboring a felon husband or for helping him escape. The common law does not require a wife to choose between fidelity to the relation of husband and wife and duty to the state. Also legislation as to mothers' pensions proceeds at least in large part upon this interest.

A second form is an interest in the security of religious institutions. In the beginning this is closely connected with the general security. A chief point of origin of the criminal law, of that part of the law by which social interests as such are directly and immediately secured, is in religion. Sacrifice of the impious offender who has affronted the gods, and exclusion from society of the impious offender whose presence threatens to bring upon his fellows the wrath of the gods, are, in part at least, the originals of capital punishment and of outlawry. Religious organization was long a stronger and more active agency of social control than political organization. In the Anglo-Saxon laws the appeals or exhortations addressed to the people as Christians are at least as important as the threats addressed to them as subjects. One of the great English statutes of the thirteenth century recites that Parliament had met to make laws "for the common Profit of holy Church, and of the Realm." It is only in relatively recent times that we have come to think of blasphemy as involving no more than a social interest in the general morals, of Sunday laws only in terms of a social interest in the general health, of heresy as less dangerous socially than radical views upon economics or politics, or of preaching or teaching of atheism as involved in a guaranteed liberty. Today what was formerly referred to this interest is usually referred to the social interest in the general morals. Questions as to the interest in the security of religious institutions have been debated in all lands.

In a third form the interest is one in the security of political institutions. This interest has weighed heavily in much twentieth-century legislation too familiar to require more than mention. When the public called for such legislation for the security of political institutions, absolute constitutional guarantees of free speech and natural rights of individual self-assertion, which in other times had moved courts to refuse to enjoin repeated and undoubted libels, lest liberty be infringed, were not suffered to stand in the way. If the individual interests involved had been conceived less absolutely and had been looked at in another light, as identified with a social interest in the general progress, they might have fared better.

Perhaps a fourth form of the interest in the security of social institutions should be added, namely, an interest in the security of economic institutions. Formerly, these were chiefly commercial. Today industrial institutions also must be taken into account. Judicial recognitions of a social interest in the security of commercial institutions are numerous. In a leading case in which it was determined that a bank note payable to bearer passed current the same as coin, Lord Mansfield grounded the judgment "upon the general course of business, and . . . the consequence to trade and commerce: which would be much incommoded by a contrary determination." More than one decision in the last generation on labor law seems to go upon an interest in maintaining the industrial regime in the face of persistent pressure from the claims of organized workingmen. Some of the policies to be considered presently under the social interest in general progress might be referred to this head.

Third, we may put the social interest in the general morals, the claim or want or demand involved in social life in civilized society to be secured against acts or courses of conduct offensive to the moral sentiments of the general body of individuals therein for the time being. This interest is recognized in Roman law in the protection of *boni mores*. It is recognized in our law by policies against dishonesty, corruption, gambling, and things of immoral tendency; by treating continuing menaces to the general morals as nuisances; and by the common-law doctrine that acts contrary to good morals and subversive of general morals are misdemeanors. It is recognized in equity in the maxim that he who comes into equity must come with clean hands. Similar provisions are to be found in the private law and in the criminal law in other lands. Obstinately held ideas of morality may in time come in conflict with ideas arising from changed social and economic conditions or newer religious and philosophical views. In such cases we must reach a balance between the social interest in the general progress, taking form in a policy of free discussion. What was said above as to free speech and writing and the social interest in security of social institutions applies here also.

Fourth, there is the social interest in conservation of social resources, that is, the claim or want or demand involved in social life in civilized society that the goods of existence shall not be wasted; that where all human claims or wants or desires may not be satisfied, in view of infinite individual desires and limited natural means of satisfying them, the latter be made to go as far as possible; and, to that end, that acts or courses of conduct which tend needlessly to destroy or impair these goods shall be restrained. In its simplest form this is an interest in the use and conservation of natural resources, and is recognized in the doctrines as to *res communes*, which may be used but not owned, by the common law as to riparian rights and constitutional and statutory provisions where irrigation is practiced, by modern game laws, by the recent doctrines as to percolating water and surface water, and by laws as to waste of natural gas and oil. There has been a progressive tendency to restrict the *ius abutendi* which the maturity of law attributed to owners. A crowded and hungry world may yet weigh this interest against individual claims to free action still further by preventing destruction of commodities in order to keep up prices, or even cutting off the common-law liberty of the owner of land to sow it to salt if he so desires. At times overproduction of agricultural products has led to proposals for restriction of the owner's *ius utendi* by regulation of what crops he may raise. At other times there are projects for administrative appointment of receivers of agricultural land cultivated or managed by the owner "in such a manner as to prejudice materially the production of food thereon . . ." Restrictions with respect to housing proceed on another aspect of this same social interest.

A closely related social interest is one in protection and training of dependents and defectives. It might from one point of view be called an interest in conservation of the human assets of society. In one form it was recognized long ago in the common-law system by the jurisdiction of the chancellor, representing the king as *parens patriae*, over infants, lunatics, and idiots. This jurisdiction has had a significant development in recent times in the juvenile court, and an extension to youthful offenders beyond the period of infancy is being urged. Again, there has been an extension of the idea of protection and training of dependents, on one hand to the reformation of mature delinquents, and on another hand to protection of the mature who are yet economically more or less dependent. This has gone a long way in recent times in social security or social insurance legislation and in small loan legislation. The latter has had a historical background in the interference of equity to prevent oppression of debtors and necessitous persons. Also after the first world war there was legislative recognition of a social interest in rehabilitation of the maimed. Much of the legislation referred to runs counter to the insistence upon abstract individual liberty in the juristic theory of the last century. It was formerly often pronounced arbitrary and so unconstitutional by courts whose dogmatic scheme could admit no social interest other than the general security. There has been a significant widening of the field of legally recognized and secured social interests. But for the most part the claims or demands here considered are better treated in connection with the social interest in the individual life.

Fifth, there is the social interest in general progress, that is, the claim or want or demand involved in social life in civilized society, that the development of human powers and of human control over nature for the satisfaction of human wants go forward; the demand that social engineering be increasingly and continuously improved; as it were, the self-assertion of the social group toward higher and more complete development of human powers. This interest appears in three main forms, an interest in economic progress, an interest in political progress, and an interest in cultural progress. The social interest in economic progress has long been recognized in law and has been secured in many ways. In the common law it is expressed in four policies: the policy as to freedom of property from restrictions upon sale or use, the policy as to free trade and consequent policy against monopoly, the policy as to free industry, which has had to give much ground in recent legislation and judicial decision, and the policy as to encouragement of invention, which is behind patent legislation and there comes in conflict with the policy as to free trade. All of these policies have important consequences in everyday law. It may be thought that some of them should be classified rather as forms of a social interest in the security of economic institutions. As I read the cases, however, these demands have pressed upon courts and jurists from the standpoint of their relation to economic progress. If that relation fails, they are not likely to maintain themselves. Likewise the law has long recognized a social interest in political progress. In American bills of rights, and in written constitutions generally, a policy of free criticism of public men, public acts, and public officers, and a policy of free formation, free holding, and free expression of political opinion are guaranteed as identified with individual rights. Moreover, at common law, the privilege of fair comment upon public men and public affairs recognizes and secures the same interest. But the third form, the social interest in cultural progress, has not been recognized in the law so clearly. It may be said to involve four policies: a policy of free science, a policy of free letters, a policy of encouragement of arts and letters, and a policy of promotion of higher learning. The first two have made their way more slowly because of conflict or supposed conflict with the security of religious and political institutions.

Closely connected with the interest in cultural progress is a social interest in aesthetic surroundings, which recently has been pressing for legal recognition. Fifty years ago, Sir Frederick Pollock could say with assurance that our law ignored aesthetic relations, and, comparing the English with the French in this respect, could quote Hood's lines:

Nature which gave them the goût
Only gave us the gout.

In the United States, courts and legislatures were long engaged in a sharp struggle over billboard laws and laws against hideous forms of outdoor advertising. For a time also the interest pressed in another way in connection with town planning legislation. It is significant that the courts are now ready to admit a policy in favor of the aesthetic as reasonable and constitutionally permissible.

Last and in some ways most important of all, as we now are coming to think, there is the social interest in the individual life. One might call it the social interest in the individual moral and social life, or in the individual human life. It is the claim or want or demand involved in social life in civilized society that each individual be able to live a human life therein according to the standard of the society. It is the claim or want or demand that, if all individual wants may not be satisfied, they be satisfied at least so far as is reasonably possible and to the extent of a human minimum. Three forms of this social interest have been recognized in common law or in legislation: individual self-assertion, individual opportunity, and individual conditions of life. The first, the interest in free self-assertion, includes physical, mental, and economic activity. In Spencer's scheme of natural rights, they appear as a "right of free motion and locomotion," a "right of free exchange and free contract," deduced as a sort of free economic motion and locomotion, a "right of free industry," deduced expressly as a modern outgrowth of free motion and locomotion, as a right of free economic activity, a "right of free religious belief and opinion" and a right of free political belief and opinion, the two last being deduced also as modern developments of the same natural right of free motion and locomotion. These are deduced from a "law of equal freedom" which is taken to have been discovered by observation of social phenomena and verified by further observation. Without the aid of his "law of equal freedom" he might have found them by observation of the policies set forth in the law books. The old common-law policy in favor of freedom, the doctrine that one may justify by his natural liberty of action, except where his action takes the form of aggression and so threatens the general security, and in part the policy of free industry, are examples of recognition of a social interest in individual physical self-assertion. The policy in favor of free speech and free belief and opinion, although related also to the social interest in political progress, must be referred in part to a social interest in individual mental self-assertion. Policies favoring free trade and free industry are in part referable to a social interest in free economic self-assertion.

But the most important phase of the social interest in individual self-assertion, from the standpoint of modern law, is what might be called the social interest in freedom of the individual will – the claim or interest, or policy recognizing it, that the individual will shall not be subjected arbitrarily to the will of others. This interest is recognized in an old common-law policy which is declared in the Fifth and Fourteenth Amendments. If one will is to be subjected to the will of another through the force of politically organized society, it is not to be done arbitrarily, but is to be done upon some rational basis, which the person coerced, if reasonable, could appreciate. It is to be done upon a reasoned weighing of the interests involved and a reasoned attempt to reconcile them or adjust them. This policy obviously expresses political and juristic experience of what modern psychology has discovered as to the ill effects of repression. For example, it is more and more recognized today in our penal legislation and in our treatment of offenders. It has come to be recognized particularly of late as a result of pressure upon courts and lawmakers for security in the relation of employer and employee. It is coming to be recognized also in juristic thought in another connection as sociological theories of property replace metaphysical theories. There are many signs of a growing feeling that complete exclusion of all but him whom the law pronounces owner from objects which are the natural media of human existence or means of human activity, must be measured and justified by a reasoned attempt to harmonize them or to save as much as we may with the sacrifice of as little on the part of the excluded, no less than on the part of the owner, as we may.

I have called a second form the social interest in individual opportunity. It is the claim or want or demand involved in social life in civilized society that all individuals shall have fair or reasonable (perhaps, as we are coming to think, we must say equal) opportunities – political, physical, cultural, social, and economic. In American thinking we have insisted chiefly on equal political opportunities, since in the pioneer conditions in which our institutions were formative other opportunities, so far as men demanded them, were at hand everywhere. But a claim to fair physical opportunities is recognized in public provision of parks and playgrounds and in public provisions for recreation; the claim to fair cultural opportunities is recognized by laws as to compulsory education of children (although the social interests in general progress and in dependents are also recognized here) as well as by state provisions for universities and for adult education; the claim to fair social opportunities is recognized by civil rights laws; and the claim to fair economic opportunities is recognized, for example, in the legal right to "freedom of the market," and in the so-called "right to pursue a lawful calling," which is weighed with other social interests in regulating training for and admission to professions.

In a third form, a interest in individual conditions of life, the social interest in the individual life appears as a claim that each individual shall have assued to him the conditions of at least a minimum human life under the circumstances of life in the time and place. I have said minimum, which certainly was all that was recognized until relatively recent times. But perhaps we should now say reasonable or even equal. A claim for equal conditions of life is pressing and we can't put the matter as to what is recognized with assurance as we could have done a generation ago. Moreover, the scope of generally asserted demands with respect to the individual life is obviously growing. The Roman law recognized a policy of this sort, and it has long been recognized in American legislation. In weighing individual interests in view of the social interest in security of acquisitions and security of transactions, we must also take account of the social interest in the human life of each individual, and so must restrict the legal enforcement of demands to what is consistent with a human existence on the part of the person subjected thereto. The Roman law imposed such a limitation in a number of cases in what is called the *beneficium competentiae.* At common law there were restrictions on what could be taken in distress for rent, and the thirteenth-century statute providing for execution by writ of *elegit* exempts the debtor's oxen and beasts of the plow and half of his land. In the United States and recently in continental Europe, this policy is given effect in homestead laws and in exemptions from execution. In the latter, the social interest in the family as a social institution is also a factor. But nineteenth-century opposition to homestead and exemption laws, and in Europe to the *beneficium competentiae*, is significant. The nineteenth century sought to treat such cases as if they involved nothing more than the individual interests of the parties to the debtor-creditor relation, or, if a social interest was considered, sought to think only of the general security, which here takes the form of security of transactions. Other recognitions of this interest may be seen in restrictions on the power of debtors or contractors to saddle themselves with oppressive burdens, as in the doctrines of equity heretofore referred to, as in usury laws, and more recently in "loan shark" legislation. A notable instance in recent judicial decision may be seen in the English doctrine as to covenants not to exercise the calling for which one has trained himself. Statutes forbidding contracts by laborers to take their pay in orders on company stores, and as to conditions and hours of labor, minimum wage laws, child labor laws, and housing laws, are recognitions of the same interest.

Again, when the law confers or exercises a power of control, we feel that the legal order should safeguard the human existence of the person controlled. Thus the old-time sea law, with its absolute power of the master over the sailor, the old-time ignominious punishments, that treated the human offender like a brute, that did not save his human dignity – all such things are disappearing as the circle of recognized interests widens and we come to take account of the social interest in the individual life and to weigh that interest with the social interest in the general security, on which the last century insisted so exclusively.

Such in outline are the social interests which are recognized or are coming to be recognized in modern law. Looked at functionally, the law is an attempt to satisfy, to reconcile, to harmonize, to adjust these overlapping and often conflicting claims and demands, either through securing certain individual interests, or through delimitations or compromises of individual interests, so as to give effect to the greatest total of interests or to the interests that weigh most in our civilization, with the least sacrifice of the scheme of interests as a whole.

Pound first developed his theory of interests in 1914 [*Outlines of Lectures in Jurisprudence* 56-59 (2nd ed. 1914)], revised it in 1921 ["A Theory of Social Interests"

(1921) 15 Proc. Amer. Soc. Soc'y 16], and published the definitive version in the 1943 article reproduced above. His treatment of social interests in *Jurisprudence*, III 268-324 (1959) is merely a reproduction of the 1943 article.

The five stages of legal history, which are somewhat obliquely stated above but which are emphasized in earlier writings, are: (1) primitive law – the end of law in this stage is to keep the peace, especially to prevent the blood-feud; (2) strict law – the end is certainty and uniformity (Roman law or in England the fourteenth and fifteenth centuries); (3) equity and natural law – in this stage there is a loosening of strict law by moral ideas; (4) maturity of law – certainty returns as a paramount end, but this time accompanied by security of expectations and equality as additional ends; (5) socialization of law – in this stage there is an infusion of a sociological conception of morals. For a fuller development of the stages of legal history, see Patterson, *Jurisprudence* 513-516 (1953).

Roscoe Pound, 1870-1964

MY PHILOSOPHY OF LAW

I think of law as in one sense a highly specialized form of social control in a developed politically organized society – a social control through the systematic and orderly application of the force of such a society. In this sense it is a regime – the regime which we call the legal order. But that regime operates in a systematic and orderly fashion because of a body of authoritative grounds of or guides to determination which may serve as rules of decision, as rules of or guides to conduct, and as bases of prediction of official action, or may be regarded by the bad men, whose attitude is suggested by Mr. Justice Holmes as a test, as threats of official action which he must take account of before he acts or refrains from action. Moreover, it operates through a judicial process and an administrative process, which also go by the name of law – a development and application of the authoritative grounds of or guides to determination by employing a received and so authoritative technique by the light of received and so authoritative ideals. The idea of system and order and predictability lies behind every meaning which has been given to the term law – to all of what the analytical jurist calls analogous uses of the term – and every application of the word until the rise in recent times of absolutist ideas which would apply the term to whatever is done by those who wield the powers of a politically organized society simply because, and no matter how, they do it.

When, therefore, one asks himself what is the task of the law, what is the end to which this regime, maintained by politically organized societies, adjusting relations and ordering conduct through a judicial and an administrative process, and carried on by employing a body of recognized or established precepts, applied by an authoritative technique in the light of authoritative ideals – when one asks himself what all this complicated machinery is for, the answer must be that the end, whatever it is, is the end of social control of which law in all three of its meanings is a specialized form. But we cannot neglect that question, difficult of answer and far reaching in the implications of the answer as it may be. For received ideas as to the answer, traditionally established, are an important item in the received grounds of or guides to determination of controversies and are decisive in the choice of starting points for legal reasoning, the interpretation of legal precepts and the application of legal standards.

A prevailing type of philosophical thought today, going upon Kantian epistemology, tells us we cannot answer this question. No doubt we cannot answer it absolutely. But law in all its meanings is a practical matter. If we cannot give an answer which will be absolutely demonstrable to every one and wholly convincing to the philosopher, it does not follow that we may not have a good workable blueprint of what we are trying to do and be able to make a good practical approximation to what we seek to achieve. There are many practical activities the postulates of which will not bear critical logical examination if we demand of them an absolute correspondence of phenomena to theory, but nevertheless serve their practical purposes very well. If, as is now taught, we live in a curved universe in which there are no planes and straight lines and right angles and perpendiculars, it does not follow that we must give up surveying which does its work satisfactorily on the basis of such postulates. If we cannot make a watertight domonstration of the end to which the legal order is directed in practice, if we cannot attain that end completely, the history of civilization shows we can make a continually closer practical approximation, and that it is because of this practical approximation that the legal order and the body of authoritative grounds of or guides to determination have been able to develop and maintain themselves.

What we are seeking to do and must do in a civilized society is to adjust relations and order conduct in a world in which the goods of existence, the scope for free activity, and the objects on which to exert free activity are limited, and the demands upon those goods and those objects are infinite. To order the activities of men in their endeavor to satisfy their demands so as to enable satisfaction of as much of the whole scheme of demands with the least friction and waste has not merely been what lawmakers and tribunals and jurists have been striving for, it has also been put in one way or another by philosophers as what we ought to be doing. Life in accord with nature or measured by reason (that is, in accord with an ideal in which the perfect man seeks only what as such he ought to have, and renders to others as perfect men what they ought to have) reconciling wills of free men in action by a universal law giving a maximum scope for free activity to each, reconciling of what used to be called instincts in action, bringing about a maximum of happiness, satisfying the wants of each so far as compatible with satisfying the wants of all – these are different ways of putting this practical task which the courts and lawyers have been going about doing in a practical way from the time when the rise of political organization of society led to courts and lawyers as agents of organized social control.

If, as lawyers must, we look at law, in all of its senses, functionally with respect to its ends, as that end is at bottom the end of social control, our science of law cannot be self-sufficient. Ethics has to do with another great agency of social control covering much of the ground covered by the legal order and having much to tell us as to what legal precepts ought to be and ought to bring about. Security which the law, in an adjustment of relations, has continually to seek to keep in balance with the individual life, is in special degree called for by the economic order which is the subject of another social science. We cannot ignore it in a science of law, but just as some sought to merge jurisprudence in ethics, there are those who would refer everything in law in all of its senses to economics, with no more warrant. Again, there is the science of politics. Since the legal order is a regime of social control through politically organized society, the science which organizes our knowledge of such societies cannot be ignored, although jurists in the English-speaking world have been wont to give it an exaggerated importance in their interpretation of legal history and their accounts of legal institutions. Sociology has for a time gone off into methodology and is more concerned with demonstrating that it is a separate science, by developing its separate method, than with organizing our knowledge of the phenomena of human association. But the science of society did much for the law a generation ago and can do so again particularly in what has been called social psychology. History is not to be overlooked. The history of civilization has much to tell us of how law has operated to maintain and further civilization, how it has grown out of civilization, how it has been adapted to new types of civilization, and perhaps how at times it has hindered, as at other times it has furthered, civilization. Finally, there is psychology, with much to tell us not only about the claims and demands we must be busied to reconcile or adjust, but also about the bases of the conduct we seek to order and the underlying bases of the processes, judicial and administrative, as well as the lawmaking process, by which the legal order is maintained and the precepts by which those processes are to be guided are devised and formulated.

From Roman times, except for analytical jurists in the nineteenth century, philosophy has been recognized as something indispensable for the jurist. In a great part of the history of juristic thought it has been misused to frame ideal systems of legal precepts of supposed universal validity for times, places, and men. But it has a task of the first importance in organizing and criticizing the ideal element in the body of authoritative grounds of and guides to determination. When it seeks to do more than that, and, on the one hand, furnish a universal plan or absolute starting points or charts for all times and places, or on the other hand, to tell us that we can't do anything but observe the unfolding of an idea by its intrinsic power or the orbit of development according to fixed laws, as beyond our control as the revolutions of the planets, or that we are inevitably caught in a mess of irreducible antinomies so that we can do no more than let things work themselves out, the lawyer has learned to cease to follow the philosopher and to go on upon the basis of experience developed by reason and reason tested by experience. The philosophical jurisprudence of the seventeenth and eighteenth centuries held that everything in the science of law could be achieved by a sheer exercise of reason. Philosophy was the one necessary instrument of the jurist. The metaphysical jurisprudence of the nineteenth century held that philosophy could demonstrate the idea that was realizing itself in legal development or the orbit of legal evolution, but after showing us these necessary paths from which there was no escape, it could not help us. Much of philosophy of law today is equally assured that we cannot do much toward making law in all its senses achieve its end better. These give-it-up philosophies and the juristic skepticism to which they lead, or which they aid and abet, may serve for philosophies of law. They will not be of help as philosophical jurisprudence.

In the nineteenth century jurists were concerned chiefly with three problems: the nature of law, the interpretation of legal history, and the relation of law and morals.

As to the nature of law, as I see it our difficulties lie in the different meanings for which we have been using the one word. In the languages of Continental Europe the word we translate as law has a meaning for which we have no word in English and conveys an idea very hard for us to understand, which can only be indicated by some such awkward phrase as right-plus-law or what-is-right-backed-by-law. But if we read critically the books in our own tongue we soon perceive that "law" may mean any one of the three things I indicated at the outset and that some address themselves to the nature of the legal order, some to the nature of the body of authoritative grounds of or guides to decision, and some to the process of adjudication or the process of administration, and assume that a theory of the one will of course do for the other two. Moreover, the oldest of the meanings as employed by jurists, namely, the body of authoritative guides to decision, usually thought of down to Kant and very generally since as a body of rules of conduct, is composite. Instead of being, as Bentham took it to be, an aggregate of laws, that is, of rules in the strict sense, such as the provisions of a penal code, it is made up of precepts, an authoritative technique of developing and applying the precepts, and a body of received ideals as to the end or purpose of the legal order, and hence to what legal precepts ought to be and how they ought to be applied. These received ideals are just as authoritative as the traditionally received precepts and are often much more obstinate and manifestly are longer lived than the rules which were all that the analytical jurist could see in the last century.

But this is not all. The precept element in law in the second sense has no less than four constituents: rules in the strict sense, principles, precepts defining conceptions, and precepts prescribing standards. If all of these could be called rules in a wider sense, yet conceptions and standards, which play very important roles in the administration of justice, are not rules in any sense. Indeed, much harm has been done in American constitutional law by trying to reduce the standard of due process of law to a body of rules analogous to rules of property.

By rules I mean precepts attaching a definite detailed legal consequence to a definite detailed state of facts or situation of fact. Such rules were the staple of ancient codes and are found today chiefly in criminal law, in commercial law, and in the law of property.

By principles I mean authoritative starting points for legal reasoning. They do not attach any definite detailed consequence to any definite, much less detailed, state or situation of fact. They furnish a basis for reasoning when a stituation not governed by a precise rule comes up for consideration as to what provision should be made for it. By legal conceptions I mean authoritatively defined categories into which cases may be put with the result that certain rules and principles and standards become applicable. Such things as trust, sale, bailment, will occur to one at once in this connection. Legal standards are defined measures of conduct, to be applied according to the circumstances of each case, entailing liability to respond for resulting injury in case the limits of the standard are departed from. There is no definite state of facts provided for and no definite detailed consequence is prescribed. Examples are the standard of due care, the standard of fair conduct of a fiduciary, the standard of reasonable facilities imposed on a public utility.

When it is perceived how much we have been seeking to embrace in the one word "law," it will be seen why so much of the discussion as to the nature of law in the last century was so futile.

With the passing of the era of history, for such was the nineteenth century, the interpretation of legal history is no longer taken to be the key to the science of law, and economics and psychology have arisen to furnish universal solvents instead. As to the relation of law and morals, we have again to contend with difficulties due to the use of one word with more than one meaning in a connection in which the contest will not distinguish, because the writer does not. When we write of the relation of law and morals we may mean the relation of the legal order to a received body of ethical custom in a time and place or to an organized body of principles as to what conduct ought to be, not actually obtaining anywhere, but arrived at by speculation instead of by observation. Or we may mean the relation of the body of received grounds of or guides to decision to either or both of what are put under the name "morals." Or we may mean the relation of the judicial or of the administrative process or of both to either or both of the things for which the word "morals" has been used. It is not unlikely that we may try to reason about the relation of the three to the two as if there were one idea on each side as there is one word. What we can say is that if for convenience we think of the body of speculative principles as morals, each of these, as well as law in each of its senses, is an agency of social control. Partly their spheres overlap and in the common area they reinforce or ought to reinforce each other. Partly they deal with matters exclusively in their own domain, where nevertheless they may and do influence each other. But beyond this general statement one cannot go without distinguishing the different meanings of each word.

Today, in my judgment, the most important problem which confronts the jurist is the theory of interests. A legal system attains the ends of the legal order (1) by recognizing certain interests, individual, public, and social; (2) by defining the limits within which these interests shall be recognized legally and given effect through legal precepts; and (3) by endeavoring to secure the interests so recognized within the defined limits. I should define an interest, for the present purpose, as a demand or desire which human beings either individually or in groups or in associations or in relations, seek to satisfy, of which, therefore, the ordering of human relations must take account. This needs to be put psychologically, but we must avoid the controverted questions of group psychology. It is not group demands or desires, but the strivings of men in (or perhaps one should say through) groups and associations and relations to satisfy certain demands or desires. The legal order or the law does not create these interests. There is this much truth in the old idea of a state of nature and theory of natural rights, namely, that interests in this sense would exist if there were no legal order but were some other form of social control, and no body of authoritative guides to conduct or decision. Conflicts or competition between interests arise because of the competition of individuals with each other, the competition of groups or societies of men with each other, and the competition of individuals with such groups or societies, in the endeavor to satisfy human wants. The law, then, does not create these interests. But it classifies them and recognizes a larger or smaller number. Also it defines the extent to which it will give effect to these interests which it recognizes. It may do this in view of other interests. These other interests may be directly recognized and limited or secured, for example, by creating a legal right enforceable by action at law, or by a legal power such as the power of the wife to pledge the husband's credit for necessaries, so that the limits of the right or power must be fixed. For example, the right of reputation is limited by the privilege of confidential communication, and the power of the wife is limited to cases of living apart without her fault. Or the extent to which it will give effect to recognized interests may be limited in view of other interests which get only indirect recognition through limitations imposed on expressly recognized interests. For example, at common law the interest of the child is indirectly recognized by limiting the father's privilege of correction. Or the extent to which legally recognized interests are given effect may be limited in view of the possibilities of effectively securing them through the legal order. Next, the legal order devises means for securing interests when recognized and within the defined limits.

Hence in determining the scope and subject matter of the legal system we have to consider five things: (1) we must take an inventory of the interests which press for recognition and must generalize them and classify them; (2) we must select and determine the interests which the law should recognize and seek to secure; (3) we must fix the limits of securing the interests so selected – this, for example, is the whole problem in the secondary boycott cases; (4) we must consider the means by which the law may secure interests when recognized and delimited, that is, we must take account of the limitations upon effective legal action which may preclude complete recognition or complete securing of interests which otherwise we seek to secure, as, for example, in the case of the rights of husband and wife to consortium as against each other; (5) in order to do these things we must work out principles of valuation of interests. The chief importance of these principles is in determining what interests to recognize, or, in other words, in selection of interests to be recognized. But we must use these principles also in fixing the limits of securing recognized interests, and fixing upon the means of securing interests, and in judging of the weight to be accorded in any given case to the practical limitations upon effective legal action.

We are told nowadays that it is impossible to find a measure of values. But some such measure will be used as different ones have been used in different stages of legal development in the past. Moreover, a practical one, as pointed out above, has long been used and has worked reasonably well. It is when courts and lawmakers have departed from this to follow philosophical theories not based on scientifically developed experience that difficulties have arisen. The practitioner of the last generation was distinctly ahead of the jurists if we judge his practice and their theories by the direction which the law has been taking in the last three decades. Bringing to bear upon these problems scientific scrutiny of experience in finding how to deal effectively with concrete cases, being cautious about generalizations and universal formulas, useful as they are when enough concrete observation is behind them, if not a method of jurisprudence, is the method of Anglo-American law and has been the method which has enabled that system of law to go round the world. If we are inclined to scoff at the practitioner, let us remember the warning of William James that the worst enemies of a subject are the professors thereof.

Benjamin N. Cardozo, 1870-1938
Judge of New York Supreme Court and of the New York Court of Appeals, then Chief Justice of New York, and finally Associate Justice of the United States Supreme Court.

THE NATURE OF THE JUDICIAL PROCESS

LECTURE I. INTRODUCTION. THE METHOD OF PHILOSOPHY

. . . The common law does not work from pre-established truths of universal and inflexible validity to conclusions derived from them deductively. Its method is inductive, and it draws its generalizations from particulars. The process has been admirably stated by Munroe Smith: "In their effort to give to the social sense of justice articulate expression in rules and in principles, the method of the law-finding experts has always been experimental. The rules and principles of case law have never been treated as final truths, but as working hypotheses, continually retested in those great laboratories of the law, the courts of justice. Every new case is an experiment; and if the accepted rule which seems applicable yields a result which is felt to be unjust, the rule is reconsidered. It may not be modified at once, for the attempt to do absolute justice in every single case would make the development and maintenance of general rules impossible; but if a rule continues to work injustice, it will eventually be reformulated. The principles themselves are continually retested; for if the rules derived from a principle do not work well, the principle itself must ultimately be re-examined". . . .

In this perpetual flux, the problem which confronts the judge is in reality a twofold one: he must first extract from the precedents the underlying principle, the *ratio decidendi*; he must then determine the path or direction along which the principle is to move and develop, if it is not to wither and die.

The first branch of the problem is the one to which we are accustomed to address ourselves more consciously than to the other. Cases do not unfold their principles for the asking. They yield up their kernel slowly and painfully. The instance cannot lead to a generalization till we know it as it is. That in itself is no easy task. For the thing adjudged comes to us oftentimes swathed in obscuring dicta, which must be stripped off and cast aside. Judges differ greatly in their reverence for the illustrations and comments and side-remarks of their predecessors, to make no mention of their own. All agree that there may be dissent when the opinion is filed. Some would seem to hold that there must be none a moment thereafter. Plenary inspiration has then descended upon the work of the majority. No one, of course, avows such a belief, and yet sometimes there is an approach to it in conduct. I own that it is a good deal of a mystery to me how judges, of all persons in the world, should put their faith in dicta. A brief experience on the bench was enough to reveal to me all sorts of cracks and crevices and loopholes in my own opinions when picked up a few months after delivery, and reread with due contrition. The persuasion that one's own infallibility is a myth leads by easy stages and with somewhat greater satisfaction to a refusal to ascribe infallibility to others. But dicta are not always ticketed as such, and one does not recognize them always at a glance. There is the constant need, as every law student knows, to separate the accidental and the non-essential from the essential and inherent. Let us assume too that the principle, latent within it, has been skillfully extracted and accurately stated. Only half or less than half of the work has yet been done. The problem remains to fix the bounds and the tendencies of development and growth, to set the directive force in motion along the right path at the parting of the ways.

The directive force of a principle may be exerted along the line of logical progression; this I will call the rule of analogy or the method of philosophy; along the line of historical development; this I will call the method of evolution; along the line of the customs of the community; this I will call the method of tradition; along the lines of justice, morals and social welfare, the *mores* of the day; and this I will call the method of sociology.

I have put first among the principles of selection to guide our choice of paths, the rule of analogy or the method of philosophy. In putting it first, I do not mean to rate it as most important. On the contrary, it is often sacrificed to others. I have put it first because it has, I think, a certain presumption in its favor. Given a mass of particulars, a congeries of judgments on related topics, the principle that unifies and rationalizes them has a tendency, and a legitimate one, to project and extend itself to new cases within the limits of its capacity to unify and rationalize. It has the primacy that comes from natural and orderly and logical succession. Homage is due to it over every competing principle that is unable by appeal to history or tradition or policy or justice to make out a better right. All sorts of deflecting forces may appear to contest its sway and absorb its power. At least, it is the heir presumptive. A pretender to the title will have to fight his way. . . .

. . . The judge who moulds the law by the method of philosophy may be satisfying an intellectual craving for symmetry of form and substance. But he is doing something more. He is keeping the law true in its response to a deep-seated and imperious sentiment. Only experts perhaps may be able to gauge the quality of his work and appraise its significance. But their judgement, the judgement of the lawyer class, will spread to others, and tinge the common consciousness and the common faith. In default of other tests, the method of philosophy must remain the organon of the courts if chance and favor are to be excluded, and the affairs of men are to be governed with the serene and impartial uniformity which is of the essence of the idea of law. . . .

LECTURE II. THE METHODS OF HISTORY, TRADITION AND SOCIOLOGY

. . . Three of the directive forces of our law, philosophy, history and custom, have now been seen at work. We have gone far enough to appreciate the complexity of the problem. We see that to determine to be loyal to precedents and to the principles back of precedents does not carry us far upon the road. Principles are complex bundles. It is well enough to say that we shall be consistent, but consistent with what? Shall it be consistency with the origins of the rule, the course and tendency of development? Shall it be consistency with logic or philosophy or the fundamental conceptions of jurisprudence as disclosed by analysis of our own and foreign systems? All these loyalties are possible. All have sometimes prevailed. How are we to choose between them? Putting that question aside, how do we choose between them? Some concepts of the law have been in peculiar sense historical growths. In such departments, history will tend to give direction to development. In other departments, certain large and fundamental concepts, which comparative jurisprudence shows to be common to other highly developed systems, loom up above all others. In these we shall give a larger scope to logic and symmetry. A broad field there also is in which rules may, with approximately the same convenience, be settled one way or the other. Here custom tends to assert itself as the controlling force in guiding the choice of paths. Finally, when the social needs demand one settlement rather than another, there are times when we must bend symmetry, ignore history and sacrifice custom in the pursuit of other and larger ends.

From history and philosophy and custom, we pass, therefore, to the force which in our day and generation is becoming the greatest of them all, the power of social justice which finds its outlet and expression in the method of sociology.

The final cause of law is the welfare of society. The rule that misses its aim cannot permanently justify its existence. "Ethical consideration can no more be excluded from the administration of justice which is the end and purpose of all civil laws than one can exclude the vital air from his room and live." Logic and history and custom have their place. We will shape the law to conform to them when we may; but only within bounds. The end which the law serves will dominate them all. There is an old legend that on one occasion God prayed, and his prayer was "Be it my will that my justice be ruled by my mercy." That is a prayer which we all need to utter at times when the demon of formalism tempts the intellect with the lure of scientific order. I do not mean, of course, that judges are commissioned to set aside existing rules at pleasure in favor of any other set of rules which they may hold to be expedient or wise. I mean that when they are called upon to say how far existing rules are to be extended or restricted, they must let the welfare of society fix the path, its direction and its distance. We are not to forget, said Sir George Jessel, in an often quoted judgment, that there is this paramount public policy, that we are not lightly to interfere with freedom of contract. So in this field, there may be a paramount public policy, one that will prevail over temporary inconvenience or occasional hardship, not lightly to sacrifice certainty and uniformity and order and coherence. All these elements must be considered. They are to be given such weight as sound judgment dictates. They are constituents of that social welfare which it is our business to discover. In a given instance we may find that they are constituents of preponderating value.

In others, we may find that their value is subordinate. We must appraise them as best we can. . . .

Social welfare is a broad term. I use it to cover many concepts more or less allied. It may mean what is commonly spoken of as public policy, the good of the collective body. In such cases, its demands are often those of mere expediency or prudence. It may mean on the other hand the social gain that is wrought by adherence to the standards of right conduct, which find expression in the *mores* of the community. In such cases, its demands are those of religion or of ethics or of the social sense of justice, whether formulated in creed or system, or immanent in the common mind. . . .

The courts, then, are free in marking the limits of the individual's immunities to shape their judgements in accordance with reason and justice. That does not mean that in judging the validity of statutes they are free to substitute their own ideas of reason and justice for those of the men and women whom they serve. Their standard must be an objective one. In such matters, the thing that counts is not what I believe to be right. It is what I may reasonably believe that some other man of normal intellect and conscience might reasonably look upon as right. . . .

LECTURE III. THE METHOD OF SOCIOLOGY. THE JUDGE AS LEGISLATOR.

. . . Scholars of distinction have argued for a more subjective standard. "We all agree," says Professor Gray, "that many cases should be decided by the courts on notions of right and wrong, and, of course, everyone will agree that a judge is likely to share the notions of right and wrong prevalent in the community in which he lives; but suppose in a case where there is nothing to guide him but notions of right and wrong, that his notions of right and wrong differ from those of the community – which ought he to follow – his notions, or the notions of the community? Mr. Carter's theory ["Origin and Sources of Law," J. C. Carter] requires him to say that the judge must follow the notions of the community. I believe that he should follow his own notions." The hypothesis that Professor Gray offers us is not likely to be realized in practice. Rare indeed must be the case when, with conflicting notions of right conduct, there will be nothing else to sway the balance. If, however, the case supposed were here, a judge, I think, would err if he were to impose upon the community as a rule of life his own idiosyncrasies of conduct or belief. Let us suppose, for illustration, a judge who looked upon theatre-going as a sin. Would he be doing right if, in a field where the rule of law was still unsettled, he permitted this conviction, though known to be in conflict with the dominant standard of right conduct, to govern his decision? My own notion is that he would be under a duty to conform to the accepted standards of the community, the *mores* of the times. . . .

My analysis of the judicial process comes then to this, and little more: logic, and history, and custom, and utility, and the accepted standards of right conduct, are the forces which singly or in combination shape the progress of the law. Which of these forces shall dominate in any case must depend largely upon the comparative importance or value of the social interests that will be thereby promoted or impaired. One of the most fundamental social interests is that law shall be uniform and impartial. There must be nothing in its action that savors of prejudice or favor or even arbitrary whim or fitfulness. Therefore in the main there shall be adherence to precedent. There shall be symmetrical development, consistently with history or custom when history or custom has been the motive force, or the chief one, in giving shape to existing rules, and with logic or philosophy when the motive power has been theirs. But symmetrical development may be bought at too high a price. Uniformity ceases to be a good when it becomes uniformity of oppression. The social interest served by symmetry or certainty must be balanced against the social interest served by equity and fairness or other elements of social welfare. These may enjoin upon the judge the duty of drawing the line at another angle, of staking the path along new courses, of marking a new point of departure from which others who come after him will set out upon their journey.

If you ask how he is to know when one interest outweighs another, I can only answer that he must get his knowledge just as the legislator gets it, from experience and study and reflection; in brief, from life itself. Here, indeed, is the point of contact between the legislator's work and his. The choice of methods, the appraisement of values, must in the end be guided by like considerations for the one as for the other. Each indeed is legislating within the limits of his competence. No doubt the limits for the judge are narrower. He legislates only between gaps. He fills the open spaces in the law. How far he may go without traveling beyond the walls of the interstices cannot be staked out for him upon a chart. He must learn it for himself as he gains the sense of fitness and proportion that comes with years of habitude in the practice of an art. Even within the gaps, restrictions not easy to define, but felt, however impalpable they may be, by every judge and lawyer, hedge and circumscribe his action. They are established by the traditions of the centuries, by the example of other judges, his predecessors and his colleagues, by the collective judgment of the profession and by the duty of adherence to the pervading spirit of the law. . . .

You may say that there is no assurance that judges will interpret the *mores* of their day more wisely and truly than other men. I am not disposed to deny this, but in my view it is quite beside the point. The point is rather that this power of interpretation must be lodged somewhere, and the custom of the constitution has lodged it in the judges. If they are to fulfill their function as judges, it could hardly be lodged elsewhere. Their conclusions must, indeed, be subject to constant testing and retesting, revision and readjustment; but if they act with conscience and intelligence, they ought to attain in their conclusions a fair average of truth and wisdom. The recognition of this power and duty to shape the law in conformity with the customary morality is something far removed from the destruction of all rules and the substitution in every instance of the individual sense of justice, the *arbitrium boni viri*. That might result in a benevolent despotism if the judges were benevolent men. It would put an end to the reign of law. The method of sociology, even though applied with greater freedom than in the past, is heading us toward no such cataclysm. The form and structure of the organism are fixed. The cells in which there is motion do not change the proportions of the mass. Insignificant is the power of innovation of any judge, when compared with the bulk and pressure of the rules that hedge him on every side. Innovate, however, to some extent, he must, for with new conditions there must be new rules. All that the method of sociology demands is that within this narrow range of choice he shall search for social justice. . . .

In *The Growth of the Law* 60 (1924) Cardozo estimates: "Nine-tenths, perhaps more, of the cases that come before a court are predetermined – pre-determined in the sense that they are predestined – their fate established by inevitable laws that follow them from birth to death."

Learned Hand, 1872-1961
Judge of United States Circuit Court of Appeals, Second Circuit.

THE SPEECH OF JUSTICE

Conservative political opinion in America cleaves to the tradition of the judge as passive interpreter, believing that his absolute loyalty to authoritative law is the price of his immunity from political pressure and of the security of his tenure. Therefore, since he should have no aim but to understand the law as he finds it, conservative opinion finds it monstrous to require of him results which shall suit the changing popular aspirations, which, being unformulated, must be vague, undifferentiated, and fragmentary. His is the role of a faithful administrator whose success depends upon his interpretation of the written word, not of the full heart. In its passionate adherence to this tradition such opinion is not disinterested; it would as eagerly encourage judicial initiative, if the laws were framed by labor unions, as it insists upon rigid obedience in a system framed for the most part for the protection of property and for the prevention of thoroughgoing social regulation. Under such a system nothing seems to it more subversive of ordered liberty than to permit the judge to make a personal interpretation of the uncertain and distracted yearnings of a suppositious public opinion.

This attitude is in part right and in part wrong. Much of the law is indeed written in formal shape, the authoritative emanation of the state through agencies to which the judge is confessedly inferior. Beyond the limits of such ambiguity as the words may honestly carry the judge surely has no duty but to understand, and to bring to his understanding good faith and dutiful acquiescence. For the results he may not justly be held accountable; to hold him is to disregard the social will, which has imposed upon him that very quiescence that prevents the effectuation of his personal notions. There is a hierarchy of power in which the judge stands low; he has no right to divinations of public opinion which run counter to its last formal expressions. Nevertheless, the judge has, by custom, his own proper representative character as a complementary organ of the social will, and in so far as conservative sentiment, in the excess of caution that he shall be obedient, frustrates his free power by interpretation to manifest the half-framed purposes of his time, it misconceives the historical significance of his position and will in the end render him incompetent to perform the very duties upon which it lays so much emphasis. The profession of the law of which he is a part is charged with the articulation and final incidence of the successive efforts towards justice; it must feel the circulation of the communal blood or it will wither and drop off, a useless member.

When Plato tried to define justice, he found he could not stop short of building a commonwealth. No concept would answer which did not compromise the sum of the citizen's relations to the state at large. Yet we know that such a definition does not define until it be filled with purposes which the people feel and the state sets out to realize. Ulpian might take as the constitutive principle of justice the steady and eternal purpose to give each man his own, but no *a priori* concepts can determine in advance what each man's own shall be, and the form of justice will be without content till we fill it with the ardor of life. It can from time to time become realized in fragmentary compromises, the ingenious expedients of those who can penetrate and satisfy the cravings of the time, but it will submit to no eternal rationalistic, any more than any other manifestation of the human soul.

Two conditions are essential to the realization of justice according to law. The law must have an authority supreme over the will of the individual, and such an authority can arise only from a background of social acquiescence, which gives it the voice of indefinitely greater numbers than those of its expositors. Thus, the law surpasses the deliverances of even the most exalted of its prophets; the momentum of its composite will alone makes it effective to coerce the individual and reconciles him to his subserviency. The pious traditionalism of the law has its roots in a sound conviction of this necessity; it must be content to lag behind the best inspiration of its time until it feels behind it the weight of such general acceptance as will give sanction to its pretension to unquestioned dictation. Yet with this piety must go a taste for courageous experiment, by which alone the law has been built as we have it, an indubitable structure, organic and living. It is in this aspect that the profession of the law is in danger of failing in times like our own when deep changes are taking place in the convictions of men. It is not as the priest of a completed revelation that the living successors of past lawmakers can most truly show their reverence or continue the traditions which they affect to regard. If they forget their pragmatic origin, they omit the most pregnant element of the faith they profess and of which they would henceforth become only the spurious and egregious descendants. Only as an articulate organ of the half-understood aspirations of living men, constantly recasting and adapting existing forms, bringing to the high light of expression the dumb impulses of the present, can they continue in the course of the ancestors whom they revere.

Yet the conditions of the enterprise have changed. Until within a very few decades the American bench and bar could utter justice without misgiving or constraint. Differences of course there were, but the self-conscious elements of society were homogeneous and the divergences not fundamentally distracting. At least, such genuine distraction as there was was latent, class grievances were inaudible, justice might be vague but it was consistent. Lawyers got by a kind of natural right the authority to interpret justice, since they were in a broad sense genuine representatives of all that could achieve representation. Nor was it different in Great Britain. When Lord Mansfield made the modern commercial law of England, he had no need to force his native convictions; he spoke with authority because the resultant values in his mind substantially accorded with that of all other men who ever conceived that their scale of values could gain an effective recognition.

All this has changed; the profession is still drawn, and so far as we can see, will always be drawn, from the propertied class, but other classes have awakened to conscious control of their fate, their demands are vocal which before were dumb, and they will no longer be disregarded. If justice be a passable accommodation between the vital and self-conscious interests of society, it has taken on a meaning not known before. But the profession has not yet learned to adapt itself to the change; the most difficult of adjustments has not been made, an understanding of and sympathy with the purposes and ideals of those parts of the common society whose interests are discordant with its own. Yet nothing can be more certain than that its authority as interpreter of customary law must in the end depend upon its power to learn precisely that adaptation. As mediator it must grasp from within the meaning of each phase of social will; it must divine the form of what lies confused and unexpressed and must bring to light the substance of what is half surmised. To adjust and to compromise, to balance and to value, one must first of all learn to know, not from the outside, but as the will knows. This is the condition of the continued high position of the lawyer; without this he must degenerate to a mere rational automation, expounding a barren scholasticism which his society will quickly learn to value at its true worth.

It may be said that this fate is in any event inevitable, that the obvious purport of the present is towards an increasing body of minute formularies which leave no option and permit no latitude. Yet one must not be too hasty to confuse cause with effect. A large part of the tendency towards such meticulous prolixity rests in the very inability of the profession to show a more enlightened sympathy with the deeper aspirations of the time. Moreover, as we are coming now to learn, no human purpose possesses itself so completely in advance as to admit of final definition. Life overflows its moulds and the will outstrips its own universals. Men cannot know their own meaning till the variety of its manifestations is disclosed in its final impacts, and the full content of no design is grasped till it has got beyond its general formulation and become differentiated in its last incidence. It should be, and it may be, the function of the profession to manifest such purposes in their completeness if it can achieve the genuine loyalty which comes not from obedience, but from the according will, for interpretation is a mode of the will and understanding is a choice.

In so far as we have realized that definition must follow application, the movement has been to intrust broad powers to administrative commissions, which thus become charged with the execution of wide legislative purposes, and which establish upon them a customary law through the slow accretion of their own precedents. Such functions should more properly lie with courts, who by training and experience ought to be better fitted for their discharge. The movement reflects a suspicion of courts in the end resting upon that very scrupulousness to the written word which has been their undoing. Yet they stand in a dilemma, because, while no ritualistic piety can save them from the necessity of an active partisanship amid the contests of their time, their partiality must endure the final test of a genuine social ideal which shall be free from class prejudice. Like every public functionary, in the end they are charged with the responsibility of choosing but of choosing well. Courage and insight alone can in the end win confidence and power. Democracy must learn to value and to trust such qualities or democracy cannot disentangle its true purposes and realize its vaguely formed ideals; but democracy is quick to understand those who respond to its fundamental feelings, and is ruthless in casting aside those who seek cover behind the protection of the written word, for which it may, and even in the same breath, itself profess reverence.

The profession of the law has its fate in its own hands; it may continue to represent a larger, more varied social will by a broader, more comprehensive interpretation. The change must come from within; the profession must satisfy its community by becoming itself satisfied with the community. It must assimilate society before society will assimilate it; it must become organic to remain a living organ. No political mechanism designed to accomplish this by fear will succeed, if the inward disloyalty of purpose remain. The lawyer must either learn to live more capaciously or be content to find himself continuously less trusted, more circumscribed, till he becomes hardly more important than a minor administrator, confined to a monotonous round of record and routine, without dignity, inspiration, or respect. There can be no ambiguity in the answer of those who are worthy of the traditions and the power of a noble calling.

In an address to Yale Law Graduates in 1931, Judge Hand referred to the law as "no more than the formal expression of that tolerable compromise that we call justice, without which the rule of the tooth and claw must prevail. [*The Spirit of Liberty* 68 (Dilliard ed. 1959)]. In praise of Hand's philosophy of judicial self-restraint see Mendelson, "Learned Hand: Patient Democrat" (1962) 76 *Harv. L. Rev.* 322.

Julius Cohen, Reginald A. H. Robson, and Alan Bates

PARENTAL AUTHORITY: THE COMMUNITY AND THE LAW

Why was this Study Undertaken?

THE MORAL INGREDIENT IN LAW

In the shaping of normative standards for the resolution of conflicts, law-makers have sought guidance from prevailing notions of right and wrong, from concepts of justice and injustice, or – to use a more generic term – from principles of morality, whencesoever they might stem. This is evident in legislative law-making, where the function of policy-formulation is open and undisguised, and where the emphasis admittedly is upon the *making* and not the *discovery* of law. It is less evident, but nevertheless the case with respect to judicial law-making – less evident, because many of the conceptual devices that have been employed by courts, e.g., "negligence," "proximate cause," "due process," "consideration" and the like, have lent themselves so readily to the manipulation of logical form as to shield the law-*making* function of courts from public view and give plausibility to the fiction that judges do not make, but merely apply the law. Both the logical form and the fiction were given dignity by the school of analytic jurisprudence which flourished under John Austin's guidance in England a century ago and took root in a significant area of American jurisprudential thought. Under the theory advanced by this school, the key problems for the jurist are twofold: (1) the discovery of the legal norms, and (2) the development of their logical implications. Evaluation or criticism of the law by reference to non-legal norms is deemed beyond the ambit of appropriate juristic activity. However, the limitation of the analytical school in confining the judicial process to these two functions became apparent with the realization that many legislative standards are vague and ambiguous and, therefore, defy discovery and logical application until judges, by a legislative process of their own, pour specific content into them. Moreover, there are large areas in which the law, though clear, expressly gives broad discretionary powers to judges in the disposition of litigious controversies. Here, too, judges *create* rather than find or discover the law. In choosing between competing law analogies in situations not foreseen in the early development of law, in the application of principles of equity, in dealing with such broad constitutional concepts as "due process of law" and "interstate commerce," in selecting from among competing maxims of interpretation where statutory language is unclear, in pouring specific content into such statutory standards as "reasonable" and "fair," in the exercise of discretionary functions relating to sentencing and the imposition of fines or to the custody of children, it is apparent that judges do more than discover and apply the law. In effect, they are creating it, albeit interstitially, and in so doing, concern themselves with notions of right and wrong, of justice and injustice – in brief, with principles of morality. The insistence of the analytic jurists that the legal skin be cut away completely from the body of moral principles that give it nourishment was, of course, predicated on the ideal notion of a fully developed legal system, in which the legislative and judicial functions are completely separated. Ideally, morality was for the legislative branch, and law was for the courts. Even Austin, however, was quick to recognize that his image of a fully developed legal system, with a complete separation of legislative and judicial functions, was a theoretical construct and that, in practice, with the lines of function often blurred, a resort to moral principles in the decisional process of judges was inevitable. His distinguished American disciple, John Chipman Gray, also acknowledged moral principles to be a source that judges could legitimately tap when formal legal guides were unavailing.

The movement away from analytic jurisprudence – epitomized by Holmes's famous statement, "The life of the law is not logic, but experience" – was spurred on by the recognition of the need to place the moral ingredient in the forefront rather than in the background of juristic thought. Not only did this grow out of the recognition of the creative role of judges, but also out of the need to include within the province of law the problem of the justness of the legal norms themselves. In those juristic formulations which view law in relation to the achievement of human goals, law is regarded less as a self-contained entity seeking internal consistency than as a discipline in which not only the efficacy of law as an instrumental means but the ends of law themselves are placed under constant scrutiny and surveillance. This would seem to be implicit in the formulations of Pound, of his forebears Kohler and Von Jhering, and of the many-bannered realists – whether pragmatists, empiricists, experimentalists, functionalists or the like – who, in their many different ways, have joined in emphasizing the significance of the teleogical as distinguished from the merely logical in law. . . .

ASCERTAINING THE COMMUNITY'S MORAL SENSE – IN PRACTICE

. . . Despite lip service to the need to treat the moral sense as an observable datum; and despite exhortations to employ "the spirit of science" in the task of observation, judicial law-makers have relied mainly upon intuitive hunch, on the vagaries of "judicial notice," on the predilections of the groups identified with the social origin of the law-makers, on crude personal observation, on a "best guess," or some such other esoteric method for divining the *Zeitgeist*. It is not that there is an unawareness of the unreliability of these methods. Mr Justice Cardozo's observation that "In every court there are likely to be as many estimates of the *'Zeitgeist'* as there are judges on its bench," and Judge Frank's wry remark that "Usually a person who talks of 'opinion of the world at large' is really referring to the 'few people with whom I happen to converse,' " evidence a lively alertness to the problem.

It is, however, one thing to be aware of the problem; it is another thing to be stoically resigned to the necessity of utilizing these crude devices for estimating the community's moral sense because of the belief that more reliable measuring rods are unavailable. Such seems to be the position of Judge Learned Hand. In endeavoring to implement the statutory standard of "good moral character" which is involved in naturalization proceedings, Judge Hand felt that it was incumbent upon him to consult not his own subjective feelings, but rather "the moral feelings now prevalent in the country" or "the generally accepted moral conventions current at the time." In another instance, he used the expression " 'common conscience' prevalent at the time." His test, then, for "good moral character" was objective – but how to ascertain it? Judge Hand reluctantly concluded that the "common conscience" is something that has to be "divined," because "it is impossible in practice to ascertain what, in a given instance, it does demand." Two reasons are advanced for this: (1) inasmuch as each moral situation is unique, general principles would be of no utility; and (2) even though, theoretically, a poll could be taken to determine whether "those who would approve the specific conduct would outnumber those who would disapprove," it would be "fantastically absurd to try to apply it." Because of this, Judge Hand found himself resigned to "the best guess we can make of how such a poll would result."

Both reasons are worth examining closely, because they have been given currency in modern juristic thought. The alleged uniqueness of moral situations has served to justify not only the use of the "best guess," but also the resistance to any attempt to place restrictions upon the purely subjective in judicial judgment. There are those who, in resisting efforts to encompass the unique within a larger framework, sense in such efforts a great danger of overstressing the element of likeness in moral problems. Nonetheless, uniqueness *per se* is not a sufficient ground for denying the legitimacy of a generalizing function that extracts and organizes *similarities* from admittedly different phenomena. Physical phenomena are certainly not any less apt to be unique than are moral judgments, but no one would seriously contend that, because of this the physical sciences are to be shorn of their elemental power to group and classify. In the moral realm, the inclusion or exclusion of a unique situation under a more general rubric is dependent on the relative importance of the purposes which society, through its law-making authorities, desires to effectuate. All humans, for example, are presumed to have uniquely different fingerprints, but if X and Y, who in this sense are unique, each loot and kill, should they be treated as similar in the eyes of the criminal law, or should they be treated differently? This depends on the ends which society seeks to achieve. The search for the moral sense of the community is, in essence, therefore, a search for insights into social purpose. It is an attempt to ascertain which unique factors (dissimilarities) should be taken account of or rejected as unimportant, and which common factors (similarities) should be grouped together for purposes of regulation and control. Should all parents, for example, be treated as if they were the same in the eyes of the law for purposes of caring for their children, or should the requirements of parental care be dependent upon the unique quality of each parent? The method, as can readily be seen, is that of analogy – the weighing of the importance of similarities and dissimilarities in the light of social need and purpose. It is not new to the lawman. For, if it be true that much of judicial law itself grows by inductive case-by-case generalization by analogical reasoning, how can this be done without assuming the very existence of those common elements which are extracted from uniquely dissimilar cases?

Now, granted that such a poll as suggested by Judge Hand would not yield any general principles covering *all* moral situations; granted, also, that it would be impracticable to poll the community concerning *each* specific moral issue raised in litigious controversies, would it not be more reliable to develop analogically from a poll of sentiment of *several* concrete moral issues, concerning which the views of the community are relevant, than it is to develop analogically from a surmise or "guess" by a judge as to the nature of the community sentiment regarding those issues? Take the situation in the *Johnson* case. Johnson had failed to support his legal wife; for years he had been living with a paramour. Was he of "good moral character" within the meaning of the naturalization statute? Judge Hand held in the negative because of his belief that it conformed to his "best guess" of what the "common conscience" would be on the facts of the case. Now, suppose that Judge Hand were confronted with another case, the facts of which varied slightly from the *Johnson* case. Assume, too, that the facts in the *Johnson* case are from *a* to *m*, and that the new case has additional facts, *n* and *o*, which Judge Hand, by analogical reasoning, dismisses as differences that are nonessential. Would he not be on firmer ground in the second case if he had at his disposal an accurate poll of the community's reaction to the situation in the Johnson case rather than having to rely upon his "guess" of what the moral sense of the community would be with respect to it? We think he would be. For if he erred in his judgment in the first case, the error would be repeated in the second, in the third and in the other analogical extensions that would follow.

To insist that there is danger of overstressing moral likenesses, if such a method were utilized, overlooks the fact that there is also danger in overstressing uniqueness. Granted that abstract uniformity often results in injustice, thus inviting correction by a method of equity or individualization, it is well to remember that equality before the law is also a desired end, and that the absence of general standards encourages favoritism and partiality, which are elements of lawlessness. If a person whose feet must be fitted for shoes has a triple E width and a narrow heel – all well and good, he should be fitted! This should not militate against the need for providing regular shoe widths and lengths for more normal feet, or for striving, as does scientific endeavor, to place under a more general rubric those elements which initially are regarded as being unique.

The second reason offered to justify the divining rod as a method for asertaining the community's moral sense is an underlying skepticism toward the application of modern polling techniques to the problem. Judge Hand, in seeking to determine the meaning of "good moral character" in the naturalization statute searched vainly for *objective* guidance from the community itself. Had Professor Edmond Cahn been deciding the case, he would have differed with Judge Hand on the ground that "the act of individual judgment must belong to him who bears the name of judge." Though differing as to the role of the judge, both would, however, seem to shun the application of empirical method to the moral realm – but for different reasons. Judge Hand seems to be pointing to the impracticality of undertaking an elaborate polling operation each time a case comes up involving a determination of "the common conscience." This is less a criticism of the reliability of polling methods than it is an observation concerning the infeasibility – perhaps in terms of expense and energy – of their application to a single case. To grant this, however, does not mean that the method could not be applied to a legal standard which could be relevant to many cases. If it is considered feasible to undertake lengthy and costly legislative investigations of labor racketeering, monopolies, campaign expenditures, and housing, it is difficult to comprehend why it would be infeasible to undertake reliable polls of the sentiment of the community in selected areas of activity – for example, areas in which the law in flux seeks guidance from the community; areas in which greater harmony is sought between legal norms and the community's moral sense. Indeed, on the basis of the cost of the experiment undertaken in conjunction with the present study – involving, as it does, an area of considerable scope and magnitude – it is not unreasonable to assume that it would involve less of an outlay than would many of the "hearing" types of legislative investigations undertaken in the ordinary course of legislative business. This is not to suggest that the feasibility of such an undertaking is limited only to the legislative forum. Granted that the institutional structure of the judiciary does not at present include the luxury of a research staff as a permanent adjunct, there are many research sources – the bar, the schools, foundations – that could be galvanized into action once the courts suggest the need for this type of inquiry.

Professor Cahn's objection takes a somewhat different turn. It is presumably based on the notion that the moral ingredient is such that to attempt to apply an empirical measuring rod to it would somehow dissolve its special quality into a "conglomerate mass." This does not mean, however, that observable data in the field of morals need necessarily dissolve the quality of a moral decision. On the contrary, it might enhance and illuminate it. Assume, for example, that a judge has the awesome discretion to choose a life sentence or hanging as the fate of a condemned man. Would the fact that he was influenced in his decision by knowledge – that, say, 99% of the community deeply abhorred capital punishment – necessarily reduce the quality of his moral judgment in the case? Would he necessarily abdicate any responsibility for "individual judgment" if he merely chose to *consider* this factor in his deliberations?

The *extent* to which the moral sense of the community should or should not be reflected in legal decisions is, of course, another matter. On this there is a wide divergence of respectable views, concerning which we do not here venture any opinion. There are many who would find most unattractive the thought that law-makers ought to be bound to follow the prevailing moral sense of the community, no matter how that standard is determined. Pointing, for example, to segregation in the South, many undoubtedly would insist that law-makers use "higher" standards that those which prevail in the community. Others, on the contrary, would insist upon greater adherence to prevailing moral standards in the interest not only of their concept of justice, but of the preservation of the very fabric of law and order itself. Theoretically, then, if not actually, one extreme would require that the legal order not take into account the moral sense of the community; the other would urge that the law mirror the community's moral sense. Clearly, one's choice of positions on either extreme end, or on any of the intermediate points of the scale, is a matter of juristic philosophy, concerning which there can be honest differences of opinion. Which position is the more "proper" or "just" is a serious problem, but not one to which our inquiry is addressed. For the purposes of our undertaking, however, it is our position that *if* the moral sense of the community is relevant to the law-making process, either as a norm for the law-maker to consider, or as a norm to follow, it need not be left wholly to conjecture, to hunch or to intuition; and that modern social science techniques could more reliably be utilized for the task. In so stating we do not propose to enter into any discussion concerning the comparative merits either of Professor Cahn's position, or of the views of those who, with Judge Hand, recognize the need objectively to ascertain the community's moral sense. From a strictly "if-then" vantage point, we merely suggest that *if* legal theorists and legislative and judicial law-makers *choose* to regard the moral sense of the community as a significant factor in the law-making process, it would seem incumbent upon them to obtain as reliable an estimate of this empirical fact as is possible – no matter how or to what extent it would be utilized in any particular formulation of law or theory of justice. Otherwise they would be subject to error.

By showing how juries may erroneously apply the wrong facts to a good or proper legal principle, Judge Frank pointed up how really insecure is the security of those who assume that a just cause is won because the legal rule is on their side. However, if Judge Frank's skepticism towards the fact-finding activities of juries is warranted, equally warranted should be a skepticism towards that law-making activity which seeks anchorage in community sentiment but is insecurely anchored in hunch or guess.

DEFINING THE AREA OF THE STUDY

The fundamental concepts

Let us then take those hypothetical law-makers who, for whatever reason, are imbued with a juristic theory which seeks a high degree of harmony between law and the moral sense of the community. Assume that they are insecure in the role suggested by Edmund Burke in his famous letter to the Bristol constituents – that is, as representatives or spokesmen of the community's moral sense. Assume, further, that they are earnestly in search of a method more reliable than conjecture, hunch or intuition that would permit them to gauge the extent to which legal norms are in harmony or at variance with the moral sense of the community. What assistance could be given them? It was this challenging problem that became the focal point of an inter-disciplinary project involving research both in law and in the social sciences. What follows, therefore, is an account of how that challenge was met. It is an account of a pilot experiment which purports to represent *a* method, not *the* method for meeting the problem. It does not deal with *all* aspects of the moral sense, but just a *single*, although significant, dimension of it. It does not assume that the views in the community are homogeneous; rather it endeavors to explore the extent to which both homogeneity and heterogeneity of views are present. It pertains to *existing* legal norms, but the method could as readily be applied to those which are *proposed*; it relates to law at the *judicial* stage, although it could be applied to the *legislative* as well. And, although it singles out legal norms in only one field of law, and is limited in jurisdictional scope to only one geographic area, it nevertheless is intended as a pilot study for possible application beyond the immediate narrow limits to which it is necessarily confined.

Operational Terms. At the very outset, it was necessary to give operational meaning to the term "community." For the purposes of the study, it was defined as the adult population of the state of Nebraska, excluding inmates of mental institutions, reformatories and penitentiaries. From this "community," a representative sample was chosen.

The legal norms of the jurisdiction which could have been chosen for the experiment were virtually boundless in scope. There was strong attraction, however, to the field of family law, especially as it concerns the varied legal relationships between parent and child. First of all, there was reason to believe that, in this field, law-makers would wish to achieve a high degree of congruence between legal norms and the felt convictions of the community. Secondly, the area of child-parent relationships has, for some time, been a common hunting ground for both lawyers and sociologists. Although each group heretofore has been looking for a different game, it was thought that familiarity with the terrain would make a joint hunting party more attractive, encourage greater communication between specialists in different disciplines, and thereby extend the scope of mutual interest. Moreover, sociological and other literature suggested that changing community attitudes towards many aspects of child-parent relationships were not reflected in law.

Out of this vast area of law, a series of specific legal norms were isolated for the experiment. These are detailed in Chapter III. Broadly speaking, however, they deal with situations concerning the issue of parental versus governmental control over children; with the question of the extent of the child's freedom from parental authority; with the legal obligations of parent to child, and of child to parent; and with the extent of the legal involvement of the parent where relationships between children and third parties are brought into play.

The norms that were isolated represented the choices that the courts in the jurisdiction probably would have made – by virtue of existing statutes, precedents or analogies – if the specific situations were presented to them in litigious form. They are legal norms, then, in a Holmesian sense, that is, predictions of what the courts would in fact do. They are not what has been commonly referred to as "law-in-action," *i.e.*, the unofficial norms of those who establish certain expectations in the *enforcement* of the law. It is not to be assumed, moreover, that they represent areas of activity which are in frequent litigation. Indeed, some might be, and some might not be at all. They are treated here in the more traditional sense – as law ready to be applied if and when the occasion calls.

Granted the demarcation of the geographic bounds of the community, and the selection of the legal norms, the difficult problem remained of how to identify and measure the so-called "moral sense." In dealing with a problem in the realm of morals, we were aware that we were invading an area that in name, at least, has long been the domain of the ethical philosophers. The question raised by Hume's predecessors, Shaftesbury and Hutcheson, as to whether there is a moral sense that operates in the moral field as does, say, the senses of taste, smell and sight in the physical, was long debated and still remains the subject of modern philosophical discourse. Serious controversies are still being waged over the intrinsic meaning of a moral judgment – whether it states an objective fact such as the color "red," or is merely a grunt, expressive of some desire, aversion, love or hate; whether its mood is imperative and not indicative, and whether, if imperative, it can be reduced to fact terms. The so-called naturalists have one view, the intuitionists another, the subjectivists and emotivists still another. Basically, these are meta-ethical theories, which seek analytically to explain the function of the moral judgment in human discourse. However, our concern with things moral as they relate to the community was, for the purposes of our undertaking, entirely of a different order. Our objective was not to search for the intrinsic meaning of moral judgment, but to isolate and measure a moral ingredient that is operationally defined, for it was clear at the outset that, because of the variety of vague uses of the term *moral sense* an operational definition was required. Following the views of Carnap and Hempel, this meant that, for purposes of the study, it was necessary to *stipulate* a more precise meaning for the term.

The moral sense could have been defined in terms of what the community in fact *does*. This would have led to an approach somewhat along the lines suggested by Ehrlich in his sociological studies of the "living law," by Underhill Moore in his institutional and parking studies, by the Kinsey group in their work on sex behavior and by Jacobs and Angell in their socio-legal study of husband-wife relationships – all of whom sought insight into *existing* patterns of practice. It was also basically the approach of Llewellyn and Hoebel in their study of the law-ways of the Cheyenne Indians, for they sought, through the reports of the actual case controversies, to reconstruct what the legal norms *were* and, through them, perhaps infer what they still *are*. In all these studies the sights were on the "is" or the "was" side of the behavior pattern. To borrow an expression from Professor F.S.C. Northrop, their emphasis was upon "the normative 'is' of the living law." The focal point for our study is also a normative "is," but it is an "is" not of the *living law*, but of the community's feelings in what the law *ought* to be. It was our view that although a knowledge of what exists in practice would be helpful to the hypothetical law-maker, it would not provide him with a secure guide for determining whether the community would desire to have existing practice or custom crystallized into law. To put it more succinctly: If it were established that war among people is customary, it would not necessarily follow that people therefore believed that war, legally, ought to exist. The fact that people might customarily practice theft or tax-evasion would not necessarily mean that they would want the practices to be the norm for law. Ehrlich himself recognized this distinction when he carved out the area of his investigations. He differentiated "between the actual customs by which people live and their moral views, which may be very different from their actual customs," the latter being on a "lower grade of morality" than the abstract moral principles themselves. With Ehrlich, it was "the actual practice of the community, and not its abstract moral standard" that was sought. With us it was the "abstract moral standard" of what the law *ought* to be that was sought – simply on the assumption that this is what the hypothetical law-maker would want to know in facing the question of whether existing practice or custom should be permitted to continue.

In contrast to Ehrlich's interest in the "is" of "living law," our study more closely approximated the approach of Stouffer in his recent inquiry into attitudes toward Communist activities. There the search was also for "ought" attitudes in the community, although it was not primarily directed to attitudes concerning what the *law* ought to be. Community attitudes concerning what the *law* should be were central to our study. When each respondent was asked whether the law ought to allow (or prevent) certain conduct in situations involving child-parent relationships, we were seeking to explore the extent to which the community desired to have an authoritative arm of government, with power to impose sanctions, control or regulate such conduct. Moreover, we were not seeking to ascertain just how the community actually behaves in these situations. By dealing solely with "ought" attitudes concerning what the law should be, and not with actual behavior, our study obviates the criticisms that have been leveled in social science literature against attempts in some attitude studies to treat verbal responses as indices of actual behavior.

An operational distinction having been assumed between what *is* or *was* and what the community thinks *ought* to be, further refinement of the behavioral *ought* became necessary. Dewey's distinction between that which is *desired* and that which is *desirable* and the Parsons-Shils-Kluckhohn differentiation between the *cathectic* and the *evaluative* modes of behavior suggested to us that we should undertake to infer the moral sense not merely from short-term, narrow types of value responses from representatives of the community, but from responses that were more reasoned and considered in a context of wider and more perduring goals. Accordingly, instead of inviting quick, "yes-no" type of answers to problem situations involving child-parent relationships, an interview schedule was developed which sought (1) to alert each respondent to a consideration of consequences that would be likely to flow from alternative choices; (2) to elicit from each considered, as distinguished from off-the-cuff, responses; and (3) to obtain from each the reasons for the responses. The community, in effect, was asked what legal norms should be established for resolving the conflicts in the situations chosen for the study. The moral sense thus was to be inferred from the considered choices (expressed verbally) which the members of the community felt the law-making authorities *ought* to make if, in the given situations, they were confronted with alternative courses of action.

It is clear that this choice of operational definition provided lenses only for seeing a moral sense that is inferred from reactions to hypothetical rather than from live emotionally charged situations. The respondents were not actually put in a position of responsibility to act as would a judge in actual litigious situations; nor did the questions asked necessarily relate to issues which they themselves actually experienced. We were not unmindful of the Isocratic maxim that has been urged for the testing of the moral decision, *i. e.*, that we "should test justice when a man is in want, temperance when he is in power, continence when he is in the prime of youth." We recalled, as well, Hume's counter-advice: that in considering the moral character of an act, we should assume the role of the benevlent, impartial spectator, seeking reactions as to what we ourselves would feel. How the community would have reacted to the situations were they live and real, rather than hypothetical, what the reactions would have been had the community actually faced the situations and at the same time been put into a position of responsibility to judge them, we do not venture to surmise. This is a matter that needs testing; it is useless to guess. To have chosen these narrower lenses –

assuming that they could have been fashioned – would, at the most, have permitted observation of the moral sense of only a few members of the community – *i. e.,* those who experienced the responsibility of actual choices when confronted with actual conflict situations. This would not have advanced the supposed law-maker's goal of ascertaining the moral sense of the *community.* When he asks: "How would the community react to a certain issue if it were squarely faced with it?" we have assumed that he is seeking an answer to a problem put abstractly and hypothetically; we have also assumed that he would not be satisfied with inferring the moral sense of the entire community from any one of its many complex parts.

Much thought was given to the problem of measuring the intensity of the responses of those in the community who were interviewed concerning what the law ought to be in the various situational contexts. The decision to exclude this dimension of the moral sense from the confines of our study was motivated by several considerations. Aside from the difficulties that were envisaged in creating a meaningful and reliable instrument for measuring the intensity of conviction, the incorporation of the element of intensity into each of the questions in the Interview Schedule would have required a drastic reduction in the scope of the issues concerning which the community views were sought. To incorporate this without reducing the number of questions originally planned for the Interview Schedule would have so lengthened the time span of the interview as to have made it virtually impossible to administer. To shorten the number of issues in the Interview Schedule in order to accommodate the dimension of intensity within a manageable time limit for the interview would have decreased the opportunity to scrutinize broader and more general areas of law-controlled activities.

Objectives of the study

With the terms *community, law* and *moral sense* operationally defined, our next task was to crystallize the major objectives of the study. What information should the research seek to obtain? What facts would be significant? The answers to these inquiries may themselves be put in question form, since they quickly demarcate the bounds of our undertaking. The data sought related to five problems that it was our purpose to explore. Briefly:

(1) To what extent is the law in the selected areas of child-parent relationships in agreement or at variance with the view of the community?

(2) How homogeneous are the views in the community concerning the law? In other words, is there *a* moral sense of the community, or are there *many* moral senses?

(3) What bearing do such socio-economic factors as age, income, sex, education, religion, have on the views of people in the community concerning the law?

(a) To what extent does the law coincide with the views of categories of persons identified by these socio-economic factors?

(b) Is there any marked difference in the views of people in different group stratifications?

(4) What reasons are given by those in the community for the views held concerning the law?

(5) To what extent do the findings of social science support the judgments of the community concerning the consequences of the adoption or rejection of specific legal norms? . . .

The findings

Within the confines of the specific areas of inquiry that were carved out for our undertaking, what, then, in summary, are our findings? Briefly, we discovered: There are at least twice as many issues concerning which the community views are in disagreement with the law as there are of those on which the community views and the law are in harmony. Of the 17 issues examined, the community and the existing law would disagree as to ten, agree as to five, and perhaps evenly divide as to one; and if, on the last issue of the group of 17, on which the law of the jurisdiction has not yet crystallized, the courts would follow what seems to be the preponderant judicial view throughout the country, there would be an additional instance of a variance between the community's views and the law.

The community does not display the same degree of homogeneity with respect to all the issues presented to it. There are wide variations in the degree of consensus within the community. On some issues, there is virtual unanimity; on others, the divisions within the community, in varying degrees, are quite evident. For some questions the predominant view was held by a substantial majority; for others by a bare majority, and for still others, by less than a majority.

The majority in the community would favor greater legal restrictions on parental authority over the child than the law presently requires. Out of eleven general areas in which the issue of parental authority was raised, a majority would impose greater restrictions upon parents in eight of them than the law does at present; it would be as ready as the present law to restrict parental control with respect to two of them; and it would agree with the law in not restricting such authority only in one instance.

Child autonomy may be conceived as a set of claims which the child can assert, and a set of obligations which he is required to meet. In the specific areas covered, a majority in the community would have the law grant more legally enforceable claims to pre-adolescent children than it now permits. In the smaller number of cases in which we raised the question of legally enforceable obligations of the pre-adolescent child, a majority of the community was in favor of relaxing the requirements of the existing law.

With respect to the question of granting autonomy to the child, the law, by and large, does not distinguish between the pre-adolescent and the adolescent child; with few exceptions, it tends to lump children under 21 into one large, generic category – no matter what the gradations in age. The community, on the other hand, recognizes the need to have the law accord increasing degrees of autonomy as the age of the adolescent child increases – autonomy not only as to claims, but as to obligations as well. To a substantial portion of the community, the age of 18 marks the boundary line between adolescence and adulthood.

Except in the case of marriage, the law does not differentiate between boys and girls in the recognition of claims and the imposition of legal obligations. With respect to this, a majority of the community – on all the issues considered – is in agreement with the position of the law.

To a majority of the community, the problem of the support of indigent parents and indigent, emancipated children is primarily a matter for the family, and secondarily a matter for the government. In this, the community is in accord with the prevailing law.

By and large, there are no *substantial* differences between the views of the members of various social groupings within the community toward the issues we studied, based on such factors as sex, residential area, religion, age, income, parenthood, schooling and occupation. However, in several instances, the small differences in the views of respondents identified with different socio-economic groups do exhibit consistent patterns.

On none of the selected issues involving parent-child relationships does the law *consistently* reflect the views of any particular social group among the ones we studied in the community rather than those of any other.

Of the reasons given for the views expressed by the respondents concerning the issues posed in the Interview Schedule, the predominant one is concern for the welfare of the child. Parental authority is regarded as a means to an end, and there is little hesitance to employ the arm of the law to curb it when its existence is perceived as being detrimental to the welfare of the child. There is comparatively little sentiment against the intrusion of law or government in what has, for so long a time, been considered the private domain of the family; there is considerable feeling in favor of increased autonomy for the child – especially for the older child. . . .

Implications of our findings

TOOL FOR THE LAW-MAKER

For those law-makers whose juristic philosophy stakes out as an objective a high degree of harmony between the existing law and the moral sense of the community, our findings make it clear that, in the area of parent-child relationships, such harmony exists only to a very limited extent. In fact, with respect to the specific issues that were raised in this area, the law and community opinion were more often in disagreement than in agreement. Those who would desire in a practical way to narrow the gap between the law and the community's moral sense will find detailed and accurate information in our study on the extent of agreement or disagreement between the law and the views of the community. There is also information which identifies the precise areas in which harmony or variance are present.

We realize, of course, that our data do not provide information as to the views of the community on all the issues involving parent-child relationships. By grouping the discrete questions in terms of their common denominators – some, for example, dealt with different aspects of the autonomy of the child, others with the financial support of the family, and so forth – we did endeavor to ascertain the predominant views of the community on more general issues than those raised by the discrete questions themselves. Accordingly, our data include information that will enable law-makers to make reasonable inferences as to what community opinion would probably be on a more specific matter based upon our conclusions as to what the views of the community are with respect to the more general issue. For example, we do not have the views of the community on whether the law should hold the child responsible for criminal acts which he might commit, or whether the parents should be held accountable. However, we did conclude from our data that the majority of the community felt that the law should grant a fair degree of autonomy to the child, particularly when he reaches adolescence, and also thought the law should make an older child responsible for his *civil* wrongs. We suggest, therefore, that this information would give law-makers a more informed basis for dealing analogically with the problem of the child's legal responsibility for criminal acts. Our findings yielded other general clusters of community sentiment from which similar analogical extensions could be made.

THE PROBLEM OF RESPECT FOR THE LAW

Our data showing disagreements between the views of the community and the law suggest questions concerning the possible effects of such a divergence upon the law itself. How far can the two be at odds before the enforcement of the law is adversely affected? To what extent do disagreements between the law and community opinion engender hostility and disrespect toward the particular law and toward law in general? An important instance of the consequences of such a situation was the experience of the country with the Prohibition Amendment. The answer to these questions is obviously not a simple one, and is not within the purview of our undertaking. Our findings do, however, prompt inquiry into the extent to which respect for and obedience to law are affected by such considerations as: the importance of the issue for the community, the frequency with which the issue arises, the complexity of the issues and the degree of consensus within the community concerning the issue.

THE PROBLEM OF COMPETING MORAL SENSES

Our data indicate that there are a number of issues where there is almost complete agreement in the community as to what the law should be; in these cases, those who feel that the law should be related to the views of the community would have little difficulty in implementing their objective. However, our data also show that there are many issues where community opinion concerning the law's attitude is almost evenly divided between opposing points of view, and still others where the most popular view of what the law should be represents the opinions of less than a majority of the community. In contrast to the situations where there is a high degree of consensus within the community, these data showing substantial disagreement among the population as to what the law should be create certain problems that must be faced by those advocating community opinion as the standard to which the law should seek to conform. How is a "community view" to be defined for this purpose? Should law conform to this standard only where there is a high degree of consensus among the population? If so, what should be the law in those areas where there are differences of opinion within the community? Or, if a lower degree of consensus is acceptable, where should the line be drawn? Should law only conform to community opinion where a majority of the population holds the same view, or should it be in harmony with the most popular point of view in the community, even though a majority of the population holds different opinions? These are questions of considerable magnitude as well as of practical importance. Our findings merely point up these questions; they do not purport to answer them. They should, however, help illuminate some of the implications of a juristic theory that seeks a high degree of harmony between law and *the* moral sense of the community.

THE "GROUP CONFLICT" THEORY

In much of the literature of current political and juristic theory, group conflicts over competing group values are regarded as the key to much of political behavior. It was this "group conflict" theory which helped to shape our original assumption that it would be possible, in the area of parent-child relationships, to isolate the group or groups whose views were consonant with the norms of the existing law, and that, as between the various stratified groups, there would be considerable variance in the attitudes concerning what the law should be. Typical of the expressions found in the literature of the "group conflict" theory is the following: "What may be called public policy is the equilibrium reached in this group struggle at any given moment, and it represents a balance which the contending factions or groups constantly strive to weight in their favor." Accordingly, it was felt that an analysis of the relationship between the views of the respondents and the various socio-economic groups with which they are identified would give us some insight into the power structure of the community and isolate the elements in the community whose influence was likely to be felt in the particular area of law. For, the result of conflict between the socio-economic groups that were studied, and therefore point up the need to re-examine the bounds of the operative claims of the "group conflict" theory as it relates to the creation of legal norms.

THE COMMUNITY'S MORAL SENSE AND THE LAW VERSUS THE FINDINGS OF SCIENCE

There are those who would view with concern the application of a juristic formula which erects the moral sense of the community as a norm for the law. This is a political or philosophical issue with which our undertaking is not concerned – our interest, as we have pointed out, being solely with the "then" or implementation phase of an "if-then" proposition. However, it is worth noting that one reason that has been advanced in opposition to this juristic formula is the fact that the community's moral sense might run counter to the findings of science. Those who offer this criticism would prefer to have both the law and the community's moral sense bow ultimately to science as the higher standard. In designing our project, we regarded the answers people gave to our questions as to what the law should be as *means* for achieving certain *ends*, the latter represented by the reasons they gave for their responses. The purpose of this kind of analysis was to try to identify those instances: where there was agreement between the law and the community, both as to the ends to be achieved and the means for achieving them, and where there was agreement between the law and the community as to ends but disagreement as to means. In both such situations, the relevant consideration for many would be the verdict of social science as to the relative effectiveness of alternative means for achieving the mutually desired ends. While we do not claim to have made a completely exhaustive search of the vast social science literature in the field of family behavior, we do feel confident in stating that, although there is some material that is tangentially related, there is a dearth of material of a sufficiently high degree of reliability that is directly and specifically relevant to the particular problems that we covered. We have an illustration here of the point made in the preface concerning inter-disciplinary research between law and the social sciences that, while both disciplines may be interested in the same general area, *i. e.*, the family, up to the present time each field has had a different focus of interest. In the absence of sufficiently reliable scientific data, action, if there must be action, must proceed on the basis of guess. In such a circumstance, the choice is not between reliable knowledge and no knowledge, but between two guesses as to the consequences of the law taking one path instead of another – the law-makers' guess, and the guess that is embodied in the expression of the community's moral sense. When one guess is no more intelligent than the other, the choice between them, when a choice must be made, would put the law-maker's political philosophy to a crucial and revealing test.

Concluding Observations

In undertaking our study, it has not been our function to advocate the acceptance or rejection of any juristic theory involving the moral sense of the community. Our primary task has been to fashion a more reliable instrument which may be utilized by those for whom the moral sense of the community is an essential ingredient in juristic formulations of what the law ought to be. At the same time, we did endeavor to obtain reliable information concerning the community's moral sense in specific areas of parent-child relationships. As we bring this report to a close, we hope that we have, in some measure, succeeded in these objectives. It is also our hope that our undertaking represents a method of inquiry that will have the potential for illuminating other dark corners of the law, that both our research procedures and substantive findings will have relevance for the social under this theory, law is a sort of treaty of peace – the end product of a series of power skirmishes between the competing groups within the community. Our negative findings suggest that the law in the area of parent-child relationships is not scientist, particularly for the sociologist specializing in the field of the family, and that our experiences with cooperative, interdisciplinary research will be a spur to further ventures of this kind.

Professor Underhill Moore's famous parking study was conducted with the assistance of Professor Charles C. Callahan: "Law and Learning Theory: A Study in Legal Control" (1943) 53 Yale L. J. 1-136. Moore's various studies are subjected to critical analysis by Professor F. S. C. Northrop in "Underhill Moore's Legal Science" (1950) 59 Yale L. J. 196 and again in *The Complexity of Legal and Ethical Experience* 31-33, 59, 77 (1959).

Charles D. Raab, 1939 –
Lecturer in Politics, University of Edinburgh.

SUGGESTIONS FOR A CYBERNETIC APPROACH TO SOCIOLOGICAL JURISPRUDENCE (1965)

Benjamin Cardozo's lectures on the nature of the judicial process, along with some of the writings of Roscoe Pound, contain the seeds of a sociological approach to jurisprudence, as compared with earlier theories of what the judicial process should be like. Having found the methods and values of historical and logical jurisprudence wanting in several respects, the proponents of a sociological jurisprudence seek a jurisprudential theory which would bring to the attention of participants in the judicial process the relation of their decision-making to the society in which they operate. Holding that law is a means to social justice, and not an end in itself, Pound asserted that

> We must seek the basis of doctrines, not in Blackstone's wisdom of our ancestors, not in the apocryphal reasons of the beginnings of legal science, not in their history, useful as that is in enabling us to appraise doctrines at their true value, but in a scientific apprehension of the relations of law to society and of the needs and interests and opinions of society of today.

Cardozo pointed out that the usual principles upon which judges had been accustomed to making their decisions were not infallible; frequently, they offered no guide at all. Although "*stare decisis* is at least the everyday working rule of our law," and despite the need for reliance on statutory prescription as the source for judgment,

> It is true that codes and statutes do not render the judge superfluous, nor his work perfunctory and mechanical. There are gaps to be filled. There are doubts and ambiguities to be cleared. There are hardships and wrongs to be mitigated if not avoided.

Thus, sociological jurisprudence has been offered as a source of judgment in filling the gaps that occur. It recognized a creative element in decisionmaking – the judge is often called upon to legislate where he cannot uncover a just rule for the particular case at hand, in the interests of "social justice."

The process of creative decision-making may be viewed as a problem in judicial steering, involving the functions of intelligence and appraisal to a high degree.[1] As such, it raises important questions about the capabilities and consequences of judicial steering. By focusing on these capabilities and consequences,

[1] An interesting discussion of the use of these and other functions is found in Lasswell, *Technique of Decision Seminars,* 4 Midwest J. Pol. Sci. 213 (1960).

we may talk about the inputs and outputs, and the intelligence and appraisal functions, of the creative, sociologically-oriented decision-making process. This article will attempt to provide a framework for assessing them. It will use some of and concepts of a cybernetic model of communication and control,[2] since this approach is highly suggestive of parallels with the process of creative jurisprudence. While this article will not search for the answers, it will try to phrase some of the questions that arise from this view of sociological jurisprudence.

I

Judicial steering is behavior in connection with a goal, and with changes in goals. The method of sociological jurisprudence is to employ a principle "along the lines of justice, morals and social welfare, the *mores* of the day." Immediately it can be seen that this goal is fixed in its form, for each time-period, yet changing in its substance, over time. The problem of judicial steering would be simplified if social conditions remained fixed. However, since social *stasis* is not the case, there exists the dual difficulty of keeping the law in correspondence with social mores at any specific time, and also of keeping the law flexible for change in accordance with changes in mores. In Cardozo's judgment,

> The difference from age to age is not so much in the recognition that law shall conform itself to an end. It is rather in the nature of the ends to which there has been need to conform.

According to this view, that philosophy of law is "just" which seeks the enduring ideal "in and out of the positive law – out of what it is and of what it is becoming." The function of courts is therefore to keep doctrine abreast of social habits – the "living law." Thus, "law" and "social mores" are considered as abstractions for two sets of processes, and the new jurisprudential philosophy is aimed at correlating them in practice. Notions of growth, communication, information, and control are implicit in the sociological approach. If the possibility and existence of discrepancies between law and social welfare are brought to our attention, we are led to ask questions about the capability of the judicial process to narrow these gaps by its judgments. We seek to assess the performance of the system, in regard to its fixed and changing goals. Briefly, we seek to assess its ability to learn and grow.

In our thinking about goal-directed performance of a judicial decision-making process, we might seek for analogous processes in other systems which also exhibit goal-seeking and goal-changing behavior. Hence we employ a model whose resemblance to the judicial process, as conceived by advocates of a sociological jurisprudence, is suggestive by analogy of the kinds of characteristics that such a process would need in order to perform its prescribed functions with a high degree of efficiency. As we explicate the model, its similarity to many of the considerations of Cardozo will appear quite striking. However, the usefulness of a descriptive model from the social or biological sciences for talking about the judicial process is not exhausted when we describe this process; it also may introduce a fresh perspective from which the judicial process is not usually discussed. Very often, the use of a relevant model enables us to appraise the performance of a system, not only in connection with remedial suggestions, but in regard to our concern with improving our understanding of judicial behavior in a context of other processes outside the legal system.

The tone of this orientation is reflected in a recent article by Philip Selznick.

[2] The cybernetic approach is explained in Norbert Wiener, The Human Use of Human Beings (2d ed. 1954); Karl W. Deutsch, The Nerves of Government: Models of Political Communication and Control (1963); Wladyslaw Sluckin, Minds and Machines (rev. ed. 1960).

He suggests several questions which in effect are concerned with the decision capabilities of the law-in-society, and with the limits of law as an instrument of social control. Selznick complains of a lack of research which would facilitate answers to these questions of performance-criteria of the judicial system:

> In this country, the premises of sociological jurisprudence achieved a rather quick and general victory. . . . This victory, such as it is, has had but little to do with the actual researches of sociologists. . . . It is a point of view, an approach, a sensitivity that has been accepted. . . .
>
> But research has been wanting. This is the kind of problem that can be approached in many ways, but it surely demands both a broad theoretical perspective and an emphasis on social needs and institutional potentialities.

It is hoped that the present approach will provide one such perspective as an aid to assessing the judicial process' potentialities.

Cardozo's image of the judicial process resembles that of

> self-controlling machines which react to their environment, as well as to the results of their own behavior; that store, process, and apply information; and that have, in some cases, a limited capacity to learn.

Thus, a "sociological" judicial process is affected by inputs of new information from the social setting in which it operates, by other stored information from its "memory," and by the feedback of information about the effects its own decisions have had and are likely to have on social processes and values. If it is to keep abreast of social mores, it must have a capacity to learn, and to put into practice what it learns.

The judicial system has a "will," that is

> a pattern of relatively *consolidated preferences and inhibitions, derived from . . . past experiences . . ., consciously labeled . . ., and applied to* guide actions, to restrict the subsequent experiences. . . .

We may assess the judicial will by examining its stored memory; that is, its previous decisions, the doctrines set forth in previous cases, and the statutes by which it is guided. The view of Cardozo is that there always must be a presumption in favor of statute or precedent, except where the statute clearly does not apply, and where the precedent is inconsistent with present-day standard of social justice. A judicial decision must be "in character," and reflect the accumulated preferences as contained in the memory of the system. However, there are dangers in over-reliance on the past – dangers which can only be reduced by a predisposition to learn and employ information from the present, from outside the will of the judicial system.

> We must keep within those interstitial limits which precedent and custom and the long and silent and almost indefinable practice of other judges through the centuries of the common law have set to judge-made innovations. But within the limits thus set, within the range over which choice moves, the final principle of selection for judges, as for legislators, is one of fitness to an end. . . .
>
> Uniformity ceases to be a good when it becomes uniformity of oppression. The social interest served by symmetry or certainty must then be balanced against the social interest served by equity and fairness or other elements of social welfare.

Several considerations flow from this:

1. What is the "will" of the judicial system?
2. To the extent that this depends on its memory, how efficient is the system's memory, such that it does not drift and lose the capacity to direct the system's behavior as an autonomous process?

3. How are past decisions, cases, and dicta stored and classified?
4. How speedily are they capable of being retrieved for purposes of decision-making in the present?
5. What are the probabilities of novel recombination of past information which might more closely suit novel conditions?
6. How much is known about the system's past, and how might this self-knowledge be improved by better techniques of classification and retrieval?
7. How is new information incorporated into the memory, stored, combined with the old, and retrieved; that is, how does the system learn?
8. What are the costs, in time, money, and physical and human resources, of an improved classification-and-retrieval system?
9. How might particular precepts, already existing in precedent although below the conscious attention of participants in the process, be "rediscovered" and employed with relevance to present conditions?
10. If "will" represents

> the set of *internally labeled decisions and anticipated results, proposed by the application of data from the system's past and by the blocking of incompatible impulses or data from the system's present or future*

how might a more effective scanning of precedent increase the probability of intake of impulses from the present or future, in order to up-date the will?
11. To what extent is the judge's hand bound by precedent?
12. At what point in the decision process does the decision harden by the rejection of certain kinds of information, among them new data from the social sciences?
13. Recognizing Cardozo's concern for the limits ("inhibitions") within which the judge must be held, how would an increased consciousness of the judicial past more precisely and pragmatically define these limits?
14. What are the probabilities of these limits changing with increased intake of information, and in which directions?

Each of these matters refers to one of two kinds of "feedback." One is the concept of "goal-seeking feedback"; that is, the responses of the judicial system are to be modified in the light of an evaluation of new information incorporated into the system. The system "zeroes in" on the goal of alignment with social mores in a given period, and the increased information comes from its own precedent as well as from new material added to its memory. The other concept is that of "goal-changing feedback." While the *formal* goal remains constant in the view of sociological jurisprudence, the *substantive* changes in social custom over time require a judicial flexibility in specific policies in order to meet the new requirements of these specific changes in social life. Hence, within the overall (strategic) goal, specific short-run (tactical) goals are set up, sought, and constantly modified through time. The modifications in social phenomena, then, would demand similar modifications in the process and content of judicial decision-making, and also in its machinery. Whether or not the system is able to achieve its long-run goal of social justice may depend on the following:

1. The rate and extent of change in the various areas of social life in relation to the position of the system (*i. e.*, "load").
2. The difference in time between the changes and the system's awareness of them; also, the difference in time between awareness and response (*i. e.*, "lag").
3. The amount of corrective response made by the system (*i. e.*, "gain").
4. The amount of anticipation of social changes before they occur, and the ability of the system to prepare its responses to them (*i. e.*, "lead").

All of these considerations, and several more in the same line of inquiry relate to what Deutsch refers to as "fourth-order purposes," in which he includes

> states offering high probabilities of the *preservation of a process* of purpose-seeking, even beyond the preservation of any particular group or species of nets.

Essentially, the chief question here is: how does a sociologically-oriented judicial process provide for its own growth? Growth, in Deutsch's terms, might mean

> an application of learning capacity toward an increase in openness, that is, an increase in the range, diversity, and effectiveness of an organization's *channels of intake* of information from the outside world . . . an increase in the organization's ability to make effective responses to its environment in accordance with its needs, . . . an increase in the range and diversity of goals the organization is able to follow.

Philip Selznick has pointed out the possible range of applicability of sociological research to the problems of law. Thus, it would be worthwhile to bring to the intelligence-process of the judicial system studies of

> The effect upon legal doctrines and instituions of a number of sociological phenomena, including socialization, value systems, stratifications, collective behavior, and demographic trends. . . .

The following questions relate to the extent to which social-scientific knowledge might enter into the decision process of the judiciary:

1. How great are the predispositions of participants to make use of social science information?
2. How capable are they of handling it meaningfully?
3. What kinds of information are made available by social scientists?
4. What are the costs of this information?
5. In which areas of the law is such information likely to be of value?
6. What is the present and expected availability and employment of this information in those areas?
7. How is the use of sociological data likely to affect judicial behavior, and what have been the results thus far, in terms of social justice?
8. Where does this new input of information stand in relation to the limits set by precedent?

Thus, we may suggest the need for continuous data on changes in the several value processes of society, in order to increase the system's awareness of the recurrence of fissures between its decisions and social phenomena; further, a decrease in the inertia of the system, in order to keep pace with these changes by increasing the propensity of participants to change patterns of decisions where they are no longer applicable; in addition, an increased ability to forecast probable social behavior, and, in turn, to select an appropriate course of action in accordance with projections.

II

So far, we have been considering the inputs to a judical decision-making process, in connection with the goal of sociological jurisprudence; shaping the law to fit customary morality. We have indicated ways of ascertaining the system's capabilities of searching statute and precedent, that it might learn the limits beyond which creative judicial decisions may not go. We have also questioned the system's capabilities to incorporate new data into its memory for application at decision-points. A further set of input-information needs to be specified. This consists of the information that can be obtained about the effects and the subjective perception of law as a means of social control in the society in which it operates, and, further, about variations in the influence of law in different social processes, and variations in perspectives among different participants in them. It is possible that the prescriptions of the legal system loom larger in the perspectives of some groups or individuals than in the perspectives of others, and influence their behavior accordingly. An important sociological task, of great relevance to judicial decision-makers, might be to identify trends in the different perceptions of the efficacy of legal prescriptions in the behavior of people as these individuals or groups differ on social class, economic, psychological and education variables, among others. Another valuable set of data might be the relative strength and distribution over the population of other means of social control, such as a family, school, church, etc. It would be helpful to know the relative strength of law as a means of social control alongside these other instruments of public order, as a guide for policy.

Participants in the judicial process might profitably become concerned with the likely consequences of particular types of decisions, for different categories of people, in order to obtain a more accurate picture of the role of a creative judicial process acting as a social control. Some questions in this area of investigation might be:

1. What techniques are available for tracing and predicting these consequences in society?
2. What are the likely consequences of different types of decisions?
3. What are the inhibitions and possibilities of effecting social changes by means of innovative decisions?
4. What are the different public images of the judicial process, as compared with public images of other social-control mechanisms?
5. What other means of control exist, and for whom, in the absence of an excercise of judicial control?
6. In which social processes are other methods of social regulation more effective and more acceptable as promoters of justice?
7. How might information about matters such as those above be gathered, incorporated, and used in the process of judicial decision-making?
8. What are the implications of such usage for setting the limits to and outlining the areas of possible creativity for the system?

Thus, in order to improve the steering performance of the system, and especially its "lead" capacity, the system must be able to evaluate and predict not only social trends, but also social changes brought about by the system's own policies and actions. Deutsch contends that "The amount of lead . . . depends on the efficiency of predictive processes available to the . . . system.

In addition, perception of the likely effects of decisions in advance would help eliminate possible tendencies for the system to be overloaded with cases, provided that this predicted information were employed in such a way as to keep the incidence of litigation down in areas where social justice can be accomplished without the use of courts to resolve conflicts.

Considering now the functions of intelligence and appraisal, important tasks in the former would be the gathering of goal-statements, trend reports, and condition analyses about social phenomena and processes which might come into the purview of the legal system in future litigation. In addition, projection of trends into the future would better enable judicial decision-makers to foresee future conflicts among social value-practices, and would facilitate the selection of policy alternatives in order to influence future outcomes in the interests of the goal of social justice. The appraisal function would be concerned with evaluating the results of past decisions and those in the present in the light of this goal, providing a feedback of information about the performance of the process so that selection and revision of policies for the future is made on an informed basis.

We are interested in the rationalization of power practices, insofar as the legal system participates in them by the invocation and application of sanctions. Rationalization

> involves two requirements: that the practice is economical with respect to all the values in the situation; and that it has been technicalized, that is, freed from sanctions unrelated to conditions. . . . These results accrue, not adventitiously, but as a consequence of a process of taking thought.

Another way of putting it is that we seek to reduce, by application of a feedback network of intelligence and appraisal, the system's oscillations in the process of achieving the goals indicated in sociological jurisprudential philosophy, over time.

It thus may be relevant to consider a judicial system of prevention, as part of what has been referred to by Lasswell as "the politics of prevention:"

> The problem of politics is less to solve conflicts than to prevent them; less to serve as a safety valve for social protest than to apply social energy to the abolition of recurrent sources of strain in society.

In this sense, a well-selected decision today may perhaps reduce the work-load of the system tomorrow, and may also prevent the genesis of dangerous social strains tomorrow. The short-run work of the system would be the resolution of conflicts that are brought before it, not only in the sense of immediate contests between litigants but also the wider value-conflicts they may contain. Resolution in the short-run might, however, best be the result of an informed process in which the system is alerted to the future and attempts to prevent certain maladaptations in the longer run. Thus, well-thought-out resolution might be an aspect of a preventive strategy, considering the future.

Therefore, the "load" on the system may be decreased by an improvement in the capability of "lead." This can in principle be accomplished by efficient predictability of social trends, and perhaps of social crises; also, by an awareness of the probable results of judicial action in social processes. However, a third possibility is that "load" is reducible by an improvement in the predictability of judicial decisions themselves – an increase in the certainty of law.

III

The certainty of judicial behavior and the predictability of decisions are important considerations and values for which sociological jurisprudence has implications. In the opinion of Cardozo, "We must not throw to the winds the advantages of consistency and uniformity to do justice in the instance. Innovation, therefore, must be carefully guarded. A judicial system which follows a philosophy of conformity to statute or precedent may be highly predictable; no doubt, even a sociologically-oriented judicial system, in the major share of its work, conforms to its past and is thus predictable to a high degree. The judicial system, then, is serving a social purpose even when not carrying out adequately the functions of intelligence (the gathering of information from without) or appraisal (assessing the results of its own behavior) insofar as its decisions are in accord with the expectations of people who must base important parts of their own decisions upon what is likely to be considered legal, and on probable results of lawsuits. Public order is likely to be fostered, in one sense, when the behaviour of the legal system is unambiguous to those in contact with it. As Norbert Wiener states,

> Besides the general principles of justice, the law must be so clear and reproducible that the individual citizen can assess his rights and duties in

advance, even where they appear to conflict with those of others. He must be able to ascertain with a reasonable certainty what view a judge or a jury will take of his position. If he cannot do this, the legal code, no matter how well intended, will not enable him to lead a life free from litigation and confusion.

However, we are not solely concerned with the effects of certainty on public order, on the ability of people acting in social processes to plan their activities in accordance with what they know is likely to be declared illegal. We are also concerned with the effects of certainty on the system itself, on its steering capacity, on its "load," and on its role as an agency for effecting social justice beyond simply public order.

The notions of judicial steering, of goal-seeking and goal-changing, are not in themselves destructive of predictability, nor do they necessarily imply a reduction in the ability of participants in social processes to calculate future judicial outcomes. There is even a sense in which the application of intelligence and appraisal in the making of decisions may tend to decrease the uncertainty of what responses the judicial system will make when it decides cases. For example, by placing decision-making on a more informed, rationalized basis, amenable to public scrutiny by scientific techniques of observation and analysis, we may reduce the scope in which a judge acts out his own biases or psychological idiosyncrasies in decision-making, or at least reduce the unpredictability of these factors. As Wiener says,

> The judges, those to whom is confided the task of the interpretation of the law, should perform their function in such a spirit that if Judge A is replaced by Judge B, the exchange cannot be expected to make a material change in the court's interpretation of customs and of statutes.

Thus, if possible bases for decision-making that judges may refer to in the absence of relevant precedents are a body of sociological research about social phenomena, together with a scientific appraisal of the social results of various types of decisions, these may perhaps increase the probability that different judges can arrive at the same decision. If this information were also available to lawyers, they might have a more rational basis for predicting likely outcomes of litigation. Developing techniques of predicting judicial decisions, as Kort and Nagel have attempted, might be useful in helping restore certainty even though judges relax their reliance in a will governed by the past.

Certainty requires, in addition, agreement on the ends that law is to serve, among the participants in the decision-making process. It depends in part upon the ability to communicate the fact that particular ends are being sought to those outside the process who are basing their activities and choices, to some extent, on what the legal system is likely to regard as legitimate, and what illegitimate and hence subject to sanction. Therefore, better channels of communication between the judicial system and society may be called for, on the assumption that participants in social processes are better able to steer *their* courses with an increase intake and employment of knowledge about the likely position of the legal system, whether or not the latter is constant or changing. A "movable" or goal-changing judiciary might require improvements in the methods available to legal specialists in society to predict the probable direction and rate of change in the goals of the judicial system; in principle, however, certainty need not be threatened by an innovative judicial process.

IV

From the point of view of sociological jurisprudence, justice is not equated with simple correspondence of the law to social practices, because social practices are often in conflict with one another. When a judge is called upon to "legislate" in the absence of rules, he needs some guide byond conformity to social norms in order to steer his behavior. In this sense, law is not merely what the sociologists say it is; although, as we have suggested, sociological jurisprudence must consider outside preferences and values embodied in social phenomena. The judicial system also has its own preferences, in some part implied by the information fed back to it by its memory, from present society, and from a predictable future. The power of the system can be measured by its ability to enforce social compliance with its preferences, without having to review those preferences. Power, in this sense, is connected closely with will. But power need not be blind if the will is subject to revision through time. Power operating from a hardened will can be effective in short-run situations, where temporary "relative" goals are chosen within the "absolute," continuing goal of effecting social justice, and where immediate decision-making capabilities are applied to achieve them. In the short run at least, there exists the problem of *selection* of substantive social purposes to be fostered from among those that compete for indulgence by the system, and of *rejection* of those considered undesirable – incompatible with a view of social welfare. As Pound remarks,

> They [jurists at the start of the present century] began to think of the end of law, not as a maximum of self-assertion, but as a maximum satisfaction of wants. Hence for a time they thought of the problem of ethics, of jurisprudence, and of politics as chiefly one of valuing; as a problem of finding criteria of the relative value of interests. In jurisprudence and politics they saw that we must add practical problems of the possibility of making interests effective through governmental action, judicial or administrative.

For jurists adopting this orientation,

> Attention was turned from the nature of law to its purpose, and a functional attitude, a tendency to measure legal rules and doctrines and institutions by the extent to which they further or achieve the ends for which the law exists, began to replace the older method of judging law by criteria drawn from itself.

From the position of sociological jurisprudence, we are concerned with reducing the propensity of the system to operate on pre-set and unchangeable programming determined only by its will. Thus, in temporary commitments, we ask whether or not the system has reduced its capacity to grow in the future, to alter its specific goals and to maintain its selectivity from among several alternatives by the reception and use of further information. The intention of sociological jurisprudence is not the demise of judicial autonomy, nor of necessary constraints on the judiciary, but the rationalization of preferences, the ability to choose, and the realization on the part of decision-makers that the law and society have a present and a future as well as a past. In Pound's view,

> When we think of law as existing to secure social interests, so far as they may be secured through an ordering of men and of human relations through the machinery of organized political society, it becomes apparent that we may reach a practicable system of compromises of conflicting human desires here and now, by means of a mental picture of giving effect to as much as we can, without believing that we have a perfect solution for all time and for every place.

Of course, we must recognize with Pound that "difficulties arise chiefly in connection with criteria of value." In the absence of an "ultimate" criterion of value, we may agree with Pound's working hypothesis that the jurist should address himself to the problem of

> securing all social interests as far as he may, of maintaining a balance or

harmony among them that is compatible with the securing of all of them. This may require a process of informed creativity which Deutsch has discussed in connection with the political system as a whole, but which appears germane in application to the legal process.

> If we define the core area of politics as the area of enforceable decisions, or more accurately, of all decisions backed by some combination of a significant probability of voluntary compliance with a significant probability of enforcement, then politics becomes the method *par excellence* for securing preferential treatment for messages and commands and for the reallocation of human or material resources. Politics thus appears as a major instrument for either retarding or accelerating social learning. . . .

From this standpoint, the caveat is that the judicial system act so as not to retard social growth in the sense of diversity and change of social wants and individual desires, and where possible, to promote this growth through policy. Referring back to Pound, sociological jurisprudence prefers

> to think of law as a social institution to satisfy social wants – the claims and demands and expectations involved in the existence of civilized society – by giving effect to as much as we may with the least sacrifice, so far as such wants may be satisfied or such claims given effect by an ordering of human conduct through politically organized society.

To the extent that society undergoes growth in its corpus of wants over time, what is sought is, "in short, a continually more efficacious social engineering."

To the extent, also, that a steering problem is deeply involved in this engineering, this paper has attempted to cast some light on the "possibility of improved tools" for a more effective execution of this task.

Richard D. Schwartz, 1925-
Professor of Sociology, Northwestern University

FIELD EXPERIMENTATION IN SOCIOLEGAL RESEARCH (1959)

The need for sociolegal research has been repeatedly stressed. To make law a more effective instrument of policy, the argument runs, it is necessary to understand why it develops, what forms it takes, and especially what are its consequences. Repetition of these well-worn questions is not enough. Indeed, concentration on eloquent and suggestive paraphrases may substitute for the much tougher, but potentially more rewarding, business of digging for the answers.

Yet, for obscure reasons, there is great hesitation about undertaking and supporting such research. Social scientists talk among themselves of the hostile reception that their prospective and complete research receives at the hands of lawyers. Lawyers shake their heads over the insignificant product that social science effort seems to yield. Such general indictments are not very helpful. They may create harmony at home by directing aggression elsewhere, but I doubt that they will contribute to our progress.

Nevertheless, the temptation to engage in interdisciplinary polemic is almost irresistible. My first thought in preparing this paper was to compare the legal profession to the medieval clergy. There are some striking parallels. The lawyers have great power in our society, as did the churchmen of yore. The legal profession draws to itself the most intelligent and capable people in the society, trains them in the skills of doctrinal disputation, and certifies their capacity to decide normative questions on the basis of explicit but unverified assumptions about the nature of reality. Efforts to test these assumptions empirically are turned aside on the premise that common knowledge and logical reasoning provide a satisfactory epistemology, or one that at any rate is superior to the scientific method.

The analogy hinges, however, on the dubious premise that legal resistance to social science is based on arrogance rather than on reasonable doubt as to the utility for law of social science research. Until such doubts are resolved, it would be unfair to say that legal resistance to social science is irrational. The lawyers I know – they are, to be sure, a biased sample – have shown little evidence of irrational resistance. If anything, some lawyers (not my friends) have at times been too eager to accept the substantive conclusions of social scientists without inquiring into the adequacy of the methods and findings on which these conclusions are based. Reliance on Kinsey and on some of the sources cited in footnote eleven of the Desegregation Cases are painful illustrations of this tendency. Greater methodological sophistication on the part of lawyers should make it possible for them to select and interpret sound empirical findings, while rejecting invalid and irrelevant ones. In the present state of the social sciences, however, I am afraid that such selection would not leave us much. Our problem, as I understand it, is to explore ways in which we can increase the supply of scientifically valid and legally relevant empirical research.

It seems to me that there are three principal ways in which social science can ultimately yield findings which are relevant to law. First, it can enlarge the range of *alternative policies* envisioned by legal policy-makers. Second, it can seek to explain *decisions* representing choices among alternative policies. Third, it can examine, in terms of some specified criteria, the *consequences* of each of the alternatives.

Given our existing knowledge, it seems to me that we would be wise to focus on the last of these, the problem of consequences. By so doing, we may achieve a better basis for conceptualizing and exploring alternative legal policies. Concentration of our efforts on consequences and alternatives may also provide time for the development of methodolgical innovations capable of application to legal decision-making.

In examining the consequences of alternative legal policies, what kinds of research will be most useful? Our methods should, in so far as possible, give us the most accurate information about the widest range of relevant consequences, with the least disturbance to the existing social order, and with the largest increment to general knowledge concerning the nature of man and society. My present view is that field experimentation – as contrasted with case studies, survey research, and laboratory experimentation – holds the greatest promise of meeting these criteria. By a field experiment, I mean the controlled introduction of stimuli into situations that existed without experimental instigation, under circumstances where the differential effects of those stimuli can be accurately measured. All of the other methods mentioned earlier are useful in preparing for and supplementing field experiments and in substituting for them where field experiments are impossible. Of course, a case can be made for the primacy of the other methods. But the field experiment seems to me to provide a model of the type of research that promises most for the empirical study of the consequences of law. Because it does, I shall try to present the case for this method.

I

Taking a leaf from the law teacher's book, let us proceed by way of a case study of sociolegal research design. At present, I am working with Jerome H. Skolnick, a fellow-sociologist at the Yale Law School, on factors contributing to individual compliance with income tax laws. The subject has some obvious advantages. For one thing, it has a practical side. According to the sample audit of 1948, a billion and a half dollars were lost during that year because of underestimations on personal returns of taxes owed to the Government. The amount that the audit failed to disclose may add appreciably to the total sum; subsequent inflation and tax law changes may boost it further. Even accepting the 1948 figure, consider the possible advantages of a more effective tax collecting policy. If our advice could increase payment by one per cent and if we received contingent fees of, say, five per cent, the return for one year's work would be $750,000. Forgive me for sounding mercenary, but I can not help thinking what a wonderful endowment that would make for an Institute of Sociolegal Research. Seriously, though, there is merit in doing research – especially this kind of research – on a subject of practical concern to lawmakers, law enforcers, law violators, and (that residual category) law abiders. Pervasive interest in the topic increases the chances of obtaining cooperation all around.

What type of study is most appropriate to this subject? Let us begin with impressionistic methods, proceed to survey research, and then examine experimental possibilities.

First, we might introspect about our own reasons for complying with income tax laws. This might yield some interesting hypotheses, but little more. We, as a group, probably violate the tax laws too infrequently to permit examination of the range from complete compliance to complete violation. We might come up with many (perhaps disproportionately many) instances of avoidance, but we would yield disappointingly little by way of evasion. Since the policy objective calls for eliminating evasion, our design would lack information on that segment of taxpaying behavior which matters most.

To avoid that difficulty, we might arrange to interview tax evaders. The easiest way to find such a group is to interview convicted tax offenders in prison. This has been done with embezzlers and could undoubtedly be easily arranged with tax evaders. One may wonder whether the imprisoned tax evaders are a representtive sample of all tax evaders. Does the fact of their being caught make them less responsive to threat of sanction, less well-advised, more involved with the underworld, and so forth? It should be noted also that tax evaders in prison may be appreciably different from those whose crimes have not been publicly exposed and whose liberty is undisturbed. If such differences exist, they might lead us to erroneous conclusions concerning the nature of the average uncaught tax evader and thence to mistakes in our policy recommendations as to the best ways of making the unknown evader comply.

Perhaps we should survey the entire taxpaying population to obtain representative samples of evaders, avoiders, and strict compliers. A national random sample of taxpayers would require an enormous effort. It would have made Alfred Kinsey turn pale – which would have been no mean trick. Kinsey himself settled for quota sampling, meaning that he filled each of his categories with volunteers in the order in which they presented themselves. By so doing, he estimates that he reduced the cost per subject to about three per cent of previous interview studies. From his own evidence, however, the resultant sample appears to overrepresent the domineering, sexually more active elements in the white American and Canadian male population that he studied. It may be that he had no real choice, since the turndown rate among randomly sampled citizens who were asked to talk about their sex lives might be enormous; exceeded only, perhaps, by the turndown rate of those chosen at random to be questioned about their tax evasions.

Some ways are available for dealing with the sampling problem. One might begin by trying to obtain a random or even a 100 per cent sample of some segment of the population that was particularly amenable to being surveyed, for instance, a professional society such as the American Sociological Association, whose members are professionally committed to the value of such research. If several such groups could be obtained, we might assume that we had not an unbiased sample of the taxpayer universe, but a sample whose biases we could specify. Or, to put it another way, we could ascertain what universe we *had* accurately sampled and compare it to the one originally sought. For our purposes, a subuniverse of business and professional men might turn out to be as valuable as a sample of the entire universe of taxpayers, since much of the entire universe consists of working men whose opportunities for evasion are limited.

Assuming that we have properly sampled an interesting universe, what then? We might try to get information from the subjects directly. Since questionnaires have a way of not being returned, interviews would be a better, though costlier, method. What would we want to know? First of all, it would be necessary to identify the dependent variable, tax compliance or evasion. Since that is likely to be an embarrassing subject, we might put it toward the end of the interview or disguise it by asking only such data as income, deductions, exemptions, and tax payments – from which we might later calculate the amount that should have been paid and compare it with the amount reportedly paid. We might even get information bearing on intent, which would provide a basis for estimating whether or not the failure to pay would qualify as fraud.

Several devices could increase the validity of the findings. It is possible to provide a series of internal consistency checks. We know something about ways of establishing rapport and increasing motivation to tell the truth. Of special importance in this kind of interview would be the assurance of complete anonymity. Since information on illegal conduct would be uncovered, the researchers and their records could be subpoenaed to aid in tax fraud prosecution. It is interesting to note in this connection that no privilege has been established for researchers, no matter how valuable their work may be to society. In the specific case of tax research, where the Government avowedly has something to gain, Internal Revenue Service officials said regretfully that the Service was unable to commit itself in writing to any kind of privilege. Justice Department officials were less circumspect. Asked about a possible informal immunity from subpoena, a Deputy Assistant Attorney General exclaimed, "You guys are mad!" Parenthetically, one might ask whether changes in the machinery of government are not worth consideration where these might be expected to contribute to an appraisal of, and consequent increase in, governmental effectiveness. It certainly does not make it easy or pleasant for a researcher to know that his records might be subpoenaed. Nevertheless, the problem of anonymity can be handled with some additional effort by destroying all records of the identity of the subject or by making sure through a third party that the interviewer is never aware of the subject's identity. Though my colleague, Professor Abraham S. Goldstein, says that conceptually such procedures might fall within the broad ambit of conspiracy to defraud the Government, he assures me that, as a practical matter, (as a matter of living law, that is) anonymity of subjects can in this way probably be preserved.

Once data concerning tax evasion has been obtained, their validity should be checked. This is much more difficult than determining their internal consistency. In dealing with reports of behavior where the motive for distortion is strong, substantiation is especially crucial. Chances are that verbal reports of what the subject paid the Government would be reasonably accurate. They might be checked by obtaining carbon copies of returns or by securing the individual's permission to look at the filed return. Another possibility involves obtaining employment-without-compensation with the IRS in order to have legal access to the returns. The latter course unfortunately entails a legal obligation to report to tax officials every instance of fraud known by the employee, a requirement that might well conflict with the researcher's obligation to his subjects.

A more serious problem arises in checking the validity of information as to what the subject *ought* to have paid. One method would be to request a fully anonymous communication following the interview, in which the subject would indicate whether he had consciously distorted and, if so, in what ways and for what reasons. This technique would also provide a basis for selecting and evolving superior techniques of interviewing, by permitting rough comparisons among diverse interview methods. Another check on validity might be obtained by securing independent information on given items of income, such as dividends from a particular company or questionable fellowships, and relating this information to interview responses. The problem with such methods is that the dishonest subject is likely to reveal whatever is a matter of public record and distort those items that are unknown to interviewer and auditor alike.

A final possible way of securing validity involves coordination of the survey with IRS auditing activities, so that the determination of evasion might be left entirely in government hands. If a survey could be arranged in advance, without forewarning the subjects of an eventual audit, this might provide the surest way thus far mentioned of relating background information to a valid index of tax compliance. It is doubtful, of course, that government officials would be able to permit such an arrangement.

These problems have been discussed in some detail to give some idea of the difficulties entailed in survey research. Even among the methods mentioned, some would have to be discarded on grounds of impracticality, immorality, or illegality. Probably remaining would be a residue of questionable information, better perhaps than anything now available, but falling short of desired standards of scientific accuracy. The same can be said for methods of ascertaining other information in the survey, notably information concerning factors contributing to tax evasion – that is, the independent variables. If, for instance, taxpaying is viewed as a type of decision-making, it would be necessary to examine such factors as the background of the decision-makers, their existing statuses and roles, their values and expectations, and their decision-making orientations. All of these are likely to present validity problems in one form or another, often in ways that are much more complex than the validity problem discussed.

Assuming that valid data could be obtained, the problem of analysis would then arise. Survey data of this kind would require a comparison of compliers and evaders in terms of numerous characteristics. The principal difficulty posed by such an analysis lies in isolating the effect of any given independent variable. It is not enough to show that a particular variable, such as education, is correlated with evasion. This relationship might occur solely because of the relationship of education to income and the relationship of income to evasion. Indeed, if we were to hold income constant (by examining the relationship between education and evasion at various income levels), we might discover that education correlated inversely with evasion – that is, that well-educated people at a given level of income evaded taxes less frequently than poorly-educated ones at the same income level. Alternatively, it might turn out that the inverse relationship just mentioned existed at high income levels but that it was reversed at lower income levels, where better-educated people might be more likely to evade.

Several difficulties inhere in this type of analysis. It is impossible to locate all of the relevant factors or to control for them by randomization. Even with known relevant factors, simultaneous statistical control requires extremely large samples. Using 12,000 cases, Kinsey was unable to exercise simultaneous control over more than seven of the twelve factors that he considered relevant. To control a limited number of factors at a time is to run the risk that the relationship then observed between the independent and dependent variables is the result of a rampant additional factor, control of which would destroy the apparent relationship.

Finally, survey analysis poses problems of statistical criteria. It has been cogently argued that tests of significance are appropriate primarily in experimental situations. Their function there is to specify the likelihood that the differences appearing between the experimental and control groups after administration of the experimental variable are *not* the result of chance in selection from a common universe. If the experiment is to show statistically significant results, it must produce an effect greater than might have occurred by any plausible chance. Though the same phrases have been used in the context of survey research, it is doubtful that they are legitimately applied there, since random selection of the two compared groups was not employed in the first place. If application of these tests is not legitimate, then the question arises as to how an objective measure can be obtained that would provide meaningful standardized criteria of the magnitude of differences obtained from survey analysis.

One further point should be raised concerning the utility of the survey. Even if we could specify the relations between variables, would we be able to use such information in recommending policies? As a source of hypotheses, yes. As a basis for prediction, I think not. Unless we have some way of ascertaining the effect of a given policy in action, our capacity to verify the hypotheses will necessarily be limited.

II

From survey analysis, then, we can hope at best to obtain interesting but unverified hypotheses. What is needed is a rigorous way of testing them. The most accurate way of verifying a hypothesis is the controlled experiment. I shall not attempt to describe this method in detail, since I assume a familiarity with it in general terms. Its use in social science research has not yet been extensive enough to permit detailed and critical discussion of its values and limitations in the study of human behavior. The ultimate evaluation of experimentation will have to depend on many more examples than are now available. Nevertheless, logical considerations combined with limited experience can take us part of the way.

Suppose we wanted to study experimentally the relative effects of threats and incentives on tax compliance. What would this require? Principally, three things: first, a valid measure of tax compliance; second, a way of giving or not giving measurable amounts of threat or incentive to individual taxpayers; and third, conditions under which changes in tax compliance could not be attributed to any factors other than the direct or indirect action of the independent variable.

All of these conditions can best be achieved, I believe, by controlled experimentation. This means at a minimum that the independent variable should be administered to randomly-selected individuals and withheld from randomly-selected individuals. Where experimental and control groups of adequate size are randomly-selected and subjected to conditions similar in all regard except the independent variable, it is possible to assume that the differences they show will be primarily owing to the operation of the independent variable. This method tends to minimize the impact of a number of other factors that might otherwise affect the result. Suppose we urged a randomly-selected sample of taxpayers to pay their taxes for patriotic reasons, but provided no comparison with a similar group receiving a threat or receiving no communication. A subsequent increase in tax payment in that group might be the result of several factors, such as a rising income level, a change in the moral climate of the country, an increase in the Soviet threat, a tendency of taxpayers to become increasingly honest with age and experience, and a statistical effect resulting from having so high a proportion of noncompliers in the original sample that more changes can occur by chance in the direction of compliance than in the direction of noncompliance. If, on the other hand, we had a randomly-selected control group that we could observe over the same period, it would be plausible to assume that all such effects would operate on that group as well. Accordingly, the difference between taxpaying in the two groups would give a measure of the effectiveness of the communication.

To achieve maximum validity, however, such studies should generally be carried out in field rather than in laboratory settings. Laboratory situations are typically limited to a very specialized sample, those who volunteer or can be coerced into participation. These subjects, moreover, are placed under conditions that by definition vary from those of ordinary life. To the extent that they perceive these differences, their reactions may differ markedly from what might be expected in real life situations.

These problems are illustrated in the very important University of Chicago jury studies, which have been designed and executed by a topnotch experimental sociologist, Fred Strodtbeck. In the Chicago studies, the problem of sample representativeness is neatly handled by drawing subjects from regular jury panels. The second problem (the problem of realism) is partially dealt with by having a real judge impress on the jurors the importance of their task. A source of external invalidity (*i. e.*, incapacity to generalize experimental results to the real world) remains, however, in the jurors' knowledge that they are judging an unreal proceeding and that their decisions will not have consequences for the parties. This source of invalidity may well be reinforced by the procedure of presenting a recorded trial rather than showing real people in action. An effort to ascertain the degree of invalidity is made by obtaining postexperimental reports concerning the feelings of reality of which subjects were aware. Such statements, while providing some evidence of validity, are not conclusive, since they are subject to two kinds of distortion: conscious (*e.g.*, from a desire to please the investigator) and unconscious (*e.g.*, a lack of subjective awareness of the effects that identification might have had in actual jury duty). Another technique for checking validity involves comparisons between deliberations of actual juries and experimental ones. This scientifically promising effort ran into practical difficulties whose outcome is well known.

A third source of external invalidity in laboratory experiments derives from sampling particular types of decisions from the universe of possible decisional situations in the real world. Unless this sampling is representative of the universe, serious limitations may be imposed on the capacity for valid generalization. Thus, the Chicago jury studies on the *M'Naghten* and *Durham* rules are limited to one or two fact situations, whose representativeness for all actual uses of the rules is doubtful. A possible solution would involve systematic variations of fact situations in order to approximate the universe, but this would entail many additional experiments or a limitation on the valuable practice of replicating particular trials.

These limitations on external validity make it unwise to depend entirely on the laboratory for experimental research. For some topics, such as the jury studies, laboratory experiments may be the only method possible. Moreover, with great skill, adequate simulation of field conditions might conceivably be obtained. But it is difficult to see how the laboratory could or should be adapted to the study of tax compliance. A tax service might be set up, but to the extent that it simulated a real advisory service, it would approach the field experiment. If it failed to, the subjects might well diverge widely from their ordinary motives and expectations. In any case, a public tax service would attract a rather specialized sample of taxpayers whose differences from the universe would be difficult to specify.

To avoid these problems, one might undertake, with government cooperation, a full-scale field experiment on tax compliance. From the universe of sixty million individual federal income taxpayers, we would randomly select several large samples. To each of these would be sent one or more communications from various sources (*e. g.*, IRS, a citizens' organization, a tax advisory service) – communications containing different kinds of content (*e.g.*, anxiety-arousing warnings and appeals to social and individual incentives of various kinds). Effects of these diverse patterns of communication could be observed by obtaining *group* data on the increase in tax payments of various kinds over the preceding year and as compared with other groups that had received other or no communications. By obtaining such group data, we could avoid any knowledge of individual returns. The group distributions would provide a quantitative measure (complete with means and standard deviations) of increased compliance with the law. This measure could be related to the single isolated independent variables to which that group had been subjected.

It is not necessary for this purpose to detail the proposed research design further. Suffice it to say that the method seems to fulfill the requirements of a field experiment. If it worked – and one never knows until research is completed whether it will – our results should be free of many of the difficulties faced in survey research and laboratory experimentation. We would have a quantitative measure of the dependent variable, without the need for elaborate validation. The independent variables could be administered in a variety of patterns, representing alternative enforcement policies. The relative effectiveness of each could be determined for the short and long run, in regard to specific types of payment and for general compliance. Factors could be patterned to determine how the combined effects compared with the sum of their individual effects. Undoubtedly, the method would raise new problems that are difficult to foresee. For instance, initial receipt of tax communications by *isolated* individuals would probably have very different effects than might be expected from repeated or widespread use of such messages. Theories of social interaction and cultural development give us hypotheses as to what these differences would be, but these would require verification by continuing research.

In addition, administration of these messages might have a variety of consequences (*e.g.*, effects on bond buying, attitude to Government, letters to Congress) other than their direct effects on tax compliance. These side-effects would, of course, have to be anticipated and studied if the experiment were to provide fully adequate guidance for policy decisions.

From the viewpoint of social science theory, such research should yield interesting results. Accurate indices of law-abiding behavior would be available. It would be possible to test the duration, generality, and uniformity of the effect of different kinds of sanctions and sanctioners on such behavior. Further elaborations should make it possible to test the interaction of experimental stimuli with dispositional factors pre-existing in the subjects. The design may be used for quantitative tests drawn from such diverse theorists as Weber, Durkheim, Hull, and Freud. It should be noted that findings would be limited, for ethical and legal reasons, to communications likely to have a neutral or positive effect on tax compliance. Nevertheless, the range of alternatives permissible within that requirement would justify the study in theoretical terms.

It is my belief that empirical studies that can yield precise results on determinants of behavior are extremely important for the development of both social science and law. After a hundred or a thousand studies of this kind, we shall be in a far better position to construct a systematic general theory and to use law as an effective instrument of control. For the present, we need to know, within narrow ranges of data, what works how.

In this kind of research, the interest of the social scientist coincides with that of the problem-oriented lawyer. Both need to know the precise effects of particular policies. The lawyer can help to locate appropriate problems, specify the criteria (including main and side effects) as to whether given policies work, and arrange the legal and administrative conditions necessary for field experimentation. The social scientist can set up the experimental design and provide the analysis of data. Elucidation of alternative policies is a task to which both disciplines might contribute, the lawyer in terms of the feasible, the social scientist in terms of the theoretically interesting and counterintuitive. Such a differentiation is likely to blur over time, since each of the participants may find himself more capable of contributing as he acquires knowledge of the other's specialty. There is probably real value, however, in each participant retaining and strengthening his original specialized knowledge and role conception.

Of course, field experimentation cannot automatically be applied to every legal problem. Designing a field experiment in any legal area requires methodological training, extensive planning, and good luck. Perhaps as this and other exact methods are developed in sociolegal research, standardized procedures will emerge that will make such research easier. For the present, however, the planning of valid research takes time and energy. If such research succeeds, the results for law and social science should be well worth the effort.

Besides the Chicago jury studies, perhaps the most important law-social-science partnership has been the Columbia Project for Effective Justice. Its director, Columbia Law Professor Maurice Rosenberg, described it as follows in 1963 ["Researching Law in Action" (1963) 7 *Colum. L. Alumni Bull*, 12-15]:

> "In 1956 the Columbia University Project for Effective Justice was organized to make systematic studies of law in action – so to speak, to compare law in action with law in the books. Since then the Project has made several large-scale surveys of civil litigation, drawing on the work of sociologists as well as lawyers; and upon statistics, experimentation and computers as well as upon traditional lawyer skills and resources. The main Project efforts to date have been concentrated on investigating proposed plans for rolling back trial delay in the civil courts, to see whether and how they work. . . . Judges and lawmakers from all parts of the country increasingly consult the Project for help in planning research in vital sectors of the administration of justice. During the last few weeks its counsel has been asked on such diverse programs as: possible revision of jurisdictional and venue lines in the federal court system; a study of free press and fair trial; and evaluation of proposals to introduce pretrial examiners and auditors in several state court systems. These inquiries come to the Project for careful work.
>
> "The first problem the Project tackled was excessive trial delay, a subject of nationwide concern. Research on court delay led directly to intensive investiga-

tion of the dynamics of personal injury litigation, for negligence suits comprise about two-thirds of the business of major civil courts through-out the country. A group of field studies in New York, Arkansas, Massachusetts and Pennsylvania disclosed that personal injury actions are subject to discernible dynamic principles; and that many of the widely advertised "remedies" for court delay do not on close analysis justify claims made for them by their sponsors, while others do.

"In addition to its independent research, the Project sponsored a joint undertaking with the Association of the Bar of the City of New York to learn why some people injured in automobile accidents make claims and bring lawsuits while others similarly situated do not. The results have been published in a book entitled "Who Sues in New York City?" by Roger B. Hunting and Gloria S. Neuwirth. The staff has completed preliminary work on a set of recommendations to cut down trial delay in handling personal injury cases and these will be presented in 1963.

"The most exciting Project research effort to date has been the controlled test of the impact of the pretrial conference procedure on personal injury cases in New Jersey. The work was done in cooperation with the Supreme Court of New Jersey and is believed to be a unique application of experimental methods to evaluate the functioning of a major procedural rule. Beginning in 1960, under a special court rule requested by the Project, the pretrial conference procedure, instead of being applied to every case in turn on a mandatory basis, was applied to every other case, to provide a "control" of its functioning. After nearly three years in the collection of data on 3,000 cases as they followed their courses through the litigation process, the Project has prepared its preliminary findings and evaluations. At a seminar co-sponsored by the Project at Princeton, New Jersey, on September 5-7, 1962, the trial and appellate judges of New Jersey were given a report of the findings. Chief Justice Joseph Weintraub then created a committee of judges to work with a group from the Project to investigate carefully the changes which should be made in New Jersey procedures upon the basis of the Project's test and findings. This task of harnessing the findings is to begin in December, 1962.

"The Project's chief new task is a study of the functioning of pretrial discovery rules in federal civil cases. A comprehensive field study of federal discovery is desired by the Advisory Committee on Civil Rules (Dean Acheson, chairman), created in 1960 under the aegis of the United States Supreme Court to study the Federal Rules of Civil Procedure and to suggest needed revisions. The Acheson Committee believes that evaluation of the discovery rules in their present form requires empirical research rather than reliance solely on traditional library analysis. The Chief Justice of the United States has declared his support for this approach and for the Project's undertaking the study. The discovery program will occupy the major energies of the Columbia Project's staff until 1964. It is being carried out under generous grants from The Ford Foundation and the Walter E. Meyer Research Institute of Law, Inc.

"The field investigation, by interview, mail questionnaire, courtroom observation, docket studies, etc., is designed to produce the facts about discovery in its day to day use and to determine the impact of discovery procedures upon the litigation process – its relation to other pretrial procedures, to promoting settlements, more efficient trials, and fairer trials."

For opposing views on the value of social science for law see Fahr, "Why Lawyers Are Dissatisfied With the Social Sciences" (1961) 1 *Washburn L. J.* 161, and Geis, "The Social Sciences and the Law" (1962) 1 *Washburn L. J.* 569. In "Law and the Behavioral Sciences: The Case for Partnership" (1963) 47 *J. Am. Jud. Soc.* 109, Professor Harry Jones, then Director of Research of the American Bar Foundation, describes a colloquium on research in judicial administration marking the initiation of a new program in judicial administration at the Universty of Denver College of Law.

A stimulating article, "What Law Can Do for Social Science" *Law and Sociology*

91-123 (Evan ed. 1962) by Professor Thomas A. Cowan emphasizes that the relationship is one of mutual benefit. Professor Cowan writes (94): "The law can help the process of social investigation (1) by sharpening up the social scientific model [through the lawyer's training in the art of verbal inquiry]; (2) by supplying the social scientist's kit with another investigative tool, the art of cross-examination; (3) by providing him with a method of control, namely, legal coercion; (4) by making available to him an immense reservoir of value judgments on human behavior in the history of law itself and in its present body of empirical rules of decision."

Chapter V

The Judicial Process

Perhaps the most striking characteristic of the common law is the tension between its two conflicting attitudes to legal generalizations: on the one hand, there is the cautious case by case approach, which in tendency limits the generalization to the instant case; and on the other hand, there is the attitude towards precedent expressed in the doctrine of stare decisis, the principle of following the decided cases of the past, which in tendency extends the generalization over a wide area of the law. The interplay of these opposing tendencies makes possible a legal system capable of both stability and change. Possibly the common law appears to the nonlegal observer to be as changeless as the laws of the Medes and Persians, and perhaps he feels that the only release from its rigid embrace is to be found in statutory enactment, but anything more than a cursory study will show that even apart from statutory reform, the common law of today is far from a carbon copy of the common law of the nineteenth century. The law changes as society changes, in some fields so rapidly that Cardozo calculated that the life span of a case is about a single generation.

A study of the judicial process in the twentieth century must be in large measure an account of the conflict between the traditional conception and the new approach of American Legal Realism. The traditional theory of the common law, as laid down by such masters as Coke and Blackstone, was that the judge did not make the law but merely found it. In this view there was little of creativity about the judicial role, for the judge has merely to look in the opinions of his predecessors for principles from which to deduce the proper rule for the case at hand. It was recognized that sometimes no precedents directly in point could be found, and in this event the judge was expected to chart new lands, in the sense that he might extend the old principles by analogy. But he was at most a judicial Christopher Columbus, discovering what was already existent, though previously unknown. He was never a Thomas Edison, bringing into being something which had not hitherto been. At its most extreme this theory looked on the judge as a logical automaton who needed to know merely how to deduce conclusions from premises.

Holmes was not the only jurisprudent to take issue with the old view, but he may well have been the first. It was not until the first decade of the twentieth century that Roscoe Pound entered the fray against the traditionalists, and Holmes' lecture, "The Path of the Law" was delivered two years before François Gény published his *Méthode d'interprétation et sources en droit privé* in 1899 and brought a similar viewpoint to bear on the French civil law. Moreover, along with Pound, Holmes was more responsible than anyone else for the propagation in the common-law world of the new theory that law is not an end in itself but merely a means to social ends. Indeed Holmes had already written in his book, *The Common Law,* published in 1881:

> "The life of the law has not been logic: it has been experience. The felt necessities of the time, the prevalent moral and political theories, intuitions of public policy, avowed or unconscious, even the prejudices which judges share with their fellow men, have had a good deal more to do than the syllogism in determining the rules by which men should be governed" (p. 1).

It was, however, his formulation of the problem in terms of prediction in his 1897 speech which was to have the profoundest effect on later jurisprudents. The realists under Karl Llewellyn, acknowledging Holmes as their spiritual father, took as their starting point his denunciation of the fallacy of logical form in the second part of his essay.

Professor Hessel Yntema, himself a part of the realist explosion of the late 'twenties and early 'thirties, has recently written a mature reflection on the realism movement ["American Legal Realism in Retrospect" (1960) 14 *Vand. L. Rev.* 317, 323]. In his view there were four characteristic hypotheses of the movement: (1) the conception of law as a means to politics and values; (2) the conception of law in society, as a part of life; (3) the conception of change in both law and society and consequently a critique of legal rules on the basis of social context; and (4) the conception of legal research as a scientific enterprise open to critical scepticism and accompanied by objective description of detail, accurate formulation of solutions, and the use of appropriate techniques. In retrospect Professor Yntema is willing to abandon the early stress on behaviorism which led to the drawing of a sharp distinction between what courts say and what they do, for he feels that judicial opinions are as much facts as judicial actions and that the appropriate distinction is one of degree rather than of kind. He also disallows even the temporary divorce between *is* and *ought* which Llewellyn adopted, on the ground that, although law itself must always be normative, the scientific study of law is rather descriptive.

The question may well be raised whether American legal realism is a movement that died a generation ago. Certainly the excitement of the early days has not been sustained in the last three decades. But the early excitement was in part the result of the personal impact upon their audience of Llewellyn's vehemence and of Frank's down-to-earth matter-of-factness, manifested in such Frank titles as "Are Judges Human?" (1931), "If Men Were Angels" (1942), and "Say It With Music" (1948), for legal realism was a movement in which, despite the scientific intention, personality mattered a great deal. The writing, however, did not stop, for both Frank and Llewellyn continued to publish until their deaths in 1957 and 1962 respectively. Moreover, the last few years have witnessed a new realist interest in the problem of law and morals, as manifested by Professor Harry Jones' perceptive study in which he draws the conclusion that "the moral dimension of law is to be sought . . . in the process of responsible decision". Undoubtedly this position is taken under existentialist as well as under realist influence, but it does raise the fundamental question whether realism can cease to be merely a process theory that can be tacked onto any substantive theory of law and itself become an autonomous substantive viewpoint.

Moreover, in the last few years the influence of realism has just begun to make itself felt among natural lawyers and positivists, two groups which until recently felt they were essentially committed to the traditional attitude of judicial quietism. Professor H. L. A. Hart displayed some positivist adaptation to the realist stimulus in his debate with Professor Fuller and natural lawyers such as Dean O'Meara and Rev. Thomas E. Davitt, S. J. [*The Elements of Law* (1957)] have shown a keen awareness of realist insights. [For another naturalist appreciation of realism, see MacGuigan, "The Problem of Law and Morals in Contemporary Jurisprudence" (1962) 8 *Catholic Law.* 293].

However, in a deeper sense it is irrelevant to ask whether legal realism has survived, because since the 'thirties realist attitudes (perhaps in slightly tamed form) have dominated American and Canadian jurisprudence to the point of becoming current coin. If legal realism is no longer recognizable as a distinct movement, it is because we all, to a greater or lesser degree, have become realists. [On realism generally, see Gilmore, "Legal Realism: Its Cause and Cure" (1961) 70 *Yale L. J.* 1037, and Burrus, "American Legal Realism" (1962) 8 *How. L. J.* 36].

A. CASES

LONDON STREET TRAMWAYS COMPANY, LIMITED v. LONDON COUNTY COUNCIL.

House of Lords. (1898) 78 L.T. 361; [1898] A.C. 375.

Sir R. T. Reid Q. C. and *Seward Brice Q.C.* (*J.R. Paget* with them) for the appellants. This is in substance a petition to reconsider and overrule the decisions of this House in the *Edinburgh Street Tramways* and the *London Street Tramways* cases upon the construction of s. 43 of the Tramways Act, 1870. There are certain differences, between the present facts and the facts in those cases, which are set out in the appellants' case, but they are comparatively unimportant. The question is the same and arises upon the construction of the same statute. It is therefore desired to argue as a preliminary point the general question whether the House is bound by its own decision on a point of law in a previous case, and if that is determined in the appellants' favour, then to argue that the above decisions in 1894 were erroneous, for reasons which were not presented to the House in those cases. Upon the general question there is a conflict of authority. . . .

Freeman Q.C. and Hon. *Alfred Lyttleton* for the respondents were not heard.

EARL OF HALSBURY L.C. My Lords, I think your Lordships are very much indebted to Sir Robert Reid and his learned junior for the candour with which this question has been raised. It would undoubtedly have been extremely inconvenient if, after hearing the case argued for a considerable time, the fact had been pointed out to us that there was a decision of this House which was conclusive upon the point. By the candour of the learned counsel who very properly raised the question in the first instance, it has now been admitted that there is upon this very question a decision of this House.

My Lords, for my own part I am prepared to say that I adhere in terms to what has been said by Lord Campbell and assented to by Lord Wensleydale, Lord Cranworth, Lord Chelmsford and others, that a decision of this House once given upon a point of law is conclusive upon this House afterwards, and that it is impossible to raise that question again as if it was res integra and could be reargued, and so the House be asked to reverse its own decision. That is a principle which has been, I believe, without any real decision to the contrary, established now for some centuries, and I am therefore of opinion that in this case it is not competent for us to rehear and for counsel to reargue a question which has been recently decided.

My Lords, the only trace of authority for the proposition submitted to us by the learned counsel is that of Lord St. Leonards, and I give full effect to the argument of the learned counsel when I say that no doubt Lord St. Leonards did in the most unqualified manner lay down the proposition for which he contends. Whether that noble and learned Lord was altogether satisfied with his own reasoning I am not prepared to say. When I find the proposition coupled with such qualifications and such a preamble as Lord St. Leonards has introduced in his judgment, I entertain some doubt whether the noble and learned Lord was perfectly satisfied in his own mind as to the logic of his reasoning. Whether he was or was not, the main point is that this House has on more than one occasion acted upon the principle to which I have referred.

My Lords, no more conspicuous case could arise, I think, than what occurred in the case of *Beamish* v. *Beamish* [(1861) 9 H.L.C. 274]. In that case some of the learned Lords were of opinion that *Reg.* v. *Millis* [(1844) 10 Cl. & F. 534].

was wrongly decided, but nevertheless they acquiesced in that decision – that is to say, they held themselves bound by that decision in the subsequent case of *Beamish* v. *Beamish* and treated that decision of your Lordships' House as conclusive upon the question then under appeal.

My Lords, it is totally impossible, as it appears to me, to disregard the whole current of authority upon this subject, and to suppose that what some people call an "extraordinary case," an "unusual case," a case somewhat different from the common, in the opinion of each litigant in turn, is sufficient to justify the rehearing and rearguing before the final Court of Appeal of a question which has been already decided. Of course I do not deny that cases of individual hardship may arise, and there may be a current of opinion in the profession that such and such a judgment was erroneous; but what is that occasional interference with what is perhaps abstract justice as compared with the inconvenience – the disastrous inconvenience – of having each question subject to being reargued and the dealings of mankind rendered doubtful by reason of different decisions, so that in truth and in fact there would be no real final Court of Appeal? My Lords, "interest rei publicae" that there should be "finis litium" at some time, and there could be no "finis litium" if it were possible to suggest in each case that it might be reargued, because it is "not an ordinary case," whatever that may mean. Under these circumstances I am of opinion that we ought not to allow this question to be reargued.

My Lords, I only wish to say one word in answer to a very ingenious argument which the learned counsel set before your Lordships. It is said that this House might have omitted to notice an Act of Parliament, or might have acted upon an Act of Parliament which was afterwards found to have been repealed. It seems to me that the answer to that ingenious suggestion is a very manifest one – namely, that that would be a case of a mistake of fact. If the House were under the impression that there was not such an Act as was suggested, of course they would not be bound, when the fact was ascertained that there was not such an Act or that the Act had been repealed, to proceed upon the hypothesis that the Act existed. They would then have ascertained whether it existed or not as a matter of fact, and in a subsequent case they would act upon the law as they found it to be, although before they had been under the impression, on the hypothesis I have put, either on the one hand that an Act of Parliament did not exist, or on the other hand that an Act had not been repealed (either case might be taken as an example) and acted accordingly. But what relation has that proposition to the question whether the same question of law can be reargued on the ground that it was not argued or not sufficiently argued, or that the decision of law upon the argument was wrong? It has no application at all.

Under these circumstances it appears to me that your Lordships would do well to act upon that which has been universally assumed in the profession, so far as I know, to be the principle, namely, that a decision of this House upon a question of law is conclusive, and that nothing but an Act of Parliament can set right that which is alleged to be wrong in a judgment of this House. For these reasons, my Lords, I move your Lordships that this appeal be dismissed with costs.

LORDS MCNAGHTEN, MORRIS and JAMES OF HEREFORD concurred.

Since 1898 the House of Lords has never entertained the argument that a decision of the House could be reversed. However, in *Bourne* v. *Keane* [1919] A. C. 815 the House overruled a case almost a century old holding that a bequest of personal estate for Masses for the dead is void as a gift to superstitious uses. The overruled case was not a decision of the House of Lords itself, and so the question of overruling one of its own decisions did not arise. Nevertheless the strict doctrine of stare decisis places great stress on the importance of upholding well established doctrines. Lord Wrenbury in a strong dissent upheld the principle of maintaining authoritative opinion or judicial decision of long standing: "It is a principle which recognizes the importance of certainty and finality – and which, under circumstances, refuses to disturb after a certain lapse of time a doctrine 'whether,' to use Lord Herschell's words, 'it rests upon any sound basis or not' " (925). The four-man majority in effect placed the avoidance of undesirable social consequences above the importance of certainty and finality. Lord Birkenhead, L.C., wrote: "In my view it is undoubtedly true that ancient decisions are not to be lightly disturbed when men have accepted them and regulated their dispositions in reliance upon them. And this doctrine is especially deserving of respect in cases where title has passed from man to man in reliance upon a sustained trend of judicial opinion. But this, my Lords, is not the present case. . . . I cannot conceive that it is my function as a judge of the Supreme Appellate Court of this country to make error perpetual in a matter of this kind. The proposition crudely stated really amounts to this, that because members of the Roman Catholic faith have wrongly supposed for a long period of time that a certain disposition of their property was unlawful, and have abstained from making it, we, who are empowered and bound to declare the law, refuse to other members of that Church the reassurance and the relief to which our view of the law entitles them. My Lords, I cannot and will not be a party to such a proposal" (860).

The attitude of the Supreme Court of the United States towards the binding authority of its own decisions is quite different from the strict House of Lords view. Past decisions are regarded with respect but not with subservience, and while stare decisis is the everyday rule there is generally no hesitation in departing from it when a social interest is to be served thereby. In *Washington* v. *Dawson & Co.* (1924) 264 U.S. 219, 238 fn. 21, Brandeis J. lists ten instances in which the Court has overruled itself. In *Burnet* v. *Coronado Oil & Gas Co.* (1932) 285 U.S. 393, 406 fn. 1, 407 fn. 2, 409 fn. 4 he expands the list to some 40 instances in which previous decisions were overruled or qualified, and he quotes *Hertz* v. *Woodman* (1910) 218 U.S. 205, 212 to the effect that "The rule of *stare decisis,* though one tending to consistency and uniformity of decision, is not inflexible. Whether it shall be followed or departed from is a question entirely within the discretion of the court, which is again called upon to consider a question once decided" (405-406). For a brief discussion as to when a court should exercise its discretion to overrule, see Note (1920) 34 *Harv. L. Rev.* 74. Blaustein and Field, " 'Overruling' Opinions in the Supreme Court" (1958) 57 *Mich. L. Rev.* 151 report that the Supreme Court overruled itself 90 times between 1810 and 1957.

So firmly is the power of overruling established that its exercise is usually taken as a matter of course: see, e.g. *Graves et al* v. *New York ex rel. O'Keefe* (1939) 306 U.S. 466 and *United States* v. *Darby* (1941) 312 U.S. 100. However, occasionally a particular overruling draws a strong protest from a dissenting judge. Roberts J. was twice moved to protest in 1944. In *Mahnich* v. *Southern S.S. Co.* (1944) 321 U.S. 96, 112-113 he declared: "The evil resulting from overruling earlier considered decisions must be evident. In the present case, the court below naturally felt bound to follow and apply the law as clearly announced by this court. If litigants and lower federal courts are not to do so, the law becomes not a chart to govern but a game of chance; instead of settling rights and liabilities it unsettles them. . . . But the more deplorable consequences will inevitably be that the administration of justice will fall into disrepute. Respect for tribunals must fall when the bar and the public come to understand that nothing that has been said in prior adjudication has force in a current controversy." And in *Smith* v. *Allright* (1944) 321 U.S. 649, 669 he added: "The reason for my concern is that the instant decision, overruling that announced about nine years ago, tends to bring adjudications of this tribunal into the same class as a restricted railroad ticket, good for this day and train only. I have no assurance, in view of current decisions, that the opinion anounced today may not shortly be repudiated and overruled by justices who deem they have new light on the subject. In the present term the court has overruled three cases."

One of the most famous cases of overruling, *Erie Railroad Co.* v. *Tompkins* (1938) 304 U.S. 64 overruling *Swift* v. *Tyson* (1842) 41 U.S. (16 Pet.) 1, illustrates a problem peculiar to the United States, viz. the relationship of federal and state courts. In *Swift* v. *Tyson* the Supreme Court had established the duty of federal courts to apply state law only when it was distinctively local in character; in the area of the general provisions of the common law the federal courts had the duty of ascertaining the law independently of the understanding of the general law by the state courts. *Erie Railroad Co.* v. *Tompkins* held that in areas reserved by the Constitution to the states, the federal courts were bound to apply state case law as well as state statute law.

Dr. Goodhart, "Case Law in England and America" (1929) 15 *Cornell L.Q.* 173, 186-191 assigns five reasons for the freer attitude towards stare decisis in the United States than in England: (1) the pressure on jurists resulting from the 350 volumes of annual law reports (as compared with the five or six in England) creates a desire for decisions based on principles rather than on precedents; (2) it has been found desirable to keep law flexible in constitutional questions and such questions have a predominant position in American law; (3) social and economic conditions are changing rapidly in the United States, whereas in England they are more or less static; (4) the American casebook method tends to undermine precedent and so does the comparative law method of the "national" law schools; (5) the restatements of the American Law Institute, by formulating an ideal law, tend to break down the acceptability of precedent.

Australian practice as to stare decisis is less rigid than the English. Judges of the High Court of Australia have from time to time persisted in their dissents with ultimate success: see McWhinney, "Judicial Concurrences and Dissents: A Comparative View of Opinion-writing in Final Appellate Tribunals" (1953) 31 *Can. Bar Rev.* 595, 603. On the Australian attitude to English precedents, see Howard, "Australia and the House of Lords" [1963] *Crim. L. R.* 675.

In civil law systems, of course, there is no principle of stare decisis because it would encroach on the exclusive authority of statutory law. Nevertheless, in practice there is a strong tendency for the courts to follow precedents, especially those of the higher courts. On precedent in the French system, see David and de Vries, *The French Legal System* 114-121 (1958).

QUINN v. LEATHEM.

House of Lords. [1900-03] All E.R. Rep. 1; [1901] A.C. 495.

EARL OF HALSBURY L. C.: My Lords, in this case the plaintiff has by a properly framed statement of claim complained of the defendants, and proved to the satisfaction of a jury that the defendants have wrongfully and maliciously induced customers and servants to cease to deal with the plaintiff, that the defendants did this in pursuance of a conspiracy framed among them, that in pursuance of the same conspiracy they induced servants of the plaintiff not to continue in the plaintiff's employment, and that all this was done with malice in order to injure the plaintiff, and that it did injure the plaintiff. If upon these facts so found the plaintiff could have no remedy against those who had thus injured him, it could hardly be said that our jurisprudence was that of a civilized community, nor indeed do I understand that any one has doubted that, before the decision in *Allen* v. *Flood* [(1898) A.C. 1], in this House, such fact would have established a cause of action against the defendants. Now, before discussing the case of *Allen* v. *Flood* and what was decided therein, there are two observations of a general character which I wish to make, and one is to repeat what I have very often said before, that every judgment must be read as applicable to the particular facts proved, or assumed to be proved, since the generality of the expressions which may be found there are not intended to be expositions of the whole law, but governed and qualified by the particular facts of the case in which such expressions are to be found. The other is that a case is only an authority for what it actually decides. I entirely deny that it can be quoted for a proposition that may seem to follow logically from it. Such a mode of reasoning assumes that the law is necessarily a logical code, whereas every lawyer must acknowledge that the law is not always logical to all. My Lords, I think the application of these two propositions renders the decision of this case perfectly plain, notwithstanding the decision of the case of *Allen* v. *Flood*.

Now, the hypothesis of fact upon which *Allen* v. *Flood* was decided by a majority in this House was that the defendant there neither uttered nor carried into effect any threat at all: he simply warned the plaintiff's employers of what the men themselves, without his persuasion or influence, had determined to do, and it was certainly proved that no resolution of the trade union had been arrived at at all, and that the trade union official had no authority himself to call out the men, which in that case was argued to be the threat which coerced the employers to discharge the plaintiff. It was further an element in the decision that there was no case of conspiracy or even combination. What was alleged to be done was only the independent and single action of the defendant, actuated in what he did by the desire to express his own views in favour of his fellow members. It is true that I personally did not believe that was the true view of the facts, but, as I have said, we must look at the hypothesis of fact upon which the case was decided by the majority of those who took part in the decision. My Lords, in my view what has been said already is enough to decide this case without going further into the facts of *Allen* v. *Flood*, but I cannot forbear accepting with cordiality the statement of them prepared by two of your Lordships, Lord Brampton and Lord Lindley, with so much care and precision.

Now, in this case it cannot be denied that if the verdict stands there was conspiracy, threats, and threats carried into execution, so that loss of business and interference with the plaintiff's legal rights are abundantly proved, and I do not understand the very learned judge who dissented to have doubted any one of these propositions, but his view was grounded on the belief that *Allen* v. *Flood* had altered the law in these respects, and made that lawful which would have clearly been actionable before the decision of that case. My Lords, for the reasons I have given I cannot agree with that conclusion. I do not deny that if some of the observations made in that case were to be pushed to their logical conclusion it would be very difficult to resist the Chief Baron's inflexible logic; but, with all the respect which any view of that learned judge is entitled to command and which I unfeignedly entertain, I cannot concur. This case is distinguished in its facts from those which were the essentially important facts in *Allen* v. *Flood*. Rightly or wrongly, the theory upon which judgment was pronounced in that case is one whereby the present is shewn to be one which the majority of your Lordships would have held to be a case of actionable injury inflicted without any excuse whatever. . . .

[The concurring judgments of LORD MACNAGHTEN, LORD SHAND, LORD BRAMPTON, LORD ROBERTSON, and LORD LINDLEY are omitted].

The House of Lords had a great deal of difficulty around the turn of the century with the area of business competition. See the discussion in Friedmann, *Law and Social Change in Contemporary Britain* 112-122 (1951) of their attempts to find a solution. It is worth noting that Lord Halsbury was one of the three dissenting judges in *Allen* v. *Flood*.

YOUNG v. BRISTOL AEROPLANE COMPANY, LIMITED.

English Court of Appeal. [1944] 2 All E.R. 293; [1944] 1 K.B. 718.

LORD GREENE M.R. read the judgment of the court: In considering the question whether or not this court is bound by its previous decisions and those of courts of co-ordinate jurisdiction, it is necessary to distinguish four classes of case. The first is that with which we are now concerned, namely, cases where this court finds itself confronted with one or more decisions of its own or of a court of co-ordinate jurisdiction. The second is where there is such a conflicting decision. The third is where this court comes to the conclusion that a previous decision, although not expressly overruled, cannot stand with a subsequent decision of the House of Lords. The fourth (a special case) is where this court comes to the conclusion that a previous decision was given per incuriam. In the second and third classes of case it is beyond question that the previous decision is open to examination. In the second class, the court is unquestionably entitled to choose between the two conflicting decisions. In the third class of case the court is merely giving effect to what it considers to have been a decision of the House of Lords by which it is bound. The fourth class requires more detailed examination and we still refer to it again later in this judgment.

For the moment it is the first class which we have to consider. Although the language both of decision and of dictum as well as the constant practice of the court appears to us clearly to negative the suggested power, there are to be found dicta, and, indeed, decision, the other way. So far as dicta are concerned, we are, of course, not bound to follow them. In the case of decisions we are entitled to choose between those which assert and those which deny the existence of the power. . . .

It remains to consider the quite recent case of *Lancaster Motor Co. (London) v. Bremith, Ltd.* [(1941) 1 K.B. 675.], in which a court consisting of the present Master of the Rolls, Clauson L.J. and Goddard L.J., declined to follow an earlier decision of a court consisting of Slesser L.J. and Robber L.J. [in *Gerard* v. *Worth of Paris Ltd.* [1936] 2 All E.R. 905.]. This was clearly a case where the earlier decision was given per incuriam. It depended on the true meaning (which in the later decision was regarded as clear beyond argument) of a rule of the Supreme Court to which the court was apparently not referred and which it obviously had not in mind. The Rules of the Supreme Court have statutory force and the court is bound to give effect to them as to a statute. Where the court has construed a statute or a rule having the force of a statute its decision stands on the same footing as any other decision on a question of law, but where the court is satisfied that an earlier decision was given in ignorance of the terms of a statute or a rule having the force of a statute the position is very different. It cannot, in our opinion, be right to say that in such a case the court is entitled to disregard the statutory provision and is bound to follow a decision of its own given when that provision was not present to its mind. Cases of this description are examples of decision given per incuriam. We do not think that it would be right to say that there may not be other cases of decisions given per incuriam in which this court might properly consider itself entitled not to follow an earlier decision of its own. Such cases would obviously be of the rarest occurrance and must be dealt with in accordance with their special facts. Two classes of decisions per incuriam fall outside the scope of our inquiry, namely, those where the court has acted in ignorance of a previous decision of its own or of a court of co-ordinate jurisdiction which covers the case before it – in such a case a subsequent court must decide which of the two decisions it ought to follow; and those where it has acted in ignorance of a decision of the House of Lords which covers the point – in such a case a subsequent court is bound by the decision of the House of Lords.

On a careful examination of the whole matter we have come to the clear conclusion that this court is bound to follow previous decisions of its own as well as those of courts of co-ordinate jurisdiction. The only exceptions to this rule (two of them apparent only) are those already mentioned which for convenience we here summarize: (1.) The court is entitled and bound to decide which of two conflicting decisions of its own it will follow. (2.) The court is bound to refuse to follow a decision of its own which, though not expressly overruled, cannot, in its opinion, stand with a decision of the House of Lords. (3). The court is not bound to follow a decision of its own if it is satisfied that the decision was given per incuriam. . . .

[See Mason, "Stare Decisis in the Court of Appeal" (1956) 19 M. L. R. 136.]

STUART v. BANK OF MONTREAL and STUART
Supreme Court of Canada. 1909. 41 S.C.R. 516.

DAVIES: J.: The only question argued before us on this appeal was whether conveyances or securities given by a married woman of or upon her separate property to or for the benefit of her husband can be upheld as against her in the absence of independent advice before executing the documents, the beneficial assignee having knowledge at the time of her marital relationship. Or, put it in another way, whether under English authorities the wife stands towards her husband within those confidential relationships which, in cases where conveyances or securities are made or given by one to or for the benefit of the other, the law, on grounds of public policy, requires shall have the protection of independent advice in order to be upheld.

In the case of *Cox* v. *Adams* [35 S.C.R. 393] this court had to consider the question very fully. A majority of the court, of which I was one, was, after full consideration of the authorities, of the opinion that the wife was within those confidential relationships and gave judgment accordingly. Mr. Justice Sedgewick, while expressly concurring in the opinions delivered by Mr. Justice Girouard and myself, held also that the securities in question in that case were avoided as against the wife by fraud, and, because of this, an attempt has been made in the courts below to distinguish *Cox* v. *Adams* from the case now before us. where no fraud is charged. But that additional ground adopted by Mr. Justice Sedgewick for the conclusion he reached cannot, in my judgment, weaken the authority of that case or make it less binding upon us than it, otherwise, would be. The learned justice fully agreed with the ground on which Mr. Justice Girouard and I, myself, rested our judgments, that the wife was within those confidential relationships.

As I am of the opinion that the decision of this court in *Cox* v. *Adams* is binding on us, I would allow this appeal with costs and dispose of the case in the manner proposed by Chief Justice Moss in the Court of Appeal.

DUFF J. – In the determination of this appeal we are, I think, concluded by *Cox* v. *Adams*. . . .

It is true that the judgment of Sedgewick J. and, perhaps, also that of Girouard J., rested upon another ground as well; but "it is," said Lord Macnaghten, in *New South Wales Taxation Commissioners* v. *Palmer*, at page 184:

> impossible to treat a proposition which the court declares to be a distinct and

sufficient ground for its decision as a mere dictum because there is another ground upon which, standing alone, the case might have been determined.

Some question is raised, whether or not we are entitled to disregard a previous decision of this court laying down a substantive rule of law. This court is, of course, not a court of final resort in the sense in which the House of Lords is because our decisions are reviewable by the Privy Council; but only in very exceptional circumstances would the Court of Exchequer Chamber or the Lords Justices, sitting in appeal, (from which courts there was an appeal as of right to the House of Lords), have felt themselves at liberty to depart from one of their own previous decisions. That is also the principle upon which the Court of Appeal now acts: *Pledge* v. *Carr*; and the Court of Appeal, in any province where the basis of the law is the common law of England, would act upon the same view. Quite apart from this, there are, I think, considerations of public convenience too obvious to require statement which make it our duty to apply this principle to the decisions of this court. What exceptional circumstances would justify a departure from the general rule, we need not consider; because there was, in the circumstances in which *Cox* v. *Adams* was decided, nothing in the least degree exceptional. Mr. Shepley, with his usual candour, admitted frankly, what indeed is indisputable, that under the rule laid down in the passage quoted above from the judgment of Davies J. the appellant must succeed.

I would allow the appeal with costs; the action should be disposed of in the manner proposed by Moss C.J.O.

ANGLIN J.: There are instances in which judges of this court have considered themselves free to decline to follow its earlier decisions with which they did not agree. In the *Burrard Election Case*, Gwynne J. (dissenting) expressed his opinion that the Supreme Court is competent to overrule a judgment of the court differently constituted, if it clearly appears to be erroneous. In *Stephens* v. *McArthur*, at page 460, Patterson J. (dissenting) said

> "it is indisputable that, as a matter of principle, the reasons given by the court for its judgment in any case may properly be reconsidered, and, if found to be erroneous, corrected, when a similar question arises in another case;"

and he indicated that the Supreme Court of Canada should, in this matter, be governed rather by the rules which prevail in intermediate appellate tribunals – such as the English Court of Appeal – than by those which now govern such a final appellate tribunal as the House of Lords.

In the *Stanstead Election Case* this court refused to hold itself bound by a previous judgment dismissing an appeal upon an equal division: *Megantic Election Case*; but there is no case in which the court has refused to follow a previous judgment in which a majority concurred. The nearest approach to such a position is that taken by Strong C.J. in *The Queen* v. *Grenier*, where he says, at page 53:

> "Since the case of *Robertson* v. *The Grand Trunk Railway Co.*, it would seem that *Vogel's Case* can scarcely be considered as a binding authority and, at all events, I should not hesitate to reconsider it if a similar question arose. . . ."

The Supreme Court of Canada occupies a somewhat peculiar position. From it no appeal lies as of right. By special leave an appeal may be had to the Judicial Committee. In the great majority of the cases which it hears it is a final appellate tribunal; in other cases, it occupies the position of an intermediate appellate court. But, whether it be regarded as final or intermediate, in view of the current of recent decisions to which reference has been made, the attitude of this court towards its previous decisions upon questions of law should, in my opinion, be the same. Of course, if the Privy Council should determine that the law is not what this court has declared it to be, the view of this court must be deemed to be overruled. A decision of the House of Lords should, likewise, be respected and followed though inconsistent with a previous judgment of this court. In the event of an irreconcilable conflict upon a question of law between a decision of this court and a subsequent decision of the English Court of Appeal – should such a case arise – in view of what was said by the Privy Council in *Trimble* v. *Hill*, the duty of this court would require most careful consideration. (See *Jacobs* v. *Beaver.*) But we should not, in my opinion, hesitate now to determine that, in other cases, unless perhaps in very exceptional circumstances, a previous deliberate and definite decision of this court will be held binding, if it is clear that it was not the result of some mere slip or inadvertence. . . . It is of supreme importance that people may know with certainty what the law is, and this end can only be attained by a loyal adherence to the doctrine of *stare decisis*. I see no good reason why this doctrine should not be applied, and many very cogent reasons why it should prevail in this court. As tersely put by Pratt J. in *Rex* v. *Inhabitantes de Haughton*:

> "Little respect will be paid to our judgments if we overthrow that one day which we have resolved the day before."

The case at bar is, no doubt, an important case. It may be in one sense "Not an ordinary case." It may be that the application to it of the principle of the decision in *Cox* v. *Adams* will do some injustice to the present respondents. But, to quote the Earl of Halsbury, in *London Street Tramways Co.* v. *London County Council*, at page 380,

> "what is an occasional interference with what is, perhaps, abstract justice as compared with the inconvenience – the disastrous inconvenience – of having each question subject to being re-argued and the dealings of mankind rendered doubtful by reason of different decisions. . . ."

[FITZPATRICK C.J. concurred with DUFF J. The dissenting judgment of IDINGTON J. is omitted].

THE QUEEN (EX REL. A.-G. CAN.) v. SUPERTEST PETROLEUM CORP. LTD.

Exchequer Court of Canada [1954] 3 D.L.R. 245.

THORSON P.: The principles to be applied in determining the amount of compensation to be paid to the owner of expropriated property have been discussed in many cases but it would not be correct to say that they are wholly settled. It is established, of course, that the owner is to receive its money equivalent, that is to say, its worth to him in money, that, while his property is changed in form, it is not diminished in amount and that its money equivalent is estimated on its value to him and not on its value to the purchaser: *vide Re Lucas & Chesterfield Gas & Water Bd.*, [1909] 1 K.B. 16 at p. 29. But there are differences in the statements of the tests of value to be used.

Before I deal with these tests I must refer to the second last paragraph of the reasons for judgment of the Supreme Court of Canada in *Woods Mfg. Co.* v. *The King*, [1951], 2 D.L.R. 465, S.C.R. 504, 67 C.R.T.C. 87, which reads as follows: "There is this to be added. It is fundamental to the due administration of justice that the authority of decisions be scrupulously respected by all Courts upon which they are binding. Without this uniform and consistent adherence the administration of justice becomes disordered, the law becomes uncertain, and the confidence of the public in it undermined. Nothing is more important than that the law as pronounced, including the interpretation by this Court of the decisions of the Judicial Committee, should be accepted and applied as our tradition requires; and even at the risk of that fallibility to which all Judges are liable, we must maintain the complete integrity of relationship between the Courts. If the rules in question are to be accorded any further examination or review, it must come either from this Court or from the Judicial Committee."

This is a remarkable statement. While there will be general agreement with most of its sentiments it is subject to objection on several counts. It was neither necessary nor relevant to the decision in the case. Consequently, its admonitions, being *obiter dicta*, have no binding effect. That being so, the easier course to follow would be to let them pass without comment but, in view of the circumstances, it would not be proper to do so.

The implications in the statement have caused me deeper concern than I care to express. For, while the reason for making it is not apparent on its face, there is no doubt that it was because of the fact that I have disagreed with some of the opinions expressed by individual Judges of the Supreme Court of Canada in certain expropriation cases.

If there is implied in the statement, as appears to be the case, an imputation that by disagreeing with the opinions referred to I have not shown proper respect for the authority of the Supreme Court of Canada and that my disagreements have tended to the administration of justice becoming disordered, the law becoming uncertain and the confidence of the public in it being undermined there is the simple answer that there is no foundation or justification for any such imputation.

Here I may perhaps be permitted to interject what I hope will not be considered too personal a note. Prior to my appointment I was made aware of the fact that there was criticism of the Exchequer Court of Canada on the ground that many of its awards in expropriation cases were excessive. In an attempt to remove this ground of criticism I have since my appointment to the presidency of the Court set myself rigidly against excessive awards. It was, and is, my opinion that in measuring the amount of money which the owner of expropriated property should receive as the equivalent in value of the property taken from him it is just as important to ensure that the Crown, which has lawfully taken the property for public purposes, is not required to pay more for it than it is worth as it is to make sure that its owner receives its fair value. The duty of determining the equivalence in money of the value of the expropriated property demands fairness to the expropriating public as well as to the owner of the property and an excessive award is a breach of this duty.

In the course of attempting to make awards that would be as fair to the Crown as to the owner I sought, as carefully as I could, to apply what I considered, in my view of the decisions, a fair test of the value to the owner of the expropriated property under consideration and it was in the search for such a test that the disagreements to which I have referred occurred. They were intended to be impersonal and objective and were expressed in the belief, as Joseph H. Choate, a great American lawyer, once put it, that it is "only on the anvil of discussion that the spark of truth can be struck out". There was no vestige of disrespect for the Supreme Court of Canada or any of its Judges in any of my remarks and any imputation or suggestion to the contrary is quite unjustified.

But there is a more serious objection to the statement than that which I have mentioned. This is to the *dictum* in its last sentence, which reads as follows: "If the rules in question are to be accorded any further examination or review, it must come either from this Court or from the Judicial Committee." The meaning of the *dictum* is not clear. But if it purports to prohibit this Court from any further examination of judgments dealing with the difficult quesion of the value of expropriated property and the tests by which it is to be measured it seeks to impose a restriction on the judicial independence and freedom of the Court to which it has hitherto not been subject.

There are several reasons for objecting to the *dictum*. In the first place, the Court could not, in my opinion, properly perform its duty if it were to cease its inquiry as suggested. I doubt whether there is any concept in the whole field of law that is more elusive than that of value. There has been a long and ceaseless search by Judges and others charged with the valuation of property to ascertain the proper tests by which the amount of such value can be ascertained in any given case. And the search must continue for the factors of value that should be taken into account are not static. On the contrary, there is a continuing shift in their respective weights as the circumstances under which they arise alter.

Moreover, the restriction sought to be imposed is not required under even the strictest view of the doctrine of *stare decisis* and it is certainly not in accord with the spirit that has permitted Judges, even of Courts of first instance, to make a useful contribution to the administration of justice by pointing out defects in the law as they become manifest and recommending legislative action for their remedy when reform by judicial decision has become impossible. Under the circumstances, I respectfully suggest that the ends of justice will be better served by the continued freedom of inquiry of this Court than by the prohibition of it. . . .

It was held by the Supreme Court of Canada in the *Woods Case* that an allowance of 10% for compulsory taking should be added to the value of the land and buildings expropriated. However, in *Drew* v. *The Queen* (1961) 29 D. L. R. (2d) 114 in the Supreme Court of Canada Judson J. held for 6 of 9 judges that as there is no statutory basis for an allowance for compulsory taking, and no rule of law requiring it, it should not be awarded. The Court, without in terms overruling *Woods*, thus approved the position which had been adopted by Thorson P.

BROWN v. BOARD OF EDUCATION

Supreme Court of the United States, 1954.
347 U.S. 483, 74 S.Ct. 686.

Appeal from the United States District Court for the District of Kansas.

MR. CHIEF JUSTICE WARREN delivered the opinion of the Court: These cases come to us from the States of Kansas, South Carolina, Virginia, and Delaware. They are premised on different facts and different local conditions, but a common legal question justifies their consideration together in this consolidated opinion.

In each of the cases, minors of the Negro race, through their legal representatives, seek the aid of the courts in obtaining admission to the public schools of their community on a nonsegregated basis. In each instance, they had been denied admission to schools attended by white children under laws requiring or permitting segregation according to race. This segregation was alleged to deprive the plaintiffs of the equal protection of the laws under the Fourteenth Amendment. In each of the cases other than the Delaware case, a three-judge federal district court denied relief to the plaintiffs on the so-called "separate but equal" doctrine announced by this Court in *Plessy* v. *Ferguson*, (1896) 163 U.S. 537. Under that doctrine, equality of treatment is accorded when the races are provided substantially equal facilities, even though these facilities be separate. In the Delaware case, the Supreme Court of Delaware adhered to that doctrine, but ordered that the plaintiffs be admitted to the white schools because of their superiority to the Negro schools.

The plaintiffs contend that segregated public schools are not "equal" and cannot be made "equal" and that hence they are deprived of the equal protection of the laws. Because of the obvious importance of the question presented, the Court took jurisdiction. Argument was heard in the 1952 Term, and reargument was heard this Term on certain questions propounded by the Court.

Reargument was largely devoted to the circumstances surrounding the adoption of the Fourteenth Amendment in 1868. It covered exhaustively consideration of the Amendment in Congress, ratification by the states, then existing practices in racial segregation, and the views of proponents and opponents of the Amendment. This discussion and our own investigation convince us that, although these sources cast some light, it is not enough to resolve the problem with which we are faced. At best, they are inconclusive. The most avid proponents of the post-War Amendments undoubtedly intended them to remove all legal distinctions among "all persons born or naturalized in the United States." Their opponents, just as certainly, were antagonistic to both the letter and the spirit of the Amendments and wished them to have the most limited effect. What others in Congress and the state legislatures had in mind cannot be determined with any degree of certainty.

An additional reason for the inconclusive nature of the Amendment's history, with respect to segregated schools, is the status of public education at that time. In the South, the movement toward free common schools, supported by general taxation, had not yet taken hold. Education of white children was largely in the hands of private groups. Education of Negroes was almost nonexistent, and practically all of the race were illiterate. In fact, any education of Negroes was forbidden by law in some states. Today, in contrast, many Negroes have achieved outstanding success in the arts and sciences as well as in the business and professional world. It is true that public education had already advanced further in the North, but the effect of the Amendment on Northern States was generally ignored in the congressional debates. Even in the North, the conditions of public education did not approximate those existing today. The curriculum was usually rudimentary; ungraded schools were common in rural areas; and compulsory school attendance was virtually unknown. As a consequence, it is not surprising that there should be so little in the history of the Fourteenth Amendment relating to its intended effect on public education.

In the first cases in this Court construing the Fourteenth Amendment, decided shortly after its adoption, the Court interpreted it as proscribing all state-imposed discriminations against the Negro race. The doctrine of "separate but equal" did not make its appearance in this Court until 1896 in the case of *Plessy* v. *Ferguson*, supra, involving not education but transportation. American courts have since labored with the doctrine for over a half a century. In this Court, there have been six cases involving the "separate but equal" doctrine in the field of public education. In *Cumming* v. *County Board of Education*, 175 U.S. 528, and *Gong Lum* v. *Rice*, 275 U.S. 78, the validity of the doctrine itself was not challenged. In more recent cases, all on the graduate school level, inequality was found in that specific benefits enjoyed by white students were denied to Negro students of the same educational qualifications. *Missouri ex rel. Gaines* v. *Canada*, 305 U.S. 337; *Sipuel* v. *Oklahoma*, 332 U.S. 631; *Sweatt* v. *Painter*, 339 U.S. 629; *McLaurin* v. *Oklahoma State Regents,* 339 U.S. 637. In none of these cases was it necessary to reexamine the doctrine to grant relief to the Negro plaintiff. And in *Sweatt* v. *Painter*, supra, the Court expressly reserved decision on the question whether *Plessy* v. *Ferguson* should be held inapplicable to public education.

In the instant cases, that question is directly presented. Here, unlike *Sweatt* v. *Painter*, there are findings below that the Negro and white schools involved have been equalized, or are being equalized, with respect to buildings, curricula, qualifications and salaries of teachers, and other "tangible" factors. Our decision, therefore, cannot turn on merely a comparison of these tangible factors in the Negro and white schools involved in each of the cases. We must look instead to the effect of segregation itself on public education.

In approaching this problem, we cannot turn the clock back to 1868 when the Amendment was adopted, or even to 1896 when *Plessy* v. *Ferguson* was written. We must consider public education in the light of its full development and its present place in American life throughout the Nation. Only in this way can it be determined if segregation in public schools deprives these plaintiffs of the equal protection of the laws.

Today, education is perhaps the most important function of state and local governments. Compulsory school attendance laws and the great expenditures for education both demonstrate our recognition of the importance of education to our democratic society. It is required in the performance of our most basic public responsibilities, even service in the armed forces. It is the very foundation of good citizenship. Today it is a principal instrument in awakening the child to cultural values, in preparing him for later professional training, and in helping him to adjust normally to his environment. In these days, it is doubtful that any child may reasonably be expected to succeed in life if he is denied the opportunity of an education. Such an opportunity, where the state has undertaken to provide it, is a right which must be made available to all on equal terms.

We come then to the question presented: Does segregation of children in public schools solely on the basis of race, even though the physical facilities and other "tangible" factors may be equal, deprive the children of the minority group of equal educational opportunities? We believe that it does.

In *Sweatt* v. *Painter*, supra, in finding that a segregated law school for Negroes could not provide them equal educational opportunities, this Court relied in large part on "those qualities which are incapable of objective measurement but which make for greatness in a law school." In *McLaurin* v. *Oklahoma State Regents*, supra, the Court, in requiring that a Negro admitted to a white graduate school be treated like all other students, again resorted to intangible considerations: ". . . his ability to study, to engage in discussions and exchange views with other students, and, in general, to learn his profession." Such considerations apply with added force to children in grade and high schools. To separate them from others of similar age and qualifications solely because of their race generates a feeling of inferiority as to their status in the community that may affect their hearts and minds in a way unlikely ever to be undone. The effect of this separation on their educational opportunities was well stated by a finding in the Kansas case by a court which nevertheless felt compelled to rule against the Negro plaintiffs:

"Segregation of white and colored children in public schools has a detrimental effect upon the colored children. The impact is greater when it has the sanction of the law; for the policy of separating the races is usually interpreted as denoting the inferiority of the Negro group. A sense of inferiority affects the motivation of a child to learn. Segregation with the sanction of law, therefore, has a tendency to retard the educational and mental development of Negro children and to deprive them of some of the benefits they would receive in a racially integrated school system."

Whatever may have been the extent of psychological knowledge at the time of *Plessy* v. *Ferguson*, this finding is amply supported by modern authority. [1] Any language in *Plessy* v. *Ferguson* contrary to this finding is rejected.

We conclude that in the field of public education the doctrine of "separate but equal" has no place. Separate educational facilities are inherently unequal. Therefore, we hold that the plaintiffs and others similarly situated for whom the actions have been brought are, by reason of the segregation complained of, deprived of the equal protection of the laws guaranteed by the Fourteenth Amendment. This disposition makes unnecessary any discussion whether such segregation also violates the Due Process Clause of the Fourteenth Amendment.

Because these are class actions, because of the wide applicability of this decision, and because of the great variety of local conditions, the formulation of decrees in these cases presents problems of considerable complexity. On reargument, the consideration of appropriate relief was necessarily subordinated to the primary question – the constitutionality of segregation in public education. We have now announced that such segregation is a denial of the equal protection of the laws. In order that we may have the full assistance of the parties in formulating decrees, the cases will be restored to the docket, and the parties are requested to present further argument on Questions 4 and 5 previously propounded by the Court for the reargument this Term. The Attorneys General of the United States is again invited to participate. The Attorneys General of the states requiring or permitting segregation in public education will also be permitted to appear as *amici curiae* upon request to do so by September 15, 1954, and submission of briefs by October 1, 1954.

It is so ordered.

On the question of relief see (1955) 349 U.S. 294.

The relevant part of the Fourteenth Amendment to the U.S. Constitution is as follows: "No State shall make or enforce any law which shall abridge the privileges or immunities of citizens of the United States, nor shall any State deprive any person of life, liberty, or property without due process of law; *nor deny to any person within its jurisdiction the equal protection of the laws.*"

On the reaction to *Brown* see Clark, "The Desegregation Cases: Criticism of the Social Scientist's Role (1959-1960) 5 *Vill. L. Rev.* 224.

[1] K. B. Clark, Effect of Prejudice and Discrimination on Personality Development (Midcentury White House Conference on Children and Youth, 1950); Witmer and Kotinsky, Personality in the Making (1952), c. VI; Deutscher and Chein, The Psychological Effects of Enforced Segregation: A Survey of Social Science Opinion, 26 *J. Psychol.* 259 (1948); Chein, What are the Psychological Effects of Segregation Under Conditions of Equal Facilities?, 3 *Int. J. Opinion and Attitude Res.* 229 (1949); Brameld, Educational Costs, in Discrimination and National Welfare (McIver, ed., 1949), 44-48; Frazier, The Negro in the United States (1949), 674-681. And see generally Myrdal, An American Dilemma (1944). [Footnote by the Court.]

HYNES v. NEW YORK CENT. R. CO.

(Court of Appeals of New York. 1921. 131 N. E. 898; 231 N. Y. 229.)

CARDOZO J.: On July 8, 1916, Harvey Hynes, a lad of 16, swam with two companions from the Manhattan to the Bronx side of the Harlem River, or United States Ship Canal, a navigable stream. Along the Bronx side of the river was the right of way of the defendant, the New York Central Railroad, which operated its trains at that point by high-tension wires, strung on poles and cross-arms. Projecting from the defendant's bulkhead above the waters of the river was a plank or springboard, from which boys of the neighborhood used to dive. One end of the board had been placed under a rock on the defendant's land, and nails had been driven at its point of contact with the bulkhead. Measured from this point of contact the length behind was 5 feet; the length in front 11. The bulkhead itself was about 3½ feet back of the pier line as located by the government. From this it follows that for 7½ feet the springboard was beyond the line of the defendant's property and above the public waterway. Its height measured from the stream was 3 feet at the bulkhead, and 5 feet at its outermost extremity. For more than five years swimmers had used it as a diving board without protest or obstruction.

On this day Hynes and his companions climbed on top of the bulkhead, intending to leap into the water. One of them made the plunge in safety. Hynes followed to the front of the springboard, and stood poised for his dive. At that moment a cross-arm with electric wires fell from the defendant's pole. The wires struck the diver, flung him from the shattered board, and plunged him to his death below. His mother, suing as administratrix, brings this action for her damages. Thus far the courts have held that Hynes at the end of the springboard above the public waters was a trespasser on the defendant's land. They have thought it immaterial that the board itself was a trespass, an encroachment on the public ways. They have thought it of no significance that Hynes would have met the same fate if he had been below the board and not above it. The board, they have said, was annexed to the defendant's bulkhead. By force of such annexation, it was to be reckoned as a fixture, and thus constructively, if not actually, an extension of the land. The defendant was under a duty to use reasonable care that bathers swimming or standing in the water should not be electrocuted by wires falling from its right of way. But to bathers diving from the springboard, there was no duty, we are told, unless the injury was the product of mere willfulness or wantonness – no duty of active vigilance to safeguard the impending structure. Without wrong to them, cross-arms might be left to rot; wires highly charged with electricity might sweep them from their stand and bury them in the subjacent waters. In climbing on the board, they became trespassers and outlaws. The conclusion is defended with much subtlety of reasoning, with much insistence upon its inevitableness as a merely logical deduction. A majority of the court are unable to accept it as the conclusion of the law.

We assume, without deciding, that the springboard was a fixture, a permanent improvement of the defendant's right of way. Much might be said in favor of another view. We do not press the inquiry for we are persuaded that the rights of bathers do not depend upon these nice distinctions. Liability would not be doubtful, we are told, had the boy been diving from a pole, if the pole had been vertical. The diver in such a situation would have been separated from the defendant's freehold. Liability, it is said has been escaped because the pole was horizontal. The plank when projected lengthwise was an extension of the soil. We are to concentrate our gaze on the private ownership of the board. We are to ignore the public ownership of the circumambient spaces of water and of air. Jumping from a boat or a barrel, the boy would have been a bather in the river. Jumping from the end of a springboard, he was no longer, it is said, a bather, but a trespasser on a right of way.

Rights and duties in systems of living law are not built upon such quicksands.

Bathers in the Harlem River on the day of this disaster were in the enjoyment of a public highway, entitled to reasonable protection against destruction by the defendant's wires. They did not cease to be bathers entitled to the same protection while they were diving from encroaching objects or engaging in the sports that are common among swimmers. Such acts were not equivalent to an abandonment of the highway, a departure from its proper uses, a withdrawal from the waters, and an entry upon land. A plane of private right had been interposed between the river and the air, but public ownership was unchanged in the space below it and above. The defendant does not deny that it would have owed a duty to this boy if he had been leaning against the springboard with his feet upon the ground. He is said to have forfeited protection as he put his feet upon the plank. Presumably the same result would follow if the plank had been a few inches above the surface of the water instead of a few feet. Duties are thus supposed to arise and to be extinguished in alternate zones or strata. Two boys walking in the country or swimming in a river stop to rest for a moment along the side of the road or the margin of the stream. One of them throws himself beneath the overhanging branches of a tree. The other perches himself on a bough a foot or so above the ground. Hoffman v. Armstrong, 48 N. Y. 201, 8 Am. Rep. 537. Both are killed by falling wires. The defendant would have us say that there is a remedy for the representatives of one and none for the representatives of the other. We may be permitted to distrust the logic that leads to such conclusions.

The truth is that every act of Hynes from his first plunge into the river until the moment of his death was in the enjoyment of the public waters, and under cover of the protection which his presence in those waters gave him. The use of the springboard was not an abandonment of his rights as bather. It was a mere by-play, an incident, subordinate and ancillary to the execution of his primary purpose, the enjoyment of the highway. The by-play, the incident, was not the cause of the disaster. Hynes would have gone to his death if he had been below the springboard or beside it. Laidlaw v. Sage, 158 N. Y. 73, 97, 52 N E. 679, 44 L. R. A. 216. The wires were not stayed by the presence of the plank. They followed the boy in his fall, and overwhelmed him in the waters.

The defendant assumes that the identification of ownership of a fixture with ownership of land is complete in every incident. But there are important elements of difference. Title to the fixture, unlike title to the land, does not carry with it rights of ownership usque ab coelum. There will hardly be denial that a cause of action would have arisen if the wires had fallen on an aeroplane proceeding above the river, though the location of the impact could be identified as the space above the springboard. The most that the defendant can fairly ask is exemption from liability where the use of the fixture is itself the efficient peril. That would be the situation, for example, if the weight of the boy upon the board had caused it to break and thereby throw him into the river. There is no such casual connection here between his position and his injuries. We think there was no moment when he was beyond the pale of the defendant's duty – the duty of care and vigilance in the storage of destructive forces.

This case is a striking instance of the dangers of "a jurisprudence of conceptions" (Pound, Mechanical Jurisprudence, 8 Columbia Law Review, 605, 608, 610), the extension of a maxim or a definition with relentless disregard of consequences to "a dryly logical extreme." The approximate and relative become the definite and absolute. Landowners are not bound to regulate their conduct in contemplation of the presence of trespassers intruding upon private structures. Landowners are bound to regulate their conduct in contemplation of the presence of travelers upon the adjacent public ways. There are times when there is little trouble in marking off the field of exemption and immunity from that of liability and duty. Here structures and ways are so united and commingled, superimposed upon each other, that the fields are brought together. In such circumstances, there is little help in pursuing general maxims to ultimate conclusions. They have been framed alio intuitu. They must be reformulated and readapted to meet exceptional conditions. Rules appropriate to spheres which are conceived of as separate and distinct cannot both be enforced when the spheres become concentric. There must then be readjustment or collision. In one sense, and that a highly technical and artificial one, the diver at the end of the springboard is an intruder on the adjoining lands. In another sense, and one that realists will accept more readily, he is still on public waters in the exercise of public rights. The law must say whether it will subject him to the rule of the one field or of the other, of this sphere or of that. We think that considerations of analogy, of convenience, of policy, and of justice, exclude him from the field of the defendant's immunity and exemption, and place him in the field of liability and duty. Beck v. Carter, 68 N. Y. 283, 23 Am. Rep. 175; Jewhurst v. City of Syracuse, 108 N. Y. 303, 15 N. E. 409; McCloskey v. Buckley, 223 N. Y. 187, 192, 119 N E. 395.

The judgment of the Appellate Division and that of the Trial Term should be reversed, and a new trial granted, with costs to abide the event.

HOGAN, POUND, and CRANE, JJ., concur.

HISCOCK, C. J., and CHASE and MCLAUGHLIN, JJ., dissent.

Judgments reversed, etc.

[Cf. *Thompson* v. *Bankstown Corp.* (1953) 87 *C.L.R.* 619.]

ROSENSTIEL v. ROSENSTIEL

(Court of Appeals of New York. 1965. 209 N.E. 3d 709; 16 N.Y. 2d 64; 262 N.Y.S. 2d 86.)

Consolidated actions for annulment and separation.

BERGEN, JUDGE.

I. Rosenstiel v. *Rosenstiel*

The defendant wife's former husband Felix Ernest Kaufman in 1954 obtained a divorce from her in a district court at Juarez in Chihuahua, Mexico. Plaintiff and defendant were married in New York in 1956 and this action by the husband seeks to annul that marriage on the ground the 1954 divorce is invalid and that, therefore, the defendant wife was incompetent in 1956 to contract a marriage.

In seeking the divorce in Mexico Mr. Kaufman went to El Paso, Texas, where he registered at a motel and the next day crossed the international boundary to Juarez. There he signed the Municipal Register, an official book of residents of the city, and filed with the district court a certificate showing such registration and a petition for divorce based on incompatibility and ill treatment between the spouses.

After about an hour devoted to these formalities, Mr. Kaufman returned to El Paso. The following day his wife, the present defendant, appeared in the Mexican court by an attorney duly authorized to act for her and filed an answer in which she submitted to the jurisdiction of the court and admitted the allegations of her husband's complaint. The decree of divorce was made the same day. The judgment is recognized as valid by the Republic of Mexico.

The Divorce Law of the State of Chihuahua provides that the court may exercise jurisdiction either on the basis of residence or of submission. Article 22 provides that the Judge "competent to take cognizance of a contested divorce" is the Judge "of the place of residence of the plaintiff" and of a divorce "by mutual consent", the Judge "of the residence of either of the spouses".

For the purposes of article 22, the statute further provides that the residence "shall be proven" by the "certificate of the Municipal Register" of the place (art. 24). Article 23, which has application to Wood v. Wood, provides that judicial competence "may also be fixed" by express or tacit submission.

After a trial at Special Term in the present husband's action for annulment, the court, holding that New York would not recognize the Mexican decree, granted judgment for the plaintiff and annulled the marriage; the Appellate Division reversed this judgment and dismissed the complaint. . . .

There is squarely presented to this court now for the first time the question whether recognition is to be given by New York to a matrimonial judgment of a foreign country based on grounds not accepted in New York, where personal jurisdiction of one party to the marriage has been acquired by physical presence before the foreign court; and jurisdiction of the other has been acquired by appearance and pleading through an authorized attorney although no domicile of either party is shown within that jurisdiction; and "residence" has been acquired by one party through a statutory formality based on brief contact. In cases where a divorce has been obtained without any personal contact with the jurisdiction by either party or by physical submission to the jurisdiction by one, with no personal service of process within the foreign jurisdiction upon, and no appearance or submission by, the other, decision has been against the validity of the foreign decree.

Although the grounds for divorce found acceptable according to Mexican law are inadmissible in New York, and the physical contact with the Mexican jurisdiction was ephemeral, there are some incidents in the Mexican proceedings which are common characteristics of the exercise of judicial power.

The former husband was physically in the jurisdiction, personally before the court, with the usual incidents and the implicit consequences of voluntary submission to foreign sovereignty. Although he had no intention of making his domicile there, he did what the domestic law of the place required he do to establish a "residence" of a kind which was set up as a statutory prerequisite to institute an action for divorce. This is not our own view in New York of what a bona fide residence is or should be, but it is that which the local law of Mexico prescribes.

Since he was one party to the two-party contract of marriage he carried with him legal incidents of the marriage itself, considered as an entity, which came before the court when he personally appeared and presented his petition. In a highly mobile era such as ours, it is needful on pragmatic grounds to regard the marriage itself as moving from place to place with either spouse, a concept which underlies the decision in Williams v. State of North Carolina I, 317 U.S. 287, p. 304, 63 S.Ct. 207, 87 L.Ed. 279; see, especially, Justice Frankfurter's concurrence.

The voluntary appearance of the other spouse in the foreign court by attorney would tend to give further support to an acquired jurisdiction there over the marriage as a legal entity. In theory jurisdiction is an imposition of sovereign power over the person. It is usually exerted by symbolic and rarely by actual force, e. g., the summons as a symbol of force; the attachment and the civil arrest, as exerting actual force.

But almost universally jurisdiction is acquired by physical and personal submission to judicial authority and in legal theory there seems to be ground to admit that the Mexican court at Juarez acquired jurisdiction over the former marriage of the defendant.

It is true that in attempting to reconcile the conflict of laws and of State interests in matrimonial judgments entered in States of the United States, where the Constitution compels each to give full faith and credit to the judgments of the others, a considerable emphasis has been placed on domicile as a prerequisite to that compulsory recognition. But domicile is not intrinsically an indispensable prerequisite to jurisdiction.

The duration of domicile in sister States providing by statute for a minimal time to acquire domicile as necessary to matrimonial action jurisdiction is in actual practice complied with by a mere formal gesture having no more relation to the actual situs of the marriage or to true domicile than the formality of signing the Juarez city register. The difference in time is not truly significant of a difference in intent or purpose or in effect.

The State or country of true domicile has the closest real public interest in a marriage but, where a New York spouse goes elsewhere to establish a synthetic domicile to meet technical acceptance of a matrimonial suit, our public interest is not affected differently by a formality of one day than by a formality of six weeks.

Nevada gets no closer to the real public concern with the marriage than Chihuahua. New York itself will take jurisdiction of a matrimonial action without regard to domicile or residence if it happened, by mere fortuity, that the marriage was contracted here, even between people entirely foreign to our jurisdiction.

A leading New York decision on the recognition of a divorce granted in a foreign nation where we are under no constituional compulsion to give full faith and credit is Gould v. Gould, 235 N.Y. 14, 138 N.E. 490 [1923] and there the court sustained a judgment of divorce in France between parties not domiciled in France at a time when the husband, who instituted the French action, was domiciled in New York. Indeed, the New York law was applied by the French court because "the plaintiff Gould" was a resident of New York.

The decision is not a clear precedent for the case now at bar; there are differences, e. g., the parties had substantial personal ties with France; the ground for the French divorce was the New York law; and this court laid down a number of precautionary warnings about the scope of its decision and what it was leaving open.

Still the fact is that this court accepted as valid a judgment affecting marital status of a New York domiciliary granted by a court in a foreign nation, without requiring domiciliary status in that nation; and this aspect of the decision does have relevance here since it is not helpful on the question of French jurisdiction that the French court acted on its conception of New York law. It applied New York law for the very reason that Gould was not a domiciliary of France but of New York.

The opinion in Caldwell v. Caldwell, 298 N.Y. 146, 81 N.E. 2d 60, dealing with divorces obtained on no personal presence or submission by either party in Mexico, the "mail-order decree", discusses domicile, but the question was not decisive of that case.

A balanced public policy now requires that recognition of the bilateral Mexican divorce be given rather than withheld and such recognition as a matter of comity offends no public policy of this State.

The order should be affirmed, with costs.

II. Wood v. *Wood*

Although the Mexican decree of divorce in Wood v. Wood was entered under a provision of the Chihuahau Divorce Law (art. 23) which does not require proof of registration as a resident and which allowed jurisdiction to be taken by submission, the personal appearance in Chihuahua before the court of one party and the appearance through a duly authorized attorney by the other requires for the purposes of New York public policy decision in this case be consistent with that in Rosenstiel.

On the wife's appeal from an affirmance of the dismissal of her complaint for separation based on cruelty, it is enough to say that if the facts as found and affirmed are accepted it was not error as a matter of law to dismiss the complaint.

The order should be affirmed, with costs, to plaintiff.

DESMOND, Chief Judge (concurring in part): Although for reasons hereafter stated I would not void past-granted Chihuahua divorces, I emphatically reject the proposition that New York State must continue to recognize these one-day decrees awarded to our residents in manner and on theories repugnant to our basic ideas.

There is no justification in positive law, public policy, natural justice or morals for a validation by this court of the practice of some of the citizens of our State of going to Mexico for divorces of the sort attacked on these appeals. My vote against recognizing them for the future is based on these self-evident propositions:

1. Divorce decrees rendered in foreign countries and purporting to dissolve New York marriages are entitled to recognition and effect in New York State only when such recognition is consistent with the public policy of our State. The Gould case is illustrative. There the New York courts upheld a divorce granted in France but only because the parties had actually lived for years in their Paris home and the decree was granted after an actual court contest without collusion and on a ground recognized in New York, that is, adultery.

2. Mexican "bilateral" divorces where one party crosses a bridge from El Paso, Texas, spends a day in Juarez and, by arrangement, the other appears by attorney, followed by a *pro forma* one-hour court appearance with no real hearing, or persuasive evidence or independent judicial determination lack almost all the elements which New York State considers requisites for a valid divorce. The residence requirements of the State of Chihuahua are minimal and inadequate to form a recognizable domiciliary jurisdictional base since in Mexico and contrary to our views neither spouse need have a true or real domicile in Mexico. Domicile as the law uses the term means a fixed, permanent and principal home to which a person wherever temporarily located always intends to return (Black's Law Dictionary, 4th ed.).

3. No attention is paid in Juarez divorces to the principle, fundamental with us, that marriage is an institution in which the public as a third party has a vital interest. The Mexican State does not concern itself with maintenance of the marriage or reasons for its dissolution. In these latter respects the one-day judgments here attacked differ in no essential respect from the mail-order writs described in Caldwell v. Caldwell, 298 N.Y. 146, 81 N.E.2d 60.

4. Such decrees are blatantly and obviosly the fruit of consensual divorce arrangements and as such are forbidden by New York public policy statute (now General Obligations Law, Consol. Laws, c. 24–A, § 5–311; see Caldwell v. Caldwell, 298 N.Y. 146, 150, 81 N.E.2d 60, 62–63, supra; Viles v. Viles, 14 N.Y.2d 365, 251 N.Y.S.2d 672, 200 N.E.2d 567).

5. Although there is a line of lower court decisions in the State upholding these "Chihuahua" decrees they are, so we are told and so it would seem, refused recognition everywhere else. Approval of these lower court decisions puts our State in the uneasy and inappropriate position of sole acceptor of Mexican "quickie" divorces. The suggestion in the majority opinion that these trial court and Appellate Division decisions, together with the fact that Mexico has issued divorces to New Yorkers, plus the fact of advices by New York attorneys to their clients, force this court into a totally wrong public policy is a suggestion that answers itself. We are forgetting that the public policy of this State as to divorce "exists to promote the permanency of the marriage contracts and the morality of the citizens of the state" (Hubbard v. Hubbard, 228 N.Y. 81, 85, 126 N.E. 508, 509).

Of course, it is in the modern manner to shrug off all this, to ask what is the difference between a one-day "domicile" in Juarez and a six weeks' "domicile" in Reno, to pile scorn and ridicule on New York's one-ground divorce law as archaic, cruel or worse. The approach is too facile. For 160 years New York as a State has recognized one cause only for divorce (Domestic Relations Law, § 170) and has refused to approve the practice of its domiciliaries going to other jurisdictions to evade our laws by obtaining divorces after short sojourns and on grounds not cognizable here. This official position of our State stands not on mere parochialism but on some of the oldest and deepest-felt sentiments of humanity. As Lord Mansfield wrote long ago: "Matrimony was one of the first commands given by God to mankind after the Creation, repeated again after the Deluge, and ever since echoed by the voice of nature to all mankind." Seventy-seven years ago in Maynard v. Hill, 125 U.S. 190, 205, 8 S.Ct. 723, 31 L.Ed. 653, supra, the United States Supreme Court referred to marriage as creating the most important relation in life and as having more to do with the morals of a civilized people than any institution, and pointed out that while marriage is in a sense a contract, it "partakes more of the character of an institution regulated and controlled by public authority, upon principles of public policy, for the benefit of the community" (Justice Field at pp. 205 and 213 of 125 U.S. p. 730 of 8 S.Ct.). There can be no doubt that this speaks the public policy of our State to be changed only by the people through Constitution or statute. No court is licensed to write a new State policy, however attractive or convenient. As to divorces gotten in other States of the Union we are constrained to recognition by modern constructions of the Federal full faith and credit clause. But when asked to recognize divorces rendered in foreign countries we as a court have neither right nor need to look beyond our own declared and unmistakable State policy.

As to analogizing the one-day Mexican divorce to the six weeks' Nevada decree, the first and ready answer is that judgments from other States are given faith and credit here because the Federal Constitution so commands. The second answer is a substitution of the true analogy, that is, between one-day foreign divorces, as between which there is no logical or real difference at all.

It is suggested, too, that a Juarez divorce is some sort of official "act of State" of a sovereign foreign power and, as such, safe from our scrutiny or ban. That might be so as to Mexico divorcing her own citizens. But our recognition of any foreign judgments is a mere act of official courtesy, implying no surrender of our own sovereignty. There is no compulsion. Were we to give credit to these Mexican judgments we would as a court be turning our backs on New York's restrictive divorce policy and allowing the divorce of our own citizen-residents by a foreign government having no interest in the marriage *res*.

For these reasons I vote for a declaration that such divorces are void, but I am not bound to and do not vote to give this ruling any more than prospective effect. I cannot shut my eyes to the realities. Tens of thousands of such purported divorces have been granted to New Yorkers who acted on advice of attorneys who relied on 25 years of decisions by the New York lower courts. No social or moral purpose would now be served by ruling that marriages long ago dissolved are still in existence, and the result would be destructive to the present homes, marriages and lives of those who remarried on the strength of Juarez decrees. This court has a clear right to give our ruling prospective effect only and justice and fairness dictate that we should do so and refuse to allow these plaintiffs or others to attack collaterally such past-rendered Mexican "one-day" divorces.

None of the other points made by counsel requires discussion herein.

In each case the order should be affirmed, with costs, but with the clear understanding that divorces of this sort granted after the date of the decision of these appeals will be void in New York State.

SCILEPPI, Judge (dissenting): I agree with the Chief Judge inasmuch as he would hold that these divorces are void; however, I would permit the present appellants to succeed on this appeal.

As we analyze the cases in this area, we must be ever mindful that we are not dealing with a decree of a sister State, but with one of a foreign nation. Decrees of a foreign nation are not only not entitled to full faith and credit, but are not even entitled to prima facie validity despite any allegation of jurisdiction which may appear on the face of the judgment (Rosenbaum v. Rosenbaum, 309 N.Y. 371, 375, 130 N.E.2d 902, 903). *The sole criterion by which these decrees may be judged is whether they contravene our public policy. . . .*

. . . New York requires that there be a relationship of substantial permanence between the decree rendering nation and the subject matter of the action, the marital *res*. Lack of jurisdiction over the subject matter of a controversy cannot, of course, be cured by the mere personal appearance of the parties (Matter of Lindgren's Estate, 293 N.Y. 18, 55 N.E. 849, 153 A.L.R. 936; Solotoff v Solotoff, 269 Appl Div. 677, 53 N.Y.S.2d 510).

Would the public policy of our State be served by departing from that well-established rule? I do not believe so. Illustrative of the many cases emphasizing the vital stake which the State has in every marriage contract is Fearon v. Treanor, 272 N.Y. 268, pp. 272-273, 5 N.E.2d 815, p. 816, 109 A.L.R. 1229, wherein this court stated:

"Marriage is more than a personal relation between a man and woman. It is a status founded on contract and established by law. It constitutes an institution involving the highest interests of society. It is regulated and controlled by law based upon principles of public policy affecting the welfare of the people of the State. . . .

"There are, in effect, three parties to every marriage, the man, the woman and the State. Trammel v. Vaughan, 158 Mo. 214, 59 S.W. 79, 51 L.R.A. 854. * * * The Domestic Relatons Law provides in great detail when and how marriage may be entered into, how the relation may be dissolved, the grounds for divorce and annulment, the rights and liabilities of husband and wife, the age at which the relation may be entered into and the class of persons who are disqualified from marrying.

"From time immemorial the State has exercised the fullest control over the marriage relation, justly believing that happy, successful marriages constitute the fundamental basis of the general welfare of the people."

Faced with this overwhelming interest of the State in the marital relationship, an interest which our State still maintains even in a "highly mobile era", we should not discard the rule that jurisdiction over the subject matter of a divorce action requires a substantial relationship between the decree rendering jurisdiction and the marital *res*.

It is anomalous, indeed, that we are today upholding a one-day Mexican divorce decree while several of our sister States, which afford grounds for divorce not afforded by us, have refused to recognize such a decree. As recently as 1963, New Jersey, in Warrender v. Warrender, 79 N.J. Super. 114, 190 A.2d 684, affd. on op. below 42 N.J. 287, 200 A.2d 123, declared that a decree of divorce rendered in Juarez upon the personal appearance of the plaintiff and appearance by attorney of the defendant was void. The court observed that "there is no basis for according greater recognition to a Mexican divorce on a one-day appearance than to the mail-order variety. . . ."

I am convinced that, with the decision in this case, this court has rekindled the spark still burning in the breasts of some that so-called Mexican mail-order decrees may one day be recognized as valid in this State. I agree with the Chief Judge that there is no distinction of substance between mail-order decrees and the decrees which have received the stamp of approval in the cases before us. Indeed, if the Mexican courts are jurisdictionally empowered to sever the matrimonial bonds of New York residents upon what the majority concedes to be a most flimsy jurisdictional basis, I fail to see why they are not jurisdictionally empowered to sever those bonds by mail with the virtue at least of its resultant economic benefit of avoiding the necessity of even a one-day trip. . . .

I agree with the majority that "our public interest is not affected differently by a formality of one day than by a formality of six weeks" and that "Nevada gets no closer to the real public concern with the marriage than Chihuahua." But—and this distinction is crucial in the case of a sister State—we are *compelled* to give full faith and credit to its decrees. In the case of a foreign country we are not compelled to do so and should not voluntarily recognize its decrees.

So-called "realities of life" and "contemporary experience", assuming that such considerations may be accurately assessed, which I doubt, are not reliable bases for determining public policy. That some, perhaps many, choose to treat their marriage contract with the same indifference that they would a commerical contract does not mean that we should indorse such conduct.

In addition to abandoning the requirement that a court which affects the marital status of our citizens should have subject matter jurisdiction, the majority has chosen to ignore the basic concepts and value judgments which permeate our Domestic Relations Law. The Legislature has seen fit to permit divorce in this State only because of the adultery of the defendant (Domestic Relations Law, § 170). This is certainly indicative of a design to restrict the availability of divorce and in so doing to preserve the family unit. Such preservation is considered vital and indispensable to the welfare and stability of the family, the ultimate goal being a climate conducive to the better development of our society. This court has a duty not to sanction the casual and consensual dissolution of the marriage contract by two of the three parties interested therein. This is especially true in light of the clear public policy announced in section 5–311 of the General Obligations Law, and in Viles v. Viles, 14 N.Y.2d 365, 251 N.Y.S.2d 672, 200 N.E.2d 567. To recognize these divorces is to disregard the traditionally solemn nature of the marriage contract (see Fearon v. Treanor, 272 N.Y. 268, 5 N.E.2d 815, 109 A.L.R. 1229, supra), legislative pronouncements (e.g., Domestic Relations Law, 170; General Obligations Law, 5–311), and decisions of this court (e.g., Viles v. Viles, supra; Caldwell v. Caldwell, 298 N.Y. 146, 81 N.E.2d 60, supra).

I am fully aware that a vast number of our citizens, relying upon the pronouncements below, have remarried, established families, acquired property, and engaged in many activities, personal and financial, as husband and wife. To accord this decision traditional retroactive effect would indeed have a profoundly convulsive and disruptive effect on our State, and on our citizens, who acted in good faith reliance on the law as enunciated below. However, to hold this divorce valid merely because our lower courts have been recognizing similar ones as such, and because many have placed reliance on those decisions, is no answer to the public policy considerations presented in this case. If this divorce is void, we should say so regardless of these prior decisions in our lower courts. Nonetheless, I also recognize that there are public policy considerations which should be taken into account concerning parties who have already obtained such divorces in reliance upon those decisions. Therefore, again as a matter of public policy, I would hold that, although Mexican divorce decrees of this type are void, this decision should not be applied retroactively. It is certainly within our power as the highest court in the State to give a decision such effect and not violate the Federal Constitution. I point out that this is a case where there are overriding and compelling reasons of public policy for refusing to give retrospective effect. I note that no one is being injured and no established rights are being impaired by such a disposition. . . .

In sum, for reasons of public policy, I would give this decision prospective effect only but would permit the appellants here to reap the benefits of the appeal. . . . "At least two compelling reasons exist for applying the new rule to the instant case while otherwise limiting its application to cases arising in the future. First, if we were to merely announce the new rule without applying it here, such announcement would amount to mere *dictum*. Second, and more important to refuse to apply the new rule here would deprive appellant of any benefit from his effort and expense in challenging the old rule which we now declare erroneous. Thus there would be no incentive to appeal the upholding of precedent since appellant could not in any event even benefit from a reversal invalidating it." This view was adopted by the Wisconsin Supreme Court in Kojis v. Doctors Hosp., 1 Wisc.2d 367, 374, 107 N.W.2d 131, 292, supra. Of course, parties to cases which have already been decided and which have already upheld their divorces could obtain no benefit from the consideration afforded these appellants.

The order of the Appellate Division vacating the judgment of annulment and reinstating Mrs. Rosenstiel's injunction action restraining Mr. Rosenstiel from seeking marital relief outside this jurisdiction should be reversed.

In Wood v. Wood decided herewith, I would modify the order of the Appellate Division to the extent of granting the defendant's counterclaim for annulment. In all other respects I would affirm.

DYE, FULD and VAN VOORHIS, JJ., concur with BERGAN, J.

BURKE, J., taking no part in each action: order affirmed.

One of the strongest endorsations of judicial legislating ever given came from President Theodore Roosevelt in a Message to Congress, December 8, 1908:

"The chief lawmakers in our country may be, and often are, the judges, because they are the final seat of authority. Every time they interpret contract, property, vested rights, due process of law, liberty, they necessarily enact into law parts of a system of social philosophy; and as such interpretation is fundamental, they give direction to all law-making. The decisions of the courts on economic and social questions depend upon their economic and social philosophy; and for the peaceful progress of our people during the twentieth century we shall owe most to those judges who hold to a twentieth century economic and social philosophy and not to a long outgrown philosophy, which was itself the product of primitive economic conditions." Holmes J. was more cautious: "I recognize without hesitation that judges must and do legislate, but they do so only interstitially; they are confined from molar to molecular motions. A common-law judge could not say, I think the doctrine of consideration a bit of historical nonsense and shall not enforce it in my court" [*Southern Pacific Co.* v. *Jensen* (1917) 244 U.S. 205, 221]. The view of Chief Justice Hughes, *The Supreme Court of the United States* 230 (1928) was that "a federal statute finally means what the [Supreme] Court says it means."

AERO SPARK PLUG CO., INC. v. B. G. CORPORATION

(United States Court of Appeals, Second Circuit, 1942. 130 F. 2d 290.)

Appeal from the District Court of the United States for the Southern District of New York.

Patent infringement suit by the Aero Spark Plug Company, Incorporated, and another, against the B. G. Corporation. From a final decree of the District Court for the Southern District of New York dismissing on the merits the complaint, plaintiffs appeal.

CHASE, Circuit Judge: The decree was based upon two grounds, non-infringement and invalidity of Claim 2, which is the only claim in issue.

Kasarjian's patent involves spark plugs for use in airplane engines. The usual aviation spark plug assembly has a core in the center consisting of a metal rod or spindle. The lower end of this spindle constitutes one of the electrodes at the spark gap, and therefore the whole must be insulated from the other electrode known as the ground electrode. Because of the intense heat in aviation engines, mica is used as an insulator. Several thin laminations of mica are first wound around the spindle. This is known as the mica "cigarette." About midway on this "cigarette" is a tight-fitting brass bushing to hold it in place on the spindle. Above the bushing, and sometimes both above and below it, is placed a stack of mica washers the inner circumference of which fits snugly around the "cigarette." This constitutes the insulation of the center electrode.

An extremely high voltage is required in aviation engines to create a satisfactory spark in the cylinder because of the high compression of the explosive mixture. It has been found that occasionally a plug would miss fire because there would be a parasitic discharge or flashing within the insulation rather than at the spark gap where resistance was high. This flashing occurred in the slight air space between the mica "cigarette" and the mica washers, and the explanation for it was that in some plugs this air between the "cigarette" and washers became ionized from the leakage of the high voltage electricity and the ionization deprived the air of its usually good insulating properties with the result that there was less resistance offered the discharge through this path than across the spark gap. All this was known to the prior art, and it was while seeking to eliminate parasitic discharge that Kasarjian invented the new construction which he patented. . . .

Assuming, without deciding, that claim 2 is valid, we agree that infringement has not been shown. The general structure of the accused plug is that of the conventional aviation spark plug, but in it the parasitic discharge is prevented by placing a refractory substance at only two places, one just above and one just below the brass bushing which holds the mica "cigarette" in place. In actual practice this is done by placing a small amount of the refractory cement in the shape of a doughnut around the "cigarette" at either end of the bushing. The washers are then pressed on and the whole is then compressed as part of the usual assembly method. The theory is that these refractory "doughnuts" will act as an insulating barrier to prevent either the leakage of electricity or parasitic discharge regardless of the presence of air which in the patented construction has been excluded. No effort is made to fill the air spaces completely and that result is not attained. The purpose and the final end of both methods are to prevent flashing, but with that their similarity ends. To eliminate harmful air is one thing and to make the residual air in such spaces harmless is quite another and so different a method that it does not infringe. . . .

Since there is no infringement even if the patent be valid, we do not decide the question of validity. See S. S. Kresge Co. v. Davies, 8 Cir., 112 F.2d 708, 711. But cf. dissent in Exhibit Supply Co. v. Ace Patents Corp., 315 U.S. 126, 137, 62 S.Ct. 513, 86 L.Ed. 736.

Affirmed.

FRANK, Circuit Judge (concurring). I concur. But I think we should also hold the patent invalid. That issue was squarely raised in the court below and in this court. When such an issue is raised, and when the patent is invalid, I think it is our duty so to decide. . . .

As we said recently in Picard v. United Aircraft, 2 Cir., May 28, 1942, 128 F.2d 632, 636, "there is more at stake [in a patent case] than the issues between the two parties." The decision of my colleagues relieves appellee, but leaves appellant free to sue others as alleged infringers, putting them to the expense – notoriously great in patent suits – of defending themselves. It is well known, too, that threats of such suits, because of that expense, often induce alleged infringers to accept licenses on onerous terms rather than to engage in litigation. As the exercise of a patent monopoly is publicly injurious when an invalid patent remains at large, the public interest is, therefore, deeply involved. And as, under the existing patent statute and decisions, no one, on behalf of the public, can institute a suit to have a patent declared invalid, we should, I think, avail ourselves of this opportunity to wipe out the patent here.

That it is invalid seems clear, in the light of Picard v. United Aircraft, supra. The appellee's brief in the instant case states that the patentee hit on the use of the refractory material "only as a last resort," and adds, "Indeed, as it proved to be, it was not a problem solvable by deduction but only by experimentation; and, as often happens, it was solved in the end by trying something that did not seem practicable." That statement brings the patentee's method directly within the description of what this court, the other day, held not to constitute invention. See Picard v. United Aircraft, supra, where we said (per Judge L. Hand) that nothing is an invention which is the product of "the slow but inevitable progress * * * through trial and error" and of "the exercise of persistent and intelligent search for improvement." There was here no "new display of ingenuity beyond the compass of the routineer"; Kirsch Mfg. Co. v. Gould Mersereau Co., 2 Cir., 6 F.2d 793, 794.

It is true that, in ordinary private litigation, courts sometimes confine their decisions narrowly, and, if one point is sufficient to support a decision, other points are not discussed. Even if that could be said to be the usual practice, it loses much of its pertinence in patent cases. A patent is a "public franchise," a legalized monopoly. To allow a patent to remain apparently valid when the issue of invalidity is raised and the court sees that the patent is invalid, is to ignore the paramount public interest. Because no representative of the public may institute a suit to have a patent held invalid, and because the courts have no staff of independent experts to aid them in patent suits, the courts must, in most cases, rely on the litigants in ascertaining the prior art. But when, in a patent suit, the court is aware of a prior art which shows no invention, and that issue is raised by one of the parties, the public interest would seem to require that the court should so decide. . . .

It is no adequate answer to say that courts should not concern themselves with the protection of persons not parties to suits pending before them. The fact is that courts daily do so concern themselves, and in circumstances where the desirability of doing so is far less obvious than here and the means far less effective. Because I think that to hold invalid a patent which is obviously void is a matter of a major public importance, I think it desirable to elaborate that point:

Perhaps the central theme in most discussions of the judicial process is the obligation of judges to consider the future consequences of their specific decisions. Such discussions usually stress the "rule" or precedent aspect of decisions. Thus Dickinson, in 1927, paraphrasing (it may be unconsciously) Aristotle's remarks made almost twenty-two hundred years earlier, writes, "One danger in the administration of justice is that the necessities of the future and the interest of parties not before the court may be sacrificed in favor of present litigants"; he thinks it imperative that judges should "raise their minds above the immediate case before them and subordinate their feelings and impressions to a practice of intricate abstract reasoning, . . . centering their attention on a mass of considerations which lie outside the color of the case at bar."

Although much can be said for that attitude – of considering a decision primarily with reference to its significance in future cases – it is sometimes given too much weight. Excessive concentration of attention, by some upper court judges, on the formulation in their opinions of so-called legal rules, with an eye chiefly to the impact of those rules on hypothetical future cases not yet before the court, sometimes results in their allotting inadequate attention to the interests of the actual parties in the specific existing cases which it is the duty of the courts to decide. Such judges never quite catch up with themselves; for, in cases which actually occur, they are deciding future cases that may never occur. Legal history shows that such an attitude leads to judicial pronouncements which, at times, are none too happy in their effects on future cases. For the future develops unanticipated happenings; moreover, it does not stay put, it refuses to be trapped.

The intended consequences of efforts to govern the future often fail; the actual consequences – which may be good or evil – are, frequently, utterly different. Results are miscalculated; there is an "illusion of purpose." Of course, present problems will be clarified by reference to future ends, but, as I have elsewhere suggested, such ends, although they have a future bearing, must obtain their significance in present consequences, otherwise those ends lose their significance. For, it is the nature of the future that it never arrives. "Tomorrow today will be yesterday." Any future, when it becomes the present, is sure to bring new and unexpected problems. There is much wisdom in Valery's reference to the "anachronism of the future."

And the paradox is that when judges become unduly interested in the future consequences of their rulings, they are (as Walter Bingham pointed out years ago) doing precisely what they say they must avoid – they are deciding not real but hypothetical cases, with no one present to speak for the imaginary contestants. The interests of the parties to cases actually before the court are thus sacrificed to the shadowy unvoiced claims of supposititious litigants in future litigation which may never arise; and the judicial process becomes the pursuit of an elusive horizon which is never reached. No one – except perhaps those judges – is satisfied, since the interests of the parties to real present cases are overlooked, and the interests of the parties in subsequent cases are often inadequately determined in their absence. No doubt it expands the ego of a judge to look upon himself as the guardian of the general future. But his more humble yet more important and immediate task is to decide individual, actual, present cases. The exaggerated respect paid today to upper court judges, as distinguished from trial court judges, is both a cause and a result of this over-emphasis on the rule-aspect of decisions. Such judicial legislation as inheres in formulating legal rules is inescapable. But courts should be modest in their legislative efforts to control the future, since they cannot function democratically, as legislative committees and administrative agencies can, by inviting the views of all who may be affected by their prospective rules. And, because they do not learn those views, and must largely rely on their own imaginations, they should be cautious about attempting, in present cases, to project their formulations too far and too firmly into the days yet to come. To cope with the present is none too easy, in part because the present is only a moving line dividing yesterdays and tomorrows, so that reflections on what will happen are unavoidable elements of current problems. But, although continuity, both backwards and forwards, is to some extent a necessity, judges should not shirk the present aspect of today's problems in favor of too much illusory tinkering with tomorrow's. The future can become as perniciously tyrannical as the past. Posterity-worship can be as bad as ancestor-worship.

Dean Leon Green's tentative analysis of the factors which affect upper court decisions helps to reveal the extent to which the judges of those courts, when deciding cases, often interest themselves in the future at the expense of the present. He refers to (1) the "administrative" factor, (2) the "ethical or moral" factor, (3) the "economic" factor (4) the "prophylactic or preventive" factor, and (5) the "justice" factor (the "merits" of the particular case). The "administrative" factor, for instance, relates to "the workability" of a rule, its "ease and certainty of performance" in the future. Thus we find courts saying that, if recovery were allowed "in this class of cases, it would naturally result in a flood of litigation in cases where the injury complained of may be easily feigned without detection"; or that "in practice it is impossible satisfactorily to administer any other rule"; or that a rule "is an arbitrary exception, based upon a notion of what is practicable." The "prophylactic" factor, bred of a desire of judges "to fashion rules for a healthy future," is frequently operative, for "judges are inveterate prophets and legislators"; they "scale their penalties, they impose damages, both punitive and exemplary, not merely for the individual offender's lesson, but as a preventive of future harms"; they "spend much time fashioning prophylactic rules both of substantive and procedural design in their efforts to purify the social stream through the judicial process." Those and similar factors are undeniably important. But it is not always fortunate when judges tend first to consider such factors before turning their attentions to the parties to the particular actual cases which they are called upon to decide.

The elaborate (and sometimes fatuous) concern with the future potentialities of expressions in judicial opinions, which accompany and justify specific decisions is, in considerable measure, due to uncritical veneration of the doctrine of "standing by the precedents"; for, if an opinion does, in truth lay down rules which must thereafter be followed by the courts themselves in later cases, the responsibility in deciding existing controversies is far greater than that of being fair to the parties to those controversies, for then a judge is playing the important role of legislator. That responsibility, however, can be too much underscored.

Stare decisis, within limits, has undeniable worth. . . . But precedent-worship has been so unreflective that there has been insufficient inquiry into its practical workings. There is need to apply to it more of that constructive scepticism voiced by Wigmore twenty-five years ago. We have paid too little heed to the way in which John Chipman Gray – a successful practising lawyer in the field of real property where, above all, precedent has been traditionally sanctified – challenged the fundamental thesis of stare decisis when he said that few men, in the conduct of their practical affairs, actually rely on past judicial rulings. Perhaps his scepticism went too far. Yet, in the twenty years which have elapsed since he issued that challenge, few persons have met it, and most lawyers and many judges go on declaiming that life would be unbearably uncertain if courts did not adhere to their earlier formulations of "rules" and "principles." We know virtually nothing of the extent to which men do, in fact, rely on past judicial utterances. If, as is often said, stare decisis is bottomed on something like estoppel, courts should not be too hesitant about changing their previous formulations when change is highly desirable, in the absence of proof of actual reliance by the litigant who opposes such a change. It might be well to hold that such reliance will be presumed but that that presumption is rebuttable. And, in any event, such changes, as Wigmore suggested, can be made prospective, and not retroactive, where there is any likelihood that there was reliance. If the sanctity of stare decisis were thus moderately diminished, and if authorities were employed as they were by the much abused scholastics, i.e., only when shown to be reasonable, upper court judges might lose some of their prestige, but they could, by reducing their Jovian aloofness, devote more time to the interests of litigants in specific actual cases and less to the possible future harm of "just" decisions of those actual controversies.

Fortunately, wise judges have devised escapes from improvidently formulated rulings. For instance, the courts have recognized the fact that chance circumstances – such as the peculiar interests of the parties to a suit or the laziness or incompetence of their lawyers – may prevent the adequate presentation of all aspects of a case and thus induce judicial neglect of those aspects, with resultant inadequacy in the judicial generalizations. So the Supreme Court has wisely said, "Questions which merely lurk in the record, neither brought to the attention of the court nor ruled upon, are not to be considered as having been so decided as to constitute precedents."

But, no matter what is done, the problem of deciding cases so that decisions will not be hurtful, as precedents, to future litigants, is not too easy of solution. It is surprising, then, that my colleagues, who like all judges, seek, every day, as they must, to solve that difficult problem, refuse, in the case at bar, to tackle a problem the solution of which is far simpler and with results far more easily foreseeable: Here the question is not of the future consequences, on litigants in possible future suits, of a general rule articulated in an opinion accompanying a decision, but of how a decision as to the specific rights of a particular person before the court may affect others not in court against whom that same person may, in the future, attempt to assert those very rights. It resembles the question of revoking the license to drive an automobile of a man who has been proved to be an incompetent driver: In deciding whether that specific man should be permitted to drive in the future, it is necessary to consider those who may be injured by his future conduct if his license is not revoked, and the precedential effect of the decision on future litigation, not relating in any way to that specific man, is, relatively, unimportant. The public interest in his later activities should be a paramount consideration. His potential future victims are not present, and, for that very reason, their interests should be a major concern of the tribunal called upon to render decision.

Consequently, if we must here choose between deciding that the patent is not valid or is not infringed – a choice I think we are not required to make – our choice should be the former. By such a choice, we will do no harm to the patent system. It is under fire today, and may not survive attack unless its major abuses are removed. Among such abuses is the persistence of cancerous "spurious" patents. To shift the metaphor, they are vicious Zombis. Their attacks on the public interest bring the patent system into disrepute.
SWAN, Circuit Judge, joined in the opinion of CHASE, Circuit Judge.

RICKETTS v. PENNSYLVANIA R. CO.

(United States Court of Appeals, Second Circuit, 1946. 153 F.2d 757.)

[The majority opinion of L. Hand, J. and the dissenting opinion of Swan, J., have been omitted. Footnotes to Judge Frank's concurring opinion have also been omitted. Ed.]

An action under section 51 of 45 U.S.C.A. by Sydney George Ricketts against the Pennsylvania Railroad to recover damages for injuries suffered while in employ of defendant. From a judgement of the District Court in favor of plaintiff, defendant appeals.

Affirmed.

FRANK, Circuit Judge (concurring): Plaintiff, as a result of a railroad accident which occurred while he was working as an employee of the Pennsylvania Railroad Company, suffered personal injuries which turned out to be so serious that the jury returned a verdict in his favor for $7,500, which the Railroad Company does not contest – except on one ground, i. e., that his claim was barred by a release he gave the company on payment to him of one-tenth that sum, or $750. That smaller sum represents merely the approximate amount of his lost earnings up to the date of the release. When he signed the release, he could not read it because of the effects of the accident, and without negligence on his part – since he relied on his own lawyer who mis-informed him – he understood that it purported to be only a receipt for payment of those lost earnings.

Judge HAND says (and I entirely agree) that the evidence sufficiently shows that the lawyer acted beyond his authority. Accordingly, it is as if a non-lawyer, carefully selected by plaintiff, had erroneously interpreted the release to him. The case thus comes within the category, described by Williston, of non-negligent unilateral mistakes preventing the formation of valid contracts. Accepting Williston's analysis, Judge HAND's rationale seems to me to be impregnable.

But I am not content to rest the decision on that analysis, because I think that that analysis leads to needless complexities which will confront us in future cases. The Supreme Court recently, in a case (cited by Judge HAND) relating to a release by a seaman, Garrett v. Moore-McCormack Co., 317 U.S. 239, at page 248, 63 S.Ct. 246, 87 L.Ed. 239, note 17, has broadly hinted that the courts should treat non-maritime employees, with respect to releases of personal injury claims, just as they treat seamen. I think we should take that hint, and, in doing so, should reject many of the finespun distinctions made by Williston and expressed in the Restatement of Contracts. Since I believe that not only is an important social policy involved but also that a good opportunity offers itself to uncomplicate an excessively complicated set of legal rules, I shall state, in some detail, my reasons for this conclusion.

In the early days of this century a struggle went on between the respective proponents of two theories of contracts, (a) the "actual intent" theory – or "meeting of the minds" or "will" theory – and (b) the so-called "objective" theory. Without doubt, the first theory has been carried too far: Once a contract has been validly made, the courts attach legal consequences to the relation created by the contract, consequences of which the parties usually never dreamed – as, for instance, where situations arise which the parties had not contemplated. As to such matters, the "actual intent" theory induced much fictional discourse which imputed to the parties intentions they plainly did not have.

But the objectivists also went too far. They tried (1) to treat virtually all the varieties of contractual arrangements in the same way, and (2), as to all contracts in all their phases, to exclude, as legally irrelevant, consideration of the actual intention of the parties or either of them, as distinguished from the outward manifestation of that intention. The objectivists transferred from the field of torts that stubborn anti-subjectivist, the "reasonable man"; so that, in part at least, advocacy of the "objective" standard in contracts appears to have represented a desire for legal symmetry, legal uniformity, a desire seemingly prompted by aesthetic impulses. Whether (thanks to the "subjectivity" of the jurymen's reactions and other factors) the objectivists' formula, in its practical workings, could yield much actual objectivity, certainty, and uniformity may well be doubted. At any rate, the sponsors of complete "objectivity" in contracts largely won out in the wider generalizations of the Restatement of Contracts and in some judicial pronouncements.

Influenced by their passion for excessive simplicity and uniformity, many objectivists have failed to give adequate special consideration to releases of claims for personal injuries, and especially to such releases by employees to their employers. Williston, the leader of the objectivists, insists that, as to all contracts, without differentiation, the objective theory is essential because "founded upon the fundamental principle of the security of business transactions."

He goes to great lengths to maintain this theory, using a variety of rather desperate verbal distinctions to that end. Thus he distinguishes between (1) a unilateral non-negligent mistake in executing an instrument (i. e., a mistake of that character in signing an instrument of one kind believing it to be of another kind) and (2) a similar sort of mistake as to the meaning of a contract which one intended to make. The former, he says, renders the contract "void"; the latter does not prevent the formation of a valid contract. Yet in both instances "the fundamental principle of the security of business transactions" is equally at stake, for there has been the same "disappointment of well-founded expectations." More than that, Williston concedes that a mistaken idea of one party as to the meaning of a valid contract (Williston's second category) "may, under certain circumstances, be ground for relief from enforcement of the contract." But he asserts that (a) such a contract is not "void" but "voidable," and (b) that the granting of such relief is no exception to the objective theory, because this relief "is in its origin equitable," and "equity" does not deny the formation of a valid contract but merely acts "by subsequently . . . rescinding" it. His differentiation, moreover, of "void" and "voidable" has little if any practical significance: He says that a "voidable" contract will be binding unless the mistaken party sets up the mistake as a defense; but the same is obviously true of agreements which (because of unilateral mistakes affecting their "validity") he describes as "wholly void."

It is little wonder that a considerable number of competent legal scholars have criticized the extent to which the objective theory, under Williston's influence, was carried in the Restatement of Contracts. . . .

In other realms of thought, attempted over-simplification has yielded complexities in practice. So here, as appears from the following.

Fortunately, most judges are too common-sensible to allow, for long, a passion for aesthetic elegance, or for the appearance of an abstract consistency, to bring about obviously unjust results. Accordingly, courts not infrequently have departed from the objective theory when necessary to avoid what they have considered an unfair decision against a person who, for a small sum, signed a release without understanding either the seriousness of his injury or the import of the words of the release, provided (1) he was not "negligent" and (2) the other party (the releasee) had not, in reliance on the release, importantly "changed his position." Some courts, in some of the mistake cases, frankly abandon the "objective" test, saying boldly that a non-negligent unilateral mistake justifies cancellation or rescission of a contract. As New York, a lively center of commerce, at least to some extent allows relief for such unilateral mistakes, it should be obvious that, contrary to Williston & Co., any deviation from the objective theory is not fatal to the functioning of business.

Some courts, however, escape marring the verbal symmetry of the objective theory, while actually abandoning it, thus: They say that a mistake by one party about a striking fact (sometimes called "palpable") must be deemed to have been known to the other party, that even if the evidence fails to show that he knew it, yet he had "reason to know it" and is therefore to be treated as if he did: so that there results, by this device, which comes close to a fiction, a "mutual mistake of fact." . . .

Two approaches have been suggested which diverge from that of Williston and the Restatement but which perhaps come closer to the realities of business experience. (1) The first utilizes the concept of an "assumption of risk": The parties to a contract, it is said, are presumed to undertake the risk that the facts upon the basis of which they entered into the contract might, within a certain margin, prove to be non-existent; accordingly, one who is mistaken about any such a fact should not, absent a deliberate assumption by him of that risk, be held for more than the actual expenses caused by his conduct. Otherwise, the other party will receive a windfall to which he is not entitled. (2) The second suggestion runs thus: Business is conducted on the assumption that men who bargain are fully informed as to all vital facts about the transactions in which they engage; a contract based upon a mistake as to any such fact as would have deterred either of the parties from making it, had he known that fact, should therefore be set aside in order to prevent unjust enrichment to him who made the mistake; the other party, on this suggestion also, is entitled to no more than his actual expenses. Each of those suggestions may result in unfairness, if the other party reasonably believing that he has made a binding contract, has lost the benefit of other specific bargains available at that time but no longer open to him. But any such possibility of unfairness will seldom, if ever, exist in the case of a release of liability for personal injury whatever the nature of the mistake (i.e., whether it fits into one or the other of Williston's categories).

In short, the "security of business transactions" does not require a uniform answer to the question when and to what extent the non-negligent use of words should give rise to rights in one who has reasonably relied on them. That the answer should be favorable to the relier when the words are used in certain kinds of contracts, does not mean that it should also be when they are used in a release of a claim for personal injury; and there may be still further reasons for an unfavorable answer when the claim is by an employee against his employer.

In all likelihood, it is because the courts have sensed the differentiated character of releases of personal injury claims that the "modern trend," as Wigmore describes it, "is to . . . develop a special doctrine . . . for that class of cases, liberally relieving the party who signed the release. Surely much is to be said for that liberality, especially in a case where an employee has given a release of personal injury liability, without the fullest comprehension of what he was about, for a relatively small sum which turns out to be wholly inadequate.

In the admiralty cases, such relief has long been accorded seamen; the courts, calling them "wards of admiralty," have regarded them, in many of their dealings with their employers, as necessitous persons, under strong economic pressures, who because of their helplessness, are to be protected from hard bargains, just as "equity," for similar reasons, protects mortgagors and beneficiaries of spendthrift trusts. The usual non-maritime employees, because they are under similar economic pressures, are no less helpless in their trafficking with their employers. . . .

It is not surprising, then, that many courts – although without such direct expressions as those which adorn the seaman cases – have in fact in the release cases manifested, although obliquely, a not dissimilar guardianship of employees of large corporations. As already noted, the Supreme Court recently gave a broad hint that the admiralty doctrine is not as exceptional as is sometimes supposed; see Garrett v. Moore-McCormack Co., 317 U.S. 239, 248, 63 S.Ct. 246, 87 L.Ed. 239; note 17. For reasons previously indicated, I think we should take that hint. It seems to me that the time has come to give up the elaboration of distinctions found in the judicial opinions relieving non-admiralty employees of their releases. I believe that the courts should now say forthrightly that the judiciary regards the ordinary employee as one who needs and will receive the special protection of the courts when, for a small consideration, he has given a release after an injury. As Mr. Justice Holmes often urged, when an important issue of social policy arises, it should be candidly, not evasively, articulated. In other contexts, the courts have openly acknowledged that the economic inequality between the ordinary employer and ordinary individual employee usually means the absence of "free bargaining." I think the courts should do so in these employee release cases. And the federal courts, I think, should so hold in respect to liability pursuant to the Federal Employers Liability Act. I think, therefore, that we should treat the plaintiff here as we would if he were a seaman.

Such a ruling will not produce legal uncertainty but will promote certainty – as anyone can see who reads the large number of cases in this field, with their numerous intricate methods of getting around the objective theory. Such a ruling would simply do directly what many courts have been doing indirectly. It is fairly clear that they have felt, although they have not said, that employers should not, by such releases, rid themselves of obligations to injured employees, obligations which society at large will bear – either, by taxes, through the government or, by donations, through private charitable organizations. . . .

B. READINGS

John Dewey, 1859-1952

LOGICAL METHOD AND THE LAW

Human conduct, broadly viewed, falls into two sorts: particular cases overlap, but the difference is discernible on any large scale consideration of conduct.

Sometimes human beings act with a minimum of foresight, without examination of what they are doing and of probable consequences. They act not upon deliberation but from routine, instinct, the direct pressure of appetite, or a blind 'hunch.' It would be a mistake to suppose that such behavior is always inefficient or unsuccessful. When we do not like it, we condemn it as capricious, arbitrary, careless, negligent. But in other cases, we praise the marvellous rectitude of instinct or intuition; we are inclined to accept the offhand appraisal of an expert in preference to elaborately calculated conclusions of a man who is ill-informed. There is the old story of the layman who was appointed to a position in India where he would have to pass in his official capacity on various matters in controversy between natives. Upon consulting a legal friend, he was told to use his common sense and announce his decisions firmly; in the majority of cases his natural decision as to what was fair and reasonable would suffice. But, his friend added: "Never try to give reasons, for they will usually be wrong."

In the other sort of case, action follows upon a decision, and the decision is the outcome of inquiry, comparison of alternatives, weighing of facts; deliberation or thinking has intervened. Considerations which have weight in reaching the conclusion as to what is to be done, or which are employed to justify it when it is questioned are called "reasons." If they are stated in sufficiently general terms they are "principles." When the operation is formulated in a compact way, the decision is called a conclusion, and the considerations which led up to it are called the premises. Decisions of the first type may be reasonable: that is, they may be adapted to good results; those of the second type are reasoned or rational, increasingly so, in the degree of care and thoroughness with which inquiry has been conducted and the order in which connections have been established between the considerations dealt with.

Now I define logical theory as an account of the procedures followed in reaching decisions of the second type, in those cases in which subsequent experience shows that they were the best which could have been used under the conditions. This definition would be questioned by many authorities, and it is only fair to say that it does not represent the orthodox or the prevailing view. But it is stated at the outset so that the reader may be aware of the conception of logic which underlies the following discussion. If we take an objection which will be brought against this conception by adherents of the traditional notion, it will serve to clarify its meaning. It will be said that the definition restricts thinking to the processes antecedent to making a decision or a deliberate choice; and, thereby, in confining logical procedure to practical matters, fails to take even a glance at those cases in which true logical method is best exemplified: namely, scientific, especially mathematical, subjects.

A partial answer to this objection is that the especial topic of our present discussion is logical method in legal reasoning and judicial decision, and that such cases at least are similar in general type to decisions made by engineers, merchants, physicians, bankers, etc., in the pursuit of their callings. In law we are certainly concerned with the necessity of settling upon a course of action to be pursued, giving judgment of one sort or another in favor of adoption of one mode of conduct and against another. But the scope of the position taken will appear more clearly if we do not content ourselves with this *ad hoc* reply.

If we consider the procedure of the mathematician or of any man of science, as it concretely occurs, instead of considering simply the relations of consistent implication which subsist between the propositions in which his finally approved conclusions are set forth, we find that he, as well as an intelligent farmer or business man or physician, is constantly engaged in making decisions; and that in order to make them wisely he summons before his mental gaze various considerations, and accepts and rejects them with a view to making his decision as rational as possible. The concrete subject with which he deals, the material he investigates, accepts, rejects, employs in reaching and justifying his decision, is different from that of farmer, lawyer, or merchant, but the course of the operation, the form of the procedure, is similar. The scientific man has the advantage of working under much more narrowly and exactly controlled conditions, with the aid of symbols artfully devised to protect his procedure. For that reason it is natural and proper that we should, in our formal treatises, take operations of this type as standards and models, and should treat ordinary "practical" reasonings leading up to decision as to what is to be done as only approximations. But every thinker, as an investigator, mathematician, or physicist as well as "practical man," thinks in order to determine *his* decisions and conduct – his conduct as a specialized agent working in a carefully delimited field.

It may be replied, of course, that this is an arbitrary notion of logic, and that in reality logic is an affair of the relations and orders of relations which subsist between propositions which constitute the accepted subject-matter of a science; that relations are independent of operations of inquiry and of reaching conclusions or decisions. I shall not stop to try to controvert this position, but shall use it to point the essential difference between it and the position taken in this article. According to the latter, logical systematization with a view to the utmost generality and consistency of propositions is indispensable but is not ultimate. It is an instrumentality, not an end. It is a means of improving, facilitating, clarifying the inquiry that leads up to concrete decisions; primarily that particular inquiry which has just been engaged in, but secondarily, and of greater ultimate importance, other inquiries directed at making other decisions in similar fields. And here at least I may fall back for confirmation upon the special theme of law. It is most important that rules of law should form as coherent generalized logical systems as possible. But these logical systematizations of law in any field, whether of crime, contracts, or torts, with their reduction of a multitude of decisions to a few general principles that are logically consistent with one another while it may be an end in itself for a particular student, is clearly in last resort subservient to the economical and effective reaching of decisions in particular cases.

It follows that logic is ultimately an empirical and concrete discipline. Men first employ certain ways of investigating, and of collecting, recording and using data in reaching conclusions, in making decisions; they draw inferences and make their checks and tests in various ways. These different ways constitute the empirical raw material of logical theory. The latter thus comes into existence without any conscious thought of logic, just as forms of speech take place without conscious reference to rules of syntax or of rhetorical propriety. But it is gradually learned that some methods which are used work better than others. Some yield conclusions that do not stand the test of further situations; they produce conflicts and confusion; decisions dependent upon them have to be retracted or revised. Other methods are found to yield conclusions which are available in subsequent inquiries as well as confirmed by them. There first occurs a kind of natural selection of the methods which afford the better type of conclusion, better for subsequent usage, just as happens in the development of rules for conducting any art. Afterwards the methods are themselves studied critically. Successful ones are not only selected and collated, but the causes of their effective operation are discovered. Thus logical theory becomes scientific.

The bearing of the conception of logic which is here advanced upon legal thinking and decisions may be brought out by examining the apparent disparity which exists between actual legal development and the strict requirements of logical theory. Justice Holmes has generalized the situation by saying that "the whole outline of the law is the resultant of a conflict at every point between logic and good sense – the one striving to work fiction out to consistent results, the other restraining and at last overcoming that effort when the results become too manifestly unjust." This statement he substantiates by a thorough examination of the development of certain legal notions. Upon its surface, such a statement implies a different view of the nature of logic than that stated. It implies that logic is not the method of good sense, that it has as it were a substance and life of its own which conflicts with the requirements of good decisions with respect to concrete subject matters. The difference, however, is largely verbal. What Justice Holmes terms logic is formal consistency, consistency of concepts with one another irrespective of the consequences of their application to concrete matters-of-fact. We might state the fact by saying that concepts, once developed have a kind of intrinsic inertia on their own account; once developed the law of habit applies to them. It is practically economical to use a concept ready at hand rather than to take time and trouble and effort to change it or to devise a new one. The use of prior ready-made and familiar concepts also gives rise to a sense of stability, of guarantee against sudden and arbitrary changes of the rules which determine the consequences which legally attend acts. It is the nature of any concept, as it is of any habit to change more slowly than do the concrete circumstances with reference to which it is employed. Experience shows that the relative fixity of concepts affords men a specious sense of protection, of assurance against the troublesome flux of events. Thus Justice Holmes says, "The language of judicial decision is mainly the language of logic. And the logical method and form flatter that longing for certainty and for repose which is in every human mind. But certainty generally is an illusion." From the view of logical method here set forth, however, the undoubted facts which Justice Holmes has in mind do not concern logic but rather certain tendencies of the human creatures who use logic; tendencies which a sound logic will guard against. For they spring from the momentum of habit once forced, and express the effect of habit upon our feelings of ease and stability – feelings which have little to do with the actual facts of the case.

However, this is only part of the story. The rest of the story is brought to light in some other passages of Justice Holmes. "The actual life of the law has not been logic: it has been experience. The felt necessities of the times, the prevalent moral and political theories, intuitions of public policy, avowed or unconscious, even the prejudices which judges share with their fellow-men, have had a good deal more to do than the syllogism in determining the rules by which men should be governed." In other words, Justice Holmes is thinking of logic as equivalent with the syllogism, as he is quite entitled to do in accord with the orthodox tradition. From the standpoint of the syllogism as the logical model which was made current by scholasticism there is an antithesis between experience and logic, between logic and good sense. For the philosophy embodied in the formal theory of the syllogism asserted that thought or reason has fixed forms of its own, anterior to and independent of concrete subject-matters, and to which the latter have to be adapted whether or no. This defines the negative aspect of this discussion; and it shows by contrast the need of another kind of logic which shall reduce the influence of habit, and shall facilitate the use of good sense regarding matters of social consequence.

In other words, there are different logics in use. One of these, the one which has had greatest historic currency and exercised greatest influence on legal decisions, is that of the syllogism. To this logic the strictures of Justice Holmes apply in full force. For it purports to be a logic of rigid demonstration, not of search and discovery. It claims to be a logic of fixed forms, rather than of methods of reaching intelligent decisions in concrete situations, or of methods employed in adjusting disputed issues in behalf of the public and enduring interest. Those ignorant of formal logic, the logic of the abstract relations of ready-made conceptions to one another, have at least heard of the standard syllogism: All men are mortal; Socrates is a man; therefore, he is mortal. This is offered as the model of all proof or demonstration. It implies that what we need and must procure is first a fixed general *principle*, the so-called major premise, such as 'all men are mortal,' then in the second place, a fact which belongs intrinsically and obviously to a class of things to which the general principle applies: Socrates is a man. Then the conclusion automatically follows: Socrates is mortal. According to this model every demonstrative or strictly logical conclusion 'subsumes' a particular under an appropriate universal. It implies the prior and given existence of particulars and universals.

It thus implies that for every possible case which may arise, there is a fixed antecedent rule already at hand; that the case in question is either simple and unambiguous, or is resolvable by direct inspection into a collection of simple and indubitable facts, such as, 'Socrates is a man.' It thus tends, when it is accepted, to produce and confirm what Professor Pound has called mechanical jurisprudence; it flatters that longing for certainty of which Justice Holmes speaks; it reinforces those inert factors in human nature which make men hug as long as possible any idea which has once gained lodgment in the mind.

In a certain sense it is foolish to criticise the model supplied by the syllogism. The statements made about men and Socrates are obviously true, and the connection between them is undoubted. The trouble is that while the syllogism sets forth the results of thinking, it has nothing to do with the *operation* of thinking. Take the case of Socrates being tried before the Athenian citizens, and the thinking which had to be done to reach a decision. Certainly the issue was not whether Socrates was mortal; the point was whether this mortality would or should occur at a specified date and in a specified way. Now that is just what does not and cannot follow from a general principle or a major premise. Again to quote Justice Holmes, "General propositions do not decide concrete cases." No concrete proposition, that is to say one with material dated in time and placed in space, follows from any general statements or from any connection between them.

If we trust to an experimental logic, we find that general principles emerge as statements of generic ways in which it has been found helpful to treat concrete cases. The real force of the proposition that all men are mortal is found in the expectancy tables of insurance companies, which with their accompanying rates show how it is prudent and socially useful to deal with human mortality. The "universal" stated in the major premise is not outside of and antecedent to particular cases; neither is it a selection of something found in a variety of cases. It is an indication of a single way of treating cases for certain purposes or consequences in spite of their diversity. Hence its meaning and worth are subject to inquiry and revision in view of what happens, what the consequences are, when it is used as a method of treatment.

As a matter of fact, men do not begin thinking with premises. They begin with some complicated and confused case, apparently admitting of alternative modes of treatment and solution. The problem is not to draw a conclusion from given premises; that can best be done by a piece of inanimate machinery by fingering a keyboard. The problem is to *find* statements, of general principle and of particular fact, which are worthy to serve as premises. As matter of actual fact, we generally begin with some vague anticipation of a conclusion (or at least of alternative conclusions), and then we look around for principles and data which will substantiate it or which will enable us to choose intelligently between rival conclusions. No lawyer ever thought out the case of a client in terms of the syllogism. He begins with a conclusion which he intends to reach, favorable to his client of course, and then analyzes the facts of the situation to find material out of which to construct a favorable statement of facts, to *form* a minor premise. At the same time he goes over recorded cases to find rules of law employed in cases which can be presented as similar, rules which will substantiate a certain way of looking at and interpreting the facts. And as his acquaintance with rules of law judged applicable widens, he probably alters perspective and emphasis in selection of the facts which are to form his evidential data. And as he learns more of the facts of the case he may modify his selection of rules of law upon which he bases his case.

I do not for a moment set up this procedure as a model of scientific method; it is too precommitted to the establishment of a particular and partisan conclusion to serve as such a model. But it does illustrate, in spite of this deficiency, the particular point which is being made here; namely, that thinking actually sets out from a more or less confused situation, which is vague and ambiguous with respect to the conclusion it indicates, and that the formation of both major premise and minor proceed tentatively and correlatively in the course of analysis of this situation and of prior rules. As soon as acceptable premises are given and of course the judge and jury have eventually to do with their becoming accepted – and the conclusion is also given. [sic] In strict logic, the conclusion does not follow from premises; conclusions and premises are two ways of stating the same thing. Thinking may be defined either as a development of premises or development of a conclusion; as far as it is one operation it is the other.

Courts not only reach decisions; they expound them, and the exposition must state justifying reasons. The mental operations therein involved are somewhat different from those involved in arriving at a conclusion. The logic of exposition is different from that of search and inquiry. In the latter, the situation as it exists is more or less doubtful, indeterminate, and problematic with respect to what it signifies. It unfolds itself gradually and is susceptible of dramatic surprise; at all events it has, for the time being, two sides. Exposition implies that a definitive solution is reached, that the situation is now determinate with respect to its legal implication. Its purpose is to set forth grounds for the decision reached so that it will not appear as an arbitrary dictum, and so that it will indicate a rule for dealing with similar cases in the future. It is highly probable that the need of justifying to others conclusions reached and decisions made has been the chief cause of the origin and development of logical operations in the precise sense; of abstraction, generalization, regard for consistency of implications. It is quite conceivable that if no one had ever had to account to others for his decisions, logical operations would never have developed, but men would use exclusively methods of inarticulate intuition and impression, feeling; so that only after considerable experience in accounting for their decisions to others who demanded a reason, or exculpation, and were not satisfied till they got it, did men begin to give an account to themselves of the process of reaching a conclusion in a justified way. However this may be, it is certain that in judicial decisions the only alternative to arbitrary dicta, accepted by the parties to a controversy only because of the authority or prestige of the judge, is a rational statement which formulates grounds and exposes connecting or logical links.

It is at this point that the chief stimulus and temptation to mechanical logic and abstract use of formal concepts come in. Just because the personal element cannot be wholly excluded, while at the same time the decision must assume as nearly as possible an impersonal, objective, rational form, the temptation is to surrender the vital logic which has actually yielded the conclusion and to substitute for it forms of speech which are rigorous in appearance and which give an illusion of certitude.

Another moving force is the undoubted need for the maximum possible of stability and regularity of expectation in determining courses of conduct. Men need to know the legal consequences which society through the courts will attach to their specific transactions, the liabilities they are assuming, the fruits they may count upon in entering upon a given course of action.

This is a legitimate requirement from the standpoint of the interests of the community and of particular individuals. Enormous confusion has resulted, however, from confusion of *theoretical* certainty and practical certainty. There is a wide gap separating the reasonable proposition that judicial decisions should possess the maximum possible regularity in order to enable persons in planning their conduct to foresee the legal import of their acts, and the absurd because impossible proposition that every decision should flow with formal logical necessity from antecedently known premises. To attain the former result there are required general principles of interpreting cases – rules of law – and procedures of pleading and trying cases which do not alter arbitrarily. But principles of interpretation do not signify rules so rigid that they can be stated once for all and then be literally and mechanically adhered to. For the situations to which they are to be applied do not literally repeat one another in all details, and questions of degree of this factor or that have the chief weight in determining which general rule will be employed to judge the situation in question. A large part of what has been asserted concerning the necessity of absolutely uniform and immutable antecedent rules of law is in effect an attempt to evade the really important issue of finding and employing rules of law, substantive and procedural, which will actually secure to the members of the community a reasonable measure of practical certainty of expectation in framing their courses of conduct. The mechanical ease of the court in disposing of cases and not the actual security of agents is the real cause, for example, of making rules of pleading hard and fast. The result introduces an unnecessary element of gamble into the behaviour of those seeking settlement of disputes, while it affords to the judges only that factitious ease and simplicity which is supplied by any routine habit of action. It substitutes a mechanical procedure for the need of analytic thought.

There is of course every reason why rules of law should be as regular and as definite as possible. But the amount and kind of antecedent assurance which is actually attainable is a matter of fact, not of form. It is large wherever social conditions are pretty uniform, and when industry, commerce, transportation, etc., move in the channels of old customs. It is much less wherever invention is active and when new devices in business and communication bring about new forms of human relationship. Thus the use of power machinery radically modifies the old terms of association of master and servant and fellow servants; rapid transportation brings into general use commercial bills of lading; mass production engenders organization of laborers and collective bargaining; industrial conditions favor concentration of capital. In part legislation endeavors to reshape old rules of law to make them applicable to new conditions. But statutes have never kept up with the variety and subtlety of social change. They cannot at the very best avoid some ambiguity, which is due not only to carelessness but also to the intrinsic impossibility of foreseeing all possible circumstances, since without such foresight definitions must be vague and classifications indeterminate. Hence to claim that old forms are ready at hand that cover every case and that may be applied by formal syllogizing is to pretend to a certainty and regularity which cannot exist in fact. The effect of the pretension is to increase practical uncertainty and social instability. Just because circumstances are really novel and not covered by old rules, it is a gamble which old rule will be declared regulative of a particular case, so that shrewd and enterprising men are encouraged to sail close to the wind and trust to ingenious lawyers to find some rule under which they can get off scot free.

The facts involved in this discussion are commonplace and they are not offered as presenting anything original or novel. What we are concerned with is their bearing upon the logic of judicial decisions. For the implications are more revolutionary than they might at first seem to be. They indicate either that logic must be abandoned or that it must be a logic *relative to consequences rather than to antecedents*, a logic of prediction of probabilities rather than one of deduction of certainties. For the purposes of a logic of inquiry into probable consequences, general principles can only be tools justified by the work they do. They are means of intellectual survey, analysis, and insight into the factors of the situation to be dealt with. Like other tools they must be modified when they are applied to new conditions and new results have to be achieved. Here is where the great practical evil of the doctrine of immutable and necessary antecedent rules comes in. It santifies the old; adherence to it in practice constantly widens the gap between current social conditions and the principles used by the courts. The effect is to breed irritation, disrespect for law, together with virtual alliance between the judiciary and entrenched interests that correspond most nearly to the conditions under which the rules of law were previously laid down.

Failure to recognize that general legal rules and principles are working hypotheses, needing to be constantly tested by the way in which they work out in application to concrete situations, explains the otherwise paradoxical fact that the slogans of the liberalism of one period often become the bulwarks of reaction in a subsequent era. There was a time in the eighteenth century when the great social need was emancipation of industry and trade from a multitude of restrictions which held over from the feudal estate of Europe. Adapted well enough to the localized and fixed conditions of that earlier age, they became hindrances and annoyances as the effects of methods, use of coal and steam, showed themselves. The movement of emancipation expressed itself in principles of liberty in use of property, and freedom of contract, which were embodied in a mass of legal decisions. But the absolutistic logic of rigid syllogistic forms infected these ideas. It was soon forgotten that they were relative to analysis of existing situations in order to secure orderly methods in behalf of economic social welfare. Thus these principles became in turn so rigid as to be almost as socially obstructive as "immutable" feudal laws had been in their day.

That the remarks which have been made, commonplace as they are in themselves, have a profound practical import may also be seen in the present reaction against the individualistic formulae of an older liberalism. The last thirty years has seen an intermittent tendency in the direction of legislation, and to a less extent of judicial decision, towards what is vaguely known as "social justice," toward formulae of a collectivistic character. Now it is quite possible that the newer rules may be needed and useful at a certain juncture, and yet that they may also become harmful and socially obstructive if they are hardened into absolute and fixed antecedent premises. But if they are conceived as tools to be adapted to the conditions in which they are employed rather than as abolute and intrinsic "principles," attention will go to the facts of social life, and the rules will not be allowed to engross attention and become absolute truths to be maintained intact at all costs. Otherwise we shall in the end merely have substituted one set of formally absolute and immutable syllogistic premises for another set.

If we recur then to our introductory conception that logic is really a theory about empirical phenomena, subject to growth and improvement like any other empirical discipline, we recur to it with an added conviction: namely, that the issue is not a purely speculative one, but implies consequences vastly significant for practice. I should indeed not hesitate to assert that the sanctification of ready-made antecedent universal principles as methods of thinking is the chief obstacle to the kind of thinking which is the indispensable prerequisite of steady, secure and intelligent social reforms in general and social advance by means of law in particular. If this be so infiltration into law of a more experimental and flexible logic is a social as well as an intellectual need.

[On Dewey's logic see Brodbeck, "The New Rationalism: Dewey's Theory of Induction" (1949) 46 *J. Phil.* 780; Mayerhoff, (1950) 47 *J. Phil.* 353; and White, "Experiment and Necessity in Dewey's Philosophy" (1959) 19 *Antioch Rev.* 329].

Herman Oliphant, 1884-1939
Professor of Law, Columbia University

A RETURN TO STARE DECISIS
(1927)

. . . Our part in shaping the future of legal scholarship thus recognized makes this an appropriate time and gathering to consider what seems to be a most profound change which has been slowly and imperceptibly creeping into our treatment of problems in Anglo-American law, a fundamental change which merits careful study in order that we may recognize its presence, measure its extent, and judge its consequences. Let me anticipate my conclusions by asserting that we are well on our way toward a shift from following decisions to following so-called principles, from *stare decisis* to what I shall call *stare dictis*; by saying that this shift has far reaching and unfortunate consequences for both the art of judicial government and the science of law and by proposing a return toward the ancient doctrine of *stare decisis*.

Support for this position will be found by examining that doctrine. It asserts not one thing, but two. For one thing, it asserts that prior decisions are to be followed, not disregarded. But it also asserts that we are to follow the prior decisions and not something else.

Most discussions of the doctrine of *stare decisis* have emphasized the first of these two assertions. In those we are told of the advantages and disadvantages of the doctrine. It has been pointed out how, on the one hand, it makes the law applicable to future transactions certain and the future decisions of judges predictable; and again, how it gives us justice according to law and not according to the whims of men. On the other hand, it has been shown that to follow it gives us a measure of inflexibility in our law resisting changes needed to meet changing conditions. We are all familiar with these and other broad implications of this branch of the doctrine and have considered the necessary choice between conflicting advantages which its acceptance or rejection involves. The vigor of this branch of the ancient doctrine has been weakened but little. Something in the cases is being followed. This whole aspect of the matter is mentioned here only to be set to one side.

The drift in our methods of dealing with legal problems which is upon us and is the subject of this discussion, concerns more intimately the second branch of the rule dealing with what it is in prior decisions which is to be followed. It is to be carefully noted that, when *stare decisis* is hereinafter mentioned, only this branch of the doctrine is referred to. It is in this quarter that innovation has been at work and is carrying us farther and farther toward treating this ancient doctrine as if it were *stare dictis* instead of *stare decisis*.

There seems to have been little critical study of this phase of the doctrine, – of just what it is in prior decisions which is to be followed. General statements that the decision is to be looked for, that dicta are of slight weight and offer no certain guide can be turned to at many places in the books and are familiar to all. Students beginning their law study are told these things in a general way and then are left to an apprenticeship among the cases to discover largely for themselves their fuller meaning. Yet this matter is the one most vital and difficult factor conditioning the soundness of their scholarship. It is because the word *decision* may mean any one of many things that it is perilous to leave the matter thus unarticulated.

In the first place, a court, in deciding a case, may throw out a statement as to how it would decide some other case. Now if that statement is a statement of another case which is as narrow and specific as the actual case before the court, it is easily recognized as dictum and given its proper weight as such. In the second place the court may throw out a broader statement, covering a whole group of cases. But so long as that statement does not cover the case before the court, it is readily recognized as being not a decision, much less the decision of the case. It is dictum, so labeled and appraised. But in the third place, a court may make a statement broad enough to dispose of the case in hand as well as to cover also a few or many other states of fact. Statements of this third sort may cover a number of fact situations ranging from one other to legion. Such a statement is sometimes called the *decision* of the case. Thereby the whole ambiguity of that word is introduced and the whole difficulty presented.

If a more careful usage limits the word *decision* to the *action* taken by the court in the specific case before, it, *i.e.*, to the naked judgment or order entered, the difficulty is not met; it is merely shifted. *Stare decisis* thus understood becomes useless for no decision in that limited sense can ever be followed. No identical case can arise. All other cases will differ in some circumstance, – in time, if no other, and most of them will have differences which are not trivial. *Decision* in the sense meant in *stare decisis* must, therefore, refer to a proposition of law covering a group of fact situations of a group as a minimum, the fact situation of the instant case and at least one other.

To bring together into one class even this minimum of two fact situations however similar they may be, always has required and always will require an abstraction. If Paul and Peter are to be thought of together at all, they must both be apostles or be thought of as having some other attribute in common. Classification is abstraction. An element or elements common to the two fact situations put into one class must be drawn out from each to become the content of the category and the subject of the proposition of law which is thus applied to the two cases.

But such a grouping may include multitudes of fact situations so long as a single attribute common to them all can be found. Between these two extremes lies a gradation of groups of fact situations each with its corresponding proposition of law, ranging from a grouping subtending but two situations to those covering hosts of them. This series of groupings of fact situations gives us a parallel series of corresponding propositions of law, each more and more generalized as we recede farther and farther from the instant state of facts and include more and more fact situations in the successive groupings. It is a mounting and widening structure, each proposition including all that has gone before and becoming more general by embracing new states of fact. For example, A's father induces her not to marry B as she promised to do. On a holding that the father is not liable to B for so doing, a graduation of widening propositions can be built, a very few of which are:

1. Fathers are privileged to induce daughters to break promises to marry.
2. Parents are so privileged.
3. Parents are so privileged as to both daughters and sons.
4. All persons are so privileged as to promises to marry.
5. Parents are so privileged as to all promises made by their children.
6. All persons are so privileged as to all promises made by anyone.

There can be erected upon the action taken by a court in any case such a gradation of generalizations and this is commonly done in the opinion. Sometimes it is built up to dizzy heights by the court itself and at times, by law teachers and writers, it is reared to those lofty summits of the absolute and the infinite.

Where on that gradation of propositions are we to take our stand and say "This proposition is the decision of this case within the meaning of the doctrine of *stare dicisis*?" Can a proposition of law of this third type ever become so broad that, as to any of the cases it would cover, it is mere dictum?

That would be difficult enough if it ended there. But just as one and the same apple can be thrown into any one of many groups of barrels according to its size, color, shape, etc., so also there stretches up and away from every single case in the books, not one possible gradation of widening generalizations, but many. Multitudes of radii shoot out from it, each pair enclosing one of an indefinite number of these gradations of broader and broader generalizations. For example, a contract for wages contains a stipulation that it shall be non-assignable by the employee. A court holds that the laborer can assign any way and that his assignee can sue the employer for the wages regardless of the stipulation. This holding can serve as the apex of many triangles of generalizations. At the base of one will be a broad generalization treating the claim as property and asserting the alienability of property; at the base of another will be an equally broad generalization having to do with contractual stipulations opposed to public policy and the base of a third will be similarly wide generalization concerning the liquidation of claims in the labor market. Others could be enumerated and other cases similarly analyzed. That is not needed, for we all know of at least one case appearing in the casebooks of more than one subject upon which securely rests more than one inverted pyramid of favorite theory.

A student is told to seek the "doctrine" or "principle" of a case, but which of its welter of stairs shall he ascend and how high up shall he go? Is there some one step on some one stair which is *the* decision of the case within the meaning of the mandate *stare decisis*? That is the double difficulty. Each precedent considered by a judge and each case studied by a student rests at the center of a vast and empty stadium. The angle and distance from which that case is to be viewed involves the choice of a seat. Which shall be chosen? Neither judge nor student can escape the fact that he can and must choose. To realize how wide the possibilities and significant the consequences of that choice are is elementary to an understanding of *stare decisis.* To ask whether there exists a coercion of some logic to make that choice either inevitable or beneficent, searches the significance of *stare decisis* in judicial government and the soundness of scholarship in law. This question is real and insistent. It is one which should be asked explicitly and faced squarely. . . .

Of course, complete particularity in our treatment of legal problems is not possible. If states of fact are not grouped at all, no decision can be followed since no two cases are identical. Some abstraction and generalization is unavoidable, and considerable distance is desirable. If we are to see and to judge the play, others must carry the ball. The shift from *stare decisis* has not been from absolute particularity to absolute generality but from greater particularity to greater generality. But the difference, though one of degree, has been great enough to alter the very texture of our work even though the outlines of its design seem still unchanged. Moreover, perfect modernity in the laws' treatment of life's problems is not desirable were it possible. This factor concerns not the distance, but the angle of our view of those problems. That angle should not shift with each move of the play. Unless the common law is to be capricious, it must lag a bit. It must lag enough for the fitful actions of men to disclose trends of customary practice.

But all this granted, there has been such a shift in our work on cases from particularity to generality of treatment and such a shift of life from the grooves of our present long-standing abstractions, that our scholarship becomes loose and unreal. No longer coerced to think in exact procedural moulds, and few substitute devices to compel particularity in thinking having been set up, our minds are free to wander. The former discipline of a more rigorous *stare decisis* is replaced by the current license of *stare dictis*. Our categories of thought have become unreal by life having left them behind and no alert sense of actuality checks our reveries in theory. . . .

But there is a constant factor in the cases which is susceptible of sound and satisfying study. The predictable element in it all is what courts have done in response to the stimuli of the facts of the concrete cases before them. Not the judges' opinions, but which way they decide cases will be the dominant subject matter of any truly scientific study of law. This is the field for scholarly work worthy of best talents because the work to be done is not the study of such tough things as the accumulated wisdom of men taught by immediate experience in contemporary life, – the battered experiences of judges among brutal facts. The response of their intuition of experience to the stimulus of human situations is the subject-matter having that constancy and objectivity necessary for truly scientific study. When we pin our attention to this, we may more freely criticize what courts have said but we shall more cautiously criticize what they have done realizing, as we shall, that they were exposed to the impact of more of the facts than we.

This surer thing for scholarly purpose is also the inner secret of what is soundest in the enfeebled *stare decisis* in judicial government of today. With eyes cleared of the old and broad abstractions which curtain our vision, we come to recognize more and more the eminent good sense in what courts are wont to do about disputes before them. Judges are men and men respond to human situations. When the facts stimulating them to the action taken are studied from a particular and current point of view, which our present classification prevents, we acquire a new faith in *stare decisis*. From this viewpoint we see that courts are dominantly coerced, not by the essays of their predecessors but by a surer thing, – by an intuition of fitness of solution to problem, – and a renewed confidence in judicial government is engendered. To state the matter more concretely, the decision of a particular case by a thoughtful scholar is to be preferred to that by a poorly trained judge, but the decision of such a judge in a particular case is infinitely to be preferred to a decision of it preordained by some broad "principle" laid down by the scholar when this and a host of other concrete cases had never even occurred to him.

One sampling of this proposed subject-matter of a real science of law must suffice. There are two lines of old cases involving the validity of promises not to compete. They are considered in square conflict. But when the opinions are ignored and the facts re-examined all the cases holding the promises invalid are found to be cases of employees' promises not to compete with their employers after a term of employment. Contemporary guild regulations not noticed in the opinions made their holding eminently sound. All the cases holding the promises valid were cases of promises by those selling a business and promising not to compete with the purchasers. Contemporary economic reality made these holdings also eminently sound. This distinction between these two lines of cases is not even hinted at in any of the opinions but the courts' intuition of experience led them to follow it with amazing sureness and the law resulting fitted life. That is a sample of the stuff capable of scientific study. . . .

Arthur L. Goodhart, 1891-
Formerly Professor of Jurisprudence, Oxford University; now Master, University College, Oxford University

DETERMINING THE RATIO DECIDENDI OF A CASE (1930)

In discussing the nature of a precedent in English law Sir John Salmond says:

"A precedent, therefore, is a judicial decision which contains in itself a principle. The underlying principle which thus forms its authoritative element is often termed the *ratio decidendi.* The concrete decision is binding between the parties to it, but it is the abstract *ratio decidendi* which alone has the force of law as regards the world at large."

The rule is stated as follows by Professor John Chipman Gray:

"It must be observed that at the Common Law not every opinion expressed by a judge forms a Judicial Precedent. In order that an opinion may have the weight of a precedent, two things must concur: it must be, in the first place, an opinion given by a judge, and, in the second place, it must be an opinion the formation of which is necessary for the decision of a particular case; in other words, it must not be *obiter dictum.*"

Both the learned authors, on reaching this point of safety, stop. Having explained to the student that it is necessary to find the *ratio decidendi* of the case, they make no further attempt to state any rules by which it can be determined. It is true that Salmond says that we must distinguish between the concrete decision and the abstract *ratio decidendi*, and Gray states that the opinion must be a necessary one, but these are only vague generalizations. Whether it is possible to progress along this comparatively untrodden way in a search for more concrete rules of interpretation will be discussed in this paper.

The initial difficulty with which we are faced is the phrase "*ratio decidendi*" itself. With the possible exception of the legal term "malice," it is the most misleading expression in English law, for the reason which the judge gives for his decision is never the binding part of the precedent. The logic of the argument, the analysis of prior cases, the statement of the historical background may all be demonstrably incorrect in a judgment, but the case remain a precedent nevertheless. It would not be difficult to cite a large number of leading cases, both ancient and modern, in which one or more of the reasons given for the decision can be proved to be wrong; but in spite of this these cases contain valid and definite principles which are as binding as if the reasoning on which they are based were correct.

In *Priestley* v. *Fowler* the famous or infamous doctrine of common employment was first laid down. Of this case it has been well said, "Lord Abinger planted it, Baron Alderson watered it, and the Devil gave it increase." Yet the case is still law in England (although limited in effect by the Employers Liability Act of 1880) in spite of the fact that the two reasons on which Lord Abinger based his judgment are palpably incorrect. The first reason is that any other rule would be "absurd." This argument is always a dangerous one upon which to base a judgment and in this instance, it is, unfortunately, the rule in *Priestly* v. *Fowler* which has proved to be not only absurd but also unjust. The second reason given by Lord Abinger is that by his contract of service a servant impliedly consents to run the risk of working with negligent fellow-servants. In fact, of course, a servant does not consent to run the risk; the implication was invented by the judge himself.

In *Hochster* v. *Delatour* the defendant engaged the plaintiff on April 12 to enter his service on June 1, but on May 11 he wrote to him that his services would not be needed, thus renouncing the agreement. On May 22 the plaintiff brought an action, and the court held that he was not premature in doing so. Lord Campbell, C.J., said: "It is surely much more rational . . . that, after the renunciation of the agreement by the defendant, the plaintiff should be at liberty to consider himself absolved from any future performance of it, retaining his right to sue." But, as Professor Corbin has pointed out, even though this statement is entirely correct, "it does not follow therefrom that the plaintiff should be allowed to sue *before the date fixed for performance* by the defendant". It is clear that, after repudiation, the other party need not perform his part nor remain ready and willing to perform it, but why should he be given the immediate right to sue for damages which will only arise when the threatened breach actually occurs? Lord Campbell's *non sequitur* has not, however, prevented *Hochster* v. *Delatour* from becoming a leading case in the law of contract, for although the reasoning of the judgment may be at fault, we have no difficulty in finding in it a general rule which will apply to similar cases.

For that matter, by what may seem a strange method to those who do not understand the theory of the Common Law, it is precisely some of those cases which have been decided on incorrect premises or reasoning which have become the most important in the law. New principles, of which their authors were unconscious or which they have misunderstood, have been established by these judgments. Paradoxical as it may sound, the law has frequently owed more to its weak judges than it has to its strong ones. A bad reason may often make good law. Street has put this clearly in his *Foundations of Legal Liability*:

"The dissenting opinion of Coleridge, J., in *Lumley* v. *Gye* (1853), like the dissenting opinions of Cockburn, C.J., in *Collen* v. *Wright* (1857), and of Grose, J., in *Pasley* v. *Freeman* (1789), is exceedingly instructive, for it brings into clear relief the fact that the decision of the majority embodied a radical extension of legal doctrine, not to say an actual departure from former precedents. Nothing better illustrates the process by which the law grows. That situation which to one judge seems to be only a new instance falling under a principle previously recognized, will to another seem to be so entirely new as not to fall under such principle. It will not infrequently be found that the judge of greatest legal acumen, the greatest analyzer, is the very one who resists innovation and extension. This, indeed, is one of the pitfalls of much learning."

Our modern law of torts has been developed to a considerable extent by a series of bad arguments, and our property law is in many instances founded on incorrect history. To state this is not, however, to question the authority of that law. It is clear, therefore, that the first rule for discovering the *ratio decidendi* of a case is that it must not be sought in the reasons on which the judge has based his decision.

This view is in conflict with two often-quoted dicta which, by force of repitition, have almost become maxims of the law: "The reason of a resolution is more to be considered than the resolution itself," by Holt, C.J., and "The reason and spirit of cases make law; not the letter of particular precedents," by Lord Mansfield, C.J. But, however true these dicta may have been of the law at the time they were pronounced, it is clear, as Professor Allen has shown, that they are not in accord with the modern English doctrine of precedent.

Having stated its reasons for reaching a certain conclusion, the court frequently sums up the result in a general statement of the law on the point at issue. Can we find the principle of the case in this proposition of law, this comprehensive expression of the rule involved, which students underline with such enthusiasm in their casebooks? Thus in the chapter on Judgments in Halsbury's *The Laws of England*, the rule is given as follows:

"It may be laid down as a general rule that that part alone of a decision of a court of law is binding upon courts of coordinate jurisdiction and inferior courts which consists of the enunciation of the reason or principle upon which the question before the court has really been determined. This underlying principle which forms the only authoritative element of a precedent is often termed the *ratio decidendi*."

Professor Morgan of the Harvard Law School, in his valuable book *The Study of Law*, says:

"Those portions of the opinion setting forth the rules of law applied by the court, the application of which was required for the determination of the issues presented, are to be considered as decision and as primary authority in later cases in the same jurisdiction."

If these statements are to be understood in their literal sense, it is respectfully submitted that the words are misleading, for it is not the rule of law "set forth" by the court, or the rule "enunciated" as Halsbury puts it, which necessarily constitutes the principle of the case. There may be no rule of law set forth in the opinion, or the rule when stated may be too wide or too narrow. In appellate courts, the rules of law set forth by the different judges may have no relation to each other. Nevertheless each of these cases contains a principle which can be discovered on proper analysis.

So also a case may be a precedent, involving an important principle of law, although the court has given judgement without delivering an opinion. At the present time, although occasionally an appellate court will affirm without opinion a case which involves an interesting point, we rarely find a case of any importance in which an opinion has not been written. In the past, however, especially during the Year Book period, we find a great number of cases in which there were no opinions and in which the principle therefore must be sought elsewhere. . . .

Since, therefore, the principle of the case is not necessarily found in either the reasoning of the court or in the proposition of law set forth, we must seek some other method of determining it. Does this mean that we can ignore the opinion entirely and work out the principle for ourselves from the facts of the case and the judgment reached on those facts? This seems to be the view of a certain American school of legal thought represented by Professor Oliphant. According to him it is what the judge does and not what he says that matters. He writes:

"But there is a constant factor in the cases which is susceptible of sound and satisfying study. The predictable element in it all is what courts have done in response to the stimuli of the facts of the concrete cases before them. Not the judges' opinions, but which way they decide cases, will be the dominant subject matter of any truly scientific study of law."

Undoubtedly this theory has the attractiveness of simplicity. No longer will we have to analyze the sometimes lengthy and difficult opinions of the judges; all that we are concerned with are the facts and the conclusion. The judge who writes an opinion will be wasting both his own time and ours, for it is not what he says but what he does that matters. We can ignore the vocal behaviour of the judge, which sometimes fills many pages, and concentrate upon his nonvocal behaviour which occupies but a few lines.

Unfortunately I believe that there is a fallacy in Professor Oliphant's argument which will prevent our following this convenient course. The fallacy lies in suggesting that the facts of a case are a constant factor, that the judge's conclusion is based upon the fixed premise of a given set of facts. We do not have to be philosophers to realize that facts are not constant but relative. The crucial question is "What facts are we talking about?" The same set of facts may look entirely different to two different persons. The judge founds his conclusions upon a group of facts selected by him as material from among a larger mass of facts, some of which might seem significant to a layman, but which, to a lawyer, are irrelevant. The judge, therefore, reaches a conclusion upon the facts as he sees them. It is on these facts that he bases his judgment, and not on any others. It follows that our task in analyzing a case is not to state the facts and the conclusion, but to state the material facts as seen by the judge and his conclusion based on them. It is by his choice of the material facts that the judge creates law. A congeries of facts is presented to him; he chooses those which he considers material and rejects those which are immaterial, and then bases his conclusion upon the material ones. To ignore his choice is to miss the whole point of the case. Our system of precedent becomes meaningless if we say that we will accept his conclusion but not his view of the facts. His conclusion is based on the material facts as he sees them, and we cannot add or subtract from them by proving that other facts existed in the case. It is, therefore, essential to know what the judge has said about his choice of the facts, for what he does has a meaning for us only when considered in relation to what he has said. A divorce of the conclusion from the material facts on which the conclusion is based is illogical, and must lead to arbitrary and unsound results.

The first and most essential step in the determination of the principle of a case is, therefore, to ascertain the material facts on which the judge has based his conclusion. Are there any rules which will help us in isolating these material facts? It is obvious that none can be found which will invariably give us the desired result, for if this were possible then the interpretation of cases, which is one of the most difficult of the arts, would be comparatively easy. The following tentative suggestions may, however, prove of some aid to the student faced with his first case-book.

If there is no opinion, or if the opinion does not contain a statement of the facts, then we must assume that all the facts given in the report are material except those which on their face are not. Thus the facts of person, time, place, kind, and amount are presumably immaterial unless stated to be material. As a rule the law is the same for all persons, at all times, and at all places within the jurisdiction of the court. For the purposes of the law a contract made between A and B in Liverpool on Monday involving the sale of a book worth £10 is identical with a similar contract made between C and D in London on Friday involving the sale of a painting worth £100,000.

Where there is an opinion but the facts are not stated in it we must examine the report with great care, for the reporter may have left out an essential point. It is for this reason in particular that it is useful to compare the various reports of the same case if there is any doubt as to the principle involved in it. The well known case of *Williams* v. *Carwardine* has troubled generations of law students because the report usually referred to is the one in 4 Barnewall and Adolphus at page 621. The facts, as given there, merely show that the defendant offered a reward for certain information and that the plaintiff gave the information for motives unconnected with the reward. It is not stated that the plaintiff knew of the offer. But in the report of the case in 5 Carrington and Payne the following colloquy is given at page 574:

"Denman, C.J. – Was any doubt suggested as to whether the plaintiff knew of the handbill at the time of her making the disclosure?

Curwood (for the defendant). She must have known of it, as it was placarded all over Hereford, the place at which she lived."

By omitting a material fact, *viz.*, knowledge of the offer of the reward, the report in Barnewall and Adolphus makes nonsense of the case. This is not infrequent in those cases in which the facts are stated by the reporter, for, either owing to a misunderstanding of the point involved or a zeal for compression, he may have left out an essential fact. At the present time, however, the absence of an opinion, or of an opinion which states the facts, is so infrequent that it is unnecessary to discuss this situation at greater length.

If there is an opinion which gives the facts, the first point to notice is that we cannot go behind the opinion to show that the facts appear to be different in the record. We are bound by the judge's statement of the facts even though it is patent that he has misstated them, for it is on the facts as he, perhaps incorrectly, has seen them that he has based his judgment. The difficulty in the much discussed revocation-of-offer case, *Dickinson* v. *Dodds*, is due chiefly to the fact that the reporter in his introductory statement says, "The plaintiff was informed by a Mr. Berry that Dodds had been offering or agreeing to sell the property to Thomas Allen," while, when we turn to the judgments, we find that James, L.J. says:

"In this case, beyond all question the plaintiff knew that Dodds was no longer minded to sell the property to him as plainly and clearly as if Dodds has told him in so many words, 'I withdraw the offer.' This is evident from the plaintiff's own statement in the bill."

Mellish, L.J., states the facts as follows:

"Then Dickinson is informed by Berry that the property has been sold by Dodds to Allen. Berry does not tell us from whom he heard it, but he says that he did hear it, that he knew it, and that he informed Dickinson of it." If we take the reporter's facts, the conclusion reached in *Dickinson* v. *Dodds* is astonishing; if we accept, as we are bound to do, the facts as given in the judgments the conclusion seems a reasonable one.

Two other cases illustrate this point in an interesting manner. In *Smith* v. *London and South Western Ry.*, Kelly, C.B., Channell, B., and Blackburn J., each assumed as a fact "that no reasonable man would have foreseen that the fire would get to the plaintiff's cottage." We lose the whole point of their judgments if we attempt to explain them by showing that a reasonable man should have foreseen that the fire might reach the cottage. Similarly in *In Re Polemis and Furness, Withy & Co.* the Court of Appeal was bound by the arbitrators' finding of fact that a reasonable man would not have anticipated that a plank falling into the hold of a steamer filled with petrol vapour might cause an explosion. This finding of fact is probably incorrect, but we cannot ignore it if we are to determine the true principle of the judgments based on it. As has already been said, if we are not bound by the facts as stated by the judge it would be wholly illogical to be bound by his conclusion on those facts.

Moreover, such a course would be most inconvenient, for it would then become necessary when citing an important case to go through the record so as to be certain that the facts as given by the court were correct. In view of the vast number of precedents existing on almost any disputed point of law the task of the common law lawyer is sufficiently difficult at the present time; if he must also consult the record in every case to determine the actual facts his work will be overwhelming. The emphasis which American law libraries are now placing on collecting the whole records in the leading cases may prove to be a dangerous one, for such collections tend to encourage a practice which is inconvenient in operation and disastrous in theory.

Although it is comparatively rare to find any real conflict between the facts given in the opinion and those in the record, it is of frequent occurrence to find that the facts in the opinion fail to include some of the facts in the record. Under these circumstances there are two possible explanations of the omission: (1) the fact was considered by the court but was found to be immaterial, or (2) the fact in the record was not considered by the court as it was not called to its attention by counsel or was for some other reason overlooked. Which of the two explanations is the correct one will depend upon the circumstances of the particular case. If counsel have referred to the fact in the course of their arguments this is strong evidence that the fact has not been overlooked but has been purposely omitted. For this reason the practice in the Law Reports of giving a short summary of counsel's speeches is of particular value. But if it is clear that a certain fact, however material it may have been, was not considered by the court, then the case is not a precedent in future cases in which a similar fact appears. Thus in the leading case of *Dunlop Tyre Co.* v. *Selfridge & Co.* no mention was made by either the judges or counsel of the possible fact that a trust had been created, and Professor Corbin has argued with great force that this case cannot, therefore, be held to be a precedent in any case in which the fact of a trusteeship is shown to exist. In *Fisher* v. *Oldham Corporation* McCardie, J., in discussing the *ratio decidendi* of *Bradford Corporation* v. *Webster*, said:

"It is obvious, however, that the point which I am dealing with might there have been raised by the defendants. But, *mirabile dictu,* no such point was even mentioned to the learned judge . . . The learned Judge, therefore, never even considered the point that is now before me for decision."

It must be noted, however, that the burden of showing that a fact has been overlooked is a heavy one, for as a rule a material fact does not escape the attention of counsel and of the court.

Having, as a first step, determined all the facts of the case as seen by the judge, it is then necessary to discover which of these facts he has found material for his judgment. This is far more difficult than the first step, for the judge may fail to label his facts. It is only the strong judge, one who is clear in his own mind as to the grounds for his decision, who invariably says, "on facts A and B and on them alone I reach conclusion X." Too often the cautious judge will include in his opinion facts which are not essential to his judgment, leaving it for future generations to determine whether or not these facts constitute a part of the *ratio decidendi*. The following guides may, however, be followed in distinguishing between material and immaterial facts.

(1) As was stated above in discussing the principle of a case in which there is no opinion, the facts of person, time, place, kind, and amount are presumably immaterial. This is true to an even greater extent when there is an opinion, for if these facts are held to be material particular emphasis will naturally be placed upon them.

(2) All facts which the court specifically states are immaterial must be considered so. In *People* v. *Vandewater* the defendant, who was charged with maintaining a public nuisance, kept an illicit drinking place. There was proof that the house was actually disorderly as the evidence showed that persons became intoxicated on the premises and left them in that condition. The majority of the New York Court of Appeals, speaking by Lehman, J., held that the fact that acts of annoyance and disturbance had occurred was immaterial. The learned judge said:

"It is the disorderly character of the illicit drinking place which constitutes the offense to the public decency. That offense arises from the nature of the acts habitually done upon the premises and the injury to the morals and health of the community which must naturally flow therefrom, apart from the annoyance or disturbance of those persons who might be in the neighborhood."

This case strikingly illustrates the distinction between the view that a case is authority for a proposition based on all its facts, and the view that it is authority for a proposition based on those facts only which were seen by the court as material. If we adopt the first view, then the majority judgment is only a dictum, not binding in any future case in which the facts do not show actual disorder. Under the second view the court has specifically stated that the fact of disorder is immaterial. The case is, therefore, a binding precedent in all future cases in which either orderly or disorderly illicit drinking places are kept. The case can be analyzed as follows:

Facts of the Case

Fact 1. *D* maintained an illicit drinking place.
Fact II. This illicit place was noisy and disorderly.
Conclusion. *D* is guilty of maintaining a nuisance.

Material Facts as seen by the Court

Fact 1. *D* maintained an illicit drinking place.
Conclusion. *D* is guilty of maintaining a nuisance.

By specifically holding that Fact II was immaterial, the court succeeded in creating a broad principle instead of a narrow one.

(3) All facts which the court impliedly treats as immaterial must be considered immaterial. The difficulty in these cases is to determine whether a court has or has not considered the fact immaterial. Evidence of this implication is found when the court, after having stated the facts generally, then proceeds to choose a smaller number of facts on which it bases its conclusion. In *Rylands* v. *Fletcher* the defendant employed an independent contractor to make a reservoir on his land. Owing to the contractor's negligence in not filling up some disused mining shafts, the water escaped and flooded the plaintiff's mine. The defendant was held liable. Is the principle of the case that a man who builds a reservoir on his land is liable for the negligence of an independent contractor? Why then is the case invariably cited as laying down the broader doctrine of "absolute liability"? The answer is found in the opinions. After stating the facts as above, the

judges thereafter ignored the fact of the contractor's negligence, and based their conclusions on the fact that an artificial reservoir had been constructed. The negligence of the contractor was, therefore, impliedly held to be an immaterial fact. The case can be analyzed as follows:

Facts of the Case

Fact I. *D* had a reservoir built on his land.
Fact II. The contractor who built it was negligent.
Fact III. Water escaped and injured *P*.
Conclusion. *D* is liable to *P*.

Material Facts as Seen by the Court

Fact I. *D* had a reservoir built on his land.
Fact III. Water escaped and injured *P*.
Conclusion. *D* is liable to *P*.

By the omission of Fact II, the doctrine of "absolute liability" was established.

It is obvious from the above cases that it is essential to determine what facts have been held to be immaterial, for the principle of a case depends as much on exclusion as it does on inclusion. It is under these circumstances that the reasons given by the judge in his opinion, or his statement of the rule of law which he is following, are of peculiar importance, for they may furnish us with a guide for determining which facts he considered material and which immaterial. His reason may be incorrect and his statement of the law too wide, but they will indicate to us on what facts he reached his conclusion. . . .

(4) All facts which are specifically stated to be material must be considered material. Such specific statements are usually found in cases in which the judges are afraid of laying down too broad a principle. Thus in *Heaven* v. *Pender* the plaintiff, a workman employed to paint a ship, was injured because of a defective staging supplied by the defendant dock owner to the shipowner. Brett, M.R., held that the defendant was liable on the ground that:

". . . whenever one person is by circumstances placed in such a position with regard to another that every one of ordinary sense who did think would at once recognise that if he did not use ordinary care and skill in his own conduct with regard to those circumstances he would cause danger of injury to the person or property of the other, a duty arises to use ordinary care and skill to avoid such danger."

Cotton and Bowen, L. JJ., agreed with the Master of the Rolls that the defendant was liable, but the material facts on which they based their judgment were: (1) that the plaintiff was on the staging for business in which the dock owner was interested, and (2) he "must be considered as invited by the dock owner to use the dock and all appliances provided by the dock owner as incident to the use of the dock." The principle of the case cannot, therefore, be extended beyond the limitation of these material facts.

(5) If the opinion does not distinguish between material and immaterial facts then all the facts set forth in the opinion must be considered material with the exception of those that on their face are immaterial. There is a presumption against wide principles of law, and the smaller the number of material facts in a case the wider will the principle be. Thus if a case like *Hambrook* v. *Stokes,* in which a mother died owing to shock at seeing a motor accident which threatened her child, is decided on the fact that a bystander may recover for injury due to shock, we have a broad principle of law. If the additional fact that the bystander was a mother is held to be material we then get a narrow principle of law. Therefore, unless a fact is expressly or impliedly held to be immaterial, it must be considered material.

(6) Thus far we have been discussing the method of determining the principle

of a case in which there is only a single opinion, or in which all the opinions are in agreement. How do we determine the principle of a case in which there are several opinions which agree as to the result but differ in the material facts on which they are based? In such an event the principle of the case is limited to the sum of all the facts held to be material by the various judges. A case involves facts A, B and C, and the defendant is held liable. The first judge finds that fact A is the only material fact; the second that B is material, the third that C is material. The principle of the case is, therefore, that on the material facts A, B and C the defendant is liable. If, however, two of the three judges had been in agreement that fact A was the only material one, and that the others were immaterial, then the case would be a precedent on this point, even though the third judge held that facts B and C were the material ones. The method of determining the principle of a case in which there are several opinions is thus the same as that used when there is only one. Care must be taken by the student, however, to see that the material facts of each opinion are stated and analyzed accurately, for sometimes the judges think that they are in agreement on the facts when they concur only in the result.

Having established the material and the immaterial facts of the case as seen by the court, we can then proceed to state the principle of the case. It is to be found in the conclusion reached by the judge on the basis of the material facts and on the exclusion of the immaterial ones. In a certain case the court finds that facts A, B and C exist. It then excludes fact A as immaterial, and on facts B and C it reaches conclusion X. What is the *ratio decidendi* of this case? There are two principles: (1) In any future case in which the facts are A, B and C, the court must reach conclusion X, and (2) in any future case in which the facts are B and C the court must reach conclusion X. In the second case the absence of fact A does not affect the result, for fact A has been held to be immaterial. The court, therefore, creates a principle when it determines which are the material and which are the immaterial facts on which it bases its decision.

It follows that a conclusion based on a fact the existence of which has not been determined by the court, cannot establish a principle. We then have what is called a dictum. If, therefore, a judge in the course of his opinion suggests a hypothetical fact, and then states what conclusion he would reach if that fact existed, he is not creating a principle. The difficulty which is sometimes found in determining whether a statement is a dictum or not is due to uncertainty as to whether the judge is treating a fact as hypothetical or real. When a judge says, "In this case, as the facts are so and so, I reach conclusion X," this is not a dictum, even though the judge has been incorrect in his statement of the facts. But if the judge says, "If the facts in this case were so and so then I would reach conclusion X," this is a dictum, even though the facts are as given. The second point frequently arises when a case involves two different sets of facts. Having determined the first set of facts and reached a conclusion on them, the judge may not desire to take up the time necessarily involved in determining the second set. Any views he may express as to the undetermined second set are accordingly dicta. If however, the judge does determine both sets, as he is at liberty to do, and reaches a conclusion on both, then the case creates two principles and neither is a dictum. Thus the famous case of *National Sailors' and Firemen's Union* v. *Reed*, in which Astbury, J., declared the General Strike of 1926 to be illegal, involved two sets of facts, and the learned judge reached a conclusion on each. It is submitted that it is incorrect to say that either one of the conclusions involved a dictum because the one preceded the other or because the one was based on broad grounds and the other on narrow ones. On the other hand, if in a case the judge holds that a certain fact prevents a cause of action from arising, then his further finding that there would have been a cause of action except for this fact is an obiter dictum. By excluding the preventive fact the situation becomes hypothetical, and the conclusion based on such hypothetical facts can only be a dictum.

Having established the principle of a case, and excluded all dicta, the final step is to determine whether or not it is a binding precedent for some succeeding case in which the facts are prima facie similar. This involves a double analysis. We must first state the material facts in the precedent case and then attempt to find those which are material in the second one. If these are identical, then the first case is a binding precedent for the second, and the court must reach the same conclusion as it did in the first one. If the first case lacks any material fact or contains any additional ones not found in the second, then it is not a direct precedent. [It may, however, carry great weight as an analogy. Thus, if it has been held in a case that a legatee who has murdered his testator cannot take under the will, this will be an analogy of some weight in a future case in which the legatee has committed manslaughter. It is important to note that when a case is used merely as an analogy, and not as a direct binding precedent, the reasoning by which the court reached its judgment carries greater weight than the conclusion itself. The second court, being free to reach its own conclusion, will only adopt the reasoning of the first court if it considers it to be correct and desirable. In such analogous precedents the *ratio decidendi* of the case can with some truth be described as the reason of the case.] Thus, in *Nichols* v. *Marsland* the material facts were similar to those in *Rylands* v. *Fletcher* except for the additional fact that the water escaped owing to a violent storm. If the court had found that this additional fact was not a material one, then the rule in *Rylands* v. *Fletcher* would have applied. But as it found that it was a material one, it was able to reach a different conclusion.

Before summarizing the rules suggested above, two possible criticisms must be considered. It may be said that a doctrine which finds the principle of a case in its material facts leaves us with hardly any general legal principles, for facts are infinitely various. It is true that facts are infinitely various, but the material facts which are usually found in a particular legal relationship are strictly limited. Thus the fact that there must be consideration in a simple contract is a single material fact although the kinds of consideration are unlimited. Again, if A builds a reservoir on Blackacre and B builds one on Whiteacre, the owners, builders, reservoirs and fields are different. But the material fact that a person has built a reservoir on his land is in each case the same. Of course a court can always avoid a precedent by finding that an additional fact is material, but if it does so without reason the result leads to confusion in the law. Such an argument assumes, moreover, that courts are disingenuous and arbitrary. Whatever may have been true in the past, it is clear that at the present day English courts do not attempt to circumvent the law in this way.

The second criticism may be stated as follows: If we are bound by the facts as seen by the judge, may not this enable him deliberately or by inadvertence to decide a case which was not before him by basing his decision upon facts stated by him as real and material but actually non-existent? Can his conclusion in such a case be anything more than a dictum? Can a judge, by making a mistake, give himself authority to decide what is in effect a hypothetical case? The answer to this interesting question is that the whole doctrine of precedent is based on the theory that as a general rule judges do not make mistakes either of fact or of law. In an exceptional case a judge may in error base his conclusion on a non-existent fact, but it is better to suffer this mistake, which may prove of benefit to the law as a whole, however painful its results may have been to the indiidual litigant, than to throw doubt on every precedent on which our law is based.

Conclusion

The rules for finding the principle of a case can, therefore, be summarized as follows:

(1) The principle of a case is not found in the reasons given in the opinion.

(2) The principle is not found in the rule of law set forth in the opinion.

(3) The principle is not necessarily found by a consideration of all the ascertainable facts of the case and the judge's decision.

(4) The principle of the case is found by taking account (a) of the facts treated by the judge as material, and (b) his decision as based on them.

(5) In finding the principle it is also necessary to establish what facts were held to be immaterial by the judge, for the principle may depend as much on exclusion as it does on inclusion.

The rules for finding what facts are material and what facts are immaterial as seen by the judge are as follows.

(1) All facts of person, time, place, kind and amount are immaterial unless stated to be material.

(2) If there is no opinion, or the opinion gives no facts, then all other facts in the record must be treated as material.

(3) If there is an opinion, then the facts as stated in the opinion are conclusive and cannot be contradicted from the record.

(4) If the opinion omits a fact which appears in the record this may be due either to (a) oversight, or (b) an implied finding that the fact is immaterial. The second will be assumed to be the case in the absence of other evidence.

(5) All facts which the judge specifically states are immaterial must be considered immaterial.

(6) All facts which the judge impliedly treats as immaterial must be considered immaterial.

(7) All facts which the judge specifically states to be material must be considered material.

(8) If the opinion does not distinguish between material and immaterial facts then all the facts set forth must be considered material.

(9) If in a case there are several opinions which agree as to the result but differ as to the material facts, then the principle of the case is limited so as to fit the sum of all the facts held material by the various judges.

(10) A conclusion based on a hypothetical fact is a dictum. By hypothetical fact is meant any fact the existence of which has not been determined or accepted by the judge.

Goodhart's view that the choice of material facts by a judge is binding on his successors does not square with American practice. Consider, for example, the two Supreme Court cases, *McCollum* v. *Board of Education* (1948) 333 U.S. 202 and *Zorach* v. *Clauson* (1952) 343 U.S. 306. In the *McCollum* case Black J. delivered the opinion of the court (Reed J. dissenting) holding unconstitutional an arrangement whereby representatives of the Catholic, Protestant and Jewish faiths gave religious instruction in public school buildings once a week. Black J. said: "Here not only are the State's tax-supported public school buildings used for the dissemination of religious doctrines. The State also affords sectarian groups an invaluable aid in that it helps to provide pupils for their religious classes through use of the State's compulsory public school machinery" (212). Frankfurter J. (concurring) commented: "Religious education so conducted on school time and property is patently woven into the working scheme of the school" (227).

The "released time" program under consideration in the *Zorach* case did not involve the use of school property, but it did make use of school time, the New York statute in question permitting schools to release students during school hours to go to religious centers for religious instruction or devotional exercises. The court, by a 6-3 vote, held the scheme constitutional. Douglas J., giving the opinion of the court, attempted to distinguish the cases: "In the *McCollum* case the classrooms were used for religious instruction and the force of the public school was used to promote that instruction. Here . . . the public schools do no more than accommodate their schedules to a program of outside religious instruction. We follow the *McCollum* case. But we cannot expand it to cover the present released time program unless separation of Church and State means that public institutions can make no adjustments of their schedules to accommodate the religious needs of the people. We cannot read into the Bill of Rights such a philosophy of hostility to religion" (315). Black J. (dissenting) refused to accept the distinction: "I see no significant difference between the invalid Illinois system and that of New York here sustained. . . . [T]he *McCollum* decision would have been the same if the religious classes had not been held in the school buildings" (316).

Edward H. Levi, 1911-
Professor of Law, University of Chicago

AN INTRODUCTION TO LEGAL REASONING

(Reprinted from *An Introduction to Legal Reasoning* by Edward H. Levi by permission of The University of Chicago Press, Copyright 1948 by The University of Chicago.)

. . . The basic pattern of legal reasoning is reasoning by example.[1] It is reasoning from case to case. It is a three-step process described by the doctrine of precedent in which a proposition descriptive of the first case is made into a rule of law and then applied to a next similar situation. The steps are these: similarity is seen between cases; next the rule of law inherent in the first case is announced; then the rule of law is made applicable to the second case. This is a method of reasoning necessary for the law, but it has characteristics which under other circumstances might be considered imperfections.

These characteristics become evident if the legal process is approached as though it were a method of applying general rules of law to diverse facts – in short, as though the doctrine of precedent meant that general rules, once properly determined, remained unchanged, and then were applied, albeit imperfectly, in later cases. If this were the doctrine, it would be disturbing to find that the rules change from case to case and are remade with each case. Yet this change in the rules is the indispensable dynamic quality of law. It occurs because the scope of a rule of law, and therefore its meaning, depends upon a determination of what facts will be considered similar to those present when the rule was first announced. The finding of similarity or difference is the key step in the legal process.

The determination of similarity or difference is the function of each judge. Where case law is considered, and there is no statute, he is not bound by the statement of the rule of law made by the prior judge even in the controlling case. The statement is mere dictum, and this means that the judge in the present case

[1] "Clearly then to argue by example is neither like reasoning from part to whole, nor like reasoning from whole to part, but rather reasoning from part to part, when both particulars are subordinate to the same term and one of them is known. It differs from induction, because induction starting from all the particular cases proves . . . that the major term belongs to the middle and does not apply the syllogistic conclusion to the minor term, whereas argument by example does make this application and does not draw its proof from all the particular cases." Aristotle, Analytica Priora 69a (McKeon ed., 1941).

may find irrelevant the existence or absence of facts which prior judges thought important. It is not what the prior judge intended that is of any importance; rather it is what the present judge, attempting to see the law as a fairly consistent whole, thinks should be the determining classification. In arriving at his result he will ignore what the past thought important; he will emphasize facts which prior judges would have thought made no difference. It is not alone that he could not see the law through the eyes of another, for he could at least try to do so. It is rather that the doctrine of dictum forces him to make his own decision.

Thus it cannot be said that the legal process is the application of known rules to diverse facts. Yet it is a system of rules; the rules are discovered in the process of determining similarity or difference. But if attention is directed toward the finding of similarity or difference, other peculiarities appear. The problem for the law is: When will it be just to treat different cases as though they were the same? A working legal system must therefore be willing to pick out key similarities and to reason from them to the justice of applying a common classification. The existence of some facts in common brings into play the general rule. If this is really reasoning, then by common standards, thought of in terms of closed systems, it is imperfect unless some overall rule has announced that this common and ascertainable similarity is to be decisive. But no such fixed prior rule exists. It could be suggested that reasoning is not involved at all; that is, that no new insight is arrived at through a comparison of cases. But reasoning appears to be involved; the conclusion is arrived at through a process and was not immediately apparent. It seems better to say there is reasoning, but it is imperfect.[1]

Therefore it appears that the kind of reasoning involved in the legal process is one in which the classification changes as the classification is made. The rules change as the rules are applied. More important, the rules arise out of a process which, while comparing fact situations, creates the rules and then applies them. But this kind of reasoning is open to the charge that it is classifying things as equal when they are somewhat different, justifying the classification by rules made up as the reasoning or classification proceeds. In a sense all reasoning is of this type, but there is an additional requirement which compels the legal process to be this way. Not only do new situations arise, but in addition peoples' wants change. The categories used in the legal process must be left ambiguous in order to permit the infusion of new ideas. And this is true even where legislation or a constitution is involved. The words used by the legislature or the constitutional convention must come to have new meanings. Furthermore, agreement on any other basis would be impossible. In this manner the laws come to express the ideas of the community and even when written in general terms, in statute or constitution, are molded for the specific case.

But attention must be paid to the process. A controversy as to whether the law is certain, unchanging, and expressed in rules, or uncertain, changing, and only a technique for deciding specific cases misses the point. It is both. Nor is it helpful to dispose of the process as a wonderful mystery possibly reflecting a higher law, by which the law can remain the same and yet change. The law forum is the most explicit demonstration of the mechanism required for a moving classification system. The folklore of law may choose to ignore the imperfections in legal reasoning, but the law forum itself has taken care of them.

[1] The reasoning may take this form: A falls more appropriately in B than in C. It does so because A is more like D which is of B than it is like E which is of C. Since A is in B and B is in G (legal concept), then A is in G. But perhaps C is in G also. If so, then B is in a decisively different segment of G, because B is like H which is in G and has a different result than C.

What does the law forum require? It requires the presentation of competing examples. The forum protects the parties and the community by making sure that the competing analogies are before the court. The rule which will be created arises out of a process in which if different things are to be treated as similar, at least the differences have been urged. In this sense the parties as well as the court participate in the law making. In this sense, also, lawyers represent more than the litigants.

Reasoning by example in the law is a key to many things. It indicates in part the hold which the law process has over the litigants. They have participated in the law making. They are bound by something they helped to make. Moreover, the examples or analogies urged by the parties bring into the law the common ideas of society. The ideas have their day in court, and they will have their day again. This is what makes the hearing fair, rather than any idea that the judge is completely impartial, for of course he cannot be completely so. Moreover, the hearing in a sense compels at least vicarious participation by all the citizens, for the rule which is made, even though ambiguous, will be law as to them.

Reasoning by example shows the decisive role which the common ideas of the society and the distinctions made by experts can have in shaping the law. The movement of common or expert concepts into the law may be followed. The concept is suggested in arguing difference or similarity in a brief, but it wins no approval from the court. The idea achieves standing in the society. It is suggested again to a court. The court this time reinterprets the prior case and in doing so adopts the rejected idea. In subsequent cases, the idea is given further definition and is tied to other ideas which have been accepted by courts. It is now no longer the idea which was commonly held in the society. It becomes modified in subsequent cases. Ideas first rejected but which gradually have won acceptance now push what has become a legal category out of the system or convert it into something which may be its opposite. The process is one in which the ideas of the community and of the social sciences, whether correct or not, as they win acceptance in the community, control legal decisions. Erroneous ideas, of course, have played an enormous part in shaping the law. An idea, adopted by a court, is in a superior position to influence conduct and opinion in the community; judges, after all, are rulers. And the adoption of an idea by a court reflects the power structure in the community. But reasoning by example will operate to change the idea after it has been adopted.

Moreover, reasoning by example brings into focus important similarity and difference in the interpretation of case law, statutes, and the constitution of a nation. There is a striking similarity. It is only folklore which holds that a statute if clearly written can be completely unambiguous and applied as intended to a specific case. Fortunately or otherwise, ambiguity is inevitable in both statute and constitution as well as with case law. Hence reasoning by example operates with all three. But there are important differences. What a court says is dictum, but what a legislature says is a statute. The reference of the reasoning changes. Interpretation of intention when dealing with a statute is the way of describing the attempt to compare cases on the basis of the standard thought to be common at the time the legislation was passed. While this is the attempt, it may not inially accomplish any different result than if the standard of the judge had been explicitly used. Nevertheless, the remarks of the judge are directed toward describing a category set up by the legislature. These remarks are different from ordinary dicta. They set the course of the statute, and later reasoning in subsequent cases is tied to them. As a consequence, courts are less free in applying a statute than in dealing with case law. The current rationale for this is the notion that the legislature has acquiesced by legislative silence in the prior, even though erroneous, interpretation of the court. But the change in reasoning where legislation is concerned seems an inevitable consequence of the division of function between court and legislature, and, paradoxically, a recognition also of the impossibility of determining legislative intent. The impairment of a court's freedom in interpreting legislation is reflected in frequent appeals to the constitution as a necessary justification for overruling cases even though these cases are thought to have interpreted the legislation erroneously.

Under the United States experience, contrary to what has sometimes been believed when a written constitution of a nation is involved, the court has greater freedom than it has with the application of a statute or case law. In case law, when a judge determines what the controlling similarity between the present and prior case is, the case is decided. The judge does not feel free to ignore the results of a great number of cases which he cannot explain under a remade rule. And in interpreting legislation, when the prior interpretation, even though erroneous, is determined after a comparison of facts to cover the case, the case is decided. But this is not true with a constitution. The constitution sets up the conflicting ideals of the community in certain ambiguous categories. These categories bring along with them satellite concepts covering the areas of ambiguity. It is with a set of these satellite concepts that reasoning by example must work. But no satellite concept, no matter how well developed, can prevent the court from shifting its course, not only by realigning cases which impose certain restrictions, but by going beyond realignment back to the overall ambiguous category written into the document. The constitution, in other words, permits the court to be inconsistent. The freedom is concealed either as a search for the intention of the framers or as a proper understanding of a living instrument, and sometimes as both. But this does not mean that reasoning by example has any less validity in this field.

Joseph C. Hutcheson, 1879-
Judge of United States Court of Appeals, Fifth Circuit

THE JUDGMENT INTUITIVE: THE FUNCTION OF THE "HUNCH"[1] IN JUDICIAL DECISION

Many years ago, at the conclusion of a particularly difficult case both in point of law and of fact, tried by a court without a jury, the judge, a man of great learning and ability, announced from the Bench that since the narrow and prejudiced modern view of the obligations of a judge in the decision of causes prevented his resort to the judgment aleatory by the use of his "little, small dice" he would take the case under advisement, and, brooding over it, wait for his hunch.

To me, a young, indeed a very young lawyer, picked, while yet the dew was on me and I had just begun to sprout, from the classic gardens of a University, where I had been trained to regard the law as a system of rules and precedents, of categories and concepts, and the judge had been spoken of as an administrator, austere, remote, "his intellect a cold logic engine," who, in that rarified atmosphere in which he lived coldly and logically determined the relation of the facts

[1]. "A strong, intuitive impression that something is about to happen." Webster, *International Dictionary*.

of a particular case to some of these established precedents, it appeared that the judge was making a jest, and a very poor one, at that.

I had been trained to expect inexactitude from juries, but from the judge quite the reverse. I exalted in the law its tendency to formulize. I had a slot machine mind. I searched out categories and concepts and, having found them, worshiped them. . . .

I knew, of course, that some judges did follow "hunches," – "guesses" I indignantly called them. I knew my Rabelais, and had laughed over without catching the true philosophy of old Judge Bridlegoose's trial, and roughly, in my youthful, scornful way, I recognized four kinds of judgments; first, the cogitative, of and by reflection and logomachy; second, aleatory, of and by the dice; third, intuitive, of and by feeling or "hunching;" and fourth, asinine, of and by an ass; and in that same youthful, scornful way I regarded the last three as only variants of each other, the results of processes all alien to good judges.

As I grew older, however, and knew and understood better the judge to whom I have in this opening referred; as I associated more with real lawyers, whose intuitive faculties were developed and made acute by the use of a trained and cultivated imagination; as I read more after and came more under the spell of those great lawyers and judges whose thesis is that "modification is the life of the law," I came to see that "as long as the matter to be considered is debated in artificial terms, there is danger of being led by a technical definition to apply a certain name and then to deduce consequences which have no relation to the grounds on which the name was applied;" that "the process of inclusion and exclusion so often applied in developing a rule, cannot end with its first enunciation. The rule announced must be deemed tentative. For the many and varying facts to which it will be applied cannot be foreseen."

And so, after eleven years on the Bench following eighteen at the Bar, I, being well advised by observation and experience of what I am about to set down, have thought it both wise and decorous to now boldly affirm that "having well and exactly seen, surveyed, overlooked, reviewed, recognized, read and read over again, turned and tossed about, seriously perused and examined the preparatories, productions, evidences, proofs, allegations, depositions, cross speeches, contradictions . . . and other such like confects and spiceries, both at the one and the other side, as a good judge ought to do, I posit on the end of the table in my closet all the pokes and bags of the defendants – that being done I thereafter lay down upon the other end of the same table the bags and satchels of the plaintiff."

Thereafter I proceed "to understand and resolve the obscurities of these various and seeming contrary passages in the law, which are laid claim to by the suitors and pleading parties," even just as Judge Bridlegoose did, with one difference only. "That when the matter is more plain, clear and liquid, that is to say, when there are fewer bags," and he would have used his "other large, great dice, fair and goodly ones," I decide the case more or less off hand and by rule of thumb. While when the case is difficult or involved, and turns upon a hairsbreadth of law or of fact, that is to say, "when there are many bags on the one side and on the other" and Judge Bridlegoose would have used his "little small dice," I, after canvassing all the available material at my command, and duly cogitating upon it, give my imagination play, and brooding over the cause, wait for the feeling, the hunch – that intuitive flash of understanding which makes the jump-spark connection between question and decision, and at the point where the path is darkest for the judicial feet, sheds its light along the way.

And more, "lest I be stoned in the street" for this admission, let me hasten to say to my brothers of the Bench and of the Bar, "my practice is therein the same with that of your other worships."

For let me premise here, that in feeling or "hunching" out his decisions, the judge acts not differently from, but precisely as the lawyers do in working on their cases, with only this exception; that the lawyer, having a predetermined destination in view, – to win his law suit for his client – looks for and regards only those hunches which keep him in the path that he has chosen, while the judge, being merely on his way with a roving commission to find the just solution, will follow his hunch wherever it leads him, and when, following it, he meets the right solution face to face, he can cease his labors and blithely say to his troubled mind – "Trip no farther, pretty sweeting, journeys end in lovers meeting, as every wise man's son doth know."

Further, at the outset, I must premise that I speak now of the judgment or decision, the solution itself, as opposed to the apologia for that decision; the decree, as opposed to the logomachy, the effusion of the judge by which that decree is explained or excused. I speak of the judgment pronounced, as opposed to the rationalization by the judge on that pronouncement. . . .

And not only do I set down boldly that I, "even as your other worships do," invoke and employ hunches in decisions, but I do affirm, and will presently show, that it is that tiptoe faculty of the mind which can feel and follow a hunch which makes not only the best gamblers, the best detectives, the best lawyers, the best judges, the materials of whose trades are the most chancey because most human, and the results of whose activities are for the same cause the most subject to uncertainty and the best attained by approximation, but it is that same faculty which has guided and will continue to guide the great scientists of the world, and even those august dealers in certitude, the mathematicians themselves, to their most difficult solutions, which have opened and will continue to open hidden doors; which have widened and will ever widen man's horizon.

"For facts are sterile until there are minds capable of choosing between them and discerning those which conceal something, and recognizing that which is concealed. Minds which under the bare fact see the soul of the fact."

I shall further affirm, and I think maintain, that the judge is, in the exercise of this faculty, popularly considered to be an attribute of only the gambler and the short story detective, in the most gallant of gallant companies; a philosopher among philosophers, and I shall not fear to stand, unrebuked and unashamed before my brothers of the Bench and Bar. . . .

Now, what is this faculty? What are its springs, what its uses? Many men have spoken of it most beautifully. Some call it "intuition" – some, "imagination," this sensitiveness to new ideas, this power to range when the track is cold, this power to cast in ever widening circles to find a fresh scent, instead of standing baying where the track was lost. . . .

It is imagination which, from assembled facts, strikes out conclusions and establishes philosophies. "Science is analytical description. Philosophy is synthetic interpretation. The philosopher is not content to describe the fact; he wishes to ascertain its relation to experience in general, and thereby to get at its meaning and its worth. He combines things in interpretative synthesis. To observe processes and to construct means is science. To criticize and coordinate ends is philosophy. For a fact is nothing except in relation to desire; it is not complete except in relation to a purpose and a whole. Science, without philosophy, facts without perspective and valuation cannot save us from havoc and despair. Science gives us knowledge, but only philosophy can give us wisdom." Cardozo expresses it most beautifully.

"Repeatedly, when one is hard beset, there are principles and precedents and analogies which may be pressed into the service of justice, if one has the perceiving eye to use them. It is not unlike the divinations of the scientist. His experiments must be made significant by the flash of a luminous hypothesis. For the creative process in law, and indeed in science generally, has a kinship to the creative process in art. Imagination, whether you call it scientific or artistic, is for each the faculty that creates."

"Learning is indeed necessary, but learning is the springboard by which imagination leaps to truth. The law has its piercing intuitions, its tense, apocalyptic moments. We gather together our principles and precedents and analogies, even at times our fictions, and summon them to yield the energy that will best attain the jural end. If our wand has the divining touch, it will seldom knock in vain. So it is that the conclusion, however deliberate and labored, has often the aspect of a lucky find." . . .

Time was when judges, lawyers, law writers and teachers of the law refused to recognize in the judge this right and power to intuitive decision. It is true that the trial judge was always supposed to have superior facilities for decision, but these were objectivized in formulas, such as – the trial judge has the best opportunity of observing the witnesses, their demeanor, – the trial judge can see the play and interplay of forces as they operate in the actual clash of the trial.

Under the influence of this kind of logomachy, this sticking in the "skin" of thought, the trial judge's superior opportunity was granted, but the real reason for that superior position, that the trial creates an atmosphere springing from but more than the facts themselves, in which and out of which the judge may get the feeling which takes him to the desired end, was deliberately suppressed.

Later writers, however, not only recognize but emphasize this faculty, nowhere more attractively than in Judge Cardozo's lectures before the law schools of Yale University, in 1921 and Columbia University in 1927, while Max Radin, in 1925, in a most sympathetic and charming way, takes the judge's work apart, and shows us how his wheels go round.

He tells us, first, that the judge is a human being; that therefore he does not decide causes by the abstract application of rules of justice or of right, but having heard the cause and determined that the decision ought to go this way or that way, he then takes up his search for some category of the law into which the case will fit.

He tells us that the judge really feels or thinks that a certain result seems desirable, and he then tries to make his decision accomplish that result. "What makes certain results seem desirable to a judge?" he asks, and answers his question that that seems desirable to the judge which, according to his training, his experience, and his general point of view, strikes him as the jural consequence that ought to flow from the facts, and he advises us that what gives the judge the struggle in the case is the effort so to state the reasons for his judgment that they will pass muster.

Now what is he saying except that the judge really decides by feeling, and not by judgment; by "hunching" and not by ratiocination, and that the ratiocination appears only in the opinion?

Now what is he saying but that the vital, motivating impulse for the decision is an intuitive sense of what is right or wrong for that cause, and that the astute judge, having so decided, enlists his every faculty and belabors his laggard mind, not only to justify that intuition to himself, but to make it pass muster with his critics?

There is nothing unreal or untrue about this picture of the judge, nor is there anything in it from which a just judge should turn away. It is true, and right that it is true, that judges really do try to select categories or concepts into which to place a particular case so as to produce what the judge regards as a righteous result, or, to avoid any confusion in the matter of morals, I will say a "proper result."

This is true. I think we should go further, and say it ought to be true. No reasoning applied to practical matters is ever really effective unless motivated by some impulse.

"Occasionally and frequently, the exercise of the judgment ought to end in absolute reservation. We are not infallible, so we ought to be cautious." "Sometimes," however, "if we would guide by the light of reason, we must let our minds be bold."

The purely contemplative philosopher may project himself into an abstract field of contemplation where he reasons, but practical men, and in that judges must be included, must have impulses. The lawyer has them and because he has them his work is tremendously important. If a lawyer merely reasoned abstractly and without motive he would do the judge no good. But the driving impulse to bring about his client's success not only makes him burrow industriously for precedents, and as industriously bring them forth, but also makes him belabor and cudgel the brains of the listening judge to bring him into agreement.

It is this factor in our jurisprudence, and only this, that clients have lawyers and that lawyers are advocates, which has made and will continue to make it safe for judges not only to state, but sometimes to make the law. "A thorough advocate in a just cause, – a penetrating mathematician facing the starry heavens, alike bear the semblance of divinity."

If the judge sat upon the Bench in a purely abstract relation to the cause, his opinion in difficult cases would be worth nothing. He must have some motive to fire his brains, to "let his mind be bold."

By the nature of his occupation he cannot have advocacy for either side of the case as such, so he becomes an advocate, an earnest one, for the – in a way – abstract solution. Having become such advocate, his mind reaches and strains and feels for that result. He says with Elihu, the son of Barachel, the Buzite, of the family of Ram – "There is a spirit in man, and the breath of the Almighty giveth him understanding. It is not the great that are wise, nor the aged that understand justice. — Hearken to me; I also will show mine opinion. For I am full of matter; the spirit within me constraineth me. Behold my belly is as wine which hath no vent. Like new wineskins it is ready to burst."

And having travailed and reached his judgment, he struggles to bring up and pass in review before his eager mind all of the categories and concepts which he may find useful directly or by analogy, so as to select from them that which in his opinion will support his desired result.

For while the judge may be, he cannot appear to be, arbitrary. He must at least appear reasonable, and unless he can find a category which will at least "semblably" support his view, he will feel uncomfortable.

Sometimes he must almost invent a category, but he can never do quite that thing, for as we have seen, the growth of the law is interstitial, and the new category cannot be new enough wholly to avoid contact and placement in the midst of prior related categories.

But whether or not the judge is able in his opinion to present reasons for his hunch which will pass jural muster, he does and should decide difficult and complicated cases only when he has the feeling of the decision, which accounts for the beauty and the fire of some, and the labored dullness of many dissenting opinions.

All of us have known judges who can make the soundest judgments and write the dullest opinions on them; whose decisions were hardly ever affirmed for the reasons which they gave. Their difficulty was that while they had the flash, the intuitive power of judgment, they could not show it forth. While they could by an intuitive flash leap to a conclusion, just as an inventor can leap to his invention, just as often as an inventor cannot explain the result or fully understand it, so cannot and do not they.

There is not one among us but knows that while too often cases must be decided without that "feeling" which is the triumphant precursor of the just judgment, that just as "sometimes a light surprises the Christian while he sings," so sometimes, after long travail and struggle of the mind, there does come to the dullest of us, flooding the brain with the vigorous blood of decision, the hunch that there is, or is not invention; that there is or is not, anticipation; that the plaintiff should be protected by a decree, or should be denied protection. This hunch, sweeping aside hesitancy and doubt, takes the judge vigorously on to his decision; and yet, the cause decided, the way thither, which was for the blinding moment a blazing trail, becomes wholly lost to view.

Sometimes again that same intuition or hunch, which warming his brain and lighting his feet produced the decision, abides with the decider "while working his judgment backward" as he blazes his trail "from a desirable conclusion back to one or another of a stock of logical premises."

It is such judicial intuitions, and the opinions lighted and warmed by the feeling which produced them, that not only give justice in the cause, but like a great white way, make plain in the wilderness the way of the Lord for judicial feet to follow.

If these views are even partly sound, and if to great advocacy and great judging the imaginative, the intuitional faculty is essential, should there not be some change in the methods of the study and of the teaching of the law in our great law schools? Should there not go along with the plain and severely logical study of jural relations study and reflection upon, and an endeavor to discover and develop, those processes of the mind by which such decisions are reached, those processes and faculties which, lifting the mind above the mass of constricting matter whether of confused fact or precedent that stands in the way of just deciion, enable it by a kind of apocalyptic vision to "trace the hidden equities of divine reward, and to catch sight through the darkness, of the fateful threads of woven fire which connect error with its retribution?"

In "are Judges Human?" (1931) 80 *Univ. of Pennsylvania Law Review* 17, Jerome Frank launched an attack on Dean Pound on behalf of the new "realist" movement. He wrote in part (17-19):

"Holmes and his friend the bad man, to anyone who listened to them intelligently, put an end to the old fogey belief that law is rules and that rules are law. Holmes told lawyers and law teachers that, if they would go into court and look at what was going on, they would see that the primary business of courts was to render specific decisions (*i.e.*, specific judgments, orders and decrees); that law meant such specific decisions in concrete cases, not so-called legal rules and principles. 'A legal duty so-called,' he said, 'is nothing but a prediction that if a man does or omits certain things he will be made to suffer in this or that way by a judgment of the court; and so of legal right.'

"Holmes suggested, in effect, the creation of a new jurisprudence based on assumptions which flatly contradicted some of the basic assumptions of the time-honored jurisprudence.

"But Holmes' revolutionary suggestion was little heeded until recently; it was ignored for years – or at any rate, its full import was virtually overlooked.

"True, now and then, in the first two decades of this century, law teachers made pointed references to elements of the judicial process other than the rules. Notably Dean Pound was among the leaders of those who combated the naïve notion that the work of lawyers and judges ends with legal rules. But he adopted the Holmes' idea in a strange way. While brilliantly elaborating it in some limited directions, he nevertheless repressed it, obstructed its full growth. He diluted it, mingled it with the watery substance of Holmes' predecessors. Pound has done magnificent work of permanent value. But he mangled his work because he compromised the heritage from Holmes, because he refused to recognize its essentially revolutionary character, its sharp break with the past; because he tried to cover up the true nature of that break. Pound was the right wing of the Holmes' movement. It was in the highest degree unfortunate that the first vastly influential teacher to take over Holmes' insight should thus have warped it. It might almost be said that the Holmes' point of view would have been less retarded today in its consequences had Pound opposed it. For his mode of partially adopting it was to confuse and mislead those whom he influenced. And he deservedly influenced many, since, for years, he was the amazingly industrious, ingenious, erudite key-man in American legal education. Indeed, his hold on teachers of law is still so potent that anyone who hopes to bring about any fundamental changes in legal pedagogy and legal thinking in this country must cope with Pound and his disciples, must point out Pound's errors, separate his wisdom from his mistakes – *rescue Pound's lasting contributions from Pound and his uncritical adulators.*

"Pound's attitude was confusing and baffling primarily because he adhered to the traditional conception of law and by his learning and prestige strengthened it. The strange sight was presented of a follower of Holmes giving aid and comfort to the enemy. For in one of Pound's earliest and most vigorous writings he said that, 'Without entangling ourselves in the discussion as to the definition of law, we may say that *laws are general rules* recognized in the administration of justice.' Some twelve years later he wrote that *'the fundamental idea of law is that of a rule or principle underlying a series of decisions'* and described 'the three steps in the decisions of causes' as *'finding* of *rules, interpretation* of *rules,* and *application* to particular controversies of the *rules* when found and interpreted.' And still later he stated, 'Typically, judicial treatment of a controversy is a measuring of it by rule in order to reach a universal solution for a class of causes of which the cause in hand is but an illustration.' Such treatment of lawsuits he called 'justice according to law'."

Pound responded with an attack on legal realism, "The Call for a Realist Jurisprudence" (1931) 44 *Harvard Law Review* 697, 700:

"Let it be repeated. Faithful portrayal of what courts and law makers and jurists do is not the whole task of a science of law. One of the conspicuous actualities of the legal order is the impossibility of divorcing what they do from the question what they ought to do or what they feel they ought to do. For by and large they are trying to do what they ought to do. Their picture of what they ought to do is often decisive in determining what they do. Such pictures are actualities quite as much as the materials of legal precepts or doctrines upon which or with which they work. Critical portrayals of the ideal element in law, valuings of traditional ideals with respect to the actualities of the social and legal order, and the results to which they lead in the social and legal order of today, are as much in touch with reality (*i.e.,* have to do with things of at least as much significance for the legal order) as psychological theories of the behavior of particular judges in particular cases.

"There is nothing upon which the new realist is so insistent as on giving over all preconceptions and beginning with an objectively scientific gathering of facts. As the analytical jurist insisted on the pure fact of law he seeks the pure fact of fact. But facts occur in a multifarious mass of single instances. To be made intelligible and useful, significant facts have to be selected, and what is significant will be determined by some picture or ideal of the science and of the subject of which it treats. Thus preconceptions will creep in and will determine the choice of pure fact of fact as they determined the pure fact of law of the analytical jurist. The new realists have their own preconceptions of what is significant, and hence of what juristically must be. Most of them merely substitute a psychological must for an ethical or political or historical must."

Professor Fuller joined the attack on the realists with "American Legal Realism" (1934) 82 *U. Pa. L. Rev.* 429, and repeated his criticisms in *The Law in Quest of Itself* (1940). He was answered by Professor Myres McDougall, "Fuller v. The American Legal Realists: An Intervention" (1941) 50 *Yale L. J.* 827.

Karl N. Llewellyn, 1893-1962
Professor of Law, Columbia University, 1925-1951; Professor of Law, University of Chicago, 1951-1962

SOME REALISM ABOUT REALISM – RESPONDING TO DEAN POUND

Ferment is abroad in the law. The sphere of interest widens; men become interested again in the life that swirls around things legal. Before rules, were facts; in the beginning was not a Word, but a Doing. Behind decisions stand judges; judges are men; as men they have human backgrounds. Beyond rules, again, lie effects: beyond decisions stand people whom rules and decisions directly or indirectly touch. The field of Law reaches both forward and back from the Substantive Law of school and doctrine. The sphere of interest is widening; so, too, is the scope of doubt. *Beyond rules lie effects* – but do they? Are some rules mere paper? And if effects, what effects? Hearsay, unbuttressed guess, assumption or assertion unchecked by test – can such be trusted on this matter of what law is *doing*?

The ferment is proper to the time. The law of schools threatened at the close of the century to turn into words – placid, clear-seeming, lifeless, like some old canal. Practice rolled on, muddy, turbulent, vigorous. It is now spilling, flooding, into the canal of stagnant words. It brings ferment and trouble. So other fields of thought have spilled their waters in: the stress on behavior in the social sciences; their drive toward integration; the physicists' reëxamination of final-seeming premises; the challenge of war and revolution. These stir. They stir the law. Interests of practice claim attention. Methods of work unfamiliar to lawyers make their way in, beside traditional techniques. Traditional techniques themselves are reëxamined, checked against fact, stripped somewhat of confusion. And always there is this restless questing: what *difference* does statute, or rule, or court-decision, make?

Whether this ferment is one thing or twenty is a question; if one thing, it is twenty things in one. But it is with us. It spreads. It is no mere talk. It shows results, results enough through the past decade to demonstrate its value. . . .

What, then, *are* the characteristics of these new fermenters? One thing is clear. There is no school of realists. There is no likelihood that there will be such a school. There is no group with an official or accepted, or even with an emerging creed. There is no abnegation of independent striking out. We hope that there may never be. New recruits acquire tools and stimulus, not masters, nor overmastering ideas. Old recruits diverge in interests from each other. They are related, says Frank, only in their negations, and in their skepticisms, and in their curiosity.

There is, however, a *movement* in thought and work about law. The movement, the method of attack, is wider than the number of its adherents. It includes some or much work of many men who would scorn ascription to its banner. Individual men, then. Men more or less interstimulated – but no more than all of them have been stimulated by the orthodox tradition, or by that ferment at the opening of the century in which Dean Pound took a leading part. Individual men, working and thinking over law and its place in society. Their differences in point of view, in interest, in emphasis, in field of work, are huge. They differ among themselves well-nigh as much as any of them differs from, say, Langdell. Their number grows. Their work finds acceptance.

What one does find as he observes them is twofold. First (and to be expected) certain points of departure are common to them all. Second (and this, when one can find neither school nor striking likenesses among individuals, is startling) a cross-relevance, a complementing, an interlocking of their varied results "as if they were guided by an invisible hand." A third thing may be mentioned in passing: A fighting faith in their methods of attack on legal problems; but in these last years the battle with the facts has proved so much more exciting than any battle with traditionalism that the fighting faith had come (until the spring offensive of 1931 against the realists) to manifest itself chiefly in enthusiastic labor to get on.

But as with a description of an economic order, tone and color or description must vary with the point of view of the reporter. No other one of the men would set the picture up as I shall. Such a report must thus be individual. Each man, of necessity, orients the whole to his own main interest of the moment – as I shall orient the whole to mine: the workings of case-law in appellate courts. Maps of the United States prepared respectively by a political geographer and a student of climate would show some resemblance; each would show a coherent picture; but neither's map would give much satisfaction to the other. So here. I speak for myself of that movement which in its sum is realism; I do not speak of "the realists"; still less do I speak *for* the participants or any of them. And I shall orient the whole to mine: the workings of case-law in appellate courts. men together lies not in that they are *alike* in belief or work, but in that from certain common points of departure they have branched into lines of work which seem to be building themselves into a whole, a whole planned by none, foreseen by none, and (it may well be) not yet adequately grasped by any.

The common points of departure are several.

(1) The conception of law in flux, of moving law, and of judicial creation of law.

(2) The conception of law as a means to social ends and not as an end in itself; so that any part needs constantly to be examined for its purpose, and for its effect, and to be judged in the light of both and of their relation to each other.

(3) The conception of society in flux, and in flux typically faster than the law, so that the probability is always given that any portion of law needs reëxamination to determine how far it fits the society it purports to serve.

(4) The *temporary* divorce of Is and Ought for purposes of study. By this I mean that whereas value judgments must always be appealed to in order to set objectives for inquiry, yet during the inquiry itself into what Is, the observation, the description, and the establishment of relations between the things described are to remain *as largely as possible* uncontaminated by the desires of the observer or by what he wishes might be or thinks ought (ethically) to be. More particularly, this involves during the study of what courts are doing the effort to disregard the question what they ought to do. Such divorce of Is and Ought is, of course, not conceived as permanent. To men who begin with a suspicion that

change is needed, a permanent divorce would be impossible. The argument is simply that no judgment of what Ought to be done in the future with respect to any part of law can be intelligently made, without knowing objectively, as far as possible, what that part of law is now doing. And realists believe that experience shows the intrusion of Ought-spectacles *during the investigation of the facts* to make it very difficult to see what is being done. On the Ought side this means an insistence on informed evaluations instead of arm-chair speculations. Its full implications on the side of Is-investigation can be appreciated only when one follows the contributions to objective description in business law and practice made by realists whose social philosophy rejects many of the accepted foundations of the existing economic order. (*E.g.*, Handler *re* trade-marks and advertising; Klaus *re* marketing and banking; Llewellyn *re* Sales; Moore *re* banking; Patterson *re* risk-bearing.)

(5) Distrust of traditional legal rules and concepts insofar as they purport to *describe* what either courts or people are actually doing. Hence the constant emphasis on rules as "generalized predictions of what courts will do." This is much more widespread as yet than its counterpart: the careful severance of rules *for* doing (precepts) from rules *of* doing (practices).

(6) Hand in hand with this distrust of traditional rules (on the descriptive side) goes a distrust of the theory that traditional prescriptive rule-formulations are *the* heavily operative factor in producing court decisions. This involves the tentative adoption of the theory of rationalization for the study of opinions. It will be noted that "distrust" in this and the preceding point is not at all equivalent to "negation in any given instance."

(7) The belief in the worthwhileness of grouping cases and legal situations into narrower categories than has been the practice in the past. This is connected with the distrust of verbally simple rules – which so often cover dissimilar and non-simple fact situations (dissimilarity being tested partly by the way cases come out, and partly by the observer's judgment as to how they ought to come out; but a realist tries to indicate explicitly which criterion he is applying).

(8) An insistence on evaluation of any part of law in terms of its effects, and insistence on the worthwhileness of trying to find these effects.

(9) Insistence on *sustained and programmatic* attack on the problems of law along any of these lines. None of the ideas set forth in this list is new. Each can be matched from somewhere; each can be matched from recent orthodox work in law. New twists and combinations do appear here and there. What is as novel as it is vital is for a goodly number of men to pick up ideas which have been expressed and dropped, used for an hour and dropped, played with from time to time and dropped – to pick up such ideas and set about consistently, persistently, insistently to carry them through. Grant that the idea or point of view is familiar – the results of steady, sustained, systematic work with it are not familiar. Not hit-or-miss stuff, not the insight which flashes and is forgotten, but sustained effort to force an old insight into its full bearing, to exploit it to the point where it laps over upon an apparently inconsistent insight, to explore their bearing on each other by the test of fact. This urge, in law, is quite new enough over the last decades to excuse a touch of frenzy among the locust-eaters.

The first, second, third and fifth of the above items, while common to the workers of the newer movement, are not peculiar to them. But the other items (4, 6, 7, 8 and 9) are to me the characteristic marks of the movement. Men or work fitting those specifications are to me "realistic" whatever label they may wear. Such, and none other, are the perfect fauna of this new land. Not all the work cited below fits my peculiar definition in all points. All such work fits most of the points.

Bound, as all "innovators" are, by prior thinking, these innovating "realists" brought their batteries to bear in first instance on the work of appellate courts. Still wholly within the tradition of our law, they strove to improve on that tradition.

(a) An early and fruitful line of attack borrowed from psychology the concept of *rationalization* already mentioned. To recanvass the opinions, viewing them no longer as mirroring the process of deciding cases, but rather as trained lawyers' arguments made by the judges (after the decision has been reached), intended to make the decision seem plausible, legally decent, legally right, to make it seem, indeed, legally inevitable – this was to open up new vision. It was assumed that the deductive logic of opinions need by no means be either a *description* of the process of decision, or an *explanation* of how the decision was reached. Indeed over-enthusiasm has at times assumed that the logic of the opinion *could* be neither; and similar over-enthusiasm, perceiving case after case in which the opinion is clearly almost valueless as an indication of how that case came to decision, has worked at times almost as if the opinion were equally valueless in predicting what a later court will do.

But the line of inquiry via rationalization has come close to demonstrating that in any case doubtful enough to make litigation respectable the available authoritative premises – *i.e.,* premises legitimate and impeccable under the traditional legal techniques – are at least two, and that the two are mutually contradictory as applied to the case in hand. Which opens the question of what made the court select the one available premise rather than the other. And which raises the greatest doubts as to *how far* that supposed certainty in decision which derives merely from the presence of accepted rules really goes.

(b) A second line of attack has been to discriminate among rules with reference to their relative significance. Too much is written and thought about "law" and "rules," lump-wise. Which part of law? Which rule? Iron rules of policy, and rules "in the absence of agreement"; rules which keep a case from the jury, and rules as to the etiquette of instructions necessary to make a verdict stick – if one can get it; rules "of pure decision" for hospital cases, and rules which counsellors rely on in their counselling; rules which affect many (and which many, and how?) and rules which affect few. Such discriminations affect the traditional law curriculum, the traditional organization of law books and, above all, the orientation of study: to drive into the most important fields of ignorance.

(c) A further line of attack on the apparent conflict and uncertainty among the decisions in appellate courts has been to seek more understandable statement of them by grouping the facts in new – and typically but not always narrower – categories. The search is for correlations of fact-situation and outcome which (aided by common sense) may reveal when courts seize on one rather than another of the available competing premises. One may even stumble on the trail of *why* they do. Perhaps, *e.g.,* third party beneficiary difficulties simply fail to get applied to promises to make provision for dependents; perhaps the pre-existing duty rule goes by the board when the agreement is one for a marriage-settlement. Perhaps, indeed, contracts in what we may broadly call family relations do not work out in general as they do in business. If so, the rules – viewed as statements of the course of judicial behavior – as *predictions* of what will happen – need to be restated. Sometimes it is a question of carving out hitherto unnoticed exceptions. But sometimes the results force the worker to reclassify an erea altogether. Typically, as stated, the classes of situations which result are narrower, much narrower than the traditional classes. The process is in essence the orthodox technique of making distinctions, and reformulating –

but undertaken systematically; exploited consciously, instead of being reserved until facts which refuse to be twisted by "interpretation" for action. The departure from orthodox procedure lies chiefly in distrust of, instead of search for, the widest sweep of generalization words permit. Not that such sweeping generalizations are not desired – *if they can be made so as to state what judges do.*

All of these three earliest lines of attack converge to a single conclusion: *there is less possibility of accurate prediction of what courts will do than the traditional rules would lead us to suppose* (and what possibility there is must be found in good measure outside these same traditional rules). The particular kind of certainty that men have thus far thought to find in law is in good measure an illusion. Realistic workers have sometimes insisted on this truth so hard that they have been thought pleased with it. (The danger lies close, for one thinking indiscriminately of Is and Ought, to suspect announcements of facts to reflect preferences, ethically normative judgments, on the part of those who do the announcing.) ...

Indeed, the most fascinating result of the realistic report appears as one returns from trial court or the ways of laymen to the tradition-hallowed problem of appellate case-law. Criticized by those who refuse to disentangle Is and Ought because of their supposed deliberate neglect of the normative aspect of law, the realists prove the value, for the normative, of temporarily putting the normative aside. They return from their excursion into the purest description they can manage with a demonstration that the field of free play for Ought in appellate courts is vastly wider than traditional Ought-bound thinking ever had made clear. This, *within* the confines of precedent as we have it, *within* limits and on the basis of our present order. Let me summarize the points of the brief:

(a) If deduction does not solve cases, but only shows the effect of a given premise; and if there is available a competing but equally authoritative premise that leads to a different conclusion – then there is a choice in the case; a choice to be justified; a choice which *can* be justified only as a question of policy – for the authoritative tradition speaks with a forked tongue.

(b) If (i) the possible inductions from one case or a series of cases – even if these cases really had each a single fixed meaning – are nonetheless not single, but many; and if (ii) the standard authoritative techniques of dealing with precedent range from limiting the case to its narrowest issue on facts and procedure, and even searching the record for a hidden distinguishing fact, all the way to giving it the widest meaning the rule expressed will allow, or even thrusting under it a principle which was not announced in the opinion at all – then the available leeway in *interpretation of precedent* is (relatively to what the older tradition has *consciously* conceived) nothing less than huge. And only policy considerations . . . can justify "interpreting" (making, shaping, drawing conclusions from the relevant body of precedent in one way or in another. And – the essence of all – *stare decisis* has in the past been, now is, and must continue to be, a norm of change, and a means of change, as well as a norm of staying put, and a means of staying put. *The growth of the past has been achieved by "standing on" the decided cases*; rarely by overturning them. Let this be recognized, and precedent is clearly seen to be a way of change as well as a way of refusing to change. Let this be recognized, and that peculiar one of the ways of working with precedent which consists in blinding the eyes to policy loses the fictitious sanctity with which it is now enveloped *some of the time*: to wit, whenever judges for any reason do not wish to look at policy.

(c) If the classification of raw facts is largely an arbitrary process, raw facts having in most doubtful cases the possibility of ready classification along a number of lines, "certainty," even under pure deductive thinking, has not the meaning that people who have wanted certainty in law are looking for. The quest of this unreal certainty, this certainty unattained in result, is the major reason for the self-denying ordinance of judges: their refusal to look beyond words to things. Let them once see that the "certainty" thus achieved is *un*certainty for the non-law-tutored layman in his living and dealing, and the way is open to reach for *layman's* certainty-through-law, by seeking for the fair or wise outcome, so far as precedent and statute make such outcome *possible*. To see the problem thus is also to open the way to conscious discrimination – *e.g.,* between current commercial dealings and conveyancing – in which latter the *lawyer's* peculiar reliance on formulae may be assumed as of course; whereas in the former cause must be shown for making such an assumption.

Thus, as various of the self-designated realistic spokesmen have been shouting: the temporary divorce of Is and Ought brings to the reunion a sharper eye, a fuller judgment – even a wide opportunity as to that case-law which tradition has painted as peculiarly ridden by the past. That on the fact side, as to the peculiar questions, the temporary divorce yields no less gratifying results is demonstrated by the literature.

When the matter of *program in the normative aspect* is raised, the answer is: *there is none.* A likeness of method in approaching Ought-questions is apparent. If there be, beyond that, general lines of fairly wide agreement, they are hardly specific enough to mean anything on any given issue. Partly, this derives from differences in temperament and outlook. Partly, it derives from the total lack of organization or desire to schoolify among the men concerned. But partly, it is due to the range of work involved. Business lawyers have some pet Oughts, each in the material he has become familiar with; torts lawyers have the like in torts; public lawyers in public law. And so it goes. Partly also, the lack of programmatic agreement derives from the time and effort consumed in getting at facts, either the facts strictly legal or the "foreign" facts bearing on the law. Specialized interests must alone spell absence of group-program. Yet some general points of view may be hazarded.

(1) There is fairly general agreement on the importance of personnel, and of court organization, as essential to making laws have meaning. This both as to triers of fact and as to triers of law. There is some tendency, too, to urge specialization of tribunals.

(2) There is very general agreement on the need for courts to face squarely the policy questions in their cases, and use the full freedom precedent affords in working toward conclusions that effects of rules, so far as known, should be taken account of in making or remaking the rules. There is fairly general agreement that we need improved machinery for making the facts about such effects – or about needs and conditions to be affected by a decision – available to courts.

(3) There is a strong tendency to think it wiser to narrow rather than to widen the categories in which concepts and rules *either about judging or for judging are* made.

(4) There is a strong tendency to approach most legal problems as problems in allocation of risks, and so far as possible, as problems of their reduction, and so to insist on the effects of rules on parties who not only are not in court, but are not fairly represented by the parties who are in court. To approach not only tort but business matters, in a word, as matters of *general policy.*

And so I close as I began. What is there novel here? In the ideas, nothing. In the sustained attempt to make one or another of them fruitful, much. In the narrowness of fact-category together with the wide range of fact-inquiry, much.

In the technique availed of, much – for lawyers. But let this be noted – for the summary above runs so largely to the purely descriptive side: When writers of realistic inclination are writing in general, they are bound to stress the need of more accurate description, of Is and not of Ought. There lies the *common* ground of their thinking; there lies the area of new and puzzling development. There lies the point of discrimination which they must drive home. To get perspective on their stand about ethically normative matters one must pick up the work of each man in his special field of work. There one will find no lack of interest or effort toward improvement in the law. As to whether change is called for, on any *given* point of our law, and if so, how much change, and in what direction, there is no agreement. Why should there be? A *group* philosophy or program, a *group* credo of social welfare, these realists have not. They are not a group.

[In "A Realistic Jurisprudence – The Next Step" (1930) 30 *Columbia Law Review* 431 Professor Llewellyn had distinguished "real" rules and rights from "paper" rules and rights and pointed out that the problem was to determine how far a paper rule is real, how far merely paper.]

Edward S. Robinson, 1893-1937
Professor of Psychology, Yale University

LAW AND THE LAWYERS
(1935)

Chapter VIII

JUDICIAL DELIBERATION

Judicial Utterances Are Facts

An early difficulty in such an undertaking is the obvious fact that only a judge can secure a direct, introspective approach to the judicial consciousness. The judicial opinions, it is widely recognized, depart far from the original deliberative processes. The author of an appellate opinion sets forth a train of thought which seems to him a sound defense of the court's conclusion; he makes no direct effort to describe the actual deliberative processes either of his own mind or those in the minds of his colleagues.

The situation is probably not quite so hopeless as it first appears. Freud was early confronted with the objection that, during the psychoanalysis, his patients might tell him of dreams and fantasies which actually they had never had. But what of it? A lie about a dream is actually as significant as a dream that one actually has had, providing only that the lie is properly interpreted. Indeed one could even press the point and say that dreams and fantasies are always lies anyway and that that is why they are so important. In other words Freud always assumes a latent meaning or implication under every act or thought or feeling that is worthy of psychoanalytic notice. Thus one is forced to get behind the obvious contents of a patient's report whether or not it is upon its surface obviously false. Similarly the private, inarticulate deliberations of the judge can hardly be taken more literally than can their public expression. In either case there is a task of psychological interpretation.

And, after all, whatever discrepancies may exist between judicial thoughts and judicial words, it is through words alone that the lawyer can make any practical impression upon the judicial mind. Professor Gray put the matter clearly: "The student of jurisprudence is at times troubled by the thought that he is dealing not with things, but with words, that he is busy with the shape and size of counters in a game of logomachy, but when he fully realizes how these words have been passed and are still being passed as money not only by fools and on fools, but by and on some of the acutest minds, he feels that there is work worthy of being done, if only it can be done worthily."

There is, as a matter of fact, some ground for questioning the assumption that the articulate cogitations of the court, that is to say, the expressed opinions, are in any sense secondary. Descartes, in the days of an immature but vigorous physical science, saw no place within the system of physical nature for such intangibles as the ideas and passions. He therefore relegated them to a spiritual level of reality. While subsequent modern thought has not retained all of Descartes' theological tenets regarding the status of psychlogical facts, it has held fairly slavishly to the belief that, for the psychologist, the more subtle facts like toothaches and daydreams must have a primacy which objective behavior can never have. The story of the behavioristic movement in this country has had as its central theme the contradiction of this attitude and the counterclaim that overt speech and bodily movements are not psychologically insignificant simply because they are as susceptible to direct examination as are the facts of the nonpsychological sciences. The assumption, therefore, that the written judicial opinions cannot be important data for psychology is hardly in line with the present attitude of psychologists toward other similar problems. The present tendency in psychology is to begin an inquiry by examining the plainest and most accessible facts. The written discourse of the courts would thus seem to be a proper rather than a makeshift starting point for an empirical investigation of judicial deliberation.

It was in many ways a great achievement when scholars came to recognize that a man's talk is not a mirror-image of his motivation. But like most other essentially negative scientific conclusions, this one has tended to divert interest from the more constructive question as to what his talk does reflect. There has been a tendency to use too glibly such terms as *rationalization* without pushing forward to inquire what rationalization does besides affording an immediate relief to psychological tensions.

Consider first the certain fact that the expressed reasons for coming to a decision are to a degree at least indicative of the impulses that actually did play a part in reaching that decision. In many instances these reasons are more than reliable symptoms of previous thinking. They may give a psychological analysis of that thinking which could not have been found in the thinking itself. Much of what goes on in private deliberation is not only dim and fragmentary to the thinker himself; much of it must be interpreted before it can be intelligibly described. ". . . thought is reorganized and mind is reconstituted through the instrumentality of linguistic processes into human reason and logical structure." The fact that the mental attitudes of Abraham Lincoln toward the Civil War had not previously been stated just as he stated them in the Gettysburg Address by no means indicates that the was representing facts that were ineffective elements in his conduct. A man has come to a general decision with nothing but fleeting ideas and attitudes present in the immediate deliberative consciousness. For the purposes of communication, or perhaps for his personal satisfaction, he feels the need of exploring his own mind in respect to that decision. And so he talks or writes about the subject and in this talking and writing he discovers why he came to think as he did. There is no absolute guarantee that this verbal exploration will reveal the whole truth or that it will avoid the fabrication of satisfying fictions. On the other hand, there is every reason to believe that it will clarify factors that were only implicitly present in the original process of inarticulate deliberation. Whether, in his explicit statement of his reasons for concluding thus and so, a man gives a largely accurate or a largely fictitious account of himself is another one of those matters of fact. They are not always easy to settle, but certainly they can never be settled by the loose, lazy, and frequently cynical use of such terms as *unconscious complexes* and *rationalization.*

The possibility of a man discovering ideas and motives simply because he is impelled to talk about them has excellent illustration in many of those psychogenic disorders known as the psychoneuroses. In the hysterias encountered among many of the soldiers of the World War there were frequently symptoms of bodily disability, like the paralysis of a limb, which fulfilled the obvious purpose of keeping the patient out of the trenches. Functionally such a symptom represented a decision to escape the horrors of battle, but the elements in the precurrent conflict that lead to such decision were ordinarily not known to the patient himself. Yet frequently they could be made known to him by the simple procedure of telling him of his own motivation. In some cases severe psychological pressure had to be brought to bear. At first the patient might be unable to see that he was malingering, but sheer insistence upon the point would often enforce his fuller acquaintance with his own personality.

One does not need to go to psychopathology to illustrate the power of an individual to uncover meanings that have determined explicit actions. The average man who is cross to his wife because he is worried about his business does not, in the process of becoming cross, entertain his business worries as an argument in favor of displaying his temper. Yet it is fairly easy to train an individual so that he can discover the psychological bases of his own behavior.

The situation is similar in respect to those conclusions ordinarily called intellectual. We present an economist with the question as to whether the business cycle has turned. He concludes after a merely momentary hesitation that it has. Of course he may be relying upon a conclusion that has already been thoroughly thought out, but suppose that we are the first to force him to make up his mind upon this question, and suppose that after he has given us his verdict we ask him why he thinks so. He will immediately begin an exploration of his own information and conceptions which may explain his intellectual result. In that process he may think of a wide variety of *reasons* backing his conclusion, many of which were functionally present in his mental attitude toward this problem even if they did not rise to conscious thought prior to the articulation of his judgment. Or turn back to that earlier and simpler example in which we cited the reaction of a person to the question whether dogs fly. At once he answers, "no" without being aware of any of the considerations entering into the determination of that answer. Yet such considerations may be found after the fact and they are not all post-rationalizations.

In earlier pages we examined the prevalent theory that formal discourse is never more than a disguise for deep-seated impulses. If this were true, judicial opinions would hold no direct evidence of the psychological make-up of the judge. But psychologists are becoming increasingly suspicious of the instincts and urges which are supposed to be the underlying reality of overt behavior. Such instincts and urges remind us too much of the natural man of earlier political theory. There are also grounds for suspecting the reality of class prejudice and many other goblins that are assumed to be the moving spirits back of judicial discourse. We would not take such discourse at its face value, but it is at all times necessary to realize that the mere establishment of logical congruence between a judicial argument and some large division of public interest does not justify the conclusion that the utterance is a merely superficial symptom of the more general underlying trend.

We should also recall in this connection, that though the utterance of an argument in favor of a certain course of thought or action may at first be an ineffective element in the total dynamic pattern of a deliberation, such arguments soon become deep-set habits. The idea that is at first added to an argument simply as a kind of pious gesture frequently becomes a powerful motive in the mind of him who has employed it. What the judge himself recognizes as mere dicta may, by virtue of the fact that they are expressed, gradually increase in apparent relevance until they become real determinants of a later decision.

It thus appears that no utterance can be neglected simply because it can be called a rationalization. If one makes the naïve assumption that men either do or do not say what they mean, one may find ground for dismissing as irrelevant statements that are not literally true. Yet psychological sophistication permits no such easy avoidance of facts. For the psychologist all that a man does or says is proper matter for study.

While the expressed opinion of a judge may add arguments that were present in that private deliberation by means of which he first came to his conclusion, these new ideas frequently perform a direct psychological function. When one threads one's way through a host of facts and principles to a final decision one seeks not only to arrive at a decision, but also to attain conviction both for oneself and for all others who may be concerned. The concept of rationalization ordinarily implies that the actual, motivating influences of thought are being distorted into acceptable form, but these new arguments brought forward in the search for personal and social conviction may not distort anything. In the struggle for convincing expression the judge may discover notions which, though they did not influence him in his preliminary thinking, actually do so now. The jurist finds himself mentally hemmed in by formal doctrines that seem to force him to an inhumane decision. In such a case he sees clearly what his decision should be but he feels he must find a way to believe in that decision.

In many instances a happy word or phrase may be achieved which is more than mere rhetoric; it may actually constitute a discovery of fact. "The last clear chance," "the imminent danger," "the attractive nuisance" are more than metaphors. When first employed they probably came out of the struggle for conviction rather than out of the primary struggle for decision, but they nevertheless raised into prominence obviously relevant facts. When we discover an ancient phrase in an opinion on public utility regulation, the psychologist cannot afford to dismiss it summarily on the grounds of senility – on the grounds that there were no electric lights in seventeenth-century England. If the phrase is one that hides the motivation of the opinion or if it is one that is no more than coloring to the effective argument, well and good; the exposure of such misfunction or lack of function will be part of a thorough naturalistic inquiry. "Metaphors in law are to be narrowly watched, for starting as devices to liberate thought, they end often by enslaving it." But the criticism cannot be justified on the general grounds that the phrase is old. Ancient, half-forgotten words may bring to view facts crucial to a modern problem.

The present position may be summarized, then, by saying that the expressed opinion, even though it is given forth after a conclusion has been reached, is nevertheless a sound starting point in the study of judicial deliberation. Although such an opinion never reflects completely and accurately the unexpressed play of thought prior to judgment, and although its psychological significance is rarely to be found simply within the literal meaning of its statements, it needs no more interpretation than does that silent thinking which rarely can be reached by the investigator. Furthermore, in the process of justifying his decision the judge explores his own personality and he brings out to the light of day genuine attitudes of which he himself was unaware during his private deliberations. There is no denying the obvious fact that the judge's explanation of himself is often inadequate and that sometimes it actually is false. The claim is simply that the expressed opinion as an object of psychological study offers no pitfalls of unprecedented variety. We are no longer impressed with the Cartesian notion that private thought and feeling fall peculiarly within the realm of spirit and thus attain unique prestige.

An insistence upon the value of judicial opinions as objects of psychological study may give the impression that we are defending the role played by those opinions in the Great Society. But no such defense is intended. It will ultimately be the purpose of naturalistic jurisprudence to approach the talk of the judges in the same objective spirit as that in which the cultural anthropologist approaches the ceremonials of primitive society. Such a statement, of course, will produce in some minds the other conclusion that we are seeking to shake public confidence in judges by labeling their conscientious sayings as mere incantations. Here again our attitude would be misinterpreted. It will be the essence of naturalistic jurisprudence to seek a fresh perspective of judicial discourse. The old issue as to whether such discourse is or is not sincere will have to be set aside just as modern science is able to set aside the question as to whether the universe was or was not made for man. We must remember, also, that modern science has still retained an interest in human welfare and we shall expect of naturalistic jurisprudence that it will have much aid to offer in our evaluation of judicial utterance. What the empirical attitude will protect us against is the premature and overgeneralized judgment typical of the professional moralist. We shall become less interested in pinning a white or a black feather upon Mr. Justice Brandeis and we shall be more interested in the relation of his doctrinary hobbies to the clarity with which he has preached his judicial sermons. We shall become more competent to evaluate the emotional and conceptual devices of judicial discourse and to separate them from the good men and the bad men who employ them.

The Social Nature Of Individual Thinking

In our efforts to understand the process of deliberation as it occurs in the judicial mind we cannot set aside as mere argumentative devices all those elements of expression that imply an audience. The contents of the self are largely social. A man's most intimate thoughts deal with what he thinks others think about him. Whenever a man feels that his conduct is important he looks upon it as though through the eyes of another person; he stands, a spectator, upon the curb and watches himself march by. Whenever a man accepts or rejects an opinion he feels his act of judgment being judged by others. These critics who permeate a man's thinking, may be hypothetical; their evaluations may not correspond with those that actual persons would make; but they are in a very real sense social influences. In overt controversy one may distinguish between one's own opinions and those of other persons, but the segregation of self is never more than partial. One who is content with opinions that are approved by none of his fellow men assumes the grave psychic risks of paranoia.

And so the judge in his expressed opinion orders his thoughts and puts them in becoming dress not simply with the design of reducing an argumentative adversary nor yet with that of disguising his own real meaning. The atmosphere of sobriety, of modesty, of conscientious effort that he seeks to cast about his written words are frequently no more than is required for the maintenance of his own essentially social nature. Those words, if they are properly to represent himself, must also represent his colleagues, whether or not they have participated in the case, and also a larger world of men in which the court is an instrument of the good and decent life. . . .

Possibly judicial thinking of today is less self-conscious than that of earlier times. Yet it is still quite evident that the conscientious judge tries to look at his case through "the eye of the law." He still desires to come to a judge-like decision. Possibly the authorities are not showered with the compliments that would have been appropriate in a more spacious age. Nevertheless the legal concepts that enter into judicial deliberation often come associated with personalities. Thus we sometimes find a bow of respect even as a judge departs from a doctrine.

"We have great respect for the New York court and those following its lead upon this subject, but we feel constrained to hold that the decided weight of authority, both in numbers and reason, supports the contention, etc., etc. . . ."

We see that, though the mental operations of a judge may, in a sense, be peculiarly his own, their acceptance or rejection by him is always related to his estimate of the opinions of others. We have spoken mainly of his concern with the thinking of other judges, but his mind is also laden with values taken from society at large. He wants the legal institution to be what it is generally thought to be. Even a statute comes into the judicial consciousness as an opinion and purpose of the legislature, and its interpretation requires the honest judge to consider what the members of the legislature, in their own minds, sought to express.

Chapter X

LEGAL RULES

Legalisms

The Law is an expression of the larger cultural stream within which it occurs. Professor Sir M. S. Amos has summarized this generalization in vigorous language (though he admits a degree of exaggeration of a view which he is about to criticize). "On the surface there is a fleeting and trivial scum of positive enactment, representing the capricious imaginings of presumptuous individuals, while beneath there flows, unperturbed from age to age, and broadening down from precedent, the mighty current of the national jurisprudence, the *Volksrecht*, the law which has been created by, and in its turn reflects the national character. Whatever belongs to this stream is pregnant, permanent, and vital; you will divert or ignore it at your peril; whatever does not spring from this living source is impermanent, inorganic, insignificant. Any hope that institutions inspired by foreign example or by the exercise of pure reason will work, save in a lifeless and uncongenial way, must be dismissed as vain." Such a deeply imbedded institution is capable of change, but its changes are important and substantial only if they reflect some actual alteration of the culture. Such changes, which are almost always slow, are very likely to take place by means of those natural-law concepts and legal fictions that we have been discussing.

But, as Professor Amos goes on to say, we shall only partially account for the values that permeate judicial deliberation if we think of all of them as rising up into the formal law from the underlying culture. There is the question "whether we have not to recognize as holding an important place among the universal and not specifically national forces or moments in the building of law the distinctive contribution of the legal mind, the moulding, and perhaps sometimes the distorting, influence of that particular bias or bent of the intellect, which seems to spring into action in very much the same way in very different countries and in ages far apart, whenever the systematic administration of the law becomes the business of professional men." " . . .we must expect to be able to recognize, in every system of jurisprudence which has passed beyond the primitive stage, the moulding and controlling influence of a very specific cast of mind or method of thought. We shall not then be surprised if we are compelled to recognize that the group-mind, the professional psychology, of the lawyers has submerged and obscured the less concentrated influence of the primitive national character, and that, as I have suggested before, it seems at least as true to say that the lawyers through the legal system . . . have moulded the national character, as that the law is an expression of that character." Professor Amos contends that this influence of legal thinking upon public life is especially strong in England and that it is perhaps even more conspicuous in America.

These observations set a definite problem for psychological investigation. What forces determine the discrepancy between these legal values and those of common sense or the world at large?

The lawyer, in the first place, feels the necessity of organizing his rules into a consistent and integrated body of doctrine. The common man gets on quite well in tolerating sympathies that are incoherent and frequently contradictory. We have earlier had reason to point this out in connection with political opinions. Philosophers feel a need for a consistent set of political values, but not so the common man. He is well able to cherish bigamously a love for the status quo and a love for his Utopia. When the lawyer comes, in the course of history, to fit together those values that have passed from natural into formal law, he finds that there are contradictions which must be resolved. As a result, a value which has had a high position in loose, extra-legal thinking becomes legally subordinate. But since the subordination is brought about simply in the interests of a consistency not demanded by the common man, a feeling is created that the law is both arbitrary and artificial. . . .

In the development of the doctrinal law there is a special tendency, where values conflict, to give superior position to those of more general scope. As a matter of fact there could hardly be any legal theory if there were not this institutional preference for abstract rules over concrete sympathies. Yet this is one of the most frequent forces tending to separate the judicial from the popular judgment on any particular case. An endless array of judicial utterances could be cited to illustrate the sacrifice of present sympathy in the interest of a general rule which is deemed essential for the orderly conduct of the world's affairs.

"It may, under the circumstances of this case . . . be a subject of regret that effect cannot be given to the intention of Mrs. Trubcy by awarding the property to those who she desired should have it, but however clear her intention may have been, unless she did such acts as the law requires to make that intention effective, courts are powerless to afford relief."

Or consider another random case in which a wife, after the death of her husband, had drawn out the money from certain joint bank accounts. There was evidence that the husband prior to his death had told her that she might have the money.

"Without an act of delivery, an oral disposition of property, in contemplation of death, could be sustained only as a nuncupative will; and in the manner and with the limitations as evidence of deliberation and intention. It is a test of sincerity and distinguishes idle talks from serious purposes. . . . Gifts, *causa mortis,* ought not to be encouraged. They are often sustained by fraud and perjury. . . ."

Such opinions as these are frequently cited as examples of the stubborn technicality of courts and they do represent a disposition of the courts to depart from the common man's tendency to be ruled by the particulars of a given conflict. On the other hand, the general rules that the judges are here seeking to protect are not themselves foreign to the common man. He would also follow them if they did not conflict with values of more immediate emotional force. The legalism in such cases is brought about largely because the courts are forced to make a choice where the common man would be content to favor the general principle in one breath and a contradictory sympathy in another.

Legal deliberation also looks technical when its choice between social interests differs from that of the onlooker. Such a decision naturally looks like a legalism to a layman who holds it to be socially unfortunate, but actually the court would use as many or more technicalities to reach the opposite decision. . . .

Our conclusion is not that all judicial deliberation is equally technical, but merely that any decision we do not like is apt to appear legalistic to us and broad-minded to our opponents. In other words, it would seem that the presence of intricate doctrinal logic is based upon something more fundamental than the particular social perspective represented by the judge. It is a grave question, therefore, whether we are to conceive of judicial thinking as representing a struggle for mastery between logic and utility.

We might think of these legalisms in which the law does no more than make a choice where the common man would prefer inconsistency, or where the law decides against the onlooker's preference, as illusory rather than real, because the judicial thinking has not created a principle foreign to everyday life. If, indeed, lawyers were suddenly dispensed with and the public were forced to try cases, we might in many instances expect an insistence upon doctrinaire decisions which courts have in the course of long experience found methods of avoiding. The public would, in other words, violate its own values because of the importance it has learned from the courts to attach to the appearance of certainty.

We are not to suppose that the lessons of technicality taught by the judges are reluctantly learned. It is another one of those psychological paradoxes that the common man has a degree of admiration for technicality at the same time that he disclaims responsibility for such modes of thought. "Undoubtedly one cause of the tendency of scientific law to become mechanical," says Dean Pound, "is to be found in the average man's admiration for the ingenious in any direction, his love of technicality as a manifestation of cleverness, his feeling that law, as a developed institution, ought to have a certain ballast of mysterious technicality. . . . Every practitioner has encountered the lay obsession as to invalidity of a signing with a lead pencil. Every law-teacher has had to combat the student obsession that notice, however cogent, may be disregarded unless it is 'official.' Lay hair-splitting over rules and regulations goes far beyond anything of which lawyers are capable. Experienced advocates have insisted that in argument to a jury, along with a just, common sense theory of the merits, one ought to have a specious technicality for good measure."

The following story could probably be matched by many others. On the night of January 18, 1932 an elderly woman was taken ill on a New York street. She sat down on a doorstep. A policeman who was near-by came to her assistance and, seeing that she was seriously sick, he immediately went into the office of a hospital that was just across the street and requested that someone be sent out to the woman. But the man at the desk said that it was against the rules of the hospital to send anyone out. He suggested that the officer either bring the woman into the hospital or call an ambulance. The ambulance was finally summoned through a pay-station telephone, but the woman died before the ambulance arrived. When reporters interviewed the clerk at the hospital he again insisted that he could not send anyone out of the hospital.

But let us turn back to the situation in which the plain man feels that the law is disparate from his own modes of thought. In a society equipped with rapid transportation and communication the small businesses of an earlier day have become transformed into complex corporate enterprises depending upon a multitude of intangible social arrangements. This development has gone to a point beyond the average man's capacity to comprehend, and the manifold human relations created have gone far beyond the concepts and vocabulary of ordinary thought. Only jurists, who have been forced to settle conflicts that have arisen in the system, have been able to keep step with it and even they have usually been tardy in adjusting their intellectual resources to the new demands. Interlocking corporations have frequently been so set up as to confound ordinary men who try to analyze them. Only in the law, which has been pressed to carry social analysis to the limit, have conceptual instruments been devised partially adequate to the task of "piercing the corporate veil." But the important point for the present argument is that legal terms and legal concepts supply the only means of thinking about the more delicate of these rapidly multiplying social relationships. One could ask no better demonstration of this fact than the demands of modern business for the services of lawyers, not simply as its representatives in the trial court, but as the technicians of its organization.

Now the layman sometimes feels that the law has simply clouded a world that would be clear without judicial jargon. He may feel that he would be perfectly capable of organizing his own business or of writing his own will, if his handiwork was not liable to legalistic dissection. What he fails to recognize, of course, is that he would not like the results of his own authorship even if they were not criticized by the courts. He would not like their more immediate social consequences. The jurist knows that the modern social world is complicated, that one cannot think about an agreement of a group of men to make money together or of a plan for the future financial independence of one's heirs without considering a host of social possibilities that ordinary men are simply not trained to think about.

There is no point in denying that advantage is taken by lawyers of their technique of dealing with social complexities and that sometimes this advantage is unfair. A judge may swing his verdict to one party or the other because of a merely technical superiority in the argument of counsel for one side. Yet this advantage is only such as will always be taken where, of two opponents to a controversy, one is able and the other dull. The significant fact is that the existence of legal technicality applicable to the realm of business arrangements is essentially the contribution by the legal mind of a vocabulary and a manner of thought somewhere nearly adequate to the mechanism that it is designed to control. We have here, of course, the very type of situation cited by Professor Amos, in which the law is a creative force modifying rather than being modified by customary morality. If there is any criticism to be made of juristic thinking in so far as it deals with modern business enterprise, that criticism may be most pertinently aimed at a certain deficiency of technicality. The courts seem loath to leave the intellectual level of the common man and they are therefore slow to adopt terms and conceptions adequate to the commercial and industrial problems that they are called upon to solve. Yet as slow as they are in meeting such obligations, they still leave the common man behind. . . .

Benjamin N. Cardozo, 1870-1938

JURISPRUDENCE
(1932)

. . . The most distinctive product of the last decade in the field of jurisprudence is the rise of a group of scholars styling themselves realists, and content with nothing less than revision to its very roots of the method of judicial decision which is part of the classical tradition. . . .

I have said that the members of this group style themselves realists, – realists because fidelity to the realities of the judicial process, unclouded by myth or preconception, is supposed to be, in a degree peculiarly their own, the end and aim of their endeavor (Pound, The Call for a Realist Jurisprudence). I shall make bold to vary the description and speak to them hereafter as neo-realists instead. There were brave men before Agamemnon; and before the dawn of the last decade there were those in jurisprudence who strove to see the truth in the workings of the judicial process, to see it steadily and whole, and to report what they had seen with sincerity and candor. In this sense Savigny was a realist, and Jhering, and in our own land Holmes and Pound, and many others too. "Law," says Savigny, "takes actual life as its starting point." "Das Recht geht von der Wirklichkeit des Leben aus." In so far as the bond of union among the realists of the hour is the will to extend this motto of Savigny's to the workings of the judicial process, to view the process as it is, and not as a facile lip service may at times have represented it to be, there will be few so unregenerate as to remain without the fold. Perhaps the style that the faithful have appropriated to themselves may seem a bit over-pretentious. If so, the pretense may be forgiven as a reflection of a tendency now prevalent in philosophy and art and letters to speak of realism, however and wherever practised, as inherently a good and one of constant value (M. R. Cohen, Reason and Nature). On the other hand, when you pass beyond the unifying bond of a spiritual ideal and seek to find among the neo-realists a unifying bond of doctrine, the quest is not so simple. The truth indeed is that the votaries of the new faith do not constitute a school. They are representatives of a movement, an outlook, a tendency, avowing fundamental differences of emphasis and dogma (Llewellyn, Some Realism about Realism) In a critique of the new faith there is thus a constant need to separate the accident from the attribute, the tenet from the gloss. Not a little that has been said by one votary or another must be rejected, at least to my thinking, as ill-advised and exaggerated, though said with incisiveness and force and the arresting charm of novelty. The exaggeration is largely *obiter*. When it shall be excised and pruned away, there will remain a core of truth. Perhaps we may find in the end that here, as so often, the war is chiefly one of words, and that a *rapprochement* between the factions is simpler than we think. Let us not exaggerate unduly the differences that divide the forces of enlightenment and truth when there is need to present a united front to the embattled ranks and outposts of prejudice and error.

Fundamental in the thought of the neo-realists, or of most of them, is the exaltation of what is done by a judge as contrasted with what is said. They cling to the motto that "action speaks louder than words." Indeed they go beyond it, for some of them seem to tell us, not only that conduct is the louder, but that words do not speak at all. In the view of this section of the groups – a section growing swiftly in influence and numbers – law is to be found not in anything that a judge says in his opinion, but rather in what he does and only in what he does. Principles and rules and concepts are not law in and of themselves, and have no coercive power to fix the forms of law thereafter. They are nothing but tentative explanations of the implications of an actual holding embodied in a judgment. They are "ballons d'essai," experiments, not finalities. What has been said by a judge in an attempt to rationalize the holding may appear to be inadequate or mischievous if applied to the limit of its logic in novel situations. In that event the principle or rule or concept to the extent that it is found to be an incumbrance is to be jettisoned as useless. I am reminded of Bentham in his Comment on the Commentaries, a treasure only recently unearthed from among his unpublished and neglected manuscripts. "The individual judicial decisions," he says, "are acts of judges; they are acts of authority. But the rules of law are general propositions, these general propositions are conclusions drawn from the above-mentioned individual acts; and these conclusions are formed by any one who happens to bestow his thought upon the subject. If he happens to be a judge, his conclusions will naturally carry more weight with them than those of a common man." But the authority attaching to his conclusions differs in degree and not in kind. Thus the reforming jurist of a century and more ago! The neologisms of the hour – the popular novelties of thought and phrase – are sometimes older than we think.

Now, the thesis of the neo-realists in its beginnings was hardly more than a restatement of the doctrine of *stare decisis* thus formulated by Bentham, a restatement with slightly different emphasis and in modernistic forms and phrases. I do not mean to say that even in its beginnings it was a completely adequate doctrine.[1] Even in its beginnings the doctrine placed the creative potency of the judgment too far into the foreground, and cast too far into the background the significance of words. At the same time I cannot doubt that the teachings of the neo-realists were and still are of great value to jurisprudence in ridding *stare decisis* of something of its petrifying rigidity, in warning us that in many instances the principles and rules and concepts of our own creation are merely *aperçus* and glimpses of reality, and in reminding us of the need of reformulating them or at times abandoning them altogether when they stand condemned as mischievous in the social consciousness of the hour, the social consciousness which it is our business as judges to interpret as best we can. I have preached the same doctrine myself in a modest way (The Paradoxes of Legal Science) and in a still more modest way I have practised what I preached. Nothing that has since happened has brought me a different faith.

Neo-realism in its beginnings, and even now in its essence, is not to be identified with everything put forth under its banner. We are to keep in mind what I have stated, that is the slogan of a movement, not the dogma of a school. One might fancy from enthusiastic phrases here and there that the remedy for our ills is to have the law give over, once and for all, the strivings of the centuries for a rational coherence, and sink back in utter weariness to a justice that is the flickering reflection of the impulse of the moment (see the criticism of this tendency in Dickinson, Legal Rules in the Process of Decision). I am not wise enough to know whether this or something like it is to be the judicial process of the future. It is not the judicial process yet, and prophecy is not identical with exposition, though very often easier and by far more entertaining. Indeed, I can hardly bring myself to doubt, after reading the most recent and authoritative

[1] Some of its weaknesses have been exposed with admirable clarity by Professor Arthur L. Goodhart in his essay, "Determining the Ratio Decidendi of a Case."

statements of the creed of the new group, that by none of them is a saving grace attributed to the virtue of mere benevolence, undisciplined by the scrutiny of objective tests and standards. Belief in the efficacy of mere emotion is not essential to the faith whereby a sinful idolizer of precedent may be transported into the beatitude of a regenerate lover of reality (Llewellyn, Some Realism about Realism, cf. Frank, Are Judges Human?). I do, indeed, discover here and there an accent of contempt for the old ideals of symmetry and order, – a note of mere derision as if they had been supplanted altogether, made obsolete and futile by a new organon and method; but the accent and the note are not, to my thinking, of the essence of the movement. They are not the leit-motif of the symphony, but mere grace notes, so to speak, mere decorative incidents. It would be strange if they were not heard in these days when the movement is still young. Seldom can one point to stumbling sinners the road to salvation, discerned for the first time, without displaying in so doing some exuberance of manner and hyperbole of phrase. The only sad thing is that so often the road turns out not to be new, and the salvation at the end a distant and receding goal. The neo-realists have suffered at times from this missionary ecstasy. Over-zealous among the faithful, – when I call them over-zealous, I do not mean to disparage their brilliancy and power, – over-zealous ones, have not been satisfied to teach that order and certainty and rational coherence are goods to be subordinated on occasion to others more important. There has been a petulant contempt of them as if to dethrone them from the rank of idols was to prove them evil altogether. Not only are principles and rules and concepts shorn of their ancient tyranny. They are degraded altogether, stripped with contumely of every vestige of their bygone power; indeed, the process of humiliation is carried even farther, and there is taken from them the regenerative capacity to reproduce in their own image. Order in the legal system (so runs the argument) is an illusion, a mirage. The quest for it is a childish dream, the craving of the adolescent for the steadiness that came to him from the guidance of a parent; it is the unwillingness of sheltered youth to face the trials and perils of maturity and manhood. Silver-haired judges in the evenings of their days are as adolescent as the youngest neophyte, – a gospel carrying its solace as well as its reproaches. What began as a doctrine for emergencies – a weapon of peaceful revolution to be kept under lock and key, and employed with circumspection in hours of stress and strain – is turning, it seems, into a tool to be kept at one's elbow in a compartment of the desk, and plied with all the freedom of the screw-driver or the hammer in the grasp of the handy-man at home.

Now, if neo-realism means this or all that this implies, if its gospel is merely one of spasmodic self-expression, it is a false and misleading cult, unless, as I have suggested, its concern is with prophecy only, in which event I stand aloof. But in spite of the fact that at times its votaries have said things from which you might gather that they were professing such a cult or making ready to profess it, I am persuaded that these extravagances are not of the essence of the faith. What they wish to disparage, I believe, or at least to disparage chiefly, is the illusion of order and certainty and coherence which comes from sticking in the bark of congruities that are verbal rather than essential. In saying this I do not mean to acquit them of all fault. Certain it is that jurists of great distinction, critics of their teaching, have understood them to insist on something more (Pound, The Call for a Realist Jurisprudence; Bohlen, Review of Frank's Law and the Modern Mind; Dickinson, Legal Rules and the Process of Decision). They can hardly escape the charge of some obscurity of exposition if the tone and temper of their teaching have been misapprehended by readers such as these. When all these allowances are made, I am persuaded, none the less, that there has been no thought to preach a doctrine of undisciplined surrender to the cardiac promptings of the moment, the visceral reactions of one judge or another (Bohlen). Such surrender, instead of being vital to the new creed, is in fact essentially opposed to it, opposed to a creed which teaches as a basic article that generalizations of every kind, the subjective creations of the mind, must be constantly checked and restrained and reconsidered in the light of the tests and standards of objective or external verity. I put aside, therefore, as false and unessential the derision and impatience that betray themselves here and there among the priests of the new gospel of juridicial salvation. I put aside the outbursts of a solipsism condemned out of their own mouths, since it is at war with other doctrine fundamental to their teaching. One can match these excesses with doctrine more moderate, more in harmony with tradition.[2] The hyperbole and the solipsism have done damage to the cause of neo-realism by drowning other voices. Let them not deafen us to the message and to the truth that lies within it, if truth can be discerned by a willing and attentive ear.

Not a little confusion of thought has ensued, I am persuaded, from looking at the judicial process as if it had its complete and final summary in the doctrine of the binding force of precedent. Now, *stare decisis* is an important factor in the jducial process, but it is not the entire process by a long shot. The truth is that the problem which the neo-realists have set themselves to solve divides itself into two questions, which are not always kept apart. At the outset is the question whether generative force is to be withdrawn altogether from the principles and rules and concepts which are formulated by judges in the course of their opinions, whether certainty and order and coherence are to have the quality of ends at all. When that question has been answered, another and subsidiary one remains. There is still need to consider to what extent the doctrine of *stare decisis* exacts adherence to a principle, a rule, a concept, an ideal of certainty or order, after the mischiefs attendant upon conformity have made themselves apparent. These two inquiries may run into each other, but they are far from being the same, yet in much juristic writing, whether favorable to neo-realism or opposed to it, there is the assumption that they are, or at least a seeming failure to keep the two apart. It does not at all follow because conformity to a principle or a rule or a concept is a dictate of logic or consistency that therefore we are to insist upon conformity at the cost of every other good. But equally it does not follow because occasion may arise when other goods are greater, that therefore conformity and order are to be spurned by the judge as no longer goods at all. Happily, the bark of philosophers as of canines is often worse than their bite, and the neo-realist is not so indifferent to coherence as his anarchical professions might lead a critic to suppose.

Peril lurks in definitions, so runs an ancient maxim of the law. What is true of definitions is true of universals generally. The snares that are thus set may catch the heedless feet of thinkers who have been loud even as they stumbled in cries of danger unto others. So it is with the subject of our study, the theory of juristic method. Generalizations about the ways in which the judicial process works are quite as likely to be incomplete, and to stand in need of supplement or revision, as the generalizations yield by the process when in action, the output of its workings. . . .

[2] A temperate and withal a wise summary of neo-realist tendencies is to be found in the latest exposition of the new creed by one of the most brilliant of its teachers: Llewellyn, Some Realism about Realism, 44 H. L. R. 1222; also the same author's "Legal Thinking and Social Science."

If I consult my own experience, and ask what judges do in building law from day to day, I find that for the average run of cases what our predecessors have *said* is a generative force quite as much as what they have done. I do not mean what has been said by way of mere dictum, though I have no doubt that even dicta have been propagating forces and have borne a fruitful progeny; I mean what has been said as the professed and declared principle dictating the conclusion. But the average run of cases do not make up the entire body of the law. There are the exceptional cases too, the cases where the creative function is at its highest. These are the cases that have a maximum of interest for the student of legal methods. These are the cases in which neo-realism, as I view it, has its maximum of truth and also its maximum of utility. It is here that mere logic or consistency, though never negligible forces, have a minimum of compulsion. When a conclusion is felt to be unjust or inexpedient, or when the logic or supposed consistency that begat the parent precedent is itself suspect, – when a court is hard put to it, in other words, to find some avenue of escape – the actual thing done in the decision of the earlier case may assume a new importance, and many things professed may be retracted or ignored. This is so though the new case would be held to be fairly within the compass of the earlier one, within the range of its *ratio decidendi,* if the incitement to change were not so violent and compelling. "Every lawyer knows," says Llewellyn (Preface to Cases and Materials on Sales) "that a prior case may, at the will of the court, 'stand' either for the narrowest point to which its holding may be reduced, or for the widest formulation that its *ratio decidendi* will allow."

The picture of the process will be incomplete and misleading unless other distinctions are placed upon the canvas. We must distinguish between the propagating power of a principle in cases that come within its range and its propagating power in cases where its application is less direct, where it supplies a mere analogy, a signpost, a guide, but not a governing rule, even if its legitimacy in its own domain be conceded to the full. In such cases the analogy will be checked, the seminal principle drained, by many obstacles and outlets, the most important being those of expediency and justice. So also, if the range of the principle is doubtful, if there is a borderland of uncertain application, the extension will be affected by a consideration of the actual necessities of the precedent, words being at times subordinated to words. In brief, just as the law generally is permeated by distinctions of degree, so also is that branch of the law which is concerned with the significance of precedents and the significance of the forms in which precedents are cast. There is the process of distinction, which may vary from the recognition of differences that are apparent on the surface to the discovery of others that are subtle and obscure; there is the process of limitation, by which the precedent, though not annihilated altogether, is declared to be erroneous in part; and there is the process of annihilation by which it is squarely overruled. . . .

The emergent evolution of a formula into a precept is determined by its dimensions, spatial and temporal. To put the thought in other words: Considerations of space and time affect the capacity of the formula to shape the law thereafter. By considerations of space, I mean the generality or extension of the formula invoked in a particular controversy as establishing the stock of descent from which a conclusion is to be drawn. In the main, we may say, though only as a rough approximation, that obligation will vary inversely with extension. Take some of the principles of constitutional law, such a principle as the one that the due process clause of the constitution forbids a wholly arbitrary interference with liberty or property. Nearly the entire meaning of a principle so general depends upon the application. Much will therefore turn, when a specific act of legislation is in question, upon the social or juridical philosophies of the judges who constitute the court at one time or another (T. R. Powell, State Utilities and the Supreme Court). On the other hand, we must bear in mind that even in this department of the law where the expansive capacity of a principle is greatest, it is an expansive capacity within limits. The principle even here has a coercive force beyond the specific facts of the controversy in which it was announced. We misread history in a most unrealistic fashion if we say that the seeds of generations of later judgments were not in Gibbons v. Ogden and McCulloch v. Maryland....

Just as there are distinctions dependent upon extension, distinctions in space, so there are distinctions in time. The principle or the rule or the concept, even though its extension is not great, is pliable in its early stages before the bones have set. This is far from saying that its pliability continues. There comes a time when it has been fitted to a great many combinations of facts, when it has been made to rule them all, and when this has been done so often that at last its application is coincident or nearly so with its maximum extension. At that time pliability ends, and even before that time it is greatly diminished. Hypothesis is now reality. What was once but a hint has been turned into a command. By fitting itself to the instance in multitudinous variations, the formula has won authority when at first it had mere persuasion. It is law now in every sense, law by embodiment in successive judgments through the whole extent of the territory staked out at the beinning as the field of its domain.

Now, the impulse or the energy that thus pushes a formula to mastery is the driving force of order, of certainty, of rational coherence, as a juristic end and aim. The force has capacity to drive because discretion, unmeasured and unregulated, is felt to open the door to tyranny and corruption. So it is that long before a principle or a rule or a concept has become so firmly established that its title to govern is unchallenged by pretenders, long before this, it will still have made its way, slowly and hesitantly, into terrains of the law that are doubtful or disputed, will still have peopled the legal scene with forms in its own mould. Its power is not yet supreme. It must still compete with other analogies, which may be able to show themselves to be more exact, more expedient, more just. If they fail in that showing, it will have the right of way.

I have said that I prefer to give the name of law to formulas that are charged with this procreative power – to give it in advance of the hour of their final triumph – though it may turn out in the end that their lives and the lives of their expected progeny are shorter than was hoped for when the horoscope was cast. If I give them this name, I am merely preserving the analogy between the laws that are the province of jurisprudence and the predictions of orderly succession that are called the laws of nature (cf. The Growth of the Law). Lawyers have been quoting these many years the famous saying of Justice Holmes that "a legal duty so-called is nothing but a prediction that if a man does or omits certain things, he will be made to suffer in this or that way by judgment of the court." Now comes Dr. Dewey in his book, "The Quest for Certainty," and shows that the majestic laws of nature are predictions of a like order with not a little of the same chances of fallibility and error. They have lost the quality once ascribed to them of immutable sequences inherent in the constitution of the universe. What is known as the principle of indeterminacy seems to have given the finishing stroke to any such grandiose pretensions. They have been pulled down pretty near to the level of the laws declared by judges as approximate hypotheses. "In technical statement," says Dr. Dewey, "laws on the new basis are formulae for the prediction of the probability of an observable occurrence. They are designations of a relation sufficiently stable to allow of the occurrence of individualized situations – for every observed phenomenon is individual – within limits of specified probability, not a probability of error, but of probability of actual occurrence." This sounds a good deal like a statement of the kind of law that emanates from the workings of the judicial process. Law as understood and developed by the lawyers may be coming nearer to law as understood and developed by the scientists, but it is also true that the laws of science are coming nearer to the judge-made law of courts. "Mankind," the words are those of Dr. Whitehead, "never quite knows what it is after. When we survey the history of thought, and likewise the history of practice, we find that one idea after another is tried out, its limitations defined, and its core of truth elicited. . . . The proper test is not that of finality, but of progress."

So it is with law, the law, that is to say, which is the concern of jurisprudence. Its principles or rules or concepts are not always finalities. They may mark what is only a stage of progress, or at times a stage of retrogression. Even so, their implications are something more than vanities. They are to be heeded like the laws of nature till superseded by another formulation more truthful in its expression of the order of the juristic universe. What that order is the judge is to say by his judgments, for he is the appointed searcher of the juristic heavens. The order is made up of certainty and regularity, but not of these only. It is made up of expediency, too, and justice. Long habitude and a traditional technique must tell which of these component elements is to receive in any given instance the dominating place. Certainly and regularity have at least a presumption in their favor. They show us the well-worn ways, and as in conduct generally, so in law, what we have done in the past, we are likely to continue to do till the shock of a perturbing force is strong enough to jolt us out of the rut. . . .

In the business of choosing between all these competitive offerings in the legal mart, we hear a good deal now-a-days of the intuitive judgment, more picturesqely styled the hunch, as the arbiter of values (Hutcheson, The Judgment Intuitive). I do not seek to minimize its role upon the scene of the judicial process, but I think there is a good deal of misapprehension as to its significance for a philosophy of law. The thought seems to be that to prove the value of the hunch is to establish the empire of mere feeling or emotion, of arbitrary preference, and by the same token to disprove the value of conceptions, rules and principles, the value of all logic, till we are driven, like the sophist in the Greek comedy, to proclaim that Whirl is King (Irwin Edman, The Contemporary and His Soul; Lippman, A Preface to Morals). I do not mean that there was any such misapprehension in the mind of the distinguished judge and author by whom the hunch may be said to have been given its card of admission into the polite society of juristic methodology. I am fearful, however, that the newcomer's importance, even if justly rated by its sponsor, has been exaggerated by others.

Now, indubitably, the intuitive flash of inspiration is at the root of all science, of all art, and even of all conduct. I have discussed this in my lectures on the Paradoxes of Legal Science, and so have many others. I quoted Graham Wallas. Other testimony may be added, if supplement is needed. "Our fundamental units, light waves, electric current and resistance, rates of metabolism, etc., are never visible except to the eye illuminated by all sorts of ideas and rigorous deductions from them. Accidental discoveries of which popular histories of science make mention never happen except to those who have previously devoted a great deal of thought to the matter. Observation unillumined by theoretic reason is sterile. Indeed, without a well reasoned anticipation or hypothesis of what we expect to find there is no definite object to look for, and no test as to what is relevant to our search. Wisdom does not come to those who gape at nature with an empty head" (M. R. Cohen, Reason and Nature; cf. the same author's Vision and Technique in Philosophy).

The process is not different when we pass from theory to practice, from the sphere of thought to that of conduct. In a paper by Sir Austen Chamberlain, published a few months ago (Bases of British Foreign Policy, vol. 9, Foreign Affairs 535, July, 1931) we learn that the hunch has been for centuries the driving force for British statesmen in international diplomacy. "The Englishman," says Chamberlain, "distrusts logic at all times and most of all in the government of men, for instinct and experience alike teach him that men are not governed by logic, that it is unwise to treat political issues as exercises in logic and that wisdom more often lies in refraining from pressing sound arguments to their logical conclusion and in accepting a workable though illogical compromise. After all, logic lost us the Thirteen Colonies."

The doctrine of the hunch, if viewed as an attempt at psychological analysis, embodies an important truth; it is a vivid and arresting description of one of the stages in the art of thought. The hunch is the divination of the scientist, the luminous hypothesis, the apocalyptic insight, that is back of his experiments (The Paradoxes of Legal Science; Graham Wallas, The Art of Thought). If we conceive of it, however, as a summary of the complete judicial process, it is one-sided and misleading. Carried to an extreme, it is merely a transference into the realm of jurisprudence of that gospel of unfettered self-expression which has a passing vogue today in the realm of external conduct. There is nothing new about such systems or lack of systems. The French made the experiment a generation ago. What ensued forms the chapter in the history of their law which is known as "le phénomène Magnaud." The judges were to ask themselves in every instance what in the circumstances before them a good judge would wish to do, and render judgment accordingly. I have considered the episode in other writings. Its epitaph has been written by Geny with the authority of a master. We had a similar episode in our own country a decade or more ago when Judge Robinson initiated a like revolt against the existing order of jurisprudence in the State of North Dakota. What the Germans call "Die Gefühlsjurisprudencz," the jurisprudence of mere sentiment or feeling, however notable its merits does not number among them the grace of novelty.

In condemning or in extolling the ideals of certainty and order and coherence, it is important to fix their meaning. Not a little confusion of thought and speech has grown out of the failure to heed this admonition. There is such a thing as certainty and order and coherence from the standpoint of the lawyer, and such a thing as certainty and order and coherence from the standpoint of the layman. Often we confuse the two. If a choice is necessary between them, we may find it wise to prefer the kind known to the layman, for it is his conduct that is to be regulated, it is from him, not from the lawyer, for the most part, that conformity is due. If the law as declared in a judgment is made to accord with established custom or with the plain and unquestioned dictates of morality it will seldom fail that certainty is promoted, not hindered, though lawyers may espy a flaw in the symmetry of the legal sphere, a break in the elegantia juris so precious to their hearts. The layman cares little about elegantia and has never had occasion to make a survey of the legal sphere. What is important for him is that the law be made to conform to his reasonable expectations, and this it will seldom do if its precepts are in glaring opposition to the mores of the times. Genuine certainty will very often be better attained, the ideal of the legal order more fully realized, by causing these expectations to prevail, than by developing the formula of an ancient dictum to the limit of its logic. Once more it is a question of degree, a matter of more or less, an adjustment of the weights and a reading of the scales . . .

What is useful in neo-realism is its insistence upon the "margin of error," the "increase of entropy," the "principle of indeterminacy," which condition the generalizations of judge-made law just as they do the laws of physics, whose terminology I am borrowing. What is wrong in neo-realism is a tendency manifest at times to exaggerate the indeterminacy, the entropy, the margin of error, to treat the random or chance element as a good in itself and a good exceeding in value the elements of certainty and order and rational coherence, – exceeding them in value, not merely at times and in places, but always and everywhere. In emphasizing the danger of extracting principles and formulas from an aggregation of specific cases and adhering to them blindly, we must be on our guard lest we be carried over to the other extreme and left with nothing more coherent than a mass of nebulous particulars. There are times when principles and rules and concepts must be accommodated to ends, yet there must always be remembrance of the truth that of the ends to be achieved definiteness and order are themselves among the greatest and most obvious. Certainly the historic masters of the law have been the boldest in the pursuit of principles, though this is not to say that they have not also been bold in rejecting what had proved itself to be out-worn or untenable. Haldane says in his autobiography that early in his professional career there had come to him the "conviction that not only in philosophy but in science it was true that no systematic knowledge is sufficient in itself unless it leads up and points to first principles. This doctrine later became valuable to me," he says, "even as a guide in work at the bar. It did not help in the work of cross-examination. I was never good at that, nor in the conduct of *nisi prius* cases. But it was invaluable in the preparation for the presentation of great questions to the Supreme Tribunals, where the judges were keen about first principles and were looking out for help from the advocate." I take it that what is suspect and dangerous is not the search for principles, but the readiness to canonize them too quickly before their saintly character has been attested by the ages. What we need to guard against is the notion that because a principle has been formulated as the *ratio decidendi* of a given problem, it is therefore to be applied as a solvent of other problems, regardless of consequence, regardless of deflecting factors, inflexibility and automatically, in all its pristine generality. On the other hand, a blight would fall upon our law if the opinions of our judges were to be as colorless and concrete as the judgment of a French court in its recitals and conclusions. "Those who make no mistakes," we are reminded by Sir Frederick Pollock, "will never make anything, and the judge who is afraid of committing himself may be called sound and safe in his own generation, but will leave no mark on the law." We are not to forget that generalizations have their value, their fructifying virtue, in law as in science generally, though the later years may prune them or even discard them altogether. The judicial method of the future must see to it that judicial inventiveness shall not be desiccated or stunted, that generalization shall be as free and as bold as in the past, perhaps freer and bolder. Unless it can accomplish this, it is headed toward disaster. What is to be changed, if anything, is the capacity of the generalized principle, the *ratio decidendi*, to reproduce in its own image, to reproduce without restraint. Its generative power must depend upon the quality of its progeny. Like the hypotheses of science it is to be judged by its results. There must be a new system of eugenics for the pullulating precedents.

The movement to identify law with the action of the judge to the exclusion of his utterance has not developed without protest. It has found vigorous opposition in an illuminating essay by Prof. Arthur L. Goodhart, "The Ratio Decidendi". . . . The opposition has found voice again in an article by Prof. Morris R. Cohen, "Justice Holmes and the Nature of Law." Prof. Cohen, criticizing the tendency, sees in it a reflection of the behavioristic psychology. He denies that the reasons put forward in opinions as the professed grounds of a decision are to be laid aside as minor factors in determining the result. In this I quite agree, yet I am wondering whether he does not impute to his opponents a depreciation of the written word more thorough-going than they mean to teach. None of them would be willing to say that the professed reasons are of no importance. What is meant is rather this, that the reasons are to be jettisoned for the safety of the ship when the emergency is adequate, though adequacy remains as in the past a question of degree. One finds it hard to believe that the psychology of behaviorism could lead to any other doctrine. Certainly behaviorism does not depreciate the significance of speech, since one of its central teachings is the doctrine that speech, however dimly unformulated, is an indispensable preliminary to the reality of thought. The thinkers of the new movement have formulated the problem a little more sharply than their predecessors, yet the query propounded is not new. We have to face it, more or less unconsciously, every time that we decide how finely we will draw the line of distinction between one precedent and another. To what extent shall the reasons professed in an opinion be treated by the courts as invested with coercive power, and to what extent with power that is merely persuasive or advisory? In the solution of that problem the behavioristic outlook may at times help us to a clue. I dissent from the neo-realists in their depreciation of order and certainty and rational coherence as merely negligible goods, if depreciation so extreme is of the essence of their teaching. On the other hand, I am wholly one with them in their insistence that the virtues of symmetry and coherence can be purchased at too high a price; that law is a means to an end, and not an end in itself; and that it is more important to make it consistent with what men and women really and truly believe and do than what judges may at times have said in an attempt to explain and rationalize the things they have done themselves. The high priests of the new movement will have to say whether this confession makes me a realist or not. In my case, as in many others, the schism is not wide if lip service to a catechism is less important than the actualities of conduct, – as every genuine realist must concede that it is.

Felix S. Cohen, 1907-1953
U. S. Government Solicitor, private practitioner, and Visiting Professor, Yale Law School.

TRANSCENDENTAL NONSENSE AND THE FUNCTIONAL APPROACH (1935)

. . . That something is radically wrong with our traditional legal thought-ways has long been recognized. Holmes, Gray, Pound, Brooks Adams, M. R. Cohen, T. R. Powell, Cook, Oliphant, Moore, Radin, Llewellyn, Yntema, Frank, and other leaders of modern legal thought in America, are in fundamental agreement in their disrespect for "mechanical jurisprudence," for legal magic and word-jugglery. But mutual agreement is less apparent when we come to the question of what to do: How are we going to get out of this tangle? How are we going to substitute a realistic, rational, scientific account of legal happenings for the classical theological jurisprudence of concepts?

Attempts to answer this question have made persistent use of the phrase "functional approach." . . .

Fundamentally there are only two significant questions in the field of law. One is, "How do courts actually decide cases of a given kind?" The other is, "How ought they to decide cases of a given kind?" Unless a legal "problem" can be subsumed under one of these forms, it is not a meaningful question and any answer to it must be nonsense. . . .

The parallel between the functional method of modern physics and the program of realistic jurisprudence is so well sketched by a distinguished Chinese jurist [Wu] that I can only offer a quotation without comment:

> "Professor Eddington, in a recent book on "The Nature of the Physical World," observes: "A thing must be defined according to the way in which it is in practice recognized and not according to some ulterior significance that we suppose it to possess." So Professor Bridgman, in "The Logic of Modern Physics":
>
> "Hitherto many of the concepts of physics have been defined in terms of their properties." But now, "in general, we mean by any concept nothing more than a set of operations; *the concept is synonymous with the corresponding set of operations.* If the concept is physical, as of length, the operations are actual physical operations, namely, those by which length is measured; or if the concept is mental, as of mathematical continuity, the operations are mental operations, namely those by which we determine whether a given aggregate of magnitudes is continuous."
>
> Now, this way of dealing with concepts was precisely what Holmes introduced into the science of law early in the '80's. . . ."

The significance of the functional method in the field of law is clarified if we consider the bearings of this method upon four traditional legal problems: (1) The definition of law; (2) The nature of legal rules and concepts; (3) The theory of legal decisions; and (4) The role of legal criticism.

1. *The Definition of Law*

The starting point of functional analysis in American jurisprudence is found in Justice Holmes' definition of law as "prophecies of what the courts will do in fact." It is in "The Path of the Law," that this realistic conception of law is first clearly formulated. . .

A good deal of fruitless controversy has arisen out of attempts to show that this definition of law as the way courts actually decide cases is either true or false. A definition of law is *useful* or *useless*. It is not *true* or *false*, any more than a New Year's resolution or an insurance policy. A definition is in fact a type of insurance against certain risks of confusion. It cannot, any more than can a commercial insurance policy, eliminate all risks. Absolute certainty is as foreign to language as to life. There is no final insurance against an insurer's insolvency. And the words of a definition always carry their own aura of ambiguity. But a definition is useful if it insures against risks of confusion more serious than any that the definition itself contains.

"What courts do" is not entirely devoid of ambiguity. There is room for disagreement as to what a *court* is, whether, for instance, the Interstate Commerce Commission or the Hague Tribunal or the Council of Tesuque Pueblo is a court, and whether a judge acting in excess of those powers which the executive arm of the government will recognize acts as a court. There may even be disagreement as to the line of distinction between what courts *do* and what courts *say*, in view of the fact that most judicial behavior is verbal. But these sources of ambiguity in Holmes' definition of law are peripheral rather than central, and easily remedied. They are, therefore, far less dangerous sources of confusion than the basic ambiguity inherent in classical definitions of law which involve a confusion between what is and what ought to be. . . .

2. *The Nature of Legal Rules and Concepts*

If the functionalists are correct, the meaning of a definition is found in its consequences. The definition of a general term like "law" is significant only because it affects all our definitions of specific legal concepts.

The consequence of defining law as a function of concrete judicial decisions is that we may proceed to define such concepts as "contract," "property," "title," "corporate personality," "right," and "duty," similarly as functions of concrete judicial decisions.

The consequence of defining law as a hodge-podge of political force and ethical value ambiguously amalgamated is that every legal concept, rule or question will present a similar ambiguity.

Consider the elementary legal question: "Is there a contract?"

When the realist asks this question, he is concerned with the actual behavior of courts. For the realist, the contractual relationship, like law in general, is a function of legal decisions. The question of what courts *ought* to do is irrelevant here. Where there is a promise that will be legally enforced there is a contract. So conceived, any answer to the question "Is there a contract" must be in the nature of a prophecy, based, like other prophecies, upon past and present facts. So conceived, the question "Is there a contract?" or for that matter any other legal question, may be broken up into a number of subordinate questions, each of which refers to the actual behavior of courts: (1) What courts are likely to pass upon a given transaction and its consequences? (2) What elements in this transaction will be viewed as relevant and important by these courts? (3) How have these courts dealt with transactions in the past which are similar to the given transaction, that is, *identical in those respects which the court will regard as important*? (4) What forces will tend to compel judicial conformity to the precedents that appear to be in point (*e.g.* inertia, conservatism, knowledge of the past, or intelligence sufficient to acquire such knowledge, respect for predecessors, superiors or brothers on the bench, a habit of deference to the established expectations of the bar or the public) and how strong are these forces? (5) What factors will tend to evoke new judicial treatment for the transaction in question (*e.g.* changing public opinion, judicial idiosyncrasies and prejudices, newly accepted theories of law, society or economics, or the changing social context of the case) and how powerful are these factors?

These are the questions which a successful practical lawyer faces and answers in any case. The law, as the realistic lawyer uses the term, is the body of answers to such questions. The task of prediction involves, in itself, no judgment of ethical value. Of course, even the most cynical practitioner will recognize that the positive existing ethical beliefs of judges are material facts in any case because they determine what facts the judge will view as important and what past rules he will regard as reasonable or unreasonable and worthy of being extended or restricted. But judicial beliefs about the values of life and the ideals of society are *facts*, just as the religious beliefs of the Andaman Islanders are facts, and the truth or falsity of such moral beliefs is a matter of complete unconcern to the practical lawyer, as to the scientific observer.

Washed in cynical acid, every legal problem can thus be interpreted as a question concerning the positive behavior of judges.

There is a second and radically different meaning which can be given to our type question, "Is there a contract?" When a judge puts this question, in the course of writing his opinion, he is not attempting to predict his own behavior. He is in effect raising the question, in an obscure way, of whether or not liability *should* be attached to certain acts. This is inescapably an ethical question. What a judge ought to do in a given case is quite as much a moral issue as any of the traditional problems of Sunday School morality.

It is difficult for those who still conceive of morality in otherworldly terms to recognize that every case presents a moral question to the court. But this notion has no terrors for those who think of morality in earthly terms. Morality, so conceived, is vitally concerned with such facts as human expectations based upon past decisions, the stability of economic transactions, and even the maintenance of order and simplicity in our legal system. If ethical values are inherent in all realms of human conduct, the ethical appraisal of a legal situation is not to be found in the spontaneous outpourings of a sensitive conscience unfamiliar with the social context, the background of precedent, and the practices and expectations, legal and extra-legal, which have grown up around a given type of transaction.

It is the great disservice of the classical conception of law that it hides from judicial eyes the ethical character of every judicial question, and thus serves to perpetuate class prejudices and uncritical moral assumptions which could not survive the sunlight of free ethical controversy.

The Blackstonian conception of law as half-mortal and half-divine gives us a mythical conception of contract. When a master of classical jurisprudence like Williston asks the question "Is there a contract?", he has in mind neither the question of scientific prediction which the practical lawyer faces, nor the question of values which the conscientious judge faces. If he had in mind the former question, his studies would no doubt reveal the extent to which courts actually enforce various types of contractual obligation. His conclusions would be in terms of probability and statistics. On the other hand, if Professor Williston were interested in the ethical aspects of contractual liability, he would undoubtedly offer a significant account of the human values and social costs involved in different types of agreements and in the means of their enforcement. In fact. however, the discussions of a Williston will oscillate between a theory of what courts actually do and a theory of what courts ought to do, without coming to rest either on the plane of social actualities or on the plane of values long enough to come to grips with significant problems. This confused wandering between the world of fact and the world of justice vitiates every argument and every analysis.

Intellectual clarity requires that we carefully distinguish between the two problems of (1) objective description, and (2) critical judgment, which classical jurisprudence lumps under the same phrase. Such a distinction realistic jurisprudence offers with the double-barreled thesis: (1) that every legal rule or concept is simply a function of judicial decisions to which all questions of value are irrelevant, and (2) that the problem of the judge is not whether a legal rule or concept actually exists but whether it *ought* to exist. Clarity on two fronts is the result. Description of legal facts becomes more objective, and legal criticism becomes more critical.

The realistic lawyer, when he attempts to discover how courts are actually dealing with certain situations, will seek to rise above his own moral bias and to discount the moral bias of the legal author whose treatise he consults.

The realistic author of textbooks will not muddy his descriptions of judicial behavior with wishful thinking; if he dislikes a decision or line of decisions, he will refrain from saying, "This cannot be the law because it is contrary to sound principle," and say instead, "This is the law, but I don't like it," or more usefully, "This rule leads to the following results, which are socially undesirable for the following reasons * * *."

The realistic advocate, if he continues to use ritual language in addressing an unrealistic court, will at least not be fooled by his own words: he will use his "patter" to induce favorable judicial attitudes and at the same time to distract judicial attention from precedents and facts that look the wrong way (as the professional magician uses his "patter" to distract the attention of his audience from certain facts). Recognizing the circularity of conceptual argument, the realistic advocate will contrive to bring before the court the human values that favor his cause, and since the rules of evidence often stand in the way, he will perforce bring his materials to judicial attention by sleight-of-hand – through the appeal of a "sociological brief" to "judicial notice," through discussion of the background and consequences of past cases cited as precedents, through elaboration and exegesis upon admissible evidence, or even through a political speech or a lecture on economics in the summation of his case or argument.

The realistic judge, finally, will not fool himself or anyone else by basing decisions upon circular reasoning from the presence or absence of corporations, conspiracies, property rights, titles, contracts, proximate causes, or other legal deriviatives of the judicial decision itself. Rather, he will frankly assess the conflicting human values that are opposed in every controversy, appraise the social importance of the precedents to which each claim appeals, open the courtroom to all evidence that will bring light to this delicate practical task of social adjustment, and consign to Von Jhering's heaven of legal concepts all attorneys whose only skill is that of the conceptual acrobat.

3. *The Theory of Legal Decisions*

The uses of the functional approach are not exhausted by "realistic jurisprudence." "Realistic jurisprudence," as that term is currently used, is a theory of the nature of law, and therefore a theory of the nature of legal rules, legal concepts, and legal questions. Its essence is the definition of law as a function of judicial decisions. This definition is of tremendous value in the development of legal science, since it enables us to dispel the supernatural mists that envelop the legal order and to deal with the elements of the legal order in objective, scientific terms. But this process of definition and clarification is only a preliminary stage in the life of legal science. When we have analyzed legal rules and concepts as patterns of decisions, it becomes relevant to ask, "What are judicial decisions made of?"

If we conceive of legal rules and concepts as functions of judicial decisions, it is convenient, for purposes of this analysis, to think of these decisions as hard and simple facts. Just as every physical object may be analyzed as a complex of positive and negative electrons, so every legal institution, every legal rule or concept may be analyzed as a complex of plaintiff decisions and defendant decisions. But simplicity is relative to the level of analysis. For the chemist, the atom is the lowest term of analysis. But the physicist cannot stop the process of analysis with the atom or even the electron. It would be heresy to the faith of science to endow either with final simplicity and perpetual immunity from further analysis. Unfortunately, certain advocates of realistic jurisprudence, after using the functional method to break down rules and concepts into atomic decisions, refuse to go any further with the analytic process. They are willing to look upon decisions as simple unanalyzable products of judicial hunches or indigestion.

The "hunch" theory of law, by magnifying the personal and accidental factors in judicial behavior, implicitly denies the relevance of significant, predictable, social determinants that govern the course of judicial decisions. Those who have advanced this viewpoint have performed a real service in indicating the large realm of uncertainty in the actual law. But actual experience does reveal a significant body of predictable uniformity in the behavior of courts. Law is not a mass of unrelated decisions nor a product of judicial bellyaches. Judges are human, but they are a peculiar breed of humans, selected to a type and held to service under a potent system of governmental controls. Their acts are "judicial" only within a system which provides for appeals, rehearings, impeachments, and legislation. The decision that is "peculiar" suffers erosion – unless it represents the first salient manifestation of a new social force, in which case it soon ceases to be peculiar. It is more useful to analyze a judicial "hunch" in terms of the continued impact of a judge's study of precedents, his conversations with associates, his reading of newspapers, and his recollections of college courses, than in strictly physiological terms.

A truly realistic theory of judicial decisions must conceive every decision as something more than an expression of individual personality, as concomitantly and even more importantly a function of social forces, that is to say, as a product of social determinants and an index of social consequences. A judicial decision is a social event. Like the enactment of a Federal statute, or the equipping of police cars with radios, a judicial decision is an intersection of social forces: Behind the decision are social forces that play upon it to give it a resultant momentum and direction; beyond the decision are human activities affected by it. The decision is without significant social dimensions when it is viewed simply at the moment in which it is rendered. Only by probing behind the decision to the forces which it reflects, or projecting beyond the decision the lines of its force upon the future, do we come to an understanding of the meaning of the decision itself. The distinction between "holding" and "dictum" in any decision is not to be discovered by logical inspection of the opinion or by historical inquiry into the actual facts of the case. That distinction involves us in a prediction, a prophecy of the weight that courts will give to future citations of the decisions rendered. This is a question not of pure logic but of human psychology, economics and politics.

What is the meaning of a judicial decision, summed up in the words, "Judgment for the plaintiff"? Obviously, the significance of the decision, even for the parties directly involved in the case, depends upon certain predictable uniformities of official behavior, *e.g.* that a sheriff or marshall will enforce the decision, in one way or another, over a period of time, that the given decisions will be respected or followed in the same court or other courts if the question at issue is relitigated, and that certain procedures will be followed in the event of an appeal, etc. When we go beyond the merely private significance of an actual decision, we are involved in a new set of predictions concerning the extent to which other cases, similar in certain respects, are likely to receive the same treatment in the same courts or in other courts within a given jurisdiction. Except in the context of such predictions the announcement of a judicial decision is only a noise. If reasonably certain predictions of this sort could never be made, as Jerome Frank at times seems to say, then all legal decisions would be simply noises, and no better grist for science than the magical phrases of transcendental jurisprudence.

If the understanding of any decision involves us necessarily in prophecy (and thus in history), then the notion of law as something that exists completely and systematically at any given moment in time is false. Law is a social process, a complex of human activities, and an adequate legal science must deal with human activity, with cause and effect, with the past and the future. Legal science, as traditionally conceived, attempts to give an instantaneous snapshot of an existing and completed system of rights and duties. Within that system there are no temporal processes, no cause and no effect, no past and no future. A legal decision is thus conceived as a logical deduction from fixed principles. Its meaning is expressed only in terms of its logical consequences. A legal system, thus viewed, is as far removed from temporal activity as a system of pure geometry. In fact, jurisprudence is as much a part of pure mathematics as is algebra, unless it be conceived as a study of human behavior, – human behavior as it molds and is molded by judicial decisions. Legal systems, principles, rules, institutions, concepts and decisions can be understood only as functions of human behavior.

Such a view of legal science reveals gaps in our legal knowledge to which, I think, legal research will give increasing attention.

We are still in the stage of guesswork and accidentally collected information, when it comes to formulating the social forces which mold the course of judicial decision. We know, in a general way, that dominant economic forces play a part in judicial decision, that judges usually reflect the attitudes of their own income class on social questions, that their views on law are molded to a certain extent by their past legal experience as counsel for special interests, and that the impact of counsel's skill and eloquence is a cumulative force which slowly hammers the law into forms desired by those who can best afford to hire legal skill and eloquence; but nobody has ever charted, in scientific fashion, the extent of such economic influences. We know, too, that judges are craftsmen, with aesthetic ideals, concerned with the aesthetic judgments that the bar and the law schools will pass upon their awkward or skillful, harmonious or unharmonious, anomalous or satisfying, actions and theories; but again we have no specific information on the extent of this aesthetic bias in the various branches of the law. We know that courts are, at least in this country, a generally conservative social force, and more like a brake than a motor in the social mechanism, but we have no scientific factual comparison of judicial, legislative, and executive organs of government, from the standpoint of social engineering. Concretely and specifically, we know that Judge So-and-so, a former attorney for a non-union shop, has very definite ideas about labor injunctions, that another judge, who has had an unfortunate sex life, is parsimonious in the fixing of alimony; that another judge can be "fixed" by a certain political "boss"; that a series of notorious kidnappings will bring about a wave of maximum sentences in kidnapping cases. All this knowledge is useful to the practicing lawyer, to the public official, to the social reformer, and to the disinterested student of society. But it is most meager, and what little of it we have, individually, is not collectively available. There is at present no publication showing the political, economic, and professional background and activities of our various judges. Such a reference work would be exceedingly valuable, not only to the practical lawyer who wants to bring a motion or try a case before a sympathetic court, but also to the disinterested student of the law. Such a Judicial Index is not published, however, because it would be disrespectable. According to the classical theory, these things have nothing to do with the way courts decide cases. A witty critic of the functional approach regards it as a *reductio ad absur-*

dum of this approach that law schools of the future may investigate judicial psychology, teach the art of bribery, and produce graduate detectives. This is far from a *reductio ad absurdum.* Our understanding of law will be greatly enriched when we learn more about how judges think, about the exact extent of judicial corruption, and about the techniques for investigating legally relevant facts. Of course, this knowledge may be used for improper purposes, but cannot the same be said of the knowledge which traditional legal education distributes?

If we know little today of the motivating forces which mold legal decisions, we know even less of the human consequences of these decisions. We do not even know how far the appellate cases, with which legal treatises are almost exclusively concerned, are actually followed in the trial courts. Here, again, the experienced practitioner is likely to have accumulated a good deal of empirical information, but the young law clerk, just out of a first-rate law school, is not even aware that such a problem exists. Likewise, the problem of the actual enforcement of judgments has received almost no critical study. Discussion of the extent to which various statutes are actually enforced regularly moves in the thin air of polemic theory. It is usually practically impossible to find out whether a given statute has ever been enforced unless its enforcement has raised a legal tangle for appellate courts.

When we advance beyond the realm of official conduct and seek to discover the social consequences of particular statutes or decisions, we find a few promising programs of research but almost no factual studies. Today the inclusion of factual annotations in a code, showing the extent and effects of law enforcement, would strike most lawyers as almost obscene. But notions of obscenity change, and every significant intellectual revolution raises to prominence facts once obscure and disrespectable. It is reasonable to expect that some day even the impudencies of Holmes and Llewellyn will appear sage and respectable.

4. *Legal Criticism*

It is perhaps the chief service of the functional approach that in cleansing legal rules, concepts, and institutions of the compulsive flavors of legal logic or metaphysics, room is made for conscious ethical criticism of law. In traditional jurisprudence, criticism, where it exists, is found masked in the protective camouflage of transcendental nonsense: "The law *must* (or *cannot*) be thus and so, because the *nature* of contracts, corporations or contingent remainders so requires." The functional approach permits ethics to come out of hiding. When we recognize that legal rules are simply formulae describing uniformities of judicial decision, that legal concepts likewise are patterns or functions of judicial decisions, that decisions themselves are not products of logical parthenogenesis born of pre-existing legal principles but are social events with social causes and consequences, then we are ready for the serious business of appraising law and legal institutions in terms of some standard of human values.

The importance for legal criticism of clear, objective description of judicial behavior, its causes and its consequences, is coming to be generally recognized. What is not so easily recognized is the importance for objective legal science of legal criticism.

Since the brilliant achievements of Bentham, descriptive legal science has made almost no progress in determining the consequences of legal rules. This failure of scholarship, in the light of the encouraging progress of modern research into the antecedents and social context of judicial decision, calls for explanation.

Possibly this gap is to be explained in terms of an inherited assumption that statutes and decisions are self-executing, that the consequences of a law or a judgment are, therefore, clearly indicated by the language of the statute or decision itself, and that factual research is therefore a work of supererogation. Possibly this failure of research is to be explained in terms of the dominance of the private lawyer in our legal education. The private attorney is interested in the *causes* of judicial decisions, but his interest in consequences is likely to stop with the payment of a fee. I am inclined to think, however, that the failure of our legal scholarship in this direction may be attributed to a more fundamental difficulty. The prospect of determining the consequences of a given rule of law appears to be an infinite task, and is indeed an infinite task unless we approach it with some discriminating criterion of what consequences are *important*. Now a criterion of *importance* presupposes a criterion of values, which is precisely what modern thinkers of the "sociological" and "realistic" schools of jurisprudence have never had. Dean Pound has talked for many years of the "balancing" of interests, but without ever indicating which interests are more important than others or how a standard of weight or fineness can be constructed for the appraisal of "interests." Contemporary "realists" have, in general, either denied absolutely that absolute standards of importance can exist, or else insisted that we must thoroughly understand the facts as they are before we begin to evaluate them. Such a postponement of the problem of values is equivalent to its repudiation. We never shall thoroughly understand the facts as they are, and we are not likely to make much progress towards such understanding unless we at the same time bring into play a critical theory of values. In terms of such a theory, particular human desires and habits are important, and the task of research into legal consequences passes from the realm of vague curiosity to the problem form: How do these rules of law strengthen or change these important habits and satisfy or impede these important desires?

The positive task of descriptive legal science cannot, therefore, be entirely separated from the task of legal criticism. The collection of social facts without a selective criterion of human values produces a horrid wilderness of useless statistics. The relation between positive legal science and legal criticism is not a relation of temporal priority, but of mutual dependence. Legal criticism is empty without objective description of the causes and consequences of legal decisions. Legal description is blind without the guiding light of a theory of values. It is through the union of objective legal science and a critical theory of social values that our understanding of the human significance of law will be enriched. It is loyalty to this union of distinct disciplines that will mark whatever is of lasting importance in contemporary legal science and legal philosophy.

[For a discussion of Cohen's work, see "A Jurisprudential Symposium in Memory of Felix S. Cohen" (1954) 9 Rutgers L. Rev. 341].

Jerome N. Frank, 1889-1957
Judge of United States Court of Appeals, Second Circuit

CARDOZO AND THE UPPER-COURT MYTH (1948)

II

Since Cardozo, when at the bar, was principally an upper-court lawyer, and, in his long tenure on the bench, an upper-court judge (except for a few months), it would have been understandable if he had avowedly limited himself to writing of "The Nature of the Appellate Phases of the Judicial Process." In that event, these books would have deserved the all but uniform praise they have received. But I think they merit a marked criticism almost never voiced: unfortunately, Cardozo purported, without qualification, to describe the entire judicial process. Because of his reputation, the very excellence of his teachings in the narrow appellate field, to which they legitimately pertain, has tended to dampen inquiry in a far larger field where inquiry is far more necessary.

For Cardozo completely by-passed the operations of the trial courts, as if to say either that they had little significance or that their unique decisional activities and distinctive functions had no place in that process. Although, before he used the phrase, the "judicial commencement to its conclusion," Cardozo excluded, as if non-existent, the events occurring in the trial stage of thousands of cases, events which occur in trial courts but never in upper courts: the witnesses testifying, the lawyers examining and cross-examining the witnesses, the jurors listening to the witnesses and to the arguments of the lawyers, the trial judge (when sitting without a jury) passing on the credibility of the witnesses' oral testimony. The omission of all these phenomena – familiar to every trial judge, trial lawyer, and newspaper reporters who "cover the courts" – renders Cardozo's exposition, as a description of how courts work, seriously misleading. Eminently satisfactory as an account of appellate-court ways, it is bizarre as an account of trial-court ways – as bizarre as would be an account of manners at Buckingham Palace if taken as also applicable to rush-hour behavior in the New York subways. Nor was Cardozo's misdescription inadvertent. On the contrary, as we shall see, he grew irritated when his grave omission of trial-court happenings was called to his attention, and did his best to discourage efforts to correct his description.

The omission was grave for this reason: because of it, Cardozo, with seeming justification, could give credence to a gross over-estimation of the reliability and excellence of our courthouse products. "Nine-tenths, perhaps more, of the cases that come before a court," he wrote, "are predetermined – predetermined in the sense that they are predestined – their fate established by inevitable laws that follow them from birth to death." Substitute "upper court" for "court" in that sentence, and it is perhaps not too wide of the mark. It cannot possibly stand up, however, as a characterization of our entire court system. In most instances, when a case has already been decided by a trial court, a capable lawyer can accurately predict what, if an appeal is taken, will be the decision of the upper court. But (for reasons I shall presently canvass) no such easy prediction can be made of most trial-court decisions. Cardozo, by restricting the judicial process to appellate courts, presented a picture of the workings of our court system as, in the main, just, reliable, and steady. That highly inaccurate picture afforded smug satisfaction to much of the legal profession. For, if Cardozo was correct, the judicial process needed comparatively little improvement.

Now the truth is that, for most persons who become involved in litigation, what trial courts do has far more significance than has the performance of upper courts. For not only is the overwhelming majority of decisions not appealed, but in most of the relatively few that are appealed – probably not more than 6 per cent annually – the appellate courts accept as final the trial-court findings of fact. This they do because of a circumstance which accounts for and derives from a unique characteristic of our trial courts: a jury, or a trial judge in a non-jury case, can observe the demeanor of the orally testifying witnesses. The appellate judges cannot. Observation of witnesses' deportment is by no means an infallible method of determining the accuracy of their testimony; but, no better method having been devised, such observation of witnesses, whenever it is possible, is generally deemed essential in our legal system. Judge Learned Hand summarized views often previously expressed by our courts when he said that "that complex of sight and sound, from which we make our conclusions in a courtroom, is in large part eviscerated when reduced to the printed word." As Wigmore put it, "The witness' demeanor . . . is always assumed to be in evidence." A "stenographic transcript," wrote Judge Ulman, " . . . fails to reproduce tones of voice and hesitations of speech that often make a sentence mean the reverse of what the mere words signify. The best and most nearly accurate record is like a dehydrated peach; it has neither the substance nor the flavor of the fruit before it was dried."

It follows that the decisions of trial courts – in which courts alone can the witnesses be seen and heard – determine the fate of, say, 98 per cent of all litigated cases. That 98 per cent Cardozo usually disregarded. For him, a 2 per cent tail wagged a 98 per cent dog. It was as if a meteorologist had founded his studies of weather solely on weather conditions at the equator, or as if a physician had insisted that human health must be studied exclusively in terms of the health of twenty-year-old males. Cardozo, generalizing from wholly insufficient material, was guilty of an unwarranted extrapolation. He basically erred in considering the "facts" of cases as "data," as "given" to the courts. That is true, on the whole, in the appellate phase of that process. It is emphatically not true in its trial phase. The "facts" of cases (as I shall try to show) are not the facts as they actually occurred, not things which exist outside of court. They are usually processed by the trial courts, are their peculiar products. As Judge Olson recently said, "trials are commonly called law suits, but it often seems they might better be called fact suits."

Upper courts concern themselves chiefly with the legal rules and principles. So, too, did Cardozo in his books. As a consequence, for him the judicial process signified little more than the application to facts, already "found," of (1) established rules and principles, or (in occasional "exceptional cases") of (2) new rules and principles brought into being through the "creative" activities of the courts. The same was true of Cardozo's conception of "jurisprudence." His definitions of "law" – composed in part of ingredients taken from Holmes and from Pollock and Maitland – included non-legal materials, but did so only in so far as they contributed to such legal concepts or generalizations: "We shall unite in viewing as law," he wrote, "that body of principle and dogma which with a reasonable measure of probability may be predicted as the basis for judgment in pending or future controversies." I underscore "the," as it high-lights Cardozo's perspective: The "body of principle and dogma," he is saying in effect, should alone be regarded as "the basis of judgment." Nothing is said to indicate that the ascertainment of the facts of a lawsuit also enters into the making of a judgment, so that to predict future judgments one must be able to predict what facts will be ascertained in future cases.

What I am driving at grows clearer in his other definitions: "A principle or rule of conduct so established with reasonable certainty that it *will be enforced by the courts* if its authority is challenged, is . . . a principle or rule of law." Subsequently he expanded this statement into a general definition of "law." After noting that "that word stands for a good many notions," he added: "I find lying around loose, and ready to be emodied into a judgment according to some process of selection to be practised by a judge, a vast conglomeration of principles and rules and usages and moralities. If these are so established as to justify a prediction with reasonable certainty that *they will have the backing of the courts* in the event that their authority is challenged, I say that they are law. . . ." It would waste time to argue whether these definitions of the hopelessly ambiguous word "law" are preferable to one of a dozen or more others. But it is distinctly worth while to point out that his definitions contain phrases which Cardozo never bothered to explain although they shriek for elucidation. I refer to the phrases, "*will be enforced* by the courts," and "*will have the backing* of the courts." If you peer behind those words, you will be gazing at an immense legal jungle (partly explored by Wigmore, in his *Principles of Judicial Proof*, and by others in books written for practicing trial lawyers), a jungle Cardozo disdained to enter – the jungle of trials and trial-court fact-finding.

Without trial-court fact-finding, judicial "enforcement" of the legal rules seldom gets under way. For a court "enforces" or "backs up" a rule only if the court, in some specific lawsuit, holds that the facts which invoke that rule are the facts of that specific case. If, and only if, the court so holds, does it apply that rule to those facts. It follows that a rule is not "enforced" unless a trial court has "found" or purports to have "found" the pertinent facts, *i.e.,* those facts to which the rule applies. It also follows that, in almost any particular case – and therefore in almost all cases – trial-court fact-finding is fully as vital as any legal rule. To the human beings whose specific lawsuits the courts decide, the determinations of the facts have the utmost significance. If the facts are found against a party, he loses. The facts of a case, as found, furnish the ticket to the decision. "No tickee, no washee." For a legal rule is only a conditional statement. It says, "If the facts are thus and so, then these legal consequences ensue."

One would suppose, then, that a study purporting to cover the judicial process, a treatise on "jurisprudence," would include an extensive discussion of the methods of trial-court fact-finding and of the influences that affect it; would explain the multitude of factors involved in it; would emphasize its ineradicable chanciness and uncertainty in most cases, due to the unavoidable fallibility of witnesses, jurors, and trial judges.

Cardozo, however, ignored those topics, and without apologies. This is the more remarkable since, in the single brief passage in which he mentions the function of facts in litigation, he acknowledges their undeniable significance: "In what I have said," he wrote in 1924, "I have thrown, perhaps too much into the background and the shadow the cases where the controversy turns not upon the rule of law, but upon its application to the facts. Those cases, after all, make up the bulk of business of the courts. They are important for the litigants concerned in them. They call for intelligence and patience and reasonable discernment on the part of the judges who must decide them. But they leave jurisprudence where it stood before." A few lines later, he says that "jurisprudence remains untouched, regardless of the outcome" of such cases.

Truly, an astonishing attitude. "Jurisprudence," as Cardozo envisions it, stands aloof from those decisions, "important to litigants," which, according to Cardozo himself, "make up the bulk of the business of the courts." Why this snobbish aloofness on the part of "jurisprudence" when so much is at stake for our citizens? Because, in Cardozo's view, "jurisprudence" is indifferent to anything other than the legal generalizations, the legal rules and principles. Since the "judicial process," for Cardozo, is substantially co-extensive with "jurisprudence," his exposition of the nature of that process likewise cold-shoulders, as unworthy of consideration, the "bulk of the business of the courts."

Having thus artificially circumscribed the judicial process (by admittedly excluding from it the bulk of judicial business), Cardozo reaches a conclusion as to its workings which necessarily is artificial but which affords him much comfort: since (1) but a small percentage of the legal rules lack certainty, and (2) certainty in the judicial process means certainty in rules, it is demonstrable (according to Cardozo's reasoning) that (3) the extent of uncertainty in the judicial process is small. This conclusion (which is correct in respect of appellate courts but otherwise false) has a logical corollary; *i.e.,* experienced, able lawyers, Cardozo implies, can usually predict court decisions with accuracy: he declared that most rules, even those which allow courts some discretion, "have such an element of certainty that, in a vast majority of instances, prediction ceases to be hazardous for the trained and expert judgment." In other words (so Cardozo apparently maintains) competent lawyers can predict the outcome of most lawsuits before trial.

Not only that. "Law," as Cardozo defines it, shows up as largely stable, since "law" consists of the rules. Here, apparently, is cheer for the layman, since, says Cardozo, the "law" will, on the whole, conform to the layman's "reasonable expectations."

The fatal vulnerability of that thesis, – *i.e.,* that legal certainty and the predictability of decisions are measurable by, and correspond to, the certainty of the rules – can be made clear by exposing the error in one of Cardozo's remarks about facts. After noting that the issues in most lawsuits relate "not to the law, but to the facts," he adds: "In countless litigations, the law is so clear that the judges have no discretion." *But trial courts – juries or trial judges trying cases without juries – have an amazing discretion in finding the facts.* When, as happens in most trials, the testimony is oral and the several witnesses disagree concerning the facts, the trial court's discretion in the determination of the facts – based on a selection of some of the witnesses as credible and others as not – usually is utterly uncontrollable. Indeed, the jury system has often been praised just because juries, through general-verdict fact-finding, have a virtually unregulated power to nullify the legal rules; and much the same power is possessed by a trial judge who sits without a jury.

The exercise of this discretion will often paralyze prediction. In the first place, witnesses, being human, are humanly fallible. No one has discovered or invented any instrument or objective method by which a jury or trial judge can pick out those of the witnesses, if any, who accurately observe the facts in dispute, accurately remembered what they observed, and accurately (without bias or prejudice or perjury) report in court their memories of what they observed. Conventional jurisprudence, in turning its back on that difficulty, relies on an implicit postulate or axiom – the Truth-Will-Out Axiom, *i.e.,* that bias, mistakes and perjury are infrequent, abnormal, and that, when they occur in litigation, they are usually uncovered, so that they have slight effects on the outcome of lawsuits. That axiom, completely out of line with observable trial courtroom realities, should be repudiated. Once it is repudiated, it becomes obvious that, in the selection of portions of the testimony on which to rely, the jury or trial judge must make a guess. In this guessy choice, on which fact-finding is constructed, there inheres much inscrutable, un-get-at-able subjectivity: Not only are the reactions of the witnesses, to the past events about which they testify, shot through with subjectivity. So, also, are the reactions of juries or trial judges to the witnesses. For the juries and trial judges are themselves but fallible witnesses of the witnesses. Thus fact-finding encounters multiple subjectivity.

The truth, neglected by Cardozo & Co., is that the facts in dispute in a lawsuit are past events which do not walk into the courtroom; that those actual past "objective" events can be ascertained, at best, only through subjective reactions to the testifying witnesses' subjective reactions; and that, therefore, to speak of "finding" the "facts" is misdescriptive. Therefore, my description of the nature of a legal rule needs revision: a legal rule means, "If the jury or trial judge (expressly or impliedly) says that it believes the facts are thus and so, and if there is some substantial evidence to justify that statement of belief, then these legal consequences ensue."

No third person can tell whether such statements correctly report the beliefs of the juries or trial judges (*i.e.,* whether the statements match their private beliefs); for it is not permitted to examine or cross-examine juries and judges. But even if any such statement did correctly report such belief, no appellate judges could probe the belief to determine whether it matched the actual past facts, the "facts in themselves." For no one can formulate, in the form of rules, the bases of such a belief. The belief is "unruly," one might say. Long ago, Sir Henry Maine, in a passage which has largely escaped attention, pointed to the delicate task of a trial judge "in drawing inferences from the assertion of a witness to the existence of the facts asserted by him. It is in the passage from the statements of the witness to the inference that those statements are true, that judicial inquiries break down." It "is the rarest and highest personal accomplishment of a judge to make allowance for the ignorance and timidity of witnesses, and to see through the confident and plausible liar. Nor can any general rules be laid down for the acquisition of this power, which has methods peculiar to itself, and almost undefinable." Wherefore, as there is no yardstick for measuring the accuracy of a trial court's finding of facts in a case where the testimony is oral and credibility is in issue, often the discretion used in reaching that finding cannot be controlled.

You will search in vain in Cardozo's discourses on the judicial process for any mention of the huge measure of discretion vested in juries and trial judges with respect to the facts. (Indeed, nowhere did he refer to juries.) He wrote as if discretion in the judicial process consisted solely of discretion inhering in the rules or in the selection of rules. That perhaps explains why it never occurred to him to note that it is peculiarly true of jurymen and trial judges – when reacting at trials to witnesses who testify orally – that they are affected by "forces" which lie "deep below consciousness," the "likes and dislikes, the predilections and the prejudices, the complex of emotions and habits and convictions." In the upper courts, as Cardozo noted, those "forces" sometimes somewhat influence the choice of rules. In the trial courts, those "forces" influence, often immeasurably, the choice of facts which is within the wide discretion of jurors and trial judges.

Since that choice is a guess, frequently induced by inscrutable factors, the lawyer, trying to predict a decision, engages in a baffling undertaking: he is trying to predict what facts will be "found," and therefore guessing the future guess of a jury or trial judge. Moreover, before a case is tried, the lawyer's guess often must be about the future guess of a jury, or trial judge, as yet unknown to the lawyer. Necessarily, such a guess is wobbly. It would be wobbly even if all the legal rules and principles were as precise as a table of logarithms, as fixed as the North Star.

How true that it becomes obvious when one considers that in the great majority of suits (*e.g.*, negligence actions and the like) both sides agree as to the applicable rules, the disputes relating to the facts alone. In the light of such cases, it passes understanding that many distinguished legal thinkers, who are rule-obsessed (*i.e.*, who want to believe that decisions are readily foreseeable whenever the pertinent rules are precise), absurdly prattle that clear and definite rules prevent much litigation because (so say these thinkers) most men will not be so foolish as to begin suits in which the relevant rules have such definiteness. Nor can it be ignored that no legal rule, no matter how exact, precludes the injection, by one of the parties to a suit, of an issue of fact which throws open the doors to the reception of oral testimony, and thus to a choice of the "facts" by the trial judge or jury.

These choices of the "facts," resulting from the exercise of the trial courts' guessy discretion, may "leave jurisprudence untouched," but, if so, they leave it looking pretty lifeless, indeed inhuman. The legal rules and principles, the sole foundation of that artificial, ghostly, Cardozian jurisprudence, are stable for the most part, as Cardozo correctly maintains; and, often, predictions of what rules and principles the courts will employ can be fairly exact. Trained lawyers, for example, know the "jurisprudence" relevant to murder trials or automobile accident trials, and can prophesy, with a high degree of reliability, what rules will be applied in such litigation. But what of it? The layman wants to know whether those rules will be applied to the actual facts. If, in a murder case, the correct rule is applied to the wrong facts, an innocent man will be killed by the state. If a trial court, by believing a prejured witness, decides that a deed is a mortgage, the court's legal rule may be impeccable, but the wrong litigant will win.

If, as Cardozo suggests, it be the function of the courts to ensure that, in general, decisions conform to the layman's "reasonable expectations," will a layman consider that a court has discharged its obligations if the legal rules thus conform but, because of an error in fact-finding, the decision in his case does not? As I have said elsewhere: "When the actual facts of a case are not ascertained by a court, its decision may be completely erroneous while yet appearing to be correct. It matters little to a citizen, when he wrongfully loses a lawsuit, whether the decision is the product of the application of the 'wrong' legal rule to the 'right' facts, or the product of the application of the 'right' legal rule to the 'wrong' facts. It is a basic tenet of our theory of justice that cases which are substantially alike should, usually, be decided the same way – according to the same legal rules – and that cases which are substantially different should be decided differently – according to different legal rules. Defects in the ascertainment of the actual facts may result, therefore, in a denial of justice. Because of such defects, cases which, in truth, are very different may seem to the courts to be virtually identical and are decided identically. To the extent, then, that removable defects in fact-finding are not eliminated, proper and practicable individualization of cases does not occur, and avoidable injustice is done."

When one discusses legal certainty and predictability, is it not misleading to discuss merely the certainty of the rules and of predictions as to what rules courts will employ while refusing to talk of decisions? If a man, defeated in a suit because of a mistake of the trial court about the facts, goes to jail or the electric chair, or looses his business, will it solace him to learn that there was no possible doubt concerning the applicable legal principle?

Usually a client wants his lawyer to prophesy a specific decision relating to a matter in which that particular client has a specific interest. The likelihood that the lawyer will successfully predict such a decision will vary with the stage at which he is asked for his opinion:

1. When the client, having just signed a contract, asks what are his rights thereunder, at that time neither the client nor the other party to the contract has as yet taken any steps under the contract. The lawyer's prediction at this stage must include a hazardous guess as to what each of the parties will do or not do in the future. The prediction must frequently be so full of if's as to be of little practical value.

2. After events have occurred which give rise to threatened litigation, the client may inquire concerning the outcome of the suit, if one should be brought.

a. Before the lawyer has interviewed prospective witnesses, his guess is on a shaky foundation.

b. After interviewing them, his guess is less shaky. But, unless the facts are certain to be agreed upon, the guess is still dubious, if the lawyer does not know what judge will try the case; it is more so, if there may be a jury trial, since the lawyer cannot know what persons will compose the jury.

3. After the trial, but before decision, the lawyer's prophecy may be better. For he is now estimating the reaction to the testimony of a known trial judge or a known jury. Yet, if the testimony was oral, that guessing is frequently not too easy.

4. After trial and judgment by the trial court, the guess relates to the outcome of an appeal, should one be taken. It therefore usually relates solely to the rules the upper court will apply to the facts already "found" by the trial judge or jury. At this stage, a competent, trained lawyer can often predict with accuracy. Only this last prediction situation, no others, does Cardozo discuss.

Surely his discussion is altogether too restricted. And surely those interested in the judicial process ought not to disregard such factors, producing uncertainties in decisions, as, *inter alia,* the following: perjured witnesses, coached witnesses, biased witnesses, witnesses mistaken in their observation of facts as to which they testify or in their memory of their observations, missing or dead witnesses, missing or destroyed documents, crooked lawyers, stupid lawyers, stupid jurors, prejudiced jurors, inattentive jurors, trial judges who are stupid or bigoted or biased or "fixed" or inattentive to the testimony. Nor ought humane men ignore the fact that a party may lose a suit he should win because, in preparation for trial, he cannot afford to hire a detective, an engineer, an accountant, or a handwriting expert. Are we, judges and lawyers, to give no heed to such matters and, because of such heedlessness, to do nothing to improve, so far as practicable, the methods of fact-finding in trial courts?

III

None of these matters did Cardozo deign to consider in these books. In banishing such matters from the province of "jurisprudence," and, correlatively, in excluding them from the judicial process, he did a marked social disservice. For if they are thus ostracized, if eminent judges – setting an example to the bar – will not soil their hands with them, but regard them as legal bastards beyond the pale of proper professional notice, who will attend to them?

Someone may say in Cardozo's defense that he followed an established tradition, since few books or articles on jurisprudence had mentioned the vagaries of trials and the obstacles to prediction inhering in fact-finding. But, alas, Cardozo, lent his imposing authority to the strengthening of that tradition. Worse, in 1932, in his last published address on the subject, he severely criticized those writers who, about that time, were calling attention to the grave deficiencies and unfortunate consequences of that tradition. He ascribed to these writers "anarchical professions," expressions manifesting "a petulant contempt" of "order and certainty and rational coherence," an attempted "degradation of the principles, rules and concepts," "a tendency to exaggerate the indeterminacy . . . or chance element" in the decisions of cases, and an advocacy of the position that "conformity and order are to be spurned by the judge as no longer goods at all." He wholly disregarded the fact that several of those he thus criticized were trying to describe, not to praise, the current workings of the trial courts, that their purpose was to show that the description of the judicial process in conventional books on jurisprudence had grossly exaggerated the extent of legal certainty and had led to gross over-estimations of the capacity of lawyers to predict many decisions in particular lawsuits, because, no matter how certain most of the rules and principles might be, the fact-determinations in many lawsuits could not be foretold. He erroneously asserted that these writers regarded as desirable the amount of existing legal imprecision they described. He took their descriptions of existing conditions as manifestations of their aims and desires, of their ideals, their program. When they said, "This is the way things are," in effect he read them as saying, "This is the way things ought to be, the way we want them to be."

I shall dwell on this startling misreading, because it is the key to an understanding of Cardozo's attitude. At first glance, his strictures may appear to have been provoked by his irritation that the descriptions these writers gave of courthouse ways were strikingly at odds with his own relatively tranquil picture of the judicial process. I think, however, that the explanation is more complicated and runs thus: In this 1932 paper, he criticized all those persons unfortunately called "legal realists" but who might better have been labeled adherents of "constructive legal skepticism." Although they had in common a skeptical attitude towards traditional jurisprudence, by no means did they constitute a homogeneous movement, since they disagreed sharply with one another. Nevertheless, they may be roughly divided into two groups:

1. The first and larger group (of whom Llewellyn is representative) may conveniently be labeled "rule-skeptics." They resembled Cardozo in that they had little or no interest in trial courts, but riveted their attention largely on appellate courts and on the nature and uses of the legal rules. Some (not all) of this group (Oliphant being the most conspicuous here) espouse the fatuous notions of "behaviouristic psychology." Some (not all) of these "rule-skeptics" went somewhat further than Cardozo as to the extent of the existent and desirable power of judges to alter the legal rules.

2. The second and smaller group may conveniently be labeled the "fact-skeptics." They importantly diverged not only from conventional jurisprudence but also from the "rule-skeptics." So far as appellate courts and the legal rules are concerned, the views of the "fact-skeptics" as to existent and desirable legal certainty approximated the views of Cardozo, Pound, and many others not categorized as "realists." The "fact-skeptics" divergence sprang from their prime interest in the trial courts. Tracing the major cause of legal uncertainty to trial uncertainties, and claiming that the resultant legal uncertainty was far more extensive than most legal scholars (including the "rule-skeptics") admitted, the "fact-skeptics" urged students of our legal system to abandon an obsessively exclusive concentration on the rules. . . .

IV

In an address in 1931, Cardozo spoke of "the myths that gather around institutions," saying that often such "myths are really the main thing," and "greater than the reality." Maybe those observations were revelatory. For, in all his writings, Cardozo helped to perpetuate what I would call the Upper-Court Myth, the myth that upper-court opinions are "the main thing" in courthouse government. That myth I think deplorable. It bestows upon us appellate judges too much public kudos. It obscures the transcendent importance of trial courts, and the fact that trial judges encounter far greater difficulties than we do. In part, those difficulties inhere in the character of their job; in part they derive from our antiquated trial procedures. To improve the administration of justice we need, at a minimum, to overhaul our jury system; to revise our evidence rules; to give special training for the trial bench; to augment (without displacing the essential aspects of the adversary procedure) the responsibility of government for insuring that all important and practically available evidence is presented in trials. Those and other improvements will not be achieved as long as judges of great eminence, like Cardozo, continue to induce belief in the Upper-Court Myth.

It is high time that we apply to that myth all the skills of what Samuel Butler called the Art of Covery. "This," he said, "is important . . . as Discovery. Surely the glory of finally getting rid of and burying a . . . troublesome matter should be as great as that of making an important discovery."

Karl N. Llewellyn, 1893-1962

ON THE CURRENT RECAPTURE OF THE GRAND TRADITION

(Reprinted from *Jurisprudence*: *Realism in Theory and Practice* by Karl N. Llewellyn by permission of The University of Chicago Press. © 1962 by The University of Chicago).

THE CURRENT RECAPTURE OF THE GRAND TRADITION

To work: Since our reports first begin to accumulate – say 1810 – there have been two well-nigh complete revolutions in the way and theory that deal with how you supreme appellate judges have been going and ought to go about your job. You can test this cleanly by looking, say, at 1859, 1909, and 1959.

In 1859, one era and manner of your work was perhaps beginning to wane, though it was still definitely dominant – say, like a moon one or two days after full. Roscoe Pound has called this general period our "formative period" when his eye was on the rather lovely building of doctrine in that time. In a happier phrase, he has also called it our "classic period." Then he was thinking of the method.

I call it our Grand Style, or the Manner of Reason. The essence is, I think, that every current decision is to be tested against life-wisdom, and that the phrasing of the authorities which build our guiding structure of rules is to be tested and is at need to be vigorously recast in the new light of what each new case may suggest either about life-wisdom, or about a cleaner and more usable structure of doctrine. In any event, and as overt marks of the Grand Style: "precedent" is carefully regarded, but if it does not make sense it is ordinarily re-explored; "policy" is explicitly inquired into; alleged "principle" must make for wisdom as well as for order if it is to qualify as such, but when so qualified it acquires peculiar status. On the side both of case-law and of statutes, where the reason stops there stops the rule; and in working with statutes it is the normal business of the court not only to read the statute but also to implement that statute in accordance with purpose and reason.

And also, if I may return to my opening: the writing judge has neither any illusion that he is or ought to be a Pythian priest, nor has he any illusion of freedom to move as he wills. He does recognize, indeed, the duty to make a solid case on the authorities. But my reading has turned up only one judge who (according to my sniffer) was completely ready to *distort* them in the interest of *his* will. Reasonable, lawyer-like arrangement of authorities in a good cause, even if slightly skewed, – that I am not denying. What I am saying, and this is important, is that for most judges on most occasions – should I guesstimate over 90 per cent? – this was in no way under cover, and that policy – which means the *reason* of *the situation* – was a normal, overt and sometimes lengthy subject of discussion. Thus, as of 1859.

By 1909 such practice had become exceptional, the ideal of it, *even the idea* of it was all but dead, and most lawyers, indeed most sitting judges, either knew, or thought, or felt, any such way of appellate deciding to be simply wrong, and, praise be, absent. Statutes, moreover, tended to be read unfavorably, and even when seen favorably, they tended to be limited to the letter. . . .

But when you are now reminded of the fact that that way and ideal of work dominated the American appellate bench – great judges and mediocre judges alike – for more than half a century, then you should see and feel at once that the open and conscious quest for the reasonable rule *for the type-situation* which characterizes the work of the American State Supreme Court today, so far from being ground for unease, should be a basis for rich pride. What it means is that your branch of the profession has performed a truly amazing feat. Within fifty years, without conscious planning, in the teeth of the conscious image of duty and of correct craftsmanship misinculcated in your legal youth and insisted upon loudly and bitterly by the whole vocal bar, you have yet managed to work your way back to a daily way of judging which has almost recaptured the full Grand Tradition of the Common Law.

I speak of the American Supreme Bench in general; but I feel safe. I have studied New York at all periods, with closely examined mine-run samplings from 1939, 1940, 1951, and 1958. I have studied Ohio in 1844, 1939-40, 1953, and 1958. In Massachusetts, North Carolina, Pennsylvania, and Washington there have been sustained studies from fifteen or twenty years ago and then from full current samplings as well – all mine-run stuff, the reported cases taken in sequence as they appear. Nine other states, West, South, and Middle West, were studied in full current samplings. In each instance the material tested runs regardless of subject matter, accounts to "unfavorable" as well as "favorable" material, and reaches at least a majority of the judges on the court. There have also been a number of intensive borings, especially into Illinois material, to test the possibility of getting further light by approaches from other angles. Results: the historical comparisons show that the march toward recapture of the Grand Style is unmistakable, strong, steady, and increasing. The fifteen current samplings seem to me conclusive that almost no state can have escaped its influence. It is, I repeat, an amazing achievement, and it is more than time that it should become a source not only of conscious pride but of that even more effective craftsmanship which can be generated when men add to a sound feeling for the job a conscious study directed to improving the know-how of the craft.

Before moving on to a few suggestions which the best work, older or current, holds out for any work of every day, let me take a precaution against possible misunderstanding. When I speak of overt resort to and discussion of sense as an opinion-daily phenomenon of current judging among American Supreme Courts, I do *not* mean merely such discussion in regard to the *application* of the rule. Neither do I mean such discussion merely in regard to a *choice* between two so-called competing rules or principles. I refer to open, reasoned, extension, restriction or reshaping of the relevant rules, done in terms not of the equities or sense of the particular case or of the particular parties, but instead (illuminated indeed by those earthy particulars) done in terms of the sense and reason of some significantly seen *type* of life-*situation.* A short speech is no place to develop what has cost me a 500-page book. I give a single illustration. Oregon had a precedent, based on soapy window-washing water on a sloping sidewalk, that was cast in terms of "not creating a hazard or adding to the danger of pedestrians who might use the sidewalk, by placing thereon, or, if so placed, in not removing therefrom, any matter that would cause a slippery or dangerous condition." Some snow fell in Portland, was cleared from steps onto an embankment, melted and ran, and, overnight, left a small patch of ice on the sloping sidewalk. The plaintiff slipped and was injured. What the court did not was to "apply." What it did, in the light of "negligence" "principle" plus some aversion to "strict liability," and in the light of three well considered Eastern cases, was to diagnose a new significant *situation*: "snow-clearance by the abutter," and to adopt a *new rule* to further general public convenience by freeing such clearing from risks of liability merely for refreezing.

The case simultaneously brings out another of the more striking phenomena of modern advance sheets. The courts search for, and then quote in some fullness, among out-of-state opinions as well as among home opinions, cases which give not only a rule but also *a persuasive presentation of good life-reason in the light of the type life situation.* Now I shall be slow to be persuaded that it is, as yet (though God grant it may soon be), the *general* habit of the bar to dig out and brief-quote this type of opinion in particular; and rarely is the presence of any such given reason even suggested by either digest or encyclopedia. The labor of this increasingly general quest thus indicates to me one of two things: either a hunger of the writing judge for situation-reason, before he can himself be satisfied, and then, in true Common Law Grand Tradition, his hunger also for merging that situation-reason with authority; or else it shows that, as a skilled man who wishes to keep or capture votes among his brethren, he knows this kind of material to be what they will go for. This is the sweetest dilemma any disciple and preacher of the Grand Tradition can ask to be impaled on. Either horn is honey. Neither will I be put off by any judge's conviction and assertion that he never writes to capture votes, that he writes merely his best version of the facts, the law, and the sound and right decision – let votes or heavens fall where they may. No judge of such conviction can deprive me of my comfort. For he could not be a judge unless he was a lawyer. And a lawyer either is no lawyer at all, or else as he shapes up a matter he puts its best foot forward. And a lawyer – including an appellate judge writing for his own conscience (but also to get his duty done, of a right resolution of the litigation in hand) – may indeed not think consciously about the particular tribunal he has in front of him. But his lawyer's instinct does a lot of that kind of work without his having to do conscious thinking. . . .

. . . [W]hy should you not *generally*, instead of at odd moments, bring this principle of warning and this practice of two-stage to bear on the problem of overruling, as well as of any other change or warning? There is no time to develop this. I ask you only to think about three questions:

(1) If the argument and study in a case persuade you that a rule in the immediate area is ready to fall in the next wind, I am suggesting that warning of that is by any discoverable standard of decency as much needed as can possibly be the carving out of a little Swiss cheese hole in any pending decision.

(2) If the case in hand just slips in under an exception (so to speak, "on other grounds") to a rule which the argument has persuaded you no longer fits

our people: why is this not the perfect opportunity to give, in regard to a rule, the warning notice which every man of you is willing to give with regard to an exception?

You will observe that what I am here urging, to wit, the considered expression that "When we get a clean chance, we will extirpate," does not even touch the problem of the *Sunburst Oil* case.

And yet, as far as my limited reading goes, this easier and more useful method has found more resistance among you gentlemen and your brethren than has even the bold move of deciding the pending case by the old rule, while announcing a new rule (or a new approach to a statute) for the future. I think that this difference is because you have been (rightly) trained to think protection against retroactive "law" to be not only decency, but *your* office; while you have also been mistrained to think that your office has no part in prophecy. But surely *any* good case-law judgment is in its best part a combination of prophecy and of clean guidance toward fulfillment thereof. In any event:

(3) Why do not the principle of warning, and the practice and policy of two-stage operation become a standard approach to possible overruling, prospective overruling, and to the case which has, in itself, to be expected from the overruling – easing all of these, while it effectively warns the bar, and also opens up whatever may be elicited to inform the court before the final leap?

The last matter which refuses to be left without mention is that of the statutes. Here the image of 1909 – "We must accept what is written, we have only to read the [so frequently non-existent] "intent of the legislature,' we have no *power* to add," etc. – modified only by the 1959 willingness to abdicate self-will and to try to make sense – here, I say, the image of 1909 stalks not only active (though most intermittently) but vicious.

The simple basic principle which expresses both the Grand Manner and today's need is this: It is contrary to a Supreme Court's duty, and therefore to its power, to allow any statute to remain as an undigested and indigestible lump in the middle of Our Law.

Even the most formal judges of the Formal Period recognized this principle. Their response was sound in terms of office-instinct: The Law does call for wholeness. Their response was not good, in terms of measure. They refused to participate in the intrusion. They excreted what they could, via unconstitutionality. They walled off the rest by literalistic construction.

That is past, in regard to the particular. But it is still with us at odd moments, and vigorously whenever a court settles down to a sermon on its lack of power over the written word.

But in my current samplings

(a) I have found no single court which, even if it mouths the statute-image of 1909 today, cannot also be found *operating* in conflict with that image, and in an approach to the Grand Approach to statutes, on the same opinion-day or on the next.

(b) Nor have I found any court which, *judged on a sequence of cases*, is not moving with regard to statutes about as freely in the average as it is in the case-law field. This holds also for the 1939-1940 and 1944 work examined from six courts. What you get in the statutory field is a jerkier, less predictable movement: here more of a hitch, there a sudden jump, so to speak, under cover; with no adequate guidance, as to when which will occur.

That is not healthy judging. . . .

Herbert Wechsler, 1909-
Harlan Fiske Stone, Professor of Constitutional Law, Columbia University

THE NATURE OF JUDICIAL REASONING

[T]hey [the courts] cannot escape the obligation of interpreting the open-ended concepts framed as limitations upon government, like guarantees of "the freedom of speech and of the press," "due process of law," or "equal protection of the laws," even though it involves passing upon action of the other branches resting on a choice of values, as invariably action does.

These affirmations forced me to consider whether there are any standards to be followed in interpreting such open-ended clauses, criteria that both the Supreme Court and those who undertake to praise or to condemn its judgments are morally and intellectually obligated to support. Noting that the history of our politics is rich with illustration of the way in which opposing factions have felt free to manipulate their constitutional positions to advance or hinder interests they supported, be it those of capital or labor, shipping or manufacturing, slavery or abolition, radicals or businessmen, I asked if something else is not required of the courts, whose only competence to intervene derives from their sworn duty to apply the law and to regard the Constitution as the supreme law. Putting the question differently, I asked how determinations that do not derive from any true compulsion of the text or even of its earlier interpretation can be asserted to have a legal quality.

My answer was "that the main constituent of the judicial process is precisely that it must be genuinely principled, resting with respect to every step that is involved in reaching judgment on analysis and reasons quite transcending the immediate result that is achieved." Granting that "the courts decide, or should decide, only the case they have before them," I suggested that they must "decide on grounds of adequate neutrality and generality, tested not only by the instant application but by others that the principles imply"; and that it is "the very essence of judicial method to insist upon attending to such other cases, preferably those involving an opposing interest, in evaluating any principle avowed."

Reverting to Judge Hand's contention that a constitutional interpretation based on any other ground than the historical intendment of provisions having ascertainable specific content casts the courts in the role of a third legislative chamber, I asked if there is not a vital difference between legislative freedom to appraise the gains and losses in projected measures and the kind of principal appraisal, in respect of values that can reasonably be asserted to have constitutional dimension, that alone is in the province of the courts. I argued that there is a difference; and, moreover, that the difference yields a middle ground between a judicial House of Lords and the abandonment of any limitation on the other branches – a middle ground consisting of judicial action that embodies what are surely the main qualities of law, its generality and its neutrality.

If I had been content to put this general position without testing it by concrete illustration, I doubt if I would have provoked substantial disagreement, since few among us really think it proper for the courts to act by fiat rather than as organs and expositors of law, in a sense that implies a limitation of this kind. But deeming it important to delineate the point of the position by some challenging examples of its application, I selected three great cases in which the Supreme Court sustained egalitarian contentions, with which I am deeply sympathetic, upon grounds that seemed to me deficient in the quality of principled neutrality and generality for which I asked. The cases all involved the interpretation of the clause of the Fourteenth Amendment that forbids a state to deny to any person within its jurisdiction the equal protection of the laws, and each involved the overruling of an earlier decision. The first was the decision that a Negro voter excluded from the Democratic party and declared ineligible to vote in the party primary election by a resolution of the party was denied equal protection by the state. The second was the holding that a state denies equal protection if the state courts enforce a racially restrictive covenant against an owner or successor who attempts to break it. The third was the decision that state segregation of the public schools violates equal protection because it discriminates against the Negro, even though the schools for Negroes equal those for whites in every other way except the color of the students.

I shall confine myself to dealing with the covenant, where it is easiest to make the point involved. The Court's opinion rested the decision on the simple ground that the covenant embodied a discrimination and that the enforcement order of the court is action of the state. Both of these propositions are correct. Yet I submit that it is clear that they do not suffice to uphold the judgment, unless it is affirmed that a private discrimination becomes a discrimination by the state whenever it is legally enforced. But such a proposition is absurd and would destroy the law of wills and a good portion of the law of property, which is concerned precisely with supporting owner's rights to make discriminations that the state would not be free to make on the initiative of officials. Hence, I suggest that this was not a principled decision in the sense that is demanded of the courts.

In saying this, I do not, of course, deny that it would be entirely proper for a legislature to enact a law forbidding the enforcement of racially restrictive covenants, or even for a court with general jurisdiction over the reshaping of the law of contracts or of equitable remedies to declare the covenant invalid or to deny its enforcement by injunction. I not only consider such a statute or decision permissible; I consider it entirely proper. But the Supreme Court had no authority to enact such a statute or to deal generally with the law of contracts or of remedies. It claimed no such authority. Its sole competence was to give meaning to a general provision forbidding a state to deny the equal protection of the laws. Nothing in that provision accords relevance to the particular impact of restrictive covenants concerning land as distinguished from other kinds of discriminatory agreements or discriminations in the use or disposition of property. If the enforcement of the owners' discrimination made it that of the state in the case of the covenant, the tenement owner's refusal to lease, the store owner's refusal to sell, the testator's discriminatory devise must equally become the discriminatory action of the state if enforced by a state court. That is, indeed, precisely what has now been argued in the sit-in cases – that a state discriminates against Negroes if it enforces the general law of trespass against persons excluded by an owner upon racial grounds. If that proposition is unacceptable, as I believe it will prove to be, can the covenant decision be defended – or is it an *ad hoc* determination, as I argued, lacking the generality required of decisions of the courts?

Professor Wechsler is here defending and re-interpreting his thesis of "neutral principles" of the Holmes Lecture (1959) 73 *Harv. L. Rev.* 1, later incorporated in his *Principles, Politics, and Fundamental Law* (1961). His paper here is a contribution to a symposium on judicial reasoning in which the first paper was by Professor Levi. Wechsler welcomes Levi's interpretation of his thesis, viz. "that a judge who makes changes in the law must take seriously the duty of reworking the pattern of the law" [*Law and Philosophy* 274 (Hook ed. 1964)].

Joseph O'Meara, 1898-
Dean, Notre Dame Law School

NATURAL LAW AND EVERYDAY LAW (1960)

Like most terms "natural law" has had, and has, a variety of meanings. In most of its meanings it touches scarcely at all the professional concerns of the lawyer but moves, rather, on a plane widely separated from his daily cares and duties. Thus, for the most part, natural law stands aloof from the urgent here-and-now with which lawyer and judge necessarily are preoccupied; it inhabits a world apart.

Relevant in this connection is a comment by Canon Leclercq, Professor of Moral and Social Philosophy at the Catholic University of Louvain:

> . . . The term "natural law" is currently fashionable, especially among Catholics who seek a rallying point against relativism. There are, therefore, many people fond of using it, and they bring it up on any pretext, as other men use the term "sociology."

I venture to think he is right – on both counts.

In these remarks I hope to suggest an approach to natural law which will make it useful on a day-to-day basis in the perplexities by which practitioners and judges constantly are confronted. I shall talk more about the judge than about the practitioner, though I have been the latter but never the former. I make no apology, however, since, after all, it is not necessary to be a concert artist to distinguish between a baritone and a basso.

Specifically, I suggest that natural law fruitfully may be regarded as the contribution which ethics can make to law.

But "law" itself is a word of many meanings; and one of the least profitable of scholarly enterprises is the seemingly endless endeavor to prove that it really means this or that and nothing else. In fact, language being conventional, law means all the things to which it properly is applied within the confines of accepted usage. In the customary language of lawyers, it refers chiefly to constitutions, judicial decisions and legislative enactments and, more particularly, to the rules of conduct they embody. In this sense, law is an accumulation of "rules which will be enforced by the government . . . or to which it will at least provide forcible means to secure conformity."

If that is what law is and all that it is, it is hard to see how natural law in any of its meanings could make a significant contribution to it, save insofar as natural law may guide legislators in their consideration of pending measures. But I am not here concerned with legislators. I am concerned with practicing lawyers and judges, especially the latter; and it may be that the widespread habit of regarding law as an accumulation of rules is in part responsible for the ineffectiveness of natural law so far as concerns the practical affairs of professional life. How could it be otherwise if law is simply an aggregation of already existing rules? In that situation, what part is there for natural law to play, except perhaps the negative role of calling in question the moral authority of a rule when it exceeds the limits of reason?

As appears from what I have just said, I do not envisage natural law as the arbiter of legal validity. "Law is law, whether it be good or bad." But this raises a problem: what is a judge to do when the relevant legal materials (constitutions, legislative enactments, decided cases and, on occasion, executive orders, administrative rulings and the like) necessitate a result which he cannot square with his conscience, for example, the Nazi confiscation laws? I answer: resign. "Tyranny is tyranny," as Judge Learned Hand has said, "no matter what its form; the free man will resist it if his courage serves." In this Country, indeed, we cannot well deny the right of revolution without illegitimating ourselves. But, I submit, only those in private life are free to resist: it seems to me obviously inadmissible for a public official to attack what he is sworn to uphold. And this is true, in my opinion, of all forms of resistance, from civil disobedience to subversion to armed rebellion. Yes, if a judge's conscience gets in the way of performance of his official duties, the only course open to him is resignation.

Well, then, what role is there for natural law to play? What contribution can it make? Comparatively little, so far as I can see, if law be no more than an aggregation of already existing rules. But law must be regarded as a good deal more than that. It seems to me convenient and useful to think of law as a living process for the just resolution of never-ending human controversies. If law is regarded in this light, as a process of decision, it comes alive, is responsive to changing human needs; and the way is cleared for a positive contribution by natural law, as I shall attempt to show.

This, of course, presupposes that the judge is not an automaton proceeding mechanically according to predetermined rules. I shall not dwell on this, for I assume it is now generally recognized that, in many if not most litigated cases, there is no logical necessity for deciding one way rather than another; that is to say, logical application of the relevant legal materials does not require one and only one result.

It may be useful, though, to consider briefly why this should be. According to Dr. Alexis Carrel, "every man is a history unlike all others." Similarly, every lawsuit is unique; each is a history unlike all others. It does not follow that law is a wilderness of single instances. Common-law judges reason from case to case by resemblance or analogy. For the purpose in hand a case may be regarded as analogous or comparable to other cases previously decided, that is, as duplicating their significant features and thus as presenting essentially the same question. To this recurring question common-law judges habitually give the same answer their predecessors gave. That, in short, is the Doctrine of Judicial Precedent. Save in rare instances, judges are bound by this doctrine to decide every case in a way which will make a consistent pattern with the decisions in comparable cases in the past. But this involves problems of appraisal, evaluation and choice. Is this case really comparable to those urged upon him by this side or that? Does a certain circumstance present here, not present there, alter the picture essentially or only in an immaterial detail? Plaintiff's authorities present a persuasive analogy; defendant constructs a cogent argument on altogether different precedents. In short, there are two sides to every question. Thus many if not most cases that come before a court for decision present, in greater or less degree, a hitherto unsolved problem – and one which cannot be postponed to another day. For it is the judge's duty as well as his prerogative to decide. This is the Anglo-American common-law system.

I have been talking about cases which turn on prior judicial decisions, precedents; but what I have said is equally true of constitutions and statutes. One cannot simply look at a constitution – or at a statute – and find there the answers to all of the questions arising under it which a court must decide. There are persuasive reasons for deciding many of these questions one way as well as another.

In large part, indeed, constitution and statute do no more than provide alternatives or set limits on decision.

So the judge has choice thrust upon him, as Judge Hand has recognized: "Like every public functionary, in the end [judges] are charged with the responsibility of choosing but of choosing well." Creative, therefore, the judge's function inescapably is, and this involves the exercise of discretion though not, of course, unlimited discretion. The judge exercises discretion because there is no escape from doing so; but decision is never at large, discretion being limited to choosing between alternatives within the framework of our traditional approach to legal problems.

Thus the sharp distinction, commonly drawn, between the law-that-is and the law-that-ought-to-be is unrealistic, for the simple reason that the so-called law-that-*is* in important part is a myth: it is fictitious – and inhibiting and mischievous as well – so far as concerns those numerous questions I have alluded to, namely, doubtful questions.

But if this be so, if precedent and constitution and statute, instead of supplying clear-cut answers, so often point simultaneously in more than one direction, to what is a judge to turn?

Now, of course, there is no problem if the relevant legal materials do not speak to the question or speak ambiguously, or with more than one voice. In that event, obviously, if the question is to be answered, the answer must be sought elsewhere, beyond the relevant legal material – in short, outside the law. Thus in very truth legal problems are solved by recourse to non-legal considerations.

To be sure, the naive idea appears to be entertained by some British scholars that solving legal problems is a simple matter, requiring little more than precise delimitation of terms. But, as Hohfeld saw clearly, describing words by metes and bounds can do no more than sharpen issues; it cannot solve the problems on which, in the end, decision turns in doubtful cases – problems of appraisal, evaluation and choice. Solution of such problems involves a great deal more than semantics; it necessitates recourse to substantive considerations; and, since legal problems seldom if ever arise unless legal materials leave the answer in doubt, these substantive considerations must be nonlegal considerations.

But what nonlegal considerations? If decision is not to be capricious there must be some criteria of choice among possible solutions. What are the nonlegal criteria for solution of legal problems?

Mr. Justice Cardozo has suggested that the judge's duty is to conform to the "standards of the community, the *mores* of the times." But there are conflicting standard and mores at any given date. How is the judge to know which standards to follow? Should he make up a Gallup-poll approach and thus seek guidance from the multitude? Even if he should, can he? Has he the facilities necessary to do this? Of course he has not. To attempt to conduct a poll, in the words of Judge Hand, "would be fantasically absurd."

What, then, should the judge do? Should he guess what a poll would show and let that determine choice? Yes, says Judge Hand. The judge, he says, is "confined to the best guess he can make of how such a poll would result." He says that in respect of cases turning on a moral issue. No reason appears, however, why the judge should not be similarly confined in any case in which public attitudes, impulses and aspirations are thought of as decisive. But if that is all he has to go by, his conjecture of how a poll would turn out, the judge is at sea without a compass on a starless night.

Nevertheless, if Hand is right, he must take what might be called a "constructive" poll; for Hand insists that the judge is an "organ of the social will" and must be free "by interpretation to manifest the half-framed purposes of his time"; his mission is by "divination" to discover "the deeper moods of [his] time"; he must be "an articulate organ of the half-understood aspirations of living men, constantly recasting and adapting existing forms, bringing to the high light of expression the dumb impulses of the present." Only so, says Hand, "can [judges] continue in the course of the ancestors whom they revere." Then judges must be seers; and, if that be so, who is to man the bench?

But suppose judges were seers. Would that help, for example, on intricate questions of commercial law, involving sales, negotiable instruments and complicated security arrangements? Whatever dumb impulses might be able to divine would help not at all, I suggest, in such complexities nor, it seems plain, in any other technical dilemma. So, even the gift of divination would avail little in the run of cases.

But suppose a populace sophisticated enough to have opinions on technical problems. What then? Having ascertained these opinions, would the judge be bound to follow them? And every time they change must his judgment change? "Assuming it to exist at all," Judge Hand points out, "there is nothing more impalpable, nebulous and fugitive than common will, as any political doctor will agree."

Other problems must be faced if the judge is bound to follow the popular will. Must he follow the popular will of the Nation as a whole, or as it is reflected on a regional basis, or on a State or local basis? If he be an elected judge, must he think first of his constituents? Or is he bound to take a wider view? And, if so, how wide?

Assuming these questions settled, and that the opinions of the multitude on legal problems could somehow be ascertained, are we prepared to say the judge is duty bound to abide by them? Would we accept the consequences of an affirmative reply? What would happen to the Fifth Amendment? – for that matter, to the whole of the Bill of Rights, to the Constitution itself?

Enough of this. The very idea of the judge as a political barometer is obnoxious; in our Western tradition nothing could be more out of character.

Is there help from some other quarter? Yes, says Hand: the judge can appeal to his predecessors on the bench whose decisions, when he seeks to apply them in more or less altered circumstances, turn out to be equivocal. That actually is what he does, according to Judge Hand:

> . . . Although at times he says and believes that he is not doing so, *what* [the judge] *really does is to* take the language before him, whether it be from a statute or from the decision of a former judge, and *try to find out what* the government, or *his predecessor, would have done, if the case before him had been before them.* (Emphasis supplied.)

The judge cannot possibly find out how another judge, very likely a stranger to him and very likely long since dead, would have decided a case which, for that other judge, never existed. If you were somebody else, who would you be? Indeed, Judge Hand himself recognizes that "it is impossible to know" how another would have decided. Are we to believe, then, that an adult, twentieth-century judge actually spends his energies trying to solve conundrums? I find it hard to accept the notion that judges occupy their time trying to find out what "it is impossible to know," namely, how some other judge in the past would have decided a case which only now has arisen.

If, nevertheless, that really is what the judge does, as Hand says it is, how can he be the interpreter of "the half-framed purposes" and "the deeper moods of his time"? How can he be "an articulate organ of the half-understood aspirations of living men"? And if he be "an articulate organ of the half-understood aspirations of living men," how can he obey Judge Hand's admonition on other occasions to respect and follow "the law as it is" instead of "a factitious common will"?

With all respect, I can find in Judge Hand's counsel only confusion and contradiction – confusion and contradiction embroidered with the allure of style.

The question remains: where is the judge to turn for help in answering unanswered problems? He cannot shift responsibility to his judicial predecessors nor to the men and women of his time. Is there nowhere he can turn?

Dean Pound has advanced a variation of Cardozo's suggestion that judgment should conform to the "standards of the community, the *mores* of the times." Modern jurists, says Pound, "are content to search for the ideals of the age and to set them up as a guide." But the ideals of the age are always in flux. At any given time and place there are conflicting and competing ideals; and now this, now that is ascendant. How, then, are the ideals of the age to be identified? It cannot be simply a matter of "count[ing] heads, without any appraisal of the voters." If no more than that were involved, we would be back to a Gallup poll, confronting all of the difficulties I have pointed out; confronting them, moreover, in the most exaggerated form, with the inquiry broadened from the here-and-now to embrace the age.

But if the weight of numbers does not determine choice among competing ideals, the selection must be based on worth. That, however, involves a value judgment, requiring the judge to decide according to his own intellect, experience and conscience.

There is no escape, Let the judge extract all the instruction which can be got from judicial precedent. Still, the case now pending never arose before; to some extent it differs from all earlier cases. Someone must settle whether the differences are essential and, accordingly, whether the same or a different pattern of decision should be followed. Or perhaps the case can be fitted nicely into either of two competing lines of authority. Which shall it be? The judge does not usurp authority when he decides; he would default in his duty if he did not decide. *This* case must be decided *now*, and in our Anglo-American common-law system the judge is the official authorized – and required – to perform that office. Thus the judge's role necessarily is a creative one – he must legislate; there is no help for it. And, I submit, when the critical moment comes and he must say yea or nay, he is on his own; he has nothing to rely on but his own intellect, experience and conscience.

Hence, if decision is not to be capricious, it seems obvious there must be some criteria of choice among the alternatives which virtually every case presents. But what criteria of choice?

I do not now undertake to answer fully. I suggest merely that the criteria should include the principles of natural law; in other words, when the nature of the case warrants, the judge should turn for guidance to relevant ethical principles – those principles of conduct, that is, "which [are] in keeping with man's nature as it would if it were able to resolve its disharmonies and to surmount its imperfections."

These principles are, to be sure, nonspecific, and we all remember the dictum of Mr. Justice Holmes that "general propositions do not decide concrete cases." But they do, indeed they do. In Whitehead's words, "the ideals cherished in the souls of men enter into the character of their actions." For example, as he has pointed out,

> . . . Millions of men have marched to battle fiercely nerved by intense faith in law imposed by the will of inflexible Allah, Law sharing out to each

human his inevitable fate, Law sharing out to each faithful Mahometan either victory, or death and Paradise. Millions of Buddhists have shunned the intrinsic evils of such fierce Mahometan emotion relying on the impersonal immanence of Law, made clear to them by the doctrines of the Buddha.

For present purposes the principles of ethics may be compared, fruitfully it seems to me, to the polestar of the mariner – if I may talk in such terms in this day of radar. Now, the polestar is of no use if a fire breaks out aboard, and in a hundred other ways it will avail nothing whatsoever; but it helps to keep the ship on course. That, I suggest, is what these principles can do for the judge; they can help to keep the legal ship on course.

Are they absolutes? Someone is sure to ask: are these principles absolutes? That, if I may say so, is the language of debate, not of inquiry. I think it likely that many of those who argue fiercely pro and con about absolutes have not bothered to look very closely at what they are talking about. Generally they seem not to appreciate, for one thing, "the difficulty of making language express anything beyond the familiarities of daily life." So, exaggerated claims are met by sweeping denials, both sides acting as if words were as precise as mathematical symbols.

If, instead of being queried about absolutes, I am asked whether there are enduring values, I answer categorically. The position of the ethical relativist is untenable. Times and attitudes change and there is no doubt about it. But it does not follow that everything changes and all is flux. On the contrary, "under the turbulence of change there is a bedrock of unchanging values." Could Hitler's concentration camps be anything but evil – anywhere, ever? Could the compassion of the Good Samaritan be anything but good – anywhere, ever? There are some things, then, which are evil in their very nature and therefore evil at all times and in all places; similarly, there are some things which are good in their nature and therefore good at all times and in all places. It may be that the list of things essentially evil – or good – is not very extensive; and no doubt there would be dispute as to what the list should include. I venture to suggest, though, that, in his innermost being, every man acknowledges there are some things which cannot be right and some which cannot be wrong. Indeed, I suspect the area of disagreement is much smaller than the alarms of partisans would lead one to suppose.

What I have suggested offends an admonition by Judge Hand, contained in his eulogy of those who taught him in the Harvard Law School:

> . . . You cannot raise the standard against oppression, or leap into the breach to relieve injustice, and still keep an open mind to every disconcerting fact, or an open ear to the cold voice of doubt. . . .
>
> Many years ago in this place I sat under men who resisted all such allurements; men who believed that the pursuit of knowledge was enough to absorb all their powers and more. They taught me, not by precept, but by example, that nothing is more commendable, and more fair, than that a man should lay aside all else, and seek truth; not to preach what he might find; and surely not to try to make his views prevail; but, like Lessing, to find his satisfaction in the search itself. These men did not seek to rebuild the world nearer to the heart's desire; they were content to be themselves, confident that, if they were faithful in that, their light would shine, steady and far.

While these words describe primarily Hand's ideal for the scholar, my reading of the address in which they appear indicates that it is likewise his ideal for the judge.

But pure knowledge, with which alone the judge no less than the scholar should be concerned, if Hand is right, is a mirage, as Whitehead has made clear:

> . . . You cannot consider wisdom or folly, progress or decadence, except in relation to some standard of judgment, some end in view. . . .
>
> . . . the notion of "mere knowledge" is a high abstraction which we should dismiss from our minds. Knowledge is always accompanied with accessories of emotion and purpose.

The weight of history, I suggest, is likewise against Hand. The great majority of common-law judges have been active men, trained in the school of practical affairs, who believed they had a mission and took it seriously – a mission that cannot rightly be described in terms of the acquisition of knowledge. And so they had. The judge is not a eunuch on the bench any more than he is a ventriloquist's dummy. I cannot imagine a worthy judge who is not the personification of a fierce partisanship for justice. Nor am I troubled by my inability to capture and confine within a definition the animating principle of justice. Justice is an aspiration lifting men to the heights, no less potent because its spirit eludes expression in verbal formula.

But will not all this lead to personal justice? The best answer, I submit, is that it hasn't. There has been plenty of opportunity, for common-law judges have been deciding cases for a long time. And, I submit, they have been deciding doubtful questions according to their own intellect, experience and conscience – the only course, I suggest, open to a conscientious judge.

The judicial office in common-law countries is hedged about with built-in safeguards. The humility and respect for the opinions of others which characterize a worthy judge will protect him from riding his hobbies. As a great judge has pointed out, "Something of Pascal's spirit of self-search and self-reproach must come at moments to the man who finds himself summoned to the duty of shaping the progress of the law." In fact, as we all know, for whatever reason, judges tend to be conservative and

> . . . are curiously timid about innovations. A judge who will hector the bar and browbeat the witnesses and who can find a warrant in the Fourteenth Amendment for stifling a patently reasonable legislative experiment, will tremble at the thought of introducing a new exception into the hearsay rule.

And there are other, external safeguards. We are all fenced in by the age in which we live, and by the conditions, traditions and circumstances of our calling. Lawyers and judges, with few exceptions, share a common outlook; and this provides an automatic and unnoticed check on discretion, except in times of revolutionary upheaval. There are, moreover, in Cardozo's words,

> . . . restrictions not easy to define, but felt, however impalpable they must be, by every judge and lawyer [which] hedge and circumscribe his action. They are established by the traditions of the centuries, by the example of other judges, his predecessors and his colleagues, by the collective judgment of the profession, and by the duty of adherence to the pervading spirit of the law.

Congress could cut off appropriations for the other branches of government. The President could declare martial law, arrest the members of Congress and send them to a concentration camp. What restrains the President and Congress? In the final analysis, nothing but our common commitment to liberty ordered by reason under the guidance of our democratic heritage and aspirations. That, too, must be our reliance against abuse of judicial power – along with the safeguards already mentioned, the traditions and ideals of the legal profession and the watchfulness of the Bar.

This, of course, underlines the Bar's duty to subject the work of courts to constant, searching criticism – but informed criticism, not hysterical or partisan clamor.

To sum up, natural law in its usual meanings is not very helpful in the day-to-day problems of professional life. This could be remedied, I suggest, and natural law made much more fruitful if it were thought of as the contribution to law which can be made by ethics. At the same time, of course, it would be necessary to think of law as a process of decision rather than as an agglomeration of rules, a process in which the judge performs not a mechanical but a creative function. In so doing, he must of necessity rely, in the end, on his own intellect, experience and conscience. Thus he has urgent need for guides to which he can turn in his recurrent perplexities. My suggestion is that natural law, in the sense in which I am using that term, is one such guide.

Seen in this perspective, though always old, law is never old, like the Poor Old Woman in the play. "Did you see an old woman going down the path?" asked Bridget. "I did not," replied Patrick, who had come into the house just after the old woman left it, "but I saw a young girl and she had the walk of a queen."

Harry W. Jones, 1911 —

LAW AND MORALITY IN THE PERSPECTIVE OF LEGAL REALISM (1961)

American legal realism is not a systematic philosophy of law but a way of looking at legal rules and legal processes. It has nothing whatever in common with realism in general philosophy; indeed, legal realism's identifying characteristic is a sceptical temper toward generalizations. In his realist manifesto of 1931, Karl Llewellyn expressed this point of departure as a "distrust of traditional legal rules and concepts insofar as they purport to *describe* what either courts or people are actually doing" and an accompanying "distrust of the theory that traditional prescriptive rule-formulations are *the* heavily operative factor in producing court decisions." Mr. Justice Holmes, is, of course, the hero figure of the realist clan. "The prophecies of what the courts will do in fact, and nothing more pretentious, are what I mean by the law." "The life of the law has not been logic, it has been experience." "General propositions do not decide concrete cases."

One might have thought, thirty years ago, that jurisprudents of the natural law tradition would not be entirely unsympathetic with the realist thesis that there is more to legal decision-making than the orderly application of positive law generalizations. There are, to my mind, far closer affinitics between legal realism and natural law theory than exist between conventional analytical jurisprudence and the natural law tradition. In legal realism, as in natural law theory, critical intelligence is brought to bear on the positive law; neither approach is content with formal analysis of positive law concepts, and both are concerned more with justice in human affairs than with the inner doctrinal consistency of the positive legal order. What happened, however, is that an uncompromising attack was launched from the natural law camp on the legal realists, and particularly on their hero figure, Justice Holmes. Consider this natural law change: "This much must be said for Realism. If man is only an animal, Realism is correct, Holmes was correct, Hitler is correct." That was guilt by association, with a vengeance, and suggests the depth of natural law antagonism towards the realist inquiries.

If, as I believe, the natural law attack on legal realism was a misidentification of the enemy, how are we to account for it? There are several possible explanations. For one thing, the realists were asking new and different questions, attempting a long overdue analysis of the decisional process, without always making it entirely clear that this was what they were about. There was underbrush to be cleared away, notably the stubborn remnants of the old slot-machine theory of judicial decision, and the realist commitment to this limited mission was such as to create a widespread impression that the realists, as a group, were not at all interested in the problem of law and morality. This concentration of the decisional process as it *is* in act, and consequent underplaying of the legal *ought to be*, was bound to draw fire from the members of a philosophical tradition that had focussed its attention for seven hundred years on justice and righeousness in law. Further, the realist thesis included an all-out attack on what Holmes had called "the fallacy of logical form" in law, that is, on the adequacy of the syllogism as an explanation of the process of judicial decision. The historic association of Scholastic thought, including Thomist natural law, with the method of formal logic is such that a sharp dissent from the natural law quarter was perhaps inevitable.

There are indications, in recent natural law writings and in the occasional pieces of younger Thomist legal scholars, that legal realism now is regarded with far less hostility in natural law circles than was the case thirty, or even twenty, years ago, but it may still be the weight of opinion there that only a scholar of split personality can be, at once, a natural lawyer and a legal realist. This is a family disagreement within the natural law camp, but it suggests a question for those of us who, by philosophical or religious conviction, are outside the Thomist natural law tradition but share its view that moral evaluation is the great task of legal philosophy. The question is this: Does the realist perspective obscure or sharpen the moral dimension of law? Is moral evaluation of the positive legal order less searching and less effective when undertaken in a sceptical spirit towards "traditional prescriptive rule-formulations" as the controlling factor in legal decision-making?

Holmes himself is the case in point. Is his famous address, *The Path of the Law*, evidence of a split jurisprudential personality? For this essay, which sets out many of the seed ideas of American legal realism, concludes with words of high moral affirmation:

> "The remoter and more general aspects of the law are those which give it universal interest. It is through them that you not only become a great master in your calling, but connect your subject with the universe and catch an echo of the infinite, a glimpse of its unfathomable process, a hint of the universal law."

Is this "campaign oratory," or can it be that legal realism has something unique to offer on the age-old jurisprudential problem of the role of moral ideas in the functioning of law in society?

The ethical theory to be drawn from legal realism is, I suggest, that the moral dimension of law is to be sought not in rules and principles, or the higher law appraisal of rules and principles, but in the process of responsible decision, which pervades the whole of law in life. Is this a rewarding, even a respectable, approach to the enduring problem of morality in law? The best answer, I think, is that the moral insights suggested by the realist analysis have striking parallels in the literature of contemporary theology. There are sentences in Paul Tillich's *Love, Power and Justice* that might, if read out of context, be taken for quotations from one of the more advanced of the American legal realists:

> "Justice is expressed in principles and laws none of which can ever reach the uniqueness of the concrete situation. Every decision which is based on the

abstract formulation of justice alone is essentially and inescapably unjust. Justice can be reached only if both the demand of the universal law and the demand of the particular situation are accepted and made effective for the concrete situation."

It is, in fact, on the ground just stated that much present day Protestant theology is most critical of the postulates and methods of the natural law tradition. Thus Reinhold Niebuhr criticizes the "rational 'intuitions' " of natural law theory as "much too rigid and neat to give adequate moral guidance to men in the unique occasions of history" and asserts that the religious tradition to which he belongs "has too strong a sense of the individual occasion, and the uniqueness of the individual who faces the occasion, to trust in general rules." The analogy from theology to law suggests, at least, that legal realism, with its emphasis on the tensions that exist in law administration between the demands of the prescriptive rule-formulation and the appeal of the concrete problem situation, is not the irrational philosophy that it seems to those of its critics who would find all the answers to law's moral problems in higher law precepts, or in the general concepts of analytical jurisprudence, or, for that matter, in any body of abstract moral or political principles.

At the risk of belaboring the theological analogy, I summon one more witness in support of the proposition that the interplay of law and conscience is better seen in the context of the decisional process than in disputations about the "morality" or "policy" of general legal rules and principles. Martin Buber, the great Jewish existentialist theologian, has a paragraph in his *Between Man and Man* that states the task of decision more precisely and forcefully than anything I know in the literature of jurisprudence:

> "Of course there are all sorts of similarities in different situations; one can construct types of situations, one can always find to what section the particular situation belongs, and draw what is appropriate from the hoard of established maxims and habits, apply the appropriate maxim, bring into operation the appropriate habit. But what is untypical in the particular situation remains unnoticed and unanswered. . . . In spite of all similarities every living situation has, like a new-born child, a new face, that has never been before and will never come again. It demands nothing of what is past. It demands presence, responsibility; it demands you."

Let us then survey, as briefly as is manageable, how choice and decision are inevitable in the life of the law, inescapable in the life of the lawyer, whatever his role in the calling. This, unavoidably, requires an analysis of what lawyers *do* in their manifold tasks as judges, prosecutors, advocates, and counsellors.

II

"Reason is but choosing." These key words in Milton's *Areopagitica* have particular force in relation to those decisional situations in which the judge or the practising lawyer finds little guidance in established legal doctrine and yet must choose profoundly the lives of other people. Does someone ask, at this point, whether that area of inescapable choice is not closely bounded in a mature legal system? Does a judge really decide major questions in a government that is "of laws and not of men?" Is it not more accurate to say that the authoritative rules of law, for which the judge is spokesman, decide his problems for him?

Legal realism's answer is that the syllogistic form characteristic of judicial opinions operates, in many instances, to obscure policy decision in a wrapping of formal and essentially secondary explanations. A statement of Holmes is again the classic one:

> "Behind the logical form lies a judgment as to the relative worth and importance of competing legislative grounds, often an inarticulate and unconscious judgment, it is true, and yet the very root and nerve of the whole proceeding. You can give any conclusion a logical form. You always can imply a condition in a contract. But why do you imply it?"

Every lawyer of competence knows this; he is a legal realist in his practice, however passionately he may disapprove of legal realism as an explicit legal philosophy.

To limit the range of possible disagreement, I will not take an extreme realist position in this brief but necessary analysis of the common law judicial process. I am not saying that the judge is undirected, uncontrolled by the precedents and statutes, in all the cases before him, or even in most of them. Many, perhaps most, of the controversies that reach the courts can be decided without much more than a reference to existing rules. Some judges and lawyers of experience will say that at least three-fourths of the cases that come to court leave the judge no room, no leeway, for alternative decision. [Cardozo's estimate is surprising. "Nine tenths, perhaps more, of the cases that come before a court are predetermined — predetermined in the sense that they are predestined – their fate preestablished by inevitable laws that follow them from birth to death." THE GROWTH OF THE LAW 60 (1924). But, to Cardozo, the unpredetermined tenth make up the judge's "serious business." THE NATURE OF THE JUDICIAL PROCESS 21 (1921)]. I would set the figure far lower, but that is not relevant to our present inquiry. On any account of the judicial process, there is a substantial incidence of cases that can be decided, and justified with all traditional common law properties, either way. Whatever the incidence may be – a fifth, a fourth, a third – it is indisputable that the work of the judge involves the inescapability of choice and so of responsibility for externally uncontrolled decisions.

Great judges have been peculiarly sensitive to the demand of decisional responsibility in the hard or unprovided-for case. Cardozo, Holmes's only equal as an American common law judge, had this to say:

> "It is when the colors do not match, when the references in the index fail, when there is no decisive precedent, that the serious business of the judge begins."

Is it not manifest that the area of the judge's serious business is that area most worth studying to reveal the moral dimension of judicial action? If the judge, whatever his metaphysical views, takes his moral convictions seriously, they will be relevant, above all, to his serious business.

If judicial choice is inevitable even in run-of-the-mill situations, what must the burden of decision be in the great cases, in which the deciding judges have even less to work with, less to control their choice, in the pre-existing legal doctrine? What of *Brown* v. *Board of Education*, where the issue was the constitutionality of racial segregation in the public schools of an entire region of the United States? Consider what the nine participating Justices had to draw on by way of doctrinal authority: one constitutional clause, so short as to approach the cryptic, "Nor shall any State deny to any person within its jurisdiction the equal protection of the laws." The precedents? A sequence of inconclusive, manifestly distinguishable, past decisions. Can any theory of fixed principles or higher law precepts illumine the inner struggle, the turmoil of soul, through which a judge must pass in deciding a case of this magnitude? Yet it must be decided, one way or the other. The judge, unlike the pure social scientist, can not withhold his action until all the returns are in. His duty to support the Constitution includes the obligation to give concreteness to the great guide lines of American liberty –

"due process of law," "free exercise of religion," "the equal protection of the laws" – and there is no hiding place from that political and moral obligation.

The natural law tradition, at least as usually understood, has the effect of urging the judge to turn his thought from distracting social details towards the universally valid precept. It is true that a precept of great moral power was at stake in *Brown* v. *Board of Education,* the moral and religious principle that all men, as sons of God, are of equal worth and dignity. But the choice the nine Justices had to make, uncontrolled and largely unguided by technical legal doctrine, concerned the concretization of that moral precept in a context of potential violence and disaffection and in a tangled, endlessly confused cultural situation. In a case like this, the resources brought to bear must be more than those of reason alone. Steadfastness of spirit and, at the same time, a keen awareness of personal unworthiness for final moral evaluations are attributes of judicial greatness fully as important as the attribute of reason. Our institutions demand a great deal of the more or less ordinary human beings to whom judicial power is entrusted. Can the judge be better armed for the task of responsible decision than when he possesses a sense of divine judgment upon all human institutions and all human history?

American legal thought has focussed too much on judges, perhaps because the judge, to us as to Aristotle, is "living justice." Let us consider the far less frequently discussed matter of the moral responsibility of the practicing lawyer for the causes to which he gives his training and his talents. The lawyer, whether in court or as a counsellor in his office, is a professional partisan. By the nature of his calling, he works not in his own cause but in the causes of others. Does he carry personal moral responsibility for the cases he accepts, the enterprises with which he becomes identified? The conventional answer is that a lawyer is a spokesman by profession and that it is unfair to identify him personally with the clients and causes he serves. This is usually justified in terms of an appeal to professional tradition. That tradition is expressed, for American lawyers, by the Canons of Ethics of the American Bar Association. Do these Canons make the criteria for the provision or withholding of professional service so clear that the individual lawyer has no moral leeway, and hence no responsibility, in the acceptance or rejection of professional employment?

We turn to Canon 30:

> The lawyer must decline to conduct a civil cause or to make a defense when convinced that it is intended merely to harass or to injure the other party or to work oppression or wrong. But otherwise it is his *right*, and, having accepted retainer, it becomes his duty to insist upon the judgment of the Court as to the legal merits of his client's claim....

Thus far, we have the conventional explanation: the lawyer has a professional right to take any case offered to him, excepting only the quite infrequent case of pure harassment, oppression, or wrong, and it would seem to follow that he carries no personal responsibility in exercising that right. But we read on to Canon 31, which begins as follows:

> No lawyer is obliged to act either as adviser or advocate for every person who may wish to become his client. He has the *right* to decline employment.

What now of the lawyer's moral responsibility for his career decisions? Our lawyer, according to the traditional rules of the game, has a right to take the usual case offered to him, but, at the same time, he also has a right to reject it. If he is a lawyer of uncommon skill and resourcefulness, more cases will be offered than he can handle. If he is of limited talent or reputation, self-interest will exert pressures on him to accept every employment offered. The professional tradition merely blocks out an area of choice, a right to accept and a right to decline. Thus, at the heart of the lawyer's functioning, we see a power to choose and, with that right of choice, responsibility for choices made. Here, again, is professional decision seen in its inescapable moral dimension.

The thoughtful lawyer seeks always to discern a morally consistent pattern, a justifying value, in the work to which he is giving his life. He seeks this authentication of his professional existence not in one case but in the professional work of a lifetime. Have his choices, in the acceptance and rejection of offered professional employment, contributed in some way to greater justice between man and man, to the creation of a fairer and more productive economic system, to higher standards in commercial life or in family life or in the administration of the criminal law? Can any body of ethical principles symbolize this deeply felt need for professional authentication with the clarity and power of the religious concept of the "calling" or "vocation?"

So far, I have given only a few illustrations of the inevitability of responsible choice in the life of the law. They are illustrations only of a decisional process seen everywhere. No matter where we turn in an analysis of lawyers at work, we find power to choose and accompanying responsibility for choices made. Lawyers, more than any other group in our society, are the architects and engineers of our economic system. The structures of American economic development have had their origin, times without number, in major law offices. The counsellor, the office lawyer, is fully as important as the advocate in the contemporary profession and far less controlled in his choices by the rules of law. A great office lawyer uses legal sources as an artist uses pigments, to accomplish a design. He can not evade moral responsibility for the worth of that design. In the words of the 1958 report of the Joint Conference on Professional Responsibility:

> The reasons that justify and even require partisan advocacy in the trial of a cause do not grant any license to the lawyer to participate as legal adviser in a line of conduct that is immoral, unfair, or of doubtful legality. In saving himself from this unworthy involvement, the lawyer cannot be guided solely by an unreflective inner sense of good faith; he must be at pains to preserve a sufficient detachment from his client's interests so that he remains capable of a sound and objective appraisal of the propriety of what his client proposes to do.

Reason and learning are not enough; in his office, as in court, the lawyer must "possess the resolution necessary to carry into effect what his intellect tells him ought to be done."

Or consider the decisions, unpublicized and quite uncontrolled by strictly "legal" doctrine, that are made every day in the administration of criminal justice. The penal statutes tell the prosecuting attorney when he is empowered to invoke the sanctions of the criminal law. But he can not institute criminal proceedings in every case in which prosecution is technically appropriate, or the law would operate most oppressively and the courts soon be swamped beyond rescue. I have some existential knowledge of the prosecutor's task from two years spent in a law enforcement post where excellently prepared potential criminal cases poured in from field offices by the dozens. It was impossible, for reasons of court congestion and limited enforcement personnel, to institute fullfledged criminal proceedings in more than one of the ten possible criminal cases. Choice was inescapable, one case for criminal information or grand jury indictment, the other nine for such milder sanctions as treble damages, suspension order or mere formal reprimand. I realized then the soul-searching called for in devising moral criteria for the sifting of potential criminal cases. The exercise of the prosecutor's discretion, I have believed since, is even more important than the content of a penal code as a force in the administration of criminal justice.

Again, once the criminal defendant has been found guilty, leeway and responsibility characterize the duty of the sentencing judge. The statutory precept, more likely than not, leaves a wide range of permissible treatment of the offender. "Punishable by fine not to exceed $10,000 or by imprisonment from one to five years, or by both such fine and such imprisonment" is a not untypical sentencing provision of our day. The law, thought of as rule, merely fixes the outside bounds for the act of judicial choice. On what other sources shall the sentencing judge draw as he exercises the awful power conferred on him over the life and freedom of another man? Yet he must decide and, as he makes his inescapable moral evaluation of the offense and the offender, he grasps the full meaning of the chastening injunction, "Judge not, that yet be not judged."

III

In its approach to the law-morality problem, legal realism is closer, in one important sense, to the natural law position than to the position of conventional analytical jurisprudence. If the realist analysis is right, the day to day work of judges, law officers, and practicing lawyers involves processes far less orderly and far more intricate than the application of positive law generalizations to fact-situations falling more or less neatly within them. In leeway situations, the positive law *is* is not a command but, at most, an authorization of alternative decisions. The choice between alternatives, the selection of the path to be pursued, can not but be influenced by the decision-maker's *ought to be*. Legal realism, with its emphasis or the inevitability of choice and discretion in the life of the law, casts its vote – though for very different reasons – with the tradition of natural law, and against Austin and the positivists, on the old issue of the complete analytical separateness of the law that *is* from the law that *ought to be*. [The legal realist position in the *Is-Ought* relation has been widely misunderstood. In *Some Realism About Realism*, 44 Harv. L. Rev. 1222, 1236 (1931), Llewellyn listed, as one of the realist points of departure, "the *temporary* divorce of Is and Ought for purposes of study." This did not line him up with the Austinians: (1) because the divorce was to be only *temporary* – "during the investigation of the facts"; and (2) because the analytical separation that Llewellyn chiefly wished to preserve was less that between the doctrinal Is of analytical jurisprudence and the ethical Ought than it was that between the Is of law in action (what courts are doing in fact) and the normative Ought of the law in the books.

To say, as I have, that legal realism stresses the extent to which the moral *ought to be* influences practical judicial decision-making, is not, of course, to side with Professor Fuller and against Professor Nagel on the issue of their recent exchange, Fuller, *Human Purpose and Natural Law,* 3 Natural L. F. 68 (1958), Nagel, *On The Fusion of Fact and Values: A Reply to Professor Fuller, id. at* 83. The distinction between fact and value is, I think, inescapable and basic to clarity of analysis in law as elsewhere. It is simply that the dynamics of the judicial process are such that the ethical values of the decision maker are material sources of law.]

The moral appraisal of law, however, is not always or usually to be accomplished by measuring positive law general propositions against other general propositions, or principles, of asserted higher validity. Higher law critiques of formal legal doctrine do not take us very far towards an understanding of the problematic of legal decision. "Do good and avoid evil," yes, but what of the ethical relativities of an imperfect society, and how do fallible human decision-makers determine what is the better and what the worse in concrete human situations? "Act in accordance with reason," yes, but man's reason is no superhuman faculty, and just decision requires both an intellect that perceives the good and a will that perseveres resolutely in the good course intellectually perceived. When we enter the realm of the judge's "serious business," the prosecutor's discretion, the practicing lawyer's choices, we need a moral theory fully as demanding as the older natural law tradition but more directly addressed to the points of strain at which moral insights are most needed. In realist perspective, choice, decision, and responsibility for decision are central elements for a philosophy of law.

Irving Kayton, 1927 —
Associate Professor of Law, George Washington University

CAN JURIMETRICS BE OF VALUE TO JURISPRUDENCE? (1964)

Jurimetrics broadly signifies "the scientific investigation of legal problems," but so also does the philosophy of legal realism. The tools used in the investigation are that which distinguish jurimetrics from the broader jurisprudential discipline. The jurimetric tools and their applications are:

a) modern or symbolic logic for analyzing legal material;

b) digital computers, modern logic, and quantitative methods for behavioral analysis of judicial decisions; and

c) digital computers for the storage and automatic retrieval of legal literature.

Automatic legal information storage and retrieval is a significant area of jurimetrics. It holds potential (not yet certain to be completely fulfilled) for the practical and theoretical advancement of the administration of justice, as well as for the intellectual elevation and financial enhancement of the everyday practice of law. It bears only slightly on the judicial decision-making process, however, and from this point on is outside the ambit of this discussion.

Modern logic and digital computers are the stuff of which jurimetrics is made. It is not necessary to understand these tools as does a logician or a computer engineer. In order to evaluate them, all we need know is that which is essential to their new legal role. Before proceeding to an understanding of these essential features it will be well to acknowledge that there are prevalent, understandably, some emotionally determined attitudes about this new technology.

Just as the pagans ascribed human characteristics to their totems and deified the omnipotent forces of wind, sun, and lightning, so modern man, in keeping with his primitive predilections, has responded to the apparent omniscience of the computer by deifying and anthropomorphizing it. Cartoons in the "sophisticated" magazines have caricatured this human reaction. In one is shown a room-filling digital computer with a complex overlay of dials, electron tubes, wires, and flashing lights. Viewing the printed output tape of the machine is a lace-collared, spinster mathematician. The expression on her face is quizzical but pleased as she reads the words, "I love you." The viewer of the cartoon cannot but have a warm feeling at the thought that even for this nondescript woman there is someone (excuse the slip), rather, some*thing*, with deep affection for her. Although it is a whimsical use, a computer can be programmed to print out words of endearment. Its physical contact, needless to say, cannot provide a tingling of the nerve endings in a human being. Anecdotes deifying the computer, on the other hand, reflect an anxiety-provoking type of humor.

> Everything is lost to man when machines take over. To the question asked of the omniscient and infallible one [the computer] "Is there a God?", the unfaltering, self-confident reply booms forth: "There is . . . now!"

The tendency toward humorously primitive responses such as these is due to lack of familiarity (the first electronic digital computer was completed little over a dozen years ago). The largest, most complicated computer in existence is actually quite simple compared to the telephone connections between the lawyer's office phone and his client's phone a hundred miles away. Yet, today, the telephone system evokes no such emotional responses. So, too, digital computers will fall eventually into the neutral acceptance accorded the commonplace, whether or not they are ever understood by lawyers to any significant extent. More than this is required, however, if computers and their handmaiden, modern logic, are to be evaluated properly as tools for the law. One of the purposes of this exploration is to make such an evaluation, and one by-product will be a demonstration of the conceptual simplicity of both modern logic and digital computers.

Let us turn now to the heart of the matter. Cardozo longed for certainty in the judicial process. He complained that when retiring at night

> after putting forth the best that is in me, I look upon the finished product and cannot say that it is good. In these moments of disquietude, I figure to myself the peace of mind that must come, let us say, to the designer of a mighty bridge. The finished product of his work is there before his eyes with all the beauty and simplicity and inevitableness of truth.

Plaintively, he wondered if the process of human decision might not be done better with logarithms. The first half of this article will examine how closely modern logic approaches the wished-for table of logarithms which would permit a Cardozo to sleep well. The second half of the article derives its direction from Holmes' flat statement that

> the primary rights and duties with which jurisprudence busies itself . . . are nothing but prophesies . . . . The prophesies of what courts will do in fact, and nothing more pretentious are what I mean by law. . . .

This is a definition of law, of course, which is debatable in view of the hundreds, if not thousands, of books and articles published subsequently in which other definitions have been advanced. But it does structure our exploration nicely. Can digital computers be used to prophesy what courts will do with greater certainty than otherwise would be possible, and thereby make more ascertainable that which Holmes defined as law?

II

The first area of investigation, then, is modern logic. The nature of modern logic as it functions in the analysis of legal material can best be appreciated by a specific example. Set forth below is a highly contrived, hypothetical criminal case designed as a vehicle to illustrate the use of modern logic in a legal setting, not in an absolute sense, but by way of contrast to the non-symbolic analysis a lawyer would use ordinarily in such a situation. To maximize the value of this illustration, four questions are presented at the end of the case. The reader is invited to answer them; if he does, his understanding of modern logic will be enhanced by the comparison he can then make between his own processes and the techniques of modern logic which will be demonstrated in answering the questions.

Fifty thousand dollars were stolen from the Third National Bank during regular banking hours. The bank has a vault alarm system devised so that an alarm bell is controlled by four switches: D, A, V and P.

D is turned on automatically when the vault door is closed.
A is turned on automatically when the anteroom door is closed.
V is a wall switch in the vice-president's office.
P is a wall switch in the president's office.

The alarm sounds only if any of the following conditions occurs:

a) The vault and anteroom doors are both open.
b) The vault door is closed, and the vice-president's switch is on.
c) The vault door is open, and the president's switch is on.

A bank guard and an off-duty teller were standing inside the bank, near an exit, at the time the money was stolen. Both saw a man run out of the bank with a large suitcase. The man was apprehended shortly thereafter and the stolen money found in his suitcase. At his trial (the outcome of which is not important for our purposes), it was established that at the time the defendant ran out, the guard and teller were talking to each other and facing in somewhat different directions so that the guard could see both the anteroom and the vault doors, while the teller had the president's and vice-president's wall switches in view. The following exchange of questions and answers between prosecuting attorney and witness took place:

PROSECUTING ATTORNEY: Was the alarm bell ringing at the time you saw the defendant run from the bank?
GUARD: Yes!
PROSECUTING ATTORNEY: What were the states of the vault and anteroom doors at that time?
GUARD: Both were open.
PROSECUTING ATTORNEY: Teller, was the alarm bell ringing at the time you saw the defendant run from the bank?
TELLER: No!
PROSECUTING ATTORNEY: What were the states of the wall switches?
TELLER: Neither was on.

In response to questions about the alarm system, the bank president testified: "If the alarm is silent, then a door is closed, or neither wall switch is operated."

Shortly after the defendant ran from the bank, there was an explosion which made it impossible to ascertain the previous states of the switches and doors. Other than the guard and teller, no other witnesses could recall the states of the doors and switches just before the explosion. The guard, teller, and president appear to be about equally credible witnesses.

Assuming all of the above information to be true, with the exception of the quoted testimony of the guard, teller, and president, consider the following questions:

1. Was the guard's quoted testimony true?
2. Was the teller's quoted testimony true?
3. Was the president's quoted testimony true?
4. Changing the facts somewhat, suppose both the guard and teller testified that the president's and vice-president's switches were off and the anteroom door closed. The guard said also that the alarm was ringing while the teller said it was silent. Was either of them lying, and if so, which one?

I am confident that most people would agree that answering questions 2 through 4 is more than a trivial mental exercise.[1] Furthermore, you may have noticed that because of the change in testimony postulated in question 4, it is necessary to think through the problem afresh and almost as completely as was required when answering questions 1 and 2. Lastly, there is no way of proving the correctness of the answers. Here, then, are three areas in which the use of modern logic may prove advantageous: ease of solution; no need to rework or rethink the problem for changed facts; and means available for proving correctness of the answers. The disadvantages, on the other hand, will be appreciated best after the demonstration below, in which the problem is solved with the techniques of modern logic.

To George Boole, a nineteenth century mathematician, we are indebted for the symbolism and technique known as Boolean algebra. Boole's system comprises a substantial portion of modern or symbolic logic. A special aspect of Boolean algebra is our main interest; it deals with the truth and falsity of statements or propositions about things (propositional logic) and relations between classes of things (class calculus). Despite Boole's having been a mathematician and despite the "algebra" following "Boolean," it is not necessary to comprehend mathematics to understand the solution of the hypothetical criminal case in the notation of symbolic logic, or to learn Boolean algebra rigorously. Indeed, even a knowledge of simple arithmetic is superfluous in this undertaking. A knowledge of the notation for three simple, basic, logical relationships is all that is required to understand the solution of the hypothetical case.

The first notation is for the logical "or" relation, in the form

$$a = h + b$$

which is spoken: a is equal to h or b. The plus sign $(+)$ is not intended to mean addition as it does in arithmetic, but is merely a shorthand notation for the word "or." If h stands for the class of things known as horses, and b represents the class of animals having brown tails, then this expression means that a is the class of things that consists of either h or b, or both, i.e., a can be a horse or an animal with a brown tail, or both. For example, a is satisfied by a white horse, or a beaver (assuming beavers do in fact have brown tails), or a brown-tailed horse.

The second notation is the logical "and" relation in the form,

$$a = h \,.\, b$$

which is spoken: a is equal to h and b (or a equals h dot b). The dot means "and." It is often left out, and two letters together such as hb are understood to mean the same things as $h.b$. The expression a in this relationship is satisfied only by that class of things which are both h and b, i.e., brown-tailed horses.

The third important symbol is that of logical negation,

$$a = \overline{h}$$

which is spoken: a equals not h, or a equals h bar. This means that a is the negation of h and is satisfied whenever h is not, or a is equal to all things which are not horses.

[1] From a group of twelve people in an advanced graduate law school seminar in legal philosophy, ten submitted answers to these questions. Two of the ten answered all four questions correctly. Five others answered three of them correctly. The remaining two did not do as well. Each of the ten was either a professor of law or philosophy or a doctoral candidate in law. Some of the people were completely convinced that all their answers were correct those who were so positive included some who wre considerably in error.

The way in which propositional logic can be employed to answer the questions about the hypothetical criminal case may now be considered. Let the facts about the bank alarm in the hypothetical case be represented by the letters as follows:

D means: the vault door is closed;
A means: the anteroom door is closed;
V means: the vice-president's switch is on;
P means: the president's switch is on; and
X means: the alarm is sounding.

The only conditions under which the alarm sounds, as verbally expressed in the case, may now be represented in logic notation:

$$X = \overline{A} \,.\, \overline{D} + D \,.\, V + \overline{D} \,.\, P \qquad (1)$$

That expression (1) is the notational counterpart of the verbal conditions is seen from the following demonstration of the one-to-one correspondence between the words and symbols: The alarm sounds (X), only if (=), the vault and anteroom doors are both open ($\overline{A} \,.\, \overline{D}$), or (+), the vault door is closed and the vice-president's switch is on (D . V), or (+), the vault door is open and the president's switch is on ($\overline{D}$. P). The words "only if" or "if, and only if" (represented by =) also mean: if the proposition or notational expression on the left hand side of "only if" is true, then the right hand proposition is true, and if the right hand proposition is true then the left hand proposition is true.

Although it may be difficult to believe, all four questions asked about the case and every conceivable variation of them can now be answered solely by examination or manipulation of expression (1). Not another thought need be given to the words, concepts, or conditions of the case, or to their relationships. No thought need be given to whether or not implicit conditions can be derived from the combination of explicit conditions. The rules of formal logic control, and we are ensured that all that can be implied validly from the explicit statement of expression (1) will be made known and available to us. Such is the power of this discipline.

Expression (1) may be reformulated, using standard Boolean techniques, to be more readily understandable relative to the questions to be answered. This reformulation of the expression is a simple, mechanical transformation requiring no acute mental faculties, but merely a knowledge of the simple logic rules. It is carried out in Appendix A, and the necessary rules of logic are set forth and explained. The reformulation results in an expression which encompasses all possible conditions of the hypothetical case:

$$\overline{X} \,.\, (D \,.\, \overline{V} + A \,.\, \overline{P} \,.\, \overline{D} + A \,.\, \overline{P} \,.\, \overline{V}) + X(\overline{A} \,.\, \overline{D} + D \,.\, V + \overline{D} \,.\, P). \qquad (2)$$

This expression contains an X (the alarm is sounding) and an $\overline{X}$ (the alarm is silent) with various combinations of the terms D, A, V, P, or their negations, grouped with each. Thus all the conditions under which X occurs are grouped in the parentheses, conjunctively with X. Similarly, all the conditions for the alarm being silent are grouped conjunctively with $\overline{X}$, The expression

$$\overline{X} \,.\, (D \,.\, \overline{V} + A \,.\, \overline{P} \,.\, \overline{D} + A \,.\, \overline{P} \,.\, \overline{V}) \qquad (3)$$

therefore, completely defines those conditions which result in the alarm being silent, while the expression

$$X \,.\, (\overline{A} \,.\, \overline{D} + D \,.\, V + \overline{D} \,.\, P) \qquad (4)$$

completely defines those conditions which result in sounding the alarm. Without further ado, let us, as quasi-logicians, answer the four questions.

Answer to question number 1: The guard's testimony that both doors were open is consistent with his saying the alarm was ringing (this is obvious without logic notation). This follows from the $\overline{A} . \overline{D}$ term of expression (4). Therefore, he *may* have been telling the truth.

Answer to question number 2: The teller's testimony that both switches were off is consistent with his saying the alarm was silent. This follows from the $A . \overline{P} . \overline{V}$ term of expression (3). Therefore, the teller also *may* have been telling the truth. It follows, therefore, that even though the guard and teller offered contrary testimony as to whether or not an alarm was ringing, we cannot determine if either was telling the truth. But, it may be seen that the guard's $\overline{A} . \overline{D}$ testimony and the teller's $\overline{P} . \overline{V}$ are both consistent with the alarm sounding (as asserted by the guard), while the teller's assertion that the alarm was silent is incompatible with the guard's $\overline{A} . \overline{D}$ testimony.

Answer to question number 3: The president testified: "If the alarm is silent, then a door is closed or neither wall switch is operated," *i.e.*, if $\overline{X}$, then $D+A+(\overline{V} . \overline{P})$. From expression (3) it is clear that the president was telling the truth. In fact, if he had testified only that "if the alarm is silent, then a door is closed," *i.e.,* if $\overline{X}$, then $D+A$, he still would have been telling the truth.

Answer to question number 4: In this question the facts are changed. For the new state of facts, namely, $A . \overline{P} . \overline{V}$, the alarm must have been silent since this expression is conjunctively linked with $\overline{X}$ in expression (3). The teller, therefore, made a consistent statement about the state of the alarm, while the guard's statement was inconsistent since $A . \overline{P} . \overline{V}$ is not associated with X. The question asked, however, was whether or not either of them was *lying*. Lying involves more than logical inconsistency. It involves intent as well; mere inaccuracy or falsehood without the intent to deceive is not lying. A complete answer to question 4, therefore, is not actually possible by the method of formal logic analysis of testimony alone, since it cannot reach the issue of intent.

The questions are now answered to the extent that they can be answered. It is unlikely that many readers will challenge the correctness of these answers even though their own may be different. Some may suggest that the hypothetical case and the questions were posed ambiguously, or otherwise unclearly, and account in that way for having diffferent answers. Few will have the temerity to launch a frontal attack and say that the answers derived here are incorrect. This is understandable, after all, because, first, the fact of publication in itself is a safeguard against error; and, second, the rules of logic set forth above seem reasonable, and the notational development in Appendix A appears in order. But for those who do challenge directly, stronger evidence is required. Indeed, proof of the correctness of the answers may be a necessary precondition for their making the effort to follow the notational development in Appendix A. Happily, any solution obtained by propositional logic can be proven correct in a simple, nonmathematical way. This is done by constructing a truth table, which is simply a shorthand graphic demonstration of the truth or falsity of a compound proposition by an enumeration of the truth or falsity of all possible combinations of all the constituent propositions involved. The truth table for expressions (3) and (4) is shown in Appendix B and should do much to satisfy even an incorrigible skeptic.

The problem and analysis of the hypothetical case dealt with testimony or alleged facts, to the exclusion of rules of law. It was restricted, therefore, to the minor premise of the legal syllogism, which is the focus of Jerome Frank's "fact skepticism." In keeping with the spirit of Frank's contribution, let us speculate upon possible explanations for the testimony given by the guard and teller which go to the issue of the truth or falsity of the testimony, irrespective of its logical consistency. Suppose, for example, that the teller is over sixty years old and, as is sometimes the case at that age, is substantially deaf to the high end of the human-audible frequency spectrum. If the sound of the alarm is largely within this high frequency range, the residual sound that was "heard" by the teller may have been an insufficient auditory stimulation to be consciously registered on the brain, especially under the excitement of the events of the bank robbery. Another possibility is that the guard may be an alcoholic of the type which suffers from short, unpredictable, but chronic intervals of amnesia. He may have had a short memory loss during the time that the defendant ran from the bank and really did not know whether or not the alarm was sounding. Such people, often unwilling to admit even to themselves that this can happen, may attempt to fill the gaps by other means. Thus, the guard may have convinced himself that the alarm was ringing in view of other seemingly persuasive evidence in the case tending to indicate the guilt of the defendant.

In short, consistent testimony may be incorrect for many reasons, and inconsistent testimony may be correct if only because of the many conscious and unconscious factors affecting human judgment and memory. Does this mean that techniques for determining logical consistency are of no value when applied to the minor premise? Not at all. Important, but infrequent, procedural situations occur in which logical consistency not only is useful in reaching the correct factual conclusion, but is totally determinative. In some judicial and administrative proceedings the facts of the case, usually complicated, may be stipulated by the the opposing parties. Truth for the purpose of such proceedings, is nothing more than consistency. Neither the intent nor the credibility of the witnesses can be in issue, nor can the principles of fact-skepticism be called into play. For the minor premise of the legal syllogism, therefore, the usefulness of propositional logic is delineated in a small but important area of application.

The rule of law or major premise of the legal syllogism, on the other hand, provides an area of application for formal logic which is much larger and perhaps more valuable. The major premise may include constitutional provisions, statutory and case law, administrative rules, and contractually determined rules of conduct. It was suggested at the outset of the solution to our hypothetical case that the answering of questions 2 to 4 without propositional logic is more than a trivial mental exercise. Yet, in that case, there are only five operative factors or propositions to be considered. Imagine the difficulty of solution when four or five times as many propositions are involved, as may well be the case, for example, in an insurance contract. Moreover, the difficulty in using such a major premise is much more than four or five times as difficult for the unaided lawyer. The human mind is simply not efficient enough in such situations. As the number of operative factors increase, psychological considerations apparently come into play, because the job appears overwhelmingly difficult. Assistance is indicated.

> The more complex forms of inference cannot be studied until a specially devised symbolism is introduced . . . which enables us to keep different meanings distinct, to concentrate upon what is essential, to show the form of propositions, and to save labor and thought.

It was not until 1937 that a publication clearly demonstrated this in quasi-legal applications; it dealt with corporate group insurance contracts. Five different illustrative problems and solutions were given, involving five to eighteen operative factors and as many as eleven rules relating the propositions, many of which were mutually contingent in various ways, e.g., if *a* then *b, c* only if *b,* but if *c* then not *a.*

The difficulty in understanding such contractually defined relations is formidable in itself, aside from having to determine the applicability of any set of facts to the contract. Provisions in complex, prolix, and verbally involuted statutes such as the Internal Revenue Code are in the same class. In other words, aside from having to decide on the applicability of the minor premise to the major premise, it may be no small task merely to understand the relations between the propositions of the major premise. In this regard, the job is to identify and eliminate ambiguities from the major premise. For purposes of illustration, consider the declaration:

> *Professors and graduate students at the X law school conduct themselves with decorum.*

At first blush this appears to be a simple and understandable communication. But if this were part of a statute or a contract clause over which controversy had arisen, it soon would become clear that the propositions and the relationships between the propositions are ambiguous. Indeed, this short declaration could be interpreted reasonably in at lease twelve different ways. In what now should be a familiar procedure, let us assign letter symbols to the propositions or classes involved, as follows:

PL = Professors of law.
P = Professors of any subject.
GL = Graduate students in law.
G = Graduate students in any subject.
L_1 = People physically present at X law school.
L_2 = People connected with X law school in some official capacity.

The following classes of people, and perhaps others, reasonably can be said to conduct themselves with decorum:

1. $(P+G) . L_1$: Professors of any subject and graduate students in any subject who happen to be physically present at X law school.
2. $(P+G) . L_2$: Professors of any subject and graduate students in any subject who are connected with X law school in some official capacity (e.g., research associate, student, interdisciplinary instructor) even when they are not physically present at the law school.
3. $(P+G)L_1 . L_2$: The same people as in the two above cases, but only if they are connected with the law school in some official capacity *and* only when they are physically present at the school.
4. $P+G . L_1$: Professors of any subject, irrespective of their physical location or official capacity, and graduate students in any subject who are physically located at the law school.

The last eight of the suggested interpretations are set forth solely as logic expressions, thereby providing the reader with the opportunity to formulate the verbal meanings for himself

5. $P+G . L_2$ 6. $P+G . L_1 . L_2$ 7. P+GL 8. PL+GL
9. $P . G . L_1$ 10. $P . G . L_2$ 11. $P . G . L_1 . L_2$ 12. PL . GL

Taken out of context, any of these interpretations is equally likely to have been what the draftsman intended. The causal factors affecting decorous behavior may be the personalities of the people in the P, PL, G, or GL status groups, or the environmental influences operative at the law school, or the social pressures applied to people officially connected with the law school, or any combination thereof. Ambiguities of this type, if fully appreciated and identified to begin with, often can be resolved by reference to the overall context, or, during the drafting stage, can be rewritten unabiguously. Indeed, a multiplicity of phrases from article I of the United States Constitution were analyzed in similar fashion and found to be replete with ambiguity, but their meanings are reasonably clear in context. Resort to context has not always provided a solution. There are myriad reported cases where the context of a contract or statute does not provide an adequate basis for resolving the ambiguity, and the legislature's intent, or the contracting parties' intent, is then sought through parol considerations. Often enough, there is no clear evidence of legislative intent or apparent manifestation of mutual contractual intent. The court, having no real alternative, imposes its own interpretation upon the ambiguous phrase under the fiction of having divined, by some means, the intent of the draftsmen.

III

It is obvious, by now, that in the use of propositional logic for the analysis of the major premise, ambiguity is necessarily identified and guidelines are necessarily provided for its resolution. Symbolic logic can function in no other way. The question then arises: May the major premise not be more useful if its ambiguities are left undisturbed? Are there contracts, statutes, cases, or administrative rules in which ambiguity is desirable? Would not each concrete demonstration of ambiguity and its resolution tend to rigidify the law and eventually destroy the very flexibility which has made the common law viable? After all, legal words of art often have meanings which have changed or been added to over the years as a consequence of decision, staute, or both. Would not the fixing of meaning in an absolute sense, and the fixing of the way the term may be related to other terms, bring about ossification of the judicial system? Despite the dangers of generalization, it is submitted that all these questions should be answered in the negative. Information brought to bear in a rational pursuit is always better than ignorance or confusion. The elimination of ambiguities, rather than ossify the law, would produce an optimum condition for the purposeful, intelligent, and efficient development of the law. In short, knowing what we are talking about, irrespective of its correctness, is always the best point of departure to additional knowledge, or to a better formulation. To illustrate and particularize this point, let us consider the case law doctrine of "clear and present danger."

The constitutional provision that "Congress shall make no law . . . abridging freedom of speech has been judicially held a relative rather than absolute prohibition. Inroads are permitted under the "clear and present danger" test which was given form and substance in Holmes' dissenting opinion in *Abrams v. United States* [(1919) 250 U.S. 616]. Holmes argued that the prohibition should give way only when

> the expressions of opinions . . . so imminently threaten[s] immediate interference with the lawful and pressing purposes of the law that an immediate check is required to save the country . . . . Only the emergency that makes it immediately dangerous to leave the correction of evil counsels to time warrants making any exception. . . .

This definition suggests two major operative factors. One is time. Is the danger a present one, *i.e.,* does it "imminently threaten immediate interference"? The second factor is the nature of the danger or evil. Will it destroy the country if carried out? In Figure 1, the applicability of Holmes' "clear and present danger" test is represented by a graph. The horizontal or x axis is the estimated time that would elapse before the evil could be carried out. The vertical or *y* axis is the magnitude or gravity of the evil. Point y_1, on the *y* axis, represents an evil sufficiently great to invoke the doctrine (assuming the time requirement is met), *i.e.,* destruction of the government by violence. Point x_1, on the *x* axis, represents a

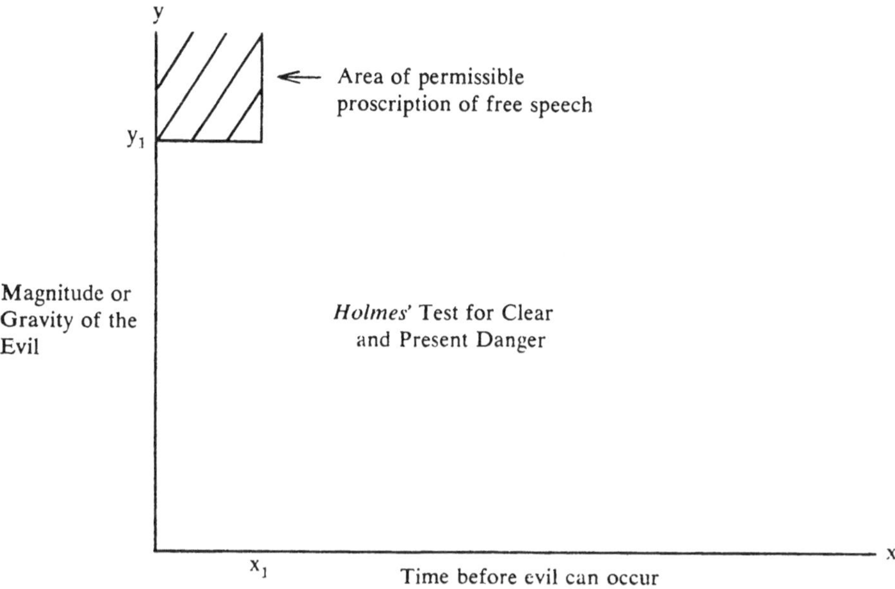

Figure 1

period of time in which the evil can be perpetrated, which is so short that the doctrine would be invoked (assuming the magnitude of the evil requirement is met), *i.e.,* the threat is immediate. Any greater evil or any more immediate threat justifies invoking the doctrine, a fortiori. Holmes' definition, however, pushes each factor just about to its extreme, as is seen by the fact that very little of the *y* axis extends above point y_1, the point of destruction of the government by force, and very little of the *x* axis exists to the left of point x_1, the point of immediate threat. Reasonable men will differ over where precisely to place point x on the *x* axis, *i.e.,* the number of seconds, minutes, days, weeks, or months which must elapse before something is no longer immediate. Similarly, there can be reasonable differences over the location of y_1, the kind of acts which are sufficient to place the government in danger of destruction. In short, Holmes' doctrine is imprecise or vague, but basically unambiguous.

Brandeis, joined by Holmes in his concurring opinion in *Whitney v. California,* [(1927) 274 U.S. 357] effectively lowered to the point to y_2, on the *y* axis, and moved the point to the right to x_2, on the *x* axis. For Brandeis, the danger is not present "unless the incidence of the evil apprehended is so imminent that it may befall before there is opportunity for full discussion." The threat, therefore, need no longer be "immediate." Furthermore, since imminence is a function of "opportunity for full discussion," the precise amount of permissible time, in turn, may be a function of the state of development of the communications technologies. The evil for Brandeis is relaxed to the danger of "serious injury to the state." Figure 2 represents the Brandeis test for "clear and present danger." It should be noted that the permissible area of deprivation of free speech is much enlarged in Figure 2.

Last, we consider Learned Hand's definition of clear and present danger as adopted by the Supreme Court in *Dennis* v. *United States* [(1951) 341 U.S. 494]:

> In each case [courts] must ask whether the gravity of the "evil" discounted by its improbability, justifies such invasion of free speech as is necessary to avoid the danger.

A qualitatively different standard for permissible infringement of speech is set with this definition. Although the *y* axis represents substantially the same factor as in the Holmes and Brandeis graphs, the *x* axis in the Learned Hand graph of

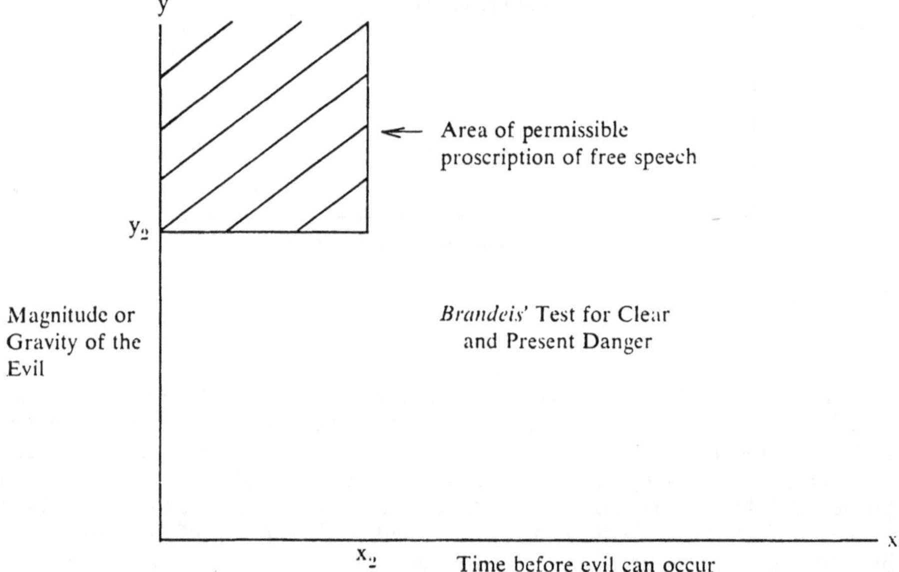

Figure 2

Figure 3 is now the probability of the evil occurring, rather than the time of its occurrence. The death of a ninety-eight year old man suffering from pneumonia is imminent and probable, while the death of a healthy twenty-five year old man, although it does not threaten imminently, is also probable. The Learned Hand representation in Figure 3 indicates that if the evil is sufficiently grave, even though the probability of occurrence is small, free speech may be proscribed. The precise shape of the curve of Figure 3 and its exact intersection (if any) with the axis will be ascertained only after sufficient litigation provides the required data. The area of permissible proscription is above the curve, but it cannot be compared quantitatively with that fixed by the Holmes and Brandeis definitions because the *x* axis of Figure 3 represents a qualitatively different factor from that in Figures 1 and 2.

Using these three undefinitive, thumb-nail analyses, it is apparent that the Brandeis definition differs from Holmes' only in degree. The degree of vagueness in the *x* and *y* factors of Holmes was altered. Some may say that these factors have been rendered more specific with more detailed guidelines in the later judicial contribution of Brandeis. Others may say that the cut-off points have

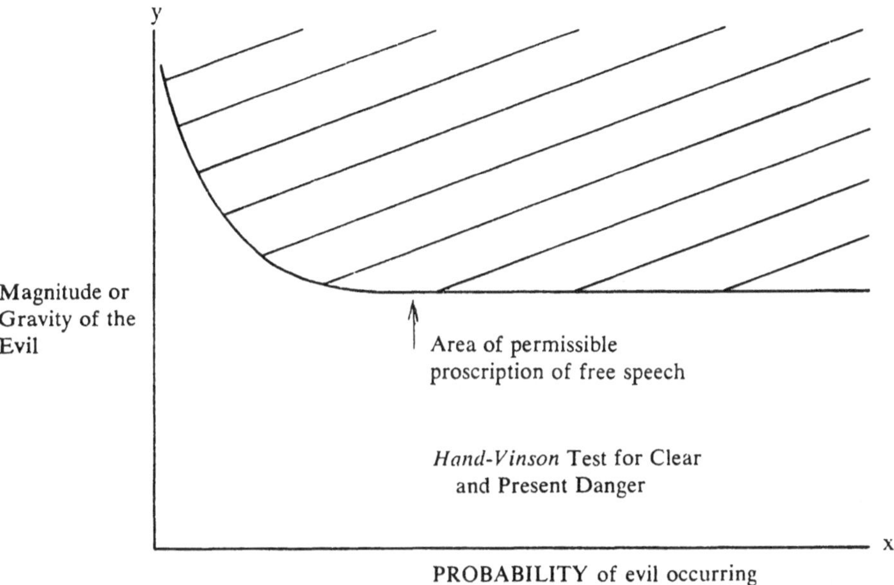

Figure 3

been shifted and nothing more. Apart from the amount of vagueness, however, the legal phrase "clear and present danger" can encompass both definitions without ambiguity. But if Hand's definition, which differs in kind, is subsumed under this phrase, then "clear and present danger" becomes an ambiguous phrase and is more misleading than clarifying as a legal term of art. For clarity and for the efficient subsequent development of the law, Hand's definition should be given another name; perhaps "clear and probable danger" is appropriate. No good for the law can come from the confusion which results by making ambiguous a term of art previously quite unambiguous, albeit vague.

When courts legislate, or reverse or modify earlier decisions, the temptation is great to "put new wine in an old cask." As if to justify his making the doctrine ambiguous, Chief Justice Vinson, when adopting Hand's definition, wrote for the majority in the *Dennis* case:

> [N]either Justice Holmes nor Justice Brandeis ever envisioned that a shorthand phrase should be crystallized into a rigid rule to be applied inflexibly without regard to the circumstances of each case.

This is sophistry. If anything, the definitions of Holmes and Brandeis were flexible enough, because of vagueness, to afford due "regard to the circumstances of each case." But Chief Justice Vinson apparently wanted to change the law qualitatively while retaining the authoritative mantle of Holmes and Brandeis over his shoulders. Thus, Chief Justice Vinson brings our discussion full circle by arguing that ambiguity is necessary if the law is to be flexible and adaptable to future cases.

As long as a contract is not so vague as to be unenforceable, and as long as a statute incorporates sufficient guidelines so as not to be unconstitutionally vague, vagueness itself in these instruments provides a sufficient and proper margin for error and a proper means for coping with changes in circumstances. Ambiguity in such instruments, on the other hand, means incomplete draftsmanship, with the completion left to the future and to the pen of an unknown judge or arbitrator. Ambiguity in a judicial decision with respect to that which is being decided is especially to be avoided, particularly in a common law system wherein law provides the metes and bounds for all law.

In the final analysis, the presence or absence of ambiguity in any legal instrument will depend upon the ability, intelligence, objectives, and conscience of the draftsman, exhortation to the contrary notwithstanding. But given the fact of ambiguity, those who must live with the instrument in which it occurs unquestionably should be able to identify it. Propositional logic as used in legal analysis provides a powerful and systematic tool to perform the identification. This tool is practical for legal instruments which are complex, lengthy, and verbally involuted, and to which reference must be made continually over an extended period of time. Tax statutes and lengthy contracts of adhesion, for example, are of this type. Detailed, time-consuming, and painstaking analysis must be performed in any event, in order to understand them and to pinpoint logical inconsistency and ambiguity. After performing such an analysis with the notation of symbolic logic, the major premise is tangible in a form like that of logic expression (2) above. No tortuous verbal rethinking need be done when changes of fact in specific cases require reapplication of the minor premise to the major premise.

Before pressing on, it may well be to summarize briefly the advantages and disadvatanges of propositional logic relative to the judicial process which, explicitly and implicitly, have been in evidence in this exploration.

Advantages:

1. It demonstrates logical inconsistency in the minor premise of the legal syllogism.

2. It demonstrates ambiguity and logical inconsistency in the major premise of the legal syllogism.

3. It provides a systematic method for identifying all relational ambiguity in the major premise.

4. Once the logic expression is obtained and formulated in the most convenient form, the premise or the problem need never be thought about again in verbal terms. All valid implicit and explicit relationships between operative factors are captured or crystallized in the logic expression.

5. Once the logic expression is obtained, all possible variations in combinations of operative facts are comprehended by the logic expression, and verbal rethinking of the premise or problem is never required.

6. The validity of any conclusion derived from the logic expression can be proven straightforwardly, with a truth table.

7. The logic analysis and the resulting expressions are just as effective and useful with vague propositions or factors as with precise factors.

8. Propositional logic is conceptually simple. To learn it requires no previous technical or mathematical knowledge. The only prerequisites are facility with language and a reasonably logical mind.

9. Its widespread use may establish terseness and simplicity of language as

standards for judicial writing: It may cause all lawyers to think more carefully before putting pen to paper.

Disadvantages:

1. It is a strange notation, with which the vast majority of lawyers are unfamiliar and against which most lawyers are prejudiced.
2. It must be learned before it can be used.
3. With respect to the minor premise, it has a very limited area of value.
4. Typographical or manipulative errors in the symbols occur easily, and because the symbolism is terse, even the slightest error may change the entire meaning of an expression.
5. Its widespread use may tend to place a premium in judicial decisions upon lean, unadorned prose. The rich literary style of a Cardozo is rare; propositional logic may discourage it altogether.

IV

At about this time the reader well may be wondering,"What does this have to do with digital computers, which were listed earlier as the second type of jurimetric tool?" The answer is: "Everything!" In addition to whatever else may have been accomplished to this point, all this time we have been examining and describing digital computers. The fact is that the logic expression:

$$X=\bar{A}\,.\,\bar{D}+D\,.\,V+\bar{D}\,.\,P \qquad (1)$$

is virtually a small digital computer. This expression literally describes, and is directly convertible into, the hardware and electronic circuits of the digital control system which would be used to control the burglar alarm system in the hypothetical case if the Third National Bank were real. True, this digital system can accomplish only the special purpose defined by logic expression (1), *i.e.*, all it can do is generate a control signal which will ring an alarm under the conditions prescribed in the hypothetical case. Even the largest, most complex digital computer in existence, however, is literally nothing more than a physical embodiment of an aggregation of thousands of different logic expressions. The United States Patent Office recently has started issuing patents for computer inventions in which the description of the computer comprises little more than hundreds of pages of logic equations. Conceptually, a digital computer is a box full of the electronic equivalent of thousands of logic equations, into which facts or data are fed, and out of which answers to questions are printed, in much the same way the four questions about the hypothetical case were answered from the logic equations. In addition, the computer has space for holding some of the input information for future use, and some of its logic equations can be rearranged by the operator of the machine.

With this understanding of computers, let us turn to their use in "the prophesies of what courts will do in fact." One serious approach, used by Lawlor for United States Supreme Court decisions in "right-to-counsel" cases, fully utilizes the techniques of propositional logic. Based upon an analysis of the "right-to-counsel" cases prior to *Gideon* v. *Wainwright*, a separate logic expression was formulated to represent the past judicial behavior of each member of the Supreme Court, and another to represent the past decisional behavior of the Court as a whole. To do this, decisions had to be made as to what were the operative factors or propositions, as seen within the confines of the written decisions, in the right-to-counsel cases, *i.e.*, what were the factors which led the Justices to hold for, or against, the petitioner who claimed that he had been deprived of his constitutional rights by denial of counsel? Based largely upon earlier work by Kort, forty-four operative propositions were selected and numbered consecutively. Some of them, for example, are:

1. The petitioner was charged with a crime subject to capital punishment.
5. The petitioner was young and immature.
10. The petitioner was interrogated in the absence of counsel and before arraignment.
17. Petitioner's request for assignment of counsel was denied.
23. The petitioner was deceived by the court or the police.
40. The accused was indigent.

Each factor selected was such that, if its presence in a case tended toward a decision for the petitioner, its absence had the opposite effect. The criterion of presence or absence of a factor is an all-or-nothing affair, in the same sense as is the truth or falsity of a proposition, thereby making these factors compatible with the operation of propositional logic.

Once the factors which were mentioned in the decisions and deemed to be controlling were isolated, a logic expression was written for each Justice which defined his voting behavior, as of that time, in right-to-counsel cases. Similarly, a logic expression was drawn for the Court as a whole. If the forty-four factors are designated f_1 through f_{44}, and some of them are grouped in sets, e.g., set S_6 includes factors 5, 6, 7, and 9, then the Boolean expression representing the Supreme Court's behavior in right-to-counsel cases prior to July 1, 1962, was defined as:

$$P \equiv [f_{12} \cdot f_{13} \cdot f_{14} + f_{44} \cdot t(1,S_3)] \cdot f_{19} \cdot [t(1,S_{11}) + t(2,S_6)]$$

where $t(1,S_3)$ means at least one factor from the set of factors S_3 and $t(2,S_6)$ means at least two factors from set S_6. Pursuant to this definition, the Court holds for the petitioner (P) if, and only if:

1) factors 12, 13, and 14 are present, or factor 44 and at least one factor from set S_3 are present; and
2) factor 19 is present; and
3) either at least one factor from set S_{11} is present or at least two factors from set S_6 are present.

This logic expression, as well as one for each Justice, was then stored in the computer; the input data fed into the computer was in the form of the presence or absence of each of the forty-four factors in specific cases of interest. Prior to the Supreme Court's decision in *Gideon* v. *Wainwright*, Lawlor's computer, using facts from that case and using the Supreme Court logic expression, predicted that the petitioner would be denied relief and *Betts v. Brady* would be upheld. Using the Justices' logic expressions, however, the computer predicted that five Justices would vote for the petitioner and four against, and *Betts v. Brady* would be overruled. In fact, the Court, in a unanimous decision, held for the petitioner and overruled *Betts v. Brady*.

Another computer prediction method in the right-to-counsel cases was developed by Kort, wherein he selected twenty-six operative factors. Unlike the later work of Lawlor, which treated the factors as true-false, yes-no, present-absent, or on-off, for use in a logic expression, Kort believed that the presence of some of the factors contributed more to a decision for the petitioner than did others. He therefore assigned a numerical weight or constant to each factor; the weight of the twenty-six factors ranges from 68.3 for the presence of "coercion or intimidation to plead guilty," down to 5.2 for "no assistance of counsel at any other phase of the proceeding" (absence of counsel at arraignment, between arraignment and trial, at trial, and at sentencing, are given higher weights). For any case, the weights of the factors present were added, and if the sum exceeded a critical cut-off region, between 370.4 and 378.2, the prediction was that the petitioner would be granted relief, while if below 370.4, relief would be denied. If the sum falls within the cut-off region, the situation is indeterminate, and no prediction is made. In terms of the operation of the computer, the weights of the twenty-six factors are stored in the machine, as are the bounds of the cut-off region; the computer is arranged to perform the sequence of logical steps necessary to add a series of decimal numbers, and to compare that sum with the cut-off figure. The inputs to the machine are the presence or absence of each of the twenty-six factors; the output is either a statement for the petitioner or against him. Using this technique, the computer failed to predict the reversal of *Betts v. Brady* in *Gideon v. Wainright.*

The computer using the logic equation for the Court and the computer using the sum of the weighted factors technique both failed miserably to predict the Court's reversal of itself. The use of a logic equation for each Justice by Lawlor was somewhat more effective, but the predicted five-to-four vote is still a far cry from the actual unanimous decision for reversal. Should we have expected otherwise? Of course not! *A reversal is by definition a logical inconsistency.* That which by stare decisis had been called black is now called white. If we have learned anything about symbolic logic and digital computers, it is that logical consistency is their pith and essence. The logic expression which was devised for the Court's behavior in the right-to-counsel cases was nothing less than a shorthand description of stare decisis in that field. Each logic expression devised for a Justice of the Court was a shorthand formulation of his past voting history in which the voting history itself was taken as consistent by definition; each Justice's logic equation was the definition of his own personal stare decisis, which is not necessarily the same as the Court's stare decisis. The reason why the computer did a better predicting job when using the several logic equations of the Justices, rather than that of the Court's was not that these equations were able to predict the pending logical inconsistency. Quite to the contrary. This individual-oriented prediction also was based upon consistency, but the composition of the Court had changed between *Betts* v. *Brady* (1942) and *Gideon* v. *Wainwright* (1963). Consequently, the technique which individuated, rather than grouped, the behavior of the Justices, past and present, was able to come closer to predicting the reversal, while still being consistent.

Does the inefficiency of present computer techniques in predicting reversals mean that little can be learned from these techniques until we advance beyond them? Not at all. Hitherto unexplored vistas in the world of the judicial decision-making process have been opened to us by even these primitive or embryonic excursions into jurimetrics.

It was found that when these techniques were formulated from the first half of chronologically arranged cases, the decisions in the later group of cases (except for reversals) were predicted at an extremely high rate. This was to be expected, because that is the way stare decisis works. Fascinating, however, is that in one field of law, Connecticut's workmen's compensation cases (and there may be others), not only were the chronologically second half of the cases predicted from the chronologically first half, but the first half could be predicted from the second half. This cannot be due to stare decisis. Either the total body of law in that field had been created full-blown in the first one or two cases and the law thereafter was totally static in that field, or there is some agency or power outside the realm of stare decisis which controlled the outcome of the cases. Perhaps this agency or power is some special form of natural law; perhaps it is some immutable but unknown form of logic or law of human nature which has been controlling or directing man's activities from the beginning of time. What an exciting area for speculation! More importantly, what a potentially fruitful area of investigation; and jurimetrics has opened it up for us.

Some irrepressible jurimetricians, however, are not content; they believe logic and computer techniques should be powerful enough to come to grips even with judicial reversals if all of the truly operative factors are brought to light. Some of them suggest that at least some of the operative factors may not be contained within the bounds of the written decisions. External factors are being investigated, harking back to the early legal realists. For example, statistical searches are going on for possible correlation between the way judges vote and the presence of emotionally or politically charged factors in the case, such as aliens, Communists, or minority groups; the way one judge votes is being examined as a function of how other judges on the same court vote.

The use of computers as a tool for investigating the judicial process is in an embryonic stage. The techniques developed thus far are primitive compared to those used in nonlegal fields to which computers have been applied. If they are ever so improved that computer prediction in law becomes more accurate more regularly than *ad hoc* human prediction, our significant accomplishment will not be that we have created a mechanical servant to take over human effort. Rather it will be that we have succeeded in discovering and isolating more of those factors which are the viscera of the judicial decision-making process than we could have without the rigorous analysis forced upon us by the logical demands of the computer.

Can jurimetrics be of value to jurisprudence? For the present, the answer is a qualified "Yes"; it is of value in limited and well-defined ways. Its potential value, however, excites and challenges the imagination. The extent to which this potential will be fulfilled, if at all, is by no means clear. The investigation may prove fruitless – if so, the sooner this is established, the better, thereby freeing the intellectual captives of jurimetrics to devote their efforts to more promising pursuits. If, however, additional constructive results for the law materialize from the use of the jurimetric tools, let us also benefit from them promptly. The plea is before the legal profession for permission and encouragement to move forward with this work. The author hopes that this article will help in eliciting the response: Permission granted!

[See generally "Law, Science and Technology: A Symposium" (1964) 33 *Geo. Wash. L. Rev.* 1-456.]

Jurisprudence In Canada

Canada has been noted neither for its jurisprudence nor its jurisprudents, but to the extent that it has had either, they have been until the last few decades positivist in doctrine and inclination. As recently as 1962, for example, Austin was cited as an authority by a Canadian court: [1962] O.R. 705, 728. Natural law theory, as always, has had its adherents, especially in French-speaking Canada, but on the whole it has had a subordinate position.

The seldom disputed hegemony of positivism seems to have been principally the result of the influence of English legal thinking and of the system of legal education, which until recently was completely under the control of the profession and for many years consisted in office studies and supervised practice carried on under the arrangement known as service under articles of clerkship, sometimes supplemented by part-time attendance at a "law school". Beginning in 1957 the Law Society of Upper Canada (Ontario) put legal training on a full three-year academic basis leading to an LL.B. degree, and law societies in other provinces which had not previously done so have taken the same step since. Recently the Law Society of Upper Canada announced that it was giving up control of its law school as well. This move marks the end of professional domination of legal education in Canada.

In the wake of these recent changes a number of new law schools have been established, and there has been a huge increase in the numbers both of law students and law teachers across the country. Whereas in the earlier days most academic lawyers were English-trained, now almost all Canadian law professors do their advanced studies at the large American law schools, and as a consequence the effects of sociological and realist thinking are beginning to be strongly felt in Canada. This American influence on Canadian law teachers began as early as the 'twenties, and among the older generation of academics is typified by such names as Wright, Laskin and Read. But until the 'fifties and 'sixties the academics were too few and conditions within the profession too unfavorable for them to make a decisive impression on the profession at large, though in individual fields such as torts there is no doubt that their impact was considerable. Now that even the positivist influence from England is much less, the time is ripe for further advance.

One of the more interesting projects currently underway in Canada is a study of the Supreme Court of Canada by political scientist Peter Russell for the federal Royal Commission on Bilingualism and Biculturalism. Professor Russell's study encompasses such areas as historical issues, contemporary issues, personnel and procedures, and, perhaps most important from the jurisprudential viewpoint, a quantitative analysis of Supreme Court decisions.

An excellent study of the judicial process is to be found in Dean Horace Read's paper, "The Judicial Process in Common Law Canada" (1959) 37 *Can. Bar Rev.* 265. Some good, but still unpublished, jurisprudential papers have been presented at meetings of the Association of Canadian Law Teachers. See also MacGuigan, "The Privy Council and the Supreme Court: a Jurisprudential Analysis" (1966) 4 *Alta. L. Rev.*; McWhinney, "Judicial Concurrences and Dissents: A Comparative View of Opinion-writing in Final Appellate Tribunals" (1953) 31 *Can. Bar Rev.* 595; Wright, "Should the Profession Control Legal Education" (1950) 3 *J. Legal Ed.* 1; Meyer, "Jurimetrics: The Scientific Method in Legal Research" (1966) 44 *Can. Bar Rev.* 1.

Edward McWhinney, 1924-
Professor of Law, University of Toronto

LEGAL THEORY AND PHILOSOPHY OF LAW IN CANADA (1959)

The most interesting and striking feature of jurisprudence in Canada at the present day is that there has not developed, as yet, anything that might be characterized as a distinctively "Canadian" jurisprudence. On the one hand, until very recent years, the pervasive intellectual influence in Canadian law – especially in the English-speaking, Common Law, provinces, but even, to a certain extent, in the predominantly French-speaking, Civil Law, province of Quebec, too – was an essentially second-hand, derivative, English influence. And again, at a more practical, empirical, level, in spite of the obvious opportunities for cross-fertilization between the Quebec Civil Law and the jurisprudence of the Common Law provinces, it is clear that there has been very little mutual inter-action or inter-change over the years; and so there is, today, in Canada, a dualism of legal systems and nothing as yet in the way of a blended or fused jurisprudence that might incorporate the best elements of the principles, practice, and procedure of the two separate bodies of law.

That English substantive law ideas and general intellectual attitudes should be so largely dominant in Canadian law, even today, is hardly surprising. The Canadian Constitution, in its formal origins at least, is a statute of the United Kingdom Parliament, – The British North America Act of 1867. The Common Law of the English-speaking provinces is, in its historical roots, "received" English Common Law, brought over (according to the conventional legal fiction) to North America by the first English settlers to the extent that its substantive provisions were applicable to conditions in the new colonies. And until as late as 1949 the final appellate tribunal for Canada was an essentially English court sitting in London, – the Judicial Committee of the Privy Council, the highest appellate tribunal of the old British colonial Empire. . . .

Granted, however, the force and validity of many of the criticisms, from English Canada, of the record of the Privy Council and particularly of its work in the public law area, what is not so well known is that those same decisions enjoy some greater acceptance and even approval in French Canada at the present day. One may censure, as being an absurdly academic exercise in English, Austinian, positivist, jurisprudence, the Privy Council's official conception of the Canadian Constitution as an ordinary statute, to be interpreted according to the ordinary (restrictive) canons of statutory construction. One may also suggest (again in an American Legal Realist vein) that to achieve their particular end-results the hall-mark decisions on the Canadian Constitution required some distortion by the Privy Council of the constitutional text. But those same end-results seem to have corresponded, to a very considerable extent, with French Canadian preference, from the 1890's onwards, for a pluralistic, decentralized type of federal polity, in which, (whatever the historical intentions of 1867), the old weighting towards the centre would be replaced by a weighting towards the provinces, and a new era of Provincial Rights ushered in. In a vaguely intuitive way, the Privy Council, especially in the Watson-Haldane eras of its work, seems to have responded to Quebec sentiments in favour of decentralization and Provincial separatism; and so, in fact, in despite of the avowed value-neutralism of its main judicial authors, the dominant judicial construction of the Canadian Constitution to the present day has been a policy-type (Provincial Rights-oriented) interpretation. Its acceptance and support by French Canada, even though achieved, doctrinally, through the "Constitution-as-an-English-statute" fiction and without formal adverting, in the official opinions of the court, to Quebec's special interests or to general concepts of philosophic pluralism, represents, no doubt, another example of what a percipient observer, Baudouin, has characterized as Quebec's adoption of English techniques as a means of *cultural* self-defence.

In the area of Code interpretation, the Privy Council's "statutory construction" approach has evoked much less satisfaction in French Canada, more especially when it has been used, in significant areas, to make over the Code into a Common Law image. One wonders whether a better sense of tactics might not, for example in the Delicts area, have allowed the Privy Council to reach the same end-results as were in fact reached by the judges but by the politically stronger method of recourse to (metropolitan) French materials. The answer, probably, is that the thought never occurred to the Privy Council, and that even if it had it would have been asking too much of a tribunal whose members were generally unacquainted with Geny, Duguit, Durkheim, and others of their character and sympathies, to indulge in systematic reference to French materials, whether *doctrines* or *jurisprudence*.

Of course, a similar tactical problem may well confront the Canadian Supreme Court in its new phase of juridicial independence from the United Kingdom. . . .

The intellectual attitudes of a court, whether in the exercise of judicial review of a written constitution or more generally in the interpretation of Code, statute, or common law, are, of course, of tremendous practical significance in its day-by-day work. The dominant philosophy of law of the Privy Council of modern times has been baldly positivist, in the best English sense. This has involved both the denial that judges *ought* to make law in the sense of consciously moulding policy in cases coming before them, and also an insistence that, operationally, (that is, as a question of actual working fact), it is possible, and has been possible in the past, to limit the judges to a purely mechanical role of "finding" the law. At bottom, the positivist approach to law rests on an assumption that the legal system of Canada is a closed and static body of propositions, – that it has all the answers, so to speak, legal logic, on this view, being a logic of antecedents, and not of consequences.

Now the English positivist philosophy of law has also been the prime Canadian philosophy of law, at least until the last generation or so. This has been so because positivism was the Privy Council's official philosophy, and the Privy Council was both the intellectual style-leader and the final source of authoritative judicial decisions for Canada; and also because the normal outlet for graduate work for Canadian law teachers, for so many years, was in United Kingdom universities in which, indeed, the positivist philosophy had had its roots. Beginning in the 1930's, however, the positivist approach began to be challenged by a younger group of Canadian jurists. The challenge seems to have had some purely indigenous origins[1], the critics of the Privy Council and its dominant positivist approach responding (much as in the United States, a few years earlier, the American Legal Realists had responded) to the gap between what the judges had actually decided and what they said they had decided in their opinions. But this nativistic Canadian Legal Realist impulse was supplemented, in its attack on the

[1] I am thinking here especially of that very vigorous and imaginative group of public lawyers, – Dean W. P. M. Kennedy of the University of Toronto, Vincent MacDonald of Dalhousie University, and Frank Scott of McGill University. In the more esoteric field of Conflicts of Laws, Dean John D. Falconbridge of the Osgoode Hall Law School devised new and challenging theories whose influence was soon felt outside Canada.

old legal order, by the marked reception in Canada of a general body of American ideas hostile to the basic positivist creed. From the mid-1920's onwards, there had been a general switch in the locus of graduate training in law for law teachers in English Canada[2], a product in part, perhaps, of the post-World War I opening up of research and scholarship funds in law in the United States. Instead of to England as heretofore, the young Canadian law teacher began to make his way to the great graduate legal centres of the United States – to Harvard, Yale, Columbia, Michigan, and Chicago. Some of these men elected to stay on permanently in the United States, but others returned to Canada and they brought back with them the special techniques of legal instruction, the special thought-ways, and the special value-structure, of the American law school of the between-the-two-Wars era. Sometimes this process of absorption and taking over of American legal ideas was not fully conscious even in the minds of those who were themselves active in bringing the "reception" about. In its *best* form, this "reception" of American legal ideas involved an acceptance of the proposition that judges can, and do, and should, make law in the process of decision-making. Concomitantly, this involved the recognition of the purely instrumental character of legal rules and doctrine, and the abandonment of any quest for an absolute meaning in the words of the constitutional text or for the historical intentions of the Founding Fathers, as governing rules in constitutional interpretation. It also involved a conception of society as being in a state of flux, and of the criterion of "good"-ness in law as being the extent to which it reflected and fulfilled the changing aspirations, demands, and interests, pressed in society – an essentially relativistic philosophy of law which, (in so far as there existed in most branches of the common law and of public law in the Canada of the 1930's a rather considerable gap or time-lag between the positive law and the society it was supposed to reflect), gave a certain dynamism and impetus to legal change.

Of course these basic propositions, first, as to the true nature of the judicial process, and, secondly, as to the necessary and proper relationship or symbiosis between law and society, are essentially the teachings of the American Realist and Sociological schools of law. Ideally, one would like to think that these new ideas were propagated in Canada in the 1930's through the medium of the formal law school courses on jurisprudence and philosophy of law. In fact the main influence seems to have come in the regular law school course work in the ordinary substantive law subjects – Torts, Contracts, Conflicts of Laws, Constitutional Law; and even there, the new ideas were introduced less through explicit *ex cathedra*-type pronouncement, than indirectly, – in the interstices of the case method of instruction, newly introduced into Canada by the American-trained teachers. Just as, in Langdell's day in the United States, the new case method introduced a new fluidity in the teacher and student's approach to legal principles and destroyed once and for all the old conception of law as a body of closed dogma, so in Canada also it helped to shatter altogether the "legal-certainty myth". One cannot stress too much, as a prime causal factor in the revolution in legal thought-ways in Canada from the 1930's onwards, the effect of introduction of this new technique, *qua* technique, in overthrowing the old

[2] Dean Horace Read of Dalhousie Law School, himself one of the pioneers, in the 1920's, of the trek of the young Canadian law graduates to the graduate legal centres of the United States, has looked into the statistics and finds that whereas, up to World War II, the bulk of Canadian law teachers were still English-trained, today the overwhelming majority of them have taken graduate degrees (whether the LL.M. or S.J.D. degree) in the United States. McWhinney, "New Frontiers in Jurisprudence in Canada", 10 Journal of Legal Education 331, 332-3 (1958).

English positivist philosophy of law and its built-in cult of certainty in law. And transcending the technique as such was the fact that the new case-books produced by the American-trained teachers as basic tools for their new case method of instruction – mimeographed as these case-books were for intra-mural use and so (incidentally and without conscious design) evading American copyright laws – borrowed uninhibitedly from the existing American case-books in the field which were generally organized on a problem-solving basis so as to point up the need for adjustment of law to society, and were thus in accord with the teachings of the Sociological school. This societal, relativist, emphasis in Canadian philosophy of law, in the law schools from the 1930's onwards, is the more interesting and even surprising because not preceded or even accompanied in the college philosophy departments, (as it had been, so markedly, preceded, in the case of the United States), by any strong emphasis on pragmatism and instrumentalism after the fashion of William James and John Dewey, – the college philosophy departments in Canada until comparatively recent years being still substantially dominated by Scottish idealism.

I do not wish to suggest that, in the case of English Canada, the revolution was completely "American" inspired or "American" derived. There is, as I have noted, sufficient evidence of a protest sentiment, among purely Canadian-trained scholars of the 1920's and the 1930's, at the gap between the Privy Council decisions on the Canadian Constitution and the more obvious needs, as they themselves conceived them, of Canadian society of the time, and also sufficient irritation at the obvious spuriousness of the declaratory, "law-finding", thesis of the judicial function maintained officially by the Privy Council, to suggest that an indigenous Canadian Realist movement might have succeeded, anyway, irrespective of American influences: how often, indeed, in looking at the handful of colourful, poetic, iconoclasts in Canadian legal scholarship of a generation ago[1] is one struck by the equivalences to the exciting "Young Turk" group among the American Realists of a decade earlier – I am thinking here especially of Jerome Frank and Karl Llewellyn among the American Realists, their Canadian counterparts coming very readily to mind.

Nor do I wish to suggest, either, that the revolution came *uno ictu* or that it is necessarily complete even at the present day. Legal education in English Canada has been locked so long in the embrace of a narrow vocationalism that a great deal of the intellectual energies of law professors in the last few decades has been absorbed in the fight for the removal of professional, Bar Association, control from the schools and the placing of legal education on a full-time, University, basis. Urgent reforms like the modernization of curriculum, the building up of foreign law collections in the law school libraries, the establishment of graduate and research programmes, and the institution of competitive, "merit", systems in the recruitment and promotion of law school faculties and the granting of academic leave for research purposes, have had perforce to wait on the settlement of theses questions.

But, by and large, the fact still remains that whereas, as late as a generation ago, legal education in English Canada was English in substance, and positivist in philosophy, and rather static in content and tone, – today it is basically American, realist-sociological, and essentially fluid.

[1] Any listing of the Canadian "Legal Realist" group, whether of essentially indigenous intellectual origins or else American-inspired and influenced, would certainly have to include W. P. M. Kennedy, Sidney Smith, Norman A. M. MacKenzie, Cecil Wright, John Willis, Frank Scott, Vincent MacDonald, Horace Read, George Curtis. McWhinney, "English Legal Philosophy and Canadian Legal Philosophy", 4 McGill L.J. 213 (1958).

By contrast, French Canada has tended to remain separate and aloof in its traditions of legal education – neither English nor American, and no longer even subject to substantial (metropolitan) French influences. One of the most fascinating questions for the future of Canadian legal education, taken as a whole, may well be what changes, if any, will result from the exposure of French Canada to the general Realist, Pragmatist, and Sociological drives in philosophy of law, now that the French Canadian law schools are so vigorously encouraging their young teachers and graduates to undertake research work outside Canada and now that a regular flow of high-calibre French-Canadian students is proceeding to the great graduate centres of the United States.

The situation on the Canadian Supreme Court is even more interesting. One is here reminded strongly of Karl Mannheim's inspired comment upon the "contemporaneity of the non-contemporaneous" in present-day society; for strong vestiges of the old Austinian positivism still remain in the Canadian Supreme Court's day-by-day work, the residue no doubt of the era of the Canadian Supreme Court's hierarchical subordination to the Privy Council. There is still, as a formal matter at least, a rather mechanical deference to *stare decisis*; a refusal as yet to admit the Brandeis Brief as a technical device for bringing social and economic facts before the court; an occasional tart exclusion of counsel's attempt to refer to foreign case law. As against that, the court increasingly since 1949, and most notably in the great civil liberties decisions of the last few years, has shown a real awareness of the important role of a court as a community policy-maker; and some of the judicial opinions filed in those cases are notable for the evidence they afford of wise judicial statesmanship. In view of the substantial practical barriers to the effectuation of policy in Canada – the absence of any effective self-operating machinery for the amendment of the constitution; the lack of any developed tradition of law reform committees that can assume some continuing responsibility for recommending reform of the private law; the attrition (in Canada quite as much as in other Western countries) of the general Legislative Process, – legal change in Canada in the future must probably come, in the main, from the judiciary through creative judicial interpretation, or not at all. Hence the immense practical importance of the contemporary emphasis on the Judicial Process, and on competing theories of judicial interpretation, especially where those theories are of an activist, instrumentalist, character.

Among the problems remaining, in the development, for the first time, of an indigenous, autonomous, Canadian jurisprudence must be, first of all, problems of a jurisdictional, machinery, character. The amount and complexity of the business before the Canadian Supreme Court is now approaching the stage where the court must either, as the United States Supreme Court did years before, devise some permissible limits to the number of matters that the court must take, or else cease to be able to perform its main functions intelligently and usefully. It is a matter, really, of adequate time and opportunity for judicial research prior to the arriving at decision, and, more important, of adequate time for judicial reflection on great policy issues. The American method of limiting the amount of the Supreme Court's business, in effect through control of the *certiorari* proceeding and the federal appeals system, involves the existence of a hierarchy of inferior federal courts and of delegation to those courts (more strictly, *retention* for final decision in those courts) of a great bulk of matters that otherwise would have to be decided by the Supreme Court. In Canada, the dualism of private law systems at least presents an alternative mode of approach to control of the quantity (and quality) of Supreme Court business through possible division of the court into *bancs* and the allocation, for example, of matters arising under the Quebec Civil Code, to a special Civil Law *banc*. This would have the advantage of meeting the occasional Quebec complaint that matters arising under the Quebec Civil Code can be determined by a tribunal whose majority is untrained in the Civil Law; it would have, however, the disadvantage – not fully satisfied by the existence even of a *plenum* or full court for appeal purposes – of depriving members of the court of the inestimable benefits, in a plural society, of full and constant exposure to the problems from both main streams of law.

In the area of values, it must be confessed that our problems are just beginning. After more than a generation of almost unchallenged supremacy in the United States, the general pragmatist-relativist-societal emphasis has been tested in action and found by many jurists to be wanting as a philosophy of law for a crisis age, as the agonies of the Cold War, McCarthyism, and the internal security drive, have brought a new concern in the United States in questions of a necessary minimum moral content for law. Even allowing for the time lag as between general trends and changes in American legal ideas and general trends and changes in Canadian legal ideas, it is very likely that the same social-political factors that have produced the contemporary focus on fundamentalist aspects of law in the United States will produce at least some similar tendencies in Canada too, – quite apart from the extra factor, in the case of Canada, of the Catholic affiliations of a large section of the population, which itself conduces to an interest in ultimate values in law.

Adding to the practical difficulties in the quest for values in law in Canada is the special complexity of the Canadian federal form of government, and the plural character of the ethnic-cultural composition of the Canadian population. We do not have, in our constitution, an express "Full Faith and Credit" clause, and so we are only just beginning to think on such questions as what special recognition, if any, comity and the deference that one party to a federal system should extend to another, requires, say, the Province of Ontario to extend to the Quebec matrimonial property regime where that would involve, correlatively, an over-riding of the Ontario Land Titles register. Nor have we pondered as yet on the question of whether there should be, in Canada, one general common law (whether Civil Law or Common Law *stricto sensu*) or a plurality of separate and autonomous common law systems – what in the United States is called the *Erie Railroad* v. *Tompkins* rule.

This leads on, in turn, to the even more complex problem of how, in a plural society, to reconcile competing claims that spring directly from the differing ethnic-cultural groups in the population. What, to English Canada, is secular and a fit subject for governmental control, and national control at that, may, to French Canada, be sectarian and religious in character, because intimately connected with the Quebec family system and its specialized folkways, and therefore a fit subject only for Provincial control, if even that. Hence the debate over Social and Health Insurance, Federal Aid to Education, and similar matters. More explosively, what may seem to English Canada, with its known preference for an "Open Society", a simple matter of Provincial governmental denial of free speech, may, to the rather different *mores* of Quebec, appear as a necessary attempt by the Provincial government to protect the Roman Catholic Church against insulting or abusive attack. Even in the case of the United States, which maintains its formal "Wall of Separation" between Church and State and which, in a general sense, therefore, is much more of an "Open Society" than is perhaps Canada, it has been recognized for some time that certain types of speech must rank low in the hierarchy of values; though no final test has emerged as yet in the majority decisions of the United States Supreme Court in this area. Each case must be judged, so to speak, in its special fact-context. Thereby, we may have at least an intermediate answer to the problem of value-choice. Concrete examination of techniques actually employed by legislative or executive authority to implement a particular value in a particular context may well reveal that the methods of control employed are quite disproportionate to the results to be achieved, and that these controls would inflict too severe a deprivation on speech and other well-regarded values, where alternative, more moderate, controls are available. Thus consideration of *means* used by executive-legislative authority may properly shape and condition judicial approval of *ends* sought to be attained by executive-legislative authority. The liberating emphasis on techniques enables postponement of attempts at final resolution of conflicts over fundamental values until such time as, in case by case development, those values can be tested empirically – in action. If this particular solution to the problem of value-choice seems unduly tentative it must be remembered that Canada is a growing society, not a static one, and so further trial-and-error experimentation and consequent modification, reconciliation, or synthesis, can be expected in the area of values quite as much as in anything else.

Samuel Freedman, 1908-
Judge of the Court of Appeal, Manitoba

JUDGES AND THE LAW
(1962)

This evening is dedicated and set aside as Judges' Night. That circumstance suggests, if indeed it does not dictate, the selection of a topic. My theme tonight is "Judges and the Law". Of judges then I will speak, and of the law, of the role of the one in the development of the other, of the method and manner of the judicial function. Not in the spirit of counsel for the defence do I speak, nor indeed as the devil's advocate, but rather as one who has a deep reverence for law and the judicial process, for the ancient and honourable profession to which you and I are devoted and to which we proudly give our allegiance.

What is the role of judges in the development of law? I put the question with full awareness that some would deny to the judge any role in the making or development of law. On that view – and it is one which in every generation has had the support of at least some judges – the judge has no function except to state or to expound the law. Let me say at once, this is not a point of view that I share. I would ascribe to the judicial function a more creative role. I am, of course, conscious of the fact that this is in no sense a novel or revolutionary approach. Rather it has had the endorsation of many distinguished writers, scholars, jurists, and judges. In their number I include, of course, the name of Benjamin Cardozo. That great American judge was a person in whom law and literature were wedded in a most felicitious union; a man of whom it could have been said (as it was said of Lord Morley) – that he was sometimes on the losing side, sometimes on the wrong side, but never on the side of wrong. You remember that when the question of choosing a successor to the great Mr. Justice Holmes had to be resolved, the existing composition of the court called for an appointment of a Westerner and hence militated against Cardozo's chances. But President Hoover on good advice none the less took Cardozo from his post of Chief Judge of the Court of Appeals of New York and elevated him to the

Supreme Court – an act which evoked the observation that President Hoover ignored geography and made history. I make no apology for selecting an American judge for tribute in this context, for in the words of Pericles, all the world is the sepulchre of great men.

Forty-one years ago Cardozo illumined this whole subject with a series of lectures which are known to us today under the title of "The Nature of the Judicial Process". There Cardozo declared that there was an area – not great in extent but vital in significance – in which the judge functioned as a legislator, in which the true nature of his enterprise was not discovery but creation. He told us, you remember, that in a large number of cases both the law and its application are plain; that in a second category of cases the rule of law was certain, its application alone doubtful; and that these two categories together involved perhaps 90% of the matters with which a judge would have to deal. He then pointed out that the residue of 10% represented the serious business of a judge. "It is when the colours do not match, when the references in the index fail, when there is no decisive precedent, that the serious business of the judge begins". It is here where a decision one way or the other will advance or retard the law.

Some, fearful of admitting that judges ever make law, would deny to them even in this relatively limited area the right of judicial creativeness. If law is to be molded, reshaped, or altered, the legislator and not the judge is the proper instrument for the process. Judicial innovation, they tell us, is a threat to the stability of the law. I do not believe that these fears are soundly based.

In the first place, whenever the judge encounters a case on which the law has not yet spoken – cases of first impression, that is to say – the judge cannot escape the role of adaptation or creation. So it was when the aeroplane first appeared on the scene, necessitating a consideration for the first time of air law; so it might be today with respect to damage through nuclear fallout.

In the second place, I think that the dangers of judical creativeness can be too easily magnified. If Pollock was right that judges are of two kinds, those marked by judicial caution and those possessed of judicial valour, I venture to say that caution will usually win the day. Let us admit that as a group judges have traditionally been characterized by a certain conservatism, an attitude of mind which is a kind of built-in safeguard against excessive innovation. Judges are not famous for reform. When, a century and a half ago, there was a movement to cut down the shamefully large number of offences which were punishable by death, it was the judges – I need only mention the names of Lord Eldon and Lord Ellenborough – who tried to block the way. In 1836 for the first time in England a full right to have counsel was afforded to accused persons. We are told that the measure was opposed by twelve of the fifteen judges. In our own century the establishment of the Court of Criminal Appeal in England in 1908 was opposed by the judges, fortunately without success. So I do not think that we need be greatly apprehensive that to acknowledge the right of judicial creativeness will open the way to its undue exercise.

Surely the decisive answer to those who insist upon judicial caution at all times and in all circumstances lies in the nature of the common law itself, in its organic character as an instrument which is capable of growth, and which in fact has grown and developed through wise judicial use. I take one instance among many that could be cited to illustrate my point. The case of *Donoghue* v. *Stevenson* – the snail in the ginger beer bottle – is assuredly one where the law was advanced by the courage of judges in breaking new ground. So the manufacturer is held liable to the consumer with whom he did not deal and whom he did not even know. It was enough, said the judges, that he ought to have had her in contemplation. "You must take reasonable care to avoid acts or omissions which you can reasonably foresee would be likely to injure your neighbour", said Lord Atkin; and in the exigencies of modern commercial life the consumer of the ginger beer must be regarded as the manufacturer's neighbour. How easy it would have been to deny the claim as involving a new basis of liability, as opening up a new area of negligence. If the law is to be changed, let parliament do it, the judges could have said. Instead Lord MacMillan asserted the view that "the categories of negligence are never closed", and so helped to create a milestone in the development of the common law.

So I say that we should end the pretense that judges never make law. Let us instead have the candour to admit that judges can and do make law and that within limits it is proper for them to do so.

This brings me to another aspect of my address – namely, the value of precedent and whether stare decisis should be accepted as a rigid and inflexible doctrine. Here we come face to face with the perennial conflict between stability and certainty on the one hand and the need of keeping law fresh and up-to-date on the other.

In certain spheres, of course, the problem does not even arise. I have in mind the compulsion upon a judge to give effect to a validly enacted statute, whether he agrees with it or not. Then too, there is the binding authority of an applicable precedent upon a lower court. If binding it must be dutifully followed, even if the tribunal does not agree with it. As Baron Alderson said: "I accede to the authority of that case . . . It does not convince me, it overcomes me." Sometimes, I need hardly remind you, lower courts refuse to be so overcome. In such cases they will seek to escape the effect of the precedent by techniques of evasion, a process which may take various forms, one of which has been called "distinguishing undistinguished precedents."

But what of the situation where a long-standing precedent confronts a court that is free to follow it or not, as it may decide? Here, too, there is conflict of opinion. Some say that even if the court thinks the case was wrongly decided it ought still to follow it. For the old case may have been treated as an authority for fifty or a hundred years. On the faith that it correctly expressed the law and in reliance upon it people may have entered into contracts, or made wills, or otherwise ordered their affairs. If, now, the court should refuse to follow that case it would be undermining the certainty and stability of the law. Admittedly there is something to be said for this point of view. But we must not overlook the other side of the case, namely, that it is no part of the function of any court to make error perpetual. Unfortunately some inconvenience and dislocation will result whichever point of view is adopted. There is no perfect answer. My own preference – and I do not delude myself into thinking that it is in any sense universally shared – is for the second viewpoint, that which gives the demands of justice a priority over those of stability or certainty. There is not much to be said, in the words of Lord Wright, for the certainty of injustice.

Do you say to me that the adoption of the second point of view will introduce confusion into the law and make it impossible for lawyers to advise their clients intelligently? Not so, I answer, or at worst, seldom so – and even then defensible. For in the first place, it will only be in the rare case, rather than in the general run of cases, that the problem will arise at all. Secondly, a precedent is seldom overruled in a sudden dramatic and unexpected way. Usually it first becomes the subject of discussion, of anxious doubt, and of criticism – both on the part of legal writers and of judges. In a word, the case is now recognized as ripe for overruling. Thirdly, and perhaps most important of all is the fact that lawyers will themselves understand that the law must keep pace with a changing society; that precedents should assist the court, not enslave it; that old rules may sometimes have to be reshaped or discarded. They will recognize, with Roscoe Pound, that the law must be stable and yet it cannot stand still, and so recognizing will take that into account when they advise.

But even if in an exceptional case a lawyer's confidence is and reliance upon a particular decision should in the ultimate result not receive the sanction and endorsement of the court; if the old decision should be rejected, is not the inconvenience that results to the particular litigant simply the price that must be paid for keeping law responsive to the needs of a society that is not stagnant? I have no doubt that for forty years many lawyers gave advice to many clients on the question of damages in accordance with the *Polemis* case. Such advice was probably given to the plaintiff in the fairly recent *Wagon Mound* case. But was that sufficient reason for the court to adhere to a rule that it now believed to be wrong? No, said the Privy Council, and I can only add that to have yielded, in the name of certainty, to the authority of a decision which the court could no longer accept, would have been to hold back the progress of the law. In the words of a legal scholar, we must use the past to press beyond it.

May I say a few words about the methods and the difficulties of arriving at a judgment. How do judges reach the conclusions they do? How indeed? the cynical may echo.

Well, there are various kinds of judges and they do not all work in the same way. Indeed there is a suspicion that some do not work at all – or at least, not enough. But, as we say to juries, suspicion does not amount to proof.

I suppose that with every judge there are two stages through which he must pass in order to arrive at his final result. The first is deciding what his decision will be; the second is to express that decision, whether it be orally or in writing. Both stages have their own difficulties, and it is simple truth to say that often the hardest part of the judge's task just begins when the case has been concluded by counsel. Then comes what is sometimes referred to as the "agony of the decision", and the phrase is not always just a colourful overstatement. How do judges meet the situation? If I may apply the remarks which Mr. Justice Frankfurter made in another connection, "Some do it with ease, some do it with anguish. Some do it with great wisdom, some have done it with less than great wisdom."

Concerning the first stage of the judge's task, I may refer to at least three methods that are acknowledged to exist.

One is "*the hunch theory*" – the phrase originating, I believe, with Judge Hutcheson, a well-known American judge. On this theory the judge acts in accordance with an intuitive sense of what is right or wrong for that cause. It is a gift whose secret is concealed from most of us.

A second, which flows naturally out of the first, is *the result-oriented decision*. Here the judge, not intuitively, but on consideration, reaches a conclusion either that the plainiff should win, or that the defendant should win, and then shapes the judgment to the result. Here the process of judicial reasoning is often backward, from conclusion to argument in support of that conclusion. Let us not condemn the method out of hand. It is the source of many decisions that are rooted in simple justice and morality. The danger to be avoided is the formation of a conclusion before adequate study of the case and then sealing off one's mind to contrary argument.

A third method consists in the relentless pursuit of facts and the relentless application of law to whatever conclusion these may lead. The proponent of this method justifies it on the basis of logic. He hews to the line of the law and follows the facts to whatever conclusion they may take him. If the process should yield a result which seems harsh, and perhaps morally unjust to one of the parties – no matter. The law must be upheld. The court, he says, is not a court of morals or of sympathy.

Here then are three methods, and I am sure they are not exhaustive.

As for the second stage in arriving at a judgment, I think it may be said that sometimes a judge finds his greatest trouble in writing his judgment, after he has made up his mind which way he will hold. Lord Tweedsmuir said of a certain judgment that "it was as flat as ditchwater and as ponderous as a tombstone." On the other hand Cardozo, whose own luminous judgments are expressed in burnished prose, speaks with admiration of the judgments of English judges which to him were – as they are to us – "a mine of instruction and a treasury of joy."

There are differences in method between the trial judge and the appellate judge. The trial judge's effort is often greater in length. He must find the facts, and as Lord MacMillan said, "The first judgment rightly covers the whole ground." May I suggest that the first essential – and this applies not alone to trial judges – is clarity. Happy the judge who can say, "I have been upheld, I have been reversed, I have been varied, but I have never suffered the ultimate indignity of being explained."

With an appellate court the result is achieved by what Lord Evershed has called a "combined judicial operation." Argument and discussions among the judges, marked by frank interchange of views, help to expose and define the real problem for determination. I am sure that every appellate judge has been a beneficiary of the process.

Where does the judge seek assistance in the law? In the law books, of course; but will you allow me to refer to a second source. I have in mind the writings of legal scholars, very often professional law teachers. I do not hold with the view that one should not cite the writings of living authors. The effect of believing that a jurist must be dead before he can become an authority is to deny the judge the assistance and support of current scholarship, which is often the best and most relevant of all. It is so often the legal scholar, trained in a particular specialty, writing objectively without fear except of error, who is able to situate a case in the context of the sphere of law with which it is concerned, and who can assess the trend of judicial decisions. Some see in him only an academic theorist. In my view such an estimate is inadequate and unjust. I do not hesitate to acknowledge the contribution of the research scholar in his study, and the debt which many of the practising bench and bar owe to his effort.

One final word on the matter of arriving at judgments. What impulses or motivations should animate the judge in coming to his decision? I think that George Bernard Shaw has given as good an answer as any; and although his words are intended for the trial judge, especially in a criminal case, they truly have application at every judicial level. You may remember them: "Anger is a bad counsellor: cast out anger. Pity is sometimes a worse: cast out pity. But do not cast out mercy. Remember only that justice comes first."

I am conscious of the fact that some of the views I have expressed tonight have taken us into areas of controversy, and that there may well be dissent therefrom. I do not believe, however, that there is likely to be any dissent concerning our reverence for law and the judicial process. Of course, sometimes that process falters and fails. The law has had and still has its blemishes, its moments of shortened vision. But I prefer to think tonight of its greater moments.

In an earlier day it is Sir John Vaughan speaking for a unanimous court in *Bushell's* case. You recall that Bushell had been a member of the jury in the famous Quaker case of 1670, when William Penn and Mead and others were charged with unlawful assembly. The jury, in spite of the threats and pressure of a misguided trial judge, acquitted the prisoners; and as a result Bushell, as foreman of the jury, was arrested. Sir John Vaughan's words in the *Bushell* case come ringing through the centuries: "The jury is the sole judge of the facts. The prisoner Edward Bushell must be discharged from custody." Surely this was a landmark in the evolution of English law. It helped to preserve the integrity of the jury system, to uphold its freedom, and to establish it as it is today – a treasured safeguard of the liberty of the individual.

It is Lord Mansfield in 1771 dealing with the habeas corpus application on behalf of the Negro slave Somersett, confined in irons on a boat temporarily resting in an English harbour. Hear Lord Mansfield: "Slavery is so odious that nothing can be suffered to support it except positive law. This case is not allowed by the law of England. Let the Negro be discharged."

These, of course, are historic instances, classics among the glories of the common law. But countless other examples exist, perhaps not so well known but no less important. Whenever liberty is invaded from any quarter it is the judicial process which in the last resort alone stands forth as the instrument, the shield, and the protector of the freedom of the individual. If it be true that in this twentieth century the ideal to strive for is the free man in a free society, surely to us as lawyers that ideal should be more meaningful than to anyone else. For the keystone of a free society is the rule of law. Upon it all freedom and security depend.

And have we not all a role to play in the preservation of the rule of law? Whenever each of us performs a function of our great profession – the solicitor in his office securing the rights of his client, whether it be by written contract, or testamentary document, or oral advice; the barrister in the courtroom upholding the cause of plaintiff or defendant in a civil contest, or of Crown or accused in a criminal trial; the judge on the bench seeking to resolve the issue by justice according to law – in all these cases each of us is moving closer to the attainment of what A. T. Mason called "the ideal of an enlarging liberty through a living law." That we have not attained this ideal is true, and we must not be satisfied with what the law has thus far achieved. But our dissatisfaction should not carry with it a note of despondency or of cynicism. Rather it should be the dissatisfaction which is purposeful because the goal is high. But let us never lose sight of that goal. And as we strive to bring its attainment nearer and nearer, let us remember the great words of Thomas Wolfe: "This glorious assurance is not only our living hope, but our dream to be accomplished."

ANALOGY, 466-9, 561, 563-6, 569
Analytical Jurisprudence, 3-4, 11-14, 40, 45, 197-200, 313-4, 460, 463, 473-4, 627, 629, 633-4; *See also* Positivism
Anarchy, 355; *See also* Obedience to Law
Anthropology, 364-7
Antigone, 302

BEHAVIORAL STUDIES, 370, 647-50; *See also* Sociological Research
Boolean Algebra, 637, 648
Brandeis Brief, 656
Brother Daniel Case, 359

CATHOLICISM, 239, 332-3, 335, 349, 382
Certainty, 76, 465-9, 540-8, 576-9, 588-97, 598, 609, 611-2, 635, 643-6, 654-5. *See also* Predictian.
Chicago Jury Studies, 501
Civil Disobedience, *See* Obedience to Law
Clear and Present Danger Test, 642-6
Codification, 396-401; *See also* Legislation
Coercion, *See* Sanction
Columbia Project for Effective Justice, 503-4
Command, 109, 110, 132-42, 179-80, 197-200
Computers, 370, 634-5
Conformity to Law, *See* Obedience to Law
Court, *See* Judicial Process, Logic, Precedent, Rules
Custom, 140-2, 161, 169, 172, 281, 467-8
Cybernetics, 486-95

DATA ANALYSIS, 370
Decalogue, 311, 429
Decision-making, *See* Judicial Process
Disobedience to Law, *See* Obedience to Law
Duties, *See* Rights

ECONOMIC REGULATION, 23-8, 255-9, 447-51; *See also* Laissez-Faire
Economics, 4, 59, 461, 463
Ethics, Ethical, *See* Morals
Ethical Elite, 388, 390, 468
Equity, 34, 36, 279-80, 290-1, 411, 450, 460

FACT-FINDING, 606-14; *See also* Jury
Fidelity to Law, *See* Obedience to Law
Field-Carter Controversy, 401
Formalism, 42-3, 45, 53-5, 71, 197, 200-5, 335, 349-54, 540-8, 597, 627-8; *See also* Logic, Precedent

GALLUP POLL, *See* Opinion Poll
German Wife's Case, 207, 214, 344-5
Good, 266-8, 427-40, 625

HISTORY, 3, 55-9, 98, 296, 393-6, 418, 422-4, 426, 460, 462-3, 467, 468
Hitler, 43, 207, 235, 625, 627
Hunch, *See* Intuition

INTENTION, *See* Purpose
Interests, Social, 27-8, 121-9, 368, 415, 445-60, 464-5, 468-9
International Law, 174, 183-6
Interpretation, 15-18, 28-33, 88-92, 94-8, 110-1, 130, 162-3, 242-3, 349-56, 469, 546, 565-6, 577, 642-6, 652-3.
Intuition, 258, 566-71, 594-5, 602, 661
Is, 99, 166, 173, 322, 326-8, 364, 574-5, 622, 624, 633; *See also* Ought

JUDICIAL ACTIVISM, 244, 369-70, 371-5, 383-4, 393, 524-32, 659
Judicial Process, 3-33, 48-62, 76, 130, 148, 158-65, 177-9, 200-5, 244, 246-51, 349-56, 460, 465-9, 470-2, 473-7, 486-95, 506-663
Judicial Valor, 244; *See also* Judicial Activism, Judicial Process
Jurimetrics, 634-50
Jury, 501, 607, 609-12, 614, 663
Justice, 3-5, 34-9, 40, 44-5, 101-3, 105, 148, 152, 219-36, 240, 279-80, 290-1, 301-10, 356-60, 414-8, 470-2, 473-7, 487, 548, 564, 572, 592, 611, 626, 627-8, 631

KENNEDY, PRESIDENT, 241
Kinsey Report, 479, 496, 497
LAISSEZ-FAIRE, 23-6, 255-9, 447-51. *See also* Economic Regulation

Law, Name of, 5, 34-9
Law, Nature of, 4-5, 70, 440-5, 462-3
Law of Nature, *See* Natural Law
Legality, 171-2, 356-61
Legalism, 39-48, 584-7
Legislation, 341-47, 547-8, 565-6; *See also* Codification, Interpretation
Living Law, 386, 405, 418-27, 479-80, 487, 663
Logic, 53-5, 98, 200-5, 465-9, 474, 522-4, 540-8, 576-97, 629, 634-50, 653, 661-2

MORALITY, *See* Morals
Morals, 3-4, 39-40, 45, 49-53, 99, 111-3, 115-21, 130, 142-8, 157-8, 161, 163-5, 166-8, 193-219, 233-5, 239-42, 246-51, 271-9, 281-4, 292-3, 300-10, 311, 317-28, 332, 333-49, 356-63, 376, 384-91, 393, 427-40, 461, 463-4, 467-9, 473-86, 487, 490, 595, 600, 604-5, 620, 624-34, 657, 661; *See also* Natural Law, Ought, Values
Mores, 39, 50, 388, 403-12, 468, 487, 565, 595, 622, 624-7

NATURAL LAW, 10-11, 12-18, 40, 101-2, 109-11, 169, 210, 215-9, 239-367, 418, 620-8, 633-4, 650
Natural Law, Contemporary, 332-3, 620-8, 633-4
Natural Rights, 8-10, 11-12, 32-3, 328-32, 447
Nazi Legal System, 204-8, 341-9, 621
Norms, *See* Rules

OBEDIENCE TO LAW, 111-13, 130, 145-6, 154-7, 205-8, 241-2, 278-80, 294, 333-56, 408-10, 620-1
Ontology, 325
Opinion Polls, 369, 387, 390, 473-86, 622-4
Ought, 99, 166-8, 173, 180-2, 200, 203-4, 206, 322, 326-8, 333, 350-6, 364, 440-1, 479-81, 485-6, 574-5, 600, 622, 628, 633, 653; *See also* Morals, Values

PHILOSOPHY, 3, 462, 466-9
Political Jurisprudence, 369-70, 623
Polls, *See* Opinion Polls
Positivism, 5, 15-18, 40, 70-238, 333-56, 370, 651-6; *See also* Analytical Jurisprudence
Precedent, 73-5, 78-80, 82, 84-5, 252-3, 259-61, 392, 465-9, 506, 508-18, 524-31, 534-6, 540-71, 576-9, 588-97, 614-20, 621-2, 630, 660-3
Prediction, 48-62, 370, 460, 546, 551, 576-9, 593, 599, 602-3, 606-14, 616-7, 627, 635, 647-50
Psychology, 4, 462-3, 521, 551-2, 579-87, 597, 613
Public Policy, 246, 248, 369, 370-5, 377-84, 447-52, 467-8, 484, 614-5
Purpose, 91, 96, 212-4, 353-6, 444, 460, 474-5, 485, 486-95, 574, 626, 642

RATIO DECIDENDI, *See* Precedent
Rationalization, 548-52, 575-6, 580-4, 589.
Realism, American Legal, 200-5, 234, 236, 369-70, 474, 506-7, 532-40, 571-614, 620-34, 650-6
Realism, Scandinavian, 226-38
Reason, 239-40, 269, 270, 272-4, 285-9, 290-1, 292, 311-2, 614-20, 629
Resistance, *See* Obedience to Law
Retroactivity, 207-8, 341-7, 349
Revolution, *See* Obedience to Law
Rights, Duties, 51-2, 133-4, 186-93, 256-7, 328-33, 406-7, 446-7
Roman Law, 37, 60, 147-8, 319-21, 394-401, 411, 419, 422, 424, 425, 453, 459
Rule, 39-48, 53-5, 131-42, 158-62, 166-93, 199-205, 214, 226-30, 282-4, 296-7, 313, 357-9, 403-27, 445, 460, 462-3, 465-9, 478-81, 534-6, 546-8, 552-79; *See also* Logic, Precedent
"Rule of Law," 62-9, 471-2

SANCTION, 49, 113, 133-5, 175-6, 181-2, 187, 208, 275, 279, 311, 402, 408-10, 502
Scandinavian Realism, *See* Realism, Scandinavian
Social Control, 460-5
Social Welfare, 467-8, 487
Sociological Jurisprudence, 3-4, 18-23, 181, 313-4, 368-505, 518-32, 605, 651, 654-6
Sociological Research, 473-86, 495-505; *See also* Behavioral Studies, Jury
Sociology, 461
Sovereignty, 103-9, 111-3, 131, 137-8, 149-57, 182-3, 443-4
Stare Decisis, *See* Precedent
State, 157-8, 161, 165, 182-3, 190, 405-8, 411-2

USAGE, LINGUISTIC, 354
Utility, Utilitarian, 113-21, 193-214

VALUES, 3, 54-5, 326-8, 368-9, 465-9, 574-5, 584-5, 600-1, 605, 614-6, 618-9, 624-7, 633, 652, 654, 657-8; *See also* Morals, Ought

WELFARE STATE, 62-9

www.ingramcontent.com/pod-product-compliance
Lightning Source LLC
LaVergne TN
LVHW080153090826
844660LV00050B/1257

* 9 7 8 1 4 8 7 5 7 7 4 3 8 *